PHILIP'S

STREET ATLAS
Staffordshire

C000311500

First published in 1995 by

Philip's, a division of
Octopus Publishing Group Ltd
2-4 Heron Quays, London E14 4JP

Second colour edition 2002
Third impression with revisions 2004

ISBN 0-540-08117-5 (spiral)

© Philip's 2004

o|s Ordnance Survey®

This product includes mapping data licensed
from Ordnance Survey® with the permission of
the Controller of Her Majesty's Stationery Office.
© Crown copyright 2004. All rights reserved.
Licence number 100011710.

Printed and bound in Spain
by Cayfosa-Quebecor

Contents

III **Key to map symbols**

IV **Key to map pages**

VI **Route planning**

VIII **Administrative and Postcode boundaries**

1 **Street maps** at 3½ inches to 1 mile

282 **Street maps of centres of Stoke-on-Trent, Longton and Newcastle-under-Lyme** at 7 inches to 1 mile

285 **Town maps** of Congleton, Macclesfield, Buxton, Chesterfield, Derby and Matlock

288 **Index** of towns and villages

289 **Index** of streets, hospitals, industrial estates, railway stations, schools, shopping centres, universities and places of interest

Digital Data

The exceptionally high-quality mapping found in this atlas is available as digital data in TIFF format, which is easily convertible to other bitmapped (raster) image formats.

The index is also available in digital form as a standard database table. It contains all the details found in the printed index together with the National Grid reference for the map square in which each entry is named.

For further information and to discuss your requirements, please contact Philip's on 020 7644 6932 or james.mann@philips-maps.co.uk

Key to map symbols

III

(22a)	**Motorway** with junction number
	Primary route – dual/single carriageway
	A road – dual/single carriageway
	B road – dual/single carriageway
	Minor road – dual/single carriageway
	Other minor road – dual/single carriageway
	Road under construction
	Pedestrianised area
DY7	**Postcode boundaries**
	County and unitary authority boundaries
	Railway
	Railway under construction
	Tramway, miniature railway
	Rural track, private road or narrow road in urban area
	Gate or obstruction to traffic (restrictions may not apply at all times or to all vehicles)
	Path, bridleway, byway open to all traffic, road used as a public path

The representation in this atlas of a road, track or path is no evidence of the existence of a right of way

58	
230	**Adjoining page indicators**
237	

The map area within the pink band is shown at a larger scale on the page indicated by the red block and arrow

Walsall	**Railway station**
	Private railway station
	Bus, coach station
	Ambulance station
	Coastguard station
	Fire station
	Police station
+	**Accident and Emergency entrance to hospital**
H	**Hospital**
+	**Place of worship**
i	**Information Centre** (open all year)
P	**Parking**
P&R	**Park and Ride**
PO	**Post Office**
Ⓧ	**Camping site**
	Caravan site
	Golf course
	Picnic site
Prim Sch	**Important buildings, schools, colleges, universities and hospitals**
River Medway	**Water name**
	River, stream
	Lock, weir
	Water
	Tidal water
	Woods
	Houses
Church	**Non-Roman antiquity**
ROMAN FORT	**Roman antiquity**

Abbr.	Full	Abbr.	Full
Acad	**Academy**	Mkt	**Market**
Allot Gdns	**Allotments**	Meml	**Memorial**
Cemy	**Cemetery**	Mon	**Monument**
C Ctr	**Civic Centre**	Mus	**Museum**
CH	**Club House**	Obsy	**Observatory**
Coll	**College**	Pal	**Royal Palace**
Crem	**Crematorium**	PH	**Public House**
Ent	**Enterprise**	Recn Gd	**Recreation Ground**
Ex H	**Exhibition Hall**	Resr	**Reservoir**
Ind Est	**Industrial Estate**	Ret Pk	**Retail Park**
IRB Sta	**Inshore Rescue Boat Station**	Sch	**School**
		Sh Ctr	**Shopping Centre**
Inst	**Institute**	TH	**Town Hall/House**
Ct	**Law Court**	Trad Est	**Trading Estate**
L Ctr	**Leisure Centre**	Univ	**University**
LC	**Level Crossing**	Wks	**Works**
Liby	**Library**	YH	**Youth Hostel**

■ The small numbers around the edges of the maps identify the 1 kilometre National Grid lines ■ The dark grey border on the inside edge of some pages indicates that the mapping does not continue onto the adjacent page

The scale of the maps on the pages numbered in blue is 5.52 cm to 1 km • 3½ inches to 1 mile • 1: 18103

0	¼	½	¾	1 mile
0	250 m	500 m	750 m	1 kilometre

The scale of the maps on pages numbered in red is 11.04 cm to 1 km • 7 inches to 1 mile • 1: 9051.4

0	220 yards	440 yards	660 yards	½ mile
0	125 m	250 m	375 m	½ kilometre

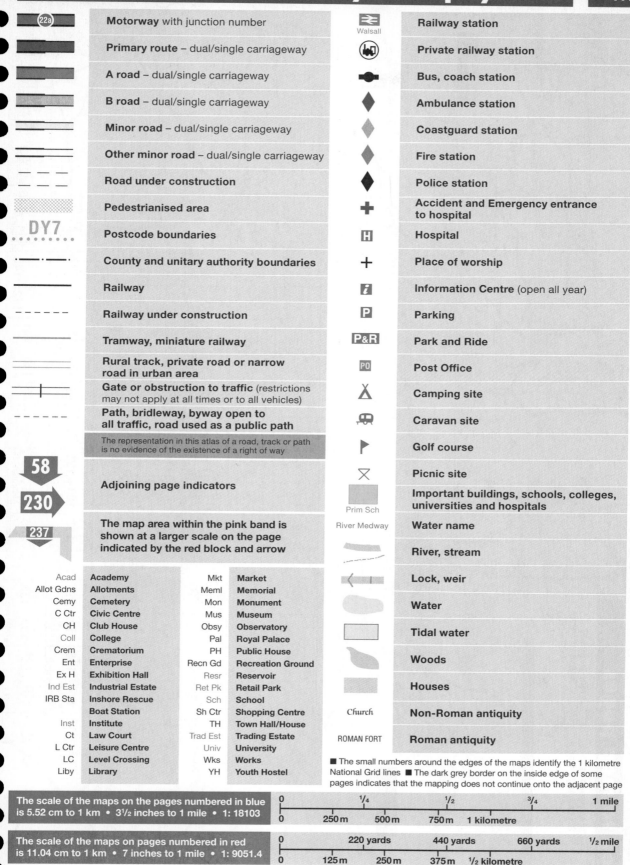

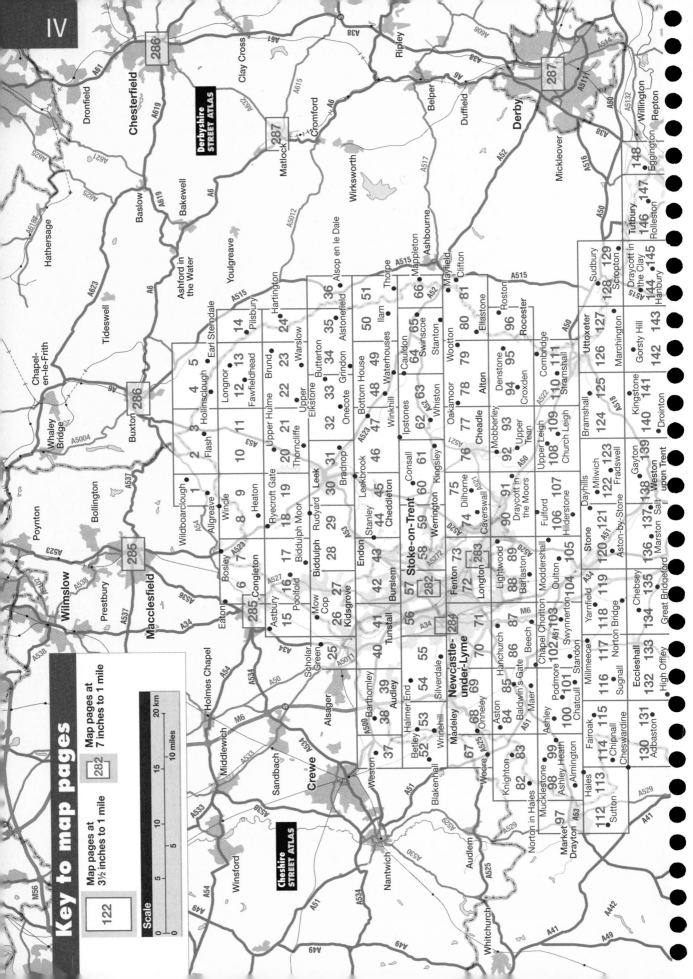

IV

Key to map pages

Map pages at 3½ inches to 1 mile
122

Map pages at 7 inches to 1 mile
282

Scale
0   5   10   15   20 km
0   5   10   15   20 miles
5   10 miles

Cheshire STREET ATLAS

Derbyshire STREET ATLAS

286   287

Dronfield   Chesterfield   Clay Cross   Ripley

Hathersage   Baslow   Bakewell   Cromford   Belper   Duffield   Derby   Mickleover

148
147 148
146 147
144 145 146
Tutbury Rolleston
128 129
Sudbury Scropton
126 127
Uttoxeter Marchington
Gorsty Hill
142 143
Kingstone 141
140 141
Drointon
139
138 139
137 138
136 137
Weston Salt upon Trent
135 136
Marston
134 135
Chebsey
133 134
Eccleshall
132 133
High Offley
131
130 131
Adbaston
Cheswardine

Chapel-en-le-Frith   Whaley Bridge   Buxton   286   285

Wildboarclough   Allgreave

Poynton   Wilmslow   Prestbury   Macclesfield   285

Bollington   Bosley   Congleton   285

Holmes Chapel   Middlewich   Sandbach

Alsager   Crewe   Nantwich

Market Drayton   Whitchurch   Audlem

Tideswell   Ashford in the Water   Youlgreave   Hartington

5   14   24   36   51
4   13   23   35   50   66   81
3   12   22   34   49   65   80   96
2   11   21   33   48   64   79   95   111
1   10   20   32   47   63   78   94   110
9   19   31   46   62   77   93   109   127
8   18   30   45   61   76   92   108   126   146
7   17   29   44   60   75   91   107   125   145
6   16   28   43   59   74   90   106   124   144
15   27   42   58   73   89   105   123   143
26   41   57   72   88   104   122   142
25   40   56   71   87   103   121   141
39   55   70   86   102   120   140
38   54   69   85   101   119   139
37   53   68   84   100   118   138
52   67   83   99   117   137
82   98   116   136
97   115   135

Earl Sterndale   Longnor   Pilsbury   Warslow   Alsop en le Dale   Swinscoe   Wootton   Ellastone   Denstone   Rocester   Roston   Combridge   Stramshall   Bramshall

Hollinsclough   Flash   Fawfieldhead   Brund   Upper Elkstone   Butterton   Grindon   Alstonefield   Ilam   Cauldon   Stanton   Oakamoor   Alton   Croxden   Church Leigh   Milwich   Fradswell   Gayton

Winkle   Heaton   Upper Hulme   Thorncliffe   Onecote   Bottom House   Waterhouses   Whiston   Cheadle   Upper Tean   Mobberley   Upper Leigh   Dayhills   Aston-by-Stone

Ryecroft Gate   Leek   Bradnor   Ipstones   Kingsley   Caverswall   Draycott in the Moors   Fulford   Hilderstone   Stone   Aston-by-Stone

Rudyard   Leekbrook   Cheddleton   Consall   Werrington   Dilhorne   Fenton   Barlaston   Moddershall   Oulton   Swynnerton   Chebsey

Biddulph Moor   Stanley   Endon   Stoke-on-Trent   282   284   Longton   Lightwood   Barlaston   Chapel Chorlton   Standon   Yarnfield   Norton Bridge

Biddulph   Poolfold   Mow Cop   Kidsgrove   Tunstall   Burslem   Newcastle-under-Lyme   Hanford   Beech   Podmore   Swynnerton   104   105   Millmeece   Sugnall

Astbury   Eaton   Scholar Green   Barthomley   Audley   Silverdale   Hanchurch   Baldwin's Gate   Maer   Chatcull   Fairoak   Chipnall

Halmer End   Silverdale   Madeley   Ashley   Almington   Adbaston

Wrinehill   Betley   Onneley   Woore   Knighton   Muckleston   Ashley Heath   Hales   Sutton   Market Drayton   Norton in Hales

Weston   Blakenhall

Leicestershire **STREET ATLAS**

Warwickshire **STREET ATLAS**

Birmingham & West Midlands **STREET ATLAS**

Worcestershire **STREET ATLAS**

Shropshire **STREET ATLAS**

Burton upon Trent

166 167
164 165
162 163
160 161
158 159
156 157
154 155
152 153
150 151
149

168 169
170 171
172 173
174 175
176 177
178 179
180 181
182 183
184 185 186

187
188 189
190 191
192 193
194 195
196 197
198 199
200 201
202

203 204 205
206 207 208 209
210 211 212 213
214 215
216 217 218 219

220 221
222 223 224 225
226 227
228 229 230 231
232 233 234 235 236

237
238 239 240 241
242 243 244 245
246 247 248 249
250 251

252 253 254 255
256 257 258 259
260 261 262

263
264 265 266
267 268 269 270 271
272 273 274 275
276 277 278 279
280 281

Stafford

Cannock

Tamworth

Birmingham

Coventry

Nuneaton

Melbourne
Newton Solney
Swadlincote
Ashby-de-la-Zouch
Measham
Ibstock
Newton Regis
Clifton Campville
Netherseal
Shuttington
Wood End
Atherstone
Coleshill
Bedworth
Kenilworth
Dorridge
Solihull
Castle Bromwich
Sutton Coldfield
Little Aston
Aldridge
Walsall
Smethwick
Rowley Regis
Halesowen
Hagley
Kidderminster
Bromsgrove
Stourport on Severn
Bewdley
Blakedown
Cookley
Kinver
Stourbridge
Stourton
Wordsley
Kingswinford
Enville
Six Ashes
Romsley
Claverley
Bobbington
Swindon
Himley
Sedgley
Dudley
Wombourne
Seisdon
Trysull
Lower Penn
Wolverhampton
Perton
Tettenhall
Codsall
Oaken
Boningale
Albrighton
Tong
Bishops Wood
Brewood
Kiddemore Green
Coven
Featherstone
Essington
Willenhall
Bilbrook
Pattingham
Rudge
Burnhill Green
Shifnal
Madeley
Dawley
Telford
Wellington
Shawbury
Much Wenlock
Bridgnorth
Donnington
Weston under Lizard
Ivetsey Bank
Blymhill
Lapley
Stretton
Wheaton Aston
High Onn
Orslow
Church Eaton
Apeton
Bradley
Haughton
Gnosall
Outwoods
Norbury
Sutton
Woodseaves
Forton
Newport
Edgmond
Chetwynd Aston
Pickstock
Ranton
Seighford
Derrington
Ingestre
Hixon
Great Haywood
Abbots Bromley
Admaston
Colton
Brocton
Acton Trussell
Coppenhall
Bednall
Penkridge
Cannock
Huntington
Hatherton
Gailey
Norton Canes
Shareshall
Hammerwich
Burntwood
Hednesford
Chorley
Farewell
Longdon Green
Elmhurst
Fradley
Lichfield
Wall
Little Hay
Shenstone
Stonnall
Brownhills
Little Wyrley
Pye Green
Slitting Mill
King's Bromley
Handsacre
Armitage
London
Ridware
Hamstall
Yoxall
Rugeley
Rangemore
Newborough
Newchurch
Barton-under-Needwood
Anslow
Tatenhill
Walton-on-Trent
Orgreave
Alrewas
Whittington
Hopwas
Hints
Fazeley
Middleton
Wiggington
Harlaston
Elford
Edingale
Thorpe Constantine
Roughley
Sutton Coldfield

A42 A511 A444 A5 A69 A460 A453 A4600 A446 A452 A41 A42 A40 A34 A435 A449 A458 A456 A491 A448 A450 A451 A442 A454 A464 A518 A5 A38 A513 A515 A51 A460 A34 A461 A462 A123 A40 A5190 A454 A159 A454 A4117 A456 A449 A458 A469

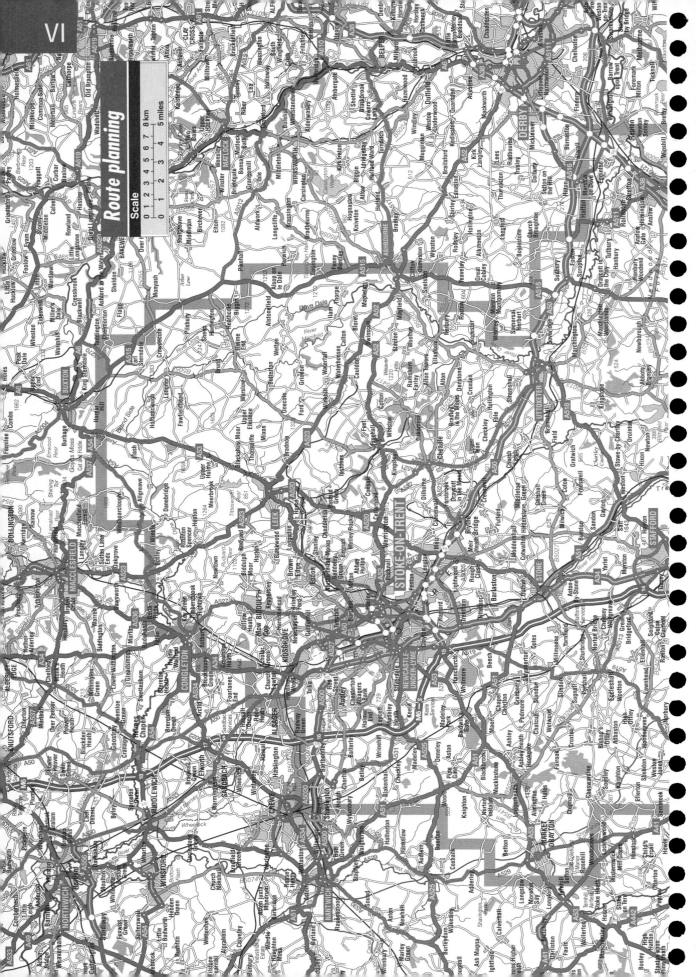

Route planning

Scale

0 1 2 3 4 5 6 7 8 km

0 1 2 3 4 5 miles

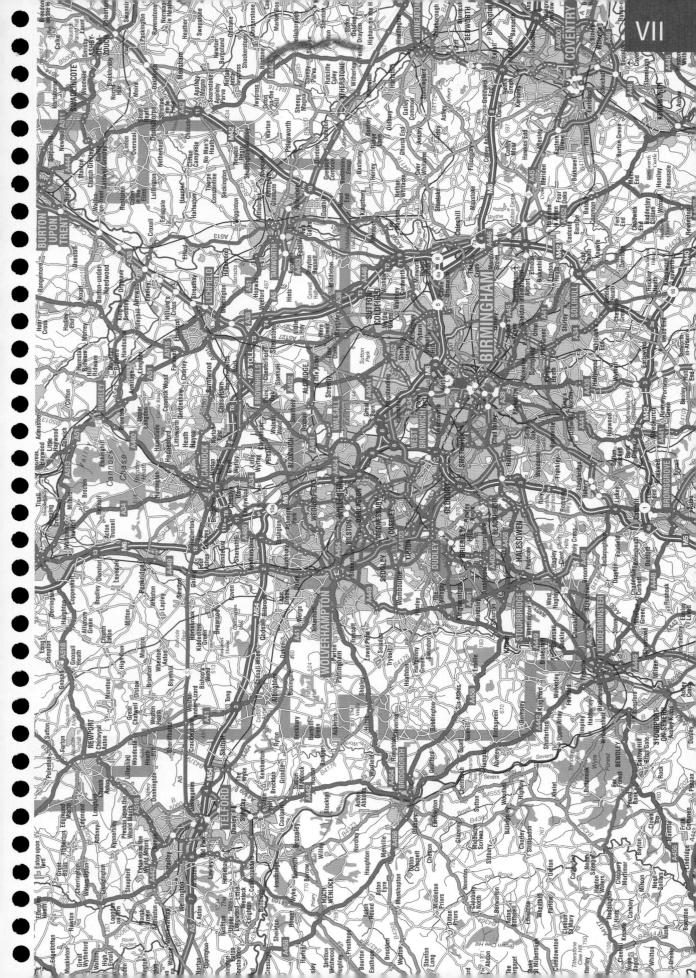

SJ | SK

Cheshire

Derbyshire

Shropshire

Telford and Wrekin

Shropshire

Worcestershire

S t a f f o r d s h i r e

City of Stoke-on-Trent

Staffordshire Moorlands

Newcastle-under-Lyme

Stafford

East Staffordshire

Cannock Chase

Lichfield

South Staffordshire

Tamworth

Dudley

Sandwell

Walsall

Warwickshire

SJ | SK
SO | SP

Flash
Wincle
Longnor
Hartington
Warslow
Biddulph
Leek
Alstonefield
Kidsgrove
Cheddleton
Weston
Betley
Stoke-on-Trent
Werrington
Kingsley
Newcastle-under-Lyme
Mayfield
Woore
Cheadle
Alton
Baldwin's Gate
Barlaston
Rocester
Norton in Hales
Swynnerton
Church Leigh
Ashley
Yarnfield
Stone
Uttoxeter
Market Drayton
Eccleshall
Sudbury
Weston
Marchington
Stafford
Abbots Bromley
Tutbury
Egginton
Gnosall
Haughton
Burton upon Trent
Brocton
Newport
Yoxall
Rugeley
Longdon
Alrewas
Wheaton Aston
Penkridge
Cannock
Fradley
Netherseal
Weston under Lizard
Lichfield
Featherstone
Burntwood
Newton Regis
Albrighton
Shenstone
Codsall
Brownhills
Tamworth
Drayton Bassett
Pattingham
Aldridge
Claverley
Wombourne
Sedgley
Kinver
Blakedown

CW12, SK11, SK17, DE6, CW1, ST8, ST13, CW2, ST7, ST6, ST9, CW5, ST1, ST2, CW3, ST4, ST3, ST11, ST5, ST12, ST15, ST14, TF9, ST21, ST18, DE6, DE65, ST16, DE13, DE15, ST20, DE14, DE11, TF10, ST17, WS15, DE12, TF11, ST19, WS13, B79, WV10, WV9, WS12, WS11, WS7, WS14, B78, WV8, WS6, B77, WV11, WS8, WV7, WS3, WS4, WS9, B74, B75, WV6, WV3, WV2, WV4, WV5, DY3, DY1, DY6, WV15, DY7, DY8, DY12, DY11, DY10

Major administrative and Postcode boundaries

County and unitary authority boundaries
District boundaries
Postcode boundaries
Area covered by this atlas

Scale
0   5   10   15 km
0   5   10 miles

Birmingham
City of Wolverhampton

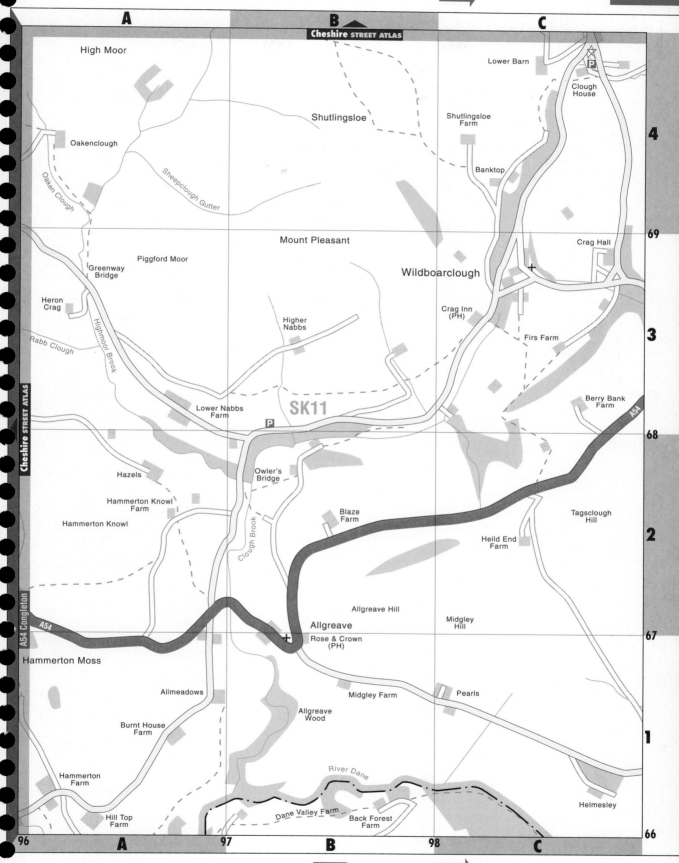

Cheshire STREET ATLAS

High Moor

Oakenclough

Oaken Clough

Shutlingsloe

Sheepclough Gutter

Lower Barn

Shutlingsloe Farm

Clough House

P

4

Banktop

Mount Pleasant

69

Greenway Bridge

Piggford Moor

Wildboarclough

Crag Hall

Heron Crag

Highmoor Brook

Higher Nabbs

Crag Inn (PH)

Firs Farm

3

Rabb Clough

Lower Nabbs Farm

SK11

Berry Bank Farm

A54

P

68

Hazels

Owler's Bridge

Clough Brook

Blaze Farm

Heild End Farm

Tagsclough Hill

2

Hammerton Knowl Farm

Hammerton Knowl

Allgreave Hill

Midgley Hill

A54 Congleton

A54

Allgreave

Rose & Crown (PH)

67

Hammerton Moss

Allmeadows

Midgley Farm

Pearls

Burnt House Farm

Allgreave Wood

1

Hammerton Farm

River Dane

Helmesley

Hill Top Farm

Dane Valley Farm

Back Forest Farm

66

Cheshire STREET ATLAS

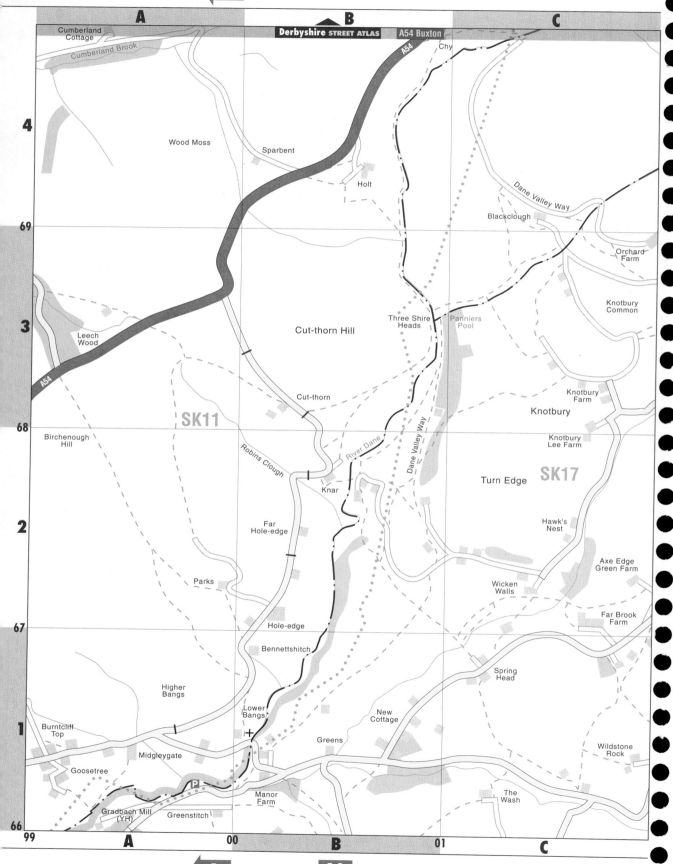

Derbyshire STREET ATLAS   A54 Buxton

Cumberland
Cottage

Cumberland Brook

A54

Chy

Wood Moss

Sparbent

Holt

Dane Valley Way

Blackclough

Orchard
Farm

4

69

Leech
Wood

A54

Cut-thorn Hill

Three Shire
Heads

Panniers
Pool

Knotbury
Common

Knotbury
Farm

Knotbury

3

Birchenough
Hill

SK11

Cut-thorn

Robins Clough

River Dane

Knar

Dane Valley Way

Knotbury
Lee Farm

SK17

Turn Edge

68

Far
Hole-edge

Hawk's
Nest

Axe Edge
Green Farm

2

Parks

Hole-edge

Wicken
Walls

Far Brook
Farm

Bennettshitch

67

Spring
Head

Higher
Bangs

Lower
Bangs

New
Cottage

Burntcliff
Top

Greens

Wildstone
Rock

1

Midgleygate

Goosetree

P

Manor
Farm

The
Wash

Gradbach Mill
(YH)

Greenstitch

66

99

A

00

B

01

C

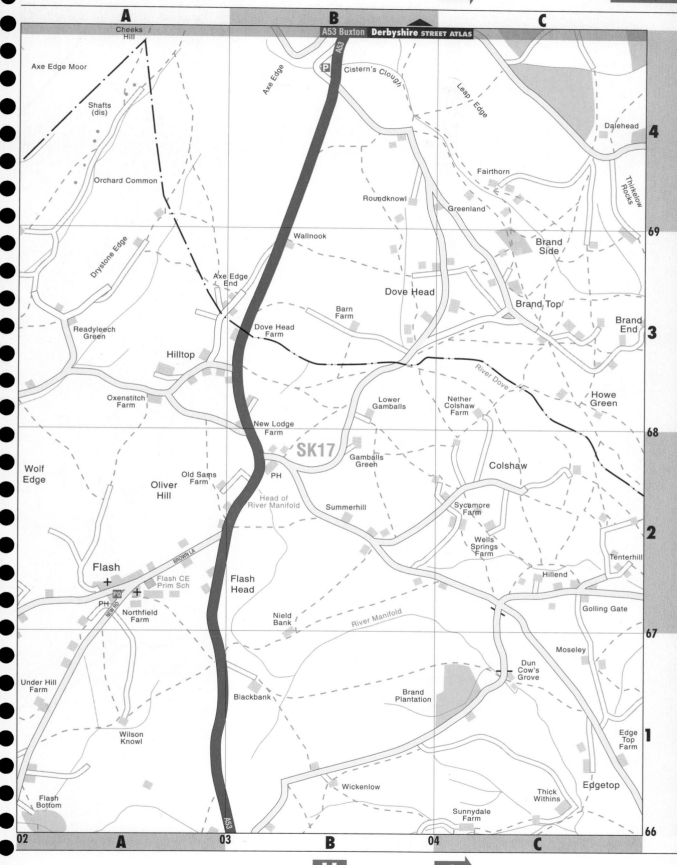

A53 Buxton **Derbyshire** STREET ATLAS

Cheeks Hill

Axe Edge Moor

Shafts (dis)

Axe Edge

Cistern's Clough

Leap Edge

Dalehead

4

Orchard Common

Fairthorn

Thirkelow Rocks

Roundknowl

Greenland

69

Drystone Edge

Wallnook

Dove Head

Brand Side

Axe Edge End

Barn Farm

Brand Top

Brand End

3

Readyleech Green

Dove Head Farm

River Dove

Hilltop

Oxenstitch Farm

Lower Gamballs

Nether Colshaw Farm

Howe Green

New Lodge Farm

SK17

68

Wolf Edge

Old Sams Farm

PH

Gamballs Green

Colshaw

Oliver Hill

Head of River Manifold

Summerhill

Sycamore Farm

Flash

BROWN LA

Wells Springs Farm

Tenterhill

2

Flash CE Prim Sch

Flash Head

Hillend

PO

Golling Gate

PH

Northfield Farm

NEW RD

Nield Bank

River Manifold

67

Under Hill Farm

Moseley

Dun Cow's Grove

Blackbank

Brand Plantation

Edge Top Farm

1

Wilson Knowl

Wickenlow

Edgetop

Flash Bottom

Sunnydale Farm

Thick Withins

A53

66

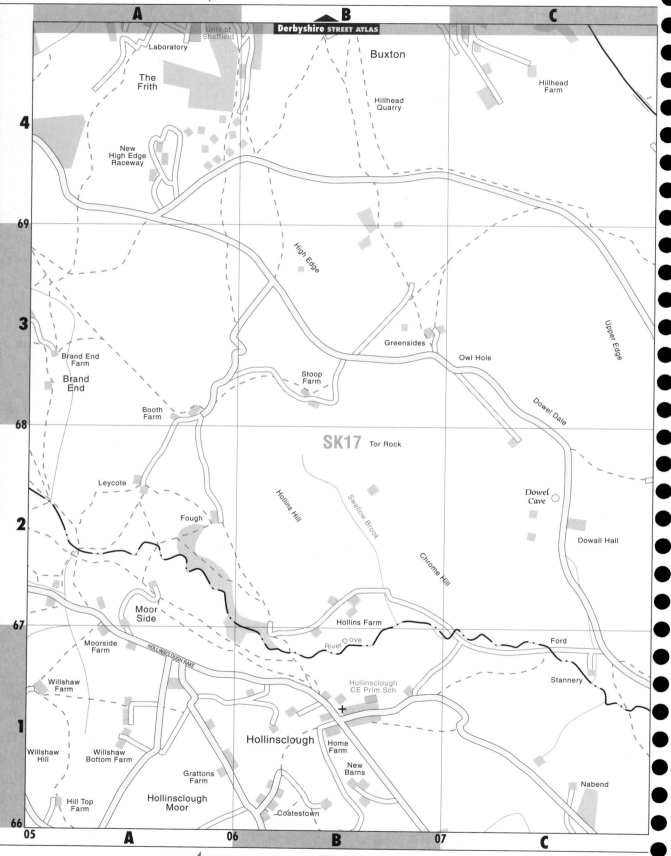
A

B

C

Derbyshire STREET ATLAS

Laboratory

Univ of Sheffield

Buxton

The Frith

Hillhead Quarry

Hillhead Farm

4

New High Edge Raceway

69

High Edge

Upper Edge

3

Brand End Farm

Brand End

Greensides

Owl Hole

Dowel Dale

Stoop Farm

68

Booth Farm

SK17

Tor Rock

Leycote

Hollins Hill

Swallow Brook

Dowel Cave

Dowall Hall

2

Fough

Chrome Hill

Moor Side

Hollins Farm

67

Moorside Farm

River Dove

Ford

HOLLINSCLOUGH RAKE

Stannery

Willshaw Farm

Hollinsclough CE Prim Sch

1

Hollinsclough

Home Farm

Willshaw Hill

Willshaw Bottom Farm

New Barns

Nabend

Grattons Farm

Hill Top Farm

Hollinsclough Moor

Coatestown

66

05

A

06

B

07

C

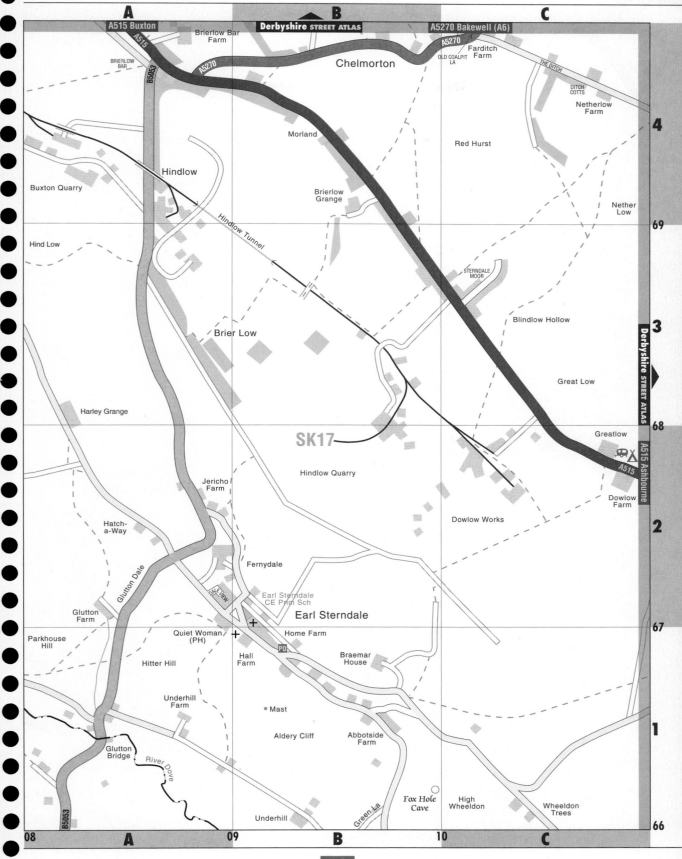

A515 Buxton
A5270 Bakewell (A6)

A
B
C

Brierlow Bar Farm

BRIERLOW BAR

B5053

A5270

OLD COALPIT LA

Farditch Farm

THE DITCH

Chelmorton

DITCH COTTS

Netherlow Farm

4

Morland

Red Hurst

Hindlow

Buxton Quarry

Brierlow Grange

Nether Low

Hind Low

Hindlow Tunnel

69

Brier Low

STERNDALE MOOR

Blindlow Hollow

3

Derbyshire STREET ATLAS

Harley Grange

Great Low

68

SK17

Greatlow

A515 Ashbourne

Jericho Farm

Hindlow Quarry

Dowlow Farm

Hatch-a-Way

Dowlow Works

2

Glutton Dale

Fernydale

Glutton Farm

DALE VIEW

Earl Sterndale CE Prim Sch

Earl Sterndale

67

Parkhouse Hill

Quiet Woman (PH)

Home Farm

PO

Braemar House

Hitter Hill

Hall Farm

Underhill Farm

Mast

1

Aldery Cliff

Abbotside Farm

Glutton Bridge

River Dove

Fox Hole Cave

High Wheeldon

Wheeldon Trees

B5053

Underhill

Green La

66

08
A
09
B
10
C

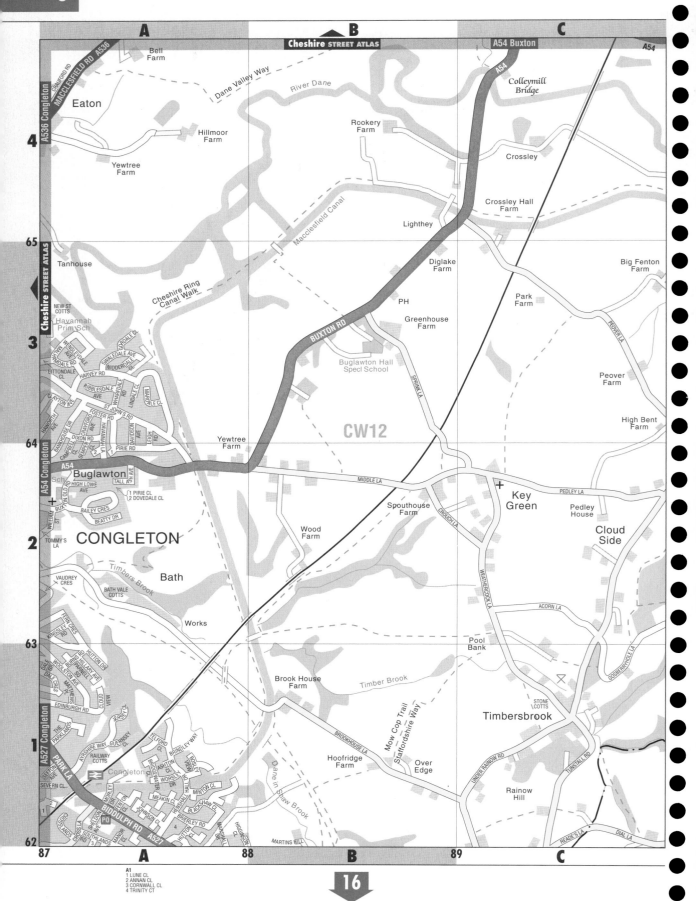

A54 Buxton

A54

Colleymill Bridge

Bell Farm

Dane Valley Way

River Dane

Eaton

Rookery Farm

Crossley

Hillmoor Farm

Yewtree Farm

Crossley Hall Farm

Macclesfield Canal

Lighthey

Diglake Farm

Big Fenton Farm

Tanhouse

Cheshire Ring Canal Walk

PH

Park Farm

PEOVER LA

NEW ST COTTS

Havannah Prim Sch

Buxton Rd

Greenhouse Farm

Peover Farm

WENSLEYDALE AVE
TINTAGEL CL
SWALEDALE AVE
NIDDERDALE CL
RIBBLESDALE AVE
WHARFDALE RD
LINDALE CL
MARPLE CL

Buglawton Hall Specl School

SPRINK LA

High Bent Farm

HARVEY RD
ST JOHN'S RD

CW12

Yewtree Farm

CLAYTON AVE
HANDMOUSE DR
CRAWFORD ST
DIXON RD
CAMPBELL LN
SEABERT
DAVIDSON RD
LEIGH
PIRIE RD

A54

Buglawton

MIDDLE LA

Key Green

PEDLEY LA

CROUCH LA

Spouthouse Farm

Pedley House

1 PIRIE CL
2 DOVEDALE CL

BAILEY CRES
BEATTY DR

Cloud Side

CONGLETON

TOMMY'S LA

Wood Farm

WEATHERCOCK LA

Bath

Timbers Brook

ACORN LA

VAUDREY CRES

BATH VALE COTTS

Works

Pool Bank

GOSBERRYHOLE LA

FERN CRES
KINGSLEY RD
HUTTON DR
HILLARY AVE
BURNS AVE
WOOLSTON AVE
MATTHEWS

Timber Brook

Brook House Farm

STONE COTTS

DALE
CLOUD VIEW
EDINBURGH RD
JERSEY CL

Timbersbrook

THE PARKLANDS

GUERNSEY CL
TELFORD
BRINDLEY WAY
POCKET
BRIDGEWATER
ASHTON
WORSLEY

Mow Cop Trail
Staffordshire Way

UNDER RAINOW RD

A527 Congleton

PARK LA

RAILWAY COTTS

BROOKHOUSE LA

Hoofridge Farm

Over Edge

TUNSTALL RD

SEFTON AVE

Congleton

MEAKIN CL
BLACKSHAW RD
BIVERLEY RD

Dane in Shaw Brook

Rainow Hill

SEVERN CL

BIDDULPH RD

A527

MARSHALL

HIGHERTON

MARTINS HILL

READE'S LA

DIAL LA

A1
1 LUNE CL
2 ANNAN CL
3 CORNWALL CL
4 TRINITY CT

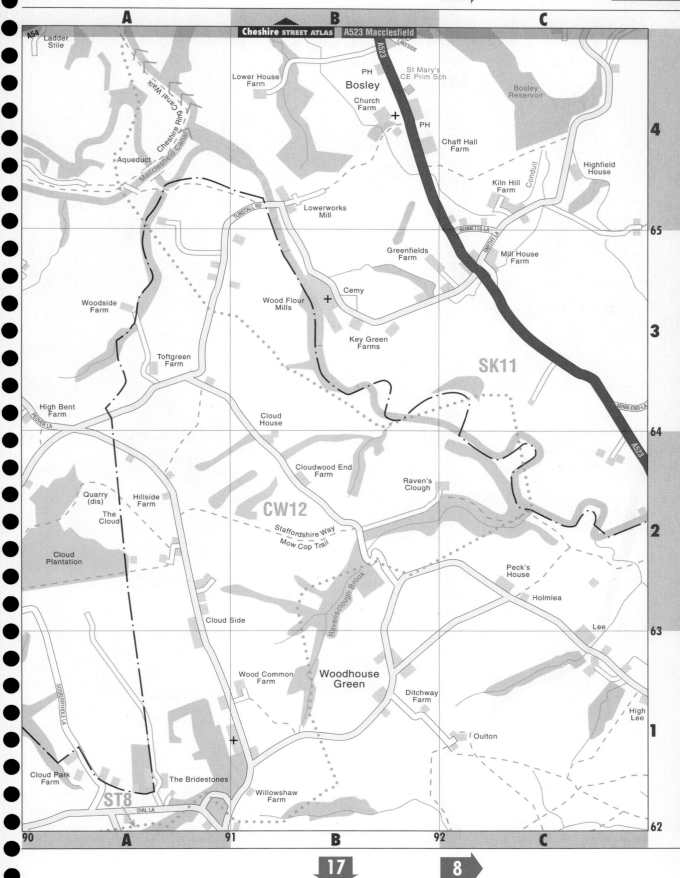

Cheshire STREET ATLAS A523 Macclesfield

A · B · C

A54
Ladder
Stile

Cheshire Ring Canal Walk

Macclesfield Canal

Aqueduct

Lower House
Farm

PH
Bosley

St Mary's
CE Prim Sch

Bosley
Reservoir

Church
Farm

PH

Chaff Hall
Farm

Highfield
House

Kiln Hill
Farm

Conduit

4

Woodside
Farm

TUNSTALL RD

Lowerworks
Mill

BENNETTS LA

Mill House
Farm

SMITH LA

65

Greenfields
Farm

Wood Flour
Mills

Cemy

Key Green
Farms

SK11

Toftgreen
Farm

3

High Bent
Farm

PEVER LA

Cloud
House

Cloudwood End
Farm

Raven's
Clough

MINN-END-LA

A523

64

Quarry
(dis)

Hillside
Farm

The
Cloud

CW12

Staffordshire Way
Mow Cop Trail

Peck's
House

2

Cloud
Plantation

Holmlea

Lee

Ravensclough Brook

Cloud Side

63

Wood Common
Farm

Woodhouse
Green

Ditchway
Farm

High
Lee

GOSBERRYHOLE LA

Oulton

1

Cloud Park
Farm

The Bridestones

ST8

DIAL LA

Willowshaw
Farm

62

90 · A · 91 · B · 92 · C

7

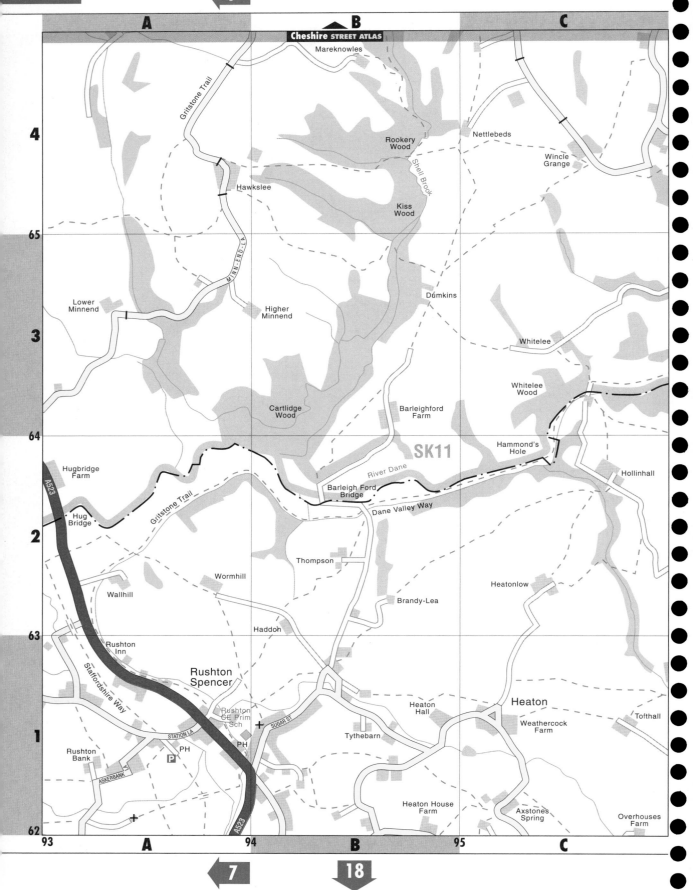

Cheshire STREET ATLAS

Mareknowles

4

Rookery Wood

Nettlebeds

Wincle Grange

Shell Brook

Hawkslee

Kiss Wood

65

MINN-END-LA

Dumkins

Lower Minnend

Higher Minnend

Whitelee

3

Whitelee Wood

Cartlidge Wood

Barleighford Farm

64

SK11

Hammond's Hole

Hugbridge Farm

River Dane

Hollinhall

A523

Gritstone Trail

Barleigh Ford Bridge

Hug Bridge

Dane Valley Way

2

Thompson

Wormhill

Heatonlow

Wallhill

Brandy-Lea

Haddon

63

Rushton Inn

Staffordshire Way

Rushton Spencer

Heaton

Heaton Hall

Weathercock Farm

Tofthall

Rushton CE Prim Sch

STATION LA

SUGAR ST

1

Tythebarn

Rushton Bank

PH

P

PH

ASKERBANK

Heaton House Farm

Axstones Spring

Overhouses Farm

62

A523

7   18

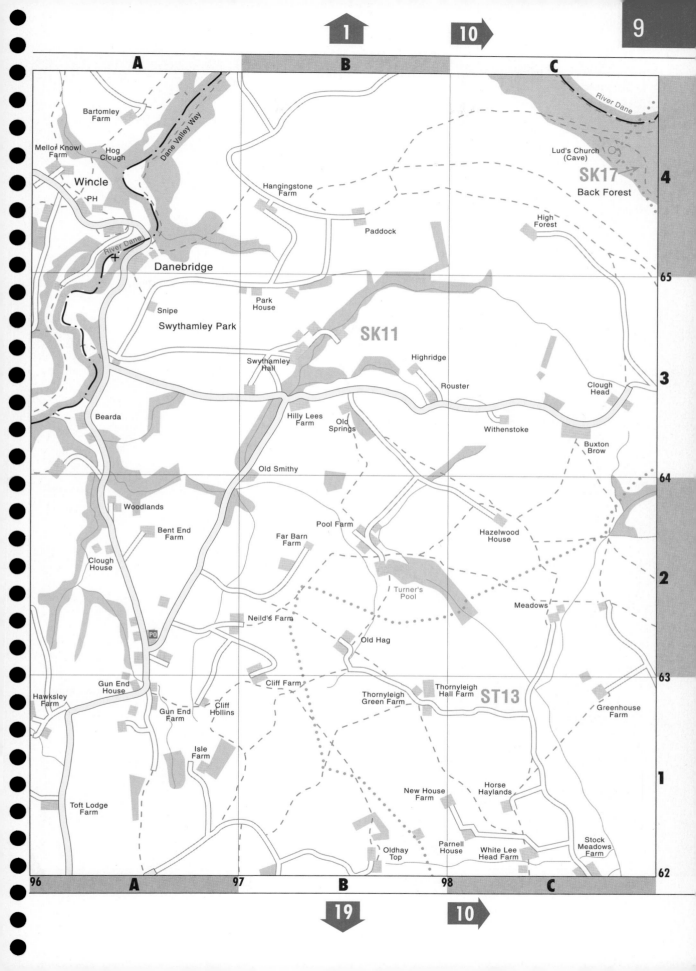

A   B   C

Gradbach

SK11

Bradley Howel

Green Gutter Head

Middle Edge

Sniddles

Gradbach Hill

Little Hillend

4

Sniddles Head Farm

Gradbach Wood

Cloughead

Moss Top

65

Black Brook

SK17

Black Forest

Moss End Farm

Gib Torr Rocks

Goldsitch Moss

SK11

3

Roach End

Goldsitch House

Blackbank

Bald Stone

64

Newstone Farm

Brownsett

Shaw Bottom

Hazel Barrow

2

Shawside

Shafts (dis)

Shaw House

Roche Grange

ST13

Shawtop

63

Harpersend

Roach Side Farm

Five Clouds

The Roaches

Newsett Farm

Blue Hills Farm

1

Summerhill

Pheasants Clough

Ramshaw Rocks

Roach House

P

Rockhall

Well Farm

A53

62

99   A   00   B   01   C

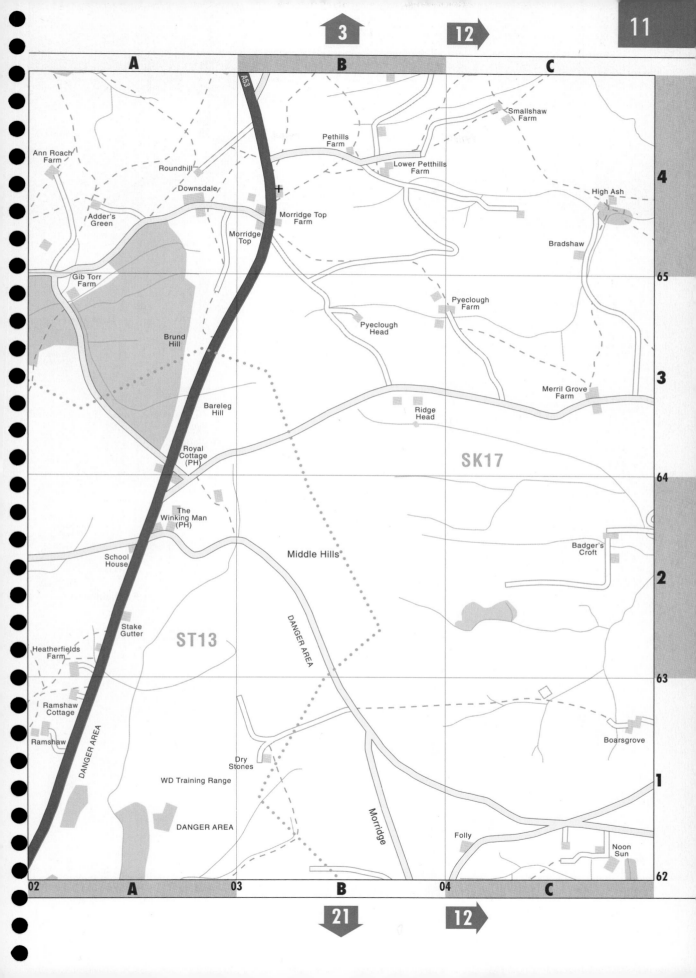

11
4

A   B   C

The New

Moss Carr

Tunstead

4

Ball Bank House Farm

Fawside Edge

Hole Carr

River Manifold

65

Fawside

Marnshaw Head

Millmoorhead Wood

Blackstone Edge

Barrow Moor

Wood Cottage

3

Lower House

Hardings Booth

The Hills

Top House Farm

Barrow Sitch

The Hocker

SK17

64

Oakenclough Hall

Hillend

Shining Ford

The Lane

School Clough

Oakenclough Brook

2

The Slack

Sycamore Farm

The Green

Holly Grove Farm

Fawfieldhead

Belfield House

Hallhill

Fair View

Newtown

Hawk's Yard

Bank House

63

The Bent

Mount Pleasant

1

Boosley Grange

Lady Edge

Shawfield Wood

Round Knowl

Brow Cottage

Smedley Sytch

Blake Brook

62

05   A   06   B   07   C

11
22

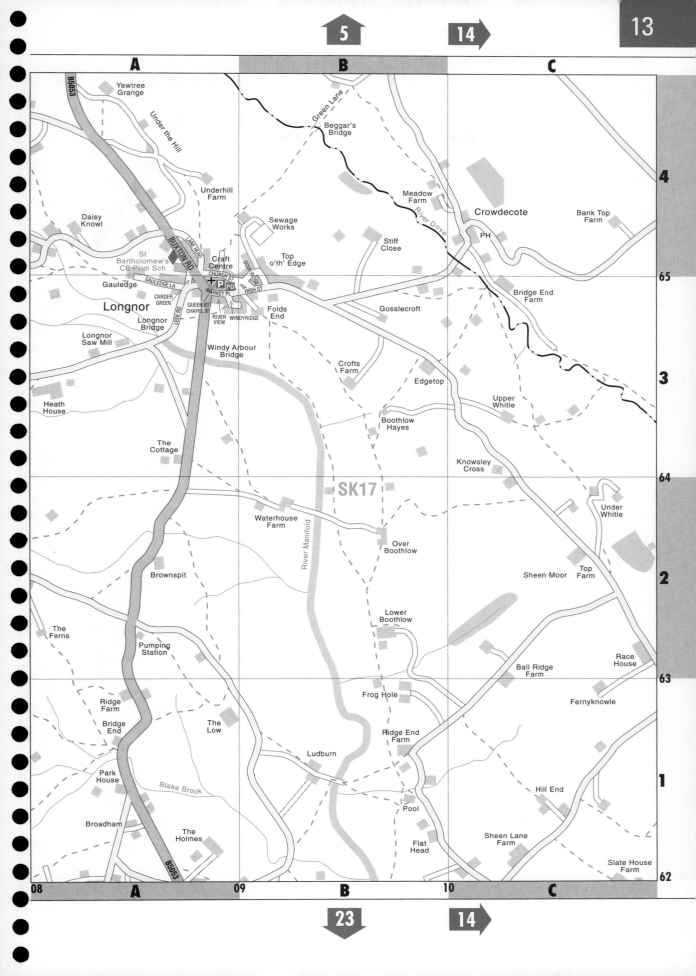

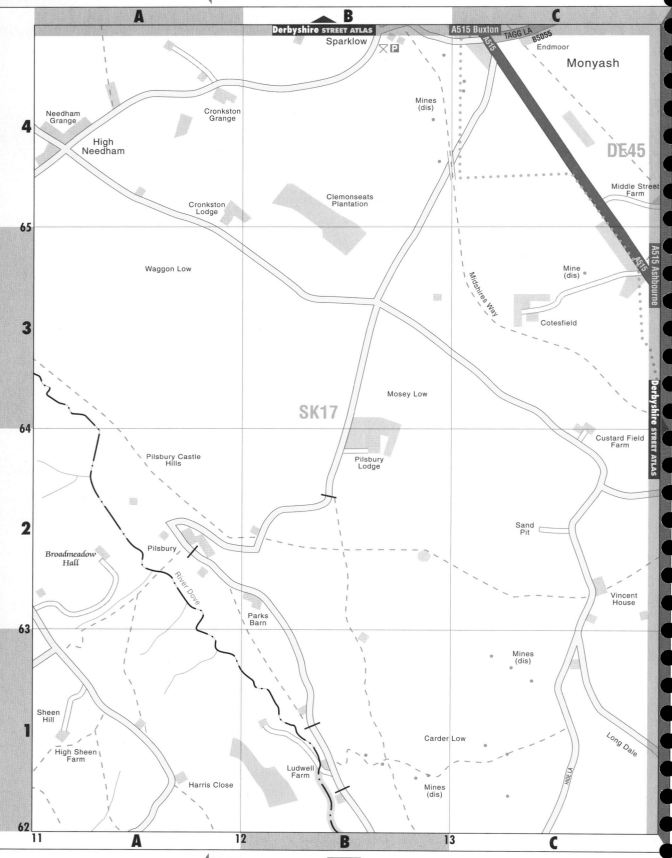

A   **B**   **C**

Derbyshire STREET ATLAS

Sparklow

A515 Buxton   TAGG LA   B5055

Endmoor

Monyash

Mines (dis)

DE45

Needham Grange

Cronkston Grange

High Needham

Cronkston Lodge

Clemonseats Plantation

Middle Street Farm

4

65

Waggon Low

Midshires Way

Mine (dis)

Cotesfield

A515 Ashbourne

3

Mosey Low

SK17

Derbyshire STREET ATLAS

64

Pilsbury Castle Hills

Pilsbury Lodge

Custard Field Farm

Broadmeadow Hall

Pilsbury

River Dove

Sand Pit

Vincent House

2

Parks Barn

63

Sheen Hill

Mines (dis)

1

High Sheen Farm

Carder Low

Long Dale

HIDE LA

Harris Close

Ludwell Farm

Mines (dis)

62

11   **A**   **12**   **B**   **13**   **C**

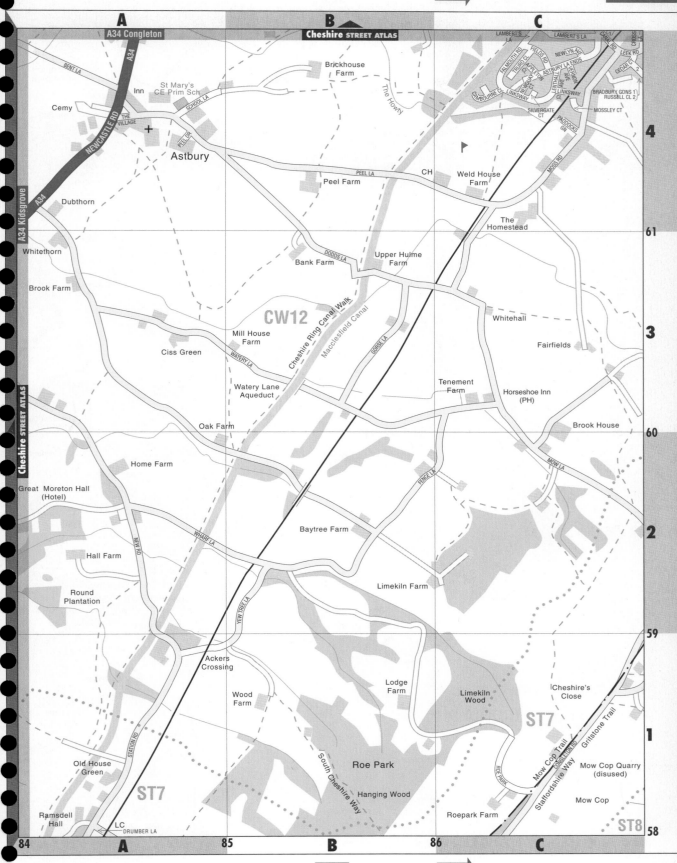

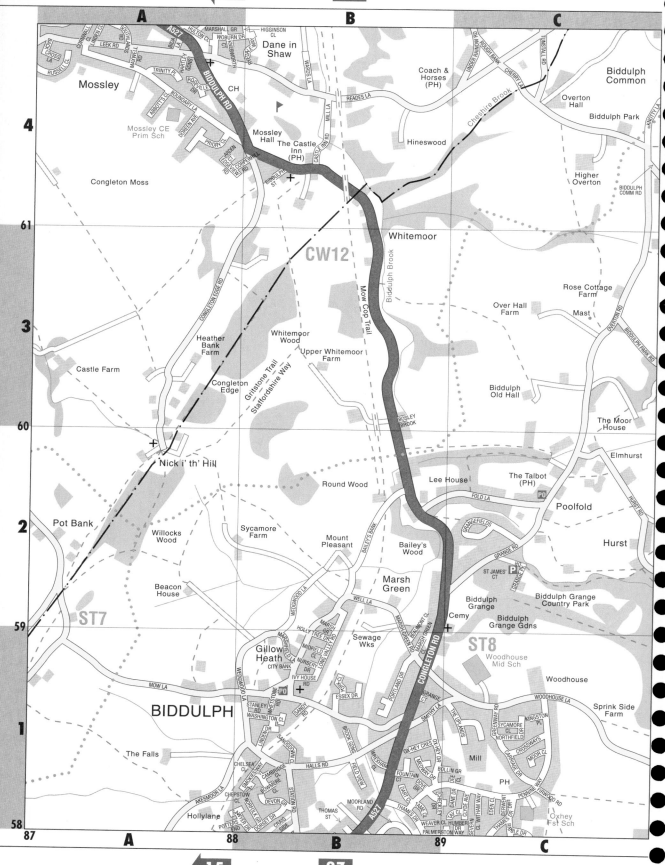

A · B · C

Mossley

Dane in Shaw

Coach & Horses (PH)

Biddulph Common

Overton Hall

Biddulph Park

Mossley CE Prim Sch

Mossley Hall

The Castle Inn (PH)

Hineswood

Higher Overton

Congleton Moss

61

Whitemoor

CW12

Rose Cottage Farm

Over Hall Farm

Mast

Heather Bank Farm

Whitemoor Wood

Upper Whitemoor Farm

3

Castle Farm

Congleton Edge

Gritstone Trail — Staffordshire Way

Biddulph Old Hall

60

The Moor House

Elmhurst

Nick i' th' Hill

Round Wood

Lee House

The Talbot (PH)

Poolfold

Pot Bank

Willocks Wood

Sycamore Farm

Mount Pleasant

Bailey's Wood

Hurst

2

ST7

Beacon House

Marsh Green

Biddulph Grange

Biddulph Grange Country Park

59

Gillow Heath

Sewage Wks

Cemy

Biddulph Grange Gdns

ST8

Woodhouse Mid Sch

Woodhouse

BIDDULPH

Mow La

Ivy House

City Bank

Woodhouse La

Sprink Side Farm

1

The Falls

Mill

PH

Hollylane

Oxhey Fst Sch

58

87 · A · 88 · B · 89 · C

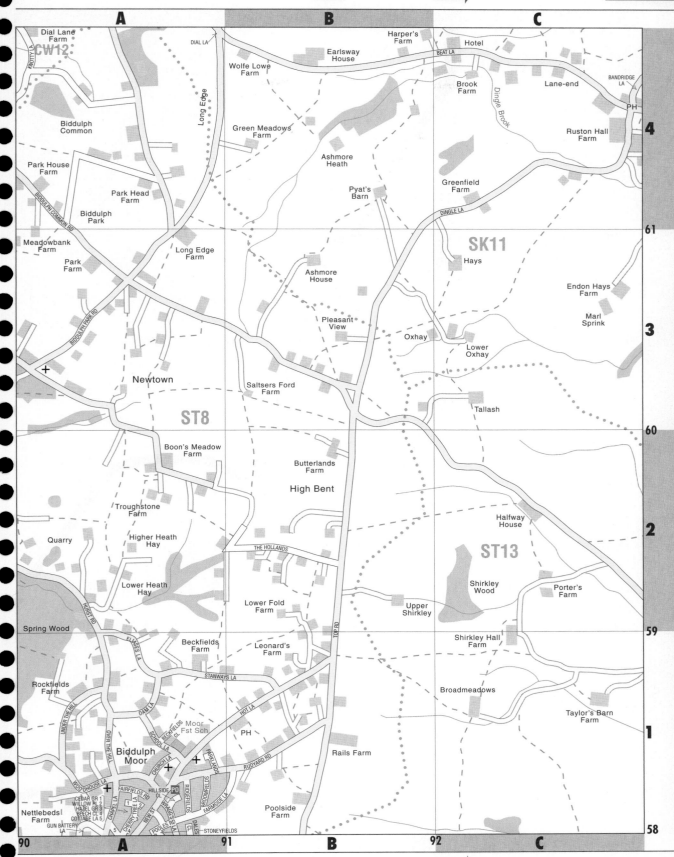

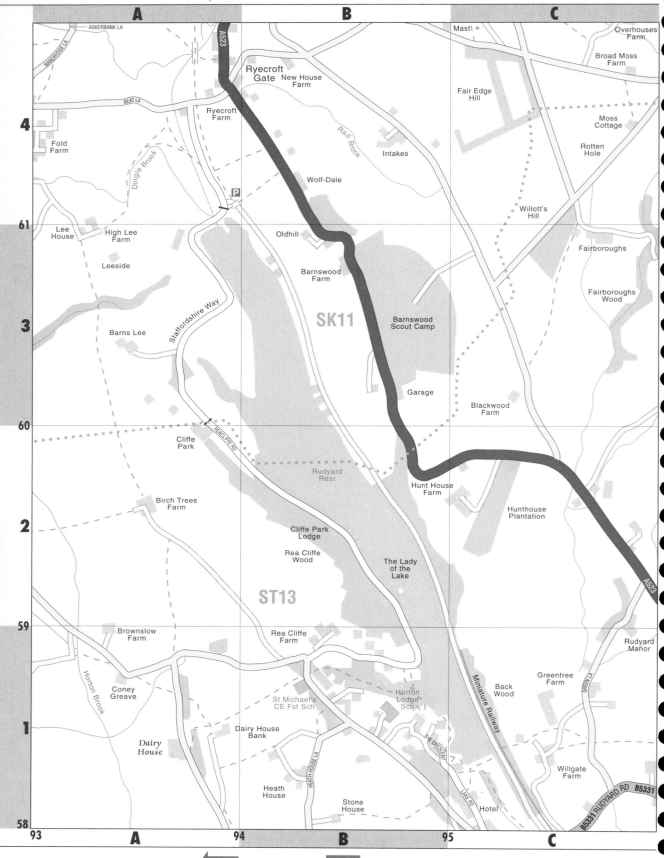

A B C

ASKERBANK LA

BANDRIDGE LA

A523

Ryecroft
Gate

New House
Farm

Mast

Overhouses
Farm

Broad Moss
Farm

BEAT LA

Ryecroft
Farm

Fair Edge
Hill

Moss
Cottage

4

Fold
Farm

Rad Brook

Intakes

Rotten
Hole

Wolf-Dale

P

Dingle Brook

61

Lee
House

High Lee
Farm

Oldhill

Willott's
Hill

Fairboroughs

Leeside

Barnswood
Farm

Fairboroughs
Wood

Staffordshire Way

SK11

Barnswood
Scout Camp

3

Barns Lee

Blackwood
Farm

Garage

60

Cliffe
Park

REACLIFFE RD

Rudyard
Resr

Hunt House
Farm

Birch Trees
Farm

Hunthouse
Plantation

2

Cliffe Park
Lodge

Rea Cliffe
Wood

The Lady
of the
Lake

A523

ST13

59

Brownslow
Farm

Rea Cliffe
Farm

Rudyard
Manor

Horton Brook

Coney
Greave

St Michael's
CE Fst Sch

Horton
Lodge
Sch

Back
Wood

Greentree
Farm

GREEN LA

Miniature Railway

1

Dairy House
Bank

THE CRESCENT

Willgate
Farm

Dairy
House

HEATH HOUSE LA

LAKE RD

B5331 RUDYARD RD B5331

Heath
House

Stone
House

Hotel

58

93   A   94   B   95   C

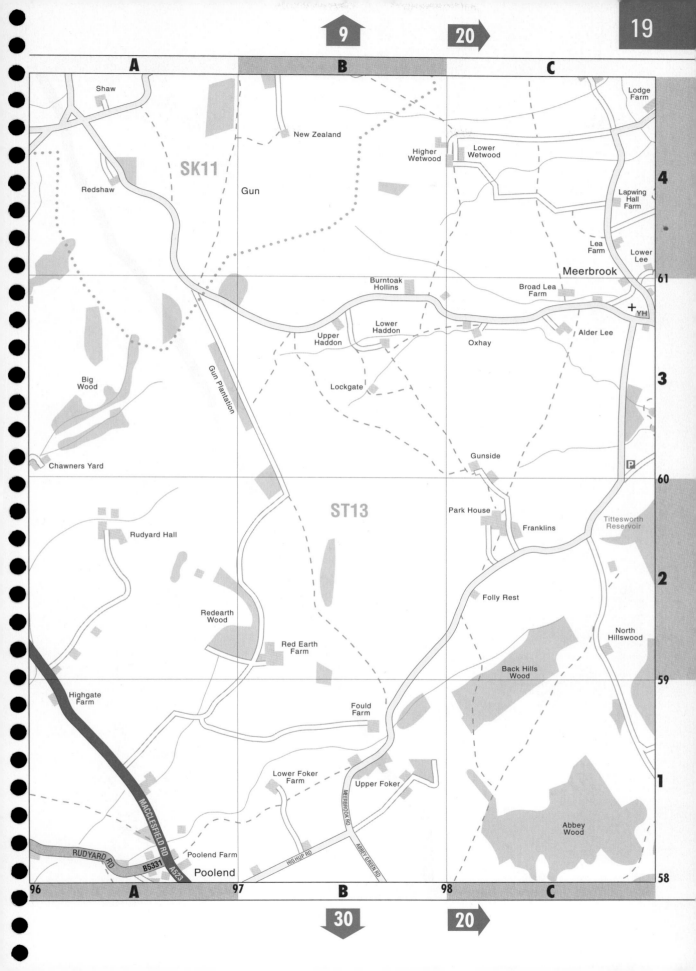

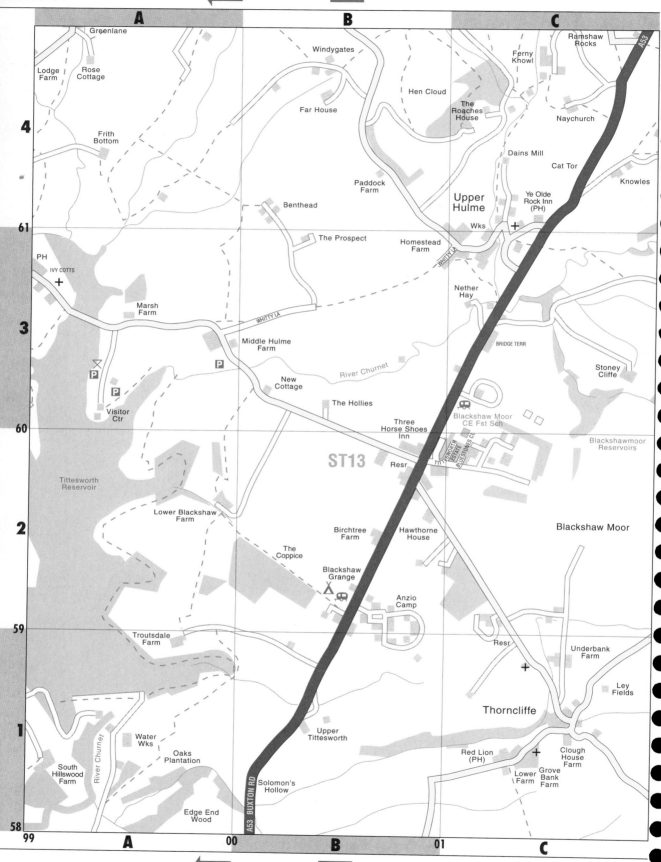

A **B** **C**

Greenlane

Lodge Farm

Rose Cottage

Windygates

Far House

Hen Cloud

The Roaches House

Ferny Khowl

Ramshaw Rocks

Naychurch

A53

4

Frith Bottom

Paddock Farm

Dains Mill

Cat Tor

Knowles

Benthead

Upper Hulme

Ye Olde Rock Inn (PH)

61

The Prospect

Homestead Farm

Wks

WHITTY LA

PH

IVY COTTS

Marsh Farm

WHITTY LA

Nether Hay

BRIDGE TERR

3

Middle Hulme Farm

River Churnet

Stoney Cliffe

P

P

P

New Cottage

The Hollies

Visitor Ctr

Three Horse Shoes Inn

Blackshaw Moor CE Fst Sch

Blackshawmoor Reservoirs

60

ST13

Resr

TITTESWORTH ESTATE
BLUESTONES CL

Tittesworth Reservoir

Lower Blackshaw Farm

Birchtree Farm

Hawthorne House

Blackshaw Moor

2

The Coppice

Blackshaw Grange

Anzio Camp

59

Troutsdale Farm

Resr

Underbank Farm

Ley Fields

Thorncliffe

1

Water Wks

Upper Tittesworth

Red Lion (PH)

Clough House Farm

South Hillswood Farm

Oaks Plantation

A53 BUXTON RD

Solomon's Hollow

Lower Farm

Grove Bank Farm

Edge End Wood

58

99 **A** **00** **B** **01** **C**

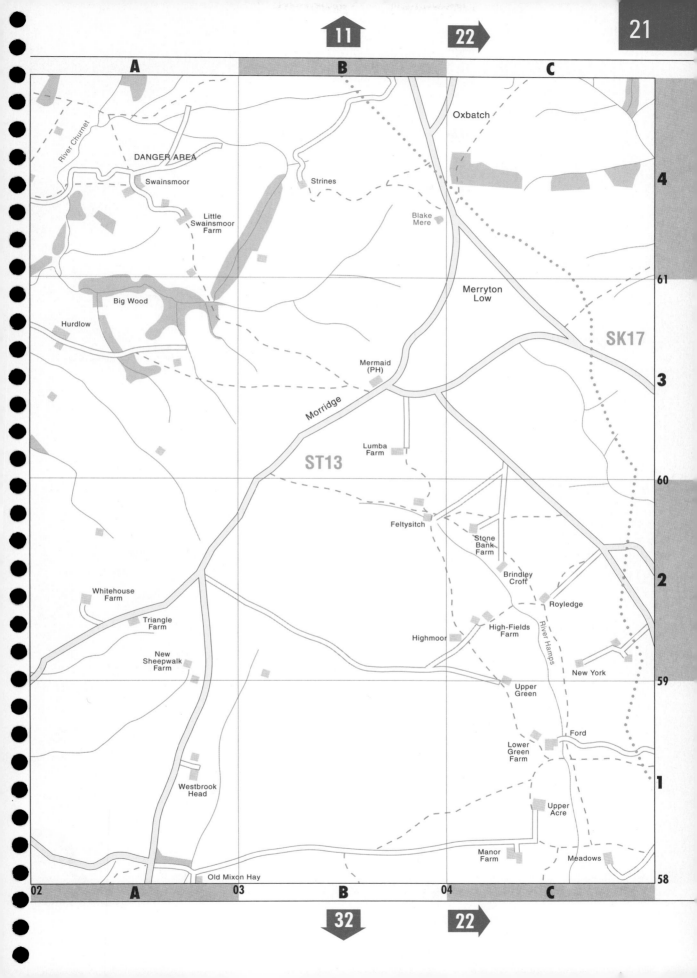

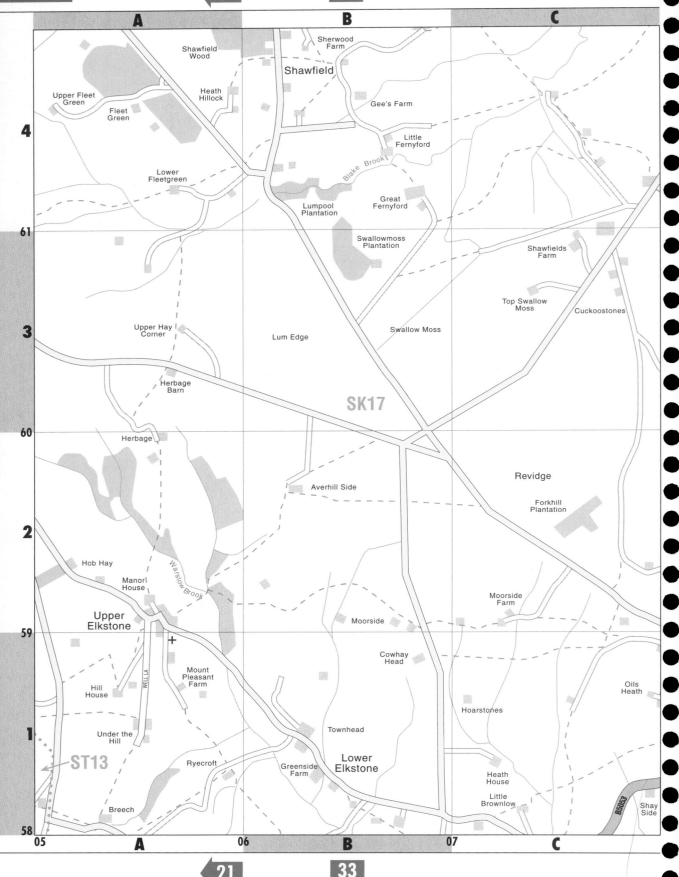

A B C

4

61

3

60

2

59

1

58

05 A 06 B 07 C

SK17

ST13

Shawfield Wood
Sherwood Farm
Shawfield
Upper Fleet Green
Fleet Green
Heath Hillock
Gee's Farm
Little Fernyford
Lower Fleetgreen
Blake Brook
Lumpool Plantation
Great Fernyford
Swallowmoss Plantation
Shawfields Farm
Top Swallow Moss
Cuckoostones
Upper Hay Corner
Lum Edge
Swallow Moss
Herbage Barn
Herbage
Revidge
Averhill Side
Forkhill Plantation
Hob Hay
Warslow Brook
Manor House
Moorside Farm
Upper Elkstone
Moorside
Cowhay Head
Oils Heath
WELL LA
Hill House
Mount Pleasant Farm
Hoarstones
Under the Hill
Townhead
Ryecroft
Greenside Farm
Lower Elkstone
Heath House
B5053
Breech
Little Brownlow
Shay Side

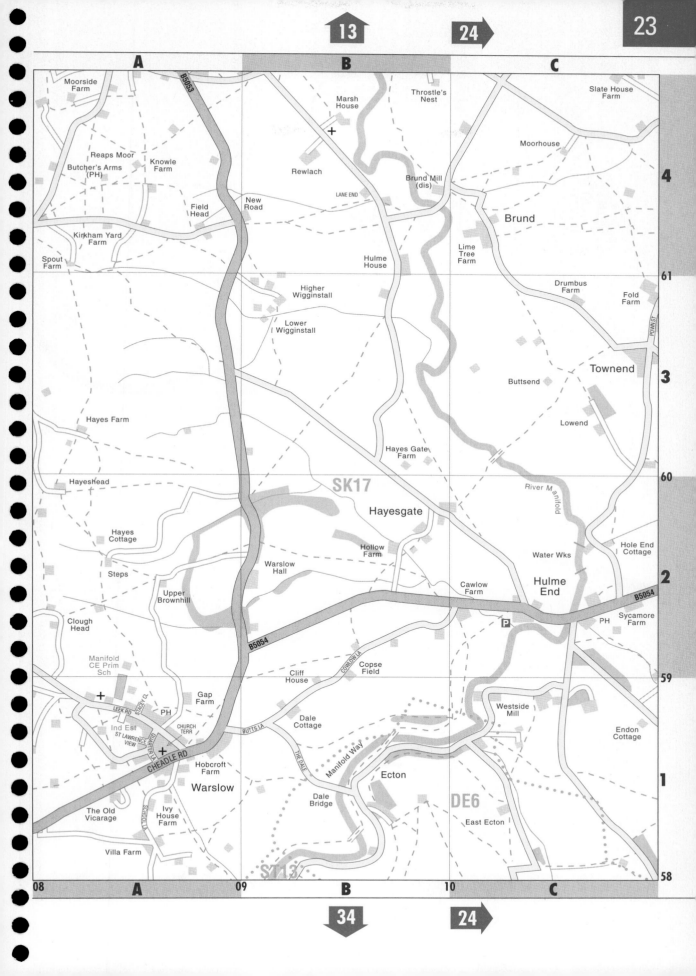

A B C

Moorside
Farm

B5053

Marsh
House

Throstle's
Nest

Slate House
Farm

Moorhouse

Reaps Moor

Butcher's Arms
(PH)

Knowle
Farm

Rewlach

Brund Mill
(dis)

Brund

4

Field
Head

New
Road

LANE END

Hulme
House

Lime
Tree
Farm

Kirkham Yard
Farm

Drumbus
Farm

Fold
Farm

Spout
Farm

Higher
Wigginstall

61

Lower
Wigginstall

PUMM ST

Townend

3

Hayes Farm

Buttsend

Lowend

Hayes Gate
Farm

Hayeshead

SK17

River Manifold

60

Hayesgate

Hayes
Cottage

Hollow
Farm

Water Wks

Hole End
Cottage

Steps

Warslow
Hall

Hulme
End

2

Upper
Brownhill

Cawlow
Farm

B5054

Clough
Head

PH

Sycamore
Farm

Manifold
CE Prim
Sch

B5054

COWLOW LA

Copse
Field

P

Cliff
House

59

Gap
Farm

LEEK RD

STACEY CL

PH

CHURCH
TERR

BUTTS LA

Dale
Cottage

Westside
Mill

Endon
Cottage

Ind Est

ST LAWRENCE
VIEW

QUARTER LA

CHEADLE RD

Hobcroft
Farm

THE DALE

Manifold Way

Ecton

DE6

1

The Old
Vicarage

LYCHGATE

Ivy
House
Farm

Dale
Bridge

East Ecton

Villa Farm

ST13

58

Warslow

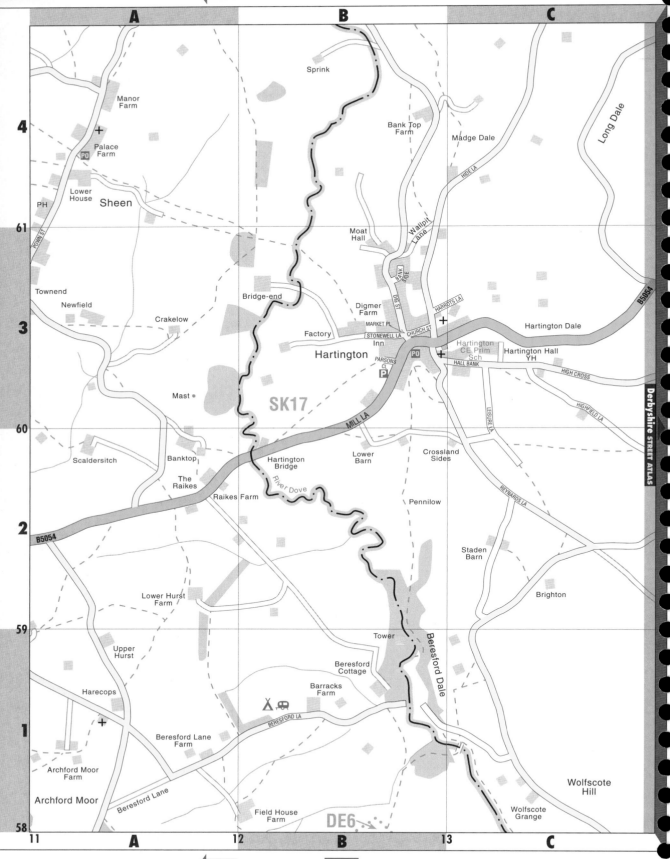

Derbyshire STREET ATLAS

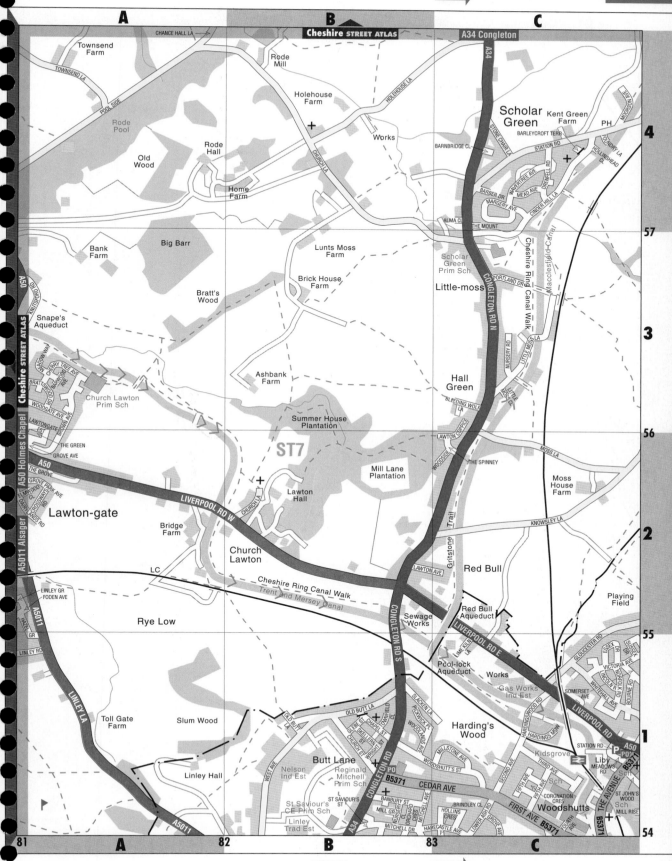

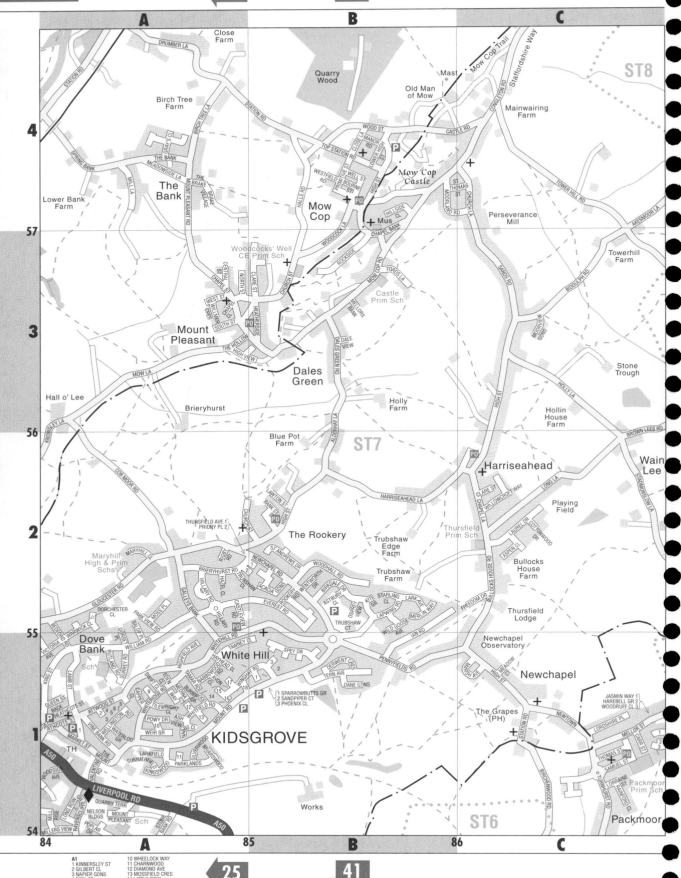

A   **B**   **C**

ST8

Close Farm

DRUMBER LA

Quarry Wood

Old Man of Mow

Mast

Mow Cop Trail

Staffordshire Way

STATION RD

Birch Tree Farm

CONGLETON RD

Mainwairing Farm

Castle Rd

WOOD ST

4

THE BANK

MEADOWSIDE LA

The Bank

Mow Cop Castle

TOWER HILL RD

ST THOMAS CHURCH LA

Mow Cop

Perseverance Mill

Lower Bank Farm

57

Mus

Towerhill Farm

AKESMOOR LA

Woodcocks' Well CE Prim Sch

ROCKSIDE

Castle Prim Sch

BIDDULPH RD

3

Mount Pleasant

HEATHERSIDE

Stone Trough

Dales Green

MOW LA

Holly Farm

HOLLY LA

Hollin House Farm

Hall o' Lee

Brieryhurst

56

Blue Pot Farm

ST7

PO

Harriseahead

BROWN LEES RD

Wain Lee

KNOWSLEY LA

COB MOOR RD

HARRISEAHEAD LA

CLARE ST

Playing Field

STADMORSLOW LA

2

Thursfield Ave 1
Priory Pl 2

The Rookery

Trubshaw Edge Farm

Thursfield Prim Sch

Bullocks House Farm

Maryhill High & Prim Schs

Trubshaw Farm

Thursfield Lodge

55

Dove Bank

White Hill

Newchapel Observatory

Newchapel

1

1 SPARROWBUTTS GR
2 SANDPIPER CT
3 PHOENIX CL

JASMIN WAY 1
HAREBELL GR 2
WOODRUFF CL 3

The Grapes (PH)

KIDSGROVE

A50

LIVERPOOL RD

Works

Packmoor Prim Sch

54

ST6

Packmoor

84   **A**   85   **B**   86   **C**

A1
1 KINNERSLEY ST
2 GILBERT CL
3 NAPIER GDNS
4 PEEL CT
5 BANK CT
6 HIGHERLAND CT
7 WESLEY GDNS
8 VICTORIA CT
9 SWALLOW CL
10 WHEELOCK WAY
11 CHARNWOOD
12 DIAMOND AVE
13 MOSSFIELD CRES
14 LITTLE ROW
15 BRIGHTS AVE
16 BIRCHES WAY
17 SILVERMINE CL
18 MAGPIE CRES

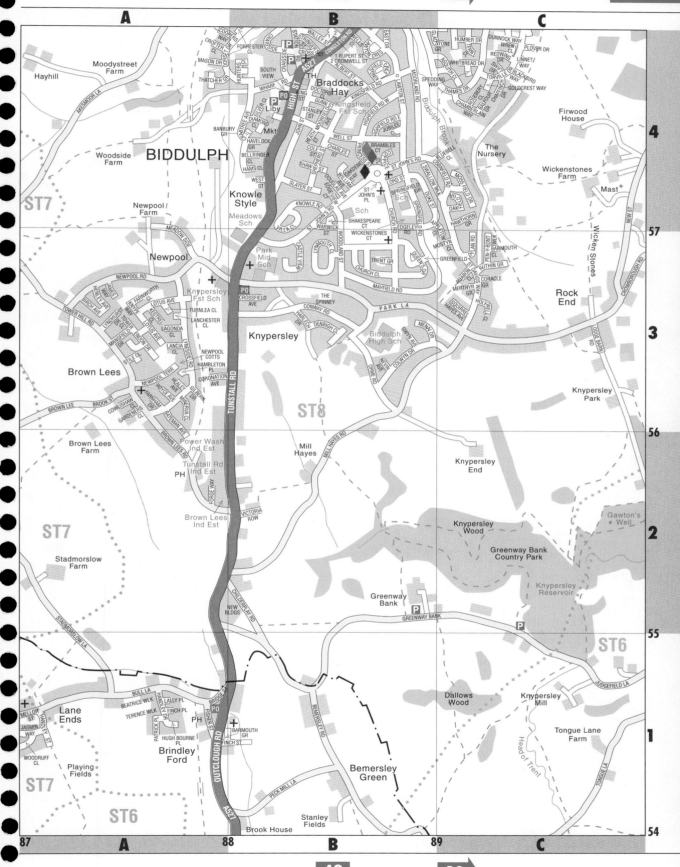

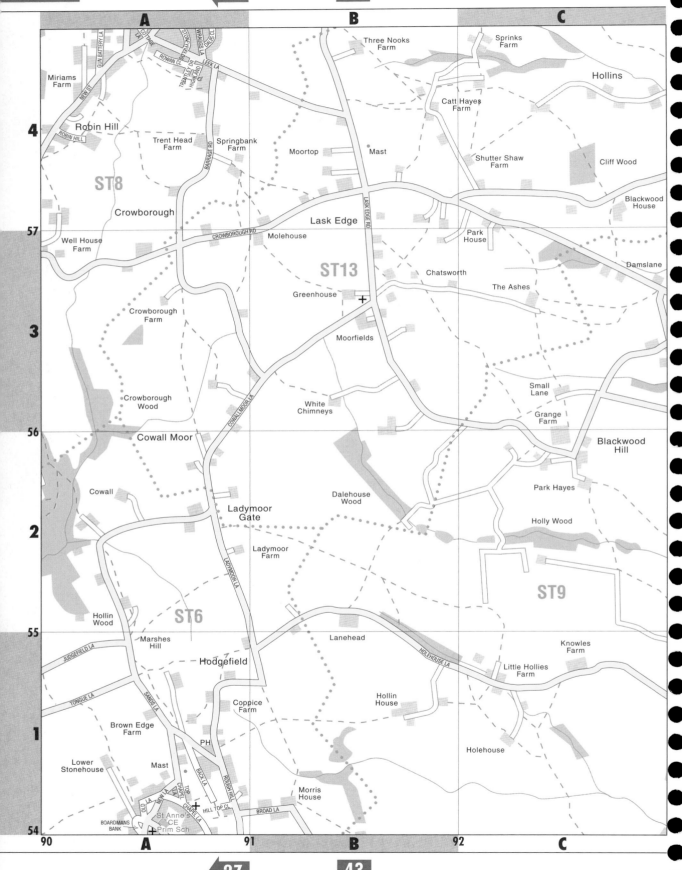

A B C

GUN BATTERY LA
NEW ST
COTTAGE LA
STONE EDGE RD
WRAGGS LA
DALES CL
LEEK LA
ROWAN CL
HIGHLAND CL
BRADLEY DR
OLD
Miriams Farm
Robin Hill
ROBIN HILL
Trent Head Farm
Springbank Farm
BARRAGE RD
Three Nooks Farm
Moortop
Mast
Sprinks Farm
Hollins
Catt Hayes Farm
Shutter Shaw Farm
Cliff Wood
Blackwood House

ST8
Crowborough
Lask Edge
LASK EDGE RD
CROWBOROUGH RD
Well House Farm
Molehouse
ST13
Park House
Chatsworth
Damslane
Greenhouse
The Ashes
Crowborough Farm
Moorfields
Small Lane
Crowborough Wood
White Chimneys
Grange Farm
Blackwood Hill
Cowall Moor
COWALL MOOR LA
Dalehouse Wood
Park Hayes
Cowall
Ladymoor Gate
Holly Wood
LADYMOOR LA
Ladymoor Farm
ST9
Hollin Wood
ST6
Marshes Hill
Lanehead
Knowles Farm
JUDGEFIELD LA
Hodgefield
HOLEHOUSE LA
Little Hollies Farm
TONGUE LA
SANDS LA
Coppice Farm
Hollin House
Brown Edge Farm
PH
Lower Stonehouse
Mast
BACK LA
ROUGH HILL
Holehouse
OLD LA
NEW LA
CHAPEL LA
TOP
HILL TOP CL
Morris House
BROAD LA
St Anne's CE Prim Sch
BOARDMANS BANK

90 91 92

4

57

3

56

2

55

1

54

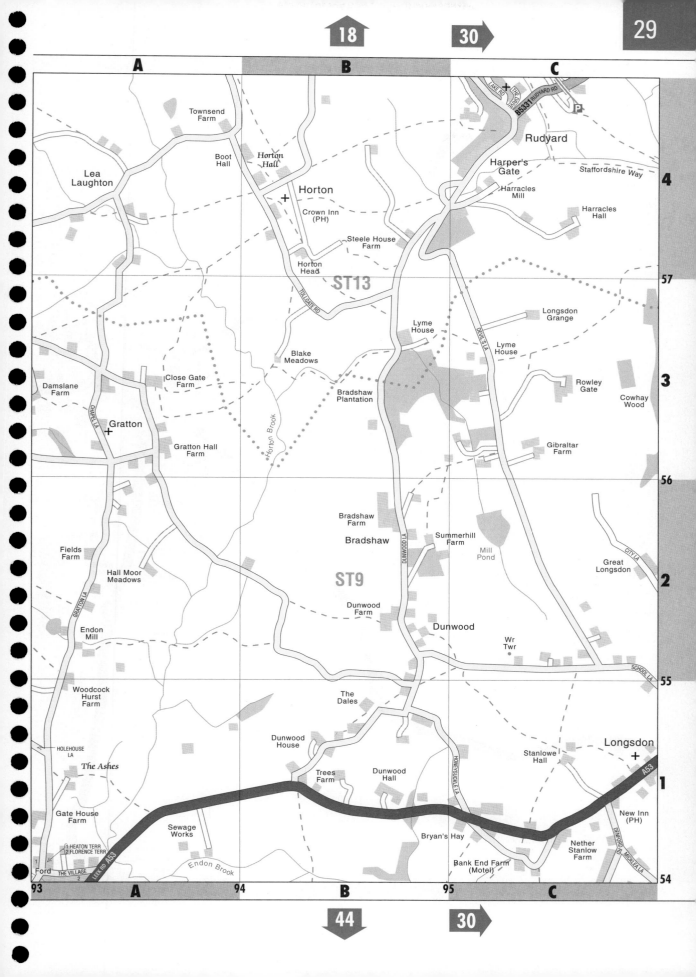

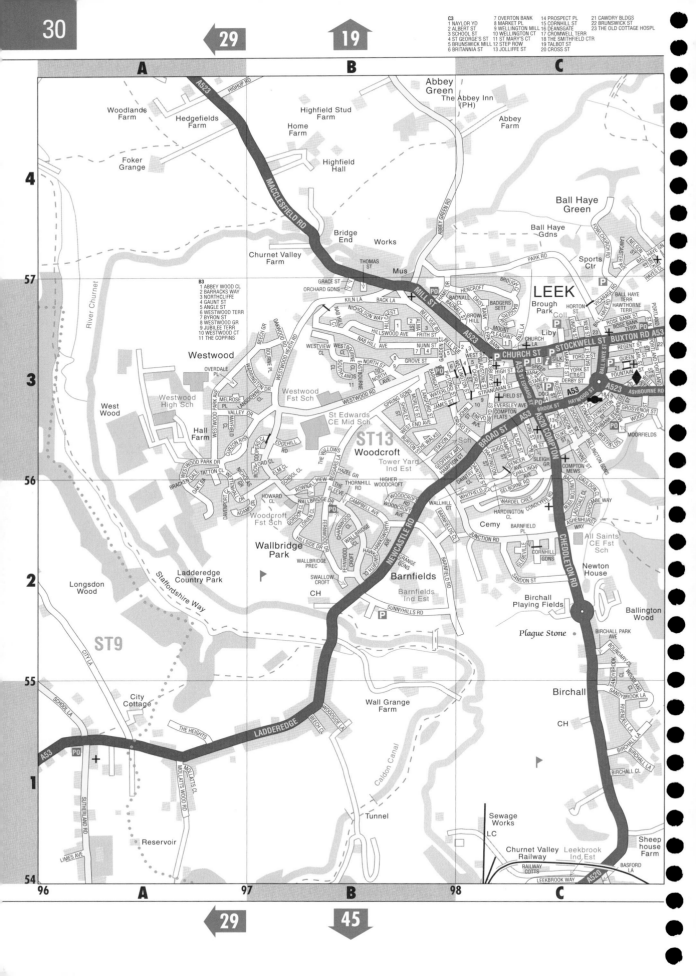

A   **B**   **C**

Wardle Barn Farm
Haregate Wood
Leek Moorside
Ankers Lane Farm
Easing Moor Farm
Ashes Farm
HAREGATE RD
HORSECROFT GR
THORNCLIFFE VIEW
CHURNET VIEW
Churnet View Mid Sch
ROCHE AVE
PRIORY AVE
HORSECROFT VIEW
PRINCE DR
QUEENS DR
RAMSHAW VIEW
GALES AVE
PRINCESS AVE
WINDSOR DR
Edge End Farm
Easing Moor
Easing LA
Moss Rose Inn (PH)
A53
THORNCLIFF RD
Easing Farm
STEESHORPH AVE
ARGLES RD
FURMSTON PL
PROVOST
WESTMINSTER RD
NOVI LA
ABBOTTS RD
SCH
O HARE PL
Sch
PO
Haregate
Easing Villa
Hollystones
Cartledge
Coltsmoor Farm
57
BUXTON RD
HALL AVE
HAIG RD
BEATTY RD
CARLTON TERR
MILNER TERR
VICTORIA ST
MOUNT RD
Freshwinds
Lark Hall
BALL HAYE DR
HARPER TERR
PUMP ST
PRINCE ST
SHAW ST
TREEBANK AVE
WOODFIELD CT
ASHDALE RD
MOUNT SIDE GDNS
ASHDAL CT
Dee Bank Farm
STILE HOUSE LA
SHIRBURN RD
SPRINGFIELD CT
SPRINGFIELD DR
SPRINGFIELD RD
FOUNTAIN ST
PARKER ST
DAIRY LA
EAST ST
Leek High Sch
Springfield Sch
Hare House
Holly House
Holly House
3
KNIVEDEN LA
LOCKERBIE CL
PITCHER'S CL
LOWTHER PL
MEADOW CL
MONTAGU DR
HILL VIEW
PEAK VIEW
PICKWOOD
FAIRY VIEW RD
PROSPECT DR
THORNFIELD DR
MOORL RD
ABBEY GRN RD
HIGH VIEW
STAFFORD DR
Stile House Farm
Beeley Barn
Mast
Kniveden
Leek Morlands
ST13
56
MILLTOW WAY
MULBERRY WAY
ASHBOURNE RD
Pickwood Cottage
Padwick Farm
Poolhall
Twillow Heath
Holly Dale
Ballington Grange Farm
Home Farm
Lowe Hill Farm
Wildgoose Farm
Buckley Farm
Brook Farm
DOUSE LA
2
SCHOOL LA
Bradnop
Lowe Hill
Meadow View
PORTERS LA
55
Cliff Farm
Hollybush
Fairfields Farm
Middle Cliff
Ashenhurst Cottage
Ivy Cottage
Birchall Wood
Ashenhurst Mill
Throstles Nest
1
Longshaw Farm
COOK'S LA
A523
Jackfield Plantation
Ashenhurst Hall Farm
Egg Well
54

A   **B**   **C**
99   00   01

31
21

A **B** **C**

4

Old Mixon
Hay

EASING LA

Cave

Westbrook

New Mixon
Hay

Mixon
Grange

Mixon
Mines

Dunlea
Farm

Mixon

57

Wormlow
Farm

Dale
House

Morridge

Harvey
Gate

Newhouse
Farm

River Hamps

3

White Lea
Farm

ST13

Wellington
Farm

Rue Hayes
Farm

56

Waterhouse

High
Cross

Onecote Lane
Head

DOUSE LA

Cemy

Onecote
Grange

2

Intake
Farm

Onecote Lane
End

Onecote

55

Newhouse
Farm

B5053

Moor
Top

Birdsgrove
Farm

Lower Moorside
Farm

Cliffhead

Weatherworth
Farm

Willowmeadow

Moorside

WETLEY LA

Hopping
Head

1

Morridge
Side

Garstones

Slate
House

New
Farm

COOKS LA

Town Field
Farm

A523

Lane-end

Astonsitch

Hobmeadows

B5053

54

02 **A** 03 **B** 04 **C**

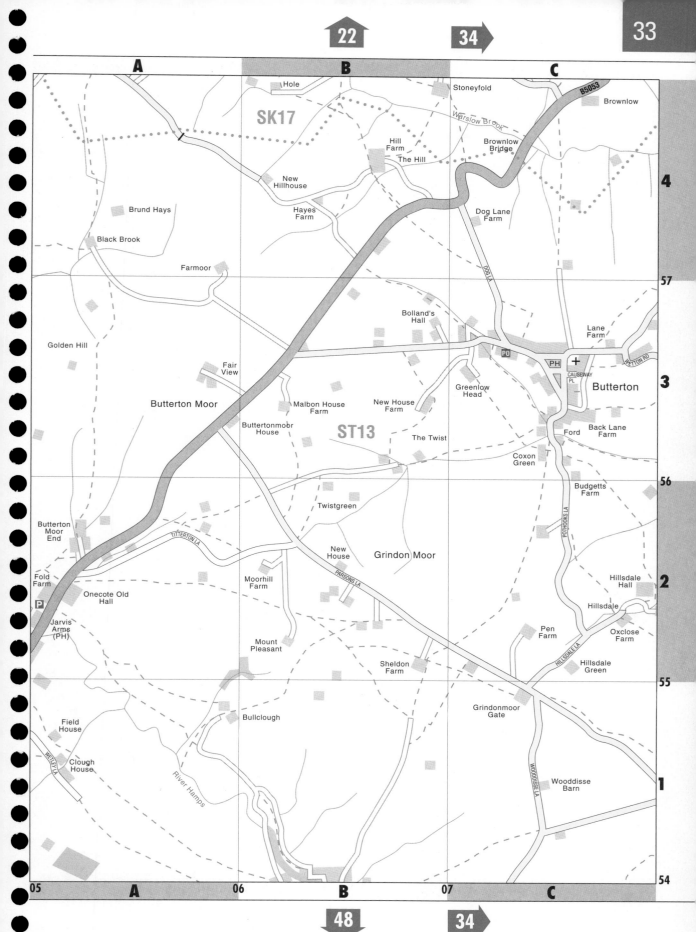

A B C

Hole
Stoneyfold
SK17
B5053
Brownlow
Warslow Brook
Hill Farm
The Hill
Brownlow Bridge
New Hillhouse
4
Brund Hays
Hayes Farm
Dog Lane Farm
Black Brook
DOG LA
57
Farmoor
Bolland's Hall
Lane Farm
Golden Hill
PO
PH
WETTON RD
Fair View
Greenlow Head
CAUSEWAY PL
Butterton
3
Butterton Moor
Malbon House Farm
New House Farm
ST13
The Twist
Ford
Back Lane Farm
Buttertonmoor House
Coxon Green
56
Budgetts Farm
Twistgreen
POTHOOKS LA
Butterton Moor End
TITTERTON LA
New House
Grindon Moor
Hillsdale Hall
2
Fold Farm
Moorhill Farm
PARSONS LA
Pen Farm
Hillsdale
P
Onecote Old Hall
HILLSDALE LA
Oxclose Farm
Jarvis Arms (PH)
Mount Pleasant
Sheldon Farm
Hillsdale Green
55
Grindonmoor Gate
Field House
Bullclough
WETLEY LA
Clough House
WOODDISSE LA
Wooddisse Barn
1
River Hamps

05 A 06 B 07 C 54

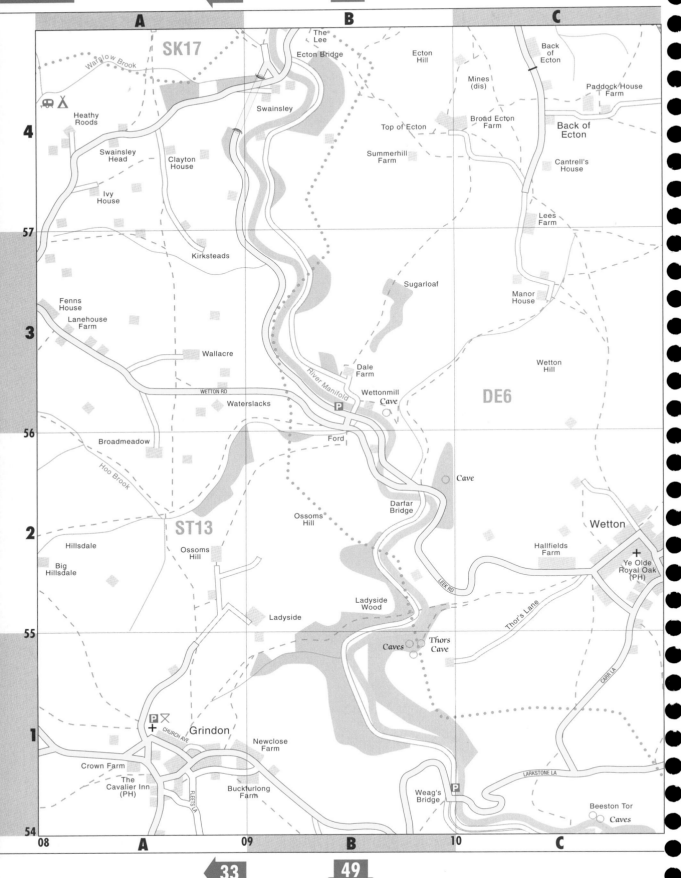

SK17

The Lee
Ecton Bridge
Ecton Hill
Back of Ecton
Mines (dis)
Paddock House Farm
Heathy Roods
Swainsley
Top of Ecton
Broad Ecton Farm
Back of Ecton
Warslow Brook
Swainsley Head
Clayton House
Summerhill Farm
Cantrell's House
Ivy House
Lees Farm
Kirksteads
Sugarloaf
Manor House
Fenns House
Lanehouse Farm
Wallacre
Wetton Hill
DE6
WETTON RD
River Manifold
Dale Farm
Wettonmill
Cave
Waterslacks
Broadmeadow
Ford
Hoo Brook
Cave
ST13
Ossoms Hill
Darfar Bridge
Wetton
Hillsdale
Ossoms Hill
Hallfields Farm
Ye Olde Royal Oak (PH)
Big Hillsdale
Ladyside Wood
Ladyside
Thor's Lane
LEEK RD
Caves
Thors Cave
CARR LA
Grindon
CHURCH AVE
Newclose Farm
Crown Farm
The Cavalier Inn (PH)
FLEETS LA
Buckfurlong Farm
Weag's Bridge
LARKSTONE LA
Beeston Tor
Caves

08   A   09   B   10   C

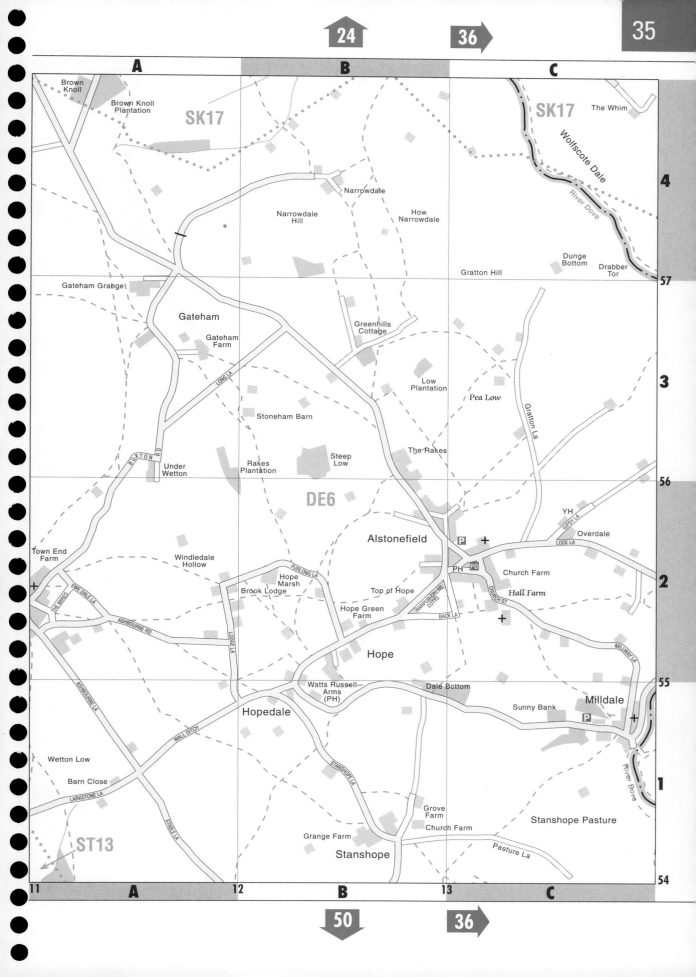

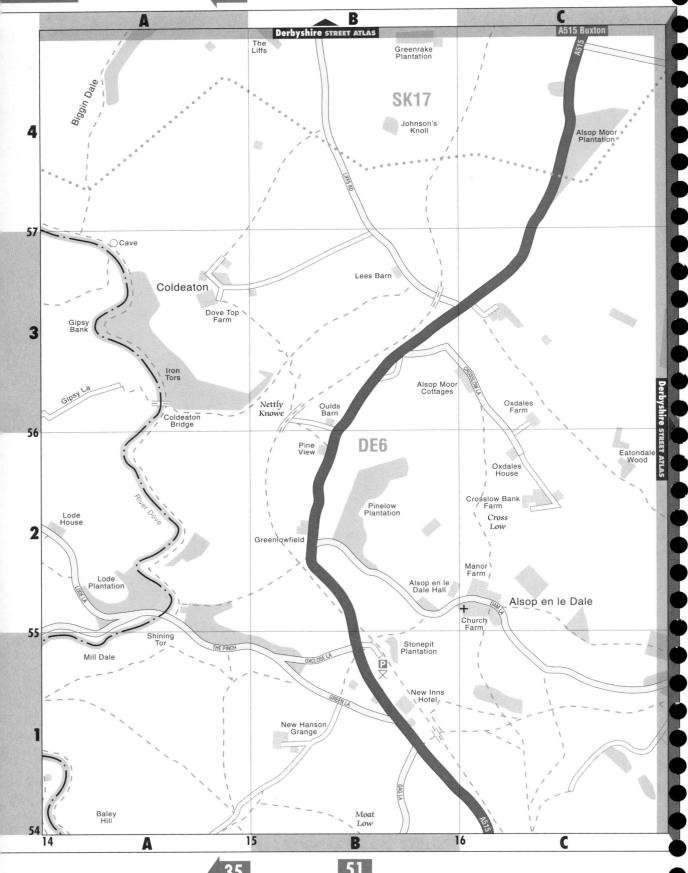

Derbyshire STREET ATLAS

A515 Buxton

The Liffs

Greenrake
Plantation

SK17

Johnson's
Knoll

Alsop Moor
Plantation

4

Biggin Dale

LIFFS RD

A515

○ Cave

57

Coldeaton

Lees Barn

Dove Top
Farm

Gipsy
Bank

3

Iron
Tors

Gipsy La

Coldeaton
Bridge

Nettly
Knowe

Oulds
Barn

Alsop Moor
Cottages

CROSSLOW LA

Oxdales
Farm

Pine
View

56

DE6

Oxdales
House

Eatondale
Wood

River Dove

Pinelow
Plantation

Crosslow Bank
Farm

Cross
Low

Lode
House

2

Greenlowfield

Manor
Farm

Lode
Plantation

Alsop en le
Dale Hall

Alsop en le Dale

LODE LA

DAM LA

✚
Church
Farm

55

Shining Tor

THE PINCH

OXCLOSE LA

Stonepit
Plantation

Mill Dale

GREEN LA

P
⚔

New Inns
Hotel

1

New Hanson
Grange

GAG LA

Baley
Hill

Moat
Low

A515

54

Derbyshire STREET ATLAS

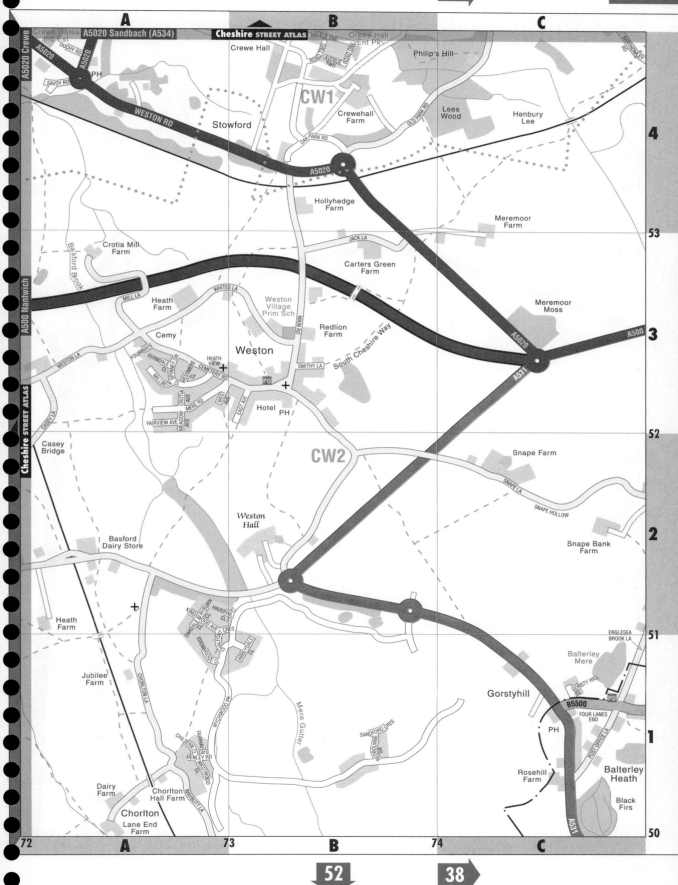

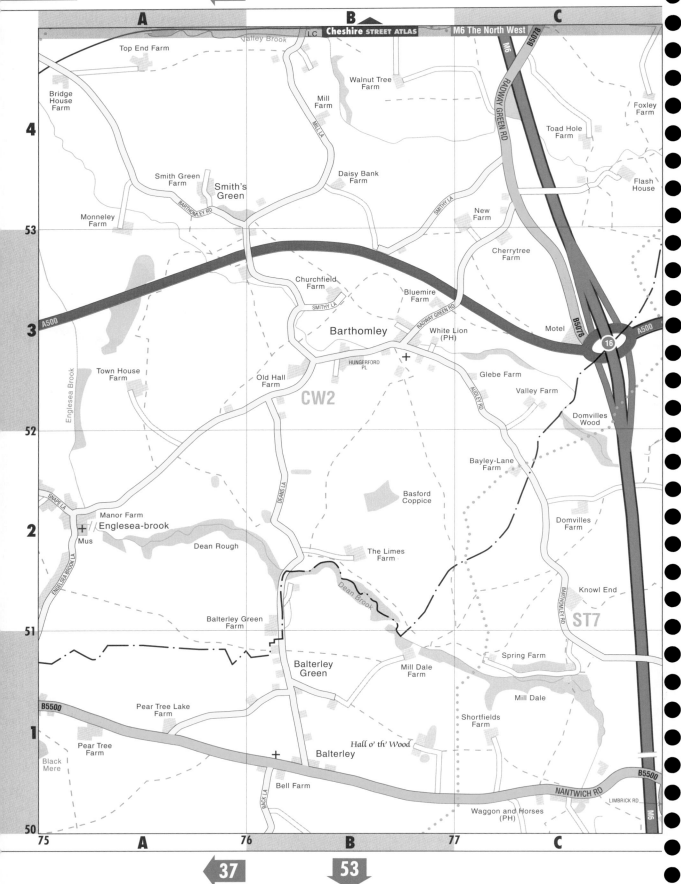

A
B
C

Top End Farm

Valley Brook

Walnut Tree
Farm

B5078

M6

Foxley
Farm

4

Bridge
House
Farm

Mill
Farm

MILL LA

RADWAY GREEN RD

Toad Hole
Farm

Flash
House

Smith Green
Farm

Daisy Bank
Farm

Smith's
Green

New
Farm

53

BARTHOMLEY RD

SMITHY LA

Monneley
Farm

Cherrytree
Farm

Churchfield
Farm

Bluemire
Farm

B5078

3

A500

SMITHY LA

Barthomley

RADWAY GREEN RD

White Lion
(PH)

Motel

A500

16

Englesea Brook

Town House
Farm

HUNGERFORD
PL

Glebe Farm

Valley Farm

Old Hall
Farm

CW2

AUDLEY RD

Domvilles
Wood

52

Bayley-Lane
Farm

SNAPE LA

Manor Farm

Englesea-brook

DEANS LA

Basford
Coppice

Domvilles
Farm

2

Mus

Dean Rough

The Limes
Farm

ENGLESEA BROOK LA

Dean Brook

Knowl End

BARTHOMLEY RD

ST7

Balterley Green
Farm

51

Spring Farm

Balterley
Green

Mill Dale
Farm

Mill Dale

B5500

Pear Tree Lake
Farm

Shortfields
Farm

1

Pear Tree
Farm

Hall o' th' Wood

Balterley

B5500

Black
Mere

BACK LA

Bell Farm

NANTWICH RD

M6

LIMBRICK RD

Waggon and Horses
(PH)

50

75
A
76
B
77
C

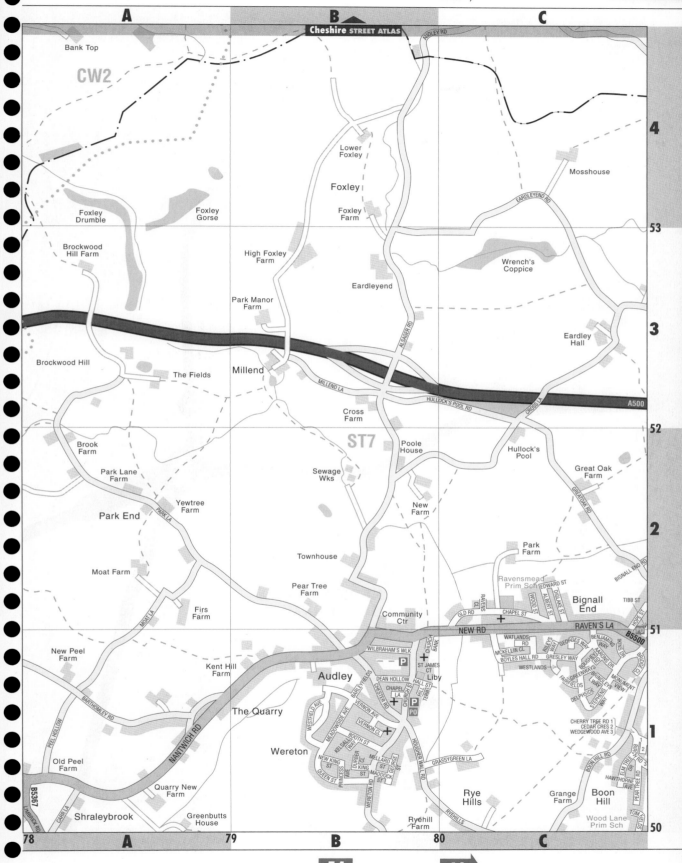

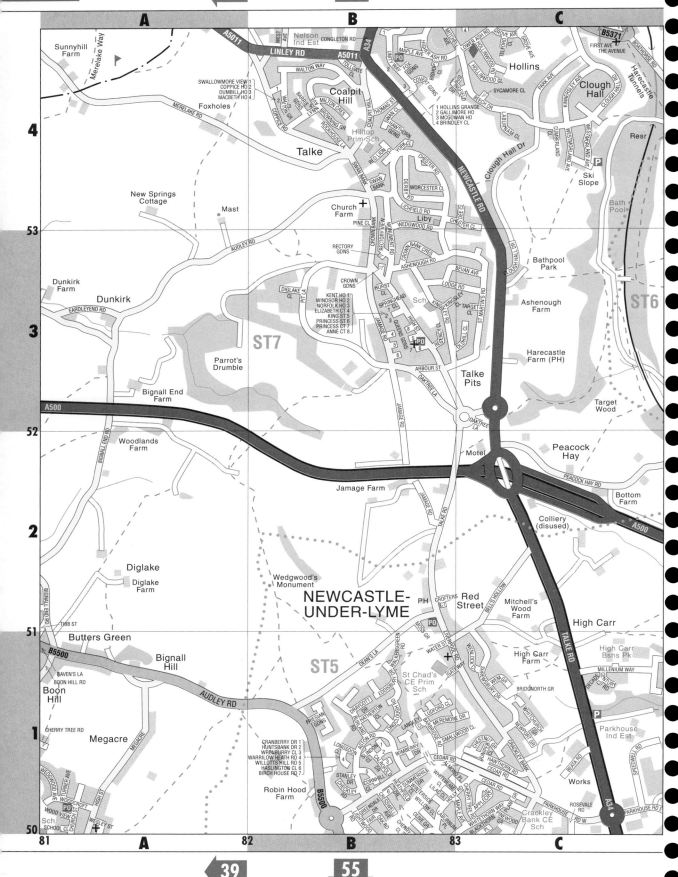

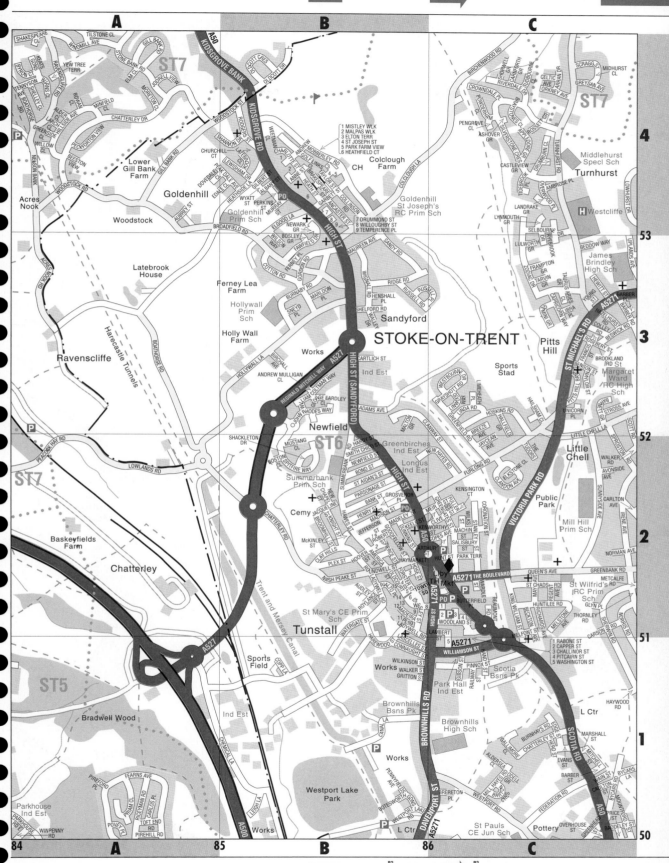

B2
1 ATHELSTAN ST
2 HOLLAND ST
3 PHOENIX ST
4 CALVER ST
5 PARADISE ST
6 PICCADILLY ST
7 McGOUGH ST
8 FARNDALE ST
9 SIMISTER CT

B2
10 COLUMBINE WLK
11 KNIGHTSBRIDGE WAY
12 CORBETT WLK
13 MAYFAIR GDNS
14 CORINTH WAY
15 PERSIA WLK

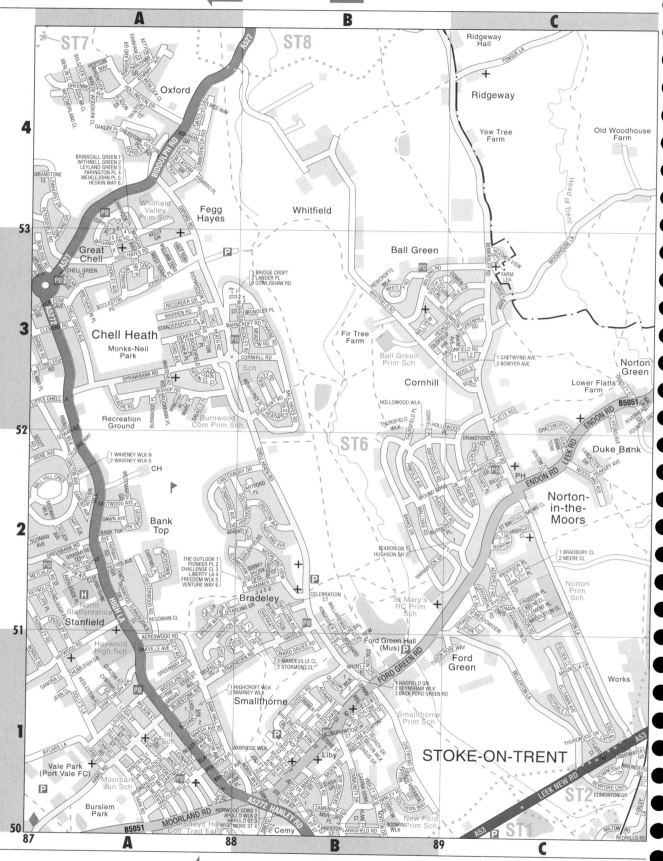

ST7

Oxford

ST8

Ridgeway
Hall

Ridgeway

A

B

C

4

Yew Tree
Farm

Old Woodhouse
Farm

BRINSCALL GREEN 1
WITHNELL GREEN 2
LEYLAND GREEN 3
FARINGTON PL 4
MEIKLEJOHN PL 5
HESKIN WAY 6

Whitfield Valley
Prim Sch

Fegg
Hayes

Whitfield

Ball Green

53

Great
Chell

1 BRIDGE CROFT
2 LANDER PL
3 COWLISHAW RD

Fir Tree
Farm

Ball Green
Prim Sch

Norton
Green

3

Chell Heath

Monks-Neil
Park

Cornhill

Lower Flatts
Farm

ENDON RD
B5051

Duke Bank

52

Recreation
Ground

Burnwood
Com Prim Sch

ST6

HOLLOWOOD WLK

ENDON RD

Norton-
in-the-
Moors

1 WAVENEY WLK N
2 WAVENEY WLK S

CH

2

Bank
Top

THE OUTLOOK 1
PIONEER PL 2
CHALLENGE CL 3
LIBERTY LA 4
FREEDOM WAY 5
VENTURE WAY 6

St Bartholomews

1 BRADBURY CL
2 MEERE CL

Norton
Prim
Sch

Bradley

St Mary's
RC Prim
Sch

H

North
Staffordshire

Stanfield

Haywood
High Sch

1 MANDEVILLE CL
2 STORMONT CL

Ford Green Hall
(Mus)

Ford
Green

Works

51

1

1 HIGHCROFT WLK
2 MARNEY WLK

Smallthorne

1 HADFIELD GN
2 KEYNSHAM WLK
3 BACK FORD GREEN RD

Smallthorne
Prim Sch

STOKE-ON-TRENT

Vale Park
(Port Vale FC)

Moorpark
Jun Sch

Libr

LEEK NEW RD

ST2

Burslem
Park

New Ford
Prim Sch

50

B5051
Sneyd Hill
Golf Trad Est

MOORLAND RD

1 HORWOOD GDNS 1
2 APOLLO WLK 2
3 HAROLD ST 3
4 WHATMORE ST 4

Cemy

A5272 HANLEY RD

ST1

87

A

88

B

89

C

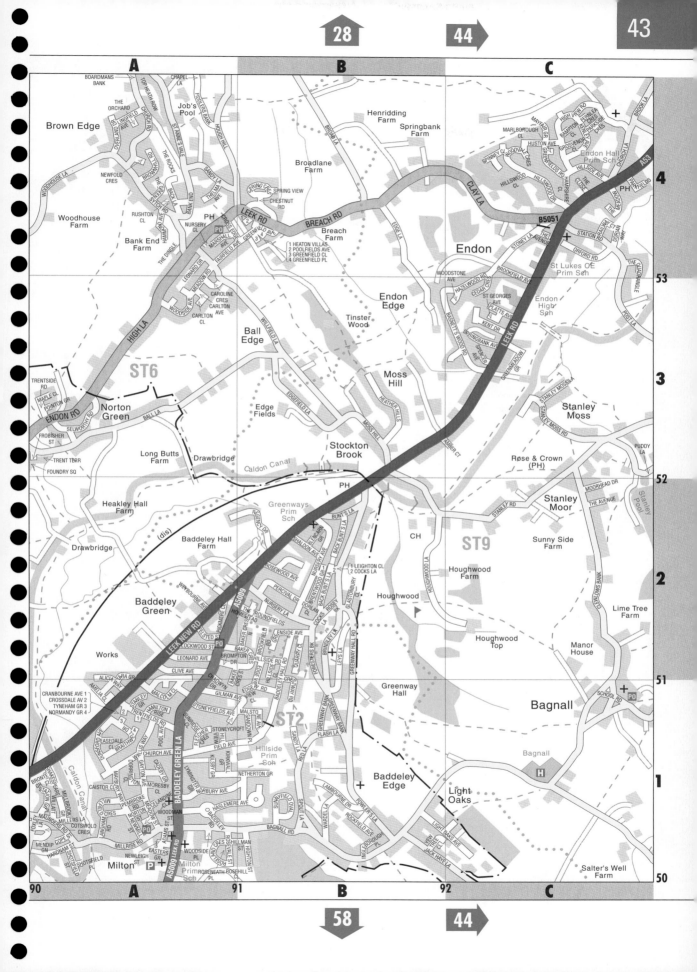

43
29

A   **B**   **C**

BROOKSIDE DR
BROOK LA
LEEK RD
A53
A53
1 BROOK CL
2 FORGE SIDE
3 EMBERS WAY
4 THE PRIORY

Denford
MICKLEA LA
DENFORD RD
SANDY LA

Manor Farm

Caldon Canal

Hazelhurst Aqueduct

HOLLY BUSH COTTAGES

4

Hayes Farm
PARK LA

Little Hollinhurst

Hollinhurst

Hazelhurst
Holly Bush (PH)

Denford Farm

Cumberledge Park

Lawn Farm

HUNTLEY RD

Deep Hayes Country Park

53

Park Farm

Reynolds Hay Farm

Cats Edge

Ladygreen

POST LA
STANLEY BANK

Travellers Rest (PH)

Acres Barn

Moss House

BLACK BANK RD

Lee House

3

Dogcroft Farm

Newhouse Farm

Clough House

ST9

PUDD LA

Stanley

Whistonshaw

Rose Bank Farm

ST13

52

Stanley Head Outdoor Education Centre

TOMKIN RD

Colford Farm

COALPITFORD LA

P

BRUND LA

Stanley Pool

Wood Lane Farm

Ford Farm

2

Cliff Wood

Tompkin

KNOWSLEY RD

Bigwood

Big Susan's Wood

Bagnall Grange Farm

OLD MILL LA

P

Knowsley Farm

Old Mill Lane

51

Pool Meadows

OLD MILL LA

Moor Hall

Bagnall

SPRINGS BANK

Ford

Cicely Haughton Sch

Rownall Cottage Farm

1

Spring Bank

Little Lawn Farm

THORNYEDGE RD

Birch Wood

Far Rownall Farm

THORNYEDGE RD

Newhouse Farm

Thornyedge

Rownall Farm

Bramhouse Farm

50

93   **A**   94   **B**   95   **C**

43
59

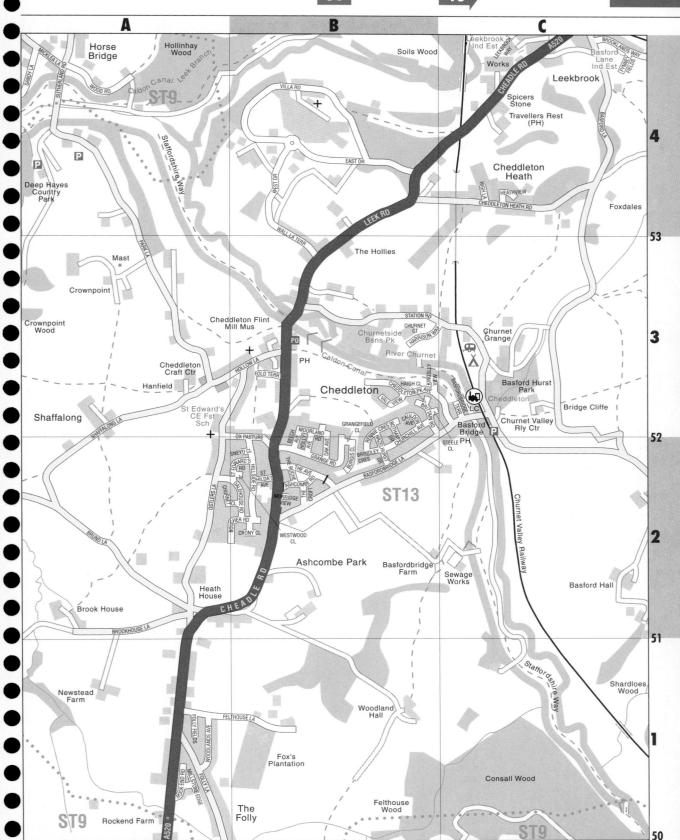

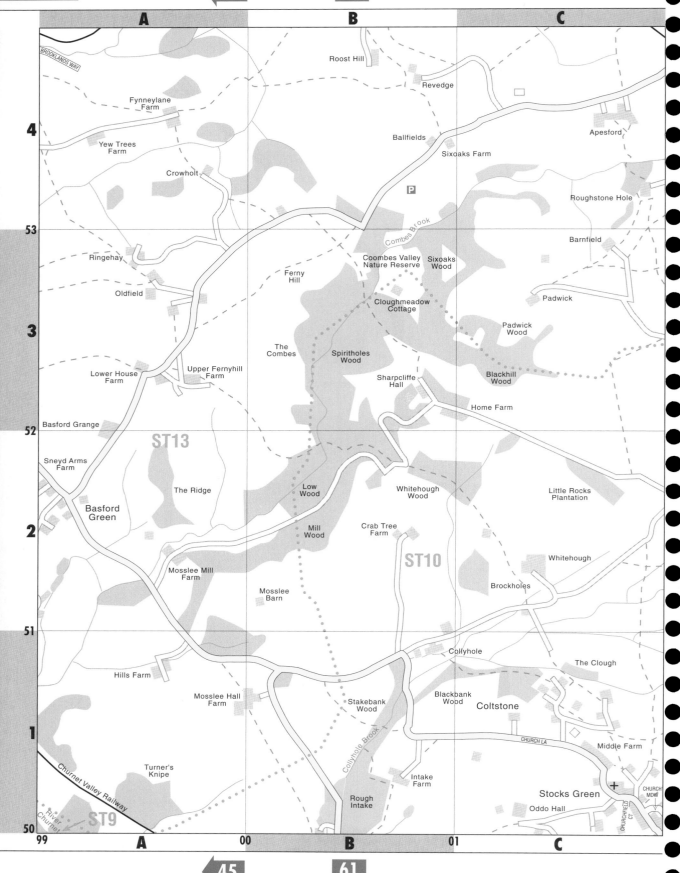

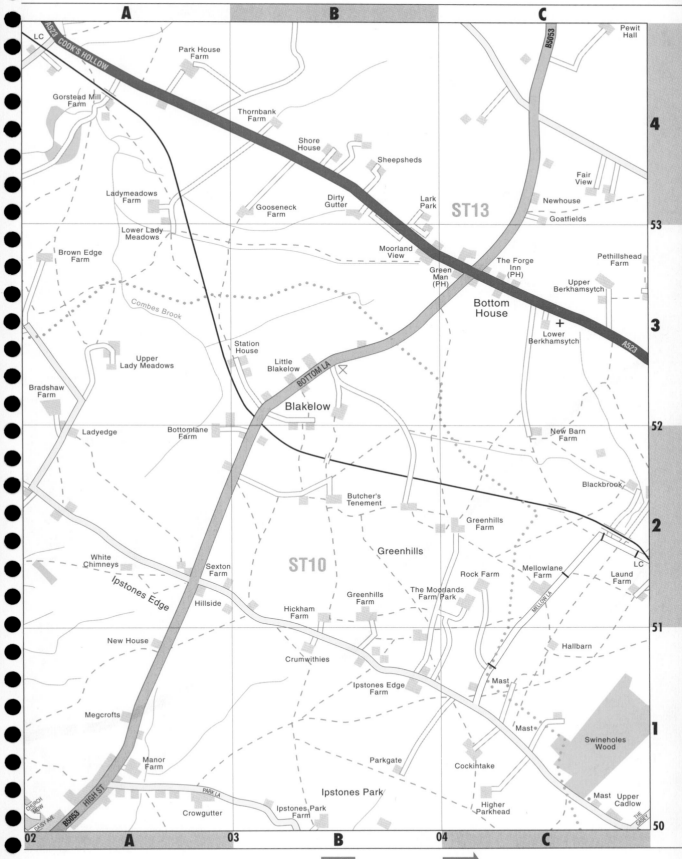

A   B   C

LC
A523 COOK'S HOLLOW
Park House Farm
Gorstead Mill Farm
Thornbank Farm
Shore House
Sheepsheds
B5053
Pewit Hall

4

Ladymeadows Farm
Gooseneck Farm
Dirty Gutter
Lark Park
ST13
Fair View
Newhouse
Goatfields

53

Lower Lady Meadows
Brown Edge Farm
Moorland View
Green Man (PH)
The Forge Inn (PH)
Pethillshead Farm
Upper Berkhamsytch

Combes Brook
Bottom House
Lower Berkhamsytch
A523

3

Upper Lady Meadows
Station House
Little Blakelow
BOTTOM LA
Bradshaw Farm

Ladyedge
Bottomlane Farm
Blakelow
New Barn Farm

52

Butcher's Tenement
Blackbrook

White Chimneys
Greenhills Farm
Greenhills

2

Ipstones Edge
Sexton Farm
ST10
Rock Farm
Mellowlane Farm
Laund Farm
LC

Hillside
Greenhills Farm
The Moorlands Farm Park
MELLOW LA

New House
Hickham Farm
Hallbarn

51

Crumwithies
Ipstones Edge Farm
Mast

Megcrofts
Mast
Swineholes Wood

1

Manor Farm
Parkgate
Cockihtake
Mast
Upper Cadlow

CHURCH ROW
DAISY AVE
B5053 HIGH ST
PARK LA
Crowgutter
Ipstones Park Farm
Ipstones Park
Higher Parkhead
THE CASEY

50

02   A   03   B   04   C

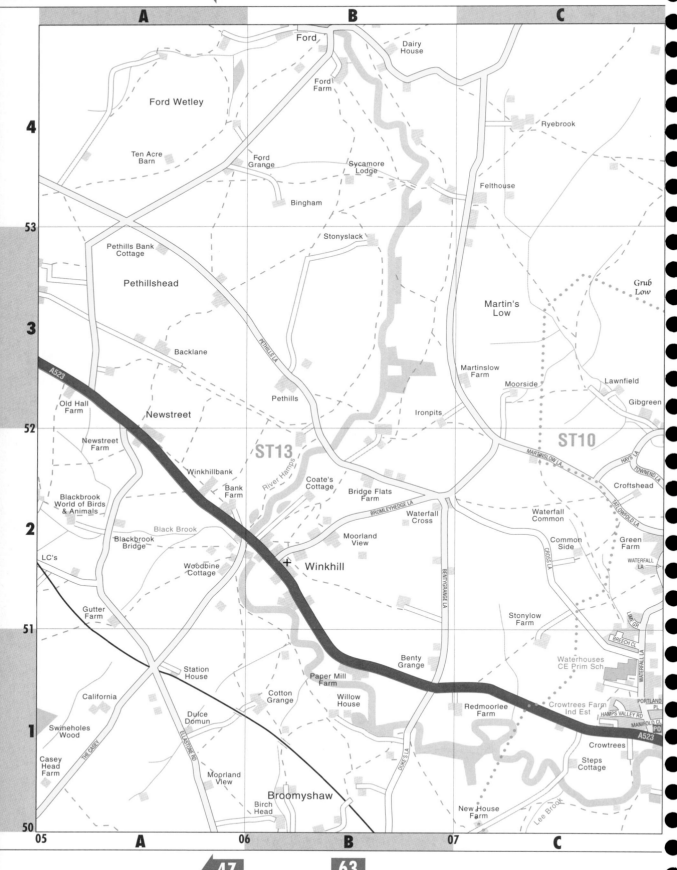

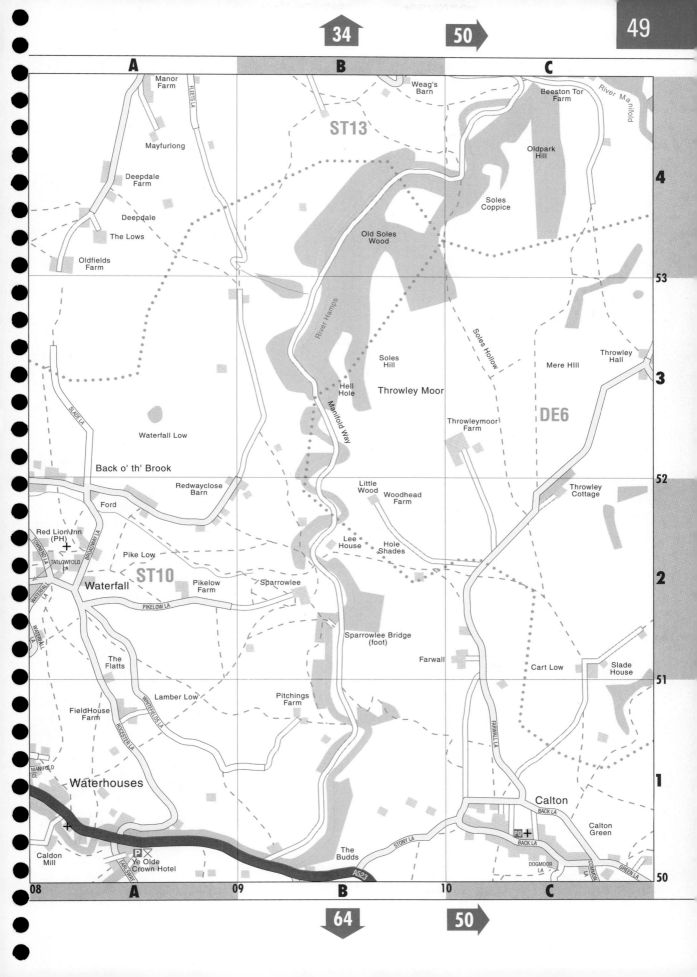

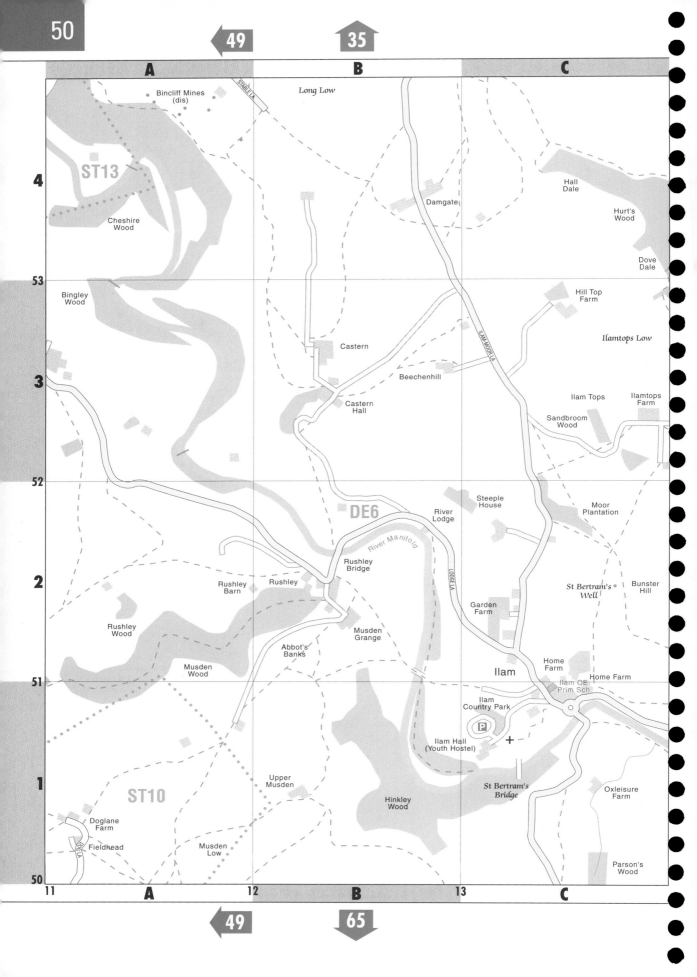

A **B** **C**

Bincliff Mines (dis)

Long Low

ST13

4

Cheshire Wood

Damgate

Hall Dale

Hurt's Wood

Dove Dale

53

Bingley Wood

Hill Top Farm

Ilamtops Low

Castern

ILAM MOOR LA

Beechenhill

3

Castern Hall

Ilam Tops

Ilamtops Farm

Sandbroom Wood

52

DE6

River Lodge

Steeple House

Moor Plantation

River Manifold

Rushley Bridge

2

Rushley Barn

Rushley

Rushley Wood

Musden Grange

LODGE LA

Garden Farm

St Bertram's Well

Bunster Hill

Abbot's Banks

Home Farm

Home Farm

Ilam

51

Musden Wood

Ilam CE Prim Sch

Ilam Country Park

P

Ilam Hall (Youth Hostel)

+

1

ST10

Upper Musden

Hinkley Wood

St Bertram's Bridge

Oxleisure Farm

Doglane Farm

LA 900

Fieldhead

Musden Low

Parson's Wood

50

11

A

12

B

13

C

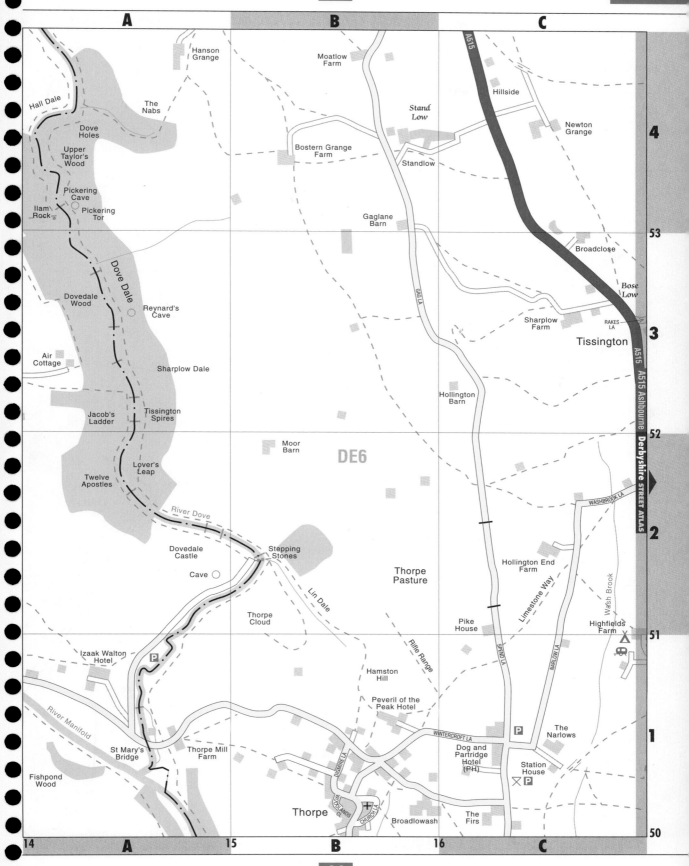

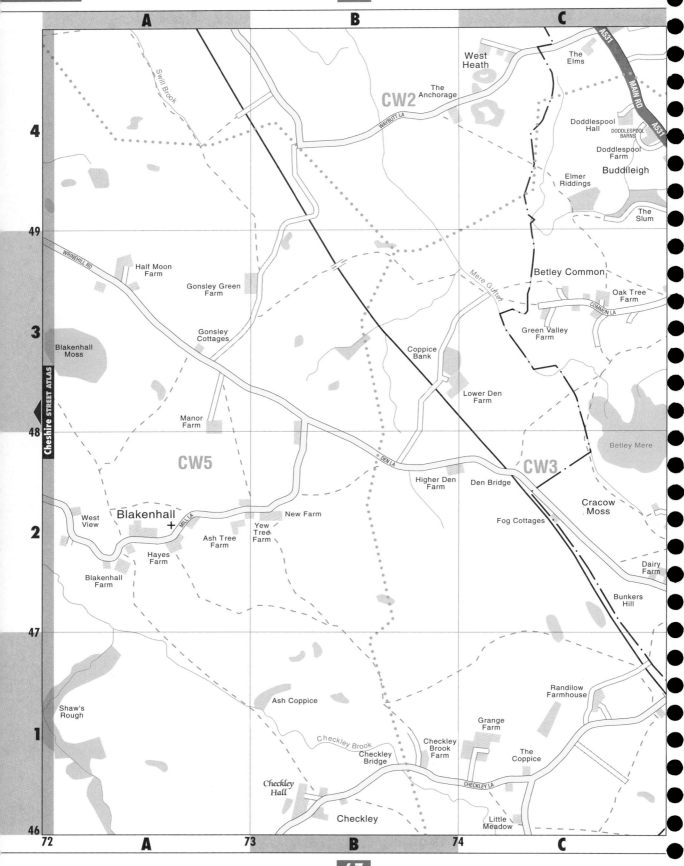

Cheshire STREET ATLAS

A | B | C

4

West Heath

CW2

The Anchorage

WAYBUTT LA

The Elms

A531

MAIN RD

A531

Doddlespool Hall

DODDLESPOOL BARNS

Doddlespool Farm

Buddileigh

Elmer Riddings

The Slum

Swill Brook

49

WRINEHILL RD

Half Moon Farm

Gonsley Green Farm

Mere Gutter

Betley Common

Oak Tree Farm

COMMON LA

3

Blakenhall Moss

Gonsley Cottages

Coppice Bank

Green Valley Farm

48

Manor Farm

CW5

Lower Den Farm

DEN LA

Higher Den Farm

Den Bridge

CW3

Betley Mere

Cracow Moss

2

West View

Blakenhall

MILL LA

New Farm

Ash Tree Farm

Yew Tree Farm

Hayes Farm

Fog Cottages

Dairy Farm

Blakenhall Farm

Bunkers Hill

47

Shaw's Rough

1

Ash Coppice

Checkley Brook

Checkley Bridge

Checkley Brook Farm

Grange Farm

Randilow Farmhouse

The Coppice

CHECKLEY LA

Checkley Hall

Checkley

Little Meadow

46

72 | A | 73 | B | 74 | C

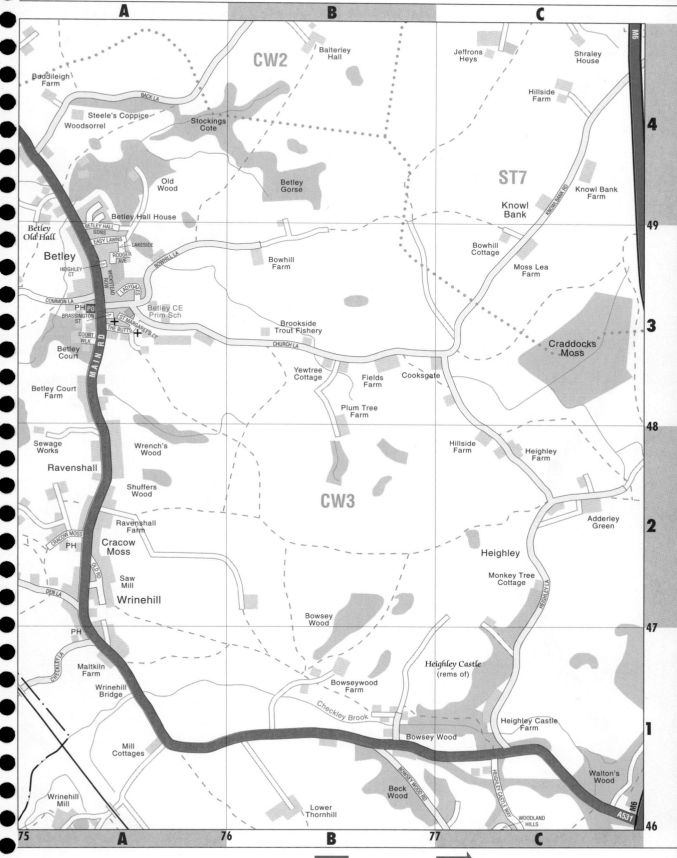

A   **B**   **C**

Rising Sun Inn (PH)

Shraleybrook

Wynbrook

RYEHILLS

MILES GREEN RD   PEGGY'S BANK   TOMFIELDS

APEDALE Sch RD

Dean Brook

Wynbank Farm

Miles Green Farm

Miles Green

LIMBRICK RD

KNOWLBANK RD

B5367

WERETON RD

STATION RD

WYNBANK CL

PH

HEATHCOTE RD

4

Golden Hay Farm

Yewtree

Hollins Farm

VICTORIA AVE

ST5

SHRALEYBROOK RD

Halmerend Hall

HOLDING CRES

Sir Thomas Boughey High Sch

P

STATION WLK

Halmer End

Chapel Farm

Co-OPERATIVE LA

Burgess's Wood

49

PH

WESLEY PL

HARRISON CL

HAYESWOOD LA

LINLEY CL

PO

Church Farm

Mast

Minnie Farm

HIGH ST

The Drive

PODMORE LA

HILL CRES

PODMORE AVE

ROBERTS CL

Hayes

3

RED HALL LA

ST7

The Richard Heathcote Prim Sch

Gresley Arms (PH)

PO

Alsagers Bank

Mast

Pheasant Hall

Industrial Estate

Hayes Wood

B5367 HIGH LA

Waste Farm

48

Craddock Moss Farm

Red Hall Farm

Scot Hay

SCOT HAY RD

CW3

2

Bullthorns Wood

HARRISON AND WOODBORN COTTS

ST5

CHURCH VIEW

LEYCETT RD

BANKFIELD GR

CRACKLEY LA

Pool End Farm

SCOT HAY RD

47

Mast

The Gladings

Walton's Wood

Lane Farm

LEYCETT LA

Leycett

Banktop Farm

DROITWICH CL

HARPDOATE WAY

STRETTON LODGE RD

BATH RD

PEEBLES CL

MOFFAT

WOODHALL PL

CHELTENHAM GR

CHEDDAR DR

ILKLEY PL

P

MALVERN AVE

REDHEATH CL

Haying Wood

1

Finney Green

Upper Farm

HOLLYWOOD LA

PEPPER ST

Wks

B5044

UNDERWOOD RD

Tunnel

Redheath Plantation

M6

A531

Sunnybank

AGGER HILL

Agger Hill Farm

Lower Farm

QUARRY BANK

46

78   **A**   79   **B**   80   **C**

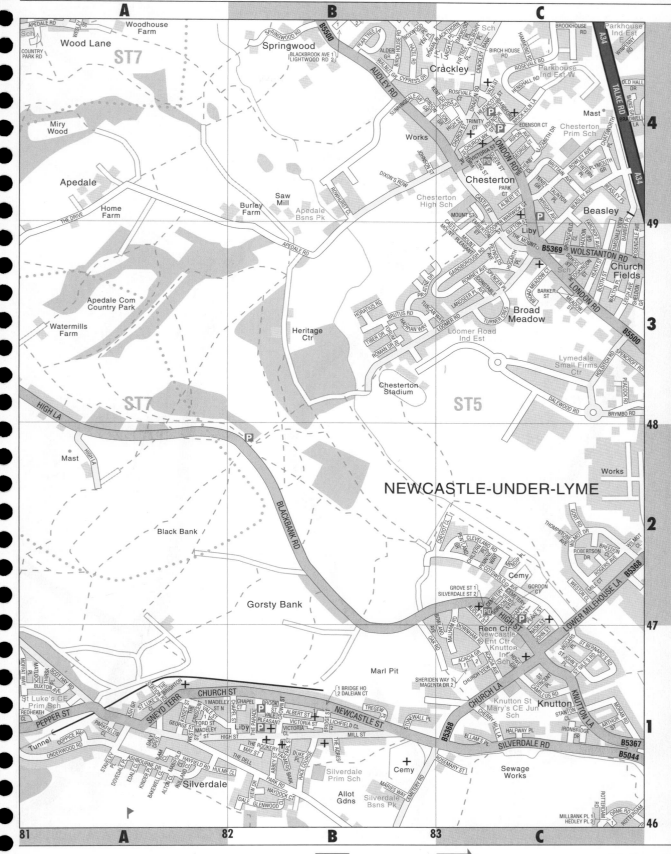

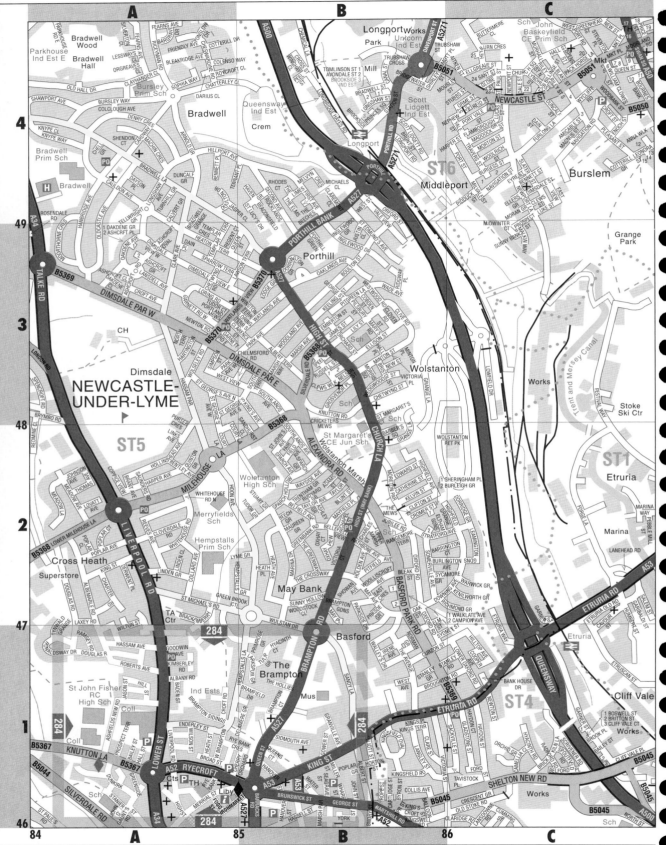

For full street detail of the highlighted area see page 284.

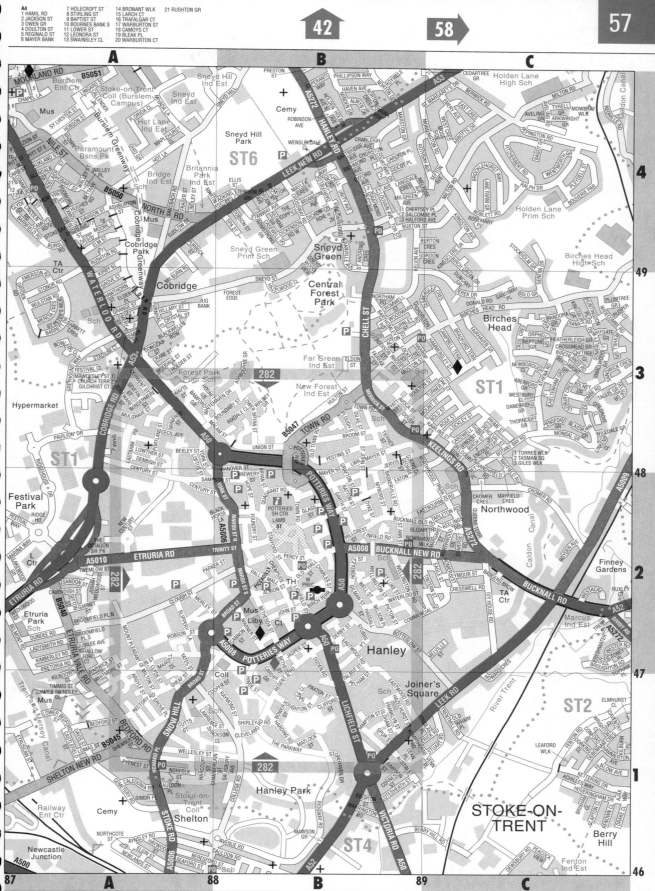

For full street detail of the highlighted area see page 282.

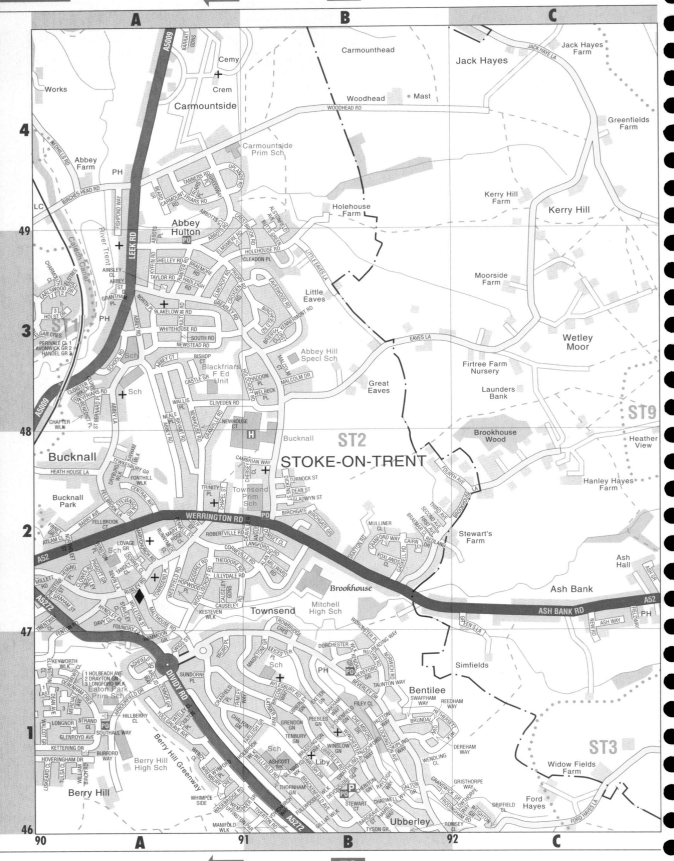

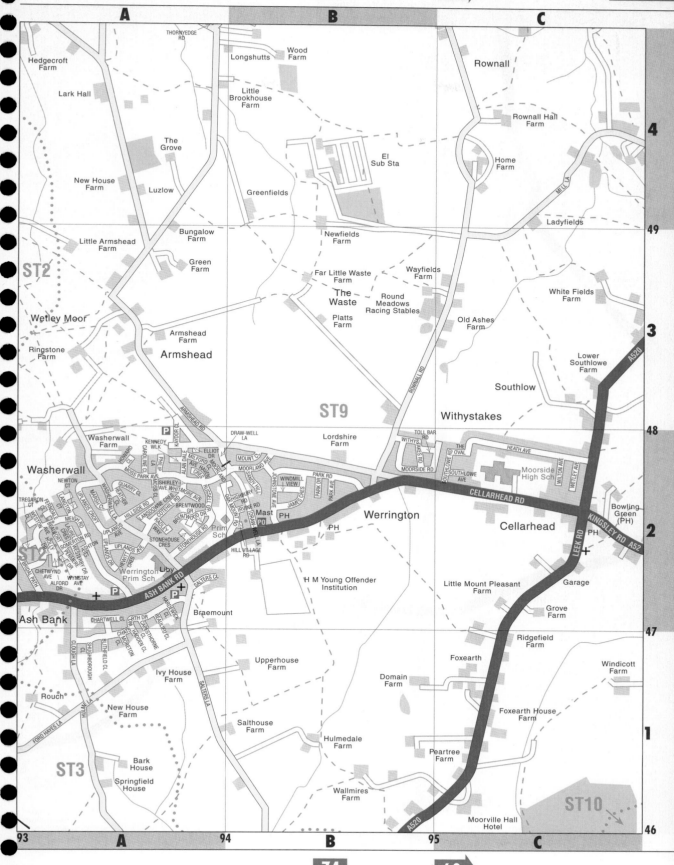

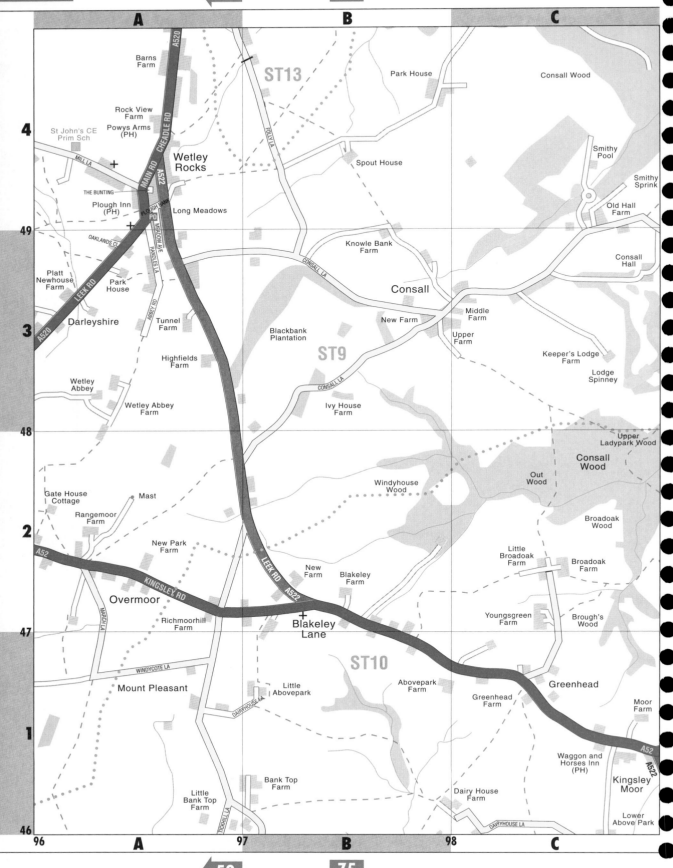

A B C

Barns Farm

A520

ST13

Park House

Consall Wood

Rock View Farm

Powys Arms (PH)

CHEADLE RD

FOLLY LA

Smithy Pool

St John's CE Prim Sch

4

Wetley Rocks

Spout House

Smithy Sprink

MILL LA

MAIN RD

A522

THE BUNTING

Old Hall Farm

Plough Inn (PH)

Long Meadows

PLOUGH BANK

PD

49

MEADOW AVE

Knowle Bank Farm

Consall Hall

OAKLANDS CL

CONSALL LA

Platt Newhouse Farm

RANDLES LA

Consall

LEEK RD

Park House

ABBEY RD

Tunnel Farm

New Farm

Middle Farm

3

A520

Darleyshire

Blackbank Plantation

ST9

Upper Farm

Keeper's Lodge Farm

Highfields Farm

CONSALL LA

Lodge Spinney

Wetley Abbey

Ivy House Farm

Wetley Abbey Farm

48

Upper Ladypark Wood

Consall Wood

Gate House Cottage

Out Wood

Mast

Windyhouse Wood

Rangemoor Farm

Broadoak Wood

2

A52

New Park Farm

LEEK RD

Little Broadoak Farm

Broadoak Farm

KINGSLEY RD

New Farm

Blakeley Farm

A522

Overmoor

Youngsgreen Farm

Brough's Wood

MARCH LA

Richmoorhill Farm

Blakeley Lane

47

ST10

WINDYCOTE LA

Abovepark Farm

Greenhead

Mount Pleasant

Little Abovepark

Greenhead Farm

Moor Farm

DAIRYHOUSE LA

1

Waggon and Horses Inn (PH)

A52

Bank Top Farm

Dairy House Farm

Kingsley Moor

A522

Little Bank Top Farm

TICKHILL LA

DAIRYHOUSE LA

Lower Above Park

46

96 A 97 B 98 C

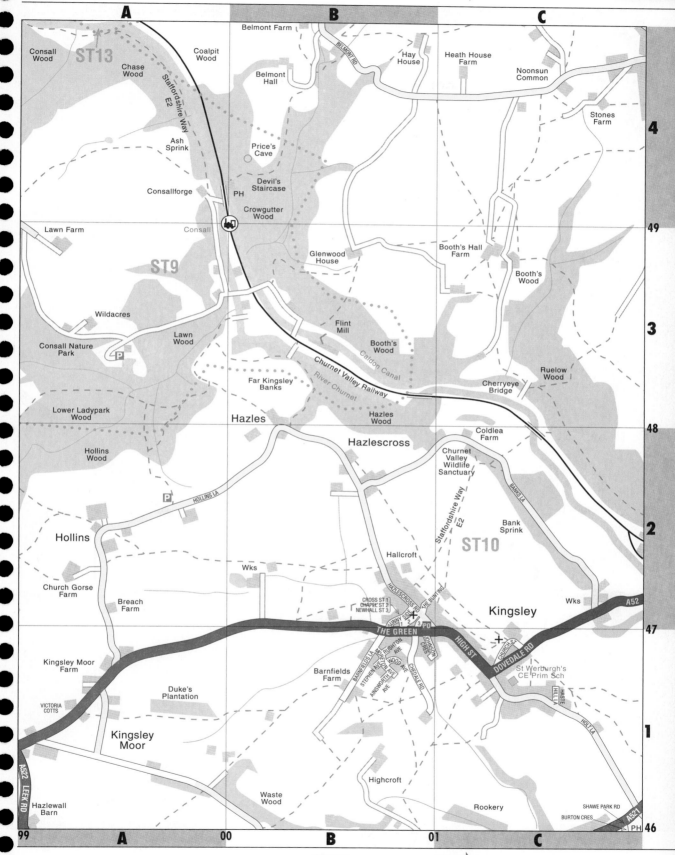

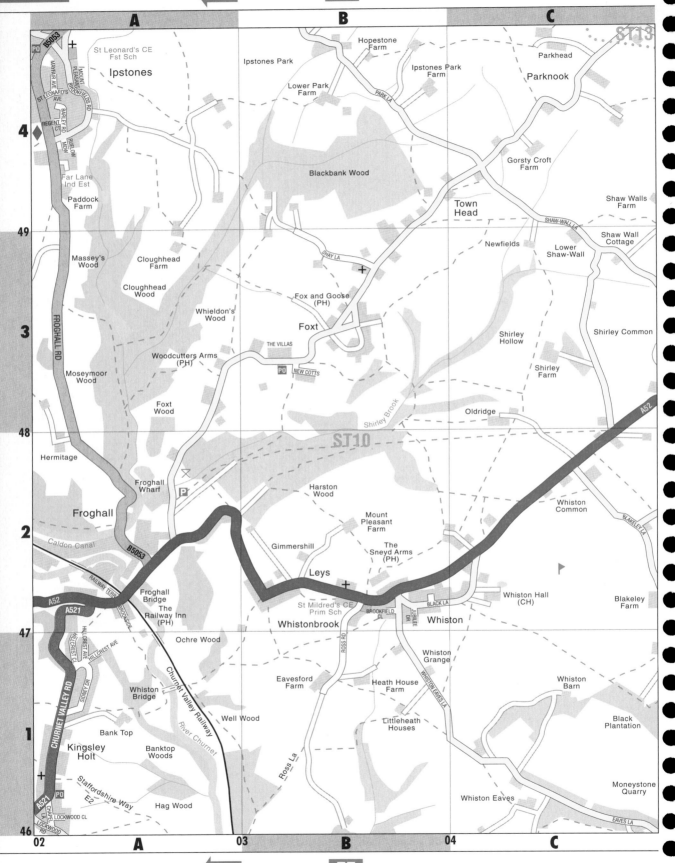

ST13

A

PO
B5053
St Leonard's CE
Fst Sch
Ipstones
MAYFAIR AVE
MOUNT PLEASANT
BROOKFIELDS RD
ST LEONARD'S
AVE
BARLEY RD
REGENT CT
BUELOW
MDW

4 ◆

Far Lane
Ind Est

Paddock
Farm

FROGHALL RD

49

Massey's
Wood

Cloughhead
Farm

Cloughhead
Wood

Whieldon's
Wood

Moseymoor
Wood

3

Woodcutters Arms
(PH)

Foxt
Wood

THE VILLAS

PO
NEW COTTS

B

Ipstones Park

Lower Park
Farm

Hopestone
Farm

Ipstones Park
Farm

PARK LA

Blackbank Wood

SHAY LA

Fox and Goose
(PH)

Foxt

Shirley Brook

ST10

C

Parkhead

Parknook

Gorsty Croft
Farm

Shaw Walls
Farm

SHAW-WALL LA

Town
Head

Newfields

Lower
Shaw-Wall

Shaw Wall
Cottage

Shirley
Hollow

Shirley Common

Shirley
Farm

Oldridge

A52

Whiston
Common

BLAKELEY LA

48

Hermitage

Froghall
Wharf

P

Froghall

2

Caldon Canal

B5053

RAILWAY TERR

Froghall
Bridge
The
Railway Inn
(PH)

A52
A521
BROOKSIDE

Harston
Wood

Gimmershill

Mount
Pleasant
Farm

Leys

St Mildred's CE
Prim Sch

Whistonbrook

The
Sneyd Arms
(PH)

BROOKFIELD
CL

BLACK LA

JUBILEE DR

Whiston

Whiston Hall
(CH)

Blakeley
Farm

47

Ochre Wood

HILLCREST CL
HILLCREST AVE

SIMON DR

Whiston
Bridge

Churnet Valley Railway

River Churnet

Well Wood

Eavesford
Farm

ROSS RD

Heath House
Farm

Whiston
Grange

WHISTON EAVES LA

Whiston
Barn

Whiston
Barn

Black
Plantation

CHURNET VALLEY RD

1

Kingsley
Holt

Bank Top

Banktop
Woods

Littleheath
Houses

Ross La

Staffordshire Way
E2

Hag Wood

A521
PO
CHAPEL LA
LOCKWOOD CL
LOCKWOOD
RD

46

Whiston Eaves

Moneystone
Quarry

EAVES LA

02   **A**   03   **B**   04   **C**

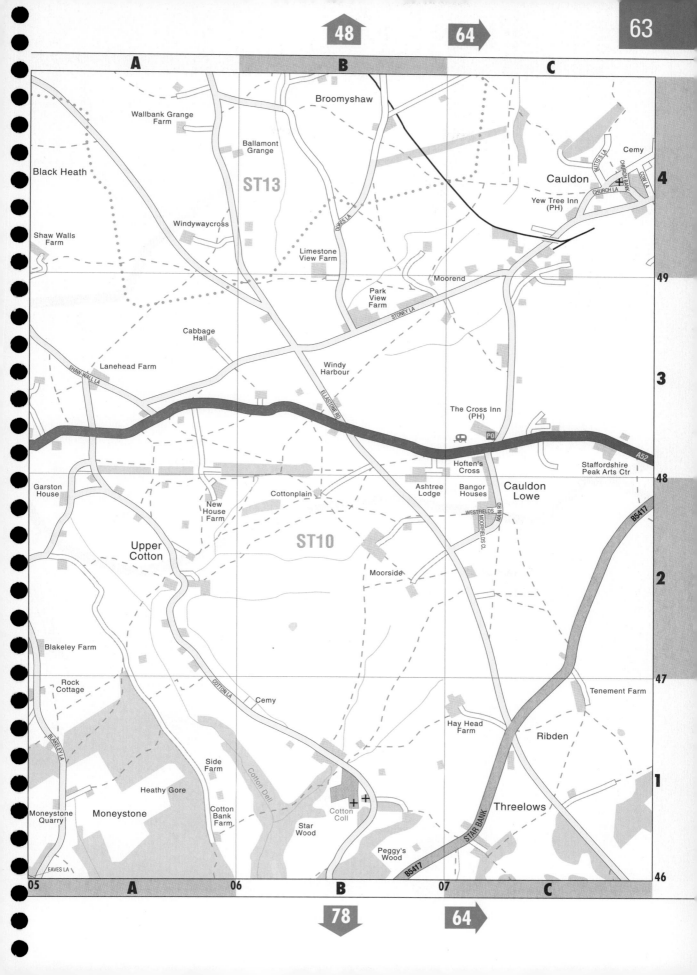

A B C

Broomyshaw

Wallbank Grange Farm

Ballamont Grange

ST13

Cemy

Cauldon

Black Heath

Windywaycross

Yew Tree Inn (PH)

Shaw Walls Farm

Limestone View Farm

Moorend

49

Park View Farm

STONEY LA

Cabbage Hall

Windy Harbour

3

Lanehead Farm

SHAW-WALL LA

ELLASTONE RD

The Cross Inn (PH)

PO

A52

Hoften's Cross

Staffordshire Peak Arts Ctr

48

Garston House

New House Farm

Cottonplain

Ashtree Lodge

Bangor Houses

Cauldon Lowe

B5417

Upper Cotton

ST10

WESTFIELDS

MOORFIELDS CL.

MAIN RD

Moorside

2

Blakeley Farm

Rock Cottage

COTTON LA

Cemy

Tenement Farm

Hay Head Farm

Ribden

47

BLAKELEY LA

Side Farm

Cotton Dell

Star Wood

Cotton Coll

STAR BANK

Threelows

1

Moneystone Quarry

Heathy Gore

Moneystone

Cotton Bank Farm

Peggy's Wood

B5417

EAVES LA

05 A 06 B 07 C 46

63
49

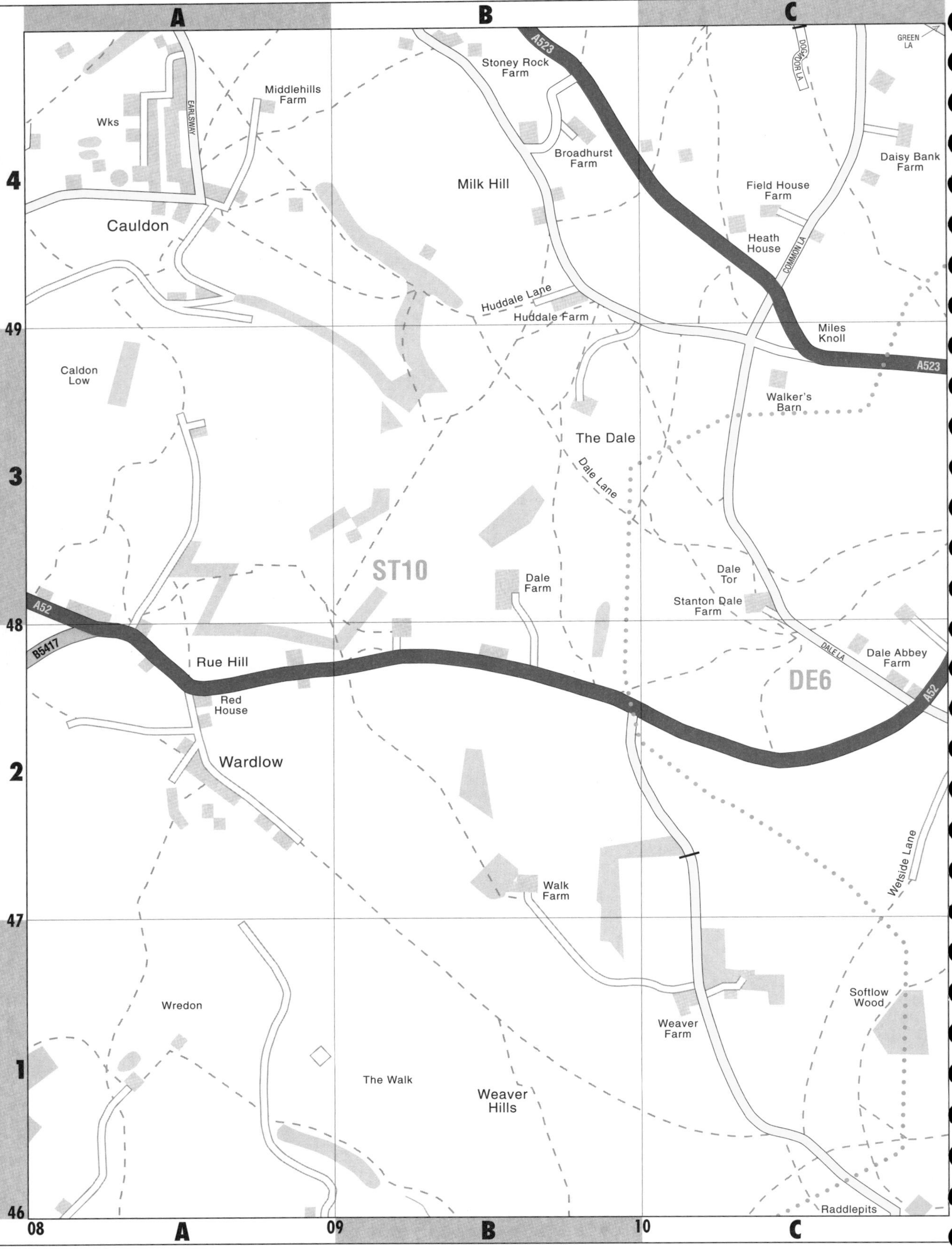

A   B   C

A523

Stoney Rock Farm

Middlehills Farm

EARLSWAY

Wks

Broadhurst Farm

DOGGAR LA

GREEN LA

Daisy Bank Farm

Field House Farm

4

Milk Hill

Heath House

COMMON LA

Cauldon

Huddale Lane

Huddale Farm

Miles Knoll

49

A523

Caldon Low

The Dale

Walker's Barn

Dale Lane

3

ST10

Dale Farm

Dale Tor

Stanton Dale Farm

DALE LA

A52

48

Rue Hill

Dale Abbey Farm

B5417

Red House

DE6

A52

Wardlow

2

Walk Farm

Wetside Lane

47

Wredon

Softlow Wood

Weaver Farm

1

The Walk

Weaver Hills

Raddlepits

46

08   A   09   B   10   C

63
79

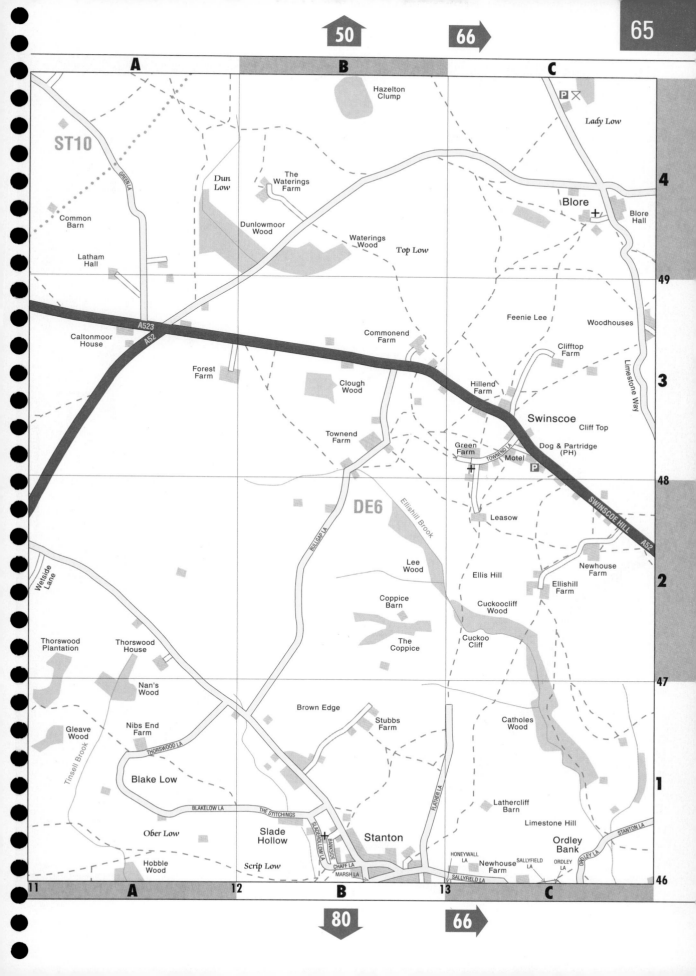

ST10

A B C

Hazelton
Clump

P ✕

Lady Low

Common
Barn

Dun
Low

The Waterings
Farm

Blore

✝

Blore
Hall

4

GREEN LA

Dunlowmoor
Wood

Waterings
Wood

Top Low

49

Latham
Hall

Feenie Lee

Woodhouses

A523

Caltonmoor
House

A52

Commonend
Farm

Clifftop
Farm

Limestone Way

3

Forest
Farm

Clough
Wood

Hillend
Farm

Swinscoe

Cliff Top

Townend
Farm

Green
Farm

✝

TOWNEND LA

Dog & Partridge
(PH)

Motel

P

48

DE6

Ellishill Brook

BULLGAP LA

Leasow

SWINSCOE HILL

A52

Wetside
Lane

Lee
Wood

Ellis Hill

Newhouse
Farm

2

Coppice
Barn

Cuckoocliff
Wood

Ellishill
Farm

Thorswood
Plantation

Thorswood
House

The
Coppice

Cuckoo
Cliff

47

Nan's
Wood

Brown Edge

Stubbs
Farm

Catholes
Wood

Gleave
Wood

Nibs End
Farm

THORSWOOD LA

FLAHER LA

1

Blake Low

Lathercliff
Barn

Limestone Hill

STANTON LA

BLAKELOW LA

THE STITCHINGS

SLADE HOLLOW LA

BANKSIDE

Ordley
Bank

ORDLEY LA

Ober Low

Slade
Hollow

✝

Stanton

HONEYWALL
LA

Newhouse
Farm

SALLYFIELD
LA

ORDLEY
LA

Hobble
Wood

Scrip Low

CHAFF LA

MARSH LA

SALLYFIELD LA

46

Tinsell Brook

11 A 12 B 13 C

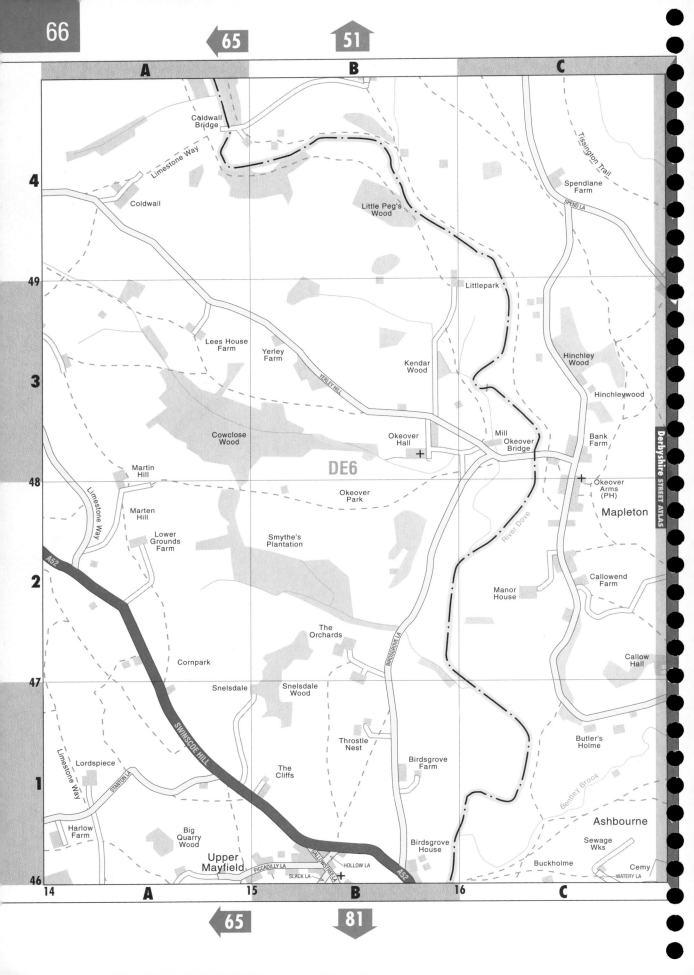

A   B   C

Coldwall Bridge

Limestone Way

Tissington Trail

Spendlane Farm

SPEND LA

4

Little Peg's Wood

Coldwall

49

Littlepark

Lees House Farm

Yerley Farm

Kendar Wood

Hinchley Wood

Hinchleywood

YERLEY HILL

3

Cowclose Wood

Okeover Hall

Mill
Okeover Bridge

Bank Farm

Martin Hill

DE6

Okeover Arms (PH)

48

Limestone Way

Marten Hill

Okeover Park

River Dove

Mapleton

Lower Grounds Farm

Smythe's Plantation

Callowend Farm

A52

Manor House

2

Cornpark

The Orchards

BIRDSGROVE LA

Callow Hall

47

Snelsdale

Snelsdale Wood

SWINSCOE HILL

Throstle Nest

Butler's Holme

Limestone Way

Lordspiece

The Cliffs

Birdsgrove Farm

Bentley Brook

1

STANTON LA

Harlow Farm

Big Quarry Wood

Upper Mayfield

PICCADILLY LA

GALLOWSTREE LA

HOLLOW LA

Birdsgrove House

Ashbourne

Sewage Wks

Buckholme

Cemy

SLACK LA

A52

WATERY LA

46

14   A   15   B   16   C

Derbyshire STREET ATLAS

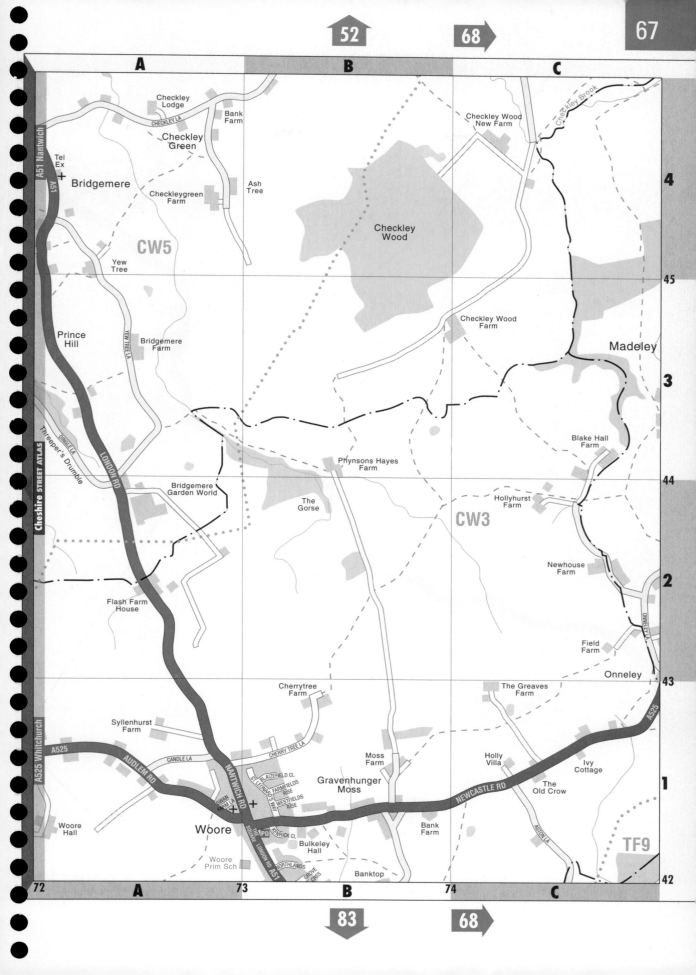

A **B** **C**

Checkley
Lodge

Bank
Farm

CHECKLEY LA

Checkley
Green

Ash
Tree

Checkleygreen
Farm

Tel
Ex +

Bridgemere

Checkley Wood
New Farm

Checkley
Brook

CW5

Yew
Tree

Checkley
Wood

Prince
Hill

Threeper's Drumble

DINGLE LA

Bridgemere
Farm

YEW TREE LA

LONDON RD

Checkley Wood
Farm

Madeley

4

45

3

Blake Hall
Farm

Bridgemere
Garden World

Phynsons Hayes
Farm

Hollyhurst
Farm

The
Gorse

CW3

44

Newhouse
Farm

Flash Farm
House

Field
Farm

2

Onneley

43

Cherrytree
Farm

The Greaves
Farm

ONNELEY LA

A525

Syllenhurst
Farm

A525 Whitchurch

A525

AUDLEM RD

CANDLE LA

CHERRY TREE LA

Moss
Farm

Holly
Villa

Ivy
Cottage

NEWCASTLE RD

The
Old Crow

1

NANTWICH RD

BL AIZEFIELD CL
ST LEONARD'S WAY
FARMFIELDS
RISE
WESTFIELDS
RISE

Gravenhunger
Moss

Woore
Hall

SWAN
FARM LA +
+

Woore

PO
KENRICK CL

Bank
Farm

ASTON LA

TF9

Woore
Prim Sch

THE SQUARE
LONDON RD
A51

NORTHLANDS
GROVE
CRES

Bulkeley
Hall

Banktop

42

72 **A** 73 **B** 74 **C**

Cheshire STREET ATLAS

67
53

A B C

4

Wrinehill
Hall

River Lea

Higher
Thornhill

Windy
Arbour

Lowermill
House

Madeley
Manor

Manor Park
Farm

Little
Madeley

Park
House

M6

A525

Grafton's
Wood

The Lum

Pond
Bay

Works

NEWCASTLE RD

Middle
Madeley

45

Wrinehill
Wood

Bower End
Farm

Moss House
Farm

THE BRIDLE PATH
APPLE CROFT
PEAR TREE DR
HEATHER GLADE
FERN DENE

POOLSIDE

PH

Greyhound
CT

Madeley
High Sch

WOODSIDE
THORNHILL DR
HOLM OAK DR
NEW RD
HEIFER DR
BECK RD
HERON
KINGFISHER
SALISBURY
DALTRY WAY
ELKINGTON
RISE

COLLEGE CL
BONGSEY WOOD RD
HEIGHEY CASTLE WAY
HEIGHEY CASTLE PARK CL
HILL ST
HIDDEN HILLS
WOODLY WAY

ARBOUR CL
MEADOWS RD
BECH
GREEN
GARNERS WALK

3

Wood
Farm

Beechfields

BOWER END LA

Moor Hall
Farm

Beech Wood

CW3

Barhill
Wood

Sir John Offley
CE Prim Sch

Birches
Farm

BIRCHES FARM MEWS

PASTORAL CL
KNIGHT LA
HUNGERFORD LA

CASTLE LA

POST
OFFICE SQ

ALMSHOUSES

44

Yewtree
Farm

ONNELEY LA

Field
House

Sandfield
House

Monument

Works

RED LA

STATION RD

MANOR RD

NETHERSET HEY LA

2

Bar Hill
Farm

Bar Hill

BAR HILL

Bar Hill
House Farm

Red Lane

Mast

Cemy

River Lea

Wheatsheaf Inn
(PH)

CH

Upper Bitterns
Wood

Hey House

43

A525

Onneley

STATION RD

Peak's Farm

Manor
Farm

Onneley Hall
Farm

New
Terrace

Lower Bitterns
Wood

1

TF9

Lea Head
Manor

Aston Cliff

Old Madeley
Manor
(rems of)

42

75 A 76 B 77 C

69
55

A   B   C

4

45

3

44

2

43

1

42

81   82   83

A   B   C

A525
BOGS COTTS
PH
Job's Wood
PARK RD
CEMETERY RD
CARAVAN CTR
KEELE RD
Playing Fields
Keele L Ctr
THE COVERT
CHURCH PLANTATION
Church Plantation
Keele Univ
Obsy
Home Farm
KEELE RD
Bear's Rough
LARCHWOOD
Paddock Farm
Clock House
Keele Hall
HORWOOD
PLANTATION PK
SPRINGPOOL
Springpool Wood
Barker's Wood
Hands Wood
Brickkiln Plantation
Pie Rough
ST5
M6
LYMES RD
Penfields Wood
Bentilee Wood
Lymes Farm
The Lymes
Lymes Farm
WHITMORE RD
Seabridge Hall
Park Farm
Seabridge
Park Manor
Butterton House
Shutlanehead
The Spinney
Butterton
Langleys
Church Wood
PARK RD
Cudmore Fishery
Pleck Farm
Wilkinspleck
A53

ST MARTIN'S RD 1
HEDLEY PL 2
ST ANDREW'S DR
WESLEY PL
ORME RD
WAIN AVE
ST PATRICK'S DR
BAGGOTT
JENKINSON CL 1
CASTLE RIDGE 2
POOLFIELDS CL 3
ORION CT 4
POOLFIELD AVE 5
CARRYER
GREENOCK CL
OBAN
RENFREW CL
ROTHESAY CT
BERWICK WLKS
FALKIRK GRANGE
ROTHESAY AVE
LANARK WLKS
THISTLEBERRY AVE
THE THISTLES
ANTHONY'S CRES
EMERY AVE
Sch
GALLOWSTREE LA
MONACO PL
LUCERNE VENICE CT
VICHY CL
OSTEND CL
PARIS AVE
LISBON PL
PO
Newcastle Com High Sch
WESTLANDS DR
SHEPO AVE
SHEVO CRES
WEDGEWOOD AVE
Westlands Prim Sch
TURIN DR
GENEVA DR
BERNE AVE
COMO PL
MILAN DR
LUGANO
VIENNA PL
GENEVA DR
NAPLES DR
CH
A53
LYNTON RD
CAMBORNE CRES
SUTHERLAND DR
REPTON DR
LEYS DR
RUSSALL AVE
RUGBY CL
WINCHESTER DR
SEDBERGH CT
ETON AVE
HARROWBY DR
HERM CL
SARK CL
FOREST CL
JERSEY CL
ALLENSWAY
SEABRIDGE LA
RUSHTON 1
FAIROAK 2
ELMHURST 3
HARTWELL 4
SCH WAY
SEABRIDGE LA
RIDGMONT RD
BAMFORD RD
SHEPPO RD
ALDERNEY DR
CASTEL
CHERBOURG CL
GUERNSEY CL
FERMAIN
FIVE OAKS CL
ST HELIER CL
ALLTHORPE WLK
BORDEAUX WLK
1 HAVELET DR
2 ALLENBY CT
3 BEAUMONT CT
4 THE BRIDLE PATH
5 DAVENPORT WAY

For full street detail of the highlighted area see page 284.

56

72

71

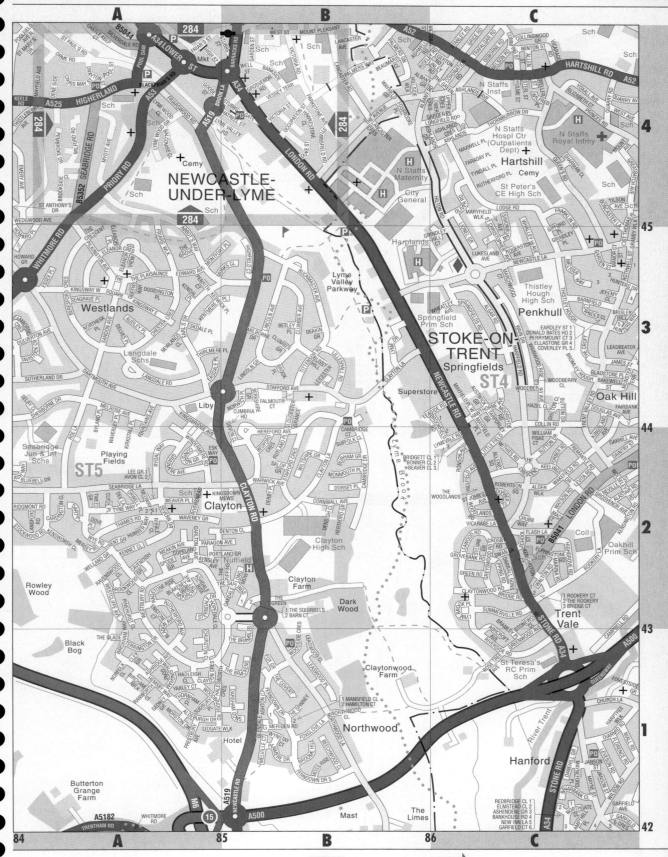

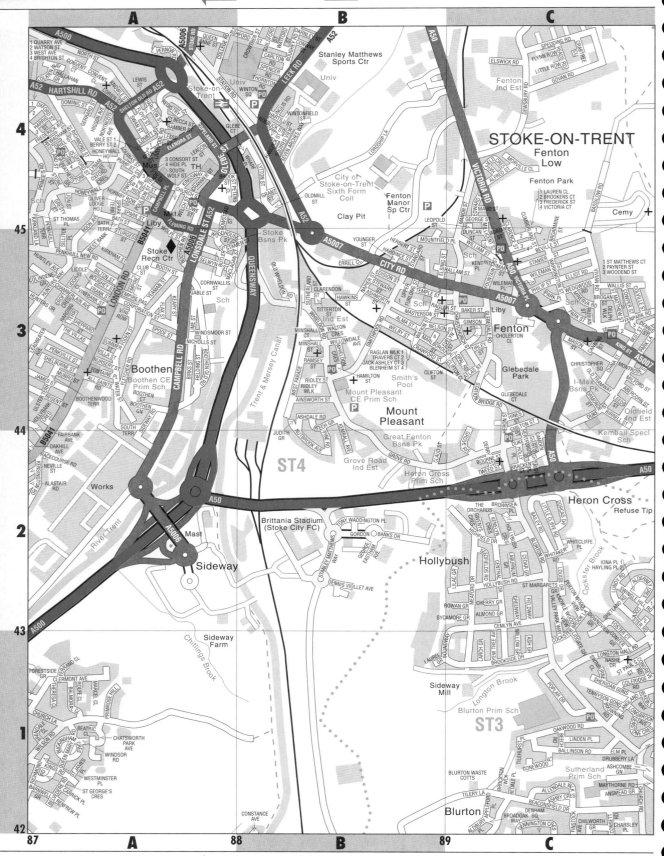

STOKE-ON-TRENT
Fenton
Low

Fenton Park

Cemy

Fenton

Glebedale
Park

Boothen

Mount
Pleasant

ST4

Works

River Trent

Mast

Sideway

Brittania Stadium
(Stoke City FC)

Hollybush

Heron Cross
Refuse Tip

Sideway Farm

Chillings Brook

Sideway
Mill

Longton Brook

Blurton Prim Sch

ST3

Blurton

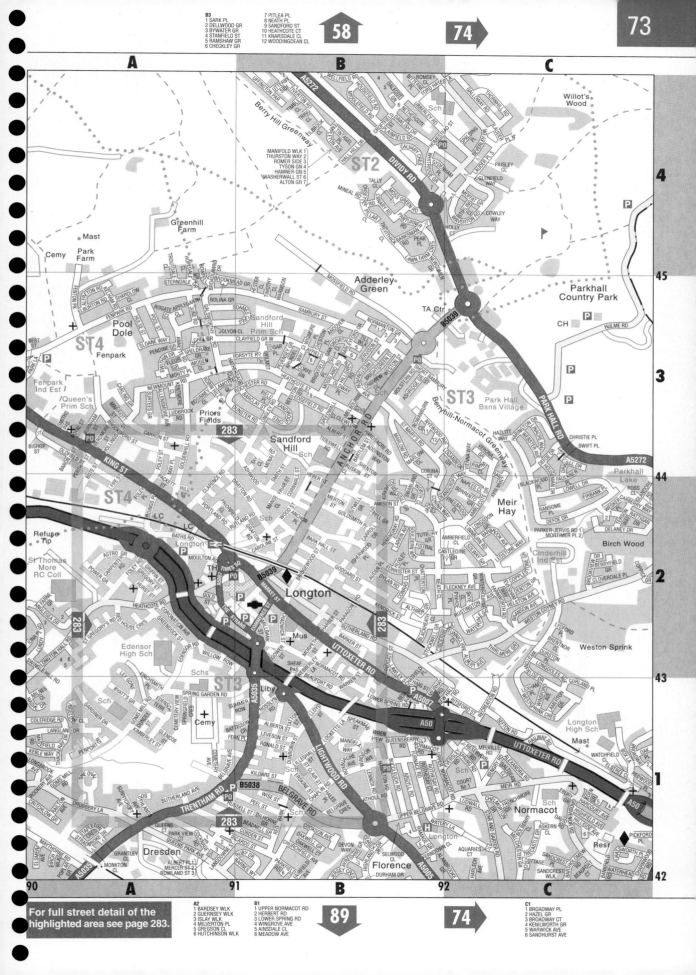

B3
1 SARK PL
2 DELLWOOD GR
3 BYWATER GR
4 STANFIELD ST
5 RAMSHAW GR
6 CHECKLEY GR

7 PITLEA PL
8 NEATH PL
9 SANDFORD ST
10 HEATHCOTE CT
11 KNARSDALE CL
12 WOODINGDEAN CL

58

74

For full street detail of the highlighted area see page 283.

A2
1 BARDSEY WLK
2 GUERNSEY WLK
3 ISLAY WLK
4 MILVERTON PL
5 GREGSON CL
6 HUTCHINSON WLK

B1
1 UPPER NORMACOT RD
2 HERBERT RD
3 LOWER SPRING RD
4 WINGROVE AVE
5 AINSDALE CL
6 MEADOW AVE

89

74

C1
1 BROADWAY PL
2 HAZEL GR
3 BROADWAY CT
4 KENILWORTH GR
5 WARWICK AVE
6 SANDHURST AVE

73
59

A **B** **C**

ST9

Creswell's Piece

HULME LA

Stonehouse Farm

THE COTTS

Hulme

The Candlesticks (PH)

Hall Farm

Malthouse Farm

Captain's Barn

MALTHOUSE LA

SALTERS LA

A520

Winterfield Farm

Smallbrook Farm

WINTERFIELD LA

LEEK RD

Blythe Lea

Sheepwash Farm

Ford

Sheepwash

45

Ward Hill Farm

Visitor Ctr

Boltongate Farm

Parkhall Ctry Pk

Roughcote

Tickhill Farm

P

CARNATION CL

ASTER CL

DAHLIA CL

EAST ST

LYNN ST

SELBY ST

IRIS CL

LILAC CL

LIME CL

LAVENDER CL

MAIN ST

FLINT ST

GATE ST

CROSS ST

BATH ST

FERNLEA GR

COUPE DR

HORTON DR

COALVILLE PL

3

Caverswall Common

Hardiwick Farm

Weston Coyney

Sch

FOXGLOVE CL

DIMMEL DR

WEST ST

Cocking Farm

River Blythe

ENGLESEA AVE

OSWALD AVE

PARK AVE

EDWAL DR

THE CLOSE

HEATHCOTE RISE

WELDON AVE

STRATHMORE CL

HOLYHEAD CRES

Sch

ROUGHCOTE LA

44 PARK HALL RD A5272

ST3

HEYSHAM CL

Intakes Farm

ST11

ST10

TICKHILL LA

MANNIN GR

ROSS CL

TAME WLK

CARBERRY WAY

IBSEN CL

GEOFFREY PK

PARK HALL CRES

PO

THE MOAT

HALL DR

HAYNER GR

FITZGERALD PL

PALACH AVE

CAVERSWALL RD

COLIN CRES

Green Farm

CARRADINE GR

MIDARD GR

NEW KINGSWAY

PRINCESS DR

QUEENS WLK

FIELD VIEW

YORK RD

HALLDEARN AVE

THE GREEN

Yewtree Farm

HANDLEY BANKS

WESTON RD

PARTON GR

COYNEY GR

SPRINKWOOD GR

AKRON CRES

DALE VIEW

DAWN VIEW

VALLEY VIEW

TERRY CL

MICHAEL CL

NATHAM CL

LONG IRON

TREVOR DR

Cookshill Hall

Tunstall Sytch

2

Weston Sprink

COPPICE GR

PARKHEAD CRES

PADWORTH GR

Weston Coyney Jun Sch

TILLER GR

BRINDON CL

MYRTLE AVE

MILL CL

Cookshill

VICARAGE CRES

WESTON COYNEY RD

PARKHEAD DR

LANSBURY GR

CLYNES WAY

HENDERSON GR

GATE

WEBB

MANN

HIGH ST

THE HOLLOW

43

WHITCOMBE RD

BIRD RD

GOODWIN RD

ODGER

SNOWDEN

MAXTON WAY

TAWNEY CL

CROSSEN

St Peter's CE Prim Sch

THE DAMS

PO

DILHORNE LA

Caverswall

The Red House PH

THE SQUARE

St Filumena's RC Prim Sch

Castle

STOKE-ON-TRENT

BROADWAY

CHERRY HILL AVE

THE GRANGE

BROOKHOUSE RD

TILSON AVE

HARVEY RD

WESTWOOD RD

WOOD CL

BLATCHFORD CL

BONDFIELD ROW

BURNS

BEVERIDGE AVE

BROOKWOOD DR

THE WOOD

SCHOOL LA

GABLE COTTS

OAK PL

ELMS

YARNFIELD CL

WOODVILLE RD

MAPLE PL

THE SQUARE

LEA PL

MEADOW CL

PENNINGTON

Pinewood Prim Sch

1

LOMBARDY GR

GIBSON PL

MEIR VIEW

BRIGHT ST

ROWNALL PL

KENNILWORTH

OCCLESHAW CL

SOUTH WLK

BRIARWOOD PL

KRANWOOD CL

DENEWOODS PL

Wood House Farm

Caverswall Park

BLITHE BRIDGE RD

EAST GR

PENFLEET AVE

STANTON RD

KINGSLEY RD

BECKET AVE

LYME RD

BRAMWOOD AVE

LIPPING

WILLWOOD GR

Meir

UTTOXETER RD

Meir Prim Sch

GEORGE AVE

CAVERSWALL LA

Foxfield Steam Rly

P PO

SANDON RD

EDNAM

GRANGEWOOD RD

HARTWELL RD

MOLLISON

A520

A50

APPLEWOOD CRES

EDENHURST AVE

LC

Mast

Caverswall Road

42

93 **A** **94** **B** **95** **C**

73
90

A1
1 DENEHURST CL
2 ROWNHALL PL
3 CORNELIOUS ST
4 SMITHS BLDGS
5 REDWOOD PL
6 BROADWAY CT
7 QUEENSWAY CT
8 PICKFORD PL
9 CHATSWORTH PL
10 SARACEN WAY
11 CROSSLAND PL W
12 COBHAM PL

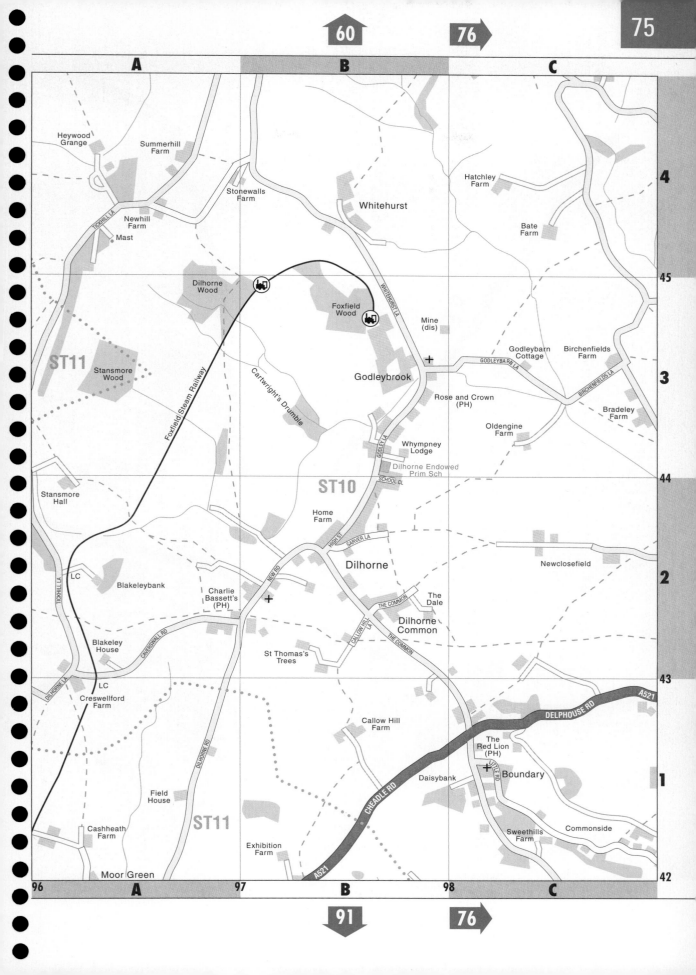

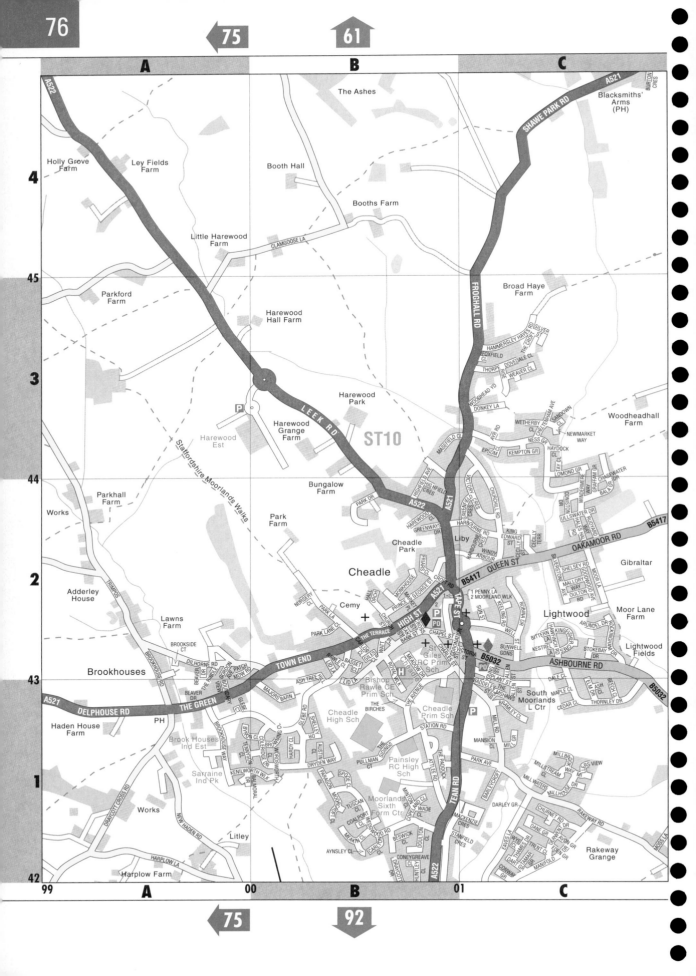

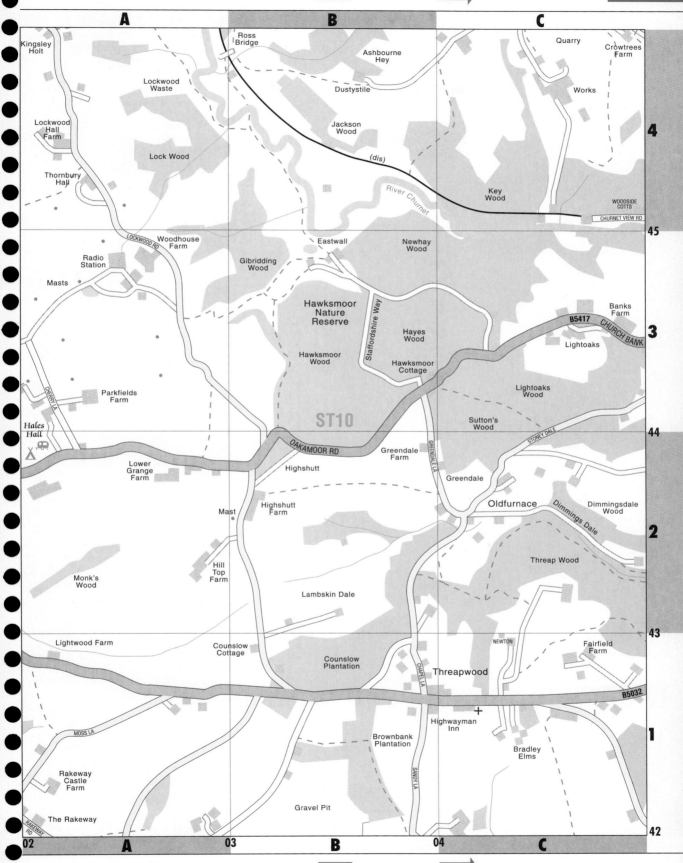

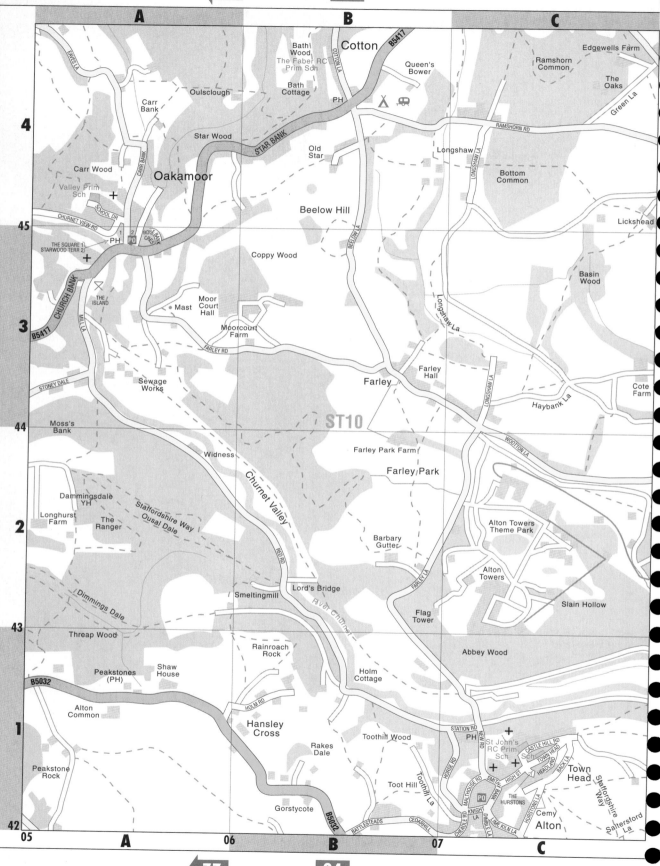

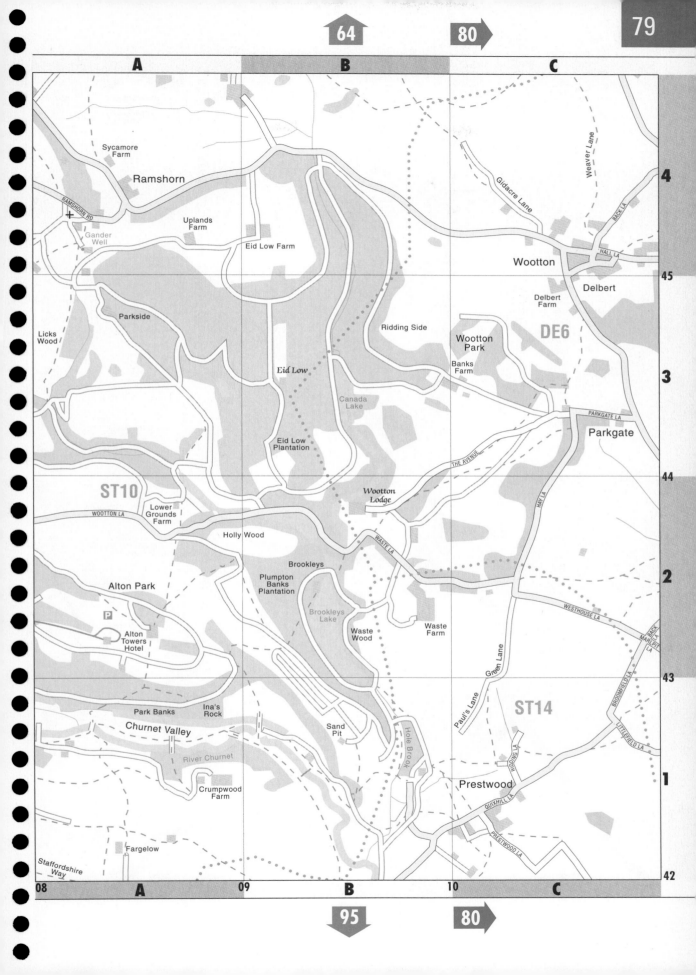

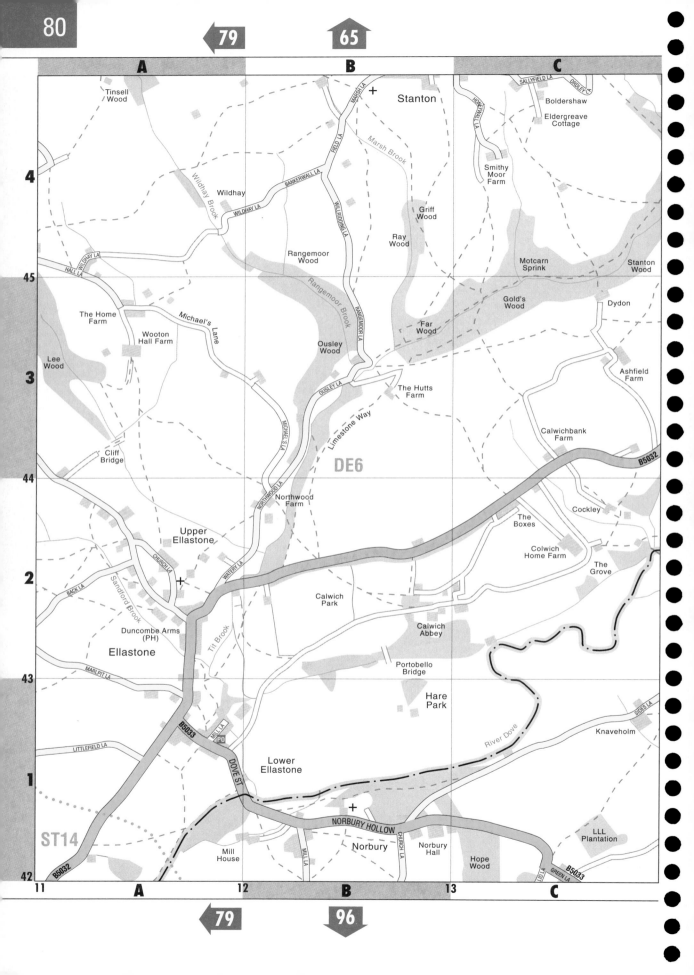

A
B
C

Tinsell
Wood

Stanton

SALLYFIELD LA
ORDLEY LA

Boldershaw

Eldergreave
Cottage

HONEYWALL LA

MARSH LA

FIELD LA

Marsh Brook

Smithy
Moor
Farm

Wildhay Brook

4

Wildhay

BANKERWALL LA

WILDHAY LA

Griff
Wood

WILLRIDDING LA

Ray
Wood

Motcarn
Sprink

Stanton
Wood

HALL LA

WILDHAY LA

45

Rangemoor
Wood

Rangemoor Brook

Gold's
Wood

Dydon

The Home
Farm

Michael's
Lane

Ousley
Wood

Far
Wood

Ashfield
Farm

Wooton
Hall Farm

RANGEMOOR LA

OUSLEY LA

The Hutts
Farm

Calwichbank
Farm

B5032

Lee
Wood

3

Limestone Way

MICHAEL'S LA

DE6

Cliff
Bridge

44

NORTHWOOD LA

Northwood
Farm

Cockley

The
Boxes

The
Grove

Upper
Ellastone

Colwich
Home Farm

CHURCH LA

WATERY LA

BACK LA

Calwich
Park

2

Sandford Brook

Duncombe Arms
(PH)

Calwich
Abbey

Tit Brook

Ellastone

Portobello
Bridge

MARLPIT LA

43

Hare
Park

SIDES LA

River Dove

Knaveholm

LITTLEFIELD LA

B5033

MILL LA

PO

DOVE ST

Lower
Ellastone

1

MILL LA

ST14

NORBURY HOLLOW

CHURCH LA

LLL
Plantation

B5032

Mill
House

Norbury

Norbury
Hall

Hope
Wood

LUD LA

GREEN LA

B5033

42

11

A

12

B

13

C

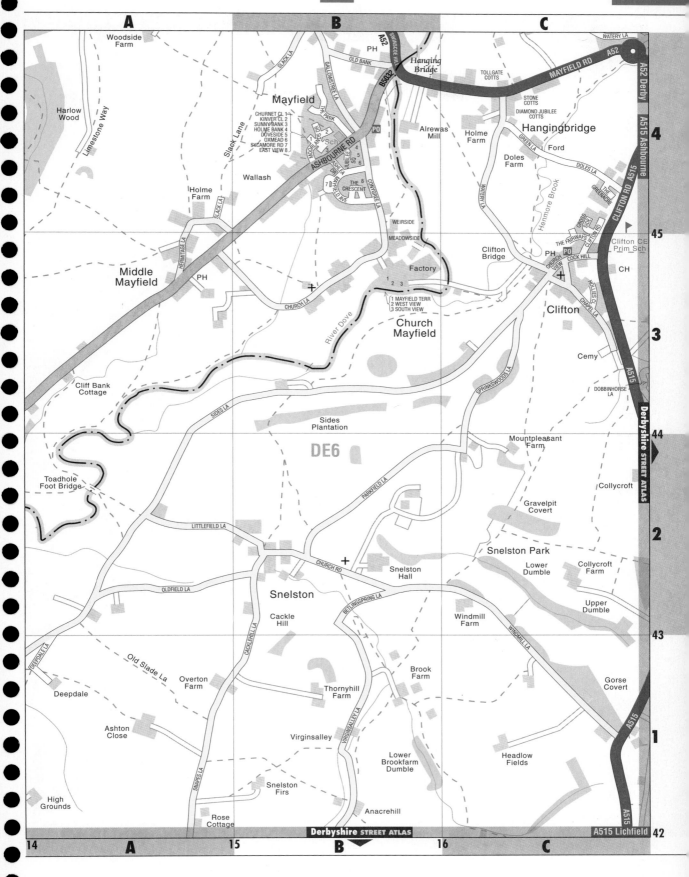

A B C

66

81

Woodside Farm

Harlow Wood

Limestone Way

SLACK LA

OLD BANK

A52

SWINSIDE HILL

Hanging Bridge

GALLOWSTREE LA

B5032

PH

Mayfield

ASHBOURNE RD

A52

MAYFIELD RD

TOLLGATE COTTS

Alrewas Mill

STONE COTTS

DIAMOND JUBILEE COTTS

Hangingbridge

WATERY LA

A52 Derby

A515 Ashbourne

CHURNET CL 1
KINVER CL 2
SUNNYBANK 3
HOLME BANK 4
DOVESIDE 5
OXMEAD 6
SYCAMORE RD 7
EAST VIEW 8

HK PARK

MOORLANDS CL

Sch

PO

Holme Farm

Holme Farm

Wallash

Slack Lane

ASHLEA

DRIVE

JUBILEE CL

CONYGREE LA

THE CRESCENT

Green La

Ford

Doles Farm

DOLES LA

CLIFTON RD

THE GREENACRE

WATERY LA

Henmore Brook

CROSS SIDE

CLIFTON RD

THE FAIRWAYS

Clifton CE Prim Sch

Hermitage La

SLACK LA

Holme Farm

PH

Middle Mayfield

CHURCH LA

WEIRSIDE

MEADOWSIDE

Factory

1 2 3

Clifton Bridge

CHURCH VIEW

PH

PO

Cock Hill

HOLLIES CT

CHAPEL LA

CH

Clifton

River Dove

1 MAYFIELD TERR
2 WEST VIEW
3 SOUTH VIEW

Church Mayfield

Cemy

A515

DOBBINHORSE LA

Cliff Bank Cottage

SIDES LA

SPRINKSWOODS LA

Derbyshire STREET ATLAS

Toadhole Foot Bridge

Sides Plantation

DE6

Mountpleasant Farm

Collycroft

PARKFIELD LA

Gravelpit Covert

LITTLEFIELD LA

CHURCH RD

Snelston Hall

Snelston Park

Lower Dumble

Collycroft Farm

OLDFIELD LA

CACKLEHILL LA

Snelston

Cackle Hill

BETTLINGSPRING LA

Windmill Farm

WINDMILL LA

Upper Dumble

DEEPDALE LA

Old Slade La

Overton Farm

Thornyhill Farm

VIRGINSALLEY LA

Brook Farm

Gorse Covert

Deepdale

Ashton Close

SNAPES LA

Virginsalley

Lower Brookfarm Dumble

Headlow Fields

A515

High Grounds

Snelston Firs

Rose Cottage

Anacrehill

Derbyshire STREET ATLAS

A515 Lichfield

14 A 15 B 16 C

42 1 2 43 3 44 45 4

Derbyshire STREET ATLAS

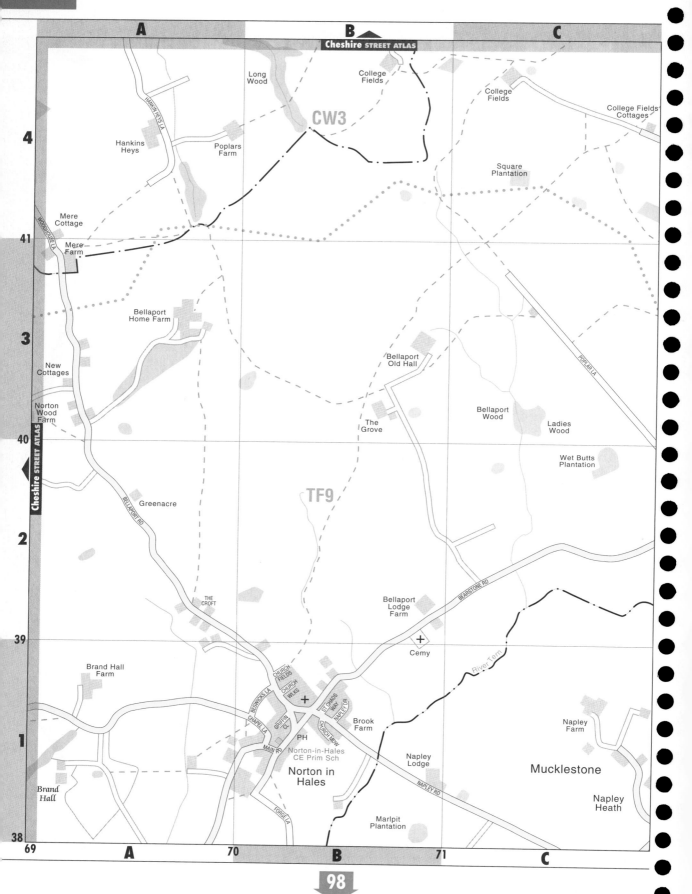

CW3

Long Wood

College Fields

College Fields

College Fields Cottages

Hankins Heys

Poplars Farm

Square Plantation

Mere Cottage

Mere Farm

WOODHOUSE LA

HANKIN HEYS LA

Bellaport Home Farm

Bellaport Old Hall

POPLAR LA

New Cottages

Bellaport Wood

Ladies Wood

Norton Wood Farm

The Grove

Wet Butts Plantation

TF9

Greenacre

BELLAPORT RD

THE CROFT

Bellaport Lodge Farm

BEARSTONE RD

Cemy

River Tern

Brand Hall Farm

CHURCH FIELDS

CHURCH WLKS

BESWICKS LA

CHAPEL LA

GRIFFIN CL

ST CHADS WAY

NAPLEY DR

CHURCH MDW

Brook Farm

Napley Farm

MAIN RD

PH

Norton-in-Hales CE Prim Sch

Napley Lodge

Mucklestone

Brand Hall

Norton in Hales

FORGE LA

NAPLEY RD

Napley Heath

Marlpit Plantation

4

41

3

40

2

39

1

38

Cheshire STREET ATLAS

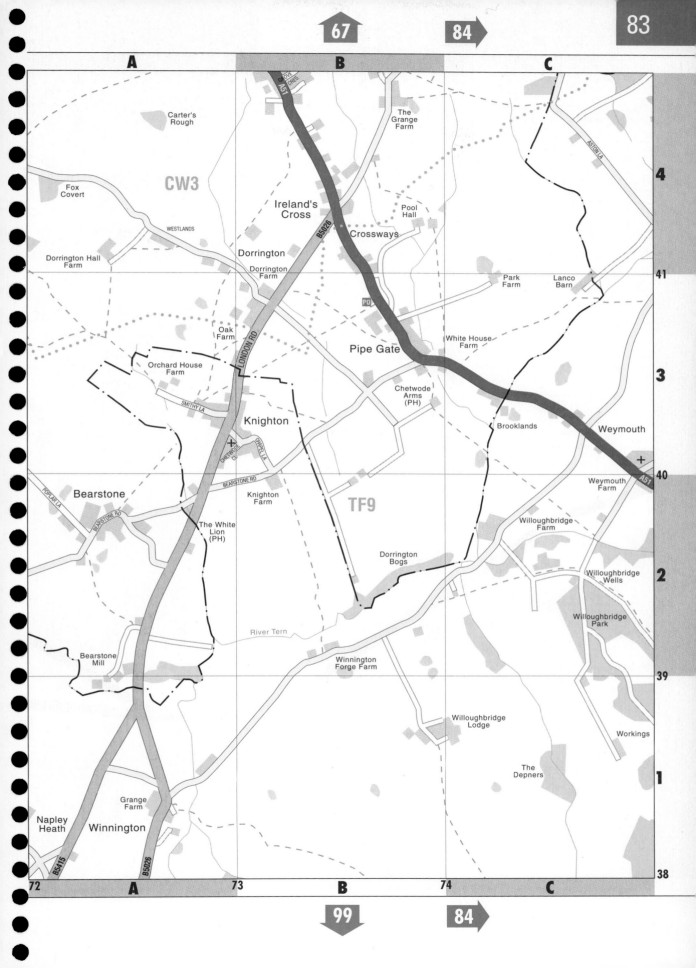

83
68

A **B** **C**

Radwood Copse

CW3

4

Rock House Farm

Lunts Farm

Radwood Hall Farm

ASTON LA

SCHOOL LA

Aston

41

Yew Tree Farm

HOLLOWAY LA

Radwood Farm

CAMP HILL

3

Minnbank

Bank Farm

Holloway Pit Holes

Holloway Farm

Holloway Lane Farm

Mast

Minnbank Farm

MAERWAY LA

Maerway Lane Farm

Camp Wood

Greenfields

Willoughbridge

40

The Dorothy Clive Garden

ST5

Sidway Hall Farm

TF9

Maer Hills

2

Willoughbridge Bogs

Sidway

BADGER LA

WOOD LA

A53

39

Sidway Mill Farm

River Tern

THE CROFT

Blackbrook

White Farm

Swan with Two Necks (PH)

Park House

A53

The Bogs

1

Lower Bogs Plantation

Hungersheath Farm

WHARMADINE LA

Maer Moss Farm

Workings

PARK LA

NEWCASTLE RD.

MOSS LA

38

A53

ROCK

The Wellings

75   **A**   76   **B**   77   **C**

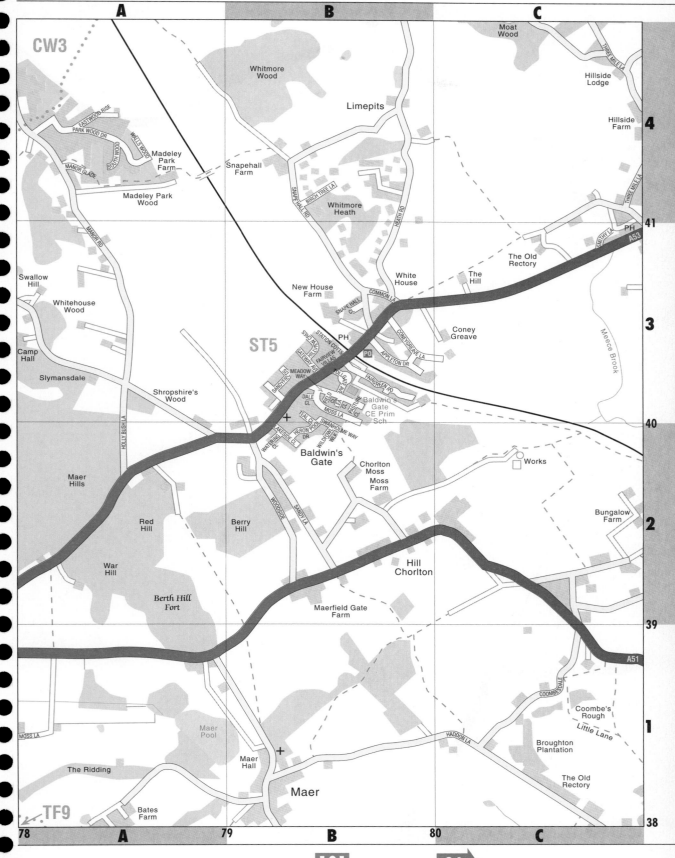

A B C

A5182
A53

Holbrook's Wood

New Hayes Farm

Rook Hall Farm

PARK RD

A5182

TRENTHAM RD

Acton

Acton Hall Farm

4

WHISPER LA

Whitmore Hall

The Rookery

Actonhill Farm

Model Farm

41

A53

Whitmore

Little Paddocks

Hobgoblin Gate

Hanchurch Hills

3

Newhouse Farm

Hanchurch Heath

ST5

40

Swynnerton Old Park

HARLEY THORN LA

Water Tower

Hanchurch Hills Circular Wlks

BENT LA

Shelton under Harley Farm

ST4

DRAYTON RD

P

Cloud End

Byatt's Common

2

Keepers Cottage

Shelton under Harley

Harley Thorns

Springfields

DOG LA

Nursery Common

39

Stableford Bridge

Cock Inn (PH)

Stableford

A51

Common Lane

1

Rowe Farm

STABLEFORD BANK

The Rowe

Hatton Common

Hatton Rough

Little Lane

Bluebell Bank

ST21

38

81 82 83

A B C

A51

71
88

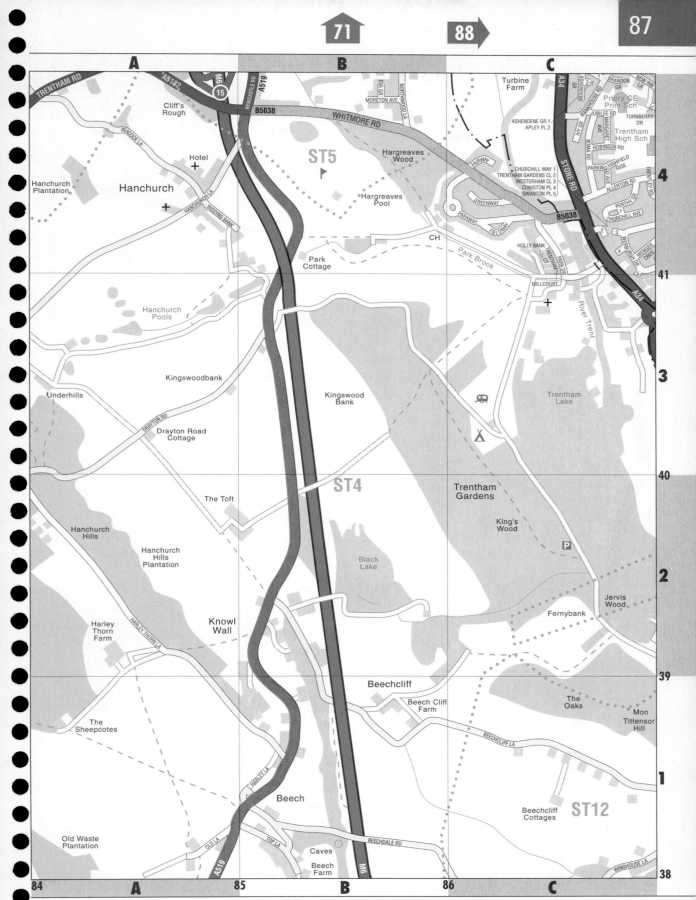

103
88

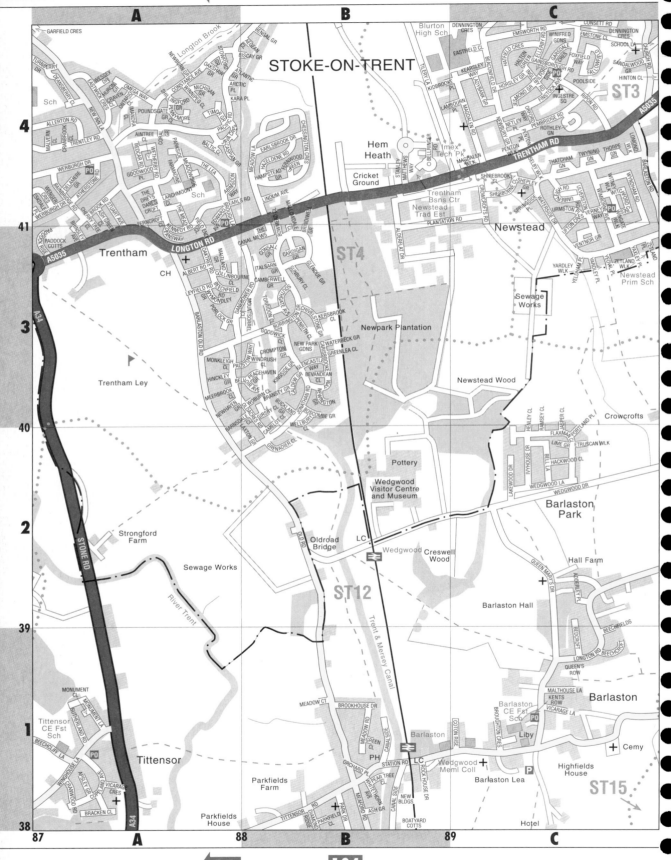

STOKE-ON-TRENT

ST3

ST4

Newstead

Trentham

Newpark Plantation

Newstead Wood

Crowcrofts

Trentham Ley

Pottery

Wedgwood Visitor Centre and Museum

Barlaston Park

Strongford Farm

Oldroad Bridge

Creswell Wood

Hall Farm

Sewage Works

Wedgwood

ST12

River Trent

Barlaston Hall

Monument Cl

Tittensor CE Fst Sch

Barlaston CE Fst Sch

Barlaston

Liby

Cemy

Tittensor

Barlaston Meml Coll

Highfields House

Parkfields Farm

Barlaston Lea

ST15

Parkfields House

Hotel

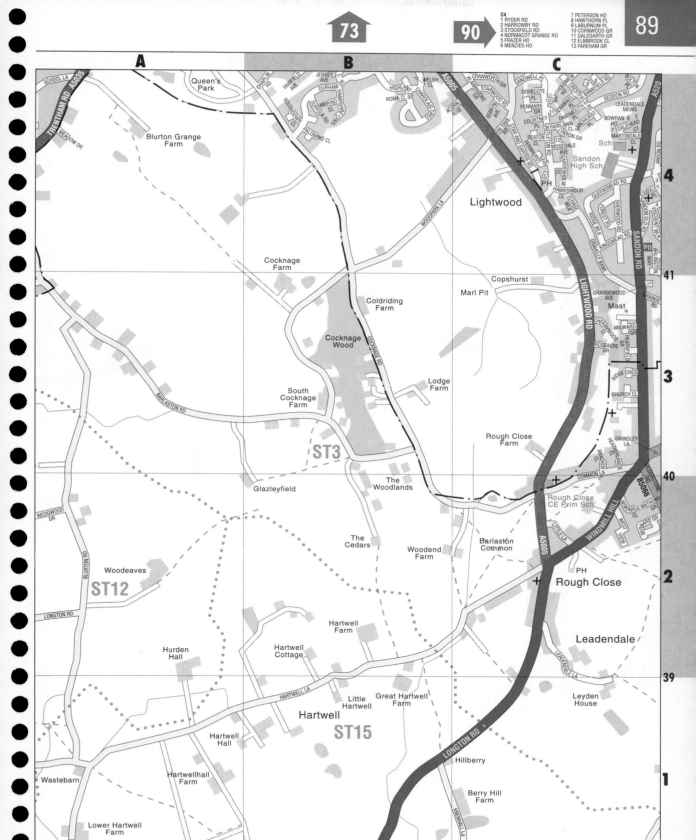

73

90 →

C4
1 RYDER RD
2 HARROWBY RD
3 STOCKFIELD RD
4 NORMACOT GRANGE RD
5 FRAZER HO
6 MENZIES HO

7 PETERSON HO
8 HAWTHORN PL
9 LABURNUM PL
10 CORNWOOD GR
11 DALEGARTH GR
12 ELMBROOK CL
13 FAREHAM GR

89

A

B

C

School La
Trentham Rd A5035
Queen's Park
Meadow Dr
Blurton Grange Farm

Chapla Vn
Fairfield Ave
Durham Dr
Hampshire Cres
Merino Cl
Suffolk Rd
Southdown Cl
Palomino Cl
Jersey Ave
Highland Dr
Roma Cl
Welsh Cl
Chalais Dr
Acorn Rise

A5005
Cranworth Gr
Alverstone Gr
Sterling Ave
Starwood Gr
Sandwell Pl
Dovecote
Penmark Gr
Courtney Pl
Fairlawn
Seaton Pl
Fenwick
Cranwell Gr
Castleton Gr
Sandhurst
Dartmouth Gr
Ashton Gr
Mosedale Ave
Gardenham
Hawksmoor
Bowran
Martindale
Dalehead
Seddon Rd
Leadendale Mews
Sandon High Sch
Sch
PH
A520
Mason Rd

Woodpark La
4

Cocknage Farm
Lightwood
Copshurst
Marl Pit
Grangewood Ave
Lightwood Rd
Mast
Sherwood Gr
Roseacre Gr
Heathfield
Milward Gr
Grange Rd
Loxley
Arlington
Sandon Old Rd
Viscount Wk
Way
41

Coldriding Farm
Cocknage Wood
Cocknage Rd
Ridge Cres
Church Cl
3

Barlaston Rd
South Cocknage Farm
Lodge Farm
Rough Close Farm
Grindley La
Heathlands
Bracken Cl
ST3

Glazleyfield
The Woodlands
Rough Close CE Prim Sch
Common La
40
Windmill Hill
B5066
Hillstone Dr
West
Anthony
Ford Pl

Wedgwood Dr
The Cedars
Woodend Farm
Barlaston Common
A5005
Little La
Leadendale La
Rough Close
PH
Little La
ST12
Blurton Rd
Longton Rd
Woodeaves
Leadendale
2

Hartwell Farm
39
Hurden Hall
Hartwell Cottage
Leyden House
Leyden
House

Hartwell La
Little Hartwell
Great Hartwell Farm
Hartwell
ST15
Hartwell Hall
Longton Rd
Hillberry
1
Wastebarn
Hartwellhall Farm
Berry Hill Farm
Knenhall La

Lower Hartwell Farm
Lower Cullamoor
Middle Cullamoor
A520
Old Rd
Far Croft
Knenhall La
38

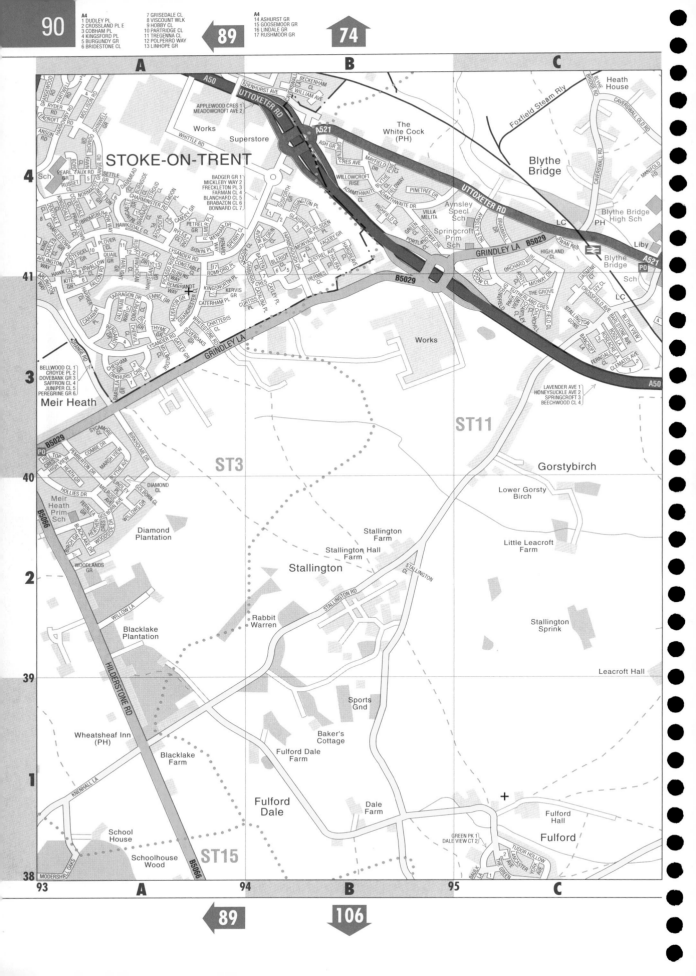

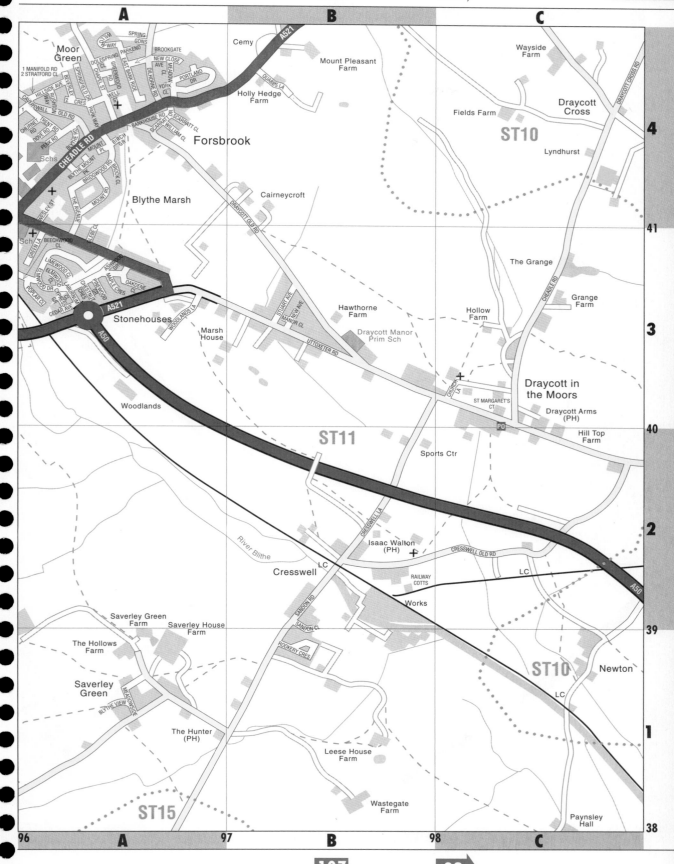

91
76

A   B   C

Harplow

DRAYCOTT CROSS RD

HARPLOW LA

Sand & Gravel Pit

Huntley Wood

HUNTLEY LA

MANIFOLD DR

Plantation House

DRAYCOTT DR 1
HUNTLEY CL 2

DANDILLION AVE

LITLEY DR

CROXDEN

TEAN RD

A522

EAVES LA

The Eaves

SMITHY LA

The Crown (PH)

4

Huntley

Mobberley

Seven Acre Wood

41

Coneygreave

Gorsty Hill Farm

Coneygreaves Farm

ST11

3

Teanford

Anchor Inn (PH)

TENFORD LA

Gorstyhill

BREACH LA

The Breach

River Tean

WENTLOWS AVE

WENTLOWS RD

CHEADLE RD

REDHILL DR

CAVANDUST RD

Gorsty Hall

ST10

WILLOW CL

40

The Rocks

KILN CROFT

GORSTY HILL RD

ASHLEY

AINTREE RD

BOXWOOD RD

BARNFIELD RD

Totmonslow

COPLOW AVE

DRAYCOTT RD

HOLBORN ROW

PARKLANDS RD

Sch

GREAT WOOD RD

OAKHILL CL

WALL FIELD CL

GARDEN VILLAGE

THE ISLAND

RIVERSIDE RD

ST THOMAS'S RD

OLD RD

NEW RD

HIGH ST

PO

P

HOLLINGTON RD

2

Oak Hill Farm

MEADOW WAY

HALL LA

Upper Tean

Great Wood Prim Sch

HOLLINSCROFT AVE

VICARAGE RD

VICARAGE CRES

FURLONG CL

CARTERS AVE

CARLING AVE

RYECROFT CL

CHESTNUT CL

Cemy

LC

FURLONG DR

HAWTHORNE CL

SORREL AVE

HONEYSUCKLE CL

A50

Midway Farm

Daisy Farm

39

Benthouse Farm

Hall Green

Hall Green Farm

UTTOXETER RD

River Tean

Lower Tean

HEATH HOUSE LA

TEANHURST RD

HEYBRIDGE CL

GOLDHURS CL

BIRCHENDO... CL

TEANVALE RD

1

Highfields Farm

MILL LA

PH

NIGHTINGALE CL

LEIGH LA

A522

ST11

Heybridge

Tean Leys

Hey Bridge

38

99   A   00   B   01   C

A50

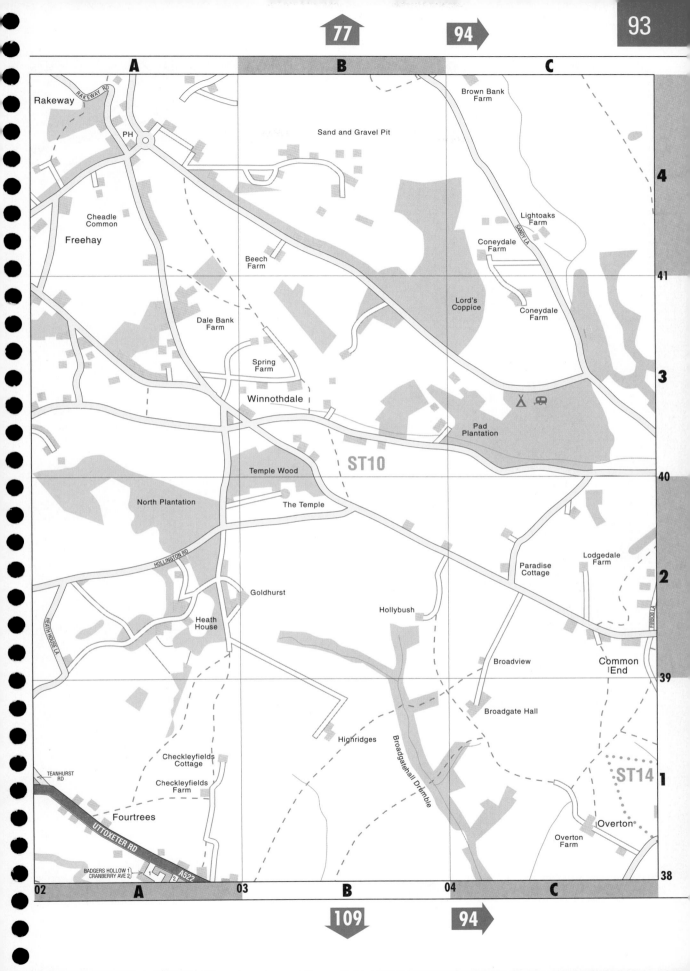

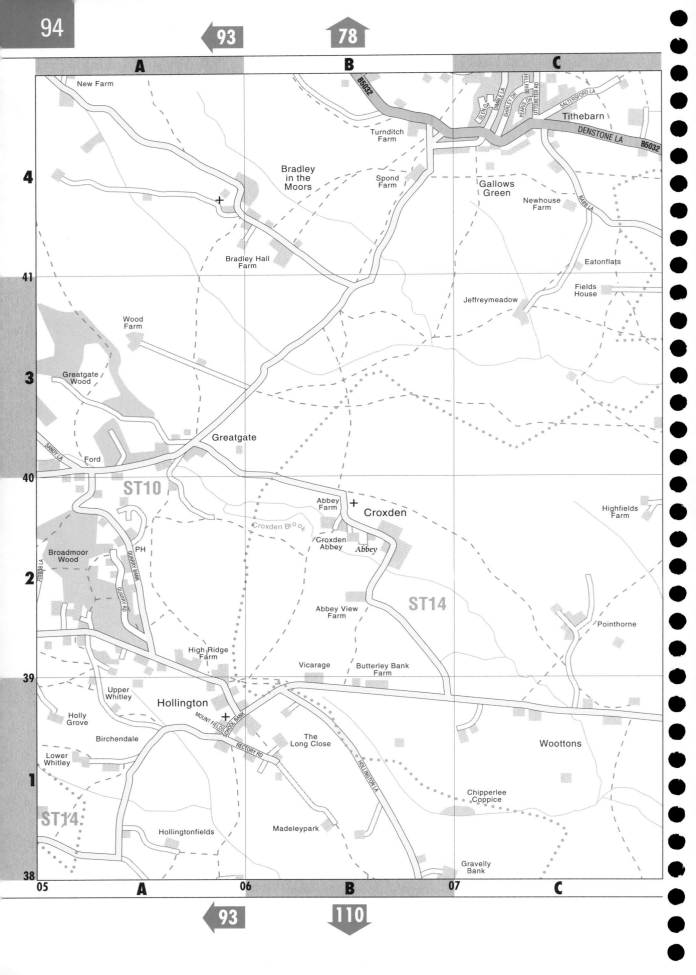

A B C

New Farm

Turnditch
Farm

B5032

GLEN DR
DIMBLE LA
SHIRLEY DR
PEARIS DR
BENSMITH
UTTOXETER RD
SALTERSFORD LA

Tithebarn

DENSTONE LA B5032

Bradley in the
Moors

Spond
Farm

Gallows
Green

Newhouse
Farm

MABB LA

4

+

Eatonflats

Bradley Hall
Farm

41

Jeffreymeadow

Fields
House

Wood
Farm

SANDY LA

Greatgate
Wood

3

Greatgate

Ford

40

ST10

Abbey
Farm

+ Croxden

Croxden Brook

Croxden
Abbey

Abbey

ST14

Highfields
Farm

Broadmoor
Wood

PH

QUARRY BANK
QUARRY RD
FERBOB LA

2

Abbey View
Farm

Pointhorne

High Ridge
Farm

Vicarage

Butterley Bank
Farm

39

Upper
Whitley

Hollington

MOUNT FIELDS
SCHOOL BANK
RECTORY RD

+

Woottons

Holly
Grove

Birchendale

The
Long Close

Lower
Whitley

1

HOLLINGTON LA

Chipperlee
Coppice

ST14

Hollingtonfields

Madeleypark

Gravelly
Bank

38

05 A 06 B 07 C

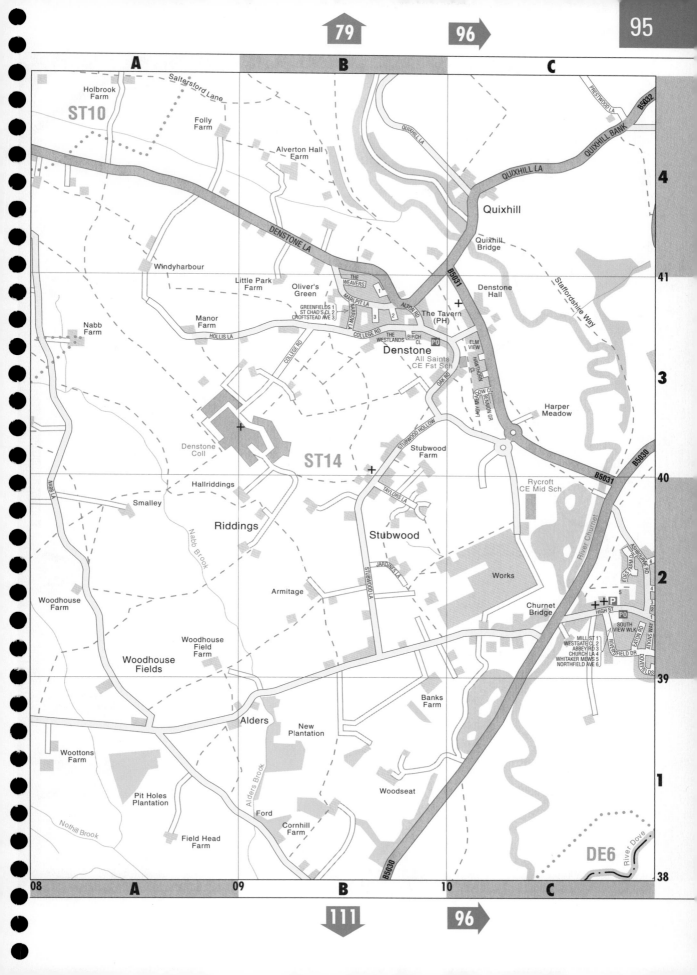

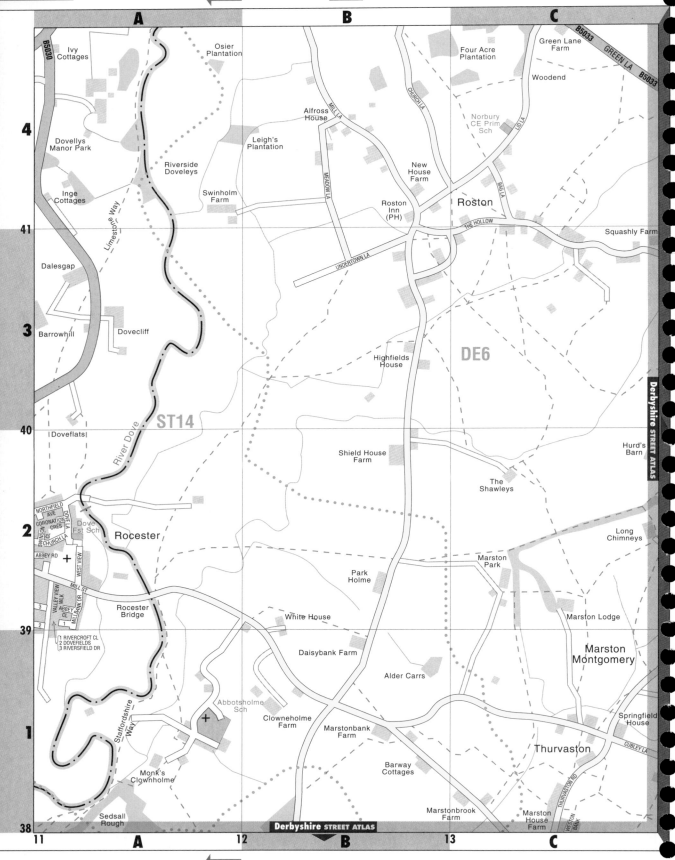

A

B

C

B5030

Ivy Cottages

Osier Plantation

Four Acre Plantation

Green Lane Farm

B5033

Woodend

GREEN LA B5033

4

Dovellys Manor Park

Riverside Doveleys

Leigh's Plantation

Alfross House

MILL LA

CHURCH LA

New House Farm

Norbury CE Prim Sch

LIO LA

Inge Cottages

Swinholm Farm

Roston Inn (PH)

Roston

41

Dalesgap

THE HOLLOW

B846 LA

Squashly Farm

UNDERTOWN LA

3

Barrowhill

Dovecliff

Highfields House

DE6

ST14

Doveflats

River Dove

Limestone Way

40

Shield House Farm

Hurd's Barn

The Shawleys

Long Chimneys

NORTHFIELD AVE

DOVE LA

CORONATION CRES

SWINSCOL RD

CHURCH LA

Dove Fst Sch

Rocester

Marston Park

2

ABBEY RD

WEST VIEW

MILL ST

Park Holme

Marston Lodge

MILLBANK DR

VALLEY VIEW WLK

ABBEY CL

Rocester Bridge

White House

Marston Montgomery

39

3

2

1

1 RIVERCROFT CL
2 DOVEFIELDS
3 RIVERSFIELD DR

Daisybank Farm

Alder Carrs

Springfield House

Staffordshire Way

Abbotsholme Sch

Clowneholme Farm

Marstonbank Farm

Thurvaston

CUBLEY LA

1

Monk's Clownholme

Barway Cottages

THURVASTON RD

Sedsall Rough

Marstonbrook Farm

Marston House Farm

WESTON BANK

38

11

A

12

B

13

C

Derbyshire STREET ATLAS

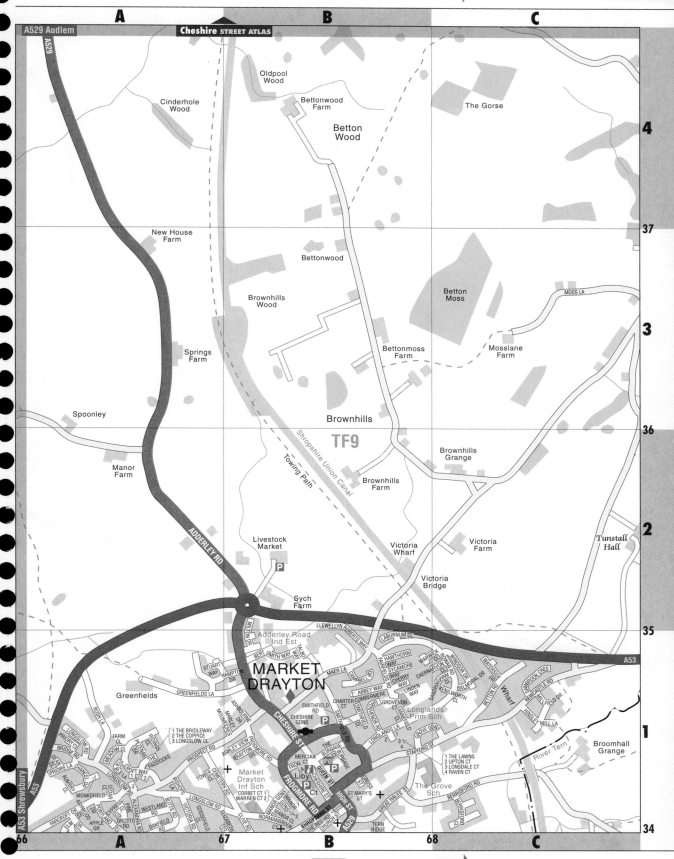

A529 Audlem

Cheshire STREET ATLAS

A529

A53 Shrewsbury

Oldpool Wood

Cinderhole Wood

Bettonwood Farm

Betton Wood

The Gorse

4

New House Farm

Bettonwood

37

Brownhills Wood

Betton Moss

MOSS LA

Springs Farm

Bettonmoss Farm

Mosslane Farm

3

Spoonley

Brownhills

TF9

Brownhills Grange

36

Manor Farm

Shropshire Union Canal

Towing Path

Brownhills Farm

Victoria Wharf

Victoria Farm

Tunstall Hall

2

Livestock Market

P

Victoria Bridge

ADDERLEY RD

Sych Farm

Victoria Wharf

35

Adderley Road Ind Est

LLEWELLYN ROBERTS WAY

LABURNUM CL

A53

MARKET DRAYTON

Wharf

Greenfields

GREENFIELDS LA

MARKET DRAYTON

Longlands Prim Sch

River Tern

Broomhall Grange

1

CHESHIRE ST

Market Drayton Inf Sch

Library

FROGMORE RD

QUEEN ST

HIGH ST

ST MARY'S ST

The Grove Sch

Berrisford Rd

1 THE LAWNS
2 UPTON CT
3 LONSDALE CT
4 RAVEN CT

A529

34

97
82

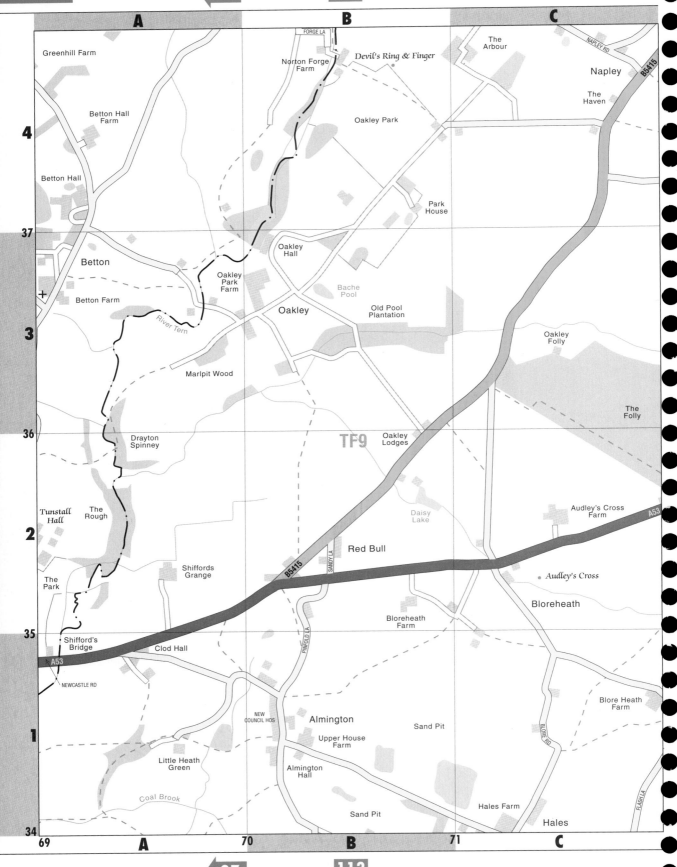

A   B   C

Greenhill Farm

Betton Hall
Farm

4

Betton Hall

37

Betton

Betton Farm

3

River Tern

Marlpit Wood

Drayton
Spinney

36

Tunstall
Hall

The Rough

2

The
Park

Shiffords
Grange

35

Shifford's
Bridge

Clod Hall

A53

NEWCASTLE RD

1

Little Heath
Green

Coal Brook

34

69   70   71

A   B   C

FORGE LA

Norton Forge
Farm

Devil's Ring & Finger

Oakley Park

Oakley
Hall

Bache
Pool

Oakley
Park
Farm

Oakley

Old Pool
Plantation

Park
House

The Arbour

NAPLEY RD

Napley

B5415

The Haven

Oakley
Folly

The
Folly

TF9

Oakley
Lodges

Daisy
Lake

Audley's Cross
Farm

A53

B5415

SANDY LA

Red Bull

Audley's Cross

Bloreheath

Bloreheath
Farm

PINFOLD LA

NEW
COUNCIL HOS

Almington

Upper House
Farm

Sand Pit

Almington
Hall

Sand Pit

BLORE RD

Blore Heath
Farm

Hales Farm

FLASH LA

Hales

97
113

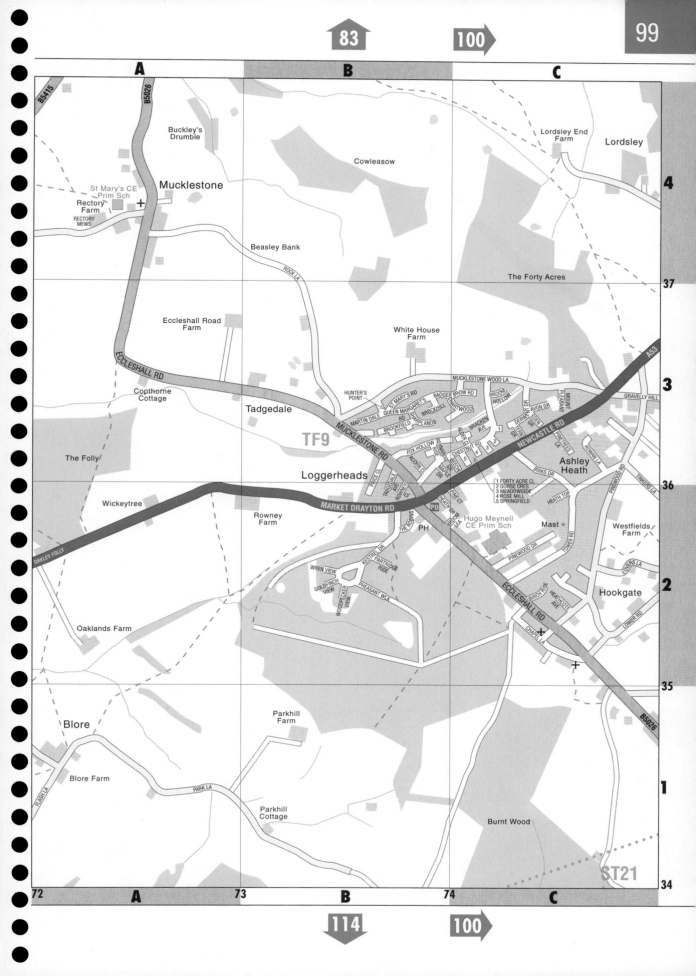

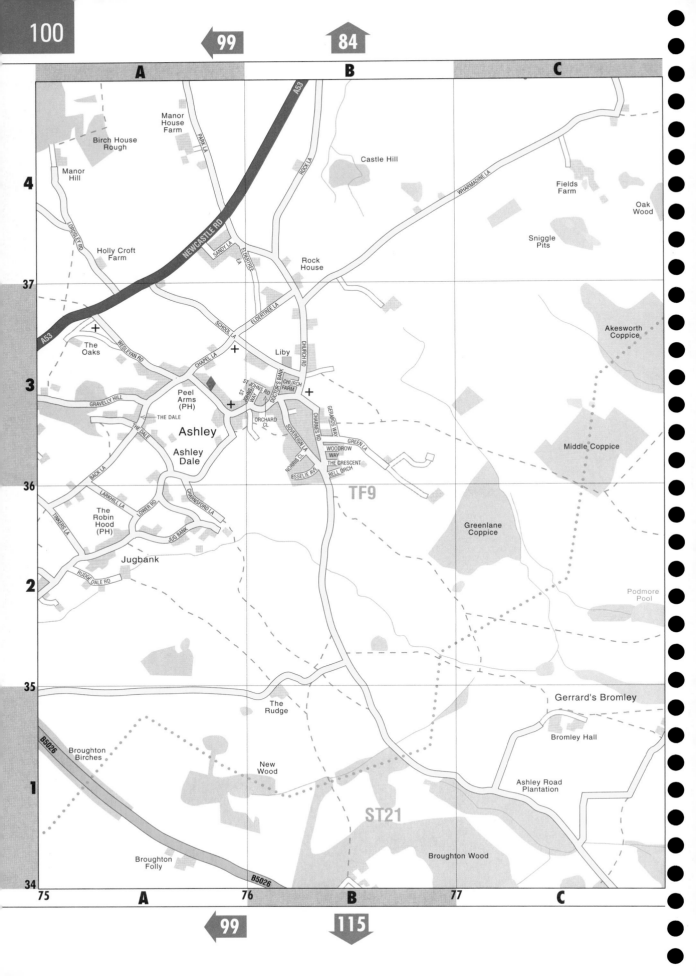

A · B · C

4

37

3

36

2

35

1

34

75 · A · 76 · B · 77 · C

Manor House Farm

Birch House Rough

Manor Hill

Holly Croft Farm

PARK LA

SANDY LA

ELNERTREE LA

NEWCASTLE RD

A53

A53

LOWGLEY RD

The Oaks

WESLEYAN RD

CHAPEL LA

SCHOOL LA

ELDERTREE LA

ROCK LA

Rock House

Castle Hill

WHARMADINE LA

Fields Farm

Oak Wood

Sniggle Pits

Akesworth Coppice

Liby

CHURCH RD

ST JOHNS RD

ST JOHNS WAY

DOCTOR'S BANK

CHURCH FARM

Peel Arms (PH)

GRAVELLY HILL

THE DALE

Ashley

ORCHARD CL

SOVEREIGN LA

CHARNES RD

GERARDS WAY

GREEN LA

Middle Coppice

Ashley Dale

THE DALE

BACK LA

NORRIS CT

ESSELIE AV

WOODROW WAY

THE CRESCENT

BELL ORCH

TF9

LARKHILL LA

LOWER RD

CHARNSFORD LA

The Robin Hood (PH)

TINKERS LA

JUG BANK

Jugbank

Greenlane Coppice

Podmore Pool

RUDGE DALE RD

B5026

Broughton Birches

The Rudge

New Wood

Gerrard's Bromley

Bromley Hall

Ashley Road Plantation

ST21

B5026

Broughton Folly

Broughton Wood

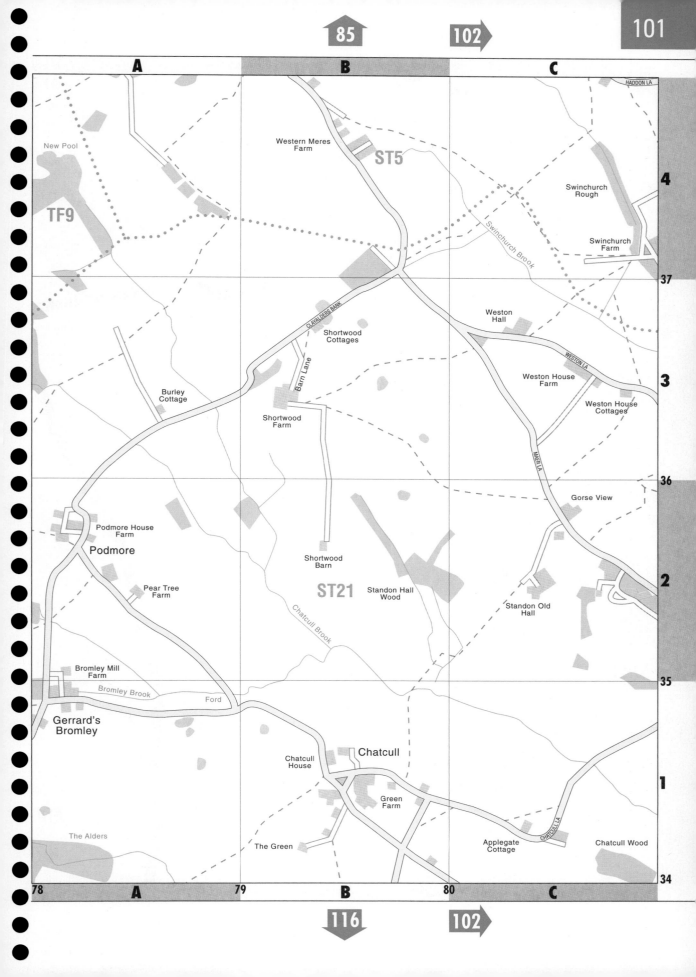

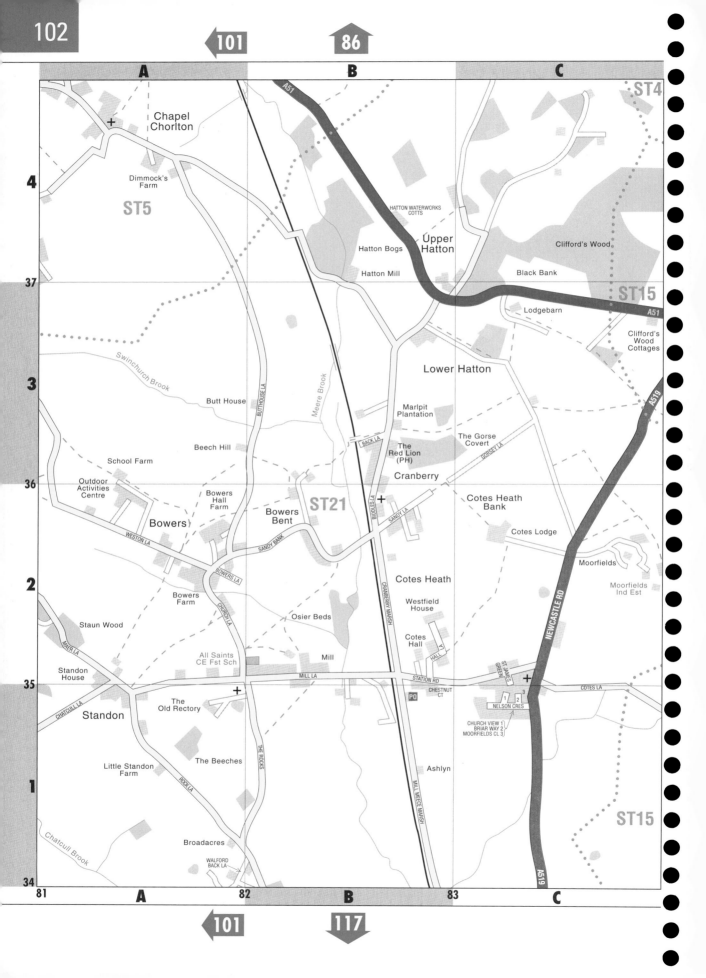

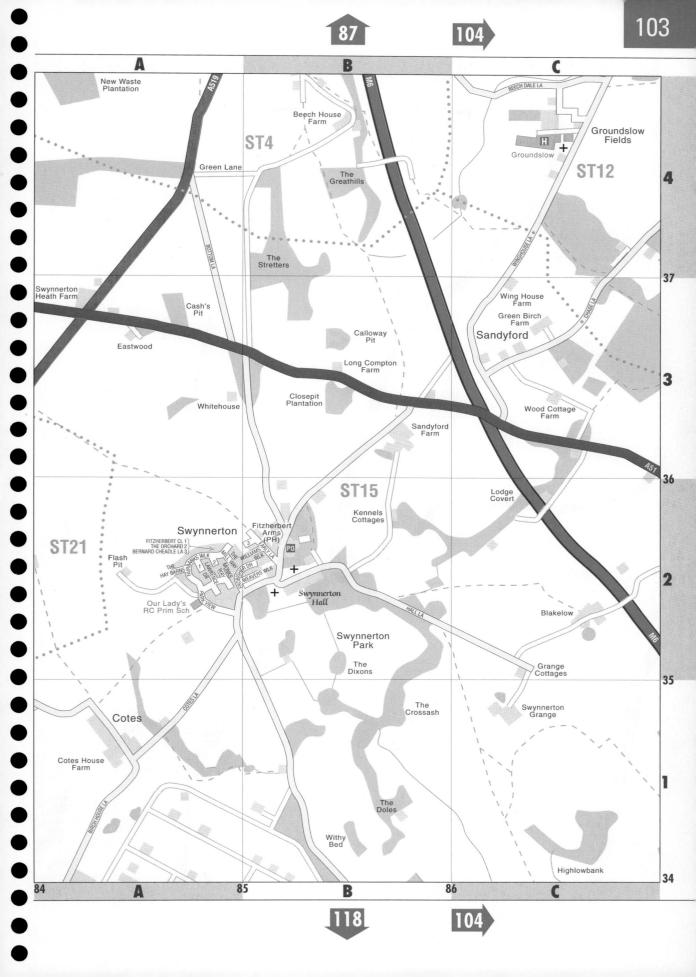

A B C

Barton Land

TITTENSOR RD

Heyfields

HEYFIELDS COTTS

ST12

RIDGE CL
DIAMOND RIDGE
DIAMOND CL
PARK DR
SILVER RIDGE

STONE RD
A34

4

Inn

CH

Downs Banks

Tittensor Chase

Spring Vale

37

Tittensor Chase

Warren House Farm

MEAFORD RD

CHASE LA

Saxon's Lowe

3

Hilltop

Firs Cottage

Power Station (dis)

Turnover Bridge

Ford

Meaford Farm

WASH DALE LA

36

A51

Bury Bank Farm

Bury Bank

BANKSIDE

River Trent

ST15

Siddall's Bridge

Outlanes Mill Farm

A34

The Darlaston (PH)

A51

P

Meaford Hall

Meaford

Trent and Mersey Canal

Meaford Old Hall Farm

2

Marlpit House

Burybank

JERVIS LA

George and Dragon (PH)

Turnover Bridge

Edge Hill

Common Plot

M6

The Drumble

Darlastonwood Farm

BARNTON EDGE
ANDERTON VIEW
BENTLEY CL
RENDEL CL
BRINDLEY CL
RUDYARD CL

PIKE LA
NAVIGATION LOOP
MARION ST
MILLENNIUM WAY

Works

LC

MOUNT RD

Mount Ind Est

Stonefield

35

Darlaston Wood

WHITEBRIDGE
SUMMIT CT
CANAL ST
CENTRE RD
CHESTNUT GR
FIELD HOUSE ST

MOUNT AVE
MOUNT CRES
BERKELEY ST
VICTOR RD
KENT GR
MEAFORD AVE

1

Darlaston Park

Home Farm

THE FILLYBROOKS

NEWCASTLE RD
B5027

Whitebridge Ind Est
Stone
STATION APP

LC

TRINITY DR
ALMA ST
REGENT ST
STATION RD
B5315

34

Darlaston Grange

YARNFIELD LA
A34
TRENT RD
HARTLEY DR
MEAFORD RD

St Dominic's Priory Sch

B5027
NEWCASTLE ST

87 A 88 B 89 C

C1
1 RANGELEY VIEW
2 DARWIN CL
3 DIXON CL
4 CHESTNUT CT
5 EDWARD ST
6 ALEXANDRA ST
7 KING'S AVE
8 NORTHESK ST
9 DOMINIC ST
10 MARGARET ST

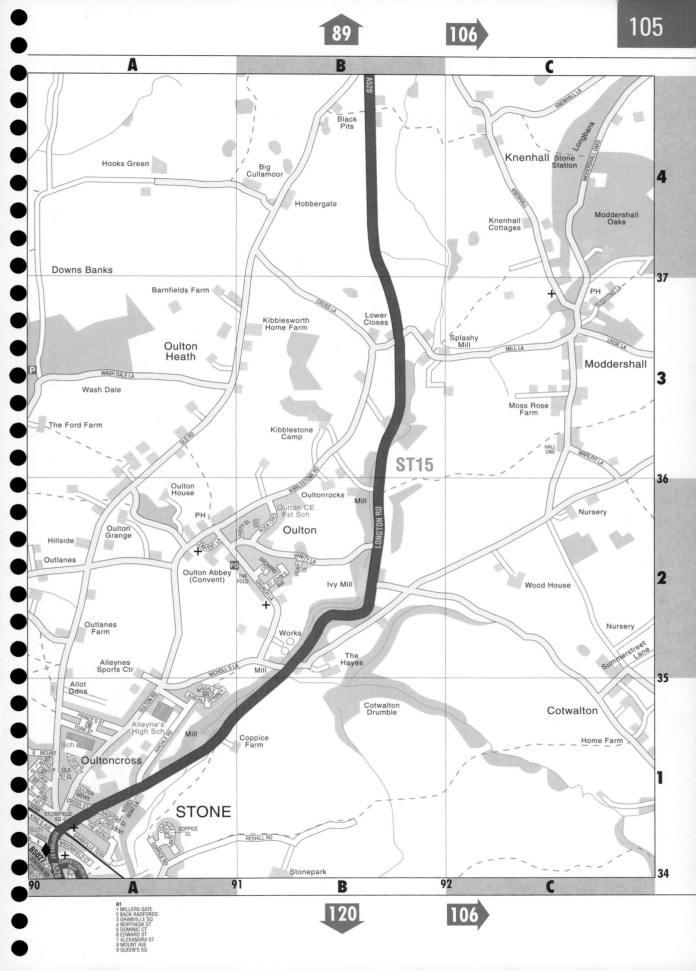

A | B | C

Black Pits

A520

Knenhall Lane

Longbank

Hooks Green

Big Cullamoor

Knenhall Stone Station

Moddershall Oaks

4

Hobbergate

Knenhall Cottages

Modershall Oaks

Knenhall La

Downs Banks

37

Barnfields Farm

Cross La

Lower Closes

Splashy Mill

PH

Bushtons La

Leese La

Kibblesworth Home Farm

Mill La

Moddershall

3

Oulton Heath

Wash Dale La

P

Wash Dale

Old Rd

Kibblestone Camp

Moss Rose Farm

The Ford Farm

Kibblestone Rd

ST15

Hall End

Marlpit La

36

Oulton House

Oultonrocks

Mill

Nursery

Vanity Cl

Rock Cres

Oulton CE Fst Sch

PH

Convent La

Oulton

Longton Rd

Hillside

Oulton Grange

Orchard Cl

Vanity La

Vicar's Cl

St John's Ave

Wood House

2

Outlanes

PO

The Fold

Church La

Ivy Mill

Nursery

Oulton Abbey (Convent)

Works

Summerstreet Lane

Outlanes Farm

Nicholl's La

Mill

The Hayes

35

Alleynes Sports Ctr

Airdale Gr

Airdale Spinney

Cotwalton Drumble

Cotwalton

Allot Gdns

Prince's St

York St

Oulton Rd

Alleyne's High Sch

Mill

Coppice Farm

Home Farm

Sch

8 Mount St

Arthur St

Victoria St

Albert St

Field

Lotus Ct

Old Rd Cl

Oulton Mews

Cross St

1

Oultoncross

Airdale Rd

Mill

STONE

Radford Cl

Goat La

Mount Ave

Kings Ave

Stonefield Sq

The Avenue

Crescent

Coppice Gdns

Coppice Cl

Sch

B5021

Bradford St

A520

Christchurch

Granville Terr

Broomfield Ct

Granville Ct

Station Rd

Redhill Rd

Coppice Rd

Stonepark

34

A | 91 | B | 92 | C

A1
1 MILLERS GATE
2 BACK RADFORDS
3 GRANVILLE SQ
4 NORTHESK ST
5 DOMINIC CT
6 EDWARD ST
7 ALEXANDRA ST
8 MOUNT AVE
9 QUEEN'S SQ

105
90

A **B** **C**

4

Moddershall
Grange

Idlerocks
Farm

Idlerocks

Idlerocks

Stallington
Heath

Broom's
Farm

Fulford

Townend

CHERRY CL

BAULK LA

KINGFISHER CRES

RICHVIEW

FULFORD RD

TOWNEND

HILLSIDE CL

SAVERLEY GREEN RD

MEADOW

Fulford
Prim Sch

PO

ST11

Crossgate

Longlane
Head
Farm

Greensitch
Farm

Spot
Acre

Spot Acre
Spinney

Mossgate

Flats

Mosslane

37

Nurseries

Spotgate Inn
(PH)

MOSS LA

BALAAM'S LA

Nursery

Rushlade

3

LEESE LA

The Spot

HILDERSTONE RD

The
Leasows

Bird in Hand
(PH)

Farthings

Spot
Farm

36

Spot
Grange

ST15

The
Hurstage

2

High Elms

Manor House
Farm

CHESSWELL RD

Home Farm

HALL LA

35

Sewage
Works

Hilderstone
Hall

DINGLE LA

BARNES
CROFT

BREMPTON
CROFT

THE MEADOWS

ROEBUCK CT

LEA
FARM

FARM VIEW

Crossgate
Barn

Newfields

Hall Wood

1

Hilderstone

SANDON RD

Roebuck Inn
(PH)

Hall Farm

Peakshill
Wood

Wooliscroft

EASTHOLME

WHITEYCH LA

B5066

34

93 **A** 94 **B** 95 **C**

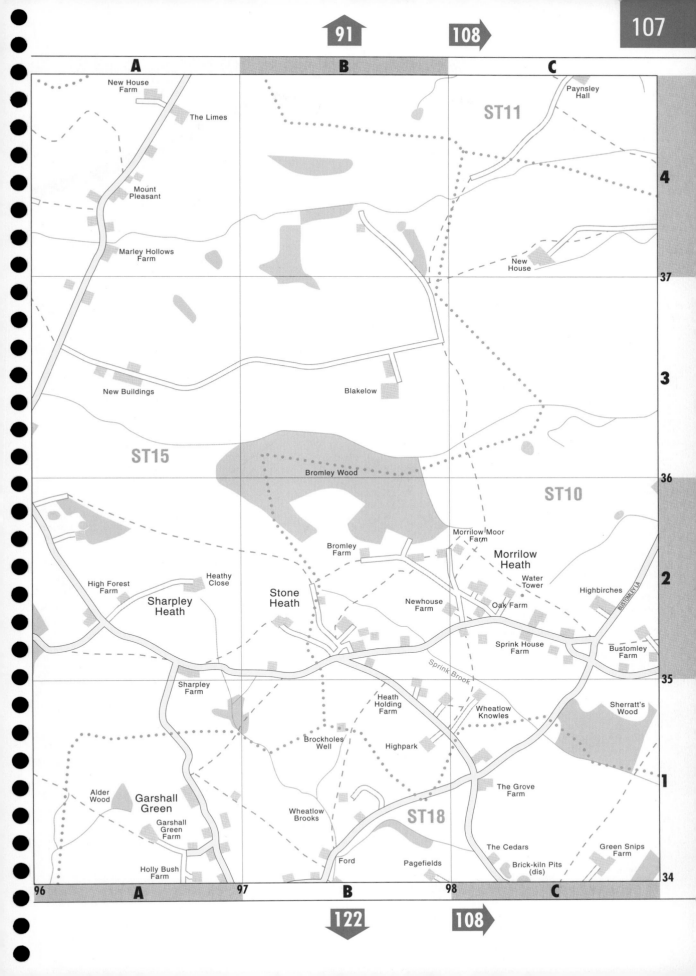

A
B
C

New House Farm
The Limes

ST11

Paynsley Hall

4

Mount Pleasant

Marley Hollows Farm

New House

37

New Buildings

Blakelow

3

ST15

Bromley Wood

36

ST10

Morrilow Moor Farm

Bromley Farm

Morrilow Heath

High Forest Farm

Heathy Close

Water Tower

Highbirches

2

Sharpley Heath

Stone Heath

Newhouse Farm

Oak Farm

Spink House Farm

Bustomley Farm

35

Sharpley Farm

Heath Holding Farm

Wheatlow Knowles

Sherratt's Wood

Brockholes Well

Highpark

Alder Wood

Garshall Green

The Grove Farm

1

Wheatlow Brooks

ST18

Garshall Green Farm

The Cedars

Green Snips Farm

Holly Bush Farm

Ford

Pagefields

Brick-kiln Pits (dis)

34

96
A
97
B
98
C

Sprink Brook

BUSTOMLEY LA

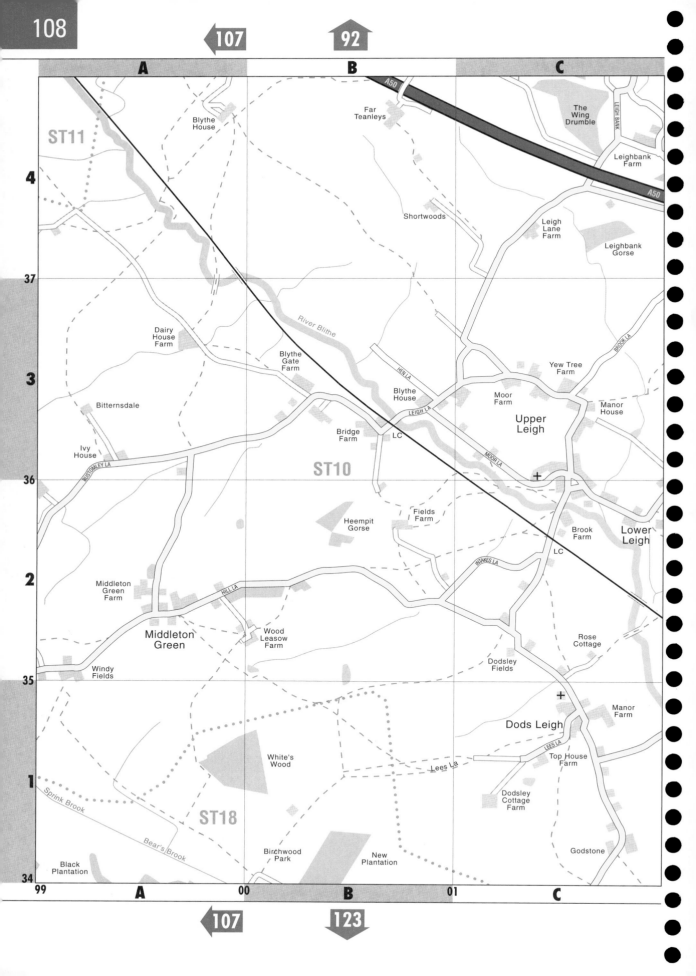

ST11

4

37

3

36

ST10

2

35

1

ST18

34

99   A   00   B   01   C

Blythe
House

Far
Teanleys

A50

The
Wing
Drumble

LEIGH BANK

Leighbank
Farm

Shortwoods

A50

Leigh
Lane
Farm

Leighbank
Gorse

River Blithe

Dairy
House
Farm

Blythe
Gate
Farm

HEN LA

Blythe
House

Moor
Farm

Yew Tree
Farm

BROOK LA

Bitternsdale

LEIGH LA

Upper
Leigh

Manor
House

Bridge
Farm

LC

Ivy
House

BUSTOMLEY LA

MOOR LA

Heempit
Gorse

Fields
Farm

Brook
Farm

Lower
Leigh

Middleton
Green
Farm

HILL LA

INTAKES LA

LC

Middleton
Green

Wood
Leasow
Farm

Dodsley
Fields

Rose
Cottage

Windy
Fields

Manor
Farm

Dods Leigh

White's
Wood

LEES LA

Top House
Farm

Lees La

Sprink Brook

Dodsley
Cottage
Farm

Bear's Brook

Birchwood
Park

New
Plantation

Godstone

Black
Plantation

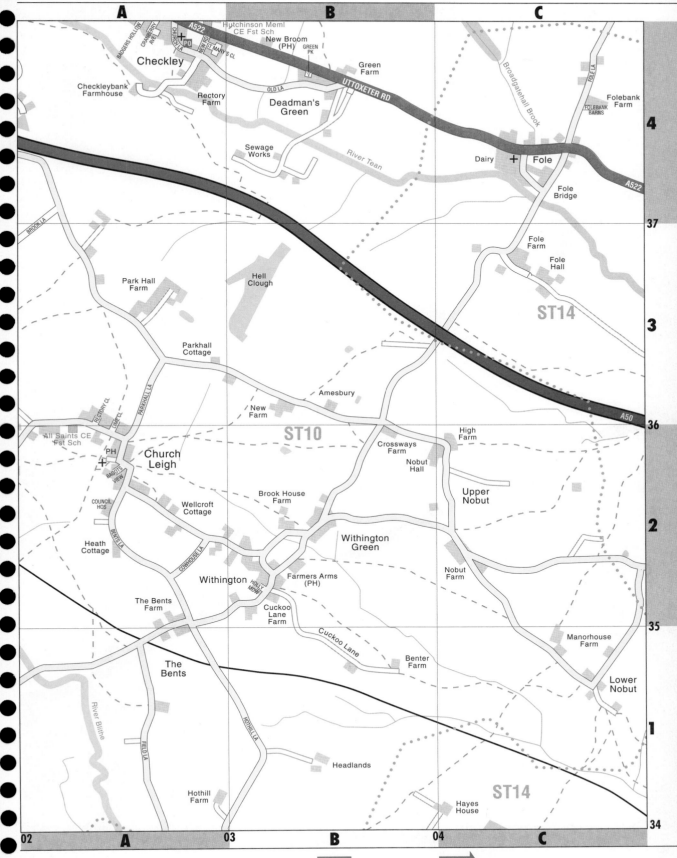

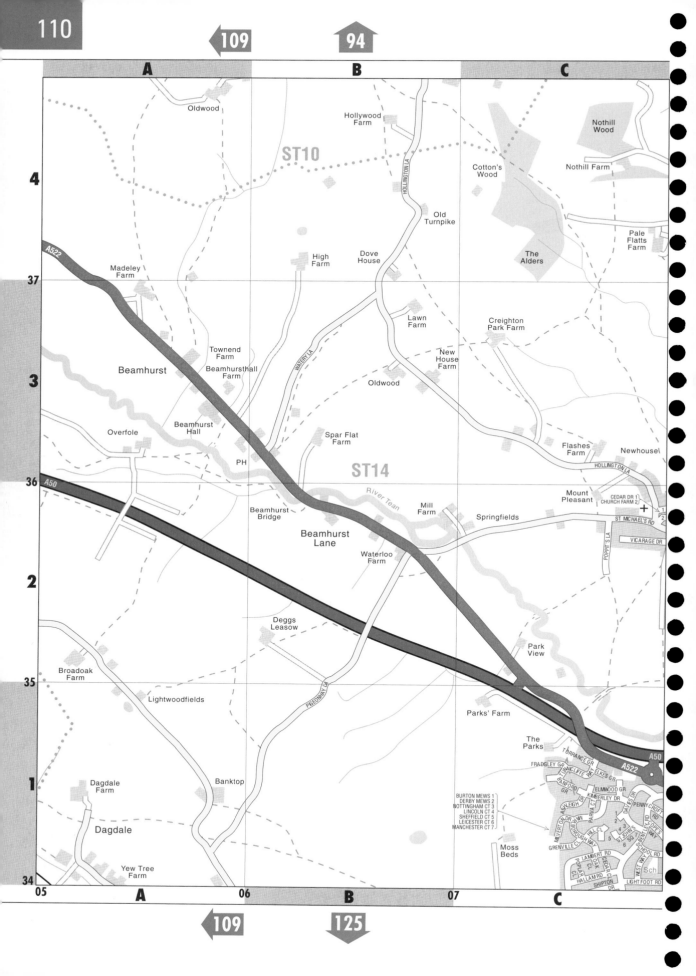

A   B   C

4

ST10

Oldwood

Hollywood Farm

Nothill Wood

Cotton's Wood

Nothill Farm

HOLLINGTON LA

Old Turnpike

Pale Flatts Farm

A522

Madeley Farm

37

High Farm

Dove House

The Alders

Lawn Farm

Creighton Park Farm

Townend Farm

Beamhursthall Farm

Beamhurst

WATERY LA

New House Farm

3

Oldwood

Beamhurst Hall

Spar Flat Farm

Flashes Farm

Newhouse

Overfole

HOLLINGTON LA

PH

36

A50

River Tean

Mount Pleasant

CEDAR DR 1
CHURCH FARM 2

Beamhurst Bridge

Beamhurst Lane

Mill Farm

Springfields

ST MICHAEL'S RD

POPPIT'S LA

VICARAGE DR

Waterloo Farm

2

Deggs Leasow

Park View

Broadoak Farm

35

Lightwoodfields

PIGEONHAY LA

Parks' Farm

The Parks

TORRANCE GR

A50

FRADGLEY GR

NICLIFFE WAY

ELKES GR

A522

BANFORD GR

ELMWOOD GR

PENNYCROFT RD

1

Dagdale Farm

Banktop

KIMBERLEY DR

DALLEY CR

BURTON MEWS 1
DERBY MEWS 2
NOTTINGHAM CT 3
LINCOLN CT 4
SHEFFIELD CT 5
LEICESTER CT 6
MANCHESTER CT 7

SCHOOL RD

Dagdale

GRENVILLE CL

Moss Beds

LAMBERT RD

Sch

Yew Tree Farm

WEST WY

SHIPTON DR

HALLAM RD

LIGHT FOOT RD

34

05   A   06   B   07   C

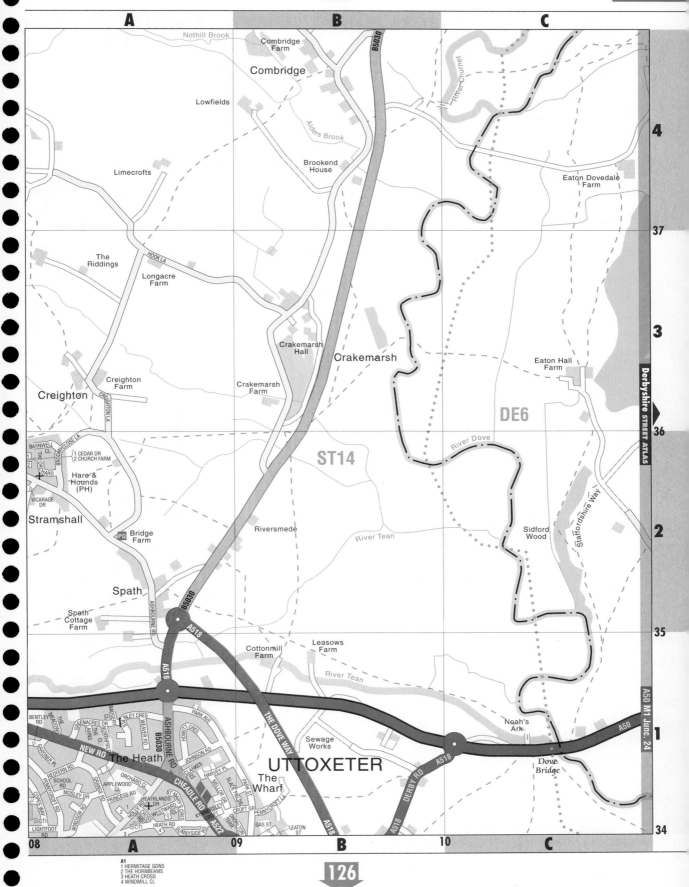

A1
1 HERMITAGE GDNS
2 THE HORNBEAMS
3 HEATH CROSS
4 WINDMILL CL

97

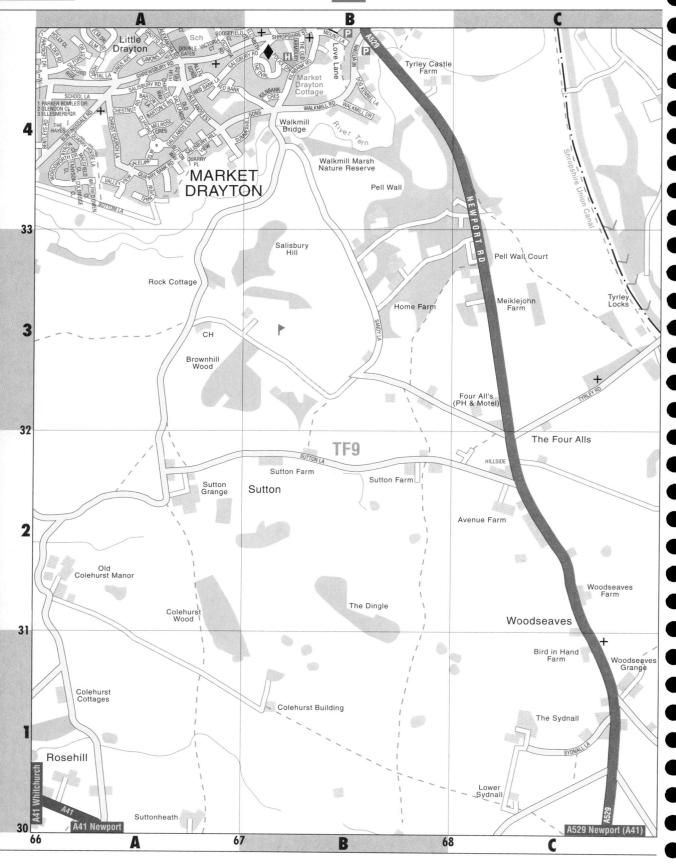

Little Drayton

MARKET DRAYTON

Tyrley Castle Farm

Shropshire Union Canal

Walkmill Bridge

Walkmill Marsh Nature Reserve

Pell Wall

Newport Rd

Tyrley Locks

Salisbury Hill

Pell Wall Court

Rock Cottage

Home Farm

Meiklejohn Farm

CH

Brownhill Wood

Four All's (PH & Motel)

Tyrley Rd

TF9

The Four Alls

Hillside

Sutton Farm

Sutton Farm

Sutton Grange

Sutton

Avenue Farm

Old Colehurst Manor

Woodseaves Farm

Colehurst Wood

The Dingle

Woodseaves

Bird in Hand Farm

Woodseaves Grange

Colehurst Cottages

Colehurst Building

The Sydnall

Rosehill

Sydnall La

A41 Whitchurch

A41

A41 Newport

Suttonheath

Lower Sydnall

A529

A529 Newport (A41)

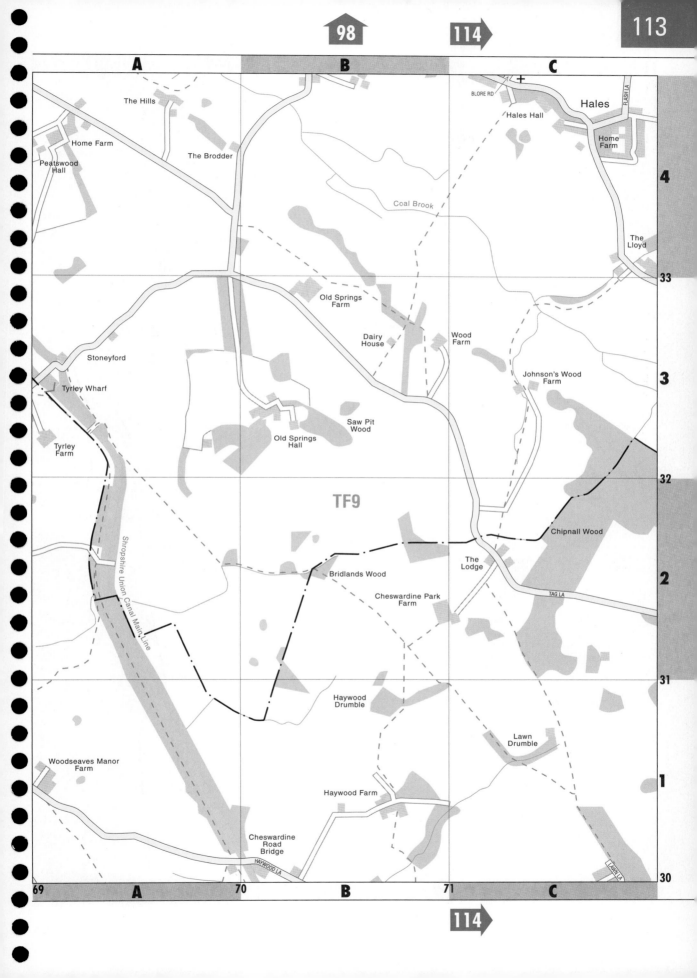

113

99

A

B

C

ST21

Park Springs

Burnt Wood

Burntwood
Farm

4

Lloyd
Drumble

Keeper's
Lodge

Smith's Rough

Bishop's Wood

Park
Springs
Farm

Knowleswood

The
Lloyd
Farm

33

The
Nook
Farm

Glass
Houses

Goldenhill
Farm

Dales
Wood

The
Lees

Coal Brook

3

Chipnall Lees

Heatherdale
Farm

Chipnall
Mill
Farm

32

TF9

Lipley
Heath
Farm

Chipnallhall
Farm

Chipnall Farm

Rushymoss
Wood

Lipley
Farm

2

Bishop's Wood

TAG LA

Chipnall

MOSS LA

Lipley

Moss
Lane
Farm

31

Cheswardine Hall

Sycamore
Cottage

1

Lipley Hall
Farm

Lipley
Cottages

Greaves
Plantation

Lipley
Villa

Marsh
House

30

72

A

73

B

74

C

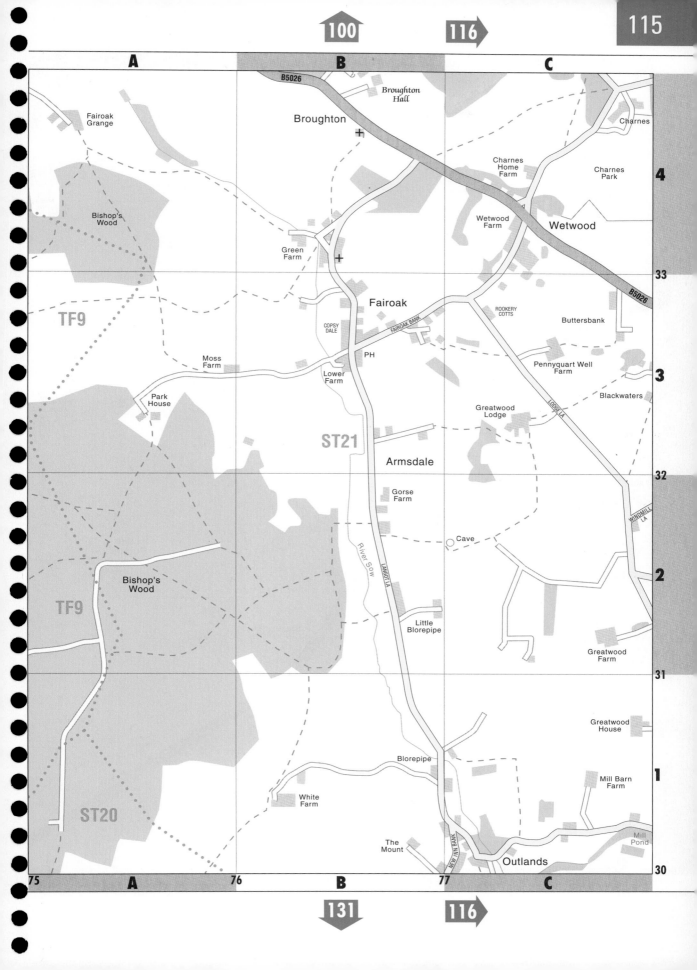

115
101

A **B** **C**

Charnes Old Hall

Brooklyn Farm

Whittington

Chatcull Wood

Whittington Farm

Brockton Brook

Foxley

4

Fir Grove

Midley Pits

33

SHUT LA

Newhouse Farm

B5026

Villa Farm

PH

CHURCH LA

Croxtonbank

Highlanes

Corner Farm

HIGHLANES

Highlanes Farm

3

THE HIGHFIELDS

Twr

PO

Arnhill Cottage

Croxton

32

WINDMILL LA

Windmill

Cutleyhorn La

THE COUNCIL HOS

The Cedars

ST21

Holts Farm

Little Sugnall

Woodwall Green

Villa Farm

Top Farm

Little Sugnall Farm

2

GINGER LA

Russia Tree Farm

Sugnall Hall

Marsh Farm

31

Redgreet

Sugnall

SUGNALL BSNS CTR

Redgreet Farm

Home Farm

The Cottage

Woodlands Farm

1

Big Wood

Sugnall Park

Broughton Pool

B5026

Offleybrook

Jackson's Coppice

30

78   **A**   79   **B**   80   **C**

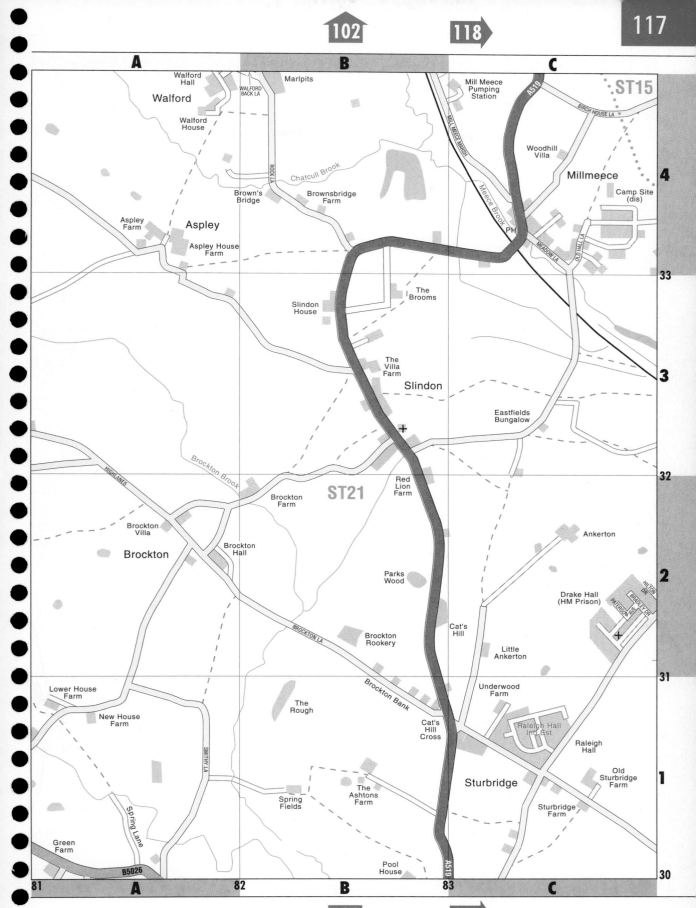

ST15

A B C

Walford Hall
Walford
Marlpits
Mill Meece Pumping Station
A519
BIRCH HOUSE LA
Walford House
WALFORD BACK LA
Woodhill Villa
Millmeece

4

Brown's Bridge
Brownsbridge Farm
Chatcull Brook
ROCK LA
Aspley Farm
Aspley
Aspley House Farm

MEECE BROOK
MILL MEECE MARSH
PH
MEADOW LA
OLD HALL LA
Camp Site (dis)

33

Slindon House
The Brooms

The Villa Farm
Slindon

3

Eastfields Bungalow

Brockton Brook
HIGHLANES
Brockton Farm
Red Lion Farm
ST21
+

32

Brockton Villa
Brockton
Brockton Hall
Ankerton

Parks Wood
Drake Hall (HM Prison)
HILTON DR
BRADLEY DR
PATERSON AVE

2

BROCKTON LA
Brockton Rookery
Cat's Hill
Little Ankerton

Lower House Farm
Brockton Bank
Underwood Farm
Raleigh Hall Ind. Est.

31

New House Farm
The Rough
Cat's Hill Cross
Raleigh Hall

SMITHY LA
Spring Fields
The Ashtons Farm
Sturbridge
Old Sturbridge Farm

1

Spring Lane
Sturbridge Farm

Green Farm
B5026
Pool House
A519

30

81 A 82 B 83 C

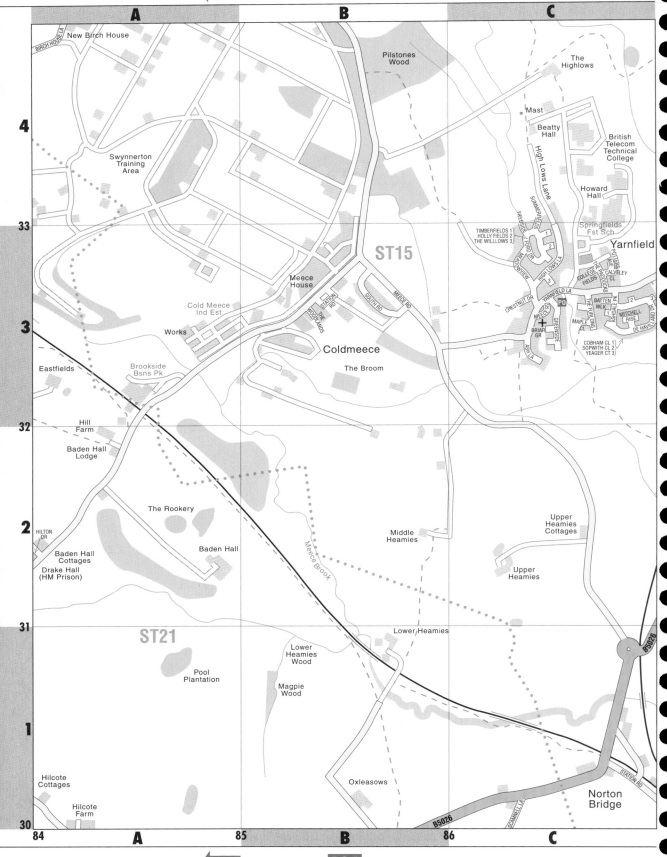

Birch House La

New Birch House

Swynnerton Training Area

Pilstones Wood

The Highlows

Mast

Beatty Hall

British Telecom Technical College

High Lows Lane

Howard Hall

Springfields Fst Sch

TIMBERFIELDS 1
HOLLY FIELDS 2
THE WILLLOWS 3

Yarnfield

ST15

Meece House

Cold Meece Ind Est

Works

Coldmeece

The Broom

Eastfields

Brookside Bsns Pk

Hill Farm

Baden Hall Lodge

The Rookery

Baden Hall

Middle Heamies

Upper Heamies Cottages

Upper Heamies

Hilton Dr

Baden Hall Cottages

Drake Hall (HM Prison)

Pool Plantation

Meece Brook

ST21

Lower Heamies Wood

Magpie Wood

Lower Heamies

Oxleasows

Norton Bridge

Hilcote Cottages

Hilcote Farm

Station Rd

B5026

B5026

Scammell La

COBHAM CL 1
SOPWITH CL 2
YEAGER CT 3

Yarnfield La

Chestnut Dr

Meece Rd

South Rd

Meece Rd

Station Rd

The Woodlands

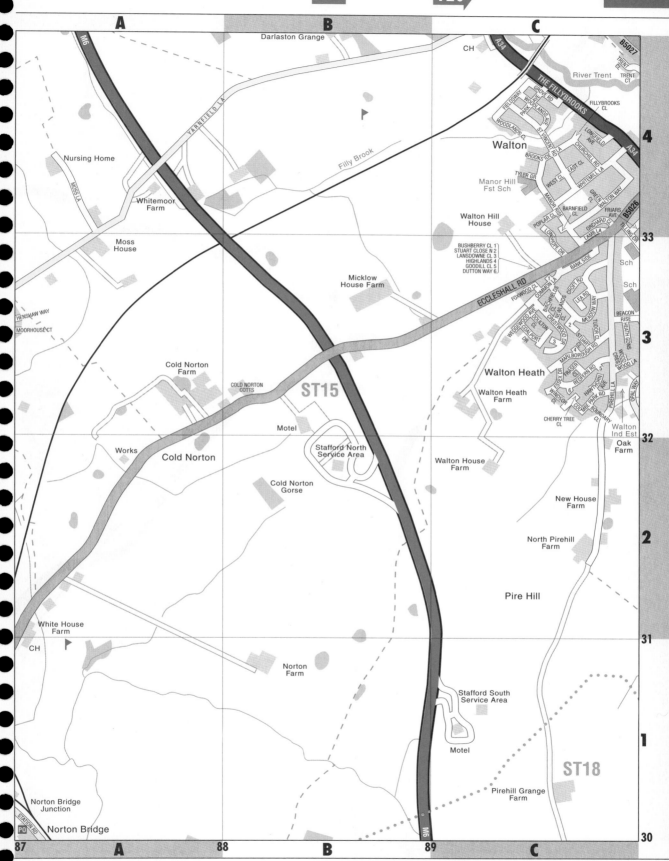

A B C

Darlaston Grange

CH

A34

B5027

River Trent

TRENT CL

TRENT CT

THE FILLYBROOKS

FILLYBROOKS CL

M6

YARNFIELD LA

Filly Brook

Nursing Home

FIELDSWAY

GROVE RD

WOODLANDS AVE

PARK AVE

WOODLANDS CL

ST VINCENT RD

LONGFIELD AVE

A34

4

Whitemoor Farm

MOSS LA

Walton

BROOKSIDE RD

WEST CL

EAST CL

CHURCHILL RD

WHITEMILL LA

TYLER GR

Manor Hill Fst Sch

GREEN CL

WALTON WAY

B5026

33

Moss House

Walton Hill House

POPLAR CL

MANOR RISE

BARNFIELD CL

ORCHARD CL

FRIARS AVE

LONGHOPE DR

LAMB LA

TIMMOR DR

HENSHAW WAY

MOORHOUSE CT

Micklow House Farm

BUSHBERRY CL 1
STUART CLOSE N 2
LANSDOWNE CL 3
HIGHLANDS 4
GOODILL CL 5
DUTTON WAY 6.

BANK SIDE

ECCLESHALL RD

Sch

Sch

3

FOXWOOD CL

WEDGEWOOD AVE

COALPORT DR

COMMON LA

BIRCHMEAD DS

NEWLANDS

CROFT RD

CHESTWOOD

LEA RD

MEADOW LA

STUART

TUDOR CL

BEACON RISE

HEATH GDNS

WOOD LA

WOOD CRES

Cold Norton Farm

COLD NORTON COTTS

ST15

Walton Heath

FRASER CL

MARLBOROUGH RD

REPERTH RD

HAWTHORN AVE

PIREHILL LA

VESSEY OF WAY

Motel

Walton Heath Farm

WINDSOR GR

COMBE PARK RD

WALTON WAY

Works

Cold Norton

CHERRY TREE CL

WALTON BOUNDARY

Walton Ind Est

32

Stafford North Service Area

Cold Norton Gorse

Walton House Farm

Oak Farm

New House Farm

North Pirehill Farm

2

Pire Hill

31

White House Farm

CH

Norton Farm

Stafford South Service Area

Motel

1

ST18

Pirehill Grange Farm

Norton Bridge Junction

STATION RD

PO

Norton Bridge

M6

30

87 A 88 B 89 C

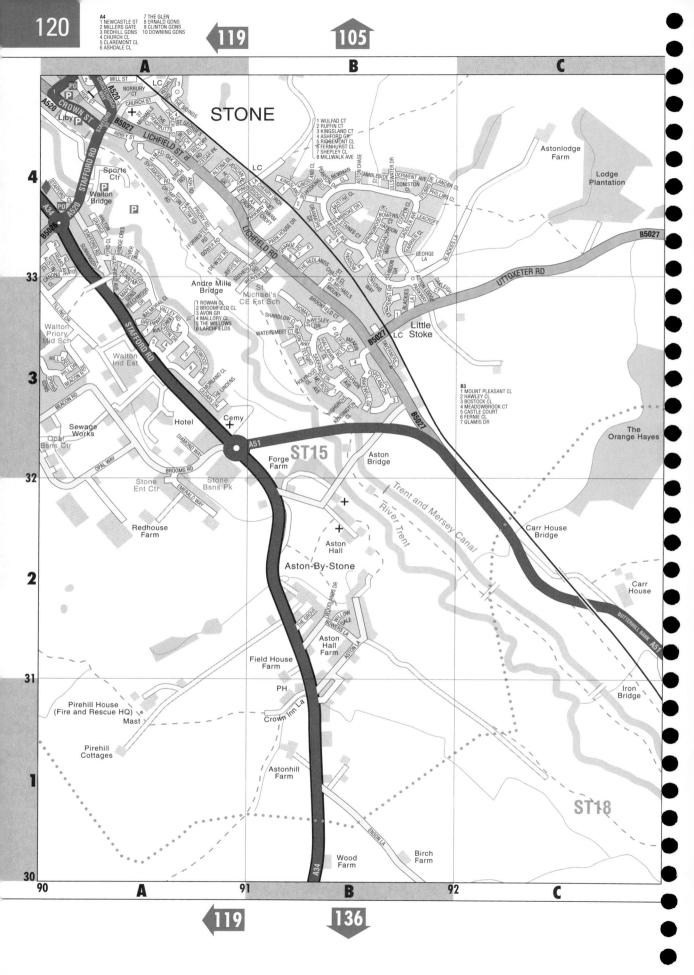

106
122

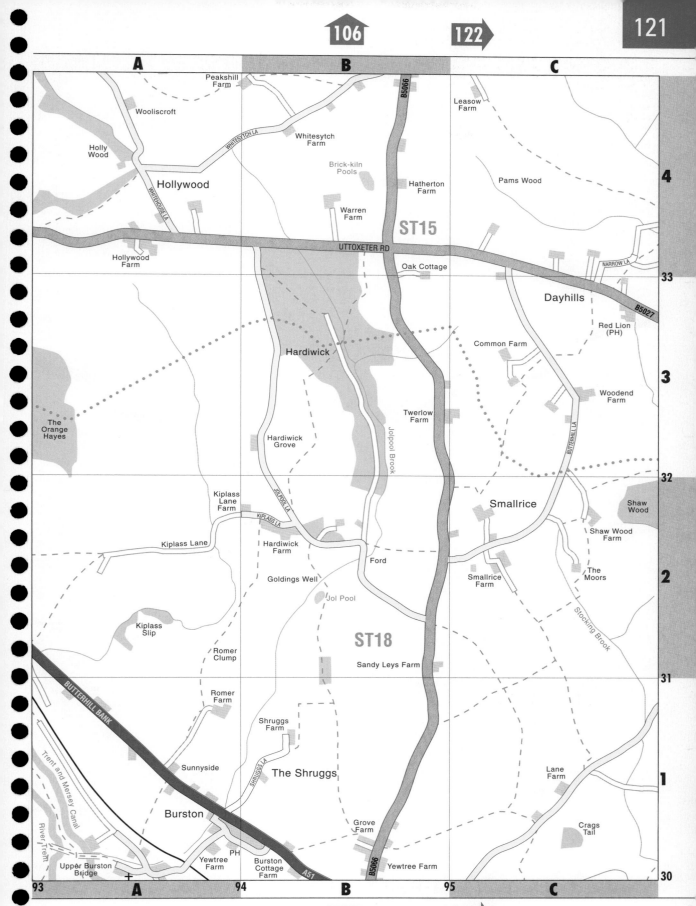

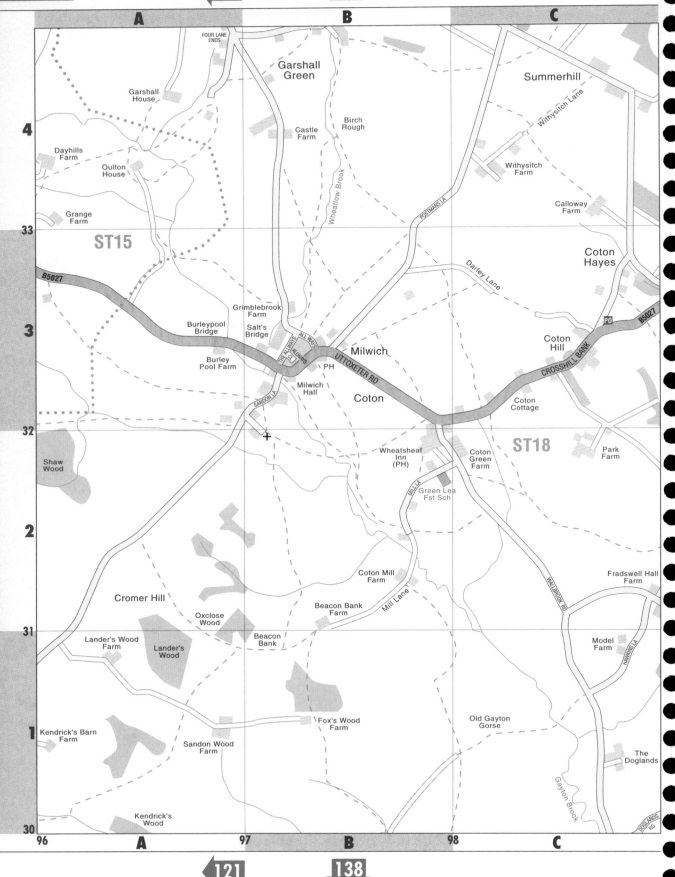

A   B   C

4

Garshall
Green

Summerhill

Garshall
House

Castle
Farm

Birch
Rough

Withysitch Lane

Withysitch
Farm

Dayhills
Farm

Oulton
House

Calloway
Farm

Wheatlow Brook

POSTMANS LA

Grange
Farm

33

ST15

Coton
Hayes

B5027

Darley Lane

Grimblebrook
Farm

Coton
Hill

PO

B5027

Burleypool
Bridge

Salt's
Bridge

3

Milwich

CROSSHILL BANK

Burley
Pool Farm

THE ALLWAYS PH
ALL WAYS

UTTOXETER RD

PH

Coton

Coton
Cottage

SANDON LA

Milwich
Hall

ST18

32

Wheatsheaf
Inn
(PH)

Coton
Green
Farm

Park
Farm

Shaw
Wood

MILL LA

Green Lea
Fst Sch

2

Coton Mill
Farm

Fradswell Hall
Farm

Cromer Hill

Oxclose
Wood

Beacon Bank
Farm

Mill Lane

WALLBROOK RD

31

Lander's Wood
Farm

Beacon
Bank

Model
Farm

HAWKINS LA

Lander's
Wood

1

Kendrick's Barn
Farm

Fox's Wood
Farm

Old Gayton
Gorse

The
Doglands

Sandon Wood
Farm

Gayton Brook

DOGLANDS RD

30

96   A   97   B   98   C

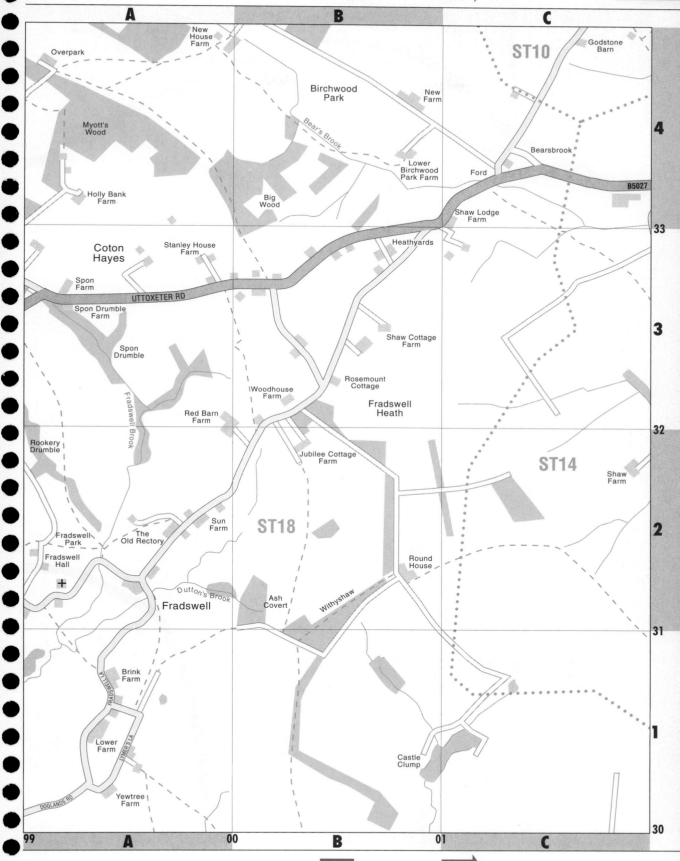

123
109

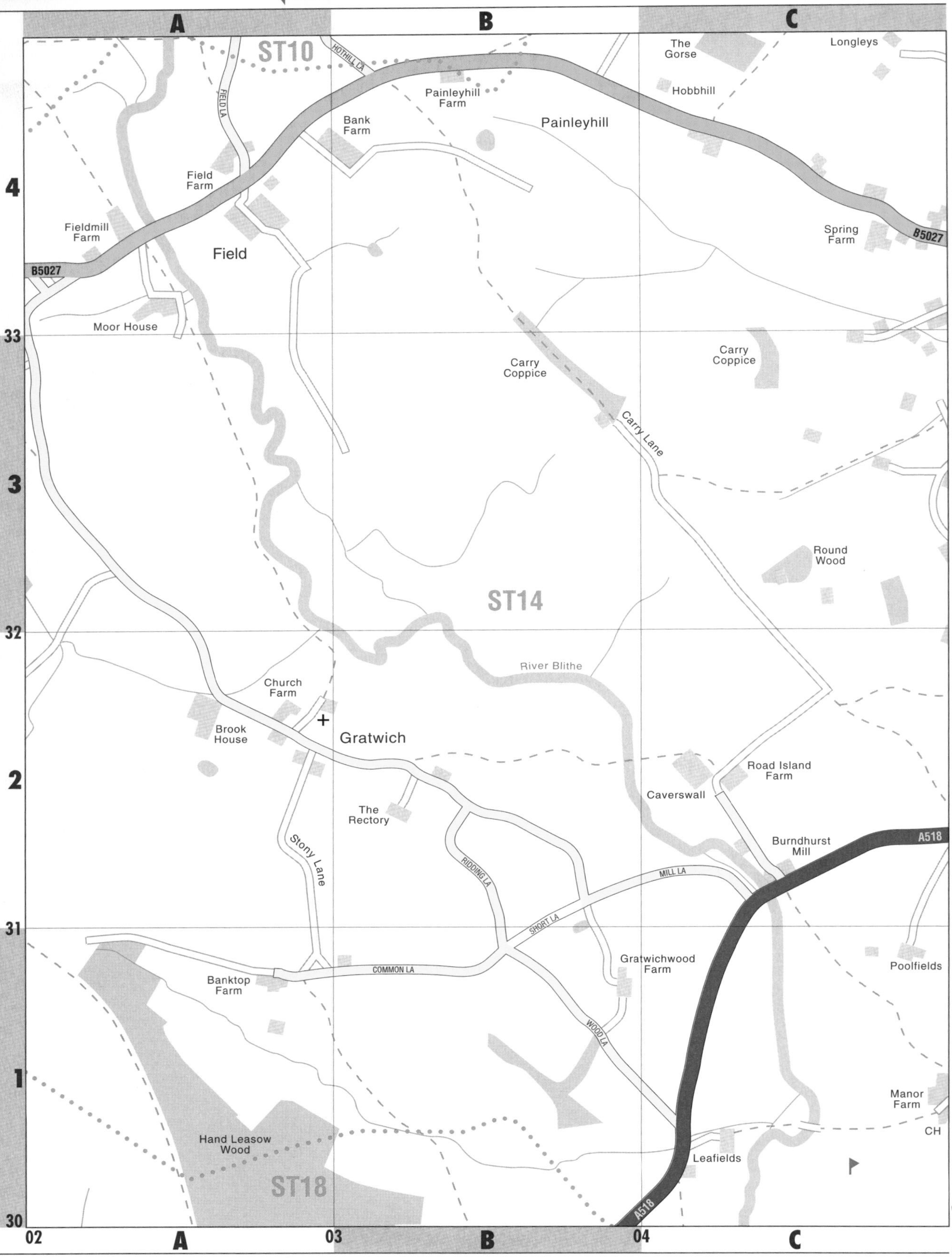

A   **B**   **C**

ST10

HOTHILL LA

FIELD LA

Painleyhill Farm

Bank Farm

Painleyhill

The Gorse

Longleys

Hobbhill

4

Field Farm

Field

Fieldmill Farm

Spring Farm

B5027

B5027

Moor House

33

Carry Coppice

Carry Coppice

Carry Lane

3

Round Wood

ST14

32

River Blithe

Church Farm

Brook House

+ Gratwich

Road Island Farm

Caverswall

2

The Rectory

Burndhurst Mill

A518

Stony Lane

RIDDING LA

SHORT LA

MILL LA

31

Banktop Farm

COMMON LA

Gratwichwood Farm

Poolfields

WOOD LA

1

Manor Farm

CH

Hand Leasow Wood

Leafields

ST18

A518

30

02   **A**   03   **B**   04   **C**

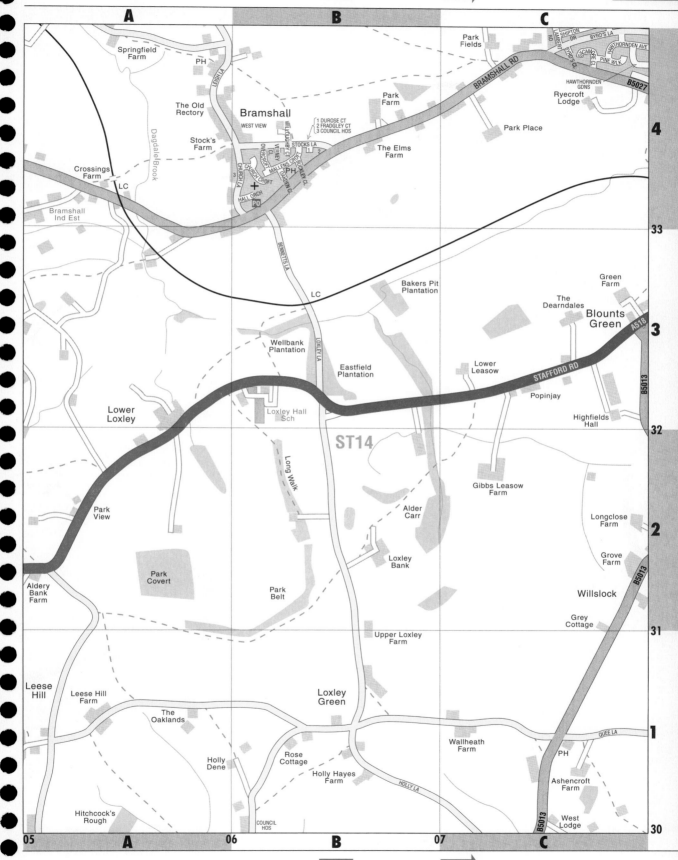

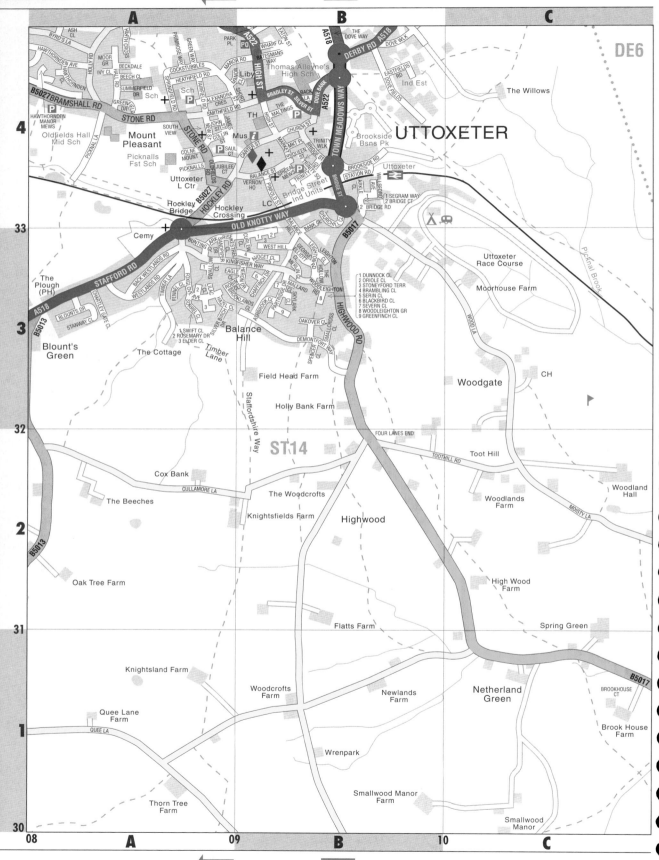

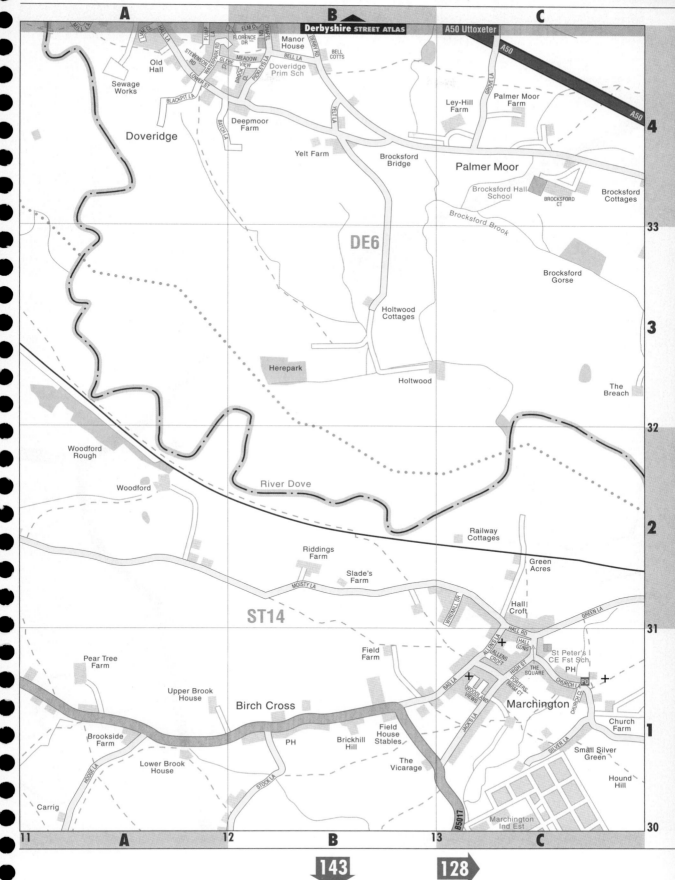

128
143
128

Derbyshire STREET ATLAS

A50 Uttoxeter

MEZL LA
LYKE CL
HALL LA
PUMP
ELM CL
FLORENCE DR
CHAPEL
Manor House
DERBY RD
BELL COTTS
GROVE LA
Old Hall
STEVENSON RD
WATERPARK RD
GLEBE CL
BROCK CL
MEADOW VIEW
PICKLEY'S LA
BELL LA
Doveridge Prim Sch
Ley-Hill Farm
Palmer Moor Farm
A50
Sewage Works
LOWER ST
Deepmoor Farm
Doveridge
BLACKPIT LA
BATCH LA
YELT LA
Brocksford Hall School
BROCKSFORD CT
Brocksford Cottages
Yelt Farm
Brocksford Bridge
Palmer Moor

DE6

Brocksford Brook

33

Brocksford Gorse

Holtwood Cottages

3

Herepark

Holtwood

The Breach

32

Woodford Rough

River Dove

Woodford

2

Railway Cottages

Green Acres

Riddings Farm

Slade's Farm

MOISTY LA

Hall Croft

GREEN LA

ST14

WINDMILL DR

HALL RD

St Peter's CE Fst Sch

31

Field Farm

ALLENS LA
ALLENS CROFT
HIGH ST
HALL GDNS
THE SQUARE
PH
CHURCH LA
PO

Pear Tree Farm

BAGS LA

PORTERS FARM CT

Upper Brook House

Birch Cross

WOODLAND VIEWS

Marchington

CHURCH CL

Brookside Farm

PH

Brickhill Hill

Field House Stables

JACKS LA

Church Farm

1

HODGE LA

Lower Brook House

STOCK LA

SILVER LA

Small Silver Green

The Vicarage

Hound Hill

Carrig

B5017

Marchington Ind Est

30

11
A
12
B
13
C

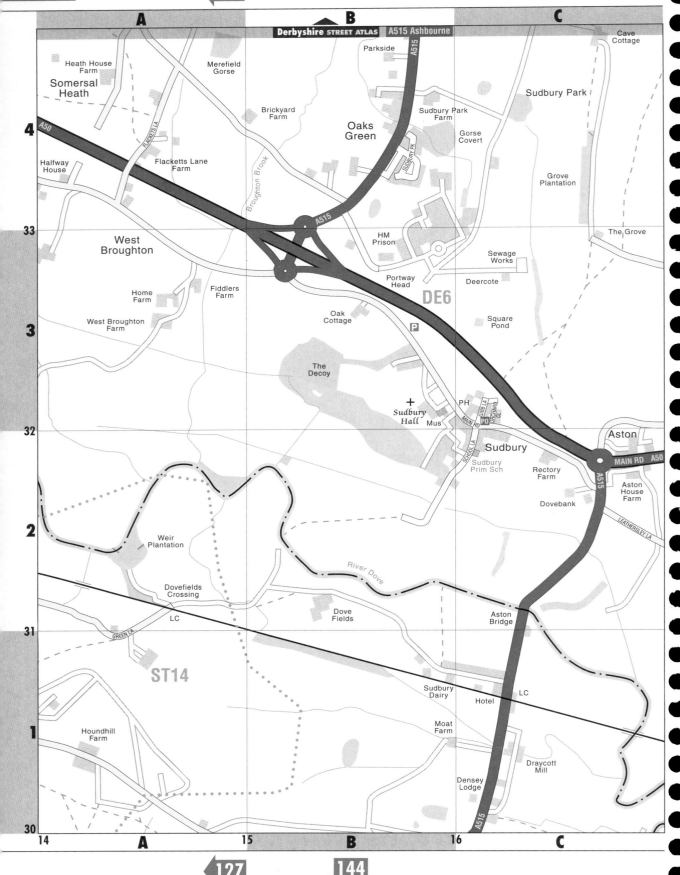

Derbyshire STREET ATLAS   A515 Ashbourne

Cave
Cottage

Heath House
Farm

Merefield
Gorse

Somersal
Heath

Parkside

A515

Sudbury Park

Brickyard
Farm

Oaks
Green

Sudbury Park
Farm

Gorse
Covert

A50

Flacketts Lane
Farm

Grove
Plantation

Halfway
House

FLACKETTS LA

A515

HM
Prison

The Grove

West
Broughton

Sewage
Works

Portway
Head

Deercote

DE6

Home
Farm

Fiddlers
Farm

Oak
Cottage

Square
Pond

West Broughton
Farm

P

The
Decoy

Sudbury
Hall

Mus

PH

GIBB LA

ORCHARD CL

Aston

Sudbury

MAIN RD   A50

MAIN RD

A515

SCHOOL LA

Sudbury
Prim Sch

Rectory
Farm

Aston House
Farm

Weir
Plantation

River Dove

Dovebank

LEATHERSLEY LA

Dovefields
Crossing

LC

Dove
Fields

Aston
Bridge

GREEN LA

ST14

Sudbury
Dairy

LC

Houndhill
Farm

Hotel

Moat
Farm

Draycott
Mill

Densey
Lodge

A515

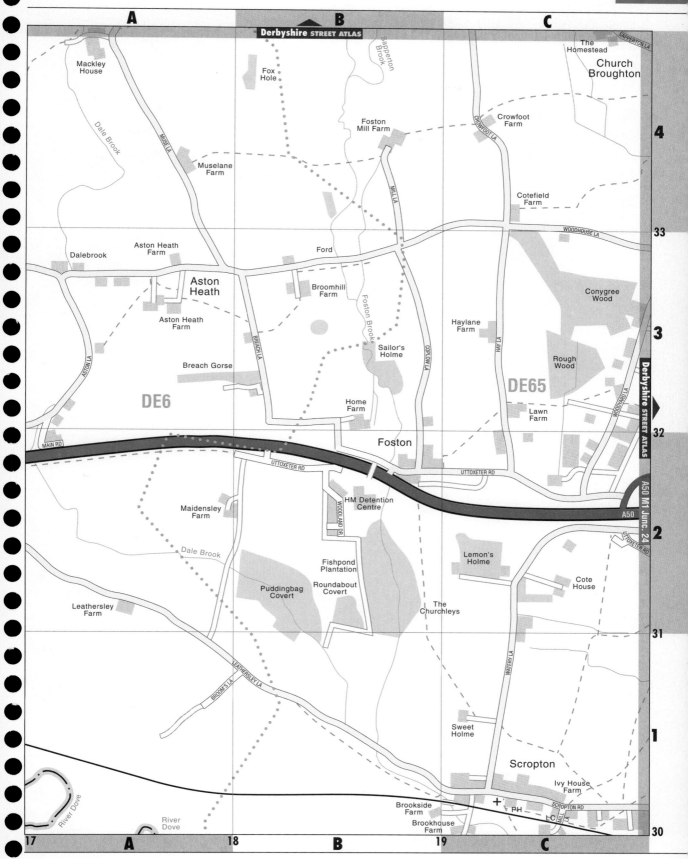

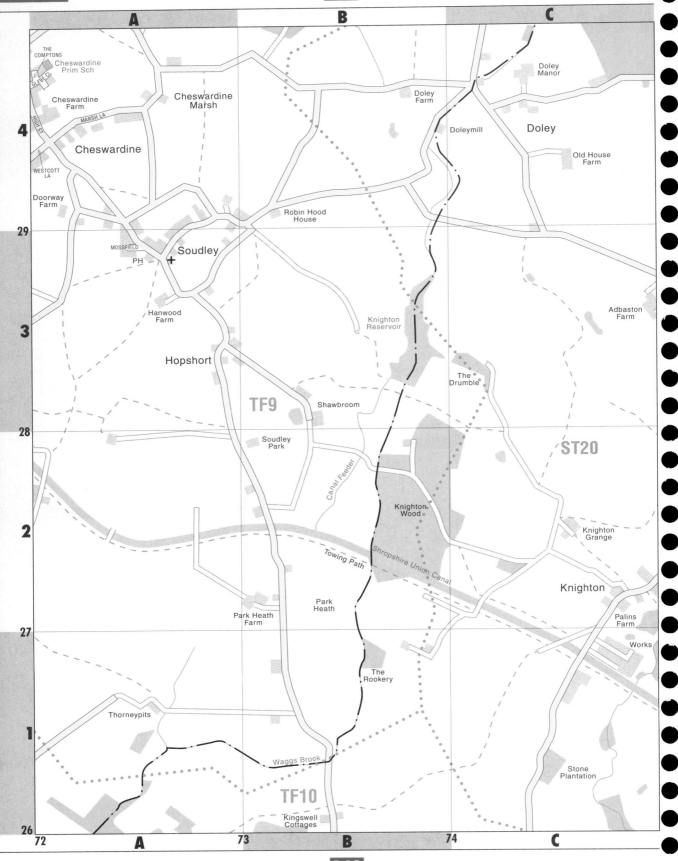

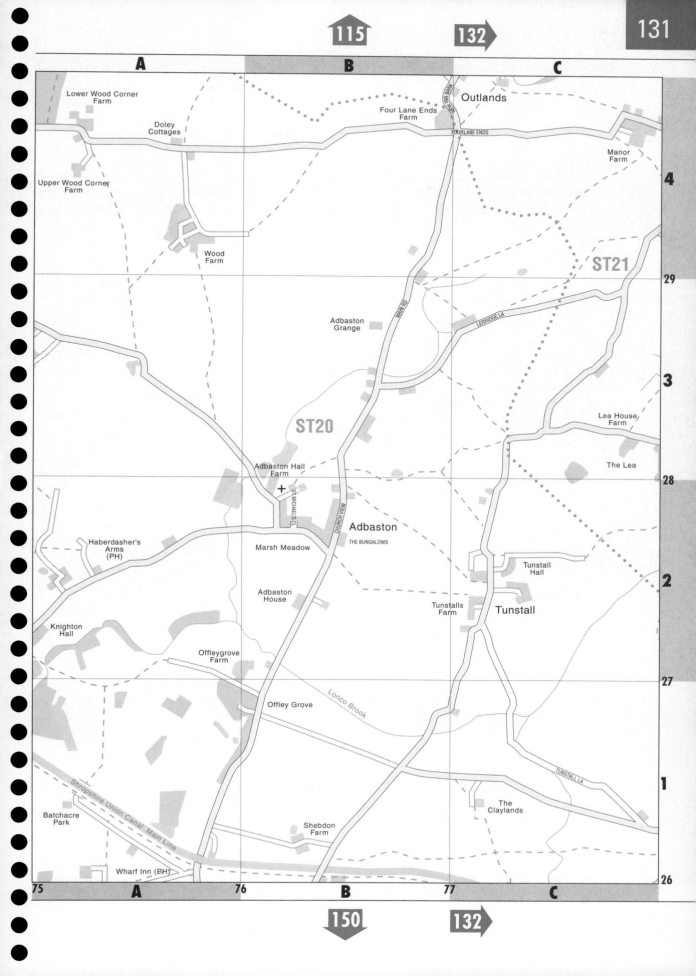

115
132

A   B   C

Lower Wood Corner
Farm

Doley
Cottages

Four Lane Ends
Farm

Outlands

FOURLANE ENDS

Manor
Farm

Upper Wood Corner
Farm

4

ST21

29

Wood
Farm

MAIN RD

Adbaston
Grange

LERRIDGE LA

3

ST20

Lea House
Farm

The Lea

28

Adbaston Hall
Farm

ST MICHAELS CL

CHURCH VIEW

Adbaston

THE BUNGALOWS

Haberdasher's
Arms
(PH)

Marsh Meadow

Tunstall
Hall

2

Adbaston
House

Tunstalls
Farm

Tunstall

Knighton
Hall

Offleygrove
Farm

27

Offley Grove

Lonco Brook

TUNSTALL LA

1

Shropshire Union Canal Main Line

Batchacre
Park

Shebdon
Farm

The
Claylands

Wharf Inn (PH)

26

75   A   76   B   77   C

150
132

A **B** **C**

4

Brown Jug (PH)

Offleybrook

Walk Mill

Walk Mill

Cop Mere

Pershall Pool

Bishop's Offley

Offleyrock

Offleyhay

PO

Star Inn (PH)

Villa Farm

White House Farm

MERE RISE

SANDY LA

Copmere End

Marsh House

29

Offleymarsh

Brann Farm

Rufford

The Drumble

Peafield Covert

3

Lea Knowl

Windsend

The Manor

Little Horsley

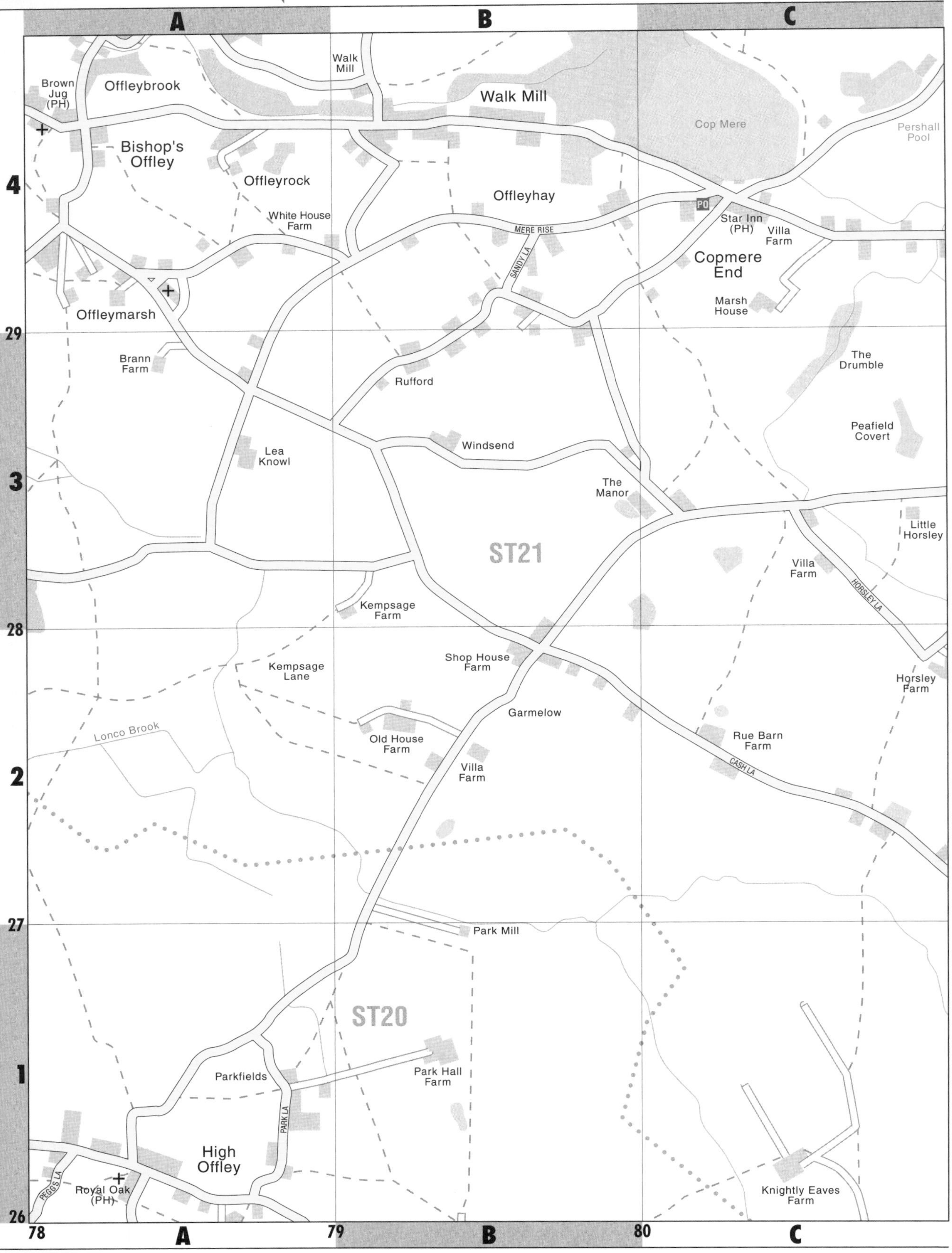

ST21

Villa Farm

HORSLEY LA

28

Kempsage Farm

Shop House Farm

Horsley Farm

Kempsage Lane

Garmelow

Rue Barn Farm

Lonco Brook

Old House Farm

CASH LA

2

Villa Farm

27

Park Mill

ST20

1

Parkfields

Park Hall Farm

PARK LA

High Offley

PEGGS LA

Royal Oak (PH)

Knightly Eaves Farm

26

78 **A** 79 **B** 80 **C**

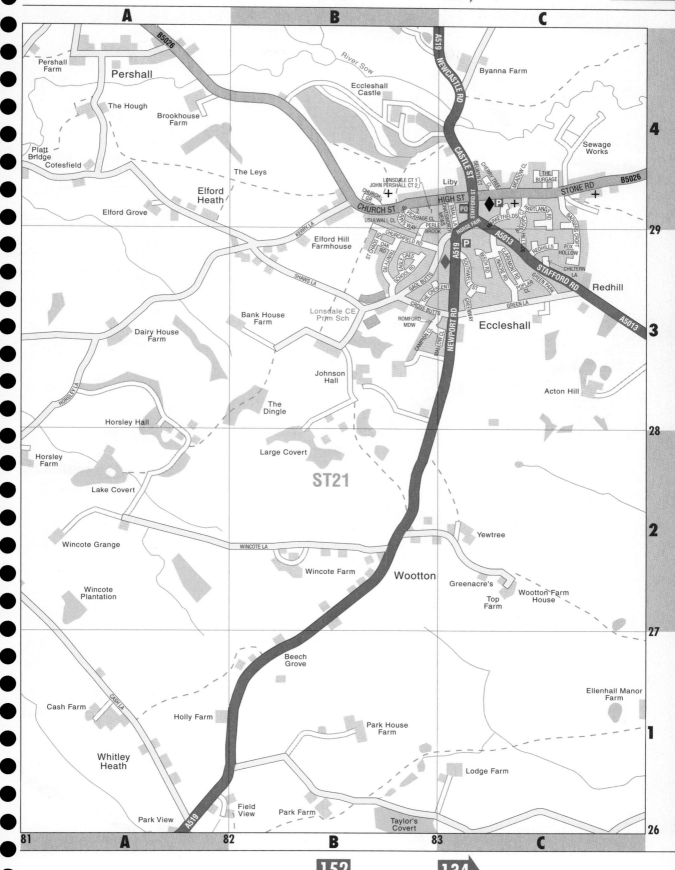

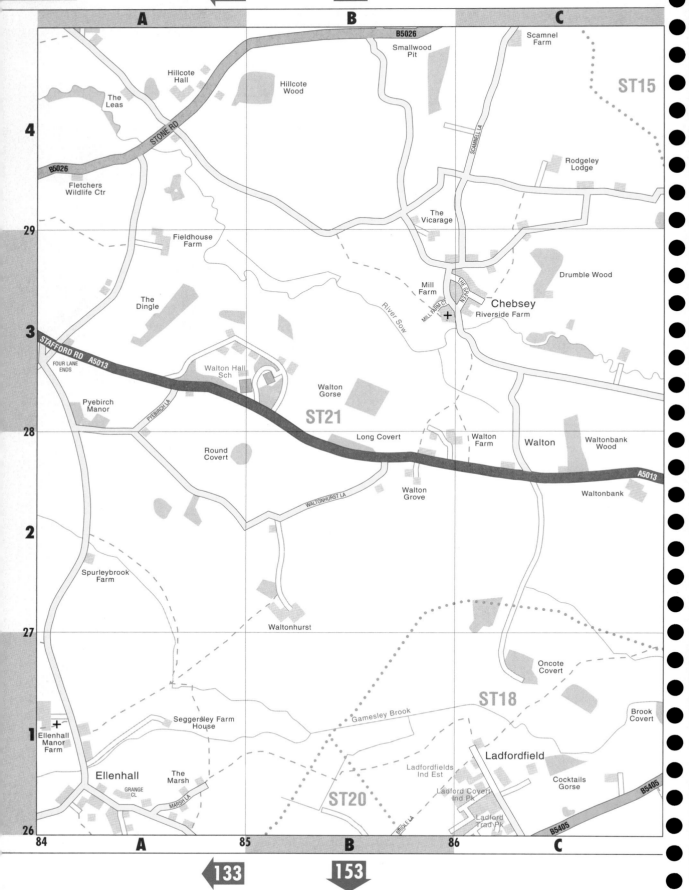

133
118

A   **B**   **C**

B5026

Smallwood Pit

Scamnel Farm

ST15

Hillcote Hall

Hillcote Wood

The Leas

STONE RD

Rodgeley Lodge

SCAMNEL LA

4

B5026

Fletchers Wildlife Ctr

Fieldhouse Farm

The Vicarage

29

Drumble Wood

The Dingle

Mill Farm

River Sow

THE GREEN

Chebsey

Riverside Farm

3

STAFFORD RD   A5013

FOUR LANE ENDS

Walton Hall Sch

Walton Gorse

ST21

Pyebirch Manor

PYEBIRCH LA

28

Long Covert

Walton Farm

Walton

Waltonbank Wood

Round Covert

A5013

WALTONHURST LA

Walton Grove

Waltonbank

2

Spurleybrook Farm

27

Waltonhurst

Oncote Covert

ST18

Brook Covert

Gamesley Brook

Seggersley Farm House

1

Ellenhall Manor Farm

Ladfordfield

Ladfordfields Ind Est

Cocktails Gorse

B5405

Ellenhall

The Marsh

GRANGE CL

MARSH LA

ST20

Ladford Covert Ind Pk

BRIDLE LA

Ladford Trad Pk

B5405

26

84   **A**   85   **B**   86   **C**

133
153

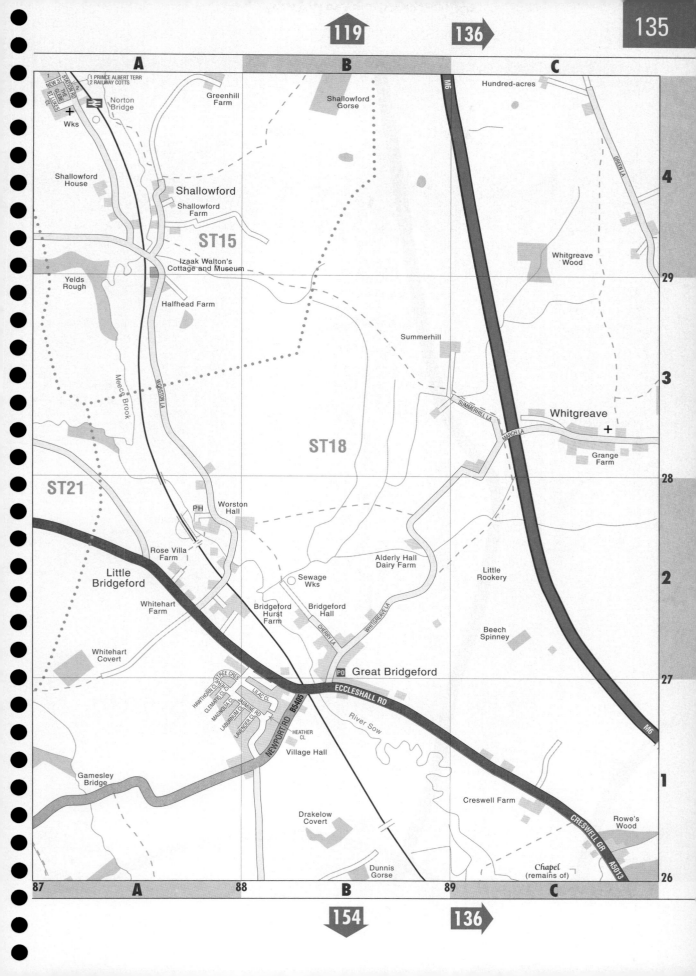

135
120

A **B** **C**

Peasley Bank

Newhouse Farm

Spring Farm

Far Enson Farm

ENSON LA

Elmhurst

4

New Plantation

Yarlet Bank Farm

Yarlet Hall

Yarlet Sch

Yarlet Hall Farm

Yarlet Hill

New Ensonmoor Farm

29

Meadow Farm

Grove Farm

Greenwood

Greyhound Inn (PH)

GREEN LA

3

Yarlet

Top Farm

Park Farm

YARLET LA

Black Plantation

Whitgreave

New Farm

Manor Farm

WHITGREAVE LA

Grange Farm

28

Upper Farm

ST18

Woodhill Farm

Marston

Church Farm

Whitgreave Manor

Marston Farm

Brook Farm

2

Newbuildings Cottage

27

STONE RD

Redhill Farm

MARSTON LA

Newbuildings Farm

Marstongate Farm

Marston Brook

M6

Little Gorse

ST16

RAF Stafford

1

New Plantation

CHAULDEN RD 1
BUCKLAND RD 2
ASHRIDGE WLK 3
MARSWORTH WAY 4

BEACONSIDE

A513

Creswell Grove

M6

A513

A34

A34

ALDERSHAW CL
AMBLEFIELD WAY
LAWNSFIELD WLK

ALDBURY CL
PARKSIDE AVE
FELDEN CL
PITTSTONE CL

Stafford Common

COMMON RD

A513

26
90 **A** **91** **B** **92** **C**

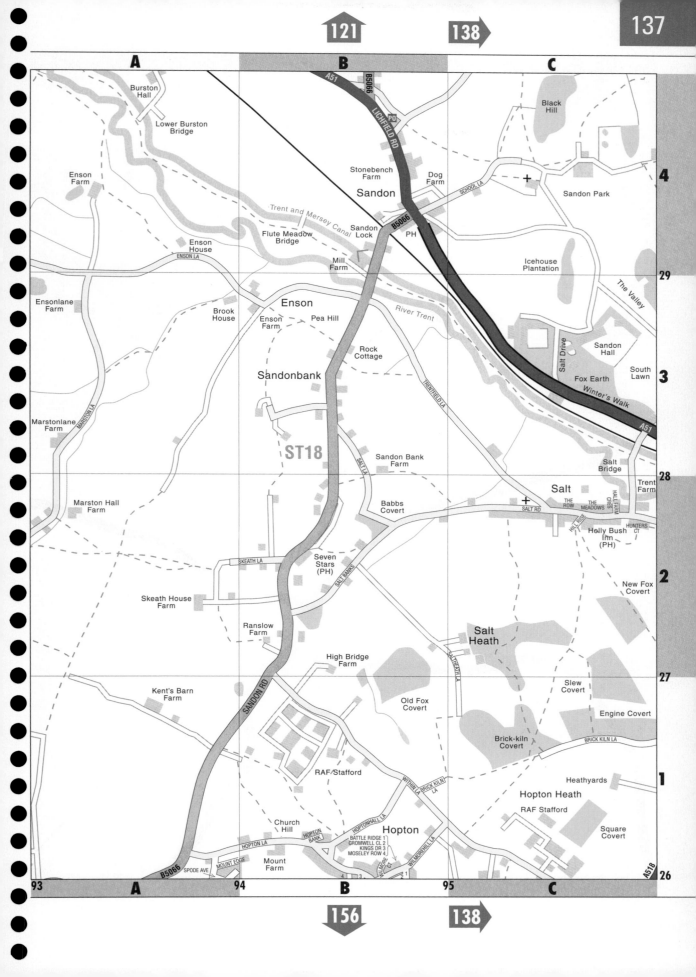

A B C

4

29

3

28

2

27

1

26

Burston Hall
Lower Burston Bridge
Enson Farm
Ensonlane Farm
ENSON LA
Enson House
Brook House
Flute Meadow Bridge
Trent and Mersey Canal
Enson
Enson Farm
Pea Hill
Rock Cottage
Sandonbank
ST18
MARSTON LA
Marstonlane Farm
Marston Hall Farm
SKEATH LA
Skeath House Farm
SALT LA
SALT BANKS
Sandon Bank Farm
Babbs Covert
Seven Stars (PH)
Ranslow Farm
Kent's Barn Farm
SANDON RD
High Bridge Farm
RAF/Stafford
Church Hill
HOPTON LA
HOPTON BANK
Mount Farm
Mount Edge
MOUNT EDGE
SPODE AVE
B5066

A51
B5066
LICHFIELD RD
PO
Stonebench Farm
Sandon
Dog Farm
SCHOOL LA
Black Hill
Sandon Park
Icehouse Plantation
Sandon Lock
B5066
PH
Mill Farm
River Trent
TRENTFIELD LA
Salt Drive
Sandon Hall
Fox Earth
South Lawn
Winter's Walk
The Valley
A51
Salt Bridge
Trent Farm
Salt
HALL FARM
THE ROW
THE MEADOWS
CRES
HUNTERS CT
HILL RISE
SALT RD
Holly Bush Inn (PH)
New Fox Covert
Salt Heath
SALT HEATH LA
Old Fox Covert
Slew Covert
Engine Covert
Brick-kiln Covert
BRICK KILN LA
Heathyards
Hopton Heath
RAF Stafford
Square Covert
WITHIN LA
BRICK KILN LA
WILMOREHILL LA
Hopton
BATTLE RIDGE 1
CROMWELL CL 2
KINGS DR 3
MOSELEY ROW 4
WILLOW CT
A518

93 94 95

A B C

137
122

A **B** **C**

4

Stonehouse Farm

Sandon Wood

WALLBROOK RD

DOGLANDS RD

Wetmoor Wood

Hartleygreen Farm

Hartley Green

Brick-kiln Pit

PARKSIDE LA

Parkside Farm

High Clump

Upper Park

Stocking Brook

Wetmoor Farm

29

Beech Banks

Vicarswood

Brook Farm

Gayton Brook

Gayton Mill Farm

Barker's Lane

Gayton

3

Chair Plantation

VICARAGE BANK

CHERRY LA

MOOR LA

Sandon Home Farm

Moat Farm

Church La

Gayton Hotel (PH)

Oak Leigh

Moor Leys Farm

Pitt's Column

Monument Plantation

A51

ST18

28

WADDEN LA

Wadden Farm

A518

2

Willowmore Banks

SAND LA

LC

Trent and Mersey Canal

Sandhill Bridge

BOAT LA

A518

Weston

Ox Hill

Leatop House

Weston Bank

Weston Bridge

Weston Hall

River Trent

PH Sewage Works

SPENCER CT

BRIDGE CT

MEADOWBANK

AVE

GREEN BARN CT

SALT WORKS LA

PELLFIELD CT

OLD SCHOOL LA

THE BULL RING

OLD RD

GREEN RD

WELLANDS

MANOR CL

HELONG CL

FERRERS RD

PO

THE GREEN

St Andrew's CE Prim Sch

OUTWARDS

GN

OUTWOODS

LONDON RD

Outwoods Farm

Amerton Brook

STAFFORD RD

27

The Green

1

BRICK-KILN LA

A518

Brinepit Bridge

A51

SHIRLEYWICH

AMERTON LA

26

96 **A** 97 **B** 98 **C**

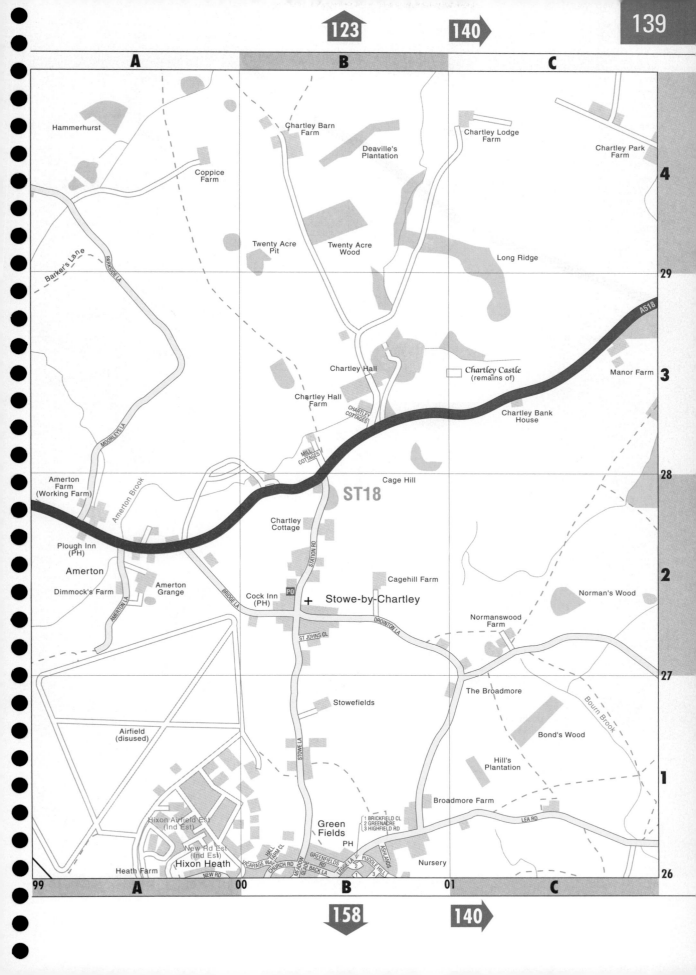

139
124

A   **B**   **C**

Newbuildings
Farm

Bowgage
Farm

A518

Chartley Park
Farm

Hand Leasow
Wood

4

Wanfield Hall
Coppice

ST14

Grindley

The General's
Farmhouse

Highfields
Farm

Wanfield
Hall

Keeper's
Pool

Wood
Farm

29

Grindley
Farm

Small
Farm

A518

Gillerd's
Rough

Blythebridge
Mill

COUNCIL
HOUSES

Keeper's Cottage
Farm

GRINDLEY BANK

BLYTHEBRIDGE BANK

Oakcroft
Farm

3

The Blythe

Stoney Brook

Blythe Inn
(PH)

Anglesea
Coppice

Chartley Moss

ST18

Drointon
Wood

Blythebridge
Hall

HILTHURST LA

28

Hardings
Wood

Moss Rise
Farm

Meadowhurst

River Blithe

2

Wood
Pit

Black
Hough

Lower
Booth

Plough
Farm

BOOTH LA

27

Upper
Booth

Yew Tree
Farm

Ivy House
Farm

Lower
Farm

Drointon

Upper
Farm

Brookside

1

Newton
Gorse

Callowhill

HEATH LA

Lea
Heath

WS15

Dapple
Heath

LEA RD

HILLCREST

Charity
Farm

Dapple Heath
Plantation

26

02   **A**   03   **B**   04   **C**

139
159

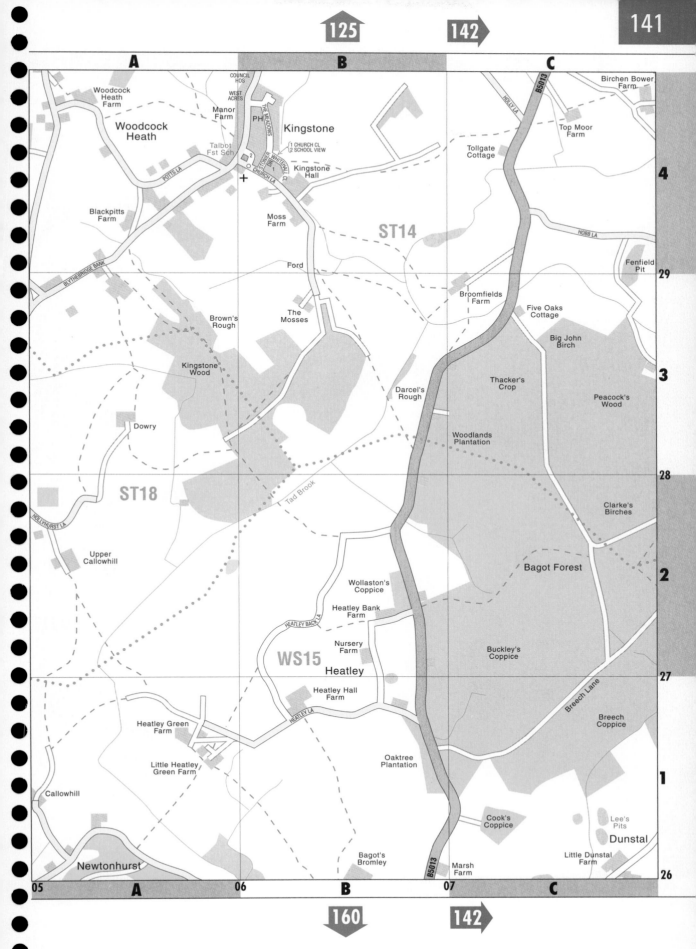

125
142
160
142

A B C

Woodcock Heath Farm
Woodcock Heath
Blackpitts Farm
POTTS LA
Manor Farm
WEST ACRES
COUNCIL HOS
PH
THE MEADOWS
Talbot Fst Sch
CHURCH LA
WHITEHALL CL
Kingstone
1 CHURCH CL
2 SCHOOL VIEW
Kingstone Hall
Moss Farm

HOLLY LA
B5013
Birchen Bower Farm
Top Moor Farm
Tollgate Cottage
ST14
HOBB LA
Fenfield Pit

4

BLYTHEBRIDGE BANK
Ford
Broomfields Farm
Five Oaks Cottage
Big John Birch

29

Brown's Rough
The Mosses
Kingstone Wood
Darcel's Rough
Thacker's Crop
Peacock's Wood

3

Dowry
Woodlands Plantation

ST18
HOLLYHURST LA
Tad Brook
28
Clarke's Birches

Upper Callowhill

Bagot Forest

2

Wollaston's Coppice
Heatley Bank Farm
HEATLEY BACK LA
Nursery Farm
WS15
Heatley
Buckley's Coppice
Breech Lane

27

Heatley Hall Farm
HEATLEY LA
Heatley Green Farm
Breech Coppice

Little Heatley Green Farm
Oaktree Plantation

1

Callowhill
Cook's Coppice
Lee's Pits
Dunstal
Little Dunstal Farm

Newtonhurst
Bagot's Bromley
B5013
Marsh Farm

26

05 A 06 B 07 C

A **B** **C**

Hanging Wicket Farm

Smallwood Manor

Spring Cottage

Holly Tree Farm

Hawkshill Farm

4

Scounslow Green

ST14

New Thorntree Farm

Twenty Acres

Roper's Hill Farm

Gorsty Hill Farm

HOBB LA

Gorsty Hill

Moat Spring Farm

29

Floyer's Coppice

Knypersley Hall

Marlpit House Farm

Glasshouse Farm

THORNEY LANES

3

High Trees Farm

Hill's Wood

Buttermilk Hill

Staffordshire Way

Felthouses Wood

Parkstile

Bagot Forest

Dixon's Hill

28

Birch Coppice

2

Bagot's Park

Park Lodge

Dun's Field

DE13

New Pool

Black Field

Story Brook

27

Squitch Bungalow

Storybrook Plantation

Bates' Pool

Blake's Plantation

Gadsby's Plantation

WS15

Parkside

Hart's Coppice

1

Squitch House

Ash Brook

Cockshutt Close

Hart's Farm

Park Farm

Dunstal Pool

Long Lands

Moors Farm

26

A **B** **C**

08 09 10

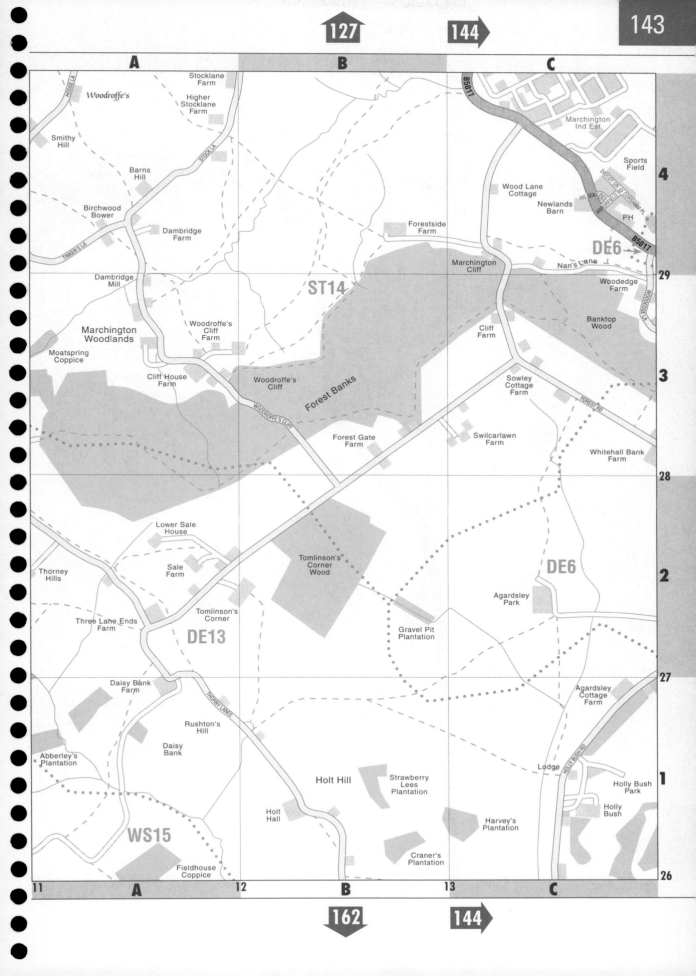

Woodroffe's
Stocklane Farm
Higher Stocklane Farm
Smithy Hill
Barns Hill
Birchwood Bower
Dambridge Farm
HODGE LA
STOCK LA
TINKER'S LA

4

Marchington Ind Est
B5017
Wood Lane Cottage
Sports Field
Newlands Barn
PH
HIL SEA CRES
DIDCOT DR
CORSHAM PL
ABBORFIELD
DE6
B5017

Dambridge Mill
Forestside Farm
Marchington Cliff
Nan's Lane
Woodedge Farm

ST14

29

Marchington Woodlands
Moatspring Coppice
Woodroffe's Cliff Farm
Cliff House Farm
Woodroffe's Cliff
Forest Banks
WOODROFFE'S CLIFF
Cliff Farm
Sowley Cottage Farm
Banktop Wood
FOREST RD
WOODEDGE LA

3

Forest Gate Farm
Swilcarlawn Farm
Whitehall Bank Farm

28

Lower Sale House
Sale Farm
Thorney Hills
Three Lane Ends Farm
Tomlinson's Corner Wood
Tomlinson's Corner
DE13
Gravel Pit Plantation
Agardsley Park
DE6

2

Daisy Bank Farm
Rushton's Hill
Daisy Bank
Abberley's Plantation
THORNEY LANES
Holt Hill
Strawberry Lees Plantation
Agardsley Cottage Farm
Lodge
Holly Bush Park
HOLLY BUSH RD

27

Holt Hall
Harvey's Plantation
Holly Bush

1

WS15
Fieldhouse Coppice
Craner's Plantation

26

11
12
13
A
B
C

A   **B**   **C**

ST14

Moreton

The Firs

Saltbrook Cottage

Moreton Farm

MORETON LA

Hall Flats

Salt Brook Meadow Farm

Ford

Coton in the Clay

Hitchett Hill

ASHE'S LA

PH

STATION RD

A515

SALTBROOK LA

Grange Byre

Coton Hall

4

Coton Hall Farm

B5017

DEEP CUT RD

WOODLANDS RISE

Draycott House

STUBBY LA

TUB'S HILL

MAIN RD

PH

Riddings Lane

29

Woodedge

WOODEDGE LA

Park Farm

Draycott in the Clay

SWAN RD

GYPSUM WAY

HOLLOW

RIDDINGS LA

Rough Hays

ST14

BANKTOP RD

Bank Farm

Bank Top

FOUNTAIN RD

PIPE HAY LA

HAY

Pipehay Farm

3

Banktop Wood

B5017

Wood Gate

POST

St Augustine's F'st Sch

Forest Farm

Bullspark Wood

DE6

Lathbury's Hill

Greaves

28

Hadley Cottages

FOREST RD

Greaves Wood

GREAVES LA

Foxholes Farm

Foxholes

Six Roads End Farm

Bott's Coppice

2

Hadley House

Hadley Farm

Saw Mill

SIX ROADS END

Hanbury Grange

Western Cottages

WOOD LA

HOLLY BUSH RD

Eland Lodge

Howitt House Sch

27

Brick-kiln Rough

B5017

A515

Newlodge Farm

New Farm

KNIGHTSFIELD RD

Knightsfield Farm

DE13

Hanbury Woodend

1

Eland Brook

Carrion Rough

Parson's Brake

CHAPEL LA

Sycamore Farm

PH

Elton Covert

Woodside Bungalow

Parsonsbrake Farm

B5017

Brickyard Cottages

26

14   **A**   15   **B**   16   **C**

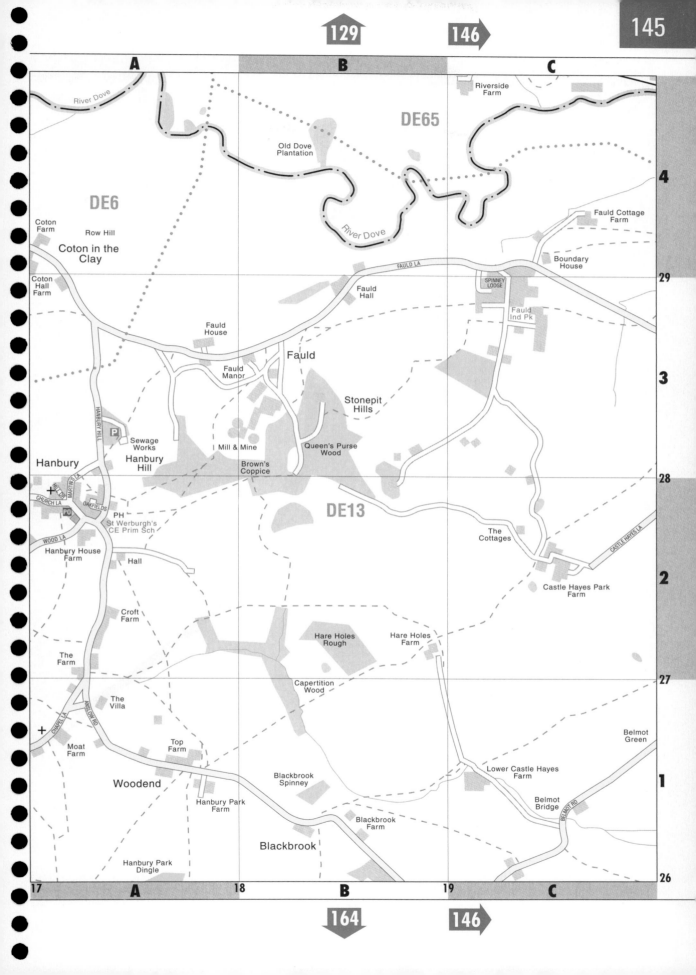

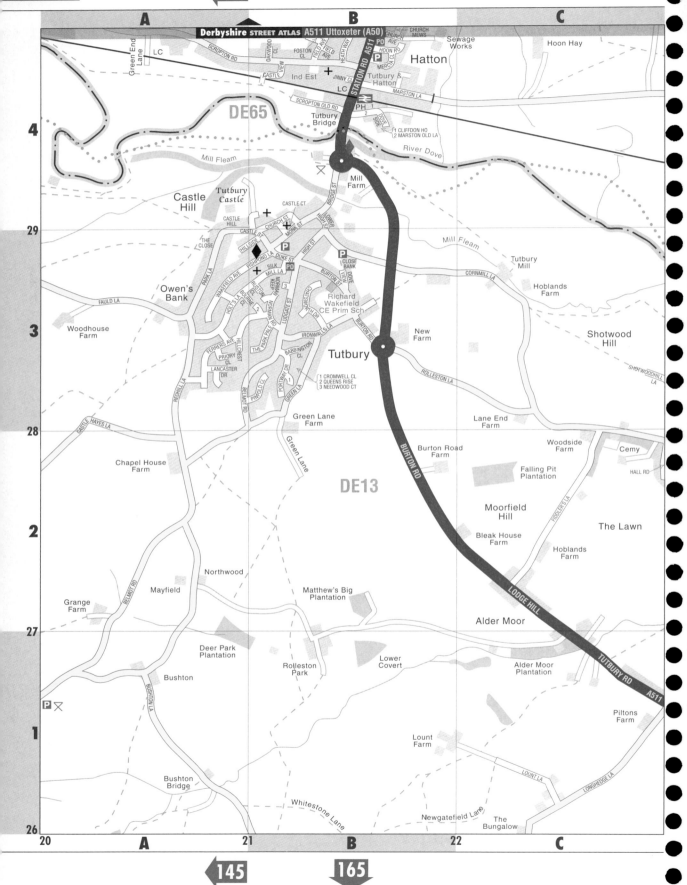

145

Derbyshire STREET ATLAS A511 Uttoxeter (A50)

Green End Lane

LC

SCROPTON RD
OAKWOOD CL
FOSTON CL
FIELD AVE
HEATH WAY
STATION RD A511
CHURCH MEWS
CHURCH AVE
PO
HOON RD
MERCIA
Sewage Works

Hoon Hay

Hatton

CASTLE VIEW
Ind Est
JINNY CT
Tutbury & Hatton
LC
MARSTON LA

SCROPTON OLD RD
PH
1 CLIFFDON HO
2 MARSTON OLD LA

DE65

Tutbury Bridge

Mill Fleam

River Dove

4

Castle Hill

Tutbury Castle

CASTLE CT
Mill Farm

Mill Fleam

CASTLE HILL
CASTLE ST
CHURCH ST
MONK ST
LOWER HIGH ST
BRIDGE ST

29

THE CLOSE
HILLSIDE
P
HIGH ST
CLOSE BANK
DOVE VIEW
P

Tutbury Mill

Hoblands Farm

CORNMILL LA

Owen's Bank

FAULD LA
PARK LA
WAKEFIELD AVE
HOLT'S LA
BELMONT CL
DUKE ST
SILK MILL LA
NORMANDY KEEP
BURTON ST
Richard Wakefield CE Prim Sch
BURTON RD

Shotwood Hill

3

Woodhouse Farm

FERRERS AVE
PRIORY CL
HILCREST
THE PARK
PINFOLD CL
PALE
LUDGATE ST
CHAINSWOOD
IRONWALLS LA
New Farm

SHOTWOODHILL LA

LANCASTER DR
REDHILL
BELMOT RD
PINFOLD CL
PORTWAY DR
BABBINGTON CL
GREEN LA
Tutbury

ROLLESTON LA

1 CROMWELL CL
2 QUEENS RISE
3 NEEDWOOD CT

Lane End Farm

28

CASTLE HAYES LA
Green Lane Farm

Chapel House Farm

Woodside Farm
Cemy

HALL RD

Green Lane

Burton Road Farm

Falling Pit Plantation

DE13

BURTON RD
Moorfield Hill

The Lawn

2

BELMOT RD
Northwood
Bleak House Farm

RIDDERS LA
Hoblands Farm

BUSHTON LA
Mayfield
Matthew's Big Plantation

LODGE HILL
Alder Moor

Grange Farm

27

Deer Park Plantation

Rolleston Park

Lower Covert

Alder Moor Plantation

TUTBURY RD A511

Bushton

P

1

Lount Farm

Piltons Farm

Bushton Bridge

LOUNT LA

LONGHEDGE LA

26

Whitestone Lane

Newgatefield Lane

The Bungalow

20 A 21 B 22 C

145   165

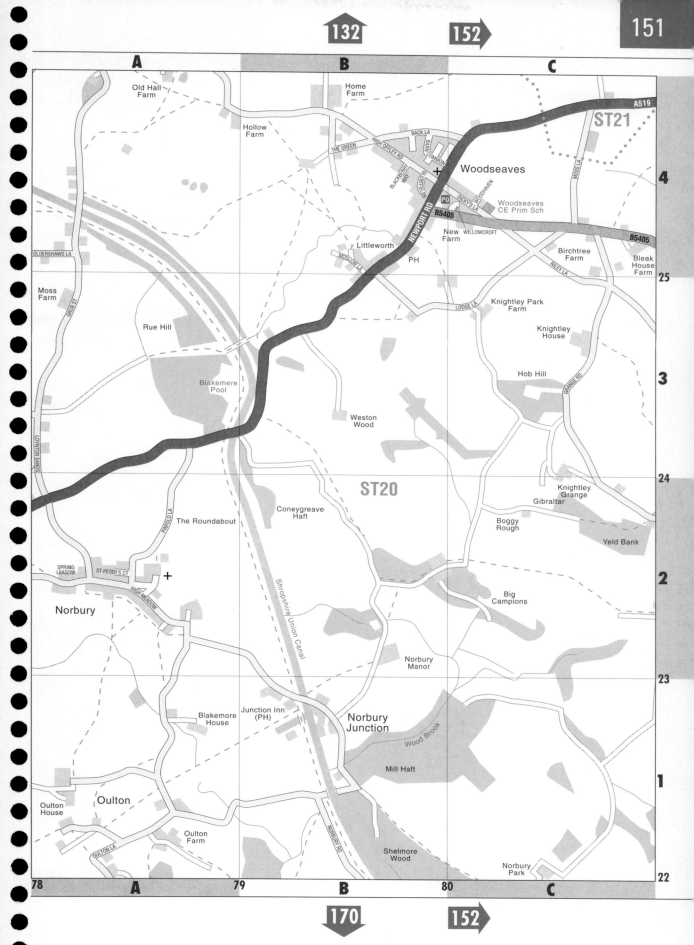

151 133

A **B** **C**

A519

A519

ST21

Taylor's
Covert

4

Knightley
Gorse

Bond's
Covert

Walton's
Rough

Gorse Covert

B5405

25

Knightley

Yewtree
Farm

Hilltop
Farm

Lawnhead

Woodhill
Farm

Depot

Addison's
Covert

B5405

The
Triangle

Common
Belt

3

RILEY LA

Rose Tree
Farm

Ashwoodhead
Farm

Ash
Wood

Wavell Lane

Ranton
Abbey

Old
Farm

LOWER RD

24

Green
Farm

ST20

Humphrey's
Wood

Yeld
Bank
Farm

GRANGE RD

Lower
Knightley

Simpkin's
Covert

Woise
Lane

2

Knightley
Green

New
Covert

Big
Wood

Woodside

Knightley
Dale

GNOSALL RD

Yewtree
Farm

Hollies Brook

Hollybank
Farm

Knightley
Hall

Prospect
Hill

23

Bellingham's
Covert

Ash's
Covert

Brough
Hall

1

Nut
Wood

KNIGHTLEY RD

Moor End
Farm

Hell
Hole

Hollies
Common

22

81 **A** 82 **B** 83 **C**

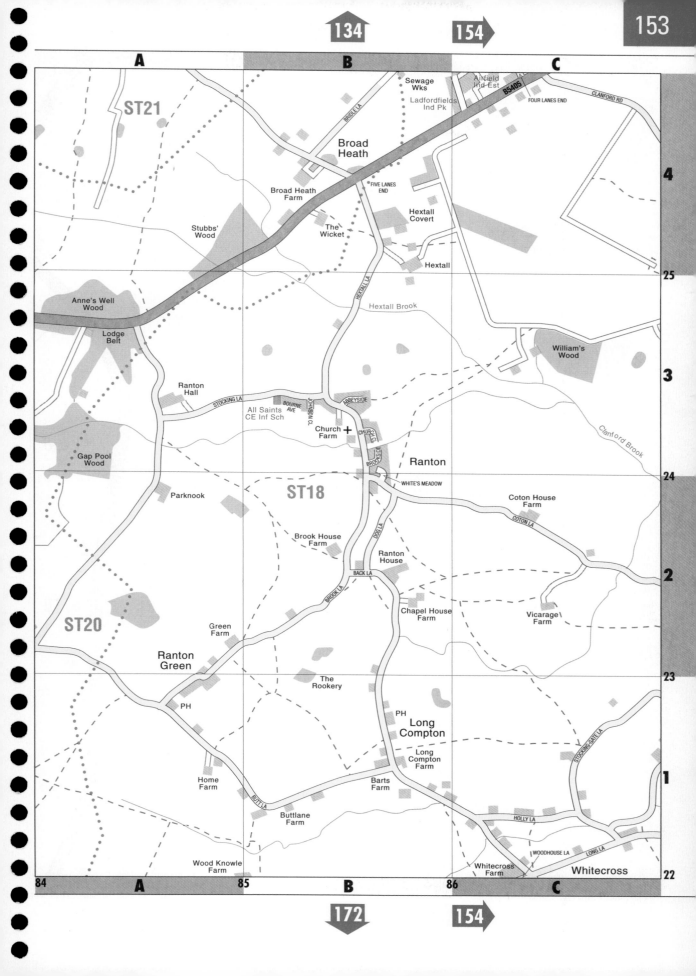

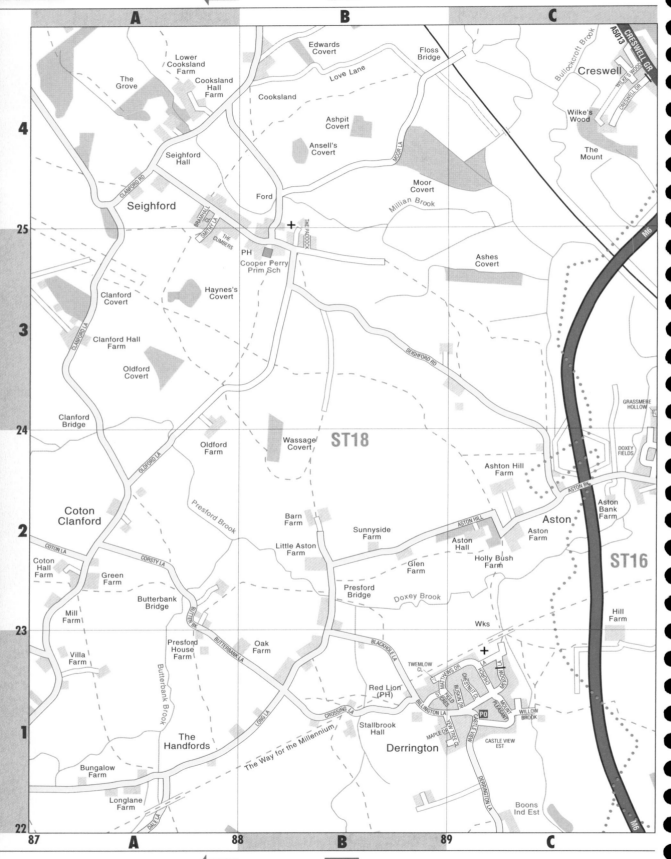

A B C

4

25

3

24

ST18

2

23

1

22

87 A 88 B 89 C

Creswell

CRESWELL GR

A5013

Bullockcroft Brook

WILKE'S WOOD

CRESWELL DR

Wilke's
Wood

The
Mount

M6

Ashes
Covert

GRASSMERE
HOLLOW

DOXEY
FIELDS

Ashton Hill
Farm

ASTON BK

Aston
Bank
Farm

Aston

Aston
Farm

ST16

Hill
Farm

Lower
Cooksland
Farm

The
Grove

Cooksland
Hall
Farm

Edwards
Covert

Love Lane

Floss
Bridge

Cooksland

Ashpit
Covert

Ansell's
Covert

MOOR LA

Moor
Covert

Millian Brook

Seighford
Hall

Seighford

Ford

THE PADDOCK

BRAIRHALL CL

SMITHY LA

THE CUMBERS

PH

Cooper Perry
Prim Sch

Clanford
Covert

Haynes's
Covert

CLANFORD RD

Clanford Hall
Farm

Oldford
Covert

CLANFORD LA

Clanford
Bridge

Oldford
Farm

OLDFORD LA

Wassage
Covert

SEIGHFORD RD

Aston Hill
Farm

Aston
Hall

Holly Bush
Farm

Barn
Farm

Little Aston
Farm

Sunnyside
Farm

ASTON HILL

Coton
Clanford

COTON LA

Coton
Hall
Farm

Green
Farm

CORSTY LA

Butterbank
Bridge

Presford Brook

Glen
Farm

Presford
Bridge

Doxey Brook

Wks

Mill
Farm

BUTTERBANK LA

BUTTER BK

Oak
Farm

BLACKHILL LA

TWEMLOW
CL

Villa
Farm

Presford
House
Farm

Butterbank Brook

LONG LA

Red Lion
(PH)

BILLINGTON LA

ST GEORGES

MATTHEWS DR

CHESTNUT CT

RUSKIN DR

LA

HOPTON

MT. PLEASANT

PO

WILLOW
BROOK

CASTLE VIEW

The
Handfords

CROSSING LA

The Way for the Millennium

Stallbrook
Hall

Derrington

MAPLE DR

YEW TREE CT

CASTLE VIEW
EST

Bungalow
Farm

Longlane
Farm

DALE LA

DERRINGTON LA

Boons
Ind Est

M6

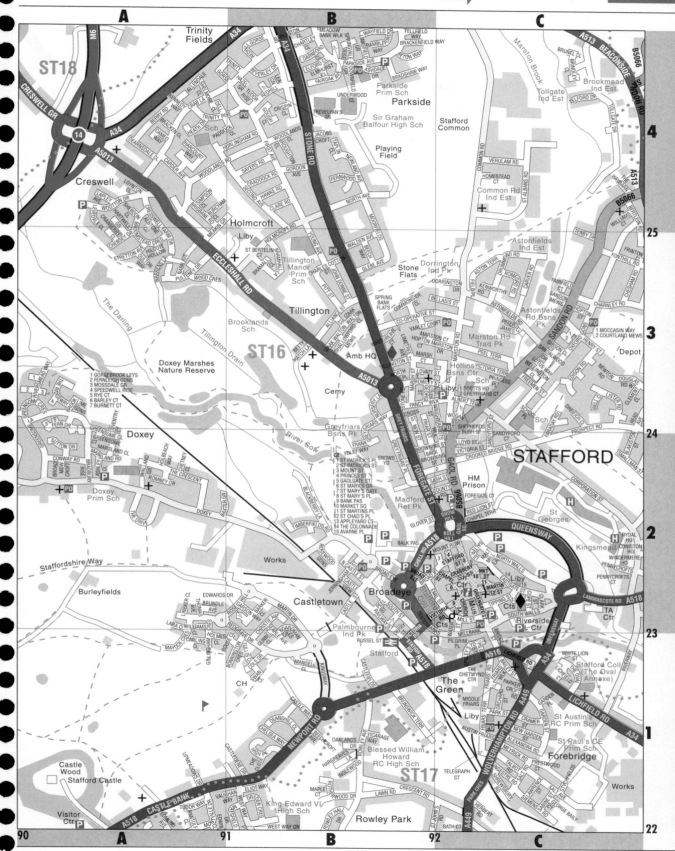

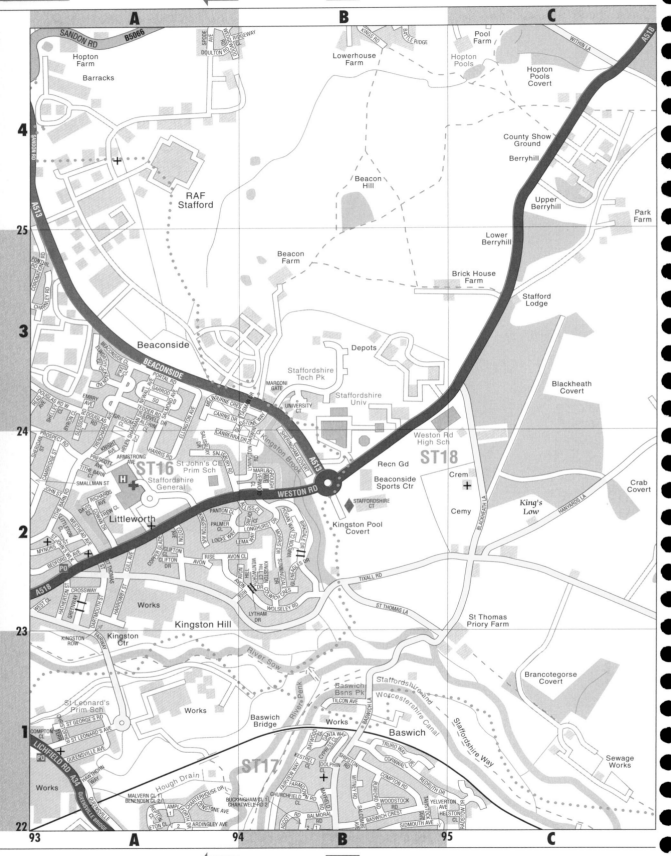

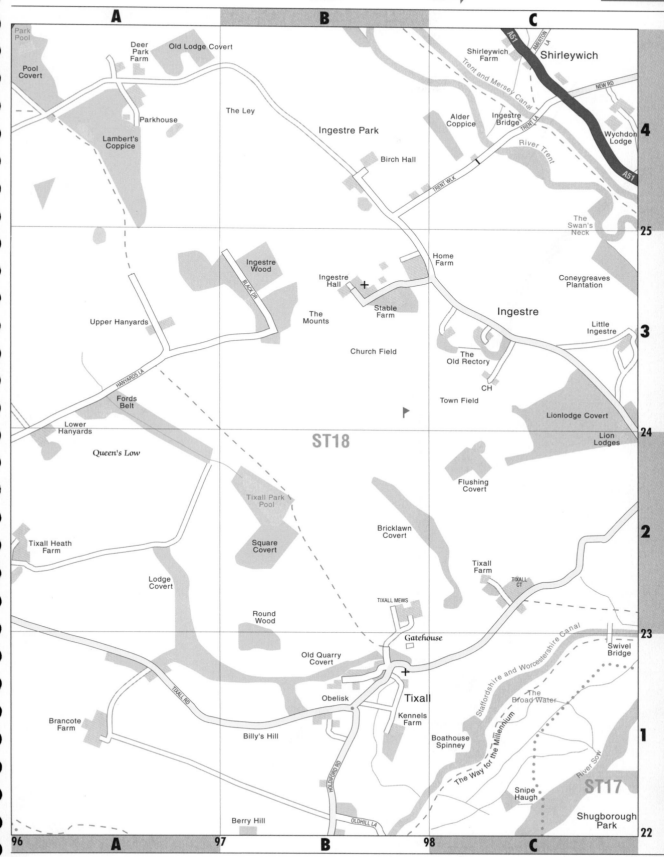

A
B
C

Park Pool
Deer Park Farm
Old Lodge Covert
Pool Covert
The Ley
Ingestre Park
Parkhouse
Lambert's Coppice
Shirleywich Farm
Shirleywich
Trent and Mersey Canal
AMERTON LA
A51
NEW RD
Alder Coppice
Ingestre Bridge
TRENT LA
River Trent
Wychdon Lodge
A51
Birch Hall
TRENT WLK
4

The Swan's Neck
25

Ingestre Wood
BLACK DR
Ingestre Hall
Home Farm
Coneygreaves Plantation
Upper Hanyards
The Mounts
Stable Farm
Ingestre
Little Ingestre
3
HANYARDS LA
Church Field
The Old Rectory
CH
Fords Belt
Lower Hanyards
Town Field
Lionlodge Covert
Lion Lodges
24

Queen's Low
ST18
Flushing Covert

Tixall Park Pool
Tixall Heath Farm
Square Covert
Bricklawn Covert
Tixall Farm
TIXALL CT
2

Lodge Covert
Round Wood
TIXALL MEWS
Staffordshire and Worcestershire Canal
Swivel Bridge
23
Gatehouse
Old Quarry Covert
Tixall
The Broad Water
Brancote Farm
TIXALL RD
Obelisk
Kennels Farm
Boathouse Spinney
The Way for the Millennium
River Sow
ST17
1
Billy's Hill
HOLDIFORD RD
Snipe Haugh
Berry Hill
OLDHILL LA
Shugborough Park
22

96
A
97
B
98
C

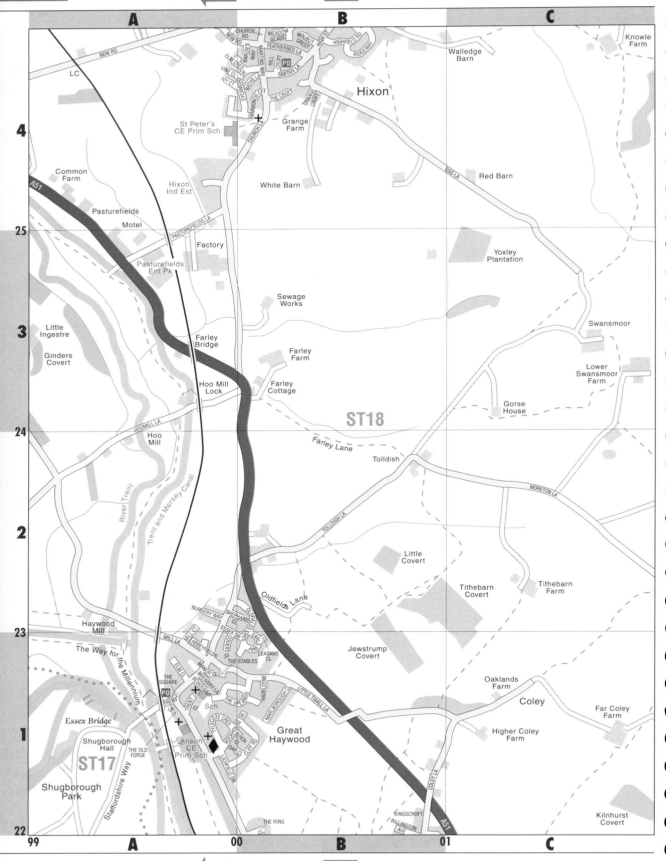

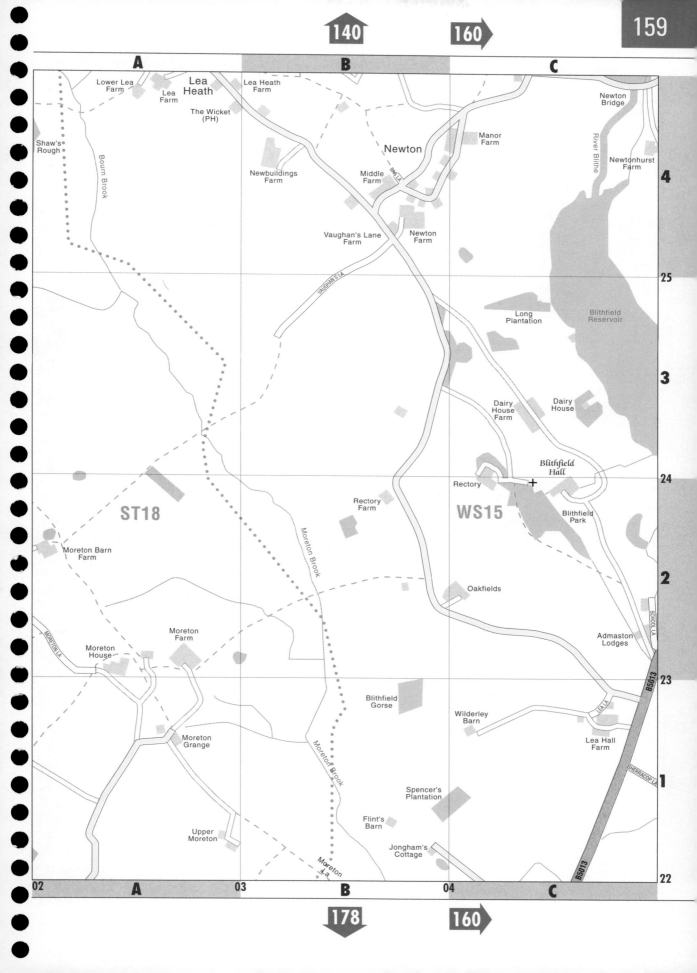

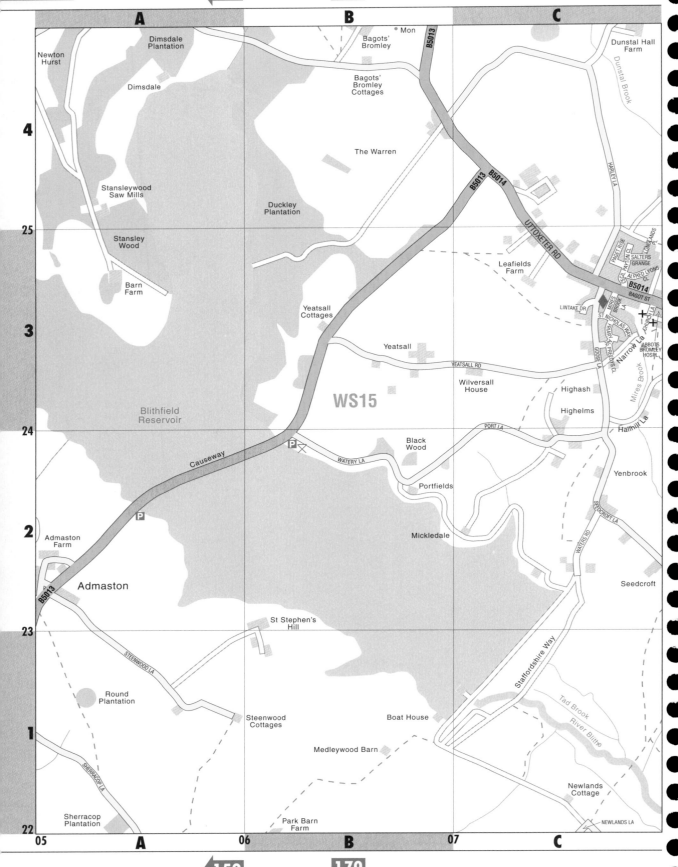

159
141

A B C

Newton Hurst

Dimsdale Plantation

Dimsdale

Bagots' Bromley

• Mon

B5013

Dunstal Hall Farm

Bagots' Bromley Cottages

Dunstal Brook

The Warren

4

Stansleywood Saw Mills

Duckley Plantation

B5013 B5014

HARLEY LA

Stansley Wood

25

UTTOXETER RD

Leafields Farm

PAGET RISE
PAXTON CL
LONG LANDS
SALTERS GRANGE
ALFRED LYONS CL

Barn Farm

Yeatsall Cottages

B5014
BAGOT ST

LINTAKE DR

3

Yeatsall

Yeatsall

YEATSALL RD

Wilversall House

Highash

ST NICHOLAS WK
SHIRE BROOK LA
FRIAR ST PRESTONS CL
GOOSE LA
Narrow La
ABBOTS BROMLEY HOSPL

Blithfield Reservoir

WS15

Highelms

Mires Brook

24

Causeway

P

WATERY LA

Black Wood

PORT LA

Hallhill La

Yenbrook

Portfields

2

Admaston Farm

P

Mickledale

SEEDCROFT LA

WATERS RD

Admaston

B5013

Seedcroft

23

St Stephen's Hill

STEENWOOD LA

Staffordshire Way

Round Plantation

Tad Brook

River Blithe

Steenwood Cottages

Boat House

1

Medleywood Barn

Newlands Cottage

SHERRACOP LA

Sherracop Plantation

Park Barn Farm

NEWLANDS LA

22

05

159
179

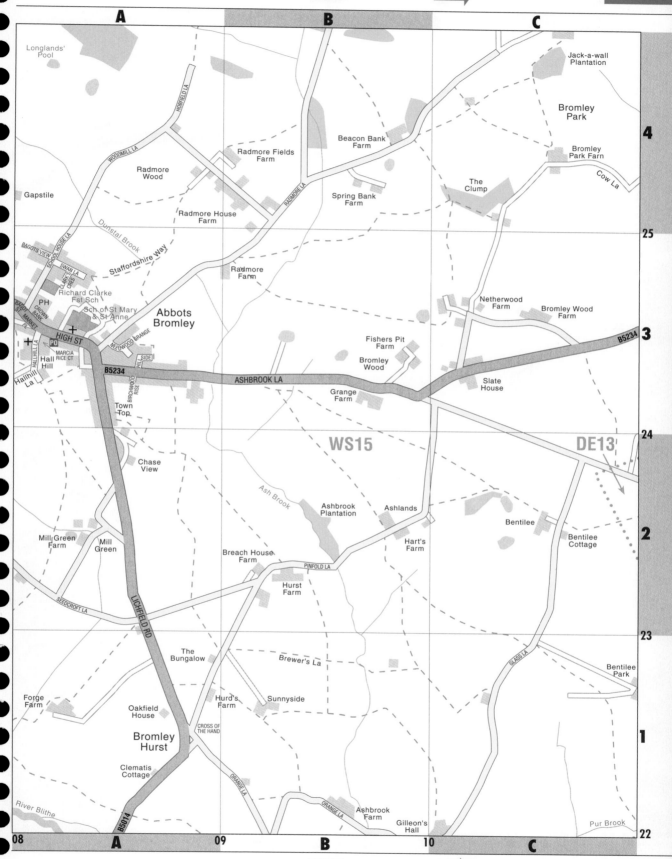

A B C

Longlands' Pool

Gapstile

Radmore Wood

Radmore Fields Farm

HOBFIELD LA

WOODMILL LA

SCHOOL HOUSE LA

BAGOTS VIEW

SWAN LA

CLARKES CRES

Dunstal Brook

Staffordshire Way

Radmore House Farm

RADMORE LA

Radmore Farm

Beacon Bank Farm

Spring Bank Farm

Jack-a-wall Plantation

Bromley Park

Bromley Park Farm

COW LA

The Clump

Netherwood Farm

Bromley Wood Farm

Richard Clarke Fst Sch

Sch of St Mary & St Anne

Abbots Bromley

PH

CROWN BANK

BAGOT
MARKET
ST PL

HIGH ST

PO

MARCIA RICE CT

NEEDWOOD GRANGE

HILL SIDE

Hall Hill

Halhill La

HALLHILL LA

B5234

Town Top

BIRCHWOOD RISE

ASHBROOK LA

Grange Farm

Fishers Pit Farm

Bromley Wood

Slate House

B5234

Chase View

WS15

DE13

Mill Green Farm

Mill Green

Ash Brook

Ashbrook Plantation

Ashlands

Hart's Farm

Bentilee

Bentilee Cottage

Breach House Farm

PINFOLD LA

Hurst Farm

SEEDCROFT LA

LICHFIELD RD

The Bungalow

Brewer's La

GLASS LA

Bentilee Park

Forge Farm

Oakfield House

Hurd's Farm

Sunnyside

CROSS OF THE HAND

Bromley Hurst

Clematis Cottage

ORANGE LA

River Blithe

B5014

ORANGE LA

Ashbrook Farm

Gilleon's Hall

Pur Brook

4

25

3

24

2

23

1

22

08 09 10

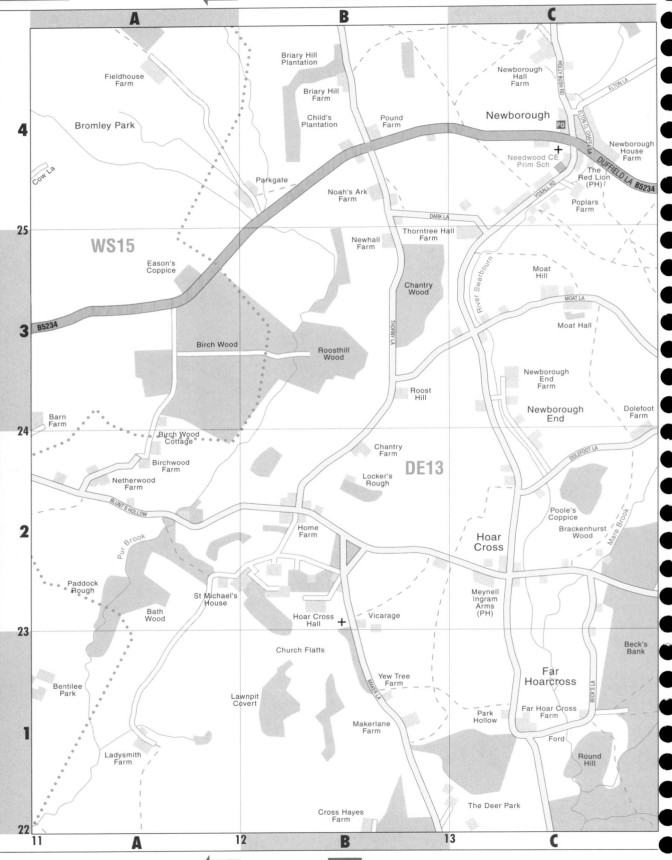

A B C

4

25

WS15

3 B5234

24

2

23

1

22

11 A 12 B 13 C

Fieldhouse Farm

Bromley Park

Cow La

Parkgate

Eason's Coppice

Birch Wood

Roosthill Wood

Barn Farm

Birch Wood Cottage

Birchwood Farm

Netherwood Farm

BLUNT'S HOLLOW

Pur Brook

Paddock Rough

Bath Wood

St Michael's House

Bentilee Park

Ladysmith Farm

Briary Hill Plantation

Briary Hill Farm

Child's Plantation

Pound Farm

Noah's Ark Farm

Newhall Farm

Thorntree Hall Farm

DARK LA

Chantry Wood

THORNY LA

Roost Hill

Chantry Farm

Locker's Rough

DE13

Home Farm

Hoar Cross Hall

Vicarage

Church Flatts

Yew Tree Farm

Lawnpit Covert

MAKER LA

Makerlane Farm

Cross Hayes Farm

Newborough Hall Farm

HOLLY BUSH RD

ELTON LA

Newborough

ELTON CL CHAPEL LA

PO

DUFFIELD LA B5234

Needwood CE Prim Sch

YOXALL RD

The Red Lion (PH)

Poplars Farm

Newborough House Farm

River Swarbourn

Moat Hill

MOAT LA

Moat Hall

Newborough End Farm

Newborough End

Dolefoot Farm

DOLEFOOT LA

Poole's Coppice

Brackenhurst Wood

Mare Brook

Hoar Cross

Meynell Ingram Arms (PH)

Far Hoarcross

Beck's Bank

BECK'S BANK

Far Hoar Cross Farm

Park Hollow

Ford

Round Hill

The Deer Park

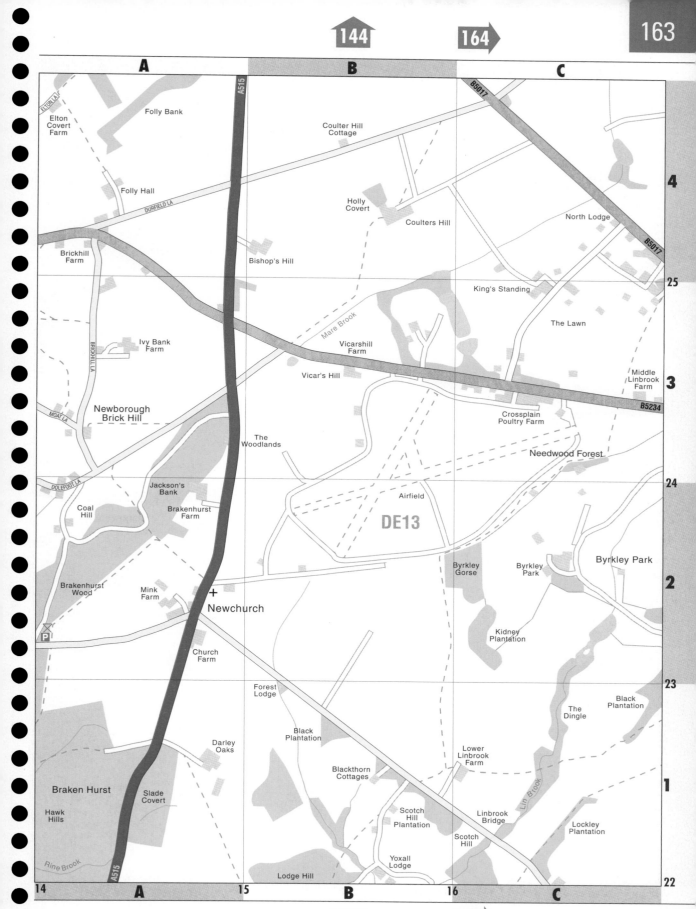

ELTON LA
Elton Covert Farm
Folly Bank
A515
B5017
Coulter Hill Cottage

4

Folly Hall
DURFIELD LA
Holly Covert
Coulters Hill
North Lodge
B5017

Brickhill Farm
Bishop's Hill
King's Standing
25

BRICKHILL LA
Ivy Bank Farm
Mare Brook
Vicarshill Farm
The Lawn

MOAT LA
Newborough Brick Hill
Vicar's Hill
Crossplain Poultry Farm
Middle Linbrook Farm
B5234
3

The Woodlands
Needwood Forest

DOLEFOOT LA
Jackson's Bank
Airfield
24

Coal Hill
Brakenhurst Farm
DE13
Byrkley Gorse
Byrkley Park
Byrkley Park
2

Brakenhurst Wood
Mink Farm
Newchurch
Kidney Plantation

P
Church Farm
23

Forest Lodge
Black Plantation
The Dingle
Black Plantation

Darley Oaks
Black Plantation
Lower Linbrook Farm
1

Braken Hurst
Slade Covert
Blackthorn Cottages
Lin Brook
Linbrook Bridge
Lockley Plantation

Hawk Hills
Scotch Hill Plantation
Scotch Hill

Rine Brook
A515
Yoxall Lodge
Lodge Hill
22

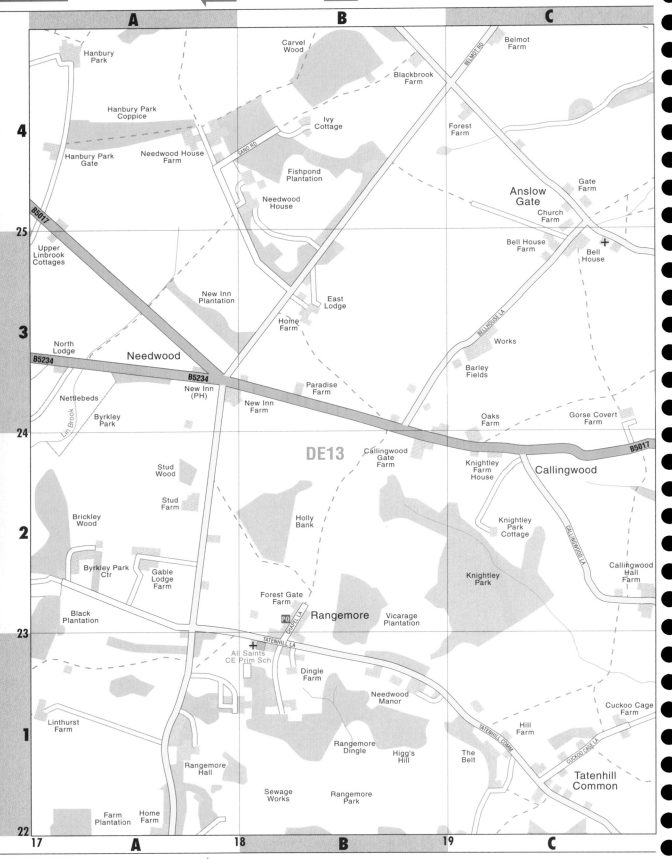

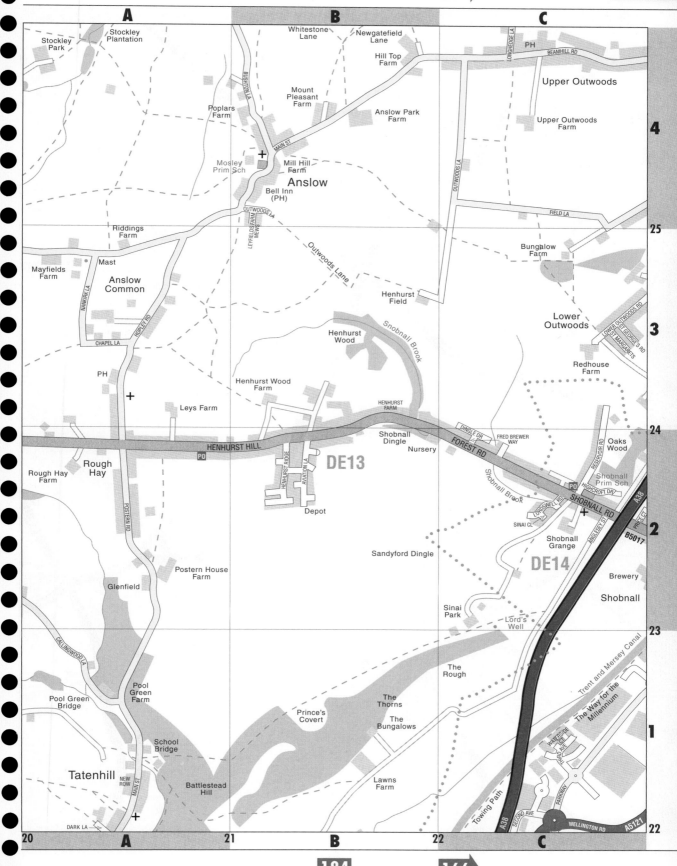

A map page showing the areas of Anslow, Tatenhill, Shobnall, Lower Outwoods, and Upper Outwoods.

Labels visible on the map include:

Stockley Plantation, Stockley Park, Whitestone Lane, Newgatefield Lane, Hill Top Farm, Longhedge La, PH, BEAMHILL RD, Upper Outwoods, Upper Outwoods Farm, Poplars Farm, Mount Pleasant Farm, Anslow Park Farm, BUSHTON LA, MAIN ST, Mosley Prim Sch, Mill Hill Farm, Anslow, Bell Inn (PH), OUTWOODS LA, OUTWOODS LA, FIELD LA, Riddings Farm, LEYFIELDS FARM MEWS, Outwoods Lane, Bungalow Farm, Mayfields Farm, Mast, MANKIRK LA, HOPLEY RD, Anslow Common, Henhurst Field, Lower Outwoods, LOWER OUTWOODS RD, ST GEORGE'S RD, ST MARGARETS, CHAPEL LA, PH, Henhurst Wood, Snobnall Brook, Redhouse Farm, Henhurst Wood Farm, Leys Farm, HENHURST HILL, Henhurst Farm, Shobnall Dingle, Nursery, DINGLE DR, FOREST RD, FRED BREWER WAY, RESERVOIR RD, Oaks Wood, PO, DE13, HENHURST RIDGE, AVIATION LA, Depot, Shobnall Brook, Shobnall Prim Sch, HIGHCROFT DR, SHOBNALL RD, A38, Rough Hay Farm, Rough Hay, POSTERN RD, SINAI CL, LORDSWELL RD, Shobnall Grange, ANGLESEY ST, PRINCESS, B5017, Sandyford Dingle, DE14, Brewery, Glenfield, Shobnall, Postern House Farm, Sinai Park, Lord's Well, The Rough, Trent and Mersey Canal, CALLINGWOOD LA, Pool Green Farm, Prince's Covert, The Thorns, The Bungalows, The Rough, WATERSIDE, THIRD AVE, The Way for the Millennium, Pool Green Bridge, School Bridge, PARKWAY, Tatenhill, NEW ROW, MAIN ST, Battlestead Hill, Lawns Farm, Towing Path, SECOND AVE, WELLINGTON RD, A5121, A38, DARK LA

Grid references: 4, 25, 3, 24, 2, 23, 1, 22 (right side); 20, 21, 22 (bottom); A, B, C (top and bottom)

165 147

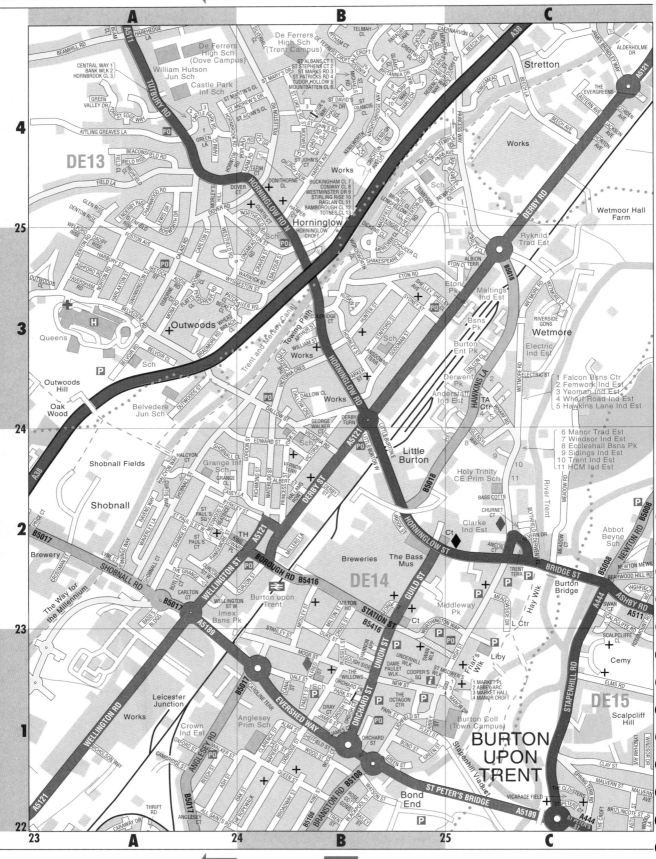

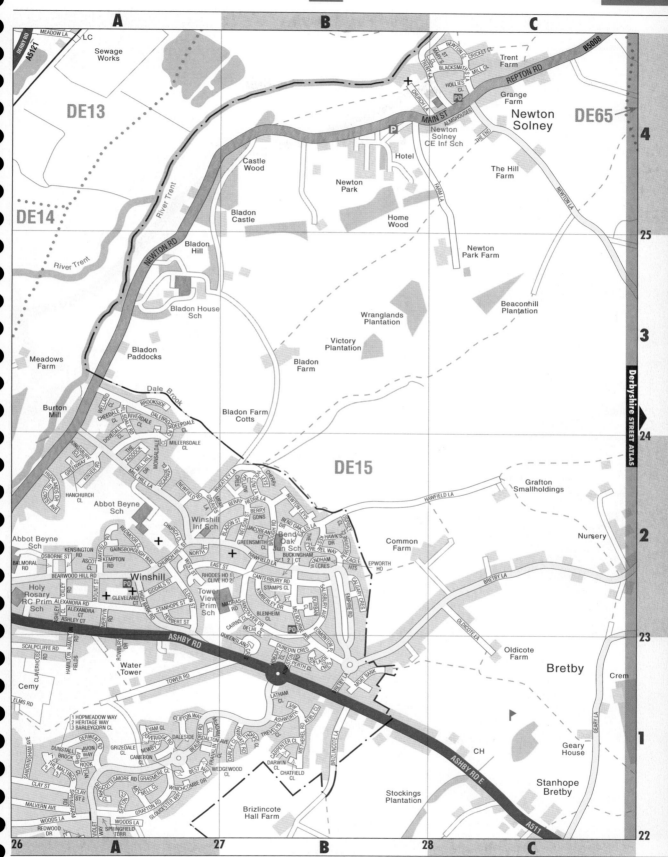

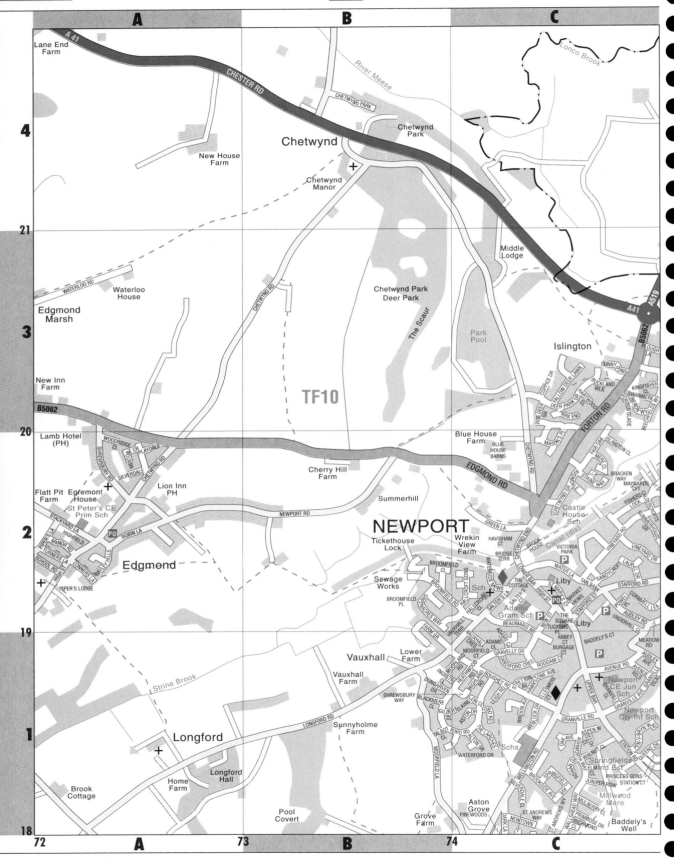

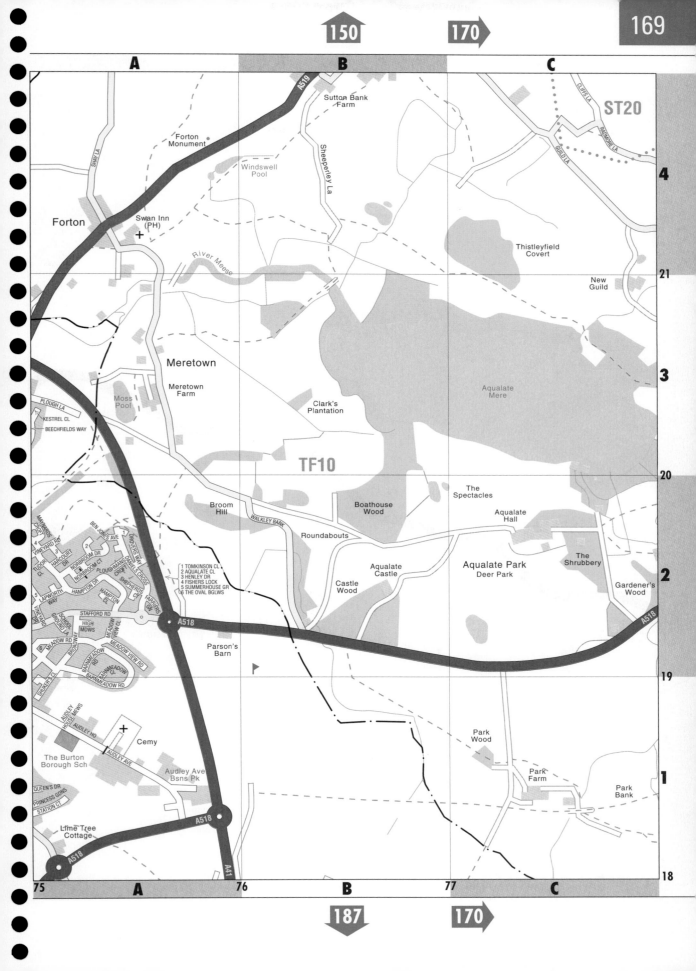

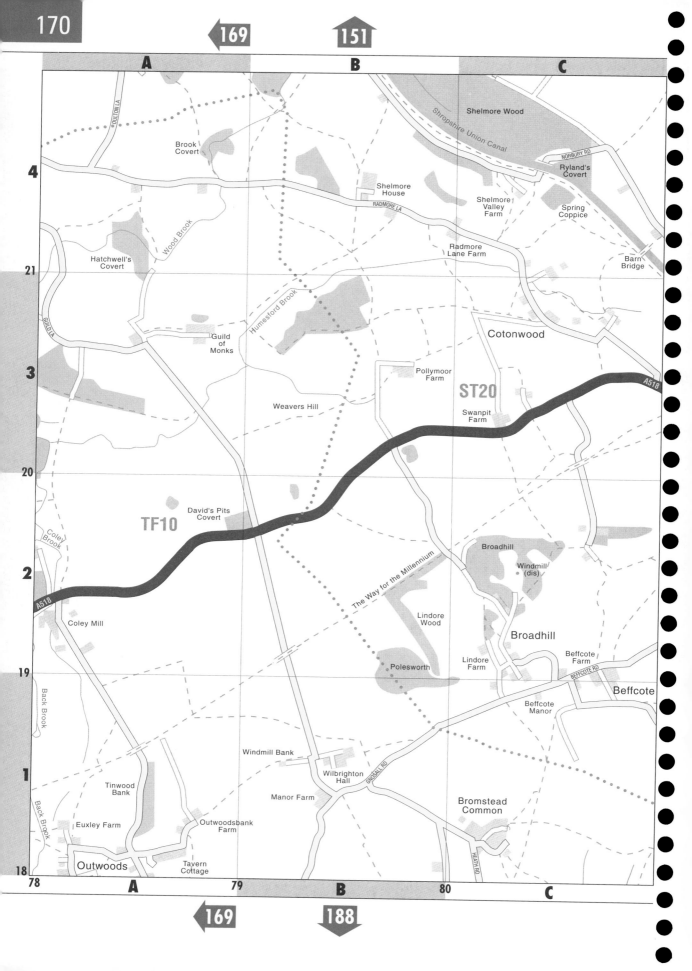

A B C

4

21

3

20

2

19

1

18

78 A 79 B 80 C

OULTON LA

Brook
Covert

Shropshire Union Canal

Shelmore Wood

NORBURY RD

Ryland's
Covert

Shelmore
House

RADMORE LA

Shelmore
Valley
Farm

Spring
Coppice

Wood Brook

Hatchwell's
Covert

Radmore
Lane Farm

Barn
Bridge

GUILD LA

Humesford Brook

Guild
of
Monks

Cotonwood

Weavers Hill

Pollymoor
Farm

ST20

Swanpit
Farm

David's Pits
Covert

TF10

Coley
Brook

Broadhill

Windmill
(dis)

The Way for the Millennium

A518

Coley Mill

Lindore
Wood

Broadhill

Lindore
Farm

Beffcote
Farm

BEFFCOTE RD

Polesworth

Beffcote

Back Brook

Beffcote
Manor

Windmill Bank

Wilbrighton
Hall

GNOSALL RD

Tinwood
Bank

Manor Farm

Bromstead
Common

Back Brook

Euxley Farm

Outwoodsbank
Farm

HEATH RD

Outwoods

Tavern
Cottage

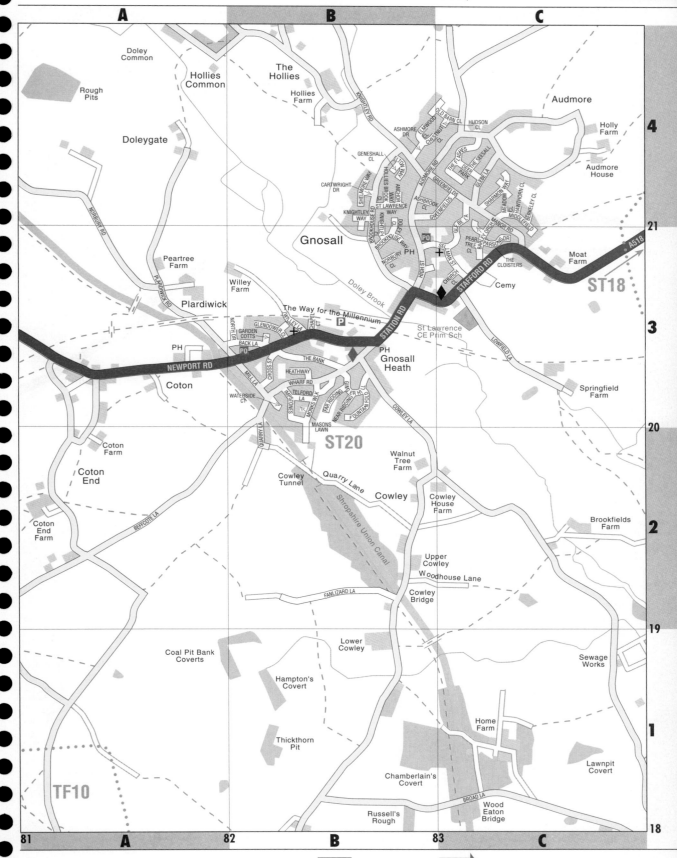

171
153

ST20

A **B** **C**

The Sheppy Farm

Whitecross

Bleak House
Farm

WOODHOUSE LA

Shutt Heath
Farm

Shut
Heath

Brazenhill

SHARMANS LA

STATION RD

Woodhouse
Farm

Brazenhill
Farm

4

Ivy House
Farm

Hurst
Farm

BRAZENHILL LA

P

Leasows
Farm

Parkhead
House

Mayo
Farm

21

A518

The Way for the Millennium

HAWTHORN
CL

STEPS GDNS

Pear Tree Bank
Farm

Old Park
House

Shropshire Inn
(PH)

MEADOW DR

POPLAR CL

MOAT HOUSE DR

CHURCH CL

BROOK END

ST GILES GR†

Upper Reule
Farm

New Park
House

The Old Hall

Grassy
La

Haughton
St Giles CE
Prim Sch

Haughton
Farm

PO

RECTORY LA

OAK
CLOSE

GNOSALL RD

BACK LA

3

Reule
Covert

PARK CL

BROOK (BLD)

JOLLY LA

PRINCE AVE

ASH DR

ASH DR

WATERY LA

Haughton

A518

Middle
Covert

ST18

20

Ox Leasow
Covert

Black
Hough

Booden
Farm

Allimore Brook

Hough
Farm

Lower Reule
Farm

Birches
Gorse

The
Black Hough
Farm

Hanging Pits
Farm

2

Wheatcroft
Covert

ST20

Allimore
Green

Reulemill
Pools

Apeton Bank
Covert

19

Alstone Hall
Farm

ALSTONE LA

Alstone
Farm

Apeton
Slang

Lower
Alstone

1

Church Eaton Brook

Apeton Brook

Alstone
Cottages

Apeton

Ford

Upper
Barton

18

84 **A** **85** **B** **86** **C**

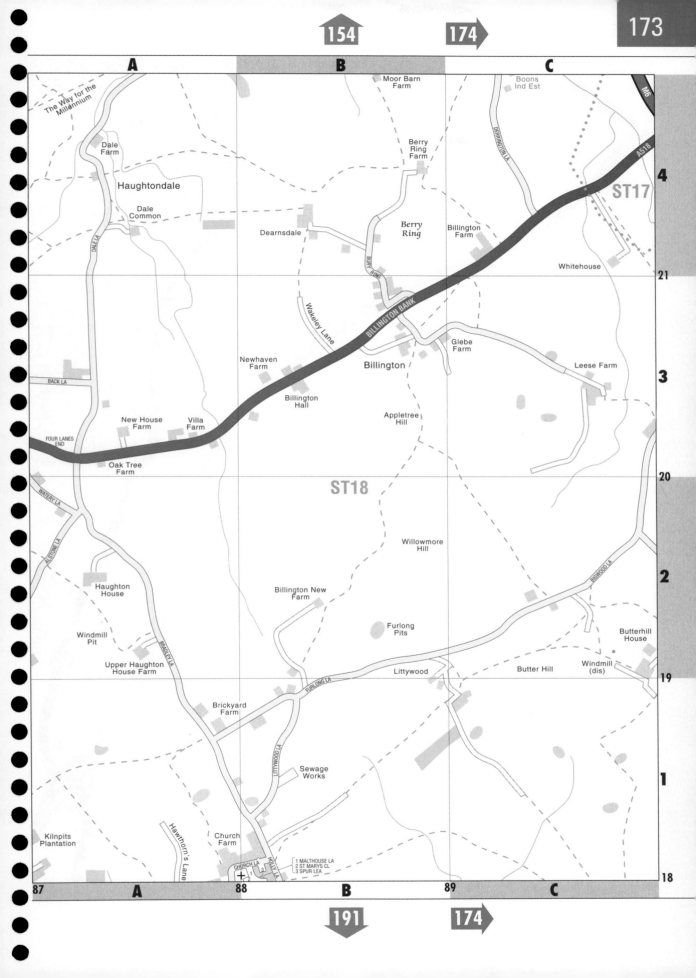

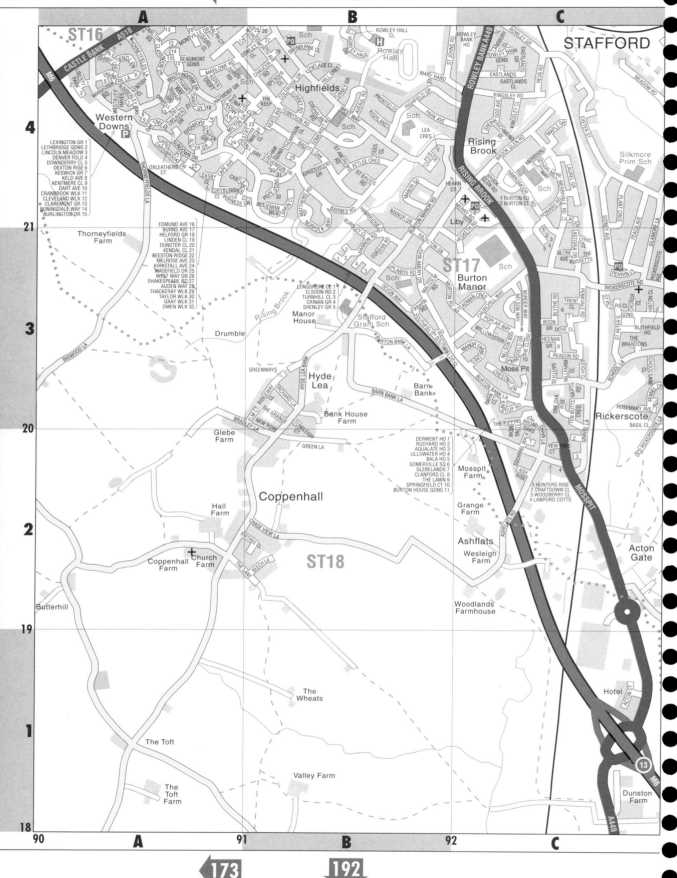

173
155

STAFFORD

ST16

A518

CASTLE BANK

M6

Western
Downs

P

Highfields

4

Lexington Gr 1
Lethbridge Gdns 2
Lincoln Meadow 3
Denver Fold 4
Downderry Cl 5
Dexton Rise 6
Keswick Gr 7
Keld Ave 8
Kentmere Cl 9
Dart Ave 10
Cranbrook Wlk 11
Cleveland Wlk 12
Claremont Gr 13
Boningdale Way 14
Burlington Dr 15

Rowley Hall
Rowley Hall

Sch

H

Rowley Hall
Cl

Rowley
Bank Ho

ROWLEY BANK A449

RISING BROOK

Eastlands
Eastlands
Cl

Kingsley Rd

Rising
Brook

Sch

Silkmore
Prim Sch

21

Thorneyfields
Farm

Edmund Ave 16
Burns Ave 17
Helford Gr 18
Linden Cl 19
Dunster Cl 20
Kendal Cl 21
Beeston Ridge 22
Melrose Ave 23
Kirkstall Ave 24
Masefield Dr 25
West Way Gn 26
Shakespeare Rd 27
Auden Way 28
Thackeray Wlk 29
Taylor Wlk 30
Gray Wlk 31
Owen Wlk 32

ST17

Burton
Manor

Liby

Sch

P
O

Rickerscote Rd

P
O

3

Rising Brook

Drumble

BIGWOOD LA

Longshore Cl 1
Elsdon Rd 2
Turnhill Cl 3
Crinan Gr 4
Shenley Gr 5

Manor
House

Stafford
Gram Sch

BURTON BANK LA

Moss Pit

Rickerscote

THE
BRANDONS

ROSEMARY AVE

Greenways

Hyde
Lea

Barn
Bank

BARN BANK LA

Barn
Bank

BURTON BANK LA

Bank House
Farm

20

Glebe
Farm

BRADLEY LA

THE GRANGE

NEW ROW

ORCHARD LA

STONELEIGH

GREEN LA

Derwent Ho 1
Rudyard Ho 2
Aqualate Ho 3
Ullswater Ho 4
Bala Ho 5
Somerville Sq 6
Glebelands 7
Clanford Cl 8
The Lawn 9
Springfield Ct 10
Burton House Gdns 11

Yew Tree
Ct

Coppenhall

Mosspit
Farm

1 Hunters Rise
2 Craftdown Cl
3 Woodberry Cl
4 Lawford Cotts

2

Hall
Farm

CHASE VIEW LA

FIRTREE CL

ST18

Grange
Farm

Ashflats

Wesleigh
Farm

Acton
Gate

Coppenhall
Farm

Church
Farm

BEECH LA

THE LANE

Butterhill

Woodlands
Farmhouse

19

Hotel

ACTON CT

The
Wheats

1

The Toft

13

M6

A449

The
Toft
Farm

Valley Farm

Dunston
Farm

18

90
91
92

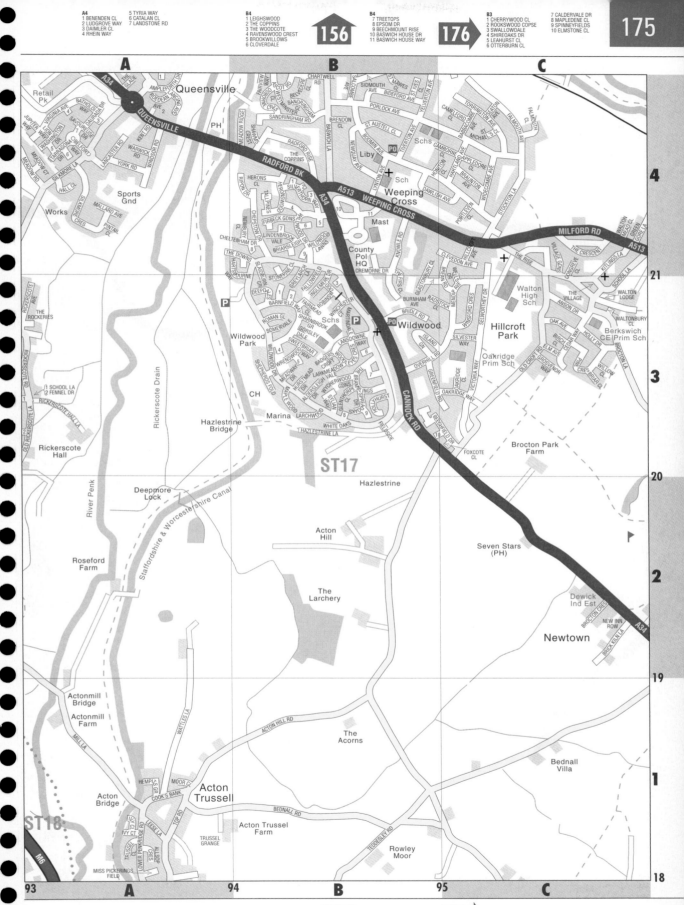

A4
1 BENENDEN CL
2 LUDGROVE WAY
3 DAIMLER CL
4 RHEIN WAY

5 TYRIA WAY
6 CATALAN CL
7 LANDSTONE RD

B4
1 LEIGHSWOOD
2 THE COPPINS
3 THE WOODCOTE
4 RAVENSWOOD CREST
5 BROOKWILLOWS
6 CLOVERDALE

156

176

B4
7 TREETOPS
8 EPSOM DR
9 BEECHMOUNT RISE
10 BASWICH HOUSE DR
11 BASWICH HOUSE WAY

B3
1 CHERRYWOOD CL
2 ROOKSWOOD COPSE
3 SWALLOWDALE
4 SHIREOAKS DR
5 LEAHURST CL
6 OTTERBURN CL

7 CALDERVALE DR
8 MAPLEDENE CL
9 SPINNEYFIELDS
10 ELMSTONE CL

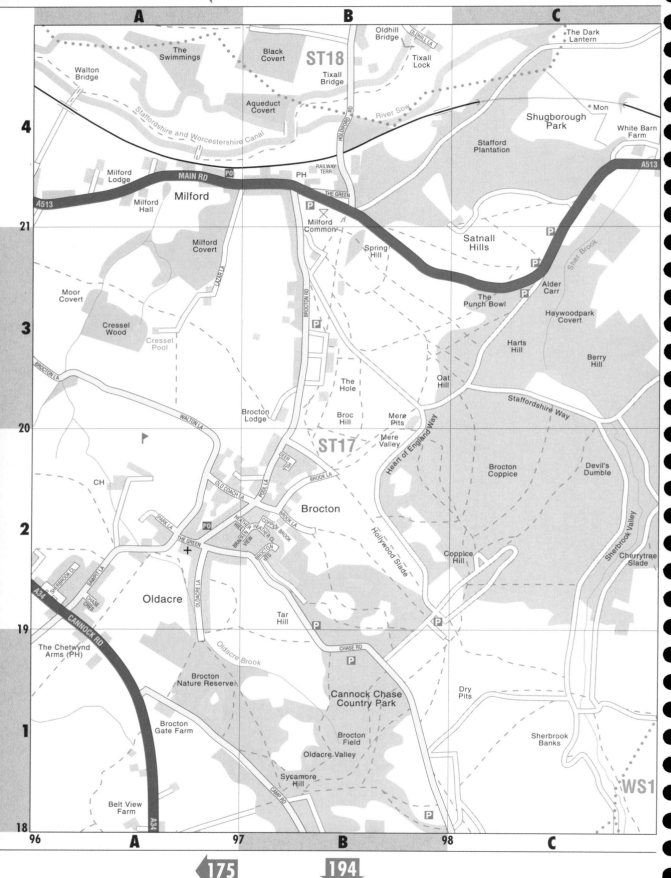
A   B   C

Oldhill Bridge
Tixall Lock
OLDHILL LA
The Dark Lantern

The Swimmings
Black Covert
ST18
Tixall Bridge
Mon
Shugborough Park
White Barn Farm

Walton Bridge
Aqueduct Covert
River Sow
Stafford Plantation

Staffordshire and Worcestershire Canal

4

A513
Milford Lodge
MAIN RD
Milford
PO
PH
RAILWAY TERR
THE GREEN
A513

Milford Hall
Milford Common
P
Satnall Hills
P

21

Milford Covert
Spring Hill
P
Alder Carr
Sher Brook

Moor Covert
P
The Punch Bowl
Haywoodpark Covert

Cressel Wood
Harts Hill
Berry Hill

3

BROCTON RD
LOCKAR LA

Cressel Pool
BROCTON LA

WALTON LA
Brocton Lodge
P
The Hole
Broc Hill
Oat Hill
Staffordshire Way

20

CH
DEER HILL
ST17
Mere Pits
Mere Valley
Heart of England Way
Brocton Coppice
Devil's Dumble

OLD COACH LA
POOL LA
BROOK LA
Brocton

PARK LA
THE GREEN
HEATHER HILL
HEATHER VIEW
COPPICE BROOK
BRACKEN
BROCTON PITS

2

SHERBROOK CL
SAWPIT LA
+
Hollywood Slade
Coppice Hill
Sherbrook Valley
Cherrytree Slade

A34
CHASE CRES
Oldacre
OLDACRE LA
Tar Hill
P

19

CANNOCK RD
Oldacre Brook
CHASE RD
P

The Chetwynd Arms (PH)
Brocton Nature Reserve
P
Dry Pits
Sherbrook Banks

1

Brocton Gate Farm
Cannock Chase Country Park
Brocton Field
Oldacre Valley
WS1

Belt View Farm
A34
Sycamore Hill
CAMP RD
P

18

96   97   B   98   C
A

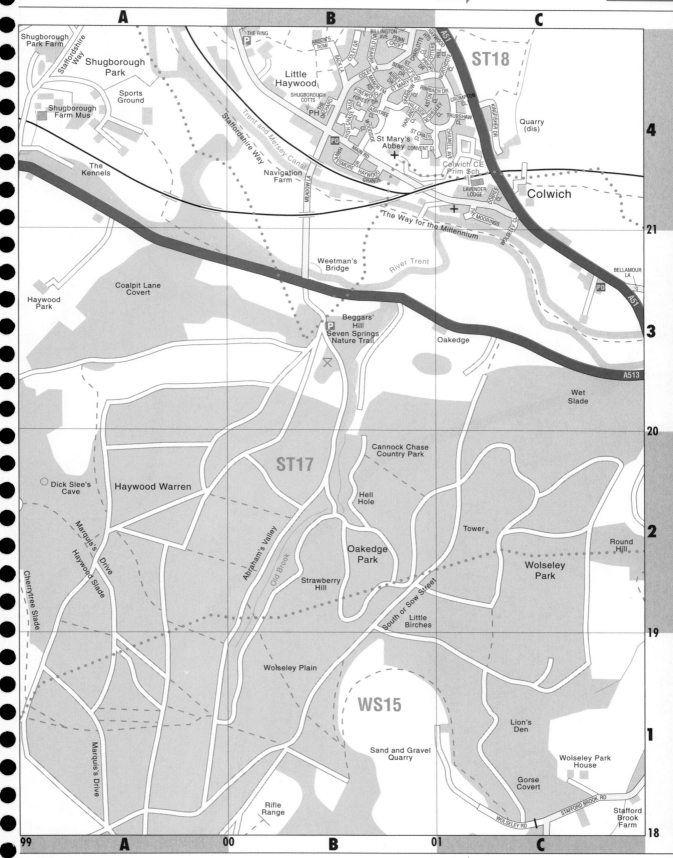

177 159

A | B | C

4

Bishton Farm

ST18

Bishton Lane Farm

Moreton Lane

Lount Farm

Hamley Cottage Farm

Hamleyheath

MOOR LA

Bellamour

B5013

21

Wilmour Farm

Bishton
Bishton Hall
St Bedes Sch

The Taft

Taft Bridge

BELLAMOUR LA

Colwich Lodge

Bellamour Lodge Farm

Boughey Hall Farm

St Mary's CE Prim Sch

SCHOOL LA

BELLAMOUR LA

COACHMAN'S WLK

3

A51

A513

PH

Wolseley Garden Park

ST17

Trent and Mersey Canal

Staffordshire Way

Wharf Cottage

WS15

Chapel Hill

Sewage Works

Long Covert

Stafford Brook

River Trent

Pumping Station

COLTON RD

Rydal Estate

2

THE BEECHES
THE BEECHES

SHUGBOROUGH RD

Allen Birt Wlk

ALBANY DR

BRINDLEY
BANK RD

The Way for the Millennium

RUGELEY

Rugeley Trent Valley

Bower House

HIGHLAND WAY

COCKETT
DALWELL
RISE

WILLIAM
MORRIS

SPRINGFIELDS RD

WATSON

OLD FELTON RD
MERSEY RD

ORCHARD

Trent Valley Trad Est

COLTON RD

19

CRESTWOOD

FINCHES HILL

PINE VIEW

ROSE WAY

GORSEY BARN
WAY

CATKIN WLK

BRACKEN WAY

Sch

CHAPELSIDE

ARTHUR
WOOD PL

SCHOOL RD

FERNWOOD
DR

PORTOBELLO

SWALLOW CL

A51

WOLSELEY RD

Playing Field

RISWORTH
RD

LEYLAND DR

BISHOPS GRANGE

COLTON RD

HORSESHOE DR 1
HUTCHINSON CL 2
DAFFODIL WLK 3
LANSDOWNE WAY 4
HURSTBOURNE CL 5
REDMOND CL 6

ANTLER
CDR

PENK DR

WAVERLEY
GDNS

Pump Lane

LANEHEAD
WLK

URFIELD WAY

MOSS GN

JOSEPH DIX DR

SPEECHLEY

CAMPBELL

CHADSFIELD
RD

OLD CHANCE
RD

DEANERY

CHURCHFIELD
CL

STATION RD

Boston Ind Est

RIVERSIDE

P

CHURCH LA

STAG
BRIDGE

THISTLE CL

DAYTON CL

MELROSE
DR

HAWTHORNE

GREEN CL

Sch

WILSON
KEYS CT

Power Station Rd Ind Est

1

Etchinghill

STAFFORD BROOK RD

ETCHING HILL RD

OAKFIELD CL

HENLEY GRANGE

MOUNT RD

WHITWORTH

RUTHERGLEN

CHERWOOD

BAYSWATER RD

BURNFIELD
DR

GREENFIELDS DR

JUBILEE
RD

WESTERN SPRINGS RD

FORTESQUE LA

JOHN ST

VARDEN
CT

Aelfgar
Ho

TA
Ctr

LATROK

P

P

ANSON ST

Liby

P

Ct

TANNERY CL

LEATHERMILL LA

SHOOTING BUTTS RD

WEST BUTTS RD

EAST BUTTS RD

OAKWOOD

CHASELEY RD

STONEHOUSE RD

KELVEDON

RIDER'S WAY

BRINKHURN

THE OAKLANS

BRIAR
WAY

BRAMBLE
WAY

MORLAND

PARK VIEW TERR

GARDEN
VIEW

FRANK BEE

GREEN LA

Aelfgar
Inf Sch

Sheep Fair

ELMORE LA

BOW ST

BEES LA

VICARS CROFT

Sneydlands

18

PENKRIDGE BANK

STEPPING STONES

HAGLEY RD

BANK TOP

CROSSLEY
STONE

ALBION ST

A51

B5013

02 | A | 03 | B | 04 | C

177 196

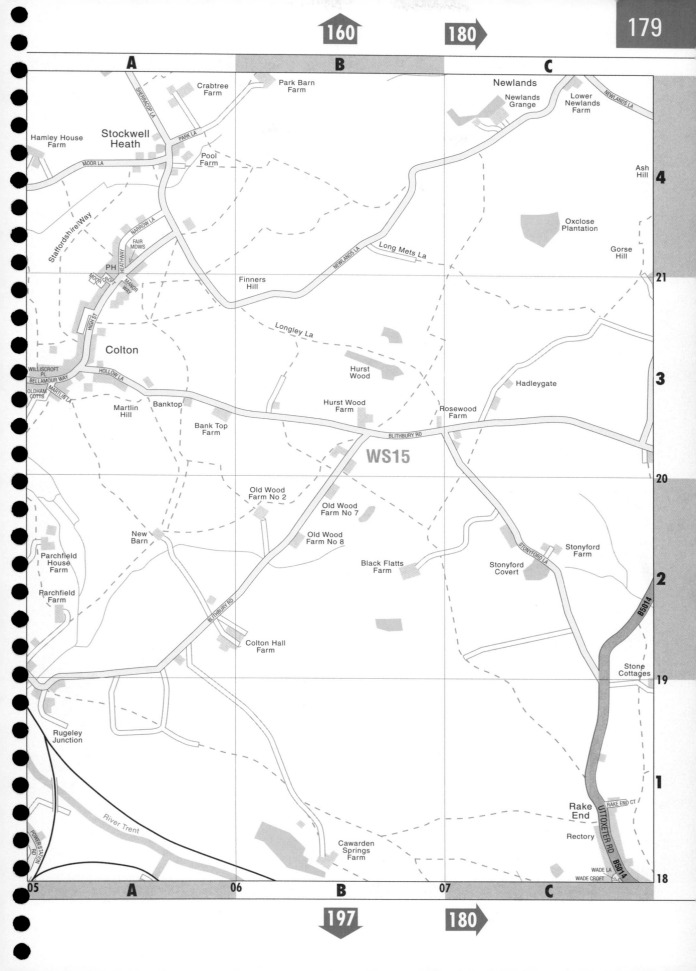

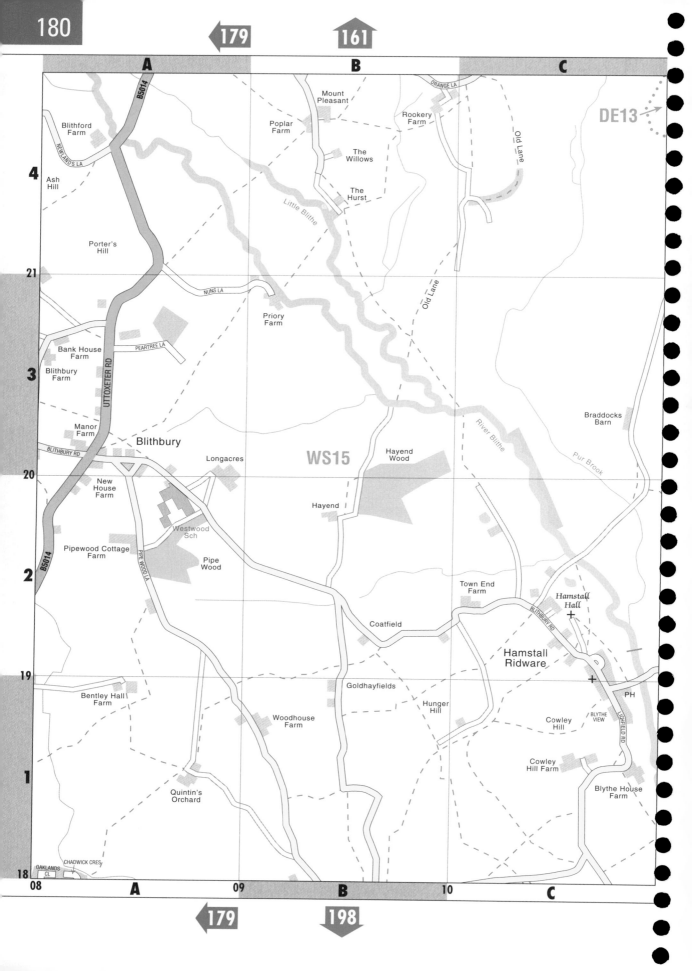

179
161

A   **B**   **C**

DE13

ORANGE LA

Mount
Pleasant

Rookery
Farm

Poplar
Farm

Blithford
Farm

Old Lane

The Willows

4

Ash
Hill

The
Hurst

Little Blithe

NEWLANDS LA

B5014

Porter's
Hill

Old Lane

21

NUNS LA

Priory
Farm

Bank House
Farm

PEARTREE LA

Braddocks
Barn

3

Blithbury
Farm

UTTOXETER RD

River Blithe

Pur Brook

Manor
Farm

BLITHBURY RD

Blithbury

Longacres

WS15

Hayend
Wood

20

New
House
Farm

Hayend

Town End
Farm

Hamstall
Hall

BLITHBURY RD

Westwood
Sch

PIPE WOOD LA

Pipewood Cottage
Farm

Pipe
Wood

Coatfield

Hamstall
Ridware

2

B5014

Goldhayfields

PH

19

Bentley Hall
Farm

Hunger
Hill

Cowley
Hill

BLYTHE
VIEW

LICHFIELD RD

Woodhouse
Farm

Cowley
Hill Farm

1

Quintin's
Orchard

Blythe House
Farm

OAKLANDS
CL

CHADWICK CRES

18

08   **A**   09   **B**   10   **C**

179
198

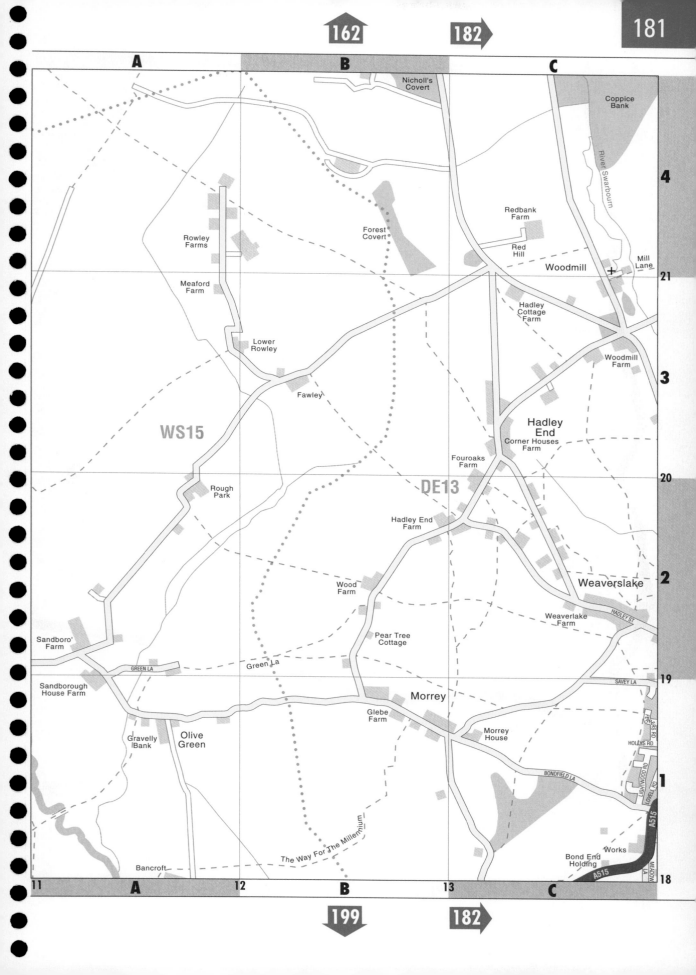

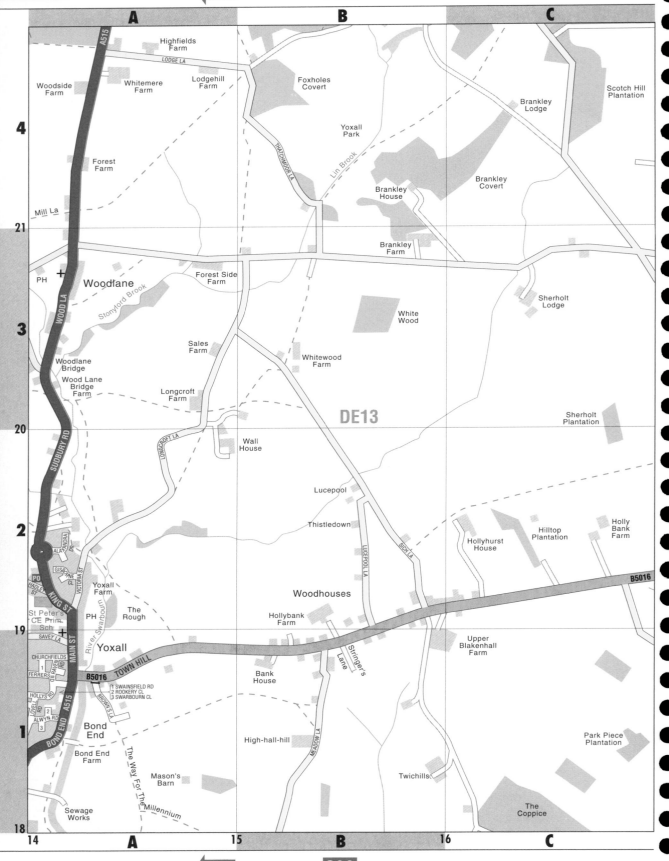

A B C

Highfields Farm

LODGE LA

Woodside Farm

Whitemere Farm

Lodgehill Farm

Foxholes Covert

Brankley Lodge

Scotch Hill Plantation

4

Yoxall Park

Forest Farm

THATCHMOOR LA

Lin Brook

Brankley House

Brankley Covert

Mill La

21

Brankley Farm

PH

Woodlane

Forest Side Farm

Sherholt Lodge

Stonyford Brook

White Wood

3

WOOD LA

Sales Farm

Whitewood Farm

Woodlane Bridge

Wood Lane Bridge Farm

Longcroft Farm

Sherholt Plantation

SUDBURY RD

DE13

20

LONGCROFT LA

Wall House

Lucepool

Sherholt Plantation

Thistledown

Hilltop Plantation

Holly Bank Farm

Hollyhurst House

LUCEPOOL LA

SICH LA

2

ALEXANDRA DR

GISBORNE CL

VICTORIA ST

B5016

PO

Yoxall Farm

Woodhouses

HADLEY ST

KING ST

The Rough

Hollybank Farm

Upper Blakenhall Farm

St Peter's CE Prim Sch

PH

Stringer's Lane

SAVEY LA

River Swarbourn

MAIN ST

19

Yoxall

TOWN HILL

CHURCHFIELDS

FERRERS RD

OLD RD

RAVEN RD

Bank House

MEADOW LA

HOLLYS RD

B5016

1 SWAINSFIELD RD
2 ROOKERY CL
3 SWARBOURN CL

LODGE RD

ALWYN RD

BROWNS CL

1

Bond End

High-hall-hill

Park Piece Plantation

Bond End Farm

The Way For The

Mason's Barn

Twichills

Sewage Works

Millennium

The Coppice

18

14 A 15 B 16 C

B5016

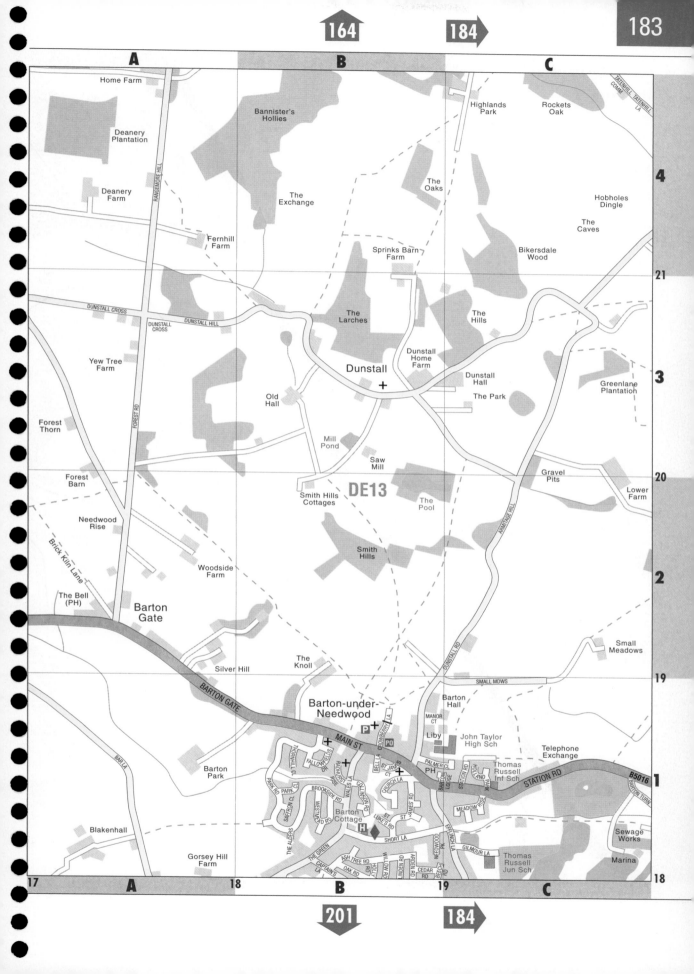

Home Farm

Deanery Plantation

Deanery Farm

Fernhill Farm

RANGEMORE HILL

Bannister's Hollies

The Exchange

Highlands Park

Rockets Oak

TATENHILL TATENHILL COMM
TATENHILL LA

The Oaks

Hobholes Dingle

The Caves

Sprinks Barn Farm

Bikersdale Wood

DUNSTALL CROSS

DUNSTALL HILL

Dunstall Cross

Yew Tree Farm

The Larches

Dunstall

The Hills

Dunstall Home Farm

Dunstall Hall

Greenlane Plantation

FOREST RD

Old Hall

The Park

Forest Thorn

Mill Pond

Saw Mill

Smith Hills Cottages

DE13

Gravel Pits

Lower Farm

Forest Barn

Needwood Rise

The Pool

ARMITAGE HILL

Brick Kiln Lane

Woodside Farm

Smith Hills

The Bell (PH)

Barton Gate

Small Meadows

Silver Hill

The Knoll

DUNSTALL RD

SMALL MDWS

SMALL MDWS

BARTON GATE

Barton-under-Needwood

Barton Hall

Manor Ct

Liby

John Taylor High Sch

Telephone Exchange

BAR LA

Barton Park

MAIN ST

P

PO

PALMER CL

PH

Thomas Russell Inf Sch

STATION RD

STATION RD

B5016

BARTON TURN

Blakenhall

Barton Cottage

H

SHORT LA

Meadow Rise

NEEDWOOD PK

Sewage Works

Gorsey Hill Farm

THE ALDERS

THE GREEN

CAPTAIN'S LA

ASH TREE RD

OAK RD

HOLLY

WILLOW RD

LINDEN

ARDEN RD

CEDAR RD

BEECH

GILMOUR LA

EFFLINCH LA

Thomas Russell Jun Sch

Marina

183
165

A B C

DARK LA
Tatenhill
PH
MAIN ST
Manor
Farm
CORONATION
COTTS
MANOR
CROFT
TATENHILL LA
THE GROVE
Yews
Bridge
THE WOODLANDS
Lawns Farm
Cottage
BRANSTON RD
Branston
Lock
A38
SECOND AVE
WELLINGTON RD
A5121
EIGHTH AVE
SPRING RD
CLEWLEY RD
WARWICK RD
HARCOURT RD
Bean's
Covert
ELM CT

4

Robinson's
Plantation
Brookfields
Farm
Branston
Bridge
PH
TATENHILL LA
Branston
LYNWOOD
CL
LYNWOOD RD
MERLIN CRES
HARWOOD AVE
FESTIVAL RD
CLAYS LA
COTSWOLD RD
MAPLE WAY
BRIDGEFORD AVE
CHERRY
FENTWELL RD
LINGFIELD
RD
WETHERBY CT
LEAMINGTON RD
SEDGEFIELD
RD
EPSOM RD
Branston
A5121
B5108
MAIN ST
BURTON
RD
WARREN LA
LANSDOWNE
RD
B5108

Rykneld
Prim Sch
PO
COURT
FARM LA
MAIN ST
OLD RD
CHURCH RD
OLD RD
BRAMELL
RIVERSIDE DR
Hotel

21

HAYTHOCK WAY
WOODBINE WAY

Branston
Water Park

DE14

Nature
Reserve

3

Tatenhill
Lock
The Way for the Millennium
Trent & Mersey Canal
Works
Gallow
Bridge
Ppg Sta

Black Meadow
Wood

20

Works
Works
Works
DE13
Gorse
Hall
LICHFIELD RD
DE15
Drakelow
Power Station

2

Gorsehall
Plantation
Works
River Trent
DE15

Newbold Manor
Farm
Tucklesholme
Farm
Sewage
Works
Warren Farm
Warren
Hill

19

Graycar
Bsns
Pk
Walton
Bridge
DE12

1

B5016
STATION RD
Motel
Rylance
Farm
Graycar
Bsns
Pk
Barr
Hall
Walton-on-Trent
WHARF
HOS
BARTON TURN
B5016
Barton
Turn
STATION LA
RIVERSIDE
MEWIES CL
Inn
P
LADLE END
PO
MAIN ST
BELLS END RD
ORCHARD
COTON RD
LEEDHAMS
CROFT
HARBIN RD

18

A38

20 21 22

A B C

183
202

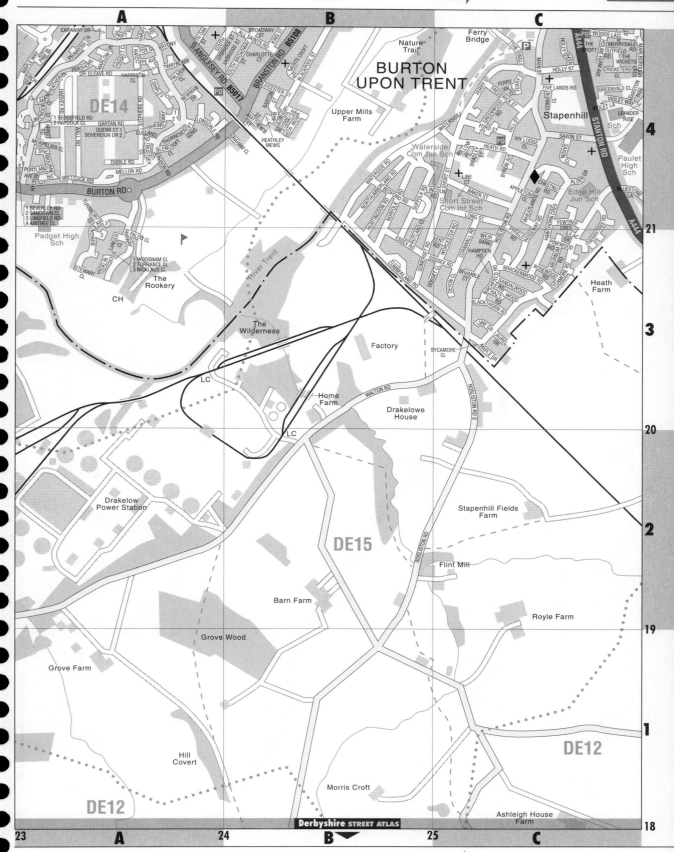

A B C

BURTON
UPON TRENT

DE14

Stapenhill

4

Padget High
Sch

21

The Rookery

CH

The
Wilderness

3

Factory

Heath
Farm

Home
Farm

Drakelowe
House

20

DE15

Drakelow
Power Station

Stapenhill Fields
Farm

2

Flint Mill

Barn Farm

Royle Farm

19

Grove Wood

Grove Farm

1

DE12

Hill
Covert

DE12

Morris Croft

Ashleigh House
Farm

18

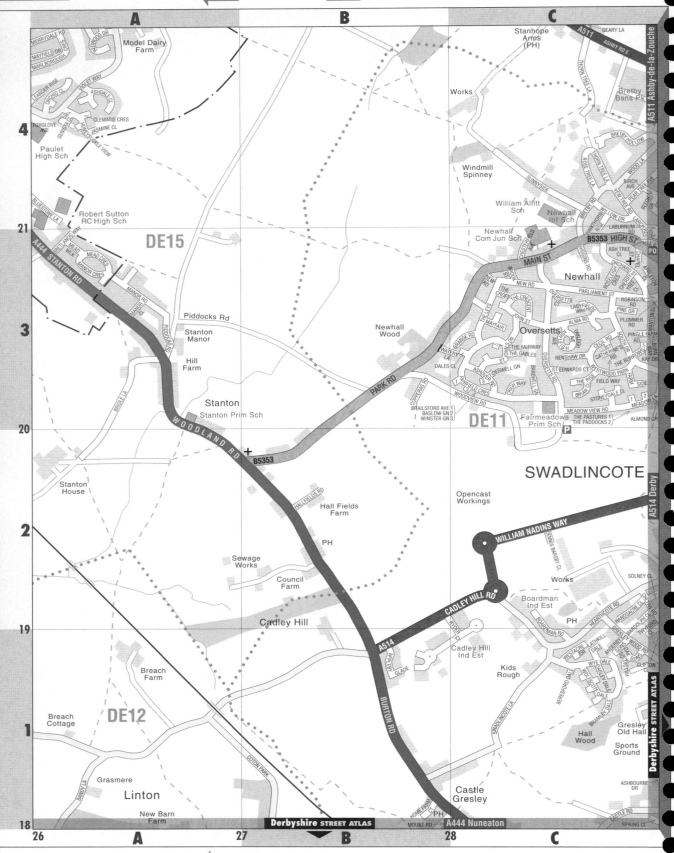

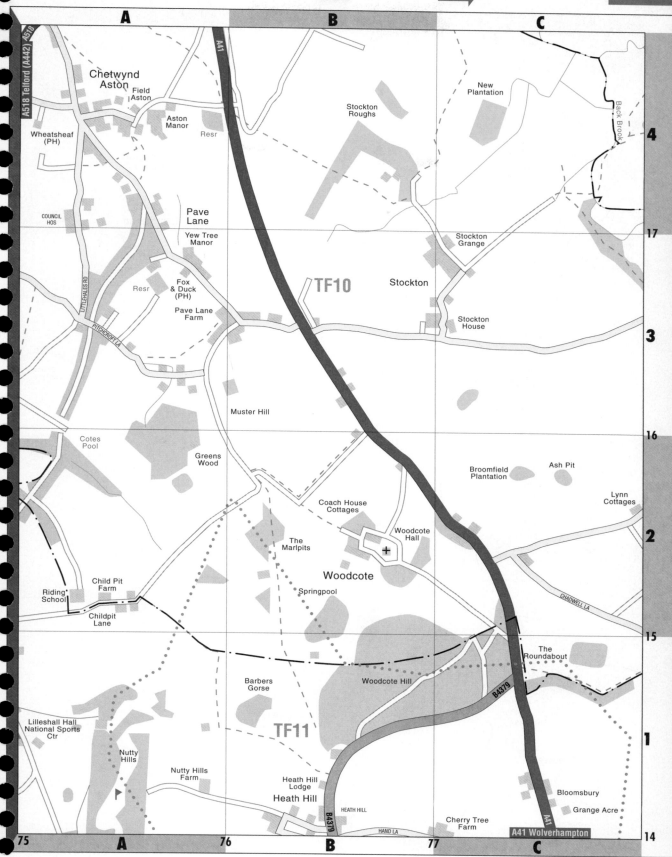

A   B   C

A518 Telford (A442) A518

Chetwynd Aston

Field Aston

Aston Manor

Resr

Wheatsheaf (PH)

COUNCIL HOS

LITTLEHALES RD

Pave Lane

Yew Tree Manor

Resr

Fox & Duck (PH)

Pave Lane Farm

PITCHCROFT LA

Muster Hill

Cotes Pool

Greens Wood

Child Pit Farm

Riding School

Childpit Lane

Lilleshall Hall National Sports Ctr

Nutty Hills

Nutty Hills Farm

Heath Hill Lodge

Heath Hill

B4379

HEATH HILL

HAND LA

The Marlpits

Barbers Gorse

Coach House Cottages

Springpool

Woodcote

Woodcote Hall

Woodcote Hill

TF11

A41

TF10

Stockton Roughs

New Plantation

Back Brook

Stockton Grange

Stockton

Stockton House

Broomfield Plantation

Ash Pit

Lynn Cottages

CHADWELL LA

The Roundabout

B4379

Cherry Tree Farm

A41 Wolverhampton

Bloomsbury

Grange Acre

4

17

3

16

2

15

1

14

75   A   76   B   77   C

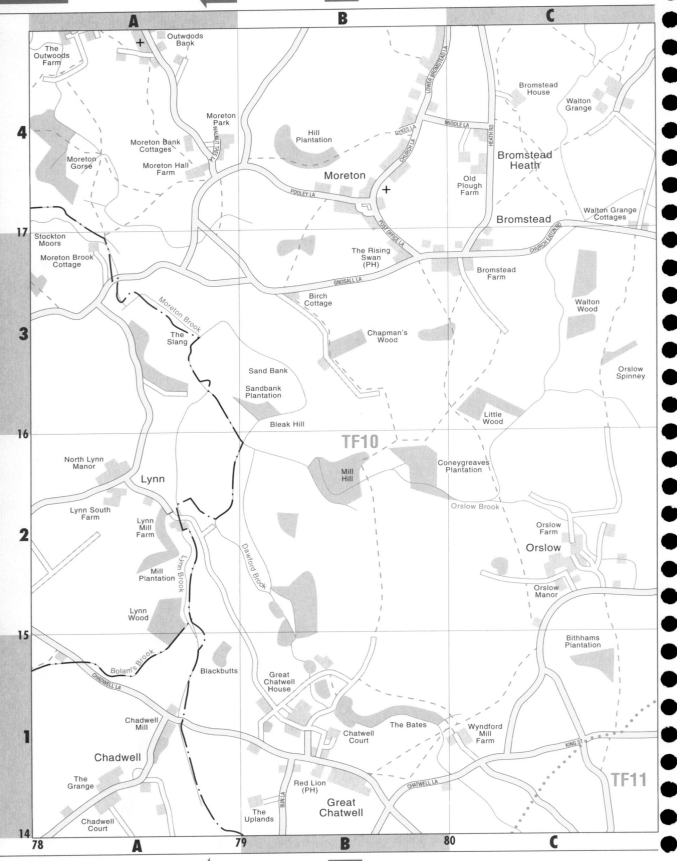

187
170

A
B
C

The Outwoods Farm
Outwoods Bank

Moreton Park

Moreton Bank Cottages
Moreton Hall Farm
Moreton Gorse

WALNUT TREE LA

Hill Plantation

LOWER BROMSTEAD LA
DYKES LA
CHURCH LA
MIDDLE LA
HEATH RD

Bromstead House
Walton Grange

Moreton

POOLEY LA
Old Plough Farm

Bromstead Heath

4

Stockton Moors
Moreton Brook Cottage

POST OFFICE LA

The Rising Swan (PH)

Bromstead

Walton Grange Cottages

CHURCH EATON RD

17

Moreton Brook

GNOSALL LA
Birch Cottage
Bromstead Farm
Walton Wood

The Slang

Chapman's Wood

Orslow Spinney

3

Sand Bank
Sandbank Plantation
Bleak Hill
Little Wood

16

North Lynn Manor

TF10

Lynn
Mill Hill
Coneygreaves Plantation

Lynn South Farm
Lynn Mill Farm

Orslow Brook

Orslow Farm

Orslow

2

Mill Plantation

Lynn Brook

Dawford Brook

Orslow Manor

Lynn Wood

15

Bithhams Plantation

Bolam's Brook
CHADWELL LA
Blackbutts
Great Chatwell House

Chadwell Mill

The Bates
Wyndford Mill Farm

KING ST

1

Chadwell
Chatwell Court
Red Lion (PH)
Great Chatwell
CHATWELL LA
TF11

The Grange
BUN LA
The Uplands

Chadwell Court

14

78
A
79
B
80
C

187
203

A
B
C

The Hall
Farm

Barlands La

Goosemoor

INTAKE LA

Daisybank
Plantation

4

Bank
Cottage

Intake
Plantation

Turnover Bridge
Plantation

Homers
Farm

JOAN EATON'S
CROSS

Shropshire Union Canal

17

Walton
Fields

CHURCH EATON RD

Taylor's
Plantation

High Onn
Wharf Farm

High Onn
Bridge

Stoney
Plantation

St Edith's
Well

3

High Onn
Wood

High
Onn

TF10

High
Onn
Manor

Hollowdine
Pits

16

ST20

The Home
Farm

Little
Onn

Rail Pit
Plantation

The Uplands

Little Onn
Hall

Keeper's
Cottage

Tinker
Pits

2

Calvescroft
Plantation

Gorse
Covert

15

Airfield
(dis)

SWEETPLACE LA

KING ST

Marston Brook

1

TF11

New House
Farm

BIRCHMOOR LA

Marston
Farm

Elm Tree
Farm

Burnt
Witheys

Aquamoor

Fox Inn
(PH)

14

81
A
82
B
83
C

A **B** **C**

BROAD LA

Brookhouse
Farm

Wood
Eaton

Barlands
La

INTAKE LA

Church
Eaton

ST EDITHA'S
CT

Church Eaton
Prim Sch

ALLEYS LA

WOOD EATON RD

ASHLEY
ASHCROFT

HIGH ST

SWAN CT

SMITHY
CROFT

CO. RD

PARKERS CL.

MALTHOUSE LA

PH

THE DINCROFTS

4

LITTLE ONN RD

Barton
Covert

ALSTONE LA

Middle
Covert

Greenfields
Farm

Church Eaton
Common

Church Eaton
Green

ST18

17

Green
Farm

Shredicote
Wood

ST20

Park Hall
Farm

Stafford La

Church Eaton Brook

3

Woollaston
Farm

Red House
Farm

Wollaston
Cottages

16

Rusty
Pits

Woollaston

Shropshire Union Canal

Bagnallditch

Upper
Woollaston
Covert

2

Airfield
(disused)

Ryehill
Bridge

SLAB LA

Little
Onn
Gorse

Longnor Gorse
Farm

Gorse La

Mitton Lodge
Farm

15

Port
Coppice

The
Rookery

Barn
Cottage

ST19

1

Shushions
Manor

Wheaton Aston Brook

Longnor
Hall

Longnor Brook

Longnor

Stonyford
Bridge

14
84 **A** 85 **B** 86 **C**

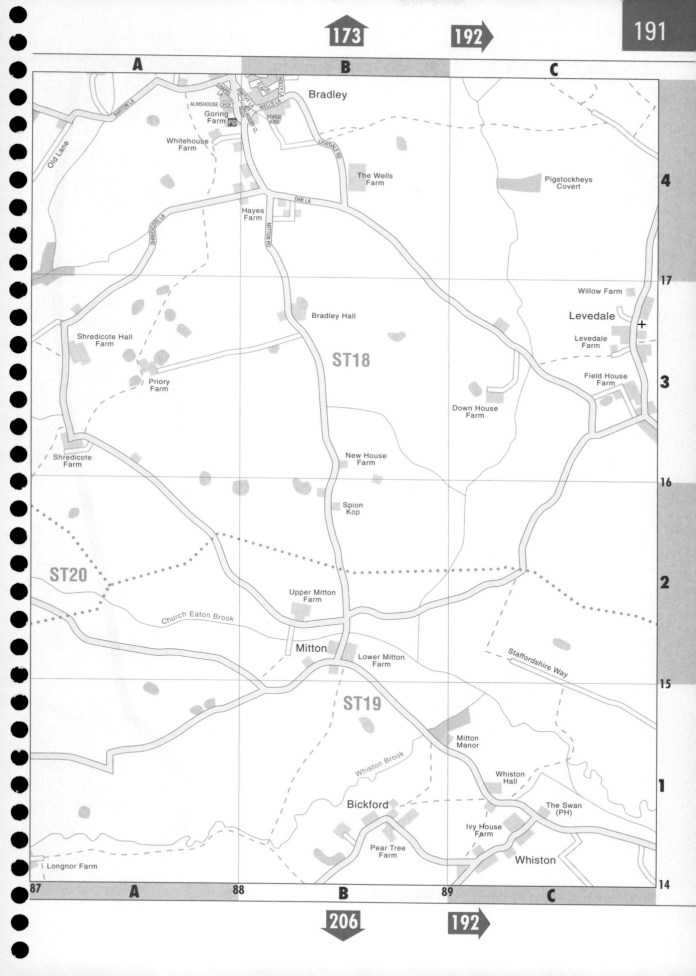

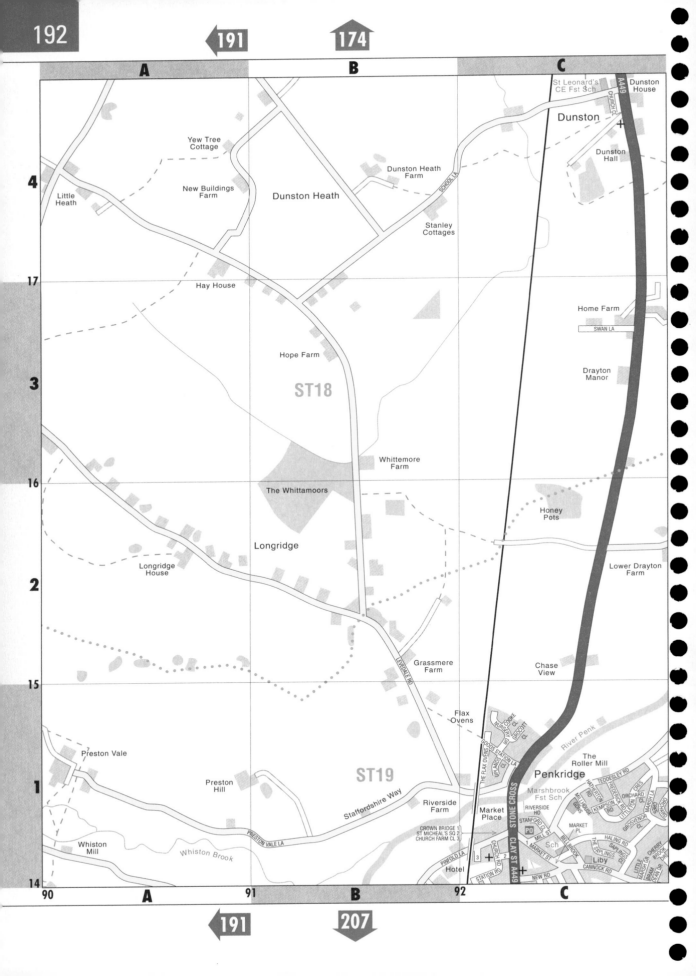

191
174

A   B   C

St Leonard's CE Fst Sch

Dunston House

Dunston

A449

CHURCH CL

Yew Tree Cottage

Dunston Hall

Dunston Heath Farm

New Buildings Farm

Dunston Heath

4

Little Heath

Stanley Cottages

SCHOOL LA

Home Farm

SWAN LA

17

Hay House

Drayton Manor

Hope Farm

3

ST18

Whittemore Farm

The Whittamoors

Honey Pots

16

Lower Drayton Farm

Longridge

Longridge House

2

Chase View

15

Grassmere Farm

LEVEDALE RD

Flax Ovens

River Penk

Preston Vale

THE FLAX OVENS

GOODS STATION LA

NURSERY RD

CROOKE CL

UPLANDS CL

GROCOTT CL

The Roller Mill

Penkridge

TEDDESLEY RD

Preston Hill

1

ST19

Staffordshire Way

Riverside Farm

Market Place

Marshbrook Fst Sch

RIVERSIDE HO

STANFORD CL

MILL ST

HATHERTON

MITHORNE

FREDERICK CL

LITTLETON

ORCHARD CL

GROSVENOR CL

MARSH LA

KEMPSON RD

HALING CL

STONE CROSS

CLAY ST A449

PO

MARKET PL

THE SAPLINGS

Whiston Mill

PRESTON VALE LA

CROWN BRIDGE 1
ST MICHEAL'S SQ 2
CHURCH FARM CL 3

PINFOLD LA

Hotel

CHURCH ST

MARSH ST

MARKET ST

BELBROOK

Sch

BRAM DR

DEAN DR

LITTLE

CHERRY BROOK

NEW RD

CANNOCK RD

Liby

Whiston Brook

14

90   A   91   B   92   C

191
207

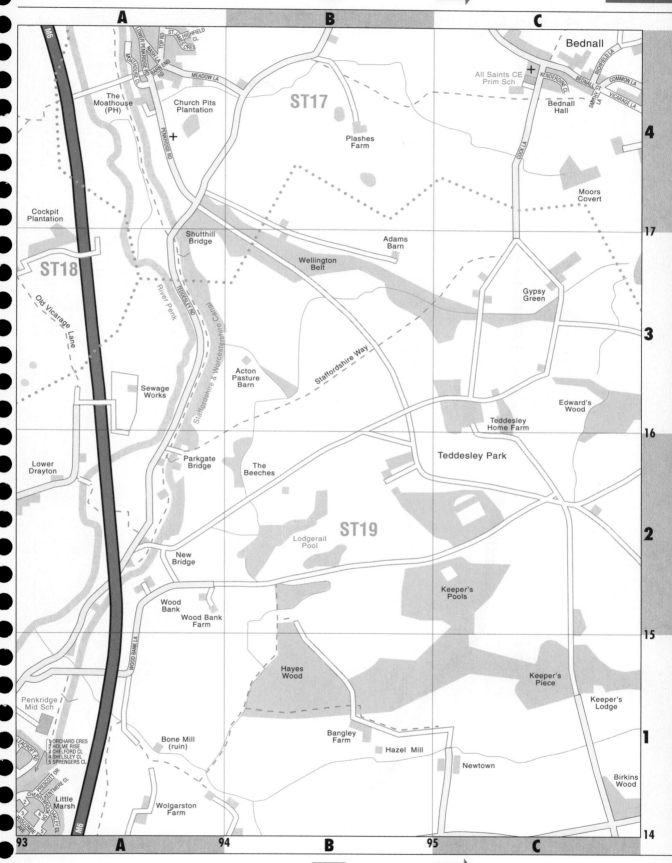

A B C

Bednall

Richfield La
Common La
Vicarage La
Bednall Ct
Smith La
Kenderdine Ct
All Saints CE Prim Sch
Bednall Hall

Top Rd
St James Cres
Nash La
Highfield Cl
Lower Penkridge Rd
Moathouse Cl
Barn End
MEADOW LA

The Moathouse (PH)
Church Pits Plantation

ST17

Plashes Farm

Penkridge Rd

Cockpit Plantation

Moors Covert

Shutthill Bridge

Adams Barn

Wellington Belt

ST18

River Penk

Teddesley Rd

Old Vicarage Lane

Staffordshire & Worcestershire Canal

Gypsy Green

Cock La

Acton Pasture Barn

Staffordshire Way

Sewage Works

Edward's Wood

Teddesley Home Farm

Parkgate Bridge

Lower Drayton

The Beeches

Teddesley Park

ST19

Lodgerail Pool

New Bridge

Keeper's Pools

Wood Bank

Wood Bank Farm

Wood Bank Rd

Hayes Wood

Keeper's Piece

Penkridge Mid Sch

1 ORCHARD CRES
2 HOLME RISE
3 CHELFORD CL
4 SHELSLEY CL
5 SPRENGERS CL

LEACROFT RD

Bone Mill (ruin)

Bangley Farm

Hazel Mill

Keeper's Lodge

Newtown

Birkins Wood

PRESCOTT DR
CHERRYBROOK DR
KENTMERE CL
OAKLEY CL
WISCOMBE AVE

Little Marsh

Wolgarston Farm

4

17

3

16

2

15

1

14

193
176

A   **B**   **C**

RICHFIELD LA

Staffordshire Way

JOYCE'S LA

Staffordshire Way

A34

VICARAGE LA

COMMON LA

Bednall Head

ST17

Bednall Head Farm

4

Bednall Belt Plantation

Womere

Brocton Field

WS15

CHASE RD

P

Heart of England Way

Bog Moor

Ansons Bank

P

Picnic Area

17

Bogmoor Farm

Spring Slade

Cannock Chase Country Park

Heart of England Way

Springslade Pool

Grenvilles's Wood

CAMP RD

P

Meml

3

Five Oak Hill Plantation

Dark Slade

Springslade Lodge

Mast

Vivian's Wood

Dark Slade Wood

Edward's Wood

WS12

16

Warren Plantation

Warren Hill

P

Cemy

Deer Slade

Badger Slade Wood

Cemy

2

Teddesley Park

Benty Hill Plantation

P

Badger Slade

PENKRIDGE BANK

Coppice Farm

Broadhurst Green

ST19

Bright's Plantation

Pottal Slade

BROADHURST GREEN RD

BROADHURST GN

Radio Twr

15

Pottal Valley

Gravel Pit

Great Horsenal Slade

Badger's Hills

PYE GREEN RD

BRINDLEY RD

1

Pottal Covert

Pottal Pool

STAFFORD RD A34

PLANTATION RD 1
SPRUCE RD 2
FISHER ST 3

Yew Tree Farm

Masts

Pye Green

14

96   **A**   **97**   **B**   **98**   **C**

193
209

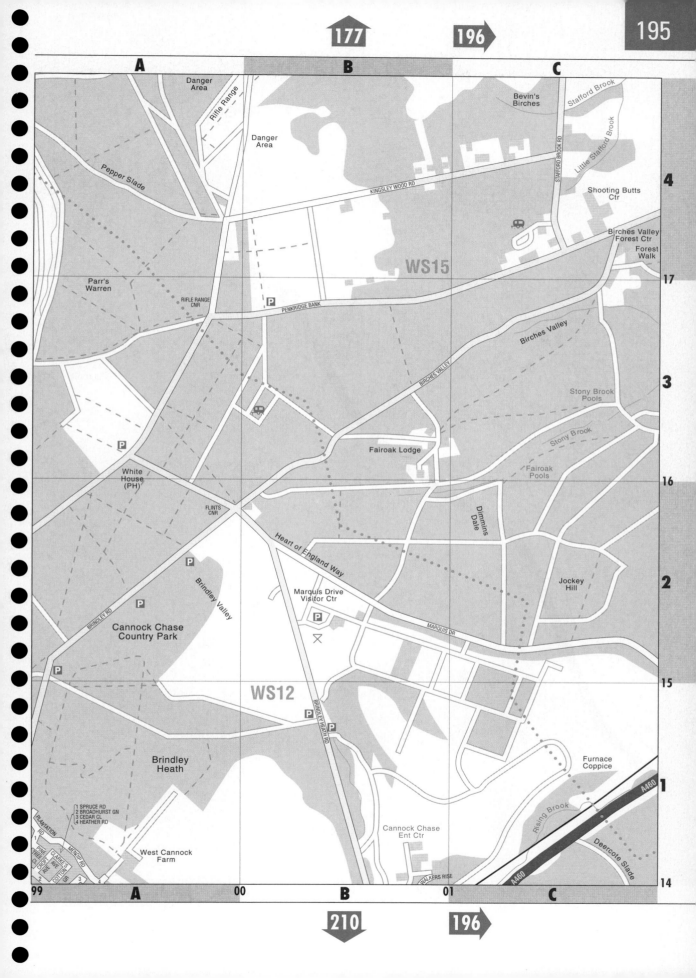

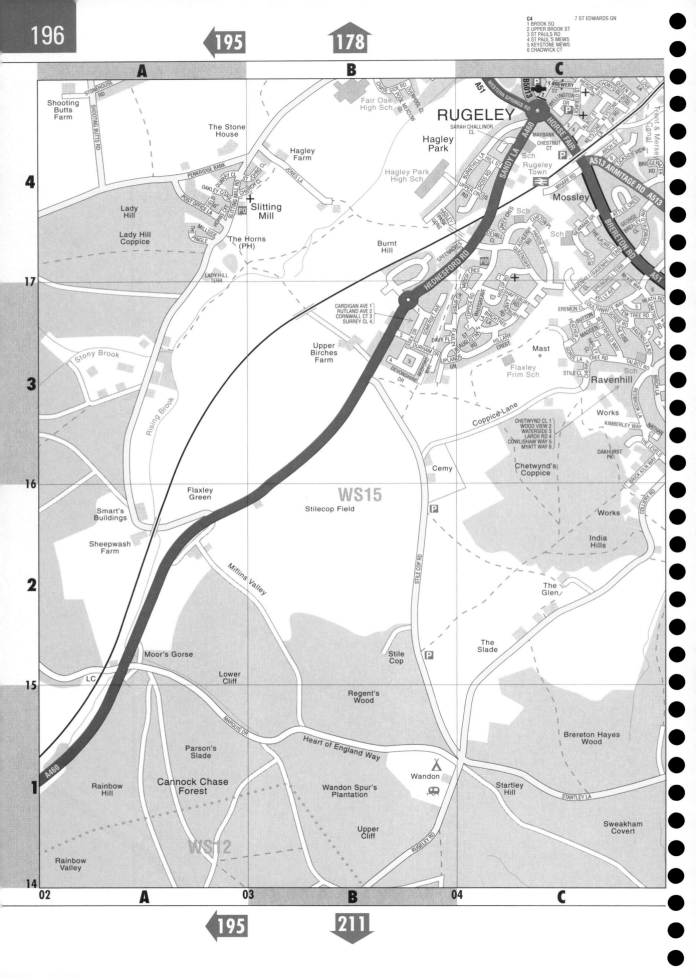

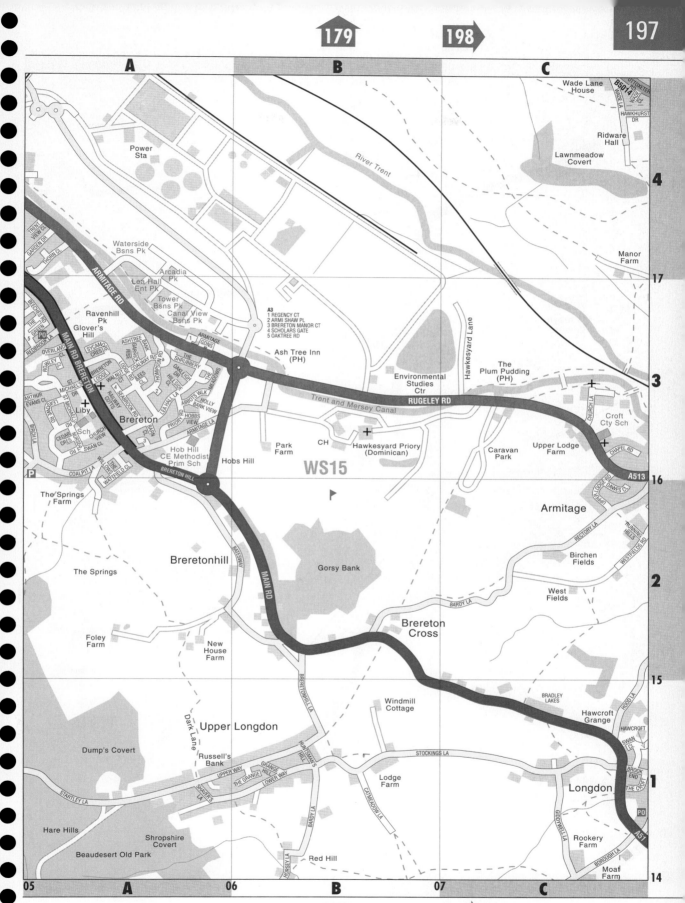

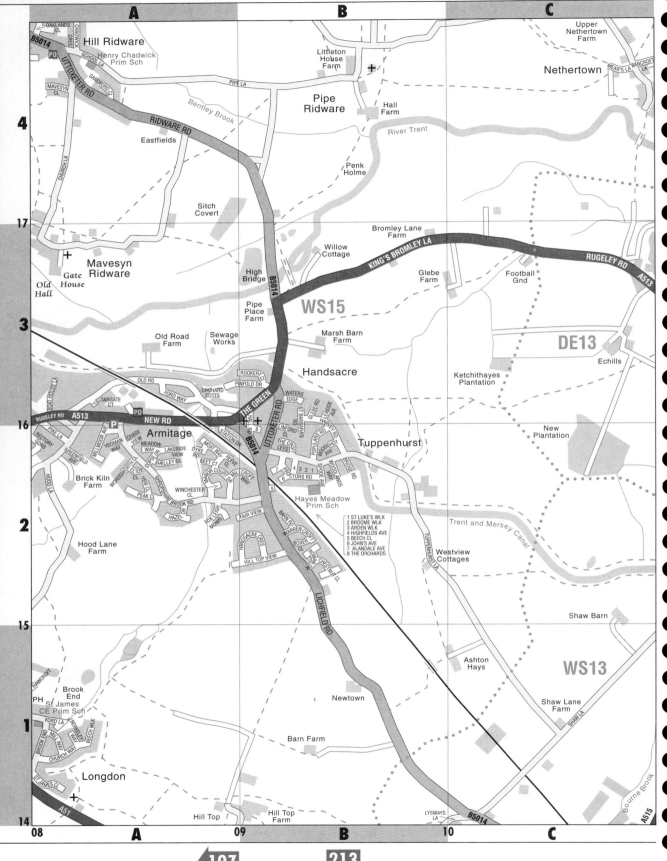

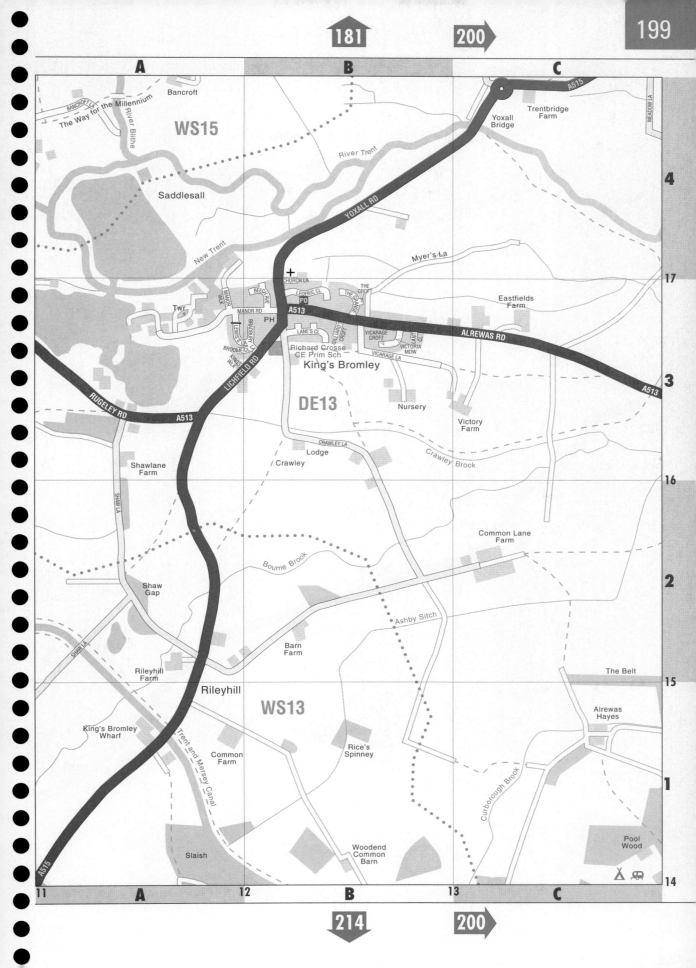

199
182

A   B   C

4

MEADOW LA

The Coppice

Parkhill
Plantation

The
Faggness

The Way for the Millennium

River Swarbourn

Wychnor
Park

The
Ashes

17

River Trent

Lodges

3

Lawn
Bank

A513

ALREWAS LA

DE13

Lupin
Farm

Lupin

Lupin
Farm

Orgreave

Orgreave
Hall

16

Overley
Farm

Wellfield
Farm

Lodge

Gas
Comp
Sta

Overley

STAFFOLD LA

COTON CL

Mill

2

CHURCH RD

Alrewas

MANOR RD

MILL END LA

Manor
Farm

BUTTS

MAYS
WLK

CL FT

THE
MOORINGS

MAIN ST

15

KINGS BROMLEY RD

Pyford Brook

PH

WALF...

CHASEVIEW RD

WALFIELD RD

CHURCHILL
CRES

Bagnall
Lock

NOON
CROFT

Trent and Mersey Canal

1

Alrewas Hayes
Cottages

Common
Lock

Bagnall

THE
CRICKETERS

MR KINS

DAISY LA

A513

OAKFIELD RD 1
SOMERVILLE RD 2

DAISY LA

Fradley
Resr

Hunt's
Lock

Keeper's
Lock

SALE LA

The Sale
Farm

WS13

LONG LA

Blackheath

PH

Lock

Sandy
Hill
Farm

COWHILL LA

14

14   A   15   B   16   C

199
215

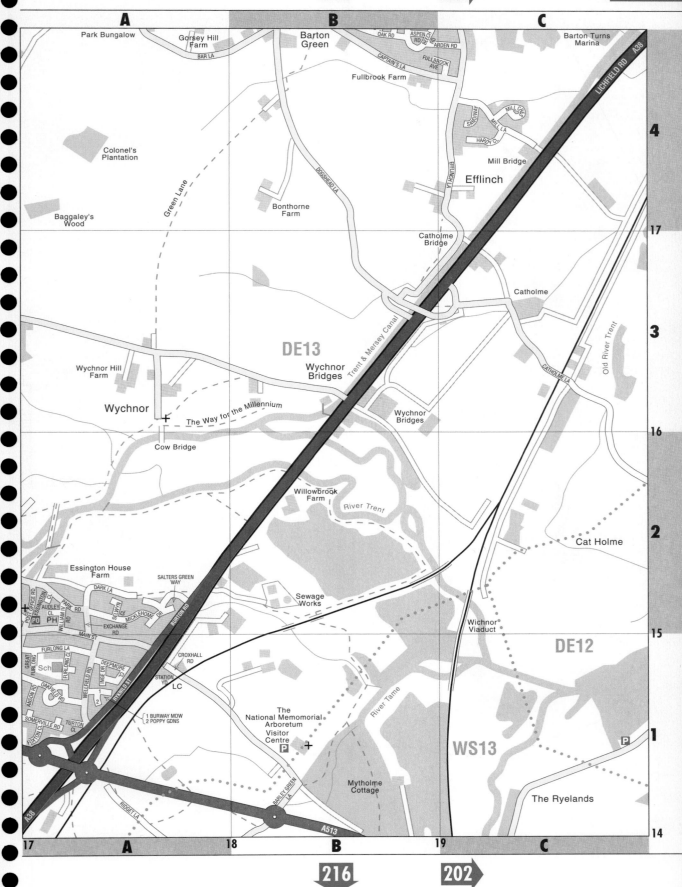

201
184

A **B** **C**

A38

LICHFIELD RD

LEEDHAMS CROFT

← BELLS END RD

Fairfield

Walton Hall

STANDING BUTTS CL

Walton-on-Trent CE Prim Sch

ROSLISTON RD

Fatholme Farm

Old Hall

The Dumps

Marlpit Spinney

Walton Hill Farm

Old Barn Farm

4

Borough Hill

Coppershill Spinney

17

Borough Holme

Ryelands Lodge

Walton Wood

COTGH RD

Oaklands Farm

River Trent

3

DE13

Sand and Gravel Pit

Borough Fields Farm

Ryelands Plantation

16

DE12

CATHOLME LA

Donkhill Cottages

Catton Farm Cottages

2

Cat Holme

The Rough

Catton Hall

Cherry Holme

Summerfields

King's Covert

15

Donkhill Plantation

Donkhill Farm

Mansditch Farm

Catton Park

Catton Wood

1

Croxall Wood

Pessall Brook

Pessall La

B79

Homestall Wood

14

20 **A** **21** **B** **22** **C**

201
217

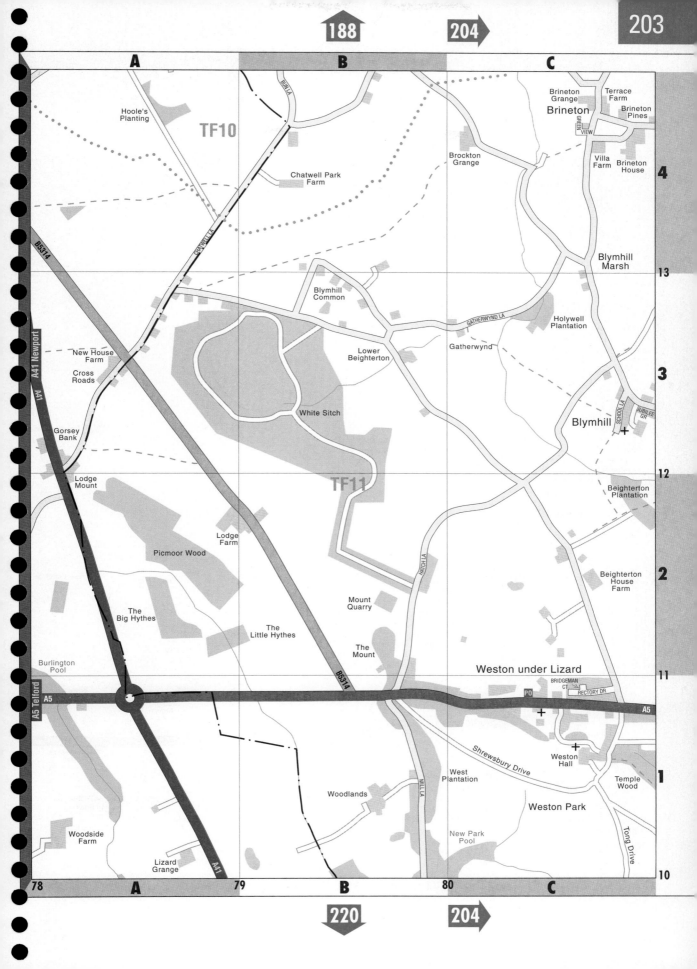

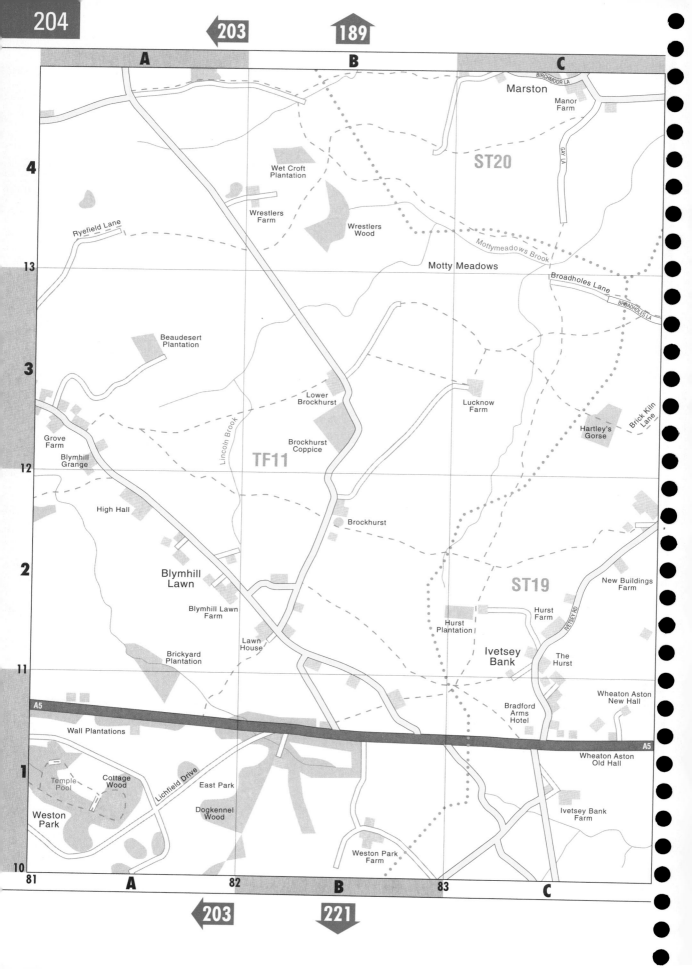

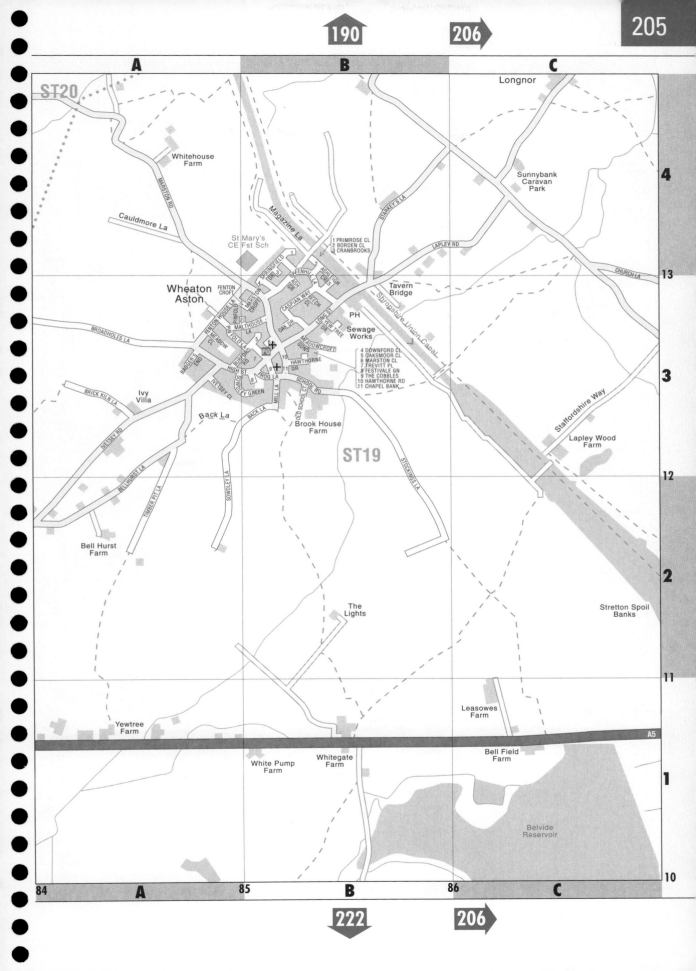

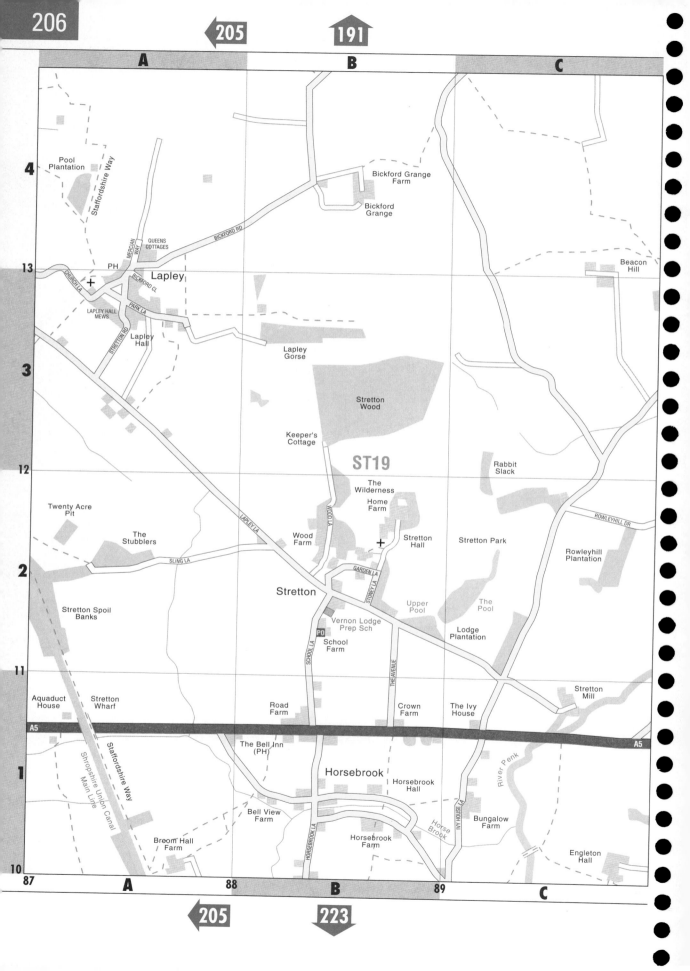

A B C

4

Pool Plantation

Staffordshire Way

Bickford Grange Farm

Bickford Grange

Beacon Hill

13

CHURCH LA

MERCIAN WAY

QUEENS COTTAGES

PH

BICKFORD RD

Lapley

BICKFORD CL

LAPLEY HALL MEWS

PARK LA

STRETTON RD

Lapley Hall

Lapley Gorse

3

Stretton Wood

Keeper's Cottage

ST19

12

Twenty Acre Pit

The Stubblers

LAPLEY LA

SLING LA

Wood Farm

WOOD LA

The Wilderness

Home Farm

Stretton Hall

Stretton Park

Rabbit Slack

ROWLEYHILL DR

Rowleyhill Plantation

2

Stretton Spoil Banks

Stretton

GARDEN LA

STONEY LA

Upper Pool

The Pool

Vernon Lodge Prep Sch

SCHOOL LA

PO

School Farm

THE AVENUE

Lodge Plantation

11

Aquaduct House

Stretton Wharf

Road Farm

Crown Farm

The Ivy House

Stretton Mill

A5

A5

Staffordshire Way

Shropshire Union Canal Main Line

1

The Bell Inn (PH)

Horsebrook

Horsebrook Hall

River Penk

IVY HOUSE LA

HORSEBROOK LA

Bell View Farm

Horse Brook

Bungalow Farm

Engleton Hall

Broom Hall Farm

Horsebrook Farm

10

87 A 88 B 89 C

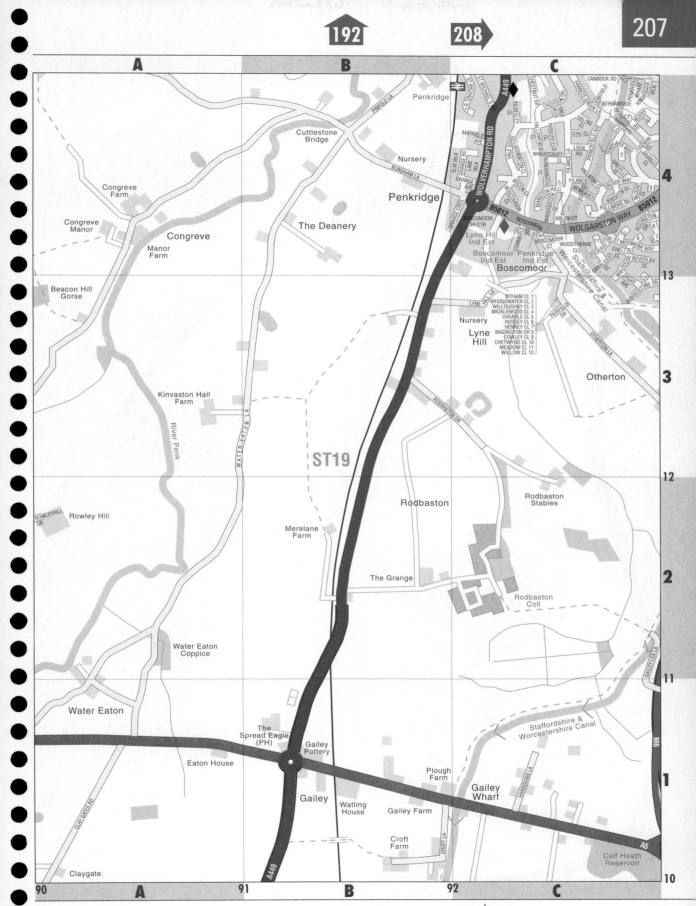

A B C

Penkridge

Cuttlestone
Bridge

Nursery

PINFOLD LA

BUNGHAM LA

Penkridge

4

Congreve
Farm

Congreve
Manor

Congreve

Manor
Farm

The Deanery

Beacon Hill
Gorse

WOLVERHAMPTON RD

A449

ST MICHAELS RD
ST PATRICKS RD

MAYFIELD
AVE

ELM WLK
LIME WLK
GRANGE RD

GRANGE
AVE

VALE GDNS

OTHERTON CL

GRANGE CRES

B5012

BOSCOMOOR
SH CTR

Lyne Hill
Ind Est

Boscomoor
Ind Est

Penkridge
Ind Est

Boscomoor

CHESTNUT DR

CROYDON
RISE

FALLOWFIELD

FRANCIS GREEN LA

CANNOCK RD

STREAMSIDE
CL

Sch

COMMERCE

B5012

BOSCOMOOR
CT

WOODTHORNE
CL

Staffordshire &
Worcestershire Canal

WOLGARSTON WAY

B5012

13

Nursery

Lyne
Hill

LYNE HILL LA

BITHAM CL 1
BRIDGEWATER CL 2
WILLOUGHBY CL 3
MICKLEWOOD CL 4
CHEADLE CL 5
HUSSEY CL 6
HENNEY CL 7
NAGINGTON DR 8
COWLEY CL 9
CHETWYND CL 10
MEADOW CL 11
WILLOW CL 12

FAIRFIELD
DR

OTHERTON LA

Otherton

3

Kinvaston Hall
Farm

WATER EATON LA

River Penk

RODBASTON DR

ST19

12

Rowleyhill
ROWLEYHILL
DR

Rowley Hill

Merelane
Farm

Rodbaston

Rodbaston
Stables

Rodbaston
Coll

2

The Grange

Water Eaton
Coppice

11

Water Eaton

The
Spread Eagle
(PH)

Gailey
Pottery

Eaton House

CLAY GATES RD

Gailey

Watling
House

Gailey Farm

Croft
Farm

CROFT LA

Staffordshire &
Worcestershire Canal

GAILEY LEA LA

Plough
Farm

HARRISONS LA

Gailey Wharf

Calf Heath
Reservoir

M6

A5

1

A449

Claygate

10

90 A 91 B 92 C

207
193

A
B
C

B5012
CANNOCK RD
GREENWAYS
ELRIC CL
ATHELSTAN CL
SAXON RD
BROC...
ELMDON...
NORMAN RD
L Ctr
Wolgarston High Sch
KENILWORTH CL
WOLGARSTON WAY
M6
4
B5012
FRANCIS CL
DRUIDS WAY
OVERDON CL
TIDDWENA WA
PAGET CL
BRUNEL CL
DERIDGE
BERKELEY
ASTON CL
BOYDEN CL
BRINGTONE...
SALMON DR
MALLARD WAY
MOOR HALL LA
Moor Hall Cottages
NAGINGTON DR

Quarry Heath

Pillaton Farm

Newlands Wood

Pillaton Hall Farm

Pillaton

13
Pillaton Old Hall +

Marina

Mansty Farm

3
Airfield

OTHERTON LA

ST19

Mansty Wood

12
Staffordshire & Worcestershire Canal

Horsemoor Wood

MICKLEWOOD LA

Micklewood

2
Fullmoor Wood

Fullmoor Lodge

Hatherton Wood

B5012

11
Gailey Lea Farm

GAILEY LEA LA

WS11

1
Gailey Upper Reservoir

Hatherton Hall Farm

Hatherton

CHURCH LA

A5
12
M6
A5
Gailey Lower Reservoir
Church Farm

10
A5

93
A
94
B
95
C

207
225

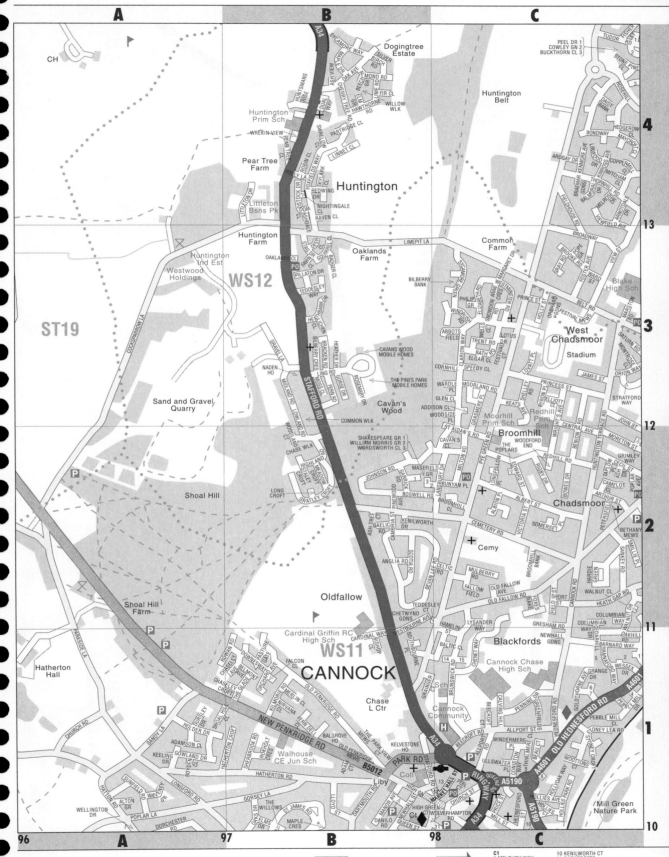

C1
1 MELBURY WAY
2 MELCHESTER WLK
3 STONEYFIELDS CL
4 MILLBROOK CL
5 EXONBURY WLK
6 STRATHMORE PL
7 HAWKESVILLE DR
8 CRANFORD PL
9 WEAVING GDNS
10 KENILWORTH CT
11 BACKCROFTS
12 MARKET PL
13 CANNOCK SH CTR
14 HANOVER PL
15 GEORGIAN PL

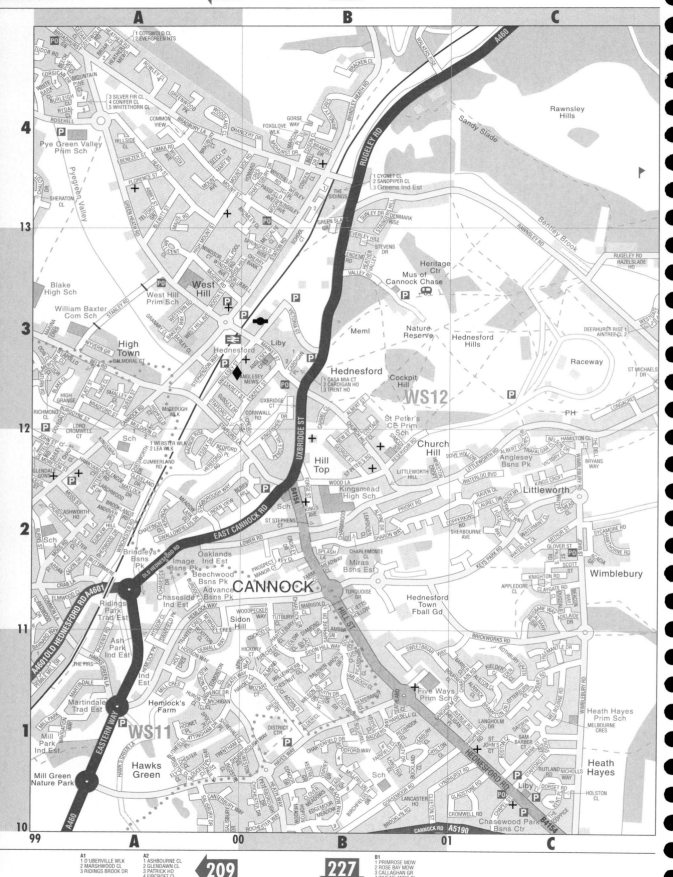

A1
1 D'UBERVILLE WLK
2 MARSHWOOD CL
3 RIDINGS BROOK DR

A2
1 ASHBOURNE CL
2 GLENDAWN CL
3 PATRICK HO
4 FIRCROFT CL
5 VERMONT GN
6 MEADOW HILL DR

B1
1 PRIMROSE MDW
2 ROSE BAY MDW
3 CALLAGHAN GR
4 WHEATLANDS CL
5 SPINDLEWOOD CL
6 LAWNSWOOD CL
7 GREEN MDWS
8 THISTLEDOWN DR
9 BUCKINGHAM PL

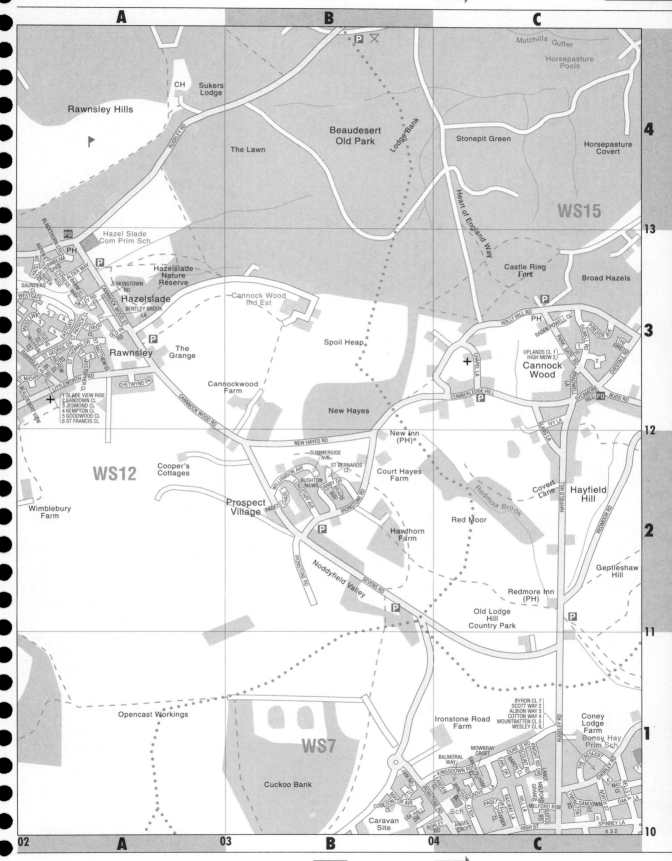

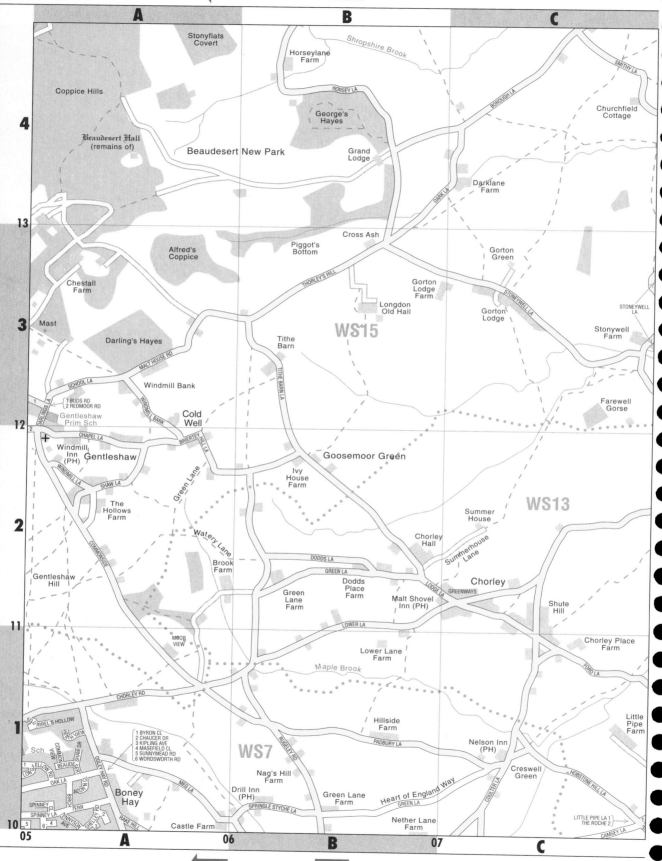

A   B   C

Stonyflats Covert
Shropshire Brook
Horseylane Farm
HORSEY LA
Coppice Hills
George's Hayes
4
Beaudesert Hall (remains of)
Beaudesert New Park
Grand Lodge
BOROUGH LA
SMITHY LA
Churchfield Cottage
DARK LA
Darklane Farm
13
Cross Ash
Piggot's Bottom
Gorton Green
Alfred's Coppice
THORLEY'S HILL
Gorton Lodge Farm
STONEYWELL LA
STONEYWELL LA
Chestall Farm
Longdon Old Hall
WS15
Gorton Lodge
Stonywell Farm
3
Mast
Darling's Hayes
Tithe Barn
MALT HOUSE RD
SCHOOL LA
Windmill Bank
TITHE BARN LA
Farewell Gorse
1 BUDS RD
2 REDMOOR RD
WINDMILL BANK
12
Gentleshaw Prim Sch
Cold Well
BRIERTEY
CHAPEL LA
HILL LA
Goosemoor Green
Windmill Inn (PH)
Gentleshaw
Ivy House Farm
WS13
GREEN LANE
Summer House
The Hollows Farm
Summerhouse Lane
WINDMILL LA
SHAW LA
Chorley Hall
2
Gentleshaw Hill
Watery Lane
Brook Farm
DODDS LA
GREEN LA
Dodds Place Farm
Chorley
COMMONSIDE
LODGE LA
GREENWAYS
Shute Hill
Green Lane Farm
Malt Shovel Inn (PH)
11
MOOR VIEW
LOWER LA
Chorley Place Farm
FORD LA
Maple Brook
Lower Lane Farm
CHORLEY RD
Hillside Farm
Little Pipe Farm
1
SQUIRREL'S HOLLOW
PADBURY LA
Nelson Inn (PH)
WS7
Creswell Green
1 BYRON CL
2 CHAUCER DR
3 KIPLING AVE
4 MASEFIELD CL
5 SUNNYMEAD RD
6 WORDSWORTH RD
RUGELEY RD
Sch
COMMON VIEW
BEAUDE
OAK LA
ACORN CL
Nag's Hill Farm
MEG LA
Drill Inn (PH)
Green Lane Farm
Heart of England Way
GREEN LA
COULTER LA
HOBSTONE HILL LA
Boney Hay
SPINNEY
SPINNEY LA
TENNYSON AVE
SHELLEY RD
RAKE HILL
Castle Farm
SPRINGLE STYCHE LA
Nether Lane Farm
LITTLE PIPE LA 1
THE ROCHE 2
10
05   A   06   B   07   C
CAMSEY LA

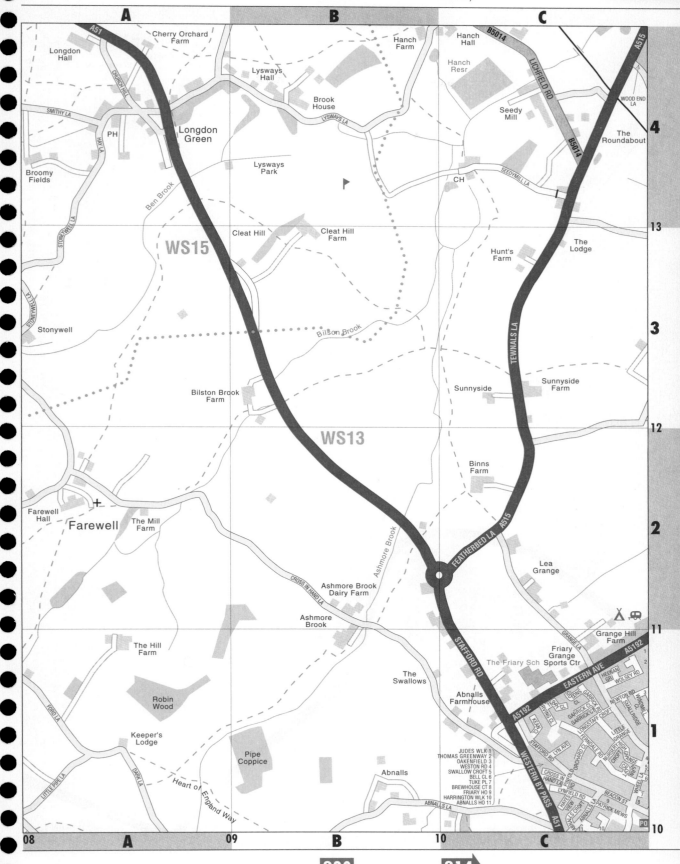

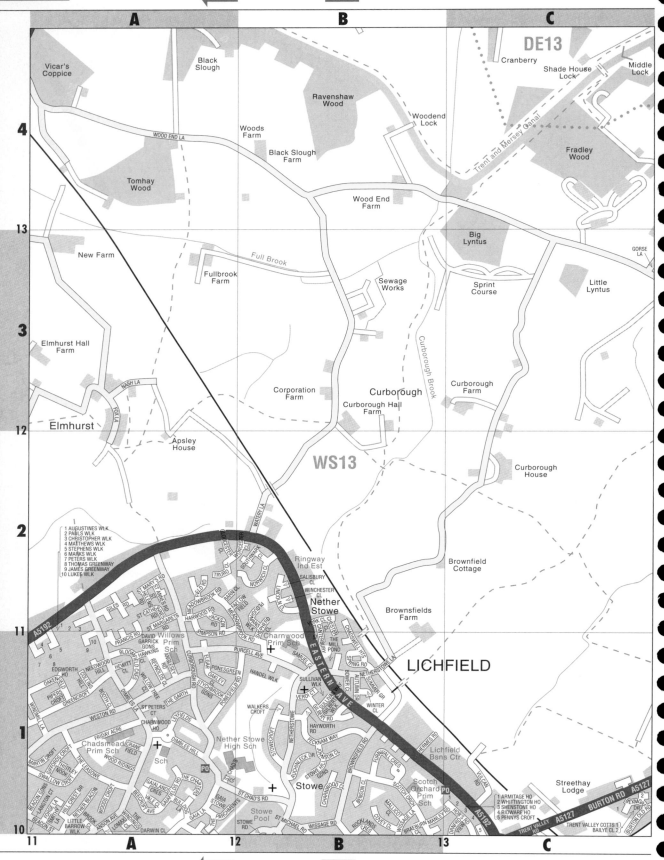

A   **B**   **C**

DE13

Vicar's Coppice

Black Slough

Cranberry

Shade House Lock

Middle Lock

Ravenshaw Wood

Woodend Lock

Trent and Mersey Canal

WOOD END LA

Woods Farm

Black Slough Farm

Fradley Wood

4

Tomhay Wood

Wood End Farm

Big Lyntus

13

New Farm

Full Brook

Fullbrook Farm

Sewage Works

Sprint Course

GORSE LA

Little Lyntus

3

Elmhurst Hall Farm

Curborough Brook

Curborough

Curborough Farm

NASH LA

FOX LA

Corporation Farm

Curborough Hall Farm

Curborough House

12

Elmhurst

Apsley House

WS13

WATERY LA

2

1 AUGUSTINES WLK
2 PAULS WLK
3 CHRISTOPHER WLK
4 MATTHEWS WLK
5 STEPHENS WLK
6 MARKS WLK
7 PETERS WLK
8 THOMAS GREENWAY
9 JAMES GREENWAY
10 LUKES WLK

Ringway Ind Est

Brownfield Cottage

SALISBURY CL

WINCHESTER CL

Nether Stowe

Brownsfields Farm

A5192

Charnwood Prim Sch

EASTERN AVE

LICHFIELD

11

Willows Prim Sch

Charnwood Prim Sch

THE MILL POND

Lichfield Bsns Ctr

Nether Stowe High Sch

Streethay Lodge

1

Chadsmead Prim Sch

Stowe

Scotch Orchard Prim Sch

1 ARMITAGE HO
2 WHITTINGTON HO
3 SHENSTONE HO
4 RIDWARE HO
5 PENNYS CROFT

BURTON RD

A5127

Stowe Pool

A5192

A5127

TRENT VALLEY COTTS 1
BAILYE CL 2

10

11   **A**   **12**   **B**   **13**   **C**

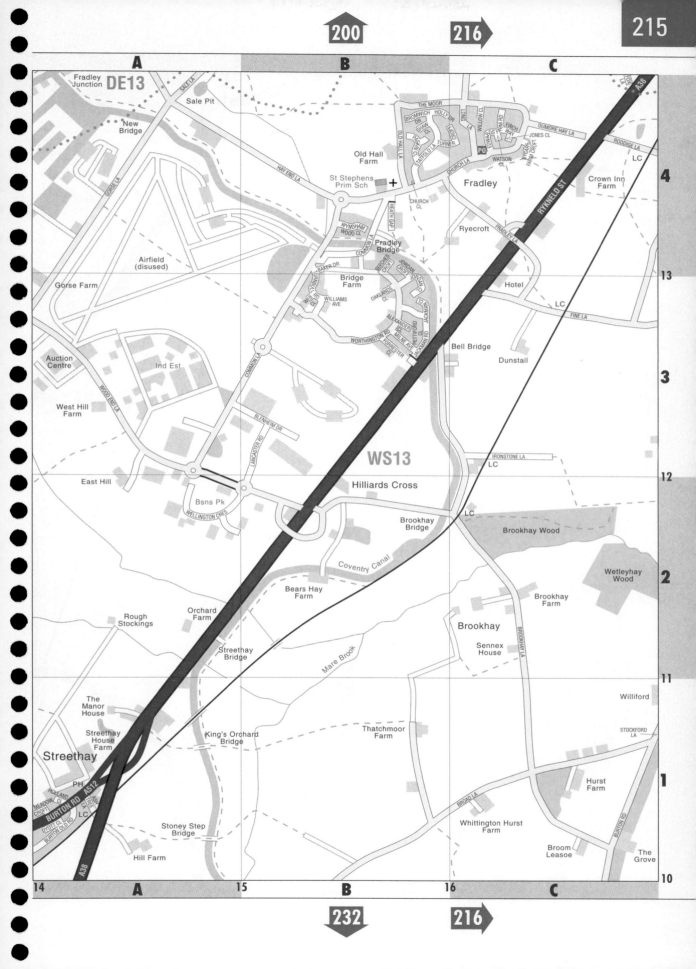

215
201

A **B** **C**

DE13

RIDGET LA

BARLEY GREEN LA

A513

Chetwynd or
Salter's Bridge

Croxall

CROXALL RD

Dovecote

The
Hall

Roddige

Whitemoor
Haye

Brown's
Island

4

RODDIGE LA

WS13

Broadfields

Oakley
Farm

River Mease

13

Croxall
Mill

3

River Tame

A513

New Buildings
Farm

Sittles

Lady
Walk

Elford
Park

12

STOCKFORD LA

Sand & Gravel
Pit

Park
Farm

The
Bungalow

2

Bisphill
Plantation

B79

11

Greendales
Farm

A513

Home
Farm

BROADHOUSE LA

Elford

Howard
Prim Sch

OLD HALL DR

THE GARDENS

CHURCH RD

THE SQUARE

PH
PO

CROFT CL

THE BECK

Raddle
Farm

1

ETDES LA

The Hill

BURTON RD

THE SHRUBBERY

Old
Orangery

A513

10

17 **A** **18** **B** **19** **C**

215
233

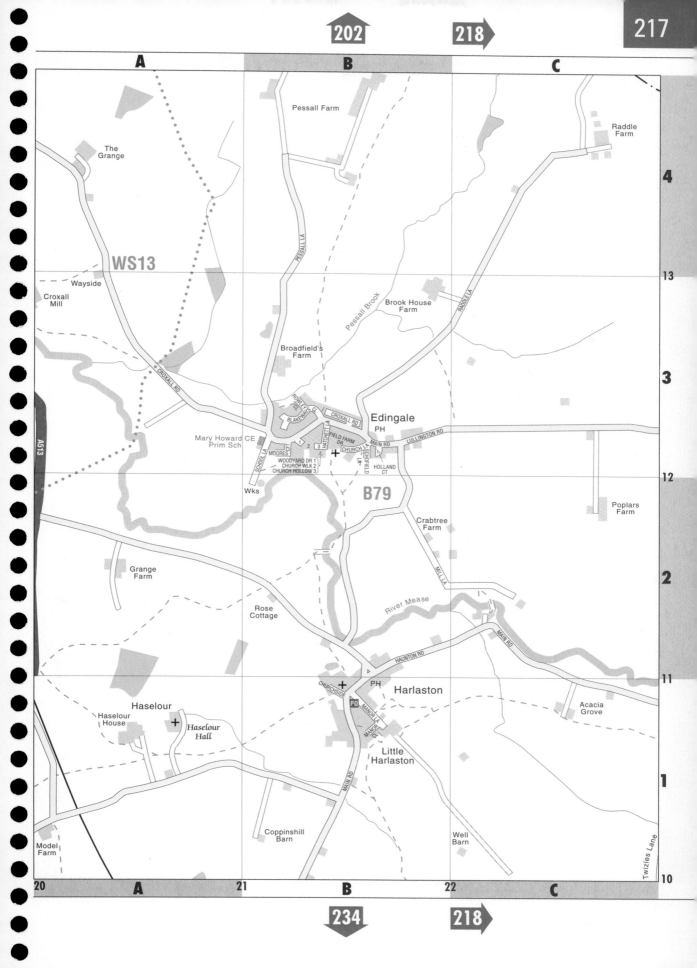

202
218
234
218

A513

WS13

The Grange

Wayside

Croxall Mill

CROXALL RD

Pessall Farm

PESSALL LA

Raddle Farm

RANDLE LA

Pessall Brook

Brook House Farm

Broadfield's Farm

ROWLEY'S CL

BLAKEWAYS CL

HATCHETT LA

CROXALL RD

Edingale
PH

FIELD FARM DR

CHURCH LA

MAIN RD

LULLINGTON RD

Mary Howard CE Prim Sch

SCHOOL LA

MOORES

WOODYARD DR 1
CHURCH WLK 2
CHURCH HOLLOW 3

SCHOFIELD

LA

HOLLAND CT

Wks

B79

Poplars Farm

Crabtree Farm

MILL LA

Grange Farm

Rose Cottage

River Mease

MAIN RD

HAUNTON RD

Haselour

Haselour House

Haselour Hall

CHURCHSIDE

PO

PH

Harlaston

MANOR LA

MANOR CL

Acacia Grove

Little Harlaston

MAIN RD

Model Farm

Coppinshill Barn

Well Barn

Twizles Lane

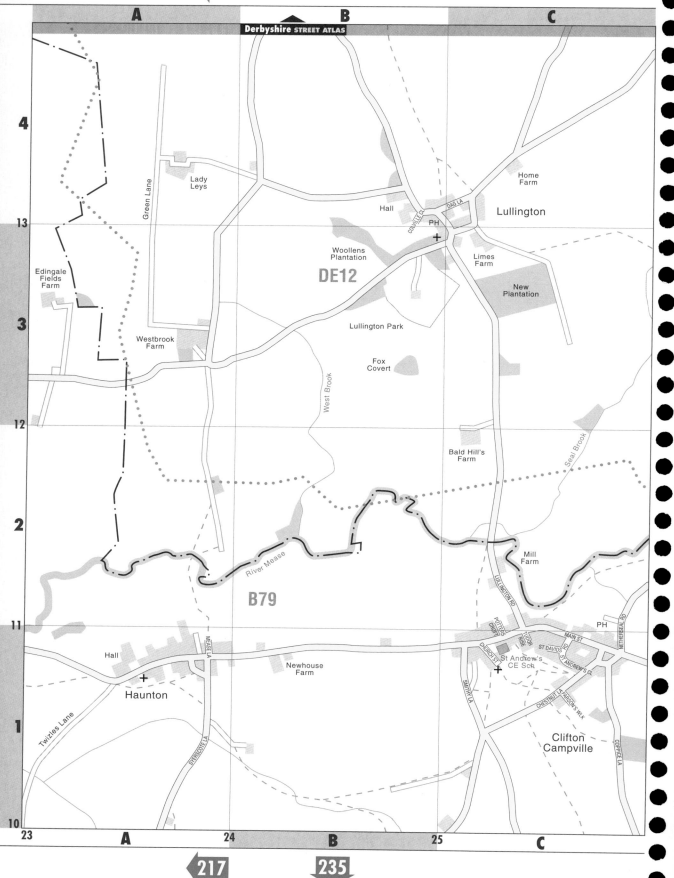

Derbyshire STREET ATLAS

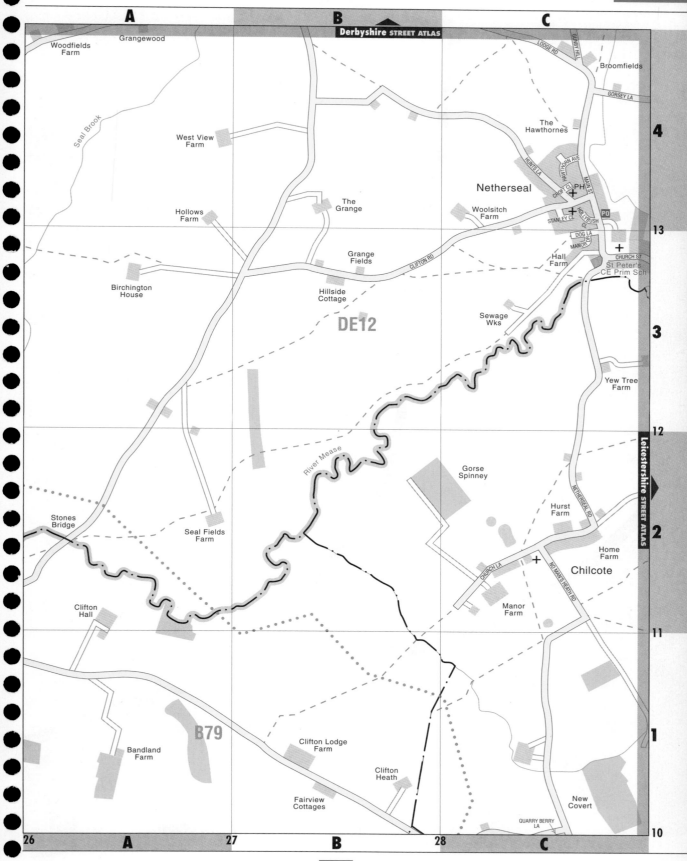

Woodfields Farm

Grangewood

Broomfields

LODGE RD

GUNBY HILL

GORSEY LA

The Hawthornes

4

Seal Brook

West View Farm

HINTS LA

HAWTHORN AVE

MAIN ST

Netherseal

CROFT CL

PH

The Grange

Woolsitch Farm

HOLLYBUSH CL

STANLEY CL

PO

Hollows Farm

13

Grange Fields

CLIFTON RD

MANOR DR

DOG LA

Birchington House

Hillside Cottage

Hall Farm

CHURCH ST

St Peter's CE Prim Sch

DE12

Sewage Wks

3

Yew Tree Farm

12

River Mease

Gorse Spinney

NETHERSEAL RD

Leicestershire STREET ATLAS

Hurst Farm

Stones Bridge

Seal Fields Farm

Home Farm

2

CHURCH LA

NO MANS HEATH RD

Chilcote

Clifton Hall

Manor Farm

11

B79

1

Bandland Farm

Clifton Lodge Farm

New Covert

Clifton Heath

Fairview Cottages

QUARRY BERRY LA

10

203

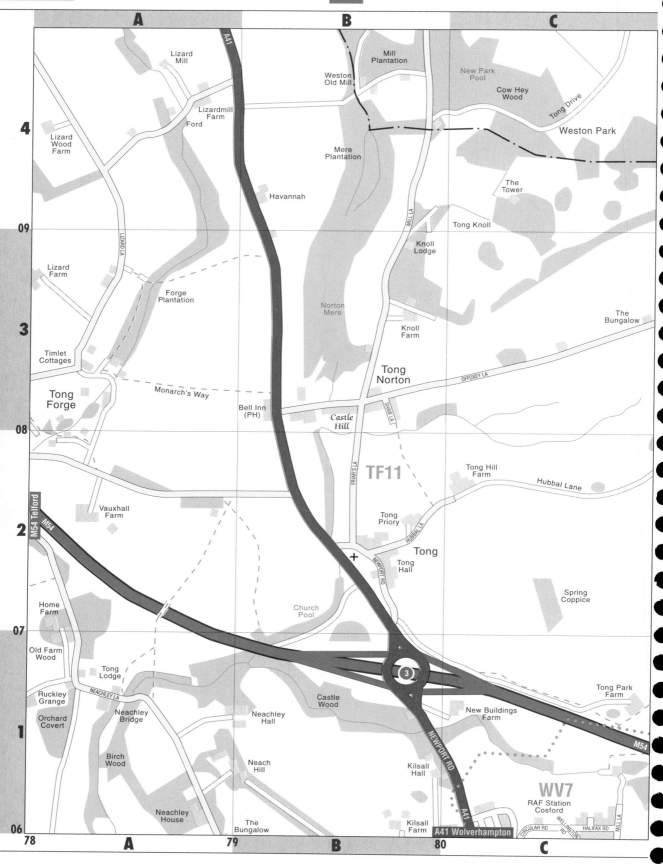

A   B   C

4

Lizard Mill
Weston Old Mill
Mill Plantation
New Park Pool
Cow Hey Wood
Tong Drive
Weston Park

Lizardmill Farm
Ford
Lizard Wood Farm

Mere Plantation

The Tower

Havannah

09

Tong Knoll

LIZARD LA

Knoll Lodge

MILL LA

3

Lizard Farm
Forge Plantation
Norton Mere
Knoll Farm
The Bungalow

Timlet Cottages
Tong Forge
Monarch's Way
Tong Norton
OFFOXEY LA

SHAW LA

08

Bell Inn (PH)
Castle Hill
TF11

FRIAR'S LA

Tong Hill Farm
Hubbal Lane

Vauxhall Farm
Tong Priory

HUBBAL LA

Tong

2

M54 Telford
M54

Spring Coppice

Home Farm
Church Pool

Tong Hall

NEWPORT RD

07

Old Farm Wood
Tong Lodge
Castle Wood

NEACHLEY LA

Tong Park Farm

Ruckley Grange
Neachley Bridge
Neachley Hall
New Buildings Farm

M54

1

Orchard Covert
Birch Wood
Neach Hill
Kilsall Hall
NEWPORT RD
WV7
RAF Station Cosford

Neachley House
The Bungalow
Kilsall Farm
A41 Wolverhampton
CIRCULAR RD
WELLINGTON RD
HALIFAX RD
MILL LA

06

78   A   79   B   80   C

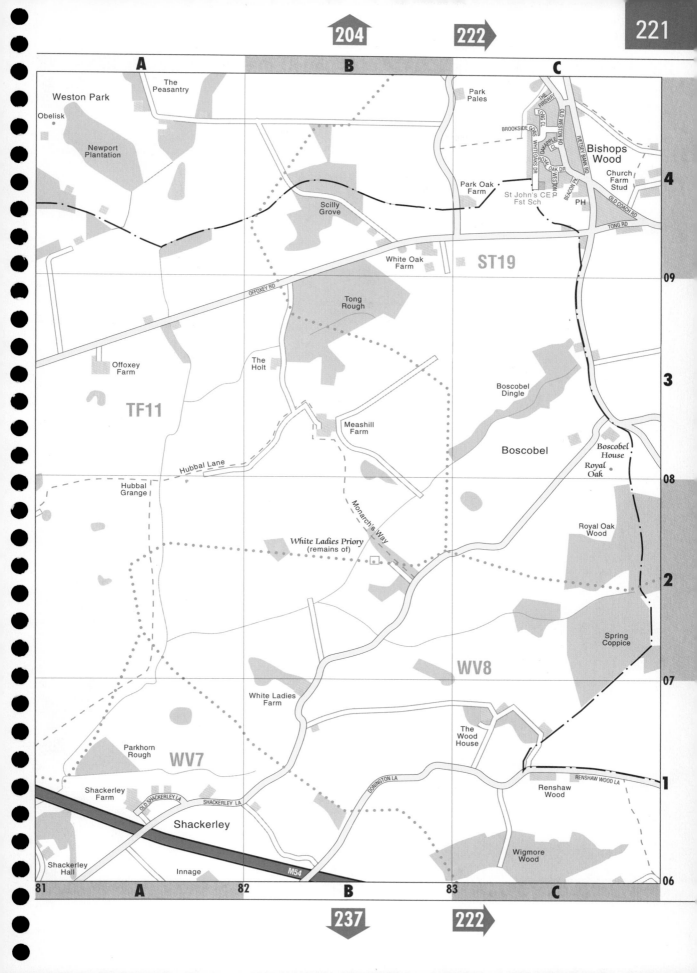

Weston Park
The Peasantry
Obelisk
Newport Plantation

Park Pales
Park Oak Farm
BROOKSIDE GDNS
THE FIRSWAY
LONG CL
OLD WESTON RD
WHITEOAKS DR
APPLE TREE ROW
ROYAL OAK DR
WESTON RD
IVETSEY BANK RD
BEACON TK
OLD COACH RD
Bishops Wood
Church Farm Stud
St John's CE Fst Sch
PH
Tong Rd

Scilly Grove

White Oak Farm

ST19

OFFOXEY RD

Tong Rough

Offoxey Farm

TF11

The Holt

Boscobel Dingle

Meashill Farm

Boscobel

Boscobel House
Royal Oak

Hubbal Lane

Hubbal Grange

Monarch's Way

Royal Oak Wood

White Ladies Priory
(remains of)

Spring Coppice

WV8

White Ladies Farm

The Wood House

Parkhorn Rough

WV7

Renshaw Wood

RENSHAW WOOD LA

Shackerley Farm
OLD SHACKERLEY LA
SHACKERLEY LA

Shackerley

DONINGTON LA

Wigmore Wood

Shackerley Hall
Innage
M54

09 4 3 08 2 07 1 06

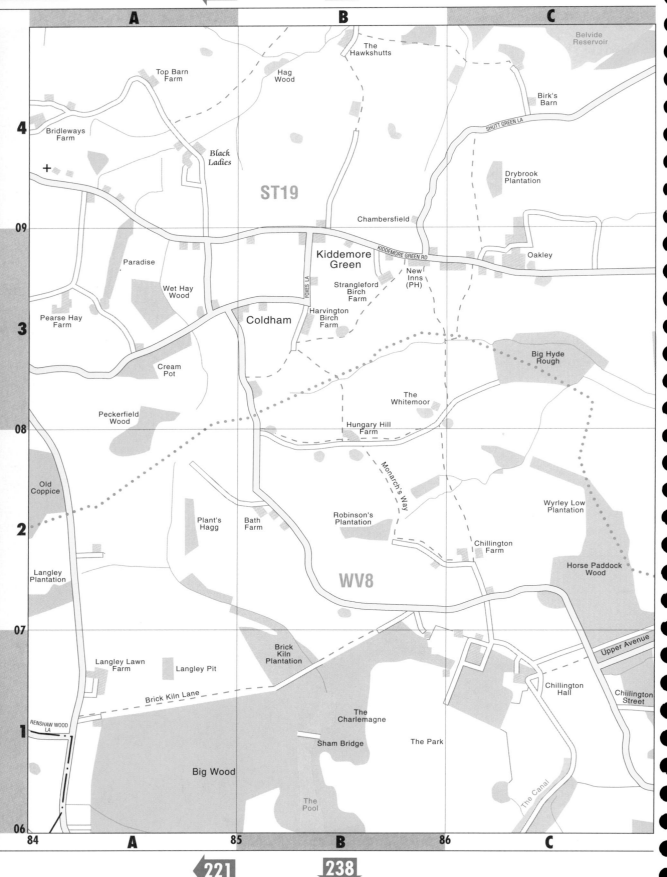

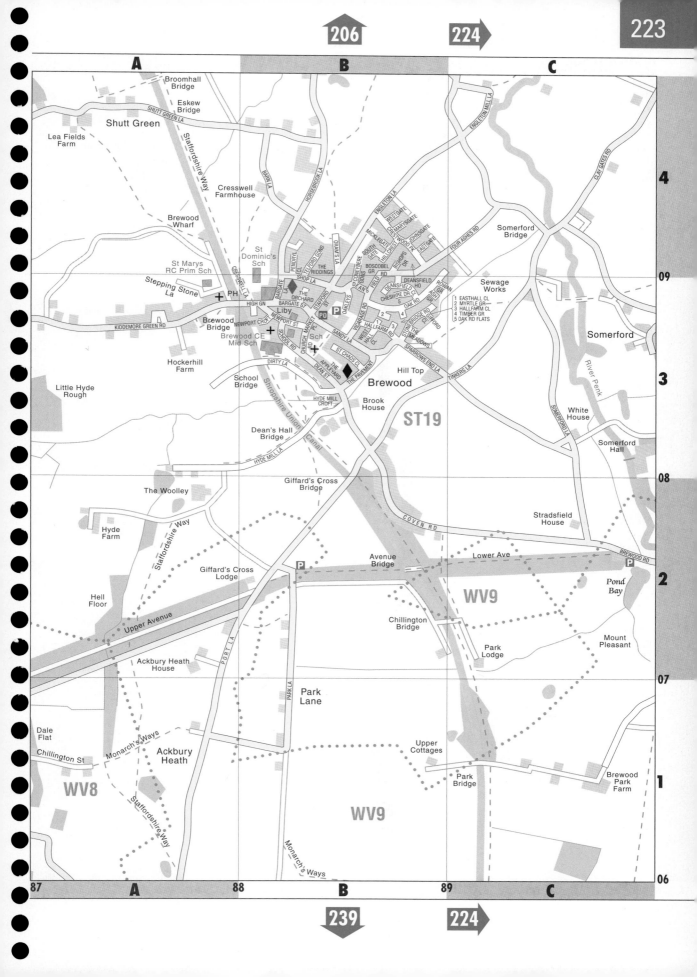

Broomhall Bridge
Eskew Bridge
Shutt Green
SHUTT GREEN LA
Lea Fields Farm
Staffordshire Way
Cresswell Farmhouse
BARN LA
HORSEBROOK LA
Brewood Wharf
St Dominic's Sch
St Marys RC Prim Sch
St CRESSWELL LA
Stepping Stone La
HIGH GN
PH
KIDDEMORE GREEN RD
Brewood Bridge
Newport Croft
Brewood CE Mid Sch
Hockerhill Farm
Little Hyde Rough
School Bridge
SCHOOL RD
DIRTY LA
Dean's Hall Bridge
HYDE MILL LA
The Woolley
Staffordshire Way
Hyde Farm
Giffard's Cross Lodge
Hell Floor
Upper Avenue
Ackbury Heath House
PORT LA
PARK LA
Dale Flat
Chillington St
Monarch's Ways
Ackbury Heath
Staffordshire Way
WV8
Monarch's Ways
Park Lane
Park Lane

Shropshire Union Canal

St
PENKRY CL
SHOP LA
BARGATE
BARGATE ST
STAFFORD ST
TELFORD GDNS
THE RIDDINGS
DRAM'S LA
OAKLEY'S
SANDY LA
Liby
THE ORCHARD
P
PO
Newport St
CHURCH MARKET PL
St St
DEAN ST
THE APPLEYARD
ENGLETON LA
WESTGATE
CRESTWOOD
DR
MICKLEGATE
SOUTH
GATE
HILLCREST
JOHNSGATE
EASTGATE
CONEYBERE
COUNTY
GDNS
BISHOPS
DR
BOSCOBEL
GR
RD
DEAN'S
FIELD
DEANSFIELD
CL
DEANSFIELD HO
ROWAN
GR
OAK RD
CHESHIRE DR
VICARAGE RD
WEST
HALL
HALLFARM RD
THE
MEADOWS
STONEBRIDGE RD
SPARROWS END LA
GIFFORD
CL
FOUR ASHES RD
Somerford Bridge
ENGLETON MILL LA
CLAY GATES RD
Sewage Works
1 EASTHALL CL
2 MYRTLE GR
3 HALLFARM CL
4 TIMBER GR
5 OAK RD FLATS
Somerford
River Penk
Brewood
Hill Top
TINKERS LA
ST19
Brook House
HYDE MILL CROFT
SOMERFORD LA
White House
Somerford Hall
Giffard's Cross Bridge
COVEN RD
Stradsfield House
Avenue Bridge
Lower Ave
BREWOOD RD
P
Giffard's Cross Lodge
WV9
Pond Bay
Chillington Bridge
Park Lodge
Mount Pleasant
Upper Cottages
Park Bridge
Brewood Park Farm
WV9

4
09
3
08
2
07
1
06

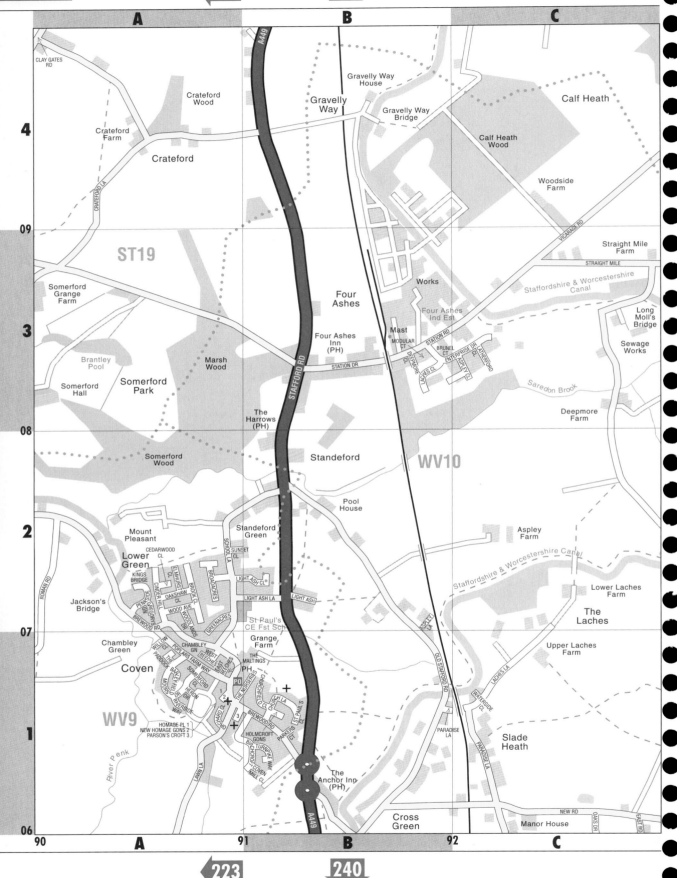

A **B** **C**

CLAY GATES RD

Crateford Wood

Crateford Farm

Crateford

CRATEFORD LA

4

Gravelly Way House

Gravelly Way

Gravelly Way Bridge

Calf Heath

Calf Heath Wood

Woodside Farm

A449

09

ST19

VICARAGE RD

Straight Mile Farm

STRAIGHT MILE

Somerford Grange Farm

Four Ashes

Works

Staffordshire & Worcestershire Canal

Long Moll's Bridge

3

Brantley Pool

Marsh Wood

Four Ashes Inn (PH)

STATION DR

Mast

MODULAR CT

Four Ashes Ind Est

STATION RD

DEEPMORE

LACHES CL

BRUNEL CT

ENTERPRISE DR

ASH CT

RUTHERFORD

Sewage Works

Somerford Hall

Somerford Park

STAFFORD RD

Saredon Brook

Deepmore Farm

08

Somerford Wood

The Harrows (PH)

Standeford

WV10

2

Mount Pleasant

Lower Green

CEDARWOOD CL

Standeford Green

SCHOOL LA

SUNSET CL

Pool House

Aspley Farm

KINGS BRIDGE

ELMHURST CL

CINDER HILL

BROADACRES

LIGHT ASH CL

Staffordshire & Worcestershire Canal

ROMAN RD

Jackson's Bridge

PENK RISE

GREGORY'S WAY

BREWOOD RD

OAKSHAW

WOOD AVE

WOODLANDS

GREENACRES

LIGHT ASH LA

LIGHT ASH

ASPLEY

Lower Laches Farm

The Laches

07

Chambley Green

Coven

WV9

WILLOW CL

THE POPLARS

CHAMBLEY GN

WEST ST

BEECHES

FARM WAY

St Paul's CE Fst Sch

Grange Farm

THE MALTINGS PH

CHURCHFIELD CL

ASH LA

BREWOOD RD

ST PAUL'S CL

Upper Laches Farm

LACHES LA

OLD STAFFORD RD

WATERSIDE CL

PO

BAKERS FIELD CL

MOORS DR

HERON DR

RIVERSIDE WAY

CHAPEL CL

SOMERFORD

THE SQUARE

WORCESTER

PANKERS CT

ST PAUL'S CL

Slade Heath

PARADISE LA

1

River Penk

HOMAGE PL 1
NEW HOMAGE GDNS 2
PARSON'S CROFT 3

HOLMCROFT GDNS

BIRCHCROFT

TURNPIKE WY

COVEN

MILL CL

The Anchor Inn (PH)

Paradise LA

PARADISE LA

LAWN LA

A449

Cross Green

Manor House

NEW RD

OAKS DR

EAST RD

06

90 **91** **92**

A **B** **C**

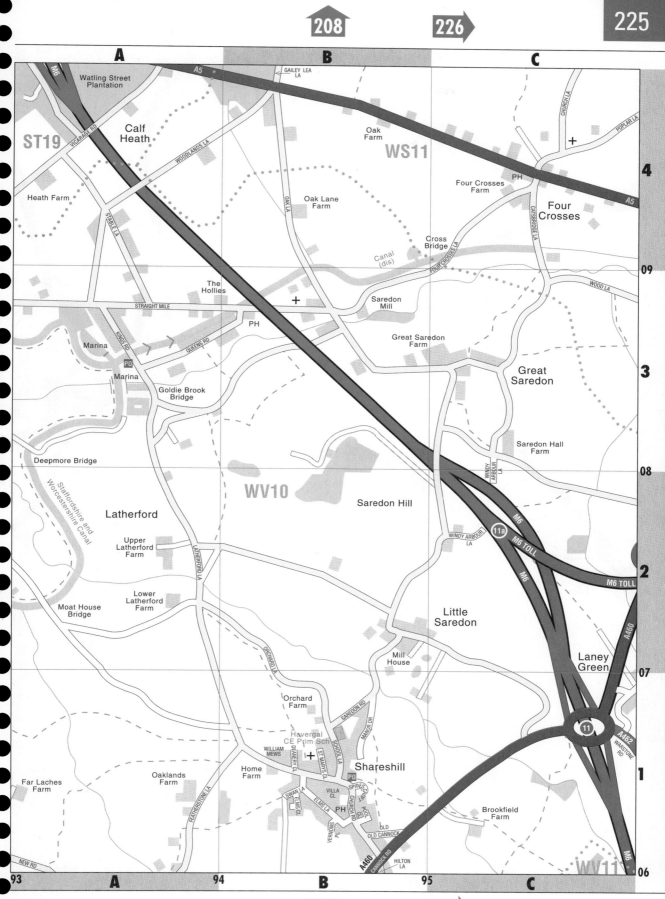

A B C

Watling Street Plantation

M6

A5

GAILEY LEA LA

Oak Farm

WS11

CHURCH LA

POPLAR LA

ST19

VICARAGE RD

Calf Heath

WOODLANDS LA

4

Four Crosses Farm

PH

Four Crosses

CATSBRIDGE LA

A5

Heath Farm

STABLE LA

OAK LA

Oak Lane Farm

Cross Bridge

FOUR CROSSES LA

09

The Hollies

STRAIGHT MILE

Canal (dis)

Saredon Mill

WOOD LA

PH

Great Saredon Farm

Great Saredon

Marina

KINGS RD

QUEENS RD

PH

Saredon Mill

3

Marina

PO

Goldie Brook Bridge

Saredon Hall Farm

Deepmore Bridge

WINDY ARBOUR LA

08

Staffordshire and Worcestershire Canal

WV10

Saredon Hill

Latherford

M6

11a

M6 TOLL

Upper Latherford Farm

LATHERFORD LA

WINDY ARBOUR LA

M6

M6 TOLL

2

Moat House Bridge

Lower Latherford Farm

Little Saredon

A460

Laney Green

07

Mill House

ORCHARD LA

Orchard Farm

SAREDON RD

MANOR DR

11

A462

WARSTONE RD

Havergal CE Prim Sch

SCHOOL LA

1

Far Laches Farm

FEATHERSTONE LA

Oaklands Farm

Home Farm

WILLIAM MEWS

DEANERY CL

PO

ST MARYS CL

Shareshill

SWAN LA

ELMS CL

ELMS LA

VILLA CL

SPIRES CROFT

PH

CHURCH RD

POOL CL

Brookfield Farm

NEW RD

VERNONS PL

OLD

OLD CANNOCK

A460

CANNOCK RD

HILTON LA

WV11

M6

06

93 A 94 B 95 C 06

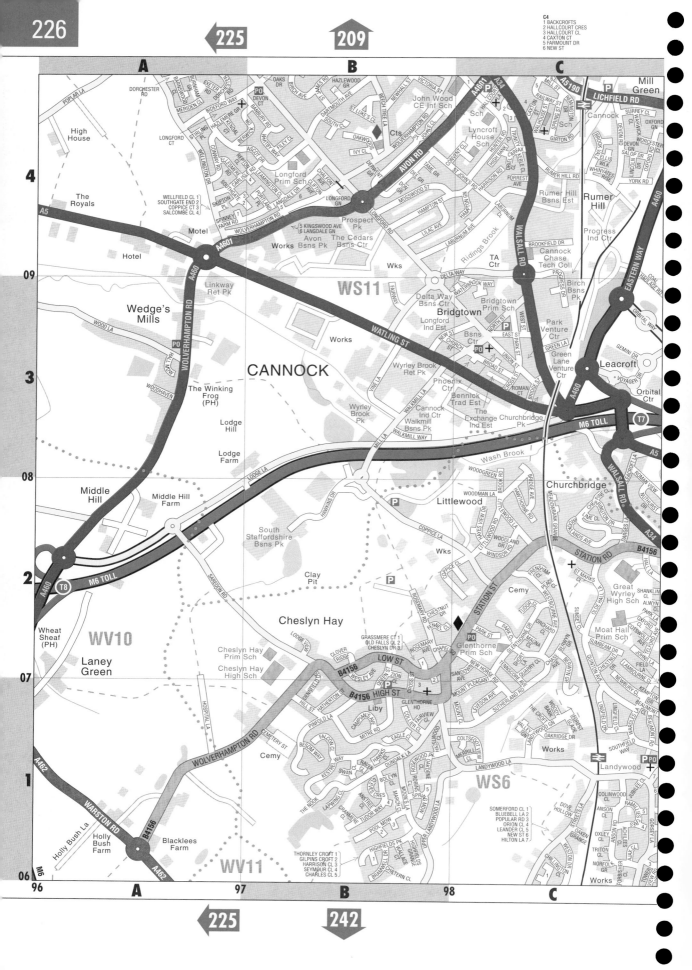

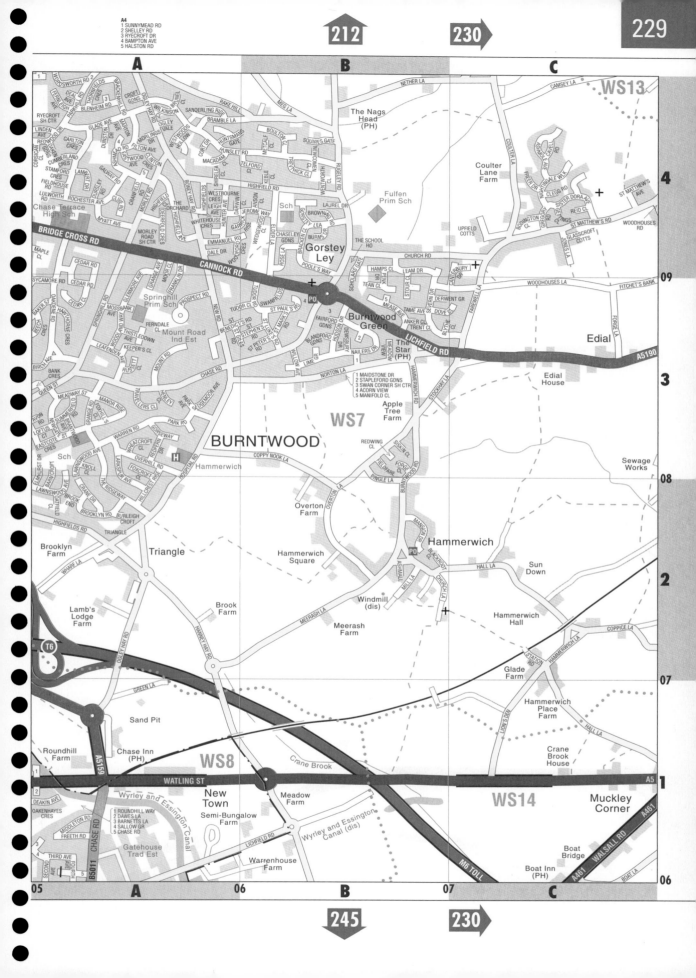

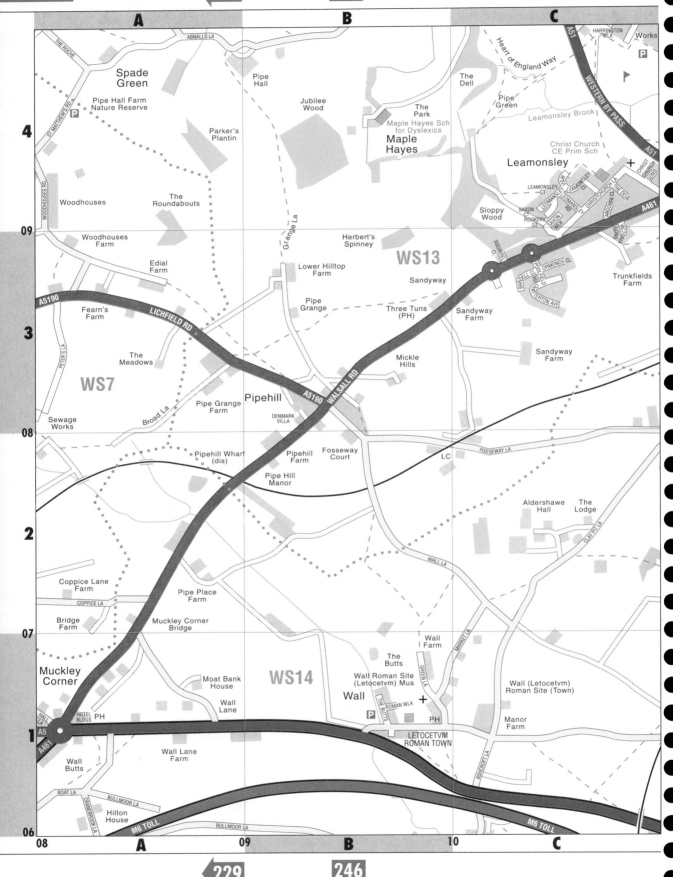

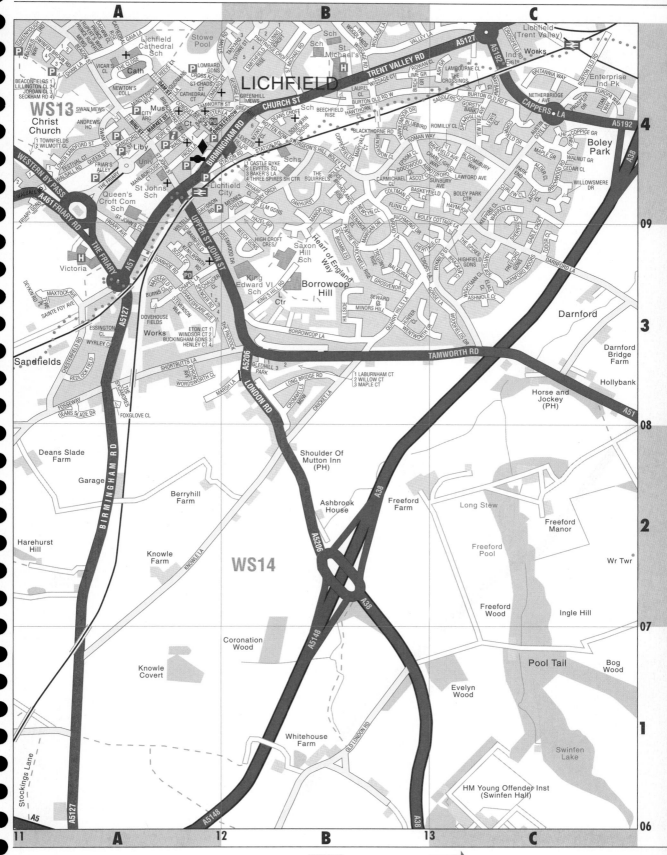

B4
1 HOULBROOKE HO
2 WILLIAM LUNN'S HOMES
3 THE CHEQUERS
4 DRAKE CROFT
5 MALLARD CROFT
6 MERCIAN CT

214

232

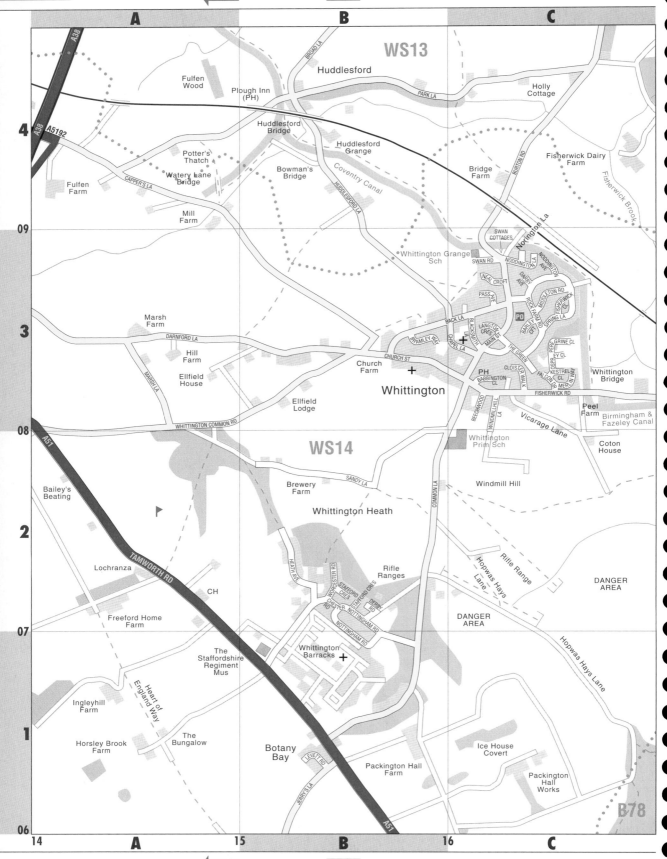

231
215

WS13

Huddlesford

Fulfen
Wood

Plough Inn
(PH)

Holly
Cottage

Huddlesford
Bridge

PARK LA

BROAD LA

Potter's
Thatch

Huddlesford
Grange

Bridge
Farm

Fisherwick Dairy
Farm

Fulfen
Farm

CAPPER'S LA

Watery Lane
Bridge

Bowman's
Bridge

Coventry Canal

BURTON RD

Fisherwick Brook

HUDDLESFORD LA

Mill
Farm

Notington La

SWAN
COTTAGES

Whittington Grange
Sch

SWAN RD

NODDINGTON
VY

NODDINGTON AVE

NEAL CROFT

DARBY AVE

MIDDLETON RD

FISHERWICK

Marsh
Farm

DARNFORD LA

PASS AVE

PO

ROCK FARM CFT

SPRING LA

Hill
Farm

MARSH LA

BACK LA

BRAMLEY WAY

BLACKSMITH LA

LANGTON CRES

MAIN ST

THE GREEN

BARLEY CFT

PERCY CL

GRINE CL

Ellfield
House

CHAPEL LA

Whittington
Bridge

CHURCH ST

Church
Farm

PH

BABBINGTON
CL

CLOISTER WALK

FALCON CL

KESTREL
CL

MERLIN WAY

Ellfield
Lodge

Whittington

BEECHWOOD

WINDMILL HILL

FISHERWICK RD

Peel
Farm

Birmingham &
Fazeley Canal

WHITTINGTON COMMON RD

WS14

Vicarage Lane

Coton
House

Whittington
Prim Sch

SANDY LA

Brewery
Farm

COMMON LA

Windmill Hill

Bailey's
Beating

Whittington Heath

Rifle Range

DANGER
AREA

TAMWORTH RD

A51

Lochranza

Hopwas Hays
Lane

CH

HEATH AVE

WORCESTER RD

STAFFORD CRES

STAFFORD CRES

Rifle
Ranges

DANGER
AREA

Freeford Home
Farm

CHESTER RD

NOTTINGHAM RD

DERBY
RD

Hopwas Hays Lane

The
Staffordshire
Regiment
Mus

NOTTINGHAM RD

Whittington
Barracks

Ingleyhill
Farm

Heart of England Way

Ice House
Covert

Horsley Brook
Farm

The
Bungalow

Botany
Bay

LEVETT RD

Packington Hall
Farm

Packington
Hall
Works

JERRY'S LA

A51

B78

14   A   15   B   16   C   06

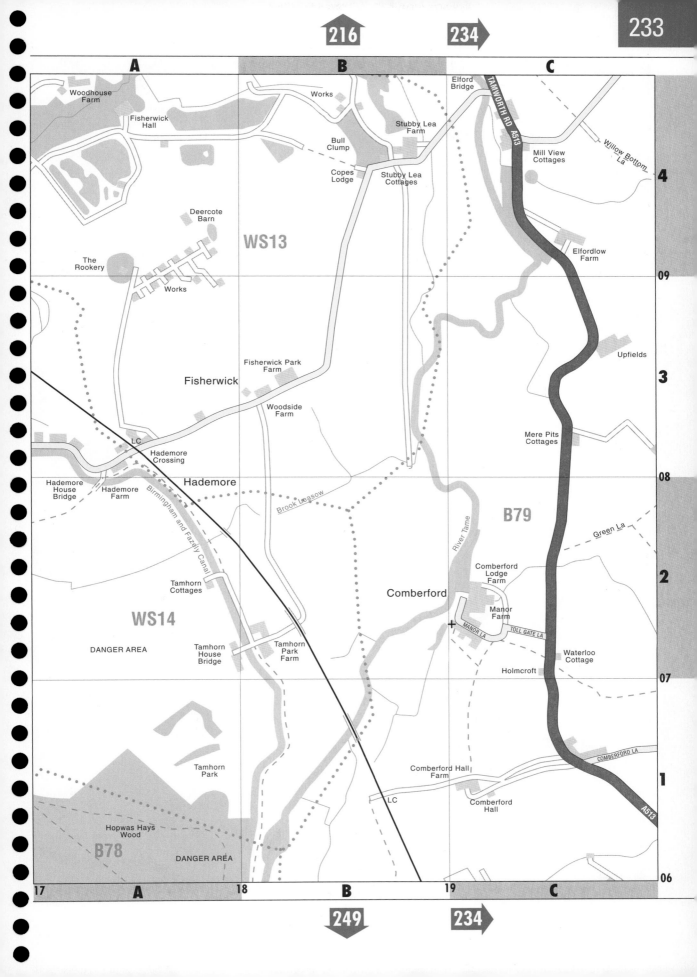

233
217

A **B** **C**

Fishpits Barn

Twizles La

4

Willow Bottom La

Portway

Dunimere Farm

Hogs Hill

PORTWAY LA

09

3

Birdsley Farm

Green La

Winterdyne Farm

Mere Pits

08

Wiggington Fields Farm

B79

Cherryfield Cottages

Hanging Hill

2

Syerscote Manor

Watergate Cottage

07

Wigginton Manor

Syerscote Barn

COMBERFORD LA

SYERSCOTE LA

PH

Wigginton

1

St Leonard's CE Prim Sch

Bridge Cottages

World's End Cottages

MAIN RD

WALRAND CL

Arkall Farm

Amington Hall Cottages

A513

Rawlett Sports Ctr

SILL GREEN

Rawlett High Sch

ASHBY RD

B5493

06

20 **A** **21** **B** **22** **C**

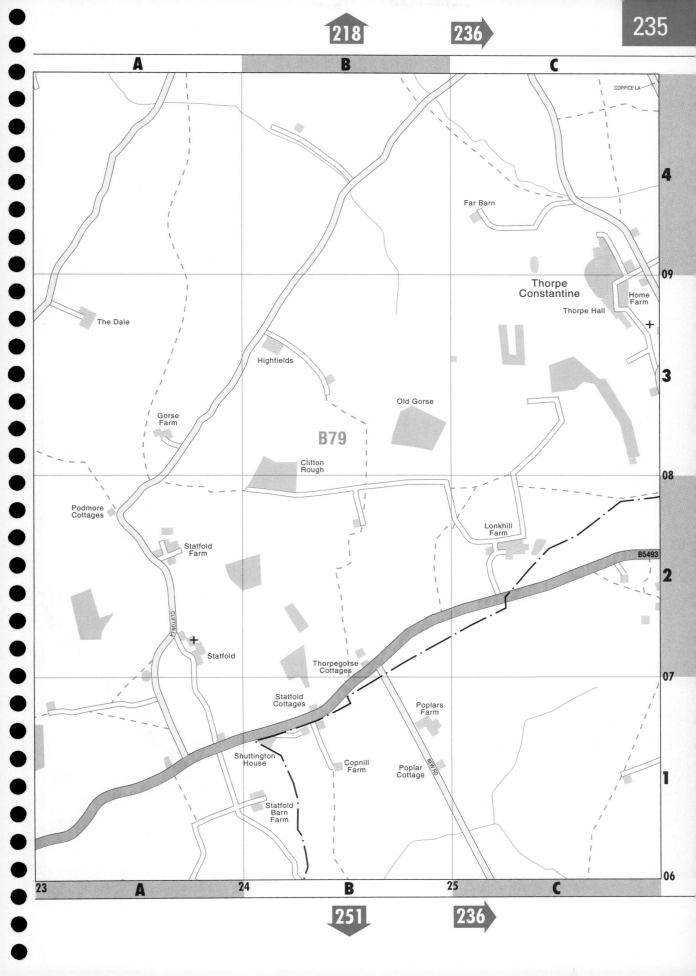

COPPICE LA

4

Far Barn

09

Thorpe
Constantine

The Dale

Home
Farm

Thorpe Hall

+

Highfields

3

Old Gorse

Gorse
Farm

B79

Clifton
Rough

08

Podmore
Cottages

Lonkhill
Farm

B5493

Statfold
Farm

2

CLIFTON LA

+

Statfold

Thorpegorse
Cottages

07

Statfold
Cottages

Poplars
Farm

Shuttington
House

Copnill
Farm

Poplar
Cottage

NEW RD

1

Statfold
Barn
Farm

06

235
219

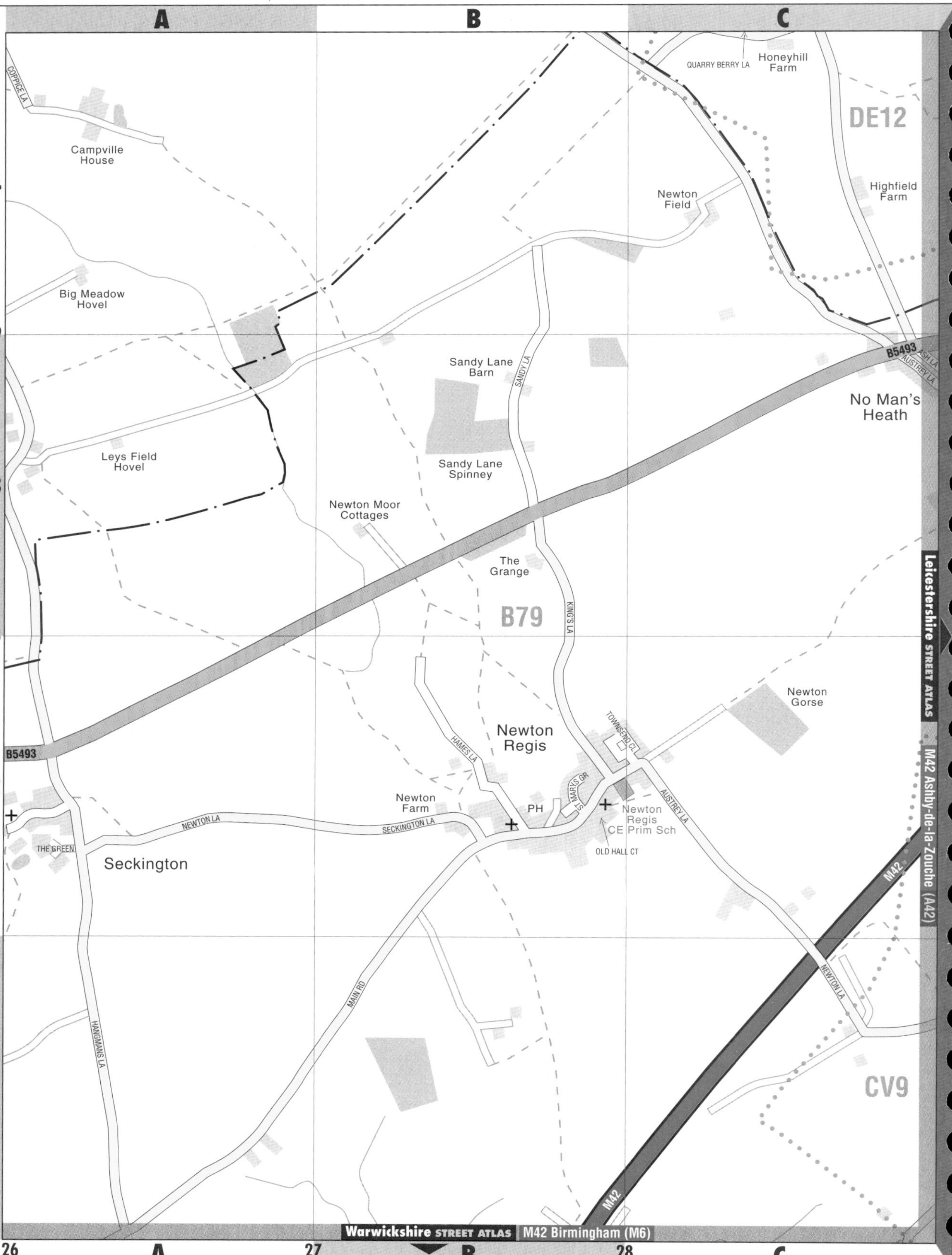

A
B
C
4
09
3
08
2
07
1
06
26
27
28
COPPICE LA
Campville House
Big Meadow Hovel
Leys Field Hovel
QUARRY BERRY LA
Honeyhill Farm
DE12
Newton Field
Highfield Farm
Sandy Lane Barn
SANDY LA
B5493
ASH LA
AUSTREY LA
No Man's Heath
Sandy Lane Spinney
Newton Moor Cottages
The Grange
B79
KING'S LA
Newton Gorse
TOWNSEND CL
Newton Regis
HAMES LA
ST MARYS GR
PH
Newton Farm
NEWTON LA
SECKINGTON LA
Newton Regis CE Prim Sch
OLD HALL CT
THE GREEN
Seckington
M42
NEWTON LA
MAIN RD
HANGMANS LA
CV9
Leicestershire STREET ATLAS
M42 Ashby-de-la-Zouche (A42)
Warwickshire STREET ATLAS
M42 Birmingham (M6)

235

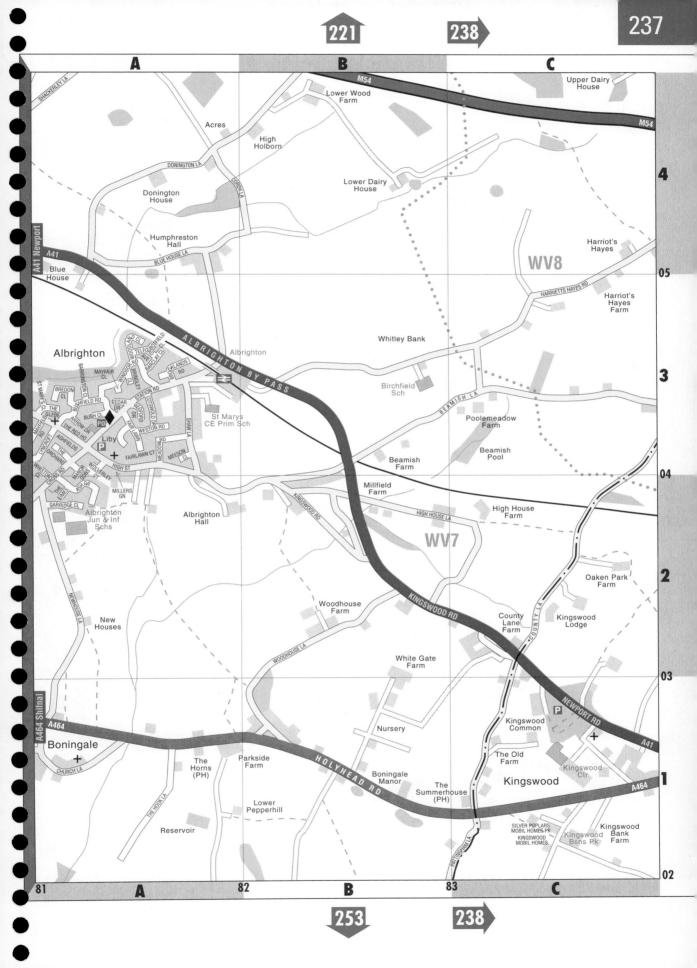

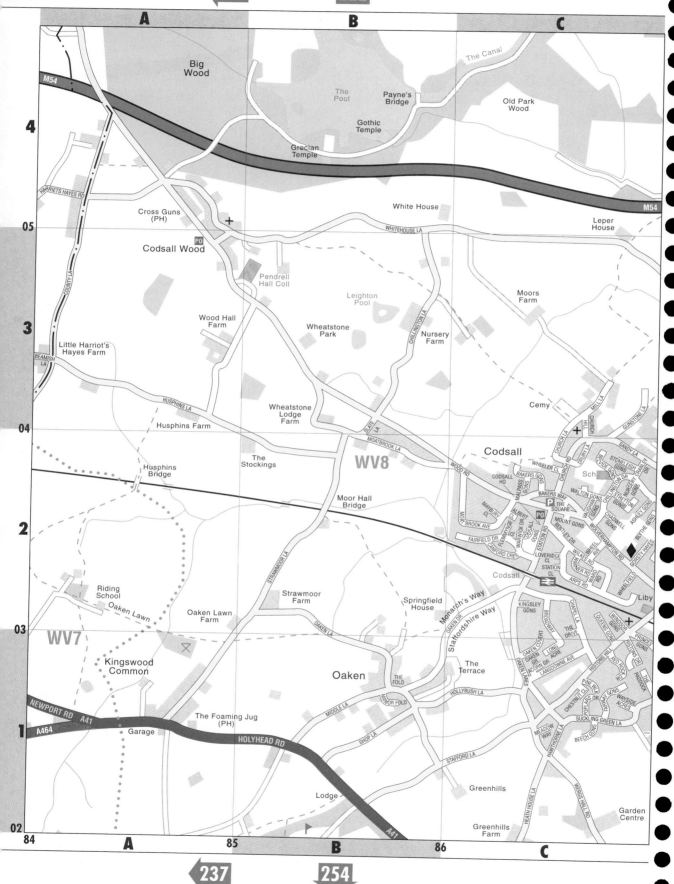

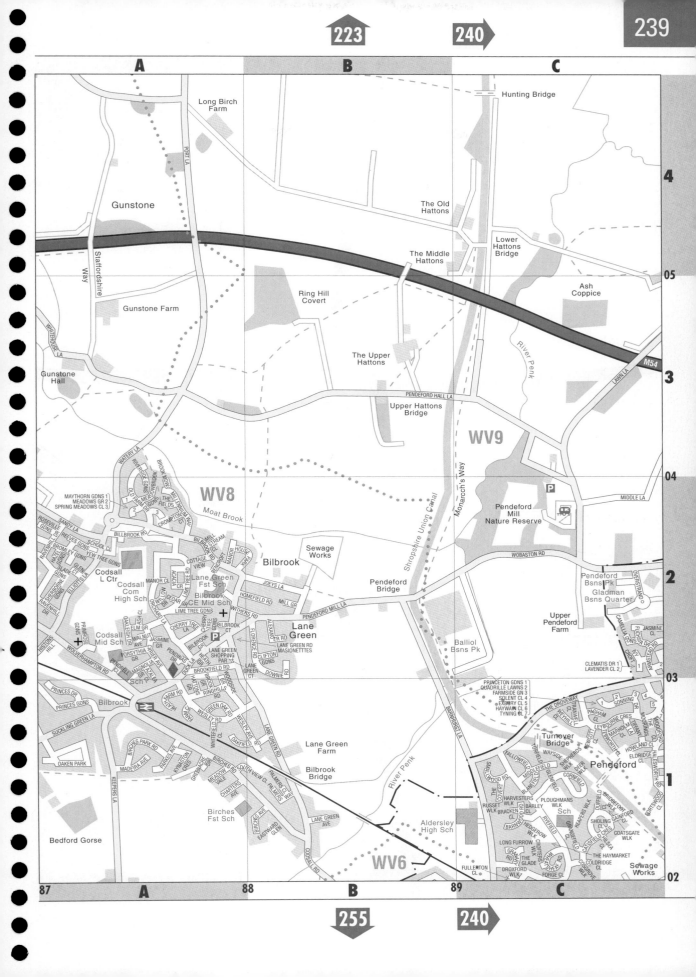

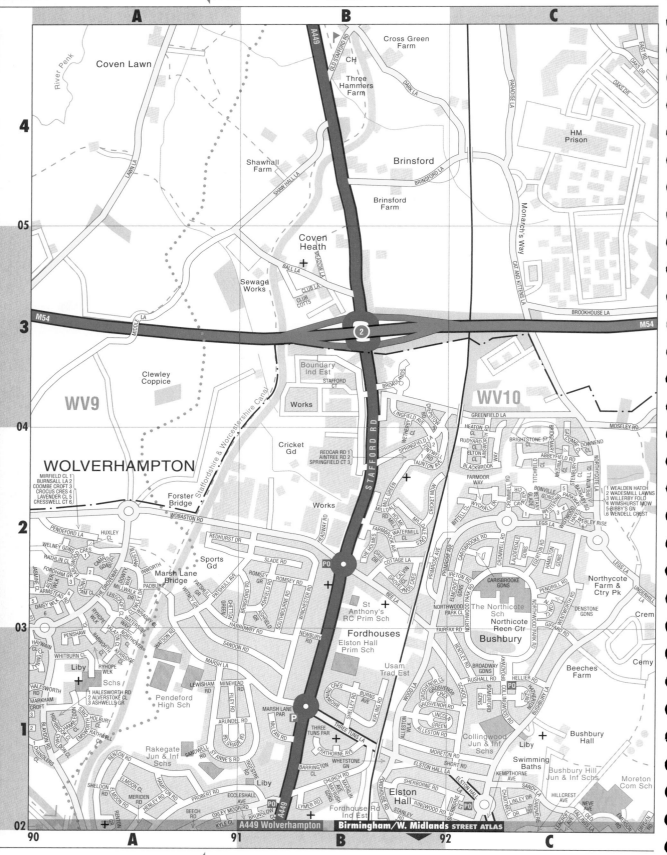

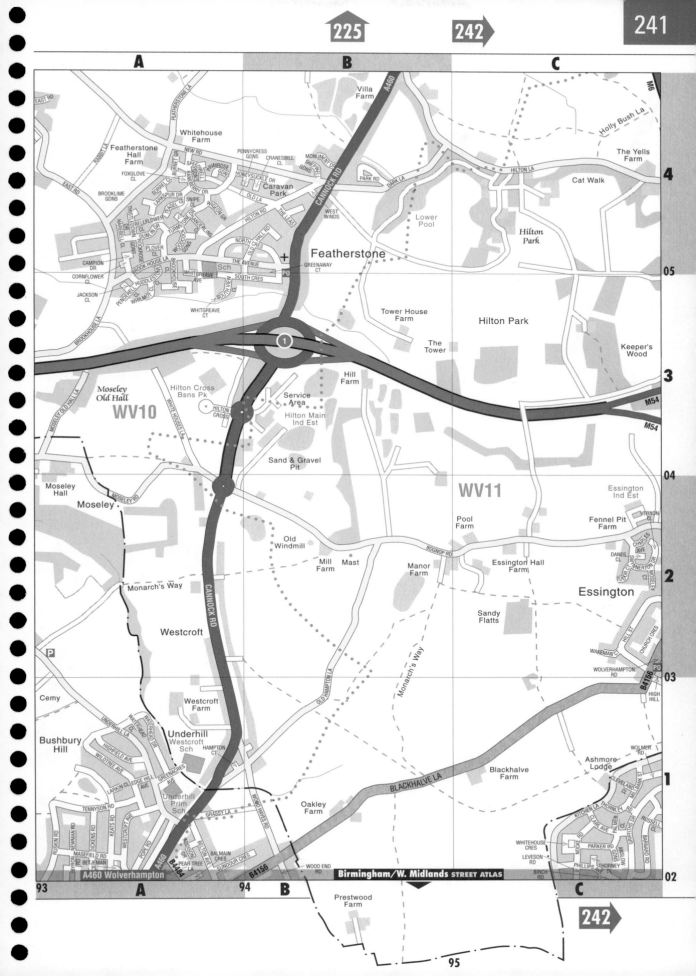

A   B   C

4

05

3

M54

M54

04

WV11

2

Essington

03

1

02

Villa Farm
A460
Holly Bush La
M6
The Yells Farm
Whitehouse Farm
NEW RD
PENNYCRESS GDNS
CRANESBILL CL
SHEPHELL GDNS
MONUMENT DR
HILTON LA
Cat Walk
Featherstone Hall Farm
RABBIT LA
FEATHERSTONE LA
BURNET GR
SPEEDWELL
HONEYSUCKLE DR
PARK RD
DARK LA
Hilton Park
FOXGLOVE CL
SORREL CL
PRIMROSE GDNS
CANNOCK RD
Lower Pool
BROOKLIME GDNS
LARKSPUR DR
BILBERRY DR
OLD LA
Caravan Park
WEST WINDS
CAMPION DR
THISTLEDOWN
DUNLIN DR
TEASEL CRES
SNIPE CL
WIGEON GR
HILTON RD
THE LEASES
Featherstone
CORNFLOWER CL
BELLFLOWER
ROCK ROSE
WOODCOCK GDNS
RINGER PLING
NORTH CRES
HALL RD
THE AVENUE
Sch
GREENAWAY CT
JACKSON CL
PENDEREL CL
HUDDLESTON CL
BROOK HOUSE LA
BROOKHOUSE
WHITGREAVE AVE
SOUTH VIEW
SOUTH CRES
PO
Tower House Farm
Hilton Park
WHILMOT CL
WHITGREAVE CT
The Tower
Keeper's Wood
BROOKHOUSE LA
Moseley Old Hall
Hilton Cross Bsns Pk
Hill Farm
MOSELEY OLD HALL LA
WHITE HOUSE LA
WV10
HILTON CROSS
Service Area
Hilton Main Ind Est
Moseley Hall
MOSELEY RD
Sand & Gravel Pit
Essington Ind Est
Moseley
Old Windmill
Pool Farm
Fennel Pit Farm
VERNON CL
CHARLES AVE
BOGNOP RD
DANES CL
TUSK CT
CANNOCK RD
Mill Farm
Mast
Manor Farm
Essington Hall Farm
MOSELEY CT
Monarch's Way
Essington
HILL ST
Westcroft
Sandy Flatts
WAKEMAN
CHURCH CRES
Cemy
WOLVERHAMPTON RD
B4156
P
Westcroft Farm
Monarch's Way
HIGH HILL
Bushbury Hill
UNDERHILL LA
WATERHEAD LA
WATERHEAD DR
Underhill
Westcroft Sch
HAMPTON CT
GREENACRES AVE
OLD HAMPTON LA
Blackhalve Farm
WOLMER RD
Ashmore Lodge
HIGHFIELD AVE
WILDTREE AVE
LODGE HILL
Blackhalve Farm
CLEVELAND CL
MILLBANK ST
LARKIN CL
Underhill Prim Sch
GRASSY LA
WOOD HAYES RD
BLACKHALVE LA
KITCHEN LA
THORNLEY RD
CLARE AVE
PALMER CL
RUSSELL CL
TENNYSON RD
WESTCROFT AVE
Oakley Farm
MOCK RD
PARKER RD
BARNARD RD
RUSKIN RD
NEWMAN RD
KEATS RD
DICKENS RD
POPE RD
BELTON AVE
MADISON AVE
BALMAIN CRES
SUNDOUR CRES
WHITEHOUSE CRES
LEVESON RD
PHILLIPS AVE
THORNEY CL
PHILLIPS AVE
BYRON
MASEFIELD RD
BETJEMAN PL
PEAR TREE LA
WOOD END RD
BIRCH CL
A460 Wolverhampton
A460
B4484
B4156
Prestwood Farm

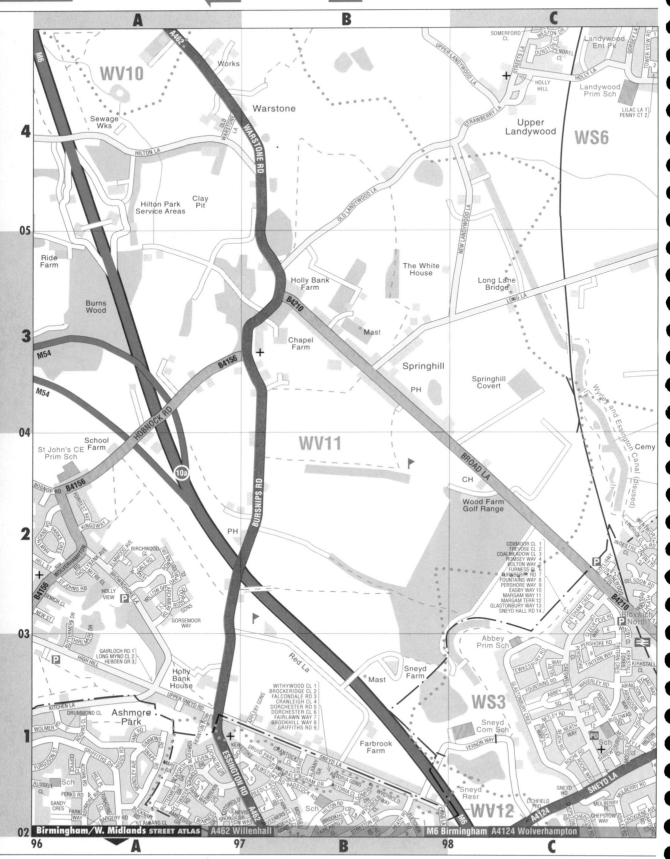

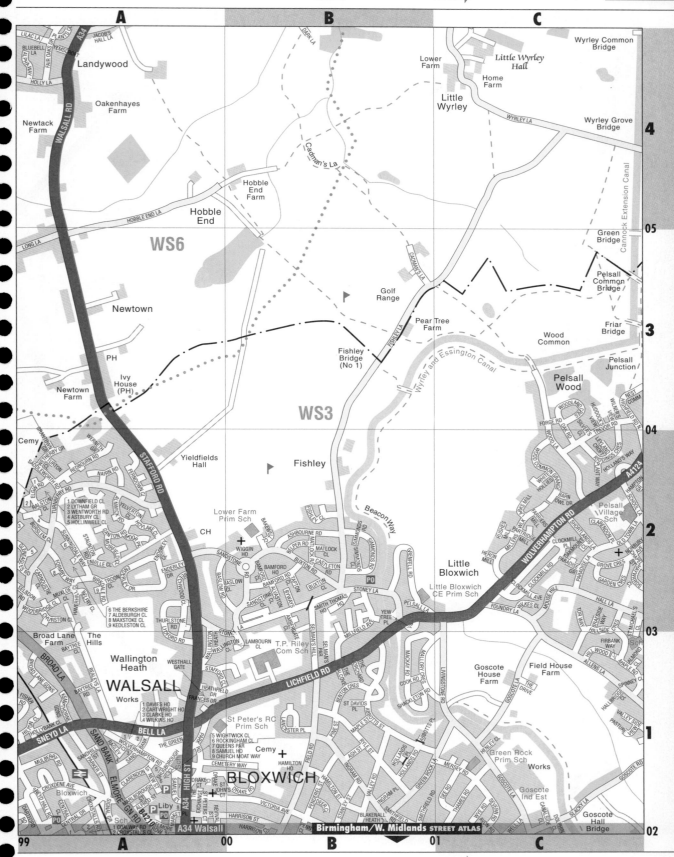

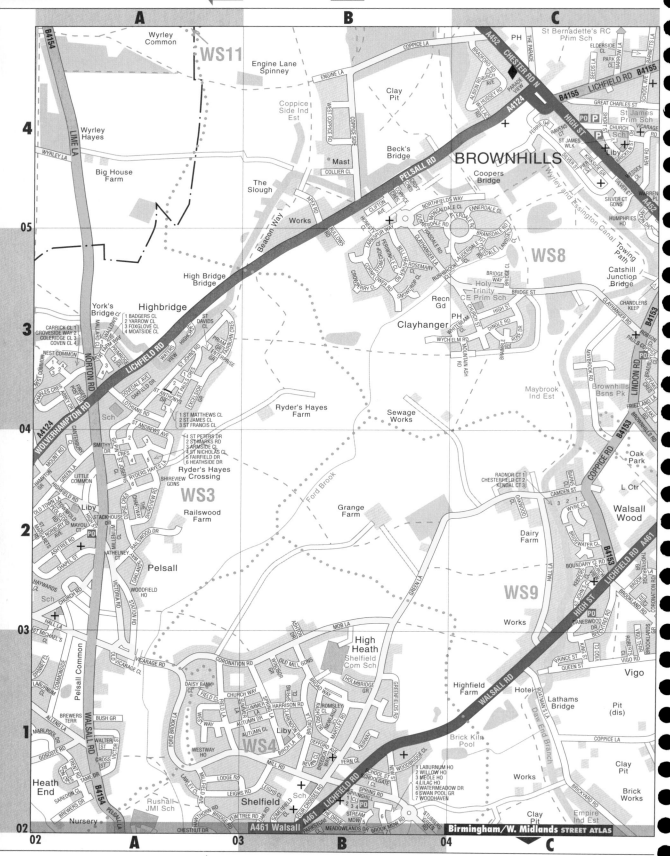

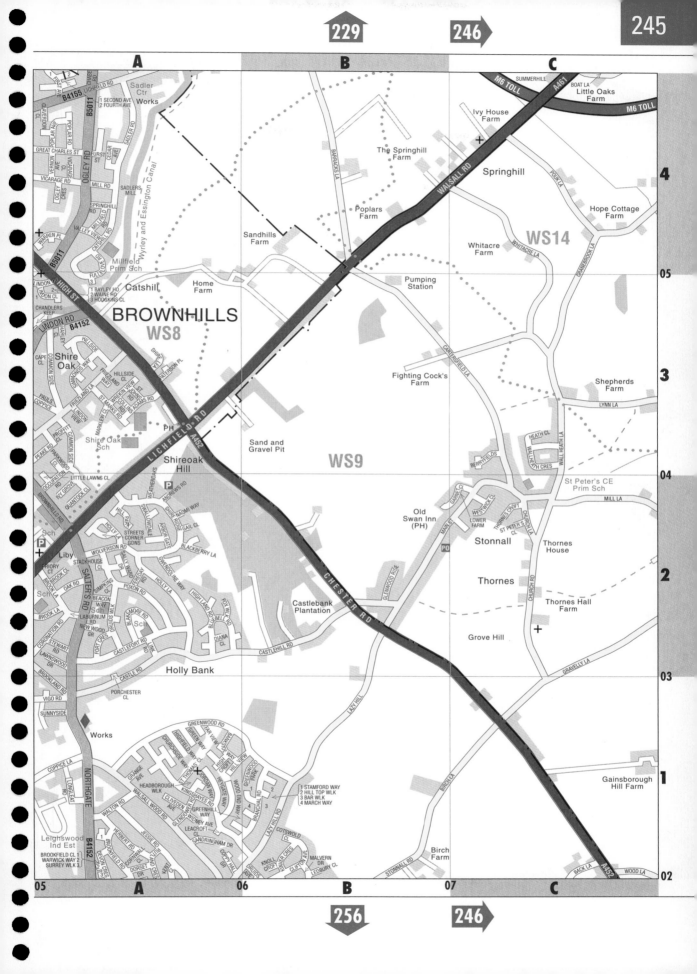

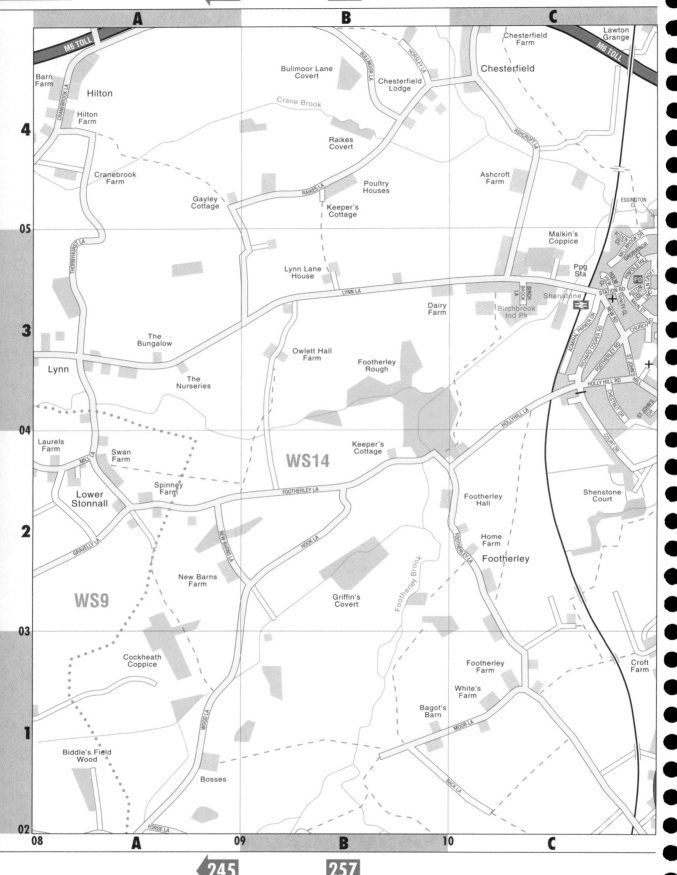

A B C

M6 TOLL

Barn Farm
Hilton
Hilton Farm
CRANEBROOK LA
Cranebrook Farm
THORNYHURST LA

4

Bullmoor Lane Covert
BULLMOOR LA
Chesterfield Lodge
HORSLEY LA
Chesterfield Farm
Chesterfield
ASHCROFT LA
M6 TOLL
Lawton Grange

Crane Brook
Raikes Covert
RAIKES LA
Gayley Cottage
Poultry Houses
Keeper's Cottage
Ashcroft Farm
ESSINGTON CL

05

Malkin's Coppice
RYDEN CL
MILLBROOK CL
GROSVENOR CL
Lynn Lane House
Ppg Sta
HOLM CL
TRINITY CL
STATION RD
ASTON CL
LINCH CROFT
PINFOLD HILL

LYNN LA
LYNN LA
Dairy Farm
BIRCH BROOK CL
BIRCHBROOK
Birchbrook Ind Pk
Shenstone
MAIN ST
NEW RD
CHURCH RD

3

The Bungalow
Owlett Hall Farm
Footherley Rough
ADMIRAL PARKER DR
RICHARD COOPER RD
FOOTHERLEY RD
ST JOHN'S HILL

Lynn
The Nurseries
Holly Hill Rd
HOLLY HILL RD
CHESTNUT DR
ST JOHN'S CR

04

Laurels Farm
MILL LA
Swan Farm
Keeper's Cottage
WS14
HOLLYHILL LA
Shenstone Court
COURT DR

Spinney Farm
Lower Stonnall
FOOTHERLEY LA
Footherley Hall

2

GRAVELLY LA
NEW BARNS LA
HOOK LA
Home Farm
FOOTHERLEY LA
Footherley

WS9
New Barns Farm
Griffin's Covert
Footherley Brook

03

Cockheath Coppice
Footherley Farm
Croft Farm

WOOD LA
White's Farm

1

Biddle's Field Wood
Bagot's Barn
MOOR LA
BACK LA

Bosses

02

FORGE LA

08 A 09 B 10 C

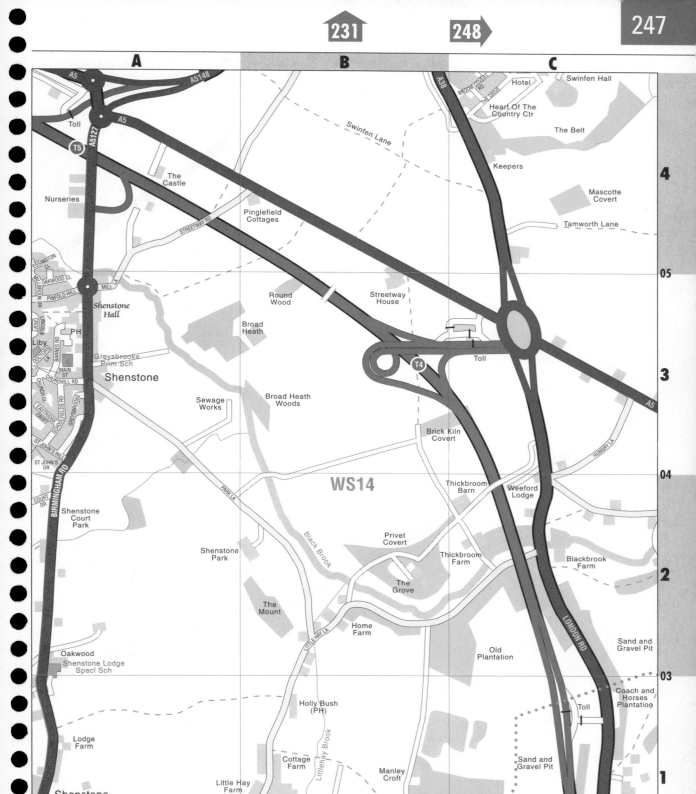

A
B
C

4

05

3

04

WS14

2

03

1

02

11
12
13

A
B
C

Swinfen Hall
Hotel
Heart Of The Country Ctr
The Belt
Keepers
Mascotte Covert
Tamworth Lane
Swinfen Lane
Round Wood
Streetway House
Pinglefield Cottages
The Castle
Nurseries
Toll
T5
A5127
A5148
A5
Shenstone Hall
Shenstone
Greysbrooke Prim Sch
PH
Liby
Broad Heath
Broad Heath Woods
Sewage Works
Brick Kiln Covert
Thickbroom Barn
Weeford Lodge
Toll
T4
Shenstone Court Park
Shenstone Park
The Mount
Home Farm
Privet Covert
Thickbroom Farm
Blackbrook Farm
The Grove
Black Brook
PARK LA
Oakwood
Shenstone Lodge Specl Sch
Old Plantation
Sand and Gravel Pit
Coach and Horses Plantation
Toll
Lodge Farm
Holly Bush (PH)
Cottage Farm
Manley Croft
Sand and Gravel Pit
Shenstone Woodend
Little Hay Farm
Little Hay
Green Barn
Manley Wood
Windmill (dis)
Wood End Farm
A5127
LITTLE HAY LA
GREEN BARNS LA
Littlehay Brook
M6 TOLL
A38
B75
LONDON RD
A5
BIRMINGHAM RD
STREETWAY RD

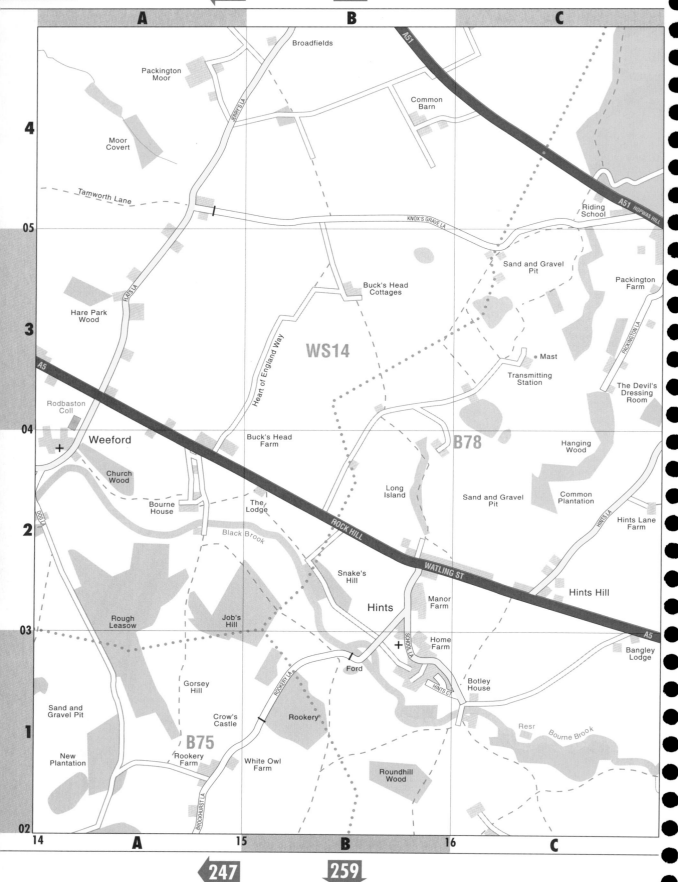

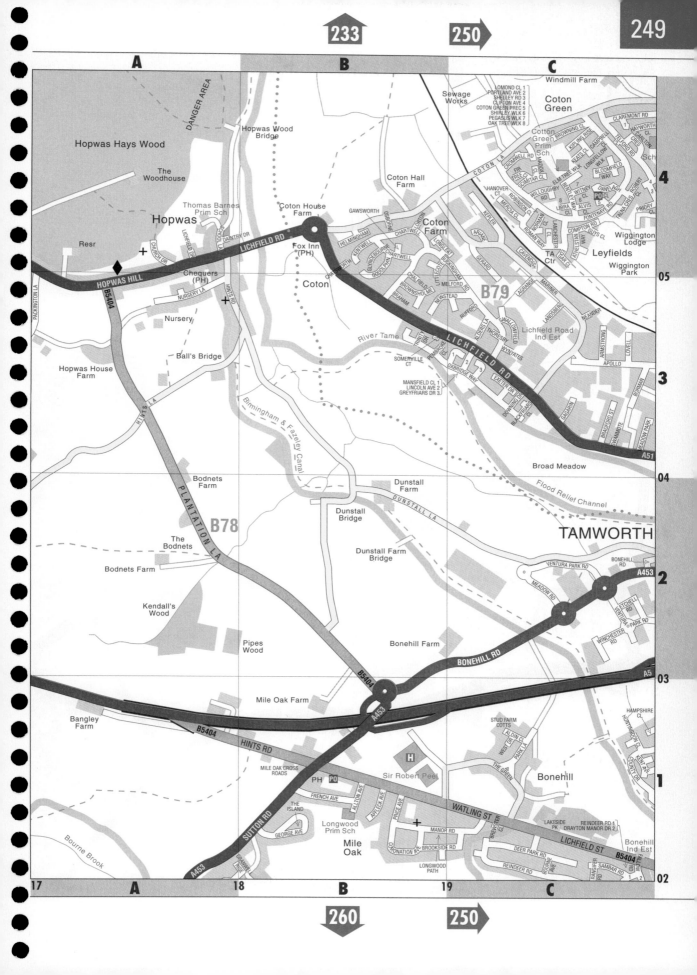

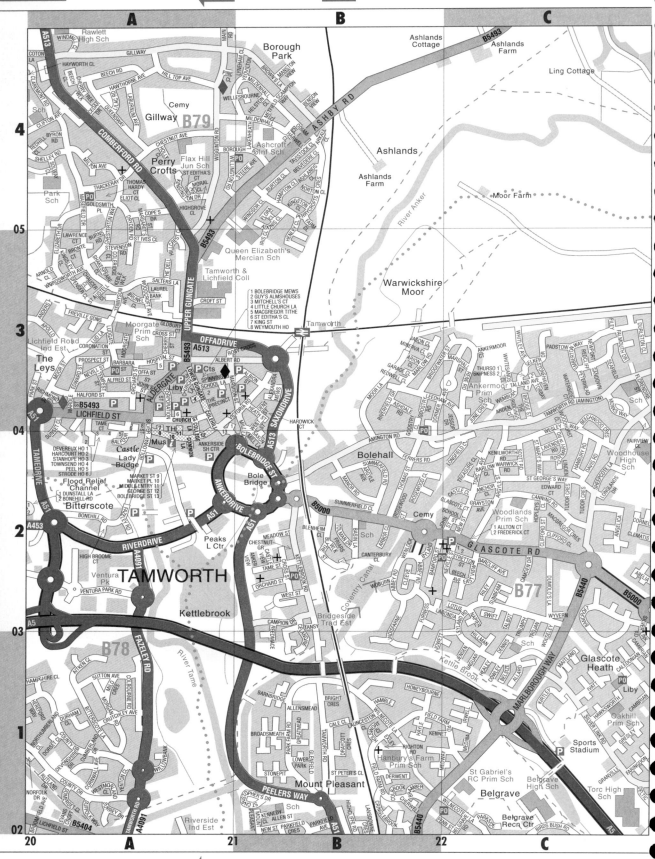

249
234

A   B   C

Rawlett High Sch

Borough Park

Ashlands Cottage

B5493

Ashlands Farm

Ling Cottage

Gillway

B79

Ashlands

Ashlands Farm

Moor Farm

4

Perry Crofts

Flax Hill Jun Sch

River Anker

Warwickshire Moor

05

Queen Elizabeth's Mercian Sch

Tamworth & Lichfield Coll

The Leys

Lichfield Road Ind Est

Moorgate Prim Sch

1 BOLEBRIDGE MEWS
2 GUY'S ALMSHOUSES
3 MITCHELL'S CT
4 LITTLE CHURCH LA
5 MACGREGOR TITHE
6 ST EDITHA'S CT
7 KING ST
8 WEYMOUTH HO

3

OFFADRIVE

A513

Tamworth

Ankermoor Prim Sch

ALDERGATE

B5493

LICHFIELD ST

04

Castle

Bolehall

Woodhouse High Sch

Mus

Woodlands Prim Sch

1 ALLTON CT
2 FREDERICK CT

Castle Lady Bridge

Bole Bridge

BOLEBRIDGE ST

B5000

Cemy

Flood Relief Channel

Bitterscote

ANKERDRIVE

A51

B77

GLASCOTE RD

2

RIVERDRIVE

A4091

TAMWORTH

Peaks L Ctr

Coventry Canal

Ventura Pk

Ventura Park Rd

Kettlebrook

Bridgeside Trad Est

B5440

Glascote Heath

03

B78

FAZELEY RD

River Tame

Kettle Brook

MARLBOROUGH WAY

Glascote Heath

A5

Liby

Oakhill Prim Sch

1

Mount Pleasant

Hanbury's Farm Prim Sch

St Gabriel's RC Prim Sch

Belgrave High Sch

Sports Stadium

Belgrave

Torc High Sch

PEELERS WAY

Riverside Ind Est

Belgrave Recn Ctr

02

B5404

A4091

A51

B5440

A5

20   A   21   B   22   C

249
261

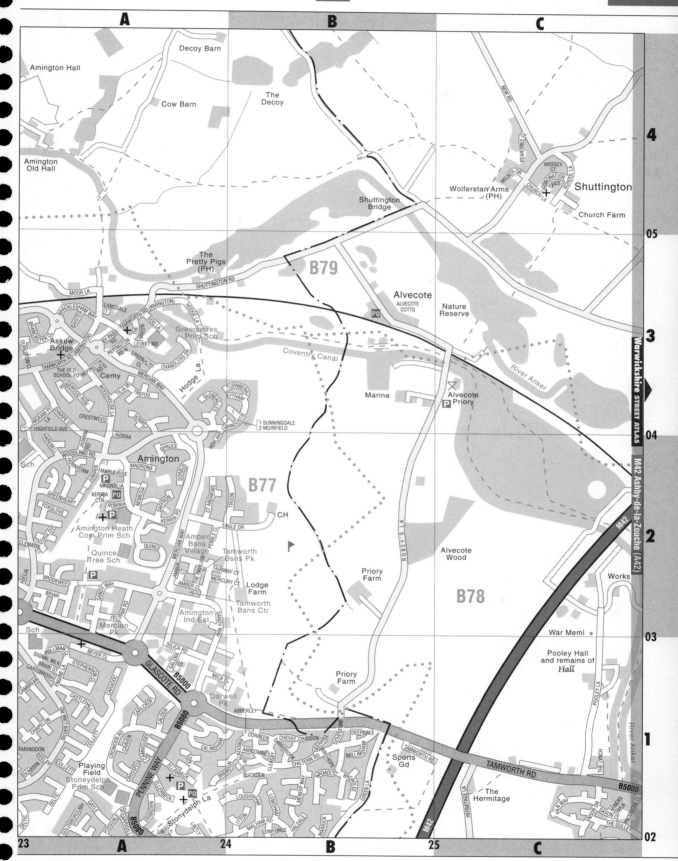

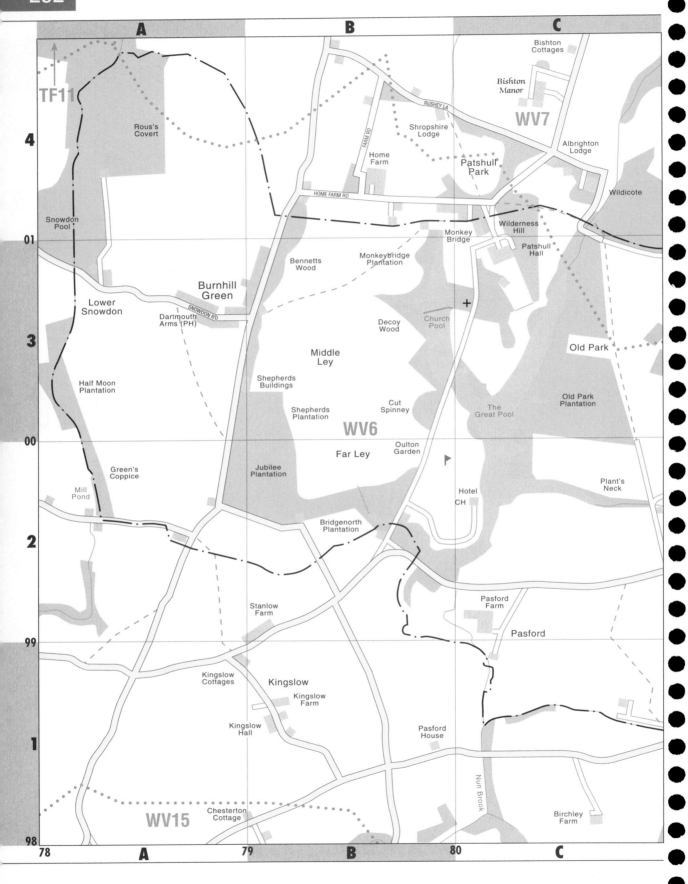

TF11

Rous's Covert

A 4

Snowdon Pool

Lower Snowdon

01

Burnhill Green

SNOWDON RD

Dartmouth Arms (PH)

Half Moon Plantation

A 3

Green's Coppice

Mill Pond

A 2

99

Kingslow Cottages

Kingslow Hall

WV15

1

98

78   A   79

Home Farm

FARM RD

HOME FARM RD

Bennetts Wood

Shepherds Buildings

Middle Ley

Shepherds Plantation

WV6

Far Ley

Jubilee Plantation

Stanlow Farm

Kingslow

Kingslow Farm

Chesterton Cottage

B   79

Monkeybridge Plantation

Monkey Bridge

Decoy Wood

Cut Spinney

Oulton Garden

Bridgenorth Plantation

Pasford House

Nun Brook

B

Bishton Cottages

Bishton Manor

RUSHEY LA

Shropshire Lodge

Patshull Park

Wilderness Hill

Patshull Hall

Church Pool

Old Park

Old Park Plantation

The Great Pool

Hotel
CH

Pasford Farm

Pasford

Plant's Neck

Birchley Farm

WV7

Albrighton Lodge

Wildicote

C

80   C

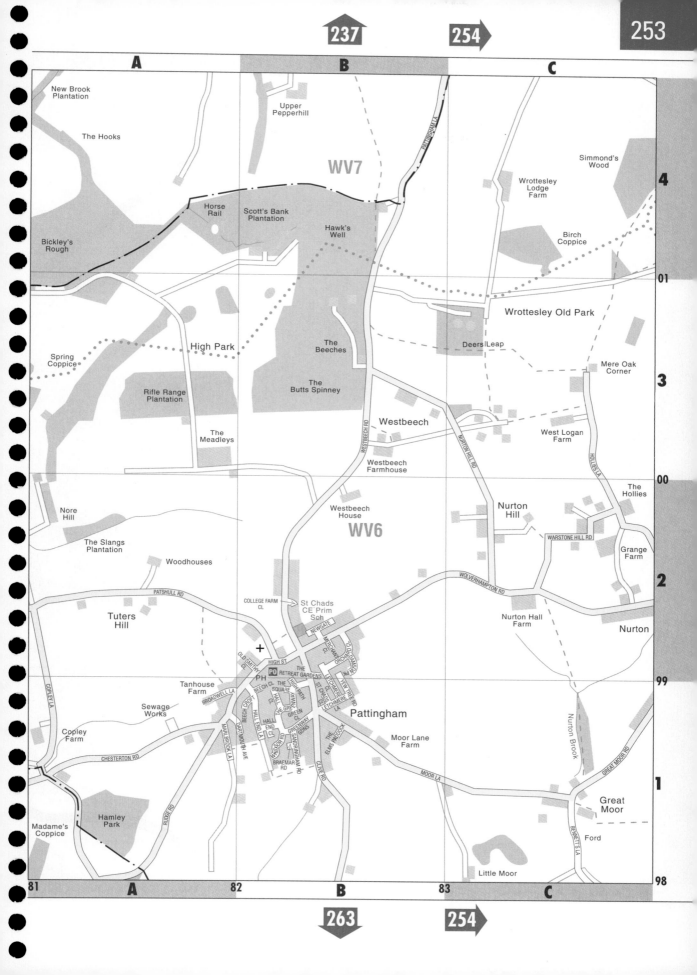

253 238

A B C

WV7

Simmond's Wood

Wrottesley Hall

The Bradshaws

Bull Ride

CH

Inland Pool

Wrottesley Park

Heath House Farm

HEATH HOUSE RD

WERGS HALL RD

HOLYHEAD RD

A41

WERGS RD

Wergs Hall

WV8

4

01

River Penk

The Grange

Wergs

WESTCROFT RD

Salt's Pool

Smith's Rough

SCAMPTON CL 1
HUDSON GR 2
TANGMERE CL 3
LIVINGSTONE DR 4

BOWEN
COOKE
AVE

FOWLER
DR

WROTTESLEY RD W

Dippons Lane

Cranmoor

3

Cranmoor Lodge

HAWKSTONE CT

TURNBERRY GR

WENTWORTH GR

COLLET DR

DEAN
AVE

STEVENSON DR

BRUNEL DR

EDNAM RD

WROTTESLEY RD

MERE OAK
RD

MERIDEN
RD

CROFTON
RD

IONIA DR

MERCIA DR

Dippons Lane

HEPWORTH CL 1
LOWRY CL 2
MOORE CL 3
THIRLMERE GR 4
WASTWATER CT 5
BUTTERMERE CT 6
CHARTLEY CL 7
KENILWORTH RD 8

SUNNINGDALE AVE

RH STEPHEN
GR

MOOR PK

FRANKLIN CT

FR BIGGIN

SHALBURY

COSFORD
GR

OFFA'S DR

ATHELSTAN
CL

GUTHRUM
CL

CYNGTON

PENDA GR

GAINSBOROUGH DR

REYNOLDS

00

TROON
CT

BELFRY

ANSON
CL

SHACKLET

COOK
CL

CABOT
GR

DARWIN

STANLEY
CL

BROWNING
CT

MILTON CT

WORDSWORTH
DR

SANDOWN DR

SEDGEFIELD
GR

INGFIELD

THE PARKWAY

Perton

WROTTESLEY PARK RD

PORTRUSH RD

LYTHAM
RD

CLOVERDALE

COLERIDGE DR

CHURCH RD

EPSOM
CL

ASCOT

HAYDOCK

THE
PASTURES

CUNNINGHAM

Liby

SPENCER AVE

Sch

ENNERDALE RD

RICHMOND DR

THE PADDOCK 1
FALLOWFIELD 2
THE CARTWAY 3
THE WINDROW 4
THE SADDLESTONES 5
MEADOW CROFT 6
WORCESTER GR 7

COULTER GR

MELROSE
AVE

ELGIN
CT

TINTERN
CT

CHEPSTOW
CL

RYDAL CL

CONWAY
GR

ARUNDEL

KELSO
GDNS

EDBURGH
CT

CROWLAND
AVE

CHESHIRE
GR

TRENT CL

CHURN

GRASMERE

TINTAGEL

LANCASTER RD

WELLS
CL

CANTERBURY DR

SEVERN DR

AVON

HAMBLE GR

SOMERBY DR

DEE GR

ST MAWES
RD

KINGSWAY

OATLANDS

MALLORY RD

CHERITON
AVE

ADVAL TON

STOKESAY

CORFE

LYMEY DR

WREN AVE

WYKEHAM
GR

PAXTON

FOSTER
GR

ROWTON
GR

ROCKINGHAM DR

WINCHBY RD

HOPTON CL

RICHMOND DR

STOCKBRIDGE

2

WOLVERHAMPTON
RD

HOLMES LA

GREAT MOOR RD

Nurton Brook

Staffordshire Way

Monarch's Way

Perton Orchard

WV6

BUTTERFIELD
CL

CH

NASH
AVE

EDGE HILL DR

TURNHAM GREEN

ROUDLOW

BERKELEY
CL

WARWICK
GR

Boundary Farm

PERTON RD

BOUNDARY WAY

CRANBROOK

OLD LA

99

Nurton Bk

PATTINGHAM RD

Old Perton

Sling Wood

Perton Court

PERTON RD

PERTON BROOK VALE

THE
HIGHFIELDS

RAVENSHILL RD

QUAIL GREEN

ROOKWOOD
DR

WIGHTWICK BK

1

Freehold Wood

Middle Wood

Perton House

South Perton Farm

JENNY WALKERS LA

Wightwick Hall Sch

Wightwick

Cherringham

TANGMERE DR

FAITH HILL

WIGHTWICK
HALL RD

MAYSWOOD DR

Wightwick Manor

BRIDGNORTH RD

A454

WV3

A454

SABRINA RD

CASTLECROFT LA

HEADLAND
RD

98

84 A 85 B 86 C

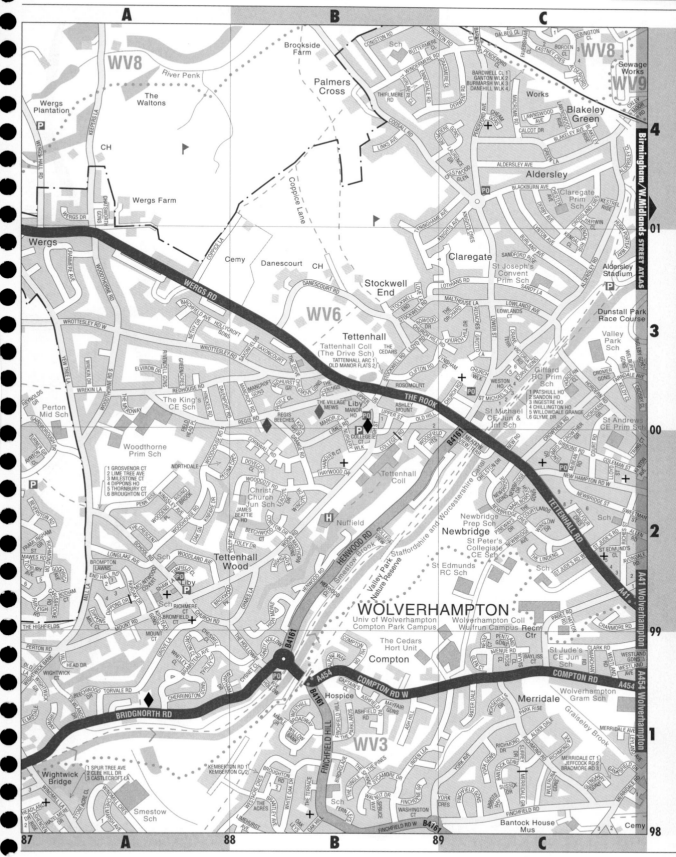

C2
1 ALBERT RD
2 BROMFORD DALE
3 SLADE HILL
4 ST JUDE'S CT
5 THE CEDARS
6 BRIMFIELD PL
7 BALFOUR CT
8 NEWBRIDGE MEWS
9 GRAFTON CT

245

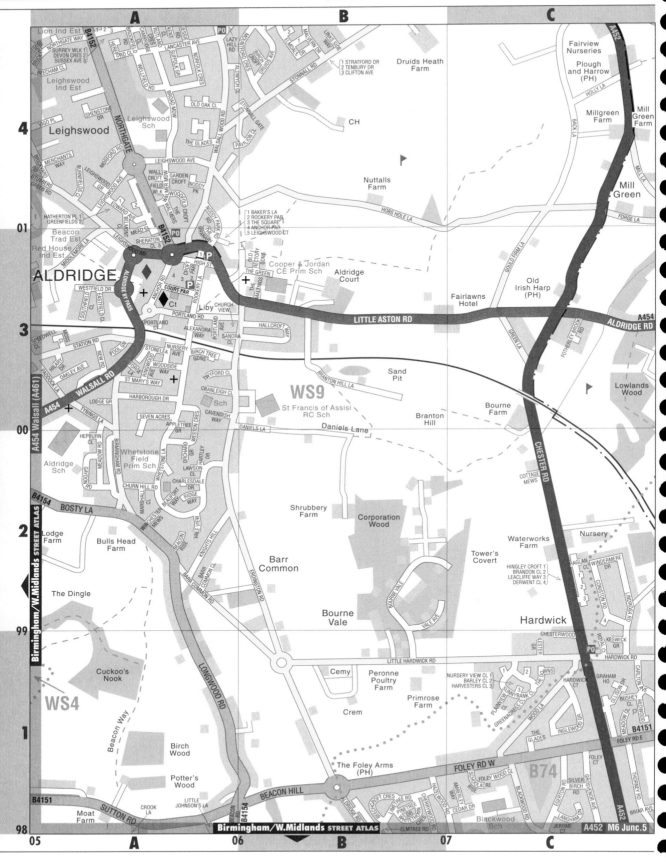

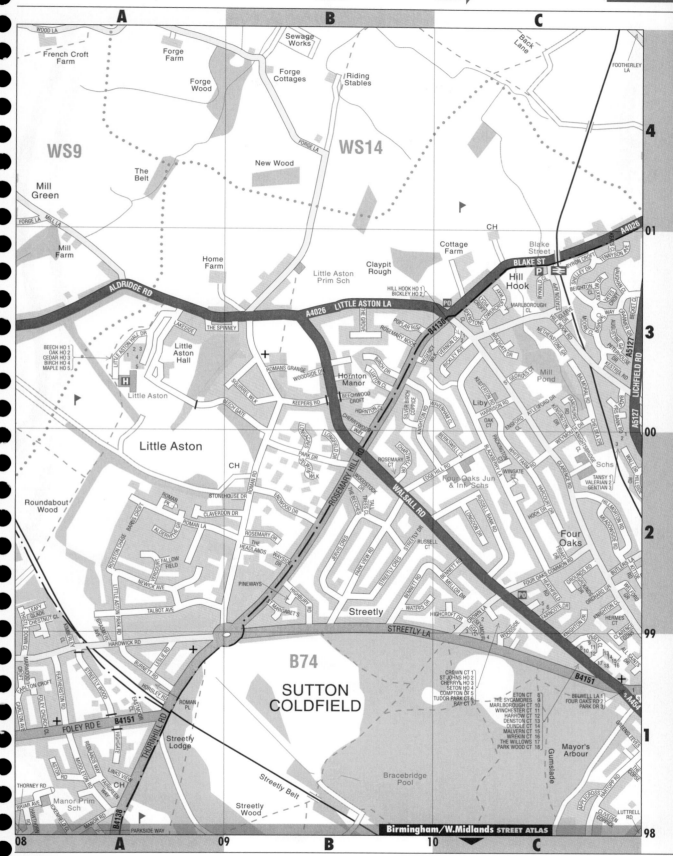

A   B   C

4

01

3

B74

00

2

99

1

98

11   A   12   B   13   C

Joburns Cottages
Alder Farm
Brookfield
GREEN BARNS LA
LITTLE HAY LA
WS14
The Highwayman (PH)
Camp Farm
Blossom Hill Farm
WOODLAND CT
SMARTS AVE
BLAKE ST
WATFORD GAP RD
Biddles Farm
Watford Gap
BIRMINGHAM RD
A5127 LICHFIELD RD
PO
Hovel Covert
Black Fir Wood
Green Wood
M6 TOLL
LONDON RD
A38
Weeford Park Farm
CAMP RD
Pine Tree Cottage
Springhill Farm
HILLWOOD COMMON RD
Hill Common
Hill Farm
Mast
Television Station
Manorial Farm
Manorial Wood
Springhill Plantation
Hill Wood
HILL WOOD RD
Spreading Tree Hill
A5127
Hill
KEATING GDNS
WARDLE CL
STRINGER
DUNTON CL
DUNTON CL
WESTFIELD
BEECH CL
HIGHOVER CL
MANOR
LAWNEY DR
GLANVILLE DR
CROCKFORD DR
OAKLAND
HILLSIDE RD
GREELEY CL
HATHAWAY RD
HAYCROFT DR
SHERBOOT LA
Hill Wood Farm
Hillside Farm
MAYALL DR
LOXLEY RD
HOMESTEAD DR
ST JOHN'S LE
WOODS LE
ARLINGTON CL
WORCESTER LA
Dale Farm
Little Sutton Prim Sch
1 PLOUGHMANS PL
2 TILLER GR
3 SOWERS CT
4 COMBINE CT
Woodside Farm
Piggery
CANWELL GATE
DUTTONS LA
WEEFORD RD
TURF PITTS LA
Hilltop Farm
A38
THORNHILL LA
B4151
M6 TOLL
1 CHEVIOT CT
2 CHILTERN CT
3 BREDON CT
4 COTSWOLD CT
B75
RANDLE DR
CARTWRIGHT RD
EDWARDS RD
HURST RD
ST BLAISE RD
WORCESTER RD
REDNILL VIEW
WILLMOTT CL
CLARENDON LA
MARLPIT LA
Roughley
HARVEST FIELDS WAY
RECROSS LA
RABONE LA
BISHOPS
SLADE RD
1 MARLPIT RISE
2 WEEFORD DELL
3 WHEATCROFT CL
LICHFIELD RD
BUTLERS LA
HENLEY DR
THE DELLE COTES
KINGS CT
BRENTHALL WALCOT RD
BOLDINGTON RD
DUNCALFE DR
DUGDALE CRES
PUSEY CL
GIBBONS RD
TOWER RD
WILMCOTE DR
GRANGE LA
GRANGE AVE
WILLMOTT CL
PH
BRADWELL CROFT
BIDDLCOTE GR
BUCKTON CL
AVON RD
FOX HILL RD
Mere Green
Butlers Lane
SARA CL
HARLAND RD
HOLLY
RED CL
CHURCH TERR
Mere Green Comb Sch
FARM
BOROUGH
ST JAMES
WHEATLEY CL
MERE GREEN RD
ROUGHLEY DR
COBURN DR
HOLTE DR
PEROTT DR
SHARRAT FIELD
MERE POOL RD
SHEPHERDS POOL RD
MORLAND
QUINTON DR
WARING RD
CHANNELS DR
HAYDON
Arthur Terry Sch
HOBART CT
BALFOUR CT
KITTOE RD
BEXTON CL
PO
Liby
CARLTON HO
MERE DR
CREMORNE RD
ARLESCOTE CL
HARVEY DR
Little Sutton Rd
LITTLE SUTTON RD
Moor Hall Prim Sch
ROYAL LA
HOLTE DR
ESSEX RD
CLIVE
FERRERS CL
Fox Hill Farm
B4151
BELWELL LA
1 DEVONSHIRE CT
2 HARBOROUGH CT
3 TUDOR CT
CARLTON
KINGSLEIGH CROFT
CREMORNE WLK
JORDAN RD
STREATHER RD
HAREWELL CL
HEATHCROFT RD
BROCKHURST RD
WYRLEY RD
P
Hotel
SUTTON COLDFIELD
A454
NURSERY LA
ALSTER
LE MORE
MINSTER DR
THE FORDROUGH
Beechcroft CT
Ley Hill
JORDAN RD
DOWER RD
DEVEREUX RD
TRINITY RD
LEY HILL RD
GROSVENOR RD
Moor Hall
CH
MOOR HALL DR
Fox Hill Farm
Ashfurlong Hall
HARTOPP RD
CRESSINGTON DR
LITTRELL RD
THE COPSE
FOUR OAKS RD
PINE LEIGH
BIDGEWOOD DR
LOCKHART DR
Coppice Sch
A5127 Sutton Coldfield
Birmingham/W.Midlands STREET ATLAS
A453 Sutton Coldfield
A454
A5127
A453 TAMWORTH RD

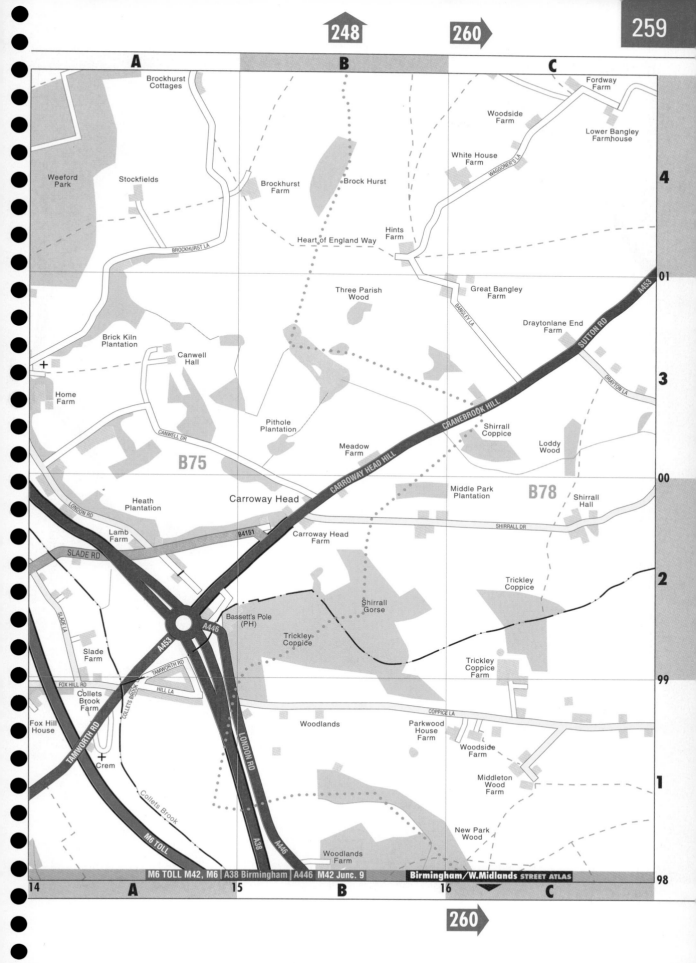

A | B | C

Brockhurst Cottages

Weeford Park

Stockfields

Brockhurst Farm

Brock Hurst

Fordway Farm

Woodside Farm

Lower Bangley Farmhouse

White House Farm

WAGGONER'S LA

4

BROCKHURST LA

Heart of England Way

Hints Farm

01

Three Parish Wood

Great Bangley Farm

A453

Brick Kiln Plantation

Canwell Hall

BANGLEY LA

Draytonlane End Farm

SUTTON RD

DRAYTON LA

3

Home Farm

CANWELL DR

CRANEBROOK HILL

Shirrall Coppice

Loddy Wood

Pithole Plantation

CARROWAY HEAD HILL

B75

Meadow Farm

Middle Park Plantation

B78

Shirrall Hall

00

Carroway Head

Heath Plantation

LONDON RD

B4151

Carroway Head Farm

SHIRRALL DR

Lamb Farm

SLADE RD

Trickley Coppice

2

Shirrall Gorse

SLADE LA

A453

A446

Bassett's Pole (PH)

Trickley Coppice

Trickley Coppice Farm

Slade Farm

TAMWORTH RD

HILL LA

99

FOX HILL RD

COLLETS BROOK

Collets Brook Farm

COPPICE LA

Fox Hill House

TAMWORTH RD

Woodlands

Parkwood House Farm

Woodside Farm

Crem

LONDON RD

Middleton Wood Farm

1

Collets Brook

New Park Wood

M6 TOLL

A38

A446

Woodlands Farm

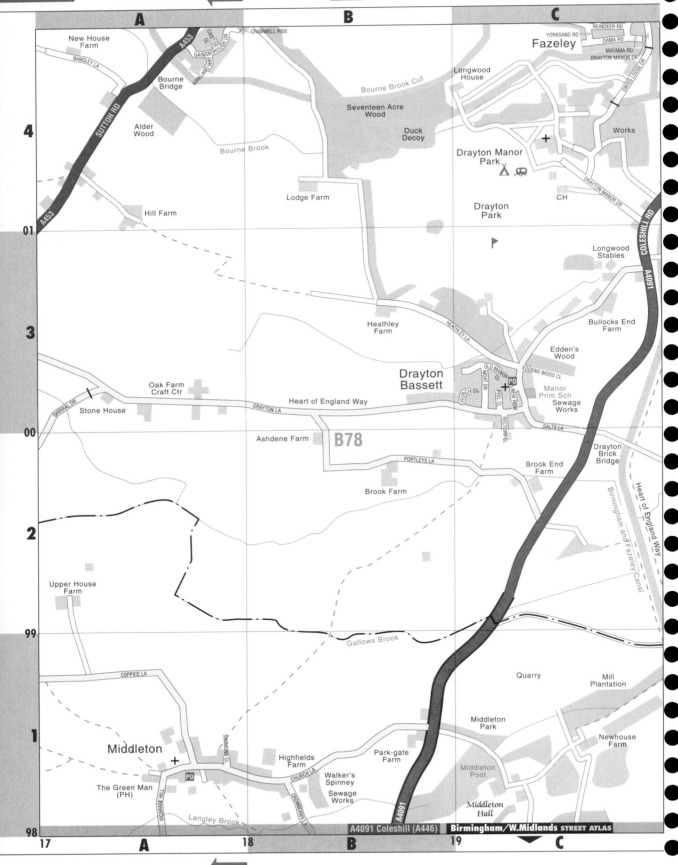

New House Farm

BANGLEY LA

Bourne Bridge

A453

SUTTON RD

A453

KIRKLAND WAY

GAINSBOROUGH DR

CASTOR CL

CRANWELL RISE

Alder Wood

Hill Farm

Bourne Brook

Bourne Brook Cut

Seventeen Acre Wood

Duck Decoy

Lodge Farm

Fazeley

YORKSAND RD

REINDEER RD

DAMA RD

MAYAMA RD

DRAYTON MANOR DR

SWISS LODGE DR

Longwood House

Works

Drayton Manor Park

CH

DRAYTON MANOR DR

Drayton Park

Longwood Stables

COLESHILL RD

A4091

Heathley Farm

HEATHLEY LA

Bullocks End Farm

Edden's Wood

EDDENS WOOD CL

Drayton Bassett

OLD MANOR CL

MOAT DR

CH CL

PEEL CL

NEW ROW

PO

Manor Prim Sch

Sewage Works

RECTORY CL

SALTS LA

Drayton Brick Bridge

Oak Farm Craft Ctr

SHIRRAL DR

Stone House

Heart of England Way

DRAYTON LA

Ashdene Farm

B78

Portley's La

PORTLEYS LA

Brook Farm

Brook End Farm

Birmingham and Fazeley Canal

Heart of England Way

Upper House Farm

Gallows Brook

COPPICE LA

Quarry

Mill Plantation

Middleton

SIMMONS CL

Highfields Farm

CHURCH LA

Park-gate Farm

Middleton Park

Newhouse Farm

Walker's Spinney

Sewage Works

Middleton Pool

The Green Man (PH)

VICARAGE HILL

PO

CRONEBERRY LA

A4091

Middleton Hall

Langley Brook

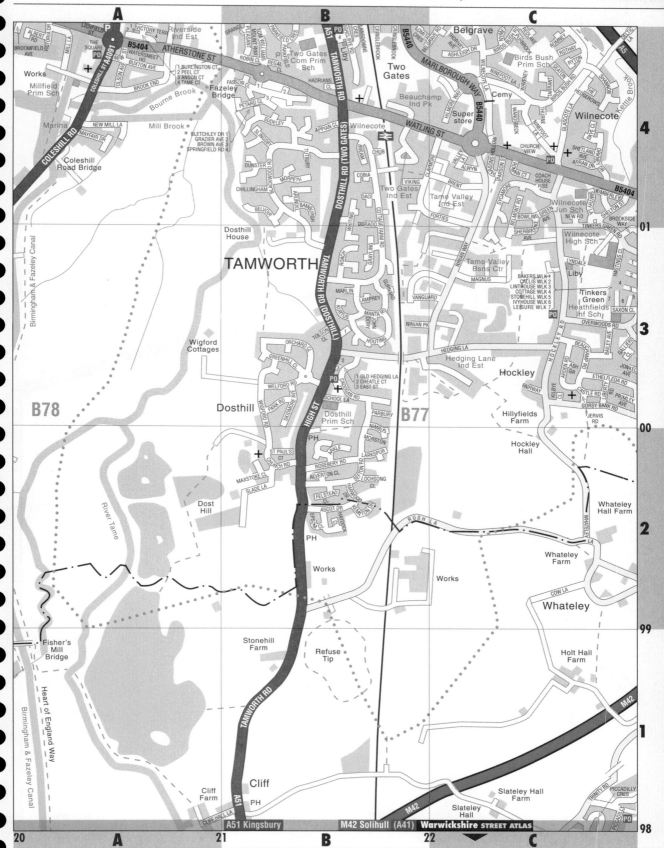

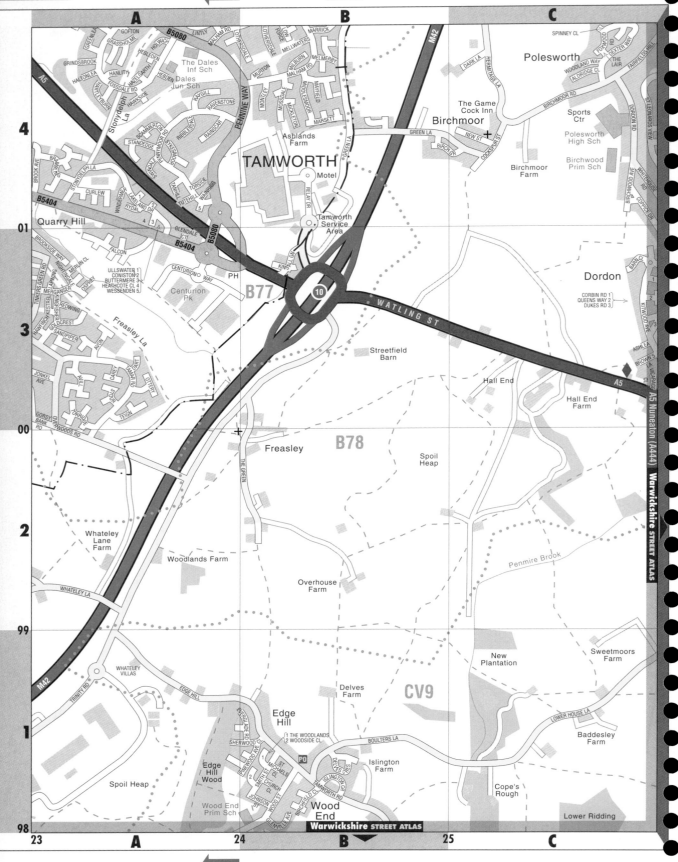

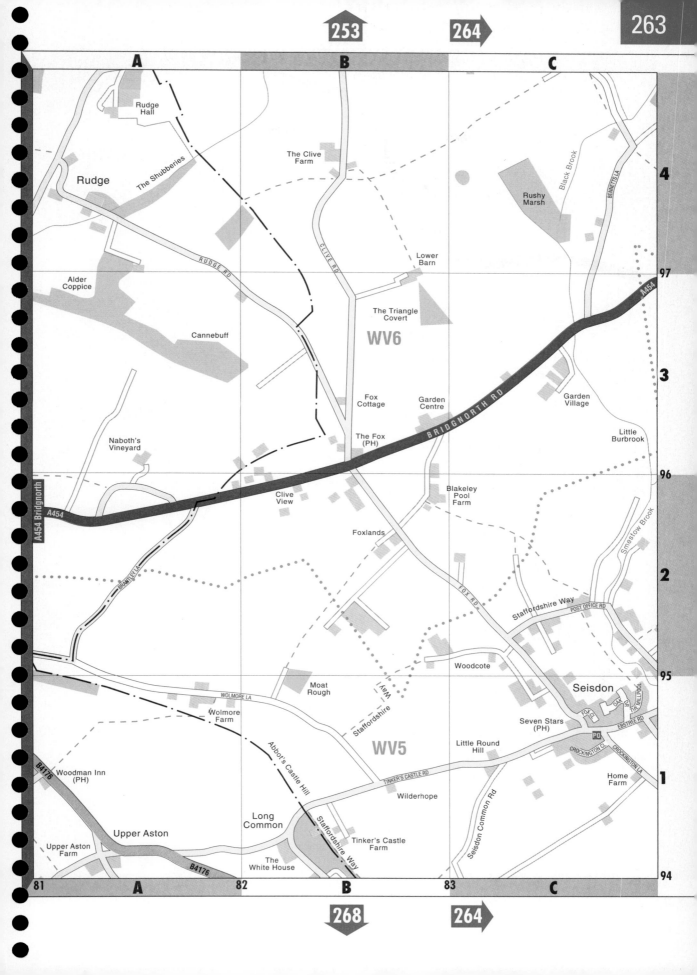

A   B   C

Rudge Hall

The Clive Farm

Black Brook

The Shubberies

Rudge

Rushy Marsh

BENNETTS LA

4

CLIVE RD

RUDGE RD

Lower Barn

Alder Coppice

97

A454

The Triangle Covert

WV6

Cannebuff

3

Fox Cottage

Garden Centre

BRIDGNORTH RD

Garden Village

Little Burbrook

The Fox (PH)

Naboth's Vineyard

Blakeley Pool Farm

96

A454 Bridgnorth

Clive View

Smeslow Brook

BROMLEY LA

A454

Foxlands

FOX RD

2

Staffordshire Way

POST OFFICE RD

Woodcote

Moat Rough

95

Seisdon

WOLMORE LA

Staffordshire Way

Wolmore Farm

Seven Stars (PH)

FOX LA

OAK DR

THE MILLPOOL

EBSTREE RD

Little Round Hill

PO

B4176

Abbot's Castle Hill

WV5

Woodman Inn (PH)

CROCKINGTON CL

CROCKINGTON LA

Home Farm

1

TINKER'S CASTLE RD

Wilderhope

Seisdon Common Rd

Upper Aston

Long Common

Staffordshire Way

Tinker's Castle Farm

Upper Aston Farm

B4176

The White House

94

263
254

A **B** **C**

JENNY WALKERS LA

A454

CASTLECROFT
POOL HALL CRES
POOL HALL RD
Sewage
Works
Perton Mill
Farm

WV6

BRIDGNORTH RD

CASTLECROFT LA

CASTLECROFT RD

WV3

4

Pool Hall
Mops Farm
Bridge

Ford

SHOP LA

Trescott

A454

RAGLAN LA

97

Langlade
Farm

LANGLEY RD

Langley
Hall

Trescott
Grange

Twin Oaks
Farm

Valley Park

MARKET LA

3

Furnace
Grange

Staffordshire and Worcestershire Canal

WV4

PH

Home
Farm

Staffordshire Way

DIMMINGSDALE RD

GREYHOUND LA

Pear Tree
Farm

SPRING HILL LA

Manor
Farm

96

Old Smithy
Farm

EBSTREE RD

Holly Bush
(PH)

PERSTONE LA

Monarch's Way

DENE RD

Lower
Penn

The
Lindens

Orton
House

2

WV5

BLACKPIT LA

ORTON LA

Orton

SHOWELL LA

TRYSULL HOLLOWAY

Orton
Hall
Farm

95

POST OFFICE RD

BEECH HURST GDNS

THE HOLLOWAY

EBSTREE RD

EBSTREE MDW

Sand Pit

Awbridge
Farm

Awbridge
Bridge

FLASH LA

Meadow
Cottage

The Grotto

UNION LA

CHURCH LA

Smestow Brook

1

The
Hall

SEISDON RD

BELL RD

Manor
House

WHITE ROW

WD HOUSE RD

Trysull

Monks
Path

Monkspath
Farm

TRYSULL RD

Clee
View

CROCKINGTON LA

BEECHOUSE LA

PH

94

84 **A** 85 **B** 86 **C**

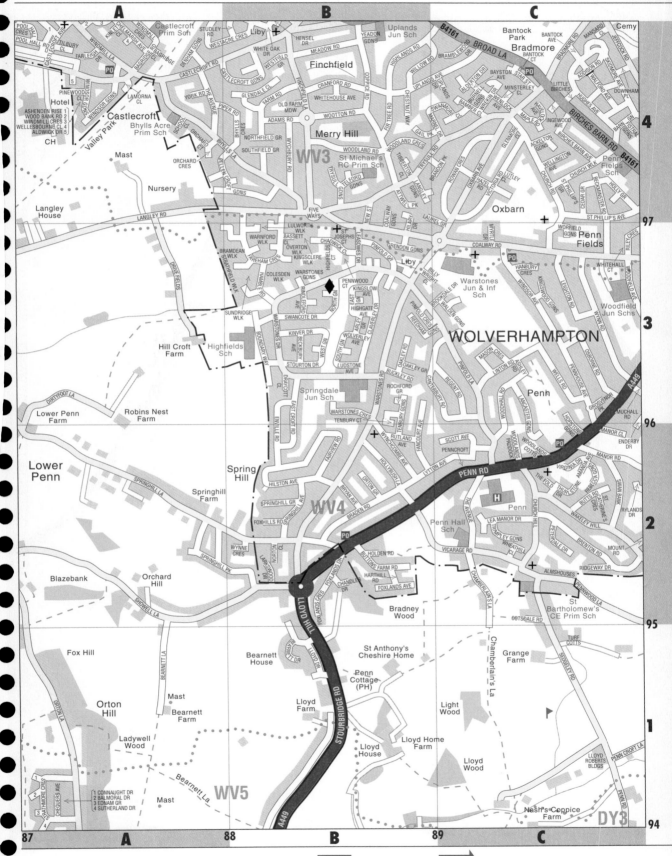

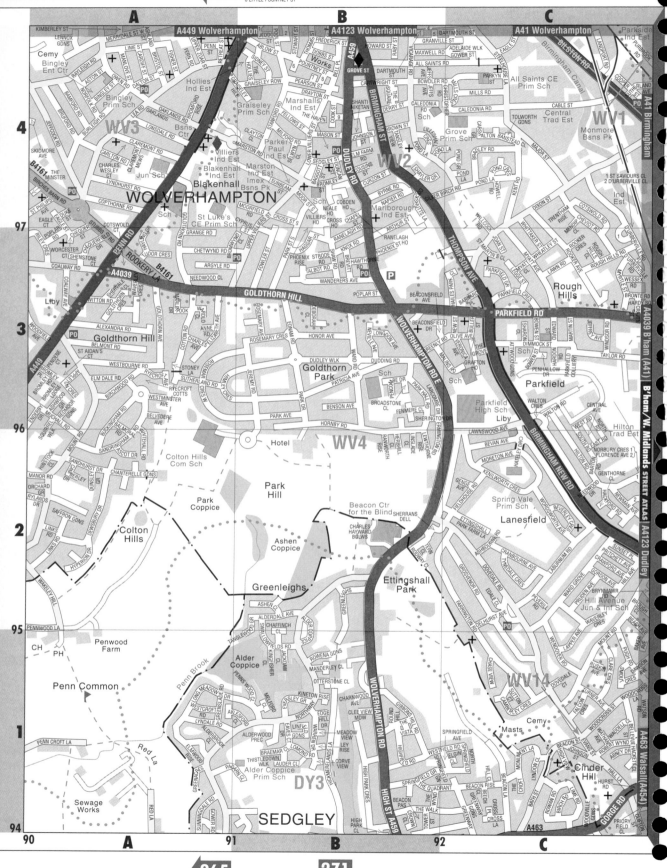

B4
1 PAUL ST
2 BLOOMSBURY ST
3 ST JOHNS RET PK
4 GORDON ST
5 GRANVILLE CL
6 LITTLE POUNTNEY ST
7 KING EDWARD'S ROW
8 STEVENS GATE
9 RAINBOW ST

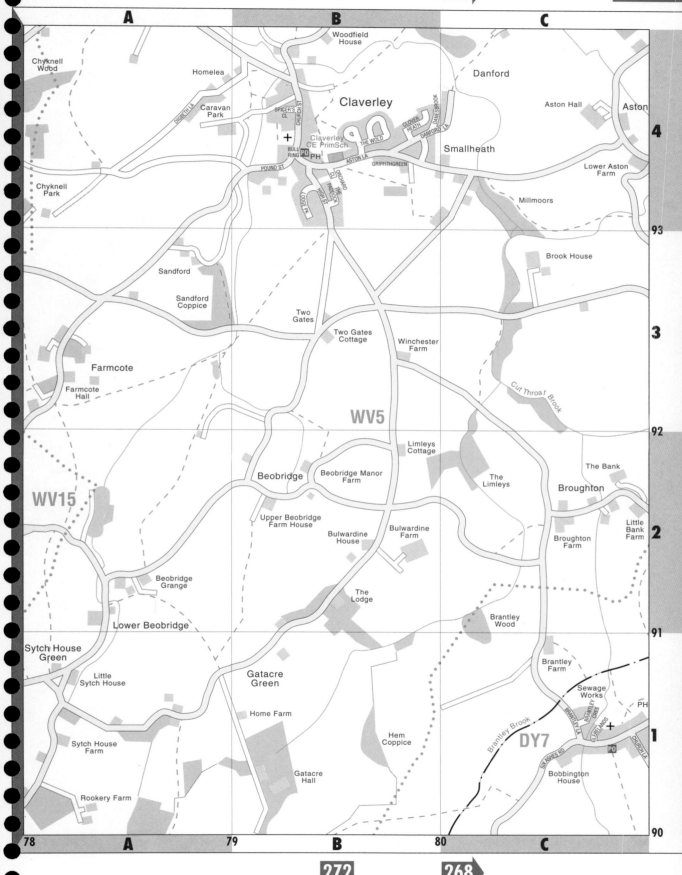

267
263

A **B** **C**

B4176

White House Farm

Long Common

Seisdon Common Rd

The Wellings

WV5

4

The Bungalow

Abbot's Castle Hill

Staffordshire Way

Gorse La

The Wellings

Shellfields Farm

The Dwellings

93

Upper Whittimere Cottage

Clan Park Farm

Gay Hills

Admoor Cottage

Draycott

Vineyard

Sand Pit

Upper Whittimere Farm

The Eaves

B4176

3

Heathton

Whittimere

Old Gate Inn (PH)

TOM LA

War Stone

Heathton House

Swan Cottage

Gayton

Staffordshire Way

NEW RD

92

Cranmere

The Royal Oak (PH)

Blackhill Plantation

PEAR TREE LA

Halfpenny Green

DY3

Ferndale Farm

2

White Cross Farmhouse

Blakelands

Blacklands Farm

+

Manor Farm

Gospel Ash

SIX ASHES RD

Blacklands Plantation

DY7

Yew Tree Farm

91

White Cross

Saltershall Farm

Wolverhampton Bsns Airport

Claire Hayes

GOSPEL ASH RD

Corbett Prim Sch

FOREST LA

Forest Cottage

Bobbington

Crab Mill Farm

CRAB LA

Twin Oaks

Leaton Cottage

WATER LA

Forest Covert

1

Dogkennel Covert

CHURCH LA

Leaton Lodge

Gorse Covert

Highgate Farm

DY3

Staffordshire Way

P

Highgate Country Park

UTLEY LA

Leaton Hall

WHITE HOUSE LA

90

81 **A** 82 **B** 83 **C**

267
273

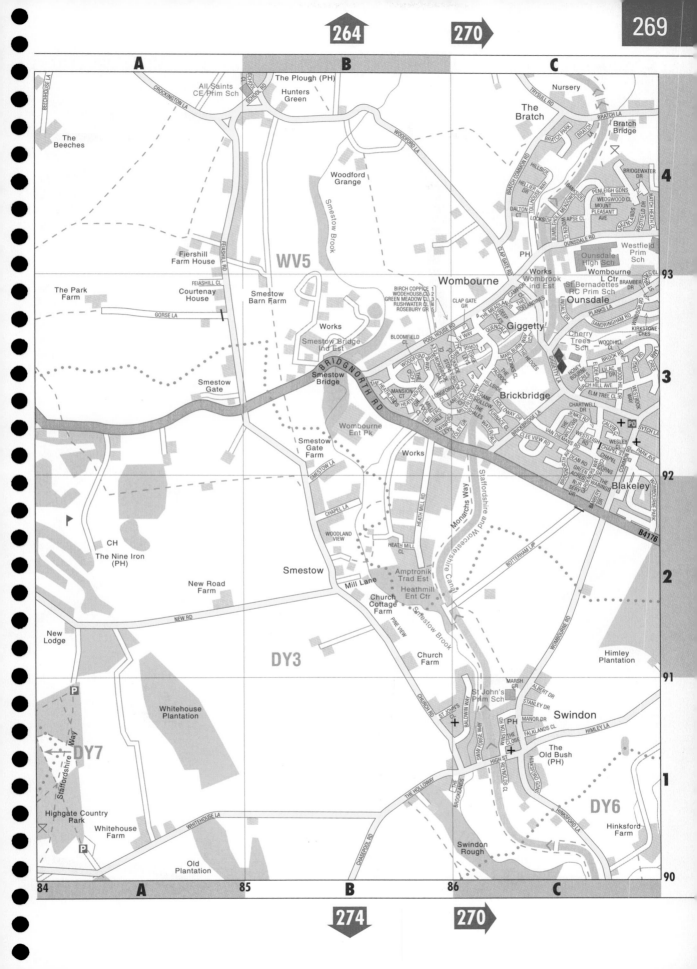

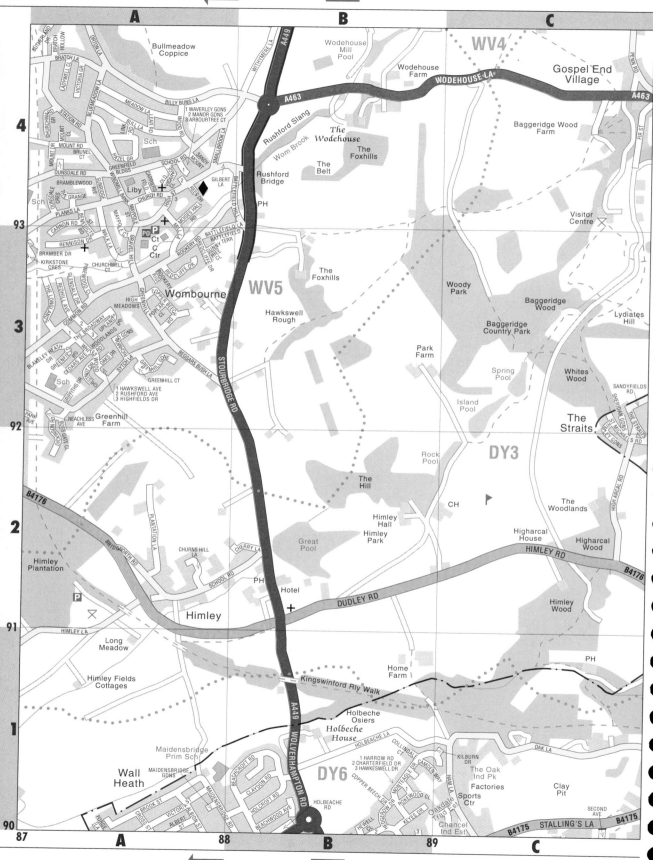

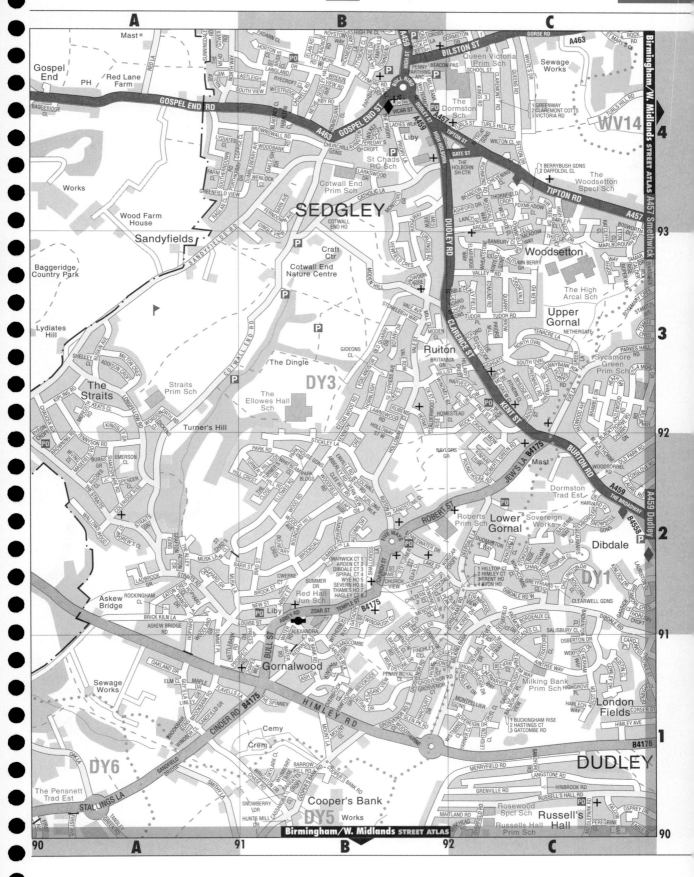

Birmingham/W. Midlands STREET ATLAS

267

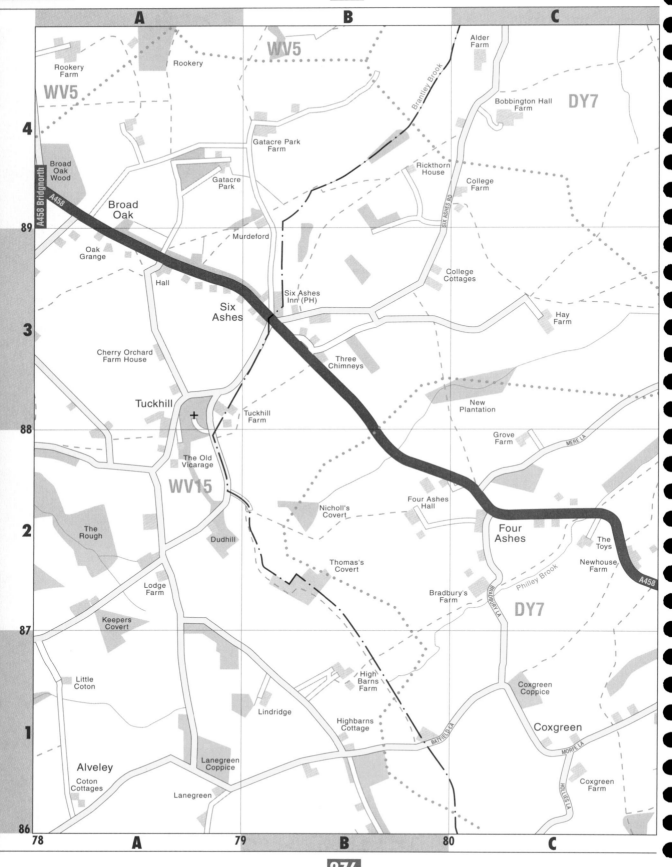

A   B   C

WV5

Rookery
Farm

Rookery

WV5

DY7

Broad
Oak
Wood

Gatacre Park
Farm

Alder
Farm

Bobbington Hall
Farm

4

A458 Bridgnorth
A458

Broad
Oak

Gatacre
Park

Rickthorn
House

College
Farm

89

Oak
Grange

Murdeford

SIX ASHES RD

Hall

Six Ashes
Inn (PH)

College
Cottages

Six
Ashes

Hay
Farm

3

Cherry Orchard
Farm House

Three
Chimneys

New
Plantation

Tuckhill

Tuckhill
Farm

Grove
Farm

MERE LA

88

+

The Old
Vicarage

Four Ashes
Hall

WV15

Nicholl's
Covert

Four
Ashes

The
Toys

The
Rough

Dudhill

Newhouse
Farm

A458

2

Thomas's
Covert

Bradbury's
Farm

PHILLEY BROOK

DY7

Lodge
Farm

BRADBURY LA

Keepers
Covert

87

Little
Coton

High
Barns
Farm

Coxgreen
Coppice

Lindridge

Highbarns
Cottage

Coxgreen

1

BATFIELD LA

MORFE LA

Alveley

Lanegreen
Coppice

Coton
Cottages

HOLLIES LA

Coxgreen
Farm

Lanegreen

86

78   A   79   B   80   C

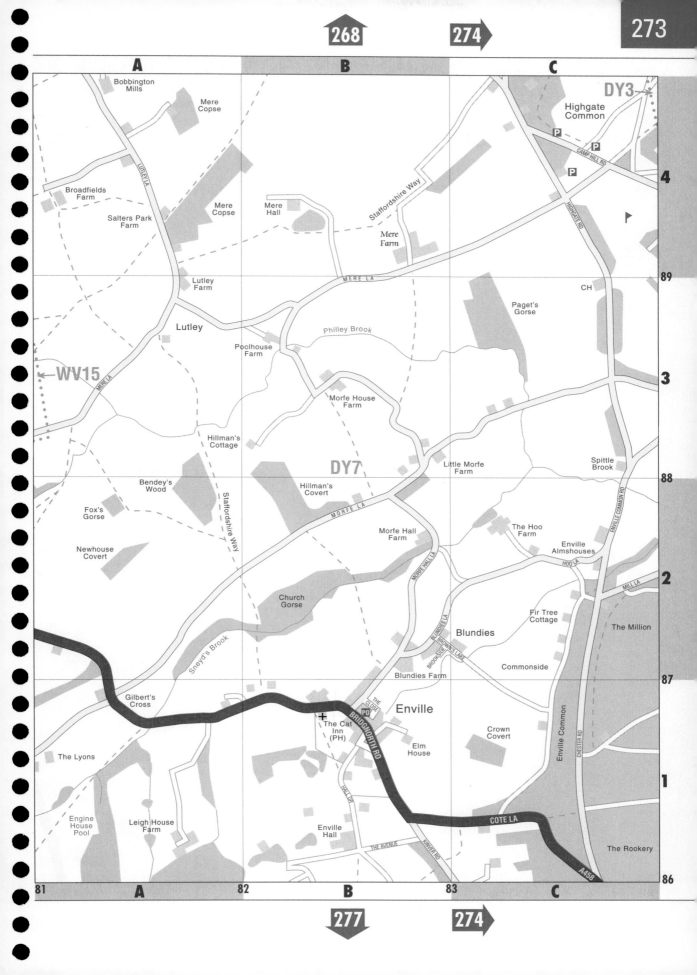

A
B
C

Bobbington Mills

Mere Copse

DY3

Highgate Common

P
P
CAMP HILL RD
P

HIGHGATE RD

Broadfields Farm

LUTLEY LA

Mere Copse

Mere Hall

Staffordshire Way

4

Salters Park Farm

Mere Farm

Lutley Farm

MERE LA

CH

89

Lutley

Paget's Gorse

Philley Brook

Poolhouse Farm

WV15

MERE LA

Morfe House Farm

3

Hillman's Cottage

Little Morfe Farm

Spittle Brook

Bendey's Wood

DY7

Hillman's Covert

88

Fox's Gorse

MORFE LA

ENVILLE COMMON RD

Staffordshire Way

Morfe Hall Farm

The Hoo Farm

Enville Almshouses

Newhouse Covert

MORFE HALL LA

HOO LA

MILL LA

2

Fir Tree Cottage

The Million

Church Gorse

BLUNDIES LA

Blundies

Sneyd's Brook

BROWN'S LANE

BROOKSIDE

Commonside

87

Gilbert's Cross

Blundies Farm

THE CLOSE

Enville

Enville Common

CHESTER RD

The Lyons

PO

The Cat Inn (PH)

BRIDGNORTH RD

Elm House

Crown Covert

1

Engine House Pool

Leigh House Farm

HALL DR

Enville Hall

KINVER RD

COTE LA

The Rookery

THE AVENUE

A458

86

81
82
83

A
B
C

273
269

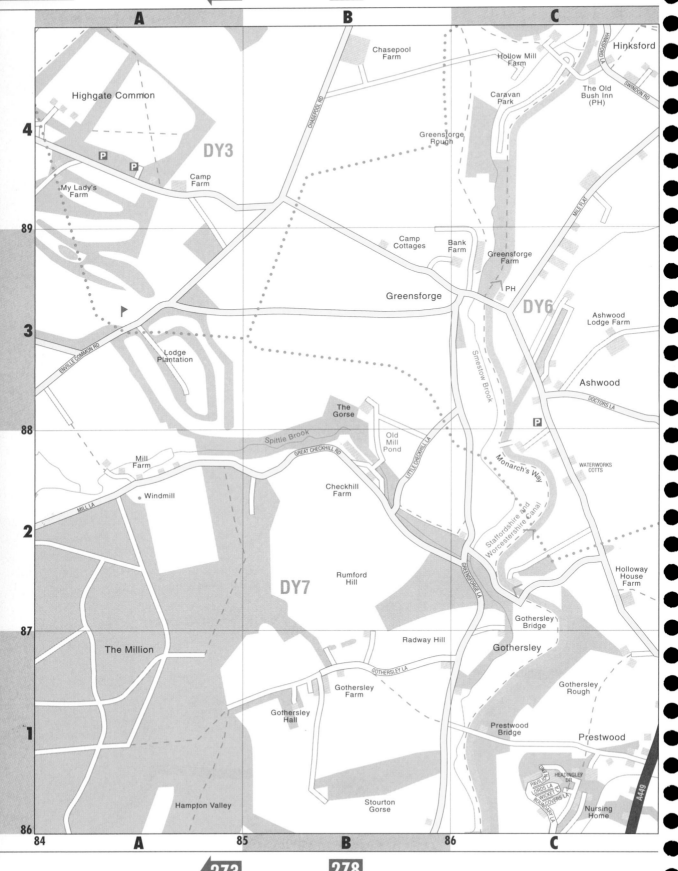

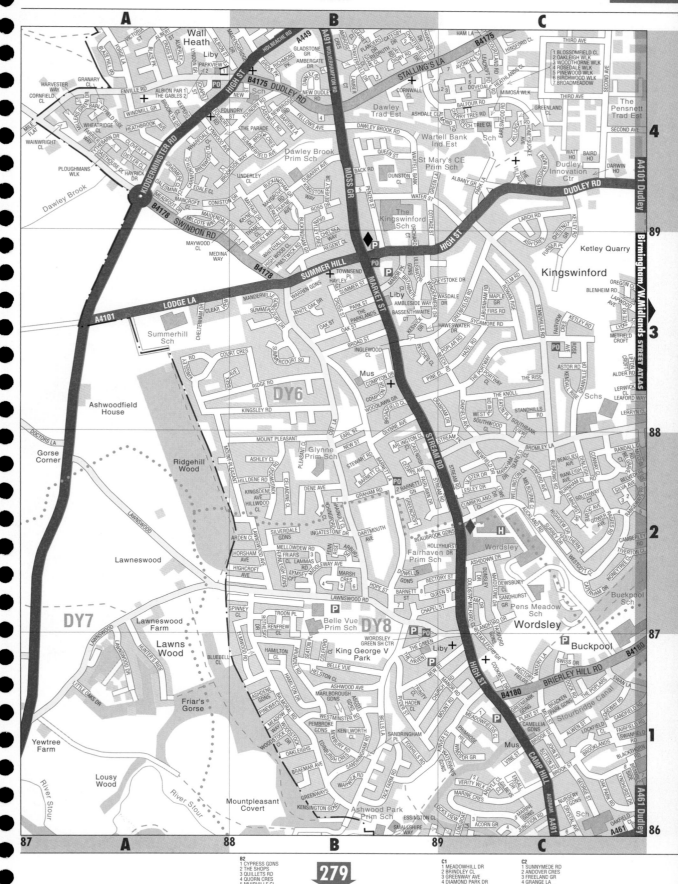

270

279

B4
1 CHARTERFIELDS SH CTR
2 FRANCIS CL
3 TRESHAM RD
4 CORRIN GR
5 WATERFORD RD

B2
1 CYPRESS GDNS
2 THE SHOPS
3 QUILLETS RD
4 QUORN CRES
5 MUIRVILLE CL
6 QUALE GR
7 ROSE COTTAGE DR
8 CROSS ST

C1
1 MEADOWHILL DR
2 BRINDLEY CL
3 GREENWAY AVE
4 DIAMOND PARK DR
5 SWEETBRIER DR
6 MAGNOLIA WAY
7 WHITETHORN RD
8 DEWBURY RD

C2
1 SUNNYMEDE RD
2 ANDOVER CRES
3 FREELAND GR
4 GRANGE LA
5 MADELEY RD

272

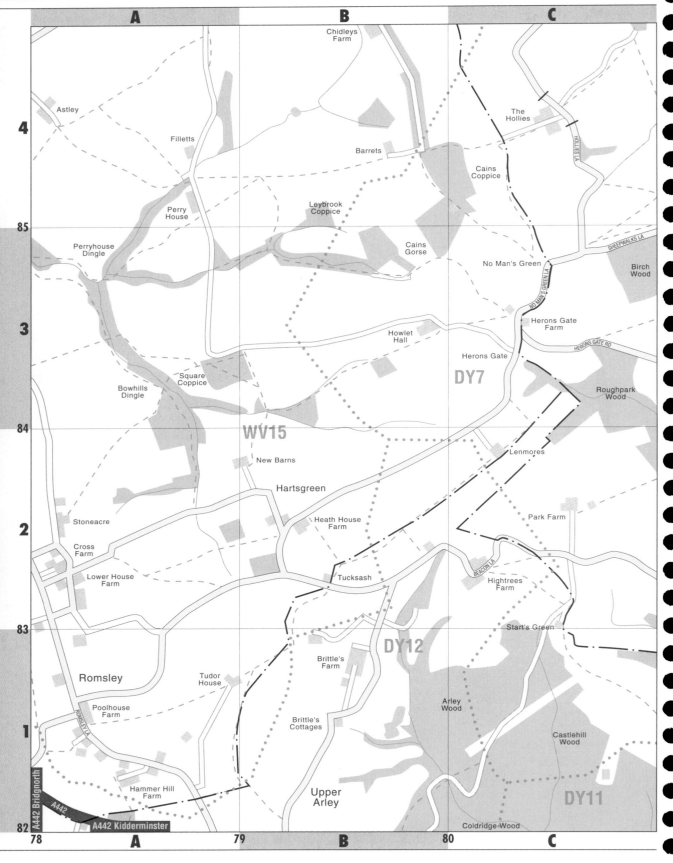

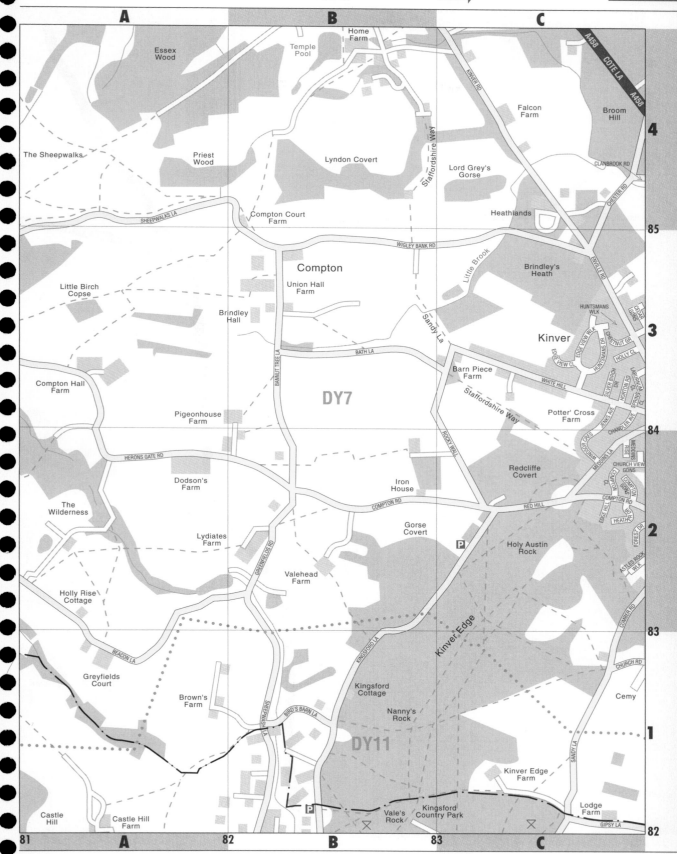

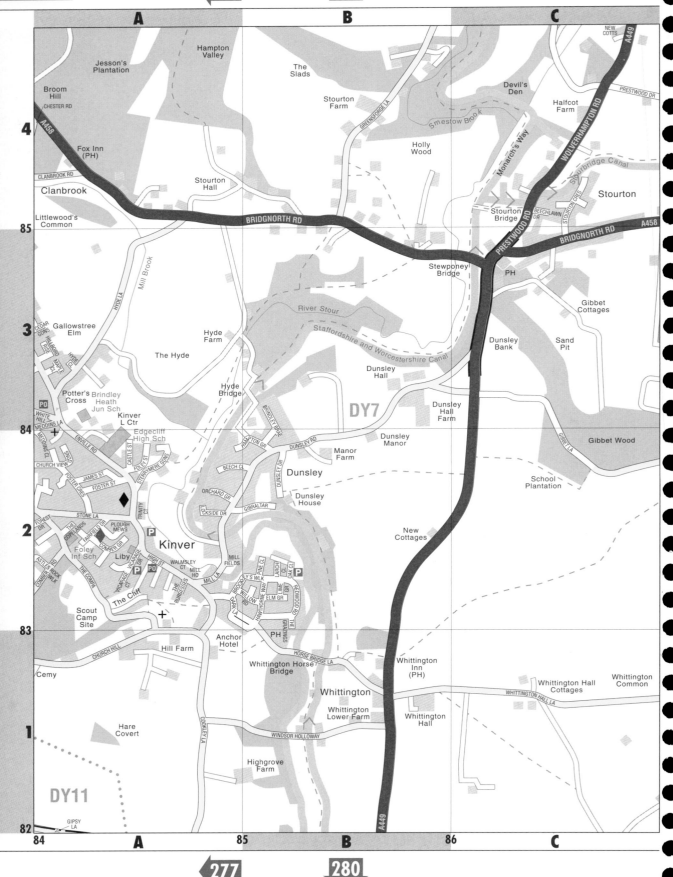

C4
1 THE JUNCTION
2 CRYSTAL AVE
3 SURREY HO
4 WILTSHIRE HO
5 DEVON HO
6 LANCASTER HO
7 HANOVER HO
8 ALLAN CL
9 CORBETT HO

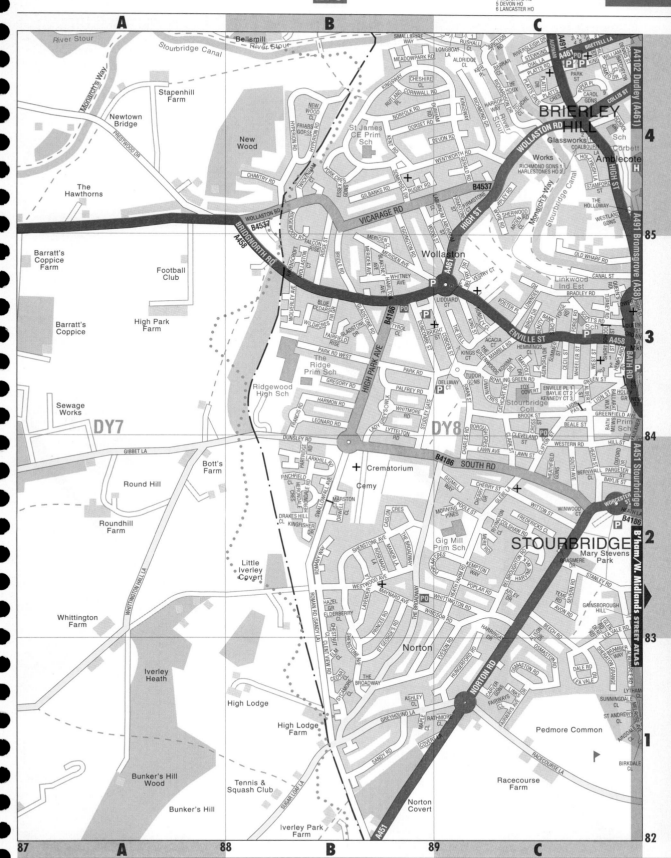

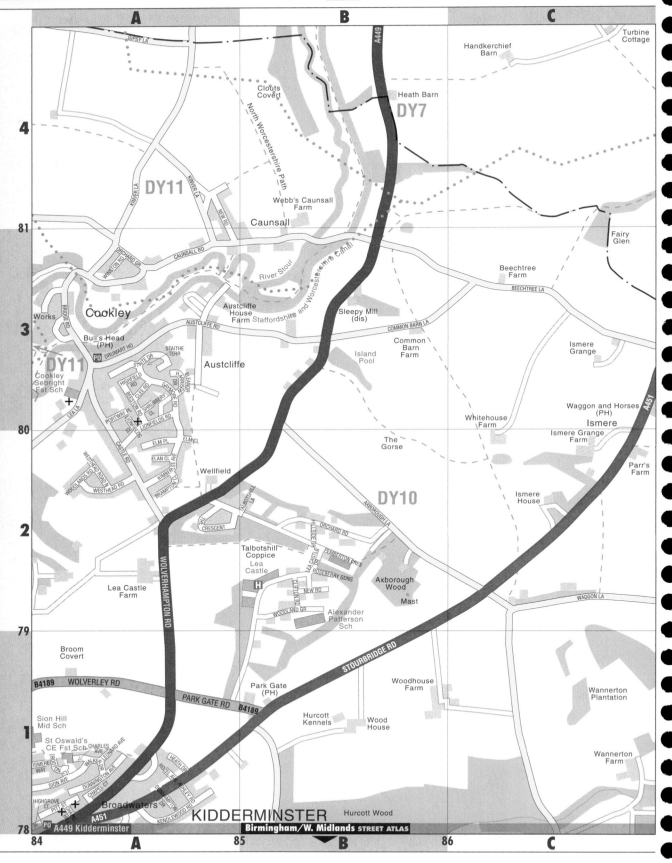

KIDDERMINSTER

Cookley

Austcliffe

DY11

DY7

DY10

Broadwaters

Caunsall

Ismere

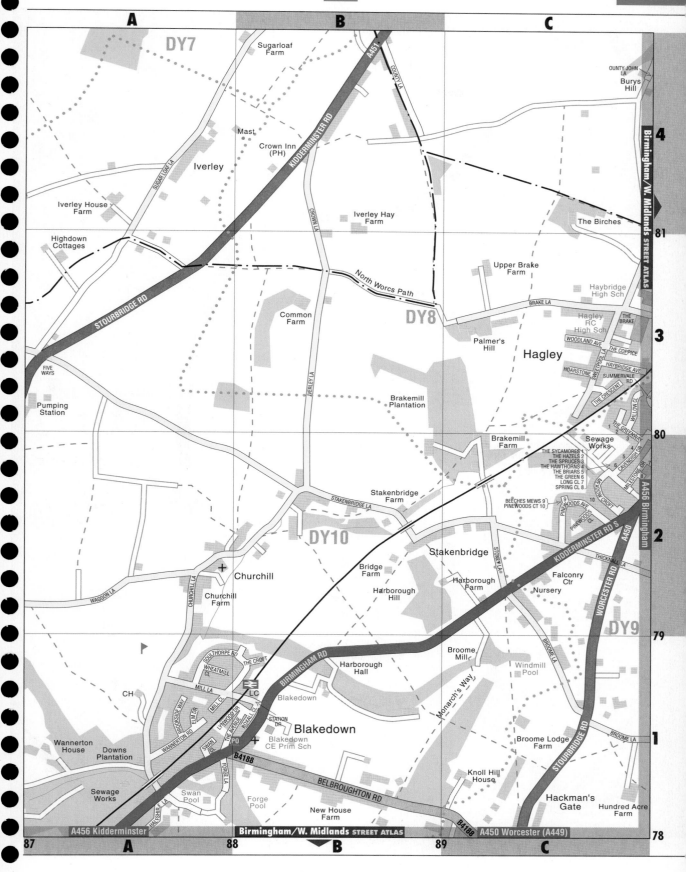

A   B   C

DY7

Sugarloaf
Farm

A451

COUNTY LA

OUNTY JOHN
LA

Burys
Hill

Mast

Crown Inn
(PH)

KIDDERMINSTER RD

Iverley

CROWN LA

Iverley Hay
Farm

The Birches

4

81

Iverley House
Farm

SUGAR LOAF LA

Upper Brake
Farm

Haybridge
High Sch

Highdown
Cottages

STOURBRIDGE RD

North Worcs Path

BRAKE LA

DY8

Hagley
RC
High Sch

THE
BRAKE

Common
Farm

WOODLAND AVE

THE COPPICE

Palmer's
Hill

Hagley

3

HOARSTONE

SWEETPOOL LA

HAYBRIDGE AVE

SUMMERVALE
RD

FIVE
WAYS

IVERLEY LA

Brakemill
Plantation

THE CRESCENT

WILLOW RD

THE GREENWAY

Pumping
Station

Brakemill
Farm

Sewage
Works

80

THE SYCAMORES 1
THE HAZELS 2
THE SPRUCES 3
THE HAWTHORNS 4
THE BRIARS 5
THE GREEN 6
LONG CL 7
SPRING CL 8.

CATCHROAD RD

MEADOW CROFT

STAKENBRIDGE LA

Stakenbridge
Farm

BEECHES MEWS 9
PINEWOODS CT 10

PINEWOODS AVE

PINEWOODS
CL

KIDDERMINSTER RD S

A450

DY10

Bridge
Farm

STONEY LA

Stakenbridge

THICKNALL LA

WORCESTER RD

2

79

+

Churchill

WAGGON LA

CHURCHILL LA

Churchill
Farm

Harborough
Hill

Harborough
Farm

Nursery

Falconry
Ctr

DY9

CH

SOULTHORPE RD

WHEATMILL
CL

THE CROFT

MILL LA

MILL CL

ELM DR

Blakedown

Harborough
Hall

BIRMINGHAM RD

Broome
Mill

Monarch's Way

BROOME LA

Windmill
Pool

BROOME LA

Wannerton
House

BROOKSIDE WAY

WANNERTON RD

LYNWOOD DR

THE AVENUE

ROXALL CL

Station
Dr

LC

Blakedown

PO

FORGE LA

SWAN CL

+

Blakedown
CE Prim Sch

B4188

Broome Lodge
Farm

STOURBRIDGE RD

Downs
Plantation

BELBROUGHTON RD

Knoll Hill
House

Hackman's
Gate

1

78

Sewage
Works

HALSHIRE LA

Swan
Pool

Forge
Pool

New House
Farm

B4188

Hundred Acre
Farm

Birmingham/ W. Midlands STREET ATLAS

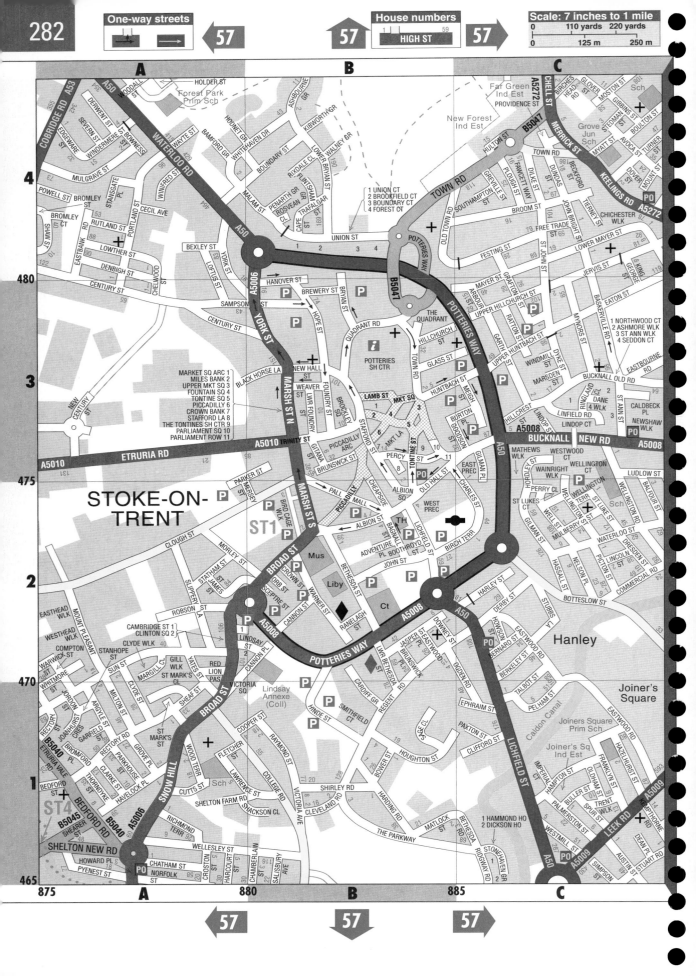

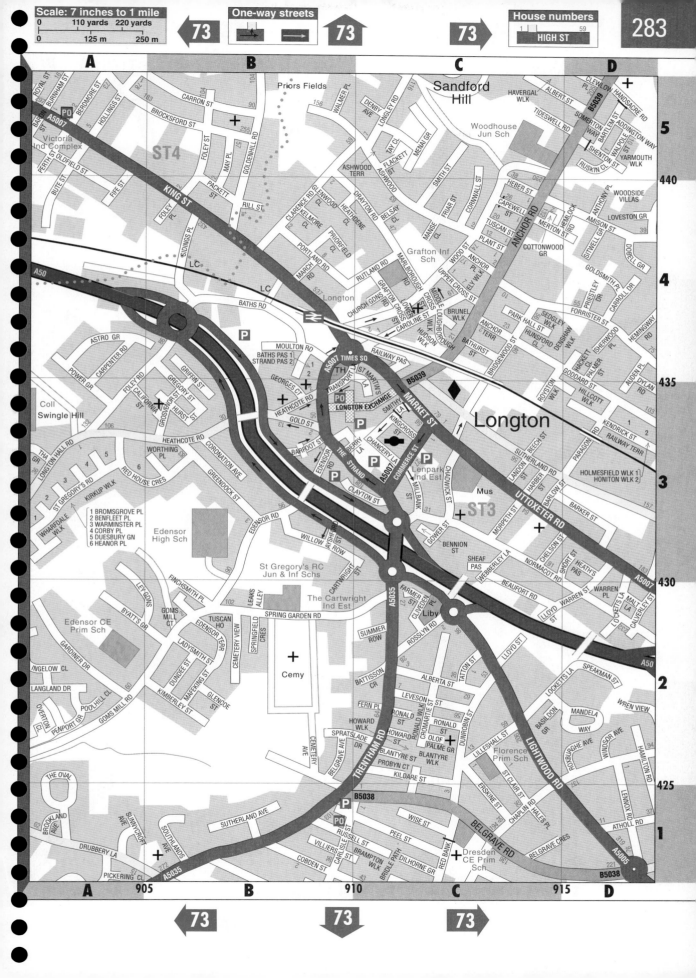

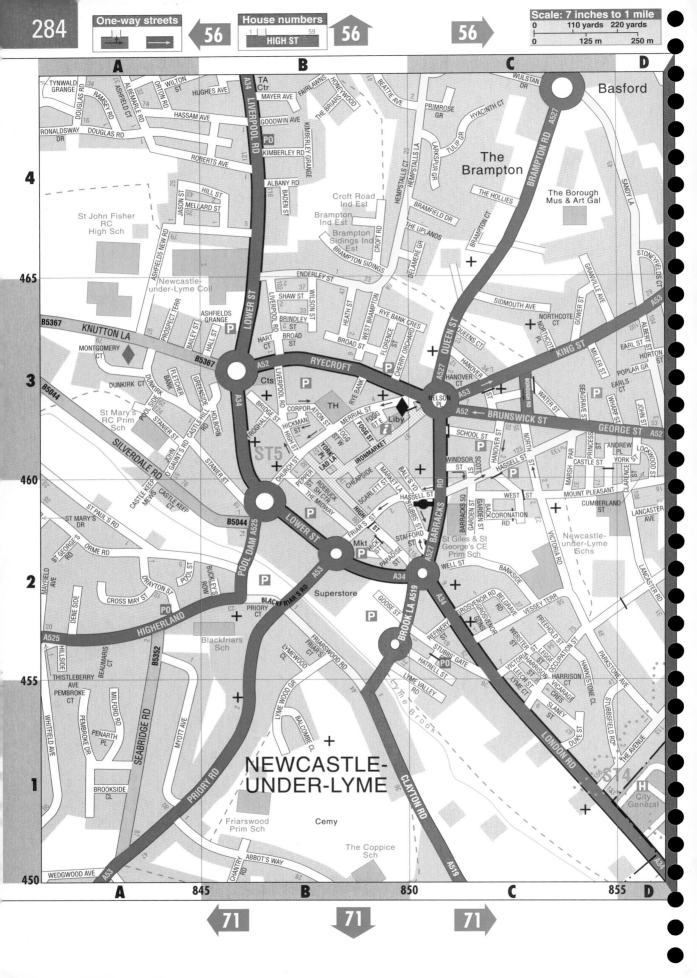

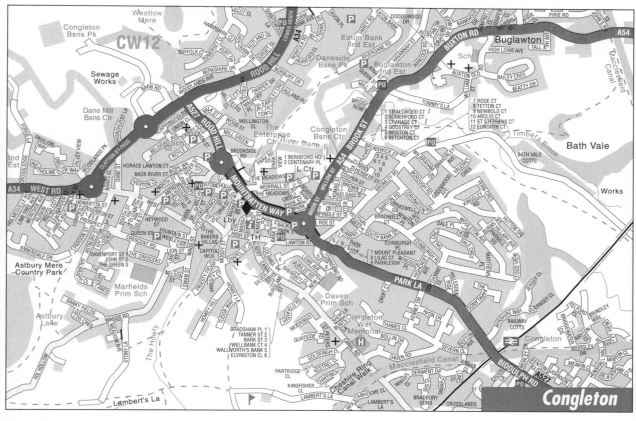

Congleton

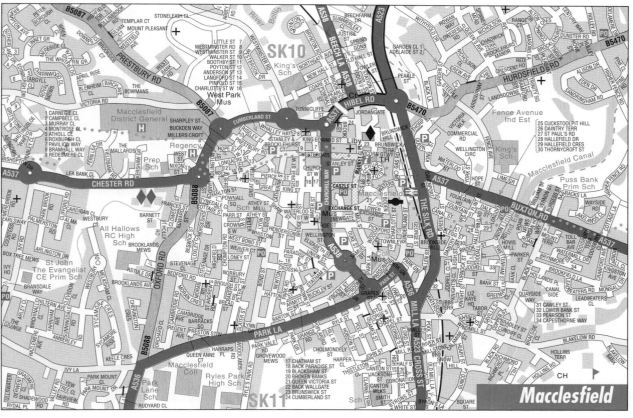

Macclesfield

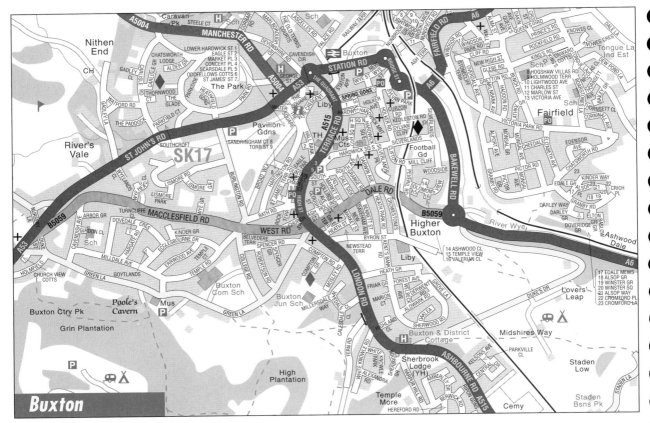

Buxton

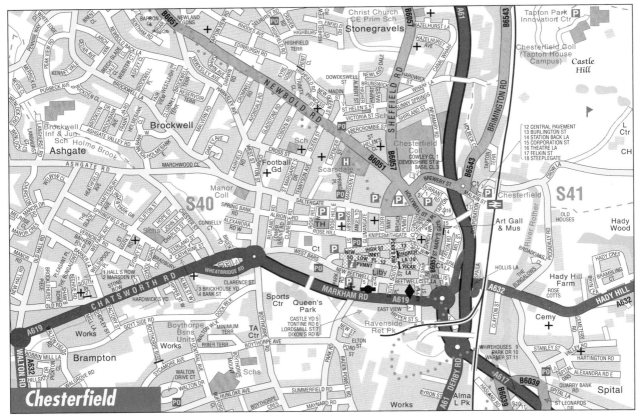

Chesterfield

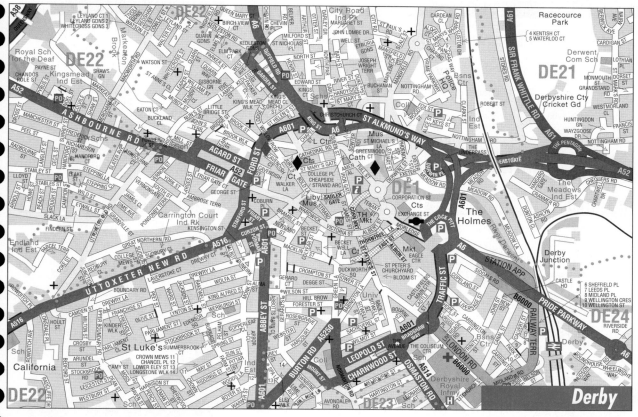

Derby

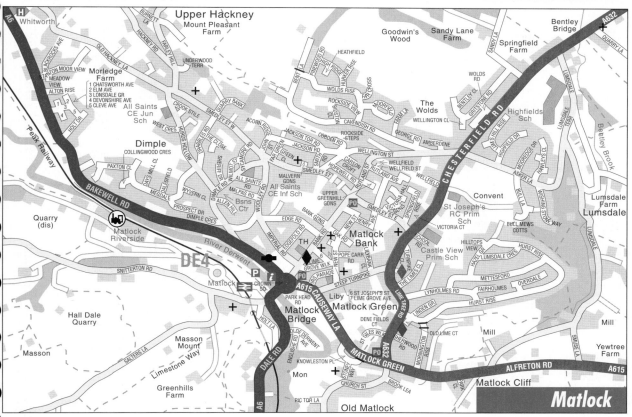

Matlock

Index

Church Rd **6** Beckenham BR2..........**53** C6

Place name May be abbreviated on the map	**Location number** Present when a number indicates the place's position in a crowded area of mapping	**Locality, town or village** Shown when more than one place has the same name	**Postcode district** District for the indexed place	**Page and grid square** Page number and grid reference for the standard mapping

Public and commercial buildings are highlighted in magenta   **Places of interest** are highlighted in blue with a star★

Abbreviations used in the index

Acad	**Academy**	Comm	**Common**	Gd	**Ground**	L	**Leisure**	Prom	**Prom**
App	**Approach**	Cott	**Cottage**	Gdn	**Garden**	La	**Lane**	Rd	**Road**
Arc	**Arcade**	Cres	**Crescent**	Gn	**Green**	Liby	**Library**	Recn	**Recreation**
Ave	**Avenue**	Cswy	**Causeway**	Gr	**Grove**	Mdw	**Meadow**	Ret	**Retail**
Bglw	**Bungalow**	Ct	**Court**	H	**Hall**	Meml	**Memorial**	Sh	**Shopping**
Bldg	**Building**	Ctr	**Centre**	Ho	**House**	Mkt	**Market**	Sq	**Square**
Bsns, Bus	**Business**	Ctry	**Country**	Hospl	**Hospital**	Mus	**Museum**	St	**Street**
Bvd	**Boulevard**	Cty	**County**	HQ	**Headquarters**	Orch	**Orchard**	Sta	**Station**
Cath	**Cathedral**	Dr	**Drive**	Hts	**Heights**	Pal	**Palace**	Terr	**Terrace**
Cir	**Circus**	Dro	**Drove**	Ind	**Industrial**	Par	**Parade**	TH	**Town Hall**
Cl	**Close**	Ed	**Education**	Inst	**Institute**	Pas	**Passage**	Univ	**University**
Cnr	**Corner**	Emb	**Embankment**	Int	**International**	Pk	**Park**	Wk, Wlk	**Walk**
Coll	**College**	Est	**Estate**	Intc	**Interchange**	Pl	**Place**	Wr	**Water**
Com	**Community**	Ex	**Exhibition**	Junc	**Junction**	Prec	**Precinct**	Yd	**Yard**

Index of localities, towns and villages

Abbots Bromley 161 A3
Acton Trussell 175 A1
Adbaston 131 B2
Admaston 160 A2
Albrighton 237 A3
Aldridge 256 A3
Alrewas 200 C1
Alsop en le Dale 36 C2
Alstonefield 35 B2
Alton 78 C1
Alveley 272 A1
Anslow 165 B4
Armitage 198 A2
Ashley 100 A3
Astbury 15 A4
Audley 39 B1
Bagnall 43 C1
Barlaston 88 C1
Barthomley 38 B3
Barton Turn 184 A1
Barton-under-Needwood183 B1
Betley 53 A3
Biddulph 27 A4
Blakedown 281 B1
Blakenhall 52 A2
Blore 99 A1
Blymhill 203 C3
Blythe Bridge 90 C4
Bobbington 268 A1
Boscobel 221 C3
Bosley 7 B4
Bradley 191 B4
Bradnop 31 C2
Branston 184 C1
Bretby 167 C1
Brewood 223 B3
Bridgemere 67 A4
Brierley Hill 279 C4
Brocton 176 B2
Brownhills 245 A3
Bucknall 58 A2
Burntwood 229 B3
Burslem 56 C4
Burton upon Trent 166 C1
Butterton 33 C3
Buxton 4 B4
Cannock 209 B1
Caverswall 74 C1
Chapel Chorlton 102 A4
Cheadle 76 B2
Chebsey 134 C3
Cheddleton 45 B3
Chell Heath 42 A3
Chelmorton 5 B4
Cheslyn Hay 226 B2

Cheswardine 130 A4
Chetwynd 168 B4
Chetwynd Aston 187 A4
Chilcote 219 C2
Chorlton 37 A1
Church Broughton 129 C4
Church Eaton 190 A4
Church Leigh 109 A2
Claverley 267 B4
Clifton 81 C3
Clifton Campville 218 C1
Codsall 238 C2
Colton 179 A3
Colwich 177 C4
Congleton 6 A2
Consall 60 B3
Cookley 280 A3
Coppenhall 174 B2
Cotton 78 B4
Croxden 94 C2
Denstone 95 B3
Dilhorne 75 B2
Dordon 262 C3
Doveridge 127 A4
Draycott in the Clay . . .144 B3
Draycott in the Moors . . .91 C3
Drayton Bassett 260 B3
Dudley 271 C1
Dunstall 183 B3
Earl Sterndale 5 B2
Eaton 6 A4
Eccleshall 133 C3
Edgmond 168 A2
Edingale 217 C3
Egginton 148 A3
Elford 216 B1
Ellastone 80 A2
Ellenhall 134 A1
Elmhurst 214 A3
Endon 43 C4
Enville 273 B1
Essington 241 C2
Farewell 213 A2
Fawfieldhead 12 C2
Fazeley 260 C4
Featherstone 241 B4
Fenton 72 C3
Flash 3 A2
Forsbrook 91 A4
Forton 169 A4
Foston 129 B2
Fradswell 123 A2
Gayton 138 C3
Gnosall 171 B3
Gorstyhill 37 C1

Great Chatwell 188 B1
Great Wyrley 227 A2
Grindon 34 A1
Hademore 233 A4
Hagley 281 C3
Hamstall Ridware 180 C2
Hanbury 145 A2
Hanchurch 87 A4
Hanley 57 B2
Harlaston 217 B1
Hartington 24 B3
Hatton 146 B4
Haughton 172 C4
Heath Hill 187 B1
Heaton 8 C1
Hilderstone 106 A1
Hill Ridware 198 A4
Hilton 147 C4
Himley 270 A2
Hints 248 B3
Hixon 158 B4
Hollinsclough 4 B1
Hopton 137 B1
Hopwas 249 A4
Huntington 209 B4
Ilam 50 C2
Ingestre 157 C3
Ipstones 62 A4
Keele 69 C4
Kidderminster 280 A1
Kidsgrove 26 C1
King's Bromley 199 B3
Kingsley 61 C2
Kingstone 141 B4
Kingswinford 275 C3
Kinver 278 A2
Lawton-gate 25 A2
Leek 30 C3
Lichfield 231 B4
Linton 186 A1
Little Aston 257 A2
Longdon 197 C1
Longford 168 A1
Longnor 13 A3
Longsdon 29 C1
Longton 73 B2
Lower Penn 265 A4
Lullington 218 C4
Madeley 67 C3
Maer 85 B1
Mapleton 66 C2
Marchington 127 C1
Market Drayton 97 B2
Marston 136 C2
Marston Montgomery . . .96 C1

Marston on Dove 147 A4
Mayfield 81 B4
Meerbrook 19 C4
Meir 74 A1
Middleton 260 A1
Millmeece 117 C4
Milwich 122 B3
Monyash 14 C4
Mount Pleasant 26 A3
Mow Cop 26 B4
Mucklestone 99 A4
Netherseal 219 C4
Newborough 162 C4
Newcastle-under-Lyme . .71 A4
Newport 168 B2
Newton Regis 236 B2
Newton Solney 167 C4
Norbury 151 A2
Norton Canes 227 C3
Norton in Hales 82 B1
Norton-in-the-Moors . . .42 C2
Oakamoor 78 A4
Onecote 32 C2
Packmoor 26 C1
Pattingham 253 B1
Penkridge 192 C1
Perton 254 B2
Polesworth 262 C4
Ranton 153 B3
Repton 148 C1
Rocester 96 C4
Rolleston 147 A2
Romsley 276 A1
Roston 96 C4
Rudge 263 A4
Rudyard 29 C4
Rugeley 196 C4
Rushton Spencer 8 A1
Salt 137 C2
Sandon 137 B4
Scholar Green 25 C4
Scropton 129 C1
Seckington 236 C2
Sedgley 271 B4
Seighford 154 A4
Seisdon 263 C1
Shareshill 225 B3
Sheen 24 A4
Shenstone 247 A3
Shuttington 251 C4
Snelston 81 B2
Stafford 155 C2
Standon 102 A1
Stanton 65 B1
Stoke-on-Trent 72 C4

Stone 120 A4
Stourbridge 279 C2
Stramshall 111 A2
Streethay 215 A1
Sudbury 128 C2
Sutton 112 B2
Sutton Coldfield 258 C1
Swadlincote 186 C2
Swindon 269 C1
Swinscoe 65 C3
Swynnerton 103 A2
Talke 40 B4
Tamworth 250 A2
Tatenhill 165 A1
The Bank 26 A4
Thorncliffe 20 C1
Thorpe 51 B1
Thorpe Constantine 235 C3
Tissington 51 C3
Tittensor 88 C3
Tixall 157 B1
Tong 220 B2
Trentham 88 A3
Tunstall 41 B2
Tutbury 146 B3
Upper Arley 276 B1
Upper Tean 92 B2
Uttoxeter 126 B4
Wall 230 B1
Walsall 243 A1
Walton-on-Trent 184 C1
Warslow 23 A1
Waterhouses 49 A1
Weeford 248 A2
Weston 37 B3
Weston 138 B2
Weston-under-Lizard . . .203 C2
Wetton 34 C2
Wheaton Aston 205 A3
Whitgreave 135 C3
Whitmore 86 A3
Whittington 232 B3
Wigginton 234 A1
Wildboarclough 1 C3
Willington 148 C3
Wincle 9 A4
Wolverhampton 266 A4
Wombourne 269 C3
Wood End 262 B3
Woodcote 187 B2
Woodhouse Green 7 B1
Woodseaves 151 C4
Woore 67 A1
Wootton 79 C4
Yoxall 182 A1

A

Aarons Dr ST7 ....39 C1
Abberley B77 ....251 B1
Abberley Rd DY3 ....271 B2
Abbey Arc DE14 ....166 C1
Abbey Cl Penkridge ST19 .208 A4
Rocester ST14 ....96 A2
Abbey Ct Bucknall ST2 ...58 A3
Newport TF10 ....168 C1
Abbey Dr Colwich ST18 ...177 B4
Walsall WS3 ....244 A3
Abbey Green Rd ST13 ....30 B4
Abbey Hill Specl Sch ST2 58 B3
Abbey Hulton Prim Sch
ST2 ....58 A3
Abbey La ST2 ....58 A3
Abbey Prim Sch WS3 ...242 C1
Abbey Rd Bucknall ST2 ...58 A3
Cheddleton ST9 ....60 A3
Sedgley DY3 ....271 B2
Tamworth B77 ....250 B2
Abbey Sq WS3 ....242 C1
Abbey St Bucknall ST2 ...58 A3
Burton u T DE14 ....166 B1
Cannock WS11 ....210 A4
Newcastle-u-L ST5 ....55 B1
Sedgley DY3 ....271 B2
Stone ST15 ....120 A4
Abbey Way TF9 ....97 B1
Abbey Wood Cl ☐ ST13 ..30 B3
Abbeydale Cl CW2 ....37 B1
Abbeyfield Rd WV10 ....240 C2
Abbeyfields ST18 ....158 A1
Abbeyside ST18 ....153 B3
Abbot Beyne Sch DE15 ..167 A2
Abbot's Rd ST13 ....31 A4
Abbot's Way ST5 ....71 A3
Abbots Bromley Hospl
WS15 ....160 C3
Abbots Field WS11 .....209 C3
Abbots Pl ST2 ....58 A3
Abbots Rd ST2 ....58 A3
Abbots Way WV3 ....255 C1
Abbots Wlk
Rugeley WS15 ....197 A3
Stafford ST16 ....155 C1
Abbotsford Rd WS14 ....231 C4
Abbotsholme Sch ST14 ...96 A1
Abbott's Cl CW12 ....16 A4
Abbotts Ct ST2 ....58 A4
Abbotts Dr ST1 ....57 C4
Abbotts Pl WS3 ....243 B1
Abbotts St WS3 ....243 B1
Abelia B77 ....250 C2
Aberford Gr ST1 ....57 C3
Abingdon Rd WS3 ....242 C1
Abingdon Way
Trentham ST4 ....88 A4
Walsall WS3 ....242 C1
Ablon Ct ST19 ....207 C4
Ablow St WV2 ....266 B4
Abnalls Croft WS13 ....213 C1
Abnalls Ho WS13 ....213 C1
Abnalls La WS13 ....213 C1
Abney Dr WV14 ....266 C1
Acacia Ave ST5 ....55 C1
Acacia Cres WV8 ....239 A2
Acacia Ct DY8 ....279 C3
Acacia Gdns ST7 ....26 B2
Acacia Gr Cannock WS12 210 C2
Newcastle-u-L ST5 ....55 C1
Achilles Cl WS6 ....226 C1
Achilles Way ST7 ....57 C1
Ackelton Gdns WV3 ....265 C4
Acorn Cl Ashley TF9 .....99 B3
Burntwood WS7 ....212 A1
Cannock WS11 ....210 B1
Great Wyrley WS6 .....227 A1
Acorn Gr
Brierley Hill DY8 ....275 C1
Codsall WV8 ....238 C1
Acorn La CW12 ....6 C2
Acorn Rd WV11 ....242 A1
Acorn Rise ST3 ....89 C4
Acorn Starter Units
WS7 ....228 B4
Acorn View WS7 ....229 B3
Acres Nook Rd ST7 ....41 A3
Acres The
Newcastle-u-L ST5 ....55 B1
Wolv WV3 ....255 B1
Acreswood Rd ST6 ....42 A1
Acton Ct ST18 ....174 C1
Acton Dr DY3 ....271 A2
Acton Hill Rd ST17 ....175 B1
Acton St ST1 ....57 B3
Adam Ct WS11 ....209 B1
Adams Ave ST6 ....41 B3
Adams Cl TF10 ....168 C1
Adams Cres TF10 ....168 C1
Adams Gr ST13 ....178 C1
Adams Gram Sch TF10 .168 C2
Adams Rd
Brownhills WS8 ....245 A3
Wolv WV3 ....265 B4
Adams St
Newcastle-u-L ST5 ....56 B2
Norton-in-t-M ST6 ....43 A1
Adamson Cl WS11 .....209 A1
Adamthwaite Cl WS11 ...90 B4
Adamthwaite Dr ST11 ...90 B4
Adderley Green Inf Sch
ST3 ....73 B3
Adderley Pl ST12 ....88 C2
Adderley Rd
Market Drayton TF9 .....97 A2

Adderley Rd continued
Norton-in-t-M ST6 ....42 C2
Adderley Road Ind Est
TF9 ....97 B1
Addie Rd DE13 ....166 A3
Addington Way ST3 ....283 D5
Addison Cl WS11 ....209 C3
Addison Croft DY3 .....271 A3
Addison Gr WV11 ....241 A1
Addison Rd WV3 ....265 C4
Addison St ST1 ....57 B3
Adelaide Cres DE15 ...167 B1
Adelaide Dr WS12 .....210 C2
Adelaide St ST6 ....57 A4
Adelaide Wlk WV2 .....266 C4
Adkins St ST6 ....57 B4
Admiral Parker Dr
WS14 ....246 C3
Adonis Cl B79 ....250 B1
Adrian St ST4 ....72 C3
Advance Bsns Pk WS11 210 A2
Adventure Pl ST1 .....282 B2
Adwalton Ave WV6 ....254 C2
Aegean Cl ST4 ....88 B4
Aelfgar Ctr WS15 .....178 C1
Aelfgar Ho WS15 .....178 C1
Affleck Ave B78 ....249 B1
Agenoria Dr DY8 ....279 C3
Agger Hill ST5 ....54 B1
Ainsdale Cl ☐ Meir ST3 ..73 C1
Stourbridge DY8 ....279 C1
Ainsley Ct ST2 ....58 A3
Ainsworth Ave ST10 ....61 B1
Ainsworth Rd WV10 ....240 C2
Ainsworth St WV4 ....72 B3
Aintree Cl
Burton u T DE14 ....185 A4
Cannock WS12 ....210 C3
Trentham ST4 ....88 A4
Aintree Ho
Upper Tean ST10 ....92 C2
Wolv WV10 ....240 B2
Aintree Way DY1 ....271 C1
Airdale Gr ST15 ....105 A1
Airdale Rd ST15 ....105 A1
Airdale Spinney ST15 ..105 A1
Airfield Ind Est ST18 ..153 C4
Aitken Cl B78 ....250 A1
Aitken St ST6 ....56 C4
Ajax Cl WS6 ....226 C1
Ajax Way ST2 ....57 C1
Akesmoor La ST7,ST8 ...27 A4
Alan Dale ST9 ....59 A2
Alan Rd ST2 ....58 B2
Alanbrooke Gr ST3 .....89 C4
Alandale Ave WS15 ....198 B2
Alanley Cl ST6 ....42 B1
Alastair Rd ST4 ....71 C2
Alaxandra Dr DE13 ....182 A2
Albany Dr Cannock WS12 210 C2
Rugeley WS15 ....178 B2
Albany Gr
Kingswinford DY6 .....275 C4
Stoke-on-T ST4 ....71 B4
Walsall WV11 ....242 B1
Albany Rd
Newcastle-u-L ST5 ....284 A4
Stoke-on-T ST4 ....71 B4
Albany St ST6 ....41 B4
Albemarle Rd
Newcastle-u-L ST5 ....56 A2
Stourbridge DY8 ....279 C1
Albert Ave ST3 ....73 C2
Albert Cl WV8 ....238 C2
Albert Davies Dr WS12 .210 C2
Albert Dr DY3 ....269 C1
Albert Pl ST3 ....73 A1
Albert Rd Fazeley B78 ..261 A4
Tamworth B79 ....250 A3
Trentham ST4 ....88 A3
☐ Wolv WV6 ....255 C2
Albert St Audley ST7 ...39 C2
Biddulph ST8 ....27 B4
Burton u T DE14 ....166 B2
Cannock, Chadsmoor
WS11 ....209 C2
Cannock, Church Hill
WS12 ....210 B3
Kingswinford DY6 .....275 A4
Longton ST3 ....283 C5
Newcastle-u-L ST5 ....284 C3
Newcastle-u-L, Chesterton
ST5 ....55 C4
Newcastle-u-L, Silverdale
ST5 ....55 B1
Stone ST15 ....105 A1
Stourbridge DY8 ....279 C3
Albert Terr
Newcastle-u-L ST5 ....56 B3
Stafford ST16 ....155 C3
Alberta St ST3 ....283 C5
Albion Par DY6 ....275 A4
Albion Pl WS11 ....209 C2
Albion Rd WS8 ....244 C4
Albion Sq ST1 ....282 B2
Albion St Hanley ST1 ..282 B2
Kingswinford DY6 .....275 A4
Leek ST13 ....30 C3
Rugeley WS15 ....178 C1
Tamworth B79 ....250 B3
Albion Terr DE14 ....166 C3
Albion Way WS7 ....211 C1
Albrighton By Pass
WV7 ....237 A3
Albrighton Jun & Inf Schs
WV7 ....237 A3
Albrighton Sta WV7 ...237 A3

Albutts Rd WS11 ....228 A2
Alcester Cl ST6 ....42 A3
Alcove The WS3 ....243 N1
Aldbury Cl ST16 ....136 B1
Aldbury Pl ST3 ....72 C1
Aldeburgh Cl WS3 .....243 A2
Aldeburgh Dr ST5 ....71 A1
Alden Hurst WS7 ....228 C4
Alder Cl Ashley TF9 .....99 C3
Kidsgrove ST7 ....41 A4
Lichfield WS14 ....231 C4
Alder Coppice DY3 ....266 B1
Alder Coppice Prim Sch
DY3 ....266 B1
Alder Dale WV3 ....255 C1
Alder Gr Burton u T DE15 .185 C4
Newcastle-u-L ST5 ....55 A4
Stafford ST17 ....174 A4
Alder Rd
Kingswinford DY6 .....275 C3
Market Drayton TF9 ....112 A4
Alder Way WS12 ....211 A3
Alder Wlk ST4 ....71 C2
Alderbrook Cl
Rolleston DE13 ....147 A2
Sedgley DY3 ....266 A1
Alderdale Ave DY3 ....266 B2
Alderflat Dr ST4 ....88 B3
Alderford Cl WV8 .....255 C4
Aldergate B79 ....250 A3
Alderhay La ST7 ....26 B3
Alderhithe Gr B74 ....257 A2
Alderholme Dr ☐ DE13 .147 C1
Alderney Cl ST5 ....70 C2
Alderney Cres ST3 ....72 C2
Alders La ST9 ....249 C3
Alders The DE13 ....183 B1
Aldersea Cl ST6 ....41 C1
Aldershaw Cl ST16 ....136 B1
Aldersleigh Dr ST17 ...175 B3
Aldersley Ave WV6 ....255 C4
Aldersley Cl WV6 .....255 A3
Aldersley High Sch
WV8 ....239 B1
Aldersley Rd WV6 ....255 C3
Aldersley Stad WV6 ...255 C3
Alderson Dr DE13 .....147 C1
Alderton Dr WV3 .....265 C4
Alderton Gr ST3 ....90 A3
Alderwood Prec DY3 ..266 B1
Alderwood Rise DY3 ..271 B3
Aldin Cl B78 ....249 C1
Aldridge By Pass WS9 .256 A3
Aldridge Cl
Brierley Hill DY8 ....279 C4
Polesworth B78 ....279 C4
Aldridge Rd Aldridge B74 256 B1
Little Aston B74,WS9 ...257 A3
Aldridge Sch WS9 ....256 A2
Aldwick Dr WV3 ....265 A4
Aldwych Rd WS9 ....256 A4
Alexander Cl WS13 ....215 B3
Alexander Patterson Sch
DY10 ....280 B2
Alexander Rd WV8 ....239 B2
Alexandra Cres ST14 ...126 A4
Alexandra Ct
Burton u T DE15 ....167 A2
Sedgley DY3 ....271 B2
Alexandra Inf Sch ST3 ..73 C1
Alexandra Jun Sch ST3 .73 C1
Alexandra Mews B79 ...250 B3
Alexandra Rd
Burton u T DE15 ....167 A2
Longton ST3 ....73 C1
Market Drayton TF9 .....97 A1
Newcastle-u-L ST5 ....56 B2
Stafford ST17 ....155 C1
Wolv WV4 ....266 A3
Alexandra St ☐ ST15 ..104 C1
Alexandra Way WS9 ...256 A3
Alford Dr ST2 ....59 A2
Alfred Lyons Cl WS15 ..160 C3
Alfred St Burton u T DE14 166 B1
Fenton ST4 ....72 C4
Tamworth B79 ....250 A3
Walsall WS3 ....243 A1
Alfreton Rd ST4 ....73 A3
Algar Rd ST4 ....71 C3
Alicia Way ST7 ....43 A1
Alison Dr DY8 ....279 C2
All Saints CE Fst Sch
Church Leigh ST10 ....109 A2
Denstone ST14 ....95 C3
Leek ST13 ....30 C1
Standon ST21 ....102 B2
All Saints CE Inf Sch
ST18 ....153 B3
All Saints CE Prim Sch
Acton Trussell ST17 ...193 C4
Alrewas DE13 ....201 A1
Seisdon WV5 ....269 A4
Tatenhill DE13 ....164 B1
Wolv WV2 ....266 C1
All Saints Croft DE14 ..185 B4
All Saints Dr B74 .....258 A1
All Saints Rd
Burton u T DE14 ....185 B4
Stoke-on-T ST4 ....72 A1
Wolv WV2 ....266 B4
All Ways ST18 ....122 B3
Allan Cl ☐ DY8 ....279 C4
Allard B77 ....250 C1
Allen Birt Wlk WS15 ...178 A1
Allen Gdns TF9 ....112 A4
Allen Rd WV6 ....255 C1

Allen St Cheadle ST10 ...76 C2
Stoke-on-T ST4 ....71 C4
Tamworth B77 ....250 B1
Allen's La ST14 ....127 C1
Allenby Ct ST5 ....70 C2
Allenby Sq ST4 ....71 C2
Allendale ST16 ....155 A4
Allendale Wlk ST3 .....72 C1
Allens Croft ST14 ....127 C1
Allens La WS3 ....243 C1
Allens Rough Prim Sch
WV12 ....242 B1
Allensmead B77 ....250 B1
Allensmore Ave ST4 ....73 A3
Allensway ST5 ....70 C2
Allerdale Rd WS8 .....244 C4
Allerton Rd ST4 ....87 C4
Alleston Wlk WV10 ....240 B1
Alley The DY3 ....271 A2
Alley's La ST20 ....190 A4
Alleyne's High Sch
ST15 ....105 A1
Alleynes Sports Ctr
ST15 ....105 A2
Alliance St ST16 .....155 B3
Alliss Cl ST16 ....156 B2
Allport Rd WS11 ....209 C1
Allport St WS11 ....209 C1
Allsop Cres ST17 .....175 A1
Allthorpe Pl ST5 ....70 C2
Allton Ave B78 ....249 B1
Allton Ct B77 ....250 C2
Allways St18 ....122 B3
Allways The ST18 .....122 B3
Alma Cl ST7 ....25 C4
Alma Rd DE11 ....186 C3
Alma St Burton u T DE14 166 B1
Fenton ST4 ....72 B3
Leek ST13 ....30 B3
Stone ST15 ....104 C1
Almar Pl ST6 ....42 A3
Almond Cl
Cannock WS11 ....210 B1
Walsall WS3 ....243 C1
Almond Ct DE13 ....147 C1
Almond Gr Fenton ST3 ...72 C2
Swadlincote DE11 .....186 C3
Almond Pl ST5 ....40 C1
Almond Rd
Huntington WS12 .....209 B4
Kingswinford DY6 .....275 C4
Almshouse Croft ST18 ..191 A4
Almshouses Madeley CW3 68 C3
Newton Solney DE15 ...167 C4
Wolv WV4 ....265 C2
Alnwick Cl WS12 .....210 C1
Alnwick Rd WS3 ....243 A2
Alpha Way WS6 ....243 C1
Alpine Dr WS12 ....210 B2
Alpine Way WV3 .....255 B1
Alrewas Rd DE13 .....199 C3
Alsager Rd ST7 ....39 C3
Alsop St ST13 ....30 C3
Alston Cl Cannock WS12 210 C1
Sutton Coldfield B74 ...258 A1
Alstone Cl ST16 ....155 A4
Alstone La Bradley ST18 .172 C1
Haughton ST18 ....172 C1
Alstonefield YH ★ DE6 ..35 C2
Alstonfield Ave ST2 ....58 B3
Althorp Way DE13 ....166 B4
Althrop Gr ST3 ....73 B2
Alton Cl Newcastle-u-L ST5 55 A1
Wolv WV10 ....240 C2
Alton Gr Bucknall ST2 ...73 B4
Cannock WS11 ....209 A1
Newport TF10 ....168 C1
Alton Rd ST14 ....95 C3
Alton Towers Theme Pk ★
ST10 ....78 C2
Altona St ST1 ....120 A4
Alvaston Cl WS3 ....243 B2
Alvecote Cotts B79 ...251 B3
Alverley Cl DY6 ....275 A4
Alverstoke Cl WV9 ....240 A1
Alverton Cl B77 ....261 B2
Alvis Cl B79 ....249 C4
Alwen St DY8 ....275 C1
Alwyn B77 ....261 C4
Alwyn Cl WS6 ....227 A2
Alwyn Cres ST6 ....57 B4
Alwyn Rd DE13 ....182 A1
Amanda Ave WV4 .....265 C2
Amber Bsns Village
B77 ....251 A2
Amber Cl B77 ....251 A2
Amber Ct Endon ST9 ....43 C3
Tamworth B77 ....251 A2
Amber Gn WS11 ....210 B1
Amberfield Cl ST3 .....73 C2
Ambergate Cl WS3 ....243 B2
Ambergate Dr DY6 ....275 B4
Amberlands ST17 .....147 C1
Amberley Way B74 ....256 C1
Amblecote Dr ST3 .....73 C2
Amblecote Prim Sch
DY8 ....279 C4
Amblefield Way ST16 ..136 B1
Ambleside Cl ST15 ....120 C4
Ambleside Gr WV11 ...242 A1
Ambleside Pl ST6 ....42 A3
Ambleside Way ST7 ...275 B3
Ambrose Cres DY6 ....275 B4
Ambrose Pl ST7 ....41 C4
Amelia Cl ST2 ....43 A1
America St ST6 ....41 B2
Amerton La
Weston ST18 ....138 C1

Amerton La continued
Weston, Amerton ST18 ...139 A2
Amerton Working Farm ★
ST18 ....139 A2
Amicable St ST6 ....56 C4
Amicombe B77 ....251 B1
Amington Cl B75 .....258 B2
Amington Heath Com Prim
Sch B77 ....251 A2
Amington Ind Est B77 .251 A2
Amington Rd B77 .....250 B2
Amison St ST3 ....73 B2
Ampleforth Dr ST17 ...156 A1
Ampthill Pl ST4 ....71 C1
Amptronik Trad Est
DY3 ....269 B2
Ancaster St ST6 ....41 B4
Anchor Cl B77 ....250 C2
Anchor Par WS9 ....256 A3
Anchor Pl ST3 ....283 C4
Anchor Rd Aldridge WS9 .256 A3
Longton ST3 ....283 C4
Anchor Terr ST3 ....283 C4
Anchor Way ST20 .....171 B4
Ancient High House Mus ★
...........155 C2
Anderby Gdns DE11 ...186 C1
Anders B79 ....250 A3
Anders Sq WV6 ....254 C2
Anderson Pl ST6 ....42 C2
Anderstaff Ind Pk DE14 166 C3
Anderton View ST12 ..104 C2
Andover Cl ST3 ....73 B3
Andover Cres ☐ DY6 ..275 C2
Andover Pl WS11 .....210 A2
Andrew Mulligan Cl ST6 .41 A2
Andrew Pl ST5 ....284 D3
Andrew St ST6 ....41 B4
Andrews Ho WS13 ....231 A4
Andrews Rd WS9 .....245 A2
Aneurin Bevan Pl WS15 178 B1
Angel Croft WS7 ......211 C1
Angelica B77 ....250 C2
Angle St ☐ ST13 ....30 B3
Anglesea Dr ST3 ....73 A2
Anglesey Bsns Pk WS12 210 C2
Anglesey Cl WS7 .....228 C2
Anglesey Cres
Brownhills WS8 ....228 C1
Cannock WS12 ....210 B3
Anglesey Ct DE14 ....166 A1
Anglesey Mews WS12 ..210 B3
Anglesey Prim Sch
DE14 ....166 B1
Anglesey Rd
Brownhills WS8 ....228 C1
Burton u T DE14 ....166 A1
Lichfield WS13 ....214 A1
Anglesey St
Burton u T DE14 ....165 C2
Cannock WS12 ....210 A3
Anglia Rd WS11 ....209 B2
Angorfa Cl WS13 .....230 C4
Angus Cl ST2 ....58 B2
Anker Cl WS7 ....229 B3
Anker View B77 ....250 B2
Ankerdrive B79 ....250 A2
Ankermoor Ct B77 ....250 C3
Ankermoor Prim Sch
B77 ....250 A4
Ankerside Sh Ctr B79 ..250 A2
Anna Wlk ST6 ....56 C4
Annan Cl ☐ CW12 ....6 A1
Anne Cres WS11 ....209 C3
Anne Ct ST7 ....40 B3
Anne Rd WV4 ....266 A3
Anne St ST6 ....41 B4
Annefield Cl TF9 ....97 B1
Annette Rd ST4 ....73 A3
Anslow Gdns WV11 ...241 C1
Anslow La DE13 ....147 C1
Anslow Rd DE13 ....145 A1
Ansmead Gr ST3 ....72 C1
Anson Ave WS13 .....214 A1
Anson CE Prim Sch
ST18 ....158 A1
Anson Cl Burntwood WS7 229 B4
Great Wyrley WS6 .....226 C1
Perton WV6 ....254 C3
Anson Ct Burton u T DE14 166 C2
Fazeley B78 ....261 A4
Anson Dr ST17 ....175 C3
Anson Mews WS15 ...178 A3
Anson Rd Alrewas DE13 .201 A1
Great Wyrley WS6 .....226 C1
Meir ST3 ....90 A4
Anson St WS15 ....178 C1
Anson's Row B74 .....177 B4
Anstree Cl WS6 ....226 B1
Ansty Dr WS12 ....210 B1
Anthony Gr ST3 ....89 C2
Anthony Pl ST3 ....283 D4
Antler Dr WS15 ....178 A1
Apedale Bsns Pk ST5 ...55 B4
Apedale Com Ctry Pk ★
ST7 ....55 A3
Apedale Rd
Audley, Wood Lane ST7 ...55 B4
Newcastle-u-L ST5 ....55 B3
Apex Bsns Pk WS11 ...227 C1
Apex Rd WS8 ....244 B4
Apley Pl ST4 ....87 C4
Apley Rd DY8 ....279 C4
Apollo B79 ....249 C3
Apollo Cl WS11 ....210 A3

Aar – Apo 289

Apollo Wlk ST6 . . . . .42 B1
Appian Cl B77 . . . . .261 B4
Apple Croft CW3 . . . . .68 B4
Apple Gr TF9 . . . . .97 A1
Apple Wlk WS14 . . . . .210 B1
Appleby Gdns WV11 . . . . . .242 B1
Appleby Glade DE11 . . . . . .186 B1
Applecroft ST5 . . . . .40 C1
Applecross B74 . . . . .257 C1
Appledore Cl
  Cannock WS12 . . . . .210 C2
  Great Wyrley WS6 . . . . . . .227 A2
  Stafford ST17 . . . . .175 C4
Appledore Gr ST7 . . . . .41 C4
Appleford Pl ST3 . . . . .72 C1
Applegarth Cl ST4 . . . . .73 A3
Appleton Cl Biddulph ST8 . . .27 C3
  Burton u T DE15 . . . . .185 C4
  Congleton CW12 . . . . .15 C4
  Swadlincote DE11 . . . . . . .186 C3
Appleton Cres WV4 . . . . . . .266 A3
Appleton Dr ST5 . . . . .85 B3
Appletree Gr WS9 . . . . .256 A3
Applewood Cl ST14 . . . . . . .111 A1
Applewood Cres ST4 . . . . . .90 A4
Appleyard Ct 13 ST16 . . . . .155 C2
Appleyard The ST19 . . . . . . .223 B3
Apse Cl WV5 . . . . .269 C4
Apsley Gr ST12 . . . . .88 A1
Aqualate Cl TF10 . . . . .169 A2
Aqualate Rd ST17 . . . . .174 C3
Aquaries Ct ST3 . . . . .73 C1
Aquinas St ST4 . . . . .72 A4
Arbor Cl B77 . . . . .250 B2
Arbor Gate WS9 . . . . .245 A4
Arborfield Rd ST14 . . . . .143 C4
Arbour Cl CW3 . . . . .68 C4
Arbour Mews WS11 . . . . . . .227 C3
Arbour St Hanley ST1 . . . . . .282 C3
  Talke ST7 . . . . .40 B1
Arbourfield Dr ST2 . . . . .58 A1
Arbourtree Ct WV5 . . . . . . .270 A4
Arbury Dr DY8 . . . . .275 B2
Arcade The DY3 . . . . .271 C3
Arcadia Pk WS15 . . . . .197 A4
Arcal St DY3 . . . . .271 C4
Arch St WS16 . . . . .196 C4
Arclid Way ST2 . . . . .58 A1
Arctic Pl ST4 . . . . .88 A4
Arden Cl
  Kingswinford DY8 . . . . . . .275 B2
  Leek ST13 . . . . .31 A3
  Rugeley WS15 . . . . .178 B1
  Stourbridge DY8 . . . . .279 C4
  Tamworth B77 . . . . .250 C3
Arden Ct Congleton CW12 . . .16 A4
  Sedgley DY3 . . . . .271 B2
Arden Rd
  Barton-u-N DE13 . . . . .201 B4
  Tamworth B77 . . . . .261 C3
Ardgay Dr WS12 . . . . .209 C4
Ardingley Ave ST17 . . . . . . .156 A1
Argles Rd ST13 . . . . .31 A4
Argosy Cl ST3 . . . . .90 A4
Argyle Ave B77 . . . . .250 B2
Argyle Cl DY8 . . . . .275 C1
Argyle Rd WV2 . . . . .266 A3
Argyle St Hanley ST1 . . . . . .282 A1
  Tamworth B77 . . . . .250 C2
Argyll Cl ST11 . . . . .90 C3
Argyll Rd ST3 . . . . .73 B1
Ariane B79 . . . . .249 C4
Aries Cl ST6 . . . . .41 C3
Arion Cl B77 . . . . .250 B3
Arkall B79 . . . . .250 B4
Arkle Cl B77 . . . . .261 B2
Arkle Ct ST14 . . . . .126 B4
Arkwright Gr ST1 . . . . .57 C4
Arlescote Cl B75 . . . . .258 B1
Arley Dr DY8 . . . . .279 C2
Arley Gr WV4 . . . . .265 B3
Arlington Cl DY6 . . . . .275 C4
Arlington Way ST3 . . . . .89 C4
Armishaw Pl 2 WS15 . . . . .197 A3
Armitage Gdns WS15 . . . . . .197 A3
Armitage Hill ST13 . . . . .183 C2
Armitage Ho WS13 . . . . . . .214 C1
Armitage La WS15 . . . . .197 A3
Armitage Rd WS15 . . . . . . .197 A3
Armshead Rd ST9 . . . . .59 A3
Armside Cl WS3 . . . . .244 A2
Armstead Rd WV9 . . . . .240 A2
Armstrong B79 . . . . .249 C3
Armstrong Ave ST16 . . . . . .156 A1
Armstrong Gn ST6 . . . . .57 B4
Arnold Cl B79 . . . . .250 B4
Arnold Gr ST5 . . . . .56 A4
Arnot Rd DE14 . . . . .185 A4
Arnotdale Dr WS12 . . . . . . .209 C4
Arps Rd WV8 . . . . .238 C2
Arran Cl WS11 . . . . .210 A2
Arran Dr Chell Heath ST7 . . .41 C4
  Tamworth B77 . . . . .261 C4
Arrow Dr WV7 . . . . .237 A3
Arthur Evans Cl WS15 . . . . .197 A3
Arthur St Burton u T DE14 166 B3
  Cannock, Chadsmoor
    WS11 . . . . .209 C2
  Cannock, Wimblebury
    WS12 . . . . .210 C1
  Newcastle-u-L ST5 . . . . . .55 C1
  Stone ST15 . . . . .105 A1
  Tunstall ST6 . . . . .41 C2
  Wolv WV2 . . . . .266 B4

Arthur Terry Sch B74 . . .258 A2
Arthur Wood Pl WS15 . .178 B1
Arthurs Ct DE13 . . . . . .147 C1
Arundel B77 . . . . .261 B4
Arundel Dr ST10 . . . . . .76 C2
Arundel Gr WV6 . . . . . .254 C2
Arundel Rd
  Kingswinford DY8 . . . . .275 B1
  Wolv WV10 . . . . .240 A1
Arundel Way ST3 . . . . . .73 B3
Ascot Cl Burton u T DE15 .167 A2
  Lichfield WS14 . . . . . . .231 B4
Ascot Dr Cannock WS11 .226 B4
  Sedgley DY1 . . . . .271 C1
  Tamworth B77 . . . . . . .261 B2
  Wolv WV4 . . . . .266 A2
Ascot Gdns DY8 . . . . . .275 B1
Ascot Rd ST17 . . . . . . .156 B1
Ash Bank Rd ST2,ST9 . . .59 A2
Ash Cl Cheadle ST10 . . .76 C1
  Codsall WV8 . . . . .239 A2
  Uttoxeter ST14 . . . . . .126 A4
Ash Cres DY6 . . . . .275 C3
Ash Dr ST18 . . . . .172 C3
Ash Gr Albrighton WV7 .237 A2
  Barlaston ST12 . . . . . . .88 B1
  Blythe Bridge ST11 . . . .90 B4
  Brewood ST19 . . . . . . .223 B3
  Cannock WS11 . . . . . .209 C2
  Caverswall ST2 . . . . . . .58 C2
  Fenton ST3 . . . . .72 C1
  Lichfield WS14 . . . . . . .231 C4
  Newcastle-u-L ST5 . . . . .55 A1
  Sedgley DY3 . . . . .271 B1
  Tamworth B77 . . . . . . .261 C3
  Wheaton Aston ST19 . . .205 B3
Ash Green Cl ST4 . . . . . .88 A4
Ash Green Prim Sch ST4 88 A4
Ash Grove La DE65 . . . .148 B3
Ash Hill WV3 . . . . .255 B1
Ash La Great Wyrley WS6 .227 A2
  Newton Regis B79 . . . . .236 C3
  Swynnerton ST15 . . . . .118 C3
Ash Park Ind Est WS11 .210 A1
Ash Rd ST15 . . . . .120 A4
Ash Rise ST17 . . . . .174 C2
Ash St Burton u T DE14 .166 A1
  Walsall WS3 . . . . .243 B1
Ash Tree Cl DE11 . . . . . .186 C3
Ash Tree Ct WS11 . . . . .209 B2
Ash Tree Hill ST10 . . . . .76 B1
Ash Tree La WS13 . . . . .215 A1
Ash Tree Rd DE13 . . . . .183 B1
Ash View
  Huntington WS12 . . . . .209 B4
  Kidsgrove ST7 . . . . .26 A1
Ash Way Caverswall ST2 . .58 C2
  Newcastle-u-L ST5 . . . . .71 A2
Ashbourne Dr
  Market Drayton TF9 . . . .97 B1
  Newcastle-u-L ST5 . . . . .55 A1
  Swadlincote DE11 . . . . .186 C1
Ashbourne Gr ST1 . . . . .282 B4
Ashbourne La DE6 . . . . . .35 A1
Ashbourne Rd
  Alstonefield DE6 . . . . . .35 A2
  Cheadle ST10 . . . . .76 C2
  Leek ST13 . . . . .31 A2
  Mayfield DE6 . . . . .81 B4
  Rocester ST14 . . . . .95 C2
  Uttoxeter ST14 . . . . . . .111 A1
  Walsall WS3 . . . . .243 B2
  Wolv WV4 . . . . .266 C2
Ashbrook DE15 . . . . . . .167 A1
Ashbrook Cl
  Gnosall ST20 . . . . .171 B4
  Uttoxeter ST14 . . . . . .126 B3
Ashbrook La ST15 . . . . .161 B3
Ashburton St ST6 . . . . . .57 A4
Ashby Cres ST3 . . . . . . .72 C1
Ashby Rd
  Burton u T DE15 . . . . . .167 A1
  Tamworth B79 . . . . . . .250 A1
Ashby Rd E DE15 . . . . . .167 C1
Ashcombe Gn ST3 . . . . .72 C1
Ashcombe Rd ST13 . . . . .45 B2
Ashcombe Way ST12 . . . .30 C2
Ashcott Wlk ST2 . . . . . . .58 B1
Ashcroft Ave ST4 . . . . . .71 C1
Ashcroft Cl ST5 . . . . . . .56 A3
Ashcroft Gr ST5 . . . . . . .56 A3
Ashcroft Inf Sch B79 . . .250 B4
Ashcroft La
  Shenstone WS14 . . . . .246 C4
  Wall WS14 . . . . .246 C4
Ashcroft Oval ST5 . . . . . .56 A4
Ashcroft Pl ST5 . . . . . . .56 A3
Ashcroft Rd ST5 . . . . . . .56 A3
Ashdale Cl
  Burton u T DE15 . . . . . .186 A4
  Kingswinford DY6 . . . . .275 B4
  6 Stone ST15 . . . . . . .120 A4
Ashdale Dr ST16 . . . . . .155 B2
Ashdale Pk ST15 . . . . . .118 C3
Ashdale Rd Fenton ST4 . .72 B3
  Leek ST13 . . . . .31 A3
  Tamworth B77 . . . . . . .250 B3
Ashdale Rise ST5 . . . . . .71 A3
Ashdene Gdns DY8 . . . .275 B1
Ashdown Dr DY8 . . . . . .275 C2
Ashe's La DE6 . . . . .144 B4
Ashen Cl DY3 . . . . .266 A3
Ashenden Rise WV4 . . . .265 A4
Ashendene Gr ST4 . . . . .87 C4
Ashenhurst Way WS13 . . .30 C2
Ashenough Rd ST7 . . . . .40 B3
Ashfield Ct ST5 . . . . . . .284 A4

Ashfield Gr WV10 . . . . . .240 B2
Ashfield Rd
  Wolv Ford Houses WV10 .240 B2
  Wolv, Compton WV3 . . .255 B1
Ashfield Sq WS7 . . . . . . .58 A1
Ashfields WV7 . . . . .237 A3
Ashfields Grange ST5 . . .284 B3
Ashfields New Rd ST5 . . .284 A4
Ashflats Rd ST17,ST18 . .174 C2
Ashford Dr DY3 . . . . . . .271 C4
Ashford Gr ST15 . . . . . .120 B4
Ashford Rd DE13 . . . . . .166 A3
Ashford St ST4 . . . . .72 B4
Ashgrove WS7 . . . . .228 C3
Ashland ST18 . . . . .139 B1
Ashlands ST18 . . . . .139 B1
Ashlands Ave ST4 . . . . . .71 A4
Ashlands Cl B79 . . . . . . .250 B4
Ashlands Cres ST4 . . . . .71 C4
Ashlands Gr ST4 . . . . . . .71 A4
Ashlands Rd ST4 . . . . . . .71 C4
Ashlar Cl ST6 . . . . .42 A4
Ashlea B78 . . . . .262 C3
Ashlea Dr DE6 . . . . .81 B4
Ashleigh Ave DE11 . . . . .186 C3
Ashleigh Cres ST19 . . . .205 B4
Ashleigh Dr
  Tamworth B78 . . . . . . .261 C3
  Uttoxeter ST14 . . . . . .110 C1
Ashleigh Rd
  Rugeley WS15 . . . . . . .196 C4
  Upper Tean ST10 . . . . . .92 C2
Ashley Cl
  Kingswinford DY6 . . . . .275 B2
  Stafford ST16 . . . . .155 A2
  Stourbridge DY8 . . . . . .279 B1
Ashley Croft ST20 . . . . .190 A4
Ashley Ct DE15 . . . . . . .167 A2
Ashley Gdns WV8 . . . . . .238 C2
Ashley Gr ST5 . . . . .56 B2
Ashley Mount WV6 . . . . .255 B3
Ashley Rd
  Burntwood WS7 . . . . . .211 C1
  Kidderminster DY10 . . . .280 A1
  Walsall WS3 . . . . .242 C1
  Wolv WV4 . . . . .265 C3
Ashley View TF9 . . . . . . .97 B1
Ashmall WS7 . . . . .229 B2
Ashman St ST6 . . . . . . .42 B1
Ashmead Rd WS7 . . . . .229 A4
Ashmole Ave WS7 . . . . .229 C4
Ashmole Cl WS14 . . . . .231 C3
Ashmore Ave WV11 . . . .242 A1
Ashmore Dr ST20 . . . . . .171 B4
Ashmore Wlk ST1 . . . . .282 C3
Ashoale Cl WS12 . . . . . .209 B4
Ashover Gr ST7 . . . . . . .41 C4
Ashover Rd DE11 . . . . . .186 C3
Ashridge Ave ST5 . . . . . .71 A1
Ashridge Gr ST3 . . . . . . .73 B3
Ashridge Wlk ST16 . . . . .136 B1
Ashton Cl CW12 . . . . . . .6 A1
Ashton Ct Caverswall ST4 .59 A2
  Newcastle-u-L ST5 . . . . .71 B1
Ashton Dr WS4 . . . . . . .244 B2
Ashtree Bank WS15 . . . .197 A3
Ashtree Cl ST18 . . . . . . .177 B4
Ashtree Rd WS3 . . . . . .244 A2
Ashurst Gr 14 ST3 . . . . .90 A4
Ashwell Rd ST4 . . . . . . .71 B4
Ashwells Gr WV9 . . . . . .240 A1
Ashwood ST3 . . . . .283 C4
Ashwood Ave DY8 . . . . .275 B1
Ashwood Cl TF9 . . . . . . .97 A1
Ashwood Gr
  Forsbrook ST11 . . . . . . .91 A3
  Wolv WV4 . . . . .266 A3
Ashwood Park Prim Sch
  DY8 . . . . .275 B1
Ashwood Terr ST3 . . . . .283 C5
Ashworth Ave DE15 . . . .167 B1
Ashworth St ST4 . . . . . .72 B3
Ashworth Way TF10 . . . .168 C1
Askerbank La SK11 . . . . .8 A1
Askern Cl ST3 . . . . .73 C1
Askew Bridge Rd DY3 . .271 A2
Askew Cl DY3 . . . . .271 C3
Aspen Cft ST17 . . . . . . .174 A4
Aspen Cl B77 . . . . .26 C2
Aspen Ct WS12 . . . . . . .211 A3
Aspen Gr WS7 . . . . .228 C4
Aspen Rd DE13 . . . . . . .201 B4
Aspen Way TF10 . . . . . .168 C1
Aspley Cl WV10 . . . . . . .224 C3
Aspley La WV10 . . . . . . .224 B2
Asquith Cl ST8 . . . . .27 C1
Asquith Dr WS11 . . . . . .210 B1
Astbury Ct Kidsgrove ST7 .26 B2
  Walsall WS3 . . . . .243 C1
Astbury Lane Ends CW12 15 C4
Aster Cl ST3 . . . . .74 A3
Aster Wlk WV9 . . . . .240 A2
Astil St DE15 . . . . .166 C1
Astles Rock Wlk DY7 . . .278 A2
Aston Bk ST16,ST18 . . . .154 C2
Aston Chase ST15 . . . . .120 B4
Aston Cl Colwich ST18 . . .177 B4
  Penkridge ST19 . . . . . .208 A2
  Shenstone WS14 . . . . .246 C3
Aston Dr TF10 . . . . .168 C1
Aston Hill ST18 . . . . . . .154 C2
Aston La Claverley WV5 . .267 B4
  Maer TF9 . . . . .83 C4
  Stone ST15 . . . . .120 B4
  Sudbury DE6 . . . . .129 A3
Aston Lodge Parkway
  ST15 . . . . .120 B3

Aston Rd ST5 . . . . .40 B1
Aston St WV3 . . . . .266 A4
Aston Terr ST16 . . . . . . .155 C3
Astonfields Ind Est
  ST16 . . . . .155 C3
Astonfields Rd ST16 . . . .155 C3
Astonfields Road Bsns Pk
  ST16 . . . . .155 C3
Astor Rd Aldridge B74 . . .257 A1
  Kingswinford DY6 . . . . .275 C3
Astoria Cl WV12 . . . . . . .242 B1
Astoria Dr ST17 . . . . . . .174 C3
Astoria Gdns WV12 . . . .242 B1
Astro Gr ST3 . . . . .283 A4
Athelney Ct WS3 . . . . . .244 A2
Athelstan Cl ST19 . . . . . .208 A4
Athelstan Gr WV6 . . . . . .254 C2
Athelstan St 1 ST6 . . . . .41 B2
Athelstan Way B79 . . . . .249 C4
Athena Rd ST1 . . . . .57 C3
Atherstone Rd ST4 . . . . . .88 A4
Atherstone St B77,B78 . .261 A4
Athlestan Way DE13 . . . .147 B1
Athlone St ST6 . . . . .42 B1
Atholl Rd ST3 . . . . .283 D1
Atkins Way ST14 . . . . . . .95 C2
Atlam St ST2 . . . . .58 A2
Atlantic Gr ST4 . . . . .88 A4
Atlas St ST4 . . . . .72 C3
Attingham Dr WS11 . . . .210 A1
Attlee Cres
  Rugeley WS15 . . . . . . .196 C4
  Stafford ST17 . . . . .174 B4
Attlee Gr WS11 . . . . . . .210 B1
Attlee Rd ST10 . . . . .76 B1
Attwell Pk WV3 . . . . . . .265 B4
Attwood Gdns WV4 . . . . .266 A3
Attwood Rd WS7 . . . . . .228 B4
Attwood St ST7 . . . . . . .26 A1
Aubrey St ST6 . . . . .41 A4
Auchinleck Dr WS13 . . . .214 B1
Auckland Rd DY6 . . . . . .275 C2
Auden Ct WV6 . . . . .254 C2
Auden Pl ST3 . . . . .283 D4
Auden Way ST17 . . . . . .174 B4
Audlem Rd CW3 . . . . . . .67 C1
Audley Ave TF10 . . . . . .169 A1
Audley Ave Bsns Pk
  TF10 . . . . .169 A1
Audley Cl DE13 . . . . . . .201 A4
Audley Ho TF10 . . . . . . .169 A1
Audley House Mews
  TF10 . . . . .169 A1
Audley Pl ST5 . . . . .71 A3
Audley Rd Audley ST7 . . . .39 C4
  Barthomley CW2,ST7 . . .38 C3
  Newcastle-u-L ST7,ST5 . .40 A1
  Newport TF10 . . . . .168 C2
  Talke ST7 . . . . .40 A1
Audley St
  Newcastle-u-L ST5 . . . . .55 C2
  Tunstall ST6 . . . . .41 B2
Audmore Rd ST20 . . . . .171 B4
Audnam DY8 . . . . .275 C1
Augustine Cl ST15 . . . . .120 B4
Augustine Gr B74 . . . . . .257 C3
Augustines Wlk WS13 . . .214 A2
Aukland St ST6 . . . . .57 A4
Aulton Rd B75 . . . . .258 C1
Aumbry Cl TF9 . . . . .97 A1
Austcliffe Rd DY10 . . . . .280 A3
Austin Cl Cheadle ST10 . .76 B1
  Stone ST15 . . . . .120 A4
Austin Cote La WS14 . . .231 C1
Austin Friars ST17 . . . . .155 C1
Austin St ST1 . . . . .282 C1
Austrey La
  Newton Regis B79 . . . . .236 C2
  Newton Regis, No Man's Heath
    B79 . . . . .236 C2
Austwick Gr ST4 . . . . . . .71 C1
Autumn Berry Gr DY3 . . .271 C3
Autumn Cl WS4 . . . . . . .244 B1
Autumn Dr
  Lichfield WS13 . . . . . . .214 B1
  Sedgley DY3 . . . . .271 B2
  Walsall WS4 . . . . .244 B1
Avarne Pl 15 ST16 . . . . .155 C2
Aveling Gn ST1 . . . . .57 C4
Aveling Rd ST1 . . . . .57 C4
Avenue One CW1 . . . . . .37 B4
Avenue Rd
  Cannock WS12 . . . . . . .210 C1
  Newport TF10 . . . . .168 C1
  Stoke-on-T ST4 . . . . . . .57 B1
  Wolv WV3 . . . . .255 C1
Avenue Rd S TF10 . . . . .168 C1
Avenue The Bagnall ST9 . .43 C2
  Blakedown DY10 . . . . . .281 A2
  Cheadle ST10 . . . . .76 B1
  Cheddleton ST13 . . . . . .45 B2
  Endon ST9 . . . . .43 C4
  Enville DY7 . . . . .273 C1
  Featherstone WV10 . . . .241 A4
  Forsbrook ST11 . . . . . . .91 A1
  Kidsgrove ST7 . . . . .25 C1
  Newcastle-u-L, Basford ST5 .56 B1
  Newcastle-u-L, City General Hospl
    ST4 . . . . .71 B4
  Stone ST15 . . . . .105 A1
  Wheaton Aston ST19 . . .206 B2
  Wolv, Finchfield WV3 . . .265 A4
  Wolv, Penn WV4 . . . . . .265 C2
  Wootton DE6 . . . . .79 C4
Avenue Two CW1 . . . . . .37 B4
Averill Dr WS15 . . . . . . .178 B1
Averill Rd ST17 . . . . . . .174 B4

Aviation La DE13 . . . . . . .165 B2
Avill B77 . . . . .262 A3
Avington Cl DY3 . . . . . . .271 C4
Avion Cl ST3 . . . . .90 B4
Avoca St ST1 . . . . .282 C4
Avocet Cl ST14 . . . . .126 B3
Avon B77 . . . . .262 A3
Avon Cl Kidsgrove ST7 . . .26 A1
  Newcastle-u-L ST5 . . . . .71 A2
  Perton WV6 . . . . .254 C2
  Stafford ST16 . . . . .156 A2
Avon Cres WS3 . . . . . . .244 A1
Avon Dale TF10 . . . . . . .168 C2
Avon Gr Ashley TF9 . . . . .99 C3
  Cheadle ST10 . . . . .76 C1
  Stone ST15 . . . . .120 A3
Avon Hill ST16 . . . . .156 B2
Avon Ho DY3 . . . . .271 C4
Avon Rd Burntwood WS7 .228 C3
  Cannock WS11 . . . . . . .226 B4
  Stourbridge DY8 . . . . . .279 C2
  Walsall WS3 . . . . .243 C1
Avon Rise ST16 . . . . . . .156 A2
Avon Way
  Burton u T DE15 . . . . . .167 A1
  Marston on D DE65 . . . .147 B4
Avondale Cl DY6 . . . . . .275 C4
Avondale Rd WV6 . . . . . .255 C2
Avondale St ST6 . . . . . . .56 B4
Avonlea Gdns WS15 . . . .178 B1
Avonside Ave ST6 . . . . . .41 C2
Avonwick Gr ST1 . . . . . . .58 A3
Axborough La DY10 . . . . .280 B2
Axbridge Wlk ST6 . . . . . .42 B1
Axon Cres ST3 . . . . .74 A2
Aylesbury Rd ST2 . . . . . .58 B1
Aylesford Cl DY3 . . . . . .266 B1
Aylesford Dr B74 . . . . . .257 C3
Aynsley Ave ST5 . . . . . . .71 A2
Aynsley Cl ST10 . . . . . . .76 B1
Aynsley Rd ST4 . . . . . . .57 A1
Aynsley Specl Sch ST11 . .90 C4
Aynsley's Dr ST5 . . . . . .90 C4
Ayr Rd ST3 . . . . .76 C3
Ayreshire Gr ST3 . . . . . .73 B1
Ayrshire Way CW12 . . . . .6 A1
Ayrton Cl WV6 . . . . .255 C2
Ayshford St ST3 . . . . . . .283 B3
Azalea Cl WV8 . . . . .239 A2

B

Babbacombe Ave ST17 .175 C4
Babbington Cl
  Tutbury DE13 . . . . .146 B3
  Whittington WS14 . . . . .232 C3
Babworth Cl WV9 . . . . . .240 A1
Back Browning St ST16 155 B2
Back Bunt's La ST9 . . . . .43 B2
Back Cross La CW12 . . . .16 A4
Back Ford Green Rd ST6 42 B1
Back Garden St ST5 . . . .284 C2
Back Heathcote St ST6 . .26 A1
Back La Aldridge WS9 . . .256 C4
  Alstonefield DE6 . . . . . .35 C2
  Alton ST10 . . . . .78 C1
  Ashley TF9 . . . . .100 A3
  Betley CW2,CW3 . . . . . .53 A4
  Colwich ST18 . . . . .177 B4
  Ellastone DE6 . . . . .80 A2
  Endon, Brown Edge ST6 . .43 A4
  Endon, Hodgefield ST6 . . .28 A1
  Forton TF10 . . . . .150 B1
  Gnosall ST20 . . . . .171 B3
  Haughton ST18 . . . . . . .173 A3
  Hixon ST18 . . . . .139 B1
  Leek ST13 . . . . .30 B3
  Millmeece ST21 . . . . . .102 B3
  Ranton ST18 . . . . .153 B2
  Shenstone WS14 . . . . .246 C1
  Uttoxeter ST14 . . . . . .126 B4
  Waterhouses ST10 . . . . .49 C1
  Wheaton Aston ST19 . . .205 B3
  Whittington WS14 . . . . .232 C3
  Woodseaves ST20 . . . . .151 B4
  Wootton DE6 . . . . .79 C4
Back Radfords 2 ST15 . .105 A1
Back Rd DY6 . . . . .275 B4
Back Westlands Rd
  ST14 . . . . .126 A3
Backcester La WS13 . . . .231 A4
Backcrofts WS11 . . . . . .209 B1
Baddeley Green La ST2 . .43 A1
Baddeley Hall Rd ST2 . . .43 B2
Baddeley Rd ST2 . . . . . .43 A1
Baddeley St Burslem ST6 .41 C1
  Cheadle ST10 . . . . .76 C1
Baddly's Ct TF10 . . . . . .168 C2
Baden Powell Cl WS15 . .211 C3
Baden Rd ST6 . . . . .42 B1
Baden St ST5 . . . . .284 B4
Bader Rd WV6 . . . . .254 C2
Badger Brow Rd TF9 . . . .99 B3
Badger Cl WS12 . . . . . . .209 B3
Badger Gr ST3 . . . . .90 B4
Badger La TF9,ST5 . . . . .84 B2
Badger St DY3 . . . . .271 C4
Badger's End ST19 . . . . .205 A3
Badgers Bank Rd B74 . . .257 C3
Badgers Brow ST1 . . . . .57 C2
Badgers Cl WS3 . . . . . . .244 A3
Badgers Croft
  Eccleshall ST21 . . . . . .133 C3
  Stafford ST17 . . . . .175 B3
Badgers Hollow ST10 . . .93 A3
Badgers Rise ST13 . . . . .30 C3

Badgers Sett ST13 ......30 C3
Badgers Way WS12 ....210 B1
Badgery Cl ST14 ......111 A1
Badminton Cl DY1 ....271 C2
Badnall Cl WS3 ....30 C3
Badnall St ST13 ....30 B3
Bag La Admaston WS15 .159 B4
Marchington ST14 .....127 C1
Roston DE6 ....96 C4
Baggeridge Cl DY3 ....271 A4
Baggeridge Ctry Pk★
DY3 ....270 C2
Baggott Pl ST1 ....70 C4
Baggott St WV2 ....266 B4
Bagnall Hospl ST9 ......43 C1
Bagnall Rd Bagnall ST9 ..43 B1
Norton-in-t-M ST2 .....43 B1
Bagnall St ST1 ....282 B2
Bagot Gr ST1 ....57 C4
Bagot St WS15 ....160 C3
Bagots Oak ST17 .....174 B4
Bagots View
Abbots Bromley WS15 ..161 A3
Church Leigh ST10 ....109 A2
Bagridge Cl WV3 .....265 A4
Bagridge Rd WV3 ....265 A4
Bailey Ave B77 ....261 C3
Bailey Cl Burntwood WS7 228 B4
Cannock WS11 ....210 A2
Bailey Cres CW12 ......6 A2
Bailey Rd ST3 ....72 C2
Bailey St Burton u T DE14 166 B1
Newcastle-u-L ST5 ....284 A3
Stafford ST17 ....155 C1
Stoke-on-T ST4 ....56 C1
Bailey's Bank ST8 ......16 B2
Bailye Cl WS13 ....214 C1
Bain Ho ST17 ....174 C3
Bainbridge Rd ST4 .....88 C4
Bains Gr ST5 ....55 C4
Baird Ho DY6 ....275 C4
Baker Ave WV14 .....266 C1
Baker Cres ST2 ....43 B2
Baker Cres N ST2 ......43 B2
Baker Cres S ST2 ......43 A2
Baker Dr WS13 ....215 B4
Baker St Burntwood WS7 228 C3
Burton u T DE15 .....185 C4
Fenton ST4 ....72 C2
Baker's La Aldridge WS9 .256 A3
Lichfield WS13 ....231 A4
Norbury TF10 ....150 B2
Bakers Gdns WV8 ....238 C2
Bakers Way
Cannock WS12 ....210 A3
Codsall WV8 ....238 C2
Bakers Wlk B77 ......261 C2
Bakewell Cl
Newcastle-u-L ST5 .....55 B1
Walsall WS3 ....243 B2
Bakewell Dr ST15 ....120 B3
Bakewell Gn DE11 ....186 C3
Bakewell St ST4 ....71 C3
Bala Gr ST10 ....76 C2
Bala Ho ST17 ....174 C3
Balaam's La ST15 ....106 B3
Balance Hill ST14 ....126 B4
Balance St ST14 .....126 B4
Balcombe Cl ST4 ....284 B1
Baldwin Gr WS11 ....210 B1
Baldwin Way DY3 ....269 C1
Baldwin's Gate CE Prim Sch
ST5 ....85 B3
Balfour B79 ....250 A2
Balfour Cres WV6 ....255 C2
Balfour Ct
Sutton Coldfield B74 ..258 A2
■ Wolv WV6 ....255 C2
Balfour Gr ST8 ....27 C1
Balfour Rd DY6 ......275 C4
Balfour St
Burton u T DE13 .....166 B3
Hanley ST1 ....282 C2
Balgrove Ho WS11 ...209 B1
Balk Pas ST16 ....155 C3
Ball Green Prim Sch ST6 42 B3
Ball Haye Gn ST13 .....31 A4
Ball Haye Rd ST13 .....30 C3
Ball Haye St ST13 .....30 C3
Ball Haye Terr ST13 ....30 C3
Ball Hayes Rd ST6 .....42 B3
Ball La Brewood WV10 .240 B3
Leek ST13 ....30 C3
Norton-in-t-M ST6 .....43 A3
Ball's Yd ST5 ....284 B1
Ballarat Wlk DY8 ....279 C3
Ballington Gdns ST13 ..30 C3
Ballington View ST13 ..30 C2
Ballinson Rd ST5 ......72 C1
Balliol Bsns Pk WV9 ..239 C2
Balliol St ST4 ....72 A4
Balloon St ST4 ....56 B1
Balmain Cres WV11 ..241 A1
Balmoral Cl
Lichfield WS14 ....231 B1
Stone ST15 ....120 A3
Tamworth B79 ....250 A4
Trentham ST4 ....72 A1
Balmoral Ct WS11 ...210 A3
Balmoral Dr
Cannock WS12 ......209 C4
Cheadle ST10 ....76 A1
Market Drayton TF9 ...97 C1
Wombourne WV5 ....265 A1
Balmoral Rd
Burton u T DE15 .....167 A2
Kingswinford DY8 ...275 B1
Stafford ST17 ....156 B1

Sutton Coldfield B74 ..257 C3
Wolv WV4 ....266 A3
Balmoral View DY1 ..271 C1
Balmoral Way WS7 ...228 C4
Baltic Cl Cannock WS11 209 C1
Trentham ST4 ....88 A4
Balvenie Way DY1 ...271 C2
Bamber Cl WS3 .....265 C4
Bamber Pl ST5 ....55 C3
Bamber St ST4 ....72 A4
Bamborough Cl DE13 166 B4
Bamburgh B77 ......261 B1
Bambury St ST3,ST4 ...73 B3
Bamford Cl WS3 ....243 B2
Bamford Gr ST4 ....282 A4
Bamford Ho WS3 ...243 B2
Bamford Rd Walsall WS3 243 B2
Wolv WV3 ....266 A4
Bamford St B77 .....250 B2
Bampton Ave ◢ WS7 .229 A4
Bampton Cl ST9 ....43 C3
Banbury Dr WV5 ....269 C2
Banbury Cl WV3 ....271 C1
Banbury Gr ST8 ....27 B4
Banbury Rd WS11 ...226 B4
Banbury St ST7 ....25 B1
Bancroft B77 ....250 C2
Bancroft La
Forsbrook ST11 ....90 C1
Hamstall Ridware WS15 .199 A4
Bandridge La SK11 ....18 A4
Baneberry Dr WV10 ..241 A4
Banford Gr ST14 ....110 C1
Bangley La
Drayton Bassett B78 ..260 A4
Hints B78 ....259 C3
Bank Cl ST14 ....126 B4
Bank Cres WS7 .....228 C3
Bank Ct ◢ ST7 ....26 A1
Bank End ST5 ....43 A4
Bank Gn WV3 ....265 C4
Bank Hall Rd ST6 .....42 A1
Bank House Dr ST5 ...56 C1
Bank Rd DY3 ....271 B1
Bank Side Hartington SK17 24 B3
Stone ST15 ....119 C3
Bank St Cannock WS12 .210 C1
Cheadle ST10 ....76 B2
Kidsgrove ST7 ....26 B2
Tunstall ST6 ....41 B2
Bank The Gnosall ST20 .171 B3
The Bank ST7 ....26 A1
Bank Top WS15 .....178 B1
Bank Top Ave ST6 .....42 A4
Bank Wlk DE13 .....166 A4
Bankfield Gr ST5 ......54 C2
Bankfield Rd ST3 ......89 C4
Bankhouse Dr CW12 ....6 A3
Bankhouse Rd
Forsbrook ST11 ....91 A4
Trentham ST4 ....87 C4
Banks La ST10 ....61 C2
Bankside
Newcastle-u-L ST5 ...284 C2
Stanton DE6 ....65 B1
Stone ST15 ....104 B2
Wombourne WV5 ...269 C4
Bankside Way WS9 ..245 A1
Banksman Rd ST2 .....73 B4
Banktop Rd DE6,ST14 .144 A3
Banky Brook Cl ST6 ...42 B2
Bannut Tree La DY7 ..277 B3
Banstead Cl WV2 ....266 C4
Bantock Ave WV3 ...265 C4
Bantock Ct WV3 ....265 C4
Bantock Gdns WV3 ..255 C1
Bantock House Mus★
WV3 ....255 C1
Baptist St ◢ ST6 ......57 A4
Bar Hill CW3 ....68 B2
Bar La DE13 ....183 A1
Bar Wlk WS9 ....245 B1
Barbara St B79 .....250 A3
Barber Cl WS12 ....210 C1
Barber Dr ST7 ....25 C4
Barber Pl ST6 ....41 C3
Barber Rd ST6 ....41 C3
Barber St ST6 ....41 C1
Barber's Sq ST5 ......56 B2
Barbridge Rd ST5 .....40 B1
Barbrook Ave ST3 ....73 C2
Barclay Cl WV7 .....237 A3
Barclay St ST5 ....73 B3
Barcliff Ave B77 ....250 C2
Bardell Rd WS13 ....230 C3
Bardsey Wlk ◢ ST3 ...73 A2
Bardwell Cl WV8 ...255 C4
Bardy La Armitage WS15 .197 C2
Longdon WS15 ......197 B1
Barfoot St ST3 ....283 B3
Barford Rd ST5 ....70 C2
Bargate La ST19 ....223 B3
Bargate St ST19 ....223 B3
Bargery Rd WV11 ...242 A1
Bargrave Dr ST5 ......56 A4
Bargrave St ST2 ......58 B1
Barker Cl ST16 .....155 B2
Barker St Longton ST3 ..283 C1
Newcastle-u-L ST5 ....55 C3
Barks Dr ST6 ....42 B2
Barlaston CE Fst Sch
ST12 ....88 C1
Barlaston Cl ST16 ...155 B4
Barlaston Old Rd ST4 ..88 A3

Barlaston Rd
Barlaston ST3 ....89 A3
Longton ST3 ....88 C4
Barlaston Sta ST12 ...88 B1
Barley Cl Aldridge WS9 .256 C1
Burton u T DE14 .....166 C3
Cannock WS12 ......210 A3
Sedgley DY3 ....271 C4
Barley Croft Perton WV6 254 B2
Whittington WS14 ....232 C3
Barley Ct ST16 ......155 A3
Barley Field WV9 ...224 A1
Barley Green La WS13 .201 B1
Barley Orch ST20 ...171 C3
Barley Rd ST10 ....62 A4
Barleycorn Cl DE15 ..167 A1
Barleycroft ST10 ......76 C1
Barleycroft Terr ST7 ..25 A3
Barleyfield Rise DY6 ..275 A4
Barleyfields Audley ST7 .39 B1
Chell Heath ST6 ......42 B2
Barlow Cl ST3 ....73 B3
Barlow Cl B77 ......250 C4
Barlow St WS3 .....283 C3
Barlstone Ave ST11 ..90 C3
Barmouth Cl ST8 .....27 C3
Barmouth Gr ST8 ....27 C4
Barn Ave WS3 ......271 B4
Barn Bank La ST17,ST18 174 B3
Barn Cl Dordon B78 ..262 C3
Lichfield WS13 ......214 A2
Rugeley WS15 ......197 A3
Stafford ST17 ....174 C3
Barn Comm ST20 ...151 B4
Barn Croft
Burntwood WS7 .....229 A2
Great Wyrley WS6 ...227 A2
Barn Ct ST5 ....71 B2
Barn End Rd ST17 ...193 A4
Barn Gn WV3 ......265 C4
Barn La ST19 ....223 B4
Barn Owl Dr WS3 ...243 C2
Barn Rd WS15 .....198 B3
Barnaby Sq WV10 ..240 C2
Barnard Pl WV2 ....266 C3
Barnard Rd WV11 ...241 C1
Barnard Way WS11 .209 C1
Barnbridge B77 ....250 B1
Barnbridge Cl ST7 ...25 C4
Barncroft Rd ST6 .....42 B3
Barnes Croft WS15 ..106 B1
Barnes Rd
Shenstone WS14 ....247 A3
Stafford ST17 ......174 A3
Barnes Way ST3 ......73 B1
Barnett Cl DY6 .....275 B2
Barnett Gn DY6 ....275 B2
Barnett Gr ST6 ....41 C3
Barnett La DY6,DY8 ..275 C4
Barnetts La WS8 ....228 C1
Barnfield Cl
Lichfield WS14 ......231 A3
Stone ST15 ....119 C4
Barnfield Rd ST13 ....30 C2
Barnfield Rd Burslem ST6 .57 A4
Leek ST13 ....30 B2
Upper Tean ST10 .....92 C2
Barnfield Way
Cannock WS12 ......211 A3
Stafford ST17 ......175 B3
Barnfields Cl ST13 ....30 B2
Barnfields Ind Est ST13 .30 B2
Barnfields La ST10 ....61 B1
Barnfields Prim Sch
ST17 ....175 B3
Barngate St ST13 .....30 B3
Barnhurst La WV8 ..239 C1
Barnlea Gr ST3 ....73 A2
Barnmeadow Cl TF10 .169 A2
Barnmeadow Rd TF10 .169 A1
Barns Cl WS9 ....244 C3
Barns Croft B74 ....257 A2
Barnsdale Cl ST4 .....88 B3
Barnswood Cl WS11 .228 A4
Barnwell Cl ST4 ....111 A2
Barnwell Gr ST4 .....72 A1
Barnwood Rd WV8 ..239 C1
Baron Cl WS7 ....211 C1
Baron St ST4 ....283 A5
Baron's Way ST18 ..158 A4
Barr Common Cl WS9 .256 A2
Barr Common Rd WS9 .256 A1
Barr St DY3 ....271 B2
Barracks La WS14 ...245 B4
Barracks Rd ST5 ....284 C2
Barracks Sq ST5 ....284 C2
Barracks Way ◢ ST13 .30 B3
Barrage Rd ST8 ......28 A4
Barrar Cl DY8 ......279 C4
Barratt Gdns ST4 .....58 A4
Barratt Cres ST6 .....57 A3
Barrett Dr ST6 ....57 A3
Barrie Gdns ST7 .....40 B4
Barrington Cl
Albrighton WV7 .....237 A3
Burton u T DE13 ....147 B1
Wolv WV10 ....240 B1
Barrington Rd ST6 ....56 C2
Barrow Hill Rd DY5 ..271 B1
Barry Ave ST2 ....58 A2
Bartholomew Rd ST3 ..73 C1
Barthomley Rd
Audley ST7 ....39 A1
Barthomley CW2 .....38 A4

Barthomley Rd continued
Betley ST7 ....38 C3
Wolv WV4 ....57 B3
Bartic Ave DY6 .....275 C2
Bartlem St ST3 .....283 D5
Bartlett Cl ST19 ....207 A2
Barton Cottage Hospl
DE13 ....183 B1
Barton Cres ST6 ......41 C1
Barton Gate ST14 ...183 A1
Barton La Bradley ST18 .191 A1
Kingswinford DY6 ...275 B4
Barton Lodge DE13 ..183 B1
Barton Rd WV4 ....266 C2
Barton St DE14 ....185 B4
Barton Turn DE13 ...184 A1
Barton's Rd TF9 ....112 A4
Barton's La TF9 ....112 A4
Barwood Ave ST7 ....25 A3
Basford La ST13 .....45 C4
Basford Lane Ind Est
ST13 ....45 C4
Basford Park Rd ST5 ..56 B2
Basford Villas ST5 ....56 B1
Basfordbridge La ST13 .45 B2
Basfordbridge Terr ST13 .45 A5
Basil Cl ST14 ....174 C3
Basildon Gr ST4 ....283 C2
Basin La B77 ....250 C2
Baskerville Rd ST1 ..282 C3
Baskeyfield Cl WS14 .231 B4
Baskeyfield Pl ST6 ....42 A3
Baslow Cl WS3 ....243 A2
Baslow Gn DE11 ....186 C3
Baslow Rd WS3 ....243 A2
Basnett's Wood Rd ST9 .43 C3
Bass Cotts ST4 .....166 C2
Bass Mus The★ DE14 .166 B2
Bass's Bldgs DE14 ...166 A2
Bassenthwaite Ct DY6 .275 C2
Bassett Cl Cheadle ST10 .76 B2
Wolv WV4 ....265 B3
Bassilow Rd ST4 .....72 C4
Baswich Bsns Pk ST17 .156 B1
Baswich Crest ST17 ..156 B1
Baswich House Dr ◢
ST17 ....175 B4
Baswich House Way ◢
ST17 ....175 B4
Baswich La ST17 ....175 B4
Batch La DE6 ....127 A4
Batchelor Cl DY8 ...279 C4
Bateman Ave ST8 ....27 A3
Batemans Rd ST14 ..126 A4
Batesway WS15 ....197 B2
Batfield La DY7 .....272 B1
Bath Ct ST17 ....155 C1
Bath La DY7 ....277 B3
Bath Mews ST17 ....155 C1
Bath Rd Cannock WS11 209 C3
Newcastle-u-L ST5 ...54 C1
Stourbridge DY8 ...279 C4
Bath St ST13 ....30 C3
Meir ST3 ....74 A3
Sedgley DY3 ....266 C1
Stoke-on-T ST4 .....72 A4
Bath Terr ST4 ....72 A4
Bath Vale Cotts CW12 ..6 A2
Batholoi Way ST17 ..175 A4
Baths La ST18 ......158 B4
Baths Pas ST3 .....283 B4
Baths Rd ST3 ....283 B4
Bathurst St ST3 ....283 C4
Batkin Cl ST6 ....42 A3
Batten Cl ST3 ....90 C1
Batten Wlk ST13 ....118 C3
Battison Cres ST3 ..283 C2
Battle Ridge ST18 ..156 B4
Battlefield Hill WV5 ..270 A4
Battlefield La WV5 ..270 A3
Battlefield Terr WV5 .270 A3
Battlesteads ST10 ....78 B1
Baulk La ST11 ......106 C4
Baxter Gn ST16 ....155 A2
Bayham Wlk ST2 .....58 A2
Bayley Hills TF10 ...168 A3
Bayley Ho WS8 ....245 A3
Baylie Ct ST4 ......279 C3
Baylie St DY8 ......279 C2
Bayliss Ct ST5 ......255 C1
Bayston Ave WV3 ..265 C4
Bayswater Rd
Rugeley WS15 ......178 B1
Sedgley DY3 ....271 B1
Baytree Cl Hanley ST1 ..57 C3
Walsall WS3 ....243 A1
Baytree Rd WS3 ....243 A1
Baywood Cl ST17 ...156 B1
Beach Ave WV4,WV14 .266 C2
Beachcroft Rd DY6 ..270 A1
Beachwood Ave DY6 .270 B1
Beacon Ctr for the Blind
WV4 ....266 B2
Beacon Dr DE13 ....147 A2
Beacon Gdns WS13 .214 A1
Beacon Hill WS9 ...256 B1
Beacon La Kinver DY7 ..277 A1
Romsley WV15,DY7,DY12 276 C2
Sedgley DY3 ....266 C1
Beacon Pas DY3 ...266 B1
Beacon Pk ST19 ....221 C4
Beacon Rd Aldridge WS9 256 A1
Rolleston DE13 .....147 A4
Stone ST15 ....120 A3
Beacon Rise
Aldridge WS9 ....256 A2
Sedgley DY3 ....266 C1
Stone ST15 ....120 A3

Beacon St Lichfield WS13 213 C1
Wolv WV14 ....266 C2
Beacon Trad Est WS9 .256 A3
Beacon Way
Brownhills WS9 .....245 A3
Cannock WS12 ......210 C2
Beaconfields WS13 ..231 A4
Beaconsfield ST5 .....56 B4
Beaconsfield Ave WV4 266 C3
Beaconsfield Dr
Longton ST3 ....72 C1
Wolv WV4 ....266 C3
Beaconsfield Rd DE13 166 A4
Beaconside ST16 ...156 A3
Beaconside Cl ST16 .156 A3
Beaconside Sports Ctr
ST18 ....156 B2
Beadnall Cl ST3 ......73 B1
Beale St DY8 ....279 C3
Bealeys La WS3 ....243 A1
Beam Cl DE13 .....166 A4
Beamhill Rd DE13 ..165 C4
Beamish La WV7,WV8 .237 C3
Beard Gr ST2 ....58 A4
Bearnett Dr WV4 ...265 B1
Bearnett La WV4 ...265 A1
Bearstone Rd TF9 ...82 C2
Bearwood Hill Rd DE15 167 A3
Beasley Ave ST5 .....55 C4
Beasley Pl ST5 ....55 C4
Beat La SK11 ....17 C4
Beata Rd ST5 ....40 C1
Beaton Rd B74 ....258 A2
Beatric Cl ST4 ....72 A1
Beatrice Ct DE14 ...166 A2
Beatrice Wlk ST8 ....27 A1
Beattie Ave ST5 ....284 B4
Beatty Dr CW12 ....6 A2
Beatty Rd ST13 .....31 A3
Beau Ct WS11 .....209 C1
Beaubrook Gdns DY6 275 C2
Beauchamp Ind Pk B77 261 B4
Beauchamp B77 ....261 C3
Beaudesert WS7 ....212 A1
Beaudesert View ST11 211 A3
Beaufort Ave ST9 .....59 A2
Beaufort Ct ST3 ......73 C1
Beaufort Rd
Burton u T DE15 ....167 A1
Longton ST3 ....73 B1
Beaufort Way WS9 ..256 A2
Beaulieu Ave DY6 ..275 C2
Beaulieu Cl ST9 ......59 A2
Beaumaris Cl
Sedgley DY1 ....271 C2
Stoke-on-T ST4 ......71 B4
Beaumaris Ct ST4 ..284 A2
Beaumaris Rd TF10 .168 C2
Beaumont Cl Biddulph ST8 16 B1
Great Wyrley WS6 ...226 C1
Newcastle-u-L ST5 ...70 C2
Beaumont Gdns ST17 174 A4
Beaumont Rd
Great Wyrley WS6 ...226 C1
Tunstall ST6 ....41 C2
Beaumont Way WS11 .228 A2
Beauty Bank Cres DY8 279 C3
Beauty Bank Prim Sch
DY8 ....279 C3
Beaver Cl ST4 ....71 C2
Beaver Dr ST10 ......76 A1
Bebington Cl WV8 ..255 C4
Beck Rd CW3 ....68 C4
Beck The B79 ......216 C1
Beck's La DE13 ....162 C1
Beckbury Ave WV4 .265 B3
Beckdale Cl ST14 ..126 A4
Beckenham Cl ST3 ...90 B4
Becket Cl
Burton u T DE13 ....166 A3
Sutton Coldfield B74 ..257 C3
Beckett Ave ST3 .....74 A1
Beckfields Cl ST8 ....17 A1
Beckford St ST1 ....282 C4
Beckminster Rd WV3 .265 C4
Beckton Ave ST6 .....41 C2
Bedale Pl ST3 ....72 C1
Beddow Way ST6 .....41 C2
Bedford Ave ST16 ..156 A2
Bedford Cres ST5 ....71 B2
Bedford Pl WS12 ...210 A2
Bedford Rd
Burton u T DE15 ....185 B4
Hanley ST1 ....282 A1
Kidsgrove ST7 ....26 A2
Bedford St ST1 ......57 A1
Bedford Way WS15 .196 B3
Bedingstone Dr ST19 208 A4
Bednall Ct ST17 ....193 C4
Bednall Rd ST17 ...175 B1
Bee La WV10 ....240 B2
Beech Ave
Burton u T DE13 ....166 C4
Cheddleton ST13 .....45 B2
King's Bromley DE13 .199 B3
Tamworth B77 .....250 C3
Beech Cl Armitage WS15 .198 B2
Biddulph ST8 ....17 A1
Cheadle ST10 ....76 C1
Haughton ST18 .....172 C3
Kinver DY7 ....278 A2
Leek ST13 ....30 B1
Newport TF10 ......168 C1
Pattingham WV6 ...253 B1

Beech Cl continued
Sedgley DY3 ....266 C1
Sutton Coldfield B75 ....258 A4
Tamworth B79 ....250 A4
Uttoxeter ST14 ....126 A4
Wheaton Aston ST19 ...205 B3
Beech Cres WS7 ......258 A3
Beech Croft Madeley CW3 68 C4
Pattingham WV6 ......253 B1
Beech Ct Cannock WS12 .210 A4
Great Wyrley WS6 .....227 A2
Stone ST15 ....120 A4
Beech Dale La ST12 ...103 C4
Beech Dr
Burton u T DE13 ......166 C4
Talke ST7 ....40 C4
Beech Gate B74 ......257 B3
Beech Gdns Codsall WV8 238 C1
Lichfield WS14 ....231 B3
Beech Gr Ashley TF9 ....99 C3
Fenton ST4 ....72 B2
Huntington WS12 .....209 B4
Leek ST13 ....30 B3
Newcastle-u-L ST5 .....56 B2
Swadlincote DE11 .....186 C4
Beech Ho B74 ....257 A3
Beech Hurst Gdns WV5 264 A1
Beech La
Burton u T DE13 ......166 C4
Coppenhall ST18 ......174 B2
Beech Pine Cl WS12 ...210 A4
Beech Rd
Barton-u-N DE13 ......183 B1
Eccleshall ST21 ....133 C3
Kingswinford DY6 .....275 C3
Longton ST3 ....72 C1
Stourbridge DY8 ......279 C2
Tamworth B79 ....250 A4
Wolv WV10 ....240 A1
Beech St Burton u T DE14 166 A1
Longton ST3 ....283 C3
Beech Tree Cl DY6 ....275 C4
Beech Tree La WS11 ...226 B4
Beech Wlk WS15 .....198 A1
Beecham ST4 ....256 A4
Beechcliff La ST4,ST12 .87 C1
Beechcroft ST12 ......88 C1
Beechcroft Ave ST17 ..155 B4
Beechcroft Cres B74 ...256 B1
Beechcroft Ct B74 ....258 A4
Beechdale Rd ST4,ST12 .87 B1
Beechen Gr WS7 ......228 C4
Beeches Cl DY6 ....275 B4
Beeches Croft ST15 ...215 B4
Beeches Mews DY9 ....281 C2
Beeches Rd WS15 .....197 A3
Beeches The
Newcastle-u-L ST5 .....56 B4
Rugeley WS15 ....178 B2
Sutton Coldfield B74 ...257 B2
Beeches, Forsbrook Jun Sch
The ST11 ....91 A4
Beechfield Dr ST17 ....175 C3
Beechfield Rd ST4 .....88 C3
Beechfield Rise WS14 .231 B4
Beechfields ST12 ......88 C1
Beechfields Way TF10 .168 C3
Beechhouse La WV5 ...264 A1
Beechlawn Dr DY7 ....278 C4
Beechmere Rise WS15 .178 A4
Beechmont Gr ST1 ....57 C3
Beechmount Rise [9]
ST17 ....175 B4
Beechtree La DY10 ....280 C3
Beechtree Rd WS9 ....244 C4
Beechway ST16 ....155 B3
Beechwood WS14 .....232 C4
Beechwood Bsns Pk
WS11 ....210 A2
Beechwood Cl
Forsbrook ST11 ....91 A4
Newcastle-u-L ST5 .....71 B1
Walsall WS3 ....243 A2
Beechwood Cres B77 ..250 C4
Beechwood Croft B74 .257 B3
Beechwood Ct WV6 ...255 B2
Beechwood Dr
Stone ST15 ....120 A3
Wolv WV5 ....255 A4
Beecroft Ave WS13 ....214 A4
Beecroft Ct WS11 .....209 C1
Beecroft Hill Sch WS11 209 C1
Beecroft Rd WS11 .....209 C1
Beelow La ST10 ....78 B3
Bees La WS15 ....178 C1
Beeston Rd DY10 .....280 A3
Beeston Ridge ST17 ...174 A4
Beeston St ST3 ....73 B3
Beeston View ST7 .....41 A4
Beffcote La ST20 .....171 A3
Beggars Bush La WV5 .270 A3
Beggars La ST13 ......30 B3
Beighton Cl B74 ......257 C3
Belbroughton Rd
Blakedown DY10 ......281 B1
Stourbridge DY8 ......279 C2
Belfast Cl ST6 ....42 A1
Belfield Ave ST6 ......56 B2
Belford Pl ST4 ....56 C1
Belfort Way ST17 .....175 A4
Belfry WS3 ....243 A2
Belfry Dr DY8 ....279 C3
Belfry The
Burton u T DE13 ......147 B1
Perton WV6 ....254 B2

Belgrade Rd WV10 ....240 A1
Belgrave Ave ST3 .....283 B2
Belgrave Cres ST3 ....283 C1
Belgrave Ct DY6 ......275 C2
Belgrave High Sch B77 250 C1
Belgrave Rd Longton ST3 283 C1
Newcastle-u-L ST5 .....284 C2
Tamworth B77 ....261 C4
Bell Ave ST3 ....73 B1
Bell Cl Lichfield WS13 ..213 C1
Stafford ST16 ....155 C3
Bell Cotts DE6 ....127 B4
Bell Dr WS12 ....210 B4
Bell Heather Rd WS8 ..244 B3
Bell La Barlaston ST12 ..88 C3
Barton-u-N DE13 ......183 B1
Doveridge DE6 ....127 B4
Walsall WS3 ....243 A1
Bell Orch TF9 ....100 B3
Bell Pl WV2 ....266 B4
Bell Rd WV5 ....264 B1
Bell St DY8 ....279 C3
Bell Vue ST13 ....30 B3
Bell Vue Rd ST13 .....30 B3
Bell's Hollow ST5 .....40 C2
Bellamour La ST17,
WS15 ....178 B3
Bellamour Way WS15 .178 C2
Bellaport Rd TF9 .....82 A2
Bellasis St ST16 ......155 C3
Bellbrook ST19 ....192 C1
Belle Vue DY8 ....275 B1
Belle Vue Prim Sch
DY8 ....275 B2
Bellefield View ST5 ....56 B2
Bellen Croft Gdns WV3 265 B4
Bellerton La ST6 ......42 C1
Bellevue St WV14 .....266 C1
Bellflower Cl WV10 ...241 A4
Bellhouse La DE13 ....164 C3
Bellhurst La ST19 ....205 A3
Bellingham B77 ......251 B1
Bellringer Cl ST8 .....27 B4
Bellringer Rd ST4 .....88 B4
Bells End Rd DE12 ....184 B1
Bells La Burntwood WS7 211 C1
Kingswinford DY8 .....275 B1
Bellsize ST11 ....227 C3
Bellwood Cl ST3 ......90 A3
Belmont Ave WS11 ....209 B1
Belmont Cl Aldridge WS9 256 A4
Great Wyrley WS11 ....227 A2
Belmont Inf Sch ST1 ..57 A2
Belmont Rd Hanley ST1 .57 A2
Ipstones ST10 ....61 B4
Tamworth B77 ....261 C4
Wolv WV4 ....266 A4
Belmot Rd Anslow DE13 .164 C4
Tutbury DE13 ....145 C1
Belper Rd WS3 ....243 B2
Belsay Cl ST3 ....283 C4
Belsize B77 ....250 C1
Belt Rd WS11,WS12 ...210 A3
Belton Ave WV11 .....241 A1
Belvedere Ave WV4 ...266 A3
Belvedere Cl
Burntwood WS7 ......228 C3
Kingswinford DY6 .....275 C2
Stafford ST17 ....175 B4
Tamworth B79 ....250 B4
Belvedere Gdns WV6 ..255 C3
Belvedere Jun Sch
DE14 ....166 A3
Belvedere Rd
Burton u T DE13 ......166 A3
Trentham ST4 ....72 A1
Belvide Gdns WV8 ....238 C2
Belvoir B77 ....261 B4
Belvoir Ave ST4 ......88 B3
Belvoir Cl
Burton u T DE13 ......166 A3
Sedgley DY1 ....271 C1
Belvoir Rd DE13 ......166 A3
Belwell Dr B74 ....258 A1
Belwell La B74 ....258 A1
Bemersley Rd
Chell Heath ST8 ......27 B1
Norton-in-t-M ST6 .....42 C3
Ben Jones Ave TF10 ...169 A4
Benches Cl WS7 ......228 B3
Bencroft WV8 ....239 A4
Bend Oak Dr DE15 ....167 B2
Bend Oak Jun Sch DE15 167 B2
Benedict Pl ST2 ......58 A3
Benenden Ct ST17 ....156 A1
Benfleet Pl ST3 ......283 A3
Bengal Gr ST4 ....88 B4
Bengry Rd ST3 ....73 C1
Benion Rd WS11 .....209 C3
Benjamins Way ST7 ...39 C1
Bennett Pl ST5 ....56 A4
Bennett Rd B74 ......257 B2
Bennett St ST6 ....56 C4
Bennetts La Bosley SK11 ..7 C3
Perton WV6 ....263 C4
Uttoxeter ST14 ....125 B3
Bennick Trad Est WS11 226 C3
Bennion Gr ST14 .....95 C3
Bennion St ST3 ......283 C3
Benson Ave WV4 .....266 B3
Benson Cl Lichfield WS13 214 B1
Perton WV6 ....254 C3
Benson St ST6 ....41 C3
Benson View B79 .....250 B4
Bent La Astbury CW12 ..15 A4
Whitmore ST5 ....86 A4
Bentilee Prim Sch ST2 .73 B4
Bentley Ave ST5 ......56 A2

Bentley Brook La WS12 211 A3
Bentley Cl ST15 ......104 C1
Bentley Dr WV8 ......238 C2
Bentley Rd
Chell Heath ST6 ......42 B3
Uttoxeter ST14 ....110 C1
Wolv WV10 ....240 C1
Bentley Way B79 .....249 C4
Bentleys Rd TF9 ......112 A4
Benton Cres WS3 .....243 B1
Benton's La WS6 .....227 A1
Bents La ST10 ....109 A2
Bentygrange La ST13 ...48 B2
Beowulf Covert DE13 ..147 A1
Berdmore St ST4 .....283 A5
Beresford Cres ST5 ....71 A3
Beresford Dale DE11 ..186 C1
Beresford Dell CW3 ...68 B3
Beresford Meml CE Fst Sch
ST13 ....31 A4
Beresford St ST4 .....57 A1
Bergamot Dr ST3 .....90 A3
Berkeley Cl Gnosall ST20 171 C4
Perton WV6 ....254 C2
Berkeley Dr DY6 ......275 B4
Berkeley St Hanley ST1 .282 C2
Stone ST15 ....104 C1
Berkeley Way WS15 ...198 A1
Berkshire Cl ST5 .....71 B3
Berkshire The WS3 ...243 A2
Berkswell Cl
Sedgley DY1 ....271 C2
Sutton Coldfield B74 ...257 C2
Berkswich CE Prim Sch
ST17 ....175 C3
Bernard Cheadle La
ST15 ....103 B2
Bernard Gr ST3 ......89 C2
Bernard St ST1 ......282 C2
Berne Ave ST5 ....70 C3
Bernwall Cl DY8 ......279 C2
Berrisford Cl TF9 .....97 C1
Berrisford Rd TF9 .....97 C1
Berry Gdns DE15 .....167 B2
Berry Hedge La DE15 ..167 B2
Berry Hill WS12 ......210 B2
Berry Hill High Sch ST2 158 A2
Berry Hill Rd ST4 .....57 C1
Berry La ST3 ....283 B3
Berry Rd ST16 ....155 A4
Berry St ST4 ....72 A4
Berrybush Gdns DY3 ..271 C4
Berryfield Gr ST3 .....73 C2
Berryfields WS9 .....245 C3
Bert Smith Way TF9 ...97 B1
Bertlein Rd ST16 .....155 C4
Berwick Dr WS11 ....226 A4
Berwick Rd ST11 .....57 C4
Berwick Wlks ST5 ....70 C3
Berwyn Gr WS6 ......226 C2
Besom Way WS6 .....226 B1
Best Ave DE15 ....167 A1
Best St ST4 ....72 C3
Beswick Cl ST10 .....76 B1
Beswick Rd ST6 ......41 C3
Beswicks La TF9 ......82 B1
Bethany Mews WS11 ..209 C2
Bethell Rd ST1 ....57 B4
Bethesda Rd ST1 .....282 C1
Bethesda St ST1 .....282 B2
Betjeman Pl WV10 ....241 A1
Betjeman Wlk ST17 ...174 B4
Betley CE Prim Sch CW3 53 A3
Betley Hall Gdns CW3 ..53 A3
Betley Pl ST5 ....71 B3
Betlingspring La DE6 ..81 B2
Beton Way ST4 ......155 B4
Bettany Glade WV10 ..240 C2
Bettany Rd ST6 ......57 A4
Betton Rd TF9 ....97 C1
Betty Hatch La ST16 ..155 B3
Betty's La ST11 ......228 A2
Bevan Ave Talke ST7 ..40 C3
Wolv WV4 ....266 C2
Bevan Cl WS4 ....244 B1
Bevan Lee Rd WS11 ...209 B2
Bevan Pl CW3 ....68 C4
Bevandean Cl ST4 ....88 B3
Beveridge Cl ST3 .....74 A1
Beverley Cl ST19 .....207 C4
Beverley Cres
Forsbrook ST11 ....91 A4
Wolv WV4 ....266 C2
Beverley Dr Bucknall ST2 .58 B1
Stafford ST16 ....155 B4
Beverley Hill ST3 .....210 B3
Beverley Rd DE14 ....185 A4
Beverly Dr DY6 ......275 B4
Beverston Rd WV6 ....255 A2
Beville St ST4 ....72 C3
Bevin Ave ST2 ....58 A2
Bew St ST6 ....42 C3
Bewcastle Gr ST3 ....90 A4
Bexhill Gr ST1 ....57 C3
Bexley St ST1 ....282 A4
Bexmore Dr WS13 ....214 C1
Beyer Cl ST7 ....251 A4
Bhylls Acre Prim Sch
WV3 ....265 A4
Bhylls Cres WV3 .....265 B4
Bhylls La WV3 ....265 B4
Bibby's Gn WV10 ....240 C2
Bickford Rd ST19 .....206 A3
Bickford Rd ST19 .....206 A4
Bickley Ave B74 .....257 C4
Bickley Ho B74 ......257 C4
Bida La CW12 ....16 A4

Biddles La ST21 ......102 B2
Biddulph Common Rd
ST8 ....17 A3
Biddulph Grange Ctry Pk★
ST8 ....16 C2
Biddulph Grange Gdn★
ST8 ....16 C2
Biddulph High Sch ST8 .27 B3
Biddulph Park Rd ST8 ..17 A3
Biddulph Rd Biddulph ST7 26 C3
Chell Heath ST6 ......42 A4
Congleton CW12 .....16 A4
Biddulph St CW12 ....16 B4
Bideford Ave ST17 ....175 B4
Bideford Way WS11 ...226 A4
Biggin Cl WV6 ....254 C3
Bignall End Rd ST7 ...40 A2
Bigsbury Wlk [13] ST6 ..56 C4
Bigwood La
Bradley ST18 ....173 C2
Coppenhall ST18 .....173 C2
Bilberry Bank WS11 ...209 C3
Bilberry Cl WS15 .....178 B1
Bilberry Cres WS12 ...209 B3
Bilbrook CE Mid Sch
WV8 ....239 A2
Bilbrook Ct WV8 .....239 A2
Bilbrook Gr WV8 .....239 A2
Bilbrook Rd WV8 .....239 A2
Bilbrook Sta WV8 ....239 A1
Billinge St ST6 ....56 C4
Billington Ave ST18 ...158 B1
Billington Bank ST18 ..173 B3
Billington La ST18 ....154 B1
Billy Buns La WV5 ....270 A4
Billy Wright Cl WV4 ...265 C3
Bilston Rd WV2 ......266 C4
Bilston St DY3 ....271 C4
Bilton St ST4 ....72 A3
Bingley Ent Ctr WV3 ..266 A4
Bingley Prim Sch WV3 .266 A4
Bingley St WV3 ......266 A4
Birch Ave Biddulph ST8 ..27 A3
Brownhills WS8 ......244 C4
Burntwood WS7 ......228 C3
Cannock WS11 ....226 B4
Birch Brook La WS14 ..246 C3
Colwich ST18 ....158 B1
Denstone ST14 ....95 B3
Stafford ST17 ....175 C3
Birch Cl Burton u T DE14 .185 A4
Birch Coppice WV5 ...269 C4
Birch Croft WS9 .....256 B4
Birch Dale CW3 ......68 C3
Birch Dr Little Aston B74 .257 B3
Stourbridge DY8 ......279 C1
Birch Gr Blythe Bridge ST3 90 A2
Forsbrook ST11 ....91 A4
Lichfield WS14 ....231 B4
Polesworth B78 ......262 B4
Birch Green Gr ST1 ...57 C4
Birch Hill Ave WV5 ...269 C3
Birch Ho B74 ....257 A3
Birch House La ST15,
ST21 ....117 C4
Birch House Rd ST5 ...55 B4
Birch La Aldridge WS9 ..245 B1
Rugeley WS15 ....197 A3
Walsall WS4 ....244 B1
Birch Rd Audley ST7 ...39 C1
Essington WV11 ......241 C1
Sedgley DY3 ....266 C1
Stone ST15 ....120 A4
Birch Rise TF9 ....99 C2
Birch St ST1 ....57 C3
Birch Terr
Burntwood WS7 ......212 A1
Hanley ST1 ....282 B2
Birch Tree Gdns WS9 ..256 A3
Birch Tree La
The Bank ST6 ....26 A4
Whitmore ST5 ....85 B4
Birch Wlk ST3 ....73 A1
Birchall Ave ST6 .....41 B3
Birchall Cl ST13 ......30 C1
Birchall La ST13 ......30 C1
Birchall Park Ave ST13 .30 C2
Bircham Wlk ST5 .....71 A1
Birchbrook Ind Pk
WS14 ....246 C3
Birchcroft WV6 ....224 B1
Birchdale Cl ST10 ....92 C1
Birchdown Ave ST6 ...42 A2
Birchendale Cl ST10 ...75 C3
Birchenfields La ST10 ..75 C3
Birchenwood Rd ST6,ST7 26 C1
Birches Ave WV8 .....239 A1
Birches Barn Ave WV3 .265 C4
Birches Barn Rd WV3 ..265 C4
Birches Cl DE13 ......166 B4
Birches Farm Mews CW3 68 C2
Birches Fst Sch WV8 ..239 A1
Birches Head High Sch
ST1 ....57 C4
Birches Head Rd ST1 ..57 C3
Birches Park Rd WV8 ..239 A1
Birches The WV8 .....239 A1
Birches The ST10 ....76 B1
Birches Valley WS15 ..195 B3
Birches Valley Forest Ctr★
WS15 ....195 C3
Birches Way [16] ST7 ..26 A1
Birchfield Ave WV6 ...255 A4
Birchfield Cl CV9 .....262 B1
Birchfield Rd Bucknall ST2 58 B3
Burton u T DE15 .....185 A4
Birchfield Sch WV7 ...237 B3
Birchfields Cl ST15 ...119 C3

Birchfields Dr WS12 ..210 B1
Birchgate ST2 ....58 B2
Birchgate Gr ST2 .....58 B2
Birchglade WV3 .....255 B1
Birchlands Rd ST1 ....57 C3
Birchmoor La ST20 ...189 B1
Birchmoor Rd B78 ....262 C4
Birchover Way ST6 ...42 A4
Birchtree La WS15 ...196 C3
Birchwood Ave B78 ...262 C4
Birchwood Cl WV11 ..242 A2
Birchwood Prim Sch
B78 ....262 C4
Birchwood Rd
Lichfield WS13 ....231 C4
Wolv WV4 ....266 A3
Birchwood Rise WS15 .161 A3
Birchwood Wlk DY6 ..275 C4
Bird Cage Wlk ST1 ...282 B2
Bird Rd ST3 ....74 A1
Bird St Lichfield WS13 ..231 A4
Sedgley DY3 ....271 C3
Bird's Barn La DY11 ..277 B1
Birdhope B77 ....251 B1
Birds Bush Prim Sch
B77 ....261 C4
Birds Bush Rd B77 ....261 C4
Birdsgrove La DE6 ....66 B2
Birkdale Ave DE14 ...185 A3
Birkdale Cl DY8 ......279 C1
Birkdale Dr Kidsgrove ST7 26 B2
Stafford ST16 ....156 B2
Birkdale Rd WS3 .....243 C4
Birkholme Dr ST3 ....90 A3
Birks Dr TF9 ....99 C3
Birks St ST4 ....72 A3
Birmingham New Rd
WV4 ....266 C2
Birmingham Rd
Aldridge WS9 ....256 A2
Blakedown DY10 .....281 B1
Lichfield WS14 ....231 A2
Shenstone WS14 .....247 A2
Birmingham St WV2 ..266 B4
Birrell St ST4 ....72 C3
Biscay Gr ST4 ....88 B4
Bishop Cl WS11 .....209 B1
Bishop Ct ST4 ....58 A3
Bishop Rawle CE Prim Sch
ST10 ....76 B2
Bishop Rd ST6 ....42 A3
Bishop St ST4 ....73 A3
Bishop Stamer CE Prim Sch
ST4 ....72 A3
Bishop's Cl ST7 ......40 B4
Bishops Ct ST21 .....133 C3
Bishops Dr ST19 .....223 B4
Bishops Grange WS15 .178 C1
Bishops La TF9 ....97 A1
Bishops Mdw B75 ...258 C2
Bishops Way B74 ....257 C3
Bishton La WS15 .....178 A3
Bitham Cl ST19 ......207 C4
Bitham Ct DE13 ......147 B1
Bitham La DE13 ......147 B1
Bittell Cl WV10 ......240 C2
Bittern La ST10 ......76 C2
Bitterne Pl ST2 ......73 B4
Bitterscote La B78 ...250 A1
Black Bank Rd ST9,ST13 .140 B3
Black Dr ST18 ....157 B3
Black Horse La ST1 ...282 B3
Black La Forton TF10 ..150 C1
Kingsley ST10 ....62 B2
Blackbank Rd ST5 ....55 B2
Blackberry La
Brownhills WS9 ......245 A2
Stafford ST16 ....155 B2
Sutton Coldfield B74 ...257 C2
Blackberry Way ST20 .151 B4
Blackbird Cl ST14 ....126 B3
Blackbird Sch ST8 ....27 C4
Blackbrook Ave ST5 ..55 B3
Blackbrook Way WV10 240 C2
Blackbrook World of Birds &
Animals★ ST13 ......48 A3
Blackburn Ave WV6 ..255 C4
Blackdown B77 ......251 B1
Blackfriar's Rd ST5 ...284 B2
Blackfriars B79 ......249 C3
Blackfriars F Ed Unit
ST2 ....58 A3
Blackfriars Sch ST5 ...284 B2
Blackhalve La WV11 ..241 B1
Blackheath Cl ST5 ....73 B2
Blackheath La ST18 ..156 C2
Blackhole La ST18 ....154 B1
Blackies La ST15 .....120 B4
Blacklake Dr ST3 .....90 A2
Blackmere Cl TF10 ...168 B1
Blackpit La
Doveridge DE6 ....127 A4
Wombourne WV4 .....264 C2
Blackpool St DE14 ...185 B4
Blackroot Cl WS7 ....229 B2
Blackshaw CW12 .....6 A1
Blackshaw Moor CE Fst Sch
ST13 ....20 C3
Blacksmith La WS14 ..232 C3
Blacksmith's La
Egginton DE65 ....148 A3
Newton Solney DE15 ..167 C4
Blackthorn Ave ST4 ..228 C2
Blackthorn Cres WS12 .211 A3
Blackthorn Pl ST5 ....55 C4
Blackthorn Rd
Brierley Hill DY8 ......275 C4
Burton u T DE15 .....185 C3

Blackthorne Cl DY1 ....271 C2
Blackthorne Rd
Dudley DY1 ....271 C3
Lichfield WS14 ......231 B4
Blackwell's Row ST6 ...57 A3
Blackwood Pl ST3 ....73 C2
Blackwood Rd
Aldridge B74 ....256 C1
Tamworth B77 ....261 B4
Blackwood Sch B74 ...256 C1
Bladon Ave ST5 ......71 A2
Bladon Cl ST6 ....42 A4
Bladon House Sch
DE15 ....167 A3
Bladon St DE15 ......167 B2
Bladon View DE13 ....148 A1
Bladon's Yd DE13 ....147 A1
Blaizefield Cl CW3 ....67 B1
Blake Cl WS11 ....210 A3
Blake High Sch WS12 ..209 C3
Blake St Burslem ST6 ..56 C4
Sutton Coldfield B74 ...257 C3
Blake Street Sta B74 ..257 C3
Blakedown CE Prim Sch
DY10 ....281 B1
Blakedown Sta DY10 ..281 B1
Blakeley Ave WV6 ....255 C4
Blakeley Heath Dr WV5 270 A3
Blakeley Heath Prim Sch
WV5 ....270 A3
Blakeley La ST10 ......63 A1
Blakeley Rise WV6 ....255 C4
Blakelow La DE6 ......65 A1
Blakelow Rd ST2 ......58 A3
Blakemore Rd WS9 ....245 A2
Blakenall Heath WS3 ..243 B1
Blakeney Ave
Newcastle-u-L ST5 .....71 A2
Stourbridge DY8 ....279 B3
Blakeney Cl DY3 ......271 B4
Blakenhall Ind Est WV2 266 A4
Blakeways Cl B79 .....217 B3
Blakiston St ST16 .....155 C2
Blanchard Cl ST3 ......90 B4
Blandford Dr ST5 .....275 C4
Blandford Gdns WS7 ..229 B3
Blanefield WV8 ....239 C1
Blanford Mere Prim Sch
DY6 ....275 C4
Blantyre St ST3 ....283 C4
Blantyre Wlk ST3 .....283 C2
Blatchford Cl ST3 .....74 A1
Blaydon Ave B75 .....258 C1
Blaydon Rd WV9,WV10 240 A1
Blaze Hill Rd DY6 .....275 A4
Blaze Pk DY6 ....275 A4
Bleak House Dr WS7 ..228 B4
Bleak Pl ST6 ....57 A4
Bleak St ST5 ....56 B2
Bleakridge Ave ST5 ...56 A4
Bleeding Wolf La ST7 ..25 C3
Blencarn St ST9 ....43 C1
Blenheim Cl
Burton u T DE15 ......167 B2
Tamworth B77 ....250 B2
Blenheim Dr WS13 ....215 B3
Blenheim Rd
Burntwood WS7 ......229 A4
Kingswinford DY6 .....275 C3
Norton Canes WS11 ...228 A4
Blenheim St ST4 ......72 B3
Blenheim Way DY1 ....271 C1
Bleriot Cl ST3 ....90 B4
Blessed William Howard RC
High Sch ST17 ....155 B1
Bletchley Dr B77 .....261 B4
Blewitt St WS12 ......210 A4
Blithbury Rd
Colton WS15 ....179 A2
Hamstall Ridware WS15 .180 C1
Blithe View ST11 ......90 C3
Blithfield Cl ST9 ......59 A1
Blithfield Ho ST17 ....174 C3
Blithfield Pl WS11 .....210 A1
Blithfield Rd WS8 .....228 A1
Bloomfield Cl WV5 ....269 B3
Bloomfield Cres WS14 .214 A1
Bloomfield Dr WV12 ..242 B1
Bloomfield Way B79 ..249 C4
Bloomsbury St WV2 ...266 B4
Bloomsbury Way WS14 231 C4
Blore Rd TF9 ....98 C1
Blossomfield Cl DY6 ...275 C4
Blount Cl ST17 ....207 C4
Blounts Dr ST14 ......126 A3
Bloxwich CE Prim Sch
WS3 ....243 A1
Bloxwich North Sta
WS3 ....242 C1
Bloxwich Sta WS3 .....243 A1
Blue Cedars DY8 ......279 B3
Blue House Barns TF10 168 C2
Blue House La WV7 ....237 A4
Bluebell Cl Biddulph ST8 .27 C4
Cannock WS11 ....210 A3
Kingswinford DY8 ....275 B1
Bluebell Dr ST5 ....71 A2
Bluebell La WS6 ......227 A1
Bluebell Rd WS9 ......245 A2
Bluebird Cl WS14 .....231 B4
Bluemeadow La WV5 ..270 A4
Bluestone Ave ST5 ....42 A1
Bluestone La DE15 ....186 A4
Bluestones Cl ST13 ....20 C2
Blundies La DY7 ......273 B2
Blunt St ST5 ....56 B4
Blunt's Hollow WS15,
DE13 ....162 A2

Blurton High Sch ST3 ..88 C4
Blurton Prim Sch ST3 ..72 C1
Blurton Rd Barlaston ST12 89 A2
Fenton ST3 ....72 C2
Blurton Waste Cotts ST3 72 C1
Blythe Ave ST3 ....90 A3
Blythe Bridge High Sch
ST11 ....90 C4
Blythe Bridge Rd ST11 ..74 C1
Blythe Bridge Sta ST11 .90 C4
Blythe Cl
Burntwood WS7 ......229 B3
Blythe Gdns WV8 .....238 C2
Blythe Mount Pk ST11 ..91 A4
Blythe Rd Forsbrook ST11 .91 A4
Stafford ST17 ....174 C3
Blythe St B77 ....250 B2
Blythe View
Blythe Bridge ST11 ....91 A1
Hamstall Ridware WS15 .180 C1
Blythebridge Bank
ST14,ST18 ....140 C3
Blythfield DE14 ......116 C2
Board School Gdns DY3 271 C1
Boardman Cres ST16 ...155 B2
Boardman Ind Est DE11 186 C2
Boardman Rd DE11 ....186 C2
Boardmans Bank ST4 ..28 A1
Boat House La WS15 ...198 A3
Boat La Wall WS14 .....229 C1
Weston ST18 ....138 B2
Boathorse Rd
Kidsgrove ST7 ....41 A4
Tunstall ST6 ....41 A3
Boatman's La WS9 .....244 C1
Boatyard Cotts ST12 ...88 B1
Bodiam Cl WV6 ......255 A2
Bodicote Gr B75 ......258 C1
Bodington Cl WS7 .....229 C4
Bodington Rd B75 .....258 B2
Bodmin Ave ST17 .....175 B4
Bodmin Wlk ST6 ......42 B1
Bognop Rd WV11 .....241 B2
Bogs Cotts ST5 ....70 A4
Bogs La ST11 ....90 C3
Bolberry Cl ST3 ....73 C1
Bold St ST1 ....57 C3
Bolebridge Mews B79 ..250 A3
Bolebridge St B79 ....250 B2
Boley Cl WS14 ....231 B4
Boley Cottage La WS14 231 B1
Boley La WS14 ....231 B4
Boley Park Ctr WS14 ..231 C4
Boleyn Cl WS6 ....226 B1
Bolina Gr ST4 ....73 A3
Bollin Gr ST8 ....16 C1
Bolney Gr ST3 ....57 C3
Bolsover Cl ST6 ......42 A4
Bolton Pl ST3 ....89 C4
Bolton Way WS3 .....242 C2
Boma Rd ST4 ....87 C4
Bond End DE13 ......182 A1
Bond St Burton u T DE14 184 B1
Tunstall ST6 ....41 B2
Bondfield La DE13 ....181 C1
Bondfield Way ST3 ....74 A1
Bondway WS12 ....209 C4
Bonehill Ind Est B78 ...249 C1
Bonehill Rd B78 ......249 C2
Boney Hay Prim Sch
WS7 ....211 C1
Boney Hay Rd WS7 ....229 A4
Boningale Way ST3 ...174 A4
Bonnard Cl ST3 ......90 B3
Bonner Cl ST4 ....71 C2
Bonnington Cres ST16 .155 B1
Bonville Gdns WV10 ..240 C2
Boon Ave ST4 ....72 A4
Boon Gr ST17 ....174 C3
Boon Hill Rd ST7 ......39 C1
Boons Ind Est ST18 ...154 C1
Booth Cl WS13 ....214 A1
Booth La ST18 ....140 C2
Booth St Audley ST7 ...39 B1
Cannock WS12 ....210 A3
Newcastle-u-L ST5 .....55 C3
Stoke-on-T ST4 ....72 A3
Boothen CE Prim Sch
ST4 ....72 A3
Boothen Ct ST4 ....72 A3
Boothen Gn ST4 ......72 A3
Boothen Old Rd ST4 ...72 A3
Boothen Rd ST4 ......72 A3
Boothenwood Terr ST4 .72 A3
Boothroyd St ST1 .....282 B2
Booton Ct DY10 ......280 A1
Bordeaux Cl DY1 .....271 C2
Bordeaux Rd ST1 .....90 A4
Bordeaux Wlk ST5 ....70 C2
Borden Cl
Wheaton Aston ST19 ...205 B4
Wolv WV8 ....255 C4
Border Way ST17 .....174 C3
Bore St WS13 ....231 A4
Borman B79 ....249 C4
Borough Cres ST3 .....279 C3
Borough La WS15 .....212 C4
Borough Mus & Art Gal The*
ST5 ....284 C4
Borough Rd
Burton u T DE14 ......166 B2
Newcastle-u-L ST5 .....284 C3
Tamworth B79 ....250 B4
Borrowcop La WS14 ...231 B3
Borrowdale Rd ST6 ....42 C2
Boscobel Cl DY1 ......271 C2
Boscobel Gr ST19 ....223 B4

Boscombe Gr ST4 .....88 B3
Boscomoor Cl ST19 ...207 C4
Boscomoor Ct ST19 ...207 C4
Boscomoor Ind Est
ST19 ....207 C4
Boscomoor La ST19 ...207 C4
Boscomoor Sh Ctr ST19 207 C4
Bosinney Cl ST4 ......73 A3
Bosley Brook CW12 ...16 B3
Bosley Gr ST4 ....41 B3
Bosley View CW12 ....6 A1
Boss Gate ST4 ....270 A3
Bostock Cl 3 ST15 ...120 B3
Boston Cl Cannock WS12 210 C1
Tunstall ST6 ....41 B2
Boston Ind Est WS15 ..178 C1
Bosty La WS9 ....256 A2
Boswell Rd WS11 .....209 B2
Boswell St ST4 ....56 C1
Bosworth Cl DY3 .....271 C3
Bosworth Dr ST3 .....166 A4
Botany Bay Rd ST1 ....57 C3
Botany Dr DY3 ....271 B3
Botesworth Gdns ST6 ..41 B1
Botfield Cl WV7 ......237 A3
Botham Dr ST3 ......45 B3
Botterham La DY3 ....269 C2
Botteslow St ST1 .....282 C2
Bottom La
Ipstones ST10,ST13 ....47 B3
Market Drayton TF9 ...112 A4
Swynnerton ST15 ....103 A4
Boucher Rd ST13 .....45 B2
Boughey Rd Audley ST7 .39 C1
Newport TF10 ....168 C1
Stoke-on-T ST4 ....72 B4
Boughey St ST4 ......72 A3
Boulevard The ST6 ....41 C2
Boulters La CV9 .....262 B1
Boulton Cl WS7 ......229 C4
Boulton St Hanley ST1 .282 C4
Newcastle-u-L ST5 .....56 B3
Boundary Cl Leek ST13 .30 C2
Stone ST15 ....119 C3
Boundary Cres DY3 ...271 C1
Boundary Ct ST1 .....282 B4
Boundary Hill DY3 ....271 C3
Boundary Ind Est WV10 240 B3
Boundary La
Congleton CW12 ......16 A4
Kinver DY7 ....274 C1
Boundary Rd
Brownhills WS9 ......244 C2
Egginton DE65 ....148 B4
Newcastle-u-L ST5 .....56 B1
Boundary St Hanley ST1 282 B4
Boundary View ST10 ..76 A1
Boundary Way
Wolv WV6 ....254 C1
Wolv, Springhill WV4 ..265 B4
Bourne Ave Ranton ST18 153 B3
Tamworth B78 ....249 C1
Bourne Cl Cannock WS12 210 C1
Tutbury DE13 ....146 A3
Bourne Pl ST13 ....30 B3
Bourne Rd ST13 ......25 C1
Bourne St Fenton ST4 ..72 C2
Mow Cop ST7 ....26 B4
Bourne Vale WS9 .....256 B2
Bournes Bank ST6 ....57 A4
Bournes Bank S 10 ST6 .57 A4
Bouverie Par ST5 .....57 C4
Bow St WS15 ....178 C1
Bowden St ST6 ......42 A1
Bowdler Rd WV2 .....266 B4
Bowen St WV4 ....266 C3
Bowen-cooke Ave WV6 254 C3
Bower Cl WS15 ......214 B1
Bower End La CW3 ...68 B3
Bower La WS15 ......178 C2
Bower Norris RC Prim Sch
ST17 ....174 B4
Bower St ST1 ....282 C4
Bowers Ct ST15 .....120 B4
Bowers La Standon ST21 102 A2
Stone ST15 ....120 B2
Bowes Dr WS11 ......209 C2
Bowfell Gr ST4 ....73 A3
Bowhill La CW3 ......53 A3
Bowland Ave ST5 .....55 C1
Bowlers Cl ST6 ......57 A3
Bowling Green Ave B77 261 C4
Bowling Green Rd DY8 279 C3
Bowman Gr ST6 ......42 A4
Bowmead Cl ST4 .....88 B3
Bowmere Cl ST8 ......16 B1
Bowness Gr WV11 ....242 A1
Bowness St ST1 ......282 A4
Bowood Dr WV6 .....255 B3
Bowran Ho ST3 ......89 C4
Bowsey Wood Rd CW3 .68 C4
Bowstead St ST4 .....72 A4
Bowyer Ave ST6 .....42 A4
Box La ST13 ....73 C1
Boxer Cl WS15 ......198 B2
Boxwood Pl ST5 .....55 B4
Boxwood Rd ST10 ....92 C4
Boyden Cl Cannock WS11 209 A1
Penkridge ST19 ......208 A4
Boyles Hall Rd ST7 ...39 C1
Brabazon St ST3 .....90 B4
Bracken Ave TF9 ......99 C3
Bracken Cl
Blythe Bridge ST3 .....89 C3
Burntwood WS7 ......229 A4
Cannock WS12 ....210 B1
Lichfield WS14 ....231 C3

Bracken Cl continued
Stafford ST16 ....155 A4
Tittensor ST12 ....88 A1
Wolv WV8 ....239 C1
Bracken Dale ST13 ....155 A4
Bracken Park Gdns DY8 275 C4
Bracken Rd WS12 .....209 B3
Bracken St ST4 ....72 C2
Bracken View ST17 ...176 B2
Bracken Way
Newport TF10 ....168 C2
Rugeley WS15 ....178 B1
Brackenberry ST5 .....56 A2
Brackenbury Ave ST2 ..58 B1
Brackenfield Way ST16 155 A4
Brackenhill Rd WS7 ...229 A4
Brackens The ST5 ....71 B1
Brackenwood Rd DE15 .185 C3
Bracklesham Way B77 .251 A3
Brackley Ave ST6 .....42 A1
Bradbury Cl
Brownhills WS8 ......244 C3
Norton-in-t-M ST6 ....42 C2
Bradbury Ct WS12 ....210 A3
Bradbury La
Cannock WS12 ....210 A4
Enville DY7 ....272 C2
King's Bromley DE13 ..199 B3
Bradbury Rise ST16 ...155 A2
Braden Rd WV4 ......265 C3
Bradford Rd WS8 .....244 C3
Bradford St
Cannock WS11 ....210 A4
Tamworth B79 ....249 C3
Bradford Terr ST1 .....57 C3
Bradgate Dr B74 .....257 C3
Bradley Dr ST21 .....117 C2
Bradley La Bradley ST18 173 A2
Haughton ST18 ....173 A3
Stafford ST18 ....174 B3
Bradley Lakes WS15 ..197 C1
Bradley Rd
Stourbridge DY8 .....279 C3
Wolv WV2 ....266 C3
Bradley St
Burton u T DE15 ......185 C1
Uttoxeter ST14 ....126 B4
Bradmore Rd
Burton u T DE13 ......166 A3
Wolv WV3 ....265 C4
Bradshaw Way ST16 ..155 B4
Bradwell Croft B75 ...258 C1
Bradwell Grange ST5 ..56 A4
Bradwell Hospl ST5 ...56 A4
Bradwell La
Cannock WS15 ....211 C3
Newcastle-u-L ST5 .....56 A4
Bradwell Prim Sch ST5 .56 A4
Bradwell St ST6 ......56 B4
Braeburn WS13 ......214 B1
Braemar Ave DY8 ....275 B4
Braemar Bucknall ST2 ..58 B2
Sedgley DY3 ....266 B1
Braemar Gdns WS12 ..209 C4
Braemar Rd
Norton Canes WS11 ...228 A2
Pattingham WV6 .....253 B1
Braemore Rd WV2 ....58 A3
Braeside Way WS3 ...243 C2
Braham B79 ....249 B3
Brailsford Ave DE11 ..186 C3
Brain St B77 ....251 A4
Braithwaite Cl DY6 ...275 B3
Braithwell Dr ST2 ....43 C1
Brake La DY8 ....281 C3
Brake The Hagley DY8 .281 C3
The Bank ST7 ....26 A4
Brake Village ST7 .....26 A4
Brakespeare St ST6 ...41 B4
Bramall Cl ST16 ......155 B3
Bramber B77 ....250 B1
Bramber Way ST8 ....279 C1
Bramble Cl WS8 .....244 C3
Bramble Ct DE15 ....185 C2
Bramble Dr WS12 ....210 B4
Bramble Gn DY1 .....271 C3
Bramble Lea CW3 ....68 C3
Bramble Way WS15 ...178 B1
Brambles Ct ST8 .....27 B4
Brambles The
Lichfield WS14 ....231 B3
Newcastle-u-L ST5 .....71 B1
Norton Canes WS11 ...228 A3
Brambleside DY8 .....275 C1
Bramblewood WS5 ...270 A4
Bramblewood Dr WV3 265 C4
Brambling ST5 ......262 A4
Brambling Cl ST14 ...126 B3
Bramblings The ST17 ..175 B3
Bramdean Dr ST19 ...192 C1
Bramdean Wlk WV4 ..265 B4
Bramell Cl DE14 .....184 C4
Bramfield Dr ST5 .....284 C4
Bramhall Dr ST11 ....90 C4
Bramhall La ST16 ....155 B3
Bramley Cl ST15 .....76 C1
Bramley Dale DE11 ...186 C1
Bramley Pl ST4 ....71 C1
Bramley Way WS14 ..232 B3
Bramma Dr ST11 .....90 A4
Brammer St ST6 .....42 B2
Brampton Cl DY10 ...280 A2
Brampton Ct ST5 .....284 C4
Brampton Dr WS12 ...210 C1
Brampton Gdns ST5 ...56 B2
Brampton Ind Est ST5 .284 B4
Brampton Rd ST5 .....284 C4

Brampton Sidings ST5 .284 B4
Brampton Sidings Ind Est
ST5 ....284 B4
Brampton Wlk ST3 ...283 C1
Bramshall Ind Est ST14 125 A4
Bramshall Rd ST14 ...125 C4
Bramshaws The ST10 ..76 C1
Bramstead Ave WV6 ..255 A1
Bramwell Dr WS6 ....226 B1
Brancaster Cl B77 ....251 A3
Brandon Cl Aldridge WS9 256 C2
Sedgley DY3 ....271 C4
Brandon Gr ST4 ......87 C4
Brandon Pk WV3 .....265 C4
Brandons The ST7 ....174 C3
Bransdale Rd WS8 ....244 C3
Branson Ave ST3 .....73 C2
Branston Rd
Branston DE13,DE14 ..184 B4
Burton u T DE14 .....185 B4
Branston Water Pk
DE14 ....184 B3
Bransty Gr ST4 ....88 B3
Brant Ave ST5 ....56 A2
Brantley Ave WV3 ....255 B1
Brantley Cres DY7 ....267 C1
Brantley La
Bobbington DY7 ......267 C1
Seisdon WV5 ....263 A2
Branton Hill La WS9 ..256 B3
Brantwood Rd WS7 ...229 A3
Brassington St CW3 ...53 A3
Brassington Way ST2 ..58 B2
Bratch Common Rd
WV5 ....269 C4
Bratch Hollow WV5 ...270 A4
Bratch La WV5 ......269 C4
Bratch Pk WV5 ......269 C4
Brattswood Dr ST7 ...25 A3
Braunton Ave ST7 ....175 C4
Braystones Cl ST7 ....41 C4
Brazenhill La ST18 ...172 C4
Breach La Cheadle ST10 .92 B3
Draycott in t M ST10 ..92 B3
Foston DE6 ....129 B3
Breach Rd ST6 ....43 B4
Breadmarket St WS13 .231 A4
Bream B77 ....261 B4
Bream Way ST6 ......42 C4
Breamore Cres DY1 ...271 C2
Brean Rd ST17 ....175 C3
Brecon Way ST2 ......58 A3
Bredon Cl WV7 ......237 A3
Bredon Ct B75 ......258 A2
Breech Cl ST10 ......48 C1
Breedon Cl ST5 ......55 C2
Breedon Way WS4 ...244 B1
Breeze Ave
Norton Canes WS11 ...228 A3
Tunstall ST6 ....41 C3
Brelades Cl DY1 .....271 C1
Brempton Croft ST15 .106 B1
Brendale Cl ST4 ......72 A1
Brendon B77 ....251 A1
Brendon Cl ST17 .....175 B4
Brent B77 ....261 C4
Brentmill Cl WV10 ...240 C2
Brentnall Dr B75 ....258 A2
Brentnor Cl ST3 ......73 C2
Brenton Rd WV4 .....265 C2
Brentwood Dr ST9 ...59 A2
Brentwood Gr
Caverswall ST11 ......59 A2
Norton-in-t-M ST9 ....43 B2
Brenwood Cl DY6 ....275 A4
Brereton Hill WS15 ...197 A3
Brereton Lodge WS15 .197 A3
Brereton Manor Ct 3
WS15 ....197 A3
Brereton Pl ST6 ......41 C1
Brereton Rd WS15 ...196 C4
Breretonhill La WS15 ..197 B1
Bretby Bsns Pk DE15 ..186 C4
Bretby Hollow DE11 ..186 C4
Bretby La Bretby DE15 .167 C4
Burton u T DE15 ......167 B1
Bretby Rd DE11 ......186 C4
Bretherton Pl ST6 ....42 A3
Bretlands Way DE15 ..186 A3
Brettell La DY8 ......279 C4
Brevitt Rd WV2 ......266 B3
Brewers Dr WS3 .....244 A1
Brewers Terr WS3 ....244 A1
Brewery La ST18 .....158 A1
Brewery St Hanley ST1 .282 B3
Rugeley WS15 ....196 C4
Brewster Rd ST2 .....57 C2
Brewhouse Ct WS13 ..213 C1
Brewood CE Mid Sch
ST19 ....223 B3
Brewood Rd WV9 ....224 A2
Brewster Cl B78 .....249 C1
Brianson Ave ST6 ....57 B4
Briar B77 ....251 A2
Briar Ave B74 ....257 C4
Briar Cl Cannock WS12 210 A4
Rugeley WS15 ....178 C4
Stafford ST17 ....175 C3
Swadlincote DE11 ....186 C3
Briar Gr ST15 ....118 C3
Briar Way ST21 ......102 C1
Briarbank Cl ST4 .....71 C1
Briars The Hagley DY9 .281 C2
Newcastle-u-L ST5 ....284 C1
Briars Way WS12 ....211 B2

Briarsleigh ST17 ....**175** B4
Briarswood ST7 ....**26** A1
Briarwood Pl ST3 ....**74** A1
Brick House St **8** ST6 ....**56** C4
Brick Kiln La
 Brocton ST17 ....**175** C2
 Rolleston DE13 ....**147** A2
 Salt ST18 ....**137** C1
 Sedgley DY3 ....**271** A2
 Stoke-on-T ST4 ....**56** C1
 Wheaton Aston ST19 ....**205** A3
Brick Kiln Way WS15 ...**196** C3
Brick St DY3 ....**271** B4
Brick-kiln La ST5 ....**55** C4
Brickbridge La WS9 .....**269** C3
Brickfield Cl ST18 ....**139** B1
Brickfield Pl ST3 ....**73** B3
Brickhill La DE13 ....**163** A3
Brickiln St WS8 ....**244** C4
Brickworks Rd WS12 ....**210** C1
Brickyard Rd
 Aldridge WS9 ....**256** A4
 Brownhills WS9 ....**244** C1
Bridal Path ST2 ....**59** A2
Bridestone Cl **6** ST3 ....**90** A4
Bridge Ave WS6 ....**226** C2
Bridge Cl Audley ST7 ....**39** C1
 Brownhills WS8 ....**244** C3
 Weston ST18 ....**138** B2
Bridge Cres ST15 ....**120** A4
Bridge Croft ST6 ....**42** A3
Bridge Cross Rd WS7 ...**229** A4
Bridge Ct Stoke-on-T ST4 ..**71** C2
 Uttoxeter ST14 ....**126** B4
Bridge Farm DE13 ....**147** A2
Bridge Ho ST5 ....**55** B1
Bridge Ind Est ST6 ....**57** A4
Bridge La ST18 ....**139** A2
Bridge Rd
 Armitage WS15 ....**198** B2
 Cookley DY10 ....**280** A3
 Market Drayton TF9 ....**97** A1
 Stoke-on-T ST4 ....**71** C2
 Uttoxeter ST14 ....**126** B4
 Walsall WS4 ....**244** A1
Bridge St
 Brierley Hill DY8 ....**275** C1
 Brownhills WS8 ....**244** C3
 Burton u T, Stretton DE13 ..**147** A2
 Burton u T, Winshill DE14 ..**166** C2
 Cannock WS11 ....**226** A4
 Chell Heath ST8 ....**27** A1
 Newcastle-u-L ST5 ....**284** B3
 Newcastle-u-L, Silverdale
  ST5 ....**55** B1
 Stafford ST16 ....**155** C1
 Tamworth B77 ....**250** C3
 Tutbury DE13 ....**146** B4
 Uttoxeter ST14 ....**126** B4
Bridge Street Ind Units
 ST14 ....**126** B4
Bridge Terr
 Newport TF10 ....**168** C2
 Thorncliffe ST13 ....**20** C3
Bridge Way WS8 ....**244** C3
Bridgefoot Wlk WV8 ....**239** C1
Bridgeman Ct TF11 .....**203** C1
Bridgemary Rd WV10 ..**240** C2
Bridgemere Garden World★
 CW5 ....**67** A2
Bridges Cres WS11 ....**227** C1
Bridges Rd WS11 ......**227** C3
Bridgeside DE13 ....**147** C1
Bridgeside Trad Est
 B77 ....**250** B2
Bridgett Cl ST4 ....**71** C3
Bridgewater Cl
 Congleton CW12 ....**6** A1
 Penkridge ST19 ......**207** C4
Bridgewater Dr WV5 ...**269** C4
Bridgewater Rd WS15 .**196** C4
Bridgewater St
 Burslem ST6 ....**56** B4
 Tamworth B77 ....**250** B3
Bridgewood St ST3 ....**283** C4
Bridgford Ave DE14 ...**184** C4
Bridgnorth Ave WV5 ...**269** C3
Bridgnorth Gr ST5 .....**40** C1
Bridgnorth Rd
 Enville DY7 ....**273** B1
 Himley DY3 ....**270** A2
 Kinver DY7,DY8 ......**278** B4
 Perton WV6 ....**264** B4
 Seisdon WV6 ....**263** C3
 Stourbridge DY7,DY8 ..**279** B3
 Wolv WV6 ....**255** A1
 Wombourne WV5 ......**269** B3
Bridgtown Bsns Ctr
 WS11 ....**226** C3
Bridgtown Prim Sch
 WS11 ....**226** C3
Bridgwater Cl WS9 ....**244** C2
Bridgwood Rd ST11 ...**91** A4
Bridle La Ellenhall ST20 .**153** B4
 Swadlincote DE15 .....**186** A3
Bridle Path ST3 ....**283** C1
Bridle Path The
 Madeley CW3 ....**68** B4
 Newcastle-u-L ST5 ....**70** C2
Bridle Rd Stafford ST17 .**175** B3
 Stourbridge DY8 ......**279** B3
Bridle Wlk WS15 ....**178** A1
Bridleway The TF9 .....**97** A1
Brierley Hill Rd DY8 ....**275** C1

Brierley Rd CW12 ......**6** A1
Brierley St ST6 ....**42** B1
Brierlow Bar SK17 ......**5** A4
Briertey Hill La WS15 ..**212** A2
Brieryhurst Cl ST2 ......**58** B3
Brieryhurst Rd ST7 .....**26** A2
Bright Cres B77 ....**250** B1
Bright St Meir ST3 ......**74** A1
 Stourbridge DY8 ......**279** B3
Brighton St ST4 ....**72** A4
Brighton The ST5 ....**55** A1
Brights Ave **15** ST7 ....**26** A1
Brightstone Cl WV10 ..**240** C2
Brimfield Pl **6** WV6 ...**255** C2
Brindiwell Gr ST4 ......**88** B3
Brindley Ave WV11 ....**242** A1
Brindley Bank Rd WS15 .**178** C2
Brindley Brae DY7 .....**278** B3
Brindley Cl
 Albrighton WV7 ....**237** A3
 2 Brierley Hill DY8 ..**275** C1
 Kidsgrove ST7 ....**25** C1
 Penkridge ST19 ......**208** A4
 Stafford ST16 ....**155** C4
 Stone ST15 ....**104** C1
 Talke ST7 ....**40** B4
 Wombourne WV5 ......**269** B3
Brindley Cres
 Cannock WS12 ....**210** B4
 Cheddleton ST13 ......**45** A2
Brindley Heath Jun Sch
 DY7 ....**278** A3
Brindley Heath Rd
 Cannock WS12 ....**210** B4
 Rugeley WS12 ....**195** B1
Brindley La ST2,ST9 ...**43** B2
Brindley Mill Mus The★
 ST13 ....**30** B4
Brindley Pl ST6 ....**42** B1
Brindley Rd
 Cannock WS12 ....**194** C1
 Rugeley WS12 ....**194** C1
Brindley St ST5 ....**284** B3
Brindley Way CW12 ...**6** A1
Brindleys Bsns Pk
 WS11 ....**210** A2
Brindleys Way ST7 .....**39** C1
Brindon Cl ST3 ....**74** A2
Brinkburn Cl WS15 ....**178** A1
Brinley Way DY6 ....**275** B3
Brinscall Gn ST6 ......**42** A4
Brinsford La WV10 ....**240** B4
Brinsford Rd WV10 ....**240** B2
Brinsley Ave ST4 ......**88** A3
Brisbane Rd ST6 ......**155** A4
Brisbane Way WS12 ...**210** C2
Brisley Hill ST4 ....**71** C3
Bristol Cl WS11 ....**210** A1
Bristol St
 Newcastle-u-L ST5 ....**56** B3
 Wolv WV3 ....**266** A4
Britania Cl DE13 ......**166** B4
Britania Gn DY3 ......**271** C3
Britannia Park Ind Est
 ST6 ....**57** A4
Britannia St **6** ST13 ...**30** C3
Britannia Way WS13 ..**231** C4
Brittain Ave ST5 ......**55** C4
Brittain Rd ST13 ......**45** B3
Brittania Stadium (Stoke City
 FC) ST4 ....**72** B2
Brittle Pl ST6 ....**42** B1
Britton St ST6 ....**56** C1
Brixham Cl ST2 ....**57** C1
Brizlincote La DE15 ...**167** B1
Brizlincote St DE15 ...**166** C1
Broad Eye ST16 ......**155** B2
Broad La
 Church Eaton ST20 ...**171** C1
 Endon ST6 ....**43** B4
 Great Wyrley WS3 ....**242** C2
 Lichfield WS14 ....**231** B3
 Walsall WS4 ....**244** B1
 Whittington WS13 ....**215** C1
 Wolv WV3 ....**265** C4
Broad Lane Gdns WS3 .**243** A1
Broad Mdw WS9 ......**256** A4
Broad Mdw Croft ST5 .**155** A2
Broad Meadow Ct ST5 .**55** C3
Broad Meadow La WS6 .**227** A1
Broad Oaks ST7 ......**174** C3
Broad St Cannock WS11 .**226** C3
 Hanley ST1 ....**282** A4
 Kingswinford DY6 ....**275** B3
 Leek ST13 ....**30** C3
 Newcastle-u-L ST5 ...**284** B3
 Stafford ST16 ....**155** B2
Broad Way WS4 ....**244** B1
Broadacres WV9 ......**224** A2
Broadfield Cl DY6 .....**275** B3
Broadfield House Glass
 Mus★ DY6 ....**275** B3
Broadfield Rd ST6 ....**41** B4
Broadholes La ST19 ..**205** A3
Broadhurst Cl WS12 ..**194** C1
Broadhurst Gn WS12 ..**194** C1
Broadhurst Green Rd
 ST19,WS12 ....**194** B1
Broadhurst St ST6 ....**42** A1
Broadlands
 Burton u T DE13 .....**166** B4
 Wolv WV10 ....**240** B3
Broadlands Rise WS14 .**231** B4
Broadlawns Dr ST4 ...**73** A3
Broadlee B77 ....**251** B1
Broadmeadow DY6 ...**275** C4
Broadmine St ST4 ....**72** C3

Broadoak Way ST3 ....**72** C1
Broadoaks Cl WS11 ...**227** C3
Broadsmeath B77 .....**250** B1
Broadstone Cl WV4 ...**266** B3
Broadway Cannock WS12 **209** C3
 Codsall WV8 ....**238** C2
 Meir ST3 ....**73** C1
 Newport TF10 ....**169** A2
 Wolv, Bushbury WV10 .**240** C1
 Wolv, Compton WV3 ..**255** B1
Broadway Ct **3** ST3 ...**73** C1
Broadway Gdns WV10 ..**240** C1
Broadway La ST10 ....**49** C4
Broadway Pl **1** ST3 ..**73** C1
Broadway St DE14 ....**166** B1
Broadway The
 Dudley DY1 ....**271** C2
 Stourbridge DY8 .....**279** B2
 Wombourne WV5 .....**270** A3
Broadwell La WV6 ....**253** A1
Broc Cl ST19 ....**208** A4
Brockbank Pl ST6 ....**42** A3
Brockeridge Cl WV12 ..**242** B1
Brockhurst La ST6 ....**259** A4
Brockhurst Rd B75 ...**258** B1
Brocklehurst Way ST1 .**57** C4
Brockley Sq ST1 ......**282** B4
Brockley's Wlk DY7 ...**278** A2
Brocksford Ct DE6 ....**127** C4
Brocksford Hall Sch
 DE6 ....**127** C4
Brocksford St ST4 ....**283** B5
Brockton La ST21 .....**117** B2
Brockton Wlk ST3 ....**72** C1
Brocton Cres ST17 ...**175** C2
Brocton La ST17 ......**175** C3
Brocton Rd ST17 .....**176** B3
Brogan St ST4 ....**72** C3
Bromfield Ct WV6 ....**255** A2
Bromford Dale **2** WV6 .**255** C2
Bromford Pl ST1 ......**282** A1
Bromford Rise WV3 ...**266** A4
Bromley Cl WS12 .....**210** B4
Bromley Ct ST1 ......**282** A4
Bromley Gdns WV8 ...**239** A2
Bromley Hills Prim Sch
 DY6 ....**275** C3
Bromley Ho WV4 .....**266** A3
Bromley Hough ST4 ..**71** C3
Bromley La DY6 ......**275** C2
Bromley Lodge WV4 ..**266** A3
Bromley Pl WV4 ......**266** A3
Bromley St Hanley ST1 .**282** A4
 Wolv WV2 ....**266** B4
Bromleyhedge La ST13 .**48** B2
Brompton Dr ST2 .....**43** A2
Brompton Lawns WV6 .**255** C2
Bromsberrow Way ST3 .**90** A4
Bromsgrove Pl ST3 ...**283** A4
Bromwich Dr WS13 ...**215** B4
Bromwynd Cl WV2 ...**266** A3
Bronant Wlk **14** ST6 ..**57** A4
Bronte Cl DE14 ....**166** B4
Bronte Ct B79 ....**250** A4
Bronte Dr WS11 ......**210** B1
Bronte Gr ST2 ....**43** A4
Bronte Rd WV2 ....**266** C3
Brook Ave B77 ....**262** A4
Brook Cl Brewood WV9 .**224** A2
 Brownhills WS9 ......**245** A2
 Doveridge DE6 ....**127** B4
 Endon ST9 ....**44** A4
 Forsbrook ST11 ......**91** A4
 Lichfield WS13 ....**214** A1
 Penkridge ST19 ......**207** C4
Brook Cres DY6 ......**275** B4
Brook End
 Burntwood WS7 ......**229** A4
 Fazeley B78 ....**261** A4
 Haughton ST18 ......**172** C3
 Longdon WS15 ......**197** C1
Brook Gdns ST8 ......**16** B1
Brook Glen Rd ST17 ..**174** C4
Brook Gr WV8 ....**239** A1
Brook Ho TF10 ....**168** C2
Brook House La WV10 .**241** A4
Brook House Rd ST5 ..**55** C4
Brook Houses Ind Est
 ST10 ....**76** A1
Brook La Brocton ST17 .**176** B2
 Brownhills WS9 ......**244** C2
 Church Leigh ST10 ...**108** C3
 Endon ST9 ....**43** C4
 Great Wyrley WS6 ...**227** A2
 Newcastle-u-L ST5 ...**284** B2
 Ranton ST18 ....**153** B2
Brook Mdws WV8 ....**239** A2
Brook Meadow Rd WS4 **244** B1
Brook Pl
 Newcastle-u-L ST5 ...**71** B3
 Stoke-on-T ST6 ......**56** C1
Brook Prim Sch The
 DY8 ....**275** C1
Brook Rd
 Cheslyn Hay WS6 ....**226** C2
 Trentham ST4 ....**88** A4
 Wombourne WV5 .....**269** C3
Brook Sq **1** WS15 ...**196** C4
Brook St Biddulph ST8 .**27** A3
 Brierley Hill DY8 .....**275** C1
 Burton u T DE14 .....**166** B2
 Kingswinford DY6 ....**270** A1
 Leek ST13 ....**30** C3
 Newcastle-u-L ST5 ...**55** B1
 Sedgley DY3 ....**271** B2
 Stoke-on-T ST4 ......**72** A4

Brook St continued
 Stourbridge DY8 .....**279** C3
 Swadlincote DE11 ...**186** C3
Brook Vale WS11 .....**226** C4
Brookbank Gdns DY3 .**271** A1
Brookbank Rd DY3 ...**271** A1
Brookdale DY3 ....**271** B2
Brookdale Dr WV4 ...**265** C3
Brooke Rd WS12 .....**209** C3
Brookers Ct ST4 .....**72** C3
Brookfield TF9 ....**99** B3
Brookfield Ave ST9 ...**43** C4
Brookfield Cl ST10 ...**62** B2
Brookfield Cl Hanley ST1 **282** B4
 Haughton ST18 .....**172** C3
 Stone ST15 ....**120** B3
Brookfield Dr WS11 ..**226** C4
Brookfield Rd
 Aldridge WS9 ....**245** A1
 Codsall WV8 ....**239** A2
 Norton-in-t-M ST2 ...**43** B2
 Stoke-on-T ST4 .....**71** C3
Brookfields Rd ST10 ..**62** A4
Brookgate ST11 .....**91** A4
Brookhay La WS13 ...**215** C2
Brookhill Cl WV12 ...**242** B1
Brookhill Way WV12 .**242** B1
Brookhouse Cl WV10 .**241** A1
Brookhouse Ct ST14 .**126** C1
Brookhouse Dr ST12 .**88** B2
Brookhouse Green Prim Sch
 ST2 ....**58** B1
Brookhouse La
 Bucknall ST2 ....**58** C2
 Cheddleton ST13 ....**45** A2
 Congleton CW12 .....**6** B1
 Featherstone WV10 ..**241** A3
Brookhouse Rd
 Cheadle ST10 ....**76** A2
 Gnosall ST20 ....**171** B4
 Meir ST3 ....**74** A1
Brookhouse Way
 Cheadle ST10 ....**76** A1
 Gnosall ST20 ....**171** B4
Brookland Ave ST3 ...**283** A1
Brookland Rd
 Brownhills WS9 .....**244** C2
 Chell Heath ST6 ....**41** C3
Brooklands DY6 .....**275** C1
Brooklands Ave WS6 .**226** C2
Brooklands Cl ST14 ..**126** A4
Brooklands Gr WS9 ..**244** C2
Brooklands Rd
 Albrighton WV7 .....**237** A3
 Cannock WS11 .....**210** A2
Brooklands Sch ST16 .**155** B3
Brooklands The DY3 ..**269** C1
Brooklands Way ST13 .**45** C4
Brooklime Gdns
 Featherstone WV10 ..**241** A4
 Stafford ST16 ....**155** A3
Brooklyn Gr DY6 .....**275** A4
Brooklyn Rd
 Burntwood WS7 .....**229** A4
 Cannock WS11 .....**210** B1
Brookmead Gr ST4 ...**73** A3
Brookmead Ind Est
 ST16 ....**155** C4
Brookside Burslem ST6 .**56** B4
 Burton u T DE15 ....**167** A4
 Enville DY7 ....**273** B2
 Kingsley ST10 ......**62** A2
 Ranton ST18 ....**153** B3
 Rolleston DE13 .....**147** A2
 Sedgley DY3 ....**271** C1
Brookside Ave TF10 ..**168** C1
Brookside Bsns Ctr
 ST15 ....**118** A3
Brookside Bsns Pk
 ST14 ....**126** B4
Brookside Cl
 Newcastle-u-L ST5 ..**284** A1
 Wombourne WV5 ...**269** C3
Brookside Ct ST10 ...**76** A2
Brookside Dr Endon ST9 .**44** A4
 Fenton ST3 ....**72** C1
Brookside Gdns WS9 .**221** C4
Brookside Ind Est ST6 .**56** B4
Brookside La ST15 ...**119** C4
Brookside Rd
 Barton-u-N DE13 ....**183** B1
 Tamworth B77 ......**249** B1
 Uttoxeter ST14 .....**126** B4
Brookside Way
 Blakedown DY10 ....**281** A1
 Kingswinford DY6 ...**275** B4
 Tamworth B77 ......**262** A4
Brookview Dr ST3 ...**73** C2
Brookweed B77 .....**251** A2
Brookwillows **5** ST17 .**175** B4
Brookwood Ct ST5 ...**71** A2
Brookwood Dr ST3 ..**74** A1
Broom Hollow TF9 ..**99** C3
Broom Lea TF9 ......**99** B3
Broom St ST1 ....**282** C4
Broom's La DE6 .....**129** A1
Broome Cl DE13 ....**199** A3
Broome Hill ST5 ....**71** B4
Broome La DY9 .....**281** B1
Broome Wlk WS15 ..**198** B2
Broomfield Ave B78 .**261** A4
Broomfield Cl
 Newport TF10 ......**168** B2
 Stone ST15 ....**120** A3
Broomfield Ct ST15 .**105** A1
Broomfield La ST14 .**79** C1
Broomfield Pl TF10 ..**168** B2
Broomfield Pl N ST1 .**57** A2

Broomfield Pl S ST1 ...**57** A2
Broomfield Rd
 Newport TF10 ....**168** B2
 Norton-in-t-M ST2 ...**42** B3
Broomfields ST8 .....**17** A1
Broomhill Bank WS11 .**209** C2
Broomhill Cl WS11 ...**209** C2
Broomhill St ST6 .....**41** B2
Brooms Rd ST15 ....**120** A3
Broomstead Cres ST16 **155** A3
Broomyclose St ST14 .**111** A2
Brough Cl Leek ST13 ..**30** C3
 Wolv WV4,WV14 ...**266** C2
Brough La ST4 ......**88** A4
Brough Rd DE15 ....**167** B2
Broughton Cl ST16 ..**155** B4
Broughton Cres ST12 .**88** C1
Broughton Ct WV6 ..**255** A2
Broughton Rd
 Bucknall ST2 ....**57** C2
 Newcastle-u-L ST5 ..**56** B1
 Wolv WV3 ....**255** B1
Brow Hill ST13 ......**30** C3
Brown Ave
 Lawton-gate ST7 ...**25** A3
 Tamworth B77 ......**261** B4
Brown La SK17 ......**3** A2
Brown Lees Ind Est ST8 **27** A2
Brown Lees Rd
 Biddulph ST8 ....**27** A3
 Kidsgrove ST7 ......**26** C2
Brown St Burslem ST6 .**57** A4
 Wolv WV2 ....**266** B4
Brown's La Dordon B78 .**262** C3
 Tamworth B79 ......**250** B4
 Yoxall DE13 ....**182** A1
Brown's Lake DY7 ...**273** B2
Brownfield Rd ST3 ...**74** A1
Brownhill Rd ST6 ....**43** A4
Brownhills Bsns Pk ST6 .**41** B1
Brownhills Com Sch
 WS8 ....**228** C1
Brownhills High Sch ST6 **41** C1
Brownhills Rd
 Brownhills WS9 .....**245** A2
 Norton Canes WS11 .**228** A2
 Tunstall ST6 ....**41** B1
Brownhills West Prim Sch
 WS8 ....**228** B1
Brownhills West Sta★
 WS7 ....**228** B2
Browning Cl Cheadle ST10 **76** B1
 Tamworth B79 ......**249** C4
Browning Cres WV10 .**240** B1
Browning Gr
 Perton WV6 ....**254** C2
 Talke ST7 ....**40** B4
Browning Rd
 Burntwood WS7 ....**229** B4
 Longton ST3 ....**72** C1
 Sedgley DY3 ....**271** A2
Browning St ST16 ...**155** B2
Brownley Rd ST6 ....**42** B1
Browns Wlk WS15 ..**178** B1
Brownsea Pl **12** ST3 .**72** C2
Brownsfield Rd WS13 .**214** B1
Brownshill Bsns Pk
 WS8 ....**244** C3
Brownsholme B79 ...**249** B3
Brownshore La WV11 .**242** A1
Brownswall Rd DY3 ..**271** B4
Broxwood Pk WV6 ...**255** A2
Bruford Rd WV3 .....**266** A4
Brund La ST13 ......**45** A2
Brundall Oval ST2 ...**58** B1
Brundle Ave ST16 ...**155** A2
Brunel Cl
 Burntwood WS7 ....**229** A4
 Stafford ST16 ......**155** C4
 Tamworth B79 ......**250** A3
Brunel Ct Brewood WV10 **224** B3
 Wombourne WV5 ..**270** A4
Brunel Gr WV6 ......**254** C2
Brunel Wlk ST3 .....**283** C4
Brunslow Cl WV10 ..**240** B1
Brunswick Mill **5** ST13 .**30** C3
Brunswick Pl ST1 ...**282** B2
Brunswick Rd WS11 .**209** C1
Brunswick St Hanley ST1 **282** B1
 22 Leek ST13 ....**30** C3
 Newcastle-u-L ST5 ..**284** C3
Brunswick Terr ST16 .**155** B1
Brunt St ST6 ....**56** B4
Brutus St ST5 ....**55** B3
Bryan Ave WV4 .....**265** B2
Bryan St ST1 ....**282** B3
Bryans La WS15 ....**178** C1
Bryans Way WS12 ..**210** C2
Bryant Rd ST2 ......**58** A3
Brymbo Rd ST5 .....**55** C3
Brynmawr Rd WV4,
 WV14 ....**266** C2
Bryony DE14 ....**185** A4
Buccleuch Rd ST3 ..**73** B1
Buckden B77 ....**251** B2
Buckingham Cl
 Burton u T DE13 ....**166** B4
 Stafford ST16 ......**156** B1
Buckingham Cres ST4 .**72** A1
Buckingham Ct DE15 .**167** B2
Buckingham Gdns
 WS14 ....**231** A4
Buckingham Gr DY6 .**275** B4
Buckingham Pl **9**
 WS11 ....**210** B1
Buckingham Rd
 Tamworth B79 .....**249** C4
 Wolv WV4 ....**266** A3

Buckingham Rise DY1 ..271 C1
Buckland Cl WS12 ....210 B1
Buckland Gr ST4 ....88 B3
Buckland Rd ST16 ....136 B1
Buckland Wlk TF10 ...168 C3
Buckley Cl ST14 ......125 B4
Buckley Rd
  Chell Heath ST6 ......42 B3
  Wolv WV4 ....265 B3
Buckley's Row ST5 ....284 B2
Buckmaster Ave 71 B3
Bucknall Hospl ST2 .....58 B2
Bucknall New Rd ST1 .282 C3
Bucknall Old Rd ST1 .282 C3
Bucknall Rd Hanley ST1 ..57 C2
  Wolv WV11 ....242 A1
Buckpool Sch DY8 ....275 C2
Buckthorn Cl WS12 ...209 C4
Buckton Cl B75 ......258 C1
Buds Rd WS15 ....211 C3
Buglawton Hall Specl Sch
  CW12 ....6 B3
Buglawton Prim Sch
  CW12 ....6 A2
Buildwas Cl WS3 .....242 C1
Bull Hill ST16 ......155 C2
Bull La Chell Heath ST8 ..27 A1
  Wombourne WV5 .....270 A4
  Sedgley DY3 ....271 B4
Bull Ring Claverley WV5 .267 B4
Bull Ring The ST18 ..138 B1
Bull St DY3 ....271 B4
Bulldog La WS13 .....214 A1
Buller St Hanley ST1 .282 C1
  Wolv WV4 ....266 C3
Bullgap La DE6 ......65 B2
Bullmoor La WS14 ....230 A1
Bullocks House Rd ST7 ..26 C2
Bullows Rd WS8 .....244 B3
Bulstrode St 23 ST6 ...56 C4
Bumblehole Mdws WV5 269 C4
Bun La Blymhill TF10 ..188 B1
  Great Chatwell TF10 ..203 B4
Bungalows The ST20 ..131 B2
Bungham La ST19 ....207 B4
Bunny Hill ST5 ....71 B3
Bunt's La ST9 ....43 B2
Bunting Cl ST14 .....126 A3
Bunting The
  Cheddleton ST9 .....60 A4
  Kingsley ST10 ....61 B2
Buntingsdale Rd TF9 ..112 A4
Bunyan Pl WS11 .....209 C2
Burcham Cl ST16 ....155 A4
Burdock Cl WS11 ....210 A2
Burford Rd Stafford ST17 156 B1
  Wheaton Aston ST19 ..205 A3
Burford Way ST2 .....58 A1
Burgage Cl TF9 .....97 B1
Burgage Ct TF10 ....168 C1
Burgage The
  Eccleshall ST21 ....133 C4
  Market Drayton TF9 ..97 B1
Burgess St ST6 ......56 C4
Burgesses The DY7 ..278 A2
Burgis Cl ST13 ......45 B2
Burgoyne St WS11 ..210 A3
Burgundy Gr 5 ST3 ...90 A4
Burland Ave WV6 ....255 C3
Burland Rd ST5 .....40 B1
Burleigh Cl WS12 ...210 A4
Burleigh Croft WS7 ..229 A2
Burleigh Gr ST5 .....56 B2
Burleigh Rd WV3 ....266 C4
Burlidge Rd ST6 ....42 A3
Burlington Ave ST5 ..56 B2
Burlington Ct B78 ...261 A4
Burlington Dr ST17 ..174 A4
Burmarsh Wlk
  15 Burslem ST6 .....56 C4
  Wolv WV8 ....255 C4
Burnaby Rd ST5 .....41 B3
Burnell Gdns WV3 ...265 B3
Burnet Gr WV10 ....241 A4
Burnett Cl ST16 .....155 A4
Burnett Pl ST6 .....42 B2
Burnett Rd B74 .....257 A1
Burnfield Dr WS15 ..178 B1
Burnfields Cl WS9 ...256 A4
Burnham Ave ST5 ...175 B3
Burnham Cl DY6 ....275 C2
Burnham Gn WS11 ..226 A4
Burnham St ST4 ....283 A5
Burnhays Rd ST6 ....41 C1
Burnley St ST1 .....57 B3
Burns Ave Stafford ST17 174 A4
  Wolv WV10 ....240 A1
Burns Cl Kidsgrove ST7 ..41 A4
  Lichfield WS14 .....231 A4
Burns Dr WS7 ......229 B4
Burns Gr DY3 ......271 B4
Burns Rd Congleton CW12 ..6 A1
  Tamworth B79 ......250 A3
Burns Row ST3 .....74 A1
Burns St WS11 .....210 A4
Burnsall Cl WV9 ....240 A2
Burnside DE13 .....147 A2
Burnside Cl ST3 ....90 A4
Burnthill La WS15 ..196 C4
Burntwood Rd
  Burntwood WS7 ....229 B2
  Norton Canes WS11 .228 A4
Burntwood Recn Ctr
  WS7 ....228 C3
Burntwood Town Sh Ctr
  WS7 ....228 C4
Burnwood Com Prim Sch
  ST6 ....42 A3

Burnwood Ct ST6 .....42 B1
Burnwood Gr ST7 .....26 A1
Burnwood Pl ST6 .....42 A3
Burrington Dr ST4 ....88 B3
Burrows Rd DY6 ....275 C2
Burrows The DE11 ...186 C3
Burslem Cl WS3 ....243 A4
Burslem Ent Ctr ST6 ..57 A4
Burslem Prim Sch ST5 ..56 A4
Bursley Cl ST17 .....174 B3
Bursley Rd ST6 .....57 A4
Bursley Way ST5 ....56 A4
Bursnips Rd WV11 ..242 B2
Burt St ST4 ....74 A2
Burton Bank La
  Stafford ST17,ST18 ..174 C3
  Stafford,Mosspit ST17 ..174 C3
Burton Borough Sch The
  TF10 ....169 A1
Burton Cl ST9 ......250 B4
Burton Coll (Town Campus)
  DE14 ....166 C1
Burton Cres Hanley ST1 ..57 C4
  Kingsley ST10 ......76 C4
Burton Ct ST17 ....174 C4
Burton Ent Pk DE14 166 C3
Burton House Gdns
  ST17 ....174 C3
Burton Manor Prim Sch
  ST17 ....174 B3
Burton Manor Rd ST17,
  ST18 ....174 B3
Burton Mews ST14 ..110 C1
Burton Old Rd
  Lichfield WS14 .....231 C4
  Streethay WS13 ....214 C1
Burton Old Rd E WS14 231 C4
Burton Old Rd W WS14 231 A4
Burton Pl ST1 .....282 C3
Burton Rd Alrewas DE13 201 A2
  Burton u T DE14 ...185 A4
  Dudley DY1 ....271 C2
  Elford B79 ....216 C1
  Linton DE11 ....186 B1
  Repton DE15,DE65 ..148 C1
  Streethay WS13 ....214 C1
  Tutbury DE13 ......146 B2
  Whittington WS14 ..232 C4
  Willington DE65 ...148 C4
Burton Sq ST17 ....174 C4
Burton St Leek ST13 ..30 B3
  Tutbury DE13 ......146 B3
Burton Tech Coll (Rolleston
  Campus) DE13 ....147 A2
Burton upon Trent Sta
  DE14 ....166 B2
Burway Mdw DE13 ..201 A1
Bury Ring ST18 ....173 B3
Bush Cl WV7 ......237 A3
Bush Dr WS15 .....178 C1
Bush Gr WS3 .....244 A1
Bushberry Cl ST15 ..119 C3
Bushbury Hill Jun & Inf Schs
  WV10 ....240 C1
Bushbury La WV10 ..240 C1
Bushey Cl B74 .....256 C1
Bushfield Rd WV7 ..237 A3
Bushton La DE13 ..146 A1
Bustomley La ST10 ..108 A3
Bute St ST4 ....283 A4
Butler Ct DE14 ....166 A2
Butler St ST4 ......72 A3
Butlers La B74 ....258 A2
Butlers Lane Sta B74 258 A4
Butt La ST18 ......153 B1
Butter Bk ST18 ....154 A2
Butterbank La ST18 ..154 A1
Butterfield Dr WV6 ..254 B2
Butterfield Pl ST6 ...41 C2
Butterhill Bank ST18 121 A1
Butterhill La ST15,ST18 121 C3
Buttermere B77 ....262 A4
Buttermere Cl
  Burslem ST6 ......56 C4
  Cannock WS11 ....210 A2
  Wolv WV6 ....255 B4
Buttermere Ct WS4 ..254 C2
Buttermere Dr WV11 242 A2
Buttermere Gr WV11 242 A1
Butthouse La ST5,ST21 102 A3
Buttons Farm Rd WV4 265 B2
Butts Cl WS11 .....227 C4
Butts Croft DE13 ..200 C2
Butts Gn ST2 .....58 B3
Butts La
  Norton Canes WS11 .227 C2
  Warslow SK17 .....23 B1
Butts Rd
  Market Drayton TF9 ..97 A1
  Wolv WV4 ....265 C2
Butts The Betley CW3 ..53 A3
  Wall WS14 ....230 B1
Butts Way WS11 ...227 C2
Butts's La ST10 ....63 C4
Buxton Ave Fazeley B78 261 A4
  Newcastle-u-L ST5 ..55 A1
Buxton Cl WS3 ....243 B2
Buxton Old Rd CW12 ..6 A2
Buxton Rd
  Alstonefield DE6 ...35 A3
  Congleton CW12 ...6 B3
  Leek ST13 ....31 A4
  Longnor SK17 .....13 A4
  Walsall WS3 ......243 B2
Buxton St ST1 .....57 B4
By Pass Rd B77 ...251 A3
Byatt's Gr ST3 ....283 C4

Bycars Farm Croft
  WS13 ....215 C4
Bycars La ST6 .....42 A1
Bycars Rd ST6 ....41 C1
Byland B77 ......250 B2
Byland Pl ST5 .....71 A3
Byland Way WS3 ..242 C1
Byrd's Cl ST14 ....125 C4
Byrd's La 18 ST14 ..125 C4
Byrkley Park Ctr ★
  DE13 ....164 A2
Byrkley St DE14 ...166 A2
Byrne Rd WV2 ....266 C4
Byron Ave
  Burton u T DE15 ...185 C4
  Lichfield WS14 ....231 A3
Byron Cl Burntwood WS7 211 C1
  Cheadle ST10 .....76 A1
  Market Drayton TF9 ..112 A4
  Stafford ST17 .....156 A3
Byron Croft Sedgley DY3 271 A3
  Sutton Coldfield B74 ..257 C3
Byron Ct Kidsgrove ST7 ..41 A4
  Sutton Coldfield B74 ..258 A3
Byron Pl Cannock WS11 209 C3
  Rugeley WS15 .....178 B1
Byron Rd
  Essington WV10 ...241 A1
  Tamworth B79 ....250 A3
Byron St 7 Leek ST13 ..30 B3
  Stoke-on-T ST4 ...56 B1
Bywater Gr 3 ST3 ..73 B3
Byways WS3 ......243 B2

C

Cable St WV2 ......266 C4
Cacklehill La DE6 ...81 B1
Cadeby Gr ST2 ....43 A1
Cadley Hill Ind Est
  DE11 ....186 C1
Cadley Hill Rd DE11 ..186 C2
Cadman Cres ST6 ..42 C2
Cadman's La WS3 ..243 B3
Cadogan Rd B77 ...261 B3
Caernarvon Ave ST15 120 B3
Caernarvon Cl
  Burton u T DE13 ...166 C4
  Market Drayton TF9 ..97 C1
Caernarvon Way DY1 271 C1
Cairn Cl ST2 .....58 B2
Cairns Cl ST5 ....167 B2
Cairns Dr ST16 ...156 A3
Caister B77 ......251 A4
Caistor Cl Fazeley B78 261 A4
  Norton-in-t-M ST2 ..43 A1
Calais Rd DE13 ...166 A3
Calcot Dr WV6 ....255 C4
Caldbeck Pl ST1 ..282 C3
Calder B77 ......251 A4
Calder Rise DY3 ..271 C3
Caldercrofts TF10 ..168 C2
Caldervale Dr 7 ST17 175 B3
Caldew Gr ST4 ....88 B3
Cale Cl B77 ......250 B4
Caledonia Rd Hanley ST4 57 A1
  Wolv WV2 ....266 C4
Caledonian ST5 ...250 C1
Calgary Cres DE15 ..167 B2
California ST3 ....283 A3
Californian Gr WS7 ..228 A4
Callaghan Gr 3 WS11 210 B1
Callender Pl ST5 ..57 A4
Callingwood La DE13 164 C2
Callis Wlk B77 ...261 C3
Callow Hill La ST10 ..75 B2
Calrofold Dr ST5 ..40 B1
Calvary Cres ST2 ..73 B4
Calveley Cl ST15 ..118 C3
Calver St 4 ST6 ..41 B2
Calverley St ST3 ..283 D2
Calvert Gr ST5 ...56 A4
Calvin Cl Wolv WV10 240 B2
  Wombourne WV5 ..269 C3
Calving Hill WS11 ..209 C1
Camberley Cres WV4 266 C1
Camberley Dr WV4 ..266 C1
Camberley Rd DY6 ..275 C2
Camberwell Gr ST4 ..88 B3
Camborne Cl ST17 ..175 C4
Camborne Cres ST5 ..71 A3
Cambourne Cl CW12 ..15 C4
Cambria St WS11 ..209 B2
Cambria B77 .....251 A1
Cambrian La ST15 ..178 B2
Cambrian Way ST2 ..58 B2
Cambridge Cl
  Aldridge WS9 .....256 A4
  Biddulph ST8 .....16 B1
Cambridge Ct ST5 ..71 B2
Cambridge Dr ST5 ..71 B2
Cambridge St
  Burton u T DE14 ...166 A1
  Hanley ST1 ....282 A2
  Stafford ST16 ....156 A4
Camden Dr B77 ...250 C2
Camden St
  Brownhills WS9 ...244 C2
  Fenton ST4 ....72 C2
Camden Way DY6 ..270 B1
Camelford Ct ST17 ..175 C4
Camellia Cl ST4 ...56 C1
Camellia Gdns
  Brierley Hill DY8 ...275 C1
  Codsall WV9 ......239 C2
Camelot Cl
  2 Burton u T DE13 ..147 C1

Camelot Cl continued
  Cannock WS11 ....209 C2
  Trentham ST4 ....88 B2
Cameo Dr DY8 ....279 C4
Cameo Way ST16 ..155 A4
Cameron Cl DE15 ..167 A1
Camhouses B77 ...251 A1
Camillus Rd ST5 ..55 C1
Camoys Cl 18 ST6 ..57 A4
Camoys Rd ST6 ...57 A4
Camp Hill
  Brierley Hill DY8 ...275 C1
  Maer ST5 ....84 C3
Camp Hill Rd DY7 ..273 C4
Camp Rd Brocton WS12 194 B3
  Chell Heath ST6 ...42 B3
  Sutton Coldfield B75 ..258 B3
Campbell Ave ST13 ..30 C2
Campbell Cl
  Congleton CW12 ..6 A2
  Rugeley WS15 ....178 B1
  Tamworth B79 ....249 C4
Campbell Pl ST4 ..72 A4
Campbell Rd
  Market Drayton TF9 ..97 B1
  Stoke-on-T ST4 ...72 A3
Campbell Terr ST1 ..57 C3
Campian's Ave WS6 226 A1
Campion Ave ST5 ..56 B2
Campion Cl
  Eccleshall ST21 ...133 B3
  Wombourne WV5 ..269 C3
Campion Dr
  Featherstone WV10 241 A4
  Tamworth B77 ....250 B2
Camrose Gdns WV9 240 A2
Camsey La WS7 ...229 C4
Canal La ST6 .....41 B1
Canal Mews The ST4 ..88 B3
Canal Rd CW12 ...15 C4
Canal Side ST12 ..88 B3
Canal St Brierley Hill DY8 279 C3
  Burton u T ST6 ...56 C4
  Burton u T DE14 ...166 B2
Canal View Bsns Pk
  WS15 ....197 A3
Canalside Cl
  Penkridge ST19 ...207 C4
  Walsall WS3 ......243 C1
Canalside Rd ST15 ..104 C1
Canary Rd ST2 ...73 B4
Canaway Wlk WS15 ..178 B1
Canberra Cres ST3 ..90 B4
Canberra Dr ST16 ..156 A2
Candle La CW3 ...67 A1
Canford Cres WV8 ..238 C2
Cannel Rd WS7 ...228 B3
Canning B77 ......250 C2
Canning St ST4 ...72 C3
Cannock Wood Rd
  WS12 ....211 B3
Cannock Wood St
  WS12 ....211 B3
Cannock Chase Ctry Pk
  ★ Brocton ST17 ...176 B1
  ★ Rugeley WS12 ..195 A2
Cannock Chase Ent Ctr
  WS12 ....195 B1
Cannock Chase High Sch
  WS11 ....209 C1
Cannock Chase Tech Coll
  Cannock WS11 ....209 C1
  Cannock,Bridgtown WS11 226 C4
Cannock Com Hospl
  WS11 ....209 C1
Cannock Ind Ctr WS11 226 B3
Cannock Rd
  Brocton WS17 ....176 A1
  Burntwood, Chase Terrace
    WS7 ....228 C4
  Burntwood, Gorstey Ley
    WS7 ....228 C4
  Cannock, Heath Hayes
    WS12 ....227 B4
  Cannock, High Town
    WS11,WS12 ......210 A3
  Featherstone WV10 241 A2
  Huntington ST19 ..208 A4
  Penkridge ST19 ..192 C1
  Stafford ST17 ....175 C3
Cannock Sh Ctr 13
  WS11 ....209 C1
Cannock Sta WS11 226 C4
Cannock Wood Ind Est
  WS12 ....211 B3
Cannock Wood Rd
  WS12 ....211 A3
Cannock Wood St
  WS12 ....211 B3
Cannon Pl ST1 ....282 B2
Cannon Rd WV5 ...270 A4
Cannon St ST1 ...282 B2
Canons Cl ST15 ...120 A3
Canterbury Cl
  Lichfield WS13 ...214 B2
  Tamworth B77 ....250 B2
  Walsall WS3 ......244 A2
Canterbury Dr
  Burntwood WS7 ...229 C4
  Chell Heath ST6 ..42 A2
  Perton WV6 ......254 C2
Canterbury Rd
  Burton u T DE15 ...167 B2
  Wolv WV4 ....266 C4
Canterbury Way WS12 210 A1
Canvey Dr ST3 ....90 A4
Canwell Dr B75 ...259 A4
Cape Ave ST17 ...174 A4

Cape Cl WS8 .....245 A3
Cape St ST1 .....282 B3
Capesthorne Cl ST9 ..59 A2
Capewell St ST3 ..283 C4
Capper Cl ST7 ....26 A1
Capper St ST6 ...41 C2
Capper's La WS14 ..232 A4
Cappers La WS13,WS14 231 C4
Capricorn Way ST6 ..41 C3
Captain's Cl WV3 ..255 B1
Captain's La DE13 ..201 B4
Caradoc B77 .....251 A1
Caravan Ctr ST5 ..70 C4
Caraway Dr DE14 ..185 A4
Caraway Pl ST3 ...90 A3
Carberry Way ST3 ..74 A2
Card St ST6 ......57 A4
Carder Ave ST16 ..155 A4
Carder Gn SK17 ...13 A3
Cardiff Gr ST1 ....282 B1
Cardiff St WV3 ...266 A4
Cardigan Ave WS15 196 B3
Cardigan Gr ST4 ..88 B3
Cardigan Ho WS12 ..210 B3
Cardigan Pl WS12 ..210 B3
Cardinal Griffin RC High Sch
  WS11 ....209 B1
Cardinal Way WS11 209 B1
Cardington Cl ST5 ..71 A2
Cardoness Pl DY1 ..271 C1
Cardway ST5 .....56 A4
Cardwell St ST1 ...57 C3
Carey B77 ......262 A3
Carfax WS11 .....226 C4
Carier Ave WV8 ...239 A2
Carina Gdns ST3 ..42 B1
Carisbrooke B77 ..251 A1
Carisbrooke Dr
  5 Burton u T DE13 ..147 C1
  Stafford ST17 ....174 A4
Carisbrooke Gdns
  WV10 ....240 C2
Carisbrooke Rd
  Perton WV6 ......255 A2
  Wolv WV10 ....240 C2
Carisbrooke Way ST4 ..88 B3
Carlcroft B77 ....251 A1
Carling Cl ST16 ..155 A1
Carling Gr ST4 ...73 A3
Carlisle Rd WS11 ..226 A4
Carlisle St ST3 ...283 B1
Carlos Cl ST10 ...76 B2
Carlos Pl ST5 ....41 A1
Carlton Ave Aldridge B74 257 A4
  Chell Heath ST6 ..42 A2
  Endon ST6 ....43 A3
  Newcastle-u-L ST5 ..43 A3
Carlton Cl Cannock WS12 210 B1
  Cheadle ST10 ....76 B1
  Endon ST6 ....43 A3
Carlton Cres
  Burntwood WS7 ..229 A4
  Tamworth B79 ....249 C4
Carlton Croft B74 ..257 A1
Carlton Ct DE14 ..166 A2
Carlton Ho B75 ..258 A3
Carlton Rd Stoke-on-T ST4 72 B4
  Wolv WV3 ....266 A4
Carlton Sq ST17 ..174 A4
Carlton St DE13 ..166 A3
Carlton Terr ST13 ..31 A3
Carlyon Pl ST1 ...57 B4
Carmel Cl WS12 ...210 B3
Carmichael Cl WS14 231 B4
Carmount Rd ST2 ..58 A4
Carmountside Prim Sch
  ST2 ....58 A4
Carnation Cl ST3 ..74 A3
Carnforth Cl DY6 ..275 A4
Carnforth Gr ST5 ..41 C4
Carnoustie B77 ...251 B3
Carnoustie Cl WS3 243 A2
Carol Gdns DY8 ...279 C4
Caroline Cl ST9 ..59 A2
Caroline Cres ST6 ..43 A4
Caroline St ST3 ...283 C4
Caroline Terr DE14 ..166 B1
Carousels The DE14 166 B3
Carpenter Cl DE15 167 B1
Carpenter Rd ST3 ..283 A4
Carr Bank ST10 ..78 A4
Carr La Audley ST7 ..39 A1
  Wetton DE6,ST13 ..34 C1
Carr St ST7 ......26 C1
Carriage Dr ST8 ..16 C1
Carrick Cl WS3 ..244 A3
Carrick St ST4 ...72 A1
Carriers Fold WV5 ..270 A4
Carriers Rd DE65 ..148 B3
Carroll Dr ST3 ...283 D4
Carron St ST4 ...283 B5
Carroway Head Hill B78 259 B3
Carryer Pl ST5 ...70 C4
Carshalton Gr WV2 266 C4
Carson Rd ST6 ...41 C2
Carson Way ST16 ..155 B2
Carter St ST14 ...126 B4
Carters Croft ST10 ..92 C2
Cartersfield La WS14 245 B3
Cartlich St ST6 ...41 B3
Cartlidge St ST4 ..56 B1
Cartmel Pl ST6 ...42 B4
Cartway The WV6 ..254 B2
Cartwright Dr ST20 171 B4
Cartwright Ho WS3 243 A1

Cartwright Ind Est The
ST3 ....283 B2
Cartwright Rd B75 ....258 B2
Cartwright St
Longton ST3 ....283 B3
Wolv WV2 ....266 B4
Carver Gdns DY8 ....279 C1
Carver Rd
Burton u T DE13 ....166 B3
Stafford ST16 ....155 C3
Casa Mia Ct WS12 ....210 B3
Casewell Rd Hanley ST6 ..57 B4
Kingswinford DY6 ....275 B4
Casey La Burton u T DE14 166 A2
Weston CW2 ....37 A3
Casey The ST13 ....48 A1
Cash La ST21 ....132 C2
Caslon Cres DY8 ....279 B2
Caspian Gr ST4 ....88 A4
Caspian Way ST19 ....205 B3
Cassandra Cl DY5 ....271 B1
Castel Cl ST5 ....70 C2
Castle Acre ST17 ....174 A4
Castle Bank ST17 ....174 A4
Castle Cl Brownhills WS8 228 C1
Tamworth B77 ....250 C2
Castle Ct Tutbury DE13 ..146 B4
5 ST15 ....120 B3
Castle Dyke WS13 ....231 A4
Castle Gr ST2 ....58 A3
Castle Hayes La DE13 ..146 A3
Castle Hill DE13 ....146 A4
Castle Hill Rd Alton ST10 .78 C1
Newcastle-u-L ST5 ....284 A3
Castle House Sch TF10 .168 C2
Castle Inn Rd CW12 ....16 B4
Castle Keep Ct ST5 ....284 A2
Castle Keep Mews ST5 .284 A2
Castle La CW3 ....68 C3
Castle Mount ST5 ....55 C3
Castle Park Inf Sch
DE13 ....166 A4
Castle Park Rd DE13 ..166 A4
Castle Prim Sch ST7 ...26 B3
Castle Rd
Brownhills WS9 ....245 A1
Cookley DY10 ....280 A2
Kidsgrove ST7 ....26 B4
Swadlincote DE11 ....186 C1
Tamworth B77 ....261 C3
Castle Ridge ST5 ....70 C4
Castle Ring Fort*
WS15 ....211 C3
Castle St Brownhills WS8 228 C1
Eccleshall ST21 ....133 C4
Kinver DY7 ....278 A2
Newcastle-u-L ST5 ....284 C3
Newcastle-u-L, Chesterton
ST5 ....55 C4
Sedgley DY3 ....271 B4
Stafford ST16 ....155 B2
Tutbury DE13 ....146 B3
Castle View Biddulph ST8 .27 B3
Hatton DE65 ....146 B4
Seighford ST18 ....154 C1
Stafford ST16 ....155 B2
Tamworth B77 ....250 B2
Castle View Est ST18 ..154 C1
Castle Way ST16 ....155 B1
Castle Way The DE65 ..148 C3
Castlechurch Prim Sch
ST17 ....174 A4
Castlecroft WS11 ....227 C3
Castlecroft Ave WV3 ..265 A4
Castlecroft Gdns WV3 .265 B4
Castlecroft La WV6 ....254 C1
Castlecroft Prim Sch
WV3 ....265 A4
Castlecroft Rd WV3 ....265 A4
Castledene Dr ST16 ....155 B1
Castledine Gr ST3 ....73 C2
Castlefield St ST4 ....57 A1
Castlefields ST16 ....155 B1
Castlefort Jun Mix Inf Sch
WS9 ....245 A2
Castlefort Rd WS9 ....245 A2
Castlehall B77 ....251 A1
Castlehill Rd WS9 ....245 B2
Castleton Rd Meir ST3 ..89 C4
Walsall WS3 ....243 B2
Castleview Gr ST7 ....41 C4
Castleview Rd ST7 ....26 A2
Caswell Rd DY3 ....271 B4
Cat & Kittens La WV10 .240 C3
Catalan Cl 6 ST17 ....175 A4
Catalina Pl ST3 ....90 B3
Caterham Dr DY6 ....275 C2
Caterham Pl ST3 ....90 A3
Catesby Dr DY6 ....275 B4
Catharine Rd ST6 ....42 B3
Cathcart Rd DY8 ....279 C3
Cathedral Ct WS13 ....231 A4
Cathedral Rise WS13 ..231 A4
Catherine St ST5 ....56 B2
Catholic La DY3 ....271 B4
Catholme La DE13 ....201 C3
Catisfield Cres WV8 ..239 C1
Catkin Wlk WS15 ....178 B1
Catmeadow La WS15 ..197 B1
Caton Cres ST6 ....42 C1
Catsbridge La WS11 ..225 C4
Catshill Rd WS8 ....245 A4
Cauldon Ave
Cheddleton ST13 ....45 B3
Newcastle-u-L ST5 ....56 A4
Cauldon Cl ST13 ....30 C2
Cauldon Pl ST4 ....57 A1
Cauldon Prim Sch ST4 ..57 B1
Cauldon Rd ST4 ....57 B1
Caulton St ST6 ....41 C1
Caunsall Rd DY11 ....280 A3
Causeley Gdns ST2 ....58 A2
Causeley Rd ST2 ....58 A2
Causeway Pl ST13 ....33 C3
Cavalier Cir WV10 ....240 C2
Cavan's Cl WS11 ....209 C2
Cavendish Rd ST10 ....92 C3
Cavans Wood Mobile Homes
WS12 ....209 B3
Cavell Rd WS7 ....229 C4
Cavendish B79 ....249 C4
Cavendish Cl DY6 ....275 B2
Cavendish Dr DY9 ....281 C2
Cavendish Gr ST5 ....71 A2
Cavendish St ST1 ....57 A2
Cavendish Way WS9 ....256 A3
Caverswall La ST3 ....90 B4
Caverswall Old Rd ST11 .90 C4
Caverswall Rd
Dilhorne ST10 ....75 A2
Forsbrook ST11 ....90 C4
Meir ST3 ....74 A2
Caverswall Road Sta*
ST11 ....74 C1
Cavour St ST1 ....56 C2
Cawdry Bldgs 21 ST13 ....30 C3
Caxton Ct 4 WS11 ....226 C4
Caxton St WS11 ....226 C4
Cayley Pl ST3 ....90 B3
Cecil Ave ST1 ....282 A4
Cecil Payton Cl WS15 ..160 C3
Cecil Rd DE11 ....186 C3
Cecil St Cannock WS11 ..209 C2
Stourbridge DY8 ....279 C3
Cecilly St ST10 ....76 C2
Cecilly Terr ST10 ....76 C2
Cedar Ave
Brownhills WS8 ....245 A4
Forsbrook ST11 ....91 A3
Kidsgrove ST7 ....25 B1
Cedar Cl Burntwood WS7 229 A3
Cannock WS12 ....195 A1
Cheadle ST10 ....76 C1
Lichfield WS14 ....231 C4
Market Drayton TF9 ....97 A1
Stourbridge DY8 ....279 B1
Uttoxeter ST14 ....110 C1
Cedar Cres Audley ST7 ..39 C1
Endon ST9 ....43 C3
Rugeley WS15 ....197 A3
Cedar Ct CW12 ....15 C4
Cedar Dr Albrighton WV7 237 A3
Aldridge B74 ....256 C1
Tamworth B79 ....250 A4
Cedar Gdns DY7 ....277 C3
Cedar Gr Biddulph ST8 ..17 A1
Codsall WV8 ....239 A2
Fenton ST3 ....72 C2
Great Wyrley WS6 ....227 A2
Wolv WV3 ....265 C4
Cedar Ho B74 ....257 A3
Cedar Park Rd WV12 ..242 B1
Cedar Pk ST15 ....120 A4
Cedar Rd
Barton-u-N DE13 ....183 B1
Burntwood WS7 ....229 A4
Newcastle-u-L ST5 ....40 B1
Cedar Way ST17 ....175 C3
Cedar Wood Rd DY3 ..271 B3
Cedarhill ST10 ....78 B1
Cedarhill Dr WS11 ....209 C2
Cedars Ave
Kingswinford DY6 ....275 B2
Wombourne WV5 ....270 A3
Cedars Bsns Ctr The
WS11 ....226 B4
Cedars Dr ST15 ....120 A3
Cedars Hort Unit The
WV3 ....255 B1
Cedars The
5 Wolv WV6 ....255 C2
Wolv, Tattenhall WV6 ....255 B3
Cedartree Gr ST1 ....57 C4
Cedarwood B74 ....258 A1
Cedarwood Cl WV9 ....224 A2
Celandine B77 ....250 B1
Celandine Cl
Kingswinford DY6 ....275 B2
Norton-in-t-M ST2 ....43 A1
Celandines The WV5 ..269 C3
Celebration Ct ST6 ....42 B2
Cellarhead Rd ST9 ....59 C2
Celtic Ave ST7 ....41 C4
Celtic Rd WS11 ....209 C2
Cemetery Ave ST3 ....283 B2
Cemetery Rd
Cannock WS11 ....209 C2
Hanley ST4 ....57 A1
Market Drayton TF9 ....97 A1
Newcastle-u-L, Knutton ST5 55 C2
Newcastle-u-L, Silverdale
ST5 ....55 B1
Weston CW2 ....37 A3
Cemetery St WS6 ....226 B1
Cemetery View
Longton ST3 ....283 B2
Newcastle-u-L ST5 ....55 C2
Cemetery Way WS3 ....243 A1
Cemlyn Ave ST3 ....72 C2
Central Ave Bucknall ST2 .58 A2
Cannock WS11 ....209 C3
Wolv WV4 ....266 C2
Central Cl WS3 ....243 A1
Central Dr Fenton ST3 ....72 C2
Sedgley DY3 ....271 B1
Walsall WS3 ....243 A1
Central St ST7 ....26 A3
Central Trad Est WV2 ..266 C4
Central Way DE13 ....166 A4
Centre Rd ST15 ....104 C1
Centurion Pk B77 ....262 A3
Centurion Way B77 ....262 A3
Century Rd ST5 ....40 C1
Century St ST1 ....282 A3
Chadsfield Rd WS15 ..178 C1
Chadsmead Prim Sch
WS13 ....214 A1
Chadsmoor CE Jun Sch
WS11 ....210 A2
Chadsmoor Inf Sch
WS11 ....210 A2
Chadswell Hts WS13 ..214 B1
Chadwell Gdns WV8 ..238 C2
Chadwell La
Gnosall TF10 ....188 A1
Woodcote TF10 ....187 C2
Chadwell Way ST2 ....58 B1
Chadwick Cl WV4 ....265 B3
Chadwick Cres WS15 ..198 A4
Chadwick Ct 6 WS15 ..196 C4
Chadwick St ST3 ....283 C3
Chadwyn Dr ST2 ....43 A1
Chaff La DE6 ....65 B1
Chaffinch Cl
Cannock WS12 ....210 A2
Sedgley DY3 ....266 B1
Chaffinch Dr
Biddulph ST8 ....27 C4
Uttoxeter ST14 ....126 B3
Chain La ST17 ....174 C2
Chain St ST6 ....42 B1
Chalcot Dr WS12 ....210 A4
Chaldon Cl WV9 ....240 A1
Chalfield B79 ....249 B3
Chalfont Ave WS11 ....226 B4
Chalfont Cres CW2 ....37 A1
Chalfont Gn ST2 ....58 B1
Challenge Cl ST6 ....42 B2
Challinor Ave ST13 ....30 C3
Challinor St ST6 ....41 C2
Chamberlain Ave ST4 ..72 A3
Chamberlain St ST1 ..282 B1
Chamberlain Way ST8 ..27 C4
Chamberlain's La WV4 .265 C2
Chambley Gn WV9 ....224 A1
Chance Hall La ST7 ....25 A4
Chancel Dr TF9 ....97 A1
Chancel Ind Est DY6 ..270 C1
Chancel Inf Sch WS15 .178 C1
Chancery Dr WS12 ....210 B4
Chancery La ST3 ....283 C3
Chandler Ave DY7 ....277 C3
Chandler Dr WV4 ....265 B2
Chandlers Cl WV9 ....240 A1
Chandlers Dr B77 ....251 A3
Chandlers Keep WS8 ..245 A3
Chanterelle Gdns WV4 .266 A2
Chantry Rd Kinver DY7 .279 B4
Newcastle-u-L ST5 ....284 B1
Chapel Ave WS8 ....228 C1
Chapel Bank
Kidsgrove ST7 ....26 B3
Wheaton Aston ST19 ..205 B3
Chapel Cl
Mount Pleasant ST7 ....26 A3
Wombourne WV5 ....269 C3
Chapel Ct Gnosall ST20 .171 B3
Kidderminster DY10 ....280 A1
Newcastle-u-L ST5 ....55 B1
Chapel Dr WS8 ....228 C1
Chapel Gn DE6 ....127 B4
Chapel Hill DY10 ....280 A1
Chapel La Anslow DE13 .165 A3
Ashley TF9 ....100 A3
Ashley,Hookgate TF9 ....99 C2
Audley ST7 ....39 B1
Biddulph ST8 ....17 A1
Bradley ST18 ....191 A4
Burslem ST6 ....57 A4
Cannock WS15 ....211 C3
Cheadle ST10 ....77 B1
Clifton DE6 ....81 C3
Codsall WV8 ....238 C2
Endon ST6 ....28 A1
Hanbury DE13 ....144 C1
Kidsgrove ST7 ....26 C2
Kingsley ST10 ....62 A1
Lichfield WS14 ....231 A3
Longdon WS15 ....212 A2
Mucklestone TF9 ....83 B3
Newborough DE13 ....162 C4
Norton in Hales TF9 ....82 B1
Rolleston DE13 ....147 A2
Rudyard ST9 ....29 A3
Tatenhill DE13 ....164 B2
Whittington WS14 ....232 C3
Chapel Mus Mow Cop*
ST7 ....26 B4
Chapel Rd WS15 ....197 C3
Chapel Sq WS6 ....226 B2
Chapel St Audley ST7 ..39 C2
Brownhills, New Town
WS8 ....228 C1
Bucknall ST2 ....58 A2
Burntwood WS7 ....228 C4
Cannock WS12 ....210 C1
Cheadle ST10 ....76 B2
Forsbrook ST11 ....91 A4
Kidsgrove ST7 ....25 B1
Kingsley ST10 ....61 B2
Kingswinford DY8 ....275 B2
Chapel St *continued*
Kingswinford, Wall Heath
DY6 ....275 A4
Longnor SK17 ....13 A3
Mount Pleasant ST7 ....26 A3
Newcastle-u-L, Knutton ST5 55 C2
Newcastle-u-L, May Bank
ST5 ....56 B2
Newcastle-u-L, Silverdale
ST5 ....55 B1
Norton Canes WS11 ....227 C3
Stafford ST16 ....155 C2
Swadlincote DE11 ....186 C3
Walsall WS3 ....244 A2
Wolv WV2 ....266 B4
Wombourne WV5 ....269 C3
Chapel Terr ST16 ....155 C2
Chapel Wlk DY3 ....271 B1
Chapelon B77 ....251 A1
Chapelside WS15 ....178 B1
Chaplain Rd WS12 ....210 C1
Chaplin Rd ST3 ....283 C1
Chapter Wlk ST2 ....58 A3
Charlecote Dr DY1 ....271 C2
Charlemonte Cl WS12 ..210 B2
Charles Ave
Essington WV11 ....241 C2
Kidderminster DY10 ....280 A1
Wolv WV4 ....266 A3
Charles Cl WS6 ....226 B1
Charles Cotton Dr CW3 ..68 B3
Charles Cotton St ST16 .155 B3
Charles Cres WS3 ....244 A3
Charles Hayward Bglws
WV4 ....266 B2
Charles Rd DY8 ....279 C2
Charles St Biddulph ST8 ..27 B4
Cheadle ST10 ....76 B2
Hanley ST1 ....282 C2
Newcastle-u-L ST5 ....56 B2
Charles Wesley Ct WV3 266 A4
Charlesdale Dr WS9 ..256 A2
Charlestown Gr ST3 ....90 A4
Charlesway TF9 ....112 A4
Charlock Gr WS11 ....210 B2
Charlotte Cl ST18 ....177 B4
Charlotte Ct DE14 ....185 B4
Charlotte St ST6 ....41 B4
Charlton St ST4 ....72 A4
Charminster Rd ST3 ....90 A4
Charmouth Cl ST1 ....58 A3
Charmwood Cl WS12 ..210 B2
Charnes Rd TF9 ....100 B3
Charnley Dr B75 ....258 C1
Charnley Rd ST16 ....155 C3
Charnock Pl ST6 ....42 A4
Charnsford La TF9 ....100 A2
Charnwood 11 ST7 ....26 A1
Charnwood Ave DY3 ..266 B1
Charnwood Cl Leek ST13 .30 B2
Lichfield WS13 ....214 B1
Rugeley WS15 ....178 B1
Charnwood Ho WS13 ..214 A1
Charnwood Prim Sch
WS13 ....214 B1
Charnwood Rd
Burton u T DE13 ....166 A4
Meir ST3 ....73 C1
Charolais Cres ST3 ....89 B4
Charsley Pl ST3 ....72 C1
Charter Cl WS11 ....227 C2
Charter Ct TF9 ....97 B1
Charter Rd ST5 ....56 A2
Charterfield Dr
Cannock WS12 ....210 B1
Kingswinford DY6 ....275 B4
Charterfields Sh Ctr 1
DY6 ....275 B4
Charterhouse Dr ST17 ..156 A1
Charters Ave WV8 ....239 A1
Charters The WS13 ....214 A1
Chartley Cl
Blythe Bridge ST11 ....90 C3
Perton WV6 ....254 C2
Stafford ST16 ....155 B4
Chartley Cotts ST18 ..139 B3
Chartley Gate Cl ST14 .126 A3
Chartway The WS3 ....244 A2
Chartwell B79 ....249 B4
Chartwell Cl ST9 ....59 A2
Chartwell Dr
Sutton Coldfield B74 ....257 B2
Wolv WV10 ....240 C1
Wombourne WV5 ....269 C3
Chartwell Rd ST17 ....175 B4
Chartwood TF9 ....99 B3
Chase Ave WS6 ....226 C2
Chase Cres ST17 ....176 A2
Chase L Ctr WS11 ....209 B1
Chase La ST12,ST15 ....103 C3
Chase Park Ind Est
WS7 ....228 B4
Chase Rd Brocton ST17 ..176 B1
Brownhills WS8 ....229 A1
Burntwood WS7 ....229 A3
Sedgley DY3,DY5 ....271 B1
Chase Side Rd WS15 ..196 B4
Chase Terrace High Sch
WS7 ....229 A4
Chase Terrace Prim Sch
WS7 ....228 C4
Chase Vale WS7 ....228 C3
Chase View
Armitage WS15 ....198 A2
Wolv WV4 ....266 C1
Chase View La ST18 ..174 B2
Chase Wlk
Huntington WS12 ....209 B2
Chase Wlk *continued*
Meir ST3 ....89 C4
Chaselands WS7 ....228 B4
Chaseley Ave WS11 ..209 B1
Chaseley Cl WS15 ....178 A1
Chaseley Croft WS11 ..209 B1
Chaseley Gdns WS7 ..229 B4
Chaseley Rd WS15 ....178 A1
Chasepool Rd DY3 ....274 B4
Chaseside Dr WS11 ..210 A2
Chaseside Ind Est
WS11 ....210 A2
Chasetown Com Sch
WS7 ....228 C3
Chasetown High Sch
WS7 ....228 C2
Chasetown Ind Est WS7 228 C3
Chasetown Sta* WS7 ..228 B3
Chaseview Rd DE13 ....200 C1
Chasewater Country Pk*
WS7 ....228 B3
Chasewater Dr ST10 ....76 C2
Chasewater Heaths Sta*
WS7 ....228 B3
Chasewater Light Rly*
WS11 ....228 A2
Chasewater Water Sports
Venue* WS8 ....228 B2
Chasewater Way WS11 .227 C3
Chasewood Park Bsns Ctr
WS12 ....210 C1
Chatcull La ST21 ....101 C1
Chatfield Cl DE15 ....167 B1
Chatfield Pl ST3 ....73 B1
Chatham St ST1 ....282 A1
Chatsworth B79 ....249 B4
Chatsworth Dr
Cannock WS11 ....210 A2
Caverswall ST9 ....59 A2
Norton-in-t-M ST6 ....42 C3
Tutbury DE13 ....146 B3
Chatsworth Gdns WV6 .255 A4
Chatsworth Mews ST21 133 C4
Chatsworth Park Ave
ST4 ....72 A1
Chatsworth Pl Meir ST3 ..73 C1
Newcastle-u-L ST5 ....55 C4
Chatteris Cl ST3 ....90 A3
Chatterley Cl ST5 ....56 A4
Chatterley Dr ST7 ....41 A4
Chatterley Rd ST6 ....41 B2
Chatterley St ST6 ....41 C1
Chatterton Ave WS13 ..230 C3
Chatterton Pl ST3 ....73 B2
Chatwell La
Blymhill TF10 ....188 B1
Great Chatwell TF10,TF11 .203 A4
Chaucer Ave DY3 ....271 A3
Chaucer Cl
Burton u T DE14 ....166 B3
Lichfield WS14 ....231 A3
Tamworth B79 ....250 A3
Chaucer Dr WS7 ....212 A1
Chaucer Rd ST17 ....174 B4
Chaulden Rd ST16 ....136 B1
Chawner Cl WS7 ....211 C1
Cheadle Cl ST19 ....207 C4
Cheadle High Sch ST10 ..76 B1
Cheadle Hospl ST10 ....76 B2
Cheadle Prim Sch ST10 ..76 B1
Cheadle Rd Alton ST10 ..78 C1
Cheddleton ST13 ....45 B2
Draycott in t M ST11 ....91 C3
Forsbrook ST11 ....91 A4
Leek ST13 ....45 C4
Upper Tean ST10 ....92 B3
Uttoxeter ST14 ....111 A1
Warslow SK17 ....23 A1
Cheam Gdns WV6 ....255 C4
Cheapside Hanley ST1 ..282 B2
Newcastle-u-L ST5 ....284 B3
Cheatle Ct B77 ....261 B3
Chebsey Cl ST2 ....58 B2
Chebsey Dr ST16 ....155 A3
Checkley Dr ST8 ....16 B1
Checkley Gr 6 ST3 ....73 B3
Checkley La CW3 ....52 C1
Checkley Rd ST5 ....40 B1
Chedale Rd ST10 ....61 B1
Cheddar Dr ST5 ....54 C1
Cheddleton Craft Ctr*
ST13 ....45 A3
Cheddleton Flint Mill Mus*
ST13 ....45 B3
Cheddleton Heath Rd
ST13 ....45 C4
Cheddleton Park Ave
ST13 ....45 B3
Cheddleton Rd ST13 ....30 C2
Cheddleton Sta ST13 ....45 C3
Cheedale Cl DE15 ....167 A3
Chelford Cl ST19 ....193 A1
Chell Cl ST19 ....207 C4
Chell Gr ST5 ....56 A4
Chell Green Ave ST6 ..42 A3
Chell Green Ct ST6 ....42 A3
Chell Heath Rd ST6 ....42 B2
Chell Rd ST16 ....155 B2
Chell St ST1 ....57 B3
Chelmarsh Ave WV3 ..265 A4
Chelmorton Dr ST3 ....73 C1
Chelmsford Dr ST2 ....58 B1
Chelmsford Rd ST5 ....56 B3
Chelsea Cl ST8 ....16 B1
Chelsea Dr B74 ....257 C2
Chelsea Way
Kingswinford DY6 ....275 B3
Stafford ST16 ....155 B1

Chelson St ST3 ....283 C3
Chelston Dr WV6 ......255 C2
Cheltenham Ave ST10 ...76 C3
Cheltenham Dr
  Kingswinford DY6 ......275 A3
  Stafford ST17 ....175 B4
Cheltenham Gr
  Hanley ST1 ....57 C3
  Newcastle-u-l ST5 ....54 C1
Chelwood St ST1 ....282 A4
Chemical La ST6 ....41 B1
Chenet Way **8** WS11 ..209 C1
Chepstow Cl Biddulph ST8 16 B1
  Perton WV6 ....254 C2
Chepstow Dr ST17 ......175 B4
Chepstow Rd
  Walsall WS3 ....242 C1
  Wolv WV10 ....240 B3
Chepstow Way WS3 ....242 C1
Chequer St WV3 ....266 A3
Chequerfield Dr WV4 ..266 A3
Chequers Ave WV5 .....265 A1
Chequers Ct WS11 .....228 A3
Chequers The **3** WS13 ..231 B4
Cheriton Gn ST2 ....58 B1
Cheriton Gr WV6 ....254 C2
Cherrington Dr WS6 ...226 C2
Cherrington Gdns WV6 255 A1
Cherry Bank WS12 .....210 B3
Cherry Cl
  Blythe Bridge ST11 ....106 C4
  Burntwood WS7 ....228 C3
  Newcastle-u-l ST5 ......40 B1
Cherry Ct DE14 ....184 C4
Cherry Gn DY1 ....271 C2
Cherry Gr Fenton ST3 ...72 C2
  Stourbridge DY8 ....279 C2
Cherry Hill CW3 ....68 C3
Cherry Hill Ave ST3 .....74 A1
Cherry Hill La ST5 ......55 C1
Cherry La Cheadle ST10 ..77 A1
  Congleton CW12 ....16 C4
  Gayton ST21 ....138 C3
  Himley DY3 ....270 B2
  Seighford ST18 ....135 B2
Cherry Leys DE15 ......167 C4
Cherry Orch
  Lichfield WS14 ....231 B4
  Newcastle-u-l ST5 .....284 B3
  Stone ST15 ....120 B4
Cherry St
  Stourbridge DY8 ....279 C2
  Tamworth B79 ....250 A3
Cherry Tree Ave ST7 ....25 A3
Cherry Tree Cl
  Eccleshall ST21 ....133 C4
  Stone ST15 ....119 C3
  Swadlincote DE11 .....186 C3
  Trentham ST4 ....88 A3
Cherry Tree Gdns WV8 .239 A2
Cherry Tree La
  Biddulph ST8 ....17 A1
  Codsall WV8 ....239 A2
  Woore CW3 ....67 B1
Cherry Tree Rd
  Audley ST7 ....39 C1
  Huntington WS12 ......209 B4
  Kingswinford DY6 ......275 C4
  Newcastle-u-l ST5 ......40 C1
  Norton Canes WS11 ...228 A3
  Rugeley WS15 ....196 C3
Cherry Tree Wlk B79 ...250 A4
Cherry Trees Sch WV5 .269 C3
Cherry Way TF9 ....97 B1
Cherrybrook Dr ST19 ..193 A1
Cherryl Ho B74 ....257 C2
Cherrytree Cres ST18 ..135 A2
Cherrytree Rd DE15 ...185 C4
Cherrywood Cl **1** ST17 .175 B3
Cherrywood Gr ST3 .....89 C3
Cherrywood Rd B74 ...256 C1
Cherrywood Way ST7 ..257 B2
Chertsey Pl ST1 ....57 B4
Chervil Cl ST3 ....90 A3
Cherwell B77 ....250 C1
Cherwell Dr WS8 ......228 B1
Chesham Gr ST3 ....90 A2
Chesham Rd ST16 .....155 C3
Cheshire Dr DY8 ....279 B4
Cheshire Dr ST19 .....223 B3
Cheshire Gdns TF9 ......97 B1
Cheshire Gr WV6 ......254 C2
Cheshire St TF9 ....97 B1
Cheslyn Dr WS6 ....226 B1
Cheslyn Hay High Sch
  WS6 ....226 B2
Cheslyn Hay Prim Sch
  WS6 ....226 B2
Chessington Cres ST4 ..88 B4
Chestall Rd WS15 .....211 C3
Chester Ave WV6 ......255 C4
Chester Cl
  Cannock WS11 ....210 A1
  Lichfield WS13 ....214 B2
  Talke ST7 ....40 C4
Chester Cres ST5 ......71 A3
Chester Rd Aldridge B74 .256 C2
  Audley ST7 ....39 B1
  Brownhills WS9 ....245 B2
  Chetwynd TF10 ....168 B4
  Enville DY7 ....273 C1
  Kinver DY7 ....277 C4
  Talke ST7 ....40 B4
  Whittington WS14 .....232 B2
Chester Rd N WS8 .....228 B1
Chesterfield Ave DE11 .186 C3
Chesterfield Ct WS9 ..244 C2
Chesterfield Rd WS14 .231 A3

Chesterton High Sch
  ST5 ....55 C4
Chesterton Prim Sch
  ST5 ....55 C4
Chesterton Rd
  Burton u T DE14 ....166 B4
  Pattingham WV6 ....253 A1
Chesterton Stad ST5 ....55 B3
Chesterton Way B79 ...250 A4
Chesterwood WS9 .....256 C1
Chesterwood Rd ST6 ...42 A2
Chestnut Ave B79 .....250 A4
Chestnut Cl Aldridge B74 257 A2
  Armitage WS15 ....198 B2
  Cannock WS11 ....210 B1
  Codsall WV8 ....238 C1
  Gnosall ST20 ....171 B4
  Seighford ST18 ....154 C1
  Stourbridge DY8 ......279 B1
  Upper Tean ST10 ....92 C2
Chestnut Cres ST11 .....91 A3
Chestnut Ct
  Millmeece ST21 ....102 B1
  Rugeley WS15 ....196 C4
  Stone ST15 ....104 C1
Chestnut Dr
  Cheslyn Hay WS6 .....226 B2
  Great Wyrley WS6 .....226 C2
  Millmeece ST15 ....118 C3
  Shenstone WS14 ......246 C3
  Stafford ST17 ....174 C3
  Walsall WS4 ....244 A1
  Wombourne WV5 ......270 A3
Chestnut Gr
  Kingswinford DY6 ......275 C3
  Kinver DY7 ....277 C3
  Newcastle-u-l ST5 ......40 C1
  Penkridge ST19 ....207 C4
  Stone ST15 ....104 C1
  Tamworth B77 ....250 B2
Chestnut La B79 ....218 C1
Chestnut Rd Ashley TF9 ..99 C3
  Burton u T DE15 ......185 C4
  Endon ST6 ....43 B4
  Market Drayton TF9 ...112 A4
Chestnut Way WV3 ....265 B4
Chestow Pl ST3 ....73 B3
Cheswardine Prim Sch
  TF9 ....130 A4
Cheswardine Rd ST5 ...56 A4
Cheswell Cl WV6 ......255 A1
Chetney Cl ST16 ....155 C2
Chetton Gn WV10 .....240 A2
Chetwode Cl TF9 ....83 B3
Chetwynd Ave
  Caverswall ST2 ....59 C4
  Norton-in-t-M ST6 ......42 C3
Chetwynd Cl
  Penkridge ST19 ....207 C4
  Rugeley WS15 ....196 C3
Chetwynd Ctr The ST17 .155 C1
Chetwynd Gdns WS11 .209 B2
Chetwynd Gr TF10 ....168 C2
Chetwynd Pk
  Chetwynd TF10 ....168 B4
Chetwynd Rd
  Edgmond TF10 ....168 B3
  Newcastle-u-l ST5 ......56 A3
  Newport TF10 ....168 C2
  Wolv WV2 ....266 A3
Chetwynd St
  Chell Heath ST6 ....42 B1
  Newcastle-u-l ST5 ......56 B3
Chevening Cl DY3 .....271 C4
Chevin The DE13 ......147 B3
Cheviot B77 ....251 B1
Cheviot Cl ST5 ....55 C2
Cheviot Ct B75 ....258 A2
Cheviot Dr Chell Heath ST6 42 B2
  Rugeley WS15 ....178 A2
Cheviot Rd WV2 ......266 C4
Cheviot Rise WS12 ....210 B3
Chichester Dr WS12 ..210 B1
Chichester Wlk ST1 ...282 C4
Chieveley Cl WS15 ....178 B1
Childerplay Rd ST8 ....27 B2
Chilgrove Cl ST1 ....57 C3
Chilgrove Gdns WV6 ..255 B3
Chillingham B77 ......261 B4
Chillington Cl WS6 ...226 C1
Chillington Dr
  Codsall WV8 ....238 C2
  Sedgley DY1 ....271 C2
Chillington Hall* WV8 .222 C1
Chillington Ho WV5 ...255 C3
Chillington La WV8 ...238 B3
Chiltern Cl
  Cheslyn Hay WS6 .....226 B1
  Chorlton CW2 ....37 A1
  Sedgley DY3 ....271 B4
Chiltern Ct B75 ....258 A2
Chiltern La ST21 ......133 C3
Chiltern Pl ST5 ....55 C2
Chiltern Rd
  Swadlincote DE11 .....186 C2
  Tamworth B77 ....251 B1
Chilton St ST3 ....72 C1
Chilwell Ave ST18 ....177 C4
Chilworth Gr ST3 ......72 C1
China St ST4 ....72 C3
Chingford Cl DY8 .....275 B2
Chivelstone Gr ST4 ....88 B3
Cholerton Cl ST4 ......72 C3
Chorley Ave ST6 ....42 A3
Chorley Rd WS7 ......212 A1

Chorley St ST13 ....30 C3
Chorlton La CW2 ....37 A1
Chorlton Rd ST1 ....57 B3
Chorlton Terr ST14 ....111 B1
Christ Church CE Inf Sch
  WV6 ....255 A2
Christ Church CE Jun Sch
  WV6 ....255 A2
Christ Church CE Mid Sch
  ST15 ....105 A1
Christ Church CE Prim Sch
  WS13 ....230 C4
Christ Church Gdns
  WS13 ....230 C4
Christ Church Inf Sch
  DE14 ....166 B1
Christ Church La TF9 ..112 A4
Christchurch CE Prim Sch
  ST4 ....72 C3
Christchurch La WS13 .230 C4
Christchurch St ST4 ....72 C3
Christchurch Way WS15 .105 A1
Christie Ave ST16 .....155 B2
Christie Pl ST3 ....73 C3
Christine St ST2 ....58 A2
Christopher Rd WV2 ..266 C4
Christopher Sq ST4 ....72 C3
Christopher Terr WS17 .156 A1
Christopher Wlk WS13 .214 A2
Chub B77 ....261 B4
Chubb Way ST4 ....71 C2
Chumleigh Gr ST6 ......42 A1
Church Ave Grindon ST13 34 A1
  Norton-in-t-M ST6 .....43 A1
Church Bank Audley ST7 .39 B1
  Keele ST5 ....69 C4
  Oakamoor ST10 ....78 A3
  Waterhouses ST10 .....63 C4
Church Cl Alrewas WS13 .215 B4
  Biddulph ST8 ....27 B3
  Blythe Bridge ST13 ....89 C3
  Burton u T DE15 ......167 A2
  Coppenhall ST18 ......192 C4
  Drayton Bassett B78 ..260 C3
  Gnosall ST20 ....171 C3
  Haughton ST18 ....172 C3
  Kingstone ST14 ....141 B4
  Marchington ST14 ....127 C1
  Ranton ST18 ....153 B3
  Rugeley WS15 ....196 A4
  Shenstone WS14 ......247 A3
  4 Stone ST15 ....120 A4
  Wood End CV9 ....262 B1
Church Cres WV11 ....241 C2
Church Croft ST14 ....125 B4
Church Dr B78 ....249 A4
Church Eaton Prim Sch
  ST20 ....190 A4
Church Eaton Rd TF10 .188 C3
Church Farm TF9 .....100 B3
Church Farm Cl ST19 .192 C1
Church Fields Keele ST5 .69 C4
  Norton in Hales TF9 ...82 B1
Church Gdns ST3 .....283 C4
Church Gr ST21 ....133 B4
Church Hill
  Cannock WS12 ....210 B1
  Codsall WV8 ....238 C3
  Kinver DY7 ....278 A1
  Longdon WS15 ....213 A4
  Wolv WV4 ....265 C2
Church Hill Dr WV6 ...255 C3
Church Hill Rd WV6 ...255 B3
Church Hill St DE15 ...167 A2
Church Hollow B79 ...217 B3
Church La
  Abbots Bromley WS15 .160 C3
  Albrighton WV7 ......237 A1
  Alrewas WS13 ....215 C4
  Armitage WS15 ....197 C3
  Barton-u-N DE13 .....183 B1
  Betley CW3 ....53 B3
  Biddulph ST8 ....17 B1
  Bobbington DY7 ....268 A1
  Bradley ST18 ....173 B1
  Brewood WV9 ....224 A1
  Burntwood WS7 ......229 B2
  Cheslyn Hay WS11 ....225 C4
  Chilcote DE12 ....219 C2
  Codsall WV8 ....238 C2
  Draycott in T M ST11 ..91 C3
  Eccleshall ST21 ....116 A3
  Edingale B79 ....217 B3
  Ellastone DE6 ....80 A2
  Endon ST9 ....43 C4
  Gayton ST18 ....138 B3
  Gnosall TF10 ....188 B4
  Hanbury DE13 ....145 A2
  Hill Ridware WS15 ....198 A4
  Hixon ST18 ....158 B4
  Ipstones ST10 ....46 C1
  King's Bromley DE13 ..199 B3
  Kingstone ST14 ....141 B4
  Lawton-gate ST7 ......25 B2
  Leek ST13 ....30 C3
  Marchington ST14 ....127 C1
  Mayfield DE6 ....81 B3
  Middleton B78 ....260 B1
  Mow Cop ST7 ....25 B4
  Newcastle-u-l, Knutton ST5 55 C1
  Newcastle-u-l, Wolstanton
   ST5 ....56 B2
  Newton Solney DE15 ..167 B4
  Rocester ST14 ....96 A2
  Roston DE6 ....96 A4
  Rugeley WS15 ....178 B1

Church La continued
  Scholar Green ST7 .....25 B4
  Seighford ST18 ....154 C1
  Seisdon WV5 ....264 A1
  Shenstone WS9 ....245 C2
  Shuttington B79 ......251 C4
  Stafford ST16 ....155 C2
  Standon ST21 ....102 A3
  Stone ST15 ....105 B2
  Tamworth B79 ....250 A3
  Thorpe DE6 ....51 B1
  Trentham ST4 ....71 C1
  Upper Tean ST10 .....109 A4
  Uttoxeter ST14 ....125 B4
  Waterhouses ST10 .....63 C4
  Wheaton Aston ST19 ..206 A3
Church Lawton Prim Sch
  ST7 ....25 A3
Church Mdw
  Ipstones ST10 ....46 C1
  Norton in Hales TF9 ...82 B1
Church Mews DE65 ...146 B4
Church Moat Way WS3 .243 A1
Church of the Ascension
  Prim Sch DY6 ....275 B4
Church Plantation 70 A4
Church Rd Alrewas DE13 200 C2
  Ashley TF9 ....100 B3
  Biddulph ST8 ....27 B4
  Branston DE14 ....184 C4
  Brewood WV9 ....223 B3
  Brownhills, Catshill WS8 .244 C4
  Burntwood WS7 ......229 B4
  Burton u T DE13 ......147 C1
  Codsall WV8 ....238 C2
  Egginton DE65 ....148 A2
  Elford B79 ....216 B1
  Endon ST6 ....43 A4
  Hixon ST18 ....139 B1
  Huntington WS11 .....209 A1
  Kingswinford DY8 ....275 C1
  Kinver DY7 ....277 C1
  Longton ST3 ....88 C2
  Norton Canes WS11 ...227 C2
  Penkridge ST19 ....192 C1
  Perton WV6 ....254 C2
  Rolleston DE13 ....147 A2
  Shareshill WV10 ......225 B1
  Shenstone WS14 .....246 C3
  Shenstone, Thornes WS9 .245 C2
  Snelston DE6 ....81 B2
  Swindon DY3 ....269 B1
  Tamworth B77 ....261 B2
  Walsall WS3 ....244 A4
  Wolv, Elston Hall WV10 .240 B1
  Wolv, Penn Fields WV3 .265 C4
  Wolv, Stockwell End WV6 .255 C3
  Wolv, Tettenhall Wood
   WV6 ....255 A2
  Wombourne WV5 .....270 A4
Church Sq ST6 ....56 C4
Church St Alstonefield DE6 .39 B1
  Audley ST7 ....39 B1
  Audley, Bignall End ST7 .40 A1
  Brownhills WS8 ....244 C4
  Burntwood WS7 ......228 C3
  Cannock WS11 ....209 C1
  Cannock, Bridgmoor WS11 226 B3
  Cannock, Chadsmoor
   WS11 ....210 A2
  Cheadle ST10 ....76 B2
  Claverley WV5 ....267 B4
  Clifton Campville B79 .218 C1
  Eccleshall ST21 ....133 B4
  Hartington SK17 ....24 B3
  Kidsgrove, Butt Lane ST7 .25 C1
  Kidsgrove, The Rookery ST7 26 A2
  Kingsley ST10 ....61 C1
  Leek ST13 ....30 C3
  Lichfield WS13, WS14 ..231 B4
  Longnor SK17 ....13 A1
  Market Drayton TF9 ...97 B1
  Mount Pleasant ST7 ...26 B3
  Netherseal DE12 .....219 C3
  Newcastle-u-l, ST5 ....284 B3
  Newcastle-u-l, Chesterton
   ST5 ....55 C4
  Newcastle-u-l, Silverdale
   ST5 ....55 A1
  Rugeley WS15 ....178 C1
  Sedgley DY3 ....271 B2
  Stoke-on-T ST4 ....72 A2
  Stone ST15 ....120 A4
  Tamworth B79 ....250 A3
  Tutbury DE13 ....146 B4
  Uttoxeter ST14 ....126 B4
  Whittington WS14 ....232 B3
Church Terr Burslem ST6 .23 A1
  Warslow SK17 ....23 A1
Church Vale WS11 ....227 C2
Church View
  Adbaston ST20 ....131 B2
  Aldridge WS9 ....256 A3
  Audley ST5 ....54 C2
  Brownhills WS9 ....244 C2
  Burton u T DE13 ......166 B4
  Clifton DE6 ....81 C3
  Millmeece ST21 ....102 A3
  Newcastle-u-l ST5 .....55 C1
  Rugeley WS15 ....197 A3
  Sedgley DY3 ....271 B2
  Tamworth B77 ....261 C4
Church View Gdns DY7 .278 A4
Church Way
  Longdon WS15 ....198 A1
  Walsall WS4 ....244 A1
Church Wlk Edingale B79 217 B3
  Newcastle-u-l ST5 .....55 C4

Church Wlk continued
  Wolv, Penn Fields WV3 .265 C4
  Wolv, Stockwell End WV6 .255 C3
Church Wlks TF9 ....82 B1
Churchbridge Pk WS11 .226 C3
Churchcroft Gdns
  WS15 ....178 C1
Churchfield Ave ST3 ...73 B1
Churchfield Cl
  Brewood WV9 ....224 B1
  Stafford ST17 ....156 B1
Churchfield Ct ST14 ...46 C1
Churchfield Rd ST21 ..133 B3
Churchfields DE13 ....182 A1
Churchfields CE Jun Sch
  WS15 ....196 C4
Churchfields Prim Sch
  ST5 ....55 C3
Churchill Ave
  Cheddleton ST13 ......45 B4
  Trentham ST4 ....87 C4
Churchill Cl
  Blythe Bridge ST11 ....90 C3
  Uttoxeter ST14 ....126 B4
Churchill Cres DE13 ..200 C1
Churchill Ct ST6 ....41 B4
Churchill Gdns DY3 ...271 B4
Churchill La ST17 .....281 A2
Churchill Rd Cheadle ST10 76 C2
  Shenstone WS14 .....247 A3
  Stone ST15 ....119 C3
Churchill Way
  Stafford ST17 ....174 C2
  Trentham ST4 ....87 C4
Churchside B79 ....217 B1
Churchside Way WS9 .245 A1
Churchward Dr DE13 .147 C1
Churchward Gr WV5 ..270 A4
Churchwell Ct WV5 ...270 A3
Churn Hill Rd WS9 ....256 C1
Churnet Cl
  Cheddleton ST13 ......45 A2
  Mayfield DE6 ....81 B4
Churnet Ct
  Burton u T DE14 ......166 C2
  Cheddleton ST13 ......45 B3
Churnet Gr WV6 ......254 C2
Churnet Rd Cheadle ST10 76 C1
  Forsbrook ST11 ....91 A4
Churnet Valley Rd ST10 .62 C1
Churnet Valley Rly*
  ST13 ....30 C2
Churnet Valley Rly Ctr*
  ST13 ....45 C2
Churnet Valley Wildlife
  Sanctuary* ST10 ....61 C2
Churnet View ST13 ....31 A4
Churnet View Mid Sch
  ST13 ....31 A4
Churnet View Rd ST10 .78 A4
Churnetside Bsns Pk
  ST13 ....45 B3
Churns Hill La DY3 ...270 A2
Churston Cl
  Newcastle-u-l ST5 .....71 A1
  Walsall WS3 ....243 A2
Churston Pl ST1 ....57 B4
Cicely Haughton Sch
  ST13 ....44 C3
Cinder Hill WV9 ....224 A2
Cinder Hill La ST7 .....25 C4
Cinder Rd
  Burntwood WS7 ......228 C4
  Sedgley DY3 ....271 A1
Cinderhill Ind Est ST3 .73 C2
Cinderhill La ST3 ......73 B2
Circular Rd WV7 ......220 C1
City Arc WS13 ....231 A4
City Bank ST8 ....16 B1
City General Hospl ST4 .71 C4
City La ST9 ....30 A2
City of Stoke-on-Trent Sixth
  Form Coll ST4 ....72 B4
City Rd ST4 ....72 B3
Cl The WS13 ....231 A4
Clamgoose La ST10 ....76 B4
Clanbrook Rd DY7 ....278 A4
Clandon Ave ST6 ......41 C2
Clanford Cl ST17 .....174 C3
Clanford La ST18 .....154 A3
Clanford Rd ST18 .....154 A4
Clanway St ST6 ....41 C3
Clap Gate Gr WV5 ....269 C2
Clap Gate Rd WV5 ....269 C2
Clare Ave
  Essington WV11 ......241 C1
  Newcastle-u-l ST5 .....56 A3
Clare Cres WV14 .....266 C2
Clare Rd ST16 ....155 B4
Clare St Kidsgrove ST7 .26 C2
  Mount Pleasant ST7 ...26 B3
  Stoke-on-T ST4 ....56 B1
Claregate Prim Sch
  WV6 ....255 C4
Claremont Cl
  Newcastle-u-l ST5 .....56 B4
  5 Stone ST15 ....120 A4
Claremont Cotts DY3 ..271 C4
Claremont Gr ST17 ...174 C4
Claremont Mews WV3 .266 A4
Claremont Rd
  Eccleshall ST21 ....133 C3
  Sedgley DY3 ....271 C4
  Tamworth B79 ....250 A4
  Wolv WV3 ....266 A4

Clarence Gdns B74 .....257 C1
Clarence Rd Longton ST3 283 B4
Sutton Coldfield B74 .....257 C2
Clarence St
Burton u T DE14 ......166 B1
Fenton ST4 ....72 C3
Newcastle-u-L ST5 .....284 D3
Newcastle-u-L, Porthill ST5 56 A3
Clarendon Dr ST17 ....174 A4
Clarendon Pl WS3 ....243 C2
Clarendon Rd
Sutton Coldfield B75 ....258 B2
Walsall WS4 ....244 B4
Clarendon St Fenton ST4 72 B3
Walsall WS3 ....243 A1
Claridge Rd ST4 ......56 C1
Clarion Way WS11 ....209 C3
Clark Rd WV3 ....255 C2
Clark St Stafford ST16 ..155 C2
Stourbridge DY8 ......279 C2
Clark's Cres WS15 ....161 A3
Clarke Ho WS3 ....243 A1
Clarke Ind Est DE14 ...166 C2
Clarke St ST1 ....282 A1
Clarke's Ave WS12 ...195 A1
Clarkes Cl ST14 ......111 A1
Claud St ST4 ....72 B2
Claverdon Cl WS8 .....245 A4
Claverdon Dr B74 ....257 A2
Claverhouse Rd DE15 .167 A1
Claverley CE Prim Sch
WV5 ....267 B4
Claverley Dr WV4 .....265 B3
Clay Gates Rd ST19 ...207 A1
Clay Hills ST6 ....41 B2
Clay La ST9 ....43 C4
Clay Pit La WS14 .....230 C2
Penkridge ST19 ....192 C1
Clay St E DE15 ....167 A1
Clayalders Bank ST21 .101 B3
Claydon Cres ST5 .....71 A1
Clayfield Gr ST3 ......73 B3
Clayfield Gr W ST3 ....73 B3
Claygate Rd WS12 ....210 C2
Clayhanger Cl ST5 ....56 A4
Clayhanger La WS8 ...244 B3
Clayhanger Rd WS8 ..244 C3
Clayhanger St ST6 ...56 C4
Claymills Rd DE13 ....148 A1
Claymore B77 ....261 C4
Clays La DE14 ....184 C4
Clayton Cl WV2 ....266 B4
Clayton High Sch ST5 .71 B2
Clayton La
Newcastle-u-L ST5 .....71 B2
Stoke-on-T ST4,ST5 ....71 A1
Clayton Rd ST5 ....71 B2
Clayton St ST3 ......283 C3
Claytonwood Rd ST4 ..71 C3
Cleadon Pl ST2 ....58 A3
Clear View DY6 ......275 A3
Clearwell Gdns DY1 ..271 C2
Cleasby B77 ....251 B1
Cleave Rd DE14 ......185 A4
Clee Hill Dr WV3 .....255 C1
Clee Hill Rd DY3 .....271 C3
Clee Rd DY10 ....280 A3
Clee View Mdw DY3 ..266 B3
Clee View Rd WV5 ...269 C3
Cleeton St WS12 .....210 B1
Cleeve B77 ....250 B2
Cleeve Dr B74 ....257 C2
Cleeve Rd WS3 ......242 C2
Cleeve Way WS3 ....242 C2
Clegg Rd WS7 ....229 C4
Clematis B77 ....250 C2
Clematis Ave ST11 ...90 C3
Clematis Cl ST18 ....135 A1
Clematis Cres DE15 ..186 A4
Clematis Dr WV9 ....239 C2
Clement Cl ST16 ....155 C2
Clement St ST6 ......42 A3
Clement Rd ST6 .....42 A3
Clent View Rd DY8 ...279 B1
Clerk Bank ST13 .....30 C3
Clermont Ave ST4 ....72 A1
Clevedon Ave ST17 ..175 C4
Cleveland Cl WV11 ...241 C1
Cleveland Ct DE15 ...167 A2
Cleveland Dr WS11 ..210 A2
Cleveland Rd Hanley ST1 282 B1
Newcastle-u-L ST5 ....55 C2
Cleveland St
🔟 Burslem ST6 ......56 C4
Stourbridge DY8 .....279 C2
Cleveland Wlk ST17 ..174 A4
Cleves Cres WS6 ....226 B1
Clewley Dr WV9 .....240 A2
Clewley Rd DE14 ....184 C4
Clewlow Pl ST3 .....283 D5
Clewlows Bank ST9 ..43 C2
Clews St ST6 ....56 C4
Clews Wlk ST5 ....56 B3
Cley Gr ST5 ....71 A1
Cliff Hall La B78 ....261 A4
Cliff Rd ST18 ....158 C1
Cliff St ST6 ....42 B1
Cliff Vale Cl ST4 .....56 C1
Cliff Vale Pl ST4 .....56 C1
Cliffdon Ho DE65 ....146 B4
Cliffe Pl ST6 ....42 A4
Clifford Ave ST6 .....42 C3

Clifford Cl B77 ....250 C2
Clifford Rd TF9 ......112 A4
Clifford St Hanley ST1 .282 C1
Tamworth B77 ....250 C2
Cliffs La TF10,ST20 ...150 C1
Clifton Ave Aldridge WS9 245 B1
Brownhills WS8 ......244 B4
Cannock WS11 ......226 B4
Tamworth B77 ....250 A4
Clifton CE Prim Sch DE6 81 C3
Clifton Cl Fenton ST4 ..72 C3
Stafford ST16 ....156 A2
Swadlincote DE11 ....186 C1
Clifton Dr ST16 ......156 A2
Clifton Gdns WV8 ...239 B2
Clifton La B79 ....235 A2
Clifton Rd Clifton DE6 .81 C3
Cookley DY10 ....280 B2
Netherseal DE12 .....219 B3
Wolv WV4 ....255 B3
Clifton St Fenton ST4 ..72 C1
Newcastle-u-L ST5 ....56 B2
Sedgley WV14 ......266 C1
Stourbridge DY8 .....279 C2
Clifton Way DE15 ....167 A1
Clinton Cres WS7 ...229 A4
Clinton Gdns 🔟 ST15 120 A4
Clinton Sq ST1 ......282 A2
Clive Ave ST2 ....43 A2
Clive Cl B75 ....258 B1
Clive Ho DE15 ......167 B2
Clive Rd Burntwood WS7 229 A4
Market Drayton TF9 ...97 B1
Newcastle-u-L ST5 ....56 B3
Pattingham WV6 .....263 B4
Clive St ST6 ....41 C2
Cliveden Ave WS9 ...245 A1
Cliveden Coppice B74 257 C1
Cliveden Pl ST3 .....283 C2
Cliveden Rd ST2 .....58 A3
Clockmill Ave WS3 ..243 C2
Clockmill Pl WS3 ...243 C2
Clockmill Rd WS3 ...243 C2
Cloister Wlk Bucknall ST2 58 A3
Whittington WS14 ...232 C3
Cloisters The
Burton u T DE15 .....166 C1
Gnosall ST20 ....171 C3
Close Bank DE13 ....146 B3
Close Jun Sch The ST4 71 C4
Close La ST7 ....26 B4
Close The Endon ST9 ..43 C4
Enville WV5 ....273 B1
Madeley CW3 ....68 C4
Meir ST3 ....74 A3
Sedgley DY3 ....271 B2
Stafford, Moss Pit ST17 174 C3
Stafford, Rowley Park
ST16 ....155 B1
Swindon DY3 ....269 C1
Tutbury DE13 ....146 A3
Cloud The★ CW12 ....7 A2
Cloud View CW12 .....6 A1
Clough Hall Dr ST7 ..40 C3
Clough Hall Rd ST7 ..40 C4
Clough Hall Tech Sch
ST7 ....25 C1
Clough La ST9 ....59 A1
Clough St ST1 ......282 A2
Clovelly Wlk 🔟 ST6 ..56 C4
Clover Heath WV5 ...267 B4
Clover La DY6 ......275 A4
Clover Mdws WS12 ..210 B1
Clover Rd ST5 ....56 B3
Clover Ridge WS6 ...226 B2
Cloverdale Perton WV6 254 B2
🔟 Stafford ST17 .....175 B4
Cloverdale Pl ST3 ....73 C2
Cloverdale Rd ST5 ...56 A2
Clowes St ST2 ....58 A2
Club Cotts WV10 ....240 B3
Club La WV10 ....240 B3
Club Row DY3 ......271 C3
Club St ST4 ....72 A3
Clumber Ave ST5 ....71 B3
Clumber Gr ST5 .....71 B3
Cluny Pl ST2 ....58 A3
Clyde Ave ST8 ......16 C1
Clyde Pl ST5 ....71 A2
Clyde Rd ST6 ....57 A4
Clyde St ST1 ....282 A1
Clyde Wlk ST1 ......282 A2
Clydesdale Rd WS8 ..244 C3
Clynes Way ST3 ....74 A2
Co-operative La ST7 ..54 B4
Co-operative St ST16 155 B3
Coach House La WS15 178 C2
Coach House Rise B77 261 C4
Coachman's Wlk WS15 178 C2
Coal Haulage Rd WS11 227 B4
Coalbourn La DY8 ...279 C4
Coalburnhill Glassworks★
DY8 ....279 C4
Coalmeadow Cl WS3 242 C2
Coalpit Hill ST7 ......40 B4
Coalpit La WS15 .....197 A3
Coalpitford La ST13 ..44 C2
Coalport Cl ST10 ....76 B1
Coalport Dr ST15 ...119 C3
Coalville Pl ST3 .....74 A4
Coalway Ave WV3 ...266 A3
Coalway Gdns WV3 ..265 B4
Coalway Rd
Rugeley WS15 ....197 A3
Walsall WS3 ....243 A1
Coates Pl ST6 ....42 A4
Coatsgate Wlk WV8 .239 C1

Cob Moor Rd ST7 ....26 A2
Cobbett Rd WS7 ....228 B4
Cobbles The ST19 ...205 B3
Cobden Cl WS12 ....210 B4
Cobden Ho WV2 ....266 B4
Cobden St Longton ST3 283 B1
Newcastle-u-L ST5 ....56 B3
Stourbridge DY8 .....279 C3
Cobham Cl ST15 ....118 C3
Cobham Pl 🔟 ST3 ...90 A4
Cobia B77 ....261 B4
Cobridge Rd ST1 ....57 A3
Coburn Dr B75 ......258 B1
Cock Hill DE6 ....81 C3
Cock La ST14 ....193 C4
Cocketts Nook WS15 178 B2
Cocknage Rd Longton ST3 73 A1
Cocks La Norton-in-t-M ST9 43 B2
Norton-in-t-M ST9 .....43 B2
Cockshutts La WV2 ..266 A4
Cocksparrow La WS12,
WS19 ....209 A3
Cockspur St B78 ....262 C4
Cockster Brook La ST3 72 C2
Cockster Rd ST3 .....72 C2
Cockstubbles ST14 ..126 A4
Cockstubble Rd ST3 ..74 C1
Cocton Cl WV6 .....254 C3
Codsall Com High Sch
WV8 ....239 A4
Codsall Ho WV8 ....238 C2
Codsall L Ctr WV8 ...239 A2
Codsall Mid Sch WV8 239 A2
Codsall Rd Codsall WV8 239 B1
Wolv WV6 ....255 A4
Codsall Sta WV8 ....238 C2
Coghlan Rd ST17 ....174 A4
Colbourne Rd B78 ...250 A1
Colbrook B77 ....250 B1
Colclough Ave ST5 ..56 A4
Colclough La ST6 ...41 B4
Colclough Rd ST3 ...74 C1
Cold Meece Ind Est
ST15 ....118 A3
Cold Norton Cotts ST15 119 B3
Coldridge Cl WV8 ..239 C1
Coldstream Dr DE6 ..275 C2
Cole Dr ST16 ....155 B1
Cole St ST8 ....27 B4
Coleford Cl DY8 ....275 B1
Colehill ST9 ....250 A3
Coleman St WV6 ...255 C2
Colenso Way ST5 ...56 A4
Coleridge Cl
Market Drayton TF9 ..112 A4
Tamworth B79 ....250 A3
Walsall WS3 ....244 A3
Coleridge Ct DE14 ..166 B3
Coleridge Dr
Cheadle ST10 ....76 B1
Perton WV6 ....254 C2
Stafford ST17 ....174 B4
Coleridge Rd ST3 ...73 A1
Coleridge Rise ST3 ..271 A2
Colesden Wlk WV4 ..265 B3
Coleshill Rd B78 ....261 A4
Coleshill St B78 ....261 A4
Coley Gr ST18 ......177 B4
Coley La ST18 ......158 B1
Colin Cres ST3 ......74 A1
Colindene Gr ST4 ...72 A3
Colinwood Cl WS6 ..226 B1
Collard Ave ST5 ....56 A2
College Cl CW3 .....68 C4
College St WV6 .....255 B2
College Farm Cl WV6 253 B2
College Fields WS15 118 C3
College La B79 .....250 A3
College Rd Denstone ST14 95 B3
Hanley ST5,ST4 .....57 B1
Stoke-on-T ST1 .....282 B1
College View WV6 ..255 B2
Collet Rd WV6 ......254 C2
Collets Brook B75 ..259 A1
Collett B77 ....251 A1
Colley Rd ST6 ......41 C3
Collier Cl Brownhills WS8 244 B4
Cheslyn Hay WS6 ...226 B1
Colliery Dr WS3 ....242 C2
Colliery Rd WS15 ...196 C2
Collin Rd ST4 ....71 C3
Collin St ST14 ......126 A4
Collinbourne Cl ST4 ..88 A3
Collindale Ct DY6 ...270 B1
Collingwood Gr ST3 ..74 A1
Collingwood Jun & Inf Schs
WV10 ....240 C1
Collingwood Rd WV10 240 C1
Collins Hill WS13 ...214 A1
Collins Rd WS8 ....245 A3
Collinson Rd
Barton-u-N DE13 ....183 B1
Tunstall ST6 ....41 B4
Collis Ave ST4 ......56 B1
Collis Cl DY8 ....279 C4
Colne Mount ST4 ...126 A4
Colonnade The 🔟 ST16 155 C2
Colshaw Rd DY8 ...279 C2
Coltman Cl WS14 ...231 C4
Colton Hills Com Sch
WV4 ....266 A4
Colton Rd WS15 ....178 C2
Coltsfoot View WS6 .226 C1
Columbian Cres WS7 228 C4
Columbian Way ST1 .209 C2
Columbine Wlk 🔟 ST6 41 B2
Colville Cl DE12 ....218 B4

Colville St ST4 ......72 C3
Colwall Rd DY3 .....271 B2
Colwich CE Prim Sch
ST17 ....177 C4
Colwich Cres ST16 ..156 C2
Colwyn Dr ST8 .....27 B3
Combe Dr ST3 ......90 A3
Comber Gr DY7 ....278 A2
Comber Rd DY7 ....277 C2
Comberford La B79 .234 A3
Comberford Rd B79 .250 A4
Combermere TF9 ...97 B1
Combine Cl B75 ....258 B2
Comfrey Cl ST3 .....90 A3
Commerce Dr ST19 .207 C4
Commerce St ST3 ..283 C3
Commercial Rd ST1 .282 C2
Commercial St ST6 ..57 A4
Common Barn La DY10 280 B3
Common La
Acton Trussell ST17 ..194 A4
Alrewas WS13 ......215 B3
Betley CW3 ....52 C3
Cannock ST11 ......210 A2
Kingstone ST14 ....124 B1
Meir ST3 ....89 C2
Stone ST15 ....119 C3
Tamworth B79 ......250 C3
Waterhouses ST10 ...64 C4
Whitmore ST5 ....85 B3
Whittington WS14 ..232 B2
Common Rd
Stafford ST16 ......155 C4
Wombourne WV5 ...270 A3
Common Road Ind Est
ST16 ....155 C4
Common Side WS8 ..245 A3
Common The ST10 ..75 B2
Common View
Burntwood WS7 .....212 A1
Cannock WS12 .....210 A1
Common Wlk WS12 .209 B3
Commonside
Longdon WS15 .....212 A2
Walsall WS3 ....244 A1
Commonside Cl ST16 155 B3
Community Dr ST6 ..42 B1
Como Pl ST5 ....70 C3
Compa The DY7 ....278 A2
Compton ST13 .....30 C3
Compton Cl Kinver DY7 277 C2
Stafford ST17 ....156 A1
Compton Ct ST4 ...257 C2
Compton Dr DY6 ...275 C3
Compton Flats ST13 .30 C3
Compton Gdns DY7 .277 C2
Compton Gr DY6 ...275 B3
Compton Hill Dr WV3 255 B1
Compton Mews ST13 30 C3
Compton Park Recn Ctr
WV6 ....255 C2
Compton Rd Kinver DY7 277 B2
Stafford ST17 ....156 B1
Tamworth B79 ......249 C4
Wolv WV3 ....255 C1
Compton Rd W WV3 255 B1
Compton St ST1 ....282 A2
Comptons The TF9 ..130 A3
Condlyffe Rd ST13 ..30 C2
Condor Gr WS12 ...210 B1
Conduit Rd WS11 ..228 A2
Conduit St WS13 ...231 C4
Conewood Pl ST3 ...72 C1
Coney Gr ST3 ....74 A2
Coneybere Gdns ST19 223 B4
Coneygreave Cl ST10 76 B1
Coneygreave La ST5 .85 B3
Conford Cl ST2 .....57 C1
Congleton Edge Rd
CW12 ....16 A3
Congleton Rd
Biddulph ST8 ....16 B1
Kidsgrove ST7 ......25 B1
Mow Cop ST7 ......15 C1
Talke ST7 ....40 B4
Congleton Rd N ST7 .25 C3
Congleton Rd S ST7 .25 B2
Congleton Sta CW12 ..6 A1
Congreve Cl ST17 ..175 C4
Congreve Rd ST3 ...72 C1
Conifer Cl WS12 ...210 A4
Conifer Gr Longton ST3 .72 C1
Stafford ST17 ......174 A4
Coniston B77 ....262 A4
Coniston Cl ST15 ...120 B4
Coniston Dr Cheadle ST10 76 C2
Kingswinford DY6 ...275 A4
Coniston Gr ST5 ....71 A2
Coniston Ho ST16 ..155 C0
Coniston Pl ST4 ....87 C4
Coniston Rd
Aldridge B74 ....256 C2
Cannock WS11 .....209 C1
Coniston Way WS11 209 C1
Connaught Dr WV5 .265 A1
Connaught St ST6 ..41 B1
Conners La TF10 ...168 A2
Conrad Cl ST3 .....73 B2
Consall Gr ST4 .....88 B3
Consall La ST9 .....60 B3
Consall Nature Pk★ ST9 61 A3
Consall Sta ST9 ....61 A3
Consett Rd ST3 ....88 C4
Consort St ST4 .....72 A4
Constable Ave ST5 ..55 C3
Constable Cl ST3 ...90 A4
Constance Ave ST4 ..88 C4
Convent Cl

Burton u T DE15 ....185 C4
Cannock WS11 .....226 B4
Colwich ST18 ......177 C4
Stoke-on-T ST4 .....72 C4
Convent Ct ST4 .....72 A4
Convent La ST15 ...105 A2
Conway Cl
Burton u T DE13 ....166 B4
Kingswinford DY6 ..275 C2
Conway Gr ST10 ...76 C1
Conway Rd Biddulph ST8 27 B3
Cannock WS11 .....226 A4
Perton WV6 ....254 C2
Stafford ST16 ......155 A2
Conway St ST4 .....72 B4
Conygree La DE6 ...81 B4
Cook Cl WV6 ....254 C2
Cook Rd WS3 ......243 B1
Cook's Hollow ST13 .47 A4
Cook's La ST13 ....32 C1
Cooke Cl ST19 .....192 C1
Cookley La DY7 ....278 A1
Cookley Sebright Fst Sch
DY10 ....280 A3
Cooknell Dr ST10 ..275 C1
Cookson Ave ST3 ...73 B1
Coombe Croft WV9 .240 A2
Coombe Park Rd ST15 119 C3
Coombes Valley Nature
Reserve★ ST10 .....46 B3
Coombesdale ST5 ...85 C1
Cooper & Jordan CE Prim
Sch WS9 ....256 B2
Cooper Ave ST5 ....56 C1
Cooper Cl ST15 ....120 B4
Cooper Perry Prim Sch
ST18 ....154 C4
Cooper St Hanley ST1 .282 A1
Newcastle-u-L ST5 ...55 C3
Wolv WV2 ....266 C3
Cooper's Bank Rd DY5 271 B1
Cooper's Sq DE14 ..166 B1
Coopers Cl ST3 .....30 B3
Coopers Way ST8 ..27 A4
Cope St Norton-in-t-M ST2 43 A1
Stafford ST15 ......155 C2
Cope's Dr B79 .....250 A4
Copeland Ave
Newcastle-u-L ST5 ...71 A2
Tittensor ST12 ......88 A1
Copeland Cl ST10 ..76 B1
Copeland Dr ST15 ..120 B3
Copeland St ST4 ...72 A4
Copelands The DY7 .278 A2
Copes Ave ST6 .....41 C2
Copes Way ST14 ...111 A4
Copley La WV6 ....253 A1
Coplow Ave ST10 ..92 B3
Coplow La DE65 ...129 B3
Copp La ST6 ....41 B1
Copper Beech Dr
Kingswinford DY6 ..270 B1
Wombourne WV5 ..270 A3
Copper Glade ST16 .156 A2
Copperas Rd DE11 .186 B3
Copperfields WS14 .231 B4
Copperhill Rd CW12 .16 A4
Copperkins Rd WS12 210 C2
Coppermill Cl WS12 209 C4
Coppice Ave ST5 ...55 C1
Coppice Brook ST17 176 B2
Coppice Cl Biddulph ST8 27 B4
Burntwood WS7 ....228 B4
Cheslyn Hay WS6 ..226 B1
Sedgley DY3 ....271 B4
Stone ST15 ....105 A1
Wolv WV11 ....242 A1
Coppice Cres WS8 ..244 B4
Coppice Ct WS11 ..226 A4
Coppice Dr
Newport TF10 ......168 C3
Polesworth B78 ....262 C4
Coppice Farm Way
WV11 ....242 A1
Coppice Gdns WS15 105 A1
Coppice Gr
Lichfield WS14 .....231 C4
Meir ST3 ....74 A2
Coppice Ho ST7 ....40 B4
Coppice La Aldridge WS9 244 C1
Brownhills WS8 ....244 B4
Burntwood WS7,WS14 230 A2
Cheslyn Hay WS6 ..226 B2
Clifton Campville B79 218 C3
Middleton B75,B78 .259 B1
Wolv WV6 ....255 A3
Coppice Rd
Brownhills WS8,WS9 244 C2
Rugeley WS15 .....196 C3
Stone ST15 ....105 A1
Talke ST7 ....40 B4
Wolv WV3 ....265 B4
Coppice Sch B75 ..258 A1
Coppice Side The ST5 284 B1
Coppice Side WS8 .244 B4
Coppice Side Ind Est
WS8 ....244 B4
Coppice The
Cannock WS12 ....210 C1
Hagley DY8 ....281 C3
Hanley ST6 ....57 B4
Market Drayton TF9 .97 A1
Coppice View ST6 ..56 A2
Coppins The 🔟 Leek ST13 30 B3
🔟 Stafford ST17 ...175 B4
Copplestone Gr ST3 .73 C3
Coppull Pl ST6 ....42 A4

Coppy Hall Gr WS9 245 A1
Coppy Nook La WS7 229 B3
Copse Cres WS3 244 A2
Copse Dr WS15 198 A2
Copse The B74 257 C1
Copsy Dale ST21 115 B3
Copthorne Ave WS7 228 C2
Copthorne Rd WV3 266 A4
Coracle Gr ST8 27 C3
Coral Gr ST4 88 A4
Corbet Ct TF9 97 B1
Corbett Ho 9 DY8 279 C4
Corbett Hospl DY8 279 C4
Corbett Prim Sch DY7 268 A1
Corbett Wlk 12 ST6 41 B2
Corbin Rd B78 262 C3
Corby Pl ST3 283 A3
Corden Ave DE13 166 C4
Cordy La WV7 237 A4
Corfe Cl WV6 254 C2
Corfe Gn ST3 73 B3
Corfield Pl ST6 42 B3
Corfton Dr WV6 255 B2
Corina Ct ST3 73 B2
Corina Way ST3 73 B2
Corinth Way 14 ST6 41 B2
Cormie Cl ST6 42 A3
Corncrake Rd DY1,DY3 271 C2
Cornel B77 250 C2
Cornelious St 3 ST3 74 A1
Cornes St ST1 57 B1
Corneville Rd ST2 58 B2
Cornfield WV8 239 C1
Cornfield Cl DY6 275 A4
Cornfield Dr WS14 231 C4
Cornfield Rd ST8 27 C4
Cornflower Cl WV10 241 A4
Cornflower Rd WS8 244 B3
Cornhill WS11 209 C3
Cornhill Cl ST5 40 B1
Cornhill Gdns ST13 30 C2
Cornhill Rd ST6 42 B3
Cornhill St 15 ST13 30 C3
Cornmell Lea TF10 168 C2
Cornmill Gr WV6 254 B2
Cornmill La DE13 146 C3
Cornovian Cl WV6 254 C3
Corns Gr WV5 269 C3
Cornwall Ave
Newcastle-u-L ST5 71 B2
Tamworth B78 250 A1
Cornwall Cl
Aldridge WS9 245 A1
3 Congleton CW12 6 A1
Kingswinford DY6 275 B4
Cornwall Ct WS15 196 B3
Cornwall Dr ST17 156 B1
Cornwall Rd
Burton u T DE15 185 C3
Cannock WS12 210 A3
Stourbridge DY8 279 B4
Wolv WV6 255 B2
Cornwall St ST3 283 C4
Cornwallis St ST4 72 A3
Cornwood Gr 10 ST3 89 C4
Coronation Ave
Biddulph ST8 27 A3
Longton ST3 283 B3
Tamworth B78 249 B1
Coronation Cotts DE13 184 A4
Coronation Cres
Kidsgrove ST7 25 C1
Rocester ST14 96 A2
Shuttington B79 251 C4
Coronation Rd
Brownhills WS9 245 A2
Newcastle-u-L ST5 284 C2
Stafford ST16 156 A3
Stoke-on-T, Hartshill ST4 71 C4
Walsall WS4 244 A1
Coronation St
Cheadle ST10 76 B2
Tamworth B79 250 A3
Tunstall ST6 41 C2
Corporation St
Newcastle-u-L ST5 284 B3
Stafford ST16 155 C2
Stoke-on-T ST4 72 A3
Tamworth B79 250 A3
Corran Rd ST17 174 B3
Correen B77 251 B1
Corrin Gr 4 DY6 275 B4
Corser St DY1 271 C1
Corsham Pl ST14 143 C4
Corsican Cl WS7 229 A4
Corsican Dr WS12 210 A4
Corsty La ST18 154 A2
Cort Dr WS7 229 A4
Corve Gdns WV6 255 C3
Corve View DY3 266 B1
Coseley St ST6 42 B1
Cosford Ct WV6 254 C3
Cosgrove Wlk WV8 239 C1
Cot La DY6,DY8 275 B3
Cote La DY7 273 C1
Cotehill Rd ST9 59 A2
Cotes La Millmeece ST21 102 C1
Swynnerton ST12 103 A1
Cotesheath St ST1 57 B1
Coton Ave ST16 156 A2
Coton Green Prec B79 249 C4
Coton Green Prim Sch B79 249 C4
Coton La Ranton ST18 153 C2
Seighford ST18 154 A2
Tamworth B79 249 C4
Coton Pk DE12 186 B1
Coton Rd DE12 202 C3
Coton Rise ST12 88 C1
Cotsdale Rd WV4 265 C2
Cotswold Ave
Great Wyrley WS6 226 C2
Newcastle-u-L ST5 55 C2
Cotswold Cl
Aldridge WS9 245 B1
Cannock WS12 210 A4
Cotswold Cres ST2 43 A1
Cotswold Ct
Sutton Coldfield B75 258 A2
Wolv WV3 266 A3
Cotswold Dr WV7 237 A3
Cotswold Gr WV12 242 A1
Cotswold Rd
Branston DE14 184 C4
Cannock WS12 210 A4
Wolv WV2 266 C4
Cottage Cl
Burntwood WS7 228 C3
Cannock WS12 210 B3
Meir ST3 73 C1
Cottage Ct WS7 228 C3
Cottage Farm Rd B77 261 B4
Cottage La Biddulph ST8 28 A4
Burntwood WS7 228 C3
Wolv WV10 240 B2
Cottage Mews WS9 256 C2
Cottage St DY6 275 B4
Cottage The TF10 168 C2
Cottage View WV8 239 A2
Cottage Wlk B77 261 C3
Cotterill Dr ST5 56 A4
Cotterill Gr ST6 56 C4
Cotters Hill Cl ST18 177 B4
Cottesmore Rd DE15 167 A1
Cotton Cl DE13 200 C2
Cotton Coll ST10 63 B1
Cotton Gr WS12 195 A1
Cotton La ST10 63 A1
Cotton Rd Tunstall ST6 41 B3
Wolv WV4 266 A3
Cotton Way WS7 211 C1
Cottonwood Dr ST7 26 C2
Cottonwood Gr ST3 283 C4
Cotts The ST3 74 A4
Cotwall End Ho DY3 271 B4
Cotwall End Nature Ctr* DY3 271 B3
Cotwall End Prim Sch DY3 271 B4
Cotwall End Rd DY3 271 A3
Coulson Cl WS7 211 B1
Coulter Gr WV6 254 B2
Coulter La WS7 229 C4
Coulthwaite Way WS15 196 C3
Council Hos
Chetwynd Aston TF10 187 A4
Church Leigh ST10 109 A2
Kingstone ST14 125 B1
Kingstone, The Blythe ST18 140 C3
Uttoxeter ST14 125 B4
Council Hos The ST21 116 A2
Country Park View ST7 55 A4
County Dr B78 250 A1
County La
Codsall WV7,WV8 237 C2
Stourbridge DY7 281 B4
County Rd ST16 155 C2
Coupe Dr ST3 74 A3
Court Cres DY6 275 B3
Court Dr WS14 246 C2
Court Farm La DE14 184 C4
Court La ST5 56 A2
Court No 1 ST3 73 C1
Court Par WS9 256 A3
Court Rd WV6 255 C2
Court Wlk CW3 53 A3
Courtland Mews ST16 155 C3
Courtland Rd DY6 275 C4
Courtlands The WV6 255 C2
Courtney Pl ST3 89 C4
Courtway Dr ST1 57 B4
Cousins St WV2 266 B4
Coven Cl WS3 244 A3
Coven Mill Cl WV9 224 B1
Coven Rd ST19 223 B2
Coventry Ct ST16 155 A3
Coverdale Cl ST3 90 A4
Coverley Pl ST4 71 C3
Covers La DY7 274 C1
Covert Cl ST18 158 A1
Covert Gdns ST7 40 B4
Covert La DY8 279 B1
Covert The Keele ST5 70 A4
Newcastle-u-L ST5 71 B1
Wolv WV8 239 C1
Covey Cl WS13 214 B1
Cow La Waterhouses ST10 63 C4
Wood End B78 261 C2
Cowallmoor La ST13 28 A3
Cowan Dr ST16 156 A2
Cowen St ST6 42 C3
Cowhill La WS13 200 C1
Cowhouse La ST10 109 A2
Cowley B77 250 C1
Cowley Cl
Penkridge ST19 207 C4
Stafford ST17 174 B4
Cowley Dr DY1 271 C1
Cowley Gn WS12 209 C4
Cowley La ST20 171 B3
Cowley Way ST2 73 C4
Cowlishaw Cl ST8 27 A3
Cowlishaw Rd ST6 42 B3
Cowlishaw Way WS15 196 C3
Cowlow La SK17 23 B2
Cowper St ST4 72 C3
Coxmoor Cl WS3 242 C2
Crab La Bobbington DY7 268 B1
Cannock WS11 210 A2
Stafford ST16 155 A4
Walsall WV12 242 B1
Crabbery St ST16 155 C2
Crabtree Ave ST8 27 B4
Crabtree Cl ST4 72 C4
Crabtree Way WS15 178 B1
Crackley Bank ST5 40 C1
Crackley Bank CE Prim Sch ST5 40 C1
Crackley Bank Prim Sch ST5 55 C4
Crackley La ST5 54 C2
Cracow Moss CW3 53 A2
Craddock Rd ST16 155 B4
Craftdown Cl ST17 174 C2
Craigside ST8 27 B4
Cramer St ST17 155 C1
Cranberry Ave ST10 93 A1
Cranberry Cl ST16 155 A3
Cranberry Dr ST5 40 B1
Cranberry Marsh ST21 102 B2
Cranbourne Ave
Norton-in-t-M ST2 43 A1
Wolv WV4 266 C2
Cranbrook Cl ST4 88 A4
Cranbrook Gr WV6 254 C2
Cranbrook Wlk ST17 174 A4
Cranbrooks ST19 205 B4
Crane Dr WS7 229 A2
Crane Field WS13 214 A1
Crane Hollow WV5 269 C3
Crane St ST1 57 A3
Crane Terr WV6 255 C3
Cranebrook Hill B78 259 C3
Cranebrook La
Shenstone WS14 245 C4
Wall WS14 246 A4
Cranesbill Cl WV10 241 B4
Cranfield Pl ST2 58 A1
Cranfield Rd WS7 229 A4
Cranford Pl 8 WS11 209 C1
Cranford Rd WV3 265 B4
Cranford Way ST2 58 B2
Cranham Dr DY6 275 C3
Cranleigh Ave ST1 57 B4
Cranleigh Cl
Aldridge WS9 256 A3
Walsall WV12 242 B1
Cranleigh Way WS14 231 C4
Cranley Dr WV8 238 C2
Cranmer Gr B74 257 C3
Cranmer St ST4 72 A4
Cranmere Ave WV6 255 A3
Cranmere Cl WS6 226 B1
Cranmore Gr ST15 120 B4
Cranmore Rd WV3 255 C2
Cranswick Gr ST2 58 B1
Crantock Cl WV11 242 B1
Cranwell Gn WV5 269 C3
Cranwell Pl ST3 89 C4
Cranwell Rise B78 249 B1
Cranwood Rd ST12 88 A1
Cranworth Gr ST3 89 C4
Crateford La ST19 224 A4
Crathorne Ave WV10 240 B1
Crauford Rd CW12 6 A4
Craven B77 251 A1
Craven Cl ST4 88 A4
Craven St
Burton u T DE13 166 B3
Wolv WV2 266 C3
Crawford Ave WV4 266 C2
Crawford St ST4 72 B3
Crawley La DE13 199 B3
Crayford Ave CW12 6 A3
Craythorne Rd DE13 147 B2
Crediton Ave ST6 42 B2
Creighton La ST14 111 A3
Cremorne Dr ST17 175 B4
Cremorne Rd B75 258 A1
Cremorne Wlk B75 258 A1
Crescent Gr ST4 56 C1
Crescent Rd ST17 155 B1
Crescent The Ashley TF9 100 B3
Burntwood WS7 211 C1
Cookley DY10 280 A2
Eccleshall ST21 133 B3
Great Wyrley WS6 227 A1
Hagley DY8 281 C3
Leek ST13 31 A4
Mayfield DE6 81 B4
Newcastle-u-L, Silverdale ST5 55 A1
Newcastle-u-L, Westlands ST5 71 A3
Rudyard ST13 18 B1
Stafford ST17 175 C4
Stafford, Doxey ST16 155 A2
Stoke-on-T ST4 71 C2
Stone ST15 105 A1
Swadlincote DE11 186 C3
Wolv WV6 255 A2
Cressington Dr B74 258 A1
Cresswell Ave ST5 40 B1
Cresswell Ct WV10 240 A2
Cresswell La
Brewood ST19 223 B3
Draycott in t M ST11 91 B2
Cresswell Old Rd ST11 91 C2
Cresswell Rd Hanley ST1 57 C2
Hilderstone ST15 106 C2
Crest Cl DE13 147 C1
Crestbrook Rd ST2 58 B3
Crestfield Rd ST3 89 C4
Crestway Rd ST2 43 B1
Crestwood B77 251 A3
Crestwood Cl DE13 166 B4
Crestwood Dr ST15 119 C3
Crestwood Glen WV6 255 C4
Crestwood Pk ST19 223 B4
Crestwood Rise WS15 178 B1
Crestwood Sch The DY6 275 C3
Creswell Cres WS3 242 C1
Creswell Dr ST18 154 C4
Creswell Farm Dr ST16 155 A4
Creswell Gr ST18 154 C4
Crewe Gates Ind Est CW1 37 A4
Crewe Hall Ent Pk CW1 37 B4
Crich Way DE11 186 C3
Crichton Ave DE13 166 B4
Crick Rd ST1 57 C1
Cricket Cl DE15 167 C4
Cricket La WS14 231 B3
Cricket Mdw
Sedgley DY3 271 C2
Wolv WV10 240 B2
Cricketers Cl DE15 185 C4
Cricketers Mews ST5 56 B3
Cricketers The DE13 200 C1
Crigdon B77 251 B1
Crinan Gr ST17 174 B3
Cringlebrook B77 250 B1
Crispin Cl ST16 155 B4
Critchlow Gr ST3 73 A1
Crockford Dr B75 258 A2
Crockington Cl WV5 263 C1
Crockington La WV5 264 A1
Crocus Cres WV9 240 A2
Croft Ave Cannock WS12 195 A1
Newcastle-u-L ST5 56 A3
Croft Cl Elford B79 216 C1
Netherseal DE12 219 C4
Rolleston DE13 147 A2
Croft Cres
Brownhills WS8 244 B4
Stoke-on-T ST4 72 A3
Croft Ct ST6 42 B1
Croft Cty Sch WS15 197 C3
Croft Gdns WS7 229 A4
Croft Gr ST14 111 B1
Croft La ST19 207 B1
Croft Leys The WS15 198 B2
Croft Par WS9 256 A3
Croft Rd Cheadle ST10 76 B2
Newcastle-u-L ST5 284 B4
Stone ST15 119 C3
Croft Road Ind Est ST5 284 B4
Croft St Burslem ST6 56 C4
Tamworth B79 250 A3
Croft The
Blakedown DY10 281 B1
Burton u T DE15 166 C1
Cheadle ST10 76 C3
Cheddleton ST13 45 B2
Cheslyn Hay WS6 226 C1
Hixon ST18 158 B4
King's Bromley DE13 199 B3
Longdon WS15 197 C1
Maer ST5 84 B1
Norton in Hales TF9 82 A2
Sedgley DY3 266 C1
Stoke-on-T ST4 71 C3
Swadlincote DE11 186 C3
Wombourne WV5 269 B3
Croft Way TF9 97 A1
Crofter Cl ST8 27 A4
Crofters Ct ST5 40 B2
Crofters Wlk WV8 239 C1
Croftfield St ST2 73 B4
Croftstead Ave ST14 95 B3
Cromartie St ST3 283 C2
Cromer Cres ST1 57 C2
Cromer Gdns WV6 255 C3
Cromer Rd ST1 57 C2
Cromer St ST5 56 B2
Crompton Cl ST18 177 C4
Crompton Ct WV8 239 A2
Crompton Gr ST4 88 B3
Crompton Rd ST15 120 A4
Cromwell Cl
Hopton ST18 137 B1
Tutbury DE13 146 B3
Cromwell Ct WS6 227 A1
Cromwell Rd
Cannock WS12 210 C1
Tamworth B79 249 C4
Wolv WV10 240 C2
Cromwell St Biddulph ST8 27 B4
Hanley ST1 57 B3
Cromwell Terr 17 ST13 30 C3
Cromwells Mdw WS14 231 B3
Crony Cl ST13 45 B2
Crook La WS9 256 A1
Crooked Bridge Rd ST16 155 C2
Crosby Cl WV6 255 C3
Crosby Rd ST4 71 C2
Cross Butts ST21 133 B3
Cross Edge ST6 43 A4
Cross Hill ST6 56 C4
Cross Ho WV2 266 B4
Cross In Hand La
Farewell WS13 213 B2
Lichfield WS13 213 C1
Cross Keys WS13 231 A4
Cross La Audley ST7 39 C3
Congleton CW12 6 A1
Lichfield WS14 231 B3
Rolleston DE13 147 A1
Cross La *continued*
Sedgley DY3 266 C1
Stone ST15 105 B3
Waterhouses ST10,ST13 48 C2
Cross May St ST5 284 A2
Cross of the Hand WS15 161 A1
Cross Pl DY3 266 C1
Cross Rd Albrighton WV7 237 A2
Rugeley WS15 196 C4
Uttoxeter ST14 111 A1
Cross Side DE6 81 C4
Cross St Biddulph ST8 27 B4
Burntwood WS7 228 C4
Burton u T DE14 166 B2
Cannock, Bridgtown WS11 226 C3
Cannock, Hayes Heath WS12 210 C1
Cheadle ST10 76 B2
Cheslyn Hay WS6 226 B1
Gnosall ST20 171 B3
Kingsley ST10 61 B2
8 Kingswinford DY6 275 B2
Kingswinford, Wall Heath DY6 275 A4
Kingswinford, Wordsley DY6 275 B3
20 Leek ST13 30 C3
Market Drayton TF9 97 B1
Meir ST3 74 A3
Newcastle-u-L ST5 55 C4
Stafford ST16 155 B3
Stourbridge DY8 279 C3
Tamworth, Kettlebrook B77 250 B2
Tamworth, The Leys B79 250 A3
Tunstall ST6 56 B4
Walsall WS3 244 A1
Cross St S WV2 266 B4
Crossdale Ave ST2 43 A1
Crossfell B77 251 A1
Crossfield Ave
Biddulph ST8 27 B3
Forsbrook ST11 90 C3
Crossfield Rd WS13 231 C4
Crosshill Bank ST18 122 C3
Crossing La ST18 154 B1
Crossings The WS14 231 C4
Crossland Cres WV6 255 C4
Crossland Pl E 2 ST3 90 A4
Crossland Pl W 11 ST3 74 A1
Crosslands CW12 6 A1
Crossley Rd ST6 42 A2
Crossley Stone WS15 178 C1
Crosslow La DE6 36 C3
Crossman St DE14 166 A2
Crossmead Gr ST1 57 C3
Crossway ST16 156 A2
Crossway Rd ST6 57 B4
Crossway The ST5 56 B2
Crossways ST8 16 C1
Crossways Rd ST7 25 A2
Croston St ST1 282 A1
Crotia Ave CW2 37 A3
Crouch Ave ST6 42 A2
Crouch La CW12 6 B2
Crowberry Cl WS8 244 B3
Crowberry La
Barton-u-N DE13 183 B1
Middleton B78 260 B1
Crowborough Rd ST8, ST13 28 A3
Crowcrofts Rd ST4 88 C4
Crowden Rd B77 251 A1
Crowfoot La DE65 129 C4
Crowland Ave WV6 254 C2
Crown Bank
Abbots Bromley WS15 161 A3
Hanley ST1 282 B3
Talke ST7 40 B3
Crown Bank Cres ST7 40 B3
Crown Bridge ST19 192 C1
Crown Cl DY3 266 B1
Crown Gdns ST7 40 B3
Crown Ind Est DE14 166 A1
Crown La Kinver DY10 281 B4
Stourbridge DY8 279 C3
Sutton Coldfield B74 257 C2
Crown Specl Sch DE13 147 B1
Crown St Hanley ST1 282 B2
Newcastle-u-L ST5 55 B1
Stone ST15 120 A4
Crowndale Pl ST7 41 C4
Crowther Gr WV6 255 C2
Crowther Rd WV6 255 C3
Crowther St ST4 72 B4
Crowtrees Farm Ind Est ST10 48 C1
Croxall Rd B79,WS13 217 A3
Croxden Abbey* ST14 94 B2
Croxden Rd ST2 58 A3
Croxdene Ave WS3 243 A1
Croxhall Rd DE13 201 A1
Croxley Dr WS12 210 B2
Croxstalls Cl WS3 243 A1
Croxstalls Rd WS3 243 A1
Croyde Pl ST3 90 A3
Croydon Dr ST19 207 C4
Cruso St ST13 30 C3
Crutchley Ave B78 250 A1
Crystal Ave DY8 275 C1
Crystal St ST6 57 A3
Cubley La DE6 96 C1
Cuckoo Cage La DE13 164 C1
Cuckoo Cl WS11 210 B1

Cull Ave ST16 . . . . .156 A2
Cullamore La ST14 . . . . .126 A2
Culland Rd DE14 . . . . . .185 A4
Cumberland Cl
  Kingswinford DY6 . . . . .275 C2
  Talke ST7 . . . . .40 C4
Cumberland Cres WS7 . .229 A4
Cumberland Dr B78 . . . .250 A1
Cumberland Rd
  Burton u T DE15 . . . . . .185 B3
  Cannock WS11 . . . . . . .210 A2
Cumberland St
  Fenton ST4 . . . . .72 C3
  Newcastle-u-L ST5 . . . . .284 C3
Cumberledge Hill WS15 211 C3
Cumberpatch Ave ST6 . . .42 A4
Cumbers The ST18 . . . . .154 A3
Cumbria Ho ST5 . . . . . . .71 B3
Cumming St ST4 . . . . . . .71 C4
Cunningham Rd WV6 . . .254 C2
Curborough Rd WS13 . . .214 A1
Curland Pl ST3 . . . . .73 C1
Curlew B77 . . . . .262 A4
Curlew Cl Lichfield WS14 231 C4
  Uttoxeter ST14 . . . . . . .126 B3
Curlew Wlk WS11 . . . . .210 A2
Curtis Ct DE13 . . . . . . .166 B4
Curtis Way DE14 . . . . . .166 A2
Curtiss Pl ST3 . . . . .90 B3
Curzon Pl WS15 . . . . . .196 C4
Curzon Rd ST6 . . . . .42 A4
Curzon Rise ST13 . . . . . .30 A3
Curzon St
  Burton u T DE14 . . . . . .166 B2
  Newcastle-u-L ST5 . . . . . .56 B1
  Wolv WV2 . . . . .266 B4
Curzon St W DE14 . . . . .166 A2
Cutts St ST1 . . . . .282 C1
Cwerne Ct DY3 . . . . . . .271 B2
Cyclamen Cl DE14 . . . . .185 A4
Cygnet Cl Cannock WS12 .210 B4
  Keele CW3 . . . . .69 A4
  Wolv WV6 . . . . .255 B1
Cynthia Gr ST6 . . . . .42 A1
Cypress Ave DY3 . . . . . .271 B3
Cypress Cl
  Market Drayton TF9 . . . . .97 A1
  Stafford ST17 . . . . .156 B1
Cypress Gdns 1 DY6 . . .275 B2
Cypress Gr
  Forsbrook ST11 . . . . .91 A3
  Newcastle-u-L ST5 . . . . . .55 B4
Cypress Rise WS12 . . . .211 A3
Cyprus St WV2 . . . . . . .266 B3

D

D'Urberville Cl WV2 . . . .266 C3
D'Urberville Rd WV2 . . . .266 C3
D'Urberville Wlk 1
  WS11 . . . . .210 A1
Dace B77 . . . . .261 B4
Dace Gr ST6 . . . . .42 A2
Daffodil Cl DY3 . . . . . . .271 C4
Daffodil Wlk WS15 . . . .178 B1
Dag La DE12 . . . . .218 A2
Dahlia Cl ST4 . . . . .74 A3
Daimler Cl 3 ST17 . . . . .175 A4
Dain Pl ST5 . . . . .56 A3
Dain St ST6 . . . . .56 C4
Daintry Cl ST13 . . . . .30 C3
Daintry Dr B78 . . . . . . .249 A4
Daintry St Leek ST13 . . . .30 C3
  Stoke-on-T ST4 . . . . .71 C2
Dairy Cl ST13 . . . . .31 C3
Dairyfields Way ST1 . . . .57 B4
Dairyhouse La
  Cheadle ST10 . . . . .60 C1
  Dilhorne ST10 . . . . .60 A1
Dairylands Rd ST7 . . . . .25 A2
Daisy Ave ST10 . . . . .62 A4
Daisy Bank
  Cannock WS12 . . . . . . .209 C4
  Leek ST13 . . . . .30 C3
Daisy Bank Cl WS3 . . . .244 A1
Daisy La DE13 . . . . .200 B1
Daisy Pl ST4 . . . . .72 C2
Daisy Wlk WV9 . . . . . . .240 A2
Dalbeg Cl WV8 . . . . . . .255 C4
Dale Ave ST6 . . . . .42 C3
Dale Cl Cheadle ST10 . . .76 C1
  Whitmore ST5 . . . . .85 B3
Dale Cres CW12 . . . . .6 A1
Dale Dr WS7 . . . . .229 A4
Dale Gr CW12 . . . . .6 A1
Dale La Haughton ST18 . .173 A4
  Seighford ST18 . . . . . . .154 A1
  Stanton DE6 . . . . .64 C2
Dale Rd DY8 . . . . .279 C1
Dale St Burslem ST6 . . . .56 C4
  Burton u T DE14 . . . . . .166 B1
Dale The Ashley TF9 . . . .100 A3
  Warslow SK17 . . . . .23 B1
Dale View
  Earl Sterndale SK17 . . . . .5 A2
  Kidsgrove ST7 . . . . .26 B3
  Meir ST3 . . . . .74 A2
Dale View Ct ST11 . . . . .90 C1
Dale View Dr ST5 . . . . . .55 B1
Dalebrook Rd DE15 . . . .167 A3
Dalecot Gn ST2 . . . . .73 B4
Dalegarth Gr 1 ST6 . . . .89 C4
Dalehall Gdns 26 ST6 . . .56 C4
Dalehead Ct ST3 . . . . . . .89 C4

Dalehouse Rd ST13 . . . .45 B2
Daleian Ct ST5 . . . . .55 B1
Dalelands Est TF9 . . . . .112 A4
Dalelands W TF9 . . . . . .112 A4
Dales Cl Biddulph ST8 . . .28 A4
  Swadlincote DE11 . . . . .186 C3
Dales Green Rd ST7 . . . .26 B3
Dales Inf Sch The B77 . .262 A4
Dales Jun Sch B77 . . . . .262 A4
Daleside DE15 . . . . .167 A1
Dalesman Cl DY6 . . . . . .275 A4
Dalewood Rd ST5 . . . . . .55 C3
Dallow Cl DE14 . . . . . . .166 B3
Dallow Cres DE14 . . . . .166 B3
Dallow St DE14 . . . . . . .166 B3
Dalton Ave DE15 . . . . . .167 A1
Dalton Ct WV5 . . . . . . .269 C4
Dalton Gr ST2 . . . . .58 B1
Dalton St WV3 . . . . .266 A4
Daltry Way CW3 . . . . . . .68 C4
Daly Cres ST5 . . . . .55 A4
Dam La Alsop en le D DE6 .36 C2
  Biddulph ST8 . . . . .17 A1
Dam St WS13 . . . . .231 A4
Dama Rd B78 . . . . .260 C4
Dame Paulet Wlk DE14 .166 B1
Dampier St ST13 . . . . . . .30 C3
Dams The ST11 . . . . .74 B1
Damson Pk WV6 . . . . . .253 B2
Danby Crest ST17 . . . . .174 A4
Danby Dr WS12 . . . . . . .211 B2
Dandillion Ave ST10 . . . .92 B4
Dane Dr ST8 . . . . .16 C1
Dane Gdns ST7 . . . . .26 B1
Dane Gr ST10 . . . . .76 C1
Dane Wlk ST1 . . . . .282 C3
Danebower Rd ST4 . . . . .88 A3
Danebridge Gr ST1 . . . . .57 C3
Danehill Gr ST4 . . . . .71 C3
Danehill Wlk WV8 . . . . .255 C4
Danelagh Cl B79 . . . . . .249 C4
Danemead Ct ST3 . . . . . .90 A4
Danes Cl WV11 . . . . . . .241 C2
Danes Croft ST4 . . . . . . .88 A4
Danesbrook WV5 . . . . . .267 B4
Danescourt Rd WV6 . . . .255 B3
Danesmore Park Jun & Inf
  Sch WV11 . . . . .242 A1
Daneswood Dr WS9 . . . .244 C2
Danford Gr WV5 . . . . . .267 B4
Daniels Cross TF10 . . . .169 A2
Daniels La WS9 . . . . . . .256 B3
Danilo Rd WS11 . . . . . . .209 B1
Danta Way ST17 . . . . . .156 B1
Darby Ave WS14 . . . . . .232 C3
Darges La WS6 . . . . . . .226 C2
Darius Cl ST5 . . . . .56 A4
Dark La Alrewas DE13 . . .201 A2
  Farewell WS13 . . . . . . .213 A1
  Featherstone, Brinsford
  WV10 . . . . .240 B4
  Featherstone, Hilton Park
  WV10,WV11 . . . . .241 B4
  Great Wyrley WS6 . . . . .227 B1
  Kinver DY7 . . . . .278 A2
  Longdon WS15 . . . . . . .212 B4
  Newborough DE13 . . . . .162 B4
  Newport TF10 . . . . .168 C1
  Polesworth B78 . . . . . . .262 C4
Darley Cl DE15 . . . . . . .167 B1
Darley Dale DE11 . . . . . .186 C1
Darley St ST10 . . . . .76 C1
Darlings La WS15 . . . . . .212 A3
Darnbrook B77 . . . . . . .251 B3
Darnel Hurst Rd B75 . . .258 B2
Darnford Cl ST16 . . . . . .155 B4
Darnford La
  Lichfield WS14 . . . . . . .231 C3
  Whittington WS14 . . . . .232 A3
Darnford Moors WS14 . .231 C3
Darnford View WS14 . . .231 C1
Darnley St ST4 . . . . .72 B4
Darrall Gdns ST4 . . . . . .71 C2
Darsham Gdns ST5 . . . . .71 B1
Dart B77 . . . . .262 A3
Dart Ave ST6 . . . . .42 A2
Dart Cl ST8 . . . . .16 B1
Dart Gr ST10 . . . . .76 C1
Dart Pl ST5 . . . . .71 A2
Dartford Pl ST6 . . . . .42 B2
Dartford Rd WS3 . . . . . .242 C1
Dartmouth Ave
  Cannock WS11 . . . . . . .226 B4
  Kingswinford DY8 . . . . .275 B2
  Newcastle-u-L ST5 . . . . .71 A3
  Pattingham WV6 . . . . . .253 B1
Dartmouth Pl ST3 . . . . . .89 C4
Dartmouth Rd WS11 . . . .209 B1
Dartmouth St
  Chell Heath ST6 . . . . . . .42 A1
  Stafford ST16 . . . . .156 A2
  Wolv WV2 . . . . .266 B4
Darwell Pk ST7 . . . . . . .251 A1
Darwin Cl
  Burntwood WS7 . . . . . .229 A4
  Burton u T DE15 . . . . . .167 B1
  Cannock WS12 . . . . . . .210 C1
  Lichfield WS13 . . . . . . .231 A4
  Stafford ST16 . . . . .156 B2
  2 Stone ST15 . . . . . . .104 C1
Darwin Gr WV6 . . . . . . .254 C2
Darwin Ho DY6 . . . . . . .275 C4
Dash Gr ST6 . . . . .42 B1
Datteln Rd WS11 . . . . . .210 A2
Daurada Dr ST17 . . . . . .175 A4
Davenport Cl ST13 . . . . .30 A2
Davenport Rd WV6 . . . .255 A3
Davenport St Burslem ST6 56 B4

Davenport St continued
  Tunstall ST6 . . . . .41 C1
Davenport Way ST5 . . . .70 C2
Daventry Cl ST2 . . . . . . .57 C1
David Garrick Gdns
  WS13 . . . . .214 A1
David Rd ST3 . . . . .73 C1
Davidson Ave CW12 . . . . .6 A3
Davidson Rd WS14 . . . .231 A4
Davies Dr ST14 . . . . . . .110 C1
Davies Ho WS10 . . . . . .243 A1
Davis Cl ST16 . . . . .156 A2
Davis Rd B77 . . . . .250 C2
Davis St ST4 . . . . .57 A1
Davison St ST6 . . . . .57 A4
Davy Cl ST2 . . . . .58 A2
Davy Pl WS15 . . . . .196 B3
Dawes Cl WS15 . . . . . . .197 C2
Dawes La WS8 . . . . . . .229 A1
Dawley Brook Prim Sch
  DY6 . . . . .275 B4
Dawley Brook Rd DY6 . .275 B4
Dawley Rd DY6 . . . . . . .275 B4
Dawley Trad Est DY6 . . .275 B4
Dawlish Ave ST17 . . . . .175 B4
Dawlish Dr ST2 . . . . .58 B1
Dawn Ave ST6 . . . . .42 A2
Dawn View ST3 . . . . . . .74 A2
Dawney Dr B75 . . . . . . .258 A2
Dawson Ave WV14 . . . .266 C1
Dayson Cl ST5 . . . . .56 A4
Dayton Dr WS15 . . . . . .178 B1
Daywell Rise WS15 . . . .178 B2
De Ferrers Croft DE13 . .166 B4
De Ferrers High Sch (Dove
  Campus) DE13 . . . . . .166 A4
De Ferrers High Sch (Trent
  Campus) DE13 . . . . . .166 B4
De Havilland Dr ST15 . .118 C3
De-Wint Rd ST15 . . . . . .120 A4
Deacon Way WS15 . . . .178 C1
Deakin Ave WS8 . . . . . .228 C1
Deakin Gr ST5 . . . . .71 B3
Deakin Rd ST6 . . . . .42 A3
Deal Ave WS7 . . . . .229 A4
Dean Cl TF9 . . . . .97 A1
Dean Ct WV6 . . . . .254 C3
Dean Hollow ST7 . . . . . .39 B1
Dean Pl ST1 . . . . .282 C1
Dean Rd WV5 . . . . .269 C3
Dean St Brewood ST19 . .223 B3
  Bucknall ST2 . . . . .58 B2
  Sedgley DY3 . . . . .271 B4
Dean's La ST5 . . . . .40 B1
Deanery Cl
  Rugeley WS15 . . . . . . .178 C1
  Shareshill WV10 . . . . . .225 B1
Deans Croft WS14 . . . . .231 B4
Deans La CW2 . . . . .38 C2
Deans Slade Dr WS14 . .231 A3
Deansberry Cl ST4 . . . . .88 A4
Deanscroft Way ST3 . . . .73 C2
Deansfield Cl ST19 . . . . .223 B4
Deansfield Ho ST19 . . . .223 B4
Deansfield Rd ST19 . . . .223 B3
Deansgate 16 ST13 . . . .30 C3
Deanshill Cl ST16 . . . . .155 B1
Deansway ST4 . . . . .88 A3
Dearnsdale Cl ST16 . . . .155 A4
Deavall Way WS11 . . . . .210 A1
Deaville Rd ST2 . . . . . . .58 B2
Debenham Cres ST2 . . . .58 A1
Deborah Cl WV4 . . . . . .266 B3
Decade Cl ST5 . . . . .40 C1
Dee Cl Biddulph ST8 . . . .16 C1
  Talke ST7 . . . . .40 C4
Dee Gr WS11 . . . . .226 B3
Dee La ST5 . . . . .71 A2
Dee Rd WS3 . . . . .243 C1
Deebank Ave ST13 . . . . .31 A3
Deeley St Brewood ST19 .223 B3
Deeley B77 . . . . .251 A1
Deep Cut Rd DE6 . . . . . .144 C4
Deep Hayes Ctry Pk★
  ST13 . . . . .45 A4
Deepdale B77 . . . . .251 B1
Deepdale Cl
  Burton u T DE15 . . . . . .167 A3
  Norton-in-t-M ST6 . . . . .42 C1
Deepdale La
  Sedgley DY1 . . . . .271 C2
  Snelston DE6 . . . . .81 A1
Deepdales Stafford ST17 .175 B3
  Wombourne WV5 . . . . .269 C3
Deepmore Cl
  Alrewas DE13 . . . . .201 A1
  Featherstone WV10 . . . .224 B3
Deer Cl Huntington WS12 209 B3
  Norton Canes WS11 . . . .228 A4
  Walsall WS3 . . . . .243 C1
Deer Hill ST17 . . . . .176 B2
Deer Park Dr TF10 . . . . .168 C3
Deer Park Rd B78 . . . . .249 C1
Deer Pk ST20 . . . . .171 C4
Deer Wlk WV8 . . . . .239 C1
Deerfold Cres WS7 . . . . .229 A4
Deerhill B77 . . . . .251 B1
Deerhurst Rise ST10 . . .210 C3
Defford Ave WS4 . . . . . .244 B1
Defoe Dr ST3 . . . . .73 C2
Delafield Way WS15 . . . .178 B1
Delamere Gr
  Newcastle-u-L ST5 . . . . .284 C4
  Trentham ST4 . . . . .88 A4
Delamere La ST17 . . . . .174 A4
Delamere Rd ST3 . . . . . .73 C2
Delhi Cl DE15 . . . . .167 B2
Delhurst Ave WV4 . . . . .266 C2

Delius Gr ST1 . . . . .57 C3
Dell Cl ST16 . . . . .155 A4
Dell The Cannock WS12 .210 C2
  Lichfield WS13 . . . . . . .230 C4
  Newcastle-u-L ST5 . . . . .55 B1
  Stourbridge DY8 . . . . . .279 C3
  Tamworth B79 . . . . . . .250 A3
Dellway Ct DY8 . . . . . . .279 C3
Dellwood Gr 2 ST3 . . . .73 B3
Delph Wlk ST4 . . . . .72 C3
Delphouse Rd
  Cheadle ST10 . . . . .76 A1
  Forsbrook ST11 . . . . . . .75 C1
Delphside ST7 . . . . .39 C1
Delta Way WS11 . . . . . .226 C4
Delta Way Bsns Ctr
  WS11 . . . . .226 B3
Deltic B77 . . . . .251 A1
Delves Cres CW9 . . . . . .262 B1
Delves Pl ST5 . . . . .71 A3
Demontfort Way ST14 . .126 A3
Den La CW3,CW5 . . . . . .52 B2
Denbigh Cl Biddulph ST8 .27 B3
  Burton u T DE13 . . . . . .166 B4
  Dudley DY1 . . . . .271 C1
  Newcastle-u-L ST5 . . . . .71 B2
Denbigh St ST1 . . . . . . .282 A4
Denbury Cl WS12 . . . . . .210 B3
Denby Ave ST3 . . . . . . .283 C5
Dency Gr ST6 . . . . .42 C4
Dene Ave DY6 . . . . .275 B2
Dene Cl ST19 . . . . .207 C4
Dene Rd
  Lower Penn WV4 . . . . . .264 C2
  Stourbridge DY8 . . . . . .279 C2
Dene Side ST4 . . . . .284 C2
Denefield ST19 . . . . . . .207 C4
Denehurst 1 ST3 . . . . . .74 A1
Denewood Pl ST3 . . . . . .74 A1
Denford St WV9 . . . . . . .44 C4
Denham Gdns WV3 . . . .265 A4
Denham Sq ST3 . . . . . . .72 C1
Denleigh Rd DY6 . . . . . .275 C2
Denmark Rise WS12 . . .210 B3
Denmark Villa WS13 . . .230 B3
Dennfield Dr WS6 . . . . .226 B1
Dennington Cres ST3 . . .72 C1
Dennis B77 . . . . .250 C1
Dennis Barsby Cl DE11 .186 C2
Dennis St
  Brierley Hill DY8 . . . . . .279 C4
  Fenton ST4 . . . . .72 C3
Dennis Viollet Ave ST4 . .72 B2
Denry Cres ST5 . . . . . . .56 A4
Denshaw Wlk ST3 . . . . .283 C4
Denston Ct B74 . . . . . . .257 C1
Denstone Ave ST17 . . . .156 A1
Denstone Coll ST14 . . . .95 A3
Denstone Cres ST3 . . . . .72 C1
Denstone Gdns WV10 . .240 C2
Denstone La ST14 . . . . .95 B4
Dent St B79 . . . . .250 B3
Dentdale Cl ST3 . . . . . . .90 A4
Denton Cl ST5 . . . . .71 B2
Denton Gr ST3 . . . . .73 C2
Denton Rd DE13 . . . . . .166 A3
Denton Rise DE14 . . . . .166 A4
Denver Fold ST17 . . . . .174 A4
Denzil St ST1 . . . . .174 A4
Derby Ave WV6 . . . . . . .255 C4
Derby Mews ST14 . . . . .110 C1
Derby Pl ST5 . . . . .71 B2
Derby Rd
  Burton u T DE13,DE14 . .166 C4
  Doveridge DE6 . . . . . . .127 B4
  Egginton DE65 . . . . . . .148 B2
  Talke ST7 . . . . .40 B4
  Uttoxeter ST14 . . . . . . .111 B1
  Whittington WS14 . . . . .232 B2
Derby St Burton u T DE14 166 B2
  Hanley ST1 . . . . .282 C2
  Leek ST13 . . . . .30 C3
  Stafford ST16 . . . . .155 B2
Derby St E DE14 . . . . . .166 B2
Derby Turn DE14 . . . . . .166 B3
Dereham Way ST2 . . . . .58 B1
Derek Dr ST1 . . . . .57 C3
Derrington La
  Bradley ST18 . . . . .173 C4
  Seighford ST18 . . . . . . .154 C1
Derry St Fenton ST4 . . . .72 C2
  Wolv WV2 . . . . .266 B4
Derwent B77 . . . . .250 B1
Derwent Ave ST15 . . . . .120 B4
Derwent Cl Aldridge WS2 256 C2
  Burton u T DE14 . . . . . .166 C2
Derwent Cres ST7 . . . . .26 B1
Derwent Dr Ashley TF9 . .99 C3
  Biddulph ST8 . . . . .16 C1
  Cheadle ST10 . . . . .76 C1
Derwent Gr
  Burntwood WS7 . . . . . .229 B3
  Cannock WS11 . . . . . . .226 B4
Derwent Ho ST17 . . . . .174 C3
Derwent Pl ST5 . . . . . . .56 A2
Derwent Rd
  Burton u T DE15 . . . . . .167 A1
  Wolv WV6 . . . . .255 C4
Derwent St ST1 . . . . . . .282 A4
Devall Cl WS15 . . . . . . .196 C4
Devana Wlk ST3 . . . . . . .74 B1
Devereux Ho B79 . . . . . .250 A2
Devereux Rd B75 . . . . . .258 B1
Deveron Cl DE13 . . . . . .147 B1
Devil's La ST9,ST13 . . . .223 B3
Devon Cl Burton u T DE15 185 C3
  Newcastle-u-L ST5 . . . . .71 B2

Devon Cres WS9 . . . . . .245 A1
Devon Ct WS11 . . . . . . .226 B4
Devon Gn WS11 . . . . . . .226 C4
Devon Gr ST8 . . . . .16 B1
Devon Ho 5 DY8 . . . . . .279 C4
Devon Rd Cannock WS11 .226 C4
  Stourbridge DY8 . . . . . .279 C4
Devon Way Longton ST3 . .73 B1
  Stafford ST17 . . . . .174 B3
Devonshire Ct B74 . . . . .258 A1
Devonshire Dr
  Rugeley WS15 . . . . . . .196 B3
  Tamworth B78 . . . . . . .250 A1
Devonshire Sq ST2 . . . . .58 B1
Dewberry Rd 8 DY8 . . .275 C1
Dewick Ind Est ST17 . . .175 C2
Dewsbury Cl DY8 . . . . . .275 C4
Dewsbury Dr
  Burntwood WS7 . . . . . .229 B3
  Wolv WV4 . . . . .266 A2
Dewsbury Rd ST4 . . . . . .72 C4
Dexter Way B78 . . . . . .262 C4
Dexton Rise ST17 . . . . .174 A4
Deykin Rd WS13 . . . . . .231 A3
Dial La Biddulph CW12 . . .7 A1
  Brierley Hill DY8 . . . . . .279 C4
Diamond Ave 12 ST7 . . .26 A1
Diamond Cl
  Barlaston ST12 . . . . . . .104 B4
  Biddulph ST8 . . . . .27 B4
  Blythe Bridge ST3 . . . . . .90 A2
Diamond Gr WS11 . . . . .210 B3
Diamond Jubilee Cotts
  DE6 . . . . .81 C4
Diamond Park Dr 4
  DY8 . . . . .275 C1
Diamond Ridge ST12 . . .104 B4
Diamond Way WS15 . . . .120 A3
Diana Cl WS9 . . . . .245 A2
Diana Rd ST1 . . . . .57 C3
Diarmid Rd ST4 . . . . . . .71 C1
Dibble Rd DE14 . . . . . . .185 A4
Dibdale Ct DY3 . . . . . . .271 B2
Dibdale Rd DY1 . . . . . . .271 C2
Dibdale Rd W DY1 . . . . .271 C2
Dibdale St DY1 . . . . . . .271 C1
Dickens Cl
  Burton u T DE14 . . . . . .166 B3
  Sedgley DY3 . . . . .271 A3
Dickens Rd WV10 . . . . .241 A4
Dickens St ST2 . . . . .58 B2
Dickenson Rd E ST6 . . . .57 B4
Dickenson Rd W ST6 . . .57 B4
Dickinson Rd WV5 . . . . .270 A4
Dickinson Ho ST1 . . . . .282 C1
Dickson Rd ST16 . . . . . .156 A3
Dicky's La ST20 . . . . . . .151 A2
Didcot Dr ST14 . . . . . . .143 C4
Dig St SK17 . . . . .24 B3
Digbeth La WV5 . . . . . . .267 A4
Digby Rd DY6 . . . . .275 C2
Diglake Cl ST7 . . . . .40 B3
Diglake St ST7 . . . . .39 C2
Digmire La DE6 . . . . . . .51 B1
Dilhorne Endowed Prim Sch
  ST10 . . . . .75 B3
Dilhorne Gr ST3 . . . . . .283 C1
Dilhorne La
  Caverswall ST11 . . . . . .74 C2
  Dilhorne ST11 . . . . .75 A1
Dilhorne Rd Cheadle ST10 76 A2
  Forsbrook ST10,ST11 . . .75 A1
Dilke St ST1 . . . . .282 C4
Dill Gr ST3 . . . . .90 A3
Dimble La ST10 . . . . . . .94 B4
Dimbles Hill WS13 . . . .214 A1
Dimbles La WS13 . . . . .214 A1
Dimmelow St ST3 . . . . . .74 A3
Dimmingsdale Rd WV4 .264 C3
Dimmingsdale YH★
  ST10 . . . . .78 A2
Dimmock St WV4 . . . . .266 C3
Dimsdale Par E ST5 . . . .56 B4
Dimsdale Par W ST5 . . . .56 A4
Dimsdale St ST6 . . . . . . .56 C4
Dimsdale View ST5 . . . . .55 C3
Dimsdale View E ST5 . . .56 A3
Dimsdale View W ST5 . . .56 A3
Dingle Dr DE13 . . . . . . .165 C2
Dingle La Bridgemere CW5 67 A3
  Hilderstone ST15 . . . . . .106 C3
  Woodhouse Green SK11 . .17 C4
Dingle Rd
  Brownhills WS8 . . . . . . .244 C3
  Wombourne WV5 . . . . .269 C3
Dingle The
  Burton u T DE15 . . . . . .185 C4
  Endon ST6 . . . . .43 A4
  Wolv WV3 . . . . .255 B1
Dingle View DY3 . . . . . .271 B4
Dinham Gdns DY1 . . . . .271 C2
Dippons Dr WV6 . . . . . .255 A2
Dippons Ho WV6 . . . . . .255 A2
Dippons Mill Cl WV6 . . .255 A4
Dirty La ST19 . . . . .223 B3
Dirtyfoot La WV4 . . . . . .265 A3
District Ctr WS11 . . . . . .210 B1
Ditch Cotts SK17 . . . . . . .5 C3
Ditch The SK17 . . . . .5 C4
Dividy Rd ST2 . . . . .58 A1
Dixon Cl 3 ST15 . . . . . .104 C1
Dixon Rd CW12 . . . . .6 A3
Dixon St WV2 . . . . .266 C4
Dixon's Row ST5 . . . . . . .55 B4
Dobbinhorse La DE6 . . . .81 C3
Dobbs St WV2 . . . . .266 B4
Dobell Gr ST3 . . . . .283 D4
Dobree Cl ST17 . . . . . . .177 C4

Dobson St ST6 57 B4
Dock Rd DY8 275 C1
Doctor's Bank TF9 100 B3
Doctors Cl ST8 27 B4
Doctors La Kinver DY6 274 C3
Shenstone WS14 247 A3
Doddington Pl ST5 71 A3
Doddlespool Barns CW3 52 C4
Dodds La Astbury CW12 15 B3
Farewell WS13 212 B2
Dodslow Ave DE13 147 A2
Dog Kennel La TF9 112 B4
Dog La Butterton ST13 33 C4
Leek ST13 30 C3
Netherseal DE12 219 C3
Ranton ST18 153 B2
Swynnerton ST4,ST5 86 B2
Tamworth B77 251 A3
Waterhouses ST10 50 A1
Weeford WS14 248 A2
Dogcroft Rd ST6 42 B3
Doglands Rd ST18 123 A1
Dogmoor La ST10 64 C4
Dogshead La DE13 201 B4
Dolefoot La DE13 163 A2
Doles La DE6 81 C4
Dolespring Cl ST11 91 A4
Doley Cl ST20 171 B3
Dolly's La ST6 42 A1
Dolphin Cl Stafford ST17 156 B1
Walsall WS3 243 C1
Dominic St Stoke-on-T ST4 72 A4
9 Stone ST15 104 C1
Don Gr WS11 226 B4
Donald Bates Ho ST4 71 C3
Donald Rd ST1 57 C3
Doncaster La ST4 71 C4
Donington La
Albrighton WV7 237 A4
Boscobel WV8 221 B1
Donithorne Cl DE13 166 B4
Donkey La ST10 76 C3
Dorado B77 261 B4
Dorcas Dr ST3 72 C2
Dorchester Cl
Kidsgrove ST7 26 A2
Walsall WV12 242 B1
Dorchester Rd
Cannock WS11 209 A1
Walsall WV12 242 B1
Dorchester Wlk ST2 58 B1
Dordon Rd B78 262 C4
Doreen Ave CW12 16 A4
Dorian Way ST9 43 C4
Dorking Cl ST2 57 C1
Dorlan Cl ST9 43 B2
Dormer Ave B77 250 B3
Dormston Dr DY3 271 C4
Dormston Sch The DY3 271 C4
Dormston Trad Est DY1 271 C2
Dorothy Clive Garden The★
TF9 84 A2
Dorridge Gr ST5 56 C2
Dorrington Cl ST2 43 A1
Dorrington Dr ST16 155 C3
Dorrington Gr ST5 56 B3
Dorrington Ind Pk ST16 155 C3
Dorset Cl Bucknall ST2 58 B2
Burton u T DE15 185 C3
Tamworth B78 250 A1
Dorset Dr Aldridge WS9 245 A1
Biddulph ST8 27 A4
Dorset Pl Kidsgrove ST7 26 A1
Newcastle-u-L ST5 71 B2
Dorset Rd Cannock WS12 210 C1
Stourbridge DY8 279 B4
Dosthill Prim Sch B77 261 B3
Dosthill Rd (Two Gates)
B77 261 B4
Double Gates TF9 112 A4
Douglas Ave Biddulph ST8 27 B4
Stoke-on-T ST4 71 C3
Douglas Pl ST1 57 C1
Douglas Rd
Newcastle-u-L ST5 56 A2
Stafford ST16 156 A3
Douglas Rd W ST16 156 A3
Douglas St ST1 57 A3
Doulton Cl Cheadle ST10 76 B1
Stone ST15 119 C3
Doulton Dr ST5 56 A4
Doulton Rd ST18 156 A4
Doulton St 4 ST6 57 A4
Douse La ST13 32 B2
Dove Bank ST14 126 B4
Dove Bank Prim Sch ST7 26 A1
Dove Cl Burntwood WS7 229 B3
Stafford ST17 174 C3
Dove Fields ST14 126 B4
Dove Fst Sch ST14 96 A2
Dove Gr Biddulph ST8 16 B1
Egginton DE65 148 A3
Dove Hollow
Cannock WS12 210 C2
Great Wyrley WS6 226 C1
Dove La ST14 96 A2
Dove Lea DE13 147 A2
Dove Pl ST5 71 A2
Dove Rd ST11 91 A4
Dove Ridge SK17 13 B3
Dove Side DE65 146 B4
Dove St DE6 80 A1
Dove View DE13 146 B3
Dove Way The ST14 111 B1
Dove Wlk ST14 126 B4
Dovebank Gr ST3 90 A3
Dovecliff Cres DE13 147 C1
Dovecliff Rd DE13 147 C2
Dovecote Cl WV6 255 B2
Dovecote Pl ST3 89 C4
Dovecotes Prim Sch
WV8 239 C1
Dovecotes The B75 258 A2
Dovedale WS11 210 A3
Dovedale Ave WS3 244 A3
Dovedale Cl
Burton u T DE15 167 A3
Cheadle ST10 76 C3
Congleton CW12 6 A2
Tunstall ST6 41 A4
Dovedale Ct WV4 266 C1
Dovedale Pl ST5 55 A1
Dovedale Rd
Kingsley ST10 61 C1
Kingswinford DY6 275 C4
Wolv WV4 266 C2
Dovefields ST14 95 C2
Dovehouse Fields
WS14 231 A3
Dover Ct DE13 166 B4
Dover Rd DE13 166 A4
Dover St ST1 282 C4
Doveridge Prim Sch
DE6 127 B4
Doveridge Rd DE15 167 A1
Doveside DE6 81 B4
Dovestone B77 251 B1
Dowells Gdns DY8 275 B2
Dower Rd B75 258 A1
Downderry Cl ST17 174 A4
Downend Cl WV10 240 C2
Downesway WS11 209 B1
Downey St ST1 282 B2
Downfield Cl WS3 243 A2
Downfield Dr DY3 271 C3
Downfield Gr ST16 155 B4
Downfield Pl ST2 42 C1
Downford Cl ST19 205 B3
Downham Pl WV3 265 C4
Downham Rd ST5 55 C1
Downie Rd WV8 239 B2
Downing Ave ST5 56 C2
Downing Dr B79 249 C3
Downing Gdns 10 ST15 120 A4
Downs The Aldridge WS9 256 C1
Stafford ST17 175 B4
Downsview Gr ST3 72 C2
Dowty Way WV9 240 A2
Doxey ST16 155 A2
Doxey Fields ST16 154 C2
Doxey Prim Sch ST16 155 A2
Dragon Sq ST5 55 C4
Drake Ave ST19 207 C3
Drake Cl Bucknall ST2 57 C1
Walsall WS3 243 A1
Drake Croft 4 WS13 231 B4
Drake Ct WS3 243 A1
Drake Rd WS3 243 B1
Drakeford Ct ST6 42 C2
Drakeford Gr ST6 42 C2
Drakes Hill Cl DY8 279 B2
Draw-well La ST9 59 B2
Dray Ct DE14 166 B1
Draycott Cl WV4 265 B3
Draycott Cliff DE6 144 B3
Draycott Cres B77 250 B1
Draycott Cross Rd
Cheadle ST10 76 A1
Draycott in t M ST11 91 B4
Draycott Dr Cheadle ST10 76 B1
Newcastle-u-L ST5 40 B1
Draycott Manor Prim Sch
ST11 91 B3
Draycott Old Rd
Draycott in t M ST11 91 B4
Forsbrook ST11 91 B4
Draycott Rd ST10 92 B2
Drayton Gn ST2 58 A1
Drayton Gr TF9 97 B1
Drayton La B78 260 B3
Drayton Manor Dr
Drayton Bassett B78 260 C4
Fazeley B78 260 C4
Drayton Manor Pk★
B78 260 C4
Drayton Rd Longton ST3 283 C4
Swynnerton ST4 87 A3
Drayton St
Newcastle-u-L ST5 284 A2
Wolv WV2 266 B4
Dreieich Cl ST16 155 C3
Drenfell Rd ST7 25 C4
Dresden CE Prim Sch
ST3 283 C1
Dresden St ST1 282 C2
Dreys The ST4 88 A4
Driffield Cl ST2 58 C1
Drive Fields WV4 265 A3
Drive The Audley ST7 54 C3
Codsall WV8 238 C2
Rudyard ST13 29 C4
Stafford ST16 155 A2
Walsall WS3 243 C1
Walsall, Shelfield WS4 244 B1
Wolv WV6 255 B3
Drointon La ST18 139 B2
Droitwich Cl ST5 54 C1
Drovers Way TF10 169 A2
Droveway The WV9 239 C1
Droxford Wlk WV8 239 C1
Drubbery La ST3 283 A1
Druid Park Rd WV12 242 B1
Druids Ave WS9 256 B4
Druids Way ST19 207 C4
Druids Wlk WS9 245 A2
Drumart Ho DY10 280 A3
Drumber La ST7 26 A4
Drumburn Cl ST7 41 C4
Drummond Cl WV11 242 A1
Drummond Rd ST16 155 C3
Drummond St ST6 41 B4
Drury La WV8 238 C2
Dryburg Wlk ST2 58 A2
Dryburgh Cl ST17 174 A4
Dryden Cres ST17 155 B1
Dryden Rd Burslem ST6 57 A3
Tamworth B79 250 A3
Wolv WV10 240 C1
Dryden Way ST10 76 B1
Dual Way WS12 209 B4
Dubarry Ave DY6 275 B4
Duchy Cl DE13 166 C4
Duchy Rd CW1 37 A4
Duck La WV8 239 A2
Duck St DE65 148 A3
Duddell Rd ST6 42 B1
Dudding Rd WV4 266 B3
Dudley Innovation Ctr
DY6 275 C4
Dudley Pl 1 ST3 90 A4
Dudley Rd Himley DY3 270 B2
Kingswinford DY6 275 C4
Kingswinford, Wall Heath
DY6 275 B4
Sedgley DY3 271 C3
Wolv WV2 266 B4
Dudley St DY3 271 B4
Dudley Wlk WV4 266 B3
Dudmaston Way DY1 271 C2
Duesbury Gn ST3 283 A3
Duffield Cl WV8 239 C1
Duffield La DE13 162 C4
Dugdale Cl WS12 210 C2
Dugdale Cres B75 258 B2
Duke Bank Terr ST6 42 C2
Duke Pl ST5 55 B1
Duke Rd WS7 211 C1
Duke St Biddulph ST8 27 B4
Burton u T DE14 166 B1
Fenton ST4 72 C3
Leek ST13 30 C3
Newcastle-u-L ST5 284 C1
Sedgley DY3 271 B3
Tutbury DE13 146 B3
Wolv WV3 266 A4
Dukes La ST13,ST10 63 B4
Dukes Rd B78 262 C3
Dulverton Ave ST5 71 A3
Dumbill Ho ST7 40 B4
Dumbleberry Ave DY3 271 B4
Dumolo's La B77 250 C2
Dumore Hay La WS13 215 C4
Duncalf Gr ST5 56 A4
Duncalf St ST6 56 C4
Duncalfe Dr B75 258 A2
Duncan St Fenton ST4 72 C3
Wolv WV2 266 B4
Duncombe St DY8 279 B3
Dundalk La WS6 226 B1
Dundas St ST1 282 C4
Dundee Rd ST1 57 A2
Dundee St ST3 283 B2
Dunedin B77 251 A1
Dunedin Cres DE15 167 B1
Dungarven Dr TF10 168 B1
Dunhampton Dr DY10 280 A1
Dunkirk ST5 284 A3
Dunkirk Ct ST5 284 A3
Dunlin Dr WV10 241 A4
Dunnerdale Rd WS8 244 B4
Dunning St ST6 41 B2
Dunnington Ave DY10 280 A1
Dunnock Cl ST14 126 B3
Dunnock Way ST8 27 C4
Dunrobin St ST3 283 C2
Dunsany Gr ST1 57 C3
Dunsford Ave ST2 43 A1
Dunsley Dr
Kingswinford DY8 275 C2
Kinver DY7 278 B2
Dunsley Gr WV4 266 A2
Dunsley Rd Kinver DY7 278 B2
Stourbridge DY8 279 B2
Dunstall Brook DE15 167 A1
Dunstall Cross DE13 183 A3
Dunstall Hill DE13 183 A3
Dunstall La B78 249 B2
Dunstall Park Race Course
WV6 255 C3
Dunstall Rd DE13 183 C2
Dunster B77 261 B4
Dunster Cl ST17 174 A4
Dunster Gr WV6 254 C2
Dunster Rd ST3 73 B3
Dunston Cl
Great Wyrley WS6 242 C4
Kingswinford DY6 275 B4
Dunston Dr WS7 229 A4
Dunton Cl B75 258 A2
Dunwood Dr ST6 42 A2
Dunwood La ST9,ST13 29 B2
Durban Cl DE15 167 B2
Durber Cl Audley ST7 39 B1
Stoke-on-T ST4 71 C2
Durfield La DE13 163 A4
Durham Cl B78 250 A1
Durham Dr Meir ST3 89 B4
Rugeley WS15 196 B3
Durham Gr ST5 71 B2
Durham Rd DY8 279 B4
Durlston Cl B77 250 C3
Durose Ct ST14 125 B4
Dursley Dr WS11 209 A1
Dursley Rd WS7 229 A4
Durston Pl ST3 73 C2
Dutton Way ST15 119 C3
Duttons La B75 258 C2
Dyke Rd WS15 198 A2
Dyke St ST1 282 C3
Dykes La TF10 188 B4
Dylan Rd Biddulph ST8 27 C3
Longton ST3 73 B2
Dyott Ave WS14 232 C3
Dyott Cl WS13 215 A1

E

Eagle Cl
Cheslyn Hay WS6 226 B1
Dudley DY1 271 C1
Uttoxeter ST14 126 A3
Eagle Cres ST21 133 B3
Eagle Ct WV3 266 A4
Eagle Dr B77 251 B2
Eagle Gr WS12 210 B1
Eagle Hts DE15 167 B2
Eagle St Hanley ST1 57 C2
Wolv WV2 266 C4
Wolv, Penn Fields WV3 266 A4
Ealingham B77 251 A1
Eamont Ave ST6 42 A2
Eardley St ST4 71 C3
Eardleyend Rd ST7 39 C4
Earl Dr WS7 211 C1
Earl St Kingswinford DY6 275 B2
Leek ST13 30 C3
Newcastle-u-L ST5 284 D3
Newcastle-u-L, Silverdale
ST5 55 B1
Stafford ST16 155 C2
Earl Sterndale CE Prim Sch
SK17 5 B2
Earl's Dr ST5 71 A3
Earls Ct Burton u T DE13 166 B4
Newcastle-u-L ST5 284 D3
Earls Rd ST4 88 A4
Earls Way ST18 158 B1
Earlsbrook Dr ST4 88 B4
Earlsway ST10 64 A4
Earlswood Cres WV9 240 A2
Earlswood Dr ST1 58 A3
Earlswood Rd DY6 275 C4
Early La ST15 103 B2
Easby Cl ST17 174 A4
Easby Way WS3 242 C1
Easdale Pl ST5 71 A3
Easedale Cl ST2 43 A1
Easing La ST13 31 C4
East Ave CW2 37 B3
East Bank Ride ST11 91 A4
East Beeches WV9 224 A1
East Butts Rd WS15 178 A1
East Cannock Ind Est
WS12 210 A2
East Cannock Rd WS12 210 A2
East Cl ST15 119 C4
East Cres Hanley ST1 57 C4
Newcastle-u-L ST5 56 B2
East Croft Rd WV4 265 B3
East Dr Biddulph ST8 27 B4
Cheddleton ST13 45 B4
East Gn WV4 265 B3
East Gr ST3 74 A1
East Prec ST1 282 C3
East Rd
Featherstone WV10 241 A4
Wolv WV4 266 C2
East St Burton u T DE15 167 B2
Cannock WS11 226 C3
Leek ST13 31 A3
Meir ST3 74 A3
Sedgley DY3 271 B2
Tamworth B77 261 B3
East Terr ST6 42 A3
East View Burslem ST6 56 C4
Mayfield DE6 81 B4
Tamworth B77 250 C2
Eastbank Rd ST1 282 A4
Eastbourne Cl ST13 30 B3
Eastbourne Rd ST1 57 C2
Eastbridge Ave ST1 57 B4
Eastcote Cres WS7 229 A3
Eastdean Ave ST2 58 A1
Eastern Ave
Burton u T DE13 166 C4
Lichfield WS13 214 B1
Eastern Way WS11 210 A1
Easters Gr ST2 43 A1
Eastfield WS9 256 A3
Eastfield Cl ST3 88 C4
Eastfields Rd ST14 126 B4
Eastgate Brewood ST19 223 B4
Cannock WS12 211 A3
Eastgate St
Burntwood WS7 228 C4
Stafford ST16 155 C2
Easthall Cl ST19 223 B3
Easthead Wlk ST1 282 A2
Eastholme ST15 106 B1
Eastlands ST17 174 C4
Eastlands Cl ST17 174 C4
Eastlands Gr ST17 174 C4
Eastleigh DY3 271 B4
Eastmoor Cl B74 257 A1
Eastney Cres WV8 255 C4
Eastridge Croft WS14 247 A3
Eastward Glen WV8 239 B1
Eastwick Cres ST4 88 A4
Eastwood Ave
Burntwood WS7 229 A4
Chell Heath ST6 42 A2
Eastwood Pl ST1 282 B2
Eastwood Rd ST1 282 C1
Eastwood Rise ST5 85 A4
Easy Lawns CW3 53 A3
Eaton Cres DY3 271 A2
Eaton Park Prim Sch
ST2 58 A1
Eaton Pl DY6 275 C3
Eaton Rd ST14 95 C2
Eaton St ST1 282 C3
Eaves Court Dr DY3 266 B1
Eaves La Bucknall ST2 58 B3
Cheadle ST10 76 C1
Oakamoor ST10 78 A4
Eaveswood Rd ST2 58 B3
Ebenezer St WS12 210 A4
Ebstree Mdw WV5 264 A1
Ebstree Rd WV5 264 A2
Ebury Gr ST3 73 C1
Eccleshall Ave WV10 240 B1
Eccleshall Bsns Pk
DE14 166 C2
Eccleshall Rd Ashley TF9 99 C2
Mucklestone TF9 99 A3
Seighford ST18 135 B1
Stafford ST16 155 B3
Stone ST15 119 C3
Eccleston Pl ST6 42 A3
Edale B77 251 A1
Edale Cl
Kingswinford DY6 275 A4
Newcastle-u-L ST5 55 A1
Tunstall ST6 41 A4
Wolv WV4 266 C2
Eddens Wood Cl B78 260 C3
Eddies La B79 216 C1
Eddisbury Dr ST5 40 B1
Eden Cl Biddulph ST8 16 C1
Cannock WS12 210 C1
Kidsgrove ST7 26 A1
Eden Gr Ashley TF9 99 C3
Cheadle ST10 76 C1
Meir ST3 73 C1
Edenbridge View DY1 271 C2
Edenhurst Ave ST3 74 B1
Edenhurst Prep Sch ST5 70 C4
Edensor CE Prim Sch
ST3 283 A2
Edensor Ct ST5 55 C4
Edensor High Sch ST3 283 B3
Edensor Rd ST3 283 B3
Edensor St ST5 55 C4
Edensor Terr ST3 283 B2
Edes Farm Dr ST14 95 C2
Edgar Cl B79 249 C4
Edgar Pl ST3 73 B3
Edge Ave ST6 42 A3
Edge Hill Kinver DY7 277 C2
Wood End CV9 262 A1
Edge Hill Ave WV10 241 A1
Edge Hill Dr Perton WV6 254 C2
Sedgley DY3 266 B1
Edge Hill Jun Sch DE15 185 C4
Edge Hill Rd B74 257 B2
Edge La ST9 43 B4
Edge St ST6 41 C1
Edge View Cl Kinver DY7 277 C3
Norton-in-t-M ST2 43 B1
Edge View Ct ST8 27 B4
Edge View Rd ST2 43 B1
Edge View Wlk DY7 277 C3
Edgecliff High Sch DY7 278 A2
Edgefield La ST9 43 B3
Edgefield Rd ST3 73 B3
Edgehill Rd ST13 30 B3
Edgeley Rd ST8 27 B4
Edgemoor Mdw WS12 210 B1
Edgeview Rd CW12 16 A4
Edgeware St ST1 282 A4
Edgmond Rd TF10 168 C2
Edgworth Ho WS13 214 A1
Edinbridge Cl CW2 37 A1
Edinburgh Cres DY8 275 B1
Edinburgh Rd CW12 6 A1
Edinburgh Way DE13 166 B4
Edision St ST4 72 B3
Edison Cl WS12 210 B4
Edison Rd ST16 155 C3
Edmonton Cl WS11 210 A1
Edmonton Gr ST2 42 C1
Edmonton Pl DE15 167 B1
Edmund Ave ST17 174 A4
Edmund Rd DY3 271 C3
Ednam Gr WV5 265 A1
Ednam Pl ST3 74 A1
Ednam Rd WV4 266 B3
Edwal Rd ST3 74 A2
Edward Ave
Aldridge WS9 256 A4
Newcastle-u-L ST5 71 A3
Trentham ST4 88 A4
Edward Ct B77 250 C2
Edward Davies Rd ST6 42 B1
Edward Rd WV6 254 C3
Edward St Audley ST7 39 C2
Burton u T DE14 166 B2
Cannock WS11 209 C2
Fenton ST4 72 C4
Newcastle-u-L ST5 56 B2
6 Stone ST15 105 A1
Tamworth B79 250 A3
Wolv WV4 266 C3
Edwards Dr ST16 155 B2
Edwards Farm Rd WS13 215 C4

Edwards Rd
Burntwood WS7 ....228 C3
Sutton Coldfield B75 ....258 B2
Edwin Cl Penkridge ST19 .207 C4
Stafford ST17 ....155 A1
Efflinch La DE13 ....201 C4
Egelwin Cl WV6 ....254 C1
Egerton Rd Aldridge B74 256 C1
Stoke-on-T ST4 ....71 C4
Wolv WV10 ....240 C2
Egerton St ST1 ....57 B1
Egg La ST18 ....158 C4
Eggington Dr ST18 .....207 C4
Eggington Rd DY8 ......279 B3
Egginton Prim Sch
DE65 ....148 A3
Egginton Rd
Eggington DE65 ....148 A4
Hilton DE55 ....147 C4
Eighth Ave DE14 ....184 C4
Eights Croft WS7 ......228 B4
Elaine Ave ST2 ....42 A1
Elan Cl Cookley DY10 ...280 A2
Sedgley DY3 ....271 B2
Elan Rd DY3 ....271 B2
Elburton Rd ST4 ....73 A3
Elder Cl Cannock WS11 ..210 B1
Uttoxeter ST14 ....126 A3
Elder Gr WV5 ....269 C3
Elder La WS7 ....229 B4
Elder Pl ST6 ....57 A3
Elder Rd ST6 ....57 A3
Elderberry Cl DY8 ......279 B2
Elderside Cl WS8 ....244 C4
Eldertree La TF9 ....100 B3
Eldon St Burton u T DE15 .167 A4
Hanley ST1 ....57 B3
Eldridge Cl WV9 ....239 C1
Eleanor Cres ST5 ....71 A3
Eleanor Harrison Dr
DY10 ....280 A3
Eleanor Pl ST5 ....71 A3
Eleanor View ST5 ....71 A3
Electric Ind Est DE14 ..166 C3
Electric St DE14 ....166 C3
Elenora St ST4 ....72 A4
Elford Cl ST16 ....155 B4
Elgar Cl Cannock WS11 ..209 C3
Lichfield WS13 ....214 A1
Elgar Cres ST1 ....58 A3
Elgin Cl ST3 ....266 C1
Elgin Ct WV6 ....254 C2
Elgin Rd WS3 ....243 A2
Elgin St ST4 ....57 A1
Elgood La ST6 ....41 B4
Elias Cl WS14 ....231 C1
Eliases La ST8 ....17 A1
Eliot Cl Armitage WS15 ..198 A2
Tamworth B79 ....250 A4
Eliot Way ST11 ....155 B1
Elizabeth Ave
Rolleston DE13 ....147 A2
Wolv WV4 ....266 A3
Elizabeth Ct
Market Drayton TF9 ....112 B4
Stoke-on-T ST4 ....71 C4
Talke ST7 ....40 B3
Elizabeth Dr
Newcastle-u-L ST5 ......55 C4
Tamworth B79 ....250 A3
Elizabeth Rd WS11 ....209 C3
Elizabeth St ST1 ....57 C2
Elkes Gr ST4 ....110 C1
Elkington Cl TF10 ......168 C1
Elkington Rise CW3 ......68 C4
Elkstone Cl ST6 ....41 C2
Ellam's Pl ST5 ....55 C1
Ellastone Gr ST4 ....71 C3
Ellastone Rd ST10,ST13 ..63 B3
Elldawn Ave ST6 ....42 C1
Ellerbeck B77 ....251 A1
Ellerby Rd ST3 ....88 C4
Ellers Gr ST6 ....56 C4
Ellesmere Ct TF10 .....168 C1
Ellesmere Gr TF9 ......112 A4
Ellesmere Rd WS11 .....226 A4
Ellgreave St ST6 ....56 C4
Ellington Ave ST16 .....156 A3
Ellington Cl ST2 ....58 A1
Elliot Dr ST9 ....59 A2
Elliot Rd ST4 ....72 C3
Elliott Cl WS11 ....209 C3
Elliott St ST5 ....56 B1
Elliotts La WV8 ....239 A2
Ellis St ST6 ....57 B4
Ellison Prim Sch ST5 ....56 B3
Ellison St ST6 ....56 B3
Ellowes Hall Sch The
DY3 ....271 B3
Ellowes Rd DY3 ....271 B2
Elm Ave ST17 ....175 C3
Elm Cl Branston DE14 ...184 C4
Colwich ST18 ....158 A1
Cookley DY10 ....280 A2
Doveridge DE6 ....127 B4
Kidsgrove ST7 ....41 A4
Leek ST13 ....30 B3
Newport TF10 ....168 C1
Sedgley DY3 ....271 B1
Stourbridge DY8 ......279 B1
Elm Cres ST18 ....158 B4
Elm Ct ST18 ....174 B3
Elm Dale Rd WV4 ......266 A3
Elm Dr Blakedown DY10 .281 A1

Elm Dr continued
Bradley ST18 ....191 B4
Cheadle ST10 ....76 C1
Market Drayton TF9 ....112 A4
Elm Farm Rd WV2 ......266 B4
Elm Gdns WS14 ....231 B4
Elm Gr Codsall WV8 ....239 A2
Huntington WS12 ......209 B4
Kinver DY7 ....278 B2
Elm Pl Cookley DY10 ....280 A2
Longton ST3 ....72 C1
Elm Rd Kingswinford DY6 .275 C3
Norton Canes WS11 ....228 A3
Stone ST15 ....120 A4
Elm St Burslem ST6 .....57 A4
Newcastle-u-L ST5 ......56 B2
Elm Tree Cl WV5 ......269 C3
Elm Tree Dr ST7 ....39 C1
Elm Tree Wlk B79 .....249 C4
Elm View ST14 ....95 C3
Elm Wlk ST19 ....207 C4
Elmbridge Way DY3 ....271 C3
Elmbrook Cl 12 ST3 .....89 C4
Elmcroft Gdns WV10 ...240 C2
Elmcroft Rd ST2 ....58 A3
Elmdale Dr WS9 ....256 B4
Elmdon Cl
Penkridge ST19 ....208 A4
Wolv WV10 ....240 A1
Elmdon Pl ST3 ....90 A1
Elmdon Rd WV10 ......240 A1
Elmhurst Eggington DE65 .148 A3
Newcastle-u-L ST5 ......70 C2
Elmhurst Cl
Brewood WV9 ....224 A2
Bucknall ST2 ....57 C1
Stafford ST16 ....155 B4
Elmhurst Dr
Burntwood WS7 ....229 A2
Kingswinford DY6 .....275 C2
Elmley Gr WV6 ....254 C2
Elmore Green Prim Sch
WS3 ....243 A1
Elmore Green Rd WS3 ..243 A1
Elmore Ho WS15 ....178 C1
Elmore La WS15 ....178 C1
Elmore Row WS3 ......243 A1
Elms Cl WV10 ....225 B1
Elms Dr WS11 ....209 B1
Elms La WV10 ....225 B1
Elms Paddock The WV6 253 B1
Elms Rd ST6 ....166 C1
Elms The ST5 ....56 B4
Elms Way ST3 ....74 A1
Elmsdale WV6 ....255 A1
Elmsmere Rd ST2 ....58 A3
Elmstead Cl ST4 ....71 C1
Elmstone Cl 17 ST17 ...175 B3
Elmtree Rd B74 ....256 B1
Elmwood Ave WV11 ....242 C1
Elmwood Cl
Cannock WS11 ....210 A2
Forsbrook ST11 ....91 A3
Gnosall ST20 ....171 B4
Lawton-gate ST7 ....25 A2
Elmwood Dr ST11 ....91 A3
Elmwood Gr ST14 .....110 C1
Elmwood Rd DY8 ....275 C1
Elmwood Rise DY3 .....266 A1
Elphinstone Rd ST4 ......71 C2
Elsby Pl ST6 ....42 A3
Elsdon Rd ST17 ....174 B3
Elsmere Ave ST3 ....73 A1
Elston Hall La WV10 ....240 B1
Elston Hall Prim Sch
WV10 ....240 B1
Elstree Cl ST3 ....73 C1
Elstree Gr ST1 ....58 A3
Elswick Rd ST4 ....72 C4
Eltham Gdns ST5 ....56 B2
Elton Cl
Newborough DE13 .....162 C4
Wolv WV10 ....240 C2
Elton La DE13 ....162 C4
Elton Terr ST6 ....41 B4
Elton Way ST20 ....171 B4
Elunda Gr WS7 ....228 C3
Elviron Dr WV6 ....255 A3
Elwell Cres DY1 ....271 C3
Elworthy Cl ST16 ......156 A3
Elwyn Cl DE13 ....147 B1
Ely Cl WS11 ....210 A1
Ely Wlk ST13 ....283 C4
Embers Way ST9 ....44 A4
Emberton Cl
Newcastle-u-L, Chesterton
ST5 ....55 C3
Newcastle-u-L, Wolstanton
ST5 ....56 B3
Emberton Way B77 .....250 C3
Embleton Wlk 1 ST6 ....56 C4
Embry Ave ST6 ....156 A3
Emerald Way ST15 .....120 A2
Emerson Cl DY3 ....271 A2
Emerson Rd Burslem ST6 .57 A3
Wolv WV10 ....240 C1
Emery Ave Hanley ST1 ...57 C4
Newcastle-u-L ST5 ......71 A4
Emery St ST3 ....57 A3
Emmanuel Rd WS7 .....229 A4
Empire Ind Est WS9 ....244 C1
Empire Pas ST4 ....72 A3
Empire Rd DE15 ....167 B2
Empire St ST4 ....72 A3
Emstone Ct ST5 ....88 C4
Emsworth Cres WV9 ...240 A1
Emsworth Rd ST3 ....88 C4

Encounter Pl ST1 ....57 C3
End Hall Rd WV6 ....255 A2
End The DE15 ....167 C4
Enderby Dr WV4 ......266 A3
Enderby Rise DE13 .....166 A4
Enderley Cl WS3 ....243 A2
Enderley Dr WS3 ......243 A2
Enderley St ST5 ....284 B4
Endon Dr ST8 ....27 A3
Endon Hall Prim Sch
ST9 ....43 C4
Endon High Sch ST9 ....43 C4
Endon Rd
Norton-in-t-M, Duke Bank
ST6 ....42 C2
Norton-in-t-M, Norton Green
ST6 ....42 C3
Endwood Dr B74 ......257 B2
Engelsea Brook La CW2 ..38 A2
Engine La
Brownhills WS8 ....244 B4
Tamworth B77 ....251 A1
Englesea Ave ST3 ....74 A1
Englesea Brook Mus of
Primitive Methodism★
CW2 ....38 A2
Engleton La ST19 ......223 B4
Engleton Mill La ST19 ..223 C4
English Martyrs RC Prim Sch
ST8 ....27 C1
Ennerdale Cl
Brownhills WS8 ....244 C4
25 Burslem ST6 ....56 C4
Ennerdale Dr WV6 .....254 C2
Ennerdale Rd WV6 .....255 B4
Enoch St ST6 ....56 C4
Ensall Dr DY8 ....275 C1
Ensford Rd B74 ....257 C3
Enson La Marston ST18 ..137 A4
Stone ST15,ST18 ......120 B1
Ensor Dr B78 ....251 C1
Enstone Ct ST5 ....71 A2
Enterprise Dr WV10 ....224 B3
Enterprise Gr WS3 .....244 A3
Enterprise Ind Pk WS3 231 C4
Enville Cl WS3 ....243 A2
Enville Common Rd
DY7 ....273 C2
Enville Pl DY8 ....279 C3
Enville Rd
Kingswinford DY6 .....275 A4
Kinver DY7 ....278 A2
Sedgley DY3 ....271 B2
Wolv WV4 ....265 B2
Enville St DY8 ....279 C3
Ephraim St ST1 ....282 C1
Epping Rd ST4 ....71 C2
Epple's Yd ST1 ....155 C1
Epsom Cl Branston DE14 .184 C4
Kingsley ST10 ....76 C3
Lichfield WS14 ....231 B4
Perton WV6 ....254 C2
Tamworth B77 ....261 B2
Epsom Dr 8 ST17 .....175 B4
Epworth Ho DE15 ......167 B2
Epworth St ST4 ....72 A4
Erasmus Way WS13 ....231 A4
Erdington Rd WS9 .....256 B4
Eremon Cl WS15 ......196 C3
Eringden B77 ....251 A1
Ermington Rd WV4 ....266 B2
Ernald Gdns 8 ST15 ..120 A4
Eros Cres ST1 ....57 C3
Errill Cl ST4 ....72 B3
Erskine St ST3 ....283 C1
Esk Way ST5 ....71 A2
Eskdale Pl
Newcastle-u-L ST5 ......71 A3
Trentham ST4 ....88 A4
Eskrett St WS12 ....210 B3
Esperanto Way ST6 .....57 B4
Esselie Ave TF9 ....100 B3
Essex Ave DY6 ....275 A3
Essex Dr Biddulph ST8 ...16 B1
Cannock WS12 ....210 A2
Colwich ST18 ....158 A2
Kidsgrove ST7 ....25 C1
Rugeley WS15 ....196 C1
Essex Gdns DY8 ....279 B4
Essex Pl ST5 ....71 A3
Essex Rd Burton u T DE13 185 B3
Sutton Coldfield B75 ...258 B1
Essington Cl
Alrewas DE13 ....201 A3
Brierley Hill DY8 ......275 C1
Lichfield WS14 ....231 A3
Shenstone WS14 ......247 A4
Essington Ind Est WV11 241 C2
Essington Rd WV12 ....242 A1
Estridge La WS6 ......227 A1
Etchell Rd B78 ....249 C2
Etching Hill CE Prim Sch
WS15 ....178 B1
Etching Hill Rd WS15 ..178 A1
Ethelfleda Rd B77 .....261 C3
Ethelred Cl B74 ....258 A2
Eton Ave ST5 ....70 C4
Eton Cl Burton u T DE14 .166 C3
Sedgley DY3 ....271 C3
Stafford ST17 ....156 A1
Eton Ct Lichfield WS14 ..231 A3
Sutton Coldfield B74 ...257 C1
Eton Park Jun Sch
DE14 ....166 B4
Eton Pk DE14 ....166 C3
Eton Rd DE14 ....166 B3
Etruria Old Rd ST1 ......56 C4

Etruria Rd Hanley ST1 ..282 A3
Newcastle-u-L ST5 ......56 C2
Etruria Sta ST4 ....56 C1
Etruria Vale Rd ST1 .....57 A2
Etruria Way ST5 ....56 C1
Etruscan St ST1 ....56 C1
Etruscan Wlk ST12 .....88 C2
Ettingshall Park Farm La
WV4 ....266 C2
Ettymore Cl DY3 ....271 B4
Ettymore Rd DY3 ......271 B4
Ettymore Rd W DY3 ....271 B4
Etwall Rd DE65 ....148 A3
Europa Way WS13 .....231 C4
Eva Gr ST5 ....87 B4
Evans Croft B78 ....250 A1
Evans St Burslem ST6 ...41 C1
Wolv WV4,WV14 ......266 C1
Eve La DY1 ....271 C3
Evelyn St ST4 ....72 B3
Everest Rd ST7 ....26 C4
Everglade Rd CV9 .....262 B1
Evergreen Hts ST12 ...210 A4
Evergreens The DE13 ..166 C4
Evershed Way DE14 ....166 B1
Eversley Ave ST13 ......30 C3
Eversley Gr DY3 ....266 B1
Eversley Rd ST3 ....73 C1
Evesham Cres WS3 .....242 C2
Evesham Way ST3 ......73 C2
Eveson Rd DY8 ....279 C1
Ewe Dale La DE6 ....35 A2
Exbury Cl WV9 ....239 C1
Excelsior Gr WS3 ......244 A3
Exchange Ind Est The
WS11 ....226 C3
Exchange Rd DE13 .....201 C4
Exchange The WS3 .....243 A1
Exeter Dr B79 ....249 C3
Exeter Gn ST2 ....58 B1
Exeter Rd WS11 ....226 A4
Exeter St ST17 ....174 C4
Exley B77 ....250 B1
Exmouth Gr ST6 ....57 A4
Exonbury Wlk 6 WS11 .209 C1
Eyam Cl WS14 ....167 A1
Eynsham Ct WV6 ......255 C3
Eyre St ST6 ....56 C4
Eyrie The DE15 ....167 B2

F

Faber RC Prim Sch The
ST10 ....78 B4
Faceby Gr ST3 ....90 B4
Fair Lady Dr WS7 ......211 B1
Fair Lawn WV7 ....237 A3
Fair Mdws WS15 ......179 A4
Fair Oak TF10 ....168 C2
Fair Oak High Sch
WS15 ....196 B1
Fair Oak Rd ST5 ....40 B1
Fair Oaks Dr WS6 .....243 A4
Fair View WS15 ....198 B2
Fair View Rd ST13 ......31 A2
Fairbank Ave ST4 ....72 A3
Fairbanks Wlk ST15 ...103 A3
Fairburn Cres WS3 .....244 A3
Fairclough Pl ST6 ....42 A3
Fairfax Rd WV10 ......240 C2
Fairfax St ST1 ....57 B3
Fairfield Ave Endon ST6 ..43 A4
Longton ST3 ....89 B4
Newcastle-u-L ST5 ......56 B2
Rolleston DE13 ....147 B2
Fairfield Cl WS12 ......210 B1
Fairfield Cres DE11 ....186 C3
Fairfield Ct ST16 ......155 C3
Fairfield Dr Codsall WV8 .238 C2
Kinver DY7 ....278 A2
Penkridge ST19 ....207 C3
Walsall WS3 ....244 A2
Fairfield Rd
Brierley Hill DY8 ......275 C1
Uttoxeter ST14 ....126 A4
Fairfield Rise DY8 .....279 B3
Fairfields ST7 ....39 C1
Fairfields Hill B78 .....262 C4
Fairfields Rd Biddulph ST8 17 A1
Market Drayton TF9 ....97 B1
Fairford Gdns
Burntwood WS7 ....229 B3
Kingswinford DY8 .....275 C2
Fairgreen Rd ST5 ....85 B3
Fairgreen Way B74 ....257 A1
Fairham Rd DE13 ......147 C1
Fairhaven CW2 ....37 A1
Fairhaven Gr ST1 ....57 C3
Fairhaven Prim Sch
DY8 ....275 B2
Fairhills DY3 ....271 B4
Fairlady Dr WS7 ....228 B4
Fairlawn Cl Meir ST3 ....89 C4
Walsall WV12 ....242 B1
Fairlawn Ct WV7 ......237 A3
Fairlawn Dr DY6 ......275 C3
Fairlawn Way WV12 ...242 B1
Fairlawns ST5 ....284 B4
Fairlight Gr ST3 ....90 A4
Fairmead Cl ST17 .....175 B3
Fairmeadows Prim Sch
DE11 ....186 C3
Fairmount Way WS15 ..178 B1
Fairoak ST5 ....70 C2
Fairoak Ave ST16 .....155 B4
Fairoak Bank ST21 ....115 B3
Fairoak Dr WV6 ....255 A2

Fairview Ave CW2 ......37 A3
Fairview Cl
Cheslyn Hay WS6 .....226 B1
Tamworth B77 ....250 C3
Fairview Cres DY6 .....275 C3
Fairview Rd WV4 ......265 B2
Fairview Villas ST5 ......85 B3
Fairview Way ST17 ....156 B1
Fairway Burton u T DE14 .185 A3
Cannock WS11 ....226 B3
Stafford ST16,ST17 ....156 A1
Tamworth B77 ....261 C3
Trentham ST4 ....87 C4
Walsall WS4 ....244 B1
Fairway Ct B77 ....251 A2
Fairway Rd ST6 ....42 C2
Fairway The Clifton DE6 ..81 C3
Swadlincote DE11 .....186 C3
Fairways Ave DY8 .....279 C1
Fairways Cl DY8 ....279 C1
Falcon B77 ....262 C4
Falcon Bsns Ctr DE14 ..166 C3
Falcon Cl
Burton u T DE14 ......166 C3
Cannock WS11 ....209 B1
Cheslyn Hay WS6 .....226 B1
Falcon Cres WV14 .....266 C1
Falcon Dr WS14 ....232 C3
Falcon Rd ST3 ....90 A3
Falcon Rise DY8 ....279 B3
Falcon Way WV1 ......271 C1
Falcondale Rd WV12 ...242 B1
Falconry Ctr★ DY9 .....281 C2
Faldo Cl DE14 ....185 A3
Falkirk Grange ST5 ......70 C4
Falklands Cl DY3 ......269 C1
Fallow Deer Lawn TF10 168 C3
Fallow Field
Cannock WS11 ....209 C2
Lichfield WS13 ....214 A2
Little Aston B74 ......257 A2
Fallow Rd B78 ....249 C1
Fallowfield Longton ST3 ..88 C4
Perton WV6 ....254 B2
Stafford ST17 ....175 B3
Wolv WV8 ....239 C1
Fallowfield Cl ST19 ....207 C4
Fallowfields Dr DE13 ..183 A3
Falmouth Ave ST17 ....175 C4
Falmouth Cl ST17 .....175 C4
Falmouth Ct ST5 ....71 B3
Falmouth Dr B77 ......250 C3
Falmouth Rd CW12 .....15 C4
Falna Cres B79 ....249 C4
Fancourt Ave WV4 ....265 B2
Fancy Wlk ST16 ....155 B3
Fane Rd WV11 ....242 A1
Fanlizard La ST20 .....171 B2
Far Green Ind Est ST1 ...57 B3
Far Lane Ind Est ST10 ..62 A4
Far Ridding ST20 ......171 B3
Far View WS9 ....245 A1
Faraday Pl ST4 ....71 C4
Faraday Rd ST16 ......155 C3
Farcroft Ave ST5 ....55 C3
Farcroft Dr TF9 ....97 A1
Fareham Cres WV4 ....265 B3
Fareham Gr 13 ST3 .....89 C3
Farewell La WS7 ......229 C3
Faringdon B77 ....250 C1
Farington Pl ST6 ....42 A3
Farland Gr ST6 ....42 A4
Farleigh Dr WV3 ......265 A4
Farleigh Gr ST2 ....58 B1
Farleigh Rd WV6 ......255 A2
Farley La ST7 ....78 B2
Farley Rd ST10 ....78 A3
Farm Cl Burton u T DE13 .166 A4
Cannock WS12 ....210 A2
Codsall WV8 ....239 A1
Market Drayton TF9 ....97 A1
Rugeley WS15 ....178 A3
Sedgley DY3 ....271 A4
Tamworth B79 ....250 B4
Farm Ct DE13 ....166 B4
Farm Gr TF10 ....168 B2
Farm La DE15 ....167 C4
Farm Lea
Hilderstone ST15 .....106 B1
Norton-in-t-M ST6 .....42 C3
Farm Rd Albrighton WV6 .252 B4
Burton u T DE13 ....166 B4
Wolv WV3 ....265 B4
Farm Side DE11 ....186 C3
Farm View ST15 ......106 B1
Farmadine ST4 ....88 A4
Farman Cl ST3 ....90 B4
Farmbrook Ave WV10 ..240 B2
Farmdown Rd ST17 ....156 B1
Farmer St ST3 ....283 C2
Farmers Bank ST5 ......55 B1
Farmfields Rise CW3 ....67 B1
Farmoor Way WV10 ...240 C2
Farmount Dr 5 WS11 ..226 C4
Farmside Gn WV9 .....239 C1
Farmside La ST8 ....17 A1
Farmwood Cl ST3 ....74 A1
Farnborough Ct B75 ...258 B1
Farnborough Dr ST3 ....90 B4
Farncote Dr B74 ......257 C2
Farndale Ave WV6 .....255 C3
Farndale Cl 8 ST6 ......41 B2
Farne Gr ST3 ....73 A2
Farnham Dr ST8 ....27 A3
Farnworth Cl ST8 ....27 A3
Farnworth Rd ST3 ......73 C3
Farrier Cl ST15 ....120 B4
Farrier Way DY6 ......275 A4

Farriers Gn TF10 . . . . . .169 A2
Farriers Mill WS3 . . . . .243 C2
Farrington Cl ST6 . . . . . . .42 C2
Farrington Rd WV4 . . . .266 C2
Farwall La ST10 . . . . .49 C1
Farway Gdns WV8 . . . . .238 C1
Fasson Cl B77 . . . . .261 B4
Fauld Ind Pk DE13 . . . . .145 C2
Fauld La Tutbury DE13 . . .146 A3
  Tutbury, Fauld DE13 . . . .145 A4
Faulkner Cl DY8 . . . . . . .279 C2
Faversham Cl WV8 . . . . .255 C4
Faversham Rd DE13 . . . .166 A3
Fawcett Way ST1 . . . . . .282 C4
Fawfield Dr ST6 . . . . .41 B3
Fawn Cl Huntington WS12 209 B3
  Meir ST3 . . . . .90 A4
Fazeley Rd B78 . . . . .250 A1
Fearns Ave ST3 . . . . .41 A1
Fearon Gn ST6 . . . . .42 C2
Featherbed La
  Elmhurst WS13 . . . . . . .213 C2
  Hixon ST18 . . . . .158 B4
Featherston Rd B74 . . . .257 A1
Featherstone La
  Featherstone WV10 . . . .241 A4
  Shareshill WV10 . . . . . .225 A1
Fecknam Way WS13 . . . .214 B1
Federation Rd ST6 . . . . . .41 C1
Fegg Hayes Rd ST6 . . . . .42 A3
Feiashill Cl WV5 . . . . . . .269 A3
Feiashill La WV5 . . . . . . .269 A3
Felcourt Gdns ST1 . . . . . .57 C3
Felden St ST16 . . . . .136 B1
Fellbrook Ct ST2 . . . . . . .58 A2
Fellbrook La ST2 . . . . . . .58 A2
Fellfield Way ST16 . . . . .155 B4
Fellmeadow Way DY3 . . .271 C4
Fellows Ave DY6 . . . . . . .275 B4
Fellows St WV2 . . . . .266 B4
Felspar Rd B77 . . . . .251 A2
Felstead Dr B77 . . . . . . .261 B2
Felsted St ST2 . . . . .43 A2
Felthouse La ST13 . . . . . .45 A1
Femwork Ind Est DE14 . .166 C4
Fence La CW12 . . . . .15 B2
Fenlow Ave ST2 . . . . .57 C1
Fenmere Cl WV4 . . . . . . .266 B3
Fenn Rise DY8 . . . . .275 B2
Fenn St B78 . . . . .250 C1
Fennel Cl
  Cheslyn Hay WS6 . . . . . .226 B2
  Uttoxeter ST14 . . . . . . .126 A3
Fennel Dr ST17 . . . . .174 C2
Fennel Gr ST3 . . . . .90 A3
Fenpark Ind Est ST4 . . . . .73 A3
Fenpark Rd ST4 . . . . .73 A3
Fenton Cl CW12 . . . . .6 A1
Fenton Croft ST19 . . . . .205 B3
Fenton House La ST19 . .205 A3
Fenton Ind Est
  Bucknall ST2 . . . . .57 C1
  Stoke-on-T ST4 . . . . .72 C1
Fenton Pk ST4 . . . . .73 A3
Fenton Rd ST2 . . . . .57 C1
Fereday Rd WS9 . . . . . . .245 A2
Fereday's Croft DY3 . . . .271 B4
Fermain Cl ST5 . . . . .70 C2
Fern Cl WS4 . . . . .244 A4
Fern Cres CW12 . . . . .6 A2
Fern Croft WS13 . . . . . . .213 C1
Fern Dell Cl WS11 . . . . .209 B1
Fern Dene CW3 . . . . .68 B4
Fern Dr
  Great Wyrley WS6 . . . . .227 A2
  Stafford ST16 . . . . .155 C4
Fern Leys WV3 . . . . .255 B1
Fern Pl ST3 . . . . .283 C1
Fern Rd Huntington WS12 209 B3
  Wolv WV3 . . . . .266 A4
Ferncombe Dr WS15 . . . .178 B2
Ferncroft Cl ST4 . . . . .88 A4
Ferndale Cl
  Burntwood WS7 . . . . . . .229 A4
  Caverswall ST9 . . . . .59 A4
  Forsbrook ST11 . . . . .90 C3
  Weston CW2 . . . . .37 A3
Ferndale Rd
  Essington WV11 . . . . . .242 A2
  Lichfield WS13 . . . . . . .213 C1
Ferndown Ave DY3 . . . . .271 B4
Ferndown Cl Meir ST3 . . . .73 B1
  Walsall WS3 . . . . .243 A2
Ferndown Dr ST5 . . . . . . .71 B1
Ferndown Dr S ST5 . . . . .71 B1
Ferney Pl ST6 . . . . .41 B3
Fernhill Rd TF10 . . . . . . .150 B1
Fernhurst Cl ST15 . . . . . .120 B4
Fernhurst Gr ST3 . . . . . . .89 C4
Fernie Cl ST15 . . . . .120 B3
Fernlea Cres ST9 . . . . . . .43 C4
Fernlea Gr
  Blythe Bridge ST3 . . . . . .90 A2
  Meir ST3 . . . . .74 A3
Fernleigh Ave WS7 . . . . .229 A4
Fernleigh Gdns
  Kingswinford DY8 . . . . .275 B2
  Stafford ST16 . . . . .155 C4
Fernwood Cl 155 B4
Fernwood Croft WS13 . . . .30 B2
Fernwood Dr Leek ST13 . . .30 B2
  Rugeley WS15 . . . . .178 B1
Fernwood Gn ST4 . . . . . .88 B4
Ferrand Cl ST4 . . . . .72 A1
Ferrers Ave DE13 . . . . . .146 A4

Ferrers Cl B75 . . . . .258 B1
Ferrers Rd
  Tamworth B77 . . . . .250 B2
  Weston ST18 . . . . .138 B1
  Yoxall DE13 . . . . .182 A1
Ferrie Gr WS8 . . . . .244 C4
Ferry St DE15 . . . . .185 C4
Ferry Vale Cl DE15 . . . . .185 C4
Festing St ST1 . . . . .282 C4
Festival Cl ST6 . . . . .57 A3
Festival Ct
  Cannock WS11 . . . . .209 C3
  Lichfield WS13 . . . . . . .231 A4
Festival Mews WS12 . . . .209 C3
Festival Rd DE14 . . . . . .184 C4
Festival Way ST1 . . . . . . .56 C3
Festivale Gn ST19 . . . . .205 B3
Fiddler's La DE13 . . . . . .146 C2
Fiddlers Bank ST6 . . . . . .43 A4
Field Ave Hatton DE65 . . .146 A4
  Norton-in-t-M ST2 . . . . . .43 A1
Field Cl Blythe Bridge ST11 90 C3
  Burton u T DE13 . . . . . .166 A4
  Walsall WS4 . . . . .244 A1
  Whitmore ST5 . . . . .85 B3
Field Cres ST18 . . . . . . .154 B1
Field Dr DE13 . . . . .147 A2
Field End Cl ST4 . . . . .88 A4
Field Farm Dr B79 . . . . .217 B3
Field Farm Rd B77 . . . . .250 B1
Field Head Pl WV6 . . . . .255 A2
Field House Ct ST4 . . . . .104 C1
Field La Burton u T DE13 166 A4
  Church Leigh ST10 . . . . .109 A1
  Great Wyrley WS6 . . . . .226 C2
  Stanton DE6 . . . . .80 B4
  Walsall WS4 . . . . .244 A1
Field Pl Longton ST3 . . . . .73 B3
  Rugeley WS15 . . . . .196 A4
  Stafford ST16 . . . . .155 B4
Field Rd Lichfield WS13 . .214 A2
  Walsall WS3 . . . . .243 B1
Field Rise DE13 . . . . . . .166 A4
Field St Cannock WS11 . .209 C2
  Leek ST13 . . . . .30 C3
Field Terr ST15 . . . . .105 A1
Field View Biddulph ST8 . . .16 B1
  Meir ST3 . . . . .74 A3
Field Way ST11 . . . . .186 C3
Field Wlk WS9 . . . . .256 A4
Fielden Cl ST6 . . . . .42 C1
Fieldfare WS7 . . . . .229 B3
Fieldhouse Rd
  Burntwood WS7 . . . . . . .229 A4
  Cannock WS12 . . . . .209 C4
  Wolv WV4 . . . . .266 C2
Fielding St ST4 . . . . .72 A3
Fields Rd CW12 . . . . .15 C4
Fields The WV8 . . . . .239 A2
Fieldside Stafford ST17 . .175 B3
  Swynnerton ST15 . . . . . .118 C3
Fieldsway ST15 . . . . .119 C4
Fieldway
  Blythe Bridge ST11 . . . . .90 B4
  Caverswall ST2 . . . . .58 C2
  Fenton ST3 . . . . .72 C2
  Trentham ST4 . . . . .87 C4
Fife St ST4 . . . . .283 A4
Fifth Ave ST7 . . . . .25 C1
Filance Cl ST19 . . . . .207 C4
Filance La ST19 . . . . . . .207 C4
Filey B77 . . . . .250 C3
Filey Cl Bucknall ST2 . . . . .58 B1
  Cannock WS11 . . . . .226 B4
Filey Rd WV10 . . . . .240 A1
Fillybrooks Cl ST5 . . . . . .119 C4
Fillybrooks The ST15 . . . .119 C4
Filton Ave WS7 . . . . .229 A4
Finch Pl ST8 . . . . .27 A1
Finch St ST8 . . . . .27 A1
Finch Way WS13 . . . . . . .215 C4
Fincham Cl WV9 . . . . . . .240 A2
Finchdean Cl ST3 . . . . . . .90 A4
Finchdene Gr WV3 . . . . .255 B1
Finches Hill WS13 . . . . . .178 B1
Finchfield Cl DY8 . . . . . .279 B2
Finchfield Gdns WV3 . . . .255 C1
Finchfield Hill WV3 . . . . .255 B1
Finchfield La WV3 . . . . . .265 B4
Finchfield Rd WV3 . . . . . .255 C1
Finchfield Rd W WV3 . . .255 B1
Finchley Cl DY3 . . . . .271 B1
Finchsmith Pl ST3 . . . . . .283 B2
Fine La WS13 . . . . .215 C3
Finger Post Dr WS3 . . . . .244 A3
Finney Gr ST2 . . . . .58 A2
Finstock Ave ST3 . . . . . . .88 C4
Fir Cl WS12 . . . . .209 B4
Fir Gr DY8 . . . . .279 B3
Fir St DY3 . . . . .270 C4
Fir Tree Cl B79 . . . . .249 C4
Fir Tree Dr DY3 . . . . .271 C4
Fir Tree Pl ST5 . . . . .55 C4
Fir Tree Rd Meir ST3 . . . . .89 C4
  Wolv WV3 . . . . .265 B4
Firbank Pl ST3 . . . . .73 C2
Firbank Way WS3 . . . . . .243 C1
Firbeck Gdns ST17 . . . . .175 B4
Firbob La ST10 . . . . .94 A2
Fircroft Cl ST11 . . . . .210 A2
Firecrest Cl WS11 . . . . . .210 B1
Firmstone Ct DY8 . . . . . .279 C4
Firmstone St DY8 . . . . . .279 C4
Firs Cl The ST17 . . . . . . .175 B4
Firs St DY6 . . . . .275 C3
Firs The Cannock WS15 . .211 C3
  Cannock, Hawks Green
  WS11 . . . . .210 A1

First Ave Branston DE14 . .184 C4
  Brownhills WS8 . . . . . . .245 A4
  Bucknall ST2 . . . . .58 B2
  Kidsgrove ST7 . . . . .25 C1
  Newcastle-u-L ST5 . . . . . .56 B4
  Sedgley DY6 . . . . .271 A1
  Stafford ST16 . . . . .155 B4
Firsway WV6 . . . . .255 A1
Firsway The ST19 . . . . . .221 C4
Firtree Cl ST18 . . . . .174 B2
Firwood Rd ST8 . . . . .16 C1
Fisher Rd WS3 . . . . .242 C1
Fisher St Cannock WS12 . .194 C1
  Chell Heath ST8 . . . . .27 A1
  Wolv WV3 . . . . .266 A4
Fishers Lock TF10 . . . . . .168 C2
Fisherwick Cl WS14 . . . . .232 C3
Fisherwick Rd WS14 . . . .232 C3
Fishley Cl WS3 . . . . .243 B2
Fishley Rd WS3 . . . . .243 B3
Fishpond La
  Egginton DE65 . . . . .148 A3
  Tutbury DE13 . . . . .146 B3
Fishpond Way ST2 . . . . . .58 A4
Fistral Cl ST3 . . . . .73 B2
Fistral Gdns WV3 . . . . . .265 C4
Fitchet's Bank WS7 . . . . .229 C3
Fitzgerald Cl ST3 . . . . . . .74 A2
Fitzherbert Cl ST15 . . . . .103 A2
Fitzherbert Rd ST1 . . . . . .57 C4
Five Lands Rd DE15 . . . .185 C4
Five Lanes End ST20 . . . .153 B4
Five Oaks Cl ST5 . . . . . . .70 C2
Five Ways
  Blakedown DY10 . . . . . .281 A3
  Sedgley DY3 . . . . .271 B2
  Wolv WV3 . . . . .255 A4
Five Ways Prim Sch
  WS12 . . . . .210 B1
Fives Gr WS7 . . . . .228 B4
Flackets La DE6 . . . . . . .128 A4
Flackett St ST3 . . . . .283 C5
Flamborough Gr ST6 . . . . .56 C4
Flanders Dr DY6 . . . . . . .275 B4
Flash CE Prim Sch SK17 . . .3 A2
Flash La Blore TF9 . . . . . .98 C1
  Norton-in-t-M ST2 . . . . . .43 B1
  Stoke-on-T ST5 . . . . .55 A1
  Wombourne WV4 . . . . . .264 C1
Flash Ley Prim Sch
  ST17 . . . . .174 C4
Flashes The ST20 . . . . . .171 C4
Flather La DE6 . . . . .65 B1
Flats La WS14 . . . . .248 A3
Flatts Cl ST3 . . . . .166 A3
Flatts Rd ST6 . . . . .42 C3
Flavells La DY3 . . . . .271 A1
Flax Croft ST15 . . . . .120 A4
Flax Hill Jun Sch B79 . . .250 A4
Flax Ovens The ST19 . . . .192 C1
Flax St ST4 . . . . .72 A3
Flaxley Prim Sch WS15 . .196 C3
Flaxley Rd WS15 . . . . . . .196 B3
Flaxman Cl ST12 . . . . .88 C2
Fleckney Ave ST3 . . . . . . .73 C2
Fleet St DE14 . . . . .166 B1
Fleets La ST13 . . . . .49 A4
Fleming Rd ST4 . . . . .72 A4
Flemmynge Cl WV8 . . . . .238 C2
Fletcher Bank ST4 . . . . . .284 A3
Fletcher Cres ST2 . . . . . . .43 A1
Fletcher Rd
  Stoke-on-T ST4 . . . . .72 A3
  Walsall WV12 . . . . .242 B1
Fletcher St ST1 . . . . .282 A1
Fletchers Wildlife Ctr★
  ST21 . . . . .134 A4
Fletches The DE13 . . . . .147 A4
Fleur Dr ST4 . . . . .73 A3
Flinn Cl WS14 . . . . .231 B4
Flint St ST4 . . . . .74 A3
Flints Cnr WS12 . . . . . . .195 A2
Flintsham Gr ST1 . . . . . . .282 B4
Flora Cl B79 . . . . .250 B4
Florence Ave WV4 . . . . . .266 C2
Florence Dr DE6 . . . . . . .127 B4
Florence Prim Sch ST3 . .283 C2
Florence Rd Codsall WV8 239 B2
  Trentham ST4 . . . . .71 C1
Florence St
  Cannock WS12 . . . . .210 A4
  Newcastle-u-L ST5 . . . . .284 B3
Florence Terr ST4 . . . . . . .29 A1
Florendine Com Prim Sch
  B77 . . . . .250 C3
Florendine St B77 . . . . . .250 C3
Florida Cl ST6 . . . . .57 A4
Floyd St ST4 . . . . .72 A4
Flynn Row ST4 . . . . .72 C4
Foden Ave ST7 . . . . .25 A2
Foden Cl WS14 . . . . .246 C3
Foden St ST4 . . . . .72 A3
Fogg St ST5 . . . . .284 B3
Fogg St E ST5 . . . . .284 B3
Fogg St W ST5 . . . . .284 B3
Fold La ST6 . . . . .16 C2
Fold Terr ST13 . . . . .45 B3
Fold The Codsall WV8 . . .238 B1
  Stone ST15 . . . . .105 B2
  Wolv WV4 . . . . .265 C2
Fole La ST15 . . . . .109 C4
Folebank Barns ST14 . . .109 C4
Foley Ave WV6 . . . . .255 B2
Foley Church Cl B74 . . . .257 A1
Foley Cl B75 . . . . .258 C1
Foley Dr WV6 . . . . .255 B2
Foley Gr WV5 . . . . .269 C3

Foley Inf Sch DY7 . . . . . .278 A2
Foley Pl ST4 . . . . .283 B4
Foley Rd ST3 . . . . .283 A3
Foley Rd E B74 . . . . .257 A1
Foley Rd W B74 . . . . . . .256 C1
Foley St Kinver DY7 . . . . .278 A2
  Longton ST4 . . . . .283 B5
Foley Wood Cl B74 . . . . .256 C1
Folly Fields ST13 . . . . . . .45 A1
Folly La ST5 . . . . .60 B4
Fontaine Pl ST4 . . . . .72 A3
Fontenaye Rd B79 . . . . . .249 C4
Fonthill Rd ST16 . . . . . . .155 C3
Fonthill Wlk ST2 . . . . .58 A2
Fontwell Rd
  Branston DE14 . . . . .184 C4
  Wolv WV10 . . . . .240 B2
Footherley La WS14 . . . . .246 B2
Footherley Rd WS14 . . . .246 C3
Forber Rd ST4 . . . . .71 C2
Forbisher Cl WS6 . . . . . .226 C1
Ford Ave WS6 . . . . .42 A3
Ford Brook La WS3 . . . . .244 A1
Ford Cl ST15 . . . . .120 A4
Ford Dr ST15 . . . . .118 C3
Ford Green Hall (Mus)★
  ST6 . . . . .42 A1
Ford Green Rd
  Chell Heath ST6 . . . . .42 B1
  Norton-in-t-M ST6 . . . . . .42 B1
Ford Hayes La ST2,ST3 . . .58 C1
Ford La Farewell WS13 . . .212 C1
  Longdon WS15 . . . . . . .198 A1
Ford Rd TF10 . . . . .168 C3
Ford St Burton u T DE15 . .185 C4
  Leek ST13 . . . . .30 C3
  Newcastle-u-L ST5 . . . . . .55 A1
  Stoke-on-T ST6 . . . . .56 C1
Ford Way WS15 . . . . .198 A3
Fordham Gr WV9 . . . . . . .240 A2
Fordhouse Rd WV10 . . . .240 B1
Fordhouse Road Ind Est
  WV10 . . . . .240 B1
Fordrough The B74 . . . . .258 A1
Fords La ST7 . . . . .26 B3
Foregate Ct ST16 . . . . . .155 C2
Foregate St ST16 . . . . . .155 B2
Forest Cl Colwich ST18 . .177 B4
  Newcastle-u-L ST5 . . . . . .70 C2
Forest Ct ST1 . . . . .282 B4
Forest Dr DY7 . . . . .277 C2
Forest Edge ST6 . . . . .57 B3
Forest Edge Way DE13 . .166 A4
Forest Glade WS6 . . . . . .226 C1
Forest La DY7 . . . . .268 C1
Forest Park Prim Sch
  ST1 . . . . .282 A4
Forest Rd
  Burton u T DE13 . . . . . .165 C2
  Draycott in t C DE6,ST14 144 A2
  Dunstall DE13 . . . . .183 A3
  Market Drayton TF9 . . . .112 A4
  Meir ST3 . . . . .89 C4
Forest Way WS6 . . . . . . .227 A1
Foresters Bk ST2,ST9 . . . .43 B2
Forestside Gr ST4 . . . . . . .72 A1
Forge Cl Burntwood WS7 229 B3
  Wolv WV8 . . . . .239 C1
Forge La Aldridge WS9 . . .256 A3
  Aldridge, Mill Green WS9 256 C3
  Blakedown DY10 . . . . . .281 A1
  Burntwood WS7 . . . . . . .229 A3
  Burslem ST6 . . . . .56 C2
  Burton u T DE13 . . . . . .148 A1
  Kingswinford DY6 . . . . .275 A4
  Lichfield WS14 . . . . . . .214 A1
  Norton in Hales TF9 . . . . .82 B1
  Shenstone WS14 . . . . . .257 B4
Forge Leys WV5 . . . . . . .269 C3
Forge Mews WS11 . . . . . .178 C1
Forge Rd Rugeley WS15 . .178 C3
  Stourbridge DY8 . . . . . .279 C3
  Walsall WS3 . . . . .243 C2
Forge Rise ST18 . . . . . . .191 B4
Forge Side ST9 . . . . .44 A4
Forge St ST12 . . . . .210 B2
Forge Valley Way WV5 . . .269 C3
Forge Way ST8 . . . . .27 C4
Formby Ave WV6 . . . . . . .254 B2
Formby Way WS3 . . . . . .243 C2
Forrest Ave
  Cannock WS11 . . . . .226 C4
  Essington WV11 . . . . . . .242 A2
Forrester Cl
  Alrewas WS13 . . . . .215 B3
  Biddulph ST8 . . . . .27 B4
Forrester Rd ST15 . . . . . .120 A4
Forrister St ST3 . . . . .73 B2
Forsbrook CE Prim Sch
  ST11 . . . . .91 A4
Forster St ST6 . . . . .41 B2
Forsyte Rd ST3 . . . . .73 B3
Forsythia Gr WV8 . . . . . .239 A2
Fort Cres WS9 . . . . .245 A2
Fortescue La ST15 . . . . .178 C1
Forties B77 . . . . .261 C4
Forton Cl WV6 . . . . .255 A1
Forton Glade TF10 . . . . .168 C3
Forton Rd TF10 . . . . .168 C3
Forty Acre Cl TF9 . . . . . . .99 C3
Forum Rd ST5 . . . . .55 B3
Fosbrooke Pl ST4 . . . . . . .71 B4
Fossdale Rd B77 . . . . . . .262 A4
Fosseway WS14 . . . . .231 A3
Fosseway La WS13,
  WS14 . . . . .230 C2
Foster Ave WS12 . . . . . . .209 C4
Foster Cres DY7 . . . . . . .278 A2

Foster Ct ST3 . . . . .72 C3
Foster Gr WV6 . . . . .254 C2
Foster Pl DY8 . . . . .279 C3
Foster Rd CW12 . . . . .6 A3
Foster St DY7 . . . . .278 A2
Foston Ave DE13 . . . . . . .166 A3
Foston Cl DE65 . . . . .146 B4
Fotherley Brook Rd
  WS9 . . . . .256 C3
Foundry La Bucknall ST2 . .58 A1
  Scholar Green ST7 . . . . . .25 C4
  Walsall WS3 . . . . .243 C2
Foundry Rd DY6 . . . . . . .275 B4
Foundry Sq ST6 . . . . .43 A3
Foundry St Hanley ST1 . . .282 B3
  Kingswinford DY6 . . . . .275 B4
Fountain Ct Biddulph ST8 . .16 B1
  20 Burslem ST6 . . . . .56 C4
Fountain Fold ST20 . . . . .171 B3
Fountain Rd DE6 . . . . . . .144 B4
Fountain Sq ST1 . . . . . . .282 B3
Fountain St Fenton ST4 . . .72 C3
  Leek ST13 . . . . .30 C3
Fountains Ave ST5 . . . . . .71 A3
Fountains Rd WS3 . . . . . .242 C1
Fountains Way WS3 . . . . .242 C1
Four Ashes Ind Est
  WV10 . . . . .224 B3
Four Ashes Rd ST19 . . . .223 C4
Four Crosses La WV10,
  WS11 . . . . .225 C4
Four Crosses Rd WS4 . .244 B1
Four Lane Ends
  Eccleshall ST21 . . . . . . .134 A3
  Milwich ST18 . . . . .122 A4
Four Lanes End
  Betley CW2 . . . . .37 C4
  Haughton ST18 . . . . . . .173 A3
  Seighford ST18 . . . . . . .153 C4
  Uttoxeter ST14 . . . . . . .126 B2
Four Oaks Common Rd
  B74 . . . . .257 C2
Four Oaks Ct B74 . . . . . .258 A1
Four Oaks Inf Sch B74 257 C2
Four Oaks Jun Sch B74 257 C2
Four Oaks Rd B74 . . . . . .258 A1
Fourlane Ends ST20,
  ST21 . . . . .131 C4
Fourth Ave
  Brownhills WS8 . . . . . . .229 A4
  Bucknall ST2 . . . . .58 C2
  Kidsgrove ST7 . . . . .25 C1
Fourways CW2 . . . . .37 A3
Fowlchurch Rd ST13 . . . . .30 C4
Fowler Cl WV6 . . . . .254 C3
Fowler St WV2 . . . . .266 B3
Fowler's La ST7 . . . . .43 B1
Fox Cl Burton u T DE14 . .185 A4
  Seisdon WV5 . . . . .263 C1
Fox Covert DY8 . . . . .279 C3
Fox Gdns ST7 . . . . .40 B4
Fox Gr ST5 . . . . .71 B1
Fox Hill Rd B75 . . . . .258 C1
Fox Hollow Ashley TF9 . . .99 B3
  Eccleshall ST21 . . . . . . .133 C3
  Wolv WV6 . . . . .255 B1
Fox La Alrewas DE13 . . . .200 C1
  Elmhurst WS13 . . . . . . .214 A3
Fox Leigh Mdws WS15 . .198 A2
Fox Rd WV5 . . . . .263 C2
Fox Wlk WS9 . . . . .245 A2
Foxcote Cl ST17 . . . . . . .175 C3
Foxcroft Cl WS7 . . . . . . .229 A3
Foxes La ST19 . . . . .222 B3
Foxes Rake WS11 . . . . . .209 C2
Foxfield Cl ST10 . . . . .76 C3
Foxfield Steam Rly
  ★Blythe Bridge ST11 . . . . .90 C4
  ★ Dilhorne ST10,ST11 . . . .75 A3
Foxfield Way ST3 . . . . . . .88 C4
Foxfields Way WS12 . . . .209 B4
Foxglove B77 . . . . .251 A2
Foxglove Ave
  Burton u T DE15 . . . . . .186 A4
  Uttoxeter ST14 . . . . . . .126 A3
Foxglove Cl
  Featherstone WV10 . . . .241 A4
  Lichfield WS14 . . . . . . .231 A3
  Meir ST3 . . . . .74 A3
  Rugeley WS15 . . . . .178 B1
  Walsall WS3 . . . . .244 A3
Foxglove La ST5 . . . . .71 B1
Foxglove Rd DY1 . . . . . . .271 C2
Foxglove Wlk WS12 . . . . .210 B1
Foxhill Cl WS12 . . . . .210 B1
Foxhills Cl WS7 . . . . .229 A3
Foxhills Rd
  Kingswinford DY8 . . . . .275 B1
  Wolv WV4 . . . . .265 B2
Foxland Ave WS6 . . . . . . .227 A2
Foxlands Cl ST2 . . . . .58 B2
Foxlands Cres WV4 . . . . .265 B2
Foxlands Dr Sedgley DY3 271 B3
  Wombourne WV4 . . . . . .265 B2
Foxley Cl ST3 . . . . .43 A1
Foxmeadow Cl DY3 . . . . .271 C4
Foxtail Way WS12 . . . . . .210 C2
Foxton Cl DE13 . . . . .201 A1
Foxwood Cl ST15 . . . . . .119 C3
Foxwood Rd B78 . . . . . . .262 C4
Fradgley Ct ST14 . . . . . . .125 B4
Fradgley Gr ST14 . . . . . . .110 C1
Fradley La WS13 . . . . . . .215 C4
Fradswell La ST18 . . . . . .123 A1

Framlingham Gr WV6 255 A2
Frampton Gr ST6 41 C3
Frances Dr WS3 243 A1
Francis Cl
2 Kingswinford DY6 275 B4
Penkridge ST19 208 A4
Francis Green La ST19 207 C4
Francis Rd
Lichfield WS13 214 A1
Stourbridge DY8 279 B3
Francis St ST6 41 C3
Frank Foley Way ST16 155 B2
Frank Gee Cl WS15 178 B1
Frank Rogers Wlk
WS15 178 B1
Frank St ST4 72 A3
Franklin Cl
Burton u T DE15 167 A1
Perton WV6 254 C3
Franklin Dr WS7 229 A4
Franklin Rd ST4 71 C4
Franklyn St ST1 282 C1
Fraser Cl ST15 119 C3
Fraser St ST6 57 A4
Frayne Ave DY6 275 B4
Frazier Ho 5 ST3 89 C4
Freckleton Pl ST3 90 B4
Fred Brewer Way DE13 165 C2
Frederick Ave ST4 72 A4
Frederick Ct B77 250 C2
Frederick Rd ST19 192 C1
Frederick St
Burton u T DE15 185 C4
Fenton ST4 72 C3
Wolv WV2 266 B4
Fredericks Cl DY8 279 C2
Free Trade St ST1 282 C4
Freebridge Cl ST3 73 C2
Freedom Dr ST7 26 C2
Freedom Wlk ST6 42 B2
Freeford Gdns WS14 231 C3
Freehold St ST5 284 C2
Freeland Gr 3 DY6 275 C2
Freemantle Dr WS12 210 C1
Freemen St ST16 155 C3
Freer Dr WS7 229 C4
Freeth Rd WS8 229 A1
Fremantle Rd ST4 71 C2
Fremont Dr DY1 271 C2
French Ave B78 249 B1
Frenchmore Gr ST3 73 C1
Frensham Cl WS6 226 C2
Freshwater Gr ST2 57 C2
Freville Gdns B79 250 A3
Frew Cl ST16 156 A2
Friar St Longton ST3 283 C4
Stafford ST16 155 B3
Friar's Alley WS13 231 A4
Friar's Ct ST5 284 B2
Friar's La TF11 220 B2
Friar's St ST5 284 B2
Friars Ave ST15 120 A4
Friars Cl Cheadle ST10 76 B2
Kingswinford DY8 275 B2
Friars Gorse DY7 279 B4
Friars Pl ST2 58 A4
Friars Rd ST2 58 A4
Friars Wlk B77 250 B2
Friars' Rd ST17 155 C1
Friars' Terr ST17 155 C1
Friars' Wlk
Newcastle-u-L ST5 71 A3
Stafford ST17 155 C1
Friarswood Prim Sch
ST5 284 B1
Friarswood Rd ST5 284 B2
Friary Ave
Abbots Bromley WS15 160 C3
Lichfield WS13 231 A3
Friary Dr B74 257 C2
Friary Gdns WS13 231 A4
Friary Grange Sports Ctr
WS13 213 C1
Friary Ho WS13 213 C1
Friary Rd WS13 231 A4
Friary Sch The WS13 213 C1
Friary The WS13 231 A4
Friday Acre WS13 214 A1
Friendly Ave ST5 56 A4
Friesian Gdns ST5 40 B1
Friezland La WS8 245 A3
Friezland Way WS8 245 A3
Frinton Cl ST16 155 C3
Frith St ST13 30 B3
Frobisher Dr ST15 103 A2
Frobisher St ST6 43 A3
Frodingham Rd ST2 58 B1
Frog La Lichfield WS13 231 A4
Market Drayton TF9 97 B1
Wheaton Aston ST19 205 B3
Froghall ST5 284 B3
Froghall Rd Cheadle ST10 76 C3
Ipstones ST10 62 A3
Froghall Wharf★ ST10 62 A2
Frogmore Rd TF9 97 B1
Frome Cl DY3 271 B1
Frome Wlk ST6 42 A2
Froyle Cl WV6 255 B3
Fuchsia Dr WV9 239 C2
Fulfen Prim Sch WS7 229 B4
Fulford Prim Sch ST11 106 C4
Fulford Rd ST11 106 C4
Fullbrook Ave DE13 201 C4
Fullelove Rd WS8 245 A4
Fuller St ST6 41 C2
Fullerton Cl WV8 239 C1
Fullmore Cl ST19 207 C4
Fullwood Wlk ST2 58 B1
Fulmer Pl ST3 90 A4
Furber Pl DY6 275 C3
Furguson St WV11 242 A1
Furlong Ave ST10 92 C2
Furlong Cl Alrewas DE13 201 A1
Upper Tean ST10 92 C2
Weston ST18 138 B1
Furlong Dr ST10 92 C2
Furlong La Alrewas DE13 201 A1
Alstonefield DE6 35 B2
Bradley ST18 173 B1
Burslem ST6 56 C4
Furlong Par 4 ST6 56 C4
Furlong Pas 5 ST6 56 C4
Furlong Rd ST6 41 C2
Furlong The ST15 118 C3
Furlong Wlk DY3 271 B2
Furlongs Rd DY3 271 B3
Furmston Pl ST13 31 A4
Furnace Cl WV5 269 C3
Furnace La CW3 68 C4
Furnace Rd ST3 73 B1
Furness B77 250 B2
Furness Cl WS3 242 C2
Furness Gr ST17 174 A4
Furnival St ST6 57 A3
Furnivall Cres WS13 214 B1
Furst St WS8 245 A4
Fyfield Rd DE15 185 C3
Fynney Fields ST13 45 C4
Fynney St ST13 30 C3

G

Gable Cotts ST11 74 C1
Gable Croft WS14 231 C3
Gable St ST4 72 A3
Gables The
Kingswinford DY6 275 A4
Swadlincote DE11 186 C3
Gaelic Rd WS11 209 B2
Gag La DE6 51 B3
Gagarin B79 249 C3
Gaia La WS13 231 A4
Gaia Stowe WS13 214 A1
Gaiafields Rd WS13 214 A1
Gaialands Cres WS13 214 A1
Gail Cl WS9 245 A2
Gail Pk WV3 265 B4
Gailey Lea La ST19 208 A1
Gailey Pottery★ ST19 207 B1
Gainford Cl WV8 239 C1
Gains La WS3 227 B1
Gainsborough Dr
Fazeley B78 260 A4
Perton WV6 255 A2
Gainsborough Hill DY8 279 C2
Gainsborough Pl DY1 271 C1
Gainsborough Rd
Longton ST3 88 C4
Newcastle-u-L ST5 55 C3
Gainsborough Way
DE15 167 A2
Gainsbrook Cres WS11 227 C3
Gairloch Rd WV11 242 A1
Galahad Dr DE13 147 C1
Galena Cl B77 251 A1
Galleys Bank ST7 26 A2
Galliers Cl B77 261 C3
Gallimore Cl ST6 41 C1
Gallimore Ho ST7 40 B4
Galloway Rd ST2 73 C4
Gallowstree La
Mayfield DE6 81 B4
Newcastle-u-L ST5 70 C4
Galsworthy Rd ST4 73 A3
Galway Rd WS7 229 A4
Gamesfield Gn WV3 255 C1
Ganton Rd WS3 243 A2
Ganton Wlk WV8 255 C4
Gaol Butts ST21 133 B3
Gaol Rd ST16 155 C2
Gaol Sq ST16 155 C2
Gaolgate St 5 ST16 155 C2
Garage Cl B77 250 B3
Garbett St ST6 41 B4
Garden Cotts ST20 171 B3
Garden Cres WS3 243 C2
Garden Croft WS9 256 A4
Garden Dr WS15 197 A4
Garden La ST19 206 B2
Garden Pl Stafford ST17 155 C1
Stoke-on-T ST4 71 C4
Garden St Leek ST13 30 B3
Newcastle-u-L ST5 284 C2
Stafford ST17 155 C1
Stoke-on-T ST4 71 C3
Garden View WS15 178 B1
Garden Village
★Pattingham WV6 263 C3
Upper Tean ST10 92 B2
Garden Wlk DY3 271 B1
Gardeners Cl ST8 27 A3
Gardeners Way WV5 269 C2
Gardenholm Cl ST3 89 C4
Gardens The B79 216 B1
Gardiner Dr ST3 283 A2
Gardner Pl ST14 111 A1
Garfield Ave ST4 71 C1
Garfield Cres ST4 71 C1
Garfield Ct ST4 71 C1
Garfield St ST1 282 A1
Garibaldi St ST1 56 C2
Garlick St ST6 42 A1
Garner St Burslem ST5 56 C2
Stoke-on-T ST4 56 C1
Garners Wlk CW3 68 C4
Garnet Cl WS9 245 C2
Garnet St ST1 57 A2
Garnett Rd E ST5 56 A3
Garnett Rd W ST5 56 A3
Garret Cl DY6 275 B4
Garrick Cl Dudley DY1 271 C2
Lichfield WS13 213 C1
Garrick Ct WS13 213 C1
Garrick Rd
Cannock WS11 209 B2
Lichfield WS13 213 C1
Garrick Rise
Burntwood WS7 229 A4
Rugeley WS15 197 A3
Garridge Cl WV7 237 A2
Garrigill B77 251 A1
Garrod Sq ST16 156 A3
Garsdale Cres ST3 88 C4
Gartan Rd DE14 185 A4
Garth Cl ST17 174 C3
Garth Rd ST17 174 C3
Garth St ST1 282 C3
Garth The WS13 214 A1
Gas St ST14 111 B1
Gaskell Rd ST2 58 B2
Gatacre St DY3 271 B2
Gatcombe Cl
Burton u T DE13 147 B1
Wolv WV10 240 C2
Gatcombe Rd DY1 271 C1
Gate St Meir ST3 74 A3
Sedgley DY3 271 C4
Gatehouse Trad Est
WS8 229 A1
Gateway ST5 40 B1
Gateway Ave ST5 85 B3
Gatherwynd La TF11 203 C3
Gatley Gr ST3 90 A3
Gauledge La SK17 13 A3
Gaunt St 4 ST13 30 B3
Gawain Gr DE13 147 C1
Gawsworth B79 249 B4
Gawsworth Cl ST3 73 B3
Gay La ST20 204 C4
Gaydon Cl WV6 254 C3
Gaydon Rd WS9 256 A2
Gayle B77 251 A1
Gaymore Rd DY10 280 A3
Gayton Ave ST2 43 A1
Geary La DE15 167 C1
Gedney Gr ST5 71 A1
Geen St ST4 72 A4
Gemini Dr WS11 226 C3
Gemini Gr ST6 41 C3
Geneshall Cl ST20 171 B4
Geneva Dr Hanley ST1 57 C3
Newcastle-u-L ST5 70 C3
Genge Ave WV4 266 C2
Genista Cl DE15 186 A4
Genthorne Cl WV4 266 C2
Gentian B74 257 C2
Gentleshaw Prim Sch
WS15 212 A3
Geoffrey Ave ST13 30 B3
Geoffrey Gr ST3 74 A2
George Ave Meir ST3 74 A1
Tamworth B78 249 B1
George Baily Ct ST17 155 C1
George Brealey Cl
WS15 196 C4
George Eardley Cl ST6 41 B3
George Eastham Ave ST4 72 B2
George Elliott Cl ST14 126 B3
George La Lichfield WS13 231 B4
Stone ST15 120 B4
George St Audley ST7 39 B1
Brierley Hill DY8 275 C1
Burton u T DE14 166 B2
Cannock WS12 210 B2
Fenton ST4 72 C4
Newcastle-u-L ST5 284 D3
Newcastle-u-L, Chesterton
ST5 55 C4
Newcastle-u-L, Porthill ST5 56 B3
Newcastle-u-L, Silverdale
ST5 55 A1
Stafford ST16 155 B3
Tamworth B79 250 A2
George Walker Ct DE14 166 B3
Georges Ct ST3 283 B3
Georges Way ST7 39 C1
Georgian Pl 15 WS11 209 C1
Gerald Rd DY8 279 C4
Gerard B79 249 C4
Gerards Way TF9 100 B3
Gerrard St ST4 72 A4
Gettings Cl WS7 229 C4
Gibb La DE6 128 C3
Gibbet La DY7 279 A2
Gibbins St ST1 282 C4
Gibbons Gr WV6 255 C2
Gibbons Hill Rd DY3 266 B1
Gibbons Rd
Sutton Coldfield B75 258 A2
Wolv WV6 255 C2
Gibraltar DY7 278 B2
Gibson Cl ST16 155 C3
Gibson Gr ST5 55 B4
Gibson Pl ST3 74 A1
Gibson Rd WV6 254 C2
Gibson St ST6 41 C1
Giddywell La WS15 197 C1
Gideons Cl DY3 271 B3
Giffard RC Prim Sch
WV6 255 C3
Giffard Rd WV10 240 C1
Gifford Cl ST19 223 B3
Gifford Pl ST4 71 C3
Giffords Croft WS13 214 A1
Gig Mill Prim Sch DY8 279 C2
Giggetty La WV5 269 C3
Gigmill Way DY8 279 C2
Gilbanks Rd DY8 279 B4
Gilbern Dr ST8 27 A3
Gilbert Cl
2 Kidsgrove ST7 26 A1
Newport TF10 168 B1
Gilbert La WV5 270 A4
Gilbert Rd WS13 214 B1
Gilbert St ST6 41 B4
Gilbert Wlk WS13 214 B1
Gilbeys Cl DY8 275 C1
Gilchrist Ct ST6 57 A3
Giles Cl ST10 76 B2
Giles Rd WS13 214 A2
Giles Wlk ST1 57 C3
Gill Bank Rd ST6 41 A4
Gill Wlk ST1 282 A2
Gilliard's Croft DE13 199 B3
Gilliat Wlk ST2 58 B1
Gillingham Cres ST16 155 A1
Gillway B79 250 A4
Gilman Ave ST2 43 A1
Gilman Pl ST1 282 C3
Gilman St ST1 282 C2
Gilmour La DE13 183 C1
Gilpin Cres WS3 244 A2
Gilpins Croft WS6 226 B1
Gilwell Rd WS15 211 C3
Gimson St ST4 72 C3
Ginger Hill ST20 171 B3
Ginger La ST21 116 A2
Gipsy La Alstonefield DE6 35 C2
Cookley DY11 280 A4
Girsby Cl ST4 88 B3
Girton Rd WS11 226 C4
Gisborne Cl DE13 182 A2
Gitana St ST1 282 B3
Glade Ave WS7 229 A4
Glade The Cannock WS11 209 B1
Newcastle-u-L ST5 71 A1
Stafford ST17 175 A4
Wolv WV8 239 C1
Glades The
Aldridge, Hardwick B74 256 C1
Aldridge, Leighswood
WS9 256 A4
Gladman Bsns Quarter
WV9 239 C2
Gladstone Dr DY8 279 B3
Gladstone Gr
Biddulph ST8 27 C4
Kingswinford DY6 275 B4
Gladstone Pl ST4 71 C3
Gladstone Pottery Mus★
ST3 283 C3
Gladstone Rd
Cannock WS12 210 C1
Stourbridge DY8 279 B3
Gladstone St Leek ST13 30 C3
Stoke-on-T ST4 56 C1
Gladstone Way ST16 156 A3
Gladwyn St ST2 58 B2
Glaisher Dr ST3 90 B4
Glamis Cl DE13 166 B4
Glamis Dr 7 ST15 120 B3
Glandore Rd ST3 73 C2
Glanville Dr B75 258 A2
Glascote Ct B77 250 C2
Glascote Heath Prim Sch
B77 251 A1
Glascote La B77 261 C4
Glascote Rd B77 250 C2
Glass La WS15 161 C1
Glass St ST1 282 B3
Glasscroft Cotts WS7 229 C4
Glastonbury Cl
Norton-in-t-M ST9 43 B2
Stafford ST17 175 B3
Glastonbury Cres WS3 242 C1
Glastonbury Way WS3 242 C1
Glebe Ave ST16 155 B3
Glebe Cl
Cheswardine TF9 130 A4
Doveridge DE6 127 A4
Forsbrook ST11 91 A3
Rolleston DE13 147 A2
Glebe Ct Cheadle ST10 76 A1
Stoke-on-T ST4 72 B4
Glebe La Gnosall ST20 171 C4
Stourbridge DY8 279 C2
Glebe Prim Sch ST4 72 C3
Glebe Rd Armitage WS15 198 B3
Cheadle ST10 76 B1
Glebe St Kidsgrove ST7 25 B1
Stoke-on-T ST4 72 A4
Glebe The
Albrighton WV7 237 A3
Chebsey ST15 135 A4
Glebedale Ct ST4 72 C3
Glebedale Rd ST4 72 C3
Glebefields ST20 151 B4
Glebelands
Bobbington DY7 267 C1
Stafford ST17 174 C3
Glebeville ST13 30 C2
Gledhill Pk WS14 231 B3
Glen Cl WS11 209 C3
Glen Ct Codsall WV8 239 A2
Wolv WV6 255 C1
Glen Dr ST10 94 C4
Glen Park Rd DY3 271 B1
Glen Rd Sedgley DY3 271 C3
Glen Rd continued
Stourbridge DY8 279 C2
Glen Rise DE13 166 A4
Glen The 7 ST15 120 A4
Glencastle Way ST4 88 B3
Glencoe Rd WS11 210 A2
Glencoe St ST3 283 B2
Glencroft Cl DE14 185 A4
Glendale Cl WV3 265 B4
Glendale Ct
Newcastle-u-L ST5 71 B1
Tamworth B77 262 A3
Glendale Dr WV5 270 A3
Glendale Gdns WS11 210 A2
Glendale St ST6 57 A4
Glendawn Cl 2 WS11 210 A2
Glendene Rd WS12 210 B3
Glendon Cl TF9 112 A4
Glendower Cl ST20 171 B3
Glendower Rd WS9 245 A1
Glendue Gr ST4 88 B3
Gleneagles B77 251 A3
Gleneagles Cres ST1 57 C3
Gleneagles Dr
Burton u T DE13 147 B1
Stafford ST16 156 B2
Gleneagles Rd
Perton WV6 254 B3
Walsall WS3 242 C2
Glenfield Tamworth B77 250 B1
Wolv WV8 239 C1
Glenfield Rise DE13 166 A4
Glenfield Way ST2 73 C4
Glengarry Gdns WV3 255 C1
Glenhaven WS15 178 B1
Glenmore Ave WS7 229 A3
Glenmore Cl WV3 265 C4
Glennsyl Way DE14 166 C2
Glenroyd Ave ST2 58 A1
Glenroyd Wlk ST2 58 B1
Glenthorne Cl ST17 175 B3
Glenthorne Dr WS6 226 C2
Glenthorne Ho WS6 226 B1
Glenthorne Prim Sch
WS6 226 C2
Glenville Ave CV9 262 B1
Glenwood Cl
Longton ST3 283 B4
Newcastle-u-L ST5 55 B1
Glenwood Rise WS9 245 B2
Globe Ave ST17 174 C3
Globe St ST6 56 C4
Gloucester Cl WS13 214 A2
Gloucester Grange ST5 71 B3
Gloucester Rd ST7 25 C1
Gloucester Way
Burton u T DE15 167 A1
Cannock WS11 210 A1
Glover St Cannock WS12 210 C2
Hanley ST1 282 C4
Stafford ST16 155 B2
Glovers Cl WS12 211 A3
Glyme Dr WV6 255 C3
Glyn Pl ST6 41 C2
Glyndebourne B79 249 B4
Glynne Ave DY6 275 B3
Glynne Prim Sch DY6 275 B2
Gnosall La TF10 188 B3
Gnosall Rd
Gnosall, Beffcote TF10 170 B1
Gnosall, Knightley Dale
ST20 152 A2
Goddard St ST3 283 D4
Godfrey Rd ST2 58 A2
Godley La ST10 75 B3
Godleybarn La ST10 75 C3
Godolphin B79 249 B4
Godsall Gdns WV8 238 C2
Gofton B77 262 A4
Golborn Ave ST3 90 A2
Golborn Cl ST3 90 A2
Gold St ST3 283 B3
Goldcrest B77 262 A3
Goldcrest Way ST8 27 C4
Goldenhill Prim Sch ST6 41 B4
Goldenhill Rd ST4 283 B5
Goldenhill St Joseph's RC
Prim Sch ST6 41 B4
Goldfinch View TF9 99 B2
Goldhurst Dr ST10 92 C1
Goldsborough B77 251 A1
Goldsmith Pl
Longton ST3 283 D4
Tamworth B79 250 A4
Goldthorn Ave WV4 266 A3
Goldthorn Cres WV4 266 A3
Goldthorn Hill WV2,WV4 266 B3
Goldthorn Park Jun & Inf Sch
WV4 266 B3
Goldthorn Rd WV2,WV3 266 A4
Goldthorne Ave WS11 209 C1
Golf Links Cl ST6 41 B4
Goms Mill Ct ST3 283 B2
Goms Mill Rd ST3 283 A2
Goodfellow St ST6 41 B2
Goodill Cl ST15 119 C3
Goodman St DE14 166 B3
Goodrich Ave WV6 255 A2
Goods Station La ST19 192 C1
Goodson St ST1 282 C3
Goodwick Cl ST4 88 B3
Goodwin Ave ST5 284 B4
Goodwin Rd ST3 74 A1
Goodwood Ave ST10 76 C2
Goodwood Cl
Burton u T DE13 147 B1
Cannock WS12 211 A3
Lichfield WS14 231 B4

Goodwood Pl ST4 ....88 A4
Goose La WS15 ....160 C3
Goose St ST5 ....284 B2
Goosefield Cl TF9 ....97 A1
Goosemoor Gr 15 ST3 ...90 A4
Goostry Cl B77 ....250 B3
Goostry Rd B77 ....250 B3
Gordale Cl CW12 ....6 A3
Gordon Ave Cheadle ST10 .76 A2
Hanley ST6 ....57 B4
Stafford ST16 ....155 B4
Wolv WV4 ....266 C2
Gordon Banks Dr ST4 ...72 B2
Gordon Cl ST13 ....30 B2
Gordon Cres ST1 ....57 B4
Gordon Ct ST5 ....55 C2
Gordon Rd ST6 ....41 B3
Gordon St
Burton u T DE14 ....166 B2
Chell Heath ST6 ....42 A1
Newcastle-u-L ST5 ....55 C2
4 Wolv WV2 ....266 B4
Gorse Cres TF9 ....99 C3
Gorse Dr WS12 ....209 B3
Gorse La Alrewas WS13 .215 A4
Astbury CW12 ....15 B3
Gnosall ST20 ....152 A4
Lichfield WS14 ....231 C3
Rugeley WS15 ....196 C3
Seisdon WV5 ....269 A3
Gorse Rd Rugeley WS15 .196 C3
Sedgley DY3 ....271 C4
Gorse St ST4 ....72 C2
Gorse Way WS12 ....210 B4
Gorsebrook Leys ST16 .155 A3
Gorseburn Way WS15 ..178 B1
Gorsemoor Prim Sch
WS12 ....210 B1
Gorsemoor Rd WS12 ...210 B1
Gorsemoor Way WV11 .242 A2
Gorseway WS7 ....229 A3
Gorsey Bank ST6 ....42 C3
Gorsey La Cannock WS11 209 B1
Great Wyrley WS6 ....226 C1
Millmeece ST21 ....102 C3
Netherseal DE12 ....219 C4
Norton Canes WS3 ....227 C1
Gorsley Dale ST17 ....175 B3
Gorstey Lea WS7 ....229 B4
Gorsty Bank WS14 ....231 C4
Gorsty Hayes WV8 ....238 C2
Gorsty Hill Cl CW2 ....37 C1
Gorsty Hill Rd ST10 ....92 C3
Gorsy Bank Rd B77 ...261 C3
Gorsy La TF10 ....150 A2
Gort Rd ST5 ....55 C2
Gosberryhole La CW12 ...7 A1
Goscote Ind Est WS3 ...243 C1
Goscote La WS3 ....243 C1
Goscote Rd WS3 ....244 A1
Gosforth Gr ST3 ....90 B4
Gospel Ash Rd DY7 ....268 B1
Gospel End Rd DY3 ....271 A4
Gospel End St DY3 ....271 B4
Gothersley La DY7 ....274 B1
Gough Cl ST16 ....155 B4
Gough Side DE14 ....166 B1
Gould Firm La WS9 ...256 C3
Govan Rd ST4 ....72 C4
Gowan Ave ST6 ....42 A2
Gower Ave DY6 ....275 C2
Gower Rd Sedgley DY3 ..266 A1
Stone ST15 ....120 A4
Gower St Longton ST3 ...283 C3
Newcastle-u-L ST5 ....284 C3
Wolv WV2 ....266 C4
Gowland Dr WS11 ....209 A1
Goya Cl WS11 ....210 B1
Grace St ST13 ....30 B3
Gradbach Mill★ SK17 ....2 A1
Graffam Gr ST10 ....76 C2
Grafton Ave ST6 ....42 A1
Grafton Ct 9 WV6 ...255 C2
Grafton Gdns DY3 ....271 A2
Grafton Ho WV4 ....266 C3
Grafton Inf Sch ST3 ...283 C4
Grafton Rd
Burton u T DE15 ....167 A1
Longton ST3 ....283 C4
Grafton St ST1 ....282 C3
Graham Cl DE14 ....185 B4
Graham Ho B74 ....256 C1
Graham Rd DY6 ....275 B2
Graham St ST2 ....58 A2
Grainger Ct WS11 ....209 B1
Graiseley Hill WV2 ....266 B4
Graiseley Prim Sch
WV2 ....266 B4
Graiseley Row WV2 ...266 B4
Granary Cl
Cannock WS12 ....210 A3
Kingswinford DY6 ....275 A4
Granary Rd WV8 ....239 C1
Granary The WS9 ....256 A3
Granby Wlk ST4 ....71 C3
Granchester Cl ST3 ....90 A3
Grange Ave
Aldridge WS9 ....245 A1
Burntwood WS7 ....229 A4
Penkridge ST19 ....207 C4
Sutton Coldfield B75 ....258 B2
Grange Cl
Burton u T DE14 ....166 A2
Ellenhall ST21 ....134 A1
Tamworth B77 ....261 B4
Grange Cres ST19 ....207 C4
Grange Croft ST18 ....158 B4
Grange Ct Biddulph ST8 ...16 B1
Grange Ct *continued*
Egginton DE65 ....148 A3
Grange Dr WS11 ....209 C1
Grange Gdns ST13 ....30 B2
Grange Hill WS15 ....197 B1
Grange Inf Sch DE14 ...166 A2
Grange La
4 Kingswinford DY6 ....275 C2
Lichfield WS13 ....213 C1
Newcastle-u-L ST5 ....56 B3
Sutton Coldfield B75 ....258 B2
Grange Pk Dr ST8 ....16 C2
Grange Prim Sch ST3 ...90 A4
Grange Rd Biddulph ST8 ..16 C2
Burntwood WS7 ....229 A3
Cheddleton ST13 ....45 B2
Gnosall ST20 ....151 C3
Meir ST3 ....90 A3
Norton Canes WS11 ....228 A3
Penkridge ST19 ....207 C4
Stone ST15 ....120 B4
Swadlincote DE11 ....186 C3
Uttoxeter ST14 ....111 A1
Wolv, Blakenhall WV2 ....266 A3
Wolv, Tettenhall WV6 ....255 B2
Grange St Burslem ST6 ...57 A3
Burton u T DE14 ....166 A2
Grange The
Burton u T DE14 ....166 A2
King's Bromley DE13 ....199 B3
Longdon WS15 ....197 B1
Meir ST3 ....74 A1
Stafford ST18 ....174 B3
Wombourne WV5 ....270 A4
Grangefield Cl
Cheddleton ST13 ....45 B2
Wolv WV8 ....239 C1
Grangefields ST8 ....16 C2
Grangewood Ave ST3 ....89 C3
Grangewood Rd ST3 ...74 A1
Granstone Cl ST6 ....42 A4
Grant Cl DY6 ....275 B4
Grant St ST4 ....72 B4
Grantham Pl ST2 ....58 A3
Grantley Cl ST3 ....73 A1
Grantley Cres DY6 ....275 B4
Grantown Gr WS3 ....243 A2
Granville B77 ....250 C1
Granville Ave Hanley ST1 .57 B4
Newcastle-u-L ST5 ....284 C3
Newport TF10 ....168 C1
Granville Cl
Newport TF10 ....168 C1
5 Wolv WV2 ....266 B4
Granville Dr DY6 ....275 C3
Granville Rd Bucknall ST2 .58 A3
Newport TF10 ....168 C1
Granville Sq 3 ST15 ...105 A1
Granville St WV2 ....266 B4
Granville Terr ST15 ....105 A1
Granville Vilas TF10 ...168 C1
Grasmere Ave
Little Aston B74 ....257 A1
Newcastle-u-L ST5 ....71 A2
Perton WV6 ....254 C2
Grasmere Cl
Burton u T DE15 ....167 A1
Kingswinford DY6 ....275 A4
Wolv WV6 ....255 C4
Grasmere Dr DY8 ....279 C2
Grasmere Pl WS11 ....209 C3
Grasmere Terr ST6 ....42 A2
Grassholme B77 ....262 A4
Grassmere Ct WS6 ....226 B2
Grassmere Hollow ST16 154 C3
Grassy La WV11 ....241 A1
Grassygreen La ST7 ....39 C1
Gratley Croft WS12 ....209 B2
Gratton La ST9 ....29 A2
Gratton Rd ST2 ....58 B2
Gravel Hill WV5 ....270 A3
Gravel La
Huntington WS12 ....209 B3
Stafford ST17 ....174 C3
Gravelly Bank ST3 ....89 C4
Gravelly Dr TF10 ....168 C1
Gravelly Hill TF9 ....100 A3
Gravelly La WS9 ....245 C2
Gray Rd WS12 ....209 C3
Gray Wlk ST17 ....174 B4
Gray's Cl ST7 ....26 A4
Graycar Bsns Pk DE13 ..184 A1
Grayling B77 ....261 B3
Grayling Gr ST6 ....42 A2
Grayling Willows CW3 ...68 C3
Grayshott Rd ST6 ....41 C3
Grayston Ave B77 ....250 C2
Grazier Ave B77 ....261 B4
Grazings The DY7 ....278 B2
Greasley Rd ST2 ....58 A3
Great Charles St WS8 ..244 C4
Great Checkhill Rd DY7 274 B2
Great Fenton Bsns Pk
ST4 ....72 B2
Great Furlong DE13 ....201 A1
Great Hales St TF9 ....97 B1
Great Moor Rd WV6 ....253 C1
Great Wood Prim Sch
ST10 ....92 C2
Great Wood Rd ST10 ....92 C2
Great Wyrley High Sch
WS6 ....226 C2
Greatbatch Ave ST4 ....71 C4
Greatmead B77 ....250 B1
Greatoak Rd ST7 ....39 C2
Greaves La DE6,DE13 ..144 C2
Green Acres WV5 ....269 C3
Green Barn Ct ST18 ....138 B1
Green Barns La WS14 ..258 B4
Green Brook Ct ST5 ....56 A2
Green Cl Barlaston ST12 ..88 B1
Blythe Bridge ST11 ....90 B4
Pattingham WV6 ....253 B1
Stone ST15 ....119 C4
Green Gore La ST17 ....175 C4
Green Heath Rd WS12 .210 A4
Green La Aldridge WS9 ..256 C3
Alsop en le D DE6 ....36 B1
Ashley TF9 ....100 B3
Brownhills WS8 ....229 A1
Brownhills, High Heath
WS9 ....244 B2
Burntwood WS7 ....212 B1
Burton u T DE13 ....166 A4
Cannock WS11 ....226 C3
Clifton DE6 ....81 C4
Eccleshall ST21 ....133 C3
Farewell WS13 ....212 B2
Forsbrook ST11 ....91 A3
Forton TF10 ....150 C1
Hamstall Ridware WS15 ..181 A2
Heaton ST13 ....18 C1
Kingswinford DY6 ....275 B4
Marchington ST14 ....128 A1
Newport TF10 ....168 C2
Polesworth B77,B78 ....262 B4
Roston DE6 ....96 C4
Rugeley WS15 ....178 B1
Sedgley DY3 ....271 C3
Stafford ST18 ....174 B2
Tutbury DE13 ....146 B3
Wall WS14 ....230 B1
Walsall WS4,WS9 ....244 A2
Waterhouses DE6,ST10 ...65 A4
Whitgreave ST18 ....135 C4
Wolv WV6 ....255 C4
Green Lane Venture Ctr
WS11 ....226 C3
Green Lea Fst Sch ST18 122 B2
Green Mdws 7 WS11 ...210 B1
Green Meadow Cl WV5 .269 C3
Green Oak Rd WV8 ....239 A1
Green Pk
Blythe Bridge ST11 ....90 C1
Eccleshall ST21 ....133 C3
Upper Tean ST10 ....109 B4
Green Rd Stoke-on-T ST4 ..71 C2
Weston ST18 ....138 B1
Green Rock La WS3 ....243 B1
Green Rock Prim Sch
WS3 ....243 C1
Green Slade Gr WS12 ..210 B4
Green St Burton u T DE14 166 B1
Stourbridge DY8 ....279 C3
Green The Aldridge WS9 .256 B3
Armitage WS15 ....198 B3
Barton-u-N DE13 ....183 B1
Blythe Bridge ST11 ....90 C1
Brocton ST17 ....176 B4
Brocton, Old Acre ST17 ...176 A2
Burton u T DE13 ....147 C1
Caverswall ST11 ....74 B2
Cheadle ST10 ....76 A1
Chebsey ST21 ....134 C3
Dordon B78 ....262 B2
Endon ST6 ....43 A4
Hagley DY9 ....281 C2
Kingsley ST10 ....61 B1
Kingswinford DY8 ....275 B1
Lawton-gate ST7 ....25 A2
Newcastle-u-L, Clayton ST5 .71 B2
Rugeley WS15 ....197 A3
Seckington B79 ....236 A2
Stoke-on-T ST4 ....71 C4
Tamworth B77 ....251 A3
Tamworth, Bonehill B78 ....249 C1
Walsall WS3 ....243 A1
Weston ST18 ....138 B1
Whittington WS14 ....232 C3
Woodseaves ST20 ....151 B4
Green Valley Dr DE13 ...166 A4
Green View TF11 ....203 C4
Green Way Aldridge WS9 245 A1
Uttoxeter ST14 ....126 A4
Green's La ST2 ....58 C2
Greenacre ST18 ....139 B1
Greenacre Cl B77 ....251 A3
Greenacre Dr WV8 ....239 A1
Greenacre The DE6 ....81 C4
Greenacres
Brewood WV9 ....224 A2
Rugeley WS15 ....196 C4
Sedgley DY3 ....266 A1
Wolv WV6 ....255 A3
Greenacres Ave
Blythe Bridge ST11 ....90 B4
Essington WV10 ....241 A1
Greenacres Cl WS9 ....256 C1
Greenacres Dr ST14 ....111 A1
Greenacres Prim Sch
B77 ....251 A3
Greenacres Way TF10 ..168 B2
Greenaway Ct WV10 ...241 B4
Greenbank Gdns DY8 ..275 C1
Greenbank Rd
Chell Heath ST6 ....42 A2
Newcastle-u-L ST5 ....56 B2
Greenbirches Ind Est
ST6 ....41 B2
Greencroft
Kingswinford DY6 ....275 B2
Lichfield WS13 ....214 A1
Greendale Dr ST5 ....40 B1
Greendale La ST10 ....77 B2
Greendock St ST3 ....283 B3
Greenfield ST8 ....27 B3
Greenfield Ave
Armitage WS15 ....198 A2
Endon ST6 ....43 B4
Stourbridge DY8 ....279 C3
Greenfield Bldgs WV5 ..270 A4
Greenfield Cl ST6 ....43 B4
Greenfield Cres ST10 ....76 C2
Greenfield Dr ST14 ....126 A4
Greenfield La WV10 ....240 C3
Greenfield Pl ST6 ....43 B4
Greenfield Prim Sch
DY8 ....279 C3
Greenfield Rd
Stafford ST17 ....175 B3
Tunstall ST6 ....41 C3
Greenfield View DY3 ...271 A4
Greenfields
Aldridge WS9 ....256 A4
Cannock WS11 ....209 C1
Denstone ST14 ....95 B3
Gnosall ST20 ....171 C4
Greenfields Dr WS15 ...178 B1
Greenfields La TF9 ....97 A1
Greenfields Rd Endon ST9 43 C4
Hixon ST18 ....139 B1
Kingswinford DY6 ....275 C3
Kinver DY7 ....277 B2
Walsall WS4 ....244 B1
Wombourne WV5 ....270 A3
Greenfinch Cl ST14 ....126 B3
Greengate St ST16 ....155 C2
Greengates St ST6 ....41 C2
Greenhall Com Specl Sch
ST16 ....155 A4
Greenhead St ST6 ....56 C4
Greenheart B77 ....251 A2
Greenhill Lichfield WS13 .231 B4
Wombourne WV5 ....270 A3
Greenhill Cl B77 ....261 B3
Greenhill Ct WV5 ....270 A3
Greenhill Gdns WV5 ...270 A3
Greenhill La ST19 ....205 B4
Greenhill Mews WS13 ..231 B4
Greenhill Rd
Norton-in-t-M ST6 ....42 C3
Sedgley DY3 ....271 C3
Greenhill Way WS9 ....245 A1
Greenhough Rd WS13 .231 A4
Greenland Cl DY6 ....275 C4
Greenlands WV5 ....269 C4
Greenlea B77 ....262 A4
Greenlea Cl ST4 ....88 B3
Greenleighs DY3 ....266 B2
Greenly Rd WV4 ....266 B3
Greenmeadow Gr ST9 ....43 C3
Greenmeadows Rd CW3 .68 C4
Greenmoor Ave ST6 ....42 A4
Greenock Cl ST5 ....70 C4
Greens Ind Est WS12 ...210 B4
Greensforge La DY6,DY7 274 C2
Greenside
Newcastle-u-L ST5 ....284 A3
Swynnerton ST15 ....118 C3
Greenside Ave ST9 ....43 B2
Greenside Cl ST7 ....41 A4
Greenslade Rd DY3 ....266 A1
Greensmith Cl DE15 ....167 B2
Greensome Cl ST16 ....155 A2
Greensome Cres ST16 ...155 A3
Greensome Ct ST16 ....155 A2
Greensome La ST16 ....155 A3
Greenvale Cl DE15 ....185 C4
Greenway
Burton u T DE15 ....167 A2
Eccleshall ST21 ....133 C3
Fenton ST3 ....72 C2
Sedgley DY3 ....266 C1
Stafford ST16 ....156 A2
Trentham ST4 ....87 C4
Greenway Ave
3 Brierley Hill DY8 ....275 C1
Chell Heath ST6 ....42 A1
Stone ST15 ....120 A3
Greenway Bank
Biddulph ST8 ....27 B2
Norton-in-t-M ST2 ....43 B1
Greenway Bank Ctry Pk★
ST8 ....27 C2
Greenway Gdns
Pattingham WV6 ....253 B1
Sedgley DY3 ....266 C1
Greenway Hall Rd ST2,
ST9 ....43 B2
Greenway Pl ST2 ....58 A4
Greenway Rd ST8 ....16 C1
Greenway The
Hagley DY9 ....281 C3
Newcastle-u-L ST5 ....56 B2
Pattingham WV6 ....253 B1
Greenways Audley ST7 ...39 C1
Farewell WS13 ....212 C2
Kingswinford DY8 ....275 B1
Penkridge ST19 ....208 A4
Stafford ST18 ....174 B3
Greenways Dr ST10 ....76 B2
Greenways Prim Sch ST9 43 B2
Greenwood Ave ST4 ....71 C1
Greenwood Dr WS14 ....231 B3
Greenwood Gr ST17 ....174 B4
Greenwood Pk
Aldridge WS9 ....245 B1
Cannock WS12 ....210 A4
Greenwood Rd
Aldridge WS9 ....245 A1
Burton u T DE15 ....185 C4
Forsbrook ST11 ....91 A4
Greenwoods The DY8 ..279 C3
Gregory La ST20 ....150 B3
Gregory Rd
Burntwood WS7 ....229 C4
Stourbridge DY8 ....279 B3
Gregory St ST3 ....283 B3
Gregorys Gn WV9 ....224 A2
Gregson Cl 5 ST3 ....73 A2
Greig Ct WS11 ....210 B1
Grenadier Cl ST4 ....88 B2
Grendon Gdns WV3 ....265 B3
Grendon Gn ST2 ....58 B1
Grenfell Rd WS3 ....243 B2
Grenville Cl ST14 ....110 C1
Grenville Rd DY1 ....271 C1
Gresham Rd WS11 ....209 C2
Gresley B77 ....250 C1
Gresley Cl B74 ....258 A2
Gresley Row WS13 ....231 B4
Gresley Way ST7 ....39 C1
Gresley Wood Rd DE11 .186 C1
Gresty St ST4 ....72 A4
Gretton Ave DE13 ....147 C1
Greville Cl ST19 ....207 C4
Greville St ST1 ....282 C4
Grey Friars ST16 ....155 B3
Grey Friars Way ST16 ..155 B3
Grey Friars' Pl ST16 ...155 B2
Greyfriars Bsns Pk ST16 155 B2
Greyfriars Cl DY1 ....271 C2
Greyfriars Ct ST16 ....155 B3
Greyfriars Dr B79 ....249 C3
Greyfriars Rd ST2 ....58 A3
Greyhound Ct CW3 ....68 C3
Greyhound La
Lower Penn WV4 ....264 C3
Stourbridge DY8 ....279 B1
Greyhound Way ST1,ST6 .57 A3
Greylarch La ST17 ....175 B4
Greysan Ave ST7 ....41 C4
Greysbrooke WS14 ....247 A3
Greysbrooke Prim Sch
WS14 ....247 A3
Greystoke Dr DY6 ....275 B3
Greyswood Rd ST4 ....71 C2
Grice Rd ST4 ....71 C4
Griffin Cl Burntwood WS7 228 C4
Norton in Hales TF9 ....82 B1
Griffin St ST3 ....283 B3
Griffithgreen WV5 ....267 B4
Griffiths Dr Wolv WV11 ..242 A1
Wombourne WV5 ....270 A3
Griffiths Rd WV12 ....242 B1
Griffiths Way ST15 ....120 B3
Grimley Way WS11 ....209 C2
Grindcobbe Gr WS15 ....178 B2
Grindley Bank ST18 ....140 C3
Grindley Hill Ct ST4 ....71 C3
Grindley La ST3,ST11 ....90 A3
Grindley Pl ST4 ....71 C3
Grindsbrook B77 ....262 A4
Grisedale Cl 7 ST3 ....90 A4
Grissom Cl ST16 ....156 A3
Gristhorpe Way ST2 ....58 B1
Gritton St ST6 ....41 B1
Grizedale Cl DE15 ....167 A1
Grocott Cl ST19 ....192 C1
Grosvenor Ave
Aldridge B74 ....256 C1
Stoke-on-T ST4 ....71 C2
Grosvenor Cl Endon ST9 ..43 C4
Lichfield WS14 ....231 B3
Penkridge ST19 ....192 C1
Sutton Coldfield B75 ....258 B1
Wolv WV10 ....240 B1
Grosvenor Cres WV10 ..240 B1
Grosvenor Ct
Sedgley DY3 ....271 B1
Shenstone WS14 ....246 C3
Wolv WV6 ....255 A2
Grosvenor Gdns ST5 ....284 C2
Grosvenor Pk WV4 ....265 C3
Grosvenor Pl
Newcastle-u-L ST5 ....56 B3
Tunstall ST6 ....41 B2
Grosvenor Rd
Market Drayton TF9 ....97 B1
Meir ST3 ....73 C1
Newcastle-u-L ST5 ....284 C2
Sedgley DY3 ....271 B1
Wolv, Bushbury WV10 ....240 B1
Wolv, Ettingshall Park
WV4 ....266 C2
Grosvenor Road S DY3 .271 B1
Grosvenor St Leek ST13 ..30 C3
Longton ST3 ....283 B3
Grosvenor Way ST17 ....175 C3
Grotto La WV6 ....255 C3
Grotto Rd TF9 ....112 A4
Grounds Dr B74 ....257 C2
Grounds Rd B74 ....257 C2
Groundslow Hospl ST12 103 C4
Grove Ave Fenton ST4 ....72 C2
Kidsgrove ST7 ....25 C1
Lawton-gate ST7 ....25 A2
Grove Cl WS11 ....227 C3
Grove Cres Walsall WS3 .243 C2
Woore CW3 ....83 B4
Grove Gdns TF9 ....97 B1
Grove Jun Sch ST1 ....282 C4
Grove La Doveridge DE6 .127 C4
Norton Canes WS3 ....227 C1
Wolv WV6 ....255 A1
Grove Park Ave ST7 ....25 A2
Grove Pk DY6 ....275 B4
Grove Pl ST1 ....282 A1
Grove Prim Sch WV2 ...266 C4

Grove Prim Sch The
ST17 .174 B4
Grove Rd Fenton ST4 .72 B2
Stone ST15 .119 C4
Grove Road Ind Est ST4 .72 B2
Grove Sch The TF9 .97 B1
Grove St Burslem ST6 .57 A3
Leek ST13 .30 B3
Newcastle-u-L ST5 .55 C2
Wolv WV2 .266 B4
Grove The
Blythe Bridge ST11 .90 C3
Burntwood WS7 .228 B4
Chell Heath ST6 .42 A1
Lawton-gate ST7 .25 A2
Little Aston B74 .257 B3
Newcastle-u-L ST5 .71 A3
Stone ST15 .120 B2
Tatenhill DE13 .184 A4
Wolv WV4 .266 C3
Grovebank Rd ST4 .71 C2
Grovelands Cres WV10 .240 B2
Grovenor Ct TF9 .97 B1
Groveside Way WS3 .244 A3
Grub St ST20 .151 A3
Grunmore Dr DE13 .147 C1
Guernsey Cl CW12 .6 A1
Guernsey Dr ST5 .70 C2
Guernsey Wlk 2 ST3 .73 A2
Guild La TF10 .169 C4
Guild St DE14 .166 B2
Guildford St ST4 .72 B4
Guinevere Ave DE13 .147 C1
Gullet The B78 .251 C1
Gullick Way WS7 .228 B4
Gun Battery La ST8 .28 A4
Gunby Hill DE12 .219 C4
Gungate B79 .250 A3
Gunn St ST8 .27 B4
Gunnel Cl ST16 .155 B1
Gunstone La WV8 .238 C3
Gurnard B77 .261 B3
Guthrum Cl Perton WV6 .254 C3
Wolv WV6 .254 C1
Guy St ST2 .58 A2
Guy's Almshouses B79 .250 A3
Guy's La DY3 .271 A1
Guys Cl B79 .249 C4
Gwendoline Way WS9 .245 A2
Gwenys Cres ST3 .72 C2
Gwyn Ave ST8 .27 B3
Gypsum Way DE6 .144 B3

H

Hackett Cl Longton ST3 .283 D4
Wolv WV14 .266 C1
Hackford Rd WV4 .266 C2
Hackwood Cl ST12 .88 C2
Hadden Cl ST9 .59 A1
Haddon Gr ST5 .55 C3
Haddon La ST5 .85 C1
Haddon Pl Bucknall ST2 .58 B3
Stone ST15 .120 B4
Haden Cl DY8 .275 B1
Hadfield Gn ST6 .42 B1
Hadleigh Cl ST5 .71 A1
Hadleigh Rd ST2 .58 A3
Hadley Park Gdns WS15 196 B4
Hadley St DE13 .181 C2
Hadrian Way ST5 .55 B3
Hadrians Cl B77 .261 B4
Haggar St WV2 .266 B3
Hagley Ct DY3 .271 B2
Hagley Dr WS15 .178 B1
Hagley Park High Sch
WS15 .196 B4
Hagley RC High Sch
DY8 .281 C3
Hagley Rd WS15 .178 B1
Haig Cl WS11 .210 A3
Haig Rd ST13 .31 A4
Haig St ST3 .73 B1
Haigh Cl ST13 .45 B3
Hailes Park Cl WV2 .266 C3
Hailsham Cl ST6 .41 C3
Hainult Cl DY8 .275 B2
Halcyon Ct DE14 .166 A2
Halcyon Way DE14 .166 A2
Haldale B77 .251 B1
Hales Hall Rd ST10 .76 C2
Hales Pl ST3 .283 C1
Halesworth Cres ST5 .71 A1
Halesworth Rd WV9 .239 C1
Halford Ave ST1 .57 B4
Halford St B79 .250 A3
Halfshire La DY10 .281 A1
Halfway Pl ST5 .55 C1
Halifax Cl ST3 .90 B4
Halifax Rd WV7 .220 C1
Haling Cl ST19 .207 C4
Haling Rd ST19 .192 C1
Hall Ave ST13 .31 A4
Hall Bank SK17 .24 C3
Hall Cl Pattingham WV6 .253 B1
Stafford ST17 .175 A4
Hall Dr Enville DY7 .273 B1
Meir ST3 .74 A2
Hall End ST15 .105 C3
Hall End Cl WV6 .253 B1
Hall End La WV6 .253 B1
Hall Farm Cl ST18 .139 B1
Hall Farm Cres ST18 .137 C2
Hall Gdns ST14 .127 C1
Hall Green Ave DE13 .147 C1
Hall Hill Dr ST2 .73 B4
Hall La Brownhills WS9 .244 C2
Burntwood WS7 .229 C2
Doveridge DE6 .127 A4
Great Wyrley WS6 .227 A2
Hilderstone ST15 .106 C2
Standon ST21 .102 B2
Swynnerton ST15 .103 B2
Walsall WS3 .243 C2
Wolv WV14 .266 C1
Wootton DE6 .79 C4
Hall Mdw WS11 .226 A3
Hall Orch Cheadle ST10 .76 B2
Uttoxeter ST14 .125 B4
Hall Pl ST5 .56 B3
Hall Rd Armitage WS15 .198 B3
Marchington ST14 .127 C1
Rolleston DE13 .146 C2
Uttoxeter ST14 .126 A4
Hall St Audley ST7 .39 B1
Burslem ST6 .56 C4
Newcastle-u-L ST5 .284 B3
Sedgley DY3 .271 B4
Hall Yd ST10 .92 C2
Hallahan Cl ST15 .120 B3
Hallahan Gr ST4 .72 A4
Hallam Rd ST14 .110 C1
Hallam St ST4 .72 B3
Hallams Row DE14 .166 B2
Hallbridge Cl WS3 .243 C1
Hallcourt Cl 3 WS11 .226 C4
Hallcourt Cres 2 WS11 226 C4
Hallcourt La WS11 .226 C4
Hallcroft Cl TF10 .168 C2
Hallcroft Gdns TF10 .168 C2
Hallcroft Way WS9 .256 B3
Halldearn Ave ST11 .74 B2
Hallfarm Cl ST19 .223 B3
Hallfarm Rd ST19 .223 B3
Hallfield Gr ST6 .41 C3
Hallfields Rd DE15 .186 B2
Hallhill La WS15 .161 A3
Halls Rd Biddulph ST8 .16 B1
Mow Cop ST7 .26 B4
Halston Rd 5 WS7 .229 A4
Halton Gn ST3 .88 C4
Haltonlea B77 .262 A4
Ham La DY6 .270 C1
Hamble B77 .250 B1
Hamble Gr WV6 .254 C2
Hamble Rd WV4 .265 B3
Hamble Way ST2 .58 B1
Hambledon Cl WV9 .240 A1
Hambleton Pl ST8 .27 A3
Hambridge Cl ST17 .174 B4
Hambro Pl ST6 .42 A4
Hamelin St WS11 .209 C2
Hames La B79 .236 B2
Hamil Dr ST13 .30 B3
Hamil Rd ST6 .42 A1
Hamilton Ave DY8 .279 B3
Hamilton Cl
Cannock WS12 .210 C2
Kingswinford DY8 .275 B1
Sedgley DY3 .271 B4
Hamilton Ct ST5 .71 B1
Hamilton Dr DY8 .275 B1
Hamilton Fields DE15 .167 A1
Hamilton Gdns WV10 .240 C2
Hamilton Ho WS3 .243 B1
Hamilton Inf Sch ST1 .57 B3
Hamilton Lea WS11 .228 A3
Hamilton Rd
Burton u T DE15 .167 A1
Longton ST3 .283 D2
Hamilton Rise ST2 .43 A1
Hamilton St Fenton ST4 .72 B3
Walsall WS3 .243 B1
Hamlet The WS11 .227 C3
Hamlett Pl ST6 .42 C2
Hammersley Hayes Rd
ST10 .76 C3
Hammersley St ST1 .57 C3
Hammerton Ave ST2 .57 C1
Hammerwich Hospl
WS7 .229 A3
Hammerwich La WS7 .229 C2
Hammerwich Rd WS7 .229 B3
Hammond Ave ST6 .43 A4
Hammond Ho ST1 .282 C1
Hammond Rd ST5 .55 C4
Hammonds Croft ST18 .158 B4
Hammoon Gr ST2 .58 A1
Hamner Gn ST2 .73 B4
Hampden Ho DE15 .185 C3
Hamps Cl WS7 .229 B4
Hamps Valley Rd ST10 .48 C1
Hampshire Cl Endon ST9 .43 C4
Tamworth B78 .250 A1
Hampshire Cres ST3 .89 B4
Hampstead Gr ST4 .88 B4
Hampton Cl
Newport TF10 .169 A2
Tamworth B79 .250 B4
Hampton Ct
Essington WV10 .241 A1
Leek ST13 .30 B3
Hampton Dr
Market Drayton TF9 .97 B1
Newport TF10 .169 A2
Hampton Gn WS11 .226 C4
Hampton Gr Kinver DY7 .278 B2
Walsall WS3 .244 A2
Hampton Rd WV10 .240 A1
Hampton St
Cannock WS11 .226 B4
Hanley ST1 .282 C1
Hams Cl ST8 .27 B4
Hanbridge Ave ST5 .56 A4
Hanbury Cres WV4 .265 C3
Hanbury Hill DE13 .145 A3
Hanbury Rd
Brownhills WS8 .228 C1
Norton Canes WS11 .227 C3
Tamworth B77 .250 C2
Hanbury's Farm Prim Sch
B77 .250 B1
Hanch Hall* WS15 .213 C4
Hanchurch Cl DE15 .167 A2
Hanchurch Hills Circular
Wlks* ST4 .86 C3
Hanchurch La ST4 .87 A4
Hancock St ST4 .72 B4
Hand La TF11 .187 B1
Hand St ST6 .41 C1
Handel Ct WS11 .210 B1
Handel Gr ST1 .58 A3
Handel Wlk WS13 .214 B1
Handley Banks ST11 .74 C2
Handley Dr ST8 .27 A1
Handley St ST8 .27 A1
Handsacre Cl DE11 .186 C2
Handsacre Cres WS15 .198 B2
Handsacre Rd ST3 .283 D5
Hangmans La B79 .236 A1
Hanley Rd ST6,ST1 .57 B4
Hanlith B77 .262 A4
Hannaford Way WS11 .209 C1
Hanney Hay Rd WS7,
WS8 .229 A2
Hanover Ct
Newcastle-u-L ST5 .284 C3
Tamworth B79 .249 C4
Wolv WV6 .255 B2
Hanover Ho DY8 .279 C4
Hanover Pl 14 WS11 .209 C1
Hanover St Hanley ST1 .282 B3
Newcastle-u-L ST5 .284 C3
Hanyards La ST18 .157 A3
Harald Cl WV6 .254 C3
Harber St ST3 .283 C3
Harbin Rd DE12 .184 B1
Harborough Ct B74 .258 A1
Harborough Dr WS9 .256 A3
Harbourne Cres ST10 .76 C2
Harbourne Rd ST10 .76 C2
Harbury St DE13 .166 A3
Harcourt Ave ST3 .73 C1
Harcourt Dr
Newport TF10 .169 A2
Sedgley DY3 .271 B1
Sutton Coldfield B74 .257 C2
Harcourt Ho B79 .250 A2
Harcourt Rd DE14 .184 C4
Harcourt St ST1 .282 A1
Harcourt Way ST16 .155 A4
Hardewick Cl ST9 .59 A2
Hardie Ave WS15 .196 C4
Hardie Gn WS11 .209 C2
Hardince St ST4 .72 B3
Harding Rd ST1 .282 B1
Harding Terr ST4 .72 A3
Hardings Mdw ST7 .25 C1
Hardingswood Rd ST7 .25 C1
Hardington Cl ST13 .30 C2
Hardnam St ST2 .43 A1
Hardon Rd WV4 .266 C3
Hardwick Ct
Aldridge B74 .256 C1
Tamworth B79 .250 B3
Hardwick Rd B74 .257 A1
Hardy Cl Barton-u-N DE13 201 C4
Cheadle ST10 .76 B1
Hardy Rd ST17 .174 A4
Hardy Sq WV2 .266 C3
Hardy St ST6 .41 B2
Harebell B77 .251 A2
Harebell Cl
Cannock WS12 .210 B1
Featherstone WV10 .241 A4
Harebell Gr ST7 .26 C1
Harecastle Ave ST7 .25 C1
Haregate Rd ST13 .31 A4
Haregate Terr ST13 .31 A4
Harehedge La DE13 .166 A4
Hareshaw Gr ST6 .42 A4
Harewell Dr B75 .258 B1
Harewood Cl ST10 .76 B2
Harewood Est ST10 .76 A3
Harewood St ST6 .41 B1
Hargate Rd DE15 .167 B1
Hargreave Cl ST3 .90 B4
Hargreaves La ST17 .155 B1
Harington Dr ST3 .73 C3
Harland Cl ST18 .177 B4
Harland Rd B74 .258 A2
Harlaxton St DE13 .166 A3
Harlech Ave ST3 .73 C1
Harlech Dr ST8 .27 B3
Harlech Way
Burton u T DE13 .166 B4
Sedgley DY1 .271 C1
Harlequin Dr ST6 .42 B1
Harlestones Ho DY8 .279 C4
Harley Cl Brownhills WS8 245 A3
Rugeley WS15 .196 C3
Harley La
Abbots Bromley WS15 .160 C4
Swynnerton ST4 .87 B1
Harley St ST1 .282 C2
Harley Thorn La ST4 .87 A2
Harmon Rd DY8 .279 B3
Harmony Gn ST17 .174 A4
Harney Ct WS15 .178 B2
Harold St ST6 .42 B1
Harper Ave
Burton u T DE13 .166 B4
Newcastle-u-L ST5 .56 A2
Harper Ct DE13 .166 B4
Harper St ST6 .56 C4
Harpfield Prim Sch ST4 .71 B4
Harpfield Rd ST4 .71 C3
Harplands Hospl ST4 .71 B3
Harplow La ST10 .76 A1
Harptree Wlk ST4 .71 C1
Harpur-Crewe Cotts DE6 35 B2
Harrier Cl ST3 .90 A3
Harrietts Hayes Rd
WV8 .237 C3
Harringay Dr DY8 .279 C2
Harrington Wlk WS13 .213 C1
Harris Rd ST16 .156 A2
Harris St ST4 .72 A4
Harriseahead La ST7 .26 B2
Harrison & Woodburn Cotts
ST5 .54 B2
Harrison Cl Audley ST7 .54 B4
Burton u T DE14 .185 A4
Great Wyrley WS6 .226 B1
Walsall WS3 .243 B1
Harrison Ct ST5 .284 C1
Harrison Rd
Cannock WS11 .226 C4
Norton-in-t-M ST6 .42 C2
Sutton Coldfield B74 .257 C3
Walsall WS4 .244 B1
Harrison St
Newcastle-u-L ST5 .284 C2
Walsall WS3 .243 B1
Harrison Way ST13 .45 B3
Harrisons La ST19 .207 C1
Harrogate Gr ST5 .54 C1
Harrop St ST1 .57 B3
Harrop Way DY8 .279 C4
Harrots La SK17 .24 B3
Harrow Ct B74 .257 C1
Harrow Dr DE14 .185 B4
Harrow Pl ST15 .120 B4
Harrow Rd DY6 .270 B1
Harrowby Dr ST5 .70 C2
Harrowby Rd Meir ST3 .90 A4
Wolv WV10 .240 B1
Harrowby St ST16 .156 A2
Hart Ct ST5 .284 B3
Harthill Rd WV4 .265 B2
Hartill St ST4 .72 B4
Hartington CE Prim Sch
SK17 .24 B3
Hartington Hall YH*
SK17 .24 C3
Hartington St Leek ST13 .30 C3
Newcastle-u-L ST5 .56 A3
Hartland Ave
Chell Heath ST6 .42 B2
Stafford ST17 .175 C4
Hartlands Rd ST21 .133 C4
Hartlebury Cl WS11 .210 B1
Hartley Dr Aldridge WS9 .256 A2
Stone ST15 .104 C1
Hartley Gdns CW12 .16 A4
Hartleyburn B77 .262 A4
Hartopp Rd B74 .257 C1
Hartsbourne Way ST17 .175 B4
Hartshill Rd ST4 .71 C4
Hartslade WS14 .231 C3
Hartwell ST5 .70 C2
Hartwell Gr ST16 .155 A3
Hartwell La
Barlaston ST3,ST15 .89 B1
Great Wyrley WS6 .227 A2
Hartwell Rd ST3 .90 A4
Hartwood Cl TF10 .168 C3
Harvard Cl DY1 .271 C2
Harvest Cl DY3 .271 C3
Harvest Fields Way B75 258 C2
Harvester Way DY6 .275 A4
Harvesters Cl WS9 .256 C1
Harvesters Wlk WV8 .239 C1
Harvey Dr B75 .258 B1
Harvey Pl ST14 .111 A1
Harvey Rd
Armitage WS15 .198 B2
Burton u T DE14 .185 A4
Congleton CW12 .6 A3
Meir ST3 .74 A1
Harvine Wlk DY8 .279 C2
Harwell Cl B79 .250 B4
Harwin Cl WV6 .255 C4
Harwood Ave DE14 .184 C4
Harwood Dr B77 .261 B2
Harwood Rd WS13 .214 A2
Haslemere Ave ST2 .43 A1
Haslington Cl ST5 .40 B1
Hassall St ST1 .282 C2
Hassam Ave ST5 .284 A4
Hassam Par ST5 .56 A3
Hassell St ST5 .284 C3
Haste Hill La ST10 .61 C1
Hastings Cl B77 .261 C3
Hastings Ct DY1 .271 C1
Hatch Heath Cl WV5 .269 C4
Hatch La TF11 .203 B2
Hatchett La B79 .217 B3
Hateley Dr WV4 .266 C2
Hatfield Cres ST3 .88 C4
Hathaway Rd B74 .258 A2
Hathersage Cl ST3 .73 B3
Hatherton Cl ST5 .40 B1
Hatherton Croft WS11 .209 B1
Hatherton Gdns WV10 .240 C1
Hatherton Pl WS9 .256 A4
Hatherton Rd
Cannock WS11 .209 B1
Hatherton Rd *continued*
Penkridge ST19 .192 C1
Hatherton St
Cheslyn Hay WS6 .226 B1
Stafford ST16 .156 A2
Hatrell St ST5 .284 C2
Hatton Rd Cannock WS11 209 A1
Wolv WV6 .255 C2
Hatton Waterworks Cotts
ST21 .102 B4
Hattons Gr WV8 .239 A1
Haughton St Giles CE Prim
Sch ST18 .172 C3
Haunton Rd B79 .217 B2
Havannah Prim Sch CW12 6 A3
Havefield Ave WS14 .231 C4
Havelet Dr ST5 .70 C2
Havelock Ave WV3 .265 C4
Havelock Gr ST8 .27 B4
Havelock Pl ST1 .282 A1
Haven Ave ST6 .57 B4
Haven Cres ST9 .59 A2
Haven Gr ST5 .56 B4
Haven The
Kingswinford DY8 .275 B1
Wolv WV2 .266 B4
Havergal CE Prim Sch
WV10 .225 B1
Havergal Wlk ST3 .283 C5
Haverhill Cl Chorlton CW2 37 A2
Walsall WS3 .243 A2
Havisham Ct TF10 .168 C2
Hawcroft WS15 .197 C1
Hawes St ST6 .41 B2
Haweswater Dr DY6 .275 B3
Hawfield La
Burton u T DE15 .167 B2
Newton Solney DE15 .167 C2
Hawfinch B77 .262 A3
Hawfinch Rd ST10 .76 C2
Hawk Cl ST3 .90 A4
Hawk's Dr DE15 .167 B2
Hawke Rd ST16 .155 B4
Hawkesford Cl B74 .258 A1
Hawkesmoor Dr
Lichfield WS14 .231 B4
Perton WV6 .254 B2
Hawkesmore Dr ST18 .177 B4
Hawkestone Cl ST5 .284 C2
Hawkesville Dr 7
WS11 .209 C1
Hawkeswell Dr DY6 .270 B1
Hawkhurst Dr WS15 .197 C4
Hawkins Cl WS13 .214 A1
Hawkins Dr WS11 .226 B2
Hawkins La
Burton u T DE14 .166 C3
Fradswell ST18 .122 C1
Hawkins Lane Ind Est
DE14 .166 C3
Hawkins St ST4 .72 B3
Hawks Cl WS6 .226 B1
Hawks Green La WS11 .210 A1
Hawksdale Cl ST3 .90 A4
Hawkside B77 .262 A4
Hawksley Dr DE13 .147 A2
Hawksmoor Cl ST3 .89 C4
Hawksmoor Rd ST17 .174 C4
Hawkstone Ave TF10 .168 C1
Hawkstone Cl WV6 .254 B3
Hawkswell Ave WV5 .270 A3
Hawkswell Dr DY6 .275 B4
Hawksworth B77 .250 C1
Hawksworth Ave ST13 .30 B2
Hawksworth Cl ST13 .30 B2
Hawkyard Ct WS11 .210 A2
Hawley Cl 2 ST15 .120 B3
Haworth Ave CW12 .6 A3
Hawthorn Ave
Great Wyrley WS6 .227 A1
Netherseal DE12 .219 C4
Stone ST15 .119 C3
Hawthorn Cl
Denstone ST14 .95 C3
Gnosall ST20 .171 C4
Haughton ST18 .172 C3
Lichfield WS14 .231 B4
Seighford ST18 .135 A1
Hawthorn Cres DE15 .185 C4
Hawthorn Gdns ST7 .40 B4
Hawthorn Gr ST8 .27 C4
Hawthorn Pl 8 ST3 .89 C4
Hawthorn Rd
Aldridge B74 .257 A1
Newcastle-u-L ST5 .40 C1
Walsall WS4 .244 A1
Hawthorn Rise DE11 .186 C4
Hawthorn St ST6 .57 A3
Hawthorn Way
Market Drayton TF9 .97 B1
Rugeley WS15 .178 B1
Stafford ST17 .156 A1
Hawthornden Ave ST14 .126 A4
Hawthornden Cl ST14 .126 A4
Hawthornden Gdns
ST14 .125 C4
Hawthornden Manor Mews
ST14 .126 A4
Hawthorne Ave
Audley ST7 .39 C1
Stoke-on-T ST4 .71 C3
Tamworth B79 .250 A4
Hawthorne Cl ST10 .92 C2
Hawthorne Cres WS7 .229 A3
Hawthorne Dr ST19 .205 B3
Hawthorne Gr DY3 .271 B1
Hawthorne La WV8 .238 C1

Hawthorne Rd Cannock WS12 210 C2
Cheslyn Hay WS6 226 C2
Essington WV11 242 A2
Huntington WS12 209 B4
Wheaton Aston ST19 205 B3
Wolv WV2 266 B3
Hawthorne Terr ST13 30 C3
Hawthorne Way DY7 278 B2
Hawthorns The
Hagley DY9 281 C2
Keele ST5 69 C4
Hay Barns The ST15 103 A2
Hay End La WS13 215 B4
Hay La Ellastone DE6 79 C2
Foston DE65 129 C3
Longdon WS15 213 A4
Haybarn The ST16 155 C4
Haybridge Ave DY8 281 C3
Haybridge High Sch
DY8 281 C3
Haycroft Dr B74 258 A2
Haydock Cl
Burton u T DE14 185 A4
Kingsley ST10 76 C3
Tamworth B77 261 B2
Haydock Ct ST5 55 B1
Haydon Ct ST4 56 C1
Haydon St ST4 56 C1
Hayes Cl ST13 30 C4
Hayes Meadow Prim Sch
WS15 198 B2
Hayes St ST6 42 B1
Hayes The TF9 112 A4
Hayes View WS13 213 C1
Hayes View Dr WS6 226 C2
Hayes Way WS11,WS12 210 B1
Hayeswood La ST7 54 C3
Hayfield Cres ST4 72 C4
Hayfield Hill WS15 211 C2
Hayfield Rd ST5 55 A1
Hayhead Cl ST7 26 A1
Hayle B77 250 B1
Hayley Ct DY6 275 B3
Hayling Gr WV2 266 A3
Hayling Pl ST3 72 C2
Haymarket ST6 41 B2
Haymarket The WV8 239 C1
Haymoor WS14 231 C4
Hayner Gr ST3 74 A2
Hayrick Dr DY6 275 A4
Hays La ST10 48 C2
Haywain Cl WV9 239 C1
Haywards Cl WS3 243 C2
Haywood Dr WV6 255 B2
Haywood Grange ST18 177 B4
Haywood High Sch ST6 42 A1
Haywood Hts ST18 177 B4
Haywood La TF9 113 B1
Haywood Rd ST6 42 A1
Haywood St Leek ST13 30 C3
Stoke-on-T ST4 57 A1
Hayworth Cl B79 249 C4
Hayworth Rd WS13 214 B1
Hazel Cl Kidsgrove ST7 26 A2
Stoke-on-T ST4 71 C3
Uttoxeter ST14 126 A3
Hazel Dr Armitage WS15 198 A2
Cannock WS12 211 A3
Hazel Gdns WV8 239 A2
Hazel Gr Biddulph ST8 17 A1
Lawton-gate ST7 25 A2
Leek ST13 30 B3
Lichfield WS14 231 B4
2 Meir ST3 73 C1
Stafford ST16 155 B4
Stourbridge DY8 279 B2
Wombourne WV5 270 A4
Hazel La WS6 227 A1
Hazel Rd
Kingswinford DY6 275 C3
Newcastle-u-L ST5 55 B4
Wolv WV3 265 C4
Hazel Slade Com Prim Sch
WS12 211 A3
Hazeldene ST18 158 B1
Hazeldene Rd ST4 88 B4
Hazelgarth B77 262 A4
Hazelhurst Dr ST13 45 B2
Hazelhurst Rd ST6 41 C3
Hazelhurst St ST1 282 C1
Hazelmere Dr
Burntwood WS7 228 C2
Wolv WV3 255 A1
Hazels The DY9 281 C2
Hazelslade Ho WS12 210 C3
Hazelslade Nature Reserve*
WS12 211 A3
Hazelton Gn ST17 174 B3
Hazelwood Cl
Cheslyn Hay WS6 226 B1
Hanley ST6 57 B3
Hazelwood Gr WS11 226 B4
Hazelwood Rd
Aldridge B74 256 B1
Burton u T DE15 185 C3
Endon ST9 43 C3
Hazlemere Dr B74 258 A1
Hazlemere Gr WS11 226 A4
Hazlescross Rd ST10 61 B2
Hazlestrine La ST17 175 B3
Hazlewood Gr WS11 226 B4
Hazlewood Rd DY1 271 C3
Hazlitt Way ST3 73 C3
HCM Ind Est DE14 166 C2
Headborough Wlk WS9 245 A1
Headingley Dr DY7 274 C1
Headland Dr WV3 255 A1
Headland Way ST10 78 C1
Headlands The B74 257 B2
Headway Rd WV10 240 B2
Heakley Ave ST6 42 C2
Healey B77 250 C1
Healey Ave ST8 27 A3
Heanor Pl ST3 283 A3
Heantun Row WV11 242 A1
Hearn Ct ST17 174 B4
Heart Of The Country Ctr*
WS14 247 C4
Hearthcote Rd DE11 186 C2
Heath Ave Cheddleton ST9 59 C2
Newcastle-u-L ST5 56 B2
Whittington WS14 232 B2
Heath Cl WS14 245 C3
Heath Croft Rd B75 258 B1
Heath Cross ST14 126 A4
Heath Dr
Kidderminster DY10 280 A1
Stafford ST16 155 A4
Heath Farm Rd
Codsall WV8 239 A1
Stourbridge DY8 279 C2
Heath Gap WS13 215 B4
Heath Gap Rd WS11 209 C2
Heath Gdns ST15 119 C3
Heath Gn DY1 271 C3
Heath Gr Ashley TF9 99 B2
Blythe Bridge ST3 90 A3
Codsall WV8 239 A2
Heath Hayes Prim Sch
WS12 210 C1
Heath Hill TF11 187 B1
Heath Hill Rd WV6 254 C1
Heath House Dr WV5 269 B3
Heath House La
Bucknall ST2 58 A2
Codsall WV8 238 C1
Rudyard ST13 18 B1
Upper Tean ST10 93 A2
Heath La Admaston WS15 140 B1
Stourbridge DY8 279 C2
Heath Mill Cl WV5 269 B2
Heath Mill Rd WV5 269 B2
Heath Pl ST5 56 B2
Heath Rd
Burton u T DE15 185 C4
Gnosall TF10 188 C4
Rugeley WS15 196 C3
Uttoxeter ST14 111 A1
Walsall WV12 242 B1
Whitmore ST5 85 B4
Heath Row CW3 69 A4
Heath St Biddulph ST8 27 B4
Cannock WS12 210 A4
Newcastle-u-L ST5 284 B3
Newcastle-u-L, Broad Meadow
ST5 55 C3
Stourbridge DY8 279 C2
Tamworth B79 250 B3
Tunstall ST6 41 B4
Heath Top TF9 99 C2
Heath View
Burntwood WS7 212 A1
Cannock WS12 227 C4
Weston CW2 37 A3
Heath Way
Cannock WS11 210 A1
Hatton DE65 146 B4
Heath's Pas ST3 283 D3
Heathbank Dr WS12 209 B3
Heathbrook Ave DY6 275 A4
Heathcote Ave TF9 99 C2
Heathcote Cl B77 262 A4
Heathcote Ct 10 ST3 73 B3
Heathcote Rd Audley ST7 54 C4
Longton ST3 283 B3
Heathcote Rise ST3 74 A3
Heathcote St
Kidsgrove ST7 26 A1
Longton ST3 73 B3
Newcastle-u-L ST5 55 C4
Heathdene Cl ST3 283 B4
Heather Cl Brocton ST17 176 B2
Burton u T DE14 185 A4
Caverswall ST9 59 A2
Rugeley WS15 196 C3
Seighford ST18 135 B1
Heather Cres ST3 90 A2
Heather Dr
Huntington WS12 209 B3
Kinver DY7 277 C2
Heather Glade CW3 68 B4
Heather Hill ST17 176 B2
Heather Hills ST9 43 B3
Heather Mews WS12 210 A4
Heather Rd WS12 210 A4
Heather Valley WS12 210 B3
Heather View ST6 42 C3
Heatherlands Cl ST3 89 C3
Heatherleigh Gr ST1 57 C3
Heatherside ST7 26 B3
Heathfield Ave ST15 120 A4
Heathfield Ct ST6 41 B4
Heathfield Dr
Newcastle-u-L ST5 40 B1
Walsall WS3 243 A1
Heathfield Gdns DY8 279 C2
Heathfield Gr ST3 89 C3
Heathfield Rd
Chell Heath ST6 42 B3
Sutton Coldfield B74 257 C2
Uttoxeter ST14 126 A4
Heathfield Specl Sch
ST6 42 B3
Heathfields Inf Sch B77 261 C3
Heathland Cl WS12 210 B1
Heathlands Cl DY6 275 C4
Heathlands Dr ST14 111 A1
Heathlands The WV5 269 B3
Heathley La B78 260 C3
Heathley Mews DE14 185 B4
Heathmill Ent Ctr DY3 269 B2
Heathside Dr WS3 244 A2
Heathside La ST6 41 B4
Heathview ST13 45 C4
Heathway Colton WS15 179 A4
Gnosall ST20 171 B3
Heathwood Rd TF10 168 C1
Heatley Back La WS15 141 B2
Heatley La WS15 141 B1
Heaton Cl WV10 240 C3
Heaton Terr Endon ST9 29 A1
Newcastle-u-L ST5 56 A3
Heaton Villas ST6 43 B4
Hebden B77 262 A4
Hebden Gr WV11 242 A1
Heber St ST3 283 C4
Hedgerow Cl WS12 209 C4
Hedgerow Dr DY6 270 B1
Hedgerow Wlk WV8 239 C1
Hedgerows The B77 261 C4
Hedges The WV5 269 C3
Hedging La B77 261 C3
Hedging Lane Ind Est
B77 261 C3
Hedley Pl ST5 70 C4
Hednesford Rd
Brownhills WS8 228 B1
Cannock, Blackfords
WS11 209 C1
Cannock, Little Hayes
WS12 210 C1
Norton Canes WS11 227 C3
Rugeley WS15 196 B4
Hednesford St WS11 209 C1
Hednesford Sta WS12 210 A3
Heenan Gr
Lichfield WS13 213 C1
Stafford ST17 174 C3
Heighley Castle Way
CW3 68 C4
Heighley Ct CW3 53 A3
Heighley La CW3 53 C2
Heights The ST13 30 A1
Helen Sharman Dr
ST16 156 A3
Helford Gr ST17 174 A4
Heligan Pl WS12 210 C1
Hellier Dr WV5 269 C4
Hellier Rd WV10 240 C1
Helmingham B79 249 B4
Helston Ave ST3 73 C2
Helston Cl
Kingswinford DY8 275 B1
Stafford ST17 156 B1
Tamworth B79 250 B4
Heming Pl ST2 58 A2
Hemingway Rd ST3 73 B2
Hemlock Pk WS11 210 A1
Hemlock Rd ST3 283 D4
Hemlock Way WS11 210 A2
Hemmings Cl DY8 279 C3
Hempbutts The ST15 120 A4
Hempits Gr ST17 175 A1
Hemplands Rd DY8 279 C3
Hempstalls Ct ST5 284 B4
Hempstalls Gr ST5 56 A2
Hempstalls La ST5 284 C4
Hempstalls Prim Sch
ST5 56 A2
Hemsby Way ST5 71 A1
Hen La ST10 108 B3
Hencroft ST13 30 C3
Henderson Cl WS14 231 B4
Henderson Gr ST3 74 A1
Hendon Cl DY3 271 B1
Henhurst Farm DE13 165 B3
Henhurst Hill DE13 165 B2
Henhurst Ridge DE13 165 B2
Henley Ave ST8 27 A3
Henley Cl Barlaston ST12 88 C2
Burntwood WS7 229 A3
Tamworth B79 250 A3
Walsall WS3 243 C1
Henley Ct WS14 231 A3
Henley Dr Newport TF10 169 A2
Sutton Coldfield B74 258 A2
Henley Grange WS15 178 A1
Henley Rd Chorlton CW2 37 A1
Wolv WV10 240 A1
Henney Cl ST19 207 C4
Henry Chadwick Prim Sch
WS15 198 A4
Henry Prince CE Fst Sch The
DE6 81 B4
Henry St Stafford ST16 155 C3
Tunstall ST6 41 B2
Hensel Dr WV3 265 B4
Henshall Hall Dr CW12 6 A1
Henshall Pl ST6 41 B3
Henshall Rd ST5 55 C4
Henshaw Way ST15 119 A3
Henwood Cl WV6 255 B2
Henwood Rd WV6 255 B2
Hepburn Cl WS9 256 A2
Hepworth Cl WV6 254 C2
Herbert Rd Aldridge WS9 245 A1
2 Longton ST3 73 B1
Stafford ST17 155 C1
Herbert St
Burton u T DE15 167 A2
Fenton ST4 72 B3
Herbhill Cl WV4 266 B2
Herd St ST6 41 C1
Hereford Ave ST5 71 B2
Hereford Cl WS9 256 A4
Hereford Gr ST2 58 B1
Hereford Rd WS12 210 A2
Hereford Way B78 250 A1
Heritage Ct WS14 231 B3
Heritage Way DE15 167 A1
Herm Cl ST5 70 C2
Hermes Cl ST3 90 B4
Hermes Ct B74 257 C2
Hermes Rd WS13 214 B1
Hermit St DY3 271 B3
Hermitage Gdns 1
ST14 111 A1
Hermitage La DE6 81 A3
Heron Cl CW3 68 C4
Heron Cross Prim Sch
ST4 72 B2
Heron Dr Brewood WV9 224 A1
Penkridge ST19 208 A3
Heron Mill WS3 243 C2
Heron Pool Dr ST5 85 B2
Heron St Fenton ST4 72 C3
Rugeley WS15 196 C4
Heron Way TF10 168 C3
Herondale WS12 210 A2
Herondale Cres DY8 279 B2
Herondale Rd DY8 279 B2
Heronry The WV6 254 C1
Herons Cl ST17 175 B4
Herons Gate Rd DY7 277 A2
Heronswood ST17 175 B4
Hertford Gr ST5 71 B2
Hertford St ST4 72 C2
Hesketh Ave ST6 42 B3
Hesketh Rd ST17 174 C3
Heskin Way ST6 42 A3
Hesleden B77 262 A4
Hester Cl ST3 73 B3
Hethersett Wlk ST2 58 B1
Hever Cl DY1 271 C2
Hewell Cl DY6 270 B1
Hewitt Cl WS13 214 A1
Hewitt Cres ST9 59 A2
Hewitt St ST6 41 C3
Hewston Croft WS12 210 B2
Hexham Way DY1 271 C1
Hextall La ST18 153 B3
Heybridge Cl ST10 92 C1
Heyburn Cres ST6 56 C4
Heyfields Cotts ST12 104 A4
Heygate Way WS9 245 A1
Heysham Cl ST3 74 A2
Hick St ST5 284 B2
Hickman St ST5 284 B3
Hickmerelands La DY3 266 B1
Hickory Ct WS11 210 B1
Hidden Hills CW3 68 C4
Hide La SK17 24 C4
Hide Pl ST4 72 A4
Hide St ST4 72 A4
Higgins Rd DE11 186 C3
Higginson Cl CW12 16 B4
Higgott Cl DE14 185 A4
Higgs Rd WV11 242 A1
High Arcal Dr DY3 271 C4
High Arcal Rd DY3 270 C2
High Arcal Sch The
DY3 271 C3
High Bank WS11 226 C4
High Bank Pl ST6 42 A1
High Bank Rd DE15 167 A2
High Broome Ct B78 250 A2
High Carr Bsns Pk ST5 40 C1
High Chase Rise ST18 177 B4
High Croft WS9 245 A1
High Croft Cres WS14 231 B4
High Cross SK17 24 C3
High Gn Brewood ST19 223 B3
Cannock WS11 209 B1
High Grange
Cannock WS11 210 A3
Lichfield WS13 213 C1
High Green Ct WS11 209 B1
High Hill WV11 242 A1
High Holborn DY3 271 B4
High House La WV7 237 B2
High La Audley ST7 55 A3
Chell Heath ST6 42 A2
Endon ST6 43 A3
Leek ST13 45 C4
High Land Rd WS9 245 A2
High Lowe Ave CW12 6 A2
High Lows La ST15 118 C3
High Mdw Cannock WS15 211 C3
Norbury ST20 151 A2
High Mdws
Newport TF10 169 A2
Wolv WV6 255 B2
Wombourne WV5 270 A3
High Mount St WS12 210 A3
High Offley Rd ST20 151 B4
High Park Ave DY8 279 B3
High Park Cl DY3 271 B4
High Park Cres DY3 266 B1
High Path WV6 253 B1
High Pk ST16 155 B1
High St
Abbots Bromley WS15 161 A3
Albrighton WV7 237 A3
Aldridge WS9 256 A3
Alton ST10 78 C1
Audley ST7 40 A1
Audley, Alsagers Bank ST7 54 C3
Biddulph ST8 27 B4
Brierley Hill DY8 279 C4
Brownhills, Catshill WS8 244 C4
High St *continued*
Brownhills, Clayhanger
WS8 244 C3
Brownhills, Walsall Wood
WS9 244 C2
Burntwood WS7 211 C1
Burton u T DE14 166 C1
Caverswall ST11 74 C2
Cheadle ST10 76 B2
Cheslyn Hay WS6 226 B1
Cheswardine TF9 130 A4
Church Eaton ST20 190 A4
Claverley WV5 267 B4
Colton WS15 179 A3
Dilhorne ST10 75 B2
Eccleshall ST21 133 C4
Edgmond TF10 168 A2
Gnosall ST20 171 B3
Hixon ST18 158 B4
Ipstones ST10 47 A1
Kidsgrove, Harriseahead
ST7 26 C3
Kidsgrove, Newchapel ST7 26 C1
Kidsgrove, The Rookery ST7 26 B2
Kingsley ST10 61 C1
Kingswinford DY6 275 C3
Kingswinford, Wall Heath
DY6 275 B4
Kingswinford, Wordsley
DY8 275 C1
Kinver DY7 278 A2
Leek ST13 30 C3
Longdon WS15 197 C1
Longnor SK17 13 B3
Marchington ST14 127 C1
Market Drayton TF9 97 B1
Mow Cop ST7 26 B4
Newcastle-u-L ST5 284 B2
Newcastle-u-L, Chesterton
ST5 55 C4
Newcastle-u-L, Knutton ST5 55 C2
Newcastle-u-L, Silverdale
ST5 55 B1
Newcastle-u-L, Wolstanton
ST5 56 B3
Newport TF10 168 C2
Norton Canes WS11 228 A3
Pattingham WV6 253 B2
Rocester ST14 95 C2
Sedgley DY3 271 B4
Stone ST15 120 A4
Stourbridge DY8 279 C4
Swadlincote DE11 186 C3
Swindon DY3 269 C1
Talke ST7 40 B3
Tamworth B77 261 B3
Tunstall ST6 41 B2
Tunstall, Goldenhill ST6 41 B4
Tutbury DE13 146 B3
Upper Tean ST10 92 C2
Uttoxeter ST14 126 B4
Walsall WS3 243 A1
Walsall, Pelsall WS3 244 A2
Wheaton Aston ST19 205 A3
Wolv WV6 255 B2
Wombourne WV5 270 A4
High St (May Bank) ST5 56 B2
High St (Sandyford) ST6 41 B3
High View
Blythe Bridge ST3 90 A3
Mount Pleasant ST7 26 A3
Wolv WV14 266 C1
High View Rd Endon ST9 43 C4
Leek ST13 31 A3
High Wood Cl DY6 275 B3
Highbrook Cl WV9 240 A1
Highbury Rd
Caverswall ST9 59 B2
Sutton Coldfield B74 257 B2
Highcliffe Rd B77 261 B4
Highcroft WS3 244 A3
Highcroft Ave DY8 275 B2
Highcroft Dr
Burton u T DE14 165 C2
Sutton Coldfield B74 257 C2
Highcroft Wlk ST6 42 A1
Higher Ash Rd ST7 40 B4
Higher Woodcroft ST13 30 B2
Higherland ST5 284 A2
Higherland 6 ST7 26 A1
Highfied Dr DE15 166 C2
Highfield TF10 168 A2
Highfield Ave
Burntwood WS7 229 A4
Cheadle ST10 76 B2
Essington WV10 241 A1
Kidsgrove ST7 26 A1
Meir ST3 73 C1
Newcastle-u-L ST5 56 B2
Tamworth B77 251 A3
Highfield Cl
Acton Trussell ST17 193 A4
Blythe Bridge ST11 90 B4
Burntwood WS7 229 A4
Burton u T DE13 166 A4
Highfield Cres ST10 76 B2
Highfield Ct
Cannock WS11 210 A3
Newcastle-u-L ST5 71 B3
Highfield Dr
Colwich ST18 177 B4
Fenton ST3 72 C2
Highfield Gdns WS14 231 C3
Highfield Gr ST17 174 B4
Highfield Grange ST5 56 C2

Highfield La SK17 . . . . 24 C3
Highfield Rd
 Burntwood WS7 . . . . 229 B4
 Cannock WS12 . . . . 210 C1
 Cookley DY10 . . . . 280 A3
 Hixon ST18 . . . . 158 B4
 Sedgley DY3 . . . . 266 B3
 Walsall WS3 . . . . 244 A2
Highfield Rd E ST8 . . . . 27 B4
Highfield Rd N WS3 . . . . . . 243 C3
Highfield Rd W ST8 . . . . 27 B4
Highfield Rise ST4 . . . . 87 C4
Highfield Way WS9 . . . . . . 245 A1
Highfields
 Burntwood WS7 . . . . 229 A4
 Market Drayton TF9 . . . . . 112 A4
Highfields Ave WS15 . . . . . 198 B2
Highfields Ct WV4 . . . . 265 B3
Highfields Dr WS3 . . . . 270 A3
Highfields Grange WS6 . . . 226 B1
Highfields Pk WS6 . . . . 226 B1
Highfields Prim Sch
 WS7 . . . . 229 B4
Highfields Rd WS7 . . . . . . 228 C2
Highfields Sch WV4 . . . . . . 265 B3
Highfields The
 Eccleshall ST21 . . . . 116 A3
 Wolv WV6 . . . . 255 A4
Highgate Aldridge B74 . . . . 257 A1
 Sedgley DY3 . . . . 271 C3
Highgate Ave WV4 . . . . . . 265 B3
Highgate Cl ST6 . . . . 42 C2
Highgate Country Pk★
 DY3 . . . . 269 A1
Highgate Dr DY7 . . . . 273 C4
Highgrove Stone ST15 . . . . 120 B3
 Wolv WV6 . . . . 255 B2
Highgrove Cl
 Burton u T DE13 . . . . . . 147 B1
 Tamworth B79 . . . . 250 A4
Highgrove Pl DY3 . . . . 271 C1
Highland Cl Biddulph ST8 . . . 28 A4
 Blythe Bridge ST11 . . . . . . 90 C4
Highland Dr ST3 . . . . 73 B1
Highland Rd
 Huntington WS12 . . . . . . 209 B2
 Newport TF10 . . . . 168 C1
Highland Way WS15 . . . . . 178 B2
Highlands Stafford ST17 . . . 174 C4
 Stone ST15 . . . . 119 C3
Highlands Dr DE15 . . . . . . 167 A2
Highlands Rd WV3 . . . . . . 265 B4
Highlanes ST21 . . . . 116 A3
Highover Dr B75 . . . . 258 A2
Highton St ST2 . . . . 43 B1
Highup Rd ST13 . . . . 19 B1
Highview Dr DY6 . . . . 275 C2
Highview Rd ST11 . . . . 106 C4
Highway La ST5 . . . . 69 C4
Highwood Rd ST14 . . . . . . 126 B3
Higson Ave ST4 . . . . 72 A4
Hilary Dr Aldridge WS9 . . . . 256 C4
 Wolv WV3 . . . . 265 B3
Hilcote Hollow ST16 . . . . . 155 A3
Hilderstone Rd ST15 . . . . . 106 B3
Hill Ave WV4 . . . . 266 C2
Hill Avenue Jun & Inf Sch
 WV4 . . . . 266 C2
Hill Cl Sedgley DY3 . . . . . . 266 C1
 Uttoxeter ST14 . . . . 110 C1
Hill Cres Audley ST7 . . . . . . 54 C1
 Stone ST15 . . . . 120 A3
Hill Crest Sedgley DY3 . . . . 271 B4
 Stafford ST17 . . . . 174 B4
Hill Crest Dr WS13 . . . . . . 214 A1
Hill Croft ST18 . . . . 158 B4
Hill Dr Hanbury DE13 . . . . . 145 A2
 Stone ST15 . . . . 120 A3
Hill Hook Ho B74 . . . . 257 C3
Hill Hook Rd B74 . . . . 257 C3
Hill La Burntwood WS7 . . . 211 C1
 Church Leigh ST10 . . . . . 108 A2
 Sutton Coldfield B75 . . . . 259 A1
Hill Pk WS9 . . . . 245 A2
Hill Pl WV11 . . . . 242 A1
Hill Rise ST18 . . . . 137 C2
Hill Side DY3 . . . . 271 B4
Hill St Brierley Hill DY8 . . . . 279 C4
 Burntwood WS7 . . . . 228 B4
 Burton u T DE15 . . . . . . 185 C4
 Cannock WS12 . . . . 210 B2
 Cheslyn Hay WS6 . . . . . . 226 B1
 Essington WV11 . . . . 241 C2
 Newcastle-u-L ST5 . . . . . 284 C4
 Norton Canes WS11 . . . . 227 C3
 Rugeley WS15 . . . . 196 A4
 Sedgley DY3 . . . . 271 B3
 Stoke-on-T ST4 . . . . 72 A4
 Stourbridge DY8 . . . . . . 279 C2
 Swadlincote DE11 . . . . . . 186 C3
Hill Terr ST7 . . . . 39 B1
Hill Top Ave B79 . . . . 250 A4
Hill Top Cl ST6 . . . . 28 A1
Hill Top Cres ST3 . . . . 90 A3
Hill Top View WS15 . . . . . . 198 B3
Hill Top Wlk WS9 . . . . 245 B1
Hill View Aldridge WS9 . . . 245 A1
 Leek ST13 . . . . 31 A3
 Norton-in-t-M ST2 . . . . . . 43 A1
Hill Village Rd B75 . . . . . . 258 A2
Hill West Inf Sch B74 . . . . . 257 C2
Hill West Jun Sch B74 . . . . 257 C2
Hill Wood WS3 . . . . 243 C1
Hill Wood Rd B75 . . . . 258 A3
Hillary Ave CW12 . . . . 6 A1

Hillary Crest
 Rugeley WS15 . . . . 196 C3
 Sedgley DY3 . . . . 271 C3
Hillary Rd ST7 . . . . 26 A2
Hillary St ST6 . . . . 57 A3
Hillberry Cl ST2 . . . . 58 A1
Hillboro Rise DY7 . . . . 278 A3
Hillchurch St ST1 . . . . 282 B3
Hillcott Wlk ST4 . . . . 283 D3
Hillcrest Brewood ST19 . . . 223 B4
 Hixon WS15 . . . . 140 A1
 Leek ST13 . . . . 30 B3
 Tutbury DE13 . . . . 146 A3
Hillcrest Ave
 Burton u T DE15 . . . . . . 167 A2
 Kingsley ST10 . . . . 62 A1
Hillcrest Cl Kingsley ST10 . . 62 A1
 Tamworth B79 . . . . 250 A3
Hillcrest Rise WS7 . . . . . . 229 A2
Hillcrest St ST1 . . . . 282 C3
Hillcroft Ave ST17 . . . . 175 C4
Hillcroft Rd DY6 . . . . 275 C4
Hilldene Rd DY6 . . . . 275 B2
Hillfarm Ct ST17 . . . . 174 C3
Hillfield Ave ST4 . . . . 71 C4
Hillfield La DE13 . . . . 147 C1
Hillgreen Rd ST3 . . . . 73 B3
Hillman B77 . . . . 250 C1
Hillmorton Rd B74 . . . . . . 257 C2
Hillport Ave ST5 . . . . 56 A4
Hillrise ST10 . . . . 94 C4
Hillsdale La ST13 . . . . 33 C2
Hillsdale Rd DE15 . . . . 167 A3
Hillside
 Abbots Bromley WS15 . . . 161 A3
 Brownhills WS8 . . . . 245 A3
 Eccleshall ST21 . . . . 133 C3
 Lichfield WS14 . . . . 231 B3
 Market Drayton TF9 . . . . 112 C2
 Newcastle-u-L ST5 . . . . . 284 A3
 Tutbury DE13 . . . . 146 B3
 Wombourne WV5 . . . . . . 269 C4
 Wombourne, Brickbridge
  WV5 . . . . 269 C3
Hillside Ave Endon ST9 . . . . 43 C4
 Forsbrook ST11 . . . . 91 A4
 Kidsgrove ST7 . . . . 41 A4
 Meir ST3 . . . . 73 C1
Hillside Cl Biddulph ST8 . . . . 17 A1
 Blythe Bridge ST11 . . . . . 106 C4
 Brownhills WS8 . . . . 245 A3
 Cannock WS12 . . . . 210 A4
 Kidsgrove ST7 . . . . 26 A1
 Norton-in-t-M ST2 . . . . . . 43 B2
 Rugeley WS15 . . . . 197 A3
Hillside Cres WS3 . . . . 243 C2
Hillside Dr Colwich ST18 . . . 177 B4
 Leek ST13 . . . . 30 B2
Hillside Gdns DE11 . . . . . . 186 C1
Hillside Gr DY10 . . . . 280 B2
Hillside Prim Sch ST2 . . . . . 43 A1
Hillside Rd Caverswall ST9 . . 59 A2
 Cheddleton ST13 . . . . 45 B2
 Norton-in-t-M ST2 . . . . . . 43 B2
 Sutton Coldfield B74 . . . . 258 A2
Hillside Wlk ST4 . . . . 71 B4
Hillslde Cl WS7 . . . . 228 C3
Hillswood Ave ST13 . . . . . . 30 B3
Hillswood Cl ST9 . . . . 43 C4
Hillswood Dr ST9 . . . . 43 C4
Hilltop WS15 . . . . 196 C3
Hilltop Ave ST5 . . . . 56 C1
Hilltop Ct DY3 . . . . 271 C3
Hilltop Prim Sch ST7 . . . . . . 40 B4
Hillview Cres ST5 . . . . 85 B3
Hillway Cl WS15 . . . . 178 B1
Hillwood Cl DY6 . . . . 275 B2
Hillwood Common Rd
 B75 . . . . 258 A4
Hillwood Rd CW3 . . . . 69 A2
Hilmore Way B77 . . . . 261 C4
Hilsea Cl WV8 . . . . 239 C1
Hilsea Cres ST14 . . . . 143 C4
Hilston Ave WV4 . . . . 265 B2
Hilton Cl Stafford ST17 . . . . 174 C3
 Walsall WS3 . . . . 243 A1
Hilton Cross WV10 . . . . . . 241 A3
Hilton Cross Bsns Pk
 WV10 . . . . 241 A3
Hilton Dr ST21 . . . . 117 C2
Hilton La
 Featherstone WV10,WV11 . 241 C4
 Great Wyrley WS6 . . . . . . 227 A4
 Great Wyrley, Warstone
  WV11 . . . . 242 A4
Hilton Main Ind Est
 WV11 . . . . 241 B3
Hilton Park Service Area . . . 242 A4
Hilton Rd
 Burntwood WS7 . . . . 228 B4
 Egginton DE65 . . . . 148 A4
 Featherstone WV10 . . . . . 241 B4
 Stoke-on-T ST4 . . . . 71 C4
 Walsall WV12 . . . . 242 B1
 Wolv WV4 . . . . 266 C2
Hilton Trad Est WV4 . . . . . 266 C2
Himley Ave DY1 . . . . 271 C1
Himley Cres WV4 . . . . 266 A3
Himley Cl DY3 . . . . 271 C2
Himley Hall★ DY3 . . . . 270 A2
Himley La Himley DY3 . . . . 270 A2
 Swindon DY3 . . . . 269 C1
Himley Rd DY1,DY3 . . . . . . 271 B1
Hinbrook Rd DY1 . . . . 271 C1
Hinchco Pl ST6 . . . . 42 C2
Hinckes Rd WV6 . . . . 255 A3

Hinckley Gr ST4 . . . . 88 A3
Hinde St ST1 . . . . 282 B1
Hines St ST4 . . . . 72 C3
Hingley Croft WS9 . . . . . . 256 C2
Hinksford Gdns DY3 . . . . . 269 C1
Hinksford La DY3 . . . . 269 C1
Hinsford Cl DY6 . . . . 275 C4
Hinsley Mill La TF9 . . . . 97 C1
Hinstock Cl WV4 . . . . 266 A2
Hinton Cl ST3 . . . . 88 C4
Hints Cl B78 . . . . 248 B1
Hints La Hints B78 . . . . . . 248 C2
 Hopwas B78 . . . . 249 A3
Hints Rd Hopwas B78 . . . . 249 A3
 Tamworth B78 . . . . 249 B1
Hislop Rd WS15 . . . . 196 C3
Histons Dr WV8 . . . . 238 C1
Histons Hill WV8 . . . . 238 C1
Hitchman St ST4 . . . . 72 C3
Hixon Airfield Est (Ind Est)
 ST18 . . . . 139 C1
Hixon Ind Est ST18 . . . . . . 158 A4
**HM Young Offender Inst
 (Swinfen Hall) WS14** . . . 231 C1
Hoarstone DY8 . . . . 281 C3
**Hob Hill CE Methodist Prim
 Sch WS15** 197 A3
Hob's Rd WS13 . . . . 214 C1
Hobart Cl DE15 . . . . 167 B1
Hobart Ct B74 . . . . 258 A1
Hobart Rd WS12 . . . . 210 C1
Hobart St ST6 . . . . 57 A4
Hobb La ST4 . . . . 142 A4
Hobble End La WS6 . . . . . 243 C1
Hobbs Mew ST5 . . . . 197 A3
Hobby Cl [9] ST3 . . . . 90 A4
Hobfield La WS15 . . . . 161 A4
Hobnock Rd WV11 . . . . . . 242 A3
Hobs Hole La WS9 . . . . . . 256 B4
Hobson St ST6 . . . . 57 A4
**Hobstone Hill La ST7,
 WS13** 212 C1
Hockley Rd
 Tamworth B77 . . . . 261 C3
 Uttoxeter ST14 . . . . 126 A3
Hodge La B77 . . . . 251 A3
Hodgkins Cl WS8 . . . . 245 A3
Hodgkinson St ST5 . . . . 55 C3
Hodnet Gr ST1 . . . . 282 A4
Hodnet Pl WS11 . . . . 210 A1
Hodson Way WS11 . . . . . . 210 A1
Hogan Way ST16 . . . . 156 B2
Hogarth Pl ST5 . . . . 55 C3
Holbeach Ave ST2 . . . . 58 A1
Holbeach Way ST16 . . . . . 155 B2
Holbeache La DY6 . . . . . . 270 B1
Holbeache Rd DY6 . . . . . . 275 B4
Holborn ST5 . . . . 284 B3
Holborn Row ST10 . . . . 92 C3
Holborn Sh Ctr The
 DY3 . . . . 271 B4
Holborn The CW3 . . . . 68 C3
Holbrook Wlk ST2 . . . . 58 A1
Holbury Cl WV4 . . . . 240 A1
Holcroft Rd DY6 . . . . 270 B1
Holcroft Rd ST2 . . . . 58 B3
Holden Ave ST5 . . . . 56 B2
Holden Ave N ST6 . . . . 57 B4
Holden Ave S ST6 . . . . 57 B4
Holden Lane High Sch
 ST1 . . . . 57 C4
Holden Lane Prim Sch
 ST1 . . . . 57 C4
Holden Rd WV4 . . . . 265 B2
Holder Dr WS11 . . . . 209 A1
Holder St ST1 . . . . 57 A3
Holdiford Rd
 Brocton ST17,ST18 . . . . . 176 B3
 Tixall ST18 . . . . 157 B1
Holding Cres ST7 . . . . 54 B4
Holditch Rd ST5 . . . . 55 C3
Holecroft St [7] ST6 . . . . . . 57 A4
Holehouse La
 Endon ST6,ST9 . . . . 28 B1
 Scholar Green ST7 . . . . . . 25 B4
Holehouse Rd ST2 . . . . 58 B3
Holland Cl WS13 . . . . 215 A1
Holland Ct B79 . . . . 217 B3
Holland Pk DE13 . . . . 183 C1
Holland St [2] ST6 . . . . 41 B2
Holland's Way WS3 . . . . . . 243 C2
Hollands Pl WS3 . . . . 243 A1
Hollands Rd WS3 . . . . 243 B1
Hollands The ST8 . . . . 17 B2
Hollies Ave WS11 . . . . 209 C1
Hollies Brook Cl ST20 . . . . 171 B4
Hollies Cl Clifton DE6 . . . . . 81 C3
 Newton Solney DE15 . . . . 167 C4
Hollies Cl WS11 . . . . 209 C1
Hollies Dr ST3 . . . . 90 A2
Hollies Ind Est WV2 . . . . . 266 B4
Hollies La Enville DY7 . . . . 276 C4
 Pattingham WV6 . . . . . . 253 C2
Hollies Park Rd WS11 . . . . 209 C1
Hollies The
 Newcastle-u-L ST5 . . . . . 284 C4
 Wolv WV2 . . . . 266 B4
Hollings St ST4 . . . . 283 A5
Hollington Dr ST6 . . . . 42 A4
Hollington La ST14 . . . . . . 110 C3
Hollington Rd ST10 . . . . . . 93 A2
Hollins Bsns Ctr ST16 . . . . 155 B3
Hollins Cres ST7 . . . . 25 C1
Hollins Grange ST7 . . . . . . 40 B4
Hollins La ST10 . . . . 61 A2
Hollinsclough CE Prim Sch
 SK17 . . . . 4 B1
Hollinsclough Rake SK17 . . 4 A1

Hollinscroft Ct ST10 . . . . . . 92 C2
Hollinshead Ave ST5 . . . . . 56 A2
Hollinshead Cl ST7 . . . . 25 C4
Hollinwell Cl WV3 . . . . 243 A2
Hollinwood Cl ST7 . . . . 40 C4
Hollinwood Rd ST7 . . . . 40 C4
Hollis La ST14 . . . . 95 A3
Hollow Cres DE15 . . . . 167 B2
Hollow La
 Burton u T DE15 . . . . . . 167 B2
 Cheddleton ST13 . . . . 45 B3
 Colton WS15 . . . . 179 A3
 Draycott in t C DE6 . . . . . 144 B3
 Mayfield DE6 . . . . 66 B1
Hollow The
 Caverswall ST11 . . . . 74 C2
 Mount Pleasant ST7 . . . . . 26 A3
 Roston DE6 . . . . 96 C3
 Uttoxeter ST14 . . . . 126 B3
Holloway ST5 . . . . 250 A2
Holloway Dr WV5 . . . . 269 C2
Holloway La ST5,TF9 . . . . . . 84 B3
Holloway St DY3 . . . . 271 B2
Holloway St W DY3 . . . . . . 271 B2
Holloway The
 Brierley Hill DY8 . . . . . . 279 C4
 Seisdon WV5 . . . . 264 A2
 Swindon DY3 . . . . 269 B1
 Wolv WV6 . . . . 255 B1
Holly Ave ST13 . . . . 45 C4
Holly Bank ST4 . . . . 87 C4
Holly Bank View WS15 . . . . 197 A3
Holly Bush Cotts ST13 . . . . . 44 C4
Holly Bush La ST5 . . . . 85 A2
Holly Bush Rd DE6,DE13 . . . 143 C1
Holly Cl Kinver DY7 . . . . . . 277 C3
 Market Drayton TF9 . . . . 112 A4
 Tamworth B78 . . . . 250 A4
Holly Ct ST2 . . . . 73 C3
Holly Dr Alrewas WS13 . . . . 215 B4
 Caverswall ST2 . . . . 59 C3
Holly Fields ST15 . . . . 118 C3
Holly Gn DE15 . . . . 185 C4
Holly Gr Stone ST15 . . . . . 120 A4
 Stourbridge DY8 . . . . . . 279 C3
 Wolv WV3 . . . . 265 C4
Holly Grove La WS7 . . . . . 211 C1
Holly Grove Prim Sch
 WS7 . . . . 211 C1
Holly Hill WS6 . . . . 242 C4
Holly Hill Rd
 Cannock WS15 . . . . 211 C3
 Shenstone WS14 . . . . . . 246 C3
Holly La Aldridge WS9 . . . . 256 C4
 Bradley ST18 . . . . 173 B1
 Brownhills WS9 . . . . 245 A2
 Great Wyrley WS6 . . . . . . 242 C4
 Huntington WS12 . . . . . . 209 B4
 Kidsgrove ST7 . . . . 26 C3
 Seighford ST18 . . . . 153 C1
 Sutton Coldfield B74 . . . . 258 A2
 Uttoxeter ST14 . . . . 125 B1
Holly Mdw ST10 . . . . 109 B2
Holly Mews ST5 . . . . 69 C4
Holly Pl ST4 . . . . 72 C2
Holly Rd Barton-u-N DE13 . . 183 B1
 Newcastle-u-L ST5 . . . . . . 40 C1
Holly St Burton u T DE15 . . . 185 C4
 Cannock WS12 . . . . 209 C4
Holly Tree Dr ST8 . . . . 16 B1
Holly View WV11 . . . . 242 A2
Hollybank Ave WV11 . . . . . 242 A2
Hollybank Cl WS3 . . . . 243 A1
Hollybank Cres ST4 . . . . . . 72 A3
Hollybush Cl DE12 . . . . . . 219 C4
Hollybush Cres ST3 . . . . . . 72 C2
Hollybush La
 Brierley Hill DY8 . . . . . . 279 C4
 Codsall WV8 . . . . 238 C1
 Wolv WV4 . . . . 265 B2
Hollybush Rd ST3 . . . . 72 C2
Hollycroft Gdns WV6 . . . . . 255 A3
Hollyhill La WS14 . . . . 246 C3
Hollyhock Way DE14 . . . . . 184 C3
Hollyhurst ST17 . . . . 175 B3
Hollyhurst Dr DY6 . . . . . . 275 C2
Hollyhurst La ST18 . . . . . . 140 C1
Hollyoak Way WS11 . . . . . 209 C1
Hollys Rd DE13 . . . . 182 A1
Hollywall La ST6 . . . . 41 B3
Hollywall Prim Sch ST6 . . . . 41 B3
Hollywood La ST5 . . . . 54 B1
Holm Oak Dr CW3 . . . . 68 C4
Holm Rd ST10 . . . . 78 B3
Holm View Cl WS14 . . . . . 246 C3
Holmbridge Gr WS4 . . . . . 244 B1
Holmcroft Gdns WV9 . . . . 224 B1
Holmcroft Rd ST16 . . . . . . 155 B3
Holme Bank DE6 . . . . 81 B4
Holme Farm Ave ST5 . . . . . 185 C4
Holme Mill WV10 . . . . 240 B2
Holme Rise ST19 . . . . 193 A1
Holmes Cl ST16 . . . . 155 A1
Holmes The WV10 . . . . . . 240 B2
Holmes Way ST6 . . . . 42 A4
Holmesfield Wlk ST3 . . . . . 283 D3
Holst Dr ST1 . . . . 58 A3
Holston Cl WS12 . . . . 210 C1
Holsworth Cl B77 . . . . 250 B1
Holt Cres WS11 . . . . 210 C1
Holt La ST10 . . . . 61 C1
Holt's La DE13 . . . . 146 A3
Holte Dr B75 . . . . 258 B1
Holwich B77 . . . . 262 A4

Holy Austin Rock★ DY7 . . . 277 C2
Holy Rosary RC Prim Sch
 DE15 . . . . 167 A2
Holy Trinity CE Prim Sch
 Brownhills WS8 . . . . 244 C3
 Burton u T DE14 . . . . . . 166 C2
Holyhead Cres ST3 . . . . 74 A2
Holyhead Rd
 Albrighton WV7 . . . . 237 B1
 Codsall WV8 . . . . 238 B1
Holyoake Pl WV5 . . . . 178 B2
Holyrood Cl ST15 . . . . 120 B3
Holywell Cl ST8 . . . . 27 C3
Holywell Rise WS14 . . . . . 231 B3
Home Farm Ct DE11 . . . . . 186 B1
Home Farm Rd WV6 . . . . . 252 B4
Homefield Rd WV8 . . . . . . 239 B2
Homer Pl ST6 . . . . 42 A3
Homer Rd B75 . . . . 258 B1
Homer St ST1 . . . . 57 C2
Homestead Cl DY3 . . . . . . 271 C3
Homestead Ct WS16 . . . . . 155 C4
Homestead Dr B75 . . . . . . 258 B2
Homestead St ST2 . . . . 73 B4
Homestead The ST2 . . . . . . 43 B2
Honesty Cl WS8 . . . . 244 B3
Honeybourne B77 . . . . 250 B1
Honeybourne Cres WV5 . . . 269 C3
Honeysuckle Ave
 Forsbrook ST11 . . . . 90 C3
 Kingswinford DY6 . . . . . . 275 C4
Honeysuckle Cl ST10 . . . . . 92 C2
Honeysuckle Dr WV10 . . . . 241 B4
Honeysuckle La ST9 . . . . . . 29 C1
Honeysuckle View
 DE15 . . . . 186 A4
Honeysuckle Way WS6 . . . 227 A2
Honeytree Cl DY6 . . . . 275 C4
Honeywall ST4 . . . . 72 A4
Honeywall Ho ST4 . . . . 72 A4
Honeywall La Keele CW3 . . . 69 A2
 Stanton DE6 . . . . 80 C4
Honeywood ST5 . . . . 284 B4
Honiton Cl ST17 . . . . 175 B4
Honiton Wlk ST3 . . . . 283 D3
Honor Ave WV4 . . . . 266 B3
Hoo La DY7 . . . . 273 C2
Hood La Armitage WS15 . . 198 A2
 Longdon WS15 . . . . 197 C1
Hook Dr B74 . . . . 257 C2
Hook La Shenstone WS14 . . 246 B2
 Stramshall ST14 . . . . 111 A3
Hook La The WV7 . . . . 237 A1
Hoomill La ST18 . . . . 158 A3
Hoon Ave ST5 . . . . 56 A2
Hoon Rd DE65 . . . . 146 B4
Hoover St ST6 . . . . 41 B2
Hope St Audley ST7 . . . . . . 39 C2
 Hanley ST1 . . . . 282 B3
 Kingswinford DY8 . . . . . . 275 B2
Hopedale Cl Fenton ST4 . . . 73 B2
 Newcastle-u-L ST5 . . . . . . 71 A2
Hopley Rd DE13 . . . . 165 A3
Hopleys Cl B77 . . . . 250 C2
Hopmeadow Way DE15 . . . 167 A1
Hopstone Bank ST18 . . . . . 137 B2
Hopstone Gdns WV4 . . . . . 265 C2
Hopton Bank WV6 . . . . . . 254 C2
Hopton Ct ST16 . . . . 155 B3
Hopton La ST18 . . . . 137 B1
Hopton Mdw WS12 . . . . . . 210 B1
Hopton Rd ST16 . . . . 155 C3
Hopton Way ST4 . . . . 42 A4
Hoptonhall La ST18 . . . . . . 137 B1
Hopwas Hill B78 . . . . 249 A3
Hopwood Pl ST2 . . . . 58 A2
Hopyard Cl DY3 . . . . 271 A2
Hopyard La DY3 . . . . 271 A2
Horatius Rd ST5 . . . . 55 B3
Hordern Cl WV6 . . . . 255 C3
Hordern Gr WV6 . . . . 255 C3
Hordern Rd WV6 . . . . 255 C3
Hordley St ST1 . . . . 282 C3
Hornbeam B77 . . . . 251 A2
Hornbeam Cres WS12 . . . . 211 A3
Hornbeams The [2]
 ST14 . . . . 111 A3
Hornbrook Cl DE13 . . . . . . 166 A4
Hornbrook Rd DE13 . . . . . 166 A4
Hornby Rd WV4 . . . . 266 B3
Hornby Row ST4 . . . . 72 A4
Horninglow Croft DE13 . . . 166 B3
Horninglow Inf Sch
 DE13 . . . . 166 B3
Horninglow Rd DE14 . . . . . 166 B3
Horninglow Rd N DE13 . . . 166 B4
Horninglow St DE14 . . . . . 166 B2
Horns Croft WS15 . . . . . . 196 A4
Hornton Cl B74 . . . . 257 C3
Hornton Rd DE13 . . . . 166 A4
Horse Bridge La DY7 . . . . . 278 B1
Horse Fair
 Eccleshall ST21 . . . . 133 C4
 Rugeley WS15 . . . . 196 C4
Horse Rd ST10 . . . . 78 C1
Horsebrook La ST19 . . . . . 223 B4
Horsecroft Cres ST13 . . . . . 31 A4
Horsecroft Gr ST13 . . . . . . 31 A4
Horsehills Dr WV3 . . . . . . 255 C1
Horseshoe Dr WS15 . . . . . 178 A1
Horsey La WS15 . . . . 212 B4
Horsham Ave DY8 . . . . . . 275 B2
Horsley La
 Eccleshall ST21 . . . . 132 C3
 Wall WS14 . . . . 246 A4
Horsley Rd B74 . . . . 257 A1
Horton Ave DE13 . . . . 166 C4

Horton Cl DY3 ....271 B4
Horton Dr ST3 ....74 A3
Horton Lodge Sch ST13 .18 B1
Horton Rd DY7 ....277 C3
Horton St Leek ST13 .....30 C4
  Newcastle-u-L ST5 ....284 D3
Horwood ST5 ....70 B3
Horwood Gdns ST6 ....42 B1
Hose St ST6 ....41 B2
Hoskins Cl ST15 ....120 B4
Hoskins Rd ST6 ....41 C3
Hospital La
  Cheslyn Hay WS6 ......226 A1
  Market Drayton TF9 ...112 A4
Hospital Rd WS7 ....229 A3
Hospital St B79 ....250 A4
Hot La Biddulph ST8 ......17 B1
  Burslem ST6 ....57 A4
Hot Lane Ind Est ST6 ....57 A4
Hotel Bldgs WS14 ....230 A1
Hothill La ST10 ....109 B1
Hotel La ST10 ....109 B1
Hough Hill ST6 ....43 A4
Hougher Wall Rd ST7 ....39 B1
Houghton St ST1 ....282 B1
Houghwood La ST9 ....43 B2
Houlbrooke Ho ▮ WV6 231 B4
Houldsworth Dr ST6 ......42 A4
Housefield Rd ST2 ....73 B4
Houseman Dr ST3 ....73 C2
Houting B77 ....261 B3
Houx The DY8 ....279 C4
Hoveringham Dr ST2 .....57 C1
Howard Cl Caverswall ST9 59 A2
  Leek ST13 ....30 B2
Howard Cres
  Cannock WS12 ....210 B4
  Hanley ST1 ....57 C1
Howard Gr ST5 ....71 A3
Howard Pl Hanley ST1 ..282 A1
  Newcastle-u-L ST5 .....71 A1
Howard Prim Sch B79 ..216 B1
Howard Rd ST17 ....174 C4
  Wolv WV2 ....266 B4
Howard Wlk ST3 ....283 C2
Howdle's La WS8 ....228 C1
Howe Gr ST5 ....55 C1
Howell Rd WV2 ....266 C4
Howitt Cres ST14 ....111 A3
Howitt House Sch DE13 144 C2
Howland Cl WV9 ....239 C1
Howson St ST1 ....282 C2
Hoylake B77 ....251 A2
Hoylake Cl WS3 ....243 C3
Hoylake Rd WV6 ....254 B3
Hubbal La TF11 ....220 B3
Huddersford La WS14 ...232 B4
Huddlestone Cl WV10 ...241 B3
Huddock's View WS3 ....243 C3
Hudson Cl
  Cannock WS11 ....210 A1
  Gnosall ST20 ....171 C4
Hudson Dr WS7 ....229 B3
Hudson Gr WV6 ....254 C3
Hudson Wlk ST3 ....283 C4
Hugh Bourne Pl ST8 .....27 A1
Hugh Porter Way WV6 ..255 C3
Hughes Ave
  Newcastle-u-L ST5 ....284 B4
  Wolv WV3 ....265 C4
Hughes St ST6 ....57 A4
Hughson Gr ST6 ....42 C2
Hugo Meynell CE Prim Sch
  TF9 ....99 C2
Hugo St ST13 ....30 C3
Hulland Cl ST5 ....55 A1
Hullock's Pool Rd ST7 ...39 C3
Hulme La ST9 ....59 A1
Hulme Rd ST3 ....73 C3
Hulme St ST4 ....71 C4
Hulse St ST4 ....73 A3
Hulton Rd ST2 ....58 A3
Hulton St ST1 ....282 C4
Humber Dr ST8 ....27 C3
Humber Way ST5 ....71 A2
Humbert St ST1 ....56 C2
Humphrey St DY3 ....271 B2
Humphries Ho WS8 .....244 C4
Hungerford La CW3 ......69 A3
Hungerford Pl CW2 ......38 B3
Hungerford Rd DY8 ....279 C1
Hungry La WS14 ....247 C3
Hunsford Cl ST3 ....283 C4
Hunslet Rd WS7 ....229 A4
Hunt St ST6 ....41 C2
Huntbach St ST1 ....282 B3
Hunter Ave WS7 ....229 A4
Hunter Cl WS14 ....231 B4
Hunter Rd WS11 ....226 C4
Hunter St DE14 ....166 B4
Hunter's Point TF9 ......99 B3
Hunter's Ride DY7 .....275 C4
Hunters Cl ST8 ....27 B4
Hunters Ct ST18 ....137 C2
Hunters Dr ST4 ....71 C4
Hunters Rise ST17 .....174 C2
Hunters Way ST4 ....72 A3
Huntilee Rd ST6 ....41 C2
Huntingdon Cl B78 .....249 C1
Huntingdon Pl ST1 ......57 C3
Huntingdon Rd DE15 ...185 B4
Huntington Ind Est
  WS12 ....209 A4
Huntington Prim Sch
  WS12 ....209 B4
Huntington Terrace Rd
  WS11 ....209 C2

Huntley Ave ST4 ....72 A3
Huntley Cl ST10 ....76 B1
Huntley La ST10 ....92 B4
Huntley Rd ST13 ....44 C4
Hunts La DE12 ....219 C4
Hunts Mill Dr DY5 .....271 B1
Huntsbank Dr ST5 ....40 B1
Huntsman's Hill WS11 .197 B1
Huntsmans Dr DY7 .....277 C3
Huntsmans Gate WS7 ..229 A4
Huntsmans Rise WS12 .209 B4
Huntsmans Wlk
  Kinver DY7 ....277 C3
  Rugeley WS15 ....178 B1
Hurlingham Rd ST16 ...155 B4
Huron Cl WS11 ....210 A1
Huron Gr ST4 ....88 A4
Hurst Cl ST7 ....40 B3
Hurst Dr DE13 ....147 C1
Hurst Rd Biddulph ST8 ..17 A3
  Sedgley WV14 ....266 C1
Hurst St ST3 ....283 B3
Hurstbourne Cl WS15 ..178 B1
Hurstmead Dr ST17 ....175 B3
Hurstons La ST10 ....78 C1
Hurstons The ST10 ......78 C1
Husphins La WS8 ......238 A3
Hussey Cl ST19 ....207 C4
Hussey Rd
  Brownhills WS8 ....244 C4
  Norton Canes WS11 ..227 C3
Huston Ave ST9 ....43 C4
Hut Hill La WS6 ....227 C2
Hutchinson Cl WS15 ...178 A1
Hutchinson Meml CE Fst Sch
  ST10 ....109 A4
Hutchinson Wlk ▮ ST3 ..73 A2
Hutton Cl CW12 ....6 A1
Hutton Dr CW12 ....6 A1
Hutton Way ST2 ....58 B1
Huxley Cl WV9 ....240 A2
Huxley Pl ST3 ....73 B2
Hyacinth Ct ST5 ....284 C4
Hyacinth Rd ST4 ....56 C1
Hyde Cl DY7 ....278 A3
Hyde Ct ST17 ....174 B4
Hyde La DY7 ....278 A3
Hyde Lea Bank ST18 ...174 B3
Hyde Mill Croft ST19 ..223 B3
Hyde Mill La ST19 .....223 B3
Hylton Cl DE14 ....185 A4
Hyndley Cl ST2 ....58 A2
Hyperion Dr WV4 ......266 A2
Hyperion Rd DY7 ......279 B4
Hyssop Cl WS11 ....210 A2

I

I-Mex Bsns Pk ST4 ......72 C3
Ian Rd ST7 ....26 B1
Ibsen Rd ST4 ....74 A2
Ibstock St DE13 ....166 A3
Ickenfield Cl B74 .....257 A1
Idonia Rd WV6 ....254 C4
Ikins Dr ST7 ....39 C1
Ilam CE Prim Sch DE6 ..50 C1
Ilam Cl ST5 ....55 A1
Ilam Ctry Pk DE6 ....50 C1
Ilam-moor La DE6 ......50 C3
Ilford Side ST3 ....88 C4
Ilkley Pl ST5 ....54 C1
Illshaw WV9 ....240 A2
Imandra St ST4 ....88 A4
Imex Bsns Pk
  Burton u T DE14 .....166 A2
  Wolv WV2 ....266 B4
Imex Tech Pk ST4 ......88 B4
Imogen Cl ST4 ....73 A3
Imperial Ct ST1 ....282 C1
Impstones ST20 ....171 B3
Ingatestone Dr DY8 ...275 B2
Inge Dr DE13 ....201 A4
Ingelow Cl ST3 ....73 A1
Ingestre Cl
  Cannock WS11 ....210 A1
  Newport TF10 ....168 B1
  Walsall WS3 ....242 C2
Ingestre Ho WV6 ......255 C3
Ingestre Rd
  Stafford ST17 ....155 C1
  Wolv WV10 ....240 B1
Ingestre Sq ST3 ....88 C2
Ingewood Ave WV3 ....265 C4
Ingleborough Pl ST2 ....43 B1
Ingleby Gdns WV6 ....255 C3
Ingleby Rd ST3 ....88 C4
Inglefield Ave ST6 ......42 A1
Ingleside WS15 ....178 B1
Ingleton Gr ST3 ....90 A4
Inglewood ST17 ....155 B1
Inglewood Cl DY6 ....275 B3
Inglewood Dr ST5 ......56 B3
Inglewood Gr
  Aldridge B74 ....256 C1
  Newcastle-u-L ST5 ...56 B3
Inglis St ST4 ....72 B4
Ingram Pit La B77 ....251 A3
Ingram Pl WS3 ....243 A3
Ingram Rd WS3 ....243 B1
Inhedge St DY3 ....271 C1
Intake La ST20 ....190 A4
Intake Rd ST6 ....42 B2
Intakes La ST10 ....108 C2
Inworth WV9 ....240 A2
Iona Pl ST3 ....72 C2
Irene Ave Chell Heath ST6 .41 C2

Irene Ave *continued*
  Newcastle-u-L ST5 .....56 B1
Ireton Rd WV10 ....240 C2
Iris Cl Meir ST3 ....74 B3
  Tamworth B79 ....250 B3
Irnham Rd ST4 ....258 A1
Ironbridge Dr ST5 ......55 C1
Ironmarket ST5 ....284 B3
Ironstone Cl WS13 ....215 C3
Ironstone Rd WS13 ...211 B2
Ironwalls La DE13 ....146 B3
Irvine Rd ST9 ....59 B2
Irving Cl Lichfield WS13 .213 C1
  Sedgley DY3 ....271 A2
Irwell B77 ....250 C1
Isabel Cl ST17 ....174 A4
Isherwood Pl ST3 ....283 D4
Island Gn ST17 ....175 B3
Island The Alsacamoor ST10 78 A3
  Tamworth B78 ....249 B1
  Upper Tean ST10 ......92 B2
Islay Wlk ▮ ST3 ....73 A2
Islington Cl TF10 .....168 C2
Islington Cres CV9 ...262 B1
Ismere Way DY10 ....280 A1
Itchen Gr WV6 ....254 C2
Ivatt B77 ....250 C1
Iverley La DY10 ......281 B3
Iverley Rd ST4 ....87 C4
Ivetsey Bank Rd ST19 .221 C4
Ivetsey Cl ST19 ......205 A3
Ivetsey Rd ST19 .....204 C2
Ivy Cl Acton Trussell ST17 175 A1
  Cannock WS11 ....226 B4
  Forsbrook ST11 ....90 C3
  Uttoxeter ST14 ....126 A4
Ivy Cotts ST13 ....20 A3
Ivy Croft WV9 ....239 C2
Ivy Ct Acton Trussell ST17 175 A1
  Egginton DE65 ....148 A3
  Hixon ST18 ....158 A4
Ivy Gdns WS11 ....90 C3
Ivy Gr Brownhills WS8 .245 A2
  Burton u T DE13 .....166 B4
  Trentham ST4 ....87 C4
Ivy House La ST19 .....206 C1
Ivy House Rd Biddulph ST8 16 B1
  Hanley ST1 ....57 C2
Ivy La WS15 ....211 C3
Ivy Lodge Cl DE15 ...185 C4
Ivyhouse Dr ST12 ......88 C2
Ivyhouse Wlk B77 ....261 C3
Izaac Walton Way CW3 ..68 C3
Izaak Walton St ST16 ..155 B3
Izaak Walton St ST16 ..155 B3
Izaak Walton's Cottage &
  Mus★ ST15 ....135 A4

J

Jack Ashley Ct ST4 .....72 B3
Jack Haye La Bagnall ST2 .58 C4
  Norton-in-t-M ST2 ....43 B1
Jack La CW2 ....37 B3
Jack's La ST14 ....127 C1
Jackdaw Cl DY3 ......266 B4
Jackfield Inf Sch ST6 ...42 A1
Jackfield St ST6 ....42 A1
Jacklin Cl DE14 ....185 A3
Jackman Cl WS13 .....215 B3
Jackman Rd WS13 ....215 B3
Jackson Ave DE13 ....166 C4
Jackson Cl
  Featherstone WV10 ..241 A3
  Norton Canes WS11 ..227 C2
Jackson Rd WS13 .....214 A2
Jackson St ▮ ST6 ......57 A4
Jacob's Hall La WS6 ..227 A1
Jacobean Ct DE15 ....167 B2
Jacobs Croft ST16 ....155 B2
Jacqueline St ST6 ......41 B2
Jade Ct ST3 ....73 B2
Jade Gr WS11 ....210 B1
Jaguar B77 ....250 C1
Jamage Rd ST7 ....40 B3
James Beattie Ho WV6 .255 B2
James Brindley Cl ST1 ..57 A1
James Brindley High Sch
  ST6 ....41 C3
James Brindley Way
  DE13 ....166 C4
James Cres ST9 ....59 B2
James Ct DE14 ....166 B1
James Greenway WS13 214 A1
James Hutchens Ct
  WS7 ....228 C3
James St Burton u T DE14 166 B1
  Cannock WS11 ....209 C4
  Kinver DY7 ....278 A2
  Leek ST13 ....30 B3
  Newcastle-u-L ST5 ...56 B3
  Stoke-on-T ST4 ......72 A3
  Uttoxeter ST14 ......126 A4
James Warner Cl WS15 178 B1
James Way ST8 ....27 A3
Janet Pl ST1 ....57 C2
Janson St ST4 ....71 C1
Jardines La ST14 ....95 B2
Jasmin Way ST7 ....26 C2
Jasmine Cl
  Burton u T DE15 ....186 A4
  Wolv WV9 ....240 A2
Jasmine Ct ST11 ....90 C3
Jasmine Gr WV8 .....239 A2
Jasmine Rd
  Seighford ST18 .....135 B1
  Tamworth B77 ....251 A2

Jason Cl B77 ....250 B3
Jason St ST5 ....284 A4
Jasper Cl Barlaston ST12 .88 C2
  Newcastle-u-L ST5 ....56 A4
Jasper St ST1 ....282 B2
Java Cres ST4 ....88 A4
Jay Rd DY6 ....275 B4
Jaycean Ave ST6 ....41 C2
Jean Cl ST6 ....42 A1
Jedburgh Ave WV6 ...254 C2
Jeddo St WV2 ....266 B4
Jefferson St ST1 ....41 B2
Jeffrey Ave WV4 .....266 C3
Jeffrey Cl WS15 ......178 B2
Jeffs Ave WV2 ....266 B4
Jenkins St ▮ ST6 ......56 C4
Jenkinson Cl ST5 ....70 C4
Jenkinstown Rd WS12 .211 A3
Jenks Ave DY7 ....277 C3
Jenks Rd WV5 ....269 C3
Jennings Way DE14 ..166 A2
Jenny Walkers La WV6 254 B1
Jensen B77 ....250 C1
Jephson Rd DE14 ....185 A4
Jerbourg Cl ST5 ....70 C2
Jeremy Cl ST4 ....71 C3
Jeremy Rd WV4 ......266 B3
Jerningham St ST16 ..155 B2
Jerome Ct B74 ....256 C1
Jerome Dr WS11 .....228 A3
Jerome Prim Sch WS11 227 B3
Jerome Rd WS11 .....228 A3
Jerome Way WS7 ....229 B4
Jerry's La ST12 ....248 A4
Jersey Cl Congleton CW12 .6 A1
  Newcastle-u-L ST5 ...70 C2
Jersey Cres ST3 ....73 B1
Jervis Cres B74 ......257 B2
Jervis La ST15 ....104 B2
Jervis Rd Stone ST15 .120 A4
  Tamworth B77 ....261 C3
Jervis St ST1 ....282 C4
Jervison St ST3 ....73 B3
Jesmond Cl WS12 ....211 A3
Jesmond Gr ST3 ....88 C4
Jessie Rd WS9 ....245 A1
Jessop Dr B77 ....250 C3
Jessop Dr B77 ....250 C3
Jessop Dr B77 ....250 C3
Jew's La ST3 ....271 C2
Jinny Cl DE65 ....146 B4
Joan Eaton's Cross
  ST20 ....189 C4
Joan St WV2 ....266 C3
Joanhurst Cres ST1 ..282 A1
Jockey Field DY3 .....271 C3
Jodrell View ST7 ......41 A4
Jodrell View ST7 ......41 A4
Joeys La WS8 ....239 B2
John Amery Dr ST17 ..174 B2
John Ball Ct WS15 ...178 B2
John Bamford Prim Sch
  WS15 ....178 B1
John Baskeyfield CE Prim
  Sch ST6 ....56 C4
John Bright St ST1 ...282 C4
John Donne St ST16 ..155 B3
John O' Gaunt's Rd ST5 284 A3
John of Rolleston Prim Sch
  DE13 ....147 B2
John Offley Rd CW3 ...68 C3
John Pershall Ct ST21 133 B4
John Rhodes Way ST6 ..41 B3
John St Biddulph ST8 ...27 C1
  Brierley Hill DY5 ....275 C1
  Cannock, High Town
  WS11 ....210 A2
  Cannock, Wimblebury
  WS12 ....210 C2
  Hanley ST1 ....282 B2
  Leek ST13 ....30 C3
  Newcastle-u-L ST5 ..284 D3
  Newcastle-u-L, Knutton ST5 55 C1
  Stafford ST16 ....156 A2
  Swadlincote DE11 ...186 C3
  Tamworth B79 ....250 C2
  Uttoxeter ST14 ......126 A4
John Taylor High Sch
  DE13 ....183 C4
John Till Cl WS15 ....178 C1
John Wheeldon Prim Sch
  ST16 ....155 C3
John Wood CE Inf Sch
  WS11 ....226 C4
Johndory B77 ....261 B3
Johns Ave WS15 .....198 B2
Johns La WS6 ....227 A2
Johnsgate ST19 ......223 B4
Johnson Ave ST5 ......56 A2
Johnson Cl Congleton CW12 6 A1
  Lichfield WS13 ......214 A1
  Ranton ST18 ....153 B3
  Rugeley WS15 ......178 B1
Johnson Cres ST10 ....61 B1
Johnson Gr WS15 ....120 B4
Johnson Pl ST6 ....42 A1
Johnson Rd
  Burntwood WS7 ....228 C4
  Cannock WS11 .....209 B2
  Uttoxeter ST14 .....111 A1
Johnson St
  Newcastle-u-L ST5 ...55 B4
  Wolv, Blakenhall WV2 .266 B4
  Wolv, Cinder Hill WV14 266 C1
  Wood End CV9 ......262 B1
Johnstone Ave ST9 ....59 B2
Joiner's Square Ind Est
  ST1 ....282 C1
Joiner's Square Prim Sch
  ST1 ....282 C1

Jolley St ST6 ....42 B1
Jolliffe St ▮ ST13 ......30 C3
Jolpool La ST18 ....121 B2
Jolt La ST18 ....172 C2
Jolyon Cl ST4 ....73 A3
Jonathan Rd ST4 ....88 B3
Jones Cl Alrewas WS13 .215 C4
  Stafford ST17 ....174 B4
Jones La Burntwood WS7 229 C4
  Great Wyrley WS6 ...227 A1
  Rugeley WS15 ......196 B4
Jones Rd WV12 ....242 B1
Jonkel Ave B77 ......262 A3
Jordan Ave DE13 .....147 C1
Jordan Cl Alrewas WS13 .215 B3
  Lichfield WS13 .....231 A4
  Sutton Coldfield B75 258 A4
Jordan Croft WS13 ...215 B4
Jordan Rd B75 ....258 B1
Jordan Way
  Aldridge WS9 ....245 A1
  Stone ST15 ....120 A4
Jordon St ST1 ....282 A1
Joseph Dewsbury Cl
  WS7 ....228 C4
Joseph Dix Dr WS13 ..178 B1
Joseph St ▮ ST6 ......56 C4
Josiah Wedgwood St
  ST1 ....57 A2
Jowett B77 ....250 B1
Joyce Ave ST6 ....42 A1
Joyce's La ST17 .....194 A4
Jubilee Ave ST1 ....57 A2
Jubilee Cl Biddulph ST8 .27 B4
  Great Wyrley WS6 ..226 C1
Jubilee Ct ST14 .....126 A4
Jubilee Dr ST10 ....62 B2
Jubilee Gr TF11 .....203 C3
Jubilee Rd
  Newcastle-u-L ST5 ...56 B2
  Trentham ST4 ....87 C4
Jubilee Sq DE6 ....81 B4
Jubilee St WS15 .....178 B1
Jubilee Terr ▮ ST13 ...30 B3
Judes wlk WS13 .....213 C1
Judgefield La ST6 .....28 A1
Judith Gr ST4 ....72 B3
Jug Bank Ashley TF9 ..100 A2
  Hanley ST6 ....57 A3
Julian Cl WS6 ....227 C1
Junction Rd
  Brierley Hill DY8 ...275 C1
  Leek ST13 ....30 C2
Junction The ▮ DY8 ..279 C4
June Cres B77 ....250 C3
June Rd ST4 ....73 A3
Juniper B77 ....251 A2
Juniper Cl
  Cannock WS12 ......211 A3
  Meir ST3 ....90 A3
  Newcastle-u-L ST5 ...40 C1
Juniper Row TF10 ...168 C1
Jupiter St ST6 ....42 B1
Jupiter Way ST17 ...175 A4
Justin Cl ST5 ....56 B3

K

Kara Pl ST4 ....88 A4
Kay Dr DE11 ....186 C3
Kaydor Cl ST9 ....59 A2
Kayne Cl DY6 ....275 B4
Kean Cl WS13 ....213 C1
Kearsley Way ST3 ....88 C4
Kearyn St ST4 ....72 A3
Keates St ▮ ST6 ......56 C4
Keating Gdns B75 ...258 A2
Keats Ave Cannock WS11 209 C3
  Stafford ST17 ....174 B4
Keats Cl Sedgley DY3 .271 A3
  Sutton Coldfield B74 257 C3
  Tamworth B79 ......249 C4
Keats Gdns ST7 ....41 A4
Keats Rd WV10 ......241 A1
Keble Cl Burntwood WS7 229 B4
  Burton u T DE15 ....167 B1
  Cannock WS11 ......226 C4
Keble Way ST3 ....73 A1
Keble Wlk B79 ......250 A3
Kedleston Cl
  Burton u T DE13 ....147 B1
  Walsall WS3 ....243 A2
Kedleston Rd ST6 .....42 A1
Keele L Ctr ST5 ....70 A4
Keele Rd ST5 ....70 B4
Keele Service Area ST5 .69 C2
Keele St ST6 ....41 B2
Keele Univ ST5 ....70 A4
Keeling Dr WS11 ....209 A1
Keeling Rd ST10 ......76 C2
Keeling St ST5 ....56 B3
Keelings Dr ST4 ......71 C2
Keelings Rd ST1 ......57 C2
Keene Cl ST6 ....42 C2
Keep The ST17 ......174 B4
Keeper's Cl WS7 ....229 A3
Keepers Cl
  Brownhills WS9 ....244 C2
  Kingswinford DY6 ..275 A4
  Lichfield WS14 .....231 C4
Keepers Cl Codsall WV8 239 A4
  Wolv WV6,WV9 ....255 A4
Keepers Rd B74 .....257 B3
Keir Pl DY8 ....279 C4

Keld Ave ST17 ......174 A4
Keldy Cl WV6 ....255 C3
Kelham Rd ST4 ....73 A3
Kelly Ave WS15 ......196 C3
Kelly Gn ST6 ....42 A3
Kelmore Cl ST3 .....283 B4
Kelsall St ST6 ....42 A1
Kelsall Way ST7 ....39 B1
Kelso Gdns WV6 ....254 B2
Kelvedon Way WS15 ..178 B1
Kelveston Ho WS11 ..209 B1
Kelvin Ave ST1 ....57 B4
Kelvin Dr WS11 .....210 A4
Kelvin St ST5 ....56 B2
Kemball Ave ST4 .....72 B2
Kemball Specl Sch ST4 ..72 C3
Kemberton Cl WV3 ...255 B1
Kemberton Rd WV3 ...255 B1
Kemnay Ave ST6 .....42 A4
Kempson Rd ST19 ...192 C1
Kempthorne Ave WV10 ..240 C1
Kempthorne Gdns WS3 ..243 A1
Kempthorne Rd ST1 ..282 C1
Kempton Cl WS12 ....211 A3
Kempton Dr
  Great Wyrley WS6 ...226 C1
  Tamworth B77 ......261 B2
Kempton Gr ST10 .....76 C3
Kempton Rd DE15 ....167 A2
Kempton Way DY9 ...279 C2
Kendal Cl Stafford ST17 ..174 A4
  Wolv WV6 ....255 C3
Kendal Ct
  Brownhills WS9 .....244 C2
  Cannock WS11 ......226 A4
Kendal Gr ST2 ....58 B1
Kendal Pl ST5 ....71 A3
Kendal Rise WV6 ....255 C3
Kendall Rise DY6 ....275 C3
Kenderdine Cl ST17 ..193 C4
Kendlewood Rd DY10 ..280 A1
Kendrick St ST3 .....283 D3
Kenelyn Cres ST3 .....72 C2
Kenilworth Ave DE13 ..166 B4
Kenilworth Cl
  Kingswinford DY8 ..275 B1
  Market Drayton TF9 ..97 C1
  Penkridge ST19 ....208 A4
Kenilworth Cres WV4 ..266 C2
Kenilworth Ct 10 WS11 ..209 C1
Kenilworth Dr WS11 ..209 B2
Kenilworth Gr
  4 Meir ST3 ....73 C1
  Newcastle-u-L ST5 ..56 C2
Kenilworth Rd
  Perton WV6 ....254 C2
  Tamworth B77 .....250 C2
Kenilworth Wlk ST10 ..76 A1
Kenley Ave ST10 .....43 C4
Kenmore Ave WS12 ..209 C4
Kennedy Cl B77 .....250 B1
Kennedy Cres DY3 ..271 C2
Kennedy Ct DY8 ....279 C3
Kennedy Rd ST4 .....88 A4
Kennedy Way ST16 ..155 A4
Kennedy Wlk ST9 .....59 A2
Kennermont Rd ST2 ..58 B3
Kennet B77 ....250 B1
Kennet Cl
  Brownhills WS8 ....228 B1
  Newcastle-u-L ST5 ..71 A4
Kenrick Cl CW3 ......67 B1
Kensington Cl WS15 ..120 B3
Kensington Ct
  Stoke-on-T ST4 .....71 C1
  Tunstall ST6 ....41 C2
Kensington Dr
  Sutton Coldfield B74 ..257 C3
  Tamworth B79 .....250 A4
Kensington Gdns DY8 ..275 B1
Kensington Pl WS12 ..227 B4
Kensington Rd
  Burton u T DE15 ...167 A2
  Stoke-on-T ST4 .....72 A2
Kensworth Cl ST5 ....71 A4
Kent Ave B78 ......249 C1
Kent Cl WS9 ....245 A1
Kent Dr ST9 ....43 C3
Kent Gr Newcastle-u-L ST5 ..55 C4
  Stone ST15 ....104 C1
Kent Ho ST7 ....40 B3
Kent Pl Cannock WS12 ..210 C1
  Fenton ST4 ....72 C3
Kent Rd Burton u T DE15 ..185 C3
  Stafford ST17 .....175 A4
  Stourbridge DY8 ...279 B4
  Wolv WV2 ....266 C4
Kent St DY3 ....271 C1
Kentish Ct ST17 .....174 A4
Kentmere Cl Longton ST4 ..73 A3
  Penkridge ST19 ....193 A1
  Stafford ST17 .....174 A4
Kentmere Pl ST5 .....71 A3
Kenton Ave WV6 ....255 C2
Kents Row ST12 ......88 C1
Kentwell Pl ST5 ....249 B4
Kenworthy Rd ST16 ..155 C4
Kenworthy St ST6 ....41 C2
Kepler B79 ....249 C4
Kerria Ctr B77 .....251 A2
Kerria Rd B77 ......251 A2
Kerridge Cl WV9 ....240 A1
Kerry La T21 ....133 B3
Kersbrook Cl ST4 ....88 B3
Kervis Gr ST3 ....90 A3

Kesterton Rd B74 ...257 C3
Kesteven Wlk ST2 ....58 A2
Kestrel B77 ....262 A3
Kestrel Ave ST3 .....90 B4
Kestrel Cl Biddulph ST8 ..27 A3
  Newport TF10 .....169 A3
  Stafford ST17 .....156 B1
  Uttoxeter ST14 ....126 A3
  Whittington WS14 ..232 C3
Kestrel Dr TF9 ......99 B2
Kestrel Gr ST4 .....210 B1
Kestrel La ST10 .....76 C2
Kestrel Rd ST4 .....257 C3
Kestrel Rise WV6 ...255 C4
Kestrel Way
  Burton u T DE15 ...167 B2
  Cheslyn Hay WS6 ..226 B1
Keswick Dr DY6 ....275 B3
Keswick Gr Aldridge B74 ..256 C1
  Stafford ST17 .....174 A4
Keswick Pl ST5 .....71 A3
Ketley Rd DY6 .....275 C4
Kettering Dr ST2 ....57 C1
Kettlebank Rd DY3 ..271 A1
Kettlebrook Rd B77 ..250 B2
Ketton Cl ST3 ....42 A4
Kewstoke Cl WV12 ..242 B1
Kewstoke Rd WV12 ..242 B1
Key Cl WS12 ....210 B2
Keyes Dr DY6 ......270 B1
Keynsham Wlk ST6 ..42 B1
Keyspark Rd WS12 ..210 C2
Keystone La WS15 ..196 C4
Keystone Mews 5
  WS15 ....196 C4
Keystone Rd WS15 ..196 C4
Keyworth Wlk ST2 ...58 A1
Kibblestone Rd ST15 ..105 B2
Kibworth Gr ST1 ....282 B4
Kidbrooke Pl ST4 ....88 B4
Kiddemore Green Rd
  ST19 ....222 B3
Kidderminster Rd
  Kingswinford DY6 ..275 A4
  Kinver DY7,DY10 ...281 B4
Kidderminster Rd S
  DY9 ....281 C2
Kidsgrove Bank ST7 ..41 A4
Kidsgrove Rd ST6 ....41 B4
Kidsgrove Sta ST7 ...25 C1
Kielder Cl WS12 ....210 C1
Kilburn Dr DY6 .....270 C1
Kilburn Pl ST3 ....72 C1
Kilburn Way DE11 ..186 C3
Kilbye Cl B77 ....261 C3
Kildare St ST3 ......283 C2
Kilmorie Rd WS11 ..209 B1
Kiln Croft ST10 ......92 B2
Kiln La ST13 ....30 B3
Kiln Way B78 ......251 C1
Kilnbank Cres TF9 ..112 B4
Kilnbank Rd TF9 ....112 B4
Kildown Cl ST1 ......57 A1
Kilsby Gr ST3 ....43 A1
Kimberlee Ave DY10 ..280 A4
Kimberley B77 ......261 C4
Kimberley Cl B74 ..257 A1
Kimberley Dr
  Burton u T DE15 ...167 B2
  Uttoxeter ST14 ....110 C1
Kimberley Grange ST5 ..284 B4
Kimberley Rd Hanley ST1 ..57 A2
  Newcastle-u-L ST5 ..284 B4
Kimberley St
  Longton ST3 ......283 B2
  Wolv WV3 ....266 A4
Kimberley Way
  Rugeley WS15 .....196 C3
  Stafford ST17 .....174 A4
Kinder Pl ST5 ....55 A1
Kineton Rise DY3 ...266 B4
Kinfare Dr WV6 ....255 A2
Kinfare Rise DY3 ...271 C2
King Charles Cl ST3 ..90 A4
King Edward Pl DE14 ..166 A2
King Edward St ST10 ..76 C2
King Edward VI High Sch
  ST17 ....155 B1
King Edward VI Sch
  WS14 ....231 B3
King Edward's Row 7
  WV2 ....266 B4
King George St ST1 ..282 C4
King St Audley ST7 ..39 B1
  Biddulph ST8 ......27 B4
  Blymhill TF10,TF11 ..189 A1
  Brownhills WS9 ...244 C1
  Burntwood WS7 ...228 C3
  Burton u T DE14 ...166 B1
  Fenton ST4 ....72 C3
  Kidsgrove ST7 .....26 A1
  Leek ST13 ....30 C3
  Longton ST3,ST4 ..283 B4
  Newcastle-u-L ST5 ..284 C3
  Newcastle-u-L, Chesterton
   ST5 ....55 C4
  Newcastle-u-L, Cross Heath
   ST5 ....56 A2
  Rugeley WS15 ....196 C4
  Stourbridge DY8 ...279 C3
  Talke ST7 ....40 B3
  Tamworth B79 ....250 A3
  Yoxall DE13 ......182 A2
King William St
  Brierley Hill DY8 ..279 C4
  Tunstall ST6 ....41 C2
King's Ave
  Newcastle-u-L ST5 ..56 B3

King's Ave continued
  Stone ST15 ....105 A1
King's Bromley La
  WS15 ....198 B3
King's CE Sch The
  WV6 ....255 A3
King's Croft ST4 .....56 B1
King's Hill Rd WS14 ..231 B3
King's La B79 ......236 B3
Kingcross St ST3 ...283 C3
Kingcup Rd ST17 ...174 C3
Kingfisher B77 .....262 A3
Kingfisher Cl
  Madeley CW3 ......68 C4
  Newport TF10 .....168 C3
  Sedgley DY3 ......266 B1
Kingfisher Cres
  Blythe Bridge ST10 ..106 C3
  Cheadle ST10 ......76 C2
Kingfisher Dr
  Cannock WS12 ....210 B3
  Colwich ST18 .....177 C4
  Stourbridge DY8 ..279 B2
Kingfisher Gr ST6 ...42 B2
Kingfisher Way ST14 ..126 A3
Kingfisher Wlk ST6 ..207 C4
Kingham Cl DY3 ....271 B1
Kings Ave Cannock WS12 ..210 B2
  Market Drayton TF9 ..112 A4
Kings Bridge WV9 ..224 A2
Kings Bromley Rd DE13 ..200 C1
Kings Croft WS12 ..210 C2
Kings Ct Stourbridge DY8 ..279 C3
  Sutton Coldfield B75 ..258 A2
Kings Pl ST4 ....56 B1
Kings Rd Hopton ST18 ..156 B4
  Sedgley DY3 ......271 C4
  Shareshill WV10 ..225 A3
  Trentham ST4 ......72 A1
Kings Terr ST4 ......56 B1
Kings Wlk DE13 ....199 A3
Kingsbridge Ave ST5 ..71 A3
Kingsbury Cl DE15 ..167 A2
Kingsbury Gr ST1 ....57 C3
Kingsclere Gr ST1 ..57 C4
Kingsclere Wlk WV4 ..265 B3
Kingscroft ST8 .....158 B1
Kingsdale Cl ST3 ....90 A4
Kingsdale Croft DE13 ..166 B4
Kingsdene Ave DY6 ..275 B2
Kingsdown Mews ST5 ..71 B2
Kingsdown Rd WS7 ..211 C1
Kingsfield Cres ST8 ..27 B4
Kingsfield Fst Sch ST8 ..27 B4
Kingsfield Oval ST4 ..56 B1
Kingsfield Rd
  Biddulph ST8 ......27 B4
  Stoke-on-T ST4 ....56 B1
Kingsford Ctry Pk★
  DY11 ....277 B1
Kingsford La DY7,DY11 ..277 B1
Kingsford Pl 4 ST3 ..90 A3
Kingshayes Rd WS9 ..245 A4
Kingside Gr ST4 .....88 B3
Kingsland Ave ST4 ..71 C3
Kingsland Ct ST15 ..120 B4
Kingsland Rd ST15 ..120 B4
Kingsleigh Croft B75 ..258 A1
Kingsley Ave
  Cannock WS12 ....210 B4
  Wolv WV6 ....255 A2
Kingsley Cl Stafford ST17 ..174 C4
  Talke ST7 ....40 B3
Kingsley Gdns WV8 ..238 C2
Kingsley Gr DY3 ....271 A3
Kingsley Rd
  Burton u T DE14 ..166 B3
  Cheddleton ST9,ST10 ..60 A2
  Congleton CW12 ....6 A2
  Kingswinford DY6 ..275 A3
  Stafford ST17 .....174 C4
  Talke ST7 ....40 B3
Kingsley St ST3 .....74 A1
Kingsley View ST13 ..45 B3
Kingsley Wood Rd
  WS15 ....195 B4
Kingslow Ave WV4 ..265 B3
Kingsmead DE13 ...166 C4
Kingsmead High Sch
  WS12 ....210 B2
Kingsmead Hospl ST16 ..155 C2
Kingsmead Rd ST3 ..89 C4
Kingsnorth Pl ST3 ..90 A3
Kingston Ave Hanley ST1 ..57 C4
  Stafford ST16 .....156 A2
Kingston Cl B79 ....250 B4
Kingston Dr ST15 ..120 A3
Kingston Hill Ct ST16 ..156 B2
Kingston Pl Biddulph ST8 ..16 C1
  Norton-in-t-M ST6 ..42 C2
Kingston Rd DE15 ..167 B2
Kingston Row ST16 ..156 A2
Kingston Way DY6 ..275 B4
Kingsway
  Burton u T DE14 ..185 A4
  Cannock WS11 ....210 A4
  Essington WV11 ..242 A2
  Stafford ST16 .....155 B1
  Stoke-on-T ST4 ....72 A4
  Stourbridge DY8 ..279 B4
Kingsway E ST5 .....71 A3
Kingsway W ST5 ....71 A3
Kingswear Ave WV6 ..254 C2
Kingswell Rd ST4 ...56 B1
Kingswinford Pl ST4 ..57 B4

Kingswinford Sch The
  DY6 ....275 B4
Kingswood ST7 ......26 A1
Kingswood Ave
  Cannock WS11 ....226 B4
  Chorlton CW2 ......37 A2
Kingswood Bsns Pk
  WV7 ....237 C1
Kingswood Ctr WV7 ..237 C1
Kingswood Dr
  Great Wyrley WS6 ..227 A2
  Norton Canes WS11 ..227 C3
Kingswood Gdns WV4 ..265 C3
Kingswood Mobil Homes
  WV7 ....237 C1
Kingswood Rd
  Albrighton WV7 ...237 B2
  Kingswinford DY6 ..275 B2
Kinlet Cl WV3 ......265 A4
Kinloch Dr DY1 ....271 C2
Kinnersley Ave ST7 ..40 C4
Kinnersley St 1 ST7 ..26 A1
Kinross Ave ST3 ....209 C4
Kinsall Gn B77 .....262 B3
Kinsey St ST5 ....55 A1
Kinver Cl DE6 ....81 B4
Kinver Cres WS9 ...245 A3
Kinver Dr WV4 .....265 B3
Kinver Edge★ DY7 ..277 C2
Kinver La DY11 ....280 A4
Kinver St
  Burton u T DE15 ..167 A2
  Kinver DY7 ....277 C2
  Chell Heath ST6 ...42 B1
  Kingswinford DY8 ..275 C1
Kiplass La ST18 ....121 B2
Kipling Ave WS7 ...212 A1
Kipling Rd Sedgley DY3 ..240 B1
  Wolv WV10 ....240 B1
Kipling Rise B79 ...249 C4
Kipling Way ST2 ....58 B1
Kirby Dr DY1 ....271 C2
Kirby St ST6 ....57 A3
Kirk St ST6 ....42 B1
Kirkham St ST4 .....72 A3
Kirkland La ST4 ....72 A3
Kirkland Way ST3 ...73 B2
Kirkside Gr WS8 ...244 C4
Kirkstall Ave ST17 ..174 A4
Kirkstall Cl WS3 ....242 C1
Kirkstall Cres WS3 ..242 C1
Kirkstall Pl ST5 ....71 A3
Kirkstone Cres WV5 ..269 C4
Kirkup Wlk ST3 ....283 A3
Kirkwall Gr ST2 .....43 A1
Kirstead Gdns WV6 ..255 A2
Kirtley B77 ....250 C1
Kirton Gr WV6 .....255 B2
Kitchen La WV11 ...241 C1
Kite Gr Kidsgrove ST7 ..26 B2
  Meir ST3 ....90 A3
Kitling Greaves La
  DE13 ....166 A4
Kitlings La ST17 ...175 C4
Kittoe Rd B74 ......258 A2
Kitwood Ave B78 ..262 C3
Knarsdale Cl 11 ST3 ..73 B3
Knaves Castle Ave WS8 ..228 C1
Knebworth Ct CW12 ..16 A4
Knenhall ST15 .....105 C4
Knenhall La ST15 ..89 C1
Knight Ave ST16 ...156 A2
Knight La ST10 .....78 C1
Knight Rd WS7 .....211 C1
Knight St ST6 ......41 B2
Knightley CW3 ......68 C3
Knightley Ct ST20 ..171 B3
Knightley Rd ST20 ..171 B4
Knightley Way ST20 ..171 B4
Knighton Cl B74 ...257 C2
Knighton Ct B74 ..257 C2
Knighton Rd
  Cannock WS12 ....210 C2
  Sutton Coldfield B74 ..257 C3
Knights Ave WV6 ..255 C3
Knights Cl ST19 ...207 C4
Knights Cres WV6 ..255 C4
Knights Croft WS7 ..69 C4
Knights Ct
  3 Burton u T DE13 ..147 C1
  Norton Canes WS11 ..228 C1
Knights Hill WS9 ..245 A3
Knightsbridge Cl B74 ..257 C2
Knightsbridge Way
  Burton u T DE13 ..166 B4
  11 Tunstall ST6 ...41 B2
Knightsfield Rd DE13 ..144 C1
Kniveden La ST13 ..31 A3
Knoll Cl WS7 ......229 A3
Knoll Croft WS9 ..245 A3
Knoll The DY6 .....275 C3
Knotty La CW12 ....17 A4
Knowlbank Rd ST7 ..53 C4
Knowle La WS11 ...228 A3
Knowle Rd Biddulph ST8 ..27 B4
  Stafford ST17 ....175 B4
Knowle St ST4 .....72 A4
Knowle Wood View ST3 ..72 C2
Knowles Hill DE13 ..147 A4
Knowsley La ST7 ...25 C2
Knowsley Rd ST9 ...44 B2
Knox Rd WV2 ......266 B3
Knox's Grave La WS14,
  B78 ....248 B4
Knutsford St DY8 ..25 A3
Knutton Inf Sch ST5 ..55 C1
Knutton La ST5 ....55 C1

Knutton Rd ST5 .....56 B3
Knutton St Mary's CE Jun Sch
  ST5 ....55 C1
Knype Cl ST5 ....56 A4
Knype Way Biddulph ST8 ..27 A3
  Newcastle-u-L ST5 ..56 B4
Knypersley Fst Sch ST8 ..27 A3
Kohima Dr DY8 ....279 C3
Kurtus B77 ....261 B3
Kyffin Rd ST2 ......58 A3
Kyle Cl WV10 ......240 A1
Kynaston Cres WV8 ..239 A1
Kynnersley Croft ST14 ..111 A1

L

Laburnam Cl ST7 ....40 C4
Laburnham Ct WS14 ..231 B3
Laburnham Rd DY6 ..275 C3
Laburnum Ave
  Cannock WS11 ....226 C4
  Tamworth B79 ....250 A4
Laburnum Cl
  Cannock WS11 ....226 C4
  Forsbrook ST11 ...91 A3
  Kinver DY7 ....277 C3
  Market Drayton TF9 ..97 B1
  Seighford ST18 ...135 A1
  Stourbridge DY8 ..279 C4
  Walsall WS3 ......244 A1
Laburnum Gr
  Burntwood WS7 ..228 C3
  Fenton ST3 ....72 C2
Laburnum Ho WS4 ..244 B4
Laburnum Pl 9 Meir ST3 ..89 C4
  Newcastle-u-L ST5 ..40 C4
Laburnum Rd
  Brownhills WS9 ...245 A2
  Burton u T DE15 ..185 C3
  Swadlincote DE11 ..186 C3
  Wolv WV4 ....266 C2
Laburnum St DY8 ..279 C4
Laches Cl WV10 ...224 B3
Laches La WV10 ...224 C1
Lad La ST5 ....284 B3
Ladbrook Gr DY3 ..271 A2
Ladderedge ST13 ...30 B1
Ladderedge Ctry Pk★
  ST13 ....30 A2
Ladford Covert Ind Pk
  ST18 ....134 C1
Ladford Trad Pk ST18 ..134 C1
Ladfordfields Ind Est
  ST18 ....134 C1
Ladfordfields Ind Pk
  ST18 ....153 C3
Ladies Wlk DY3 ....271 A4
Ladle End La DE12 ..184 B1
Lady Grey's Wlk DY8 ..279 B3
Lady Hill Terr WS15 ..196 A4
Lady Meadow Cl ST14 ..95 C3
Ladybank Gr ST3 ..88 C4
Ladydale Cl ST13 ..30 C2
Ladyfields Way DE11 ..186 C3
Ladygates CW3 .....53 A3
Ladymoor La ST6 ...28 A2
Ladysmith Rd ST1 ..57 A2
Ladysmith St ST3 ..283 B2
Ladywell Cl
  Burton u T DE13 ..147 C1
  Wombourne WV5 ..270 A4
Ladywell Rd 5 ST1 ..41 B2
Ladywood Rd B74 ..258 A1
Lagonda B77 ......250 C2
Lagonda Cl ST8 ....27 A3
Lagrange B79 .....249 C3
Lair The B78 ......262 C4
Lake Rd ST13 ......18 B1
Lake St DY3 ....271 B2
Lakeland Dr B77 ..262 A4
Lakenheath B79 ..250 B4
Lakeside Betley CW3 ..53 A3
  Bosley SK11 ....7 B4
  Little Aston B74 ..257 A3
Lakeside Cl ST5 ...85 B2
Lakeside Dr WS11 ..228 A3
Lakeside Pk B78 ..249 C1
Lakeside Prim Sch B77 ..250 C1
Lakeside View WS15 ..198 A2
Lakewood Dr ST12 ..88 C2
Lakewood Gr ST1 ..57 A2
Lally Pl ST8 ....27 A1
Lamb Cres WV5 ...269 C3
Lamb La ST15 .....119 C4
Lamb St Hanley ST1 ..282 B3
  Kidsgrove ST7 ....26 A1
Lambert Ct DY6 ...275 B4
Lambert Dr WS7 ..229 A4
Lambert St ST14 ..110 C1
Lambert St ST6 ....41 C2
Lambert's La CW12 ..15 C4
Lambourn WS3 ....243 B1
Lambourn Pl ST3 ..88 C4
Lambourne Cl
  Great Wyrley WS6 ..226 C2
  Lichfield WS14 ...231 C4
Lambourne Dr ST2 ..43 B1
Lambourne Way WS11 ..228 A3
Lamerton Gr ST3 ..73 C1
Lammas Rd DY8 ..275 B2
Lammascote Rd ST16 ..155 C2
Lamorna Cl WV3 ...265 A4
Lamotte Cl ST4 ....73 A3
Lamprey B77 ......261 B3
Lanark Wlks ST5 ..70 C4
Lancaster Ave
  Aldridge WS9 .....256 A4

Lancaster Ave continued
Blythe Bridge ST11 ......90 C1
Leek ST13 ....30 C4
Newcastle-u-L ST5 ....284 D2
Lancaster Cres ST4 ......71 B4
Lancaster Dr
Norton-in-t-M ST6 ......42 C2
Tutbury DE13 ....146 A3
Lancaster Gdns WV4 ..265 C3
Lancaster Ho
6 Brierley Hill DY8 ...279 C4
Cannock WS12 ....210 B1
Lancaster Pl WS3 ......243 B1
Lancaster Rd
Alrewas WS13 ....215 B3
Newcastle-u-L ST5 ....284 D2
Stafford ST17 ....175 A4
Lance Dr WS7 ....211 C1
Lancelot Dr DE13 ......147 C1
Lanchester Cl
Biddulph ST8 ....27 A3
Tamworth B79 ....249 C4
Lancia Cl ST8 ....27 A3
Lancing Ave ST17 ....175 A4
Lander Cl ST15 ....120 B4
Lander Pl ST6 ....42 A3
Landon St ST3 ....283 C3
Landor Cres WS15 ....196 C4
Landport Rd WV2 ....266 C4
Landrake Gr ST7 ......41 C4
Landsberg B79 ....249 C3
Landseer Pl ST5 ......55 C3
Landstone Rd **7** ST17 ..175 A4
Landywood Ent Pk WS6 ..242 C1
Landywood Gn WS6 ....226 C1
Landywood La WS6 ....226 C1
Landywood Prim Sch
WS6 ....242 C1
Landywood Sta WS6 ..226 C1
Lane End SK17 ....23 B4
Lane Farm Gr ST1 ....57 C4
Lane Green Ave WV8 ..239 A1
Lane Green Ct WV8 ..239 A2
Lane Green Fst Sch
WV8 ....239 A2
Lane Green Rd WV8 ..239 A1
Lane Green Rd Masionetttes
WV8 ....239 B2
Lane Green Sh Par
WV8 ....239 A2
Lane Head SK17 ....13 A4
Lane The ST18 ....174 A4
Lane's Cl DE13 ....199 B3
Lanehead Rd ST1 .....56 C2
Lanehead Wlk WS15 ..178 B1
Lanes Cl WV5 ....269 C3
Langdale Cl WS8 ....244 C3
Langdale Cres ST1 ....57 B4
Langdale Ct B77 ......251 A3
Langdale Dr WS11 ....226 B4
Langdale Gn WS11 ....226 B4
Langdale Jun & Inf Schs
ST5 ....71 A3
Langdale Rd ST5 ......71 A3
Langer Cl DE14 ......185 A3
Langford Rd Bucknall ST2 ..58 B2
Newcastle-u-L ST5 ....71 A2
Langford St ST13 ......30 B3
Langham Gr B74 .....256 C1
Langham Rd ST2 ......43 A1
Langholm Dr WS12 ....210 C1
Langland Dr Longton ST3 ..73 A1
Sedgley DY3 ....271 B4
Langley Cl ST5 ....40 B1
Langley Gdns WV3 ....265 B4
Langley Rd
Lower Penn WV3 .....265 A4
Wolv WV3,WV4 ......265 A4
Langley St ST4 ....56 B1
Langot La ST21 ....115 B2
Langstone Rd DY1 ....271 C4
Langton Cres WS14 ....232 C3
Langton Ct Caverswall ST9 59 A2
Lichfield WS13 ......214 A1
Langtree Cl WS12 ....210 B1
Lanrick Gdns WS15 ..178 C1
Lansbury Cl ST17 ....174 C4
Lansbury Dr WS11 ....209 C2
Lansbury Gr ST3 ......74 A2
Lansbury Rd WS15 ..196 C3
Lansdell Ave ST5 ......56 A3
Lansdowne Ave WV8 ..238 C1
Lansdowne Cl Leek ST13 ..30 B3
Stone ST15 ....119 C3
Lansdowne Cres
Caverswall ST9 ....59 A2
Tamworth B77 ....261 B4
Lansdowne Inf Sch
DE14 ....166 B3
Lansdowne Rd
Branston DE14 ......184 C4
Stoke-on-T ST4 ......56 C1
Lansdowne St ST3 ....73 A1
Lansdowne Terr DE14 ..166 B3
Lansdowne Way
Rugeley WS15 ....178 B1
Stafford ST17 ....175 B3
Lant Cl DE13 ....199 B3
Lapley Ave ST16 ......155 A4
Lapley Hall Mews ST19 ..206 A3
Lapley La ST19 ....206 B2
Lapley Rd ST19 ......205 B2
Lapper Ave WV4 .....266 C1
Lapwing B79 ....262 A3
Lapwing Cl WS6 ......226 B1
Lapwing Rd ST7 ......26 B2
Lapwood Ave DY6 ....275 C4
Lapworth Way TF10 ..169 A2

Lara Cl ST16 ....155 A2
Larch Cl Kidsgrove ST7 ..41 A4
Kinver DY7 ....278 B2
Lichfield WS14 ......231 C4
Larch Ct **15** ST6 ......57 A4
Larch Gr Fenton ST3 ..72 C1
Sedgley DY3 ....271 C4
Larch Pl ST5 ....55 C4
Larch Rd
Kingswinford DY6 ....275 C4
Rugeley WS15 ....196 C3
Swadlincote DE11 ....186 C3
Larches The TF10 .....168 C1
Larchfields ST15 ......120 A3
Larchmere Dr WV11 ..242 A2
Larchmount Cl ST4 ....88 A4
Larchwood Keele ST5 ..70 A3
Stafford ST17 ....175 B3
Larchwood Dr WS11 ..210 A2
Larcombe Dr WV4 ....266 A3
Lark Ave ST7 ....26 B2
Lark Hall Inf Sch B79 ..249 A4
Lark Rise ST14 ....126 A3
Larkfield ST7 ....26 A1
Larkhill La TF9 ....100 A3
Larkhill Rd DY8 ......279 B2
Larkholme Cl WS15 ..178 A1
Larkin Ave ST3 ....73 B2
Larkin Cl Essington WV10 241 A1
Stafford ST17 ....174 B4
Larks Hill WS3 ....243 C2
Larksfield Rd ST6 .....42 B1
Larksmeadow Vale
ST17 ....175 B3
Larkspur B77 ....261 B2
Larkspur Ave WS7 ....229 A3
Larkspur Dr WV10 ....241 A4
Larkspur Gr ST5 .....284 C4
Larkspur Way WS8 ..244 B3
Larkstone La DE6,ST13 ..34 C1
Larkswood Dr
Sedgley DY3 ....271 B4
Wolv WV4 ....265 B4
Lascelles St ST6 ......41 B1
Laski Cres ST3 ....74 A1
Latebrook Cl ST6 .....41 B4
Latham Cl DE15 ......167 B1
Latham Gr ST6 ....42 A4
Latherford Cl WV10 ..224 C3
Latherford La WV10 ..225 A2
Lathkill Dale DE11 ..186 C1
Latimer Way ST2 .....58 B1
Lauder Cl DY3 ....266 B1
Lauder Pl N ST2 ......73 C4
Lauder Pl S ST2 ....73 C4
Lauderdale Cl WS8 ..244 C3
Lauderdale Gdns WV10 ..240 C2
Launceston Cl B77 ..250 B1
Laurel Bank B79 .....250 A3
Laurel Cl WS14 ......231 B4
Laurel Cres ST9 ....59 C4
Laurel Dr
Burntwood WS7 .....229 B4
Cannock WS12 ......210 A2
Kidsgrove ST7 ....26 C2
Newport TF10 ....168 C2
Laurel Gr
Burton u T DE15 .....185 C3
Fenton ST3 ....72 B1
Stafford ST17 ....174 C4
Wolv WV4 ....265 C3
Laurel Rd DY1 ....271 C2
Laurels The WS15 ....196 C4
Lauren Cl ST4 ....72 C3
Laurence Gr WV6 ....255 C3
Lauriston Cl DY1 ....271 C2
Lavender Ave ST11 ..90 C3
Lavender Cl
Burton u T DE14 .....185 A4
Codsall WV9 ....239 C2
Meir ST3 ....74 B3
Seighford ST18 ......135 B1
Lavender La ST4 ......279 B2
Lavender Lodge ST17 ..177 C4
Lavender Rd B77 ....250 C2
Laverock Gr CW3 .....68 C3
Lawford Ave WS14 ..231 C4
Lawford Cotts ST17 ..174 C2
Lawley Cl WS4 ......244 A1
Lawley St ST3 ....73 B2
Lawn Ave DY8 ....279 C4
Lawn Farm Cres ST2 ..57 C3
Lawn La Brewood WV9 ..240 A4
Cheswardine TF9 ....113 C1
Lawn Rd Stafford ST17 ..155 B1
Wolv WV2 ....266 C3
Lawn St DY8 ....279 C2
Lawn The ST17 ....174 C3
Lawnoaks Cl WS8 ....228 B1
Lawns The
Market Drayton TF9 ..97 B1
Rolleston DE13 ......147 A3
Uttoxeter ST14 ......111 A1
Lawnsfield Wlk ST16 ..136 B1
Lawnswood DY7,DY6 ..275 A2
Lawnswood Ave
Burntwood WS7 .....228 C3
Kingswinford DY8 ....275 B4
Wolv, Blakeley Green
WV6 ....255 C4
Wolv, Parkfield WV4 ..266 C3
Lawnswood Cl **6** WS11 ..210 B1
Lawnswood Dr
Brownhills WS9 .....245 A2
Kinver DY7 ....275 A1
Lawnswood Rd
Kingswinford DY8 ....275 B2

Lawnswood Rd continued
Sedgley DY3 ....271 B3
Lawnswood Rise WV6 ..255 C4
Lawrence Ct B79 .....250 A3
Lawrence Dr ST15 ..103 A3
Lawrence St Hanley ST1 ..282 A1
Stafford ST17 ....155 C1
Lawson Cl WS9 ......256 A4
Lawson Terr ST5 ......56 B4
Lawton Ave ST7 ......25 B2
Lawton Coppice ST7 ..25 C2
Lawton Cres ST8 ......27 B4
Lawton St Biddulph ST8 ..27 B4
Chell Heath ST6 ......42 A1
Kidsgrove ST7 ....26 B2
Lawtongate Est ST7 ..25 A2
Laxey Rd ST5 ....56 A2
Laxton Gr ST4 ....88 B2
Lazar La ST17 ....176 A3
Lazy Hill WS9 ....245 B1
Le More B74 ....258 A1
Lea Castle Dr DY10 ..280 B2
Lea Castle Hospl DY10 ..280 B2
Lea Cl ST5 ....85 B3
Lea Cres ST17 ....174 B4
Lea Gn ST16 ....155 B4
Lea Hall Dr WS7 ....211 B1
Lea Hall Ent Pk WS15 ..197 A3
Lea Hall La WS15 ....197 A3
Lea La Colton WS15 ..159 C1
Cookley DY10 ....280 A3
Great Wyrley WS6 ..227 A2
Lea Manor Dr WV4 ..265 C2
Lea Pl ST3 ....74 A1
Lea Rd Hixon ST18 ..139 C1
Stone ST15 ....119 C3
Wolv WV3 ....266 A4
Lea The ST4 ....88 A4
Lea Vale Rd DY8 ....279 C4
Lea Wlk WS11 ....210 A2
Leacliffe Way WS9 ..256 C2
Leacote Dr WV6 ....255 B2
Leacroft WS15 ....120 B4
Leacroft Ave WV10 ..240 C1
Leacroft Cl WS9 ......245 A1
Leacroft La WS11 ..226 C3
Leacroft Rd
Kingswinford DY6 ....275 C4
Meir ST3 ....90 A4
Penkridge ST19 .....193 A1
Leadbeater Ave ST4 ..71 C3
Leadendale La ST3 ....89 C2
Leadendale Mews ST3 ..89 C4
Leafdown Cl WS12 ..210 B3
Leafenden Ave WS7 ..229 A3
Leaford Way DY6 ....275 C3
Leaford Wlk ST2 ......57 C1
Leafy Glade B74 ....257 A2
Leafy Rise DY3 ......271 B2
Leahurst cl **5** ST17 ..175 B3
Leak Rd WS7 ....229 B4
Leamington Cl WS11 ..226 B4
Leamington Gdns ST5 ..56 C2
Leamington Rd DE14 ..184 C4
Leamansley Ct WS13 ..230 C3
Leander Cl
Burntwood WS7 .....211 C1
Great Wyrley WS6 ..226 C1
Leander Rise DE15 ..186 A4
Lear Rd WV5 ....270 A4
Leas The WV10 ......241 B4
Leasawe Ct ST18 ....158 B1
Leaside Ave WS15 ..198 B3
Leaside Rd ST4 ......71 C3
Leason Rd ST3 ....74 A1
Leason St ST4 ....72 A4
Leasowe Rd WS11 ..197 A3
Leasowe The WS13 ..214 A1
Leasowes Dr
Perton WV6 ....254 B2
Wolv WV4 ....265 B3
Leasowes Jun & Inf Schs
ST17 ....175 B4
Leaswood Cl ST5 ......71 B1
Leaswood Pl ST5 ......71 B1
Leathermill La WS15 ..178 C1
Leathersley La DE6,DE65 129 A1
Leawood Rd ST4 ......71 C2
Lebanon Gr WS7 ....228 C4
Ledbury Cl WS9 .....245 B1
Ledbury Cres ST1 .....57 C3
Ledstone Way ST3 ....73 C2
Lee Ct WS9 ....244 C2
Lee Gr ST5 ....71 A2
Leech Ave ST5 ....55 C3
Leech St ST5 ....284 C1
Leedham Ave B77 ....250 B3
Leedhams Croft DE12 ..202 B4
Leeds St ST4 ....72 C3
Leek Coll of F Ed ST13 ..30 C3
Leek Fst Sch ST13 .....31 A3
Leek High Sch ST13 ..31 B3
Leek La ST8,ST13 ....28 C1
Leek Morlands Hospl
ST13 ....31 A3
Leek New Rd
Chell Heath ST6,ST1 ..57 B4
Norton-in-t-M ST6 ....42 C1
Leek Rd Bucknall ST2 ..58 A3
Cheadle ST10 ....76 B3
Cheddleton ST9,ST10 ..60 B2
Cheddleton, Cellarhead ST9 59 C2
Cheddleton, Cheddleton Heath
ST13 ....45 B4
Congleton CW12 .....16 A4
Endon ST9 ....43 C3
Endon, Brown Edge ST9 ..43 B4

Leek Rd continued
Hanley ST1 ....57 C1
Longnor SK17 ....13 A3
Norton-in-t-M ST6 ....42 C2
Stoke-on-T ST4 ......72 B4
Warslow SK17 ....23 A1
Wetton DE6 ....34 B2
Leekbrook Ind Est ST13 ..45 C4
Leekbrook Way ST13 ..30 C1
Lees Cl WS15 ....197 A3
Lees La ST10 ....108 C1
Leese La
Acton Trussell ST17 ..175 A1
Stone ST15 ....105 C3
Leese St ST4 ....72 A4
Leet Cl WS15 ....198 A2
Legge La ST18 ....139 B1
Legge St
Newcastle-u-L ST5 ....284 C2
Wolv WV2 ....266 C3
Legion Cl WS11 .....228 A3
Legs La WV10 ......240 C2
Leicester Cl ST5 ......71 B3
Leicester Ct ST14 ..110 C1
Leicester Pl ST2 ......58 B1
Leicester St DE14 ..185 B4
Leigh Ave WS7 ......229 A4
Leigh Bank ST10 ....108 C4
Leigh Cl ST17 ....174 C3
Leigh La
Church Leigh ST10 ..108 B3
Tunstall ST6 ....41 B1
Upper Tean ST10 ....92 C1
Uttoxeter ST14 ......125 A4
Leigh Rd Congleton CW12 ..6 C3
Newport TF10 ....168 C1
Leigh St ST6 ....42 A1
Leighs Cl WS4 ......244 B1
Leighs Rd WS4 ......244 A1
Leighswood **1** ST17 ..175 B4
Leighswood Ave WS9 ..256 A4
Leighswood Cl WS11 ..227 C3
Leighswood Ct WS9 ..256 A3
Leighswood Gr WS9 ..256 A4
Leighswood Ind Est
WS9 ....256 A4
Leighswood Rd WS9 ..256 A3
Leighswood Sch WS9 ..256 A4
Leighton Cl
Norton-in-t-M ST9 ....43 B2
Sedgley DY1 ....271 C1
Uttoxeter ST14 ......126 B3
Leighton Rd
Uttoxeter ST14 ......126 B3
Wolv WV4 ....265 C3
Leisure La SK17 ....24 C3
Leisure Wlk B77 ....261 C3
Lema Way ST16 .....156 B2
Lennox Gdns WV3 ..266 A4
Lennox Rd ST3 ......283 D1
Lenpark Ind Est ST3 ..283 C3
Lenthall Ave CW12 ..15 C4
Leofric Cl DE13 ......199 B3
Leomansley Cl WS13 ..230 C4
Leomansley Rd WS13 ..230 C4
Leomansley View WS13 ..230 C3
Leonard Ave
Kidderminster DY10 ..280 A1
Norton-in-t-M ST2 ....43 A2
Leonard Dr ST6 ....43 A4
Leonard Rd DY8 .....279 B3
Leonard St
Chell Heath ST6 ......42 A1
Leek ST13 ....30 C3
Leonora St ST4 ......56 C4
Leopold St ST4 ......72 C4
Lerridge La ST20,ST21 ..131 C3
Lerryn St DY6 ....275 C4
Lerwick Cl DY6 ......275 C4
Lesley Dr DY6 ....275 C2
Leslie Rd B74 ....257 A1
Lesscroft Cl WV9 ....240 C2
Lessways Cl ST5 ......56 A4
Lessways Wlk **12** ST6 ..56 C4
Lester Gr WS9 ......256 C1
Letchmere Cl WV6 ..253 B1
Letchmere La WV6 ..253 B1
Lethbridge Gdns ST17 ..174 A4
Levedale Cl ST16 ....155 A4
Levedale Rd
Bradley ST18 ....191 B4
Penkridge ST19 .....192 B2
Levels The WS15 ....196 C3
Leven Dr WV11 ......242 A1
Leveson Ave WS6 ..226 C1
Leveson Rd
Essington WV11 .....241 C1
Trentham ST4 ....71 C1
Levett Rd Hopwas WS14 ..232 B1
Tamworth B77 ....251 A3
Levetts Fields WS14 ..231 B4
Levetts Hollow WS11 ..210 B2
Levetts Sq WS13 ....231 B4
Levington Cl WV6 ..254 C3
Levita Rd ST3 ....71 C2
Lewis Cl WS14 ......231 C4
Lewis Dr DE13 ......166 A4
Lewis St ST4 ....72 A4
Lewis's La DE13 ....199 B3
Lewisham Dr ST6 ....41 B4
Lewisham Rd WV10 ..240 A1
Lewthorne Rise WV4 ..266 B2
Lexham Pl ST3 ....73 C1
Lexington Gn ST17 ..174 A4
Ley Gdns ST3 ....283 C2
Ley Hill Rd B75 .....258 B1
Ley Rise DY3 ....266 B2
Leybourne Cres WV9 ..239 C1

Lan – Lim | **311**

Leycett La ST5 ....54 B1
Leycett Rd ST5 ......54 C2
Leyfield Rd ST4 ......88 C3
Leyfields WS13 ......214 A1
Leyfields Farm Mews
DE13 ....165 B4
Leyland Ave WV3 ....255 C1
Leyland Croft WS3 ..243 C2
Leyland Dr WS15 ....178 C1
Leyland Gn ST6 ......42 A3
Leyland Rd B77 .....250 C2
Leys Dr ST5 ....70 C2
Leys La ST2 ....43 B2
Leys The DE11 ......186 C3
Liberty La ST6 ....42 B2
Liberty Pk ST17 ....174 A4
Liberty Rd B77 ......261 C3
Libra Cl B79 ....249 C4
Libra Pl ST6 ....41 C3
Lichen Cl WS12 ....209 B3
Lichfield (Trent Valley) Sta
WS13 ....231 C4
Lichfield Bsns Ctr WS13 214 C1
Lichfield Cathedral Sch
WS13 ....231 A4
Lichfield City Sta WS14 231 A4
Lichfield Cl ST5 ......55 B1
Lichfield Ct ST17 ..155 C1
Lichfield Dr
Colwich WS13 ....158 A1
Hopwas B78 ....249 A4
Lichfield Rd
Abbots Bromley WS15 ..161 A2
Armitage WS15 ......198 B2
Branston DE13,DE14 ..184 B2
Brownhills, Gatehouse Trad Est
WS8 ....245 A4
Burntwood, Burntwood Green
WS7 ....229 C4
Burntwood, New Town
WS8,WS14 ....229 B1
Cannock WS11 ......226 C4
Hamstall Ridware WS15 ..180 C1
King's Bromley DE13 ..199 A3
Sandon ST18 ....137 B4
Stafford ST17 ....155 C1
Stone ST15 ....120 B4
Sutton Coldfield B74 ..258 A2
Talke ST7 ....40 B4
Tamworth B78,B79 ..249 C3
Walsall WS4 ....244 B1
Walsall, New Invention
WS3,WS4,WS8,WS9 ..242 C1
Walsall, Pelsall WS3 ..244 A3
Walsall, Wallington Heath
WS3 ....243 B1
Lichfield Road Ind Est
B79 ....249 C3
Lichfield St
Burton u T DE14 .....166 B1
Hanley ST1 ....282 C1
Rugeley WS15 ....196 C4
Stone ST15 ....120 A4
Tamworth B78 ....249 C3
Lid La Cheadle ST10 ..76 B2
Roston DE6 ....96 C4
Liddiard Ct DY8 .....279 C3
Liddle St ST4 ....72 A3
Lidgate Gr ST3 ......72 C1
Lidgate Wlk ST5 .....71 A1
Liffs Rd DE6,SK17 ..36 C1
Lifton Croft DY6 ....275 C3
Light Ash WV9 ......224 B2
Light Ash Cl WV9 ..224 B2
Light Ash La WV9 ..224 B2
Light Oaks Ave ST2 ..43 B1
Lightfoot Rd ST4 ....110 C1
Lightwater Gr ST2 ..42 C1
Lightwood Rd
Longton ST3 ....283 C2
Meir ST3 ....89 C3
Newcastle-u-L ST5 ....40 C3
Yoxall DE13 ....181 C3
Lilac Ave WS11 ......226 B4
Lilac Cl Meir ST3 .....74 B3
Newcastle-u-L ST5 ....40 B1
Seighford ST18 .....135 B1
Uttoxeter ST14 ......126 A3
Lilac Dr WV5 ....269 C3
Lilac Gr Burntwood WS7 ..228 C4
Burton u T DE15 .....185 C3
Fenton ST3 ....72 C2
Stafford ST17 ....174 C4
Lilac Ho WS4 ....244 B1
Lilac La WS6 ....243 A4
Lilac Rd B79 ....250 A4
Lilleshall Cres WV2 ..266 B4
Lilleshall Hall National
Sports Ctr TF10 ....187 A1
Lilleshall Rd ST5 ......71 B4
Lilleshall St ST3 .....283 C2
Lilleshall Way ST17 ..174 B4
Lillington Cl WS13 ..231 A4
Lillydale Rd ST2 ......58 A2
Lily St ST5 ....56 B3
Limbrick Rd ST7 ......39 C4
Lime Cl
Church Leigh ST10 ..109 A3
Doveridge DE6 ......127 A4
Great Wyrley WS6 ..226 C2
Meir ST3 ....74 B3
Lime Gr Barlaston ST12 ..88 C2
Burntwood WS7 .....229 B3
Burton u T DE15 .....185 C3
Kinver DY7 ....278 B2

Lime Gr *continued*
Lichfield WS14 . . . . .231 B4
Waterhouses ST10 . . . . . . .48 C2
Lime Kiln La Alton ST10 . . .78 C1
Kidsgrove ST7 . . . . .25 C1
Lime La WS3 . . . . .244 A4
Lime Rd Huntington WS12 209 B4
Sedgley DY3 . . . . .266 C1
Lime St Stoke-on-T ST4 . . . .72 A3
Wolv WS4 . . . . .266 A4
Lime Tree Ave WV6 . . . . . .255 A2
Lime Tree Gdns WV8 . . . . .239 A2
Lime Tree Rd WV8 . . . . . . .239 A2
Lime Wlk ST19 . . . . .207 C4
Limeheath Pl ST6 . . . . .41 C3
Limehurst Ave WV3 . . . . . .255 B1
Limepit La WS11,WS12 . . .209 B3
Limes Ave ST9 . . . . .30 A1
Limes Rd WV6 . . . . .255 B2
Limes The
Albrighton WV7 . . . . .237 A2
Newcastle-u-L ST5 . . . . . . .56 A1
Limes View DY3 . . . . .271 A4
Limetree Ave ST16 . . . . . . .155 B3
Limetree Rd B74 . . . . .256 B1
Limewood Cl ST11 . . . . .91 A3
Linacre Rd ST21 . . . . .133 C3
Linacre Way ST3 . . . . .73 C3
Lincoln Ave
Newcastle-u-L ST5 . . . . . . .71 B3
Tamworth B79 . . . . .249 C3
Lincoln Cl WS13 . . . . .214 B2
Lincoln Croft WS14 . . . . . .247 A3
Lincoln Ct ST14 . . . . .110 C1
Lincoln Dr WS11 . . . . .226 C4
Lincoln Gn WV10 . . . . . . .240 B1
Lincoln Gr ST5 . . . . .71 B3
Lincoln Mdw ST17 . . . . . . .174 A4
Lincoln Rd Burslem ST6 . . . .57 A4
Burton u T DE15 . . . . . . .185 B4
Kidsgrove ST7 . . . . .25 C1
Lincoln St ST1 . . . . .282 C2
Linda Rd ST6 . . . . .41 C3
Lindale Cl CW12 . . . . .6 A3
Lindale Dr WV5 . . . . .269 C3
Lindale Gr 16 ST3 . . . . .90 A4
Linden Ave WS7 . . . . .229 A4
Linden Cl Congleton CW12 16 A4
Newcastle-u-L ST5 . . . . . . .56 A2
Stafford ST17 . . . . .174 A4
Tamworth B77 . . . . .250 C2
Linden Dr ST8 . . . . .16 B1
Linden Gr ST5 . . . . .56 A4
Linden Lea WV3 . . . . .255 B1
Linden Pl ST3 . . . . .72 C1
Linden Rd DE13 . . . . .183 B1
Linden Way WS12 . . . . . . .210 A2
Linden Way TF9 . . . . .97 B1
Lindenbrook Vale ST17 . . . .175 B4
Lindens The Stone ST15 . . .120 A1
Wolv WV6 . . . . .255 C2
Lindera B77 . . . . .251 A2
Lindisfarne B77 . . . . .250 B2
Lindley Pl ST3 . . . . .90 A2
Lindley St ST6 . . . . .57 A4
Lindon Dr WS8 . . . . .245 A4
Lindon Rd WS8 . . . . .244 C3
Lindon View WS8 . . . . .245 A3
Lindop Ct ST1 . . . . .282 C2
Lindop St ST1 . . . . .282 C2
Lindops La CW3 . . . . .68 C2
Lindrick Cl WS3 . . . . .242 C2
Lindrosa Rd B74 . . . . .256 C2
Lindsay St ST1 . . . . .282 A2
Lindum Ave ST4 . . . . .88 B4
Line Ct DE15 . . . . .185 C4
Lineker Cl ST16 . . . . .155 A2
Linfield Gdns DY3 . . . . . . .266 B1
Linfield Rd ST1 . . . . .282 C1
Linford Cl WS15 . . . . .198 B2
Ling Rd WS12 . . . . .209 B3
Lingard St ST6 . . . . .57 A4
Lingfield Ave Endon ST6 . .43 A4
Wolv WV10 . . . . .240 B3
Lingfield Cl WS6 . . . . .226 C1
Lingfield Dr WS6 . . . . .226 C1
Lingfield Gr WV6 . . . . .254 C2
Lingfield Rd DE14 . . . . . . .184 C4
Linhope Gr 18 ST3 . . . . . . .90 A4
Link Rd Brownhills WS9 . . .245 A2
Wombourne WV5 . . . . . . .270 A4
Linkend Cl ST1 . . . . .57 C3
Links Ave
Newcastle-u-L ST5 . . . . . . .56 A2
Wolv WV6 . . . . .255 B4
Links Dr DY8 . . . . .279 C1
Links Rd WV4 . . . . .266 A2
Links Side Way WS9 . . . . . .256 B4
Links View B74 . . . . .257 A1
Linksfield Gr ST16 . . . . . . .155 B4
Linksway CW12 . . . . .15 C4
Linksway Cl CW12 . . . . . . .15 C4
Linkway Ret Pk WS11 . . . .226 A3
Linkwood Ind Est DY8 . . . .279 C3
Linley Dr WV10 . . . . .240 C1
Linley Gr Lawton-gate ST7 .25 A2
Sedgley DY3 . . . . .271 A1
Linley La ST7 . . . . .25 A2
Linley Rd Stoke-on-T ST4 . .71 C4
Talke ST7 . . . . .40 B4
Linley Trad Est ST7 . . . . . .25 B1
Linnburn Rd ST3 . . . . .73 C2
Linnet Cl WS12 . . . . .209 B4
Linnet Way ST8 . . . . .27 C3
Linslade Cl WV4 . . . . .266 B2

Lintake Dr WS15 . . . . . . .160 C3
Linthouse Wlk B77 . . . . . .261 C3
Lintly B77 . . . . .262 A4
Linton Rd WV4 . . . . .265 C3
Linwood Dr WS12 . . . . . . .209 C4
Linwood Way ST6 . . . . .41 C3
Lion Gr ST5 . . . . .55 C4
Lion Ind Est WS9 . . . . . . .256 A4
Lion Pas DY8 . . . . .279 C3
Lion St Rugeley WS15 . . .178 C1
Stoke-on-T ST4 . . . . .72 A4
Stourbridge DY8 . . . . .279 C3
Lion Wlk ST17 . . . . .175 A4
Lion's Den WS7,WS14 . . . .229 C1
Lionel Gr ST4 . . . . .71 C3
Lionfields Cl DY10 . . . . . . .280 A3
Lionfields Rd DY10 . . . . . .280 A3
Lisbon Pl ST5 . . . . .70 C4
Liskeard Cl ST2 . . . . .58 A1
Lister Rd ST16 . . . . .155 C3
Litley Dr ST10 . . . . .92 B4
Little Aston Hall Dr B74 257 A3
Little Aston Hospl B74 . . .257 A3
Little Aston La B74 . . . . . .257 B3
Little Aston Park Rd
B74 . . . . .257 A2
Little Aston Prim Sch
B74 . . . . .257 B3
Little Aston Rd WS9 . . . . .256 A4
Little Barrow Wlk WS13 214 A1
Little Birches WV3 . . . . . .265 C4
Little Bloxwich CE Prim Sch
WS3 . . . . .243 B4
Little Burton E DE14 . . . . .166 B2
Little Burton W DE14 . . . .166 B2
Little Checkhill La DY6,
DY7 . . . . .274 B2
Little Chell La ST6 . . . . . . .41 C3
Little Church La B79 . . . . .250 A3
Little Cliffe Rd ST3 . . . . . . .72 C2
Little Comm WS3 . . . . . . .244 A2
Little Eaves La ST2 . . . . . . .58 B3
Little Field ST4 . . . . .71 C2
Little Grange WS13 . . . . . .213 C4
Little Hardwick Rd WS9 256 B1
Little Hay La WS14 . . . . . .247 B2
Little Johnson's La
WS9 . . . . .256 A1
Little La ST3 . . . . .89 C2
Little Lawns Cl WS9 . . . . .245 A2
Little Marsh Gr ST19 . . . . .192 C1
Little Moss Cl ST7 . . . . . . .25 C3
Little Moss La ST7 . . . . . . .25 C3
Little Oaks Dr DY7 . . . . . . .275 A1
Little Onn Rd ST20 . . . . . .190 A4
Little Orch WS15 . . . . .178 C1
Little Pipe La WS13 . . . . . .213 A1
Little Pountney St 6
WV2 . . . . .266 B4
Little Rd ST10 . . . . .75 C1
Little Row
14 Kidsgrove ST7 . . . . . . .26 A1
Stoke-on-T ST4 . . . . .72 C4
Little Sutton La B75 . . . . .258 B1
Little Sutton Prim Sch
B75 . . . . .258 B2
Little Sutton Rd B75 . . . .258 B1
Little Tixall La ST18 . . . . .158 B1
Littlecote B79 . . . . .249 B4
Littlefield La
Ellastone DE6 . . . . .80 A1
Snelston DE6 . . . . .81 A2
Littlehales Rd TF10 . . . . . .187 A4
Littleton Bsns Pk WS12 209 B4
Littleton Cl ST16 . . . . .156 A2
Littleton Cres ST19 . . . . . .192 C1
Littleton Dr WS12 . . . . . . .209 B4
Littleton Way WS7 . . . . . .211 B1
Littlewood La WS6 . . . . . .226 C2
Littlewood Rd WS6 . . . . . .226 C2
Littleworth Hill WS12 . . . .210 B2
Littleworth Rd WS12 . . . . .210 C2
Litton B77 . . . . .251 B1
Littondale Cl CW12 . . . . . . .6 A3
Littywood La ST18 . . . . . . .173 B1
Liverpool Rd
Kidsgrove ST7 . . . . .26 C1
Newcastle-u-L ST5 . . . . . .284 B3
Newcastle-u-L, Cross Heath
ST5 . . . . .56 A2
Newcastle-u-L, Red Street
ST5 . . . . .40 B1
Stoke-on-T ST4 . . . . .72 A4
Liverpool Rd E ST7 . . . . . . .25 C1
Liverpool Rd W ST7 . . . . . .25 A2
Livingstone Dr WV6 . . . . . .254 C2
Livingstone Rd WS3 . . . . .243 C1
Livingstone St
Chell Heath ST6 . . . . .42 B1
Leek ST13 . . . . .30 C1
Lizard La TF11 . . . . .220 A3
Llewellyn Roberts Way
TF9 . . . . .97 B1
Lloyd Dr WV4 . . . . .265 B1
Lloyd George Gr WS11 . . .210 B1
Lloyd Hill WV4 . . . . .265 B2
Lloyd Rd WV6 . . . . .255 B1
Lloyd Roberts Bldgs
WV4 . . . . .265 C4
Lloyd St Cannock WS11 . . .209 B1
Longton ST3 . . . . .283 C1
Stafford ST16 . . . . .155 C2
Wolv WV6 . . . . .255 C2
Lochalsh Gr WV11 . . . . . . .242 A1
Lochsong Cl ST7 . . . . .261 B2
Lock Keepers Cl WS11 . . .227 C1
Lock Rd ST19 . . . . .207 C4

Locke Way ST16 . . . . .156 A2
Lockerbie Cl ST13 . . . . . . .31 A3
Lockett St ST1 . . . . .57 B3
Locketts La ST3 . . . . .283 C2
Lockfield Cl DY8 . . . . .275 C1
Lockhart Dr B75 . . . . .258 B1
Lockington Ave ST2 . . . . . .58 B1
Lockley St ST1 . . . . .57 C3
Locks View DY8 . . . . .275 C1
Lockside WV5 . . . . .269 C4
Lockside Dr B77 . . . . .278 A2
Lockside View WS15 . . . . .196 C3
Lockwood Cl ST10 . . . . . . .62 A1
Lockwood Rd ST10 . . . . . . .77 A3
Lockwood St
Newcastle-u-L ST5 . . . . . .284 D3
Norton-in-t-M ST2 . . . . . . .43 A2
Lodge Barn Rd ST8 . . . . . .27 C3
Lodge Gr Aldridge WS9 . . .256 A3
Newcastle-u-L ST5 . . . . . . .56 B3
Lodge Hill DE13 . . . . .146 C2
Lodge La Alstonefield DE6 .35 A4
Cheslyn Hay WS11 . . . . . .226 B3
Eccleshall ST21 . . . . .115 C3
Ilam DE6 . . . . .50 B2
Kingswinford DY6 . . . . . . .275 C3
Longdon WS15 . . . . .212 B2
Woodseaves ST20 . . . . . . .151 C3
Yoxall DE13 . . . . .182 A4
Lodge Pk WV5 . . . . .267 B4
Lodge Rd
Burntwood WS7 . . . . .211 C1
Netherseal DE12 . . . . . . .219 C4
Rugeley WS15 . . . . .197 A3
Stoke-on-T ST4 . . . . .71 C4
Walsall WS4 . . . . .244 A1
Lodge View WV6 . . . . .226 B3
Loftus Cl WS7 . . . . .229 A3
Loftus St ST1 . . . . .282 A4
Loganbeck Gr ST3 . . . . . . .73 C3
Lohengrin Ct 1 DE13 . . . . .147 C1
Lomas St ST4 . . . . .57 A1
Lomax Cl WS13 . . . . .214 A1
Lomax Rd WS12 . . . . .210 A4
Lombard Gdns WS13 . . . . .231 A4
Lombard St WS13 . . . . . . .231 A4
Lombardy Gr
Burntwood WS7 . . . . .228 C4
Meir ST3 . . . . .74 A1
Lomita Cres B77 . . . . .261 B4
Lomond Cl B79 . . . . .249 C4
Lomond Gr ST10 . . . . .76 C3
Lomond Rd DY3 . . . . .266 B1
Lomond Wlk ST3 . . . . .88 C2
London Rd
Bridgemere CW5 . . . . .67 A3
Lichfield WS14 . . . . .231 B1
Newcastle-u-L, Chesterton
ST5 . . . . .55 C1
Newcastle-u-L, City General Hospl
ST5 . . . . .72 A3
Sutton Coldfield B75 . . . . .259 A2
Sutton Coldfield B75 . . . . .259 B1
Weeford WS14 . . . . .247 C2
Weston ST18 . . . . .138 B1
Woore, Dorrington CW3,
TF9 . . . . .83 B3
London St ST13 . . . . .30 C3
Long Acre WV8 . . . . .238 C1
Long Bridge Rd WS14 . . . .231 B3
Long Cl DY9 . . . . .281 C2
Long Croft WS12 . . . . .209 B2
Long Furrow WV8 . . . . . . .239 C1
Long La Alrewas DE13 . . . .200 C1
Alstonefield DE6 . . . . .35 A3
Great Wyrley WS6 . . . . . . .242 C3
Haughton ST18 . . . . .154 B1
Kidsgrove ST7 . . . . .26 C2
Long Mdw
Newcastle-u-L ST5 . . . . . . .71 B2
Stafford ST17 . . . . .174 C3
Long Meadow Dr DY3 . . . .266 A1
Long Mynd Cl WV11 . . . . .242 A1
Long Row Caverswall ST11 74 B2
Kidsgrove ST7 . . . . .26 A1
Long St Burton u T DE15 .185 C4
Wheaton Aston ST19 . . . .205 B3
Long Valley Rd ST8 . . . . . .16 B1
Longacres
Cannock WS12 . . . . .210 C3
Little Aston B74 . . . . .257 C2
Longboat La DY8 . . . . .275 C1
Longbow La DE13 . . . . . . .147 B1
Longbow Gr DE13 . . . . . . .147 B1
Longbridge Hayes Rd
ST5 . . . . .56 B4
Longbrook St ST3 . . . . .72 C1
Longclough Rd ST6 . . . . . . .40 B1
Longcroft La DE13 . . . . . . .182 A2
Longdon Ave WV4 . . . . . . .266 B3
Longdon Dr B74 . . . . .257 C2
Longfellow Cl DE14 . . . . . .166 B4
Longfellow Pl WS11 . . . . . .209 C2
Longfellow Rd
Burntwood WS7 . . . . .212 A1
Sedgley DY3 . . . . .271 A3
Longfellow Wlk B79 . . . . . .249 C1
Longfield Ave WS15 . . . . .119 C4
Longfield Cl B77 . . . . .250 C2
Longfield Dr B74 . . . . .257 B2
Longfield Rd ST4 . . . . .71 C4

Longford Prim Sch
WS11 . . . . .226 B4
Longford Rd
Cannock WS11 . . . . .226 B4
Newport TF10 . . . . .168 B1
Longford Wlk ST2 . . . . .58 A1
Longhedge La DE13 . . . . . .146 C3
Longhope Dr ST15 . . . . . . .119 C3
Longhurst Dr ST16 . . . . . . .156 B2
Longlake Ave WV6 . . . . . . .255 A2
Longlands Dr B77 . . . . . . .250 C2
Longlands La TF9 . . . . .97 B1
Longlands Pl WS15 . . . . . .160 C2
Longlands Prim Sch TF9 .97 B1
Longlands The WV5 . . . . . .270 A3
Longleat Dr DY1 . . . . .271 C1
Longleat Rd WS9 . . . . .245 A1
Longley Rd ST3 . . . . .73 B3
Longmead Rd DE13 . . . . . .166 B3
Longnor Craft Ctr SK17 13 B3
Longnor Pl ST2 . . . . .58 A1
Longport Rd ST6 . . . . .56 B4
Longport Sta ST6 . . . . .56 B4
Longsdon Cl ST5 . . . . .40 B1
Longsdon Gr ST3 . . . . .73 C2
Longshaw Ave ST5 . . . . . . .56 A4
Longshaw La ST10 . . . . . . .78 C4
Longshaw St ST6 . . . . .56 B4
Longshore St ST17 . . . . . . .174 B3
Longslow Cl TF9 . . . . .97 A1
Longslow Rd TF9 . . . . .97 A1
Longstaff Ave WS12 . . . . . .211 B2
Longstaff Croft WS13 . . . .213 C1
Longton Exchange ST3 . . .283 C2
Longton Hall Rd ST3 . . . . .72 C1
Longton High Sch ST3 . . . .73 C1
Longton Hospl ST3 . . . . . . .73 B1
Longton Rd
Barlaston ST12 . . . . .88 C1
Stone ST15 . . . . .105 B2
Trentham ST4 . . . . .88 C2
Longton Sta ST3 . . . . .283 B4
Longus Ind Est ST6 . . . . . .41 B2
Longview Cl ST3 . . . . .73 B3
Longwood Path B78 . . . . . .249 B1
Longwood Prim Sch
B78 . . . . .249 B1
Longwood Rd WS9 . . . . . . .256 A1
Lonsdale CE Prim Sch
ST21 . . . . .133 B3
Lonsdale Ct
Eccleshall ST21 . . . . .133 B4
Market Drayton TF9 . . . . . .97 B1
Lonsdale Rd
Burton u T DE14 . . . . . . .185 A4
Wolv WV3 . . . . .266 A4
Lonsdale St ST4 . . . . .72 A3
Loomer Rd ST5 . . . . .55 C3
Loomer Road Ind Est
ST5 . . . . .55 C3
Lord Cromwell Ct WS11 210 A3
Lord St Biddulph ST8 . . . . . .27 B4
Chell Heath ST6 . . . . .42 B1
Lords La DY7 . . . . .274 C1
Lordship La ST4 . . . . .72 B4
Lordshire Pl ST7 . . . . .26 C1
Lordsley Rd TF9 . . . . .100 A4
Lordswell Rd DE14 . . . . . . .165 C2
Lorien Cl ST13 . . . . .30 B2
Lorien Ct ST4 . . . . .72 A4
Loring Rd ST5 . . . . .56 A3
Lorne St ST1 . . . . .282 B3
Lorne Terr S ST5 . . . . .56 B3
Lorne St Burntwood WS7 .228 C4
Chell Heath ST6 . . . . .42 A1
Lorraine St ST7 . . . . .26 C1
Lorton B79 . . . . .249 B4
Lothersdale B77 . . . . .262 B4
Lothians Rd Walsall WS3 244 A3
Wolv WV6 . . . . .255 C3
Lotus B77 . . . . .250 C2
Lotus Ave ST8 . . . . .27 A3
Lotus Ct ST5 . . . . .105 A1
Lotus Dr WS11 . . . . .209 C3
Lotus Way ST6 . . . . .155 C3
Loughborough Wlk ST3 283 C1
Loughshaw B77 . . . . .251 B1
Louise Dr ST3 . . . . .72 C2
Louise St Chell Heath ST6 .42 A1
Sedgley DY3 . . . . .271 B2
Lount La DE13 . . . . .146 C1
Louvain Ave ST1 . . . . .57 A4
Lovage Gr ST2 . . . . .58 A2
Lovatt Ave ST5 . . . . .56 A2
Lovatt Cl DE13 . . . . .147 C1
Lovatt Pl WS11 . . . . .209 C3
Lovatt St Stafford ST16 . . .155 B3
Stoke-on-T ST4 . . . . .72 A4
Love La
Great Wyrley WS6 . . . . . . .227 A2
Rugeley WS15 . . . . .178 C1
Wolv WV6 . . . . .255 C1
Lovelace Cl ST17 . . . . .174 B4
Lovell B79 . . . . .249 C3
Lovell Dr ST16 . . . . .156 A3
Lovell Rd DE13 . . . . .182 A1
Loveridge Cl WV8 . . . . .238 C2
Lovers La TF9 . . . . .99 C2
Loveston Gr ST3 . . . . .283 D4
Lovett Cl ST5 . . . . .178 B1
Loveston Gr ST3 . . . . .283 D4
Low St WS6 . . . . .226 B2
Lowdham B77 . . . . .251 B1
Lowe Dr DY6 . . . . .275 C2
Lowe St ST4 . . . . .72 A4
Lowell Dr ST3 . . . . .73 C2
Lower Ash Rd ST7 . . . . . . .25 C1
Lower Bar TF10 . . . . .168 C2
Lower Bedford St ST4 . . . . .57 A1

Lower Bethesda St ST1 . .282 B2
Lower Bromstead La
TF10 . . . . .188 B4
Lower Brook St WS15 . . . .178 C1
Lower Bryan St ST1 . . . . . .282 B4
Lower Cres ST3 . . . . .73 B3
Lower Cross St ST3 . . . . . .283 C4
Lower Farm Prim Sch
WS3 . . . . .243 B3
Lower Foundry St ST1 . . . .282 B3
Lower Hadderidge 3
ST6 . . . . .56 C4
Lower High St
Mow Cop ST7 . . . . .26 B4
Stourbridge DY8 . . . . .279 C3
Tutbury DE13 . . . . .146 B4
Lower House La CV9 . . . . .262 C1
Lower La WS13 . . . . .212 B2
Lower Mayer St ST1 . . . . .282 C4
Lower Milehouse La ST5 . .55 C2
Lower Outwoods Rd
DE13 . . . . .165 C3
Lower Oxford Rd ST5 . . . . .56 C1
Lower Penkridge Rd
ST17 . . . . .175 B1
Lower Rd Ashley TF9 . . . . .100 A3
Cannock WS12 . . . . .210 B2
Gnosall ST20 . . . . .152 A3
Lower Sandford St
WS13 . . . . .231 A4
Lower Spring Rd 3 ST3 . .73 B1
Lower St 11 Burslem ST6 . .57 A4
Doveridge DE6 . . . . .127 A4
Newcastle-u-L ST5 . . . . . .284 B3
Wolv WV6 . . . . .255 C2
Lower Villiers St WV2 . . . .266 C4
Lower Way WS15 . . . . .197 B2
Lowercroft Way B74 . . . . .257 C3
Lowerpark B77 . . . . .250 B1
Loweswater Dr ST3 . . . . . .271 B2
Lowfield Dr ST5 . . . . .56 C3
Lowfield La ST20 . . . . .171 C3
Lowforce B77 . . . . .251 B1
Lowhurst Dr ST6 . . . . .42 A4
Lowland Rd WS12 . . . . . . .209 B3
Lowlands Ave WV6 . . . . . . .255 C3
Lowlands Ct WV6 . . . . .255 C3
Lowlands Rd ST6 . . . . .41 A2
Lowndes Cl ST4 . . . . .71 C3
Lowndes Rd DY8 . . . . .279 C3
Lowry Cl WV6 . . . . .254 C2
Lowther Pl ST13 . . . . .31 A3
Lowther St ST1 . . . . .282 A4
Lowthorpe Way ST2 . . . . . .58 C1
Loxley Hall Sch ST14 . . . .125 B3
Loxley La ST14 . . . . .125 B3
Loxley Pl ST3 . . . . .89 C4
Loxley Rd B75 . . . . .258 B2
Loynton Cl ST16 . . . . .155 A4
Loynton Sands ST20 . . . . .151 A3
Lucas St ST6 . . . . .56 C4
Lucepool La DE13 . . . . . . .182 B2
Lucerne Pl ST5 . . . . .70 C4
Lud La B79 . . . . .250 A3
Ludbrook Rd ST4 . . . . .73 A3
Ludford Cl ST5 . . . . .40 C1
Ludgate B79 . . . . .250 A3
Ludgate St DE13 . . . . .146 B3
Ludgrove Way 2 ST17 . . . .175 A4
Ludlow Cl WS11 . . . . .210 B1
Ludlow St ST1 . . . . .282 C3
Ludlow Way DY1 . . . . .271 C4
Ludstone Ave WV4 . . . . . . .265 B3
Ludwall Rd ST3 . . . . .73 C1
Lugano Cl ST5 . . . . .70 C3
Luke St ST6 . . . . .56 C4
Lukes Wlk WS13 . . . . .214 A1
Lukesland Ave ST4 . . . . . . .71 C3
Lullington Rd
Clifton Campville B79 . . . .218 C2
Edingale B79 . . . . .217 B2
Lulworth Gr ST6 . . . . .41 C3
Lulworth Rd WS7 . . . . . . .229 A4
Lulworth Wlk WV4 . . . . . . .265 B3
Lundy Rd ST3 . . . . .72 C2
Lune Cl 1 CW12 . . . . .6 A1
Lunns Croft WS13 . . . . . . .231 B4
Lutley Cl WV3 . . . . .265 C4
Lutley La DY7 . . . . .273 A4
Luttrell Rd B74 . . . . .258 A1
Luxton Cl B74 . . . . .257 B3
Lydford Pl ST3 . . . . .73 C2
Lydford Rd WS3 . . . . .243 A2
Lydgate Rd DY6 . . . . .275 C3
Lydia Croft B74 . . . . .257 C3
Lydia Dr ST1 . . . . .57 C3
Lydiates Cl DY3 . . . . .271 A4
Lyme Brook Pl ST4 . . . . . . .71 C2
Lyme Ct ST5 . . . . .284 C1
Lyme Dr ST4 . . . . .71 B3
Lyme Gr ST5 . . . . .56 B2
Lyme Rd ST3 . . . . .74 A1
Lyme Valley Rd ST5 . . . . . .284 C1
Lyme Wood Gr ST5 . . . . . .284 B1
Lymedale Small Firms Ctr
ST5 . . . . .55 C3
Lymer Rd WV10 . . . . .240 B1
Lymer's La ST18 . . . . .123 A1
Lymes Rd ST5 . . . . .70 A2
Lymevale Rd ST4 . . . . .71 C4
Lymewood Cl ST5 . . . . . . .284 B2
Lymington Rd
Burntwood WS7 . . . . .211 C1
Stafford ST16 . . . . .156 B2
Lyminster Gr ST2 . . . . .43 A1
Lymsey Croft DY8 . . . . . . .275 B2
Lyn Ave WS13 . . . . .213 C1
Lynam St ST4 . . . . .72 A4

Lynam Way CW3 .68 C4
Lynch The B78 .251 C1
Lyncroft WV7 .237 A3
Lyncroft House Sch
WS11 .226 C4
Lyndale B77 .261 C3
Lyndale Rd DY3 .266 A1
Lyndham Ave DE15 .166 C1
Lyndhurst Dr Biddulph ST8 27 A3
Brierley Hill DY8 .275 C1
Lyndhurst Gr ST15 .120 B3
Lyndhurst Rd
Cannock WS12 .210 C1
Wolv WV3 .266 A4
Lyndhurst St ST6 .56 C4
Lyndon Cl DY3 .266 C1
Lyndon Gr DY6 .275 A4
Lyne Ct DE14 .166 A2
Lyne Hill Ind Est ST19 .207 C4
Lyneham Cl B79 .250 B4
Lynehill La ST19 .207 C3
Lyneside Rd ST8 .27 A3
Lynfield Rd WS13 .213 C1
Lynmouth Cl ST8 .27 B3
Lynmouth Gr ST6 .41 C4
Lynn Ave ST7 .40 B4
Lynn La WS14 .246 B3
Lynn St ST3 .74 A3
Lynsey Cl ST7 .54 C4
Lynton Ave Stafford ST17 175 B4
Wolv WV6 .255 C3
Lynton Gr ST3 .89 C4
Lynwood Ave DY6 .275 A4
Lynwood Cl DE14 .184 C4
Lynwood Dr DY10 .281 B1
Lynwood Rd DE14 .184 C4
Lyric Cl ST17 .174 C3
Lysander Rd ST3 .90 A4
Lysander Way WS11 .209 C2
Lysways La WS15 .213 A4
Lytham B77 .251 B3
Lytham Cl DY8 .279 C1
Lytham Dr ST16 .156 B2
Lytham Gr WS3 .243 A2
Lytham Rd WV6 .254 B2
Lyttelton Rd DY8 .279 B3
Lytton Ave WV4 .265 C2
Lytton St ST4 .72 B4

M

Macadam Cl WS7 .229 A4
Macbeth Ho ST7 .40 B4
Macclesfield Rd
Congleton CW12 .6 A4
Leek ST13 .30 B4
Macclesfield St ST6 .42 A1
Macdonald Cres ST3 .74 A2
Mace St ST4 .71 C2
Macgregor Cres B77 .250 C2
Macgregor Tithe B79 .250 A3
Machin Cres ST5 .56 A4
Machin St ST6 .41 C2
Macintyre St ST6 .57 A4
Mackay Rd WS3 .243 B1
Mackenzie Cres ST10 .76 C1
Maclagan St ST4 .72 A3
Macrome Rd WV6 .255 C4
Madden Cl WS15 .196 C3
Maddock St Audley ST7 .39 B1
Burslem ST6 .56 C4
Madeira Ave WV8 .239 A1
Madeira Pl ST6 .41 B2
Madeley High Sch CW3 .68 C3
Madeley Rd 5 DY6 .275 C2
Madeley St
Newcastle-u-L ST5 .55 A1
Tunstall ST6 .41 B2
Madeley St N ST5 .55 A1
Madford Ret Pk ST16 .155 B2
Madison St ST6 .41 B2
Madox Cl B79 .249 C4
Madras Rd DE15 .167 B2
Madrona B77 .251 A2
Maer La
Market Drayton TF9 .97 B1
Standon ST21 .101 C3
Maerway La ST5,TF9 .84 B3
Maesfield Cl TF9 .112 A4
Maesfield Dr ST17 .155 B1
Mafeking St ST3 .283 B2
Magdalen Rd ST3 .88 C4
Magdalen Wlk ST3 .88 C4
Magenta Dr ST5 .55 C1
Magna Cl WS6 .226 C2
Magnolia B77 .251 A2
Magnolia Cl ST18 .135 A1
Magnolia Dr ST6 .42 C1
Magnolia Gr WV8 .239 A2
Magnolia Way 6 DY8 .275 C1
Magnus B77 .261 C3
Magnus St ST6 .56 C4
Magpie Cres 18 ST7 .26 A1
Maidendale Rd DY6 .275 A4
Maidensbridge Dr DY6 .275 B4
Maidensbridge Gdns
DY6 .270 A1
Maidensbridge Prim Sch
DY6 .270 A1
Maidensbridge Rd DY6 .270 A1
Maidstone Dr
Burntwood WS7 .229 B3
Kingswinford DY8 .275 C2
Maidstone Gr ST2 .58 B1
Main Rd Adbaston ST20 .131 B3
Armitage WS15 .197 B2
Betley CW2,CW3 .53 A3
Main Rd *continued*
Cheddleton ST9 .60 A4
Colwich ST18 .177 B4
Cotton ST10 .63 C2
Draycott in t C DE6 .144 B4
Edingale B79 .217 B3
Harlaston B79 .217 B1
Newton Regis B79 .236 B1
Norton in Hales TF9 .82 B1
Stafford ST17 .176 A4
Sudbury DE6 .128 C3
Sudbury, Aston DE6 .129 A2
Weston CW2 .37 B3
Wigginton B79 .234 A1
Main Rd Brereton
WS15 .197 A3
Main St Alrewas DE13 .201 A2
Anslow DE13 .165 B4
Barton-u-N DE13 .183 B1
Branston DE14 .184 C4
Burton u T, Stapenhill
DE15 .185 C4
Burton u T, Stretton DE13 .147 C1
Clifton Campville B79 .218 C1
Egginton DE65 .148 A3
Meir ST3 .74 A3
Netherseal DE12 .219 C4
Newton Solney DE15 .167 C4
Shenstone WS14 .246 C3
Shenstone, Stonnall WS9 .245 B2
Swadlincote DE11 .186 C3
Tatenhill DE13 .165 A1
Walton-on-T DE12 .184 B1
Whittington WS14 .232 C3
Yoxall DE13 .182 A1
Mainwaring Dr B75 .258 C1
Maitland B77 .250 C1
Maitland Gr ST4 .88 A3
Maitland Rd DY1 .271 C1
Major St WV2 .266 C4
Majors Barn ST10 .76 B1
Maker La DE13 .162 B1
Malam St ST1 .282 B4
Malcolm Cl ST2 .43 A1
Malcolm Ct ST2 .58 B3
Malcolm Dr ST2 .58 B3
Malcolm Rd ST17 .174 B3
Malham Rd
Newcastle-u-L ST5 .55 C1
Tamworth B77 .251 B1
Malhamdale Rd CW12 .6 A3
Malins Rd WV4 .266 C3
Malkin Way ST6 .56 C3
Mallard Ave ST17 .175 A4
Mallard Cl
Uttoxeter ST14 .126 B3
Walsall WS3 .244 A3
Mallard Croft 5 WS13 .231 B4
Mallard Way
Chell Heath ST6 .42 B2
Penkridge ST19 .208 A3
Mallens Croft ST14 .125 B4
Mallicot Cl WS13 .214 B1
Mallorie Rd ST6 .42 B2
Mallory Cl ST15 .120 A3
Mallory Cres WS3 .243 B1
Mallory Rd WV6 .254 C2
Mallory Way ST10 .76 C2
Mallow Cl ST21 .133 C3
Mallowdale Cl ST4 .88 B3
Malpas Wlk ST6 .41 B4
Malpass Gdns WV8 .238 C2
Malt House Rd WS15 .212 A3
Malt La ST3 .283 D2
Malt Mill La ST16 .155 C2
Malthouse La
Barlaston ST12 .88 C1
Bradley ST18 .173 B1
Caverswall ST3 .74 B4
Church Eaton ST20 .190 A4
Wheaton Aston ST19 .205 B3
Wolv WV6 .255 C3
Malthouse Rd ST2 .58 A2
Maltings Ind Est DE14 .166 C3
Maltings The
Aldridge WS9 .256 B3
Brewood WV9 .224 A1
Burton u T DE15 .167 A1
Uttoxeter ST14 .126 B4
Malton Gr ST6 .41 B3
Malvern Ave
Burton u T DE15 .167 A1
Newcastle-u-L ST5 .54 C1
Malvern Cl Stafford ST17 156 A1
Trentham ST4 .88 A4
Malvern Ct B74 .257 C1
Malvern Dr Aldridge WS9 256 B4
Rugeley WS15 .178 B1
Malvern St DE15 .166 C1
Malvern View Rd DY3 .271 B2
Mamble Rd DY8 .279 C3
Manchester Ct ST14 .110 C1
Mancroft Cl DY6 .275 A4
Mancroft Gdns WV6 .255 B3
Mancroft Rd WV6 .255 B3
Mandela Way ST3 .283 D2
Manderley Cl DY3 .266 B1
Manderville Gdns DY6 .275 B3
Mandeville Cl ST6 .42 B2
Manifold CE Prim Sch
SK17 .23 A1
Manifold Cl
Burntwood WS7 .229 B3
Newcastle-u-L ST5 .55 A1
Waterhouses ST10 .48 C1
Manifold Dr ST10 .76 C1
Manifold Rd ST11 .90 C4
Manifold Wlk ST2 .58 B1
Manley Rd WS13 .214 B1
Manlove St WV3 .266 A4
Mann St ST3 .74 B2
Mannin Cl ST3 .74 A2
Manor Ave
Cannock WS11 .209 B1
Great Wyrley WS6 .227 A2
Manor Cl Codsall WV8 .239 A2
Colwich ST18 .158 A1
Congleton CW12 .6 A1
Draycott in t M ST11 .91 B3
Harlaston B79 .217 B1
Market Drayton TF9 .97 B1
Swadlincote DE15 .186 A3
Uttoxeter ST14 .126 A4
Weston ST18 .138 B1
Wolv WV4 .265 C2
Manor Court Dr WS15 .198 A2
Manor Cres DE15 .186 A3
Manor Croft
Burton u T DE14 .166 C1
Tatenhill DE13 .184 A4
Manor Ct DE13 .183 B1
Manor Ct St ST4 .71 C3
Manor Dr
Burton u T DE14 .166 C1
Netherseal DE12 .219 C3
Sedgley DY3 .271 A2
Shareshill WV10 .225 B1
Swindon DY3 .269 C1
Manor Farm Cres ST17 .174 C3
Manor Farm Rd ST18 .177 B4
Manor Fields DE13 .200 C2
Manor Fold WV8 .238 B1
Manor Gdns
Albrighton WV7 .237 A3
Market Drayton TF9 .97 B1
Wombourne WV5 .270 A4
Manor Glade ST5 .85 A4
Manor Gn ST17 .174 B4
Manor Hill Fst Sch
ST15 .119 C4
Manor Ho WV6 .255 B3
Manor House Pk WV8 .239 A2
Manor La Harlaston B79 .217 B1
Stourbridge DY8 .279 B2
Wigginton B79 .233 C2
Manor Pk DY6 .275 B3
Manor Prim Sch
Aldridge B74 .257 A1
Drayton Bassett B78 .260 C3
Manor Rd Aldridge B74 .257 A1
Edgmond TF10 .168 A2
Gnosall ST20 .171 C4
King's Bromley DE13 .199 B3
Kingswinford DY8 .275 C1
Madeley CW3 .68 C2
Mow Cop ST7 .26 B4
Swadlincote DE15 .186 A3
Tamworth B77 .250 B2
Tamworth, Mile Oak B78 .249 B1
Uttoxeter ST14 .126 A4
Whitmore ST5 .85 A4
Wolv WV4 .265 C2
Manor Rise
Burntwood WS7 .229 A3
Lichfield WS14 .231 B4
Stone ST15 .119 C4
Manor Sq ST17 .174 B4
Manor St Fenton ST4 .72 C4
Wolv WV6 .255 B3
Manor Trad Est DE14 .166 C2
Manor Way WS15 .179 A3
Manor Wlk DE13 .199 A3
Manorfield Cl ST19 .207 C4
Manorial Rd B75 .258 C2
Mansard Cl WV3 .265 C4
Manse Cl ST3 .283 C4
Mansell Cl ST16 .155 B1
Mansfield Cl
Newcastle-u-L ST5 .71 B1
Tamworth B79 .249 C3
Mansfield Dr ST8 .27 A3
Mansion Cl ST10 .76 C1
Mansion Ct WV5 .269 B3
Mansion Dr WS7 .229 B2
Manston Dr WV6 .254 C3
Manston Hill ST19 .207 C4
Manston View B79 .250 B4
Manta Rd B77 .261 B3
Manton Cl
7 Burton u T DE13 .147 C1
Swadlincote DE11 .186 C3
Maple Ave
Newcastle-u-L ST5 .40 C1
Talke ST7 .40 B4
Maple Cl Burntwood WS7 228 C4
Cheadle ST10 .76 C1
Kinver DY7 .278 A3
Norton-in-t-M ST6 .43 A3
Stourbridge DY8 .279 B1
Swynnerton ST15 .118 C3
Maple Cres
Cannock WS11 .209 B1
Forsbrook ST11 .91 A3
Maple Ct Lichfield WS14 .231 B3
Stafford ST17 .155 B1
Maple Dr Ashley TF9 .99 B3
Huntington WS12 .209 B4
Sedgley DY3 .271 A1
Seighford ST18 .154 B1
Maple Gdns ST15 .120 A3
Maple Gr
Burton u T DE15 .185 C3
Kingswinford DY6 .275 C3
Lichfield WS14 .231 C4
Stafford ST17 .174 C4
Wolv WV3 .255 B1
Maple Hayes Sch for
Dyslexics WS13 .230 B4
Maple Ho B74 .257 A3
Maple Pl ST3 .74 A1
Maple Rd Walsall WS3 .243 C1
Wolv WV3 .265 C4
Maple Rise B77 .251 A2
Maple St WS3 .243 B1
Maple Way
Branston DE14 .184 C4
Burton u T DE14 .185 A4
Maple Wood ST17 .175 B3
Mapledene Cl 8 ST17 .175 B3
Maplehurst Cl ST6 .57 A4
Marcel Cl ST4 .72 A1
March Banks WS15 .178 B1
March Cl WS6 .226 B1
March La Dilhorne ST9 .60 A2
Whitgreave ST18 .135 C3
March Rd ST3 .283 B4
March Way WS9 .245 B1
Marchant Rd WV6 .255 C1
Marchington Ind Est
ST14 .143 C4
Marchwood Ct ST4 .71 C3
Marcia Rice Ct WS15 .161 A3
Marconi Gate ST18 .156 B3
Marconi Pl WS12 .210 B4
Marcus Ind Est ST1 .57 C2
Mardale Cl CW12 .6 A3
Maree Gr WV11 .242 A1
Margam Cres WS3 .242 C1
Margam Terr WS3 .242 C1
Margam Way WS3 .242 C1
Margaret Ave ST4 .87 C4
Margaret Dr WS11 .209 C3
Margaret St Hanley ST1 .57 C2
10 Stone ST15 .104 C1
Margery Ave ST7 .25 C4
Margill Cl ST1 .282 A2
Marholm Cl WV9 .239 C1
Maries Way ST5 .55 B1
Marigold Cl WS11 .210 B2
Marina Cres WS12 .210 A3
Marina Rd ST4 .71 C2
Marina Way Burslem ST1 .57 A2
Newcastle-u-L ST1 .56 C2
Marine Cres DY8 .275 C1
Marine Gdns DY8 .275 C1
Mariner B79 .249 C3
Market Drayton Cottage
Hospl TF9 .112 B4
Market Drayton Inf Sch
TF9 .97 B1
Market Drayton Jun Sch
TF9 .112 A4
Market Drayton Rd TF9 .99 B2
Market Hall DE14 .166 C1
Market Hall St WS11 .209 C1
Market La Hanley ST1 .282 B3
Lower Penn WV4 .264 C3
Newcastle-u-L ST5 .284 B3
Wall WS14 .230 C1
Market Mews TF10 .168 C2
Market Pl
Abbots Bromley WS15 .161 A3
Brewood ST19 .223 B3
Burslem ST6 .56 C4
Burton u T DE14 .166 C1
12 Cannock WS11 .209 C1
Cheadle ST10 .76 B2
Hartington SK17 .24 B3
8 Leek ST13 .30 C3
Longnor SK17 .13 A3
Tamworth B79 .250 A2
Uttoxeter ST14 .126 B4
Walsall WS3 .243 A1
Market Sq Hanley ST1 .282 B3
Rugeley WS15 .178 C1
10 Stafford ST16 .155 C2
Market Sq Arc ST1 .282 B3
Market St Cannock WS12 .210 B3
Kidsgrove ST7 .26 A1
Kingswinford DY6 .275 B3
Leek ST13 .30 C3
Lichfield WS13 .231 A4
Longton ST3 .283 C3
Penkridge ST19 .192 C1
Rugeley WS15 .178 C1
Stafford ST16 .155 C2
Tamworth B79 .250 A2
Uttoxeter ST14 .126 B4
Marketfields ST21 .133 C4
Markham Croft WV9 .240 A1
Markham Dr DY6 .275 C2
Marklew Cl WS8 .245 A3
Marklin Ave WV10 .240 B1
Marks Wlk WS13 .214 A1
Marlborough Ave ST16 .156 B2
Marlborough Cl
Colwich ST18 .158 B1
Endon ST9 .43 C4
Sutton Coldfield B74 .257 C3
Marlborough Cres DE15 186 A4
Marlborough Ct
Lichfield WS13 .231 A4
Sutton Coldfield B74 .257 C1
Marlborough Gdns
Kingswinford DY8 .275 B1
Wolv WV6 .255 C2
Marlborough Ind Est
WV2 .266 B4
Marlborough Rd
Longton ST3 .283 C4
Sedgley DY3 .271 C3
Stone ST15 .119 C3
Marlborough St
Fenton ST4 .72 B3
Marlborough St *continued*
Walsall WS3 .243 A1
Marlborough Way
Tamworth B77 .250 C1
Uttoxeter ST14 .110 C1
Marlbrook Dr WV4 .266 A3
Marlbrook La WV6 .253 A1
Marlburn Way WV5 .269 C3
Marldon Pl ST6 .41 B3
Marley Mount Cres TF9 .97 B1
Marlin B77 .261 B3
Marlow Cl ST3 .73 B3
Marlow Dr DE14 .185 A4
Marlow Rd Longton ST3 .73 B3
Tamworth B77 .250 B3
Marlowe Rd ST17 .174 A4
Marlpit La Denstone ST14 .95 B3
Ellastone DE6 .80 A2
Stone ST15 .105 C3
Sutton Coldfield B75 .258 B2
Marlpool Dr WS3 .244 A1
Marmion St B79 .250 A3
Marnel Dr WV3 .265 C4
Marney Wlk ST6 .42 A1
Marquis Dr WS12,WS15 .195 B2
Marquis Drive Visitor Ctr*
WS15 .195 B2
Marrick B77 .251 B1
Marriott St ST4 .73 A3
Mars St ST6 .42 B1
Marsden St ST1 .282 C3
Marsett B77 .262 B4
Marsh Ave Chell Heath ST6 42 A1
Kidsgrove ST7 .26 C1
Newcastle-u-L ST5 .56 B3
Marsh Cl ST9 .59 A2
Marsh Cres DY8 .275 B2
Marsh Ct ST16 .155 B3
Marsh Gr Biddulph ST8 .16 B2
Swindon DY3 .269 C1
Marsh Green Cl ST8 .16 B1
Marsh Green Rd ST8 .16 B1
Marsh La
Cheswardine TF9 .130 A4
Ellenhall ST21 .134 A1
Lichfield WS14 .231 B3
Penkridge ST19 .192 C1
Stanton DE6 .80 B4
Whittington WS14 .232 A3
Wolv WV10 .240 A1
Marsh Lane Par WV10 .240 B1
Marsh Par ST5 .284 C3
Marsh Prim Sch ST11 .91 A3
Marsh St ST16 .155 B3
Marsh St N ST1 .282 B3
Marsh St S ST1 .282 B2
Marsh View ST3 .90 A3
Marsh Way ST5 .56 B3
Marshall Ave ST6 .43 A4
Marshall Cl WS9 .256 A2
Marshall Gr CW12 .16 A4
Marshall St Burslem ST6 .41 C1
Tamworth B77 .250 C3
Marshalls Ind Est WV2 .266 B4
Marshbrook Fst Sch
ST19 .192 C1
Marshfield La ST8 .16 B1
Marshland Gr ST6 .42 A4
Marshlands Sch ST17 .175 B3
Marshwood Cl 2 WS11 210 A1
Marsland Cl ST16 .155 A2
Marsland Rd ST16 .155 A2
Marston Cl
Stourbridge DY8 .279 B2
Wheaton Aston ST19 .205 B3
Marston Croft ST19 .205 B3
Marston Ct ST16 .155 B3
Marston Dr ST16 .155 B3
Marston Gr ST1 .57 B4
Marston Ind Est WV2 .266 B4
Marston La Hatton DE65 .146 B4
Marston ST18 .136 C1
Rolleston DE13 .147 A2
Marston Old La DE65 .146 B4
Marston Rd
Cannock WS12 .209 C3
Marston on D DE65 .147 A4
Stafford ST16 .155 C3
Wheaton Aston ST19 .205 A4
Wolv WV2 .266 B4
Marston Rise DE15 .185 C4
Marston Road Trad Pk
ST16 .155 C3
Marsworth Way ST16 .136 B1
Martham Dr WV6 .255 A1
Martin Croft WS13 .214 A1
Martin Dale TF9 .99 B3
Martin Dr ST16 .155 B2
Martin St Hanley ST6 .57 A4
Stafford ST16 .155 C2
Wolv WV4 .266 C3
Martin's La DE13 .145 A2
Martindale
Cannock WS11 .210 A1
Stafford ST17 .175 B3
Martindale Cl ST3 .89 C4
Martindale Trad Est
WS11 .210 A1
Martins Hill CW12 .6 B1
Martins Way ST18 .158 B4
Martinslow La ST10,ST13 .48 C2
Martley Rd WS4 .244 B1
Martlin La WS15 .179 A3
Marton Ave WS7 .229 A4
Marwood Croft B74 .257 A1

Mary Howard CE Prim Sch
B79 ....217 B3
Mary Rand Cl ST17 .....174 B4
Mary Rose Cl ST2 ....58 A2
Mary St WS12 ....210 A4
Marychurch CE Prim Sch
ST2 ....58 A2
Marychurch Rd ST2 ......58 A2
Maryfield Wlk ST4 ....71 C4
Maryhill ST7 ....26 A2
Maryhill High Sch ST7 ...26 A2
Maryhill Prim Sch ST7 ...26 A2
Marysgate ST19 ....223 B4
Maryvale Ct WS14 ......231 B4
Masefield Cl
Burntwood WS7 ....212 A1
Cheadle ST10 ....76 B3
Lichfield WS14 ....231 A3
Masefield Cres DE14 ...166 B4
Masefield Dr B79 ......250 A4
Masefield Gr WS11 .....209 C2
Masefield Rd
Essington WV10 ....241 A1
Longton ST3 ....73 A1
Sedgley DY3 ....271 A2
Mason Cres WV4 ....265 C3
Mason Dr ST8 ....27 A4
Mason St Fenton ST4 ....72 C3
Wolv WV2 ....266 B4
Mason's Pl TF10 ....168 C3
Masons Lawn ST20 .....171 B3
Masterson St ST4 ....72 B3
Mathews Wlk ST1 ......282 C3
Matlock Cl WS3 ....243 B2
Matlock Dr WS11 ......210 A2
Matlock Pl ST5 ....55 A1
Matlock Rd WS3 ....243 B2
Matlock St ST1 ....282 B1
Matthews Pl CW12 ....6 A1
Matthews Rd ST17 .....174 B4
Matthews Wlk WS13 ...214 A1
Maud St ST4 ....72 C4
Maunders Rd ST2 ....43 A1
Maureen Ave ST6 ....41 B3
Maureen Gr ST5 ....56 B2
Mavesyn Cl WS15 ......198 A4
Mavis Rd WS12 ....210 A4
Mavor Ave WS7 ....211 B1
Mawdesley St ST6 ....57 A3
Mawgan Dr WS14 ......231 B3
Mawson Dr ST4 ....57 B1
Maxstoke Cl
Tamworth B77 ....261 B2
Walsall WS3 ....243 A2
Maxtock Ave WS13 ....231 A3
Maxton Way ST3 ....74 A1
Maxwell St WS14 ......231 B4
Maxwell Pl ST4 ....71 C4
Maxwell Rd
Congleton CW12 ....16 A4
Wolv WV2 ....266 B4
May Ave Newcastle-u-L ST5 56 B2
Tunstall ST6 ....41 C2
May Bank Inf Sch ST5 ...56 B2
May Cl WS7 ....211 C1
May Pl Longton ST4 ....283 B5
Newcastle-u-L ST5 .....56 B1
May St Chell Heath ST6 ..42 A1
Newcastle-u-L ST5 .....55 B1
Mayall Dr ST5 ....258 B2
Mayama Rd B78 ....260 C4
Maybank WS15 ....196 C4
Maybank Cl WS14 .....231 C4
Maybrook Ind Est WS8 .244 C3
Maybrook Rd WS8 .....244 C3
Maybury Wlk WV8 .....238 C2
Maybury Way ST2 ....43 A1
Maybush Gdns WV10 ..240 B1
Maycroft Cl WS12 .....209 C4
Mayer Ave ST5 ....284 B4
Mayer Bank ⑥ ST6 .....57 A4
Mayer St ST1 ....282 C3
Mayfair DE11 ....186 C3
Mayfair Ave ST10 ....62 A4
Mayfair Cl WV7 ....237 A3
Mayfair Dr
Drayton Bassett B78 ..261 A4
Kingswinford DY6 .....275 B4
Mayfair Gdns
⑱ Tunstall ST6 ....41 B2
Wolv WV3 ....255 B1
Mayfair Gr ST9 ....43 C4
Mayfield B77 ....262 B4
Mayfield Ave Hanley ST1 .57 C3
Mayfield DE6 ....81 B4
Newcastle-u-L ST5 ....284 A4
Penkridge ST19 ....207 C4
Mayfield Cl ST13 ....30 C3
Mayfield Cres ST1 ......57 C2
Mayfield Dr
Blythe Bridge ST11 .....90 B4
Burton u T DE15 ......186 A4
Mayfield Pl ST5 ....56 B2
Mayfield Pl E ST4 ....71 C3
Mayfield Pl W ST4 ......71 C3
Mayfield Rd
Albrighton WV7 ....237 A3
Biddulph ST8 ....27 B3
Burton u T DE15 ......167 A2
Stafford ST17 ....156 B1
Mayfield Terr DE6 ......81 B3
Mayfields Dr WS8 .....228 A1
Mayflower Dr WS15 ...178 B1
Maygrove Rd DY6 .....275 B4
Maylea Cres ST6 ....57 B4

Maynard Ave DY8 .....279 B2
Maynards Croft TF10 ..169 A2
Mayne St ST4 ....71 C1
Mayneford Pl ST4 ....71 C1
Mayock Cres ST16 .....155 A1
Mayou Ct WS3 ....244 A2
Maypole Cl WV5 ......270 A3
Maypole Dr DY8 ......279 C3
Maypole St WV5 ......270 A4
Mays Wlk DE13 ....200 C2
Mayswood Dr WV6 ...254 C1
Maythorn Gdns
Codsall WV8 ....239 A2
Wolv WV6 ....255 B2
Maythorne Rd ST3 ......73 A1
Maywood Cl DY6 .....275 A3
McAdam Cl DE15 .....167 A1
McBean Rd WV5 ....255 C2
McGeough Wlk WS11 ..210 A3
McGhie St WS12 ......210 A3
McGough St ⑦ ST6 ....41 B2
Mcgowan Ho ST7 ....40 B4
Mckellin Cl ST17 ....39 C1
McKie Way WS15 .....196 C3
McKinley St ST6 ....41 B2
Mclean Rd WV10 .....240 B1
Mead Ave ST7 ....25 C4
Mead Cl WS9 ....256 A3
Mead Cres DE15 ......186 A3
Mead The Sedgley DY3 .271 A4
Trentham ST4 ....88 A4
Mead Wlk DE15 ....186 A3
Meadfoot Dr DY6 .....275 A4
Meadlands The WV5 ..269 C3
Meadow Ave
Cheddleton ST9 ....60 A3
⑥ Longton ST3 ....73 B1
Newcastle-u-L ST5 .....56 A2
Weston CW2 ....37 A3
Meadow Bank Wlk
ST16 ....155 B4
Meadow Cl Aldridge B74 256 C1
Blythe Bridge ST11 .....90 C3
Eccleshall ST21 ......133 C4
Forsbrook ST11 ....91 A4
Gnosall ST20 ....171 C4
Leek ST13 ....31 A3
Market Drayton TF9 ....97 A1
Penkridge ST19 ....207 C4
Wheaton Aston ST19 ..205 A3
Meadow Croft
Hagley DY9 ....281 B4
Huntington WS12 .....209 B2
Perton WV6 ....254 B2
Streethay WS13 ......215 A1
Meadow Dr Cheadle ST10 76 B2
Haughton ST18 ......172 C3
Longton ST3 ....89 A4
Meadow Glade WS18 ..158 B4
Meadow Gr WS6 .....227 A1
Meadow Hill Dr ⑥
WS11 ....210 A2
Meadow La
Acton Trussell ST17 ..193 A4
Blythe Bridge ST11 ...106 C4
Brewood WV10 ......240 B3
Burton u T DE13 .....167 A4
Colwich ST18 ....177 B4
Millmeece ST21 .....117 C4
Newcastle-u-L ST5 .....56 A2
Roston DE6 ....96 B4
Seighford ST18 ......154 C1
Swadlincote DE11 ....186 C3
Trentham ST4 ....88 A4
Wombourne WV5 ....270 A4
Yoxall DE13 ....200 A4
Meadow Lark Cl WS12 .210 A4
Meadow Pk B79 ......249 C3
Meadow Pl ST3 ....74 A1
Meadow Rd
Albrighton WV7 ....237 A3
Aldridge WS9 ....256 A2
Barlaston ST12 ....88 B1
Burton u T DE14 .....166 C2
Chell Heath ST6 ....42 B3
Endon ST6 ....43 A3
Newport TF10 ....169 A2
Stafford ST17 ....174 C4
Tamworth B78 ....249 C2
Wolv WV3 ....265 B4
Meadow Ridge ST17 ..175 B4
Meadow Rise DE13 ...183 C1
Meadow Side ST8 ......27 A3
Meadow St
Newcastle-u-L ST5 .....55 C3
Norton-in-t-M ST2 .....43 A4
Tamworth B77 ....250 B2
Meadow The ST9 ....43 C4
Meadow Vale WV8 ...239 A1
Meadow View
Burntwood WS7 .....229 A3
Doveridge DE6 ....127 B4
Rolleston ST18 ......147 B2
Sedgley DY3 ....266 B1
Meadow View Cl TF10 .169 A2
Meadow View Rd
Newport TF10 ....169 A2
Swadlincote DE11 ....186 C3
Meadow View Terr
WV6 ....255 C2
Meadow Way
Armitage WS15 ......198 A4
Cannock WS12 ......210 B1
Codsall WV8 ....238 C1

Meadow Way continued
Kingswinford DY8 ....275 B1
Lawton-gate ST7 ......25 A3
Stone ST15 ....119 C3
Upper Tean ST10 ......92 B2
Whitmore ST5 ....85 B3
Meadowbank Ave ST18 .138 B1
Meadowbank Grange
WS6 ....226 C2
Meadowbrook Ct ④
ST15 ....120 B3
Meadowbrook Gdns
WV8 ....239 A2
Meadowbrook Rd WS13 214 A2
Meadowcroft Ave ST3 ..90 B4
Meadowcroft Gdns
ST19 ....205 B3
Meadowfields Cl DY8 ..275 C1
Meadowhill Dr ① DY8 .275 C1
Meadowlands ST7 .....244 B1
Meadowpark Rd DY8 ..279 B4
Meadows Gr WV8 .....239 A2
Meadows Rd ST7 ......25 C1
Meadows Sch ST8 ......27 B3
Meadows The
Brewood ST19 ....223 B3
Hilderstone ST15 ....106 B1
Kingstone ST14 .....141 B4
Rugeley WS15 ......197 A3
Salt ST18 ....137 C2
Uttoxeter ST14 .....111 A1
Meadowside Ashley TF9 99 C3
Blythe Bridge ST11 ....91 A1
Mayfield DE6 ....81 B3
Trentham ST4 ....88 A4
Meadowside Ave ST7 ..39 A1
Meadowside Dr DE14 ..166 C2
Meadowside La ST7 ....26 A4
Meadowside Rd B74 ..257 C2
Meadowsweet Way
WS12 ....210 C2
Meadowview
Norton-in-t-M ST6 .....42 C2
Swynnerton ST15 ....118 C3
Meadway Cl WS12 ....210 B2
Meadway Dr ST17 ....175 B3
Meadway St WS7 .....229 A3
Meadway The WV6 ...255 A3
Meaford Ave ST15 ...104 C1
Meaford Dr ST3 ....72 C2
Meaford Rd ST12,ST15 104 B3
Meakin Ave ST5 ....71 A2
Meakin Cl Cheadle ST10 76 B1
Congleton CW12 ....6 A1
Stone ST15 ....120 B3
Meakin Gr ST16 .....155 A3
Meakin Ho ST5 ......104 C1
Mear Greaves La DE15 .167 A2
Mear's La WS15 .....198 C4
Mease Ave WS7 .....229 B3
Mease La B79 ....218 A1
Mease The DE65 ....147 C4
Meddins Cl DY7 .....278 A2
Meddins La DY7 .....277 C2
Meddins Rise DY7 ...277 C2
Medina B77 ....250 C1
Medina Cl WV10 ....240 C2
Medina Way
Kidsgrove ST7 ....26 A1
Kingswinford DY6 ...275 B3
Medway B77 ....250 B1
Medway Dr ST8 ....16 B1
Medway Pl ST5 ....71 A2
Medway Rd WS8 ....228 B1
Medway Wlk
Brownhills WS8 .....228 B1
Chell Heath ST6 ......42 A2
Meece Rd
Millmeece ST15 ....118 B3
Swynnerton ST15 ...118 C3
Meerash La WS7 .....229 B2
Meerbrook Cl ST4 .....88 B3
Meerbrook Rd ST13 ...19 B1
Meerbrook YH★ ST13 .19 C3
Meere Cl ST6 ....42 C2
Meeson Ct WV7 .....237 A3
Meg La WS7 ....212 A1
Megacre ST7 ....40 A1
Meigh Rd ST9 ....59 A2
Meigh St ST1 ....282 C3
Meiklejohn Pl ST6 .....42 A1
Meir Heath Prim Sch
ST3 ....90 A2
Meir Prim Sch ST3 .....74 A1
Meir Rd ST3 ....73 C1
Meir St ST6 ....41 C2
Meir View ST3 ....74 A1
Meirhay Rd ST3 ....73 B1
Melbourne Ave ST15 ..167 B2
Melbourne Cl DY6 ....275 C1
Melbourne Cres
Cannock WS12 ......210 C1
Stafford ST16 ....156 A3
Melbourne Rd WS12 ..210 C1
Melbourne St ST3 ....73 B3
Melbury Way ① WS11 .209 C1
Melchester Gr ST3 ....73 C1
Melchester Wlk ②
WS11 ....209 C1
Melfont St ST6 ....41 C2
Melford B79 ....249 C3
Melford Cl DY3 .....266 B1
Melford Grange WS7 ..211 C1
Melford Rise WS7 ....211 B1
Meliden Way ST4 ......71 C3
Mellard St Audley ST7 ..39 B1
Newcastle-u-L ST5 ...284 A4

Mellor Dr
Sutton Coldfield B74 .257 C2
Uttoxeter ST14 ......111 A1
Mellor Rd DE14 .....185 A4
Mellor St ST7 ....26 C1
Mellors Bank ST7 .....26 B3
Mellow La ST10,ST13 ...47 C3
Mellowdew Rd DY8 ..275 B2
Mellwaters B77 ......262 B4
Melmerby B77 ....262 B4
Melrose Ave
Blythe Bridge ST3 .....90 A2
Hanley ST1 ....57 B4
Newcastle-u-L ST5 ....71 A3
Stafford ST17 ....174 A4
Stone ST15 ....120 B3
Melrose Cres TF9 ....112 A4
Melrose Dr
Cannock WS12 ......209 C4
Perton WV6 ....254 C2
Melrose Pl ST13 ......30 A3
Melstone Ave ST6 .....41 C2
Melville Ct ST5 ....71 B1
Melville Rd ST3 ....73 C1
Melville St ST7 ....57 C2
Melvyn Cres ST6 ......56 B4
Menai Dr ST8 ....27 B3
Menai Gr ST3 ....283 C5
Mendip Ave ST17 ....175 C3
Mendip Cl Sedgley DY3 271 B2
Wolv WV2 ....266 C4
Mendip Gn ST2 ....43 A1
Mendip Pl ST5 ....55 C2
Mendip Rd WS12 ....195 A1
Mendip Way B77 ....251 A1
Mentone Cres TF10 ..168 A2
Menzies Ho ⑥ ST3 ....89 C4
Meole Ho WS4 ......244 B1
Meon Gr WV6 ....254 C2
Mercer Ave ST15 ....120 B4
Mercer St ST3 ....73 A1
Merchant Cl WV6 ....253 B2
Merchants Way ST15 ..256 A4
Mercia Cl Hatton DE65 146 B4
Tamworth B79 ......249 C4
Mercia Cres ST6 ......57 A3
Mercia Dr WV6 .....254 C2
Mercian Ct
⑥ Lichfield WS14 ...231 B4
Market Drayton TF9 ...97 B1
Mercian Pk B77 .....251 A2
Mercian Way
Tamworth B77 ......251 A2
Wheaton Aston ST19 .206 A4
Mercury Ct B77 .....251 A2
Mercury Pl ST6 ....42 B1
Mercury Rd WS11 ...210 A3
Mere Cl TF10 ....168 C2
Mere Croft WS11 ....227 C2
Mere Dr B75 ....258 A1
Mere Green Cl B75 ..258 B1
Mere Green Comb Sch
B75 ....258 A1
Mere La DY7 ....273 B3
Mere Oak Rd WV6 ..254 C3
Mere Pool Rd B75 ..258 C1
Mere Rd Stourbridge DY8 279 C2
Weston CW2 ....37 A3
Mere Rise ST7 ....132 B4
Meredith Cl DE14 ...166 A4
Meredith Rd DY3 ....271 A3
Merelake Rd ST7 .....40 A4
Meremore Dr ST5 .....40 B1
Merevale Ave ST2 .....58 A1
Merganser B77 ......262 A3
Meriden Ave ST3 ....279 B3
Meriden Cl
Cannock WS11 ......226 A4
Stourbridge DY8 ....279 B3
Meriden Rd
Newcastle-u-L ST5 ....71 B1
Wolv WV10 ....240 A1
Merino Cl ST3 ....89 B4
Merlin Cl Cannock WS11 209 B1
Chell Heath ST6 ......42 A4
Tamworth B77 ......262 A3
Uttoxeter ST14 .....126 B3
Merlin Cres DE14 ...184 C4
Merlin Gn CW3 ....68 C3
Merlin Way Kidsgrove ST7 26 B2
Whittington WS14 ..232 C3
Merrial St ST5 ......284 B3
Merrick St ST1 .....282 C4
Merridale Ave WV3 ..255 C1
Merridale Ct WV3 ...255 C1
Merridale Rd WV3 ..255 C1
Merridale St W WV3 .266 A4
Merrill Cl WS6 ......226 A1
Merrion Dr ST5 ....42 A2
Merrivale Rd ST17 ..174 C4
Merry Rd ST17 ......174 C4
Merrydale Rd DE15 ..186 A4
Merryfield Rd DY1 ..271 C1
Merryfields Sch ST5 ...56 A2
Mersey Cl WS15 ....178 C2
Mersey Rd
Newcastle-u-L ST5 ....71 A2
Walsall WS3 ....243 C1
Mersey St ST1 ......282 C4
Merthyr Gr ST8 ......27 C3
Merton Ct WS7 .....228 C3
Merton St ST3 ......283 C4
Mervyn Rd DE15 ....167 A2
Mesnes Gn WS14 ...231 B4
Metcalf WS7 ....229 C4

Metcalfe Cl WS12 ....210 B1
Metcalfe Rd ST6 ....42 A2
Metfield Cl B79 ......250 B4
Metfield Croft DY6 ...275 C1
Mewies Cl DE12 ....184 B1
Mews Cl ST2 ....58 A1
Mews The Cannock WS11 209 B1
Newcastle-u-L ST5 ....56 B2
Meynell Cl DE15 ....167 A1
Meyrick Rd ST17 ....155 C1
Mica Cl B77 ....251 A1
Michael Cl ST3 ....74 A3
Michael's La DE6 .....80 B3
Michaels Cl ST5 ......56 B4
Michigan Cl WS11 ...210 A1
Michigan Gr ST4 ......88 A4
Micklea La ST9 ....29 C1
Mickleby Way ST3 ....90 B4
Micklegate ST19 ....223 B4
Micklehome Dr DE13 201 A2
Mickleton B77 ......262 B4
Micklewood Cl ST19 ..207 C4
Micklewood La ST19 .208 C3
Middle Cross St ST3 ..283 C4
Middle Entry B79 ...250 C2
Middle Friars ST7 ...155 C1
Middle La Brewood WV9 240 A3
Codsall WV8 ....238 B1
Codsall, Coven Heath WV9 240 A3
Congleton CW12 ....6 B2
Gnosall ST20 ....188 B4
Middlefield Gnosall ST20 171 C4
Wolv WV8 ....239 C1
Middlefield Rd ST2 ....73 B4
Middlehurst Specl Sch
ST7 ....41 C4
Middlemore La WS9 ..256 A3
Middlepark Dr DY1 ..271 C1
Middlesmoor B77 ...262 B4
Middleton Cl ST6 .....42 C2
Middleton Hall★ B78 .260 C1
Middleton Rd
Aldridge B74 ....257 A1
Brownhills WS8 .....229 A1
Whittington WS14 ..232 C3
Middleway ST13 ....211 A3
Middleway Ave DY8 ..275 B2
Midfield Cl ST18 ......16 B1
Midgley Dr B74 ....258 A1
Midhurst Cl ST7 ......41 C4
Midhurst Dr WS12 ...210 B4
Midhurst Gr WV6 ...255 B3
Midland Rd WS12 ...209 B3
Midway Dr ST11 ......90 C3
Midway The ST5 ....284 B2
Midwinter Ct ST6 .....56 C3
Milan Dr ST5 ....70 C3
Milborne Dr ST5 .....71 B3
Milburn B77 ....262 B4
Milburn Rd ST6 ......57 A3
Milcote Way DY6 ...275 A4
Mildenhall B79 .....250 B4
Mile Ct ST5 ....55 C2
Mile Flat DY6 ....274 C4
Mile Oak Cross Roads
B78 ....249 B1
Milehouse La ST5 .....56 A2
Miles Bank ST11 ....282 B3
Miles Green Rd ST5 ...54 C4
Milestone Ct WV6 ...255 A2
Milestone Dr DY9 ...281 C2
Milford Ave ST9 ......59 A4
Milford Cl DY8 .....275 C2
Milford Rd
Newcastle-u-L ST5 ..284 C1
Stafford ST17 ......175 C4
Wolv WV2 ....266 B4
Milford St ST4 ....72 C3
Milgreen Ave ST1 .....57 B4
Milk St ST13 ....30 C4
Milking Bank DY1 ...271 C1
Milking Bank Prim Sch
DY1 ....271 C1
Mill Bank DY3 ......271 B4
Mill Cl Blakedown DY10 281 A1
Caverswall ST11 ......74 B2
Newton Solney DE15 167 C4
Sedgley DY3 ....271 B3
Mill Cotts ST18 ....139 B3
Mill Cres
Barton-u-N ST18 ....201 A4
Cannock WS11 .....210 A1
Mill Ct ST18 ....158 A1
Mill End La DE13 ...200 C2
Mill Farm Ct ST21 ..134 B3
Mill Fields DY7 .....278 A2
Mill Gn WV10 ......240 A1
Mill Gr Cheadle ST10 ..76 C1
Codsall WV8 ....239 B2
Kidsgrove ST7 ....25 B1
Mill Green Nature Pk★
WS11 ....209 C1
Mill Hayes Rd
Biddulph ST8 ....27 B2
Burslem ST6 ....41 C1
Mill Hill Cres ST6 ....42 A2
Mill Hill Dr DE15 ...167 A2
Mill Hill La DE15 ...167 A4
Mill Hill Prim Sch ST6 .41 C2
Mill Ho DY7 ....278 A2
Mill La
Acton Trussell ST17 .175 A1
Albrighton WV7 ....220 C4
Aldridge WS9 ......256 C4
Barthomley CW2 .....38 B4
Barton-u-N DE15 ...201 C4
Blakedown DY10 ...281 A1
Blakenhall CW5 ......52 A2

Mill La continued
Burntwood WS7 ....229 B2
Cheddleton ST9 ....59 C4
Cheslyn Hay WS11 ......226 B3
Codsall WV8 ....238 C3
Colwich ST18 ....158 A1
Congleton CW12 ....16 B4
Doveridge DE6 ....127 A4
Edingale B79 ....217 B2
Ellastone DE6 ....80 A1
Fazeley B78 ....261 A4
Foston DE65 ....129 B4
Gnosall ST20 ....171 B3
Hartington SK17 ....24 B3
Kingstone ST14 ....124 C2
Kinver DY7 ....278 C2
Kinver, Blundies DY7 ..274 A2
Little Aston WS9 ......257 A4
Madeley CW3 ....68 C4
Milwich ST18 ....122 B2
Oakamoor ST10 ....78 A3
Roston DE6 ....96 B4
Rugeley WS15 ....178 C1
Scropton DE65 ....129 C1
Shenstone WS14 ....247 A1
Shenstone, Lower Stonnall
   WS9,WS14 ....246 A2
Standon ST21 ....102 B2
Stone ST15 ....105 C4
Tamworth B79 ....250 B3
The Bank ST7 ....26 A4
Upper Tean ST10 ......92 C1
Weston CW2 ....37 A3
Weston-u-L TF11 ......220 B4
Wheaton Aston ST19 ..205 B3
Wolv WV6 ....255 A4
Wombourne WV5 ......270 A3
Mill Meece Marsh ST21 102 B1
Mill Meece Pumping Sta★
   ST21 ....117 C4
Mill Park Ind Est WS11 .210 A1
Mill Pk WS11 ....210 A1
Mill Pond The WS13 ....214 B1
Mill Pool Rd WS12 .....210 A1
Mill Rd
Brownhills, Catshill WS8 .245 A4
Cheadle ST10 ....76 C1
Walsall WS4 ....244 B1
Mill Rise ST7 ....26 A1
Mill St Cannock WS11 ..209 C1
Kingswinford DY8 .....275 C1
Leek ST13 ....30 B3
Newcastle-u-L ST5 ...55 B1
Penkridge ST19 ....192 C1
Rocester ST14 ....96 A2
Stafford ST16 ....155 C1
Stone ST15 ....120 A4
Mill Stream Cl WV8 ....239 A4
Mill View ST6 ....42 B1
Mill Waters ST15 ......76 C1
Mill Way WS15 ....198 A1
Mill Way The ST15 ....103 A2
Millbank ST16 ....155 C2
Millbank Dr ST14 ......96 A2
Millbank Pl ST5 ....55 C1
Millbank St
Essington WV11 ....241 C1
Longton ST3 ....283 C3
Millbeck Cl CW2 ......37 A3
Millbridge Cl ST3 .....90 A3
Millbrook Cl 4 WS11 ..209 C1
Millbrook Dr WS14 ....246 A3
Millbrook Gr ST2 ......43 A1
Millbrook Way ST10 ...76 C1
Millcourt ST4 ....87 C4
Millcroft Way WS15 ...198 A1
Milldale Cres WV10 ...240 B2
Milldale Rd WV10 .....240 B2
Millend La ST7 ....39 B3
Millenium Cl WS3 .....244 A2
Millenium Way
Newcastle-u-L ST5 ...40 C1
Stone ST15 ....104 C1
Millennium Way WV8 ..239 A2
Miller St ST5 ....284 C1
Millers Gate 2 ST15 ..120 A4
Millers Gn WV7 ....237 A2
Millers Green Dr DY6 ..275 A4
Millers La
Burton u T DE14 ......166 B2
Norton-in-t-M ST2 ...43 A1
Millers Vale
Cannock WS12 ....210 B1
Wombourne WV5 .....269 A4
Millers View Cheadle ST10 76 C1
Kidsgrove ST7 ....26 A1
Mllers Wlk WS3 ......243 C2
Millersdale Cl DE15 ..167 A3
Millett Rd ST2 ....58 A2
Millfield Ave
Walsall WS3 ....243 B2
Walsall, Shelfield WS4 .244 A1
Millfield Cres ST2 ....43 A1
Millfield Dr TF9 ....97 C1
Millfield Prim Sch
Brownhills WS8 ....245 A4
Fazeley B78 ....261 A4
Millfield Rd WS8 ......245 A4
Millfields Way WV5 ...269 C3
Millhouse Dr ST10 ....76 C1
Millhouse Gdns ST19 .192 C1
Millicent Cl WS12 ....210 A3
Millicent St ST2 ......72 C3
Millington St ST3 .....178 C1
Millmoor Ave WS15 ..198 A2
Millpool The WV5 .....263 C1
Millrise Rd ST3 ....43 A1
Mills Cres WV2 ....266 C4

Mills Rd WV2 ....266 C4
Millside WS15 ....196 A4
Millstone Ave ST7 .....25 C1
Millstone Edge ST13 ..45 A1
Millstream Cl ST10 ....76 C1
Milltown Way ST13 ....31 A2
Millwalk Ave ST15 ....120 B4
Millwalk Dr WV9 ......240 A2
Millward Rd ST2 ......58 B2
Millway La DE6 ....35 C2
Milne Ave ST14 ....215 B3
Milner Dr B79 ....251 C4
Milner Terr ST13 ......31 A4
Milnes St ST3 ....73 A1
Milo Cres B78 ....250 A1
Milton Ave B79 ....250 A1
Milton Cres Sedgley DY3 .271 A3
Talke ST7 ....40 B4
Milton Ct WV6 ....254 C2
Milton Dr TF9 ....97 B1
Milton Gr ST17 ....174 A3
Milton Ho DE14 ....166 B2
Milton Prim Sch ST2 ..43 A1
Milton Rd Cannock WS11 209 C2
Hanley ST1 ....57 C4
Milton St Burton u T DE14 166 B2
Hanley ST1 ....57 C4
Milvale St ST6 ....56 C4
Milverton Dr ST14 ....110 C1
Milverton Pl 4 ST3 ...73 A2
Milward Dr ST3 ....89 C3
Mimosa Wlk DY6 ......275 C4
Minard Gr ST3 ....74 A2
Minden Gr ST6 ....57 B4
Mineal Rd ST2 ....73 B4
Minehead Rd
Dudley DY1 ....271 C1
Wolv WV10 ....240 A1
Miners Wlk B78 ....251 C1
Minerva Cl Biddulph ST8 .27 A3
Tamworth B77 ....250 A1
Minerva Rd ST4 ....72 C3
Minewood Cl WS3 .....242 C2
Minfield Cl ST4 ....41 A4
Minn-End-La SK11 .....8 A3
Minors Hill WS14 .....231 B3
Minshall Ct ST4 ....72 B3
Minshall St ST4 ....72 B3
Minster St ST6 ....42 A1
Minster The WV3 .....266 A4
Minsterley Cl WV3 ...265 C4
Minsterpool Wlk WS13 .231 A4
Minton Cl Cheadle ST10 .76 B1
Congleton CW12 .....6 A1
Minton Pl ST5 ....56 B3
Minton St
Newcastle-u-L ST5 ...56 B3
Stoke-on-T ST4 ......71 C4
Miranda Gr ST6 ....42 B1
Miras Bsns Est WS12 ..210 B2
Mires The ST6 ....35 A2
Mirfield Cl WV9 ......240 A2
Miss Pickerings Field
ST17 ....175 A1
Mistley Wlk ST6 ......41 B4
Mitcham Cl WS12 .....209 C4
Mitchel Rd DY6 ....275 C2
Mitchell Ave ST7 ......25 B1
Mitchell Dr ST7 ....25 B1
Mitchell High Sch ST2 .58 B2
Mitchell Rise ST15 ...118 C3
Mitchell St ST6 ....41 C1
Mitchell's Ct B79 ....250 A1
Mitre Cl WV11 ....242 A2
Mitre Rd WS6 ....226 B1
Mitton Rd ST18 ....191 B4
Moat Bank DE15 ......167 B1
Moat Brook Ave WV8 ..238 C2
Moat Dr B78 ....260 C3
Moat Farm Way WS3 ..244 A3
Moat Hall Prim Sch
WS6 ....226 C2
Moat House Dr ST18 ..172 C3
Moat La Audley ST7 ...39 A2
Great Wyrley WS6 ....227 A1
Newborough DE13 ...162 C3
Moat The ST3 ....74 A2
Moat Way WS15 ......198 A2
Moatbrook La WV8 ....238 C2
Moathouse Cl ST17 ...193 A4
Moatside Cl WS3 .....244 A3
Mob La WS4 ....244 B2
Mobberley Rd ST6 ....41 C4
Moccasin Way ST16 ..155 C3
Moden Cl DY3 ....271 B3
Moden Hill DY3 ......271 B3
Modular Ct WV10 ....224 B3
Moffat Gr ST2 ....73 C4
Moffat Way ST5 ......55 A1
Moises Hall Rd WV5 ..270 A4
Moisty La
Marchington ST14 ...127 B2
Uttoxeter ST14 ......126 C2
Mollatts Cl ST13 .....30 A1
Mollatts Wood Rd ST13 .30 A1
Mollison Rd ST3 ......90 A4
Mona Rd DE13 ....166 A4
Monaco Pl ST5 ....70 C4
Monarch Cl DE13 ....166 B4
Moncreiff Dr DE13 ...148 A1
Monk St DE13 ....146 B4
Monkhouse St ST10 ..76 B2
Monkleigh Cl ST4 ....88 C3
Monks Cl
Newcastle-u-L ST5 ...71 C4
Wombourne WV5 .....269 C4
Monks Way

Swynnerton ST15 ......103 A2
Tamworth B77 ....250 C3
Monks Wlk ST20 ......171 B3
Monksfield TF9 ....97 A1
Monkton Cl ST3 ......73 A1
Monmore Bsns Pk WV2 266 C4
Monmouth Pl ST5 .....71 B2
Monpelier Cl DE14 ...185 A4
Monsal Gr ST1 ....57 C3
Monsaldale Cl
Brownhills WS8 ......244 B4
Burton u T DE15 ....167 A2
Monteagle Dr DE6 ....270 B1
Montford Gr DY3 .....271 B4
Montfort Rd ST5 ......41 A1
Montgomery Ct ST5 ..284 A3
Montgomery Pl ST3 ..74 A1
Montley B77 ....262 B4
Montpellier Gdns DY1 .271 C1
Montrose Cl WS11 ...209 C3
Montrose St ST4 ......72 C3
Montville Dr ST17 ...155 A1
Monty Pl ST4 ....73 A3
Monument Cl ST12 ...88 A1
Monument Dr WV10 ..241 B4
Monument La
Sedgley DY3 ....266 C1
Tittenson ST12 ......88 A1
Monument Rd ST7 ....40 B3
Monument View ST7 ..39 C1
Monyash Cl ST3 ......90 B4
Monyash Dr ST13 ....31 A3
Moon's La WS6 ......226 B1
Moor Cl
Acton Trussell ST17 ..175 A1
Biddulph ST8 ....16 C1
Burntwood WS7 .....229 A4
Moor Croft WS15 .....179 A3
Moor Fst Sch ST8 ....17 A1
Moor Furlong DE13 ..147 C1
Moor Gr ST14 ....126 A4
Moor Hall Dr B75 ....258 B1
Moor Hall La ST19 ...208 A4
Moor Hall Prim Sch
B75 ....258 B1
Moor La Cheadle ST10 .76 C2
Church Leigh ST10 ..108 C3
Colton WS15 ....179 A4
Gayton ST18 ....138 C3
Pattingham WV6 ....253 B1
Seighford ST18 .....154 B4
Shenstone WS14 ....246 C1
Tamworth, Amington B79 251 A3
Tamworth, Bolehall B77 .250 B3
Moor Pk Perton WV6 ..254 B3
Walsall WS3 ....243 A4
Moor St Burton u T DE14 166 B1
Tamworth B79 ....250 A1
Moor St S WV2 ....266 B4
Moor The WS13 ......215 B4
Moor View WS7 ......212 A1
Moorcroft (Mus)★ ST6 .57 A4
Moorcroft Ave ST5 ...71 A2
Moorcroft Cl ST10 ...76 B1
Moore Cl Perton WV6 ..254 C1
Sutton Coldfield B74 .257 C3
Moore St Burslem ST6 ..57 A4
Cannock WS12 ......210 B4
Moores Cl DE13 .....166 A3
Moores Croft B79 ...217 B3
Moorfield Ct TF10 ...168 C1
Moorfield La TF10 ...168 B1
Moorfield Prim Sch
TF10 ....168 C1
Moorfield Rd WV2 ...266 B4
Moorfields Leek ST13 ..30 C3
Stafford ST16 ....155 B4
Moorfields Cl Cotton ST10 63 C2
Moorfields Ind Est ST21 102 C1
Moorgate B79 ....250 A3
Moorgate Prim Sch
B79 ....250 A3
Moorhead Dr ST9 ....43 C2
Moorhill Prim Sch
WS11 ....209 C2
Moorhouse Ct ST15 ..119 A3
Moorhouse St ST13 ..30 C3
Moorings The
Alrewas DE13 ....200 C2
Colwich ST17 ....177 A4
Wolv WV9 ....239 C1
Moorland Ave ST9 ...59 B2
Moorland Cl
Caverswall ST9 ......59 A2
Rugeley WS15 ......178 B1
Moorland Rd Biddulph ST8 27 B4
Burslem ST6 ....57 A4
Cannock WS11 ......209 C3
Cheddleton ST13 ....45 B3
Chell Heath ST6 .....42 A1
Kidsgrove ST7 ....26 B4
Leek ST13 ....31 A3
Newport TF10 ....168 C1
Moorland View ST6 ..42 B2
Moorland Wlk ST10 ..76 B2
Moorlands Dr DE6 ...81 B4
Moorlands Farm Pk The★
ST10 ....47 B2
Moorlands Sixth Form Ctr
ST13 ....76 B1
Moorleys La ST14 ...139 A3
Moorpark Jun Sch ST6 .42 A1
Moors Dr WV9 ....224 A1
Moorside High Sch ST9 59 C2
Moorside Rd ST9 ....59 B2
Moorson Ave ST7 ...25 C4

Moorsyde Rd ST4 ....71 C3
Moorthorne Cres ST5 ..56 A3
Moorview Gdns ST7 ..26 C3
Moran Gr ST6 ....56 C4
Moran Rd ST5 ....55 C1
Mordaunt Dr B75 ....258 C1
Moresby Cl ST2 ......43 A1
Moreton Ave
Kingsley ST10 ....61 B1
Tittenson ST5 ....87 B4
Wolv WV6 ....266 C2
Moreton Cl
Caverswall ST9 ......59 A1
Kidsgrove ST7 ....41 A1
Moreton Com Sch
WV10 ....240 C1
Moreton La Colwich ST18 158 C2
Draycott in t C DE6 ..144 B4
Moreton Par ST5 ....56 B2
Moreton Rd WV10 ...240 B1
Moreton St WS11 ...209 C2
Morfe La DY7 ....273 B2
Morford Rd WS9 ....256 A4
Morgan B78 ....250 A1
Morgan Way ST6 ....42 A3
Morland Cl ST15 ....120 A3
Morley Dr CW12 .....6 A1
Morley Rd WS7 .....229 A4
Morley Road Sh Ctr
WS7 ....229 A4
Morley St Hanley ST1 ..282 A2
Leek ST13 ....30 B3
Morley's Hill ST3 ...166 A4
Morlings Dr WS7 ...229 A4
Morning Pines ST8 ..279 C2
Morningside CW3 ....68 C3
Mornington Rd ST1 ..57 C4
Morpeth B77 ....261 B4
Morpeth St ST3 .....283 C3
Morridge View ST13 ..45 B2
Morris Dr ST16 .....156 B2
Morris Sq ST5 ......56 B3
Morston B77 ....261 B4
Morston Dr ST5 .....71 A1
Morton Rd ST17 ....174 B3
Morton St ST6 ......56 C4
Morville Cl ST4 .....72 C4
Mosedale Ave ST4 ..89 C4
Moseley Ct WV11 ...241 C2
Moseley Old Hall★
WV10 ....241 A3
Moseley Old Hall La
..................241 A3
Moseley Rd WV10 ...241 A2
Moseley Row ST18 ..137 B1
Mosley Dr ST14 .....111 A1
Mosley Prim Sch DE13 165 B4
Mosley Sq DE14 ....166 B2
Moss Cl Aldridge WS9 .256 A3
Caversall ST9 ....59 A2
Huntington WS12 ...209 B3
Moss Gn WS15 .....178 B1
Moss Gr
Kingswinford DY6 ...275 B4
Newcastle-u-L ST5 ..40 B2
Moss Green Rd ST2 ..73 B4
Moss Hill ST9 ....43 B3
Moss La
Blythe Bridge ST15 ..106 C3
Cheadle ST10 ....77 A1
Cheswardine TF9 ....114 B2
Gnosall ST20 ....151 C4
Lawton-gate ST7 ....25 C2
Madeley CW3 ....68 B3
Maer ST5 ....84 C1
Norton in H TF9 ....97 C3
Stone ST15 ....119 A4
Whitmore ST5 ......85 B3
Moss Park Ave ST9 ..59 A2
Moss Pl ST7 ....26 A2
Moss Rd Cannock WS11 .210 A2
Congleton CW12 ....15 C3
Moss Rise ST5 ......71 B1
Moss Side ST1 ......57 C4
Moss St Cannock WS11 210 A2
Norton-in-t-M ST6 ...42 C3
Mossbank Ave WS7 ..229 A3
Mossdale B77 ......262 B4
Mossdale Way DY3 ..271 C4
Mossfield ST4 ......71 C4
Mossfield Cres 13 ST7 .26 A1
Mossfield Dr ST8 ...27 C4
Mossfield Rd ST3 ...73 C3
Mossland Rd ST3 ...73 C3
Mossley CE Prim Sch
CW12 ....16 A4
Mossley Cl WS3 ....242 C1
Mossley Ct CW12 ...15 C1
Mossley La WS3 ....242 C1
Mossley Prim Sch WS3 242 C1
Mosspit ST17 ....174 C3
Mossvale Gr ST16 ..155 A3
Mosswood St WS11 .226 A4
Moston St ST1 ......57 B3
Mostyn Cl ST8 ......27 C3
Mott Pl ST6 ....56 C4
Moulton Rd ST3 ....283 B4
Mount
Cannock WS12 ......210 A4
Stoke-on-T ST4 .....71 C4
Stone ST15 ....104 C1
Mount Cl Caverswall ST9 .59 B2
Cheslyn Hay WS6 ...226 C1
Sedgley DY3 ....271 B1
Wombourne WV5 ....270 A4
Mount Cres ST15 ...104 C1

Mount Ct WV6 ....255 A1
Mount Dr WV5 ......270 A1
Mount Edge ST18 ...137 A1
Mount Fields ST10 ...94 A1
Mount Gdns WV8 ...238 C2
Mount Ind Est ST15 ..104 C1
Mount La
Market Drayton TF9 ..112 A4
Sedgley DY3 ....271 B1
Mount Pl ST1 ....91 A4
Mount Pleasant
Ashley TF9 ....99 C3
Cheslyn Hay WS6 ...226 C3
Hanley ST1 ....282 A2
Ipstones ST10 ......62 A4
Kidsgrove ST7 ......26 A1
Kingswinford DY6 ...275 B2
Leek ST13 ....30 C3
Newcastle-u-L ST5 ..284 C2
Newcastle-u-L, Chesterton
   ST5 ....55 C3
Seighford ST18 ....154 C1
Tamworth B79 ......261 B4
Mount Pleasant Ave
WV5 ....269 C4
Mount Pleasant CE Prim Sch
ST4 ....72 C3
Mount Pleasant Cl 1
ST15 ....120 B3
Mount Pleasant Rd ST7 .26 A4
Mount Rd
Burntwood WS7 ....229 A3
Forsbrook ST11 ....91 A4
Kidsgrove ST7 .....26 A1
Kingswinford DY8 ..275 C1
Leek ST13 ....31 A3
Linton DE13 ....186 B1
Rugeley WS15 .....178 A1
Stone ST15 ....104 C1
Walsall WS3 ....244 A2
Wolv, Cinder Hill WV4 266 C1
Wolv, Colton Hills WV4 266 C2
Wolv, Tettenhall Wood
   WV6 ....255 A2
Wombourne WV5 ...270 A4
Mount Road Ind Est
WS7 ....229 A3
Mount Row ST15 ...155 C2
Mount Sch for Deaf The
ST4 ....71 C4
Mount Side Rd WS12 .210 B4
Mount St
Burton u T DE15 ...167 A2
Cannock WS12 .....210 A4
Hanley ST1 ....57 C3
Newcastle-u-L ST5 .55 C3
3 Stafford ST16 ...155 C2
Stone ST15 ....105 A1
Mount The Kidsgrove ST7 .26 A1
Newcastle-u-L ST5 .55 C3
Scholar Green ST7 .25 C4
Mountain Ash Rd WS8 244 C4
Mountain Pine Cl WS12 210 A4
Mountbatten Cl
Burntwood WS7 ...211 C1
Burton u T DE13 ...166 A4
Mountfield Pl ST4 ..72 B3
Mountford Cres WV9 .256 B4
Mountford St ST6 ..41 C1
Mountside Gdns ST13 .31 A3
Mountsorrel Cl ST4 ..88 C2
Mountwood Covert
WV6 ....255 A2
Mouse Hill WS3 ....243 C2
Mousley St ST6 .....56 C4
Mow Cop Rd ST7 ...26 B3
Mow La Biddulph ST7,ST8 .16 A1
Mount Pleasant ST6 .26 A1
Mowbray Croft WS7 .211 C1
Mowbray Wlk ST1 ..57 C4
Moxhull Cl WV12 ...242 B1
Moxhull Gdns WV12 242 B1
Moxley Ave ST1 ....57 B4
Mozart Ct WS11 ...210 B1
Muchal Rd WV4 ....266 A3
Mucklestone Rd TF9 ..99 B3
Mucklestone Wood La
TF9 ....99 C3
Muirfield B77 ......251 B3
Muirfield Cl WS3 ...243 A2
Muirville Cl 5 DY8 ..275 B2
Mulberry Cl TF10 ..168 C1
Mulberry Gn DY1 ..271 C3
Mulberry Pl
Newcastle-u-L ST5 .55 C1
Walsall WS3 ....242 C1
Mulberry Rd
Cannock WS11 ....209 C2
Walsall WS3 ....243 A1
Mulberry St ST1 ...282 C3
Mulberry Way ST13 .31 A2
Muldoon Cl WS11 ..210 A2
Mulgrave St ST1 ...282 A4
Mulliner Cl ST2 ....58 B2
Munro St ST4 ......72 A3
Munster Terr ST4 ..71 C3
Murhall St ST6 .....56 C4
Murray St ST6 .....41 B4
Murton B77 ....262 B4
Mus of Cannock Chase★
WS12 ....210 B3
Muse La DE6 ......129 A4
Musk La DY3 ......271 A2
Musk La W DY3 ...271 A2
Mustang Cl ST6 ....41 B2

Muxloe Cl WS3 . . . .**243** A2
Myatt Ave
  Burntwood WS7 . . . .**229** A4
  Wolv WV2 . . . .**266** C3
Myatt Cl WV2 . . . .**266** C3
Myatt St ST1 . . . .**282** C4
Myatt Way WS15 . . . .**196** C3
Mynors St Hanley ST1 . . .**282** C2
  Stafford ST16 . . . .**156** A2
Myott Ave ST3 . . . .**74** C1
Myrtle Ave Brewood WV19 .**223** B3
  Wolv WV3 . . . .**265** C3
Myrtle St WV2 . . . .**266** C3

N

Nab Hill Ave ST13 . . . .**30** B3
Nab Hill Ct ST13 . . . .**30** B3
Nabb La Alton ST10 . . . .**94** C4
  Denstone ST14 . . . .**95** A3
Nabbs Cl ST7 . . . .**26** A1
Nabbswood Rd ST7 . . . .**26** A1
Naden Ho WS12 . . . .**209** B3
Naesby Rd WV6 . . . .**254** C2
Nagination Dr ST19 . . . . . .**207** C4
Nailers Dr WS7 . . . .**229** B3
Nairn Rd WS3 . . . .**243** A2
Nankirk La DE13 . . . .**165** A3
Nanny Goat La ST15 . . . . . .**105** A1
Nantwich Rd Betley ST7 . . .**38** C1
  Woore CW3 . . . .**67** C1
Naomi Way WS9 . . . .**245** A2
Napier B77 . . . .**250** C2
Napier Gdns 3 ST7 . . . . . .**26** A1
Napier Rd WV2 . . . .**266** B4
Napier St
  Burton u T DE14 . . . .**166** B1
  Fenton ST4 . . . .**72** B1
Naples Cl ST3 . . . .**73** C2
Naples Dr ST5 . . . .**70** C3
Napley Dr TF9 . . . .**82** B1
Napley Rd TF9 . . . .**82** B1
Narlow La DE6 . . . .**51** C1
Narrow La
  Brownhills WS8 . . . .**244** C4
  Colton WS15 . . . .**179** A4
  Denstone ST14 . . . .**95** B3
  Milwich ST15 . . . .**121** C4
Narvik Cres ST6 . . . .**42** A1
  Stafford ST16 . . . .**155** A3
Nash Ave Perton WV6 . . .**254** C2
  Stafford ST16 . . . .**155** A3
Nash La
  Acton Trussell ST17 . . . . . .**193** A4
  Elmhurst WS13 . . . .**214** A3
Nash Peake St ST6 . . . .**41** B2
Nash St ST5 . . . .**55** C1
Nashe Dr ST3 . . . .**73** A1
Natham Cl ST11 . . . .**74** B2
Nathan Ct WS15 . . . .**196** C3
National Meml Arboretum
  The ★ DE13 . . . .**201** B1
Navigation Loop ST15 . .**104** C3
Navigation Rd ST6 . . . .**56** C4
Navigation St ST6 . . . .**56** C4
Navigation Way WS11 . . .**210** A1
Naylor St ST6 . . . .**41** C3
Naylor Yd 1 ST13 . . . .**30** C3
Naylors Dr DY3 . . . .**271** C2
Neachless Ave WV5 . . . . .**270** A3
Neachley La TF11 . . . .**220** A1
Neal Croft WS14 . . . .**232** C3
Neale Ho WV2 . . . .**266** B4
Neale Pl ST2 . . . .**58** A3
Neander B79 . . . .**249** C3
Near Ridding ST20 . . . . . .**171** B3
Neath Cl ST3 . . . .**73** B2
Neath Pl 8 ST3 . . . .**73** B3
Neath Rd WS3 . . . .**242** C1
Neath Way WS3 . . . .**242** C1
Needwood CE Prim Sch
  DE13 . . . .**162** C4
Needwood Cl WV2 . . . . . .**266** A3
Needwood Ct DE13 . . . . . .**146** B3
Needwood Dr WV4 . . . . . .**266** C2
Needwood Grange
  WS15 . . . .**161** A3
Needwood Hill WS13 . . . .**214** A3
Needwood Pk DE13 . . . . . .**183** B1
Needwood St DE14 . . . . . .**166** A2
Nellan Cres ST6 . . . .**42** B1
Nelson Bank ST7 . . . .**41** A4
Nelson Bldgs ST7 . . . .**26** A1
Nelson Cres ST21 . . . .**102** C1
Nelson Dr WS12 . . . .**210** C2
Nelson Ind Est ST7 . . . .**25** B1
Nelson Pl Hanley ST1 . . . . .**282** C2
  Newcastle-u-L ST5 . . . .**284** C3
Nelson Rd ST4 . . . .**71** C4
Nelson St
  Burton u T DE15 . . . .**167** B2
  Fenton ST4 . . . .**72** B3
  Leek ST13 . . . .**30** C4
  Newcastle-u-L ST5 . . . .**56** B3
Nelson Way ST17 . . . .**174** C3
Nemesia B77 . . . .**251** A2
Nene Cl DE13 . . . .**147** B1
Nene Way DE65 . . . .**147** C4
Nephew St ST6 . . . .**56** C4
Neptune Gr ST1 . . . .**57** C3
Ness Gr ST10 . . . .**76** C3
Nest Comm WS3 . . . .**243** C3
Nether Beacon WS13 . . . .**214** A1
Nether La WS7 . . . .**229** B4

Nether Stowe High Sch
  WS13 . . . .**214** A1
Netherbridge Ave WS14 .**231** C4
Netherby Rd DY3 . . . .**271** B4
Nethercote Pl ST2 . . . .**73** B4
Nethergate DY3 . . . .**271** C3
Netherseal Rd
  Chilcote DE12 . . . .**219** C2
  Clifton Campville B79 . . . .**218** C1
Netherstone Gr B74 . . . . .**257** C3
Netherstowe WS13 . . . . . .**214** B1
Netherstowe La WS13 . . . .**214** B1
Netherton Gr ST2 . . . .**43** B1
Nethy Dr WV6 . . . .**255** A3
Netley Pl ST3 . . . .**88** C4
Netley Rd WS3 . . . .**242** C1
Netley Way WS3 . . . .**242** C1
Nevada La ST6 . . . .**57** A4
Neve Ave WV10 . . . .**240** C1
Nevill St B79 . . . .**250** A3
Neville Ave WV4 . . . .**266** B3
Neville Cl DE13 . . . .**147** A2
Neville Gr Stoke-on-T ST4 . .**71** C2
  Tamworth B77 . . . .**250** C2
Nevin Ave ST8 . . . .**27** B3
Nevis Cl WV6 . . . .**255** C1
Nevis Gr WV12 . . . .**242** A1
New Ave ST11 . . . .**91** B3
New Barns La WS14 . . . . .**246** A2
  Biddulph ST8 . . . .**27** C2
New Century St ST1 . . . . .**282** A3
New Chapel Ct ST6 . . . .**41** B2
New Close Ave ST11 . . . . . .**91** A4
New Cotts Ipstones ST10 . . .**62** B3
  Kinver DY7 . . . .**278** C4
New Council Hos TF9 . . . . .**98** B1
New Dudley Rd DY6 . . . . .**275** B1
New Ford Prim Sch ST4 . . . .**42** B1
New Forest Ind Est ST1 . . .**282** C4
New Garden St ST17 . . . . .**155** C1
New Haden Rd ST10 . . . . . .**76** A1
New Hall Rd ST3 . . . .**73** C1
New Hall St ST1 . . . .**282** B1
New Hampton Rd W
  WV6 . . . .**255** C2
New Hayes Rd
  Cannock WS12 . . . .**211** B3
  Tunstall ST6 . . . .**41** C2
New Homage Gdns
  WV9 . . . .**224** A1
New Horse Rd WS6 . . . . . .**226** C2
New Inn Bank ST21 . . . . . .**131** B4
New Inn La ST4 . . . .**88** A4
New Inn Row ST17 . . . . . .**175** C2
New King St ST7 . . . .**39** B1
New Kingsway ST3 . . . .**74** A2
New La ST6 . . . .**28** A1
New Landywood La
  WS6 . . . .**242** C4
New Mill La B78 . . . .**261** A4
New Park Gdns ST4 . . . .**88** B3
New Penkridge Rd
  WS11 . . . .**209** B3
New Rd Aldridge WS9 . . . .**256** A3
  Alton ST10 . . . .**78** C1
  Armitage WS15 . . . .**198** A3
  Astbury CW12 . . . .**15** A2
  Audley ST7 . . . .**39** C2
  Bobbington ST7 . . . .**268** C2
  Brownhills WS8 . . . .**244** C4
  Burntwood WS7 . . . .**229** A3
  Caverswall ST2 . . . .**58** C2
  Cookley, Caunsall DY11 . . .**280** A4
  Cookley, Lea Castle Hospl
   DY10 . . . .**280** B2
  Dilhorne ST10 . . . .**75** B2
  Featherstone WV10 . . . . . .**224** C1
  Hixon ST18 . . . .**158** A4
  Madeley CW3 . . . .**68** C4
  Penkridge ST19 . . . .**192** C1
  Shenstone WS14 . . . .**246** C3
  Shuttington B79 . . . .**235** B1
  Swadlincote DE11 . . . .**186** C3
  Swindon DY3 . . . .**269** A2
  Tamworth B77 . . . .**261** C4
  Upper Tean ST10 . . . .**92** B2
  Upper Tean, Checkley
   ST10 . . . .**109** A4
  Uttoxeter ST14 . . . .**111** A1
  Wolv WV6 . . . .**255** C2
  Flash SK17 . . . .**3** A2
New Rd Est (Ind Est)
  ST18 . . . .**139** A1
New Row
  Drayton Bassett B78 . . . .**260** C3
  Keele CW3 . . . .**69** A4
  Stafford ST18 . . . .**174** B3
  Tatenhill DE13 . . . .**165** A1
New St Biddulph ST8 . . . . .**28** A4
  Burntwood, Chase Terrace
   WS7 . . . .**228** B1
  Burntwood, Chasetown
   WS7 . . . .**228** C3
  Burslem ST6 . . . .**56** C4
  Burton u T DE14 . . . .**166** B1
  Cannock, Bridgtown WS11 .**226** B3
  Cannock, Hill Top WS12 . .**210** A2
  6 Cannock, Mill Green
   WS11 . . . .**226** C4
  Chebsey ST15 . . . .**135** A4
  Essington WV11 . . . .**242** A2
  Fazeley B78 . . . .**261** A4
  Great Wyrley WS6 . . . . . .**227** A1
  Kingswinford DY6 . . . .**275** B2
  Kingswinford, Wall Heath
   DY6 . . . .**275** B4

New St continued
  Kingswinford, Wordsley
   DY8 . . . .**275** B1
  Leek ST13 . . . .**30** C3
  Newcastle-u-L ST5 . . . .**56** B3
  Newport TF10 . . . .**168** C2
  Polesworth B78 . . . .**262** C4
  Sedgley DY3 . . . .**271** B2
  Stafford ST16 . . . .**155** B3
  Stourbridge DY8 . . . .**279** C3
  Tamworth, Glascote Heath
   B77 . . . .**250** C2
  Tamworth, Mount Pleasant
   B77 . . . .**250** B1
  Uttoxeter ST14 . . . .**126** A4
  Walsall WS3 . . . .**243** A1
  Walsall, Shelfield WS4 . . .**244** B1
  Wolv, Merry Hill WV3 . . . .**265** B4
  Wolv, Parkfield WV4 . . . . .**266** C3
New St Cotts CW12 . . . .**6** A3
New Wood Cl DY7 . . . .**279** B4
New Wood Gr WS9 . . . . . .**245** A2
Newall Ave ST16 . . . .**156** A3
Newark Gr ST6 . . . .**41** B4
Newborough Cl ST1 . . . . . .**57** C3
Newbridge Ave WV6 . . . .**255** C2
Newbridge Cres WV6 . . . .**255** C2
Newbridge Dr WV6 . . . . . .**255** C2
Newbridge Mews 8
  WV6 . . . .**255** C2
Newbridge Prep Sch
  WV6 . . . .**255** C2
Newbridge Rd DY6 . . . . . .**275** B1
Newbridge St WV6 . . . . . .**255** C2
Newburn Gr ST4 . . . .**88** A4
Newbury Cl
  Great Wyrley WS6 . . . . . .**226** C1
  Stafford ST17 . . . .**175** B4
Newbury Dr DE13 . . . .**147** B1
Newbury Gr ST3 . . . .**88** C4
Newbury Rd
  Kingswinford DY8 . . . .**275** B1
  Norton Canes WS11 . . . . .**228** A3
  Wolv WV10 . . . .**240** B1
Newby Cl DE15 . . . .**167** A1
Newcastle Com High Sch
  ST5 . . . .**70** C4
Newcastle Int Ctr ST5 . . . .**55** C1
Newcastle La ST4 . . . .**71** C3
Newcastle Rd
  Ashley TF9 . . . .**100** A4
  Astbury CW12 . . . .**15** A4
  Eccleshall ST21 . . . .**133** C4
  Keele CW3 . . . .**69** A4
  Madeley CW3 . . . .**68** C4
  Market Drayton TF9 . . . . . .**97** C1
  Millmeece ST21 . . . .**102** C2
  Stoke-on-T ST4 . . . .**71** C3
  Stone ST15 . . . .**104** C1
  Talke ST7 . . . .**40** C4
  Tittensor ST5 . . . .**87** B4
  Woore CW3 . . . .**67** C1
Newcastle St Burslem ST6 .**56** C4
  Newcastle-u-L ST5 . . . .**55** B1
  Stone ST15 . . . .**104** C1
Newcastle-under-Lyme Coll
  ST5 . . . .**284** A3
Newcastle-under-Lyme Schs
  ST5 . . . .**284** C2
Newchapel Obsy ★ ST7 . .**26** C1
Newcomb Cl WS7 . . . .**229** B4
Newcomen Gr ST2 . . . .**73** B4
Newcott Cl WV9 . . . .**239** C1
Newcrofts Wlk ST6 . . . .**42** B3
Newfield Dr DY6 . . . .**275** C2
Newfield Rd DE15 . . . .**167** A2
Newfield St ST4 . . . .**41** B2
Newfold Cres ST6 . . . .**43** A4
Newford Cres ST2 . . . .**42** C1
Newgate WV6 . . . .**253** C2
Newgate St ST4 . . . .**229** A3
Newhall Com Jun Sch
  DE11 . . . .**186** C3
Newhall Cres WS11 . . . . .**210** A2
Newhall Gdns WS11 . . . . .**209** C1
Newhall Inf Sch DE11 . . . .**186** C4
Newhall St
  Cannock WS11 . . . .**209** B1
  Kingsley ST10 . . . .**61** B2
Newhaven Gr ST4 . . . .**88** A3
Newhay DE13 . . . .**147** C1
Newhouse Ct ST2 . . . .**58** A3
Newhouse La WV7 . . . . . .**237** A2
Newhouse Rd ST2 . . . .**58** A3
Newick Ave B74 . . . .**257** A2
Newington Gr ST4 . . . .**88** A3
Newland Ave ST16 . . . . . .**155** B4
Newland Cl WS4 . . . .**244** B1
Newlands Cl
  Newcastle-u-L ST5 . . . .**71** A3
  Penkridge ST19 . . . .**207** C4
  Stone ST15 . . . .**119** C3
Newlands Ct WS12 . . . . . .**227** C4
Newlands La
  Colton WS15 . . . .**179** B4
  Norton Canes WS12 . . . . .**227** B4
Newlands St ST4 . . . .**57** A1
Newleigh St ST2 . . . .**43** A1
Newlyn Ave CW12 . . . .**15** A2
Newlyn Cl WS14 . . . .**231** B4
Newman Ave WV4 . . . . . .**266** C2
Newman Cl ST15 . . . .**120** B4
Newman Dr DE14 . . . .**185** A4
Newman Gr WS15 . . . .**196** A4
Newman Rd WV10 . . . . . .**241** A1

Newmarket Rd WS11 . . . .**228** A2
Newmarket Way ST10 . . . .**76** C3
Newmill St ST2 . . . .**43** A1
Newmount Rd ST4 . . . .**73** A4
Newpool Cotts ST8 . . . .**27** A4
Newpool Rd ST8 . . . .**27** A4
Newpool Terr ST8 . . . .**27** A4
Newport B77 . . . .**250** C3
Newport CE Jun Sch
  TF10 . . . .**168** C1
Newport Cl DE14 . . . .**166** C4
Newport Croft ST19 . . . . .**223** B4
Newport Cty Inf Sch
  TF10 . . . .**168** C1
Newport Girls High Sch
  TF10 . . . .**168** C1
Newport Gr ST5 . . . .**40** C1
Newport La ST6 . . . .**56** C4
Newport Rd
  Albrighton TF11 . . . .**220** B1
  Chetwynd TF10 . . . .**168** B2
  Codsall WV8 . . . .**237** C1
  Eccleshall ST21 . . . .**133** C3
  Edgmond TF10 . . . .**168** B2
  Gnosall ST20 . . . .**171** A3
  Seighford ST18 . . . .**135** B1
  Stafford ST16,ST17 . . . . . .**155** B1
  Sutton TF9 . . . .**112** C3
  Tong TF11 . . . .**220** B2
  Woodseaves ST20 . . . . . .**151** B4
Newport St
  Brewood ST19 . . . .**223** B3
  Burslem ST6 . . . .**56** C4
Newquay Ave ST17 . . . . . .**175** B4
Newquay Cl CW12 . . . .**15** C4
Newshaw Wlk ST1 . . . . . .**282** C4
Newstead B79 . . . .**249** B3
Newstead Prim Sch ST3 . . .**88** C3
Newstead Rd ST2 . . . .**58** A3
Newstead Trad Est ST4 . . . .**88** B4
Newton Cl DE15 . . . .**167** C4
Newton Ct ST9 . . . .**59** A2
Newton La
  Newton Regis B79,CV9 . .**236** C3
  Newton Solney DE15 . . . .**167** C4
  Seckington B79 . . . .**236** A2
Newton Leys DE15 . . . . . .**167** B2
Newton Mews DE15 . . . . .**166** C2
Newton Rd
  Burton u T DE15 . . . .**167** A3
  Lichfield WS13 . . . .**213** C1
  Newcastle-u-L ST5 . . . .**56** A3
  Stafford ST16 . . . .**155** C1
Newton Regis CE Prim Sch
  B79 . . . .**236** B2
Newton Solney CE Inf Sch
  DE15 . . . .**167** C4
Newton St ST4 . . . .**56** C1
Newton's Coll WS3 . . . . . .**231** A4
Newtown Kidsgrove ST7 . . .**26** C1
  Market Drayton TF9 . . . . .**112** B4
  Newport TF10 . . . .**168** C1
Niall Rd ST4 . . . .**71** C1
Nicholas Gr ST13 . . . .**30** A3
Nicholas St 19 ST6 . . . .**56** C4
Nicholl's La ST15 . . . .**105** A3
Nicholls St ST4 . . . .**72** A3
Nicholls Way WS12 . . . . .**210** C1
Nicholson Way
  Burton u T DE14 . . . .**166** A1
  Leek ST13 . . . .**30** B3
Nicklaus Cl DE14 . . . .**185** A4
Nidderdale Cl CW12 . . . . . .**6** A3
Nightingale B77 . . . .**262** A3
Nightingale Cl
  Huntington WS12 . . . .**209** B4
  Upper Tean ST10 . . . .**92** C1
Nightingale Wlk WS7 . . . .**229** C4
Nile St ST6 . . . .**57** A4
Nimbus B77 . . . .**261** B4
Ninefoot La B77 . . . .**261** C4
Ninian Pk B77 . . . .**261** C3
Ninian Way B77 . . . .**261** C3
Nirvana Cl WS11 . . . .**209** A1
No Man's Green La DY7 . .**276** C3
No Man's Heath Rd
  DE12 . . . .**219** C2
No Name Rd WS7 . . . .**228** C4
Noblett Rd ST1 . . . .**57** C4
Nocke Rd WV11 . . . .**241** C1
Noddington Ave WS14 . . .**232** C3
Noddington La WS14 . . . .**232** C3
Noddy Park Rd WS9 . . . . .**256** C4
Noddy Pk WS9 . . . .**256** A4
Nook The WS6 . . . .**226** B1
Noon Croft DE13 . . . .**200** C3
Norbroom Ct TF10 . . . . . .**169** A2
Norbroom Dr TF10 . . . . . .**169** A2
Norbury Ave
  Norton-in-the-M ST2 . . . . .**43** A1
  Walsall WS3 . . . .**244** A2
Norbury CE Prim Sch
  DE6 . . . .**96** C4
Norbury Cl ST20 . . . .**171** B3
Norbury Cres WV4 . . . . . .**266** C2
Norbury Ct WS12 . . . .**210** A4
Norbury Dr CW12 . . . .**15** A4
Norbury Hollow DE6 . . . . .**80** B1
Norbury Rd ST20 . . . .**170** C4
Norfolk Cl ST5 . . . .**71** A1
Norfolk Cres WS9 . . . .**256** A4
Norfolk Dr B78 . . . .**250** A1
Norfolk Gr Biddulph ST8 . .**16** B1
  Great Wyrley WS6 . . . . . .**226** C1
Norfolk Ho ST7 . . . .**40** B3
Norfolk Rd
  Burton u T DE15 . . . .**185** C4
  Kidsgrove ST7 . . . .**25** C1

Norfolk Rd continued
  Stourbridge DY8 . . . .**279** B4
  Wolv WV3 . . . .**266** A4
Norfolk St ST1 . . . .**282** A1
Norfolk Way ST17 . . . .**174** B4
Normacot Grange Rd
  ST3 . . . .**90** A4
Normacot Rd ST3 . . . .**283** C3
Norman Ave ST6 . . . .**41** C2
Norman Cl B79 . . . .**249** C4
Norman Gr ST2 . . . .**56** B1
Norman Keep DE13 . . . . . .**146** B3
Norman Rd
  Penkridge ST19 . . . .**208** A4
  Tutbury DE13 . . . .**146** B3
Normanbrook Ct TF9 . . . . .**97** B1
Normandy Gr ST2 . . . .**43** A1
Normanton Gr ST3 . . . .**73** B3
Norris Cl TF9 . . . .**100** B3
Norris Rd ST6 . . . .**41** C2
North Ave Leek ST13 . . . . . .**30** B3
  Stafford ST16 . . . .**155** B4
North Castle St ST16 . . . . .**155** B2
North Cres WV10 . . . .**241** B4
North Dr ST20 . . . .**171** B3
North Gn WV4 . . . .**265** B3
North Oval DY3 . . . .**271** C3
North Pl Bucknall ST2 . . . . .**58** A3
  Stafford ST16 . . . .**155** B3
North Prim Sch ST6 . . . . . .**57** A4
North Rd Burslem ST6 . . . . .**57** A4
  Wolv WV4 . . . .**266** C3
North Springfield DY3 . . .**266** C1
North St Burntwood WS7 . .**211** C1
  Burton u T DE15 . . . .**167** A2
  Cannock WS11 . . . .**226** C3
  Leek ST13 . . . .**30** B3
  Mount Pleasant ST7 . . . . . .**26** A4
  Newcastle-u-L ST5 . . . .**284** C3
  Stoke-on-T ST4 . . . .**71** C4
North Staffordshire Hospl
  ST6 . . . .**42** A2
North Staffordshire Hospl Ctr
  (Outpatients Dept) ST4 .**71** C4
North Staffordshire
  Maternity Hospl ST4 . . .**71** B4
North Staffordshire Medical
  Inst ST4 . . . .**71** C1
North Staffordshire Nuffield
  Hospl The ST5 . . . .**71** B1
North Staffordshire Royal
  Infmy ST4 . . . .**71** C4
North Terr ST5 . . . .**56** A3
North Walls ST16 . . . .**155** C2
North West Terr ST6 . . . . . .**42** B1
North Wlk ST3 . . . .**74** A1
Northam Rd ST1 . . . .**57** B3
Northcliffe 3 ST13 . . . .**30** B3
Northcote Ave ST4 . . . .**72** A4
Northcote Cl ST18 . . . .**177** C4
Northcote Ct ST5 . . . .**284** C3
Northcote Pl ST5 . . . .**284** C3
Northcote St ST4 . . . .**57** A1
Northdale WV6 . . . .**255** A2
Northesk Pl ST5 . . . .**71** A3
Northesk St 4 ST15 . . . . .**105** A1
Northfield Ave ST14 . . . . . .**96** A2
Northfield Cl ST14 . . . .**111** A1
Northfield Dr ST8 . . . .**16** C1
Northfield Gr WV3 . . . . . .**265** B4
Northfields Rd DE13 . . . . .**166** B4
Northfields Way WS8 . . . .**244** B4
Northfleet St ST2 . . . .**58** A2
Northgate Aldridge WS9 . .**256** A4
  Brownhills WS9 . . . .**245** A1
Northgate Ct ST4 . . . .**71** C1
Northgate Way WS9 . . . . .**256** A4
Northicote Recn Ctr
  WV10 . . . .**240** C2
Northicote Sch The
  WV10 . . . .**240** C2
Northlands CW3 . . . .**67** B1
Northover Cl WV9 . . . .**240** C1
Northumberland Cl B78 .**250** A1
  DE15 . . . .**185** B4
Northway DY3 . . . .**266** C1
Northwood Cl ST5 . . . .**71** B1
Northwood Ct ST1 . . . . . .**282** C3
Northwood Gn ST1 . . . . . .**57** C2
Northwood Inf Sch ST1 . . .**57** C2
Northwood La
  Ellastone DE6 . . . .**80** B2
  Newcastle-u-L ST5 . . . .**71** B1
Northwood Park Cl
  WV10 . . . .**240** C2
Northwood Park Rd
  Hanley ST1 . . . .**57** C2
  Wolv WV10 . . . .**240** C2
Northycote Farm & Ctry Pk ★
  WV10 . . . .**240** C2
Northycote La WV10 . . . . .**240** C2
Norton Ave ST6 . . . .**42** A4
Norton Bridge Sta ST15 .**135** A4
Norton Canes High Sch
  WS11 . . . .**228** A4
Norton Canes Prim Sch
  WS11 . . . .**228** A3
Norton Cl Tamworth B79 . .**250** B4
  Wolv WV6 . . . .**265** B2
Norton Cres ST6 . . . .**57** B4
Norton Dr ST6 . . . .**57** B4
Norton Grange WS11 . . . .**227** C2
Norton Grange Cres
  WS11 . . . .**227** C2
Norton Green La WS11 . . .**227** C2
Norton Hall Cl ST6 . . . .**42** C4
Norton Hall La WS11 . . . .**227** B2

Norton La
Burntwood WS7 229 B3
Great Wyrley WS6 227 A2
Norton Canes WS11 227 A4
Norton-in-t-M ST6 42 C2
Norton Lakeside Sta★ WS7 228 B3
Norton Prim Sch ST6 42 C2
Norton Rd
Burton u T DE13 166 A3
Norton Canes WS11,WS12 227 C4
Stourbridge DY8 279 C1
Walsall WS3 244 A3
Norton Springs WS11 227 C3
Norton St ST2 43 A1
Norton Terr WS11 227 C3
Norton-in-Hales CE Prim Sch TF9 82 B1
Norwich Cl WS13 214 B2
Norwich Pl ST5 71 B3
Norwich Rd ST2 58 B1
Norwood Ho WS15 178 A1
Nottingham Ct ST14 110 C1
Nottingham Rd WS14 232 B2
Novi La ST13 31 A4
Nuffield Hospl WV6 255 B2
Nunn St ST13 30 B3
Nunn's Cl ST3 74 B3
Nuns La WS15 180 A3
Nurseries The WV9 224 A1
Nursery Ave
Aldridge WS9 256 A3
Norton-in-t-M ST9 43 B2
Nursery Cl Bradley ST18 191 B4
Cheadle ST10 76 B2
Endon ST6 43 A4
Kidsgrove ST7 25 B1
Nursery Croft WS13 213 C1
Nursery Dr Biddulph ST8 16 B1
Penkridge ST19 192 C1
Wombourne WV5 269 C2
Nursery Fields Prim Sch WS15 197 A3
Nursery Gdns
Brierley Hill DY8 275 C1
Codsall WV8 238 C2
Nursery La Hopwas B78 249 A3
Norton-in-t-M ST9 43 B2
Stafford ST16 155 B3
Sutton Coldfield B74 258 A1
Nursery Rd
Rugeley WS15 197 A3
Scholar Green ST7 25 C3
Nursery St ST4 72 A3
Nursery View Cl WS9 256 C1
Nursery Way ST18 158 A2
Nursery Wlk WV6 255 B2
Nurton Bk WV6 254 A2
Nurton Hill Rd WV6 253 C3
Nutbrook Ave ST4 72 B2
Nuthurst Dr WS11 226 C2
Nyewood Ave ST3 73 B3
Nymet B77 261 C4

O

O'Hare Pl ST13 31 A4
Oadby Rise DE13 166 A3
Oak Ave Cheddleton ST13 45 B2
Great Wyrley WS6 227 A1
Huntington WS12 209 B4
Newport TF10 168 C1
Stafford ST17 175 C3
Oak Cl Church Eaton ST20 190 A4
Colwich ST18 158 B1
Kinver DY7 278 B2
Uttoxeter ST14 110 C1
Oak Ct B74 257 C3
Oak Dr Seisdon WV5 263 C1
Wheaton Aston ST19 205 B3
Oak Farm Craft Ctr★ B78 260 A3
Oak Gdns ST18 172 C3
Oak Gn WV6 255 A2
Oak Hill WV3 255 B1
Oak Ho
Great Wyrley WS6 227 A1
Little Aston B74 257 A3
Oak Ind Pk The DY6 270 C1
Oak La Bradley ST18 191 B4
Burntwood WS7 212 A1
Cheslyn Hay WV10,WS11 225 B4
Kingswinford DY6 270 C1
Oak Lea ST13 30 A2
Oak Leys WV3 255 B1
Oak Mount Rd ST9 59 B2
Oak Park Rd DY8 275 C1
Oak Pl ST3 73 C1
Oak Rd Barton-u-N DE13 201 B4
Brewood ST19 223 B3
Brownhills, Holly Bank WS9 245 A2
Denstone ST14 95 B3
Eccleshall ST21 133 B3
Newcastle-u-L ST5 55 B1
Stone ST15 120 A4
Walsall WS3 243 C3
Walsall, Shelfield WS4 244 B1
Oak Rd Flats ST19 223 B3
Oak Sq DE11 186 C1
Oak St Burton u T DE14 166 B1
Cheadle ST10 76 B2
Hanley ST1 57 C3
Kingswinford DY6 275 B3
Newcastle-u-L ST5 56 B2
Oak Tree Cl ST17 174 A4
Oak Tree La ST7 40 B3
Oak Tree Wlk B79 249 C4
Oakamoor Rd ST10 77 B2
Oakapple Cl ST19 221 C4
Oakdale ST5 71 B2
Oakdale Cl CW2 37 A2
Oakdale Trad Est DY6 270 C1
Oakden Cl ST14 125 B4
Oakdene Ave ST5 56 A3
Oakdene Cl
Cheslyn Hay WS6 226 B1
Forsbrook ST11 91 A3
Newcastle-u-L ST5 56 A3
Oakdene Gr ST5 56 A3
Oakdene Rd WS7 229 A3
Oakdene Way ST8 27 B4
Oaken Covert WV8 238 C1
Oaken Dr WV8 238 C2
Oaken Gdns WS7 229 A4
Oaken Gr WV8 238 C1
Oaken Grange WS6 226 C1
Oaken La WV8 238 B2
Oaken Lanes WV8 238 C2
Oaken Pk WV8 239 A1
Oakenfield WS13 214 A1
Oakenhayes Cres WS8 228 C1
Oakenhayes Dr WS8 228 C1
Oakfield Ave DY6 275 C3
Oakfield Cl
Brierley Hill DY8 275 C1
Rugeley WS15 178 A1
Oakfield Dr WS3 244 A3
Oakfield Gr ST8 27 C4
Oakfield Rd
Alrewas DE13 201 A1
Codsall WV8 239 A1
Market Drayton TF9 97 A1
Oakfields DE13 145 A2
Oakham Way ST2 58 B1
Oakhill Ave ST4 71 C2
Oakhill Cl ST10 92 B2
Oakhill Prim Sch
Stoke-on-T ST4 71 C2
Tamworth B77 250 C1
Oakhill Rd WS11 209 C1
Oakhurst WS14 231 B4
Oakhurst Cres ST3 90 A3
Oakhurst Pk WS15 196 C3
Oakland Dr DY3 271 A1
Oakland Ho B74 258 A2
Oaklands WV3 266 A4
Oaklands Ave ST5 56 B3
Oaklands Cl
Alrewas WS13 215 B3
Cheddleton ST9 60 A3
Hill Ridware WS15 198 A4
Huntington WS12 209 B3
Oaklands Dr ST17 155 B1
Oaklands Ind Est WS12 210 A2
Oaklands Rd WV3 266 A4
Oaklands The
Church Eaton ST20 190 A4
Rugeley WS15 178 B1
Oaklands Way WS3 244 A2
Oakleigh Ave DE11 186 C3
Oakleigh Ct ST15 120 B3
Oakleigh Dr Codsall WV8 239 A2
Rugeley WS15 197 A3
Sedgley DY3 271 B4
Oakleigh Wlk DY6 275 C4
Oakleighs DY8 275 B1
Oakley Ave WS9 256 A3
Oakley Cl Lichfield WS13 214 A1
Penkridge ST19 193 A1
Oakley Copse WS15 196 A4
Oakley Folly TF9 99 A2
Oakley Gr WV4 265 B3
Oakley Pl ST6 42 A4
Oakley Rd WV4 265 B3
Oakleys ST19 223 B3
Oakmount Cl WS3 243 C2
Oakover Cl ST14 126 B3
Oakridge Cl ST17 175 C3
Oakridge Dr WS6 226 C1
Oakridge Prim Sch ST17 175 C3
Oakridge Way ST17 175 C3
Oaks Dr Cannock WS11 209 B1
Featherstone WV10 240 C4
Wombourne WV5 270 A3
Oakshaw Cl WV9 224 A2
Oakshaw Gr ST4 88 A4
Oaksmoor Cl ST19 205 B3
Oaktree Rd
Rugeley WS15 196 C3
Trentham ST4 88 A3
Oakville Ave ST6 42 A1
Oakwell Ct ST3 73 B1
Oakwell Gr ST3 73 B1
Oakwood WS15 178 A1
Oakwood Cl
Brownhills WS9 244 C2
Essington WV11 242 A2
Hatton DE65 146 B4
Shenstone WS14 247 A3
Oakwood Pl ST5 55 C4
Oakwood Rd Leek ST13 30 B3
Longton ST3 72 C1
Oakwood Sch WS9 245 A2
Oakwoods WS11 226 B4
Oasthouse Cl DY6 275 A4
Oatfield Cl WS7 229 A2
Oatlands Way WV6 254 B2
Oban Cl ST5 70 C4
Oberon Cl ST6 42 B1
Occupation Rd WS9 245 A2
Occupation St ST5 284 C2
Octagon Ctr The DE14 166 B1
Octagon Sh Pk The ST1 57 A2
Odell Gr ST6 41 C1
Odger Cl ST3 74 A1
Odiam Cl B79 250 B4
Odin Cl WS11 210 A3
Offa St B79 250 A3
Offa's Dr WV6 254 C3
Offadrive B79 250 A3
Offoxey Rd TF11 221 B3
Ogden Rd ST1 282 C2
Ogley Cres WS8 245 A4
Ogley Hay Inf Sch WS8 244 C4
Ogley Hay Rd
Burntwood WS7 212 A1
Burntwood, Triangle WS7, WS8 229 A2
Ogley Rd WS8 245 A4
Ogmore Gr ST3 90 A4
Ohio Gr ST6 57 A4
Old Armoury The TF9 112 B4
Old Bank DE6 81 B4
Old Barn Cl ST20 171 C4
Old Butt La ST7 25 B1
Old Cannock Rd WV10 225 B1
Old Castle Gr WS8 228 C1
Old Chancel Rd WS15 178 C1
Old Chapel Cl ST5 69 C4
Old Coach La ST17 176 A2
Old Coach Rd ST19 221 C4
Old Coalpit La SK17 5 C4
Old Colehurst Manor★ TF9 112 A2
Old Cottage Hospl The 23 ST13 30 C3
Old Croft Rd ST17 175 C3
Old Dalelands TF9 112 A4
Old Eaton Rd WS15 178 C2
Old Fallings La WV10 240 C1
Old Fallow Ave WS11 209 C2
Old Fallow Rd WS11 209 C2
Old Falls Cl WS6 226 B2
Old Farm Dr WV8 239 A2
Old Farm Mdw WV3 265 B4
Old Forge Cl DE65 148 A3
Old Forge The ST18 158 A1
Old Hall Ct B79 236 B2
Old Hall Dr Elford B79 216 B1
Newcastle-u-L ST5 56 A4
Old Hall La
Alrewas WS13 215 B4
Millmeece ST21 117 C4
Norton Canes WS11,WS12 227 A4
Old Hall Rd WV10 241 B4
Old Hall St ST1 282 B3
Old Hampton La WV11 241 B2
Old Hedging La B77 261 B3
Old Hednesford Rd WS11,WS12 210 A2
Old Hill WV6 255 B3
Old Knotty Way ST14 126 B4
Old La Endon ST6 28 A1
Featherstone WV10 241 B4
Swynnerton ST4 87 A1
Upper Tean ST10 109 B4
Wolv WV6 254 C1
Old Landywood La WS6 242 B4
Old Lodge Hill Ctry Pk★ WS15 211 C2
Old London Rd WS14 231 B1
Old Man of Mow★ ST7 26 B4
Old Manor Cl B78 260 C3
Old Manor Flats WV6 255 B3
Old Mill Gdns WS4 244 B1
Old Mill La Bagnall ST9 44 A2
Bagnall, Tompkin ST9 44 B2
Old Oak Cl WS9 256 A4
Old Park Rd
Cannock WS12 211 A3
Dudley DY1 271 C2
Weston CW1 37 B4
Old Penkridge Rd WS11 209 B1
Old Quarry Dr DY3 271 B3
Old Rd Armitage WS15 198 A3
Audley ST7 39 C2
Betley CW3 53 A2
Branston DE14 184 C4
Stone ST15 105 A3
Trentham ST4,ST12 88 B2
Upper Tean ST10 92 B2
Weston ST18 138 B1
Old Rd Cl ST15 105 A1
Old Rectory Gdns WS9 256 B3
Old Rectory Rd ST15 120 A4
Old Rickerscote La ST17 175 A3
Old School Cl ST18 138 B2
Old School Ct ST19 205 B3
Old School Yd The B77 251 A3
Old Shackerley La WV7 221 A1
Old Smithy Cl WV6 253 B2
Old Stafford Rd WV10 224 B1
Old Stoke Rd ST4 56 C1
Old Town La WS3 243 C2
Old Town Rd ST1 282 B4
Old Tramway ST4 72 C3
Old Vicarage Cl
Walsall WS3 244 A1
Wombourne WV5 270 A4
Old Warstone La WV11 242 A4
Old Weston Rd ST19 221 C4
Old Wharf Pl ST1 57 C1
Old Wharf Rd DY8 279 C3
Old Whieldon Rd ST4 72 B3
Oldacre La ST17 176 A2
Oldacres Rd ST4 88 B3
Oldbury Ct B79 250 A3
Oldcastle Ave ST5 56 A3
Oldcott Cres ST7 41 B4
Oldcott Dr ST7 41 B4
Oldcourt St ST6 41 B2
Olde Hall La WS6 226 C2
Oldershaws La ST20 150 C4
Oldfield Ave ST6 42 B3
Oldfield Dr ST15 120 B3
Oldfield Ind Est ST4 72 C3
Oldfield La
Egginton DE65 148 A4
Snelston DE6 81 A2
Oldfield St ST4 283 A5
Oldfields Cres ST18 158 B2
Oldfields Hall Mid Sch ST14 126 A4
Oldfields Rd ST14 126 A4
Oldford La ST18 154 A2
Oldham Cotts WS15 179 A3
Oldham St ST1 282 C1
Oldhill Cl ST7 40 C3
Oldhill La ST18 157 B1
Oldicote La DE15 167 C2
Oldmill St ST4 72 B4
Oldway Pl ST3 73 B3
Olive Ave WV4 266 C3
Olive Gr ST5 40 B1
Oliver Lodge Ho ST4 72 A4
Oliver Rd ST4 71 C4
Ollison Dr B74 256 C1
Olof Palme Gr ST3 283 C2
Omega Way ST4 88 A4
One Oak Rise ST17 174 C3
Onneley La CW3 67 C2
Onsetter Rd ST2 73 B4
Onslow Dr ST5 56 A4
Ontario Cl ST4 88 A4
Opal Bsns Ctr ST15 120 A3
Opal Rd ST4 72 C3
Opal Way ST15 120 A3
Oram's La ST19 223 B4
Orange La WS15 161 B1
Orb St ST1 282 B2
Orbital Way WS11 226 C3
Orchard Ave WS11 209 B1
Orchard Cl Ashley TF9 100 B3
Brewood WV9 224 A1
Cheslyn Hay WS6 226 C2
Claverley WV5 267 B4
Lichfield WS13 213 C1
Pattingham WV6 253 B2
Penkridge ST19 192 C1
Rugeley WS15 178 C2
Stone ST15 119 C4
Stone, Oulton ST15 105 B2
Sudbury DE6 128 C3
Tamworth B77 261 B3
Uttoxeter ST14 111 A1
Walton-on-T DE12 184 B1
Orchard Cotts WS15 198 A3
Orchard Cres
Kidsgrove ST7 25 B1
Penkridge ST19 192 C1
Wolv WV3 265 A4
Orchard Ct
Kingswinford DY6 275 B3
Wolv WV3 265 A4
Orchard Gdns
Cannock WS12 209 C3
Leek ST13 30 B3
Orchard Gr Aldridge WS9 256 A2
Cookley DY11 280 A3
Kinver DY7 278 A2
Sedgley DY3 271 A2
Sutton Coldfield B74 257 C2
Wolv WV4 266 A2
Orchard La Codsall WV8 239 A2
Shareshill WV10 225 B2
Stafford ST18 174 B3
Orchard Pk DE14 166 B1
Orchard Pl ST12 88 B1
Orchard Rd DY10 280 B2
Orchard Rise
Blythe Bridge ST11 90 C4
Market Drayton TF9 112 A4
Orchard St
Burton u T DE14 166 B1
Newcastle-u-L ST5 56 B3
Stafford ST17 155 C1
Swadlincote DE11 186 C3
Tamworth B79 250 A3
Tamworth, Kettlebrook B77 250 B2
Orchard The
Albrighton WV7 237 A3
Brewood ST19 223 B3
Colwich ST18 177 B4
Endon ST6 43 A4
Stramshall ST14 111 A2
Swynnerton ST15 103 A2
Walsall WS3 243 B1
Wolv WV6 255 C3
Orchards The
Armitage WS15 198 B2
Fenton ST3 72 C2
Orchid Cl DE15 186 A4
Orchid Gr ST4 56 C1
Ordish Ct DE14 166 B1
Ordish St DE14 166 B1
Ordley La DE6 65 C1
Oregon Cl DY6 275 C3
Oregon Gdns WS7 228 C4
Orford Rd ST9 43 C4
Orford St ST5 56 B4
Orford Way ST3 88 C4
Orgreave St ST6 57 A4
Orgreaves Cl ST5 56 A4
Oriel Cl Cannock WS11 226 C4
Sedgley DY1 271 C1
Oriel Dr WV10 240 B2
Oriel St ST4 72 A4
Oriole Cl ST14 126 B3
Orion Cl WS6 226 C1
Orion Ct ST5 70 C4
Orion St ST6 42 B1
Orion Way WS11 209 C3
Orkney Ave ST7 41 C4
Orkney Dr B77 261 C4
Orlestone Pl ST6 42 A4
Orme Rd Biddulph ST8 27 B3
Newcastle-u-L ST5 284 A2
Orme St ST6 56 C4
Ormes La WV6 255 B2
Ormonde St ST4 72 C3
Ormonds Cl WS13 230 C3
Oroxden Cl ST10 92 B4
Orpheus Gr ST1 57 C3
Orton Gr WV4 265 B2
Orton La WV4,WV5 265 A1
Orton Rd ST5 284 A4
Orwell Cl DY8 279 B2
Orwell Dr Longton ST3 73 C3
Stafford ST17 174 A4
Orwell Pl ST5 71 A2
Osberton Dr DY1 271 C1
Osborne B79 249 B4
Osborne Cres ST17 175 B4
Osborne Ct DE13 166 A3
Osborne Rd
Stoke-on-T ST4 71 C4
Wolv WV4 265 C3
Osborne St
Burton u T DE15 167 A2
Leek ST13 31 A3
Oslo Gr ST1 57 C3
Osmaston Rd DY8 279 C1
Osprey B77 262 A3
Osprey Ave ST3 90 A4
Osprey Cl
Burton u T DE15 167 B2
Whittington WS14 232 C3
Osprey Dr DY1 271 C1
Osprey Gr WS12 210 B1
Osprey Vale WS7 229 A4
Osprey View ST7 26 B2
Ostend Pl ST5 70 C4
Ostler Cl DY6 275 A4
Ostlers La ST13 45 A2
Oswald Ave ST3 74 A3
Otherton Cl ST19 207 C4
Otherton La ST19 207 C3
Otterburn Cl
Cannock WS12 210 C1
6 Stafford ST17 175 B3
Otterstone Cl DY3 266 B1
Ottery B77 262 A3
Oulton CE Fst Sch ST15 105 B2
Oulton La TF10,ST20 170 A4
Oulton Mews ST15 105 A1
Oulton Rd Cheadle ST10 76 C2
Chell Heath ST6 42 A4
Stone ST15 105 A1
Oulton Way ST16 155 A3
Oundle Ct B74 257 C1
Ounsdale Cres WV5 270 A4
Ounsdale High Sch WV5 269 C4
Ounsdale Rd WV5 269 C4
Ounty John La DY8 281 C4
Our Lady & St Benedict RC Prim Sch ST2 58 A3
Our Lady & St Werburgh's RC Prim Sch ST5 71 A2
Our Lady's RC Prim Sch ST4 72 B3
Our Lady's RC Prim Sch ST15 103 A2
Ousley La DE6 80 B3
Outclough Rd ST8 27 A1
Outfield Rd DE15 185 C4
Outlook The ST6 42 B2
Outwards Gn ST18 138 B1
Outwoods Cl
Burton u T DE13 166 A3
Weston ST18 138 B1
Outwoods La
Anslow DE13 165 B4
Burton u T DE13 165 C4
Outwoods St DE14 166 A3
Oval Bglws The TF10 169 A2
Oval The Cheddleton ST9 59 C2
Longton ST3 283 A2
Market Drayton TF9 112 B4
Stafford ST17 155 C1
Over The Hill ST8 17 A1
Overbrook Cl DY3 271 B1
Overcroft ST14 125 B4
Overdale Pl ST13 30 A3
Overfield Rd DY1 271 C1
Overhill Rd
Burntwood WS7 229 A3
Stafford ST17 175 B3
Overhouse St ST6 41 C1
Overland Cl WS15 197 A3
Overland Dr ST6 43 A4
Overpool Cl WS15 196 B4
Oversetts Ct DE11 186 C3
Oversetts Rd DE11 186 C3
Oversley Rd ST6 42 A4
Overstrand WV9 239 C2
Overton Bank 7 ST13 30 C3
Overton Cl ST3 283 A2
Overton La WS7 229 B2
Overton Rd ST8 16 C3
Overton Wlk WV4 265 B3
Overwood Pl ST7 41 C4

Overwoods Rd B77 262 A3
Owen Gr 3 ST6 57 A4
Owen Rd WV3 266 A4
Owen Wlk ST17 174 B4
Owens Cl WS15 178 C1
Ox Pasture ST13 45 B3
Ox St DY3 271 B3
Ox-Hey Cres ST8 16 B1
Ox-Hey Dr ST8 16 B1
Oxbarn Ave WV3 265 C4
Oxbarn Rd ST17 174 B3
Oxbridge Way B79 249 C3
Oxclose La DE6 36 B1
Oxford Ave ST1 57 B4
Oxford Cl WS6 226 C2
Oxford Cres ST4 72 A4
Oxford Dr DY8 279 C2
Oxford Gdns ST16 155 C3
Oxford Gn WS11 226 C4
Oxford Rd Cannock WS11 226 C4
Chell Heath ST6 42 A4
Newcastle-u-L ST5 56 B2
Oxford St
Burton u T DE14 166 A1
Stoke-on-T ST4 72 A4
Oxhay Ct ST5 56 B2
Oxhay View ST5 56 B2
Oxhey Fst Sch ST8 16 C1
Oxleathers Ct ST17 174 A4
Oxley Cl WS6 226 C1
Oxley Moor Rd
Wolv, Blakeley Green WV9 255 C4
Wolv, Oxley WV9,WV10 240 A1
Oxley Rd DE15 167 A2
Oxmead DE6 81 B4

P

Pacific Rd ST4 88 A4
Pack Horse La ST6 56 C4
Packett St ST4 283 B4
Packington Ct B74 257 C2
Packington La B78 248 C3
Packmoor Prim Sch ST7 26 C1
Padarn Cl DY3 266 B1
Padbury WV9 240 A2
Padbury La WS7 212 B1
Paddock Cl ST16 155 B4
Paddock Cotts ST4 88 A3
Paddock La
Aldridge WS9 256 A3
Great Wyrley WS6 227 A2
Paddock Rise ST4 88 A3
Paddock The
Brewood WV9 224 A1
Burton u T DE15 167 A2
Cheadle ST10 76 B1
Claverley WV5 267 B4
Codsall WV8 238 C1
Lichfield WS14 231 B3
Perton WV6 254 B2
Rolleston DE13 147 A2
Sedgley DY3 271 C3
Seighford ST18 154 B3
Wombourne WV5 269 C3
Paddocks Cl B78 251 C1
Paddocks Gn CW12 15 C4
Paddocks The
Market Drayton TF9 97 A1
Swadlincote DE11 186 C3
Swynnerton ST15 118 C3
Padget High Sch DE14 185 A4
Padstow B77 250 C3
Padstow Way ST4 88 B3
Padworth St ST3 74 A2
Paget Cl ST19 208 A4
Paget Dr WS7 211 C1
Paget Rd WV3,WV6 255 C2
Paget Rise WS15 160 C3
Paget St DE14 166 B1
Pagham Cl WV9 239 C1
Painsley RC High Sch ST10 76 B1
Paisley Cl ST2 73 C4
Paladin Ave ST3 74 A2
Palatine Dr ST5 55 B3
Pale St DY3 271 C3
Palfrey Rd DY8 279 B3
Pall Mall ST1 282 B2
Palmbourne Ind Pk ST16 155 B2
Palmer Cl
Barton-u-N DE13 183 B1
Burton u T DE14 185 A4
Essington WV11 241 C1
Stafford ST16 156 A2
Palmer St ST3 283 D4
Palmers Cl WV8 239 A1
Palmers Cross Prim Sch WV6 255 B4
Palmers Gn ST4 71 B4
Palmers Way
Codsall WV8 239 B1
Newcastle-u-L ST5 71 B4
Palmerston St
Hanley ST1 282 C1
2 Newcastle-u-L ST5 56 B3
Palmerston Way ST8 16 B1
Palomino Cl ST3 89 B4
Pandora Gr ST1 57 C3
Panton Cl ST16 156 A2
Pantulf Cl ST17 155 A1
Panturner Rd ST2 73 B4
Parade The
Brownhills WS8 228 C1
Kingswinford DY6 275 A4
Newcastle-u-L ST5 55 B1
Parade View WS8 244 C4
Paradise Gr WS3 243 C2
Paradise La
Featherstone WV10 224 C1
Walsall WS3 243 C2
Paradise St
Newcastle-u-L ST5 284 B2
5 Tunstall ST6 41 B2
Paragon Ave ST5 71 A2
Paragon Cl ST10 76 B1
Paragon Rd ST3 283 D3
Paramount Bsns Pk ST6 57 A4
Parbury B77 261 B3
Parchments The WS13 214 A1
Pargeter St DY8 279 C2
Paris Ave ST5 70 C3
Park Ave Burntwood WS7 229 A3
Cheadle ST10 76 C1
Meir ST3 74 A3
Newcastle-u-L ST5 56 B3
Norton Canes WS11 228 A3
Stafford ST17 174 B4
Stone ST15 119 C4
Talke ST7 40 C4
Uttoxeter ST14 111 A1
Wolv WV4 266 B3
Wombourne WV5 269 C3
Park Ave W ST5 56 A3
Park Bldgs DY3 271 B2
Park Cl Barton-u-N DE13 183 B1
Brownhills WS8 244 C4
Cheslyn Hay WS6 226 C2
Madeley CW3 68 C4
Park Cres ST17 155 C1
Park Croft WS7 228 B4
Park Ct ST5 55 C4
Park Dr Barlaston ST12 104 B4
Caverswall ST9 59 B2
Cheadle ST10 76 B2
Little Aston B74 257 B2
Sutton Coldfield B74 257 C1
Trentham ST4 87 C4
Wolv WV4 266 B3
Park End Lichfield WS14 231 C4
Newport TF10 168 C3
Park Farm Rd B77 250 B1
Park Farm View ST6 41 B4
Park Gate Rd
Cannock WS15 211 C3
Kidderminster DY10 280 A1
Park Hall Ave ST3 74 A2
Park Hall Bsns Village ST3 73 C3
Park Hall Cl WS15 178 B2
Park Hall Cres ST3 74 A2
Park Hall Ind Est ST6 41 C1
Park Hall Prim Sch ST3 74 A2
Park Hall Rd Longton ST3 73 C3
Wolv WV4 266 B3
Park Hall St ST3 283 C4
Park House Dr ST15 120 B4
Park La Ashley TF9 100 A4
Audley ST7 39 A2
Biddulph ST8 27 B3
Blore TF9 99 A1
Brewood ST19 223 B1
Brocton ST17 176 A2
Cheadle ST10 76 B2
Cheddleton ST13 45 A3
Colton WS15 179 A4
Congleton CW12 6 A1
Endon ST9 44 A4
Fenton ST4 72 C3
Great Wyrley WS6 227 A2
Haughton ST18 172 C3
Ipstones ST10 47 A1
Kingswinford DY6 275 C4
Shenstone WS14 247 A2
Tamworth B78 249 C1
Tutbury DE13 146 A3
Wheaton Aston ST19 206 A3
Whittington WS13 232 B4
Woodseaves ST20 132 A1
Park Lane Cl ST10 76 B2
Park Mid Sch ST8 27 B3
Park Pale The DE13 146 B3
Park Pl Fenton ST4 72 C3
Uttoxeter ST14 126 B4
Park Rd Alrewas DE13 201 A2
Barton-u-N DE13 183 B1
Burntwood, Chase Terrace WS7 228 C4
Burntwood, Triangle WS7 229 A3
Cannock WS11 209 B1
Caverswall ST9 59 B2
Chell Heath ST6 42 A1
Featherstone WV10 241 B4
Leek ST13 30 C4
Newcastle-u-L ST5 55 B1
Newcastle-u-L, Butterton ST5 70 C1
Norton Canes WS11 228 A3
Sedgley DY3 271 B2
Stourbridge DY8 279 B3
Swadlincote DE11,DE15 186 B3
Tamworth B77 261 B3
Walsall WS3 243 A1
Park Rd W DY8 279 B3
Park Rise WV3 255 C1
Park Sch B79 250 A4
Park St Brierley Hill DY8 279 C4
Burton u T DE14 166 B1
Cannock WS11 226 C3
Cheslyn Hay WS6 226 C2
Park St *continued*
Fenton ST4 72 C3
Kingswinford DY6 275 B3
Stafford ST17 155 C1
Tamworth B79 250 A3
Uttoxeter ST14 111 B1
Park St S WV2 266 B3
Park Terr ST6 41 C2
Park The DE6 81 B4
Park Venture Ctr WS11 226 C3
Park View
Blythe Bridge ST11 90 C3
Swynnerton ST15 103 A2
Park View Ct
Cannock WS11 209 B1
Longton ST3 73 A1
Park View Rd
Kidsgrove ST7 26 A2
Sutton Coldfield B74 257 B2
Park View Terr WS15 178 B1
Park Way Forsbrook ST11 91 A4
Wolv WV11 242 A1
Park Wood Ct B74 257 C1
Park Wood Dr ST5 85 A4
Parkdale DY3 271 B4
Parkend ST11 91 A4
Parker Bowles Dr TF9 112 A4
Parker Paul Ind Est WV2 266 B4
Parker Rd WV11 241 C1
Parker St
Burton u T DE14 166 B3
Hanley ST1 282 A3
Leek ST13 31 A3
Walsall WS3 243 A1
Parker's Croft Rd ST17 155 C1
Parker-Jervis Rd ST3 73 C2
Parkers Cl ST20 190 A4
Parkers Ct WV9 224 B1
Parkes Ave WV8 239 A1
Parkes Hall Rd DY1 271 C3
Parkfield Ave B77 250 B1
Parkfield Cl
Barlaston ST12 88 B1
Tamworth B77 261 B4
Parkfield Colliery WV4 266 C3
Parkfield Cres
Tamworth B77 261 B4
Wolv WV2 266 C3
Parkfield Gr WV2 266 C3
Parkfield High Sch WV4 266 C3
Parkfield Jun & Inf Sch WV4 266 C3
Parkfield La DE6 81 B2
Parkfield Rd Longton ST3 73 B1
Wolv WV2,WV4 266 C3
Parkfields Endon ST9 43 C4
Stafford ST17 174 B4
Parkfields Cl ST5 55 A1
Parkgate La DE6 79 C3
Parkhall Cty Pk★ ST3 73 C3
Parkhall La ST10 109 A3
Parkhead Cres ST3 74 A2
Parkhead Dr ST3 74 A2
Parkhead Gr ST3 74 A2
Parkhill Rd WS7 229 A4
Parkhouse Gdns DY3 271 B2
Parkhouse Ind Est ST5 40 C1
Parkhouse Ind Est E ST5 56 A4
Parkhouse Ind Est W ST5 55 C4
Parkhouse Rd E ST5 40 C1
Parkhouse Rd W ST5 40 C1
Parkhouse St ST1 282 A1
Parklands Biddulph ST8 17 A1
Kidsgrove ST7 26 A1
Parklands Rd ST10 92 C2
Parklands The
Congleton CW12 6 A1
Kingswinford DY6 275 B3
Wolv WV3 255 B1
Parks Cres WV11 242 A2
Parkside Tamworth B77 250 C1
Trentham ST4 88 A4
Parkside Ave ST16 155 B4
Parkside Cres ST9 43 C4
Parkside Dr ST5 56 B2
Parkside Gr ST5 56 B2
Parkside Ind Est WV1 266 C4
Parkside La Gayton ST18 139 A4
Huntington WS11 209 A1
Parkside Prim Sch ST16 155 B4
Parkside Way B74 257 A1
Parkstone Ave ST5 284 C2
Parkstone Cl WS4 244 B1
Parkview Ct DY6 275 A4
Parkview Dr WS8 228 C1
Parkway Branston DE14 165 C1
Stone ST15 120 B4
Trentham ST4 87 C4
Parkway The Hanley ST1 282 B1
Perton WV6 254 C2
Parkwood Ave ST4 87 C4
Parkwood Cl WS8 245 A3
Parkyn St WV2 266 C4
Parliament Row ST1 282 B3
Parliament Sq ST1 282 B3
Parliament St DE11 186 C3
Parnell Sq CW12 6 A1
Parson St B77 261 C4
Parson's Croft WV9 224 A1
Parson's Wlk B79 218 C1
Parsonage St ST6 41 B2
Parsons Cl SK17 24 B3
Parsons Dr ST20 171 C3
Parsons Hollow B77 261 C4
Parsons La ST13 33 B2
Parton Gr ST3 74 A2
Partridge Cl
Huntington WS12 209 B4
10 Meir ST3 90 A4
Partridge Croft WS13 231 B4
Partridge Dr ST14 126 B3
Partridge Mill WS3 243 C2
Partridge Rd DY8 279 B2
Partridge Ride TF9 99 B2
Parva Ct ST14 110 C1
Paskin Cl WS13 215 B4
Pass Ave WS14 232 C3
Passfield Ave WS12 210 B4
Pastoral Cl CW3 68 C3
Pasture Cl ST5 85 B3
Pasture Gate WS11 209 B1
Pasture View WS3 243 C1
Pasturefields Ent Pk ST18 158 A3
Pasturefields La ST18 158 A3
Pastures The
Perton WV6 254 B2
Swadlincote DE11 186 C3
Patch Cl DE13 166 A3
Patch Mdw Rd ST10 76 A2
Paterson Ave ST21 117 C2
Paterson Pl WS8 245 A3
Patricia Ave WV4 266 B3
Patrick Ho 3 WS11 210 A2
Patrick Mews WS13 213 C1
Patrick Pl ST8 27 A1
Patshull Ave WV10 240 A2
Patshull Gr WV10 240 A2
Patshull Ho WV6 255 C3
Patshull Rd WV6 253 A2
Patterdale Rd WS11 210 A2
Patterdale St ST6 42 A2
Pattingham La WV7 253 B4
Pattingham Rd WV6 254 B1
Paul St 1 WV2 266 B4
Paulet High Sch DE15 185 C4
Pauls Coppice WS8 245 A3
Pauls Wlk WS13 214 A2
Pavement The ST19 223 B3
Pavilion Cl WS9 256 B4
Pavilion Dr ST1 57 A3
Pavilion End DY7 274 C1
Pavilion The B77 251 A2
Pavior's Rd WS7 228 C2
Paxton Ave WV6 254 C2
Paxton St ST1 282 C1
Paynter St ST4 72 C3
Peace Cl WS6 226 C2
Peacehaven Gr ST4 88 B3
Peach Ave ST17 174 C4
Peacock Hay Rd ST7 40 C2
Peacock La ST4,ST5 87 A4
Peacock Rd ST5 55 C3
Peacock View ST4 57 C1
Peak Cl WS15 198 A2
Peak Dale Ave ST6 41 B4
Peak Dr DY3 271 C2
Peak View ST13 31 A3
Peake Cres WS8 244 C3
Peake Rd WS8 245 A3
Peake St ST5 55 C2
Peakes Rd WS15 178 A1
Peaks L Ctr B79 250 A2
Pear Pl ST2 73 B4
Pear Tree Ave DE11 186 C4
Pear Tree Cl
Barlaston ST12 88 B1
Gnosall ST20 171 C3
Huntington WS12 209 B4
Shuttington B79 251 C4
Pear Tree Com Prim Sch WS15 196 C4
Pear Tree Dr CW3 68 B4
Pear Tree La
Brownhills WS8 228 B1
Claverley WV5 268 A2
Essington WV11 241 A1
Newcastle-u-L ST5 55 B4
Pear Tree Rd ST7 39 C1
Pearis Dr ST10 94 C4
Pearl Gr ST3 90 A4
Pearson Dr ST15 120 B4
Pearson St WV2 266 B4
Peartree La WS15 180 A3
Peascroft Rd ST6 42 B2
Pebble Cl B77 251 A2
Pebble Mill Cl WS11 209 C1
Pebble Mill Dr WS11 210 A1
Pebble Mill St ST1 56 C2
Peck Mill La ST8 27 B1
Peckforton View ST7 41 A4
Pedley Gr ST6 42 B1
Pedley La CW12 6 C2
Peebles Gn ST2 58 B1
Peebles Rd ST5 54 C1
Peel Cl B78 260 C3
Peel Ct Cannock WS11 209 C1
Fazeley B78 261 A4
4 Kidsgrove ST7 26 A1
Peel Dr Astbury CW12 15 A4
Cannock WS12 209 C4
Peel Ho B79 250 A2
Peel Hollow ST7 39 A1
Peel La CW12 15 B4
Peel St Burton u T DE14 166 B1
Longton ST3 283 C1
Newcastle-u-L ST5 56 B3
Stafford ST16 155 B2
Tunstall ST6 56 B4
Peel Terr ST16 155 C3
Peelers Way B77 250 B1
Pegasus Gr ST6 42 B1
Pegasus Wlk B79 249 C4
Peggs La ST20 150 C4
Peggy's Bank ST7 54 C4
Pegroy Gr ST6 42 B1
Pelham St ST1 282 C1
Pellfield Ct ST18 138 B1
Pelsall La Walsall WS4 244 A1
Walsall, Bloxwich WS3 243 B2
Pelsall Rd WS8 244 B4
Pelsall Village Sch WS3 243 C2
Pemberton Cres DY10 280 B2
Pemberton Dr ST3 90 A3
Pembridge Rd ST3 88 C4
Pembroke Cl B79 249 B3
Pembroke Ct ST5 284 A1
Pembroke Dr
Newcastle-u-L ST5 284 A2
Stone ST15 120 B4
Pembroke Gdns DY8 275 B1
Pembroke Rd ST2 43 A1
Pen-y-Bony Wlk ST8 27 C3
Pen-y-bryn Way TF10 168 C1
Penarth Gr ST1 282 B4
Penarth Pl ST5 284 A1
Pencombe Dr WV4 266 B3
Penda Gr WV6 254 C3
Pendeford Ave WV6 255 C4
Pendeford Bsns Pk WV9 239 C2
Pendeford Cl WV6 255 C4
Pendeford Hall La WV9 239 B3
Pendeford High Sch WV10 240 A1
Pendeford La WV9 240 A2
Pendeford Mill La WV8 239 B2
Pendeford Mill Nature Reserve★ WV9 239 C2
Pendene Ct WV4 266 A3
Penderel St WS3 243 B1
Penderell Cl WV10 241 A3
Pendinas Dr WV8 239 A2
Pendine Gr ST4 73 A3
Pendle Hill WS12 210 B2
Pendrel Cl WS6 242 C4
Pendrell Cl WV8 239 A2
Pendrell Hall Coll WV8 238 B3
Pendrill Rd WV10 240 C2
Pendryl Cl ST19 223 B4
Penfleet Ave ST3 74 A1
Pengrove Cl ST7 41 C4
Penhallow Dr WV4 266 C3
Penk Dr WS7 229 B3
Penk Dr N WS15 178 B1
Penk Dr S WS15 178 B1
Penk Rd ST11 91 A4
Penk Rise WV6 255 A2
Penkhull Inf Sch ST4 72 A4
Penkhull New Rd ST4 72 A3
Penkhull Terr ST4 72 A3
Penkridge Bank WS15 195 B3
Penkridge Ind Est ST19 207 C4
Penkridge L Ctr ST19 208 A4
Penkridge Mid Sch ST19 193 A1
Penkridge Rd ST17 193 A4
Penkridge Sta ST19 207 C4
Penkridge Wharf ST19 207 C4
Penkside WV9 224 A2
Penkvale Rd ST17 174 C3
Penkville St ST4 72 A3
Penleigh Gdns WV5 269 C4
Penmark Gr ST3 89 C4
Penmere Dr
Caverswall ST9 59 A2
Newcastle-u-L ST5 71 B1
Penn Cl WS3 243 B1
Penn Croft ST18 177 B4
Penn Croft La WV4 266 A1
Penn Fields Sch WV3 265 C4
Penn Hall Sch WV4 265 C2
Penn Hospl WV4 265 C2
Penn Rd Himley DY3 270 C4
Wolv WV2,WV3,WV4 266 A3
Penn St WV3 266 A4
Penncroft WV4 265 C2
Pennell St ST2 58 A2
Pennhouse Ave WV4 265 C3
Pennine Dr
Cannock WS11 209 C1
Sedgley DY3 271 B2
Pennine Way
Biddulph ST8 16 C1
Newcastle-u-L ST5 55 C2
Tamworth B77 262 A4
Pennington Cl ST3 74 B1
Penns Wood Cl DY3 266 B1
Pennwood Ct WV4 265 B3
Pennwood La WV4 265 C2
Penny Cress Gn WS11 227 C2
Penny Ct WS6 242 C4
Penny Farthing Arc DY3 271 B4
Penny La ST10 76 B2
Penny Royal Cl DY3 271 B1
Pennycress Gdns WV10 241 B4
Pennycroft La ST14 111 B1
Pennycroft Rd ST14 111 A1
Pennycrofts ST16 155 C2
Pennycrofts Ct ST16 155 C2
Pennyfields Ave ST6 41 B1
Pennyfields Rd ST7 26 B1
Pennymoor Rd B77 262 A4
Pennymore Cl ST4 88 A4
Pennys Croft WS13 214 C1
Penport Gr ST3 283 A2
Penrhyn Ave ST6 42 A1
Penrith Cl ST4 88 B3
Penrith Ct ST5 71 A3

Pens Meadow Sch DY8 .275 C2
Pensett Trad Est The
DY6 ....271 A1
Pensford Gr ST1 ......57 C3
Pensgreave Rd DE13 ..166 A3
Penshaw Cl WV9 .....240 A1
Pensnett Trad Est The
DY6 ....275 C4
Penstone La WV4 .....264 C2
Pentire Rd WS14 .....231 B3
Pentland Gdns WV6 ..255 C1
Pentland Gr ST5 ......55 C2
Penton Pl ST3 ....88 C4
Penton Wlk ST3 ....88 C4
Penzer St DY6 ....275 B4
Peolsford Rd WS3 ....244 C3
Peover La CW12 ....6 C3
Pepper St Keele ST5 ...54 C1
Newcastle-u-L ST5 ...284 B2
Perceval St ST1 ....57 C3
Percival Dr ST9 ....43 B2
Percy St ST1 ....282 B3
Peregrine Cl
Burton u T DE15 .....167 B2
Dudley DY1 ....271 C1
Whittington WS14 ....232 C3
Peregrine Gr ST3 .....90 A3
Perivale Cl ST1 ......58 A3
Periwinkle Cl WS8 ...244 B3
Perkins St ST6 ....41 B4
Perle Brook ST21 ....133 B4
Perott Dr B75 ....258 B1
Perrin Cl ST17 ....174 C3
Perry Cl ST1 ....282 C2
Perrycrofts Cres B79 .250 B4
Perrymount Ct ST4 ....71 C3
Pershore Cl WS3 .....242 C1
Pershore Dr DE14 ....185 A4
Pershore Rd WS3 ....242 C1
Pershore Way WS3 ..242 C1
Persia Wlk 15 ST6 ....41 B2
Perth Cl DE15 ....167 B1
Perth St ST4 ....283 A5
Perthy Gr ST4 ....87 C3
Perton Brook Vale WV6 254 C1
Perton Fst Sch WV6 ..254 C3
Perton Gr WV6 ......254 C1
Perton Mid Sch WV6 .255 A3
Perton Rd WV6 ......254 C1
Perton Sandown Fst Sch
WV6 ....254 C2
Perton Wood View ST3 .72 C2
Pessall La B79 ....217 B4
Petard Ct B77 ....261 B4
Peter James Ct ST16 .155 C3
Peterdale Dr WV4 ....265 C2
Peterhead B77 ....250 C3
Peters Wlk WS13 ....214 A1
Petersfield WS11 ....209 C2
Petersfield Rd ST6 ....42 A4
Petershouse Dr B74 .257 C3
Peterson Ho 7 ST3 ...89 C4
Pethills La ST13 ......48 B3
Petrel Gr ST3 ....90 A4
Pettiford Cl WS13 ...215 B3
Pevensey Gr ST3 .....73 B3
Peverill Rd Perton WV6 .254 C2
Wolv WV4 ....266 C2
Pezenas Dr TF9 ....97 A1
Pheasant Wlk TF9 ....99 B2
Philip Gr WS11 ......209 C3
Philip La ST9 ....59 A2
Philip St ST4 ....72 C1
Phillips Ave WV11 ...241 C1
Phillips Cl ST15 ....120 B4
Phillipson Way ST6 ...57 B4
Phoenix Cl Kidsgrove ST7 .26 B1
Rugeley WS15 ......178 C1
Phoenix Ctr WS11 ...226 C3
Phoenix Rd WS11 ....210 A1
Phoenix Rise WV2 ...266 B3
Phoenix St 3 Tunstall ST6 41 B2
Wolv WV2 ....266 B3
Picasso Cl WS11 ....210 B1
Picasso Rise ST3 .....90 A4
Piccadilly Hanley ST1 .282 B2
Tamworth B78 ......261 C1
Piccadilly Arc ST1 ..282 B3
Piccadilly Cres B78 .261 C1
Piccadilly La DE6 .....66 B1
Piccadilly St 6 ST6 ...41 B2
Pickering Cl ST3 ....283 A1
Pickford Pl 8 ST3 ....74 A1
Pickleys La DE6 .....127 B4
Pickmere Cl ST3 ......43 A2
Picknal La ST14 .....126 A4
Picknalls ST14 ......126 A4
Picknalls Fst Sch ST14 .126 A4
Pickwick Pl ST7 ......25 B1
Pickwood Ave ST13 ...31 A3
Pickwood Cl ST13 ....31 A3
Picton St Hanley ST1 .282 C2
Leek ST13 ....30 B3
Piddocks Rd DE15 ...186 A4
Pidduck St ST6 ....56 C4
Pier St WS8 ....244 C4
Pierce St ST6 ....41 B2
Pigeonhay La ST14 ..110 B1
Piggott Gr ST2 ....58 B2
Pike Cl ST16 ....156 A3
Pike La WS15 ....198 A2
Pikelow La ST10 ......49 A2
Pilgrim Pl ST16 .....155 C1
Pilgrim St ST16 .....155 C1
Pilkington Ave ST5 ...71 A3

Pillar Cl ST2 ....73 B4
Pillaton Cl ST19 ....207 C4
Pillaton Dr WS12 ....209 B3
Pilsbury St ST5 ....56 B3
Pilsden Pl ST3 ....90 B4
Pimlico Ct DY3 ......271 B2
Pinch The DE6 ....36 A1
Pine Cl Burton u T DE14 .185 A4
Great Wyrley WS6 ...226 C2
Kingswinford DY6 ...275 B3
Kinver DY7 ....278 B2
Market Drayton TF9 ...97 A1
Talke ST7 ....40 A4
Tamworth B79 ......250 A4
Pine Cres ST17 ......175 C3
Pine Ct Ashley TF9 ...99 C2
Blythe Bridge ST11 ...90 B4
Pine Gr Burntwood WS7 228 C3
Swadlincote DE11 ...186 C3
Pine Leigh B74 .....258 A4
Pine Rd ST4 ....72 B2
Pine St WS3 ....243 B1
Pine Tree Cl WS12 ..195 A1
Pine View Rugeley WS15 178 B2
Swindon DY3 ....269 B2
Pine Wlk Codsall WV8 .238 C1
Uttoxeter ST14 .....125 C4
Pinehurst Cl ST5 .....71 A2
Pines Park Mobile Homes
The WS12 ....209 B3
Pines The Lichfield WS14 231 B4
Wolv WV3 ....255 B1
Pineside Ave WS15 .211 C3
Pinetree Dr Aldridge B74 256 B1
Blythe Bridge ST11 ...90 B4
Pinetrees La TF9 .....99 C3
Pineways
Kingswinford DY8 ...275 B1
Sutton Coldfield B74 257 B2
Pineways Dr WV6 ...255 C2
Pinewood
Cannock WS11 .....209 B3
Wood End CV9 .....262 B1
Pinewood Gr
Brownhills WS8 .....228 C1
Wolv WV5 ....265 A4
Wombourne WV5 ...270 A3
Pinewood Cres ST3 ...74 B1
Pinewood Dr ST18 ..177 B4
Pinewood Gr
Forsbrook ST11 ......91 B4
Newcastle-u-L ST5 ...40 C1
Pinewood Prim Sch ST4 .74 B1
Pinewood Rd Ashley TF9 .99 C3
Burton u T DE15 ....185 C3
Pinewood Wlk DY6 ..275 C1
Pinewoods TF10 ....168 C1
Pinewoods Ave DY9 .281 C2
Pinewoods Cl DY9 ..281 C2
Pinewoods Ct DY9 ..281 C2
Pinfold Ave ST6 ......42 B2
Pinfold Cl Tutbury DE13 .146 B3
Wheaton Aston ST19 .205 A3
Pinfold Cres WV4 ...265 B3
Pinfold Dr WS15 ....198 A3
Pinfold Gr WV4 .....265 B3
Pinfold Hill WS14 ...246 C3
Pinfold La
Abbots Bromley WS15 .161 B3
Blore TF9 ....98 B1
Cheslyn Hay WS6 ..226 B1
Norbury ST20 ......151 A2
Norton Canes WS11 .227 C2
Penkridge ST19 ....192 B3
Wheaton Aston ST19 .205 A3
Wolv WV4 ....265 C3
Pinfold Rd WS13 ....213 C1
Pinfold St ST14 .....126 B4
Pingle Farm Rd DE11 .186 C3
Pingle La
Burntwood WS7 ....229 B3
Stone ST15 ....120 A4
Pingle The WS15 ....196 A4
Pinhoe Pl ST3 ....73 C2
Pinnox St ST6 ....41 C1
Pintail Cl ST17 ......175 A4
Pioneer Pl ST6 ....42 B2
Pipe Hall Farm Nature
Reserve★ WS13 ...230 A4
Pipe Hay La DE6 .....144 B3
Pipe La WS15 ....198 A4
Pipe Wood La WS15 .180 A2
Piper Cl WV6 ....254 C2
Piper Pl DY8 ....279 C4
Piper Rd WV3 ....265 A4
Piper's La TF10 .....168 A2
Piper's Lodge TF10 .168 A2
Pipers Croft WS13 ..214 A1
Pippins The
Newcastle-u-L ST5 ...71 B4
Stafford ST17 ......174 C3
Pireford Pl ST5 ......41 A1
Pirehill Fst Sch ST15 .119 C3
Pirehill La ST15 ....119 C3
Pirehill Rd ST5 ......41 A1
Pirie Cl CW12 ....6 A2
Pirie Rd CW12 ....6 A2
Pit La ST7 ....40 B3
Pitcairn St ST6 ......41 C2
Pitchcroft La TF10 ..187 A3
Pitcher La ST13 ......31 A3
Pitfield Ave ST5 ......56 B2
Pitgreen La ST5 ......56 B3
Pitlea Pl 7 ST3 ....73 B3
Pitsford St ST5 ....73 C1
Pitstone Cl ST16 ....136 B1
Pitt St
Kidderminster DY10 ..280 A1

Pitt St continued
Stafford ST16 ......155 B3
Pitt St E ST6 ....57 A4
Pitt St W ST6 ....57 A4
Pitts Hill Bank ST6 ...41 C3
Plainfield Gr ST2 .....73 B4
Plainview Cl WS9 ...256 C1
Plaisaunce The ST5 ...71 A3
Plane Gr ST5 ....40 C1
Planks La WV5 ......269 C3
Plant Cres ST17 .....174 C4
Plant La WS7 ....228 C4
Plant St Cheadle ST10 .76 C1
Kingswinford DY8 ...275 C1
Longton ST3 ....283 C4
Plant Way WS3 .....243 C2
Plantation La
Hopwas B78 ....249 A2
Wombourne WV5 ...270 A2
Plantation Pk ST5 ....70 B3
Plantation Rd
Cannock WS12 .....195 A1
Longton ST4 ....88 B4
Plants Cl ST5 ....243 A4
Plardiwick Rd ST20 .171 A3
Platt St WS11 ......210 A3
Platts Ave ST9 ....43 C3
Platts Cres DY8 ....279 C4
Platts Dr DY8 ....279 C4
Platts Rd DY8 ......279 C4
Playdale TF10 ......168 A2
Pleasant Cl DY6 ....275 B2
Pleasant St ST6 ......56 C4
Pleasant View DY3 .271 B1
Plex St ST1 ....41 B2
Pleydell St ST1 ......57 C4
Plough Bank ST9 .....60 A4
Plough La TF10 .....168 C3
Plough Mews DY7 ..278 A2
Plough St ST1 ......282 C4
Ploughmans Croft TF10 169 A2
Ploughmans Pl B75 .258 B2
Ploughmans Wlk
Kingswinford DY6 ...275 A4
Lichfield WS13 .....214 B2
Wolv WV8 ....239 C1
Plover Cl
Featherstone WV10 .241 A4
Meir ST3 ....90 A4
Plover Dr ST8 ....27 C4
Plover Field CW3 .....68 B3
Plovers Rise WS15 .178 B1
Plummer Rd DE11 ..186 C3
Plumtree Gr ST1 .....57 C3
Plymouth Dr ST5 .....55 C4
Pochard Cl ST6 ......42 B1
Podmore Ave ST7 ....54 C3
Podmore La ST7 .....54 C3
Podmore St ST6 ......57 A4
Pointon Gr ST6 ......43 A3
Polesworth High Sch
B78 ....262 C4
Police Dr TF9 ....112 B4
Polperro Way 12 ST3 .90 A4
Pomona Rise ST1 .....57 B4
Pond Cres WV2 .....266 C4
Pond Gr WV2 ....266 C4
Pond La WV2 ....266 B4
Ponesfield Rd WS13 .214 A1
Ponesgreen WS13 ..214 A1
Pool Ave
Norton Canes WS11 .228 A3
Norton-in-t-M ST2 ...43 A1
Pool Cl WV10 ......225 B1
Pool Cres WS8 .....228 B1
Pool Dam ST5 ......284 B2
Pool Gn WV9 ....256 A3
Pool Hall Cres WV3 .265 A4
Pool Hall Rd WV3 ..265 A4
Pool House Rd WV5 .269 B3
Pool La Brocton ST17 .176 B2
Burntwood WS7 ....228 C2
Pool Mdw WS6 .....226 B1
Pool Meadow Cl WS15 .196 A4
Pool Rd Brownhills WS8 .228 C1
Wolv WV2 ....266 B4
Pool Side
Newcastle-u-L ST5 ...284 A3
Scholar Green ST7 ...25 A4
Pool St Fenton ST4 ...73 A3
Newcastle-u-L ST5 ...284 B2
Wolv WV2 ....266 B4
Pool View WS6 .....227 A2
Poole Dr DY8 ....279 C2
Poole's Way WS7 ...229 B4
Pooles Rd ST8 ....17 A1
Pooley La B79 ....251 C1
Polesworth B78 ....251 C1
Poolfield Ave ST5 ....70 C4
Poolfield Ave N ST5 ..71 A4
Poolfield Rd WS13 ..230 C3
Poolfields Ave ST6 ...43 B4
Poolfields Cl ST5 ....70 C4
Poolhill Cl ST3 .....283 A2
Poolside Longton ST3 ..88 C4
Madeley ST5 ....68 C3
Pope Gdns ST17 ....174 B4
Pope Gr WS12 ......209 C3
Pope Rd WV10 .....241 A1
Poplar Ave
Brownhills WS8 .....245 A4
Burntwood WS7 ....228 C4
Cannock WS11 .....209 C2
Newcastle-u-L ST5 ...56 A2
Poplar Cl Eccleshall ST21 133 C3
Forsbrook ST11 ......91 A3
Haughton ST18 .....172 C3
Newcastle-u-L ST5 ...56 A2

Poplar Cl continued
Stone ST15 ....119 C4
Uttoxeter ST14 .....110 C1
Poplar Cres DY8 ....279 B2
Poplar Ct ST5 ....56 A2
Poplar Dr Kidsgrove ST7 .26 A1
Longton ST3 ....72 C1
Poplar Gr Longton ST3 .73 A1
Newcastle-u-L ST5 ..284 C3
Poplar La Cannock WS11 209 A1
Huntington WS11 ..226 A4
Woore TF9 ....82 C3
Poplar Rd
Brownhills WS8 .....245 A4
Great Wyrley WS6 ..227 A1
Kingswinford DY6 ..275 C3
Stourbridge DY8 ...279 C2
Wolv WV3 ....266 A3
Poplar Rise B74 ....257 B3
Poplar St
Norton Canes WS11 .228 A3
Wolv WV2 ....266 B3
Poplar Way ST17 ...174 C3
Poplars Dr WV8 ....238 C1
Poplars Farm Way WV9 224 A1
Poplars Rd
Armitage WS15 ....198 B2
Burton u T DE13 ...166 B4
Poplars The
Cannock WS11 .....209 C2
Kingswinford DY8 ..275 C1
Poppit's La ST14 ...110 C2
Poppy Gdns DE13 ..201 A1
Porchester Cl WS9 .245 A1
Porlock Ave ST17 ..175 B4
Porlock Gr ST4 ....88 A3
Port La
Abbots Bromley WS15 .160 C3
Brewood WV9 ......223 A2
Port St ST6 ....56 C4
Port Vale St ST6 .....56 C4
Portal Rd ST16 .....156 A3
Porters Farm Ct ST14 127 C1
Porters La ST13 ......31 C2
Porthill ST6 ....56 B4
Porthill Gn ST5 ......56 B3
Porthill Rd ST6 ......56 B4
Porthkerry Gr DY3 .271 A4
Portland Ave
Aldridge WS9 ......256 A3
Burton u T DE14 ...185 A4
Tamworth B79 .....249 C4
Portland Cl ST11 ....90 B4
Portland Ct WS9 ...256 A3
Portland Dr Biddulph ST8 .16 B1
Forsbrook ST11 ......91 A4
Market Drayton TF9 ..97 A1
Scholar Green ST7 ..25 C3
Portland Gr ST5 ......71 A2
Portland Mews ST5 ...56 A3
Portland Pl
Barlaston ST12 ......88 C2
Cannock WS11 .....226 B4
Waterhouses ST10 ...48 C1
Portland Rd
Aldridge WS9 ......256 A3
Longton ST3 ....283 A4
Portland St Hanley ST1 .282 A4
Leek ST13 ....30 C3
Portland St N ST13 ...30 C3
Portland St S ST13 ...30 C3
Portleven Cl ST17 ..175 C4
Portleys La ST14 ....260 B2
Portobello WS15 ...178 C1
Portrush Rd WV6 ...254 B2
Portswood Cl WV9 .239 C1
Portway Cl DY6 ....275 C3
Portway Dr ST18 ...146 B3
Portway La B79 ....234 B4
Portway Pl DY10 ...280 A3
Portway The DY6 ...275 C3
Post La ST9 ....43 C3
Post Office La Betley CW2 37 C1
Gnosall TF10 ....188 B3
Rugeley WS15 .....196 A4
Post Office Rd
Alrewas DE13 ......201 A2
Seisdon WV5 ......263 C2
Post Office Sq CW3 ..68 C3
Postern Rd DE13 ...165 A2
Postmans La ST18 .122 B4
Pothooks La ST13 ...33 C2
Potteries Sh Ctr ST1 282 B3
Potteries Way ST1 ..282 C3
Potters Ave ST5 .....55 C3
Potters Croft B79 ..218 C1
Potters End ST8 .....16 B1
Potts La ST14 ......141 A4
Pouk La WS14 .....245 C4
Poulson St ST4 ......72 A4
Pound Gdns ST6 .....42 B2
Pound St WV5 .....267 B4
Poundsgate Gr ST4 ..88 A4
Pountney St WV2 ..266 B4
Povey Pl ST5 ....41 A1
Powderham Cl ST7 ...41 C4
Powell Pl TF10 ....168 C1
Powell St ST1 ......282 A4
Power Gr ST3 ......283 A4
Power Station Rd WS15 178 C1
Power Station Road Ind Est
WS15 ....178 C1
Power Wash Ind Est ST8 27 A2
Pows St SK17 ....23 C3
Powy Dr ST7 ....26 A1
Poxon Rd WS9 .....245 A2

Poynings The WV6 ..255 B3
Precinct The B79 ...250 A3
Preedys Cl WS15 ...160 C3
Prescott Ave ST16 ..156 A2
Prescott Dr ST19 ...193 A1
Prestbury Ave ST5 ...71 A1
Preston St ST6 ....57 B4
Preston Vale La ST19 .192 B3
Prestwick Rd DY6 ..275 B3
Prestwood Ct ST17 .155 C1
Prestwood Dr DY7 .279 A4
Prestwood La ST7 ...79 C1
Prestwood Rd DY7 .278 C3
Pretoria Rd ST1 .....57 A2
Priam Cl ST5 ....41 A1
Priam Gr WS3 ......244 A3
Price Ave B78 ......249 B1
Price Cl TF9 ....99 B3
Price Ct DE14 ......166 A2
Cannock WS11 .....209 C1
Price St Burslem ST6 .56 C4
Prices Rd DY3 ......271 B2
Priestley Dr ST3 ...283 C2
Prime St ST1 ....57 C3
Primitive St ST7 ......26 A4
Primley Ave B77 ...261 C3
Primrose Ave WV10 .240 B2
Primrose Cl Walsall WS3 244 A3
Wheaton Aston ST19 .205 B4
Primrose Dell CW3 ..68 B3
Primrose Dr
Burton u T DE14 ...185 A4
Newport TF10 .....168 C1
Primrose Gdns
Codsall WV8 ....239 A2
Featherstone WV10 .241 A4
Primrose Gr ST5 ...284 C4
Primrose Hill
Kingswinford DY8 ..275 C1
Trentham ST4 ....72 A1
Primrose Mdw 1 WS11 210 B1
Primrose Way ST14 .126 A4
Prince Albert Terr ST15 135 A4
Prince Ave ST18 ...172 C3
Prince Charles Ave ST3 31 A4
Prince George St ST10 .76 B2
Prince Rupert Mews
WS13 ....231 A4
Prince Rupert's Way
WS13 ....231 A4
Prince St Brownhills WS9 244 C1
Cannock WS12 .....209 C3
Leek ST13 ....31 A3
Prince's St ST15 ...105 A1
Princefield Ave ST19 .207 C4
Princefield Fst Sch
ST19 ....207 C4
Princes Dr WV8 ....239 A1
Princes Gdns WV8 .239 A1
Princes Rd Stoke-on-T ST4 71 C4
Stourbridge DY8 ...279 B2
Princes Sq ST6 ......56 B4
Princes St 4 ST6 ...155 C2
Princess Ave Audley ST7 .39 B1
Leek ST13 ....31 A4
Princess Cl WS7 ...228 C1
Princess Ct ST7 ......40 B3
Princess Dr ST3 .....74 A2
Princess Gdns TF10 .168 C1
Princess Pl ST16 ...155 C3
Princess Rd ST14 ..111 A1
Princess St Biddulph ST8 .27 B4
Burntwood WS7 ...228 C4
Burton u T DE14 ...166 B2
Cannock WS11 .....209 C4
Newcastle-u-L ST5 .284 C3
Talke ST7 ....40 B3
Princess Way DE13,DE14 166 C4
Princeton Gdns WV9 .239 C1
Princetown Cl ST3 ...90 A4
Priorfield Cl ST3 ...283 B4
Priors La TF9 ....97 A1
Priors Mill DY3 ....271 C3
Priory Ave ST13 .....31 A4
Priory CE Prim Sch ST4 .87 C4
Priory Cl Congleton CW12 .16 A4
Tamworth B79 .....249 C4
Tutbury DE13 ......146 A3
Priory Ct Brownhills WS9 245 A4
Market Drayton TF9 ..97 A1
Newcastle-u-L ST5 ..284 B2
Priory Dr ST18 .....177 B4
Priory Field Cl WV14 .266 C2
Priory Green Prim Sch
WV9 ....240 A1
Priory La DY3 ......271 B4
Priory Lands DE13 .147 C1
Priory Pl ST7 ....26 A1
Priory Rd Bucknall ST2 .58 A3
Cannock WS11 .....210 A3
Newcastle-u-L ST5 .284 B1
Rugeley WS15 .....197 A3
Stone ST15 ....120 A4
Priory The Endon ST9 .44 B4
Sedgley DY3 ....271 B4
Pritchard Ave WV4 .266 C2
Probert Rd WV10 ..240 A1
Probyn St ST3 ......283 C2
Proctors Rd WS15 .198 B2
Proffitt Cl WS8 ....245 A3
Progress Dr WS11 .226 C3
Progress Ind Ctr WS11 226 C4
Prospect Dr WS13 .231 C1
Prospect Manor Ct
WS12 ....210 B2

Prospect Pk WS11 . . . . . .**226** B4
Prospect Pl 14 ST13 . . . . .**30** C3
Prospect Rd
Burntwood WS7 . . . .**229** A3
Leek ST13 . . . .**31** A3
Market Drayton TF9 . . . . . .**97** A1
Sedgley DY3 . . . .**271** B1
Stafford ST16 . . . .**155** C3
Prospect St Burslem ST6 . . .**56** C3
Tamworth B79 . . . .**250** A3
Prospect Terr ST5 . . . . . .**284** A3
Prosper Mdw DY6 . . . . . .**275** C4
Providence St ST1 . . . . . .**282** C4
Provost Pl ST13 . . . .**31** A4
Pruden Ave WV4 . . . .**266** C2
Puddle Hill ST18 . . . .**139** B1
Puddy La ST9 . . . .**44** C4
Pudsey Dr B75 . . . .**258** B2
Pugh Rd WV4,WV14 . . . . .**266** C1
Pugin Cl WV6 . . . .**254** B2
Pullman Cl B77 . . . .**251** A1
Pullman Ct ST10 . . . .**76** B1
Pulteney Dr ST16 . . . .**155** A3
Pump Bank ST5 . . . .**69** C4
Pump La Doveridge DE6 . .**127** A4
Rugeley WS15 . . . .**178** B2
Pump St Leek ST13 . . . . . .**31** A4
Stoke-on-T ST4 . . . .**72** A4
Purbeck St ST6 . . . .**57** A4
Purbrook B77 . . . .**261** C4
Purbrook Rd WV1 . . . . . .**266** C4
Purcell Ave WS13 . . . . . .**214** B1
Pye Green Rd WS11 . . . . .**209** C2
Pye Green Valley Prim Sch
WS12 . . . .**210** A4
Pye Green Valley Primary
Sch WS12 . . . .**210** A4
Pyebirch La ST21 . . . . . .**134** A3
Pyenest St ST1 . . . .**282** A1
Pyrus Gr WS15 . . . .**196** C3

Q

Quabbs La ST11 . . . .**91** B4
Quadrangle The ST9 . . . . .**43** C1
Quadrant Rd ST1 . . . . . .**282** B3
Quadrant The
Hanley ST1 . . . .**282** B3
Sedgley DY3 . . . .**266** B1
Quadrille Lawns WV9 . . .**239** C1
Quail Gn WV6 . . . .**254** C1
Quail Gr ST3 . . . .**90** A4
Quale Gr 6 DY8 . . . .**275** B2
Quantock Cl WS8 . . . . . .**245** A2
Quarry Ave ST4 . . . .**71** C4
Quarry Bank Keele ST5 . . .**69** C4
Upper Tean ST10 . . . .**94** A2
Quarry Bank Rd
Keele ST5 . . . .**69** C4
Market Drayton TF9 . . . . .**112** A4
Quarry Berry La DE12 . . .**236** C4
Quarry Brow DY3 . . . . . .**271** C3
Quarry Cl Caverswall ST9 . .**59** A2
Cheslyn Hay WS6 . . . .**226** C2
Norton-in-t-M ST9 . . . .**43** B2
Rugeley WS15 . . . .**196** A4
Quarry Hills La WS14 . . .**231** B3
Quarry House La TF9 . . . .**112** A4
Quarry La ST20 . . . .**171** B2
Quarry Pl TF9 . . . .**112** A4
Quarry Rd Stoke-on-T ST4 . .**71** C4
Upper Tean ST10 . . . .**94** A2
Quarry Terr ST7 . . . .**26** A1
Quarter La SK17 . . . .**23** A1
Quee La ST14 . . . .**126** A1
Queen Anne St ST4 . . . . . .**72** A4
Queen Elizabeth's Mercian
Sch B79 . . . .**250** B3
Queen Margaret's Rd
TF9 . . . .**99** B3
Queen Mary Rd ST4 . . . . .**72** A1
Queen Mary's Dr ST12 . . . .**88** C2
Queen St Audley ST7 . . . . .**39** C1
Brownhills WS9 . . . .**244** C1
Burntwood WS7 . . . .**228** C3
Burslem ST6 . . . .**56** C4
Burton u T DE14 . . . .**166** B4
Cannock WS11 . . . .**209** B1
Cannock, High Town
WS11 . . . .**210** A3
Cheadle ST10 . . . .**76** C2
Cheslyn Hay WS6 . . . .**226** B2
Kidsgrove ST7 . . . .**26** A1
Kingswinford, Moss Grove
DY6 . . . .**275** B4
Kingswinford, Wordsley
DY8 . . . .**275** B2
Leek ST13 . . . .**30** C3
Lichfield WS13 . . . .**231** A4
Longnor SK17 . . . .**13** A3
Market Drayton TF9 . . . . . .**97** B1
Newcastle-u-L ST5 . . . . . .**284** C4
Newcastle-u-L, Chesterton
ST5 . . . .**55** C4
Newcastle-u-L, Porthill ST5 . .**56** A3
Rugeley WS15 . . . .**196** C4
Stourbridge DY8 . . . .**279** C3
Uttoxeter ST14 . . . .**126** B4
Queen Victoria Prim Sch
DY3 . . . .**271** B4
Queen's Ave ST6 . . . .**41** C2
Queen's Croft Com Sch
WS13 . . . .**231** A4
Queen's Dr ST8 . . . .**27** B3

Queen's Prim Sch ST4 . .**73** A3
Queen's Rd Stoke-on-T ST4 .**71** C4
Stourbridge DY8 . . . .**279** C3
Queen's Row ST12 . . . .**88** C1
Queen's Sq 9 ST15 . . . . .**105** A1
Queens Cotts ST19 . . . . . .**206** A4
Queens Ct
Burton u T DE14 . . . .**185** A4
Longton ST3 . . . .**73** A1
Newcastle-u-L ST5 . . . . . .**284** C1
Queens Gdns
Codsall WV8 . . . .**238** C2
Talke ST7 . . . .**40** B3
Queens Hospl DE13 . . . . .**166** A3
Queens Par WS3 . . . .**243** A1
Queens Park Ave ST3 . . . .**73** A1
Queens Rd Sedgley DY3 . .**271** C4
Shareshill WV10 . . . .**225** A3
Queens Rise DE13 . . . . . .**146** B3
Queens Sq WS11 . . . .**209** B1
Queens Terr ST1 . . . .**57** C2
Queens Way B78 . . . .**262** C3
Queens Wlk ST3 . . . .**74** A2
Queensberry Rd ST3 . . . . .**73** B1
Queensland Cres DE15 . . .**167** B1
Queensmead Rd ST3 . . . . .**89** C4
Queensville ST17 . . . .**175** A4
Queensville Ave ST17 . . . .**156** A1
Queensville Bridge
ST17 . . . .**156** A1
Queensway
Newcastle-u-L ST5 . . . .**71** A3
Rugeley WS15 . . . .**196** C4
Stafford ST16 . . . .**155** C4
Stoke-on-T ST4 . . . .**72** B3
Tamworth B79 . . . .**250** A4
Queensway Ct 7 ST3 . . . . .**74** A1
Queensway Ind Est ST6 . . .**56** B4
Queenswood Rd B75 . . . .**258** C4
Queenville ST17 . . . .**156** A1
Quendale WV5 . . . .**269** C3
Quillets Rd 3 DY8 . . . . . .**275** B2
Quince B77 . . . .**251** A1
Quince Tree Sch B77 . . . .**251** A2
Quinton Ave WS6 . . . . . .**226** C2
Quinton Gr ST5 . . . .**56** A2
Quinton Wlk ST6 . . . .**42** B1
Quixhill Bank ST14 . . . . . .**95** C4
Quixhill La ST14 . . . .**79** C1
Quorn Cl DE15 . . . .**167** A1
Quorn Cres 4 DY8 . . . . . .**275** B2

R

Rabbit La WV10 . . . .**241** A4
Rabone St ST6 . . . .**41** C2
Raby St WV2 . . . .**266** B4
Race Course ST5 . . . .**55** B1
Racecourse La DY8 . . . . .**279** C1
Racecourse Rd ST4 . . . . . .**72** A4
Rachel Gr ST4 . . . .**73** A3
Raddle La B79 . . . .**217** C3
Radford Bk ST17 . . . .**175** B4
Radford Cl ST15 . . . .**105** A1
Radford Dr WS4 . . . .**244** B1
Radford Rd ST4 . . . .**56** C1
Radford Rise ST17 . . . . . .**175** B4
Radford St ST15 . . . .**105** A1
Radhurst Rise DE13 . . . . .**183** B1
Radley Way ST9 . . . .**59** A2
Radmore Cl WS7 . . . .**228** B4
Radmore La
Abbots Bromley WS15 . . . .**161** B4
Gnosall TF10,ST20 . . . . . .**170** B4
Radnor Ct WS9 . . . .**244** C2
Radnor Rd DY3 . . . .**271** B4
Radnor Rise WS12 . . . . . .**210** A2
Radstock Cl ST17 . . . .**175** C3
Radstock Rd WV12 . . . . . .**242** B1
Radstone Rise ST5 . . . . . .**71** A2
Radway Green Rd CW2 . . .**38** C4
Ragees Rd DY6 . . . .**275** C2
Raglan Ave WV6 . . . .**254** C2
Raglan Cl Aldridge WS9 . .**256** C2
Burton u T DE13 . . . .**166** B4
Raglan St ST4 . . . .**72** C3
Raglan Wlk ST4 . . . .**72** B3
Ragley Cl WS3 . . . .**243** A1
Raikes La
Shenstone WS14 . . . .**246** B4
Wall WS14 . . . .**246** B4
Railswood Dr WS3 . . . . . .**244** A4
Railton Ave ST3 . . . .**73** A1
Railway Cotts
Chebsey ST21 . . . .**135** A4
Congleton CW12 . . . .**6** A1
Draycott in t M ST11 . . . . . .**91** B2
Egginton DE65 . . . .**148** A4
Leek ST13 . . . .**30** C1
Rugeley WS15 . . . .**197** A1
Railway Ct ST9 . . . .**43** C4
Railway Ent Ctr ST4 . . . . . .**57** C1
Railway La WS7 . . . .**211** C1
Railway Pas ST3 . . . .**283** C4
Railway Rd ST3 . . . .**73** C1
Railway St
Cannock WS11 . . . .**226** C4
Norton Canes WS11 . . . . .**228** A3
Stafford ST16 . . . .**155** B2
Tunstall ST6 . . . .**41** C1

Railway Terr
Brocton ST17 . . . .**176** B4
Kingsley ST10 . . . .**62** A2
Longton ST3 . . . .**283** D3
Rainbow St 9 WV2 . . . . . .**266** B4
Rainford Cl ST10 . . . .**26** C1
Rainham Gr ST6 . . . .**42** A4
Rainscar B77 . . . .**262** A4
Rake End Ct WS15 . . . . . .**179** C1
Rake Hill WS7 . . . .**229** A4
Rakegate Jun & Inf Schs
WV10 . . . .**240** A1
Rakes La DE6 . . . .**51** C3
Rakeway Rd ST10 . . . .**76** C1
Raleigh Hall Ind Est
ST21 . . . .**117** C1
Ralph Ct ST17 . . . .**174** A4
Ralph Dr ST1 . . . .**57** C4
Ralston Cl WS3 . . . .**243** A2
Ramage Gr ST3 . . . .**73** B1
Rambleford Way ST16 . . .**155** B4
Ramillies Cres WS6 . . . . .**226** C1
Ramsey Cl ST12 . . . .**88** C2
Ramsey Rd ST5 . . . .**284** A4
Ramsey St ST4 . . . .**72** B3
Ramshaw Gr 5 ST3 . . . . . .**73** B3
Ramshaw View ST13 . . . . .**31** A4
Ramshorn Rd ST10 . . . . . .**78** C4
Randall Cl DY6 . . . .**275** C2
Randle Dr B75 . . . .**258** B2
Randles La ST9 . . . .**60** A3
Ranelagh Ho WV2 . . . . . .**266** B4
Ranelagh Rd WV2 . . . .**266** B3
Ranelagh St ST1 . . . .**282** B2
Rangeley View 1 WS15 . . .**104** C1
Rangemoor La DE6 . . . .**80** B3
Rangemore Hill DE13 . . . .**183** A4
Rangemore St DE14 . . . . .**166** A2
Rangemore Terr ST5 . . . . .**56** B2
Ranger's Wlk WS15 . . . . .**178** A1
Rangeways Rd DY6 . . . . .**275** C2
Rangifer Rd B78 . . . .**249** C1
Ranleigh Ave DY6 . . . . . .**275** C2
Ranscombe Dr DY3 . . . . .**271** B1
Ransome Pl ST3 . . . .**73** C2
Ranton Park Area 3
WS11 . . . .**210** A1
Ranworth Cl ST5 . . . .**71** A1
Ranworth Rise WV4 . . . . .**266** B1
Ratcliffe Ave DE14 . . . . . .**185** A4
Ratcliffe Cl DY3 . . . .**271** C3
Rathbone Ave ST5 . . . .**56** B2
Rathlin Cl WV9 . . . .**240** A2
Rathmore Cl DY8 . . . .**279** C1
Rattigan Dr ST3 . . . .**73** C2
Ratton St ST1 . . . .**282** C3
Raven Cl Cannock WS12 . .**210** C2
Cheslyn Hay WS6 . . . .**226** B1
Huntington WS12 . . . .**209** B4
Raven Ct TF9 . . . .**97** B1
Raven Rd DE13 . . . .**182** A1
Raven's La ST7 . . . .**39** C2
Ravenhill Cl WS15 . . . . . .**196** C3
Ravenhill Dr WV8 . . . .**239** A2
Ravenhill Prim Sch
WS15 . . . .**196** C3
Ravenhill Terr WS15 . . . . .**196** C4
Ravenna Way ST3 . . . .**73** C3
Ravens Cl ST7 . . . .**39** C2
Ravens Ct WS8 . . . .**244** C4
Ravens Way DE14 . . . .**166** A2
Ravenscliffe Rd ST7 . . . . . .**41** A4
Ravenscroft DY3 . . . .**279** B3
Ravensholme WV6 . . . . . .**254** C1
Ravenslea Rd WS15 . . . . .**196** C3
Ravensmead Prim Sch
ST7 . . . .**39** C2
Ravenstone B77 . . . .**262** A4
Ravenswood Cl ST5 . . . . . .**71** A2
Ravenswood Crest 4
ST17 . . . .**175** B4
Rawle Cl ST10 . . . .**76** B2
Rawlett High Sch B79 . . .**234** A1
Rawlett Sports Ctr B79 . .**234** A1
Rawlins St ST1 . . . .**57** C3
Rawnsley Rd WS12 . . . . . .**210** C4
Ray Ct B74 . . . .**257** C2
Raygill B77 . . . .**262** A4
Rayleigh Rd WV3 . . . .**266** A4
Rayleigh Way ST2 . . . .**58** B1
Raymond Ave ST1 . . . .**57** B4
Raymond St ST1 . . . .**282** B1
Reacliffe Rd SK11,ST13 . . . .**18** A2
Read Ave ST16 . . . .**155** C3
Reades La CW12 . . . .**16** B4
Reading Way ST2 . . . .**58** B1
Reads Rd ST4 . . . .**72** C4
Reapers Wlk WV8 . . . .**239** C1
Reason Rd ST17 . . . .**174** C3
Rebecca Gdns WV4 . . . . .**265** C2
Rebecca St ST4 . . . .**72** A4
Recorder Gr ST6 . . . .**42** A3
Recreation Rd ST3 . . . .**73** C1
Rectory Cl
Church Leigh ST10 . . . . . .**109** A3
Drayton Bassett B78 . . . . .**260** C3
Rectory Dr TF11 . . . .**203** C1
Rectory Fields DY8 . . . . .**275** C1
Rectory Gdns
Armitage WS15 . . . .**198** A2
Talke ST7 . . . .**40** B3
Rectory La
Armitage WS15 . . . .**197** C2
Haughton ST18 . . . .**172** C3
Rectory Mews
Egginton DE65 . . . .**148** A2
Mucklestone TF9 . . . .**99** A4
Rectory Rd Hanley ST1 . . .**282** A1

Rectory Rd continued
Upper Tean ST10 . . . .**94** B1
Rectory St Hanley ST1 . . .**282** A1
Kingswinford DY8 . . . .**275** B2
Rectory View ST7 . . . .**40** B3
Red Bank Longton ST3 . . .**283** C1
Market Drayton TF9 . . . . .**112** A4
Red Bank La TF9 . . . .**112** A4
Red Hall La ST7 . . . .**54** B3
Red Hill DY7 . . . .**277** C2
Red Ho The WV7 . . . .**237** A3
Red House Cres ST3 . . . .**283** A3
Red House Ind Est WS9 . .**256** A3
Red La Himley DY3 . . . . . .**271** A4
Madeley CW3 . . . .**68** C3
Norton-in-t-M ST9 . . . .**43** B1
Red Lion Ave WS11 . . . . .**228** A2
Red Lion Cl ST7 . . . .**40** B4
Red Lion Cres WS11 . . . .**228** A2
Red Lion La WS11 . . . . . .**228** A2
Red Lion Pas ST1 . . . .**282** A2
Red Lion St ST16 . . . .**155** C2
Red Rd ST10 . . . .**78** B2
Red Rock Dr WV8 . . . .**238** C1
Redacres WV6 . . . .**255** C3
Redbourn Rd CW2 . . . .**37** B1
Redbridge Cl ST4 . . . .**71** C1
Redbrook Cl WS12 . . . . . .**210** B1
Redbrook La WS15 . . . . . .**196** C3
Redcar Rd Trentham ST4 . . .**88** A4
Wolv WV10 . . . .**240** B2
Redcliff B77 . . . .**250** C3
Redcliffe Dr WV5 . . . .**270** A3
Redfern Dr WS7 . . . .**229** A4
Redfern Rd Stone ST15 . . .**119** C3
Uttoxeter ST14 . . . .**111** A1
Redford Dr WV7 . . . .**237** A3
Redgrave Dr ST16 . . . . . .**155** C1
Redhall Rd DY3 . . . .**271** A1
Redheath Cl ST5 . . . .**55** A1
Redhill ST16 . . . .**155** B4
Redhill Ave WV5 . . . .**270** A3
Redhill Cl B79 . . . .**250** A4
Redhill Dr ST10 . . . .**92** C3
Redhill Gdns 3 ST15 . . . .**120** A4
Redhill Gorse ST16 . . . . .**155** B4
Redhill La DE13 . . . .**146** A3
Redhill Prim Sch WS11 . .**209** C2
Redhill Rd
Cannock WS11 . . . .**209** C2
Stone ST15 . . . .**105** B1
Redhills ST21 . . . .**133** C3
Redhills Rd ST7 . . . .**57** C4
Redhouse Cone & Mus *
DY8 . . . .**275** C1
Redhouse Rd WV6 . . . . . .**255** A3
Redhurst Dr WV10 . . . . . .**240** A2
Redlake B77 . . . .**261** C4
Redland Dr ST2 . . . .**58** B2
Redlands Th ST5 . . . .**120** B4
Redlands Way B74 . . . . . .**257** A1
Redlock Field WS14 . . . . .**231** A3
Redman Gr ST6 . . . .**57** B4
Redmine Cl ST5 . . . .**56** A2
Redmond Cl WS15 . . . . . .**178** B1
Redmoor Cl DE15 . . . .**167** A2
Redmoor Gdns WV4 . . . . .**266** A3
Redmoor Rd WS15 . . . . . .**211** C2
Rednall Dr B75 . . . .**258** B2
Redruth Cl DY6 . . . .**275** B4
Redruth Dr ST17 . . . .**156** B1
Redwell Cl B77 . . . .**250** B4
Redwing B77 . . . .**262** A3
Redwing Cl WS7 . . . .**229** B3
Redwing Dr Biddulph ST8 . .**22** C4
Huntington WS12 . . . .**209** B4
Redwood Ave
Dudley DY1 . . . .**271** C4
Stone ST15 . . . .**120** A3
Redwood Cl B74 . . . .**256** C1
Redwood Dr
Burntwood WS7 . . . .**228** C4
Burton u T DE15 . . . .**186** A4
Cannock WS11 . . . .**210** A2
Redwood Pl ST3 . . . .**73** C1
Redwood Rd DY7 . . . .**278** B2
Reedbed Cl ST6 . . . .**42** B2
Reedham Gdns WV4 . . . . .**265** B3
Reedham Way ST2 . . . .**58** B1
Reedly Rd WV12 . . . .**242** B1
Reedmace B77 . . . .**250** B1
Rees Dr WV5 . . . .**270** A4
Reeve Cl WS15 . . . .**198** A2
Reeve La WS13 . . . .**231** A4
Reeves Ave
Chell Heath ST6 . . . .**42** A2
Newcastle-u-L ST5 . . . .**56** A2
Reeves Gdns WV8 . . . . . .**239** A2
Refinery St ST5 . . . .**284** C1
Regal Cl B77 . . . .**261** B4
Regency Cl ST7 . . . .**40** B3
Regency Ct 1 WS15 . . . . .**197** A3
Regency Dr ST9 . . . .**43** B2
Regency Way DE13 . . . . . .**166** B4
Regency Wlk B74 . . . .**257** A3
Regent Ave ST6 . . . .**41** C2
Regent Cl DY6 . . . .**275** B3
Regent Ct Ipstones ST10 . . .**62** C1
Newcastle-u-L ST5 . . . .**56** A3
Regent Rd Hanley ST1 . . .**282** A1
Wolv WV4 . . . .**265** C3
Regent St Leek ST13 . . . . .**30** C1
Stoke-on-T ST4 . . . .**72** A3
Stone ST15 . . . .**104** C1
Regina Cres WV6 . . . .**255** C3
Regina St ST6 . . . .**42** B1

Reginald Mitchell Prim Sch
ST7 . . . .**25** B1
Reginald Mitchell Way
ST5 . . . .**41** B3
Reginald St 5 ST6 . . . .**57** A4
Regis Beeches WV6 . . . . .**255** B3
Regis Rd WV6 . . . .**255** B3
Registry St ST4 . . . .**72** A4
Reid Cl WS7 . . . .**229** C4
Reid St ST6 . . . .**56** C4
Reindeer Rd B78 . . . .**260** C4
Relay Dr B77 . . . .**262** B4
Rembrandt Cl WS11 . . . . .**210** B1
Rembrandt Way ST3 . . . . .**90** A3
Remer St ST6 . . . .**57** A3
Remington Dr WS11 . . . . .**226** C4
Renard Way ST3 . . . .**90** A4
Rendel Cl ST15 . . . .**104** C1
Rendermore Cl ST19 . . . .**207** C4
Rene Rd B77 . . . .**250** C3
Renfrew Cl
Kingswinford DY8 . . . .**275** B2
Newcastle-u-L ST5 . . . .**70** C4
Renfrew Pl ST4 . . . .**72** A1
Rennie Cres ST13 . . . .**45** B3
Rennison Dr WV5 . . . .**270** A3
Renown Cl ST7 . . . .**57** C1
Renshaw Dr DE11 . . . . . .**186** C3
Renshaw Wood La WV8 . .**221** C1
Renton Gr WV10 . . . .**240** A1
Renton Rd WV10 . . . .**240** A1
Repington Rd ST1 . . . .**57** C4
Repington Rd N B77 . . . .**251** A3
Repington Rd S B77 . . . . .**251** A3
Repton Ave WV6 . . . .**254** C2
Repton Cl Cannock WS11 .**226** A4
Stafford ST16 . . . .**156** A1
Repton Dr ST5 . . . .**70** C3
Repton Rd DE15 . . . .**167** C2
Reservoir Rd
Burton u T DE14 . . . .**165** C2
Cannock WS12 . . . .**210** B2
Longton ST3 . . . .**73** C1
Retreat Gdns DY3 . . . . . .**271** C4
Retreat Gdns The WV6 . .**253** B2
Retreat St WV3 . . . .**266** A4
Reva Rd ST17 . . . .**174** C4
Revival St WS3 . . . .**243** A1
Reynards La SK17 . . . .**24** C2
Reynolds Rise TF9 . . . .**99** B3
Reynolds Ave ST5 . . . .**55** C3
Reynolds Cl
Lichfield WS13 . . . .**214** A1
Swindon DY3 . . . .**269** C1
Reynolds Gr WV6 . . . .**254** C3
Reynolds Rd ST6 . . . .**42** A2
Rhein Way 4 ST17 . . . . . .**175** A4
Rhodes Cl DY3 . . . .**271** A1
Rhodes Ct ST5 . . . .**56** B4
Rhodes Ho DE15 . . . .**167** B2
Rhodes St ST1 . . . .**57** B3
Rhondda Ave ST6 . . . .**57** B4
Rialto Pl ST6 . . . .**41** B2
Ribble Cl ST5 . . . .**71** A2
Ribble Dr ST8 . . . .**16** C1
Ribblesdale B77 . . . .**262** A4
Ribblesdale Ave CW12 . . . .**6** A3
Ricardo St ST1 . . . .**73** B1
Riceyman Rd ST5 . . . .**56** A4
Richard Clarke Fst Sch
WS15 . . . .**161** A3
Richard Cooper Rd
WS14 . . . .**246** C3
Richard Crosse CE Prim Sch
DE13 . . . .**199** B3
Richard Wakefield CE Prim
Sch DE13 . . . .**146** B3
Richards Ave
Stafford ST16 . . . .**156** A2
Tunstall ST6 . . . .**41** C2
Richards Ct WS11 . . . .**227** C3
Richardson Dr DY8 . . . . . .**279** C4
Richardson Pl ST6 . . . .**42** A3
Richborough Dr DY1 . . . .**271** C2
Riches St WV6 . . . .**255** C2
Richfield La ST17 . . . .**193** C4
Richmere Ct WV6 . . . .**255** A2
Richmond Ave Hanley ST1 .**57** B4
Wolv WV3 . . . .**255** C1
Richmond Cl
Cannock WS11 . . . .**210** A3
Newport TF10 . . . .**168** C1
Stafford ST17 . . . .**174** C4
Tamworth B79 . . . .**250** A3
Richmond Dr
Lichfield WS14 . . . .**231** B4
Perton WV6 . . . .**254** C2
Wolv WV3 . . . .**255** C1
Richmond Gdns
Brierley Hill DY8 . . . .**279** C4
Wombourne WV5 . . . .**270** A4
Richmond Gr DY8 . . . .**279** C4
Richmond Pk DY6 . . . . . .**275** B4
Richmond Rd
Sedgley DY3 . . . .**271** C4
Trentham ST4 . . . .**72** A1
Wolv WV3 . . . .**255** C1
Richmond St
Burton u T DE14 . . . .**166** B2
Stoke-on-T ST4 . . . .**72** A4
Richmond Terr ST1 . . . . . .**282** A1
Rickerscote Ave ST17 . . . .**175** A4
Rickerscote Hall La
ST17 . . . .**175** A3
Rickerscote Rd ST17 . . . . .**174** C3
Ridding Bank ST7 . . . .**87** C4
Ridding La Denstone ST14 . .**79** C1
Kingstone ST14 . . . .**124** B2

Riddings Cres WS3 ....243 C2
Riddings La DE6 ......144 C3
Riddings The
 Brewood ST19 ......223 B4
 Tamworth B77 ......250 C3
Rider's Way WS15 ....178 A1
Ridge Cl ST12 ......104 B4
Ridge Cres ST3 ......89 C3
Ridge Croft ST15 ....120 B4
Ridge Hill Dr CW3 ....69 A4
Ridge Ho ST1 ......57 C2
Ridge Prim Sch The
 DY8 ......279 B3
Ridge Rd
 Kingswinford DY6 ....275 B3
 Tunstall ST6 ......41 B3
Ridge St DY8 ......279 B3
Ridge Way WS9 ....256 A2
Ridge Wlk ST3 ......89 C4
Ridgefields ST8 ......17 A1
Ridgehouse Dr ST1 ....57 A2
Ridgemont Cl ST15 ....120 B4
Ridgeway Hixon ST18 ..158 B4
 Sedgley DY3 ......271 B4
Ridgeway Cl
 Hopton ST18 ......156 A4
 Stafford ST17 ......174 B3
Ridgeway Dr WV4 ....265 C2
Ridgeway Prim Sch
 WS7 ......229 A3
Ridgeway Rd
 Brierley Hill DY8 ....275 C1
 Burton u T DE15 ....185 C4
Ridgeway The
 Burntwood WS7 ....229 A2
 Stafford ST17 ......155 A3
Ridgewood Ave DY8 ....279 B4
Ridgewood Dr B75 ....258 A1
Ridgewood High Sch
 DY8 ......279 B3
Ridgewood Rise B77 ..251 A3
Ridgmont Rd ST5 ....70 C2
Ridgway Dr ST11 ....90 B4
Ridgway Pl ST5 ......56 B3
Ridgway Rd ST1,ST4 ..57 B1
Ridings Brook Dr ⓷
 WS11 ......210 A1
Ridings Cl TF9 ......97 C1
Ridings Park Trad Est
 WS11 ......210 A1
Ridley St ST4 ......72 B3
Ridley Wlk ST4 ......72 B3
Ridware Ho WS13 ....214 C1
Ridware Rd WS15 ....198 A4
Rifle Range Cnr WS15 ..195 A3
Rigby Dr WS11 ....209 C2
Rigby Rd ST7 ......26 A2
Righton Ho B77 ....250 B1
Riley B77 ......250 B1
Riley Ave ST6 ......42 A1
Riley Cres WV4 ....266 A3
Riley La ST20 ......151 C4
Riley St N ST6 ......56 C4
Riley St S ST6 ......56 C4
Rileys Way ST7 ......39 C1
Rill St ST4 ......283 A4
Rimbach Dr ST18 ....177 B4
Rimini Cl ST3 ......73 C3
Rindle The ST10 ....76 A2
Rindleford Ave WV4 ..265 B3
Ring Rd WS7 ......228 C4
Ring The ST18 ......158 B1
Ringhills Rd WV8 ....239 A1
Ringland Cl ST1 ....282 C3
Ringway WS11 ......209 C1
Ringway Ind Est WS13 ..214 B2
Ringwood Ave WS9 ..256 A1
Ringwood Rd WV10 ..240 B1
Ripon Ave ST5 ......55 C4
Ripon Dr ST17 ......175 B4
Ripon Rd ST3 ......88 C4
Rise The
 Kingswinford DY6 ....275 C3
 Rugeley WS15 ......196 C3
 Stafford ST17 ......175 C4
 Swadlincote DE11 ....186 A3
Riseley Rd ST4 ......71 B4
Rishworth Ave WS15 ..178 C1
Rising Brook
 Stafford ST17 ......174 C4
 Wolv WV6 ......255 A2
Rising Brook High Sch
 ST17 ......174 C3
Riskin Cl ST3 ......73 B3
Rivendell Gdns WV6 ..255 A3
Rivendell La ST13 ....30 C1
River Lea Mews CW3 ..68 C3
River View SK17 ....13 A3
River Way ST15 ....120 A4
Rivercroft Cl ST14 ....96 A2
Riverdale Cl DE15 ....167 A3
Riverdale Dr ST7 ....41 C4
Riverdrive B78,B79 ..250 A2
Riverfield Gr B77 ....250 B3
Riverhead Cl ST6 ....42 C3
Riversfield Dr ST14 ....95 C2
Riverside Rugeley WS15 ..178 C1
 Walton-on-T DE12 ....184 B1
Riverside Dr DE14 ....184 C4
Riverside Gdns
 Burton u T DE14 ....166 C3
 Codsall WV8 ......239 A3
Riverside Ho ST19 ....192 C1
Riverside Ind Est B78 ..250 A1
Riverside L Ctr ST16 ..155 C2
Riverside Rd
 Stoke-on-T ST4 ......71 C1

Riverside Rd continued
 Upper Tean ST10 ......92 B2
Riverside Way WV9 ....224 A1
Riversleigh Dr DY8 ....279 C4
Riversmead ST5 ......71 A2
Riversmead Way ST16 ..155 C1
Riverway ST16,ST17 ..155 C1
Rivington Cl DY8 ....279 C2
Rivington Cres ST6 ....42 A3
Rixdale Cl ST1 ......282 B4
Roach B77 ......261 B3
Roaches The ⭐ ST13 ..10 B1
Road One CW1 ......37 B4
Road Two CW1 ......37 B4
Robert Cl DY8 ......279 C2
Robert Heath St ST6 ..42 B1
Robert St Sedgley DY3 ..271 B2
 Tunstall ST6 ......41 B2
Robert Sutton RC High Sch
 DE15 ......186 A4
Robert Wynd WV14 ..266 C1
Roberts Ave ST5 ....284 B4
Roberts Cl Audley ST7 ..54 C3
 Brownhills WS9 ......244 C1
Roberts Green Rd DY3 ..271 B1
Roberts Prim Sch DY3 ..271 B2
Robertson Dr ST5 ....55 C2
Robertson Sq ST4 ....71 C2
Robertville Rd ST2 ....58 A2
Robey's La B78 ......251 B2
Robin Cl
 Huntington WS12 ....209 B4
 Tamworth B77 ......261 B4
 Uttoxeter ST14 ......126 A3
Robin Croft ① ST6 ....56 C4
Robin Hill ST4 ......28 A4
Robin Hill Gr ST4 ....73 A3
Robin La TF10 ......168 A3
Robina Dr ST10 ......76 C2
Robinia B77 ......251 A2
Robins Cl WS6 ......226 B1
Robins Rd WS7 ......228 C4
Robins The TF9 ......99 B2
Robinson Ave ST6 ....57 B4
Robinson Cl B79 ....249 C4
Robinson Rd
 Burntwood WS7 ....228 C4
 Swadlincote DE11 ..186 C3
 Trentham ST4 ......87 C4
Robinswood ST17 ....175 B3
Robson Cl WS8 ......244 C3
Robson St ST1 ......282 A2
Rocester La ST10 ....49 A1
Roche Ave ST13 ......31 A4
Roche Rd WS3 ......242 C1
Roche The
 Burntwood WS13 ....230 A4
 Cheddleton ST13 ....45 B2
Roche Way WS3 ....242 C1
Rochester Ave WS7 ..229 A4
Rochester Rd ST3 ....73 B3
Rochester Way WS12 ..210 B4
Rochford Cl ST13 ....30 B3
Rochford Gr WV4 ....265 B3
Rochford Way ST2 ....58 B1
Rock Cres ST15 ......105 B2
Rock End Rd ST13 ....45 A4
Rock Farm Rd WS14 ..232 C3
Rock Hill B78,WS14 ..248 B4
Rock House Dr ST12 ..88 B1
Rock La Ashley TF9 ....100 B4
 Mucklestone TF9 ......99 B4
 Standon ST21 ......102 A1
Rock Rd WV14 ......271 C4
Rock St DY3 ......271 C3
Rockeries The ST17 ..175 A3
Rockfield Ave ST2 ....43 B1
Rockhouse Dr ST18 ..158 A4
Rockhouse La ST7 ....40 B4
Rockingham Cl
 Sedgley DY3 ......271 A2
 Walsall WS3 ......243 A1
Rockingham Dr
 Cheadle ST10 ......76 C2
 Perton WV6 ......254 C2
Rocklands ST5 ......56 B4
Rocklands Cres WS13 ..214 B1
Rocklands Sch WS13 ..231 B4
Rockrose Gdns WV10 ..241 A4
Rocks The Endon ST6 ..43 A4
 Standon ST21 ......102 B1
Rockside ST7 ......26 B3
Rocky Wall DY7 ....277 C2
Rodbaston Coll
 Hopwas WS14 ......248 A3
 Penkridge ST19 ......207 C3
Rodbaston Dr ST19 ..207 C3
Roddam Ct TF10 ....168 C1
Roddige La WS13 ....216 A4
Rode Hall ⭐ ST7 ....25 A4
Rodger Ave CW3 ....53 A3
Rodgers St ST6 ......41 B4
Rodway Dr WV4 ....266 B2
Roe Deer Gn TF10 ..168 C3
Roe La ST5 ......71 A2
Roe Pk CW12 ......15 C1
Roebuck Ct ST15 ....106 B1
Roebuck Sh Ctr ST5 ..284 B2
Roebuck St ST4 ......72 B4
Roedean Ave ST17 ..175 A4
Roford Ct DY3 ......271 C3
Rogate Cl ST4 ......73 C3
Rogers Ave ST5 ......55 C2
Rogers St ST1 ......282 A3
Rogerstone Ave ST4 ..71 C3
Rokewood Cl DY6 ....270 B1
Rokholt Cres WS11 ..209 B1
Rolfe Cl ST4 ......72 A1

Rolleston La DE13 ....146 B3
Rolleston Rd DE13 ..166 B4
Rolt Cl ST12 ......104 C2
Roma Cl ST3 ......89 B4
Roman Cl WS8 ......228 C1
Roman Ct Cannock WS11 ..226 C3
 Tamworth B77 ......261 C4
Roman Dr ST5 ......55 B3
Roman La B74 ......257 A2
Roman Pk B74 ......257 A2
Roman Pl B74 ......257 A1
Roman Rd Brewood WV9 ..224 A2
 Little Aston B74 ....257 B2
Roman Rd (Sandy La)
 DY8 ......279 B2
Roman View WS11 ..226 C3
Roman Way
 Lichfield WS14 ......231 B4
 Tamworth B77 ......249 C4
Roman Wlk WS14 ....230 B1
Romans Grange B74 ..257 B3
Romany Way DY8 ....279 B2
Romer Side ST2 ......73 B4
Romford Mdw ST21 ..133 B3
Romford Pl ST3 ......90 A4
Romford Rd ST16 ....155 C1
Romilly Cl Lichfield WS14 ..231 C1
 Stourbridge DY8 ....279 C3
Romney B77 ......261 C4
Romney Ave ST5 ....55 C3
Romney Dr ST16 ....155 A2
Romsey Cl ST2 ......73 B4
Romsey Gr ST17 ....240 B2
Romsey Rd WV10 ..240 B2
Romsey Way WS3 ..242 C2
Romsley Cl WS4 ....244 B1
Romsley La WV15,DY12 ..276 A1
Ronald St ST3 ......283 C4
Ronald Wlk ST3 ....283 C2
Ronaldsway Dr ST5 ..284 A4
Ronson Ave ST4 ......71 C2
Rook The WV6 ......255 B3
Rooker Ave WV2 ....266 C3
Rooker Cres WV2 ....266 C3
Rookery Ave ST3 ....73 A1
Rookery Ct
 Armitage WS15 ......198 B3
 Yoxall DE13 ......182 A1
Rookery Cotts WS21 ..115 C3
Rookery Cres ST11 ....91 B1
Rookery Ct
 Lichfield WS13 ......230 C4
 Stoke-on-T ST4 ......71 C2
Rookery La Aldridge WS9 ..256 A3
 Hints B75,B78 ......248 B1
 Stoke-on-T ST4 ......71 C2
 Wolv WV2 ......266 A3
Rookery Par WS9 ....256 A3
Rookery Rd Kidsgrove ST7 ..26 B2
 Wombourne WV5 ....270 A3
Rookery Rise WV5 ..270 A3
Rookery The
 Newcastle-u-L ST5 ....55 B1
 Stoke-on-T ST4 ......71 C2
Rookswood Copse ②
 ST17 ......175 B3
Rookwood Dr WV6 ..254 C1
Rope St ST4 ......56 B1
Roper Way DY3 ......271 C3
Roper Wlk DY3 ......271 C3
Ropewalk The DE14 ..166 B1
Rose Ave
 Burton u T DE13 ....148 A1
 Kingswinford DY6 ..275 C3
Rose Bank Cres ST10 ..78 A3
Rose Bank St ST13 ....30 C1
Rose Bank Terr ST13 ..30 C3
Rose Bay Mdw ② WS11 ..210 B1
Rose Cott Gdns DE14 ..166 B1
Rose Cottage Dr ⑦ DY8 ..275 B2
Rose Dr WS8 ......244 C3
Rose Hill ST6 ......155 B2
Rose La WS7 ......229 B4
Rose Mill TF9 ......99 C3
Rose St ST1 ......57 C3
Rose Tree Ave ST4 ....71 C1
Rose Tree La DE11 ..186 C4
Rose Way WS15 ......178 A1
Roseacre ST5 ......70 C4
Roseacre Gr ST3 ....89 C3
Roseacre La ST13 ....90 C3
Roseberry Dr CW3 ....68 C4
Roseberry Gdns DY10 ..280 B2
Rosebery Cl ST8 ....27 C3
Rosebery Rd B77 ....261 B2
Rosebery St ST6 ....41 C4
Rosebury Gr WV5 ....269 C3
Rosedale Wlk DY6 ....275 C4
Rosehill WS12 ......209 C4
Rosehill Ct ST2 ......43 A1
Roseland Cres ST2 ....43 A1
Roseleigh Cres DE11 ..186 C4
Rosemary Ave
 Cheslyn Hay WS6 ....226 B2
 Stafford ST17 ......174 C3
 Wolv WV4 ......266 B3
Rosemary Cl WS8 ....244 B1
Rosemary Cres
 Sedgley DY1 ......271 C3
 Wolv WV4 ......266 B3
Rosemary Cres W WV4 ..266 A3
Rosemary Ct B74 ..257 B2
Rosemary Dr
 Huntington WS12 ....209 B3
 Little Aston B74 ....257 B2
 Uttoxeter ST14 ......126 A3
Rosemary Hill Rd B74 ..257 B2
Rosemary La DY8 ....279 B2

Rosemary Nook B74 ..257 B3
Rosemary Pl ST1 ....57 C2
Rosemary Rd
 Cheslyn Hay WS6 ....226 B2
 Tamworth B77 ......250 C2
Rosemary St ST5 ....55 C1
Rosemount Rd DE15 ..166 C2
Rosendale Ave ST5 ....55 C3
Rosendale Rd ST5 ....56 A3
Roseneath Pl ST2 ....43 A1
Rosevale Ct ST5 ....55 C4
Rosevale Rd ST5 ....55 C4
Rosevale St ST5 ......43 A1
Roseville Dr CW12 ....16 A4
Roseville Gdns WV8 ..239 A2
Rosewood Ave ST9 ....43 B2
Rosewood Ct B77 ....250 B2
Rosewood Ct ST77 ..250 B2
Rosewood Gdns WV11 ..242 A2
Rosewood Pk WS6 ..226 B1
Rosewood Rd DE15 ..185 C3
Rosewood Specl Sch
 DY1 ......271 C1
Rosey Bk ST9 ......43 B2
Rosliston Rd
 Burton u T DE15 ....185 C4
 Swadlincote DE15 ..185 C3
 Walton-on-T DE12 ..202 C4
Rosliston Rd S DE15 ..185 C3
Rosomount WV6 ....255 B3
Ross Cl Longton ST3 ..74 A2
 Wolv WV6 ......255 C1
Ross Dr DY6 ......275 B4
Ross Rd ST10 ......62 C1
Rossall Ave ST5 ......70 C3
Rossett Gr ST7 ......41 C4
Rosslyn Rd ST3 ......283 C2
Rosvean Cl ST1 ....282 B4
Rothay B77 ......261 C4
Rothbury Gn WS12 ..210 C1
Rother Wlk ST6 ......42 A2
Rotherwood Dr ST17 ..155 B1
Rotherwood Gdns ST16 ..155 C2
Rothesay Ave ST5 ....70 C4
Rothesay Ct Longton ST3 ..73 B1
 Newcastle-u-L ST5 ....70 C3
Rothesay Dr DY8 ....275 B2
Rothesay Rd ST3 ....73 B1
Rothley Gn ST3 ......88 C4
Rothsay Ave ST5 ......57 B4
Rothwell St ST4 ......71 C3
Rotten Row WS14 ....231 B4
Rotterdam St ST5 ....55 C1
Rotterdam Rd ST5 ....55 C1
Rough Bank CW12 ....16 C4
Rough Close CE Prim Sch
 ST3 ......89 C2
Rough Hills Cl WV2 ..266 C3
Rough Hills Rd WV2 ..266 C3
Roughcote La ST11 ....74 B3
Roughley Dr B75 ....258 C2
Roughley Farm Rd B75 ..258 C2
Round Hill DY3 ......266 B1
Round House Rd DY3 ..271 C2
Roundfields ST9 ......43 B2
Roundhill Way WS8 ..229 A1
Roundway ST3 ......72 B1
Roundway Down WV6 ..254 C2
Roundwell St ST6 ....41 B2
Rouse Cl ST16 ......155 B1
Row The ST18 ......137 C2
Rowallan Rd B75 ....258 B1
Rowan Cl Biddulph ST8 ..28 A4
 Kidsgrove ST7 ......41 A4
 Lichfield WS14 ......231 B4
 Stone ST15 ......120 A3
Rowan Cres WV3 ....265 C4
Rowan Dr
 Armitage WS15 ......198 A3
 Essington WV11 ....242 A4
 Newport TF10 ......168 C1
Rowan Gl ST17 ......175 B3
Rowan Gr Brewood ST19 ..223 B4
 Burntwood WS7 ....228 C4
 Fenton ST4 ......72 C2
Rowan La TF9 ......99 C3
Rowan Pl ST5 ......57 C4
Rowan Rd Cannock WS11 ..209 B1
 Sedgley DY3 ......266 C1
 Market Drayton TF9 ..97 C1
Rowan Rise DY6 ....275 C3
Rowanburn Cl DY10 ..280 B2
Rowbury Dr DE15 ..167 A1
Rowena Gdns DY3 ..266 B1
Rowhurst Cl ST5 ....55 B4
Rowhurst Pl ST6 ....42 B1
Rowland St ST3 ......73 A1
Rowley Ave
 Newcastle-u-L ST5 ....55 C4
 Stafford ST17 ......155 B1
Rowley Bank ST17 ..174 C4
Rowley Bank Gdns
 ST17 ......174 C4
Rowley Bank Ho ST17 ..174 C4
Rowley Cl Cannock WS12 ..210 A4
 Edingale B79 ......217 B3
 Rugeley WS15 ......197 A3
Rowley Gr ST17 ....174 C4
Rowley Hall Cl ST17 ..174 B4
Rowley Hall Dr ST17 ..174 B4
Rowley Hall Hospl ST17 ..174 B4
Rowley St ST16 ......155 B3
Rowleyhill Dr ST19 ..206 C2
Rownall Pl ② ST3 ....74 A1
Rownall Rd
 Cheddleton ST9 ......59 B3
 Meir ST3 ......74 A1

Rownall View ST13 ....30 B2
Rowney Cl TF9 ......99 B2
Rowton Ave WV6 ....254 C2
Rowton St DE13 ....166 B3
Roxall Cl DY10 ......281 B1
Roxburghe Ave ST3 ..283 D2
Royal Cl B74 ......256 C1
Royal Doulton Mus ⭐
 ST6 ......57 A4
Royal Oak Dr ST19 ..221 C4
Royal St ST4 ......283 A5
Royal Wlk ST10 ......76 B2
Royal Wolverhampton Jun
 Sch The WV3 ......266 A4
Royal Wolverhampton Sch
 The WV3 ......266 A4
Royce Ave ST4 ......27 A3
Roycroft Cl ST5 ......56 A4
Royden Ave ST1 ....57 C2
Royds Cl ST18 ......172 C3
Roylance St ST6 ......41 B2
Royston Chase B74 ..257 A2
Royston Way DY3 ..271 B4
Royston Wlk ST3 ....283 C3
Royville Pl ST6 ......57 B4
Rozel Ave DY10 ....280 A1
Ruabon Cl ST8 ......27 C3
Rubens Cl DY3 ......271 B3
Rubens Way ST3 ....90 A4
Rubian St ST4 ......72 C3
Ruby Dr ST3 ......73 B1
Rudge Dale Rd TF9 ..100 A2
Rudge Rd
 Pattingham WV6 ....253 A1
 Rudge WV6 ......263 A4
Rudyard Cl Stone ST15 ..104 C1
 Wolv WV10 ......240 C2
Rudyard Gr ST5 ......56 B2
Rudyard Ho ST17 ....174 C3
Rudyard Rd Biddulph ST8 ..17 B1
 Heaton ST13 ......19 A1
 Rudyard ST13 ......29 C4
Rudyard Way ST10 ....76 C2
Ruelow Mdw ST10 ....62 A4
Ruffin Ct ST15 ......120 B4
Rufford B79 ......249 C4
Rugby Cl Burton u T DE14 ..185 B4
 Newcastle-u-L ST5 ....70 C2
Rugby Rd DY8 ......279 B4
Rugeley Rd
 Armitage WS15 ......197 B3
 Burntwood WS7 ....229 B4
 Cannock WS12 ......211 A4
 Cannock, Hednesford
  WS12 ......210 B4
 King's Bromley DE13 ..199 A3
Rugeley Town Sta
 SW15 ......196 C4
Rugeley Trent Valley Sta
 WS15 ......178 C2
Ruiton St DY3 ......271 B2
Rumer Hill Bsns Est
 WS11 ......226 C4
Rumer Hill Rd WS11 ..226 C4
Running Hills WS15 ..197 C2
Runnymede ST15 ....120 A4
Runnymede Cl ST2 ..58 A2
Rupert St ST8 ......27 B4
Rush La
 Market Drayton TF9 ..97 A1
 Tamworth B77,B78 ..261 B1
Rushall Cl DY8 ......279 C4
Rushall JMI Sch WS4 ..244 A1
Rushall Rd WV10 ....240 C1
Rushbrook Cl WS8 ....244 C3
Rushcliffe Dr ST3 ....90 A4
Rushes Mill WS3 ....243 C2
Rushey La WV7 ......252 B4
Rushford Ave WV5 ..270 A3
Rushmoor Gr ⑰ ST3 ..90 A4
Rushton ST5 ......70 C2
Rushton Ave ST10 ....61 B1
Rushton CE Prim Sch
 SK11 ......8 A1
Rushton Cl ST6 ......43 A4
Rushton Gr ㉑ ST6 ..57 A4
Rushton Mews WS12 ..211 B2
Rushton Rd ST6 ......57 A4
Rushton Way ST11 ....91 A4
Rushtons La ST15 ..105 C3
Rushwater Cl WV5 ..269 C3
Ruskin Ave Sedgley DY3 ..271 A3
 Wolv WV4 ......266 C1
Ruskin Cl ST3 ......283 D5
Ruskin Dr ST8 ......154 C1
Ruskin Pl DE14 ....166 B3
Ruskin Rd WV10 ....241 A1
Rusper Cl ST1 ......57 C3
Russel St ST5 ......155 B2
Russell Bank Rd B74 ..257 C2
Russell Cl Congleton CW12 ..16 A4
 Essington WV11 ....241 C1
Russell Ct B74 ......257 B2
Russell Gr ST1 ......59 A2
Russell Pl ST6 ......41 B3
Russell Rd ST6 ......41 B3
Russell St
 Burton u T DE14 ....166 B1
 Leek ST13 ......30 C3
 Longton ST3 ......283 B1
 Newcastle-u-L ST5 ..56 B3
Russell's Hall Rd DY1 ..271 C1
Russells Hall Prim Sch
 DY1 ......271 C1
Russet Cl ST3 ......90 A4

Russet Wlk WV8 ....**239** C1
Russett Cl WS7 ......**229** A3
Russetts The ST17 ...**174** C3
Rustington Ave ST3 ....**73** C2
Ruston Ave ST6 ....**42** A3
Ruston Cl DE13 ......**146** B3
Rutherford Ave ST5 ....**71** A2
Rutherford Pl ST4 .....**71** C4
Rutherglen Cl WS15 ...**178** B1
Ruthin Gr ST8 ....**27** C3
Ruthin Rd ST2 ....**58** B1
Rutland Ave
  Rugeley WS15 ....**196** B3
  Wolv WV4 ....**265** B2
Rutland Cl DE15 .....**185** B3
Rutland Cres WS9 ....**256** A4
Rutland Dr B78 ....**250** A1
Rutland Pl
  Newcastle-u-L ST5 ....**71** B2
  Stourbridge DY8 ......**279** B4
Rutland Rd
  Cannock WS12 ....**210** B2
  Kidsgrove ST7 ....**26** A1
  Longton ST3 ....**283** C4
Rutland St ST1 ....**282** A4
Ruxley Cl ST2 ....**57** C2
Ruxley Rd ST2 ....**58** A2
Ryburn Cl CW2 ....**37** A2
Rycroft CE Mid Sch ST14 **95** C2
Rydal B77 ....**262** A4
Rydal Cl WS12 ....**210** A4
Rydal Dr WV6 ....**254** C2
Rydal Ho ST16 ....**155** C2
Rydal Way ST5 ....**71** A2
Ryder Cl DE11 ......**186** C1
Ryder Rd ST7 ....**90** A4
Ryder St DY8 ....**275** B1
Ryders Hayes Com Sch
  WS3 ....**244** A3
Ryders Hayes La WS3 .**244** A2
Rye Bank ST5 ....**284** B3
Rye Bank Cres ST5 ...**284** B3
Rye Ct ST16 ....**155** B4
Ryebrook Dr ST6 ....**41** C3
Ryecroft ST5 ....**284** B3
Ryecroft Ave WS4 ....**266** A3
Ryecroft Cl Sedgley DY3 **271** B4
  Upper Tean ST10 ......**92** C2
Ryecroft Cotts WV4 ..**266** A3
Ryecroft Dr ⬛ WS7 ...**229** A4
Ryecroft Rd ST6 ....**42** C2
Ryecroft Sh Ctr WS7 .**229** A4
Ryedale Way CW12 ....**16** B4
Ryefield WV8 ....**239** C1
Ryehills ST7 ....**39** C1
Ryhope Wlk WV9 .....**240** A2
Rykneld Prim Sch DE14 **184** C4
Rykneld St WS13 .....**215** C4
Ryknild Cl B74 ......**257** C3
Ryknild St Alrewas DE13 **201** C3
  Lichfield WS14 ....**231** C3
Ryknild Trad Est DE14 **166** C3
Rylands Dr WV4 ......**266** A2
Ryle St WS3 ....**243** B1
Rylestone Cl ST3 ......**90** A4
Ryton B77 ....**261** C4
Ryton Way DE65 .....**147** B4

S

Sabine St ST17 ....**155** C1
Sabrina Rd WV6 .....**254** C1
Sackville St ST4 ......**56** C1
Saddler Ave ST15 ....**120** B4
Saddlers Cl WS14 ....**231** C4
Saddlestones The WV6 **254** B2
Sadler Cir WS8 ....**245** A4
Sadler Rd WS8 ....**245** A4
Sadlers Mill WS8 ....**245** A4
Saffron B77 ....**251** A2
Saffron
  Barton-u-N DE13 .....**183** B1
  Meir ST3 ....**90** A3
Saffron Gdns WV4 ...**266** A2
Sage Cl ST1 ....**282** B1
Sainte Foy Ave WS13 ..**231** A3
St Aidan's Cl DE13 ..**166** A4
St Aidan's Ct WV4 ..**266** A3
St Aidan's Rd WS11 .**209** C3
St Aidan's St ST6 .....**41** B2
St Albans Cl WV11 ..**242** A1
St Albans Ct DE13 ..**166** A4
St Albans Rd ST16 ..**155** C4
St Andrew Cl WS12 ..**211** A3
St Andrew's CE Sch
  B79 ....**218** C1
St Andrew's Cl
  Clifton Campville B79 .**218** C1
  Sedgley DY3 ....**271** A2
St Andrew's Dr
  Burton u T DE13 .....**166** B4
  Newcastle-u-L ST5 .....**70** C4
St Andrews B77 .....**251** A2
St Andrews Ave WS4 **244** A1
St Andrews CE Prim Sch
  Weston ST18 ....**138** B1
  Wolv WV6 ....**255** C2
St Andrews Cl DE13 .**279** C1
St Andrews Cres ST1 ..**57** B4
St Andrews Dr
  Kidsgrove ST7 ....**26** B2
  Perton WV6 ....**254** B3
St Andrews Rd ST17 .**174** B4

St Andrews Way TF10 ..**168** C1
St Ann St ST1 ....**282** C3
St Ann Wlk ST1 .....**282** C3
St Anne's CE Prim Sch
  ST6 ....**28** A1
St Anne's Cl WS7 ...**228** C2
St Anne's RC Prim Sch
  ST17 ....**175** B4
St Anne's Rd WV10 ..**240** A1
St Anne's Vale ST6 ...**43** A4
St Annes Rd WS13 ...**214** A2
St Anthony's Dr ST5 ..**71** A4
St Anthony's RC Prim Sch
  WV10 ....**240** B2
St Anthonys Cl WS15 .**196** C4
St Anthonys Dr WS3 .**244** A3
St Augustine's Fst Sch
  DE6 ....**144** B3
St Augustine's Rd WS15 **196** C3
St Augustines RC Prim Sch
  ST3 ....**89** C4
St Austell Cl
  Stafford ST17 ....**175** B4
  Tamworth B79 ....**250** A3
St Austin's RC Prim Sch
  ST17 ....**155** C1
St Barbara's Rd WS15 **198** B3
St Bartholomew's CE Prim
  Sch SK17 ....**13** A4
St Bartholomew's CE Prim
  Sch WV4 ....**265** C2
St Bedes Sch WS15 ..**178** A3
St Benedict Biscop CE Prim
  Sch WV5 ....**270** A4
St Benedict's Dr ST18 **177** B4
St Benedict's Rd WS7 **229** A3
St Benedicts Rd WV5 **270** A3
St Bernadette's RC Prim Sch
  WS8 ....**244** C4
St Bernadettes RC Prim Sch
  WV5 ....**269** C3
St Bernard Pl ST2 .....**58** A3
St Bernard's Rd ST5 ..**55** C1
St Bernards Cl WS12 .**211** B4
St Bertelin St ST16 ..**155** B3
St Blaise Rd B75 ....**258** B2
St Brides Cl Sedgley DY3 **271** B4
  Wombourne WV5 ....**269** C3
St Catherine's Cres
  WV4 ....**265** C2
St Catherine's Rd DE11 **186** C3
St Catherines Rd WS13 **214** A2
St Chad's CE Prim Sch
  ST5 ....**40** B1
St Chad's Cl
  Burton u T DE13 .....**166** B4
  Cannock WS11 ....**210** A2
  Denstone ST14 ....**95** B3
  Lichfield WS13 ....**214** A1
  Sedgley DY3 ....**271** B4
  Stone ST15 ....**120** B4
St Chad's Pl ⬛ ST16 .**155** C2
St Chad's Rd
  Burton u T DE13 .....**166** B4
  Lichfield WS13 ....**214** A1
St Chad's Stowe CE Prim Sch
  WS13 ....**231** B4
St Chads CE Prim Sch
  WV6 ....**253** B2
St Chads Cl
  Brewood ST19 ....**223** B3
  Colwich ST18 ....**177** B4
  Pattingham WV6 .....**253** B1
St Chads Ct WS13 ...**231** A4
St Chads RC Sch DY3 **271** B4
St Chads Rd
  Eccleshall ST21 ......**133** B3
  Tunstall ST6 ....**41** C2
St Chads Way TF9 .....**82** B1
St Christopher Ave ST4 ..**71** C4
St Christopher Cl WS12 **211** A3
St Christopher's Dr B77 **250** B1
St Christophers RC Prim Sch
  WV8 ....**239** A2
St Clair St ST3 ......**283** C2
St David Cl WS12 ...**211** A3
St David's Dr DE13 .**166** B4
St Davids Cl WS3 ...**244** A3
St Davids Pl WS3 ...**243** B1
St Davids Rd
  Clifton Campville B79 .**218** C1
  Stafford ST17 ....**174** B4
St Davids Way ST8 ...**27** C3
St Dominic's Priory Sch
  ST15 ....**104** C1
St Dominic's RC Prim Sch
  ST15 ....**105** A1
St Dominic's Sch ST19 **223** B4
St Dominics Ind Jun Sch
  ST4 ....**71** C4
St Editha's Cl B79 ..**250** A3
St Editha's Ct
  Church Eaton ST20 ...**190** A4
  Tamworth B79 ....**250** A4
St Edmund's Ave ST5 .**56** B3
St Edmund's Cl WV6 .**255** C2
St Edmunds RC Sch
  WV3 ....**255** C2
St Edward St ST13 ...**30** C1
St Edward's CE Fst Sch
  ST13 ....**45** A3
St Edward's Rd ST13 .**45** B2
St Edwards CE Mid Sch
  ST13 ....**30** B3
St Edwards Ct DE11 .**186** C3
St Edwards Gn ⬛ WS15 **196** C4

St Elizabeth's RC Prim Sch
  B79 ....**249** C4
St Filumena's RC Prim Sch
  ST11 ....**74** C1
St Francis Cl
  Burton u T DE13 .....**166** B4
  Cannock WS12 ....**211** A3
  Walsall WS3 ....**244** A3
St Francis of Assisi RC Sch
  WS9 ....**256** B3
St Francis RC Prim Sch
  WS4 ....**244** B1
St Gabriel's RC Prim Sch
  B77 ....**250** C1
St George & St Martin RC
  Prim Sch ST1 ....**282** C4
St George Dr WS12 ..**211** A3
St George's Ave N ST5 **56** A3
St George's Ave S ST5 **56** A3
St George's Ave W ST5 **56** A3
St George's Cres ST4 **72** A1
St George's Rd
  Burton u T DE13 .....**165** C3
  Newcastle-u-L ST5 ...**284** A2
  Stafford ST17 ....**156** A1
  Stone ST15 ....**120** A4
  Stourbridge DY8 ....**279** B1
St George's St ⬛ ST13 ..**30** C3
St George's Way B77 **250** C2
St Georges Ave
  Chell Heath ST6 ......**42** A2
  Endon ST9 ....**43** C3
St Georges St B74 ..**257** C3
St Georges Hospl ST16 **155** C3
St Gile's Rd ST5 .....**55** C1
St Giles & St George's CE
  Prim Sch ST5 ....**284** C2
St Giles Gr ST18 ....**172** C3
St Giles Rd WS7 ....**229** A3
St Giles' RC Prim Sch
  ST10 ....**76** B2
St Gregory's RC Jun & Inf
  Schs ST3 ....**283** A3
St Gregory's Rd ST3 **283** A3
St Helens Rd WS13 .**214** A2
St Helier Cl ST5 .....**70** C2
St Hilda's Ave ST13 ..**45** C2
St Ives Cl Stafford ST17 **175** B4
  Tamworth B79 ......**250** A3
St James CE Prim Sch
  Longdon WS15 ....**198** A1
  Stourbridge DY8 ....**279** B4
St James Cl
  Longdon WS15 ....**198** A1
  Walsall WS3 ....**244** A3
St James Cres ST17 .**193** A4
St James Ct Audley ST7 ..**39** B1
  Barton-u-N DE13 .....**183** B1
St James Gn ST21 ...**102** C2
St James Pl ST4 ......**72** A1
St James Prim Sch
  WS8 ....**244** C4
St James Rd
  Cannock WS11 ....**209** B1
  Norton Canes WS11 ..**228** B3
  Sutton Coldfield B75 .**258** B1
St James St ST1 ....**282** A2
St James Wlk WS8 ..**244** C4
St James' Ct ST8 .....**16** C2
St James' Rd DE13 .**183** B1
St James' St DY3 ...**271** B2
St John Cl B75 .....**258** B2
St John Fisher RC High Sch
  ST5 ....**284** C1
St John St Hanley ST1 .**282** C4
  Lichfield WS13 ....**231** B1
St John The Evangelist RC
  Prim Sch (Annexe) ST7 **25** C1
St John's Ave
  Newcastle-u-L ST5 .....**56** B2
  Stoke-on-T ST4 ......**71** C2
  Stone ST15 ....**105** B2
St John's CE Fst Sch
  ST19 ....**221** C4
St John's CE Prim Sch
  Cheddleton ST9 ......**60** A4
  Essington WV11 .....**242** A1
  Keele ST5 ....**69** C4
  Stafford ST17 ....**156** A2
St John's Cl
  Brownhills WS9 ......**244** C2
  Cannock WS11 ....**226** B4
  Lichfield WS13 ......**231** A3
  Swindon DY3 ....**269** B1
St John's Ct
  Burton u T DE13 .....**166** B4
  Cannock WS12 ....**210** C1
  Walsall WS3 ....**243** A1
St John's Dr
  Shenstone WS14 .....**246** C3
  Swadlincote DE11 ...**186** C3
St John's Hill WS14 .**246** C3
St John's Pl Biddulph ST8 **27** B4
  Newcastle-u-L ST5 ....**55** C1
St John's Prim Sch
  DY3 ....**269** C1
St John's RC Prim Sch
  ST10 ....**78** C1
St John's RC Prim Sch
  ST18 ....**158** A1
St John's Rd Biddulph ST8 **27** B4
  Burton u T DE13 .....**166** B4
  Cannock WS11 ....**226** C4
  Congleton CW12 .....**6** A3
St John's Sq
  ⬛ Burslem ST6 ....**56** C4
  Uttoxeter ST14 ......**110** C1
St John's St B79 ....**250** A3

St John's Wlk ST16 ..**156** A2
St John's Wood ST7 ...**25** C1
St Johns CE Prim Sch
  WS9 ....**245** A2
St Johns Cl Hixon ST18 **139** B2
  Rugeley WS15 ....**196** B4
St Johns Ho B74 ....**257** C2
St Johns Rd Ashley TF9 **100** B3
  Brownhills, Shire Oak
    WS8 ....**245** A3
  Essington WV11 .....**242** A2
  Stafford ST17 ....**174** B4
  Walsall WS3 ....**244** B1
St Johns Ret Pk ⬛ WV2 **266** B4
St Johns Sch WS3 ..**231** A4
St Johns Way TF9 ..**100** B3
St Joseph & St Theresa RC
  Prim Sch WS7 ......**228** C2
St Joseph St ST6 .....**41** B4
St Joseph's Coll ST4 ..**71** C2
St Joseph's Convent Prim
  Sch WV4 ....**255** C3
St Joseph's RC Prim Sch
  Cannock WS12 ....**210** B2
  Lichfield WS14 ....**231** B4
  Rugeley WS15 ....**196** C4
  Uttoxeter ST14 .....**126** A3
St Josephs Cl WS3 ..**244** A2
St Josephs Ct WV4 .**265** B3
St Jude's CE Inf Sch
  WV6 ....**255** C2
St Jude's CE Jun Sch
  WV3 ....**255** C2
St Jude's Ct ⬛ WV6 .**255** C2
St Jude's Rd WV6 ...**255** C2
St Jude's Rd W WV6 **255** C2
St Jude's Way DE13 .**166** B4
St Lawrence CE Prim Sch
  ST20 ....**171** C3
St Lawrence Rd WS11 **210** A1
St Lawrence View SK17 **23** A1
St Lawrence Way ST20 **171** B4
St Leonard's Ave
  Ipstones ST10 ....**62** A4
  Stafford ST17 ....**156** A1
St Leonard's CE Fst Sch
  Coppenhall ST18 ....**192** C4
  Ipstones ST10 ....**62** A4
St Leonard's CE Prim Sch
  B79 ....**234** B1
St Leonard's Prim Sch
  ST17 ....**156** A1
St Leonard's Way CW3 ..**67** B1
St Leonards View B78 **262** C4
St Lucy's Dr ST5 .....**56** B4
St Luke St ST1 ......**282** C2
St Luke's CE Prim Sch
  Hanley ST1 ....**282** C2
  Newcastle-u-L ST5 ....**55** A1
St Luke's CE Prim Sch
  WV2 ....**266** A4
St Luke's Cl
  Cannock WS11 ....**226** B4
  Newcastle-u-L ST5 ....**55** A1
St Luke's Rd
  Barton-u-N DE13 .....**183** B1
  Burntwood WS7 .....**229** B3
  Burton u T DE13 .....**166** B4
St Luke's Wlk WS15 .**198** B2
St Lukes CE Prim Sch
  ST9 ....**43** C4
St Lukes Cl ST15 ...**135** A4
St Lukes Ct ST1 ....**282** C2
St Lukes Inf Sch WV2 **266** B4
St Margaret Ward RC High
  Sch ST6 ....**41** C2
St Margaret's B74 ..**257** C2
St Margaret's CE Jun Sch
  ST5 ....**56** B2
St Margaret's Ct
  Betley CW3 ....**53** A3
  Draycott in t M ST11 ..**91** C3
  Newcastle-u-L ST5 ....**56** B3
St Margaret's Dr ST1 .**57** C4
St Margaret's Rd B79 **250** A4
St Margarets DE13 ..**165** C3
St Margarets Gr ST3 .**72** C2
St Margarets Rd
  Lichfield WS13 ....**214** A2
  Walsall WS3 ....**244** A2
St Maria Goreti RC Prim Sch
  ST2 ....**58** B1
St Mark's CE Prim Sch
  ST1 ....**282** A1
St Mark's Cl ST1 ....**282** A1
St Mark's Rd
  Burntwood WS7 .....**229** B3
  Burton u T DE13 .....**166** B4
St Mark's St ST1 ....**282** A1
St Marks Cl WS6 ...**226** C2
St Marks Rd
  Brownhills, Shire Oak
    WS8 ....**245** A3
  Walsall WS3 ....**244** B1
St Martin's Cl
  Burton u T DE13 .....**166** B4
  Wolv WV4 ....**266** C3
St Martin's La ST3 ..**283** C4
St Martin's Pl ⬛ ST16 **155** C2
St Martin's Rd
  Newcastle-u-L ST5 ....**70** C4
  Talke ST7 ....**40** C3
St Mary & St Chad CE Fst Sch
  ST19 ....**223** B3
St Mary of the Angels RC
  Prim Sch WS9 ......**256** C4
St Mary's CE Prim Sch
  Uttoxeter ST14 ......**111** A1

St Mary's CE Fst Sch continued
  Wheaton Aston ST19 .**205** B4
St Mary's CE Prim Sch
  CW12 ....**15** A4
St Mary's CE Prim Sch
  Bosley SK11 ....**7** B4
  Colton WS15 ....**178** C3
St Mary's CE Prim Sch
  DY6 ....**275** B4
St Mary's CE Prim Sch
  Mucklestone TF9 .....**99** A4
  Tunstall ST6 ....**41** B2
St Mary's Cl
  Albrighton WV7 .....**237** A3
  Newton Solney DE15 .**167** C4
  Sedgley DY3 ....**271** C4
  Upper Tean ST10 .....**109** A4
St Mary's Cres ST14 .**111** A1
St Mary's Ct ⬛ ST13 ..**30** C3
St Mary's Dr
  Burton u T, Clay Mills
    DE13 ....**147** C1
  Burton u T, Horninglow
    DE13 ....**166** B4
  Newcastle-u-L ST5 ...**284** A2
St Mary's Gate ⬛ ST16 **155** C2
St Mary's Gr ⬛ ST16 .**155** C2
St Mary's Pl ⬛ ST16 .**155** C2
St Mary's RC Prim Sch
  Cannock WS11 ....**226** C4
  Leek ST13 ....**30** C4
  Newcastle-u-L ST5 ...**284** A3
  Norton-in-t-M ST5 ...**84** B2
St Mary's Rd Ashley TF9 .**99** B3
  Colwich ST18 ....**177** B4
  Lichfield WS13 ......**214** A2
  Longton ST3 ....**73** B3
  Newcastle-u-L ST5 ....**56** B3
St Mary's St
  Market Drayton TF9 ...**97** B1
  Newport TF10 ....**168** C2
St Mary's Way
  Aldridge WS9 ....**256** A3
  Tamworth B77 ....**250** C1
St Marys & St Johns RC Jun
  & Inf Sch WV2 .....**266** B4
St Marys CE Prim Sch
  WV7 ....**237** A3
St Marys Cl Bradley ST18 **173** B3
  Shareshill WV10 .....**225** B1
St Marys Gr B79 ....**236** B2
St Marys St
  ST19 ....**223** A3
St Mathew Cl WS12 .**211** A3
St Matthew St ST3 ...**72** C3
St Matthew's Ave WS7 **229** A4
St Matthew's Rd WS7 **229** C4
St Matthew's St DE14 **185** B4
St Matthews Cl WS3 .**244** A3
St Matthews Ct ST3 ..**72** C3
St Matthews Dr ST18 **154** C2
St Mawes Cl ST17 ..**175** B4
St Mawes Rd WV6 ..**255** A2
St Michael CE Jun & Inf Sch
  WV6 ....**255** C3
St Michael Rd WS3 .**231** B4
St Michael's CE Fst Sch
  Rudyard ST13 ....**18** B1
  Stone ST15 ....**120** B4
St Michael's CE Prim Sch
  WS14 ....**231** B4
St Michael's Cl
  Adbaston ST20 ......**131** B2
  Penkridge ST19 .....**207** C4
  Stafford ST17 ....**175** C4
  Walsall WS3 ....**244** A1
St Michael's Ct WV6 **255** C3
St Michael's Dr WS15 **197** A3
St Michael's Hospl
  WS13 ....**231** B4
St Michael's RC Prim Sch
  WV3 ....**265** B4
St Michael's Rd
  Chell Heath ST6 ......**41** C3
  Newcastle-u-L ST5 ....**56** C3
  Penkridge ST19 .....**207** C4
  Rugeley WS15 ....**197** A3
  Uttoxeter ST14 .....**110** C2
St Michael's Sq ST19 **192** C1
St Michaels CE Fst Sch
  ST19 ....**192** C1
St Michaels CE Prim Sch
  WS3 ....**244** A2
St Michaels Cl
  Stone ST15 ....**120** A4
  Wood End CV9 ......**262** C4
St Michaels Dr WS12 **211** A3
St Michaels Mount
  ST15 ....**120** B3
St Michaels Rd
  Burton u T DE13 .....**166** B4
  Himley DY3 ....**270** C4
St Mildred's CE Prim Sch
  ST10 ....**62** B2
St Modwen's Cl DE13 **166** B4
St Modwen's RC Prim Sch
  DE13 ....**166** A3
St Modwen's Wlk DE14 **166** B1
St Modwena Way ST19 **207** C4
St Nicholas Ave ST6 ..**42** C4
St Nicholas CE Fst Sch
  WV8 ....**238** C2
St Nicholas Cl WS3 .**244** A2
St Nicholas Way WS15 **160** C3
St Oswald's CE Fst Sch
  DY10 ....**280** A1
St Patrick Cl WS12 ..**211** A3
St Patrick's Dr ST5 ..**70** C4

St Patrick's Pl **1** ST16 .155 C2
St Patrick's RC Prim Sch
  ST16 ....155 C3
St Patrick's St **2** ST16 .155 C2
St Patricks Rd DE13 .....166 B4
St Paul St ST6 ....56 C4
St Paul's CE Fst Sch
  WV9 ....224 B2
St Paul's CE Prim Sch
  ST17 ....155 C1
St Paul's Cl
  Brewood WV9 ....224 B1
  Cannock WS11 ....210 A1
St Paul's Ct
  Burton u T DE14 .....166 A2
  Longton ST3 ....72 C1
  Tamworth B77 ....261 B2
St Paul's Mews **4**
  WS15 ....196 C4
St Paul's Rd
  Burntwood WS7 ......229 B3
  Cannock WS12 ....210 C2
  Newcastle-u-L ST5 ...284 A2
St Paul's Sq DE14 .....166 A2
St Paul's St W DE14 ...166 A2
St Pauls CE Jun Sch ST6 .41 C1
St Pauls CE Sch WV9 ...240 A1
St Pauls Cres WS3 .....244 A3
St Pauls Rd **3** WS15 ..196 C4
St Peter & St Paul RC Prim
  Sch
  Lichfield WS13 ....214 A1
  Newport TF10 ....168 C2
St Peter's Bridge DE14,
  DE15 ....166 C2
St Peter's CE Fst Sch
  Alton ST10 ....78 C1
  Marchington ST14 ....127 C1
St Peter's CE High Sch
  ST4 ....71 C4
St Peter's CE Prim Sch
  WS12 ....210 B2
St Peter's CE Prim Sch
  Caverswall ST11 ......74 B1
  Edgmond TF10 ....168 A2
St Peter's CE Prim Sch
  ST18 ....158 A4
St Peter's CE Prim Sch
  Netherseal DE12 ......219 C3
  Shenstone WS9 ......245 C2
  Yoxall DE13 ....182 A2
St Peter's Cl
  Shenstone WS9 ......245 C2
  Tamworth B77 ....250 B1
St Peter's Collegiate CE Sch
  WV3 ....255 C2
St Peter's Ct ST20 .....151 A2
St Peter's Gdns ST17 ...174 C3
St Peter's RC Prim Sch
  Hanley ST6 ....57 A3
  Walsall WS3 ....243 A1
St Peter's Rd
  Burntwood WS7 ......229 B3
  Cannock WS12 ....210 B2
St Peter's St DE15 .....166 C2
St Peter's Wlk ST6 .....57 C4
St Peters Cl
  Stafford ST17 ....174 C3
  Stoke-on-T ST4 ......72 A4
St Peters Ct
  Burton u T DE15 .....166 C1
  Lichfield WS13 ....214 A1
  Walsall WS3 ....243 A1
St Peters Dr WS3 ......244 A2
St Phillip's Ave WS3 ...265 C4
St Phillip's Gr WV3 ....265 C4
St Saviour's CE Prim Sch
  ST7 ....25 B1
St Saviour's St ST7 ....25 B1
St Saviours Cl WV2 ....266 C3
St Stephen's Rd WS7 ..229 B3
St Stephens Ct
  Burton u T DE13 .....166 B4
  Cannock WS12 ....210 B2
St Stephens Prim Sch
  WS13 ....215 B4
St Teresa's RC Prim Sch
  ST4 ....71 C1
St Theresa's RC Prim Sch
  WV4 ....266 C3
St Thomas Aquinas RC Prim
  Sch ST4 ....56 C1
St Thomas CE Prim Sch
  ST7 ....26 A1
St Thomas Dr WS12 ...211 A3
St Thomas La ST18 ....156 B2
St Thomas More RC Coll
  ST3 ....73 A2
St Thomas More RC Prim Sch
  WS6 ....227 A2
St Thomas Pl ST4 ......71 C3
St Thomas RC Prim Sch
  ST10 ....92 C2
St Thomas St
  Kidsgrove ST7 ....26 C4
  Stafford ST16 ....156 A2
St Thomas' Cl WS9 ....245 A1
St Thomas' Rd ST10 ...92 C2
St Vincent St ST5 ......55 C1
St Vincent Rd ST15 ....119 C2
St Werburgh's CE Prim Sch
  Hanbury DE13 ....145 A4
  Kingsley ST10 ....61 C1
St Wilfrid's RC Prim Sch
  ST6 ....41 C2
St Wulstan's RC Prim Sch
  ST5 ....56 B2
Salcombe Ave ST17 ...175 B4

Salcombe Cl WS11 .....226 B4
Salcombe Pl ST1 ......57 B4
Sale La DE13 ....200 B1
Salem St ST1 ....56 C2
Sales La DE15 ....167 B2
Salisbury Ave
  Burton u T DE15 .....167 A4
  Hanley ST1 ....282 B1
Salisbury Cl
  Lichfield WS13 ....214 B2
  Madeley CW3 ....68 C4
  Sedgley DY1 ....271 C2
Salisbury Dr
  Cannock WS12 ....210 A1
  Stafford ST16 ....156 A2
Salisbury Hill View TF9 .112 A4
Salisbury Rd
  Market Drayton TF9 ..112 A4
  Stafford ST16 ....156 A2
Salisbury St Leek ST13 ..30 C3
  Tunstall ST6 ....41 C2
Salkeld Pl ST6 ....42 A3
Sallow Gr WS8 ....229 A1
Sally Ward Dr WS9 ....245 A2
Sallyfield La DE6 ......65 C1
Salmond Ave ST16 ....156 A3
Salop Dr WS11 ....226 C4
Salop Gr ST5 ....71 B2
Salop Pl ST7 ....26 A2
Salt Ave ST17 ....155 C1
Salt Banks ST18 ......137 B2
Salt La ST18 ....137 B3
Salt Rd Salt ST18 .....137 C2
  Stafford ST17 ....155 C1
Salt Works La ST18 ...138 B1
Saltbrook La DE6 .....144 C4
Saltdean Cl ST3 ......73 C1
Salter St ST16 ....155 C2
Salter's Ct TF10 ......168 C2
Salter's La TF10 ......168 C2
Salter's Rd WS9 ......245 A2
Salters Cl ST9 ....59 A2
Salters Grange WS15 ..160 C3
Salters Green Way
  DE13 ....201 A2
Salters La Caverswall ST9 .59 A1
  Tamworth B79 ....250 A3
Saltersford La ST10 ....94 C4
Saltheath La ST18 .....137 C2
Salts La B78 ....260 C2
Sam Barber Ct WS12 ..210 C1
Sambar Rd B78 ....249 C1
Sambrook Cres TF9 ...97 C1
Sampson St ST1 ....282 A3
Samuel Cl WS13 ......214 B1
Samuel Ho WS3 ......243 A1
Samuel Johnson's
  Birthplace Mus★
  WS13 ....231 A4
Samuel St Packmoor ST7 .26 C1
  Walsall WS3 ....243 A1
Sancton Gn **24** ST6 ...56 C4
Sand Bank WS3 ....243 A1
Sand Rd DE13 ....164 B4
Sandalwood Dr ST16 ..155 B4
Sandalwood Gr ST3 ...88 C4
Sandalwood Rd DE15 ..185 C3
Sandbach Rd ST6 .....57 A4
Sandcrest Pl ST3 .....73 C1
Sandcrest Wlk ST3 ...73 C1
Sanderling Cl WV10 ...241 A4
Sanderling Rise WS7 ..229 A4
Sandfield Bridge DY5 ..271 A4
Sandfield Gr DY3 .....271 A4
Sandfield Rd DY3 .....275 C1
Sandford Cl WS15 ....198 A4
Sandford Cres CW2 ...37 B1
Sandford Hill Prim Sch
  ST3 ....73 B3
Sandford Rd DY1 .....271 C1
Sandford Rise WV6 ...255 C3
Sandford St
  Lichfield WS13 ....231 A4
  9 Longton ST3 ......73 B3
  Newcastle-u-L ST5 ...55 C4
Sandgate St ST3 .....73 B2
Sandhill St WS3 ......243 A1
Sandhurst Ave **6** ST3 .73 C1
Sandhurst Cl ST5 .....56 B2
Sandhurst Dr WV4 ....266 A2
Sandhurst Gr DY8 ....275 C2
Sandhurst Pl ST3 .....89 C4
Sandhurst Rd B74 ....257 C3
Sandiford Cres TF10 ..168 C1
Sandiway DE13 ....201 C4
Sandiway Pl ST1 ......57 C3
Sandmere Rise WV10 .240 C1
Sandon Ave ST5 ......71 A3
Sandon Cl ST11 ......91 B1
Sandon High Sch ST3 ..89 C4
Sandon Ho WV6 ......255 C3
Sandon La ST18 ......122 B3
Sandon Mews ST16 ...155 C3
Sandon Old Rd ST3 ...89 C4
Sandon Rd
  Draycott in t M ST11 ..91 B2
  Hilderstone ST15 ....106 B1
  Hopton ST18 ....137 B1
  Meir ST3 ....89 C4
  Stafford ST16 ....155 C3
  Wolv WV10 ....240 A1
Sandon St Hanley ST1 ..57 A2
  Leek ST13 ....30 C2
Sandown B77 ....250 C3
Sandown Ave WS6 ....226 C2
Sandown Cl
  Burntwood WS7 .....211 C1
  Burton u T DE14 ....185 A4

Sandown Cl continued
  Cannock WS12 ....211 A3
  Kingsley ST10 ....76 C3
Sandown Dr WV6 .....254 C2
Sandown Pl ST2 ......43 B1
Sandpiper B77 ....262 A3
Sandpiper Cl WS12 ...210 B4
Sandpiper Ct ST7 .....26 B1
Sandpiper Dr ST4 .....126 A3
Sandra Cl Aldridge WS9 .256 A3
  Chell Heath ST6 .....42 A1
Sandringham Ave DE15 167 A1
Sandringham Cl
  Burntwood WS7 .....211 C1
  Market Drayton TF9 ..97 C1
  Stafford ST17 ....175 B4
Sandringham Dr WS9 .245 A1
Sandringham Pl DY8 ..275 B1
Sandringham Rd
  Kingswinford DY8 ....275 B1
  Pattingham WV6 ....253 B1
  Stafford ST17 ....175 B4
  Wolv WV4 ....266 A2
  Wombourne WV5 ....269 C3
Sands La ST6 ....28 A1
Sands Rd ST7 ....26 C3
Sandsdown Cl ST8 ....16 B1
Sandstone Cl
  Sedgley DY3 ....271 B2
  Walsall WS3 ....243 A1
Sandstone Rd WS3 ...243 B2
Sandwell Pl ST3 ......89 C4
Sandwell Rd WV10 ...240 A1
Sandwick Cres ST1 ...57 C3
Sandwood Cres ST3 ..73 B3
Sandy Bank ST21 .....102 B3
Sandy Cres WV11 ....242 A1
Sandy Gr WS8 ....228 C1
Sandy Hill ST9 ....59 B2
Sandy Hollow WV6 ...255 B1
Sandy La Ashley TF9 ..100 A4
  Blore TF9 ....98 B2
  Brewood ST19 ......223 B3
  Cannock WS11 ......209 A1
  Chapel Chorlton ST5 ..85 B2
  Codsall WV8 ....238 C2
  Eccleshall ST21 .....132 B4
  Endon ST6 ....43 A4
  Kinver DY7,DY11 ....277 C1
  Linton DE12 ....186 A1
  Longsdon ST9 ......44 C4
  Newcastle-u-L ST5 ...284 D4
  Newton Regis B79 ..236 B3
  Norton-in-t-M ST2 ..43 B1
  Rugeley WS15 ......196 C4
  Standon ST21 ......102 B2
  Stourbridge DY8 ....279 B2
  Sutton TF9 ....112 B3
  Upper Tean ST10 ...93 C4
  Weston ST18 ....138 B2
  Whittington WS14 ..232 B2
  Wolv, Claregate WV6 .255 C3
  Wolv, Elston Hall WV10 .240 C1
Sandy Mount WS5 ....270 A4
Sandy Rd Biddulph ST8 ..16 B1
  Stourbridge DY8 ....279 B1
  Tunstall ST6 ....41 B3
Sandy Way B77 ....251 A2
Sandybrook Cl ST13 ..30 C2
Sandybrook La ST13 ..30 C1
Sandycroft TF10 ......168 C2
Sandyfield Rd ST1 ....57 C3
Sandyfields ST5 ......85 B3
Sandyfields Rd DY3 ...271 A3
Sandyford Cl ST16 ...155 C2
Sandyford St ST16 ...155 C3
Sangster La ST6 ......42 B1
Sankey Cres WS15 ...196 C4
Sankey Rd WS11 .....209 C2
Sankey's Cnr WS7 ...228 C4
Sant St ST6 ....56 C4
Saplings ST19 ....192 C1
Saplings The
  Newcastle-u-L ST5 ...71 B2
  Penkridge ST19 .....192 C1
Sapperton La DE65 ...129 C4
Sapphire Dr WS11 ....210 B2
Sara Cl B74 ....258 A2
Saracen Way **10** ST4 .74 A1
Sarah Challinor Cl
  WS15 ....196 C4
Saredon Cl WS3 ......244 A1
Saredon Rd
  Cheslyn Hay WS6,WS11,
  WV10 ....226 A2
  Shareshill WV10 ....225 B1
Sargeant Ave ST6 ....42 A3
Sark Cl ST5 ....70 C2
Sark Pl **1** ST3 ......73 B3
Sarraine Ind Pk ST10 ..76 A1
Sarver La ST10 ....75 B2
Sash St ST1 ....155 C2
Saturn Rd Cannock WS11 210 A3
  Chell Heath ST6 .....42 B1
Saul Ct ST4 ....126 A4
Saunders Cl WS12 ...211 A3
Saunders Rd ST6 .....56 A2
Saverley Green Rd
  ST11 ....106 C4
Savey La DE13 ....181 C1
Savoureuse Dr ST17 ..175 A4
Savoy Rd CW1 ....37 C4
Sawpit La ST17 ......176 A2
Sawyer Dr ST8 ....16 B1
Saxifrage Dr ST15 ...120 B3
Saxon Cl Burton u T DE15 185 C4
  Great Wyrley WS6 ..227 A1
  Polesworth B78 .....251 C1

Saxon Cl continued
  Tamworth B77 ....261 C3
Saxon Ct WS13 ....230 C4
Saxon Hill Sch WS14 .231 B3
Saxon Rd ST19 ....207 C4
Saxon St ST6 ....185 C4
Saxon Wlk WS13 .....230 C4
Saxoncourt WV6 .....255 B3
Saxondrive B79 ......250 B3
Saxonfields WV6 .....255 B3
Saxton Dr B74 ....257 C3
Sayers Rd ST16 .....155 B4
Scalpcliffe Cl DE15 ...166 C2
Scalpcliffe Rd DE15 ..166 C2
Scammerton B77 .....262 A4
Scamnell La ST21 ....134 C4
Scampton Cl WV6 ...254 C3
Scampton Way B79 ..250 B4
Scarecrow La B75 ...258 C2
Scarlett St ST5 ......284 B2
Scarratt Cl ST11 .....91 A4
Scarratt Dr ST11 ....91 A4
Sceptre St ST1 ......282 B2
Schofield La B79 .....217 B3
Scholar Green Prim Sch
  ST7 ....25 C3
Scholars Gate
  Burntwood WS7 .....229 B4
  4 Rugeley WS15 ...197 A3
School Ave WS8 .....244 C4
School Bank ST10 ....94 A1
School Cl Audley ST7 ..40 A1
  Burntwood WS7 .....228 B4
  Codsall WV8 ....239 A2
  Dilhorne ST10 ......75 B2
  Leek ST13 ....30 A1
  Norton Canes WS11 .228 A3
  Seisdon WV5 ....269 B4
  Wolv WV3 ....265 A4
School Cres WS11 ...228 A3
School Cl WS12 .....210 B3
School Dr
  Brierley Hill DY8 ....279 C4
  Oakamoor ST10 .....78 A4
School Ground La TF10 169 A2
School Ho The WS7 ..229 B4
School House La WS15 161 A3
School La
  Admaston WS15 ....159 C2
  Ashley TF9 ....100 A3
  Astbury CW12 ......15 A4
  Biddulph ST8 ....17 A1
  Blymhill TF11 ....203 A3
  Bradnop ST13 ......31 C2
  Brewood WV9 ......224 A2
  Burntwood WS7 ....228 B4
  Caverswall ST3 .....74 B1
  Colton WS15 ....178 C3
  Colwich ST18 ......158 A1
  Coppenhall ST18 ...192 B4
  Edingale B79 ......217 B3
  Hill Ridware WS15 ..198 A4
  Hints B78 ....248 B1
  Hopwas B78 ....249 A4
  Longdon WS15 .....212 A3
  Longsdon ST9 ......30 A1
  Longton ST3 ....89 A4
  Maer TF9 ....84 A4
  Market Drayton TF9 ..112 A4
  Norton Canes WS3 ..227 C1
  Rolleston DE13 .....147 A2
  Sandon ST18 ......137 C4
  Shareshill WV10 ....225 B1
  Shuttington B79 ....251 C4
  Stafford, Hillcroft Park
  ST17 ....175 C4
  Stafford, Rickerscote ST17 174 C3
  Sudbury DE6 ....128 C2
  Tamworth B77 .....261 B3
  Walsall WS3 ....243 C2
  Warslow SK17 .....23 A1
  Wheaton Aston ST19 206 B2
  Wolv WV10 ....240 C1
School Lane Cl ST17 ..174 C3
School of St Mary & St Anne
  WS15 ....161 A3
School Pl ST16 ......155 C3
School Rd Bagnall ST9 ..43 C1
  Brewood ST19 ......223 B3
  Bucknall ST2 ....58 A3
  Eccleshall ST21 ....133 B3
  Edgmond TF10 .....168 A2
  Himley DY3 ....270 A2
  Norton Canes WS11 .228 A3
  Rugeley WS15 .....178 B1
  Seisdon WV5 ......264 B1
  Uttoxeter ST14 ....110 C1
  Wheaton Aston ST19 205 B3
  Wolv WV6 ....255 A2
  Wombourne WV5 ..270 A4
School St **3** Leek ST13 ..30 C3
  Newcastle-u-L ST5 ..284 C3
  Newcastle-u-L, Broad Meadow
  ST5 ....55 C3
  Sedgley DY3 ....271 C4
  Stoke-on-T ST4 .....71 C2
  Stourbridge DY8 ....279 C3
  Tamworth B77 ......250 C2
  Walsall WS4 ....244 A3
School View ST14 ...141 B4
School Wlk WS7 .....228 B4
Schoolacre Rise B74 ..256 C1
Schoolfields Rd WS14 .247 A3
Schoolgate Cl WS4 ...244 B1
Scimitar Cl B79 ......249 C4
Scot Hay Rd Audley ST7 ..54 C1
  Newcastle-u-L ST5 ..54 C2

Scotch Orch WS13 ...214 B1
Scotch Orchard Prim Sch
  WS13 ....214 B1
Scotia Bsns Pk ST6 ...41 C1
Scotia Rd Cannock WS11 209 B2
  Tunstall ST6 ....41 C1
Scott Ave WV4 ......265 C2
Scott Cl WS14 ....231 A3
Scott Lidgett Ind Est ST6 56 B4
Scott Lidgett Rd ST6 ..56 B4
Scott Rd Chell Heath ST6 .41 C3
  Tamworth B77 ......250 C2
Scott St Cannock WS12 ..210 C2
  Newcastle-u-L ST5 ..284 C3
Scott Way WS7 ......211 C1
Scott's Rd DY8 ......279 C3
Scotts Ho ST16 .....155 B3
Scragg St ST7 ....41 C4
Scrimshaw Dr ST6 ...42 B2
Scrivener Rd ST4 ....56 C1
Scropton Old Rd DE65 .146 B4
Scropton Rd
  Hatton DE65 ....146 A4
  Scropton DE65 .....129 C1
Seabridge Jun & Inf Schs
  ST5 ....71 A2
Seabridge La ST5 ....71 A2
Seabridge Rd ST5 ...284 A1
Seabrook Rd WS15 ..197 A3
Seafield B77 ....250 C3
Seafield Cl DY6 .....275 C2
Seaford St ST4 ......57 A1
Seaforth Gr WV11 ..242 A1
Seagrave Pl ST5 ....71 A3
Seagrave St ST5 ....284 C3
Searle Ave ST16 ....155 B1
Seaton B77 ....261 C4
Seaton Ave ST17 ...175 B4
Seaton Cl ST3 ......89 C4
Seaton Pl DY8 ......275 B4
Sebring Ave ST3 ...89 C4
Seckham Rd WS13 ..231 A4
Second Ave
  Branston DE14 .....165 C1
  Brownhills WS8 ....229 A1
  Bucknall ST2 ....58 B2
  Kidsgrove ST7 .....25 C1
  Kingswinford DY6 ..275 C4
  Newcastle-u-L ST5 ..56 C4
  Stafford ST16 ......155 B4
Sedbergh Cl ST5 ....70 C2
Seddon Ct ST1 ......282 C3
Seddon Rd ST3 .....271 C2
Sedgefield Cl DY1 ..271 C2
Sedgefield Gr WV6 ..254 C2
Sedgefield Rd
  Branston DE14 .....184 C4
  Burton u T DE14 ...185 A4
Sedgefield Way WS11 228 A2
Sedgeley Rd WV4 ...265 C2
Sedgemoor Ave WS7 229 A3
Sedgley Hall Ave DY3 271 B4
Sedgley St WV2 ....266 B4
Sedgley Wlk ST3 ...283 C4
Seedcroft La WS15 ..160 C2
Seedfields Rd ST3 ...72 C2
Seeds La WS8 ......244 C4
Seedymill La WS13 ..213 C4
Seesall The ST20 ...171 C4
Sefton Ave Congleton CW12 6 B4
  Hanley ST1 ....57 C4
Sefton Cl DE15 .....167 A1
Sefton Rd Longton ST3 ..73 C1
  Tamworth B77 .....261 B2
Sefton St ST1 ....57 A2
Segram Way ST14 ..126 B4
Seighford Rd ST18 ..154 B3
Seisdon Rd ST13 ...30 C2
Selborne Dr ST6 ...41 C4
Selby Cl ST5 ....71 A3
Selby St ST3 ....74 A3
Selby Way WS3 ....242 C1
Selby Wlk ST3 .....88 C4
Selker Dr B77 ......250 C3
Sellman St ST20 ...171 C3
Selman's Hill WS3 ..243 B1
Selman's Par WS3 ..243 B1
Selsdon Rd WS3 ...242 C1
Selwood Cl ST3 ....73 B1
Selworthy Dr ST17 ..175 C3
Selworthy Rd ST6 ...43 A3
Selwyn Cl Alrewas DE13 .201 A2
  Wolv WV2 ....266 B4
Selwyn St ST21 ....133 C4
Selwyn St ST4 ......72 A1
Selwyn Wlk B74 ...257 B2
Semper Cl CW12 ...6 A2
Senior Cl WV11 ....242 A2
Serin Cl ST14 ......126 B3
Seton Ho B74 ......257 C1
Setterfield Way WS15 .196 C3
Settle Gr ST3 ......90 A4
Setton Dr DY3 .....271 C4
Seven Acres WS9 ...256 A3
Seven Arches Way ST4 .72 B4
Seven Springs Nature Trail★
  ST17 ....177 B3
Sevenoaks Gr ST3 ..90 A4
Sevens Rd WS12 ...211 B2
Severn Cl Biddulph ST8 ..16 C1
  Burton u T DE15 ...147 B1
  Congleton CW12 ...6 A1
  Uttoxeter ST14 ....126 B3

Severn Dr
Brownhills WS8 . . . . .228 B1
Burntwood WS7 . . . . .229 B3
Burton u T DE14 . . . . .166 C2
Newcastle-u-L ST5 . . . . .71 A2
Perton WV6 . . . . .254 C2
Severn Ho DY3 . . . . .271 B2
Severn Rd
Stourbridge DY8 . . . . .279 C2
Walsall WS3 . . . . .243 C1
Severn St ST1 . . . . .282 A4
Seward Cl WS14 . . . . .231 B3
Seymour Ave DE14 . . . . . .166 C4
Seymour Cl WS6 . . . . .226 B3
Seymour Gdns B74 . . . . . .257 C2
Seymour St ST1 . . . . .57 C2
Shackerley La WV7 . . . .221 A1
Shackleton Dr
Perton WV6 . . . . .254 C3
Tunstall ST6 . . . . .41 B2
Shackleton Rd WS3 . . . . . .243 B1
Shackson Cl ST1 . . . . .282 B1
Shadwell Dr DY3 . . . . .271 B2
Shaffalong La ST13 . . . . .45 A3
Shaftesbury Ave ST6 . . . . .42 A1
Shaftesbury Dr WS12 . . . .210 B4
Shaftesbury Rd WS15 . . . .196 A4
Shakespeare Ave WS14 . .231 A3
Shakespeare Cl
Kidsgrove ST7 . . . . .41 A4
Norton-in-t-M ST2 . . . . .43 A1
Tamworth B79 . . . . .250 A3
Shakespeare Gr WS11 . . . .209 B2
Shakespeare Rd
Burntwood WS7 . . . . .228 C4
Burton u T DE14 . . . . .166 B3
Sedgley DY3 . . . . .271 A2
Stafford ST17 . . . . .174 B4
Shaldon Dr ST9 . . . . .43 B2
Shales The WV5 . . . . .269 C3
Shallcross La DY3 . . . . . . .271 B2
Shallowford Ct ST1 . . . . . . .57 A2
Shallowford Mews
ST16 . . . . .155 B3
Shanklin Cl WS6 . . . . .227 A2
Shannon B77 . . . . .261 C4
Shannon App DE14 . . . .166 B1
Shannon Dr
Brownhills WS8 . . . . .228 B1
Tunstall ST6 . . . . .41 B4
Shannon Rd ST17 . . . . . . .174 B3
Shannon Wlk WS8 . . . . . . .228 B1
Shanti Niketan WV2 . . . . .266 B4
Shardlow Cl Fenton ST4 . . . . .73 A3
Stone ST15 . . . . .120 B3
Sharman Cl ST4 . . . . .71 C4
Sharmon Way ST20 . . . . .171 C4
Sharnbrook Dr WS15 . . . .178 B1
Sharnbrook Gr ST17 . . . . .175 B3
Sharon Cl WV4 . . . . .266 C3
Sharon Way WS12 . . . . . .210 B2
Sharpe St B77 . . . . .251 A3
Sharplands TF9 . . . . .99 B3
Sharrat Field B75 . . . . . . .258 A4
Sharron Dr ST13 . . . . .31 A3
Shaver's La WS15 . . . . . . .197 A1
Shaw Cl WS14 . . . . .215 B4
Shaw Dr WS7 . . . . .212 A1
Shaw Gdns ST17 . . . . .174 B4
Shaw Hall La WV9 . . . . . . .240 B4
Shaw La Albrighton WV7 . . . .237 A3
King's Bromley WS15 . . . . . .198 C1
Lichfield WS13 . . . . .231 A4
Longdon WS15 . . . . .212 A2
Tong TF11 . . . . .220 B3
Wolv WV6 . . . . .255 A2
Shaw Pl ST13 . . . . .31 A3
Shaw Rd WV4 . . . . .266 B3
Shaw St Biddulph ST8 . . . . .27 B4
Hanley ST1 . . . . .282 A4
Newcastle-u-L ST5 . . . . .284 B3
Shaw's La WS6 . . . . .227 A1
Shaw-wall La Cotton ST10 62 C4
Ipstones ST10 . . . . .62 C4
Shawbury Gr WV6 . . . . . . .254 C3
Shawe Park Rd ST10 . . . . .76 C4
Shawmains La ST18 . . . . .172 C4
Shawms Crest ST17 . . . . .175 B4
Shawport Ave ST5 . . . . . . .56 A4
Shaws La ST21 . . . . .133 B3
Shay La Forton TF10 . . . . . . .150 A2
Ipstones ST10 . . . . .62 B3
Shayler Gr WV2 . . . . .266 B4
Sheaf Pas ST3 . . . . .283 C3
Sheaf St ST1 . . . . .282 A1
Shearer St ST1 . . . . .282 A1
Shebdon Cl ST16 . . . . .155 A4
Sheep Fair WS15 . . . . .178 C1
Sheep Market ST13 . . . . . . .30 C3
Sheepcote La B77 . . . . . . .250 C2
Sheepwalks La ST7 . . . . . .277 A4
Sheepwash La DY11 . . . . .277 B1
Sheffield Cl ST14 . . . . .110 C1
Sheffield St DE14 . . . . . . .166 A2
Shefford Rd ST5 . . . . .70 C2
Shelburne St ST4 . . . . .72 A3
Sheldon Ave CW12 . . . . . . .6 A1
Sheldon Gr ST5 . . . . .55 C3
Sheldon Rd WV10 . . . . . . .240 A1
Sheldrake Gr ST4 . . . . .73 A3
Shelfield Com Sch WS4 244 B1
Shelford Rd ST6 . . . . .41 B3
Shelley Ave DE14 . . . . . . .166 B3
Shelley Cl
Armitage WS15 . . . . .198 A2
Burton u T DE14 . . . . .166 B3
Colwich ST18 . . . . .177 B4
Kidsgrove ST7 . . . . .41 A4
Sedgley DY3 . . . . .271 A3
Stafford ST17 . . . . .156 A3
Shelley Dr Cheadle ST10 . . . .76 B1
Sutton Coldfield B74 . . . . . .257 C3
Shelley Rd Bucknall ST2 . . . . .58 A3
Burntwood WS7 . . . . .212 A1
Cannock WS11 . . . . .209 C3
Tamworth B79 . . . . .250 A4
Wolv WV10 . . . . .240 B1
Shelmore Cl ST16 . . . . . . .155 A4
Shelmore Way ST20 . . . . .171 B4
Shelsey Rd ST10 . . . . .76 C2
Shelsley Cl ST19 . . . . .193 A1
Shelton Farm Rd ST1 . . . .282 A1
Shelton New Rd ST4 . . . . . .56 C1
Shelton Old Rd ST4 . . . . . .72 A4
Shelton St B77 . . . . .261 C4
Shemilt Cres ST6 . . . . .42 B2
Shendon Ct ST5 . . . . .56 A4
Shenfield Gn ST2 . . . . .58 B1
Shenley Gr ST17 . . . . .174 B3
Shenstone Ave DY8 . . . . . .279 B2
Shenstone Cl B74 . . . . .257 C3
Shenstone Ct WV3 . . . . . . .266 A3
Shenstone Dr WS9 . . . . . . .256 A4
Shenstone Ho ST1 . . . . . . .282 A1
Shenstone Lodge Specl Sch
WS14 . . . . .247 A4
Shenstone Sta WS14 . . . . .246 C3
Shenton St ST3 . . . . .283 D5
Shephard Cl ST18 . . . . . . .158 B2
Shepherd Cl WS13 . . . . . .214 B2
Shepherd St ST8 . . . . .27 B4
Shepherds Bush St
ST16 . . . . .155 C3
Shepherds Ct TF10 . . . . . .169 A2
Shepherds Fold ST17 . . . . .175 B3
Shepherds Pool Rd B75 258 C1
Shepherds Wlk WV8 . . . . . .239 C1
Shepley Cl ST15 . . . . .120 B4
Shepley Gr ST3 . . . . .88 C4
Sheppard St ST4 . . . . .72 A3
Shepwell Gdns WV10 . . . .241 B4
Sheraton Cl
Aldridge WS9 . . . . .256 A3
Cannock WS12 . . . . .210 A4
Sheraton Grange DY8 . . . .279 C1
Sherborne Cl ST3,ST4 . . . . .88 C4
Sherborne Ct WV10 . . . . .240 C1
Sherborne Dr ST5 . . . . .71 C3
Sherborne Gdns WV8 . . . .239 A2
Sherborne Rd WV10 . . . . .240 B1
Sherbourne Ave WS12 . . . .210 C2
Sherbourne Dr DE14 . . . . .185 A4
Sherbrook Cl ST17 . . . . . . .176 A2
Sherbrook Rd WS11 . . . . . .209 B1
Sherbrooke Ave B77 . . . . .261 C3
Sheridan Gdns
Himley DY3 . . . . .270 C3
Longton ST3 . . . . .72 C1
Sheridan St ST16 . . . . .156 A4
Sheridan Way WS15 . . . . .120 B4
Sheriden Way ST5 . . . . .55 C1
Sheriffs Cl WS14 . . . . .231 C3
Sheriffs Way ST21 . . . . . . .133 B4
Sherifoot La B75 . . . . .258 A4
Sheringham Covert
ST16 . . . . .156 B2
Sheringham Dr WS15 . . . . .178 A1
Sheringham Pl ST5 . . . . . . .56 B2
Sherington Dr WV4 . . . . . .266 B3
Sherracop La WS15 . . . . . .160 A1
Sherrans Dell WV4 . . . . . .266 B2
Sherratt St ST6 . . . . .42 B2
Sherringham Dr WV11 . . . .242 B1
Shervale Cl WV4 . . . . .266 A3
Sherwin Rd ST6 . . . . .41 C2
Sherwood Ave ST17 . . . . .174 C4
Sherwood Cl CV9 . . . . .262 B1
Sherwood Dr WS11 . . . . . .210 A2
Sherwood Rd Meir ST3 . . . . .89 C4
Stourbridge DY8 . . . . .279 C4
Shetland Ave B77 . . . . . . .261 C4
Shetland Rd ST3 . . . . .72 C2
Shillingford Dr ST4 . . . . . . .88 A4
Shilton Cl ST4 . . . . .71 C3
Shinwell Gr ST3 . . . . .90 A4
Shipley Cl DE14 . . . . .185 A4
Shipley Pl ST6 . . . . .42 B1
Shipston Rd ST17 . . . . . . .156 B1
Shipton Cl DY1 . . . . .271 C2
Shipton Dr ST14 . . . . .110 C1
Shirburn Rd ST13 . . . . .31 A3
Shire Lea WS8 . . . . .245 A3
Shire Oak Sch WS8 . . . . . .245 A4
Shire Ridge WS9 . . . . .245 A2
Shirebrook Cl ST3 . . . . .88 C4
Shirehall Pl WS11 . . . . . . .210 A1
Shirelea Cl WS7 . . . . .229 A4
Shireoaks Dr [4] ST17 . . . .175 B3
Shireview Gdns WS3 . . . . .244 A1
Shireview Rd WS3 . . . . . . .244 A1
Shirley Ave ST9 . . . . .59 A2
Shirley Dr ST10 . . . . .94 C4
Shirley Rd ST1 . . . . .282 B1
Shirley St Burslem ST6 . . . . .56 B4
Leek ST13 . . . . .30 B3
Shirley Wlk B79 . . . . .249 C4
Shirleywich ST18 . . . . .138 C1
Shirrall Dr B78 . . . . .259 C2
Shoal Hill Cl WS11 . . . . . .209 A1
Shobnall Cl DE14 . . . . . . .166 A2

Shobnall Ct DE14 . . . . . . .166 A2
Shobnall Prim Sch
DE14 . . . . .165 C2
Shobnall Rd DE14 . . . . . . .166 A2
Shobnall St DE14 . . . . . . .166 A4
Sholing Cl WV8 . . . . .239 C1
Shoobridge St ST13 . . . . . .30 C3
Shooting Butts Rd
WS15 . . . . .196 A4
Shop La Brewood ST19 . . . .223 B3
Codsall WV6 . . . . .238 B1
Perton WV6 . . . . .264 A4
Shops The [2] DY6 . . . . . . .275 B2
Short Bambury St ST3 . . . . .73 B3
Short La Barton-u-N DE13 183 B1
Cheslyn Hay WS6 . . . . .226 C2
Kingstone ST14 . . . . .124 B1
Short Rd WV10 . . . . .240 C1
Short St Brownhills WS8 . . . .244 C4
Burton u T DE15 . . . . .185 C4
Cannock WS11 . . . . .209 C4
Longton ST3 . . . . .283 D3
Stourbridge DY8 . . . . .279 C3
Uttoxeter ST14 . . . . .126 A4
Short Street Com Inf Sch
DE15 . . . . .185 C4
Shortbutts La WS14 . . . . . .231 A3
Shortlands La WS3 . . . . . .243 C2
Shorwell Gr ST7 . . . . .41 C4
Shotsfield Pl ST2 . . . . .43 A1
Shotsfield St ST2 . . . . .43 A1
Shotwood Cl DE13 . . . . . . .147 A2
Shotwoodhill La DE13 . . . .147 A3
Showan Ave ST5 . . . . .56 B2
Showell La WV4 . . . . .265 A4
Shraleybrook Rd ST7 . . . . .54 A4
Shredicote La ST18 . . . . . .191 A4
Shrewsbury Cl WS3 . . . . . .242 C1
Shrewsbury Dr ST5 . . . . . . .40 C1
Shrewsbury Rd
Burton u T DE13 . . . . .147 C1
Edgmond TF10 . . . . .168 A2
Market Drayton TF9 . . . . . .112 A4
Stafford ST17 . . . . .155 C1
Shrewsbury Way ST13 . . . .168 C1
Shropshire Brook Rd
WS15 . . . . .198 A2
Shropshire St TF9 . . . . .97 B1
Shrubbery Cl DY10 . . . . . .280 A3
Shrubbery The
Elford DE13 . . . . .216 C1
Rugeley WS15 . . . . .197 A3
Shruggs La ST18 . . . . .121 B1
Shugborough Cl WS3 . . . . .243 A1
Shugborough Cotts
ST18 . . . . .177 B4
Shugborough Dr DY1 . . . .271 C4
Shugborough Farm Mus★
ST17 . . . . .177 A4
Shugborough Hall★
ST17 . . . . .158 A1
Shugborough Rd WS15 . . .178 B2
Shugborough Way
WS11 . . . . .210 B1
Shughborough Cl ST9 . . . . .59 A1
Shuker's Cl TF10 . . . . .169 A1
Shut La ST14 . . . . .116 A3
Shutt Green La ST19 . . . . .223 A4
Shuttington Rd B79 . . . . . .251 A3
Sich La DE13 . . . . .182 B2
Sidcot Pl ST1 . . . . .57 B4
Siddals St DE15 . . . . .167 A2
Siddons Cl WS13 . . . . .213 C1
Sides La DE6 . . . . .81 A3
Sideway Rd ST4 . . . . .72 A3
Sidings Ind Est DE14 . . . . .166 C2
Sidings Pl ST3,ST4 . . . . . . .283 B4
Sidings Rd ST15 . . . . .104 C1
Sidings The
Cannock WS12 . . . . .210 B4
Cheadle ST10 . . . . .76 B1
Stone ST15 . . . . .120 A4
Sidmouth Ave
Newcastle-u-L ST5 . . . . .284 C3
Stafford ST17 . . . . .156 B1
Sidney Ave ST17 . . . . .174 C4
Sidney Dr ST10 . . . . .62 A1
Sidney St WV2 . . . . .266 B4
Sidon Hill Way WS11 . . . . .210 B1
Siemens Rd ST17 . . . . .155 C1
Signal Gr WS3 . . . . .243 A1
Signal Wlk B77 . . . . .251 A1
Silica Rd B77 . . . . .251 A1
Silk Mill La DE13 . . . . .146 B3
Silk St ST13 . . . . .30 C3
Silkmore Cres ST17 . . . . . .175 A4
Silkmore La ST17 . . . . .175 A4
Silkmore Prim Sch
ST17 . . . . .174 C4
Sill Gn B79 . . . . .234 B1
Sillitoe Pl ST4 . . . . .72 A3
Silsden Gr ST3 . . . . .74 B3
Silva Ave DY6 . . . . .275 C2
Silver Birch Coppice
B74 . . . . .257 B3
Silver Birch Dr
Kinver DY7 . . . . .277 C3
Uttoxeter ST14 . . . . .126 A3
Silver Birch Rd
Aldridge B74 . . . . .256 C1
Huntington WS12 . . . . . . .209 B4
Norton Canes WS11 . . . . . .228 A3
Wolv WV2 . . . . .266 C4
Silver Ct ST8 . . . . .27 B4
Silver Ct WS8 . . . . .244 C4
Silver Ct Gdns WS8 . . . . . .244 C4
Silver Fir Cl WS12 . . . . . . .210 A4
Silver La ST14 . . . . .127 C1

Silver Link Rd B77 . . . . . . .250 C1
Silver Poplars Mobil Homes
Pk WV7 . . . . .237 C1
Silver Ridge ST12 . . . . . . .104 B4
Silver St Brownhills WS8 . . . .244 C4
Cheadle ST10 . . . . .76 C3
Norton-in-t-M ST6 . . . . .42 C2
Tamworth B79 . . . . .250 A3
Uttoxeter ST14 . . . . .126 B4
Silverdale TF10 . . . . .168 A2
Silverdale Bsns Pk ST5 . . . .55 B1
Silverdale Cl TF10 . . . . . . .168 C1
Silverdale Gdns DY8 . . . . .275 B2
Silverdale Prim Sch ST5 . . .55 B1
Silverdale Rd ST5 . . . . .55 C1
Silverdale St ST5 . . . . .55 C1
Silvergate Ct CW12 . . . . . . .15 C4
Silverhill Cl ST3 . . . . .166 B4
Silvermine Cl [17] ST7 . . . . .26 A1
Silvers Cl WS3 . . . . .243 C2
Silverstone Ave ST10 . . . . .76 C2
Silverstone Cres ST7 . . . . . .41 C4
Silverthorn Way ST17 . . . .175 B4
Silverton Cl ST5 . . . . .56 A4
Silverwood ST7 . . . . .26 A1
Silvester Way ST17 . . . . . .175 C3
Simcox St WS12 . . . . .210 B2
Simeon Way WS15 . . . . . .120 B3
Simister Ct [9] ST6 . . . . . . .41 B2
Simmonds Cl WS3 . . . . . . .243 B1
Simmonds Rd WS3 . . . . . .243 B2
Simmonds Way WS8 . . . . .245 A4
Simmons Cl B78 . . . . .260 A1
Simmons Rd WV11 . . . . . . .242 A1
Simon Pl ST4 . . . . .57 A1
Simonburn Ave ST4 . . . . . .71 C4
Simons Rd TF9 . . . . .112 A4
Simpkins Cl WS9 . . . . .245 A2
Simpson Cl ST16 . . . . .155 A4
Simpson Rd WS13 . . . . . . .214 A1
Simpson St Hanley ST1 . . . .282 C1
Newcastle-u-L ST5 . . . . .56 A3
Sinai Cl DE14 . . . . .165 C2
Sion Ave DY10 . . . . .280 A1
Sion Hill Mid Sch DY10 . . .280 A1
Sir Graham Balfour High Sch
ST17 . . . . .155 B4
Sir John Offley CE Prim Sch
CW3 . . . . .68 C3
Sir Robert Peel Hospl
B78 . . . . .249 B1
Sir Thomas Boughey High
Sch ST7 . . . . .54 B4
Siskin Cl WS7 . . . . .229 B3
Siskin Pl ST3 . . . . .90 A4
Sister Dora Ave WS7 . . . . .229 C4
Sitwell Gr ST3 . . . . .283 D4
Six Ashes Rd DY7 . . . . . . .272 B4
Six Roads End DE13 . . . . . .144 B2
Skeath La ST18 . . . . .137 B2
Skellern Ave ST6 . . . . .42 B2
Skellern St ST7 . . . . .25 B1
Skidmore Ave
Tamworth B77 . . . . .261 B3
Wolv WV3 . . . . .265 C4
Skipacre Ave ST6 . . . . .42 B1
Skipness B77 . . . . .250 C3
Skipton Pl WS11 . . . . .226 A4
Skye Cl Longton ST3 . . . . . . .73 C2
Tamworth B77 . . . . .261 C4
Skylark Cl
Huntington WS12 . . . . . . .209 B4
Sedgley DY5 . . . . .271 B1
Uttoxeter ST14 . . . . .126 B3
Slab La ST9,ST20 . . . . .190 A1
Slack La DE6 . . . . .81 B4
Slacken La ST7 . . . . .25 B1
Slacky La WS3 . . . . .243 C1
Slade Ave WS7 . . . . .229 A4
Slade Fields ST14 . . . . .111 A1
Slade Gdns WV8 . . . . .239 C4
Slade Hill [3] WV6 . . . . . . .255 C2
Slade La
Sutton Coldfield B75 . . . . . .259 A2
Tamworth B77 . . . . .261 B2
Waterhouses ST10,ST13 . . .49 A3
Slade Rd
Sutton Coldfield B75 . . . . . .258 C2
Wolv WV10 . . . . .240 B2
Slade View Rise WS12 . . . .211 A3
Sladehollow La DE6 . . . . . .65 B1
Slaidburn Gr Hanley ST1 . . .57 C3
Stafford ST17 . . . . .175 B4
Slaney St ST5 . . . . .284 C1
Slang La WS15 . . . . .211 C3
Slapton Cl ST2 . . . . .57 C1
Slate La WV8 . . . . .238 B3
Slater St Biddulph ST8 . . . . .27 B4
Burslem ST6 . . . . .56 C4
Sleeve The ST13 . . . . .30 B2
Sleigh Gr ST13 . . . . .30 C1
Slessor Rd ST16 . . . . .156 A4
Slindon Cl ST5 . . . . .40 B1
Sling La ST19 . . . . .206 A2
Slingsby B77 . . . . .261 B4
Slippery La ST1 . . . . .282 A2
Slitting Mill Rd WS15 . . . . .196 A4
Sloane Way ST4 . . . . .73 A3
Small La ST1 . . . . .133 C4
Small Mdws DE13 . . . . . . .183 C1
Smallbrook La WV5 . . . . . .270 A4
Smallcross Cl WS14 . . . . . .126 B3
Smalley Cl WS11 . . . . .210 A3
Smallman St ST16 . . . . . . .155 C2
Smallridge WS13 . . . . .213 C1
Smallshire Way DY8 . . . . . .279 B4
Smallthorne Prim Sch
ST6 . . . . .42 B1

Smallwood Cl ST5 . . . . .40 C1
Smallwood Gr ST1 . . . . .57 C3
Smallwood Rd WV8 . . . . . .239 C1
Smarts Ave WS14 . . . . . . .258 A4
Smedley Ct DE65 . . . . .148 A3
Smestow Bridge Ind Est
WV5 . . . . .269 B3
Smestow La DY3 . . . . .269 B2
Smestow Sch WV3 . . . . . . .255 A1
Smillie Pl WS11 . . . . .209 C2
Smith Child St ST6 . . . . .41 B2
Smith Ho WS3 . . . . .243 B4
Smith St Longton ST3 . . . . .283 C5
Wood End CV9 . . . . .262 B1
Smith's Cl WS7 . . . . .228 B4
Smithfield Cl TF9 . . . . .97 C1
Smithfield Cl ST1 . . . . .282 B1
Smithfield Ctr The [18]
ST13 . . . . .30 C3
Smithfield Rd
Market Drayton TF9 . . . . . .97 B1
Uttoxeter ST14 . . . . .126 A4
Walsall WS3 . . . . .243 B1
Smithfield Rise WS13 . . . . .231 B4
Smithpool Rd ST4 . . . . .72 B3
Smiths Bldgs [4] ST3 . . . . . .74 A1
Smiths Pas ST4 . . . . .73 A3
Smithy Bank ST10 . . . . .78 C1
Smithy Croft ST20 . . . . . . .190 A4
Smithy Dr WS3 . . . . .244 A2
Smithy La
Acton Trussell ST17 . . . . . .193 C4
Barthomley CW2 . . . . .38 B4
Biddulph ST8 . . . . .16 B1
Bosley SK11 . . . . .7 C3
Bradley ST18 . . . . .191 B4
Cheadle ST10 . . . . .92 B4
Clifton Campville B79 . . . . .218 C1
Eccleshall ST21 . . . . .117 A1
Hixon ST18 . . . . .158 B4
Lichfield WS13 . . . . .214 A1
Longdon WS15 . . . . .212 C4
Longton ST3 . . . . .283 C3
Sedgley DY5 . . . . .271 A1
Seighford ST18 . . . . .154 A4
Tamworth B77 . . . . .261 C4
Weston CW2 . . . . .37 B3
Whitmore ST5 . . . . .85 C3
Woore TF9 . . . . .83 A3
Smithyfield Rd ST6 . . . . . . .42 B2
Smokies Way ST8 . . . . .16 B1
Smout Cres WV14 . . . . . . .266 C1
Snape Hall Cl ST5 . . . . .85 B3
Snape Hall Rd ST5 . . . . . . .85 B4
Snape Hollow CW2 . . . . . . .37 C2
Snape La CW2 . . . . .37 C2
Snape Rd WV11 . . . . .242 A1
Snapes La DE6 . . . . .81 A1
Snead Cl ST16 . . . . .156 B2
Sneyd Ave Leek ST13 . . . . .30 C3
Newcastle-u-L ST5 . . . . .70 C4
Sneyd Cl ST13 . . . . .45 B2
Sneyd Com Sch WS3 . . . . .242 C1
Sneyd Cres ST5 . . . . .70 C4
Sneyd Green Prim Sch
ST6 . . . . .57 B4
Sneyd Hall Rd WS3 . . . . . .243 A1
Sneyd Hill ST6 . . . . .57 B4
Sneyd Hill Ind Est ST6 . . . .57 A4
Sneyd Ho WS3 . . . . .242 C1
Sneyd Ind Est ST6 . . . . . . .57 A4
Sneyd La Essington WV11 242 B1
Walsall WS3 . . . . .242 C1
Sneyd Pl ST6 . . . . .41 B3
Sneyd St Hanley ST6,ST1 . . .57 B3
Leek ST13 . . . . .30 C3
Sneyd Terr ST5 . . . . .55 A1
Sneyd Wood View ST6 . . . .57 B4
Sneydlands WS15 . . . . . . .178 C3
Snipe Cl WV10 . . . . .241 A4
Snow Hill Hanley ST1 . . . . .282 A4
Stafford ST16 . . . . .155 C2
Snowberry Dr DY5 . . . . . . .271 B1
Snowden Way ST3 . . . . . . .74 A1
Snowdon Rd
Cannock WS11 . . . . .209 C3
Pattingham WV6 . . . . .252 A3
Snowdon Rise DY3 . . . . . . .271 B3
Snowdon Way WV12 . . . . .242 A1
Snowdrop Cl WS8 . . . . . . .244 B3
Snows Yd ST16 . . . . .155 B2
Snowshill Gdns DY1 . . . . . .271 C2
Soames Cres ST4 . . . . .73 B3
Solent Cl WV9 . . . . .239 C1
Solney Cl DE11 . . . . .186 C2
Solway Cl B79 . . . . .250 A4
Solway Gr ST3 . . . . .73 C2
Somerfield Cl WS4 . . . . . . .244 B1
Somerford Cl
Brewood WV9 . . . . .224 A1
Great Wyrley WS6 . . . . . . .226 C1
Somerford Gdns WV10 . . . .240 C1
Somerford La ST19 . . . . . . .223 C2
Somerley Rd ST1 . . . . .57 C2
Somerset Ave
Kidsgrove ST7 . . . . .25 C1
Rugeley WS15 . . . . .196 B3
Somerset Cl B78 . . . . .250 A1
Somerset Dr DY8 . . . . .279 B4
Somerset Pl WS11 . . . . . . .209 C2
Somerset Rd
Burton u T DE15 . . . . .185 B3
Hanley ST1 . . . . .57 C2
Stafford ST17 . . . . .174 B4
Somerton Rd ST9 . . . . .59 A2
Somerton Way ST3 . . . . . . .283 D5
Somervale ST17 . . . . .175 B3
Somerville Ave ST5 . . . . . . .56 B2

Somerville Ct B79 .....249 B3
Somerville Rd DE13 ....201 A1
Somerville Sq ST17 .....174 C3
Sonning Dr WV9 ....239 C1
Sophia Way ST5 ....56 A4
Sopwith Cl ST15 ....118 C3
Sorbus B77 ....251 A2
Sorrel B77 ....251 A3
Sorrel Ave ST10 ....92 C2
Sorrel Cl Bucknall ST2 ....58 A2
Featherstone WV10 .....241 A4
Uttoxeter ST14 ....126 A3
Sorrento Gr ST3 ....73 C2
Souldern Way ST3 ....73 B2
Soulthorpe Rd DY10 ...281 A1
South Ave DY8 ....279 C2
South Broadway St
DE14 ....185 B4
South Cl WS11 ....226 B4
South Cres WV10 ......241 B3
South Dr DE11 ....186 C3
South Gn WV4 ....265 B3
South Hill DE13 ....147 B2
South Oak St DE14 .....185 A4
South Oval DY3 ....271 C3
South Pl ST6 ....42 B3
South Rd Bucknall ST2 ....58 A3
Millmeece ST15 ....118 B3
Stourbridge DY8 ....279 C2
Wolv WV4 ....266 C2
South St
Mount Pleasant ST7 ......26 A3
Norton-in-t-M ST6 ....42 B3
Stafford ST16 ....155 B2
South Staffordshire Bsns Pk
WS11 ....226 B2
South Terr
Newcastle-u-L ST5 ....56 B3
Stoke-on-T ST4 ....72 A3
South Uxbridge St
DE14 ....185 A4
South View Biddulph ST8 ..27 B4
Mayfield DE6 ....81 B3
Uttoxeter ST14 ....126 A4
South View Cl
Codsall WV8 ....239 A1
Featherstone WV10 .....241 A3
South View Rd DY3 .....271 B4
South View Wlk ST14 ....95 C2
South Walls ST16 ......155 C2
South Wlk ST3 ....74 A1
South Wolf St ST4 ....72 A4
South Wood ST5 ....85 A4
Southall Way ST2 ....58 A1
Southampton St ST1 ...282 C4
Southbank St ST13 ....30 C3
Southbank View DY6 ...275 C2
Southborough Cres ST6 .42 B2
Southbourne Pl WS11 ..209 B1
Southbourne Rd WV10 .240 B2
Southdown Cl ST3 ....89 B4
Southern Cl DY6 ....275 C2
Southern Cross WS14 ..231 B4
Southern Way ST6 ....42 B1
Southerndown Rd DY3 .271 A4
Southfield Cl WS9 ......256 A3
Southfield Gr WV3 .....265 B4
Southfield Way WS6 ....226 C1
Southfields Cl ST17 .....174 B3
Southfields Rd ST17 ...174 B3
Southgate Brewood ST19 223 B4
Cannock WS11 ....226 A4
Southgate Ave ST4 ....88 B3
Southgate End WS11 ...226 A4
Southlands Ave
Longton ST3 ....283 B1
Newcastle-u-L ST5 ....56 B3
Southlands Cl ST13 ....30 B3
Southlands Rd CW12 .....16 A4
Southlowe Ave ST9 ....59 C2
Southlowe Rd ST9 ....59 C2
Southwark Cl WS13 .....214 B2
Southway Ct DY6 ....275 C2
Southwell Est ST21 .....133 C3
Southwood Cl DY6 ......275 C3
Sovereign Dr
Burton u T DE14 ....185 A4
Sedgley DY1 ....271 C1
Sovereign La TF9 ....100 B3
Sovereign Works DY1 ..271 C2
Sowdley Gn ST19 ....205 A3
Sowdley La ST19 ....205 A2
Sowers Ct B75 ....258 B2
Spa St ST6 ....57 B4
Spalding Pl ST2 ....73 C4
Sparch Ave ST5 ....56 B2
Sparch Gr ST5 ....56 B2
Sparch Hollow ST5 ....56 B2
Spark St ST4 ....72 A4
Spark Terr ST4 ....72 A4
Sparrow Cl ST18 ....177 B4
Sparrow St ST6 ....42 B1
Sparrow Terr ST5 ....56 A3
Sparrowbutts Gr ST7 .....26 B1
Sparrows End La ST19 ..223 B3
Speakman St ST3 ....283 D2
Spearhill WS14 ....231 C4
Spedding Rd ST4 ....72 C4
Spedding Way ST8 ....27 C4
Speechley Dr WS15 .....178 B1
Speedwall St ST3 ....73 B3
Speedwell Cl WS9 ....256 A3
Speedwell Gdns WV10 ..241 A4
Speedwell Rd ST5 ....40 C1
Speedy Cl WS11 ....209 C3
Spencer Ave Endon ST9 ...43 C3
Leek ST13 ....30 C3
Spencer Cl
Burton u T DE13 ....147 B1
Sedgley DY3 ....271 A2
Uttoxeter ST14 ....126 B3
Weston ST18 ....138 B1
Spencer Pl ST5 ....55 C3
Spencer Rd
Lichfield WS14 ....231 A3
Stoke-on-T ST4 ....72 B4
Spencroft Rd ST5 ....56 A3
Spend La Mapleton DE6 ...66 C4
Thorpe DE6 ....51 C1
Spens St ST6 ....56 C4
Spenser Ave WV6 ....254 C2
Spenser Cl Stafford ST17 174 B4
Tamworth B79 ....250 A3
Sperry Cl ST3 ....90 A4
Spey Dr ST7 ....26 B1
Spiceal Mews ST14 ......126 B4
Spicer's Cl WV5 ....267 B4
Spills Mdw DY3 ....271 C3
Spindlewood Cl 5
WS11 ....210 B1
Spinney Cl
Burntwood WS7 ....212 A1
Endon ST9 ....43 C4
Kingswinford DY8 ....275 B2
Norton Canes WS11 .....227 C3
Polesworth B78 ....262 C4
Walsall WS3 ....244 A1
Spinney Dr CW2 ....37 A3
Spinney Farm Rd WS11 226 A4
Spinney La WS7 ....211 C1
Spinney Lodge DE13 ....145 C3
Spinney Rd DE14 ....184 C4
Spinney The Biddulph ST8 .27 B3
Keele CW3 ....69 A4
Lawton-gate ST7 ....25 C2
Little Aston B74 ....257 A3
Newcastle-u-L ST5 ....71 B1
Sedgley DY3 ....271 B1
Wolv WV3 ....255 B1
Spinneyfields 9 ST17 ...175 B3
Spinning School La
B79 ....250 A3
Spiral Ct DY3 ....271 B2
Spire Cl ST6 ....42 C2
Spires Croft WV10 ......225 B1
Spires The WS14 ....231 C3
Spitfire Way ST6 ....41 B2
Splash La WS12 ....210 B2
Spode Ave
Armitage WS15 ....198 B2
Hopton ST18 ....156 A4
Spode Cl ST10 ....76 B1
Spode Gr ST5 ....71 A2
Spode Pl WS11 ....210 A1
Spode St ST4 ....72 A3
Spout La ST2 ....43 B1
Spoutfield Rd ST4 ....56 C1
Spragg House La ST6 ....42 C2
Spratslade Dr ST3 ......283 B2
Spreadoaks Dr ST17 ....175 B3
Sprengers Cl ST19 ......193 A1
Spring Bank ST7 ....26 A4
Spring Bank Flats ST16 .155 B3
Spring Cl Hagley DY9 ...281 C2
Kinver DY7 ....277 C3
Swadlincote DE11 ....186 C1
Walsall WS4 ....244 B1
Spring Cres ST6 ....43 B4
Spring Garden Rd ST3 ..283 B2
Spring Gdns
Forsbrook ST11 ....91 A4
Leek ST13 ....30 B3
Stone ST15 ....120 A3
Spring La Walsall WS4 ..244 B1
Whittington WS14 ....232 C3
Spring Leasow ST20 ....151 A2
Spring Mdw WS6 ....226 B1
Spring Meadows Cl
WV8 ....239 A2
Spring Rd Lichfield WS13 214 B1
Longton ST3 ....73 C1
Walsall WS4 ....244 B1
Spring St Cannock WS11 .226 C4
Stoke-on-T ST5 ....56 B1
Spring Terr WS7 ....228 C3
Spring Terr Rd DE15 ....166 C1
Spring Vale Prim Sch
WV4 ....266 C2
Spring View ST6 ....43 B4
Springbank Ave ST9 ......43 C3
Springcroft ST11 ....90 C3
Springcroft Prim Sch
ST11 ....90 C4
Springdale Jun Sch
WV4 ....265 B3
Springfarm Rd DE15 ....167 A1
Springfield Ashley TF9 ....99 C3
Blythe Bridge ST11 ....90 C3
Springfield Ave
Newport TF10 ....168 C1
Rugeley WS15 ....196 C4
Sedgley DY3 ....266 C1
Springfield Cl Leek ST13 .31 A3
Newcastle-u-L ST5 ....55 C3
Springfield Cres ST3 ...283 B2
Springfield Ct Leek ST13 .31 A3
Stafford ST17 ....174 C3
Wolv WV10 ....240 B2
Springfield Dr
Forsbrook ST11 ....91 A4
Leek ST13 ....31 A3
Stafford ST17 ....174 C3
Wheaton Aston ST19 ....205 B4
Springfield Gr
Biddulph ST8 ....27 B4
Springfield Gr *continued*
Sedgley DY3 ....266 B1
Springfield La WV10 ....240 B2
Springfield Prim Sch
ST4 ....71 C3
Springfield Rd
Biddulph ST8 ....27 B4
Leek ST13 ....31 A3
Tamworth B77 ....261 B4
Uttoxeter ST14 ....126 A4
Springfield Rise WS12 ..210 B3
Springfield Sch ST13 ......31 A3
Springfield Terr DE15 ..167 A1
Springfields Fst Sch
ST15 ....118 C3
Springfields Ind Est
TF10 ....168 C1
Springfields Rd
Rugeley WS15 ....178 B2
Stoke-on-T ST4 ....71 C3
Springhead Cl ST7 ....40 B3
Springhead Prim Sch
ST7 ....40 B3
Springhill Ave WV4 .....265 B2
Springhill Cl WS4 ....244 B1
Springhill Gr WV4 ....265 B2
Springhill La WV4 ....265 A2
Springhill Pk WV4 ....265 A2
Springhill Prim Sch
WS7 ....229 A3
Springhill Rd
Brownhills WS8 ....245 A4
Burntwood WS7 ....229 A3
Springhill Terr WS15 ....196 C4
Springle Styche La WS7 212 B1
Springpool ST5 ....70 B3
Springs Bank ST9 ....44 A1
Springside Pl ST3 ....88 C4
Springvale Prim Sch
WS11 ....226 C4
Springvale Rise ST16 ...155 B4
Springwood Dr ST15 ....120 B4
Springwood Rd ST5 ......55 B4
Sprink La CW12 ....6 B3
Sprinkbank Rd ST6 ....42 A3
Sprinkswoods La DE6 ....81 C3
Sprinkwood Gr ST3 ....74 A2
Sproston Rd ST6 ....41 C2
Spruce B77 ....251 A2
Spruce Rd WS12 ....195 A1
Spruce Way WV3 ....255 B1
Spruce Wlk WS15 ....178 B2
Spruces The DY9 ....281 C2
Spur Lea ST18 ....173 B1
Spur St ST1 ....282 C1
Spur Tree Ave WV3 .....255 A1
Square The
Aldridge WS9 ....256 A3
Caverswall ST11 ....74 C1
Codsall WV8 ....238 C2
Colwich ST18 ....158 A1
Elford B79 ....216 B1
Fazeley B78 ....261 A4
Marchington ST14 ....127 C1
Meir ST3 ....74 A1
Newcastle-u-L ST5 ....71 A3
Newport TF10 ....168 C2
Oakamoor ST10 ....78 A3
Pattingham WV6 ....253 B1
Wolv WV2 ....266 B4
Woore CW3 ....67 B1
Squires Gate WS7 ....229 B4
Squires View ST4 ....72 B4
Squirrel Cl
Cannock WS12 ....210 B1
Huntington WS12 ....209 B3
Lichfield WS13 ....230 C3
Squirrel Hayes Ave ST8 ..27 C3
Squirrel Hayes Fst Sch
ST8 ....27 B4
Squirrel Wlk
Little Aston B74 ....257 B3
Stafford ST17 ....174 C2
Wolv WV4 ....266 A3
Squirrel's Hollow WS7 .212 A1
Squirrels The
Lichfield WS14 ....231 B4
Newcastle-u-L ST5 ....71 B2
Stable Ct DY3 ....271 C3
Stable La Alstonefield DE6 .35 A1
Market Drayton TF9 ......97 A1
Shareshill WV10,ST19 ...225 A4
Stableford Bank ST5 .....86 A1
Stables The ST18 ....158 A1
Stacey Cl SK17 ....23 A1
Stackhouse Cl WS9 .....245 A2
Stackhouse Dr WS3 .....244 A2
Stackyard La TF10 ......168 A2
Stadium Ct ST6 ....57 A3
Stadmorslow La ST7 .....26 C2
Stafford Ave ST5 ....71 B3
Stafford Brook Rd
WS15 ....195 C4
Stafford Castle★ ST16 ...155 A1
Stafford Cl Stone ST15 ..120 A4
Walsall WS3 ....243 A1
Stafford Coll ST16 ....155 B2
Stafford Cres
Newcastle-u-L ST5 ....71 B2
Whittington WS14 ....232 B2
Stafford Ct WV10 ....240 B3
Stafford Gram Sch
ST18 ....174 B3
Stafford La
Cannock WS12 ....210 A3
Codsall WV8 ....238 C1
Hanley ST1 ....282 B3
Stafford Rd
Brewood WV10 ....224 B3
Cannock WS11 ....209 B1
Eccleshall ST21 ....133 C3
Gnosall ST20 ....171 C3
Huntington WS11,WS12 .209 B3
Lichfield WS13 ....213 C1
Newport TF10 ....169 A2
Stone ST15 ....120 A3
Uttoxeter ST14 ....125 C3
Walsall WS3 ....243 A2
Weston ST18 ....138 B2
Wolv WV10 ....240 B2
Stafford St
Brewood ST19 ....223 B3
Burton u T DE14 ....166 B3
Cannock WS12 ....210 C1
Eccleshall ST21 ....133 C4
Hanley ST1 ....282 B3
Market Drayton TF9 ......97 B1
Newcastle-u-L ST5 ......284 C2
Newport TF10 ....168 C2
Stafford ST16 ....155 C2
Stone ST15 ....120 A4
Stafford Sta ST16 ....155 B1
Staffordshire Coll (North
Walls Annexe) ST16 ..155 C2
Staffordshire Ct ST18 ..156 B2
Staffordshire General Hospl
ST16 ....156 A2
Staffordshire Regiment Mus
The★ WS14 ....232 B1
Staffordshire Tech Pk
ST18 ....156 B3
Staffordshire Univ (Lichfield
Ctr) WS13 ....231 A4
Staffordshire Univ (Stafford
Campus) ST18 ....156 B3
Staffordshire Univ Stoke
Campus) ST4 ....72 B4
Stag Cl WS15 ....178 A1
Stag Cres WS11 ....228 A3
Stag Dr WS12 ....209 B3
Stagborough Way
WS12 ....210 A2
Staines Ct ST15 ....120 B4
Staite Dr DY10 ....280 A3
Staithe Terr DY10 ....280 A3
Stakenbridge La DY10 ..281 B2
Staley Croft WS12 ......209 B2
Stalling's La DY6 ....275 B4
Stallings La DY6 ....271 A1
Stallington Cl ST11 ....90 B2
Stallington Gdns ST11 ...90 C3
Stallington Rd ST11 ......90 B2
Stamer St ST4 ....72 A3
Stamford Cres WS7 .....229 A4
Stamford St DY8 ....279 C4
Stamford Way WS9 ......245 B1
Stamps Cl DE15 ....167 B2
Standard St ST4 ....72 B3
Standedge B77 ....262 A4
Standersfoot Pl ST6 ......42 A3
Standhills Rd DY6 ....275 C3
Standing Butts Cl DE12 .202 B4
Stanfield Cres ST10 ....76 B1
Stanfield Rd ST6 ....42 A1
Stanfield St 4 ST3 ....73 B3
Stanford Cl ST19 ....192 C1
Stanford Rd WV2 ....266 B4
Stanhope Ho B79 ....250 A2
Stanhope St
Burton u T DE15 ....167 A2
Hanley ST1 ....282 A1
Stanier St Fenton ST4 ....72 C3
Newcastle-u-L ST5 ......284 B3
Stanley Bank ST9 ....44 A3
Stanley Cl DE12 ....219 C4
Stanley Cres ST14 ....111 A1
Stanley Ct WV6 ....254 C2
Stanley Dr
Newcastle-u-L ST5 ....40 B1
Swindon DY3 ....269 C1
Stanley Gr
Newcastle-u-L ST5 ....56 B1
Norton-in-t-M ST2 ....43 A1
Stanley Matthews Sports Ctr
ST4 ....72 B4
Stanley Matthews Way
Fenton ST4 ....72 B2
Trentham ST4 ....88 B4
Stanley Moss La ST9 .....43 C3
Stanley Moss Rd ST9 .....43 C3
Stanley Rd Bagnall ST9 ...43 C2
Biddulph ST8 ....16 B1
Cannock WS12 ....210 A3
Newcastle-u-L ST5 ....56 C1
Stoke-on-T ST4 ....71 C4
Stourbridge DY8 ....279 C2
Wolv WV10 ....240 B1
Stanley St Biddulph ST8 ..27 B4
Burton u T DE14 ....166 B1
Leek ST13 ....30 C3
Tunstall ST6 ....41 C2
Walsall WS3 ....243 B1
Stansgate Pl ST1 ....282 A4
Stanshope La DE6 ....35 B1
Stansmore Rd ST3 ....74 A1
Stanton Ave DY1 ....271 C3
Stanton Cl ST5 ....55 C1
Stanton La DE6 ....65 C1
Stanton Prim Sch DE15 186 A3
Stanton Rd
Burton u T DE15 ....185 C4
Meir ST3 ....74 A1
Stanway Ave ST6 ....57 B4
Stanway Cl ST14 ....126 A3
Stanways La ST8 ....17 A1
Stapenhill Rd DE15 .....166 C1
Stapleford Gdns WS7 ..229 B3
Stapleford Gr DY8 ....275 C1
Stapleton Cres ST3 ....73 A1
Star & Garter Rd ST3 ....89 C4
Star Bank ST10 ....78 B4
Star St WV3 ....265 C4
Starkey's La ST19 ......205 B4
Starling Cl ST7 ....26 B2
Startley La WS15 ....196 C1
Starwood Rd ST3 ....89 C4
Starwood Terr ST10 ....78 A3
Statfold La Alrewas DE13 200 C2
Alrewas, Fradley WS13 ..215 B4
Statham St ST1 ....282 A2
Station App Stone ST15 .104 C1
Sutton Coldfield B74 ....257 C3
Station Bridge Rd ST4 ...72 C3
Station Cl WV8 ....238 C2
Station Cotts ST5 ....85 B3
Station Cres ST6 ....42 B1
Station Ct TF10 ....169 A1
Station Dr
Armitage WS15 ....198 A2
Blakedown DY10 ....281 B1
Keele ST5 ....69 B4
Penkridge WV10 ....224 B3
Station Gr ST2 ....43 A1
Station La
Rushton Spencer SK11 .....8 A1
Walton-on-T DE12 ....184 B1
Station Rd
Albrighton WV7 ....237 A3
Aldridge WS9 ....256 A3
Alton ST10 ....78 C1
Audley ST7 ....54 B4
Barlaston ST12 ....88 B1
Barton-u-N DE13 ....183 C1
Biddulph ST8 ....16 B1
Burntwood WS7 ....229 C2
Cannock WS12 ....210 B3
Cheadle ST10 ....76 B1
Chebsey ST15 ....118 C1
Cheddleton ST13 ....45 B3
Codsall WV8 ....238 C2
Endon ST9 ....43 C4
Gnosall ST20 ....171 B3
Great Wyrley WS6 ......226 C2
Haughton ST18 ....172 C4
Hixon ST18 ....139 B2
Keele ST5 ....69 C4
Kidsgrove ST7 ....25 C1
Kidsgrove, Newchapel ST7 .26 C1
Lichfield WS13 ....231 A4
Madeley CW3 ....68 C3
Madeley, Onneley CW3 ...68 A1
Millmeece ST15 ....118 B3
Mow Cop ST7 ....26 B4
Newcastle-u-L ST5 ....55 A1
Newport TF10 ....168 C1
Penkridge ST19 ....192 C1
Penkridge, Four Ashes
WV10 ....224 B3
Rolleston DE13 ....147 B2
Rugeley WS15 ....178 C1
Scholar Green ST7,CW12 ..26 A4
Shenstone WS14 ....246 C3
Stafford ST16 ....155 B1
Standon ST21 ....102 B2
Stoke-on-T ST4 ....72 A4
Stone ST15 ....104 C1
Uttoxeter ST14 ....126 B4
Walsall WS3 ....244 A2
Wombourne WV5 ....270 A4
Station Rd DE6 ....144 B4
Station St Burslem ST6 ...56 B4
Burton u T DE14 ....166 B2
Cheslyn Hay WS6 ....226 C2
Leek ST13 ....30 B3
Station View ST3 ....74 A1
Station Wlks ST7 ....54 B4
Station Yd DE13 ....201 A1
Staunton Rd WS3 ....243 A2
Staveley Cl ST2 ....58 A2
Staveley Pl ST5 ....55 A1
Steadman Cres ST17 ...174 C3
Stedman St ST1 ....282 C4
Steel St ST4 ....71 C4
Steele Ave ST6 ....42 A1
Steele Cl ST13 ....45 B3
Steelhouse La WV2 .....266 C4
Steenwood La WS15 .....160 A1
Steere Ave B79 ....250 B4
Stellar St ST6 ....42 B1
Stenbury Cl WV10 ....240 C2
Step Row 12 ST13 ....30 C3
Stephen Ave ST10 ....61 B1
Stephens Rd DE14 ......185 A4
Stephens Way ST7 ....39 C1
Stephens Wlk WS13 ....214 A1
Stephenson Cl B77 .....251 A1
Stephenson Dr WV6 ....254 C3
Stephenson Way WS12 .210 A3
Stepping Stones WS15 .178 B1
Steps Gdns ST18 ....172 C3
Sterndale Dr Fenton ST4 .73 A3
Newcastle-u-L ST5 ....71 A2
Sterndale Moor SK17 .....5 C3
Sterrymere Gdns DY7 ..278 A2
Stevens Dr WS12 ....210 B3
Stevens Gate 8 WV2 ...266 B4
Stevenson Dr ST17 .....174 B4
Stevenson Rd
Bucknall ST2 ....58 A2
Doveridge DE6 ....127 A4

Stevenson Rd continued
Tamworth B79 . . . .**250** A3
Stevenson Wlk WS14 . . . .**231** A3
Steventon Pl ST6 . . . .**56** C4
Stewart Cl DE14 . . . .**185** A3
Stewart Ct ST2 . . . .**58** B1
Stewart Rd
Brownhills WS9 . . . .**245** A2
Kingswinford DY6 . . . .**275** B2
Wolv WV2 . . . .**266** B4
Stewkins DY8 . . . .**279** C4
Stickley La DY3 . . . .**271** B2
Stile Cl Biddulph ST8 . . . . . .**27** A3
Rugeley WS15 . . . .**196** C3
Stile Cop Rd WS15 . . . . . .**196** B2
Stile House La ST13 . . . . . .**31** C3
Stirling Cl ST2 . . . .**73** C4
Stirling Pl WS11 . . . .**226** A4
Stirling Rise DE13 . . . .**166** B4
Stirling St 8 ST6 . . . .**57** A4
Stitchings The DE6 . . . .**65** B1
Stock La ST14 . . . .**143** A4
Stockbridge Cl WV6 . . . . .**254** C1
Stockfield Rd 3 ST3 . . . . . .**89** C3
Stockford La WS14 . . . . . .**216** A2
Stockhay La WS7 . . . .**229** B3
Stockholm Gr ST1 . . . .**57** C4
Stocking La ST18 . . . .**153** A3
Stocking-gate La ST18 . . .**153** C1
Stockings La
Longdon WS15 . . . .**197** B1
Wheaton Aston ST19 . . . . .**205** B3
Stocks La ST14 . . . .**125** B4
Stockton La ST17 . . . .**175** C4
Stockwell End WV6 . . . . . .**255** B3
Stockwell Gr ST3 . . . .**73** B2
Stockwell Rd WV6 . . . .**255** B3
Stockwell St ST13 . . . .**30** C3
Stockwood Rd ST5 . . . .**71** C4
Stoke Bsns Pk ST4 . . . .**72** A3
Stoke Rd ST4 . . . .**57** A1
Stoke Recn Ctr ST4 . . . . . .**72** A1
Stoke Ski Ctr ST6 . . . .**56** C3
Stoke's La WS11 . . . .**227** C4
Stoke-on-Trent Coll ST1 . . .**57** A1
Stoke-on-Trent Sta ST4 . . .**72** A4
Stokebay Dr ST10 . . . .**76** C2
Stokesay Ave WV6 . . . . . .**254** C2
Stokesay Gr ST6 . . . .**57** A4
Stokesay Rise DY1 . . . . . .**271** C2
Stone Bank Rd ST7 . . . .**41** A4
Stone Bsns Pk ST15 . . . .**120** A3
Stone Chair La ST7 . . . .**25** C4
Stone Cotts Clifton DE6 . . . .**81** C4
Congleton CW12 . . . .**6** C1
Stone Cross ST19 . . . .**192** C1
Stone Ent Ctr ST15 . . . .**120** A2
Stone La DY7 . . . .**278** A2
Stone Pine Cl WS12 . . . . . .**209** C4
Stone Rd Chebsey ST21 . . .**134** C4
Eccleshall ST21 . . . .**133** C4
Stoke-on-T ST4 . . . .**71** C1
Tittensor ST4,ST12 . . . .**88** A1
Trentham ST4 . . . .**87** C4
Uttoxeter ST14 . . . .**126** A4
Stone St ST4 . . . .**72** A4
Stone Sta ST15 . . . .**104** C1
Stoneacre Cl WV3 . . . .**255** A1
Stonebridge Rd ST19 . . . .**223** B3
Stonecrop Cl WS8 . . . .**244** B3
Stonefield Sq ST15 . . . . . .**105** A1
Stonehaven B77 . . . .**250** C3
Stonehaven Dr ST1 . . . . . .**282** C1
Stonehill Wlk B77 . . . .**261** C3
Stonehouse Cres ST9 . . . . .**59** A2
Stonehouse Dr B74 . . . . . .**257** B2
Stonehouse Rd
Caverswall ST9 . . . .**59** A2
Rugeley WS15 . . . .**178** A4
Stonelea WS9 . . . .**256** A3
Stoneleigh Ct ST18 . . . . . .**174** B3
Stoneleigh Gdns WV8 . . . .**238** C2
Stoneleigh Rd ST6 . . . .**42** C4
Stoneleigh Way DY3 . . . . .**271** B3
Stonepine Cl ST17 . . . .**175** B4
Stonepit B77 . . . .**250** B1
Stonewall Pl ST5 . . . .**55** C1
Stonewell La SK17 . . . .**24** B3
Stonewood ST4 . . . .**71** C2
Stoney Brook Leys WV5 .**269** C3
Stoney Croft WS11 . . . . . .**209** C1
Stoney Dale ST10 . . . .**77** C2
Stoney La Endon ST9 . . . . . .**43** C4
Hagley DY10 . . . .**281** C2
Walsall WS3 . . . .**243** B2
Waterhouses ST10 . . . .**63** B1
Wheaton Aston ST19 . . . . .**206** B2
Wolv WV4 . . . .**266** A3
Stoney Lea Rd WS11 . . . . .**209** C1
Stoneycroft ST2 . . . .**43** A1
Stoneydale Cl DE11 . . . . . .**186** C3
Stoneydelph Prim Sch
B77 . . . .**251** A1
Stoneyfields ST18 . . . .**28** A4
Stoneyfields Ave ST2 . . . . .**43** A1
Stoneyfields Cl 3
WS11 . . . .**209** C1
Stoneyfields Ct ST5 . . . . . .**284** D4
Stoneyford Terr ST14 . . . . .**126** B3
Stoneywell La
Longdon WS15 . . . .**213** A3
Longdon WS15 . . . .**212** B3
Stonier Dr ST14 . . . .**141** B4

Stonnall Gate WS9 . . . . . .**256** B4
Stonnall Rd WS9 . . . .**256** B4
Stonor Rd ST6 . . . .**57** A3
Stony La ST10 . . . .**49** B1
Stonydelph La B77 . . . .**262** A4
Stonyford La WS15 . . . . . .**179** C2
Stormont Cl ST6 . . . .**42** B1
Stour B77 . . . .**262** A3
Stour Cl Burntwood WS7 . .**229** B3
Hilton DE65 . . . .**147** C4
Stourbridge Coll DY8 . . . .**279** C3
Stourbridge Rd
Blakedown DY9 . . . .**281** C1
Cookley DY10 . . . .**280** B1
Himley WV5,DY3 . . . .**270** A3
Kidderminster DY10 . . . . . .**280** B1
Wombourne WV5,DY3 . . . .**270** A3
Stourton Cres DY7 . . . .**278** C4
Stourton Dr WV4 . . . .**265** B3
Stowe Hill Gdns WS13 . . .**214** B1
Stowe La ST18 . . . .**139** B1
Stowe Rd WS13 . . . .**231** B4
Stowe St WS13 . . . .**231** B4
Stowecroft WS13 . . . .**214** B1
Stowford Gr ST4 . . . .**88** A4
Stradbroke Dr ST3 . . . .**73** A1
Straight Mile WV10 . . . . . .**225** A3
Straits Gn DY3 . . . .**271** A2
Straits Prim Sch DY3 . . . . . .**271** A3
Straits Rd DY3 . . . .**271** A2
Straits The DY3 . . . .**271** A2
Strand Cl ST2 . . . .**58** A1
Strand Pas ST3 . . . .**283** B4
Strand The ST3 . . . .**283** B4
Strangman St ST13 . . . .**30** C3
Stranraer ST3 . . . .**74** A2
Stratford Ave ST5 . . . .**56** C2
Stratford Cl
Forsbrook ST11 . . . .**91** A4
Norton-in-t-M ST6 . . . .**42** C1
Sedgley DY1 . . . .**271** C1
Stratford Dr WS9 . . . .**256** B4
Stratford Way WS11 . . . . .**209** C3
Stratheden Rd ST6 . . . .**42** A1
Strathfield Wlk WV3,
WV4 . . . .**265** B3
Strathmore Cres WV5 . . . .**265** A1
Strathmore Pl 6 WS11 . . .**209** C1
Strawberry La WS6 . . . . . .**242** C4
Strawmoor La WV8 . . . . . .**238** B2
Stream Mdw WS4 . . . .**244** B1
Stream Pk DY6 . . . .**275** C2
Stream Rd DY6,DY8 . . . . . .**275** B2
Streamside Cl ST19 . . . . . .**207** C4
Streather Rd B75 . . . .**258** B3
Street The ST20 . . . .**150** C3
Streetly Cres B74 . . . .**257** B2
Streetly Dr B74 . . . .**257** B2
Streetly La B74 . . . .**257** B1
Streetly Wood B74 . . . . . .**257** A1
Streets Corner Gdns
WS9 . . . .**245** A2
Streets La WS6 . . . .**226** C1
Streetway Rd WS14 . . . . . .**247** A4
Stretton Ave
Newport TF10 . . . .**168** C1
Stafford ST16 . . . .**155** A3
Stretton Brook Sch
DE13 . . . .**147** B1
Stretton Gdns WV8 . . . . . .**238** C2
Stretton Rd
Newcastle-u-L ST5 . . . .**54** C1
Walsall WV12 . . . .**242** B1
Wheaton Aston ST19 . . . . .**206** A3
Stretton St B77 . . . .**250** C2
Strine Way TF10 . . . .**168** C2
Stringer Cl B75 . . . .**258** A4
Stringer's St ST8 . . . .**27** B4
Stringers Hill WS12 . . . . . .**210** B4
Strode Ho B79 . . . .**250** A2
Strode Rd WV2 . . . .**266** B3
Stroma Cl 14 ST6 . . . .**56** C4
Stross Ave ST6 . . . .**41** C3
Stroud Cl ST3 . . . .**90** A4
Stuart Ave
Draycott in t M ST11 . . . . . .**91** B3
Trentham ST4 . . . .**88** A4
Stuart Cl ST15 . . . .**119** C3
Stuart Cl N ST15 . . . .**119** C3
Stuart Gr ST15 . . . .**56** B2
Stuart Rd ST1 . . . .**57** C1
Stuart Way TF9 . . . .**97** A1
Stubbers Green Rd
Aldridge WS9 . . . .**256** A1
Walsall WS4 . . . .**244** B1
Stubbs Dr ST15 . . . .**120** B4
Stubbs La ST1 . . . .**282** C2
Stubbs Rd WV3 . . . .**266** A3
Stubbs St ST6 . . . .**56** C4
Stubbs' Gate ST5 . . . .**284** C2
Stubbs' St ST5 . . . .**284** C2
Stubbsfield Rd ST5 . . . . . .**284** C1
Stubby La DE6 . . . .**144** A3
Stubwood Hollow ST14 . . .**95** B3
Stubwood La ST14 . . . .**95** B2
Stud Farm Cotts B78 . . . . .**249** C1
Studley Gate DY8 . . . .**279** B3
Studley Rd WV3 . . . .**265** B4
Sturgeon's Hill WS14 . . . .**231** B4
Sturgess St ST4 . . . .**72** A3
Stychbrook Gdns WS13 . .**214** A1
Stychfields ST17 . . . .**155** C1
Suckling Green La WV8 . .**238** C1
Sudbourne Cl ST14 . . . .**41** C4
Sudbury Hall & Mus of
Childhood★ DE6 . . . . . .**128** B3
Sudbury Pk DE6 . . . .**128** B4
Sudbury Pl ST5 . . . .**71** A1

Sudbury Prim Sch DE6 . .**128** C2
Sudbury Rd DE13 . . . .**182** A2
Sudeley B77 . . . .**261** B4
Sudeley Gdns DY1 . . . . . .**271** B1
Sudgrove Pl ST3 . . . .**90** A4
Sudlow St ST6 . . . .**57** A4
Suffolk Cl ST5 . . . .**71** B2
Suffolk Gr WS9 . . . .**256** A4
Suffolk Rd
Burton u T DE15 . . . .**185** B4
Meir ST3 . . . .**89** A4
Sugar Loaf La DY10 . . . . . .**281** A4
Sugnall Bsns Ctr ST21 . . . .**116** B1
Sullivan Way WS13 . . . . . .**214** B1
Sullivan Wlk WS13 . . . . . .**214** B1
Sumbeam Dr WS6 . . . .**226** C2
Summer Dr DY3 . . . .**271** B2
Summer Gr WS13 . . . .**214** B1
Summer Hill DY6 . . . .**275** B3
Summer La Sedgley DY3 . . .**271** B2
Walsall WS4 . . . .**244** B1
Summer Row ST3 . . . .**283** C2
Summer St
Kingswinford DY6 . . . .**275** B3
Stoke-on-T ST4 . . . .**72** A3
Stourbridge DY8 . . . .**279** C3
Summerbank Prim Sch
ST6 . . . .**41** B2
Summerbank Rd ST6 . . . . . .**41** B2
Summercourt Dr DY6 . . . . .**275** B3
Summercourt Sq DY6 . . . .**275** B3
Summerfield ST7 . . . .**26** A4
Summerfield Ave DY6 . . . .**275** B4
Summerfield Cl B77 . . . . . .**250** B2
Summerfield Dr ST14 . . . .**126** A4
Summerfield Rd
Burntwood WS7 . . . .**229** A3
Tamworth B77 . . . .**250** B2
Summerfields ST15 . . . . . .**118** C3
Summergate DY3 . . . .**271** B2
Summerhill WS14 . . . .**245** C4
Summerhill Dr ST5 . . . .**40** B1
Summerhill Gdns TF9 . . . .**112** B4
Summerhill La ST5 . . . .**135** C3
Summerhill Sch DY6 . . . . .**275** A4
Summerhouse Gr TF10 . . .**168** C2
Summerside Ave WS12 . . .**211** B2
Summervale Rd DY9 . . . . .**281** C3
Summerville Rd ST4 . . . . . .**71** C2
Summit Pl DY3 . . . .**271** A1
Sun St Cheadle ST10 . . . . . .**76** C2
Hanley ST1 . . . .**282** A2
Sunbeam Dr ST4 . . . .**250** C2
Sunbeam St WV2 . . . .**266** B4
Sunbury Ave WS14 . . . . . .**231** C4
Sunbury Cl ST4 . . . .**88** B3
Sundorne Pl ST2 . . . .**58** A1
Sundour Cres WV11 . . . . . .**241** A1
Sundown Dr ST17 . . . .**174** A4
Sundridge Wlk WV4 . . . . .**265** B3
Sunfield Rd WS11 . . . .**209** A1
Suningdale Cl DE13 . . . . . .**147** B1
Sunley Dr WS12 . . . .**210** B4
Sunningdale B77 . . . .**251** B2
Sunningdale Ave WV6 . . .**254** C3
Sunningdale Cl
Chell Heath ST6 . . . .**42** A2
Stourbridge DY8 . . . .**279** C1
Sunningdale Dr ST16 . . . .**156** B2
Sunningdale Gr ST5 . . . . . .**55** B4
Sunningdale Rd DY3 . . . . .**266** A1
Sunningdale Way WS3 . . .**243** A2
Sunny Bank Burslem ST6 . . .**56** C3
Mayfield DE6 . . . .**81** B4
Sunny Gdns TF10 . . . .**168** C3
Sunny Hill Cl WV5 . . . .**270** A3
Sunny Hollow ST5 . . . .**56** B2
Sunny Side ST10 . . . .**61** B4
Sunnybank Cl WS9 . . . . . .**256** C1
Sunnybank Ct ST6 . . . .**42** A2
Sunnybank Rd DY3 . . . . . .**271** C3
Sunnycroft Ave ST3 . . . . .**283** A4
Sunnyfield Oval ST2 . . . . . .**43** B1
Sunnyhills Rd ST13 . . . .**30** B2
Sunnymead Rd WS7 . . . . .**212** A1
Sunnymede Rd 1 DY6 . . .**275** C2
Sunnyside
Brownhills WS9 . . . .**245** A1
Swadlincote DE11 . . . .**186** C4
Sunnyside Ave ST6 . . . .**41** C2
Sunnyside Rd ST14 . . . . . .**111** A1
Sunride Ave WV5 . . . .**270** A4
Sunridge Cl ST2 . . . .**43** A1
Sunrise Hill WS12 . . . .**210** A3
Sunset Cl Brewood WV9 . . .**224** A2
Great Wyrley WS6 . . . .**226** C2
Tamworth B79 . . . .**250** A3
Sunset Pl WV4 . . . .**266** C2
Sunwell Gdns ST10 . . . .**76** C2
Surrey Cl Cannock WS11 . .**226** C4
Rugeley WS15 . . . .**196** B3
Surrey Dr
Kingswinford DY6 . . . .**275** C2
Tamworth B78 . . . .**250** A1
Wolv WV3 . . . .**255** C1
Surrey Ho 3 DY8 . . . .**279** C4
Surrey Rd Kidsgrove ST7 . . .**26** A1
Stafford ST17 . . . .**174** B4
Surrey Wlk WS9 . . . .**245** A1
Surtees Gr ST4 . . . .**73** A3
Sussex Ave WS9 . . . .**256** A4
Sussex Dr Cannock WS12 . .**210** A3
Kidsgrove ST7 . . . .**25** C1
Wolv WV3 . . . .**255** C1
Sussex Pl ST3 . . . .**73** B1
Sussex Rd DE15 . . . .**185** C3

Sutherland Ave
Longton ST3 . . . .**283** B1
Wolv WV2 . . . .**266** C4
Sutherland Cres ST11 . . . . .**90** C3
Sutherland Dr
Newcastle-u-L ST5 . . . .**70** C3
Wombourne WV5 . . . .**265** A1
Sutherland Gr WV6 . . . . . .**254** C2
Sutherland Prim Sch
ST3 . . . .**72** C1
Sutherland Rd
Cheslyn Hay WS6 . . . .**226** C1
Longsdon ST9 . . . .**30** A1
Longton ST3 . . . .**283** C3
Stone ST15 . . . .**120** B4
Tittensor ST12 . . . .**88** A1
Wolv WV4 . . . .**266** A3
Sutherland St ST4 . . . .**72** B3
Sutton Ave B78 . . . .**250** A1
Sutton Cl WS15 . . . .**196** C3
Sutton Ct WV4 . . . .**266** C1
Sutton Dr Stafford ST16 . . .**155** A2
Stoke-on-T ST4 . . . .**71** C2
Sutton La TF9 . . . .**112** B2
Sutton Pl ST6 . . . .**42** A3
Sutton Rd Aldridge WS9 . . .**256** A1
Drayton Bassett B78 . . . . . .**260** A4
Tamworth B78 . . . .**249** B1
Sutton St
Brierley Hill DY8 . . . .**275** C1
Newcastle-u-L ST5 . . . .**55** C3
Sutton Way TF9 . . . .**112** A4
Swadlincote La DE11 . . . .**186** C1
Swaffham Way ST2 . . . . . .**58** C1
Swaffield Pk WS11 . . . . . .**210** A1
Swainsfield Rd DE13 . . . . .**182** A1
Swainsley Cl 13 ST6 . . . . . .**57** A4
Swaledale Ave CW12 . . . . . .**6** C3
Swallow Cl
Huntington WS12 . . . .**209** B4
9 Kidsgrove ST7 . . . .**26** A1
Meir ST3 . . . .**90** A4
Rugeley WS15 . . . .**178** B1
Uttoxeter ST14 . . . .**126** A3
Swallow Croft Leek ST13 . . .**30** C2
Lichfield WS13 . . . .**214** A1
Swallow Wlk ST8 . . . .**27** B4
Swallowdale
Brownhills WS9 . . . .**245** A2
3 Stafford ST17 . . . .**175** B3
Wolv WV6 . . . .**254** C1
Swallowfall Ave DY8 . . . .**279** B2
Swallowfield B79 . . . .**249** C3
Swallowfields Dr WS12 . .**210** A2
Swallowfields Rd DY3 . . . .**266** B1
Swallowmore View ST7 . . .**40** B4
Swallows Cl WS3 . . . .**244** A3
Swan Bank Talke ST7 . . . . . .**40** B4
Wolv WV4 . . . .**265** C2
Swan Cl Blakedown DY10 . .**281** A1
Cheslyn Hay WS6 . . . .**226** C1
Longdon WS15 . . . .**197** C1
Rugeley WS15 . . . .**197** A3
Stafford ST16 . . . .**155** B1
Talke ST7 . . . .**40** B4
Swan Corner Sh Ctr
WS7 . . . .**229** B3
Swan Cotts WS14 . . . .**232** C3
Swan Ct Burton u T DE14 . .**166** C2
Church Eaton ST20 . . . . . .**190** A4
Swan Farm La CW3 . . . . . .**67** A1
Swan La
Abbots Bromley WS15 . . . .**161** A3
Kingswinford DY8 . . . .**275** C1
Penkridge ST19 . . . .**192** C3
Shareshill WV10 . . . .**225** B1
Stoke-on-T ST4 . . . .**71** C2
Swan Mews WS13 . . . .**231** A4
Swan Pas ST11 . . . .**90** C4
Swan Pool Gr WS4 . . . . . .**244** B1
Swan Rd
Draycott in t C DE6 . . . . . .**144** B3
Lichfield WS13 . . . .**231** A4
Whittington WS14 . . . . . .**232** C3
Swan Sq ST6 . . . .**56** C4
Swan St Stoke-on-T ST4 . . .**72** A4
Stourbridge DY8 . . . .**279** C3
Swan Wlk DE14 . . . .**166** B1
Swanage Cl ST3 . . . .**90** A4
Swancote Dr WV4 . . . .**265** B3
Swanfield Rd DY8 . . . .**275** C1
Swanfields WS7 . . . .**229** B3
Swanholme Way ST5 . . . . .**85** B2
Swanland Gr ST3 . . . .**73** B2
Swanmere TF10 . . . .**168** C3
Swanmore Cl WV3 . . . .**265** C4
Swanmote B79 . . . .**249** C3
Swannington St DE13 . . . .**166** A3
Swanton Pl ST4 . . . .**87** C4
Swarbourn Cl DE13 . . . . . .**182** A1
Swaythling Gr ST2 . . . .**58** B1
Sweetbriar Way
Cannock WS12 . . . .**210** B1
Stafford ST17 . . . .**175** B3
Sweetbrier Dr 5 DY8 . . . .**275** C1
Sweetman St WV6 . . . .**255** C2
Sweetplace La ST20 . . . . . .**189** C1
Sweetpool La DY8 . . . .**281** C3
Swift B77 . . . .**250** C2
Swift Cl Kidsgrove ST7 . . . . .**26** A1
Uttoxeter ST14 . . . .**126** A3
Swift Dr ST8 . . . .**27** C4
Swift Pl ST3 . . . .**73** C3
Swin Forge Way DY3 . . . . .**269** C1
Swinburne Cl Longton ST3 . .**72** C1
Stafford ST17 . . . .**174** B4
Swindale B77 . . . .**262** A4
Swindon Rd DY6 . . . .**275** A4

Swinfen Broun Rd
WS13 . . . .**231** A4
Swinford Leys WV5 . . . . . .**269** B3
Swingle Hill Rd ST3 . . . . . .**72** C2
Swinscoe Hill DE6 . . . .**66** A1
Swinson Cl ST14 . . . .**96** A2
Swiss Dr DY8 . . . .**275** C1
Swiss Lodge Dr B78 . . . . . .**260** C4
Swithin Dr ST4 . . . .**73** A3
Swynnerton Dr WV11 . . . .**241** C2
Sycamore B77 . . . .**261** C4
Sycamore Cl Biddulph ST8 . .**16** C1
Blythe Bridge ST3 . . . .**90** A3
Burton u T DE15 . . . .**185** A3
Stourbridge DY8 . . . .**279** B1
Talke ST7 . . . .**40** C4
Uttoxeter ST14 . . . .**125** C4
Sycamore Cres WS15 . . . .**197** A3
Sycamore Dr Hixon ST18 . .**158** B4
Wolv WV3 . . . .**255** B1
Sycamore Gn
Cannock WS11 . . . .**209** C3
Dudley DY1 . . . .**271** C3
Sycamore Gr Fenton ST3 . . .**72** C2
Newcastle-u-L ST5 . . . .**56** B2
Sycamore Green Prim Sch
DY1 . . . .**271** C3
Sycamore Hill WS15 . . . . .**211** C3
Sycamore La ST17 . . . .**174** A4
Sycamore Rd
Burntwood WS7 . . . .**228** C4
Burton u T DE15 . . . .**185** C2
Cannock WS12 . . . .**210** C2
Kingswinford DY6 . . . .**275** C3
Mayfield DE6 . . . .**81** B4
Stone ST15 . . . .**120** A4
Sycamore Way
Huntington WS12 . . . .**209** B4
Market Drayton TF9 . . . . . .**97** B1
Sycamores The
Hagley DY9 . . . .**281** C2
Lichfield WS14 . . . .**231** A3
Sutton Coldfield B74 . . . . .**257** C1
Sydenham Pl ST2 . . . .**73** B4
Sydnall La TF9 . . . .**112** C1
Sydney St
Burton u T DE14 . . . .**166** B3
Newcastle-u-L ST5 . . . .**56** B1
Syerscote La
Clifton Campville B79 . . . . .**218** A1
Wigginton B79 . . . .**234** B1
Sykesmoor B77 . . . .**262** A4
Sylvan Gr ST4 . . . .**71** C2
Sylvan Way ST17 . . . .**175** B3
Sylvester St ST6 . . . .**57** A4
Sytch La WV5 . . . .**270** A3
Sytch Rd ST6 . . . .**43** A4

T

Tack Farm Rd DY8 . . . .**275** B1
Tadgedale Ave TF9 . . . .**99** B3
Tag La TF9 . . . .**113** C2
Tagg La DE45 . . . .**14** C4
Talaton Cl WV9 . . . .**240** A1
Talbot B77 . . . .**250** A4
Talbot Ave B74 . . . .**257** A2
Talbot Cl TF10 . . . .**168** B1
Talbot Fst Sch ST14 . . . . . .**141** B4
Talbot Rd Rugeley WS15 . .**196** C1
Stafford ST17 . . . .**155** C1
Wolv WV2 . . . .**266** B3
Talbot St Hanley ST1 . . . . .**282** C1
19 Leek ST13 . . . .**30** C3
Rugeley WS15 . . . .**196** C4
Talbot Way TF9 . . . .**97** B1
Talbotshill La DY10 . . . . . .**280** B2
Talke Rd
Newcastle-u-L ST5,ST7 . . . .**55** C4
Newcastle-u-L, Red Street
ST7,ST5 . . . .**40** B2
Tall Ash Ave CW12 . . . .**6** A3
Tall Trees Cl B74 . . . .**257** B2
Talland Ave B77 . . . .**250** C4
Tallis Gr ST1 . . . .**57** C3
Tallpines ST17 . . . .**175** B4
Tally Cl ST2 . . . .**73** A4
Talsarn Gr ST4 . . . .**88** B3
Tamar Cl WS8 . . . .**228** B1
Tamar Dr DY3 . . . .**271** C3
Tamar Gr Cheadle ST10 . . . .**76** C1
Perton WV6 . . . .**254** C2
Stafford ST17 . . . .**174** A4
Tamar Rd Kidsgrove ST7 . . .**26** A1
Tamworth B77 . . . .**262** A3
Tame Ave WS7 . . . .**229** B3
Tame Cl ST8 . . . .**16** B1
Tame Ct Fazeley B78 . . . . . .**261** C4
Tamworth B79 . . . .**250** A3
Tame Dr WS3 . . . .**244** A2
Tame Gr WS11 . . . .**226** B4
Tame St B77 . . . .**250** B2
Tame Valley Bsns Ctr
B77 . . . .**261** C2
Tame Valley Ind Est
B77 . . . .**261** C2
Tame Wlk ST3 . . . .**74** A2
Tamedrive B78,B79 . . . . . .**250** A2
Tamworth & Lichfield Coll
B79 . . . .**250** A3
Tamworth Bsns Ctr B77 . .**251** A2
Tamworth Bsns Pk B77 . . .**251** A2
Tamworth Castle★ B79 . . .**250** A2
Tamworth Castle Mus★
B79 . . . .**250** A2
Tamworth Cl WS8 . . . .**228** C1
Tamworth Rd Elford B79 . .**233** C4

Tamworth Rd *continued*
Fazeley B78 . . . . .261 B1
Lichfield WS14 . . . . .231 C3
Polesworth B78 . . . . .251 C1
Sutton Coldfield B75 . . . .259 A1
Tamworth B77 . . . . .250 B1
Whittington WS14 . . . . . .232 A2
Wood End CV9 . . . . .262 B1
Tamworth Rd (Amington)
B77 . . . . .250 C3
Tamworth Rd (Dosthill)
B77 . . . . .261 B3
Tamworth WS13 . . . . . . .231 A4
Tamworth Sta B79 . . . . . .250 B1
Tan Bank TF10 . . . . .168 C2
Tanfield Cl WV6 . . . . . . .255 A2
Tanglewood Gr DY3 . . . . .266 B1
Tangmere CI WV6 . . . . . .254 C1
Tanhill B77 . . . . .262 A4
Tanners Rd ST2 . . . . .58 A4
Tannery CI WS15 . . . . . .178 C1
Tansey CI ST2 . . . . .58 A2
Tansley Green Rd DY6 . . .271 C1
Tansley View WV2 . . . . . .266 B4
Tansy
Sutton Coldfield B74 . . . .257 C2
Tamworth B77 . . . . .250 C2
Tanyard WS13 . . . . .231 B4
Tape St ST10 . . . . .76 C2
Taplin CI ST16 . . . . .155 B4
Taplow PI WS11 . . . . .209 C2
Tapton CI WS3 . . . . .243 B2
Tara Gr ST2 . . . . .43 A2
Targate Ct WS15 . . . . . . .198 A3
Target CI ST2 . . . . .40 C3
Tarleton Rd ST1 . . . . .57 C3
Tarporley Gr ST4 . . . . .71 C3
Tarragon Dr ST3 . . . . .90 A3
Tarragona Dr ST17 . . . . .175 A4
Tarrant B77 . . . . .261 C4
Tarvin Gr ST6 . . . . .41 C3
Tasman Dr ST6 . . . . .156 A3
Tasman Gr WV6 . . . . . . .254 C1
Tasman Sq ST1 . . . . .57 C3
Tatenhill Comm DE13 . . .164 C1
Tatenhill La
Branston DE14 . . . . .184 B4
Tatenhill DE13 . . . . .184 A4
Tatenhill, Rangemoore
DE13 . . . . .164 B1
Tatlowfold La ST10 . . . . . .48 C2
Tattenhall Coll (The Drive Sch) WV6 . . . . .255 B3
Tattennall Arc WV6 . . . . .255 B3
Tatton CI ST13 . . . . .30 A3
Tatton St ST3 . . . . .283 C4
Taunton Ave WV10 . . . . .240 B2
Taunton PI ST5 . . . . .55 C4
Taunton Way ST2 . . . . . . .58 B1
Taurus Gr ST6 . . . . .41 C3
Taverners CI WV12 . . . . .242 B1
Taverners Dr ST15 . . . . . .120 B3
Tavistock Ave ST17 . . . . .156 B1
Tavistock CI B79 . . . . . . .250 B4
Tavistock Cres ST5 . . . . . .71 A3
Tavistock PI ST4 . . . . .56 C1
Tawney CI ST7 . . . . .26 A1
Tawney Cres ST3 . . . . .74 A1
Tay CI Biddulph ST8 . . . . .16 C1
Kingsley ST10 . . . . .76 C3
Longton ST3 . . . . .283 C5
Taylor Ave ST5 . . . . .56 B2
Taylor Rd Bucknall ST2 . . .58 A3
Wolv WV4 . . . . .266 C3
Taylor St
Newcastle-u-L ST5 . . . . . .56 B2
Tunstall ST6 . . . . .41 B4
Taylor Wlk ST17 . . . . . . .174 A4
Taylor's La WS15 . . . . . . .178 C1
Taylors La ST14 . . . . .95 B2
Taynton CI ST6 . . . . .42 A4
Teal CI ST5 . . . . .85 B3
Teal View ST6 . . . . .42 B1
Tean CI Burntwood WS7 . .229 B4
Burton u T DE15 . . . . . . .167 A1
Tean Rd ST10 . . . . .76 B1
Teanhurst CI ST10 . . . . . . .92 C1
Teanhurst Rd ST10 . . . . . .92 C1
Teasel Gr WV10 . . . . .241 A4
Tebworth CI WV9 . . . . . . .239 C1
Tedder Rd ST16 . . . . .156 A3
Teddesley Ct WS11 . . . . .209 C2
Teddesley Rd
Acton Trussell ST17,ST19 .193 A3
Penkridge ST19 . . . . .192 C1
Teddesley Way WS12 . . . .209 B3
Teign B77 . . . . .262 A3
Telegraph St ST17 . . . . . .155 C1
Telford Ave
Albrighton WV7 . . . . .237 A3
Great Wyrley WS6 . . . . . .226 C2
Telford CI
Burntwood WS7 . . . . . . .229 B4
Congleton CW12 . . . . .6 A1
Stone ST15 . . . . .120 B3
Talke ST7 . . . . .40 C4
Telford Dr ST16 . . . . .155 C4
Telford Gdns
Brewood ST19 . . . . .223 B4
Wolv WV3 . . . . .265 B4
Telford Gr ST3 . . . . .210 A4
Telford La ST20 . . . . .171 B3
Telford Rd B79 . . . . .249 C4
Telford Way ST6 . . . . .42 A1
Tellwright Gr ST5 . . . . . . .56 A4
Tellwright St ST6 . . . . .42 A1
Telmah CI DE13 . . . . .147 B1
Teme Rd DY8 . . . . .279 C2

Temperence PI ST6 . . . . . .41 A2
Tempest St B79 . . . . .250 A3
Templar Cres ST5 . . . . . . .56 A3
Templar Terr ST5 . . . . .56 A3
Templars Way ST19 . . . . .207 C4
Temple CI DE14 . . . . .166 C4
Temple St Fenton ST4 . . . .72 B3
Sedgley DY3 . . . . .271 B2
Templeton Ave ST2 . . . . . .73 B4
Ten Butts Cres ST17 . . . .174 C3
Tenacre La DY3 . . . . .271 C3
Tenbury Ct WV4 . . . . . . .265 B3
Tenbury Dr WV6 . . . . .256 A4
Tenbury Gdns WV4 . . . . .265 B3
Tenbury Gn ST2 . . . . .58 B1
Tenby Dr ST16 . . . . .155 B1
Tenby Gr ST5 . . . . .55 C4
Tenford La ST10 . . . . .92 B3
Tennant PI ST5 . . . . .56 A4
Tennscore Ave WS6 . . . . .226 C2
Tennyson Ave
Burntwood WS7 . . . . .212 A1
Kidsgrove ST7 . . . . .41 A4
Sutton Coldfield B74 . . . .257 C3
Tamworth B79 . . . . .250 A3
Tennyson CI Cheadle ST10 76 A1
Market Drayton TF9 . . . . .112 A4
Tennyson Gdns ST3 . . . . .72 C1
Tennyson Rd
Burton u T DE14 . . . . . . .166 B4
Essington WV10 . . . . .241 A1
Sedgley DY3 . . . . .271 A2
Stafford ST17 . . . . .174 B4
Tenterbanks ST16 . . . . . .155 B2
Tercel Gr ST3 . . . . .90 A4
Terence Wlk ST8 . . . . .27 A1
Tern Ave ST7 . . . . .26 B1
Tern CI Biddulph ST8 . . . . .27 C4
Wolv WV4 . . . . .266 B2
Tern Gr TF9 . . . . .99 C3
Tern Ridge TF9 . . . . .97 B1
Tern View TF9 . . . . .112 A4
Terrace The Cheadle ST10 .76 B4
Wolv WV3 . . . . .255 B1
Terrington Dr ST5 . . . . . . .71 A1
Terry CI Lichfield WS13 . . .213 C1
Meir ST3 . . . . .74 A2
Terson Way ST3 . . . . .73 C2
Tettenhall Coll WV6 . . . . .255 B2
Tettenhall Rd WV1,WV3,
WV6 . . . . .255 C2
Tettenhall Wood Sch
WV6 . . . . .255 A2
Teveray Dr ST19 . . . . .207 C4
Tewe PI ST5 . . . . .55 B1
Tewkesbury Gr ST2 . . . . . .58 A2
Tewkesbury Rd WS3 . . . . .242 C1
Tewnals La WS13 . . . . . . .213 C3
Tewson Gr ST6 . . . . .57 B4
Thackeray Dr Longton ST3 73 A1
Tamworth B79 . . . . .250 A4
Thackeray Wlk ST17 . . . .174 A4
Thames Dr Biddulph ST8 .27 C4
Cheadle ST10 . . . . .76 C1
Thames Ho DY3 . . . . .271 B2
Thames Rd
Newcastle-u-L ST5 . . . . . .71 A2
Walsall WS3 . . . . .243 C1
Thames Way ST17 . . . . . .174 A4
Thanet CI DY6 . . . . .275 B4
Thanet Gr B79 . . . . .283 A3
Thatcham Gn ST3 . . . . . . .88 C4
Thatcher Gr ST7 . . . . .27 A4
Thatchmoor La DE13 . . . .182 B4
The Richard Heathcote Prim Sch ST17 . . . . .54 C1
Thelma Ave ST6 . . . . .43 A4
Theodore Rd ST2 . . . . .58 A2
Theresa CI ST4 . . . . .72 A1
Thicknall La DY9 . . . . .281 C2
Third Ave Branston DE14 .165 C1
Brownhills WS8 . . . . .229 A1
Bucknall ST2 . . . . .58 B2
Kidsgrove ST7 . . . . .25 C1
Kingswinford DY6 . . . . . . .275 C4
Thirlmere CI
Cannock WS11 . . . . .209 C1
Wolv WV6 . . . . .255 B4
Thirlmere Dr WV11 . . . . .242 A1
Thirlmere Gr Longton ST3 73 C2
Perton WV6 . . . . .254 C2
Thirlmere PI ST5 . . . . .71 A3
Thirlmere Rd WV6 . . . . . .255 B4
Thirlmere Way ST17 . . . . .174 C4
Thirsk PI ST5 . . . . .55 A1
Thistle CI Rugeley WS15 . .178 B1
Sedgley DY3 . . . . .271 C3
Thistle Down CI B74 . . . . .257 A1
Thistledown Ave WS7 . . .229 A3
Thistledown Dr
⑧ Cannock WS11 . . . . . .210 B1
Featherstone WV10 . . . . .241 A4
Thistledown Wlk DY3 . . . .266 B2
Thistles The ST5 . . . . .70 C4
Thistley Hough ST4 . . . . . .71 C3
Thistley Hough High Sch
ST4 . . . . .71 C3
Thistley Nook ST5 . . . . . .214 A1
Thomas Alleyne's High Sch
ST14 . . . . .126 B4
Thomas Ave
Newcastle-u-L ST5 . . . . . .56 A2
Stafford ST16 . . . . .155 A2
Stone ST15 . . . . .120 B3
Thomas Barnes Prim Sch
B78 . . . . .249 A4

Thomas Greenway
WS13 . . . . .214 A1
Thomas Hardy Ct B79 . . .250 A4
Thomas Ho WS3 . . . . . . .243 B2
Thomas Russell Inf Sch
DE13 . . . . .183 C1
Thomas Russell Jun Sch
DE13 . . . . .183 C1
Thomas St Biddulph ST8 . .16 B1
Leek ST13 . . . . .30 B3
Packmoor ST7 . . . . .26 C1
Talke ST7 . . . . .40 B4
Tamworth B77 . . . . .250 B2
Wolv WV2 . . . . .266 B4
Thompson Ave WV2 . . . . .266 C3
Thompson CI ST17 . . . . . .174 A4
Thompson Rd WS15 . . . . .197 A3
Thompstone Ave ST5 . . . .55 C2
Thor CI WS11 . . . . .210 A3
Thoresby B79 . . . . .249 C3
Thoresby Croft DY1 . . . . .271 C2
Thorley's Hill WS15 . . . . .212 B3
Thorn CI WS15 . . . . .197 A4
Thorn Tree La DE11,
DE15 . . . . .186 C4
Thornbridge Gr WS9 . . . .244 C2
Thornburrow Dr ST5 . . . . .71 C4
Thornbury CI WV6 . . . . . .255 A2
Thornby Ave B77 . . . . . . .261 C4
Thorncliff Gr ST1 . . . . .57 C3
Thorncliff Rd ST1 . . . . .31 B4
Thorncliffe View ST13 . . . .31 A4
Thorndyke St ST1 . . . . . . .282 A1
Thorne PI ST3 . . . . .74 A2
Thornes Croft WS9 . . . . . .245 C2
Thornescroft Gdns
DE14 . . . . .185 A4
Thornewill Dr DE13 . . . . .147 C3
Thorney CI WV11 . . . . . . .241 C1
Thorney Lanes ST14,
DE13 . . . . .142 C3
Thorney Rd B74 . . . . .256 C1
Thorneycroft Ave ST6 . . . .42 A1
Thorneyfields La ST17 . . .174 A4
Thornfield Ave ST13 . . . . .31 A3
Thornfield Cres ST7 . . . . .229 A4
Thornfield Croft DY3 . . . .271 C4
Thornham CI ST5 . . . . .71 A1
Thornham Gn ST2 . . . . . . .58 B1
Thornhill CI DE13 . . . . . . .183 B1
Thornhill Dr ST3 . . . . .68 C4
Thornhill Rd Bucknall ST2 .73 C4
Cannock WS12 . . . . .209 C4
Leek ST13 . . . . .30 B2
Little Aston B74 . . . . .257 A1
Thornleigh DY3 . . . . .271 B3
Thornley Croft WS6 . . . . .226 B1
Thornley Dr ST10 . . . . .76 C1
Thornley Rd
Chell Heath ST6 . . . . .42 A2
Essington WV11 . . . . .241 C1
Thornley St ST6 . . . . .166 B3
Thornton Rd ST4 . . . . .72 B4
Thorny La DE13 . . . . .162 B3
Thorny Lanes DE13 . . . . .143 A1
Thornyedge Rd
Bagnall ST9 . . . . .44 A1
Bagnall, Thorneyedge ST9 .44 B1
Thornyfields La ST17 . . . .174 A4
Thornyhurst La WS14 . . . .246 A3
Thorpe Ave WS7 . . . . .228 B4
Thorpe CI
Burntwood WS7 . . . . . . .228 B4
Burton u T DE15 . . . . . . .167 B1
Thorpe Gn ST3 . . . . .88 C4
Thorpe Rise ST10 . . . . . . .76 C3
Thorpe St WS7 . . . . .228 B4
Thorswood La DE6 . . . . . .65 A1
Three Mile La ST5 . . . . . . .69 C2
Three Spires Sh Ctr
WS13 . . . . .231 A4
Three Tuns La WV10 . . . .240 B1
Three Tuns Par WV10 . . . .240 B1
Thrift Rd DE14 . . . . .185 A4
Thurlstone Dr WV4 . . . . . .265 C2
Thurlstone Rd WS3 . . . . . .243 A2
Thurlwood Dr ST6 . . . . . . .42 C1
Thurne B77 . . . . .261 C4
Thursfield Ave ST7 . . . . . .26 B2
Thursfield PI ST6 . . . . .42 B2
Thursfield Prim Sch ST7 .26 C2
Thursfield Wlk ST6 . . . . . .42 B3
Thurso B77 . . . . .250 C3
Thurston Way ST2 . . . . . . .73 B4
Thurvaston Rd DE6 . . . . . .96 C1
Thyme Gr ST3 . . . . .90 A3
Tibb St ST7 . . . . .39 C1
Tibberton CI WV3 . . . . . . .265 B4
Tiber Dr ST5 . . . . .55 B3
Tickhill La ST10 . . . . .75 A4
Tidebrook PI ST7 . . . . .41 C4
Tideswell Gn DE11 . . . . . .186 C3
Tideswell Rd ST3 . . . . . . .283 C5
Tierney St ST1 . . . . .282 C4
Tiffany La WV9 . . . . .239 C1
Tilbrook CI ST2 . . . . .73 B4
Tilbury CI WV3 . . . . .265 A4
Tilcon Ave ST18 . . . . .156 B1
Tildesley CI ST19 . . . . . . .207 C4
Tilehurst PI ST3 . . . . .72 C1
Tilery La ST3,ST4 . . . . .88 B4
Tilewright CI ST7 . . . . .26 A1
Tilia B77 . . . . .251 A3
Till Wlk ST3 . . . . .73 B3
Tiller Gr B75 . . . . .258 B2
Tillet St ST3 . . . . .74 A2
Tilling Dr ST15 . . . . .120 A3

Tillington Manor Prim Sch
ST16 . . . . .155 B3
Tillington St ST16 . . . . . . .155 B3
Tilson Ave ST17 . . . . .71 C4
Tilstone CI ST7 . . . . .41 A4
Timber Gr ST19 . . . . .223 B3
Timber La ST14 . . . . .126 A3
Timber Pit La ST19 . . . . . .205 A2
Timberfields ST15 . . . . . .118 C3
Timberfields Rd ST16 . . . .155 B2
Timble CI ST7 . . . . .73 B4
Times Sq ST3 . . . . .283 B4
Timmis St ST1 . . . . .57 A1
Timor Gr ST4 . . . . .88 A4
Timothy CI ST3 . . . . .73 B3
Tinacre Hill WV6 . . . . .254 C1
Tinker's Castle Rd WV5 . .263 B1
Tinker's La ST14 . . . . .143 A4
Tinkers Green Rd B77 . . .262 A3
Tinkers La Ashley TF9 . . .100 A2
Brewood ST19 . . . . .223 C3
Tintagel CI
Burton u T DE13 . . . . . . .147 C1
Perton WV6 . . . . .254 C2
Tintagel Dr DY1 . . . . .271 C1
Tintagel PI ST2 . . . . .73 B4
Tintern Cres WS3 . . . . . . .242 C1
Tintern Ct WV6 . . . . .254 C2
Tintern PI ST5 . . . . .55 C4
Tintern St ST7 . . . . .57 C2
Tintern Way WS3 . . . . . . .242 C1
Tipping Ave ST3 . . . . .74 A1
Tipping St ST16 . . . . .155 C2
Tipton Rd DY3 . . . . .271 C4
Tipton St DY3 . . . . .271 C4
Tirley St ST4 . . . . .72 C3
Tissington PI ST4 . . . . .90 B4
Titan Way ST13 . . . . .231 C4
Titchfield CI WV10 . . . . . .240 C2
Tithe Barn CI ST16 . . . . . .156 A2
Tithe Barn La WS15 . . . . .212 B3
Tithe Barn Rd ST16 . . . . .156 A2
Tithebarn Rd WS15 . . . . .178 C1
Tittensor CE Fst Sch
ST12 . . . . .88 A1
Tittensor Rd
Barlaston ST12 . . . . .104 A4
Newcastle-u-L ST5 . . . . . .71 B3
Titterton La ST13 . . . . .33 A2
Titterton St ST4 . . . . .72 B3
Tittesworth Ave ST13 . . . . .31 A4
Tittesworth Est ST13 . . . . .20 C2
Tiverton Ave ST17 . . . . . .175 B4
Tiverton CI DY6 . . . . .275 C4
Tiverton Rd ST2 . . . . .73 B4
Tixall Ct ST18 . . . . .157 C2
Tixall Mews ST18 . . . . . . .157 A1
Tixall Rd
Stafford ST16,ST18 . . . . .156 B3
Tixall ST18 . . . . .157 A1
Toby's Hill DE6 . . . . .144 B3
Toft End Rd ST5 . . . . .41 A1
Tolkien Way ST4 . . . . .72 A1
Toll Bar Rd ST9 . . . . .59 B2
Toll Gate La B79 . . . . .233 C2
Tolldish La ST18 . . . . .158 B2
Tollgate Ave ST5 . . . . .85 B3
Tollgate CI ST7 . . . . .40 B4
Tollgate Cotts DE6 . . . . . . .81 C4
Tollgate Dr ST16 . . . . .155 C4
Tollgate Ind Est ST16 . . . .155 C4
Tollgate Rd ST13 . . . . .29 B3
Tollhouse Way WV5 . . . . .269 C4
Tolman Dr B77 . . . . .250 B2
Tolson Ave B78 . . . . .261 A4
Tolson CI B77 . . . . .261 B3
Tolworth Gdns WV2 . . . . .266 C4
Tom Fields ST7 . . . . .39 C1
Tom La DY3,DY7 . . . . .268 C3
Tom Williams Way B77 . . .261 B4
Tomkin Rd ST9 . . . . .44 A2
Tomkinson CI TF10 . . . . . .169 A2
Tomlinson St ST6 . . . . . . .56 B4
Tommy's La ST4 . . . . .6 A2
Tonadine CI WV11 . . . . . .242 A1
Tonbridge Ave ST6 . . . . . .42 A2
Toney PI ST7 . . . . .57 C2
Tong CI ST19 . . . . .221 C4
Tong Rd ST19 . . . . .221 C4
Tongue La ST6 . . . . .27 C1
Tontine Sq ST1 . . . . .282 B3
Tontine St ST1 . . . . .282 B3
Tontines Sh Ctr The
ST1 . . . . .282 B3
Tony Waddington PI ST4 .72 B2
Toothill Rd ST14 . . . . .126 A3
Top Chapel La ST6 . . . . . .28 A1
Top Heath Row ST6 . . . . . .43 A4
Top La ST4 . . . . .87 B1
Top Rd
Acton Trussell ST17 . . . . .175 A4
Biddulph ST8 . . . . .17 B2
Top Station Rd ST7 . . . . . .26 B4
Topham PI ST2 . . . . .57 C2
Tor St ST1 . . . . .57 B4
Tor Way WS3 . . . . .243 C2
Torbay Rd ST5 . . . . .250 C3
Torc Ave B77 . . . . .250 C2
Torc High Sch B77 . . . . . .250 C1
Torfield WV8 . . . . .239 C1
Torrance CI DE14 . . . . . . .185 A3
Torrance Gr ST4 . . . . .110 C3
Torres Wlk ST1 . . . . .57 C3
Torridge B77 . . . . .262 A3
Torridge Dr ST7 . . . . .174 A4
Torridon CI ST4 . . . . .88 B3
Torridon Rd WV11 . . . . . .242 A1
Torrington Ave ST17 . . . . .175 C4

Torside B77 . . . . .262 A4
Torvale Rd WV6 . . . . .255 A1
Torville Dr ST8 . . . . .27 C4
Totnes CI DE13 . . . . .166 B4
Tower Bsns Pk WS15 . . . .197 A3
Tower CI Biddulph ST8 . . .27 A3
Market Drayton TF9 . . . . . .97 A1
Tower Hill Rd ST7 . . . . . . .26 C4
Tower Rd Ashley TF9 . . . . .99 C2
Burton u T DE15 . . . . . . .167 A1
Cannock WS12 . . . . .194 C1
Sutton Coldfield B75 . . . .258 A2
Tower Sq ST6 . . . . .41 B2
Tower St DY3 . . . . .266 B1
Tower View Prim Sch
DE15 . . . . .167 B2
Tower View Rd WS12 . . . .210 A4
Town End ST10 . . . . .76 B2
Town Head ST10 . . . . .78 C1
Town Hill DE13 . . . . .182 A1
Town Meadows Way
ST14 . . . . .126 B4
Town Rd ST1 . . . . .282 B4
Townend ST11 . . . . .106 C4
Townend La Swinscoe DE6 .65 C3
Waterhouses ST10 . . . . . .48 C2
Townfield CI ST7 . . . . .25 B1
Townfields WS13 . . . . . . .231 A4
Townfold WS3 . . . . .244 A2
Townsend Ave DY3 . . . . . .271 B4
Townsend CI B79 . . . . . . .236 B2
Townsend Ho B79 . . . . . .250 A2
Townsend La ST7 . . . . .25 A4
Townsend PI Bucknall ST2 .58 B2
Kingswinford DY6 . . . . . . .275 B3
Townsend Prim Sch ST2 .58 B2
Toy CI WS15 . . . . .178 B1
TP Riley Com Sch WS3 .243 B1
Trade St ST4 . . . . .72 A4
Trafalgar CI WS12 . . . . . .210 C2
Trafalgar Ct 16 ST6 . . . . . .57 A4
Trafalgar Gr ST4 . . . . .71 C4
Trafalgar St ST1 . . . . .282 B4
Trafford CI ST13 . . . . .31 A3
Transport La ST3 . . . . . . .283 B3
Tranter Cres WS11 . . . . . .210 A2
Tranter Rd ST2 . . . . .58 A3
Tranwell CI WV9 . . . . .239 C1
Travellers CI WS7 . . . . . . .229 A3
Travers Ct ST4 . . . . .72 B3
Travers St ST6 . . . . .56 C4
Treasure CI B77 . . . . .250 C2
Trecastle Gr ST3 . . . . .73 C1
Treetops 7 ST17 . . . . . . .175 B4
Trefoil B77 . . . . .251 A3
Tregaron Ct ST2 . . . . .59 A2
Tregenna CI 11 ST3 . . . . . .90 A4
Tregew PI ST5 . . . . .55 B1
Tregony Rise WS14 . . . . . .231 B3
Tregowan CI ST6 . . . . .42 A2
Trenance CI WS14 . . . . . .231 B4
Trenchard Ave ST16 . . . . .156 A3
Trent CI Burntwood WS7 . .229 A4
Cheadle ST10 . . . . .76 C1
Colwich ST18 . . . . .158 A1
Perton WV6 . . . . .254 C2
Stafford ST17 . . . . .174 C3
Stone ST15 . . . . .119 C4
Trent Ct ST15 . . . . .119 C4
Trent Gr Biddulph ST8 . . . .27 B3
Newcastle-u-L ST5 . . . . . .71 A2
Trent Ho Cannock WS12 . .210 A4
Sedgley DY3 . . . . .271 C2
Trent Ind Est DE14 . . . . . .166 C2
Trent La Colwich ST18 . . .158 A1
Hixon ST18 . . . . .157 C4
Newton Solney DE15 . . . .167 C4
Trent Rd Cannock WS11 . .209 C3
Forsbrook ST11 . . . . .91 A4
Stone ST15 . . . . .104 C1
Walsall WS3 . . . . .244 A1
Trent St Bucknall ST2 . . . .57 C2
Burton u T DE14 . . . . . . .166 B1
Trent Terr
Burton u T DE14 . . . . . . .166 C2
Norton-in-t-M ST6 . . . . . .43 A3
Trent Vale CE Prim Sch
ST4 . . . . .71 C2
Trent Valley Cotts
WS13 . . . . .214 C1
Trent Valley Rd
Lichfield WS13,WS14 . . . .231 B4
Stoke-on-T ST4 . . . . .71 C3
Trent Valley Trad Est
WS15 . . . . .178 C2
Trent View CI WS15 . . . . .197 A4
Trent Wlk Hanley ST1 . . . .282 C1
Ingestre ST18 . . . . .157 C4
Trentfield La ST18 . . . . . .137 B3
Trentfields Rd ST2 . . . . . . .43 A1
Trentham Bsns Ctr ST4 . .88 B4
Trentham CI WS11 . . . . . .210 A1
Trentham Ct ST4 . . . . .87 C4
Trentham Gardens CI
ST4 . . . . .87 C4
Trentham Gdns ★ ST4 . . . .87 C2
Trentham Gr ST5 . . . . .56 B2
Trentham High Sch ST4 . .87 C4
Trentham Rd
Longton ST3,ST4 . . . . .88 C4
Whitmore ST5 . . . . .86 C4
Trentham Rise WV2 . . . . .266 C4
Trentley Dr ST8 . . . . .28 C4
Trentley Rd ST4 . . . . .88 A4

Trentmill Rd ST1 . . . . . . .57 C1
Trentside Rd ST6 . . . . .43 A3
Trentway Cl ST2 . . . . .58 A2
Tresham Rd **3** DY6 . . . . .275 B4
Trevelyan's Grn ST16 . . . .155 B4
Trevelyn Cl DE15 . . . . . . .167 B1
Trevithick Cl Bucknall ST2 .73 B4
Burntwood WS7 . . . . .229 B4
Trevitt Pl ST19 . . . . .205 B3
Trevor Ave WS16 . . . . . . .227 A2
Trevor Dr ST11 . . . . .74 B2
Trevor Rd WS3 . . . . .243 C2
Trevose Cl WS3 . . . . .242 C2
Triangle WS7 . . . . .229 A2
Trimley Way ST2 . . . . .58 A1
Trimpley Gdns WV4 . . . . .265 C2
Trimpos ST10 . . . . .76 A2
Triner Pl ST6 . . . . .42 C2
Tring Cl ST2 . . . . .73 B4
Tring Ct WV6 . . . . .255 C3
Trinity Cl Cannock WS11 . .226 C4
Kingswinford DY8 . . . . . . .275 B1
Shenstone WS14 . . . . . . .246 C3
Trinity Ct
  4 Congleton CW12 . . . . . .6 A1
  Kinver DY7 . . . . .278 A2
  Newcastle-u-L ST5 . . . . . .55 C4
Trinity Dr Stone ST15 . . . .104 C1
Tamworth B79 . . . . .249 B3
Trinity Gorse ST16 . . . . . .155 A4
Trinity Pl Bucknall ST2 . . . .58 A1
Congleton CW12 . . . . .16 A4
Trinity Rd Eccleshall ST21 133 B3
Sutton Coldfield B75 . . . . .258 B1
Uttoxeter ST14 . . . . .126 B4
Trinity Rise ST16 . . . . . . .155 A4
Trinity Sq ST14 . . . . .126 B4
Trinity Wlk ST1 . . . . .282 B1
Tristram Gr DE13 . . . . . . .147 C1
Triton Cl WS6 . . . . .226 C1
Triton Wlk ST6 . . . . .42 B1
Triumph B77 . . . . .250 C2
Trojan B77 . . . . .250 C2
Troon B77 . . . . .251 B3
Troon Cl Burton u T DE13 . .147 B1
Walsall WS3 . . . . .243 A2
Troon Ct WV6 . . . . .254 B3
Troon Pl DY8 . . . . .275 B2
Troutdale Cl ST4 . . . . .73 A3
Trowbridge Cres ST2 . . . . .58 B2
Trubshaw Cl ST18 . . . . . .177 C4
Trubshaw Cross ST6 . . . . .56 B4
Trubshaw Ct ST7 . . . . .26 B2
Trubshaw Pl ST7 . . . . .26 A2
Trubshaw St ST6 . . . . .56 B4
Truro Cl Congleton CW12 . .15 C4
Lichfield WS13 . . . . .214 A3
Truro Pl Bucknall ST2 . . . . .58 A1
Cannock WS11 . . . . .227 B4
Truro Way ST17 . . . . .156 B1
Trussell Cl ST17 . . . . .175 A1
Trussell Grange ST17 . . . .175 A1
Trustley Cl DE14 . . . . . . .185 A4
Trysull Gdns WV3 . . . . . .265 B4
Trysull Holloway WV5 . . . .264 B2
Trysull Rd Wolv WV3 . . . .265 B4
Wombourne WV5 . . . . . . .269 C4
Tuckers Pl TF10 . . . . .168 C2
Tudor Ave Burntwood WS7 .229 B3
Cheslyn Hay WS6 . . . . . . .226 C2
Lichfield WS14 . . . . .231 C3
Newport TF10 . . . . .169 A2
Stoke-on-T ST4 . . . . .72 A3
Stone ST15 . . . . .119 C3
Tudor Cres
  Tamworth B77 . . . . .250 C2
  Wolv WV2 . . . . .266 A3
Tudor Ct Essington WV11 241 C2
Newcastle-u-L ST5 . . . . . . .56 A1
Sutton Coldfield B74 . . . . .258 A1
Tudor Gdns DY8 . . . . . . .279 C3
Tudor Gr ST5 . . . . .56 B2
Tudor Hollow
  Blythe Bridge ST11 . . . . . .90 C1
  Burton u T DE13 . . . . . . .166 B4
Tudor Park Ct B74 . . . . . .257 C2
Tudor Pl DY3 . . . . .271 C3
Tudor Rd Burntwood WS7 229 B3
Cannock WS12 . . . . .209 C4
Dudley DY3 . . . . .271 C3
Tudor Rise
  Clifton Campville B79 . . . .218 C1
  Stafford ST16 . . . . .155 B4
Tudor Rose Way ST6 . . . . .42 C1
Tudor Vale DY3 . . . . .271 C3
Tudor Way
  Cheslyn Hay WS6 . . . . . .226 B1
  Stafford ST16 . . . . .155 A1
Tudors The ST6 . . . . .41 C3
Tuke Pl WS13 . . . . .213 C1
Tulip Gr ST5 . . . . .284 C4
Tulley Pl ST2 . . . . .58 A2
Tullis Cl ST16 . . . . .155 B1
Tulsa Cl ST2 . . . . .58 A1
Tunbridge Dr ST5 . . . . . . .54 C1
Tunley St ST15 . . . . .104 C1
Tunnicliffe Cl ST3 . . . . . . .73 C2
Tunnicliffe Dr WS15 . . . . .178 B1
Tunnicliffe Way ST14 . . . .110 C1
Tunstall La ST20 . . . . . . .131 C1
Tunstall Rd Biddulph ST8 . .27 B3
Bosley SK11 . . . . .7 B4
Congleton CW12 . . . . .6 C1

Tunstall Road Ind Est
  ST8 . . . . .27 A2
Tuppenhurst La WS15 . . .198 B2
Turf Cl WS11 . . . . .228 A2
Turf Cotts WV4 . . . . .265 C1
Turf Pitts La B75 . . . . . . .258 C2
Turin Dr ST5 . . . . .70 C3
Turls Hill Rd DY3 . . . . . . .271 C4
Turls St DY3 . . . . .271 C4
Turnberry B77 . . . . .251 B3
Turnberry Dr ST4 . . . . . . .88 A4
Turnberry Gr WV6 . . . . . .254 B3
Turnberry Rd WS3 . . . . . .243 A2
Turnbull Rd WS13 . . . . . .215 B3
Turnbury Cl DE14 . . . . . .185 A4
Turner Ave Audley ST7 . . . .40 A1
Wolv WV4,WV14 . . . . . . .266 C1
Turner Cl WS11 . . . . .210 B1
Turner Cres ST5 . . . . .55 C3
Turner Croft WS13 . . . . . .215 B4
Turner Gr WV6 . . . . .255 A2
Turner St Hanley ST1 . . . . .57 C3
Sedgley DY3 . . . . .271 B2
Turner's Gr DY3 . . . . .271 B2
Turner's Hill Rd DY3 . . . . .271 B2
Turners La TF10 . . . . .168 A2
Turney Gr ST17 . . . . .174 B4
Turney Rd DY8 . . . . .279 C3
Turnham Gn WV6 . . . . . .254 C2
Turnhill Cl ST17 . . . . .174 B3
Turnhill Gr ST5 . . . . .56 A4
Turnhurst Rd ST6,ST7 . . . .41 C4
Turnlea Cl ST8 . . . . .27 A3
Turnock St ST2 . . . . .58 B2
Turnpike Way WV9 . . . . . .224 B1
Turnstone Dr WV10 . . . . .241 B4
Turquoise Gr WS11 . . . . .210 B2
Turton Cl Alrewas DE13 . . .201 A1
Walsall WS3 . . . . .243 A2
Tuscan Cl ST10 . . . . .76 B1
Tuscan Ho ST3 . . . . .283 B2
Tuscan St ST3 . . . . .283 C4
Tuscan Way ST5 . . . . .55 B3
Tutbury B77 . . . . .261 B4
Tutbury & Hatton Sta
  DE65 . . . . .146 B4
Tutbury Ave WV6 . . . . . . .255 C3
Tutbury Castle ★ DE13 . . .146 A4
Tutbury Cl WS11 . . . . . . .210 B2
Tutbury Gr ST2 . . . . .73 B2
Tutbury Rd DE13 . . . . . . .166 A4
Tutehill B77 . . . . .262 A4
Twayblade DE14 . . . . . . .185 A4
Tweed Gr ST5 . . . . .71 A4
Tweed St ST4 . . . . .72 C2
Twemlow Cl ST18 . . . . . .154 B1
Twemlow St ST1 . . . . .57 A2
Twentylands ST3 . . . . . . .147 B2
Twickenham Ct DY8 . . . . .279 B4
Twigg St ST2 . . . . .58 A1
Two Gates Com Prim Sch
  Tamworth B77 . . . . .250 B1
  Tamworth B77 . . . . .261 B4
Two Gates Ind Est B77 . . .261 B4
Two Oaks Ave WS7 . . . . .228 B4
Twyford Cl Aldridge WS9 . .256 A3
Swadlincote DE11 . . . . . .186 C1
Twyning Gn ST3 . . . . .88 C4
Tylecote Cres ST18 . . . . .158 A1
Tyler Gr **22** Burslem ST6 . .56 C4
Stone ST15 . . . . .119 C4
Tyndall Pl ST4 . . . . .71 C4
Tyne Cl WS8 . . . . .228 B1
Tyne Way ST5 . . . . .71 A4
Tynedale Cres WV4 . . . . .266 C2
Tyneham Gr ST2 . . . . .43 A1
Tyning Cl WV9 . . . . .240 A1
Tyninghame Ave WV6 . . . .255 B4
Tynings La WS9 . . . . .256 A3
Tynsel Parkes CE Fst Sch
  ST14 . . . . .111 A1
Tynsel Parkes Fst Sch
  ST14 . . . . .110 C1
Tynwald Grange ST5 . . . . .56 A2
Tyrell Gr ST1 . . . . .57 C4
Tyria Way **5** ST17 . . . . .175 A4
Tyrley Cl WV6 . . . . .255 A1
Tyrley Rd TF9 . . . . .112 C3
Tyrol Cl DY8 . . . . .279 B3
Tyson Gn ST2 . . . . .73 B4
Tythebarn Dr DY6 . . . . . .275 A4

U

Ubberley Gn ST2 . . . . .58 B1
Ubberley Rd ST2 . . . . .58 B1
Uffington Par ST2 . . . . . . .73 B4
Ufton Cres ST3 . . . . .88 C4
Ullswater B77 . . . . .262 A4
Ullswater Ave ST6 . . . . . . .56 C4
Ullswater Dr
  Cheadle ST10 . . . . .76 C2
  Stone ST15 . . . . .120 B4
Ullswater Gdns DY6 . . . . .275 B3
Ullswater Ho ST17 . . . . . .174 C3
Ullswater Pl WS11 . . . . . .209 C1
Ullswater Rd WV11 . . . . .242 A1
Ulster Cl WS11 . . . . .210 A2
Ulster Dr DY6 . . . . .275 C2
Ulster Terr ST4 . . . . .72 A3
Ulverston Rd ST3 . . . . . . .88 C4
Umberleigh Rd ST3 . . . . . .88 C4
Under Rainow Rd CW12 . . .6 C1
Under The Hill ST8 . . . . . .17 A1
Underhill Cl TF10 . . . . . . .168 C2
Underhill La WV10 . . . . . .241 B1

Underhill Prim Sch
  WV10 . . . . .241 A1
Underhill Wlk DE14 . . . . .166 B1
Underley Cl DY6 . . . . .275 A4
Undertown La DE6 . . . . . .96 B3
Underwood Cl ST16 . . . . .155 A4
Underwood Rd ST5 . . . . . .55 A1
Unicorn Ind Est ST5 . . . . . .56 B4
Unicorn Pl ST6 . . . . .41 C3
Union Ct ST1 . . . . .282 B1
Union La WV5 . . . . .264 B1
Union St Burntwood WS7 228 C3
Burton u T DE14 . . . . . . .166 B1
Cannock WS11 . . . . .226 C3
Hanley ST1 . . . . .282 B4
Leek ST13 . . . . .30 C3
Unity Ave ST1 . . . . .57 B4
Unity Way ST7 . . . . .40 B4
Univ of Sheffield SK17 . . . .4 A4
Univ of Wolverhampton
Compton Park Campus
  WV6 . . . . .255 C1
University Ct ST18 . . . . . .156 B3
Unwin Cres DY8 . . . . .279 C3
Unwin St ST6 . . . . .42 A2
Upfield Cotts WS7 . . . . . .229 C4
Upfield Way ST5 . . . . . . .178 B1
Uplands Ave
  Caverswall ST9 . . . . .59 A2
  Chell Heath ST6 . . . . .41 C3
  Wolv WV3 . . . . .265 B4
Uplands Cl
  Cannock WS15 . . . . .211 C3
  Penkridge ST19 . . . . . . .192 C1
Uplands Croft ST9 . . . . . . .59 A2
Uplands Dr
  Caverswall ST9 . . . . .59 A2
  Sedgley DY3 . . . . .271 B4
  Wolv WV3 . . . . .265 C4
  Wombourne WV5 . . . . . .270 A3
Uplands Gn WS15 . . . . . .196 B3
Uplands Jun Sch WV3 . . .265 B4
Uplands Rd Bucknall ST2 . .58 A4
Stafford ST17 . . . . .156 A1
Uplands The Biddulph ST8 .16 C1
Colwich ST18 . . . . .158 A1
Newcastle-u-L ST5 . . . . . .284 C1
Upmeadows Dr ST16 . . . .155 A1
Upper Bar ST19 . . . . .168 C1
Upper Belgrave Rd ST3 . . .73 B1
Upper Brook St **2**
  WS15 . . . . .196 C4
Upper Cres ST4 . . . . .71 C4
Upper Cross Rd WS15 . . . .196 C4
Upper Cross St ST3 . . . . .283 C4
Upper Furlong St ST4 . . . .72 B3
Upper Gn WV6 . . . . .255 B3
Upper Gungate B79 . . . . .250 A3
Upper Hillchurch St
  ST1 . . . . .282 C3
Upper Huntbach St ST1 282 C3
Upper Landywood La
  WS6 . . . . .226 B1
Upper Lodge Rd WS15 . . .197 C2
Upper Market Sq ST1 . . . .282 B1
Upper Marsh ST5 . . . . . . .56 B2
Upper Normacot Rd
  1 Longton, Longton ST3 . .73 B1
  Longton, Normacot ST3 . . .73 C1
Upper Sneyd Rd WV11 . . .242 A1
Upper St WV6 . . . . .255 B3
Upper St John St WS14 . . .231 A3
Upper Villiers St WV2 . . . .266 B3
Upper Way WS15 . . . . . . .197 A1
Upper Zoar St WV3 . . . . . .266 A4
Upton Ct TF9 . . . . .97 B1
Upton Pl WS15 . . . . .178 B1
Urmston Pl ST3 . . . . .88 C4
Usam Trad Est WV10 . . . .240 B1
Usulwall Cl ST21 . . . . . . .133 B3
Utterby Side ST2 . . . . .73 B4
Uttoxeter Heritage Ctr ★
  ST14 . . . . .126 B4
Uttoxeter Race Course
  ST14 . . . . .126 C3
Uttoxeter Rd
  Abbots Bromley WS15 . . .160 C3
  Alton ST10 . . . . .94 C4
  Armitage WS15 . . . . . . .198 B2
  Blythe Bridge ST11 . . . . . .90 B2
  Draycott in t M ST11 . . . . .91 B3
  Foston DE65 . . . . .129 C2
  Foston, HM Detention Ctr
    DE65 . . . . .129 B2
  Hill Ridware WS15 . . . . . .198 A4
  Hill Ridware, Blithbury
    WS15 . . . . .180 A3
  Longton ST3 . . . . .283 C3
  Meir ST3 . . . . .74 A1
  Milwich ST18 . . . . .122 B3
  Sandon ST15 . . . . .121 B4
  Stone ST15 . . . . .120 C4
  Upper Tean ST10,ST14 . . .109 B4
Uttoxeter Sta ST14 . . . . .126 B4
Uxbridge Cl DY3 . . . . . . .271 B1
Uxbridge Ct
  Burntwood WS7 . . . . . . .228 C3
  Cannock WS12 . . . . .210 B3
Uxbridge St
  Burton u T DE14 . . . . . . .166 B1
  Cannock WS12 . . . . .210 B2

V

Vale Ave Aldridge WS9 . . .256 B2
Sedgley DY3 . . . . .271 B3
Vale Cl WS13 . . . . .214 A1

Vale Gdns ST19 . . . . .207 C4
Vale Head Dr WV6 . . . . . .255 A1
Vale Park (Port Vale FC)
  ST6 . . . . .42 A1
Vale Pleasant ST5 . . . . . . .55 B1
Vale Rise ST19 . . . . .207 C4
Vale Row DY3 . . . . .271 B3
Vale St
  Newcastle-u-L, Chesterton
    ST5 . . . . .55 C4
  Newcastle-u-L, Silverdale
    ST5 . . . . .55 A1
  Sedgley DY3 . . . . .271 B3
  Stoke-on-T ST4 . . . . .72 A4
Vale View Aldridge WS9 . . .256 C2
Cheddleton ST13 . . . . .45 B3
Newcastle-u-L ST5 . . . . . .56 B4
Valentine Rd ST7 . . . . . . .26 A1
Valerian B74 . . . . .257 C2
Valerian Way ST3 . . . . . . .90 A3
Valley Dr ST13 . . . . .30 A3
Valley Gn WS6 . . . . .226 C1
Valley La Lichfield WS13 . .231 B4
Tamworth B77 . . . . .261 C4
Valley Park Nature Reserve ★
  WV6 . . . . .255 B2
Valley Park Sch WV6 . . . .255 C3
Valley Park Way ST3 . . . . .72 C2
Valley Prim Sch ST8 . . . . . .78 A4
Valley Rd Cannock WS12 . .211 A3
Cannock, Hednesford
  WS12 . . . . .210 B3
Meir ST3 . . . . .74 A2
Sedgley DY3 . . . . .271 B4
Stone ST15 . . . . .120 A3
Walsall WS3 . . . . .243 B1
Valley Side WS3 . . . . .243 C1
Valley View
  Brownhills WS8 . . . . .245 A4
  Market Drayton TF9 . . . .112 A4
Valley View Wlk ST14 . . . .96 A2
Van Diemans Rd WV5 . . . .269 C3
Van Gogh Cl WS11 . . . . . .210 A1
Vanbrugh Cl WV6 . . . . . . .254 C2
Vancouver Dr DE15 . . . . .167 B2
Vanguard B77 . . . . .261 B3
Vanity Cl ST15 . . . . .105 B2
Vanity La ST15 . . . . .105 B2
Varden Ct WS15 . . . . . . .178 C1
Vardon Cl ST16 . . . . .156 B2
Vaudrey Cres CW12 . . . . . .6 A2
Vaughan Cl B74 . . . . .257 C2
Vaughan Gdns WV8 . . . . .238 C2
Vaughan Way ST17 . . . . .155 B1
Vaughan's La WS15 . . . . .159 B3
Vauxhall Cres TF10 . . . . .168 C1
Vauxhall Terr TF10 . . . . . .168 C2
Venice Ct ST5 . . . . .70 C4
Venn Pl ST1 . . . . .57 C1
Ventnor Gr ST3 . . . . .88 C3
Venton Cl ST6 . . . . .42 C2
Ventura Park Rd B78 . . . .249 C2
Ventura Pk B78 . . . . .250 A4
Venture Way ST6 . . . . .42 B2
Vercourt B74 . . . . .257 A2
Verdi Ct WS13 . . . . .214 B1
Verdon Cl ST19 . . . . .208 A4
Verity Wlk DY8 . . . . .275 C1
Vermont Gn **5** WS11 . . . .210 A2
Verney Cl ST14 . . . . .125 B4
Verney Way ST3 . . . . .88 C4
Vernon Ave Audley ST7 . . .39 B1
Brownhills WS8 . . . . .245 A4
Congleton CW12 . . . . .15 C4
Vernon Cl Audley ST7 . . . .39 B1
Essington WV11 . . . . . . .241 C2
Sutton Coldfield B74 . . . . .257 C3
Vernon Ho ST14 . . . . . . .126 B4
Vernon Lodge Prep Sch
  ST19 . . . . .206 B2
Vernon Rd ST4 . . . . .72 A4
Vernon Terr DE14 . . . . . .166 B2
Vernon Way WS3 . . . . . . .242 C1
Vernons Pl WV10 . . . . . . .225 B1
Verona Gr ST3 . . . . .73 C2
Veronica Ave WV4 . . . . . .266 C3
Verulam Rd ST16 . . . . . . .155 C4
Verwood Cl ST16 . . . . . . .156 B2
Vesey Cl B74 . . . . .257 C1
Vessey Terr ST5 . . . . .284 C1
Vestry Ct DY8 . . . . .279 C3
Vicar St DY3 . . . . .271 B4
Vicar's Cl Lichfield WS13 . .231 A4
Stone ST15 . . . . .105 A1
Vicarage Bank ST18 . . . . .138 C3
Vicarage Cl
  Brownhills WS8 . . . . .245 A4
  Burton u T DE15 . . . . . . .167 A2
  Dordon B78 . . . . .262 C3
  Eccleshall ST21 . . . . . . .133 C4
Vicarage Cres
  Caverswall ST11 . . . . . . .74 B2
  Newcastle-u-L ST5 . . . . .284 C1
  Tittensor ST12 . . . . .88 A1
  Upper Tean ST10 . . . . . . .92 C2
Vicarage Croft DE13 . . . . .199 B3
Vicarage Ct DY7 . . . . . . .278 A2
Vicarage Dr Kinver DY7 . . .278 A2
Uttoxeter ST14 . . . . .110 C2
Vicarage Field DE15 . . . . .166 C1
Vicarage Hill B78 . . . . . . .260 A1
Vicarage La
  Acton Trussell ST17 . . . . .193 C4
  Barlaston ST12 . . . . .88 C1
  King's Bromley DE13 . . . .199 B3
  Madeley CW3 . . . . .68 C3
  Stoke-on-T ST4 . . . . .71 C2

Vicarage Rd
  Brewood ST19 . . . . .223 B4
  Brownhills, Ogley Rd WS8 .245 A4
  Cheslyn Hay ST19 . . . . . .225 A4
  Leek ST13 . . . . .30 C3
  Penkridge WV10 . . . . . . .224 C4
  Sedgley DY3 . . . . .271 C3
  Stoke-on-T ST4 . . . . .71 C4
  Stourbridge DY8 . . . . . . .279 B4
  Upper Tean ST10 . . . . . . .92 C2
  Walsall WS3 . . . . .244 A1
  Wolv WV2 . . . . .266 B4
  Wolv, Penn WV4 . . . . . . .265 C2
Vicarage Way
  Hixon ST18 . . . . .139 B1
  Stafford ST17 . . . . .155 B1
Vicars Croft WS15 . . . . . .178 C1
Vichy Cl ST5 . . . . .70 C4
Vickers Rd ST6 . . . . .42 A3
Victor St Stone ST15 . . . .104 C1
Walsall WS3 . . . . .244 A1
Victoria Ave Audley ST7 . . .54 C4
Hanley ST1 . . . . .282 B1
Kidsgrove ST7 . . . . .25 C1
Walsall WS3 . . . . .243 B1
Victoria Cl ST5 . . . . .56 B3
Victoria Com Sch DE14 . . .166 B2
Victoria Cotts ST10 . . . . . .61 A1
Victoria Cres DE14 . . . . . .166 B1
Victoria Ct Fenton ST4 . . . .72 C3
  8 Kidsgrove ST7 . . . . . .26 A1
  Market Drayton TF9 . . . .112 A4
  Newcastle-u-L ST5 . . . . . .56 B2
  Norton Canes WS11 . . . .228 A4
Victoria Dr B78 . . . . .261 A4
Victoria Gdns WS13 . . . . .230 C3
Victoria Gr WV5 . . . . .270 A4
Victoria Hospl WS13 . . . . .231 A3
Victoria Ind Complex
  ST4 . . . . .283 A5
Victoria Mdw DE13 . . . . .199 B3
Victoria Park Rd ST6 . . . . .41 C2
Victoria Pk TF10 . . . . . . .168 C2
Victoria Pl Fenton ST4 . . . .72 C3
  Newcastle-u-L, Chesterton
    ST5 . . . . .55 C4
  Newcastle-u-L, Wolstanton
    ST5 . . . . .56 B3
Victoria Rd
  Burton u T DE14 . . . . . . .166 B2
  Fenton ST4 . . . . .72 C4
  Market Drayton TF9 . . . . .97 A1
  Newcastle-u-L ST5 . . . . .284 C2
  Sedgley DY3 . . . . .271 C4
  Stafford ST16 . . . . .155 B2
  Tamworth B79 . . . . .250 B3
  Walsall WS3 . . . . .244 A2
  Wolv, Oxbarn WV3 . . . . .265 C4
  Wolv, Stockwell End WV6 .255 C3
Victoria Row ST8 . . . . . . .27 B2
Victoria Sq ST1 . . . . .282 A1
Victoria St
  Burton u T DE14 . . . . . . .166 B2
  Cannock WS11 . . . . .226 B4
  Cannock, Chadsmoor
    WS11 . . . . .209 C2
  Cannock, Hednesford
    WS12 . . . . .210 B3
  Cheadle ST10 . . . . .76 C2
  Kingswinford DY6 . . . . . .270 A1
  Leek ST13 . . . . .31 A3
  Newcastle-u-L ST4 . . . . .284 C2
  Newcastle-u-L, Chesterton
    ST5 . . . . .55 C4
  Newcastle-u-L, Silverdale
    ST5 . . . . .55 B1
  Stafford ST16 . . . . .155 C2
  Stoke-on-T ST5 . . . . .56 B1
  Stone ST15 . . . . .105 A1
  Yoxall DE13 . . . . .182 A2
Victoria Terr ST16 . . . . . .155 C3
Victoria Way ST17 . . . . . .175 C3
Victory Ave WS7 . . . . . . .228 C4
Victory Cl WS12 . . . . .210 C2
Victory Cres ST10 . . . . . . .76 C2
Victory Terr B78 . . . . .261 A4
Vienna Pl ST5 . . . . .70 C3
Vienna Way ST3 . . . . .73 C3
View St WS12 . . . . .209 C3
Viewfield Ave WS12 . . . . .209 C4
Viewfield Cres DY3 . . . . . .271 B3
Viewlands Dr WV6 . . . . . .255 A1
Viggars Pl ST5 . . . . .55 C1
Vigo Cl WS9 . . . . .244 C1
Vigo Pl WS9 . . . . .256 A4
Vigo Rd WS9 . . . . .244 C1
Vigo Terr WS9 . . . . .244 C1
Viking B77 . . . . .261 B4
Villa Cl Biddulph ST8 . . . . .27 B4
Shareshill WV10 . . . . . . .225 B1
Villa Melita ST11 . . . . .90 B4
Villa Rd ST13 . . . . .45 B4
Villa St ST4 . . . . .72 A3
Village Gdns ST17 . . . . . .175 C4
Village Mews The WV6 . . .255 B3
Village The Astbury CW12 .15 A4
Endon ST9 . . . . .29 A1
Keele ST5 . . . . .69 C4
Kingswinford DY6 . . . . . .275 C4
Stafford ST17 . . . . .175 C3
Villas The Ipstones ST10 . .62 B3
Stoke-on-T ST4 . . . . .72 A3
Villiers Ho WV2 . . . . .266 B4
Villiers Ind Est WV2 . . . . .266 A4
Villiers St ST3 . . . . .283 B1
Vincent St ST1 . . . . .57 C3
Vine Bank Rd ST7 . . . . . . .26 A1
Vine Cl ST18 . . . . .158 A4

Vine La WS11 ....226 B3
Vine Row ST4 ....72 A3
Vine St DY8 ....275 C1
Vinebank St ST4 ....72 A3
Vineyard Dr TF10 .....168 C2
Vineyard Rd TF10 .....168 C2
Violet La DE15 ....185 C4
Violet Lane Inf Sch
  DE15 ....185 C4
Violet Way DE15 ......186 A4
Virginia Ave ST17 ....175 A4
Virginia Dr WV4 .....265 C2
Virginsalley La DE6 ...81 B1
Viscount Rd WS7 ......211 C1
Viscount Wlk **8** ST3 ...90 A4
Vista The DY3 ....266 B1
Vivian Rd ST4 ....72 C3
Vowchurch Way ST2 ...58 C1
Voyager Dr WS11 .....226 C3
Vulcan Rd WS13 ......214 C1

W

Waddell Cl WV14 .....266 C3
Wadden La ST18 ......138 C2
Wade Ave ST5 ....56 B3
Wade Cl Cheadle ST10 ..76 B1
  Hill Ridware WS15 ...197 C4
Wade Croft WS15 ......179 C1
Wade La WS15 ....197 C4
Wade St Chell Heath ST6 .42 A1
  Lichfield WS13 ....231 A4
Wadebridge Rd ST2 ....58 A1
Wadesmill Lawns WV10 240 C2
Wadham St ST4 ....72 A4
Waggon La DY10 .....280 C2
Waggoner's La B78 ...259 C4
Wain Ave
  Newcastle-u-L ST5 ....70 C4
  Norton-in-t-M ST6 ....42 C3
Wain Dr ST4 ....71 C3
Wain St ST6 ....41 C1
Waine Ho WS8 ....245 A4
Wainrigg B77 ....262 A4
Wainwood Rise ST4 ...71 C3
Wainwright Cl DY6 ...275 A4
Wainwright Wlk ST1 .282 C3
Wakefield Ave DE13 ..146 A4
Wakefield Rd ST4 .....71 C4
Wakeley Hill Wolv WV4 265 C2
  Wombourne WV4 .....266 A2
Wakeman Ct WV11 ...241 C2
Walcot Cl B75 ....258 A2
Walcot Gr ST2 ....58 A1
Waldale Cl WV11 ....242 B1
Walden Ave WV3 .....155 B3
Walden Gdns WV4 ...265 C3
Wales La DE13 ....183 B1
Walford Ave WV3 ....265 C4
Walford Back La ST21 117 B4
Walford Rd DE13 ....147 B2
Walhouse CE Jun Sch
  WS11 ....209 B1
Walhouse Dr ST19 ...207 C2
Walhouse St WS11 ...226 C4
Walk La WV5 ....270 A4
Walk The DY3 ....266 B1
Walker Dr DY10 .....280 A1
Walker Rd ST6 ....41 C2
Walker St
  Burton u T DE14 ....166 A1
  Tunstall ST6 ....41 B1
Walkers Croft WS13 .214 B1
Walkers Rise ST4 ....210 B4
Walkersgreen Rd ST5 ..40 C1
Walkfield Rd DE13 ...200 C1
Walklate Ave ST5 .....56 B2
Walkley Bank TF10 ..169 B2
Walkmill Bsns Pk WS11 226 B3
Walkmill Dr TF9 .....112 B4
Walkmill La WS11 ....209 B1
Walkmill Marsh Nature
  Reserve★ TF9 ......112 B4
Walkmill Rd TF9 .....112 B4
Walkmill Way WS11 .226 B3
Walks The ST13 ......30 B3
Wall (Letocetvm) Roman Site
  (Town)★ WS14 .....230 C1
Wall Croft WS9 ......256 A4
Wall Ditch DE6 ....35 A1
Wall Dr B74 ....257 C2
Wall Heath La WS14 .245 C3
Wall La Terr ST13 .....45 B3
Wall Rd DE14 ....185 A4
Wall Roman Site (Letocetvm)
  Mus★ WS14 ....230 C1
Wallace Cl WS11 .....227 C1
Wallace Ct WS6 .....226 B1
Wallace Rd WS8 .....244 C4
Walland Gr ST21 .....155 A2
Wallbridge Cl ST13 ...30 B2
Wallbridge Dr ST13 ..30 B2
Wallbridge Prec ST13 .30 B2
Wallbrook Rd ST18 ..122 C2
Walley Dr ST6 ....41 B3
Walley Pl ST6 ....57 A4
Walley St Biddulph ST8 .27 B4
  Burslem ST6 ....57 A4
Walley's Dr ST6 ......56 B1
Wallfield Cl ST10 .....92 B2
Wallheath Cres WS14 245 C3
Wallhill Ct ST13 ......30 C2
Wallington Cl WS3 ...243 A1
Wallington Heath WS3 243 A1
Wallis Pl ST2 ....58 A3
Wallis St ST4 ....72 C3

Wallis Way ST2 ....43 A1
Wallows Wood DY3 ..271 A2
Walls Wood ST5 ......85 A4
Wallshead Way TF10 .168 C1
Walmer Mdw WS9 ...256 A4
Walmer Pl ST4 ......283 B5
Walmsley Ct DY7 ....278 A2
Walnut Ave WV8 .....239 A2
Walnut Cl Cannock WS11 209 C1
  Newport TF10 ....168 C1
Walnut Crest ST18 ..158 B4
Walnut Ct WS15 ......197 A3
Walnut Dr Cannock WS11 209 C2
  Wolv WV3 ....255 B1
Walnut Gr Lichfield WS14 231 C4
  Newcastle-u-L ST5 ....55 B4
Walnut Tree La TF10 .188 A4
Walpole St ST3 ......283 D5
Walrand Cl B79 .....234 A1
Walsall Rd Aldridge WS9 256 A3
  Brownhills, Vigo WS9 .244 C1
  Cannock WS11 ......226 C4
  Great Wyrley WS6 ...227 A1
  Lichfield WS13,WS14 .230 B3
  Norton Canes WS11 .227 C2
  Shenstone WS14 ....245 C4
  Sutton Coldfield B74 257 B2
  Walsall WS3 ....244 A1
Walsall Wood Rd WS9 256 A4
Walsall Wood Sch WS9 245 A2
Walsingham Gdns ST5 .71 A1
Walter St WS3 ....244 A1
Walton Cres Fenton ST4 .72 B3
  Wolv WV4 ....266 C3
Walton Gdns WV8 ...238 C2
Walton Gr ST7 ....40 B4
Walton Grange ST15 .120 A4
Walton Hall Sch ST21 134 A3
Walton Heath WS3 ..242 C2
Walton High Sch ST17 175 C3
Walton Ind Est ST17 .120 A3
Walton La ST17 ......176 A3
Walton Lodge ST17 .175 A3
Walton Mead Cl ST17 175 C4
Walton Pl ST5 ....55 C3
Walton Priory Mid Sch
  ST15 ....119 C3
Walton Rd Aldridge WS9 245 A1
  Stoke-on-T ST4 ......71 C2
  Swadlincote DE15 ...185 B3
  Wolv WV4 ....266 C3
Walton Way Stone ST15 119 C2
  Talke ST7 ....40 B4
Walton-on-Trent CE Prim
  Sch DE12 ....202 B4
Waltonbury Cl ST17 .175 C3
Waltonhurst La ST17 134 B2
Wanderers Ave WV2 .266 B3
Wandsbeck B77 .....261 C4
Wannerton Rd DY10 ..281 A1
Wansbeck Wlk DY3 .271 A2
Warburton Cl **20** ST6 ..57 A4
Warburton St **17** ST6 ..57 A4
Ward Gr WV4 ....266 C2
Ward Pl ST6 ....42 A3
Ward Rd Codsall WV8 238 C2
  Wolv WV4 ....266 B3
Ward St WS12 ......209 C3
Wardel Cres ST13 .....30 C2
Wardel La ST13 ....43 B1
Wardle Cl B75 ....258 A2
Wardle Pl WS11 .....209 C1
Wardle St Tamworth B79 250 A3
  Tunstall ST6 ....41 C2
Wardles La WS6 .....226 C1
Wardlow Cl WV4 ....266 A3
Wards La CW12 ......16 B4
Warings The WV5 ...269 C2
Warm Croft ST15 ...120 A4
Warminster Pl ST3 ..283 A3
Warmson Cl ST3 .....73 B2
Warner Rd WV8 ....238 C2
Warner St ST1 ......282 B2
Warnford Wlk WV4 .265 B3
Warren Cl
  Burton u T DE13 ....147 C1
  Cannock WS12 .....211 A3
  Lichfield WS14 .....231 C1
Warren Croft WS15 .198 B2
Warren Ct TF9 ....97 B1
Warren Dr DY3 .....266 B1
Warren Gdns DY6 ...275 B4
Warren La DE14 ....184 C4
Warren Pl
  Brownhills WS8 ....245 A4
  Longton ST3 ....283 D2
Warren Rd
  Burntwood WS7 ....229 A4
  Chell Heath ST6 .....42 A4
Warren St ST3 ......283 D2
Warrens La ST16 ....155 A3
Warrilow Heath Rd ST5 .40 B1
Warrington Dr ST13 ..30 B3
Warrington Rd ST1 ...57 B1
Warrington St ST4 ...72 C3
Warsill Gr ST3 ....73 B2
Warstone Hill Rd WV6 .253 C2
Warstone Rd WS6 ..242 B4
Warstones Cres WV4 265 B3
Warstones Dr WV4 ..265 B3
Warstones Gdns WV4 265 B3
Warstones Jun & Inf Sch
  WV4 ....265 C2
Warstones Rd WV4 .265 B3
Wartell Bank DY6 ...275 B4

Wartell Bank Ind Est
  DY6 ....275 B4
Warwick Ave **5** Meir ST3 .73 C1
  Newcastle-u-L ST5 ....71 B2
  Perton WV6 ....254 C2
Warwick Cl
  Branston DE14 .....184 C4
  Cannock WS11 ......226 C4
  Kidsgrove ST7 ....26 A2
  Market Drayton TF9 ..97 C1
Warwick Ct DY3 ....271 B2
Warwick Dr WV8 ...238 C2
Warwick Gr ST5 ......56 C2
Warwick Rd
  Kingswinford DY8 ..275 B1
  Stafford ST17 ......175 A4
  Tamworth B77 ......250 C2
Warwick St Biddulph ST8 .27 B4
  Burton u T DE13 ....166 B3
  Hanley ST1 ....57 A2
  Newcastle-u-L ST5 ...55 C4
Warwick Way WS11 .245 A1
Wasdale Dr DY6 ....275 C3
Wasdale Rd WS8 ....244 B3
Wash Dale La ST15 ..105 A3
Washbrook La
  Norton Canes WS11 .227 B3
  Tissington DE6 ......51 C2
Washerwall La ST9 ...59 A2
Washerwall St ST2 ...73 B4
Washford Rd DE65 ..147 C4
Washington Cl ST8 ...16 B1
Washington Ct WV3 .255 B1
Washington Dr ST17 175 A4
Washington St ST6 ...41 C1
Waste La DE6,ST10 ...79 B2
Wastwater Ct WV6 .254 C2
Wat Tyler Cl WS15 ..178 B2
Watchfield Cl ST3 ....73 C1
Water Dale WV3 ....255 C1
Water Eaton La ST19 207 B3
Water La Enville DY7 268 B1
  Newport TF10 ......168 C2
Water Rd DY3 ....271 B1
Water St Burntwood WS7 228 C4
  Kingswinford DY6 ...275 B4
  Newcastle-u-L ST5 ..284 C3
  Newcastle-u-L, Red Street
  ST5 ....40 B1
  Stafford ST16 ......155 C2
  Stoke-on-T ST4 ......72 A3
Waterbeck Gr ST4 ...88 B3
Waterbrook Cl ST19 207 C4
Waterbrook Way WS11 226 C3
Waterdale WV5 .....269 C3
Waterdale Gr ST3 ....73 C2
Waterfall La ST10 ....48 C1
Waterford Dr TF10 ..168 C1
Waterford Rd **5** DY6 .275 B4
Watergate St ST6 .....41 B2
Waterhead Cl WV10 .241 A1
Waterhead Dr WV10 241 A1
Waterhead Rd ST3 ...73 C1
Waterhouses CE Prim Sch
  ST10 ....48 C1
Watering Cl ST5 ......85 B2
Watering Trough Bank
  CW3 ....69 A4
Waterlily Cl WS12 ...210 C2
Waterloo Bvd WS12 210 C2
Waterloo Gr ST7 .....26 A1
Waterloo Rd
  Burslem ST6,ST1 ....57 A3
  Edgmond TF10 .....168 A3
Waterloo St
  Burton u T DE14 ....166 B2
  Hanley ST1 ....282 C2
  Leek ST13 ....30 B3
Watermeadow Dr WS4 .244 B1
Watermint Cl WS12 .210 C2
Waterpark Rd DE6 ..127 A4
Waters Dr B74 ......257 B2
Waters Edge WS15 .198 B3
Waters Rd WS15 ....160 C2
Waters View WS3 ...244 A3
Waterside
  Burton u T DE15 ....185 C4
  Rugeley WS15 .....196 C3
Waterside Bsns Pk
  WS15 ....197 A4
Waterside Cl
  Brewood WV10 .....224 C1
  Madeley CW3 ......68 C2
Waterside Com Jun Sch
  DE15 ....185 C4
Waterside Ct
  Branston DE14 .....165 C1
  Gnosall ST20 ....171 B3
  Tamworth B77 .....250 C3
Waterside Dr Longton ST3 88 C4
  Market Drayton TF9 ..97 C1
Waterside Mews TF10 .168 C2
Waterside Rd DE15 ..185 B4
Waterside Way
  Brownhills WS8 ....228 B1
  Wolv WV10 ....240 A2
Watersmead Cl WS12 210 C2
Watersmeet Ct ST15 120 B3
Waterstone Ho B78 .261 A4
Waterways Gdns DY8 275 C1
Waterworks Cotts DY6 274 C2
Watery La
  Abbots Bromley WS15 160 B2
  Astbury CW12 ......15 B3
  Clifton DE6 ....81 C4
  Codsall WV8 ....239 A3
  Ellastone DE6 ......80 A2
  Haughton ST18 .....172 C3

Watery La continued
  Kingswinford DY8 ..275 C1
  Lichfield WS13 ......214 B2
  Meir ST3 ....73 B1
  Scropton DE65 .....129 C1
  Swadlincote DE11 ..186 B3
  Uttoxeter ST14 .....110 B3
Watford Gap Rd WS14 258 A4
Watford St ST4 ....72 B4
Wathan Ave WV14 ..266 C1
Watkin St ST4 ....72 B3
Watkiss Dr WS15 ...178 B1
Watlands Ave ST5 ....56 B3
Watlands Rd ST7 .....39 C1
Watlands View ST5 ..56 B3
Watling St
  Brownhills WS8 ....228 B1
  Cannock WS11 .....226 B3
  Dordon B77,B78 ...262 B3
  Hints B78 ....248 B2
  Norton Canes WS11 227 B2
  Tamworth B78 .....249 C1
Watling Street Jun Mix Inf
  Sch WS8 ....228 C1
Watson Cl Alrewas WS13 215 C4
  Rugeley WS15 .....178 B2
Watson Rd Stoke-on-T ST4 71 C2
  Wolv, Cinder Hill WV14 266 C1
  Wolv, Pendeford WV10 240 A1
Watson St
  Burton u T DE14 ....166 B1
  Stoke-on-T ST4 .....72 A4
Watt Ho DY6 ....275 C4
Watt Pl ST10 ....76 B2
Wattfield Cl WS15 ..197 A3
Wattles La ST17 ....175 A4
Watts Cl ST17 ......174 A4
Waveney B77 ......261 C4
Waveney Ave WV6 .254 C2
Waveney Gr
  Cannock WS11 ....209 A1
  Newcastle-u-L ST5 ...71 A2
Waveney Wlk N ST6 ..42 A2
Waveney Wlk S ST6 ..42 A2
Wavenham Cl B74 ..257 C2
Waverley Cres
  Wolv, Cinder Hill WV4 266 C1
  Wolv, Goldthorn Hill WV4 266 A3
Waverley Gdns
  Rugeley WS15 .....178 A1
  Wombourne WV5 ...270 A4
Waverley La DE14 ..166 A2
Waverley Pl ST5 .....71 A3
Waverley Rd WS3 ..242 C1
Waverton St ST7 ....73 C4
Wavertree Ave ST7 ..25 C4
Waybutt La CW2 .....52 B4
Wayfield Dr ST16 ...155 B4
Wayfield Gr ST4 ......71 B4
Wayside WV8 ......239 C1
Wayside Acres WV8 238 C1
Wayside Ave ST5 ....56 B2
Wayside Dr B74 ....257 B2
Wayte St ST4 ......282 A4
Wealden Hatch WV10 240 C2
Wealdstone Dr DY3 271 B1
Weathercock La CW12 ..6 C2
Weatheroaks WS9 ..245 A2
Weaver Cl Biddulph ST8 .16 B1
  Cheadle ST10 ......76 C3
Weaver Dr ST17 ....174 A4
Weaver Pl ST5 ....71 A2
Weaver Rd ST14 ....111 A1
Weaver St ST1 .....282 B3
Weavers La ST15 ...120 B4
Weavers The ST14 ...95 B3
Weavers Wlk ST15 .103 B2
Weaving Gdns **9** WS11 209 C1
Web Cl WS13 ....215 B3
Webb Ave WV6 .....254 C3
Webb St ST3 ....74 A2
Webberley La ST3 ..283 C3
Webley Rise WV10 .240 C3
Webster Ave ST3 ....73 C3
Webster St ST5 ....284 C2
Webster Wlk WS11 .210 A2
Wedgewood Ave WS15 119 C3
Wedgwood Cl
  Burntwood WS7 ....229 B4
  Burton u T DE15 ...167 A1
Wedgwood Rd ST18 .156 A4
Wedgwood Ave
  Audley ST7 ....40 A1
  Newcastle-u-L ST5 284 A1
Wedgwood Cl WV6 .269 C4
Wedgwood Ct ST1 ...57 A2
Wedgwood Dr ST12 ..88 C2
Wedgwood Halt ST12 .88 B2
Wedgwood La
  Barlaston ST12 .....88 C2
  Biddulph ST8 ....16 B1
Wedgwood Meml Coll
  ST12 ....88 C1
Wedgwood Pl **17** ST6 ..56 C4
Wedgwood Rd
  Cheadle ST10 ......76 B1
  Fenton ST4 ....72 C3
  Talke ST7 ....40 B4
Wedgwood St
  16 Burslem ST6 ......56 C4
  Newcastle-u-L ST5 ..56 C4
Wedgwood Visitor Ctr &
  Mus★ ST12 ....88 B2
Weeford Dell B75 ..258 C2
Weeford Rd B75 ...258 C2
Weeping Cross ST17 175 B4
Weetman Cl ST6 .....41 B4
Weighton Gr ST2 ....58 C1

Vin – Wer 329

Weir Bank DE15 ....185 C3
Weir Gr ST7 ....26 A1
Weirside DE6 ....81 B4
Welbeck Pl ST2 ......58 B3
Welbury Gdns WV6 .255 C3
Welby St ST4 ....72 B3
Welch St ST4 ....72 A4
Weldon Ave ST3 .....74 A2
Welford Gr B74 ....257 C2
Welford Rd B77 ....261 B3
Welford Rise DE13 .166 A3
Well La Biddulph ST8 ...16 B2
  Great Wyrley WS6 ..227 A1
  Norbury TF10 ......150 B2
  Walsall WS3 ....243 C1
  Warslow SK17 ......22 A1
Well St Biddulph ST8 ..27 B4
  Cheadle ST10 ......76 C2
  Forsbrook ST11 ....91 A4
  Hanley ST1 ....282 C2
  Leek ST13 ....30 C3
  Mow Cop ST7 ......26 B4
  Newcastle-u-L ST5 .284 C2
Welland Cl DE15 ...167 A3
Welland Gr ST5 ......71 A2
Wellbury Cl ST4 ......88 B3
Weller St ST4 ....71 C4
Wellesbourne B79 ..250 B4
Wellesbourne Cl WV3 265 A4
Wellesley St ST1 ...282 A1
Wellfield Cl WS11 ..226 A4
Wellfield Rd
  Aldridge WS9 .....256 A4
  Alrewas DE13 .....201 A1
  Bucknall ST2 ......58 B1
Wellington Ave WV3 265 C4
Wellington Cl
  Kingswinford DY6 ..275 C2
  Stafford ST16 ......155 C3
Wellington Cres WS13 215 A2
Wellington Ct
  Hanley ST1 ....282 C3
  10 Leek ST13 ......30 C3
Wellington Dr
  Cannock WS11 ....226 A4
  Rugeley WS15 .....196 C4
Wellington Mill **9** ST13 .30 C3
Wellington Rd
  Albrighton WV7 ....220 C1
  Burton u T DE14 ...166 A1
  Hanley ST1 ....282 C2
  Kidsgrove ST7 ......26 A1
  Newport TF10 .....168 C1
Wellington St
  Burton u T DE14 ...166 A2
  Hanley ST1 ....282 C2
  Leek ST13 ....30 C3
  1 Newcastle-u-L ST5 ..56 B3
Wellington St W DE14 .166 A2
Wellington Terr ST1 .282 C2
Wells Cl Biddulph ST8 ..27 B4
  Cannock WS11 ....209 C1
  Perton WV6 ....254 B2
Wells Dr ST17 ......175 C4
Wells La ST18 ......191 B4
Wells Rd WV4 ......265 C3
Wellyards Cl ST18 ..138 B1
Welney Gdns WV9 .240 A2
Welsh Cl ST3 ....89 B4
Wem Gr ST5 ....40 C1
Wembley La WS7 ..228 B4
Wembury B77 ......250 C3
Wendell Crest WV10 240 C4
Wendling Cl ST2 .....58 B1
Wendover Gr ST2 ....58 B1
Wendover Rd WV4 .266 C1
Wendy Cl ST2 ....58 A1
Wenger Cres ST4 ....88 A4
Wenham Dr ST3 .....90 A4
Wenlock B77 ....250 B2
Wenlock Ave WV3 .265 C4
Wenlock Cl
  Chell Heath ST6 ....42 A4
  Newcastle-u-L ST5 ..40 C1
  Sedgley DY3 ....271 B4
Wenlock Dr TF10 ..168 C3
Wensleydale Ave CW12 ..6 A3
Wensleydale Cl ST1 ..57 B4
Wentlows Ave ST10 ..92 B3
Wentlows Rd ST10 ..92 B3
Wentworth Cl WS7 .229 B4
Wentworth Ct B75 .258 A1
Wentworth Dr
  Burton u T DE13 ...147 B1
  Kidsgrove ST7 ......26 B2
  Lichfield WS14 ....231 B3
  Stafford ST16 ......156 B2
Wentworth Gr Hanley ST1 57 C4
  Perton WV6 ....254 B3
Wentworth Rd
  Stourbridge DY8 ...279 C4
  Walsall WS3 ....242 C2
  Wolv WV10 ....240 C2
Werburgh Dr ST4 ....88 A4
Wereton Rd ST7 ......39 B1
Wergs Dr WV6 ......255 A4
Wergs Hall Rd
  Codsall WV8 ....254 C4
  Wolv WV6,WV8 ....255 A4
Wergs Rd Codsall WV8 254 C4
  Wolv WV6 ....255 A3
Werneth Gr WS3 ...243 A2
Werrington Prim Sch
  ST9 ....59 A2
Werrington Rd ST2 ..58 A2

Wesker Pl ST3 . . . . .73 C2
Wesley Ave
Cheslyn Hay WS6 . . . . . .226 B2
Codsall WV8 . . . . .239 A1
Wesley Cl
Burntwood WS7 . . . . .211 C1
Wombourne WV5 . . . . . .269 C3
Wesley Dr ST15 . . . . .120 B3
Wesley Gdns [7] ST7 . . . . . . .26 A1
Wesley Pl Audley ST7 . . . . . .54 B4
Cannock WS12 . . . . .210 B4
Newcastle-u-L ST5 . . . . . . .70 C4
Wesley Rd WV8 . . . . .239 A1
Wesley St Audley ST7 . . . . . .40 A1
Forsbrook ST11 . . . . .91 A4
Tunstall ST6 . . . . .41 B2
Wesley Way B77 . . . . .250 C2
Wesleyan Rd TF9 . . . . .100 A3
Wessenden B77 . . . . .262 A4
Wessex Cl WS8 . . . . .244 C4
Wessex Ct B79 . . . . .251 C4
Wessex Dr
Cannock WS11 . . . . .209 C1
Trentham ST4 . . . . .88 A4
Wessex Rd WV2 . . . . .266 C3
West Acres ST14 . . . . .141 B4
West Ave Kidsgrove ST7 . . . .25 C1
Newcastle-u-L ST5 . . . . . . .56 B1
Stoke-on-T ST4 . . . . .71 C4
Weston CW2 . . . . .37 A3
West Bank ST4 . . . . .72 A3
West Beeches WV4 . . . . . .224 A1
West Brampton ST5 . . . . . .284 B3
West Butts Rd WS15 . . . . .178 A1
West Cl Stafford ST16 . . . . .156 A2
Stone ST15 . . . . .119 C4
West Coppice Rd WS8 . .244 B4
West Cres ST1 . . . . .57 C4
West Dr Cheddleton ST13 . .45 B4
Tamworth B78 . . . . .249 C2
West End Ave ST13 . . . . . . .30 B3
West Gn WV4 . . . . .265 B3
West Hill ST14 . . . . .126 B3
West Hill Ave WS12 . . . . . .210 A3
West Hill Prim Sch
WS12 . . . . .210 A3
West Par ST4 . . . . .72 B3
West Prec ST1 . . . . .282 B2
West Rd WV4 . . . . .266 C3
West St Biddulph ST8 . . . . . .27 B4
Burton u T DE15 . . . . .167 A4
Cannock WS11 . . . . .226 C3
Leek ST13 . . . . .30 C4
Meir ST3 . . . . .74 A4
Mount Pleasant ST7 . . . . . .26 A3
Newcastle-u-L ST5 . . . . . .284 C2
Newcastle-u-L, Porthill ST5 .56 B4
Newcastle-u-L, Silverdale
ST5 . . . . .55 A1
Stourbridge DY8 . . . . .279 C3
Tamworth B79 . . . . .250 B3
Tamworth, Kettlebrook
B77 . . . . .250 B2
West Terr ST6 . . . . .42 A4
West View Mayfield DE6 . . . .81 B3
Newcastle-u-L ST5 . . . . . . .56 A3
Rocester ST14 . . . . .96 A2
Stone ST3 . . . . .89 C2
Uttoxeter ST14 . . . . .125 B4
West View Dr DY6 . . . . .275 C3
West Way Stafford ST17 . . .174 B4
Uttoxeter ST14 . . . . .110 C1
Walsall WS4 . . . . .244 A1
West Way Gn ST17 . . . . . . .155 B1
West Winds WV10 . . . . . . .241 B4
Westacre ST1 . . . . .57 C2
Westacre Cres WV3 . . . . . .255 B1
Westacre Dr DE11 . . . . . . .186 C1
Westacre Inf Sch WV3 . . . .255 B1
Westbeech Rd WV6 . . . . . .253 B4
Westbook Way WV5 . . . . . .269 C3
Westbourne Ave
Cannock WS11 . . . . .209 B2
Cheslyn Hay WS6 . . . . . .226 C3
Westbourne Cl ST13 . . . . . .30 B3
Westbourne Cres WS7 . . . .229 A4
Westbourne Dr ST6 . . . . . . .41 C4
Westbourne Rd WV4 . . . . .266 A3
Westbury Cl ST1 . . . . .57 C3
Westbury Hayes ST17 . . . .174 A4
Westbury Rd ST5 . . . . .71 A2
Westcliffe Ave ST5 . . . . . . .71 A2
Westcliffe Hospl ST6 . . . . . .41 C4
Westcott Cl DY6 . . . . .275 C2
Westcott La TF9 . . . . .130 A4
Westcroft Ave WV10 . . . . . .241 A1
Westcroft Rd
Perton WV6 . . . . .254 C3
Sedgley DY3 . . . . .266 A1
Westcroft Sch WV10 . . . . . .241 A1
Westerby Dr ST9 . . . . .59 A2
Westerham Cl ST4 . . . . .87 C4
Westering Parkway
WV10 . . . . .240 C2
Western Ave DY3 . . . . .271 A4
Western By Pass WS13 . . .213 C1
Western Rd
Cannock WS11 . . . . .210 A3
Stourbridge DY8 . . . . .279 C2
Western Springs Prim Sch
WS15 . . . . .178 B1
Western Springs Rd
WS15 . . . . .178 B1
Westfield Ave ST7 . . . . .39 B1

Westfield Dr
Aldridge WS9 . . . . .256 A3
Wombourne WV5 . . . . . . .269 C4
Westfield Gr WV3 . . . . .265 B4
Westfield Manor B75 . . . . .258 A2
Westfield Prim Sch
WV5 . . . . .269 C4
Westfield Rd Bucknall ST2 .58 A2
Burton u T DE13 . . . . .166 A3
Mow Cop ST7 . . . . .26 B4
Sedgley DY3 . . . . .266 C1
Westfields Cotton ST10 . . . .63 C3
Leek ST13 . . . . .30 C3
Westfields Rd WS15 . . . . . .197 C2
Westfields Rise CW3 . . . . . .67 B1
Westgate Brewood ST19 . . .223 B4
Cannock WS11 . . . . .211 A3
Westgate Cl DY3 . . . . .271 C4
Westhall Cl ST19 . . . . .223 B3
Westhall Gate WS3 . . . . . . .243 A1
Westhead Ave ST16 . . . . . .156 A2
Westhead Rd DY10 . . . . . . .280 A2
Westhead Rd N DY10 . . . . .280 A2
Westhead Wlk ST1 . . . . . . .282 A2
Westhill WV3 . . . . .255 C1
Westhouse La DE6,ST14 . . .79 C2
Westland WV3 . . . . .255 C1
Westland Gdns
Brierley Hill DY8 . . . . .279 C4
Wolv WV6 . . . . .255 C1
Westland Rd
Market Drayton TF9 . . . . . .97 A1
Wolv WV6 . . . . .255 C1
Westland St ST4 . . . . .72 A4
Westlands Audley ST7 . . . . . .39 C1
Woore CW3 . . . . .83 A4
Westlands Ave ST5 . . . . . . .70 C4
Westlands Prim Sch ST5 . .70 C3
Westlands Rd ST14 . . . . . . .126 A3
Westlands The ST14 . . . . . . .95 B3
Westleigh Rd WV5 . . . . . . .269 C3
Westmarsh Rd ST6 . . . . . . .42 A2
Westmead Rd DE13 . . . . . . .183 B1
Westmere Cl CW2 . . . . .37 A3
Westmill St ST1 . . . . .282 C1
Westminster Ave WV4 . . . .266 A3
Westminster Cl ST17 . . . . . .175 B4
Westminster Dr DE13 . . . . .166 B4
Westminster Pl ST4 . . . . . . .72 A1
Westminster Rd
Cannock WS11 . . . . .209 C3
Kingswinford DY8 . . . . . . .275 B1
Leek ST13 . . . . .31 A4
Westmorland Ave ST7 . . . . .40 C4
Westmorland Cl
Chell Heath ST6 . . . . .42 A4
Tamworth B78 . . . . .250 A1
Weston Bank ST18 . . . . . . .138 A1
Weston Cl Brewood ST19 221 C4
Cannock WS11 . . . . .210 B1
Caverswall ST2 . . . . .59 A2
Newcastle-u-L ST5 . . . . . . .55 C2
Weston Coney Rd ST3 . . . . .74 A2
Weston Coney Inf Sch
ST3 . . . . .74 A3
Weston Coney Jun Sch
ST3 . . . . .74 A2
Weston Coyney Rd ST3 . . . .73 C2
Weston Cres WS9 . . . . .256 A2
Weston Ct ST3 . . . . .74 A2
Weston Dr
Great Wyrley WS6 . . . . . . .226 C1
Meir ST3 . . . . .74 A2
Weston Ho WV6 . . . . .255 C3
Weston La Standon ST21 . .102 A2
Weston CW2 . . . . .37 A1
Weston Park Ave DE14 . . . .166 B4
Weston Pk * TF11 . . . . .203 C1
Weston Rd
Albrighton WV7 . . . . .237 A3
Hopton ST16 . . . . .156 B2
Lichfield WS13 . . . . .214 A1
Meir ST3 . . . . .74 A2
Weston CW1 . . . . .37 A4
Weston Rd High Sch
ST18 . . . . .156 B3
Weston St Leek ST13 . . . . . .31 A3
Longton ST3 . . . . .73 B3
Weston Village Prim Sch
CW2 . . . . .37 B3
Westonfields Dr ST3 . . . . . .73 C2
Westonview Ave ST3 . . . . . .73 B3
Westport Lake Rd ST6 . . . . .41 B1
Westport Rd ST6 . . . . .41 C1
Westridge DY3 . . . . .271 B4
Westsprink Cres ST3 . . . . . .73 C1
Westview Cl ST13 . . . . .30 B3
Westward Cl ST14 . . . . .111 A1
Westway Ho WS4 . . . . .244 A1
Westwick Cl WS9 . . . . .245 C2
Westwood Ave DY8 . . . . . .279 B2
Westwood Cl
Cheddleton ST13 . . . . .45 B2
Chorlton CW2 . . . . .37 A1
Westwood Ct
Hanley ST1 . . . . .282 C3
[10] Leek ST13 . . . . .30 B3
Westwood Fst Sch ST13 . . .30 B3
Westwood Gr [8] ST13 . . . . .30 B3
Westwood Heath Rd
ST13 . . . . .30 B3
Westwood High Sch
ST13 . . . . .30 A3
Westwood Holdings
WS12 . . . . .209 A3
Westwood Park Ave
ST13 . . . . .30 A3
Westwood Park Dr ST13 .30 A3

Westwood Pk DE11 . . . .186 C3
Westwood Rd Leek ST13 . . .30 B3
Meir ST3 . . . . .74 A1
Newcastle-u-L ST5 . . . . . . .56 B3
Westwood Sch WS15 . . . . .180 A2
Westwood Terr [6] ST13 . . .30 B3
Westwoods Hollow
WS7 . . . . .229 A4
Wetherall Cl WS15 . . . . . . .178 B1
Wetherby Cl
Kingsley ST10 . . . . .76 C3
Newcastle-u-L ST5 . . . . . . .55 C4
Wolv WV10 . . . . .240 B3
Wetherby Ct DE14 . . . . . . .184 C4
Wetherby Gr WS3 . . . . . . .243 A2
Wetherby Rd ST4 . . . . .88 A4
Wetherel Rd DE15 . . . . . . .167 B1
Wetley Ave ST9 . . . . .59 C2
Wetley La ST13 . . . . .33 A1
Wetmore La DE14 . . . . . . .166 C3
Wetmore Rd DE14 . . . . . . .166 C3
Wettenhall Dr ST13 . . . . . . .30 A2
Wetton Rd DE6,ST13 . . . . . .34 A3
Wexford Cl WV2 . . . . .271 C1
Weybourne Ave ST2 . . . . . .43 A4
Weyhill Cl WV9 . . . . .239 C1
Weymouth Dr B74 . . . . . . .257 C2
Weymouth Ho B79 . . . . . . .250 A3
Whalley Ave ST4 . . . . .71 C3
Wharf Cl Lichfield WS14 . . .231 B4
Uttoxeter ST14 . . . . .126 B4
Wharf Hos DE13 . . . . .184 A1
Wharf La Astbury CW12 . . . .15 A2
Brownhills WS8 . . . . .228 C2
Wharf Pl ST4 . . . . .72 B4
Burton u T DE14 . . . . .166 C3
Gnosall ST20 . . . . .171 B3
Rugeley WS15 . . . . .196 C4
Wharf Road Ind Est
DE14 . . . . .166 C3
Wharf St ST5 . . . . .284 D3
Wharf Terr CW3 . . . . .69 A4
Wharfdale Cl DY6 . . . . .275 A4
Wharfdale Rd CW12 . . . . . . .6 A3
Wharfedale Wlk ST3 . . . . . .283 A3
Wharmadine La
Ashley TF9 . . . . .100 C4
Maer ST5 . . . . .84 C1
Wharwell La WS6 . . . . .227 A1
Whateley La B77,B78 . . . . .261 C2
Whateley Villas CV9 . . . . . .262 A4
Whatmore St ST6 . . . . .42 B1
Wheat Breach Cl DE13 . . .166 A4
Wheatcroft Cl
Burntwood WS7 . . . . .229 A3
Penkridge ST19 . . . . .207 C4
Sutton Coldfield B75 . . . . .258 C2
Wheatfields ST6 . . . . .42 B2
Wheathill Cl WV4 . . . . .265 C2
Wheatlands Cl [4] WS11 210 B1
Wheatlands Rd DE15 . . . . .185 C4
Wheatley Ave ST4 . . . . .71 C3
Wheatley Cl B75 . . . . .258 B2
Wheatley La DE15 . . . . . . .167 B2
Wheatley St WV2 . . . . .266 C3
Wheatmill Cl DY10 . . . . . . .281 A1
Wheatridge Cl DY6 . . . . . . .275 A4
Wheatsheaf Rd WV8 . . . . . .239 C1
Wheatstone Cl DY3 . . . . . . .271 C3
Wheel Ave WV8 . . . . .238 C2
Wheel La WS13 . . . . .213 C1
Wheeler Cl WV8 . . . . .238 C2
Wheeler St DY8 . . . . .279 C3
Wheelfield WV8 . . . . .238 C2
Wheelock Way [10] ST7 . . . .26 A1
Whetstone Field Prim Sch
WS9 . . . . .256 A2
Whetstone Gn WV10 . . . . . .240 B1
Whetstone La WS9 . . . . . . .256 B1
Whetstone Rd ST8 . . . . .16 B1
Whieldon Cres ST4 . . . . . . .72 B3
Whieldon Rd ST4 . . . . .72 B3
Whilmot Cl WV10 . . . . .241 A3
Whimple Side ST2 . . . . .58 A1
Whimster Sq ST17 . . . . . . .174 A4
Whinberry Rise DY5 . . . . . .271 B1
Whinyates Rise WS11 . . . .226 C4
Whisper La ST4,ST5 . . . . . . .86 C4
Whiston Cl WV7 . . . . .237 A3
Whiston Eaves La ST10 . . .62 B1
Whitacre La WS14 . . . . . . .245 C4
Whitaker Mews ST14 . . . . . .95 C2
Whitaker Rd ST3 . . . . .72 C2
Whitbeam Cl DY3 . . . . .271 B2
Whitbread Dr ST8 . . . . .27 C4
Whitburn Cl WV9 . . . . .240 A1
Whitby Cl Stafford ST17 . . .174 B4
Walsall WS3 . . . . .242 C2
Whitby Way WS11 . . . . . . .226 B4
Whitchurch Dr ST5 . . . . . . .40 C1
Whitcliffe Pl ST3 . . . . .72 C1
Whitcombe Rd ST3 . . . . . . .74 A1
White Bark Cl WS12 . . . . . .210 A4
White Farm Rd B74 . . . .257 C2
White Hill DY7 . . . . .277 C3
White Hollies WS3 . . . . . . .243 C4
White Horse Rd WS8 . . . . .228 C1
White House La DY7 . . . . . .268 C3
White Houses La WV10 . . .241 A3
White Lion St ST17 . . . . . . .155 C1
White Oak Dr
Kingswinford DY6 . . . . . . .275 B3
Wolv WV3 . . . . .255 B1
White Oaks ST17 . . . . .175 B3
White Row WV5 . . . . .264 B1
White's Dr DY3 . . . . .271 C4

White's Mdw ST18 . . . . .153 B2
Whitebeam Cl
Brownhills WS8 . . . . .244 C3
Newcastle-u-L ST5 . . . . . . .40 B1
Whitebridge Ind Est
ST15 . . . . .104 C1
Whitebridge La ST15 . . . . .104 C1
Whitefield Cl WV8 . . . . . . .239 A1
Whitefields La ST10 . . . . . . .49 A1
Whitehall Ave ST7 . . . . .25 C1
Whitehall Cl ST14 . . . . .141 B4
Whitehall Ct WV3 . . . . .265 C3
Whitehall Rd
Kingswinford DY6 . . . . . . .275 B3
Wolv WV4 . . . . .266 A2
Whitehaven Dr ST1 . . . . . . .282 B4
Whitehead Rd ST6 . . . . .42 A3
Whitehill Rd ST7 . . . . .26 A1
Whitehorn Cres B74 . . . . . .256 B1
Whitehouse Ave WV3 . . . . .265 B4
Whitehouse Cres
Burntwood WS7 . . . . .229 A4
Essington WV11 . . . . .241 C1
Whitehouse La
Codsall WV8 . . . . .238 B4
Sandon ST18 . . . . .121 A4
Swindon DY7,DY3 . . . . . . .269 A1
Whitehouse Rd
Bucknall ST2 . . . . .58 A3
Newcastle-u-L ST5 . . . . . . .56 A2
Polesworth B78 . . . . .262 C4
Whitehouse Rd N ST5 . . . . .56 A2
Whitehurst La ST10 . . . . . . .75 B3
Whiteoaks Dr ST19 . . . . . . .221 C4
Whiteridge Rd ST7 . . . . .26 A1
Whites La CW2 . . . . .37 A3
Whites Wood WV5 . . . . . . .270 A4
Whitesands Cl B77 . . . . . . .250 C3
Whitesands Gr ST3 . . . . . . .90 A4
Whitesmith Cl DY3 . . . . . . .271 B4
Whitestone Rd ST3 . . . . . . .90 A4
Whitesytch La
Hilderstone ST15 . . . . . . .106 B1
Sandon ST15 . . . . .121 B1
Whitethorn Ave ST5 . . . . . .284 A1
Whitethorn Cl WS12 . . . . . .210 A4
Whitethorn Rd [7] DY8 . . . .275 C1
Whitethorn Way ST1 . . . . . .40 C1
Whitfield Ave ST5 . . . . .284 A1
Whitfield Rd
Cannock WS12 . . . . .210 B4
Kidsgrove ST7 . . . . .26 A1
Norton-in-t-M ST6 . . . . . . .42 B3
Whitfield St ST13 . . . . .30 C2
Whitfield Valley Prim Sch
ST6 . . . . .42 A4
Whitgreave Ave WV10 . . . .241 A4
Whitgreave Ct
Featherstone WV10 . . . . . .241 A3
Stafford ST16 . . . . .155 B3
Whitgreave La
Rugeley WS15 . . . . .196 C3
Seighford ST18 . . . . .135 B2
Whitgreave ST18 . . . . .136 A2
Whitgreave Prim Sch
WV10 . . . . .241 A4
Whiting B77 . . . . .261 B4
Whitley Ave B77 . . . . .250 C3
Whitley Cl WV6 . . . . .255 A1
Whitley Rd ST6 . . . . .42 B3
Whitmore Ave ST9 . . . . .59 A2
Whitmore Cl
Newcastle-u-L ST5 . . . . . . .70 C2
Stourbridge DY8 . . . . .279 B3
Trentham ST4,ST5 . . . . . . .87 B4
Whitmore St ST1 . . . . .57 A2
Whitney Ave DY8 . . . . .279 B3
Whitridge Gr ST2 . . . . .73 B4
Whittaker St WV2 . . . . .266 C3
Whittingham Dr ST17 . . . . .174 A4
Whittington Common Rd
WS14 . . . . .232 A3
Whittington Grange Sch
WS14 . . . . .232 A2
Whittington Hall La
DY7 . . . . .279 A2
Whittington Ho WS13 . .214 C1
Whittington Prim Sch
WS14 . . . . .232 C2
Whittington Rd DY8 . . . . . .279 C2
Whittle Rd ST3 . . . . .90 A4
Whitty La ST13 . . . . .20 B3
Whitworth La WS15 . . . . . .178 A1
Whygate Gr ST1 . . . . .57 C3
Wickenstones Ct ST8 . . . . .27 B4
Wicket La DY7 . . . . .274 C1
Wickets The DE15 . . . . . . .185 C4
Wickstead Row CW3 . . . . . .53 A3
Widecombe Ave ST17 . . . . .175 C4
Widecombe Rd ST1 . . . . . . .57 C2
Widney Ave WS9 . . . . .245 A1
Wigeon Gr WV10 . . . . .241 A4
Wigford Rd B77 . . . . .261 B3
Wiggin Ho WS3 . . . . .243 B2
Wigginton Rd B79 . . . . . . .250 A4
Wightman Cl WS14 . . . . . . .231 C3
Wightwick Bank WV6 . . . . .255 A1
Wightwick Cl WS3 . . . . . . .243 A1
Wightwick Ct WV6 . . . . . . .255 A1
Wightwick Gr WV6 . . . . . . .255 A1
Wightwick Hall Rd WV6 254 C1
Wightwick Hall Sch
WV6 . . . . .254 C1
Wigley Bank Rd DY7 . . .277 B3
Wigmore Pl ST3 . . . . .73 B3
Wignall St ST6 . . . . .41 B4
Wilbraham's Wlk ST7 . . . . .39 C1

Wilcox Ave WS12 . . . . . . .210 A4
Wild Goose Ave ST7 . . . . .26 B2
Wildacres DY8 . . . . .279 B3
Wildfowl Wlk ST5 . . . . .85 B2
Wildhay La DE6 . . . . .80 B4
Wilding Rd ST6 . . . . .42 B3
Wildtree Ave WV10 . . . . . . .241 A1
Wildwood Dr ST17 . . . . . . .175 B3
Wildwood Lawns ST17 . . . .175 B4
Wileman Pl ST4 . . . . .72 C3
Wileman St ST4 . . . . .72 C3
Wilfred Owen Cl TF9 . . . . .112 A4
Wilfred Pl ST4 . . . . .71 C4
Wilke's Wood ST18 . . . . . .154 C4
Wilkes Cl WS3 . . . . .243 C2
Wilkes Croft DY3 . . . . .271 B4
Wilkes Rd WV8 . . . . .238 C2
Wilkin Rd WS8 . . . . .228 B1
Wilkins Croft DE13 . . . . . . .200 C1
Wilkins Ho WS3 . . . . .243 A1
Wilkinson Cl WS7 . . . . .229 A4
Wilkinson St ST6 . . . . .41 B1
Wilks St ST6 . . . . .41 C2
Willatt Pl ST2 . . . . .43 A1
Willcock Rd
Burton u T DE14 . . . . .185 A4
Wolv WV2 . . . . .266 C3
Willdale Gr ST1 . . . . .57 C3
Willerby Fold WV10 . . . . . .240 C2
Willeton St ST2 . . . . .58 A2
Willett Ave
Brownhills WS7 . . . . .228 C3
Burntwood WS7 . . . . .228 C3
Willey La ST20 . . . . .171 B3
Willfield La ST6 . . . . .43 B3
William Allitt Sch DE11 . .186 C4
William Ave Biddulph ST8 . .27 B4
Meir ST3 . . . . .90 B4
William Baxter Com Sch
WS12 . . . . .210 A3
William Birch Rd ST2 . . .58 A1
William Cl ST11 . . . . .91 A4
William Clowes St ST6 . . .56 C4
William Coltman Way
ST6 . . . . .41 B3
William Fiske Ct ST4 . . . . .71 C2
William Hutson Jun Sch
DE13 . . . . .166 A4
William IV Rd DE13 . . . . . .201 A2
William Lunn's Homes [2]
WS14 . . . . .231 B4
William MacGregor Prim Sch
B77 . . . . .250 B2
William Mews WV10 . . . . . .225 B1
William Morris Ct WS15 178 B2
William Morris Gr
WS11 . . . . .209 C2
William Nadins Way
DE11 . . . . .186 C2
William Newton Cl
DE65 . . . . .148 A3
William Rd ST7 . . . . .26 B4
William Rushton Rd ST6 .42 B1
William Shrewsbury Prim
Sch DE13 . . . . .147 C1
William St
Burton u T DE14 . . . . .166 B3
Congleton CW12 . . . . .6 A2
Fenton ST4 . . . . .72 C3
William Terr ST6 . . . . .42 A3
Williams Ave WS13 . . . . . .215 B3
Williams Cl ST16 . . . . .155 A2
Williams Ct ST16 . . . . .155 C4
Williams Wlk ST15 . . . . . . .103 B2
Williamson Cl
Cannock WS12 . . . . .211 B2
Norton-in-t-M ST6 . . . . . . .42 C3
Williamson St ST6 . . . . . . .41 C1
Willingdon Rd B79 . . . . . . .250 A4
Williscroft Pl WS15 . . . . . .179 A3
Willmer Cres ST7 . . . . .26 A3
Willmott Cl B75 . . . . .258 B2
Willmott Rd B75 . . . . .258 B2
Willotts Hill Rd ST5 . . . . . . .40 B1
Willoughby Cl ST19 . . . . . .207 C4
Willoughby Ct ST14 . . . . . .125 B4
Willoughby Rd B79 . . . . . . .249 C4
Willoughby St ST6 . . . . .41 B4
Willow Ave WS7 . . . . .229 B3
Willow Bank WV3 . . . . .255 B1
Willow Brook ST18 . . . . . . .154 C1
Willow Cl Alrewas WS13 . . .215 C4
Brewood WV9 . . . . .224 A1
Hagley DY9 . . . . .281 C3
Kidsgrove ST7 . . . . .41 A4
Newcastle-u-L ST5 . . . . . . .40 B1
Penkridge ST19 . . . . .207 C3
Stafford ST17 . . . . .175 C3
Upper Tean ST10 . . . . .92 B3
Willow Ct WS14 . . . . .231 B3
Willow Dale ST15 . . . . .120 B2
Willow Dr Codsall WV8 . . . .239 A2
Swadlincote DE11 . . . . . . .186 C4
Willow Gr
Essington WV11 . . . . .242 A1
Fenton ST3 . . . . .72 C1
Willow Ho WS3 . . . . .244 B1
Willow La ST3 . . . . .90 A2
Willow Pl Biddulph ST8 . . . .17 A1
Burton u T DE15 . . . . .185 C4
Willow Row
Barton-u-N DE13 . . . . .183 B1
Kinver DY7 . . . . .278 B2
Stone ST15 . . . . .120 A4
Wolv WV3 . . . . .265 B4
Willow Row ST18 . . . . .283 B3
Willow Way ST11 . . . . .91 A4
Willow Wlk WS12 . . . . .209 B4

Willowbank B78 250 A1
Willowcroft ST20 151 C4
Willowcroft Rise ST11 90 B4
Willowcroft Way ST7 26 C2
Willowdale Ave ST4 72 B3
Willowdale Grange WV6 255 C3
Willowherb Cl WS11 210 B1
Willowmoor ST17 174 C3
Willowood Gr ST3 74 B1
Willows Dr ST3 90 A2
Willows Prim Sch WS13 214 A1
Willows The
Burton u T DE14 166 B1
Cannock WS11 209 B1
Leek ST13 30 B3
Rugeley WS15 197 A3
Stone ST15 120 A3
Sutton Coldfield B74 257 C1
Swynnerton ST15 118 C3
Wombourne WV5 269 C3
Willowsmere Dr WS14 231 C4
Willowtree Cl WS13 214 A1
Willridding La DE6 80 B4
Willsford Ave ST14 126 B4
Wilmcote Dr B75 258 A2
Wilmore Ct ST18 137 B1
Wilmorehill La ST18 137 B1
Wilmot Cl ST5 55 C2
Wilmot Dr ST5 55 C2
Wilmot Gr ST3 73 B3
Wilmott Cl WS13 231 A4
Wilnecote High Sch B77 261 C3
Wilnecote Jun Sch B77 261 C4
Wilnecote La B77 250 B1
Wilnecote Sta B77 261 B4
Wilner's View WS3 243 C3
Wilson Gr WS11 210 B1
Wilson Keys Ct WS15 178 C1
Wilson Rd ST4 71 C1
Wilson St Chell Heath ST6 42 A1
Newcastle-u-L ST5 284 B3
Wilson Way ST6 41 B3
Wiltell Rd WS14 231 A3
Wilton Ave ST9 59 C2
Wilton Cl DY3 271 C4
Wilton St ST5 284 A4
Wiltshire Gr ST5 71 B2
Wiltshire Ho 4 DY8 279 C4
Wimberry Dr ST5 40 B1
Wimblebury Rd WS12 210 C1
Wimborne Ave ST3 88 C4
Wimshurst Mdw WV10 240 C2
Winceby Rd WV6 254 C2
Winchcombe Cl DY1 271 C2
Winchcombe Dr DE15 167 A1
Winchester Ave ST2 58 B1
Winchester Cl
Armitage WS15 198 A2
Lichfield WS13 214 B2
Winchester Ct
Stafford ST17 175 B3
Sutton Coldfield B74 257 C1
Winchester Dr
Burton u T DE14 185 B4
Newcastle-u-L ST5 70 C2
Winchester Mews WS9 256 A2
Winchester Rd
Cannock WS11 210 A2
Tamworth B78 249 C2
Wolv WV10 240 B2
Wincote Dr WV6 255 B2
Wincote La ST21 133 B2
Windermere B77 262 A4
Windermere Dr
Aldridge B74 256 C2
Kingswinford DY6 275 B3
Windermere Ho ST16 155 C2
Windermere Pl WS11 209 C1
Windermere Rd
Newcastle-u-L ST5 71 A2
Wolv WV6 255 B4
Windermere St ST1 282 A4
Windermere Way ST10 76 C2
Windings The WS13 214 A1
Windmill Ave ST7 41 A4
Windmill Bank
Longdon WS15 212 A3
Wombourne WV5 270 A4
Windmill Cl
Farewell WS13 213 C1
Stone ST3 89 C2
Tamworth B79 250 A4
4 Uttoxeter ST14 111 A1
Windmill Cres WV3 255 A1
Windmill Dr ST14 127 C2
Windmill Gr DY6 275 A4
Windmill Hill ST3 89 C2
Windmill La
Eccleshall ST21 116 A2
Lichfield WS13 214 A1
Longdon WS15 212 A2
Snelston DE6 81 C1
Wolv WV3 255 A1
Windmill St Hanley ST1 282 C3
Sedgley DY3 271 B3
Windmill View ST9 59 B2
Windmillhill La WS14 232 C3
Windrow The WV6 254 B2
Windrush Cl Sedgley DY3 271 B2
Trentham ST4 88 B3
Windrush Rd WS11 209 C3
Windsmoor St ST4 72 A3
Windsor Ave
Cannock WS12 210 A3
Longton ST3 283 D2
Windsor Ave *continued*
Wolv WV4 265 C3
Windsor Cl
Burntwood WS7 211 C1
Sedgley DY3 271 A1
Stone ST15 119 C3
Tamworth B79 250 B4
Windsor Cres DY7 277 C2
Windsor Ct
Cannock WS12 210 A3
Lichfield WS14 231 A3
Windsor Dr
Burton u T DE15 166 C1
Leek ST13 31 A4
Market Drayton TF9 97 C1
Windsor Gdns
Codsall WV8 238 C2
Wolv WV3 265 A4
Windsor Gr
Kingswinford DY8 275 C1
Walsall WS4 244 B1
Windsor Ho ST7 40 B3
Windsor Holloway DY7 278 B1
Windsor Ind Est DE14 166 C2
Windsor Park CE Mid Sch ST14 126 A4
Windsor Rd
Albrighton WV7 237 A3
Cheslyn Hay WS6 226 C2
Pattingham WV6 253 B1
Stafford ST17 175 A4
Stourbridge DY8 279 C2
Trentham ST4 72 A1
Uttoxeter ST14 111 A1
Wolv WV4 266 C3
Wombourne WV5 269 C3
Windsor St ST5 284 C3
Windy Arbour ST10 76 C2
Windycote La ST9 60 A1
Windyridge SK17 13 A3
Winford Ave DY6 275 C2
Wingate Ct B74 257 C2
Wingate Wlk ST3 88 C4
Winghay Ct ST6 56 B4
Winghay Pl ST6 42 A3
Winghay Rd ST7 26 B1
Winghouse La ST12, ST15 103 C4
Wingrove Ave 4 ST3 73 B1
Winifred Gdns ST3 88 C4
Winifred St ST1 282 A4
Winnipeg Cl ST4 88 A4
Winpenny Rd ST5 55 C4
Winscar Croft DY3 271 B2
Winsford Ave ST3 73 C1
Winsford Cres ST17 175 C3
Winshill Inf Sch DE15 167 A2
Winslow Dr WV6 255 C2
Winslow Gn ST2 58 B1
Winstanley Cl WS15 178 B1
Winstanley Pl WS15 178 B1
Winster Gn DE11 186 C3
Winston Pl ST2 58 A2
Winston Rd
Cookley DY11 280 A3
Swindon DY3 269 C1
Winston Terr ST5 56 B3
Winter Cl WS13 214 B1
Winterbourne Gr ST3 73 C2
Wintercroft La DE6 51 C1
Winterfield La ST3 74 A4
Winterley Gdns DY3 271 C3
Winterside Cl ST5 40 B1
Winton Sq ST4 72 A4
Wintonfield St ST4 72 B4
Winwood Ct DY8 279 C2
Wiscombe Ave ST19 193 A1
Wise St ST3 283 C1
Wissage Ct WS13 231 B4
Wissage Rd WS13 231 B4
Wistmans Cl DY1 271 C1
Wistwood Hayes WV10 240 C2
Witchford Cres ST3 88 C4
Witham Way ST8 16 C1
Withern Way DY3 271 B2
Withers Rd WV8 239 A2
Withies Rd ST4 71 C2
Within La ST18 137 B1
Withington Rd ST6 42 A3
Withnell Gn ST6 42 A3
Withymere La WV5 270 B4
Withystakes Rd ST9 59 B2
Withywood Cl WV12 242 B1
Witney Cl B79 249 C4
Witney Gr WV10 240 A2
Witney Rd ST17 156 B1
Witney Wlk ST3 88 C4
Witton Rd WV4 266 A3
Witton St DY8 279 C2
Wobaston Rd
Codsall WV9 239 C2
Wolv WV9,WV10 240 A2
Woburn B77 250 B2
Woburn Cl ST4 88 B3
Woburn Dr CW12 16 A4
Wodehouse Cl WV5 269 C3
Wodehouse La WV5,DY3 270 B4
Woden Cl WV5 269 C4
Wogan St ST16 155 C3
Wold The WV5 267 B4
Wolfe St ST4 72 A3
Wolfscote Dale DE11 186 C1
Wolgarston High Sch ST19 208 A4
Wolgarston Way ST19 207 C4
Wollaston Ct DY8 279 B3
Wollaston Rd
Brierley Hill DY8 279 C4
Wollaston Rd *continued*
Kinver DY7 279 B4
Wolmer Rd WV11 242 A1
Wolmore La WV5 263 A1
Wolseley B77 250 C2
Wolseley Cl ST17 177 C4
Wolseley Rd
Newcastle-u-L ST5 56 A3
Rugeley WS15 178 C2
Rugeley, Wolseley Park WS15 177 C1
Stafford ST16 156 B2
Stoke-on-T ST4 71 C2
Wolsey Rd WS13 213 C1
Wolstanton High Sch ST5 56 B2
Wolstanton Rd ST5 55 C3
Wolstanton Ret Pk ST5 56 C2
Wolstern Rd ST3 73 B3
Wolverhampton Bsns Airport DY7 268 B1
Wolverhampton Coll Wulfrun Campus WV6 255 C2
Wolverhampton Girls High Sch WV6 255 C2
Wolverhampton Gram Sch WV3 255 C1
Wolverhampton Rd
Cheslyn Hay WV10,WS6 226 A1
Codsall WV8 239 A2
Cookley DY10 280 A2
Essington WV11 242 A2
Kingswinford DY6 270 B1
Kinver DY7 278 C4
Pattingham WV6 253 C2
Penkridge ST19 207 C4
Sedgley DY3 266 B1
Stafford ST17 155 C1
Walsall WS3 243 A1
Walsall, Pelsall WS3 243 C2
Wolverhampton Rd E WV4 266 B3
Wolverhamton Rd WS11 226 A3
Wolverley Ave
Stourbridge DY8 279 B3
Wolv WV4 265 B3
Wolverley Ct WV7 237 A3
Wolverley Rd DY10 280 A1
Wolverson Rd WS9 245 A2
Wombourne Cl DY3 271 B4
Wombourne Ent Pk DY3 269 B2
Wombourne Pk WV5 269 C2
Wombourne Rd DY3 269 C2
Wombrook Dale WV5 269 B3
Wombrook Ind Est WV5 269 C3
Wood Ave Brewood WV9 224 A2
Kingsley ST10 61 B1
Sedgley DY3 271 B2
Wood Bank La ST19 193 A1
Wood Bank Rd WV3 265 A4
Wood Common Grange WS3 243 C2
Wood Cres Stafford ST16 155 A3
Stone ST15 119 C3
Wood Ct DE14 166 B1
Wood Eaton Rd ST20 190 A4
Wood End La
Alrewas WS13 215 A3
King's Bromley WS13 214 A4
Wood End Prim Sch CV9 262 B1
Wood End Rd WV11 241 B1
Wood End Way WS9 245 A1
Wood Hayes Rd WV11 241 B1
Wood Hill Dr WV5 269 C3
Wood La Aldridge B74 256 C1
Cannock WS12 210 B2
Cheslyn Hay WS11 225 C3
Hanbury DE13 144 C2
Kingstone ST14 124 B1
Maer ST5 84 B2
Shenstone WS14 246 A1
Stone ST15 119 C3
Swadlincote DE11 186 C4
Uttoxeter ST14 126 C3
Walsall WS3 243 C2
Wheaton Aston ST19 206 B2
Wolv WV10 240 B1
Yoxall DE13 182 A3
Wood Lane Prim Sch ST7 40 A1
Wood Pl ST3 74 A1
Wood Rd Codsall WV8 238 C2
Longsdon ST9 45 A4
Sedgley DY3 271 B2
Wolv WV6 255 B2
Wombourne WV5 270 A4
Wood Ridings WS13 214 A1
Wood St Audley ST7 39 C2
Burton u T DE14 166 B1
Leek ST13 30 C3
Longton ST3 283 C4
Mow Cop ST7 26 B4
Stourbridge DY8 279 B3
Wood End CV9 262 B1
Wood Terr ST1 282 A1
Wood The ST3 74 B1
Wood View Audley ST7 40 A1
Rugeley WS15 196 C3
Woodall St ST1 57 A3
Woodbank Rd DY3 271 B4
Woodbank St ST6 56 C4
Woodberry Ave ST4 71 C3
Woodberry Cl
Stafford ST17 174 C2
Stoke-on-T ST4 71 C3
Woodbine Way DE14 184 C3
Woodbridge Cl
Walsall WS3 243 A2
Walsall, Shelfield WS4 244 B1
Woodbridge Rd ST5 71 A1
Woodcock Gdns WV10 241 A4
Woodcock La ST7 26 B3
Woodcock Rd WS15 178 B1
Woodcocks' Well CE Prim Sch ST7 26 B3
Woodcote Rd WV6 255 B2
Woodcote The 3 ST17 175 B4
Woodcroft ST7 40 A1
Woodcroft Ave Leek ST13 30 B2
Tamworth B79 250 A3
Woodcroft Fst Sch ST13 30 B2
Woodcroft Rd ST13 30 B2
Woodcross La WV14 266 C1
Woodcross St WV14 266 C1
Wooddisse La ST13 33 C1
Woodedge La ST14 143 C3
Woodend Pl WV6 255 A2
Woodend St ST4 72 C3
Woodfield Ave WV4 265 C3
Woodfield Cl WS11 227 C4
Woodfield Ct ST13 31 A3
Woodfield Dr WS11 227 C4
Woodfield Ho WS3 244 A2
Woodfield Hts WV6 255 B2
Woodfield Jun Sch WV4 265 C3
Woodfield Rd DY3 271 B2
Woodfields Dr WS14 231 C3
Woodfold Croft WS9 256 A4
Woodford Cl WV9 239 C1
Woodford Cres WS7 229 A4
Woodford End WS11 209 C2
Woodford La WV5 269 B4
Woodford Way
Cannock WS12 210 B1
Wombourne WV5 269 B3
Woodgate Ave ST7 25 A3
Woodgate St ST3 74 A1
Woodgreen WS6 226 C3
Woodhall Pl ST5 54 C1
Woodhall Rd
Kidsgrove ST7 26 B2
Wolv WV4 265 C3
Woodhaven
Cheslyn Hay WS11 226 A3
Walsall WS4 244 B1
Woodseaves ST20 151 B4
Woodhead Rd ST2 58 B4
Woodhead Yd ST10 76 C3
Woodheyes Lawns WS15 178 B1
Woodhill Cl WV5 269 C3
Woodhouse High Sch B77 250 C2
Woodhouse Jun Sch ST3 283 C5
Woodhouse La
Albrighton WV7 237 B2
Biddulph ST8 16 C1
Endon ST6 42 C3
Scropton DE65 129 C4
Tamworth B77 251 A3
Woodhouse Mid Sch ST8 16 C1
Woodhouse Rd WV6 255 A2
Woodhouse Rd N WV6 255 A2
Woodhouse St ST4 72 A3
Woodhouses La WS7 229 C3
Woodhouses Rd WS7 230 A4
Woodhurst Cl B77 250 C3
Woodingdean Cl 12 ST3 73 B3
Woodkirk Cl ST6 42 A4
Woodland Ave
Hagley DY8 281 C3
Newcastle-u-L ST5 56 B3
Norton-in-t-M ST6 42 C2
Wolv WV6 255 A2
Woodland Cl
Albrighton WV7 237 A3
Cannock WS12 210 A4
Leek ST13 30 C1
Woodland Cres
Walsall WS3 243 C3
Wolv WV3 265 B4
Woodland Ct
Huntington WS12 209 B2
Shenstone WS14 258 A4
Woodland Dr
Cheslyn Hay WS6 226 C2
Foston DE6 129 B2
Woodland Gr
Chell Heath ST6 42 A1
Cookley DY10 280 B2
Sedgley DY3 271 A2
Woodland Hills CW3 68 C4
Woodland Rd
Swadlincote DE15 186 A2
Tamworth B77 251 A2
Wolv WV3 265 B4
Woodland St Biddulph ST8 27 B3
Tunstall ST6 41 C2
Woodland View DY3 269 B2
Woodland Views ST14 127 C1
Woodland Way
Burntwood WS7 229 A3
Polesworth B78 262 C4
Woodlands Ave
Cheddleton ST13 45 A1
Kidsgrove ST7 25 B1
Stone ST15 119 C4
Woodlands Cl
Stafford ST16 155 B4
Stone ST15 119 C4
Thorpe DE6 51 B1
Woodlands Cotts WV4 265 C2
Woodlands Dr
Brewood WV9 224 A2
Stone ST15 120 B2
Woodlands Gr ST3 90 A2
Woodlands La
Cheslyn Hay WV10,WS11 225 A4
Forsbrook ST11 91 A3
Woodlands Paddock WV4 265 C2
Woodlands Prim Sch B77 250 C2
Woodlands Rd
Cookley DY10 280 A2
Stafford ST16 155 A4
Stoke-on-T ST4 71 C2
Wombourne WV5 270 A3
Woodlands The
Lichfield WS13 231 B4
Stoke-on-T ST4 71 C2
Tatenhill DE13 184 A4
Wood End CV9 262 B1
Woodlands Way WS15 198 B2
Woodlawn Gr DY6 275 B3
Woodleighton Gr ST14 126 B3
Woodleighton Rd ST14 126 B3
Woodleyes Cres ST17 175 B3
Woodman La WS6 226 C2
Woodman St ST2 43 A1
Woodmill La WS15 161 A4
Woodpark La ST3 89 B4
Woodpecker View TF9 99 B2
Woodpecker Way WS11 210 B2
Woodridge Cl TF10 168 A2
Woodroffe's Cliff ST14 143 B3
Woodrow Way TF9 100 B3
Woodruff Cl ST8 27 A1
Woods Croft WS13 214 A1
Woods La DE15 167 A1
Woodseaves CE Prim Sch ST20 151 C4
Woodsetton Specl Sch The DY3 271 C4
Woodshot Ave WS15 198 B2
Woodshutt's St ST7 25 C1
Woodside
Chapel Chorlton ST5 85 B2
Lawton-gate ST7 25 C2
Madeley CW3 68 C4
Sutton Coldfield B74 257 C1
Woodside Ave Endon ST6 43 A3
Kidsgrove ST7 26 A1
Woodside Cl
Colwich ST18 177 B4
Wood End CV9 262 B1
Woodside Cotts ST10 77 C4
Woodside Cres ST5 71 B1
Woodside Dr
Blythe Bridge ST3 90 A2
Little Aston B74 257 B3
Woodside Gr WV8 239 A1
Woodside La ST13 30 B1
Woodside Pl
Cannock WS11 209 C3
Norton-in-t-M ST2 43 A1
Woodside Villas ST3 283 D4
Woodside Way WS9 256 A3
Woodsorrel Rd DY1 271 C2
Woodstile Cl B75 258 B2
Woodstock Cl
Kingswinford DY8 275 B1
Newcastle-u-L ST5 56 B2
Woodstock Dr
Huntington WS12 209 B4
Kingswinford DY8 275 B1
Sutton Coldfield B74 257 B2
Woodstock Rd
Kidsgrove ST6 41 A4
Stafford ST17 156 B1
Woodstock St ST6 41 B4
Woodstone Ave ST9 43 C3
Woodtherne Cl ST19 207 C4
Woodthorne Cl
Rugeley WS15 178 B1
Sedgley DY1 271 B1
Woodthorne Prim Sch WV6 255 A2
Woodthorne Rd WV6 255 A3
Woodthorne Rd S WV6 255 A3
Woodthorne Wlk DY6 275 C4
Woodvale Cres ST9 43 C4
Woodview Rd DE11 186 C3
Woodville Gdns DY3 266 C1
Woodville Pl ST3 74 A1
Woodville Rd ST3 74 A1
Woodville Terr ST3 74 A1
Woodward St ST1 57 B3
Woody Bank WS6 226 C1
Woodyard Dr B79 217 B3
Woodyard La DE65 129 C3
Woolands Rise DE6 144 A4
Woolliscroft Ave ST5 56 B2
Woolliscroft Rd ST2 58 A2
Woolrich St ST6 56 C4
Woolston Ave CW12 6 A1
Woore Prim Sch CW3 67 A1
Woosnam Cl DE14 185 A3
Wootton Cl WS11 210 A1
Wootton Dr ST16 155 A4
Wootton La ST10 78 C2
Wootton Rd WV3 265 B4
Woottons Ct WS11 209 C1
Worcester Cl
Cannock WS11 226 C4
Lichfield WS13 214 B2

Worcester Cl continued
Sutton Coldfield B75 .....**258** B2
Talke ST7 ....**40** B4
Worcester Ct WV3 ....**266** A3
Worcester Gr WV6 ....**254** B2
Worcester La B75 .....**258** B2
Worcester Pl ST2 ....**58** B1
Worcester Rd
Burton u T DE15 ....**185** C3
Hagley DY9 ....**281** C2
Whittington WS14 ......**232** B2
Worcester St DY8 .....**279** C2
Wordsley Green Sh Ctr
DY8 ....**275** B1
Wordsley Hospl DY8 ..**275** C2
Wordsworth Ave
Stafford ST17 ....**174** B4
Tamworth B79 ....**250** A3
Wolv WV4 ....**266** C2
Wordsworth Cl
Armitage WS15 ....**198** A2
Burton u T DE14 ......**166** B3
Cannock WS11 ....**209** B2
Cheadle ST10 ....**76** B1
Lichfield WS14 ....**231** A3
Wordsworth Ct WV6 ...**254** C2
Wordsworth Dr TF9 ...**112** A4
Wordsworth Rd
Burntwood WS7 ....**229** A4
Sedgley DY3 ....**271** A2
Worfield Gdns WV3 ...**265** C3
Worsley Dr CW12 ....**6** A1
Worston La ST15,ST18 ..**135** A3
Worth Cl ST3 ....**73** B2
Worthing Pl ST3 ....**283** B3
Worthington Rd WS13 .**215** B3
Worthington Way DE14 .**166** B2
Wragby Cl WV9 ....**240** A2
Wragg's La ST8 ....**17** A1
Wrekin Ave TF10 ......**168** C1
Wrekin Ct B74 ....**257** C1
Wrekin Dr
Wolv, Bradmore WV3 ...**265** C4
Wolv, Wergs WV6 ....**255** A3

Wrekin Gr WV11 ....**242** A1
Wrekin La WV6 ....**255** A3
Wrekin View
Brownhills WS8 ....**245** A3
Huntington WS12 ......**209** B4
Wrekin View Rd DY3 ...**271** B4
Wren Ave WV6 ....**254** B2
Wren Cl ST8 ....**27** C4
Wren View Ashley TF9 ...**99** B2
Longton ST3 ....**283** D2
Wrenbury Cl ST5 ......**40** B1
Wrenbury Cres ST2 ....**58** A1
Wrenswood ST17 ......**175** B3
Wrexham Cl ST8 ....**16** B1
Wright Ave ST5 ....**55** C4
Wright St Kidsgrove ST7 ..**25** B1
Stafford ST16 ....**155** C3
Wright's Ave WS11 ....**209** C3
Wrighton Cl ST2 ....**57** C1
Wrighton Dr DY5 ......**271** B1
Wrinehill Rd CW5 ......**52** A3
Wrottesley Park Rd
WV6,WV8 ....**254** B3
Wrottesley Rd WV6 ....**255** A3
Wrottesley Rd W
Perton WV6 ....**254** C3
Wolv WV6 ....**255** A3
Wroxham Way ST5 .....**71** A1
Wulfad Ct ST15 ....**120** B4
Wulfric Cl ST19 ....**208** A4
Wulfruna Gdns WV3 ...**255** C1
Wulstan Dr ST5 ....**56** B2
Wulstan Rd ST6 ....**57** A3
Wyatt St ST6 ....**41** B4
Wych Elm Rd WS8 .....**244** C3
Wychall Dr WV10 ......**240** C2
Wychbold Cl WV12 ....**242** B1
Wychbold Way WV12 ..**242** B1
Wychbury Rd WV3 .....**265** B4
Wycherwood Gdns
ST17 ....**175** B3
Wychwood Pk CW2 .....**37** A1
Wycliffe Rd ST6 ....**56** C4
Wye Cl Cheadle ST10 ....**76** C1
Perton WV6 ....**254** C2
Wye Dale DE11 ....**186** C1
Wye Ho DY3 ....**271** B2

Wye Rd
Newcastle-u-L ST5 ....**71** A2
Walsall WS3 ....**243** C1
Wyggeston St DE13 ....**166** B3
Wykeham Gr WV6 .....**254** B2
Wymondley Gr ST4 .....**88** A3
Wynbank Cl ST7 ....**54** C4
Wynchcombe Ave WV4 .**265** B2
Wynd The DY3 ....**266** B1
Wyndham Cres DE15 ...**167** B2
Wyndham Rd ST3 ....**88** C4
Wyndham Wood Cl
WS13 ....**215** B4
Wynford Pl ST2 ....**58** A1
Wynn Rd WV4 ....**265** C3
Wynne Cres WV4 ......**265** B2
Wynstay Ave ST9 ....**59** A2
Wynstay Ct ST5 ....**71** B1
Wynyates B79 ....**249** C3
Wyre Cl WS9 ....**244** C2
Wyre Rd DY8 ....**279** C4
Wyrley Brook Pk WS11 .**226** B3
Wyrley Brook Ret Pk
WS11 ....**226** B3
Wyrley Cl
Brownhills WS8 ....**228** C2
Lichfield WS14 ....**231** A3
Wyrley La WS3 ....**243** C4
Wyrley Rd B75 ....**258** B1
Wyvern B77 ....**250** C2
Wyvern Gr WS12 ......**210** A3
Wyvis Cl WV6 ....**255** C1

Y

Yale St ST6 ....**56** C4
Yardley Pl ST3 ....**88** C3
Yardley St ST6 ....**42** C3
Yardley Wlk ST3 ....**88** C3
Yarlet Croft ST16 ......**155** B3
Yarlet La ST18 ....**136** B3
Yarlet Sch ST18 ....**136** B4
Yarmouth Wlk ST3 ....**283** D5
Yarnbrook Gr ST6 ......**42** C3
Yarner Cl DY1 ....**271** C1
Yarnfield Cl ST3 ....**74** A1

Yarnfield La
Stone ST15 ....**119** A4
Swynnerton ST15 ......**118** C3
Yarrow Cl WS3 ....**244** A3
Yateley Cl ST2 ....**58** A1
Yates Croft B74 ......**257** C3
Yates St ST1 ....**282** A2
Yaxley Ct ST5 ....**71** A1
Yaxley Pl ST3 ....**88** C3
Yeadon Gdns WV3 .....**265** B4
Yeager Ct ST15 ....**118** C3
Yeaman St ST4 ....**72** A3
Yeatsall Rd WS15 .....**160** C3
Yeldham Pl ST3 ....**88** C3
Yelt La DE6 ....**127** B4
Yelverton Ave ST17 ....**175** A4
Yelverton Cl WS3 ......**243** A2
Yemscroft WS6 ....**243** A4
Yenton Cl B78 ....**250** A1
Yeoman Ind Est DE14 ..**166** C3
Yeoman Way WS15 ....**198** A2
Yeovil Pl ST3 ....**88** C3
Yeovilton B79 ....**250** B4
Yerley Hill DE6 ....**66** B3
Yew Cl WS15 ....**198** A2
Yew Pl ST5 ....**55** B4
Yew Tree Ave
Lichfield WS14 ....**231** C4
Longton ST3 ....**72** C1
Yew Tree Cl
Norton Canes WS11 ....**228** A3
Norton-in-t-M ST2 ......**43** B1
Seighford ST18 ....**154** C1
Yew Tree Ct ST17 ......**174** C2
Yew Tree Dr ST19 ......**205** B3
Yew Tree Gdns WV8 ...**239** A2
Yew Tree La
Astbury CW12 ....**15** B2
Bridgemere CW5 ....**67** A3
Wolv WV6 ....**255** A3
Yew Tree Pl WS3 ....**243** B2
Yew Tree Rd
Pattingham WV6 ....**253** B1
Rugeley WS15 ....**196** C3
Swadlincote DE11 ......**186** C4
Walsall WS4 ....**244** B1
Yew Tree Terr ST7 ......**41** A4

Yewtree Cres DE15 ....**185** C4
York Ave
Blythe Bridge ST11 ......**90** C1
Wolv WV3 ....**255** C1
York Cl Biddulph ST8 ....**16** B1
Forsbrook ST11 ....**91** A4
Lichfield WS13 ....**214** B2
Talke ST7 ....**40** B4
York Cres
Stourbridge DY8 ....**279** B4
Wolv WV3 ....**255** C1
York Gdns WV3 ....**255** C1
York Pl ST5 ....**284** B3
York Rd Cannock WS11 .**226** C4
Meir ST3 ....**74** A2
Stafford ST17 ....**175** A4
Wolv WV3 ....**265** A4
York St Burton u T DE14 .**166** B2
Hanley ST1 ....**282** A4
Leek ST13 ....**30** C3
Newcastle-u-L ST5 .....**284** D3
Stone ST15 ....**105** A1
Yorkdale Cl DY3 ....**271** B2
Yorksand Rd B78 ......**260** C4
Youlgreave Ave ST2 .....**58** A1
Youlton Pl ST2 ....**58** A1
Young Ave ST16 ......**155** B3
Young St Cheadle ST10 ...**76** C2
Chell Heath ST6 ....**41** C3
Younger St ST4 ....**72** B3
Yoxall Ave ST4 ....**71** C4
Yoxall Rd
King's Bromley DE13 ...**199** B4
Newborough DE13 .....**162** C4

Z

Zamenhof Gr ST6 ......**42** B1
Zennor Gr ST2 ....**58** A1
Zetland Pl ST3 ....**88** C3
Zetland Wlk ST3 ....**88** C3
Zion Cl WS6 ....**226** B2
Zion St ST6 ....**57** A4
Zoar St DY3 ....**271** B2
Zodiac Dr ST6 ....**41** C3
Zouche Cl DY8 ....**279** C4

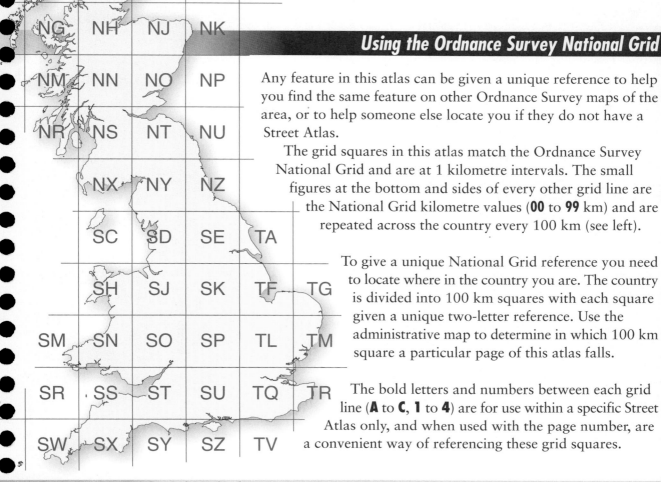

Any feature in this atlas can be given a unique reference to help you find the same feature on other Ordnance Survey maps of the area, or to help someone else locate you if they do not have a Street Atlas.

The grid squares in this atlas match the Ordnance Survey National Grid and are at 1 kilometre intervals. The small figures at the bottom and sides of every other grid line are the National Grid kilometre values (**00** to **99** km) and are repeated across the country every 100 km (see left).

To give a unique National Grid reference you need to locate where in the country you are. The country is divided into 100 km squares with each square given a unique two-letter reference. Use the administrative map to determine in which 100 km square a particular page of this atlas falls.

The bold letters and numbers between each grid line (**A** to **C**, **1** to **4**) are for use within a specific Street Atlas only, and when used with the page number, are a convenient way of referencing these grid squares.

Example   The railway bridge over DARLEY GREEN RD in grid square A1

Step 1: Identify the two-letter reference, in this example the page is in **SP**

Step 2: Identify the 1 km square in which the railway bridge falls. Use the figures in the southwest corner of this square: Eastings **17**, Northings **74**. This gives a unique reference: **SP 17 74**, accurate to 1 km.

Step 3: To give a more precise reference accurate to 100 m you need to estimate how many tenths along and how many tenths up this 1 km square the feature is. This makes the bridge about **8** tenths along and about **1** tenth up from the southwest corner.

This gives a unique reference: **SP 178 741**, accurate to 100 m.

Eastings (read from left to right along the bottom) come before Northings (read from bottom to top). If you have trouble remembering say to yourself "Along the hall, THEN up the stairs"!

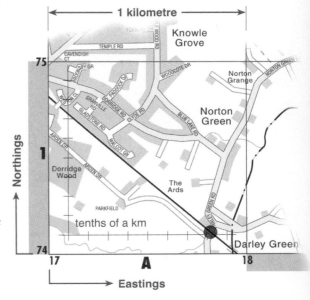

PHILIP'S MAPS

the Gold Standard for serious driving

◆ Philip's street atlases cover every county in England, plus much of Wales and Scotland.

◆ All our atlases use the same style of mapping, with the same colours and symbols, so you can move with confidence from one atlas to the next

◆ Widely used by the emergency services, transport companies and local authorities.

◆ Created from the most up-to-date and detailed information available from Ordnance Survey

◆ Based on the National Grid

BEST BUY • BEST BUY • Auto EXPRESS • BEST BUY • BEST BUY •

England	
Bedfordshire	
Berkshire	
Birmingham and West Midlands	
Bristol and Bath	
Buckinghamshire	
Cambridgeshire	Somerset
Cheshire	Staffordshire
Cornwall	Suffolk
Cumbria	Surrey
Derbyshire	East Sussex
Devon	West Sussex
Dorset	Tyne and Wear Northumberland
County Durham and Teesside	Warwickshire
Essex	Birmingham and West Midlands
North Essex	Wiltshire and Swindon
South Essex	
Gloucestershire	Worcestershire
North Hampshire	East Yorkshire Northern Lincolnshire
South Hampshire	North Yorkshire
Herefordshire Monmouthshire	South Yorkshire
Hertfordshire	West Yorkshire
Isle of Wight	
East Kent	**Wales**
West Kent	Anglesey, Conwy and Gwynedd
Lancashire	Cardiff, Swansea and The Valleys
Leicestershire and Rutland	Denbighshire, Flintshire, Wrexham
Lincolnshire	Herefordshire Monmouthshire
London	
Greater Manchester	**Scotland**
Merseyside	Edinburgh and East Central Scotland
Norfolk	
Northamptonshire	Fife and Tayside
Nottinghamshire	Glasgow and West Central Scotland
Oxfordshire	
Shropshire	

For national mapping, choose **Philip's Navigator Britain** – the most detailed road atlas available of England, Wales and Scotland. Hailed by Auto Express as 'the ultimate road atlas', this is the only one-volume atlas to show every road and lane in Britain.

How to order

Philip's maps and atlases are available from bookshops, motorway services and petrol stations. You can order direct from the publisher by phoning **01903 828503** or online at **www.philips-maps.co.uk**

For bulk orders only, phone 020 7644 6940

Breakdown cover from £35

No wonder almost 5 million motorists have found their route to Green Flag.

With Green Flag Motoring Assistance, not only could you save money on your breakdown cover, but you can rely on a totally professional, fast service, when you need it most.

- 24hr assistance, 365 days a year
- 6,000 breakdown specialists nationwide
- 39 mins average response time*
- Priority response for vulnerable callers

Green Flag ®
motoring assistance

Call 0845 246 2445
or buy online at www.greenflag.com